Saint Joseph Continuous SUNDAY MISSAL

Confraternity Version

Word-*for*-Word as Read from the Pulpit

THE HOLY SACRIFICE OF THE MASS

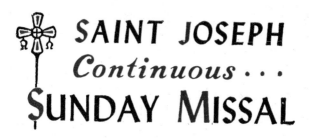

SAINT JOSEPH *Continuous . . .* SUNDAY MISSAL

A SIMPLIFIED AND CONTINUOUS ARRANGEMENT OF THE MASS FOR ALL SUNDAYS AND FEAST DAYS

with

A TREASURY OF PRAYERS

Edited and Compiled from the "Saint Joseph Daily Missal" by

REV. HUGO HOEVER, S.O.Cist., Ph.D.

CATHOLIC BOOK PUBLISHING CO.
NEW YORK

NIHIL OBSTAT:

JOHN A. GOODWINE, J.C.D.
Censor Librorum

IMPRIMATUR:

✠ FRANCIS CARDINAL SPELLMAN, D.D.
Archbishop of New York

July 1, 1957

Confraternity Version
Word-*for*-Word as Read from the Pulpit

(T-720)

Printed in U.S.A.

This New

Continuous Sunday Missal

is dedicated to

Saint Joseph

Patron

of the

Universal Church

— CONTENTS —

SUNDAY MISSAL

TREASURY OF PRAYERS

Foreword

ONE of the primary reasons for the current interest and zeal of the laity for a more active participation in the Holy Sacrifice of the Mass, is the appearance of many Missals published in the vernacular language of practically every country in the world. Thus, the layman now can "follow" the priest's gestures and motions, not only with his eyes, but can speak, in unison with him, the words which the Church bids him to say. Finally, the Missal, the Church's own Mass prayer book translated into his own language, is an indispensable aid for the layman to understand what is spoken and done by the priest while offering up the Holy Sacrifice of the Mass.

However, some of the laity find that the cross references in every Missal are a source of confusion to them while assisting at the Holy Sacrifice of the Mass. Therefore, the present Saint Joseph "Continuous" Sunday Missal was designed to eliminate all possibility of any confusion. In this Sunday Missal there are no cross references to distract the reader. The complete prayers from the beginning to the end of each Sunday or Holyday Mass are arranged to follow each other without turning pages from one part of the Missal to another part.

In presenting this New Sunday Missal, it is the fervent prayer of the editors that it will encourage a more active and zealous participation in the Holy Sacrifice of the Mass.

THE LITURGICAL YEAR

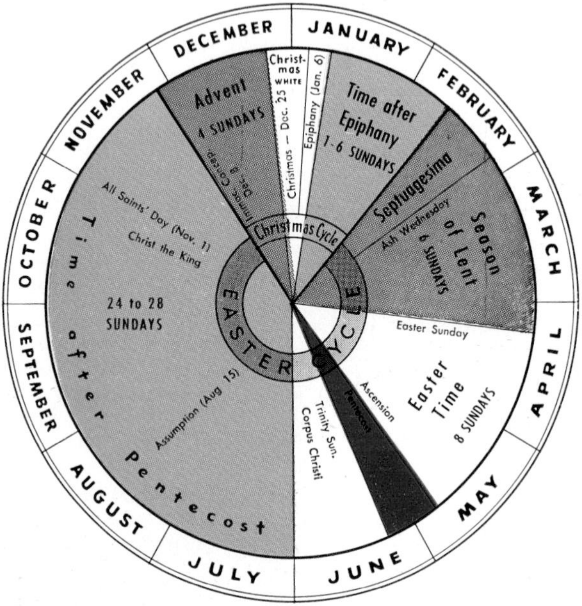

This diagram shows the divisions of the Liturgical Year into Cycles and Seasons, as well as their respective liturgical colors. As we follow this yearly round of feasts and seasons in our Missal, the Life of Jesus Christ, our Savior, unfolds in His Incarnation, Birth, Labors, Passion, Death, Resurrection, and in His unceasing Presence and Operations as the Head of the Mystical Body. Those who enter into the spirit of the different seasons of the Liturgical Year, will surely live holier and happier lives on earth and enjoy greater glory in heaven.

The HOLY SACRIFICE *of the* MASS

HOLY MASS is the highest prayer that exists. It is the real, though unbloody re-presentation of Christ's Sacrifice on the Cross. "If you wish to hear Mass as it should be heard, you must follow with eye, heart and mouth all that happens on the Altar. . . . When acting in this way you have prayed Holy Mass." (Pope Saint Pius X).

The following brief explanations and clear illustrations of the principal parts of the Holy Sacrifice of the Mass have been carefully arranged. The explanations will enable the reader to *understand* the Holy Sacrifice of the Mass better, and the colored illustrations will help him to *follow* the Mass more closely.

THE INTROIT
We Praise God

Going to the Missal the priest makes the Sign of the Cross and reads a few verses usually taken from a Psalm. This prayer is called the Introit, from the Latin *Introitus,* meaning entrance, because it used to be sung, and at Solemn Mass is still sung as the sacred ministers enter the sanctuary in procession.

THE PRAYER

Our Prayer of Petition

The priest reads the *Collect* or Prayer. He asks God for all the graces we need to save our souls. He begs God for forgiveness and help that we may be worthy to offer the Mass. The Collects are model prayers, unequaled in form and content — brief, yet forceful and charming.

THE EPISTLE

God Speaks to Us

(We Learn)

Now we ask God to teach us, that we may be ready to offer this Holy Sacrifice. He teaches us through His messengers—the Prophets, Apostles and priests. The *Epistle* is more frequently selected from the letters of the Apostles, addressed to the first Christian Churches.

THE GOSPEL

God Speaks to Us

(Our Divine Instruction)

The Gospel tells us about the life of Jesus and what He said. He is God's greatest Messenger and Teacher. Jesus becomes present among us in the Mass as our Teacher Who speaks to us in the words of life, and as the High Priest and Victim Who once offered Himself upon the altar of the Cross.

THE NICENE CREED

Our Profession of Faith

After having been taught by God through His Apostles and Jesus, we say the Creed. We tell God that we believe all He has taught us. The purpose of the beginning of the Mass (Mass of the Catechumens) is to instruct and strengthen us in our faith. The Creed contains a summary of Christian doctrine.

THE OFFERTORY

We Offer Ourselves to God

The Offertory is the first of the three important parts of the Mass (Mass of the Faithful). The priest offers bread to God. It is a sign that you want to offer yourself to God. In the Offertory and Consecration we give ourselves to God through and with our Lord; and in Holy Communion God gives Himself to us through the Body and Blood of Jesus.

THE MIXING of WINE AND WATER

Our Union with Christ

The priest pours a little wine and a drop of water into the chalice. As the water mixes and becomes one with the wine, so we should be united with Jesus by grace and love. Self-sacrifice is the drop of water in the chalice of Christ's Blood. This mingling reminds us of the purpose of redemption.

WASHING THE FINGERS

We Pray for Purity of Mind and Heart

The priest washes his hands to show that he wants God to make his soul clean. Ask God to clean your soul from sin so that you may offer this Mass well. The washing of the fingers reminds us of the great purity of soul necessary for the reception of the Body and Blood of Jesus Christ.

CANON of the MASS

We Pray for the Church

The priest calls on the Blessed Virgin Mary and all the Saints to pray for us that we may offer this Mass well. The Canon of the Mass is a fixed formula of Sacrifice and is made up of the very words of Jesus Christ, the traditions of the Apostles and the institutions of the Popes.

ELEVATION OF SACRED HOST

We Adore the Sacred Host

The Holy Spirit has worked a great miracle. The bread was changed into the Body of Jesus. When the priest lifts the Host, look at Jesus, as if He were hanging on the Cross, and tell Him you love Him. With deep faith and love say the words of St. Thomas the Apostle: "My Lord and my God!"

ELEVATION OF CHALICE

We Adore the Precious Blood

Offer the Blood of Jesus to the Heavenly Father for the forgiveness of your sins and those of the whole world. This Mass is not only a remembrance of the Passion and Death of Jesus, but also a true Sacrifice, the Sacrifice of the Cross on Calvary offered again in an unbloody manner under the appearances of bread and wine.

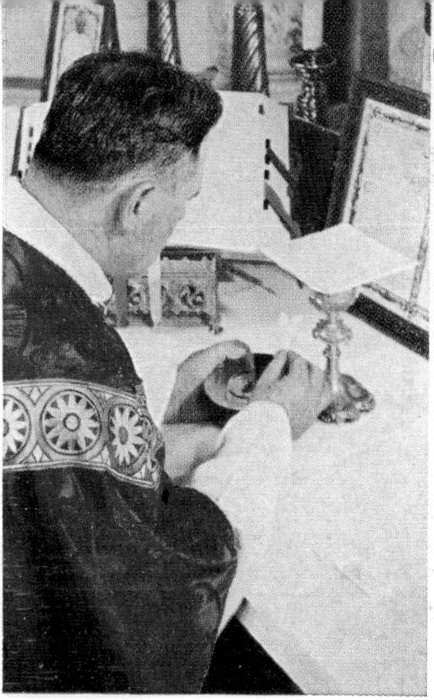

COMMUNION OF THE PRIEST

Acts of Faith

After praying to Jesus, the Lamb of God, for peace and purity of soul, the priest receives Holy Communion. The Last Supper was the observance of the paschal ceremony in which the paschal lamb was eaten in remembrance of the freeing of the Israelites from Egypt. The paschal lamb represented the Divine Redeemer Who is now our Food in Holy Communion.

COMMUNION OF THE FAITHFUL

We Receive Holy Communion

Since the people offer Jesus to God, everyone should receive Jesus in Holy Communion as God's gift to them. It is the wish of the Church that the faithful receive Communion at every Mass, in order to merit the greatest graces of the Mass.

POSTCOMMUNION

Prayer of Thanksgiving

The priest thanks God for having been so good to him. The best thanksgiving you can render for the great gift you have received in the Mass is to strive faithfully to do your daily work well, accept bravely your daily crosses, and to devote yourself, body and soul, to the service of God and His Church.

THE LAST BLESSING

We Receive God's Blessing

Before you leave, the priest gives you the blessing of the Church. He asks God the Father, the Son, and the Holy Spirit to grant you the graces and blessings you need for your soul and body. The blessing is a sacramental and as such produces a wholesome effect which can be increased by receiving the blessing devoutly.

✠

THE COMPLETE MASSES

FOR ALL

SUNDAYS AND HOLY DAYS

THROUGHOUT THE YEAR

✠

Place the Missal in the hands of the faithful so that they may take part more easily and more fruitfully in the Mass; and that the faithful, united with the Priest, may pray together in the very words and sentiments of the Church.

Pope Pius XII

720-2

"Blessed Be the Holy Trinity and Undivided Unity: We Will Give Glory to Him, Because He Has Shown His Mercy to Us." Tobias 12, 6.

"There will be signs in the sun and moon and stars . . ."

FIRST SUNDAY OF ADVENT

It is now the hour for us to rise from the sleep of sin and of religious indifference. Let us start our preparation for the blessing of Christmas with great confidence in Jesus, for those who trust in Him shall not be confounded. (PURPLE VESTMENTS)

PRAYERS AT THE FOOT OF THE ALTAR

IN THE name of the Father, ✠ and of the Son, and of the Holy Spirit. Amen.

Priest. I will go in to the altar of God.

Server. The God of my gladness and joy.

Psalm 42

DO ME justice, O God, and fight my fight against a faithless people; from the deceitful and impious man rescue me.

S. For You, O God, are my strength. Why do You keep me so far away? Why must I go about in mourning, with the enemy oppressing me?

P. Send forth Your light and Your fidelity; they shall lead me on and bring me to Your holy mountain, to Your dwelling-place.

S. Then will I go in to the altar of God, the God of my gladness and joy.
P. Then will I give You thanks upon the harp, O God, my God. Why are you so downcast, O my soul? Why do you sigh within me?
S. Hope in God! For I shall again be thanking Him in the presence of my Savior and my God.
P. Glory be to the Father, and to the Son, and to the Holy Spirit.
S. As it was in the beginning, is now, and ever shall be, world without end. Amen.
P. I will go in to the altar of God.
S. The God of my gladness and joy.
P. Our help ✠ is in the name of the Lord.
S. Who made heaven and earth.
P. I confess to almighty God, etc.
S. May almighty God have mercy on you, forgive you your sins, and bring you to life everlasting.
P. Amen.

The Server, bowing, says the "Confiteor."

I CONFESS to almighty God, to Blessed Mary, ever Virgin, to Blessed Michael the Archangel, to Blessed John the Baptist, to the Holy Apostles Peter and Paul, and to all the Saints, and to you, Father, that I have sinned exceedingly in thought, word and deed, *through my fault, through my fault, through my most grievous fault.* Therefore I beseech Blessed Mary, ever Virgin, Blessed Michael the Archangel, Blessed John the Baptist, the Holy Apostles Peter and Paul, and all the Saints, and you, Father, to pray to the Lord our God for me.
P. May almighty God have mercy on you, forgive you your sins, and bring you to life everlasting.
S. Amen.

MAY the almighty and merciful Lord grant us pardon, ✠ absolution, and remission of our sins. *S.* Amen.

P. Will You not, O God, give us life?

S. And shall not Your people rejoice in You?

P. Show us, O Lord, Your kindness.

S. And grant us Your salvation.

P. O Lord, hear my prayer.

S. And let my cry come to You.

P. The Lord be with you.

S. And with your spirit. *P.* Let us pray.

Going up to the altar, the Priest prays silently:

TAKE away from us our sins, O Lord, we beseech You, that we may enter with pure minds into the Holy of Holies. Through Christ our Lord. Amen.

WE BESEECH You, O Lord, by the merits of Your Saints (*he kisses the altar*) whose relics lie here, and of all the Saints: deign in Your mercy to pardon me all my sins. Amen.

THE INTROIT • Ps. 24, 1-4

At the right side of the altar, the Priest says:

TO YOU I lift up my soul: in You, O my God, I trust; let me not be put to shame: let not my enemies exult over me; no one who waits for You shall be put to shame. *Ps.* Your ways, O Lord, make known to me; teach me Your paths. Glory be to the Father, and to the Son, and to the Holy Spirit. As it was in the beginning, is now, and ever shall be, world without end. Amen. — To You I lift up my soul: in You, O my God, I trust; let me not be put to shame: let not my enemies exult over me; no one who waits for You shall be put to shame.

THE KYRIE

P. Lord, have mercy. *S*. Lord, have mercy. *P*. Lord, have mercy. *S*. Christ, have mercy. *P*. Christ, have mercy. *S*. Christ, have mercy. *P*. Lord, have mercy. *S*. Lord, have mercy. *P*. Lord, have mercy.

The Priest kisses the altar and turns to the people, saying:

P. The Lord be with you. *S*. And with your spirit. *P*. Let us pray.

THE PRAYER

Going to the right (Epistle) side, he says:

O LORD, we pray You, stir up Your power, and come; that by Your protection we may deserve to be rescued from the threatening dangers of our sins, and to be saved by Your deliverance. Who live and reign with God the Father, in the unity of the Holy Spirit, God, world without end. *S*. Amen.

THE EPISTLE • Rom. 13, 11-14

BRETHREN: Understand, for it is now the hour for us to rise from sleep, because now our salvation is nearer than when we came to believe. The night is far advanced; the day is at hand. Let us therefore lay aside the works of darkness, and put on the armor of light. Let us walk becomingly as in the day, not in revelry and drunkenness, not in debauchery and wantonness, not in strife and jealousy. But put on the Lord Jesus Christ. *S*. Thanks be to God.

THE GRADUAL • Ps. 24, 3. 4

NO ONE who waits for You shall be put to shame. ℣. Your ways, O Lord, make known to me; teach me Your paths.

Alleluia, alleluia. ℣. *Ps.* 84, 8. Show us, O Lord, Your kindness, and grant us Your salvation. Alleluia.

PRAYER BEFORE THE GOSPEL

Bowing down at the center of the altar, he says:

CLEANSE my heart and my lips, O almighty God, Who cleansed the lips of the Prophet Isaias with a burning coal. In Your gracious mercy deign so to purify me that I may worthily proclaim Your holy Gospel. Through Christ our Lord. Amen.

Lord, grant Your blessing. The Lord be in my heart and on my lips, that I may worthily and fittingly proclaim His holy Gospel. Amen.

THE GOSPEL • Luke 21, 25-33

Going to the left (Gospel) side of the altar, he says:

P. The Lord be with you. *S.* And with your spirit.

P. ✠ The continuation of the holy Gospel according to Saint Luke. *S.* Glory be to You, O Lord.

AT THAT time, Jesus said to His disciples: "There will be signs in the sun and moon and stars, and upon the earth distress of nations bewildered by the roaring of sea and waves; men fainting for fear and for expectation of the things that are coming on the world; for the powers of heaven will be shaken. And then they will see the Son of Man coming upon a cloud with great power and majesty. But when these things begin to come to pass, look up, and lift up your heads, because your redemption is at hand." And He spoke to them a parable. "Behold the fig tree, and all the trees. When they now put forth their buds, you know that summer is near. Even so, when you see these things coming to pass, know that the kingdom of God is near. Amen I say to you, this generation will not pass away till all things have been accomplished. Heaven and earth will pass away, but My words will not pass away." S. Praise be to You, O Christ.

P. By the words of the Gospel, may our sins be taken away.

THE NICENE CREED

At the center of the altar, he says:

I BELIEVE in one God, the Father almighty, Maker of heaven and earth, and of all things visible and invisible. And in one Lord Jesus Christ, the Only-begotten Son of God. Born of the Father before all ages. God of God; Light of Light; true God of true God. Begotten not made; of one being with the Father; by Whom all things were made. Who for us men, and for our salvation, came down from heaven. (*Here all genuflect.*) And was made Flesh by the Holy Spirit of the Virgin Mary: AND WAS MADE MAN. He was also crucified for us, suffered under Pontius Pilate and was buried. And on the third day He rose again according to the Scriptures. And ascending into heaven, He sits at the right hand of the Father. And He shall come again in glory to judge the living and the dead; and of His kingdom there shall be no end. And I believe in the Holy Spirit, Lord and Giver of life, Who proceeds from the Father and the Son. Who together with the Father and the Son is no less adored, and glorified: Who spoke by the Prophets. And I believe in One, Holy, Catholic and Apostolic Church. I confess one Baptism for the remission of sins. And I look for the resurrection of the dead. ✠ And the life of the world to come. Amen.

THE OFFERTORY

The Priest turns to the people and says:

P. The Lord be with you. *S.* And with your spirit.
P. Let us pray.

THE OFFERTORY VERSE • Ps. 24, 1-3

TO YOU I lift up my soul: in You, O my God, I trust; let me not be put to shame: let not my enemies exult over me; no one who waits for You shall be put to shame.

The Priest now uncovers the chalice, places the host on the paten and offering it up, says:

ACCEPT, O holy Father, almighty and eternal God, this spotless host, which I, Your unworthy servant, offer to You, my living and true God, to atone for my numberless sins, offenses, and negligences; on behalf of all here present and likewise for all faithful Christians living and dead, that it may profit me and them as a means of salvation to life everlasting. Amen.

He pours wine and water into the chalice, blessing the water before it is poured.

O GOD, Who established the nature of man in wondrous dignity, and still more admirably restored it, grant that through the mystery of this water and wine, we may be made partakers of His Divinity, Who has condescended to become partaker of our humanity, Jesus Christ, Your Son, our Lord. Who lives and reigns with You in the unity of the Holy Spirit, God, world without end. Amen.

Offering up the wine, the Priest says:

WE OFFER You, O Lord, the chalice of salvation, humbly begging of Your mercy that it may arise before Your Divine Majesty, with a pleasing fragrance, for our salvation and for that of the whole world. Amen.

Bowing down, the Priest says:

IN A humble spirit and with a contrite heart, may we be accepted by You, O Lord, and may our sacrifice so be offered in Your sight this day as to please You, O Lord God.

Raising his eyes and blessing the offering, he says:

COME, O Sanctifier, almighty and eternal God, and bless ✠ this sacrifice prepared for the glory of Your holy name.

WASHING THE FINGERS

I WASH my hands in innocence, and I go around Your altar, O Lord, giving voice to my thanks, and recounting all Your wondrous deeds. O Lord, I love the house in which You dwell, the tenting-place of Your glory. Gather not my soul with those of sinners, nor with men of blood my life. On their hands are crimes, and their right hands are full of bribes. But I walk in integrity; redeem me, and have pity on me. My foot stands on level ground; in the assemblies I will bless You, O Lord. Glory be to the Father, and to the Son, and to the Holy Spirit. As it was in the beginning, is now, and ever shall be, world without end. Amen.

ACCEPT, Most Holy Trinity, this offering which we are making to You in remembrance of the Passion, Resurrection, and Ascension of Jesus Christ, our Lord; and in honor of Blessed Mary, ever Virgin, Blessed John the Baptist, the Holy Apostles Peter and Paul, and of these, and of all the Saints; that it may add to their honor and aid our salvation; and may they deign to intercede in heaven for us who honor their memory here on earth. Through the same Christ our Lord. Amen.

The Priest turns toward the people and says:

Pray, brethren, that my sacrifice and yours may become acceptable to God the Father almighty.

S. May the Lord accept this sacrifice from your hands to the praise and glory of His name, for our advantage, and that of all His holy Church.

P. Amen.

THE SECRET

GRANT, O Lord, that these sacred mysteries may cleanse us by their powerful virtue, and bring us with more purity to Him, Who was the author of them. Through our Lord Jesus Christ, Your Son, Who lives and reigns with You in the unity of the Holy Spirit, God.

P. World without end. S. Amen.

PREFACE–CANON

P. The Lord be with you. S. And with your spirit.
P. Lift up your hearts.
S. We have lifted them up to the Lord.
P. Let us give thanks to the Lord, our God.
S. It is fitting and just.

IT IS fitting indeed and just, right and helpful to salvation, for us always and everywhere to give thanks to You, O holy Lord, Father almighty, everlasting God, Who with Your Only-begotten Son and the Holy Spirit are one God, one Lord; not in the unity of a single person, but in the trinity of a single nature. For that which we believe on Your revelation concerning Your glory, that same we believe of Your Son, that same of the Holy Spirit, without difference or discrimination. So that in confessing the true and everlasting Godhead, we shall adore distinction in Persons, oneness in being, and equality in Majesty. This the Angels and Archangels, the Cherubim, too, and the Seraphim do praise; day by day they cease not to cry out as with one voice, saying (*the bell is rung* 3 *times*):

HOLY, HOLY, HOLY, Lord God of Hosts. Heaven and earth are filled with Your glory. Hosanna in the highest. ✠ Blessed is He Who comes in the name of the Lord. Hosanna in the highest.

THE CANON OF THE MASS

THEREFORE, most gracious Father, we humbly beg of You and entreat You through Jesus Christ Your Son, our Lord, (*he kisses the altar*) to deem acceptable and bless these ✠ gifts, these ✠ offerings, these ✠ holy and unspotted oblations which, in the first place, we offer You for Your Holy Catholic Church, that You would deign to give her peace and protection, to unite and guard her throughout the world, together with Your servant N., our Pope, and N., our Bishop; and all true believers who cherish the Catholic and Apostolic Faith.

Commemoration of the Living

REMEMBER, O Lord, Your servants and handmaids, N. and N., (*name them*) and all here present, whose faith and devotion are known to You, on whose behalf we offer to You, or who themselves offer to You, this sacrifice of praise for themselves, families and friends, for the good of their souls, for their hope of salvation and deliverance from all harm, and who offer their homage to You, eternal, living and true God.

Commemoration of the Saints

IN THE unity of holy fellowship we observe the memory, first of all, of the glorious and ever Virgin Mary, Mother of our Lord and God Jesus Christ; next, that of Your Blessed Apostles and Martyrs, Peter and Paul, Andrew, James, John, Thomas, James, Philip, Bartholomew, Matthew, Simon and Thaddeus; of Linus, Cletus, Clement, Sixtus, Cornelius, Cyprian, Lawrence, Chrysogonus, John and Paul, Cosmas and Damian, and of all Your Saints, by whose merits and prayers grant that we may be always fortified by the help of Your protection. Through the same Christ our Lord. Amen.

Spreading his hands over the oblation, he says:

GRACIOUSLY accept, then, we beseech You, O Lord, this service of our worship and that of all Your household. Provide that our days be spent in Your peace, save us from everlasting damnation, and cause us to be numbered in the flock You have chosen. Through Christ our Lord. Amen.

O GOD, deign to bless ✠ what we offer, and make it approved, ✠ effective, ✠ right, and

wholly pleasing in every way, that it may become for our good, the Body ✠ and Blood ✠ of Your dearly beloved Son, Jesus Christ our Lord.

CONSECRATION—ELEVATION

WHO, the day before He suffered, took bread into His holy and venerable hands, and having raised His eyes to heaven, to You, O God, His almighty Father, giving thanks to You, He blessed it, ✠ broke it, and gave it to His disciples, saying: All of you take and eat of this:

FOR THIS IS MY BODY.

IN LIKE manner, when the supper was done, taking also this goodly chalice into His holy and venerable hands, again giving thanks to You, He blessed ✠ it, and gave it to His disciples, saying: All of you take and drink of this:

FOR THIS IS THE CHALICE OF MY BLOOD OF THE NEW AND ETERNAL COVENANT: THE MYSTERY OF FAITH: WHICH SHALL BE SHED FOR YOU AND FOR MANY UNTO THE FORGIVENESS OF SINS.

After replacing the chalice on the corporal, he says:

As often as you shall do these things, in memory of Me shall you do them.

Offering of the Victim

MINDFUL, therefore, O Lord, not only of the blessed Passion of the same Christ, Your Son, our Lord, but also of His Resurrection from the dead, and finally His glorious Ascension into heaven, we, Your ministers, as also Your holy people, offer to Your supreme Majesty, of the gifts be-

stowed upon us, the pure ✠ Victim, the holy ✠ Victim, the all-perfect ✠ Victim: the holy ✠ Bread of life eternal and the Chalice ✠ of unending salvation.

AND this deign to regard with gracious and kindly attention and hold acceptable, as You deigned to accept the offerings of Abel, Your just servant, and the sacrifice of Abraham our patriarch, and that which Your chief priest Melchisedec offered to You, a holy sacrifice and a spotless victim.

MOST humbly we implore You, almighty God, bid these offerings to be brought by the hands of Your holy angel to Your altar above; before the face of Your Divine Majesty; that those of us who, by sharing in the Sacrifice of this altar, shall receive the Most Sacred ✠ Body and ✠ Blood of Your Son, may be filled with every grace and heavenly blessing. Through the same Christ our Lord. Amen.

Commemoration of the Dead

REMEMBER also, O Lord, Your servants and handmaids, *N.* and *N.*, who have gone before us with the sign of faith, and rest in the sleep of peace. (*Here pray for the dead.*) To these, O Lord, and to all who rest in Christ, we beseech You to grant of Your goodness, a place of comfort, light and peace. Through the same Christ our Lord. Amen.

TO US sinners also, Your servants, trusting in the greatness of Your mercy, deign to grant some part and fellowship with Your Holy Apostles and Martyrs: with John, Stephen, Matthias, Barnabas, Ignatius, Alexander, Marcellinus, Peter, Felicitas,

Perpetua, Agatha, Lucy, Agnes, Cecilia, Anastasia, and all Your Saints; into whose company, we implore You to admit us, not weighing our merits, but freely granting us pardon. Through Christ our Lord.

THROUGH Whom, O Lord, You always create, ✠ sanctify, ✠ fill with life, ✠ bless, and bestow upon us all good things.

The Minor Elevation

THROUGH ✠ Him, and with ✠ Him, and in ✠ Him, is to You, God the Father ✠ almighty, in the unity of the Holy ✠ Spirit, all honor and glory, world without end. S. Amen.

THE COMMUNION AND THANKSGIVING

Let us pray. Prompted by saving precepts, and taught by Your divine teaching, we dare to say:

OUR FATHER, Who art in heaven, hallowed be Thy name: Thy kingdom come: Thy will be done on earth as it is in heaven. Give us this day our daily bread; and forgive us our trespasses, as we forgive those who trespass against us. And lead us not into temptation: S. But deliver us from evil. P. Amen.

DELIVER us, we beseech You, O Lord, from all evils, past, present, and to come; and by the intercession of the Blessed and glorious Mary, ever Virgin, Mother of God, together with Your Blessed Apostles Peter and Paul, and Andrew, and all the Saints, grant of Your goodness, peace in our days, that aided by the riches of Your mercy, we may be always free from sin and safe from all disturbance.

Through the same our Lord Jesus Christ, Your Son, Who lives and reigns with You in the unity of the Holy Spirit, God, world without end.

S. Amen.

P. May the peace ✠ of the Lord be ✠ always with ✠ you.

S. And with your spirit.

The Priest puts a small particle into the chalice, saying:

May this mingling and consecration of the Body and Blood of our Lord Jesus Christ help us who receive it to life everlasting. Amen.

LAMB of God, You Who take away the sins of the world, have mercy on us.

Lamb of God, You Who take away the sins of the world, have mercy on us.

Lamb of God, You Who take away the sins of the world, grant us peace.

PRAYERS BEFORE HOLY COMMUNION

Then inclining toward the altar, he says:

O LORD Jesus Christ, Who said to Your Apostles: "Peace I leave with you, My peace I give to you," regard not my sins but the faith of Your Church, and deign to give her peace and unity according to Your Will: Who live and reign, God, world without end. Amen.

O LORD Jesus Christ, Son of the living God, Who, by the will of the Father, with the cooperation of the Holy Spirit, have by Your death given life to the world, deliver me by this Your Most Sacred Body and Blood from all my sins and from every evil. Make me always cling to Your commandments, and never permit me to be separated from You. Who with the same God the Father and the Holy Spirit, live and reign, God, world without end. Amen.

LET not the partaking of Your Body, O Lord Jesus Christ, which I, though unworthy, presume to receive, turn to my judgment and condemnation; but through Your goodness, may it become a safeguard and an effective remedy, both of soul and body. Who live and reign with God the Father, in the unity of the Holy Spirit, God, world without end. Amen.

COMMUNION OF THE PRIEST

I WILL take the Bread of heaven, and call upon the name of the Lord.

Lord, I am not worthy that You should come under my roof; but only say the word, and my soul will be healed. (3 *times.*)

Making the Sign of the Cross with the Host, he says:

MAY the Body of our Lord Jesus Christ preserve my soul to life everlasting. Amen.

What return shall I make to the Lord for all He has given me? I will take the Chalice of salvation, and I will call upon the name of the Lord. Praising will I call upon the Lord and I shall be saved from my enemies.

Making the Sign of the Cross with the chalice, he says:

MAY the Blood of our Lord Jesus Christ preserve my soul to life everlasting. Amen.

The Priest reverently consumes the Precious Blood.

COMMUNION OF THE FAITHFUL

The Server and people say the "Confiteor."

P. May almighty God have mercy on you, forgive

you your sins, and bring you to life everlasting. S. Amen.

P. May the almighty and merciful Lord grant you pardon, ✠ absolution and remission of your sins. S. Amen.

Holding up a Sacred Host, the Priest says:

Behold the Lamb of God, behold Him Who takes away the sins of the world.

Lord, I am not worthy that You should come under my roof; but only say the word, and my soul will be healed. (3 *times.*)

The Priest says to each communicant:

May the Body of our Lord Jesus Christ preserve your soul to life everlasting. Amen.

The Priest purifies the chalice with wine, saying:

WHAT has passed our lips as food, O Lord, may we possess in purity of heart, that what is given to us in time, be our healing for eternity.

He purifies his fingers with wine and water, saying:

MAY Your Body, O Lord, which I have eaten, and Your Blood which I have drunk, cleave to my very soul, and grant that no trace of sin be found in me, whom these pure and holy mysteries have renewed. Who live and reign, world without end. Amen.

THE COMMUNION • Ps. 84, 13

THE Lord Himself will give His benefits: and our land shall yield its increase.

The Priest, turning to the people, says:

P. The Lord be with you. S. And with your spirit.

P. Let us pray.

THE POSTCOMMUNION

MAY we receive Your mercy in the midst of Your temple, O Lord; that we may anticipate with due honor the coming solemnities of our renewal. Through our Lord Jesus Christ, Your Son, Who lives and reigns with You in the unity of the Holy Spirit, God, world without end. *S.* Amen.

FINAL PRAYERS

The Priest turns again to the people, and says:

P. The Lord be with you. *S.* And with your spirit.
P. Let us bless the Lord. *S.* Thanks be to God.

MAY the tribute of my worship be pleasing to You, Most Holy Trinity, and grant that the sacrifice which I, all unworthy, have offered in the presence of Your Majesty, may be acceptable to You, and through Your mercy obtain forgiveness for me and all for whom I have offered it. Through Christ our Lord. Amen.

THE LAST BLESSING

He kisses the altar, and facing the people, says:

MAY almighty God bless you: ✠ the Father, and the Son, and the Holy Spirit.

S. Amen.

The Last Gospel and Prayers after Low Mass are conveniently placed inside the back cover.

While in prison, John sent two of His disciples to Christ.

SECOND SUNDAY OF ADVENT

In today's Liturgy we encounter an instant invitation to the virtue of Hope. Our hearts should be filled with joy at the thought that our Lord came to save all the nations of the world. According to St. Paul, all the sacred writers were inspired by our Lord to encourage the virtue of Hope. (PURPLE VESTMENTS)

PRAYERS AT THE FOOT OF THE ALTAR

IN THE name of the Father, ✠ and of the Son, and of the Holy Spirit. Amen.

Priest. I will go in to the altar of God.

Server. The God of my gladness and joy.

Psalm 42

DO ME justice, O God, and fight my fight against a faithless people; from the deceitful and impious man rescue me.

S. For You, O God, are my strength. Why do You keep me so far away? Why must I go about in mourning, with the enemy oppressing me?

P. Send forth Your light and Your fidelity; they shall lead me on and bring me to Your holy mountain, to Your dwelling-place.

S. Then will I go in to the altar of God, the God of my gladness and joy.
P. Then will I give You thanks upon the harp, O God, my God. Why are you so downcast, O my soul? Why do you sigh within me?
S. Hope in God! For I shall again be thanking Him in the presence of my Savior and my God.
P. Glory be to the Father, and to the Son, and to the Holy Spirit.
S. As it was in the beginning, is now, and ever shall be, world without end. Amen.
P. I will go in to the altar of God.
S. The God of my gladness and joy.
P. Our help ✠ is in the name of the Lord.
S. Who made heaven and earth.
P. I confess to almighty God, etc.
S. May almighty God have mercy on you, forgive you your sins, and bring you to life everlasting.
P. Amen.

The Server, bowing, says the "Confiteor."

I CONFESS to almighty God, to Blessed Mary, ever Virgin, to Blessed Michael the Archangel, to Blessed John the Baptist, to the Holy Apostles Peter and Paul, and to all the Saints, and to you, Father, that I have sinned exceedingly in thought, word and deed, *through my fault, through my fault, through my most grievous fault.* Therefore I beseech Blessed Mary, ever Virgin, Blessed Michael the Archangel, Blessed John the Baptist, the Holy Apostles Peter and Paul, and all the Saints, and you, Father, to pray to the Lord our God for me.
P. May almighty God have mercy on you, forgive you your sins, and bring you to life everlasting.
S. Amen.

MAY the almighty and merciful Lord grant us pardon, ✠ absolution, and remission of our sins. *S.* Amen.

P. Will You not, O God, give us life?
S. And shall not Your people rejoice in You?
P. Show us, O Lord, Your kindness.
S. And grant us Your salvation.
P. O Lord, hear my prayer.
S. And let my cry come to You.
P. The Lord be with you.
S. And with your spirit. *P.* Let us pray.

Going up to the altar, the Priest prays silently:

TAKE away from us our sins, O Lord, we beseech You, that we may enter with pure minds into the Holy of Holies. Through Christ our Lord. Amen.

WE BESEECH You, O Lord, by the merits of Your Saints (*he kisses the altar*) whose relics lie here, and of all the Saints: deign in Your mercy to pardon me all my sins. Amen.

THE INTROIT • Isa. 30, 30

At the right side of the altar, the Priest says:

PEOPLE of Sion, behold the Lord shall come to save the nations; and the Lord shall make the glory of His voice to be heard, in the joy of your heart. *Ps.* 79. O Shepherd of Israel, hearken, O Guide of the flock of Joseph! Glory be to the Father, and to the Son, and to the Holy Spirit. As it was in the beginning, is now, and ever shall be, world without end. Amen. — People of Sion, behold the Lord shall come to save the nations; and the Lord shall make the glory of His voice to be heard, in the joy of your heart.

THE KYRIE

P. Lord, have mercy. *S.* Lord, have mercy. *P.* Lord, have mercy. *S.* Christ, have mercy. *P.* Christ, have mercy. *S.* Christ, have mercy. *P.* Lord, have mercy. *S.* Lord, have mercy. *P.* Lord, have mercy.

The Priest kisses the altar and turns to the people, saying:

P. The Lord be with you. S. And with your spirit. *P.* Let us pray.

THE PRAYER

Going to the right (Epistle) side, he says:

STIR up our hearts, O Lord, to prepare the ways of Your Only-begotten Son, that we may attain to serve You with purified minds, through His advent. Who with You lives and reigns in the unity of the Holy Spirit, God, world without end. S. Amen.

THE EPISTLE • Rom. 15, 4-13

BRETHREN: Whatever things have been written have been written for our instruction, that through the patience and the consolation afforded by the Scriptures we may have hope. May then the God of patience and of comfort grant you to be of one mind toward one another according to Jesus Christ; that, one in spirit, you may with one mouth glorify the God and Father of our Lord Jesus Christ. Wherefore receive one another, even as Christ has received you to the honor of God. For I say that Christ Jesus has been a minister of the circumcision in order to show God's fidelity in confirming the promises made to our fathers, but that the Gentiles glorify God because of His mercy, as it is written, "Therefore will I praise You among the Gentiles, and will sing to Your name." And again He says, "Rejoice, you Gentiles, with His people." And again, "Praise the Lord, all you Gentiles; and sing His praises, all you peoples." And again Isaias says, "There shall be the root of Jesse, and He Who shall arise to rule the Gentiles . . . in Him the Gentiles shall hope." Now may the God of hope fill you with all joy and peace in believing, that you may abound in hope and in the power of the Holy Spirit. *S.* Thanks be to God.

THE GRADUAL • Ps. 49, 2-3. 5

FROM Sion, perfect in beauty, God shines forth. ℣. Gather His faithful ones before Him, those who have made a covenant with Him by sacrifice.

Alleluia, alleluia. ℣. *Ps. 121, 1.* I rejoiced because they said to me: "We will go up to the house of the Lord." Alleluia.

PRAYER BEFORE THE GOSPEL

Bowing down at the center of the altar, he says:

CLEANSE my heart and my lips, O almighty God, Who cleansed the lips of the Prophet Isaias with a burning coal. In Your gracious mercy deign so to purify me that I may worthily proclaim Your holy Gospel. Through Christ our Lord. Amen. Lord, grant Your blessing. The Lord be in my heart and on my lips, that I may worthily and fittingly proclaim His holy Gospel. Amen.

THE GOSPEL • Matt. 11, 2-10

Going to the left (Gospel) side of the altar, he says:

P. The Lord be with you. *S.* And with your spirit.
P. ✠ The continuation of the holy Gospel according to Saint Matthew. *S.* Glory be to You, O Lord.

AT THAT time, when John had heard in prison of the works of Christ, he sent two of his disciples to say to Him, "Are You He Who is to come, or shall we look for another?" And Jesus answering said to them, "Go and report to John what you have heard and seen: the blind see, the lame walk, the lepers are cleansed, the deaf hear, the dead rise, the poor have the gospel preached to them. And blessed is he who is not scandalized in Me." Then, as they went away, Jesus began to say to the crowds concerning John, "What did you go out to the desert to see? A reed shaken by the wind? But what did you go out to see? A man clothed in soft garments? Behold, those who wear soft garments are in the houses of kings. But what did you go out to see? A prophet? Yes, I tell you, and more than a prophet. This is he of whom it is written, 'Behold, I send my messenger before Your face, who shall make ready Your way before You.'" S. Praise be to You, O Christ.

P. By the words of the Gospel, may our sins be taken away.

THE NICENE CREED

At the center of the altar, he says:

I BELIEVE in one God, the Father almighty, Maker of heaven and earth, and of all things visible and invisible. And in one Lord Jesus Christ, the Only-begotten Son of God. Born of the Father before all ages. God of God; Light of Light; true God of true God. Begotten not made; of one being with the Father; by Whom all things were made. Who for us men, and for our salvation, came down from heaven. (*Here all genuflect.*) And was made Flesh by the Holy Spirit of the Virgin Mary: AND WAS MADE MAN. He was also crucified for us, suffered under Pontius Pilate and was buried.

And on the third day He rose again according to the Scriptures. And ascending into heaven, He sits at the right hand of the Father. And He shall come again in glory to judge the living and the dead; and of His kingdom there shall be no end. And I believe in the Holy Spirit, Lord and Giver of life, Who proceeds from the Father and the Son. Who together with the Father and the Son is no less adored, and glorified: Who spoke by the Prophets. And I believe in One, Holy, Catholic and Apostolic Church. I confess one Baptism for the remission of sins. And I look for the resurrection of the dead. ✠ And the life of the world to come. Amen.

THE OFFERTORY

The Priest turns to the people and says:

P. The Lord be with you. *S.* And with your spirit.
P. Let us pray.

THE OFFERTORY VERSE • Ps. 84, 7-8

WILL You not, O God, give us life; and shall not Your people rejoice in You? Show us, O Lord, Your kindness, and grant us Your salvation.

The Priest now uncovers the chalice, places the host on the paten and offering it up, says:

ACCEPT, O holy Father, almighty and eternal God, this spotless host, which I, Your unworthy servant, offer to You, my living and true God, to atone for my numberless sins, offenses, and negligences; on behalf of all here present and likewise for all faithful Christians living and dead, that it may profit me and them as a means of salvation to life everlasting. Amen.

He pours wine and water into the chalice, blessing the water before it is poured.

O GOD, Who established the nature of man in wondrous dignity, and still more admirably restored it, grant that through the mystery of this water and wine, we may be made partakers of His Divinity, Who has condescended to become partaker of our humanity, Jesus Christ, Your Son, our Lord. Who lives and reigns with You in the unity of the Holy Spirit, God, world without end. Amen.

Offering up the wine, the Priest says:

WE OFFER You, O Lord, the chalice of salvation, humbly begging of Your mercy that it may arise before Your Divine Majesty, with a pleasing fragrance, for our salvation and for that of the whole world. Amen.

Bowing down, the Priest says:

IN A humble spirit and with a contrite heart, may we be accepted by You, O Lord, and may our sacrifice so be offered in Your sight this day as to please You, O Lord God.

Raising his eyes and blessing the offering, he says:

COME, O Sanctifier, almighty and eternal God, and bless ✠ this sacrifice prepared for the glory of Your holy name.

WASHING THE FINGERS

I WASH my hands in innocence, and I go around Your altar, O Lord, giving voice to my thanks, and recounting all Your wondrous deeds. O Lord, I love the house in which You dwell, the tenting-place of Your glory. Gather not my soul with those of sinners, nor with men of blood my life. On their hands are crimes, and their right hands are full of bribes. But I walk in integrity; redeem me, and have pity on me. My foot stands on level ground; in the assemblies I will bless You, O Lord. Glory be to the Father, and to the Son, and to the Holy Spirit. As it was in the beginning, is now, and ever shall be, world without end. Amen.

ACCEPT, Most Holy Trinity, this offering which we are making to You in remembrance of the Passion, Resurrection, and Ascension of Jesus Christ, our Lord; and in honor of Blessed Mary, ever Virgin, Blessed John the Baptist, the Holy Apostles Peter and Paul, and of these, and of all the Saints; that it may add to their honor and aid our salvation; and may they deign to intercede in heaven for us who honor their memory here on earth. Through the same Christ our Lord. Amen.

The Priest turns toward the people and says:

Pray, brethren, that my sacrifice and yours may become acceptable to God the Father almighty.

S. May the Lord accept this sacrifice from your hands to the praise and glory of His name, for our advantage, and that of all His holy Church.

P. Amen.

THE SECRET

BE APPEASED, we beseech You, O Lord, by the prayers and offerings of our humility; and where no merit can avail, You Yourself help us with Your aid. Through our Lord Jesus Christ, Your Son, Who lives and reigns with You in the unity of the Holy Spirit, God.

P. World without end. S. Amen.

PREFACE—CANON

P. The Lord be with you. *S.* And with your spirit.
P. Lift up your hearts.
S. We have lifted them up to the Lord.
P. Let us give thanks to the Lord, our God.
S. It is fitting and just.

IT IS fitting indeed and just, right and helpful to salvation, for us always and everywhere to give thanks to You, O holy Lord, Father almighty, everlasting God, Who with Your Only-begotten Son and the Holy Spirit are one God, one Lord; not in the unity of a single person, but in the trinity of a single nature. For that which we believe on Your revelation concerning Your glory, that same we believe of Your Son, that same of the Holy Spirit, without difference or discrimination. So that in confessing the true and everlasting Godhead, we shall adore distinction in Persons, oneness in being, and equality in Majesty. This the Angels and Archangels, the Cherubim, too, and the Seraphim do praise; day by day they cease not to cry out as with one voice, saying (*the bell is rung* 3 *times*):

HOLY, HOLY, HOLY, Lord God of Hosts. Heaven and earth are filled with Your glory. Hosanna in the highest. ✠ Blessed is He Who comes in the name of the Lord. Hosanna in the highest.

THE CANON OF THE MASS

THEREFORE, most gracious Father, we humbly beg of You and entreat You through Jesus Christ Your Son, our Lord, (*he kisses the altar*) to deem acceptable and bless these ✠ gifts, these ✠ offerings, these ✠ holy and unspotted oblations

which, in the first place, we offer You for Your Holy Catholic Church, that You would deign to give her peace and protection, to unite and guard her throughout the world, together with Your servant N., our Pope, and N., our Bishop; and all true believers who cherish the Catholic and Apostolic Faith.

Commemoration of the Living

REMEMBER, O Lord, Your servants and handmaids, N. and N., (*name them*) and all here present, whose faith and devotion are known to You, on whose behalf we offer to You, or who themselves offer to You, this sacrifice of praise for themselves, families and friends, for the good of their souls, for their hope of salvation and deliverance from all harm, and who offer their homage to You, eternal, living and true God.

Commemoration of the Saints

IN THE unity of holy fellowship we observe the memory, first of all, of the glorious and ever Virgin Mary, Mother of our Lord and God Jesus Christ; next, that of Your Blessed Apostles and Martyrs, Peter and Paul, Andrew, James, John, Thomas, James, Philip, Bartholomew, Matthew, Simon and Thaddeus; of Linus, Cletus, Clement, Sixtus, Cornelius, Cyprian, Lawrence, Chrysogonus, John and Paul, Cosmas and Damian, and of all Your Saints, by whose merits and prayers grant that we may be always fortified by the help of Your protection. Through the same Christ our Lord. Amen.

Spreading his hands over the oblation, he says:

GRACIOUSLY accept, then, we beseech You, O Lord, this service of our worship and that

of all Your household. Provide that our days be spent in Your peace, save us from everlasting damnation, and cause us to be numbered in the flock You have chosen. Through Christ our Lord. Amen.

O GOD, deign to bless ✠ what we offer, and make it approved, ✠ effective, ✠ right, and wholly pleasing in every way, that it may become for our good, the Body ✠ and Blood ✠ of Your dearly beloved Son, Jesus Christ our Lord.

CONSECRATION—ELEVATION

WHO, the day before He suffered, took bread into His holy and venerable hands, and having raised His eyes to heaven, to You, O God, His almighty Father, giving thanks to You, He blessed it, ✠ broke it, and gave it to His disciples, saying: All of you take and eat of this:

FOR THIS IS MY BODY.

IN LIKE manner, when the supper was done, taking also this goodly chalice into His holy and venerable hands, again giving thanks to You, He blessed ✠ it, and gave it to His disciples, saying: All of you take and drink of this:

FOR THIS IS THE CHALICE OF MY BLOOD OF THE NEW AND ETERNAL COVENANT: THE MYSTERY OF FAITH: WHICH SHALL BE SHED FOR YOU AND FOR MANY UNTO THE FORGIVENESS OF SINS.

After replacing the chalice on the corporal, he says:

As often as you shall do these things, in memory of Me shall you do them.

Offering of the Victim

MINDFUL, therefore, O Lord, not only of the blessed Passion of the same Christ, Your Son, our Lord, but also of His Resurrection from the dead, and finally His glorious Ascension into heaven, we, Your ministers, as also Your holy people, offer to Your supreme Majesty, of the gifts bestowed upon us, the pure ✠ Victim, the holy ✠ Victim, the all-perfect ✠ Victim: the holy ✠ Bread of life eternal and the Chalice ✠ of unending salvation.

AND this deign to regard with gracious and kindly attention and hold acceptable, as You deigned to accept the offerings of Abel, Your just servant, and the sacrifice of Abraham our patriarch, and that which Your chief priest Melchisedec offered to You, a holy sacrifice and a spotless victim.

MOST humbly we implore You, almighty God, bid these offerings to be brought by the hands of Your holy angel to Your altar above; before the face of Your Divine Majesty; that those of us who, by sharing in the Sacrifice of this altar, shall receive the Most Sacred ✠ Body and ✠ Blood of Your Son, may be filled with every grace and heavenly blessing. Through the same Christ our Lord. Amen.

Commemoration of the Dead

REMEMBER also, O Lord, Your servants and handmaids, N. and N., who have gone before us with the sign of faith, and rest in the sleep of peace. (*Here pray for the dead.*) To these, O Lord, and to all who rest in Christ, we beseech You to grant of Your goodness, a place of comfort, light

and peace. Through the same Christ our Lord. Amen.

TO US sinners also, Your servants, trusting in the greatness of Your mercy, deign to grant some part and fellowship with Your Holy Apostles and Martyrs: with John, Stephen, Matthias, Barnabas, Ignatius, Alexander, Marcellinus, Peter, Felicitas, Perpetua, Agatha, Lucy, Agnes, Cecilia, Anastasia, and all Your Saints; into whose company, we implore You to admit us, not weighing our merits, but freely granting us pardon. Through Christ our Lord.

THROUGH Whom, O Lord, You always create, ✠ sanctify, ✠ fill with life, ✠ bless, and bestow upon us all good things.

The Minor Elevation

THROUGH ✠ Him, and with ✠ Him, and in ✠ Him, is to You, God the Father ✠ almighty, in the unity of the Holy ✠ Spirit, all honor and glory, world without end. S. Amen.

THE COMMUNION AND THANKSGIVING

Let us pray. Prompted by saving precepts, and taught by Your divine teaching, we dare to say:

OUR FATHER, Who art in heaven, hallowed be Thy name: Thy kingdom come: Thy will be done on earth as it is in heaven. Give us this day our daily bread; and forgive us our trespasses, as we forgive those who trespass against us. And lead us not into temptation: S. But deliver us from evil. P. Amen.

DELIVER us, we beseech You, O Lord, from all evils, past, present, and to come; and by

the intercession of the Blessed and glorious Mary, ever Virgin, Mother of God, together with Your Blessed Apostles Peter and Paul, and Andrew, and all the Saints, grant of Your goodness, peace in our days, that aided by the riches of Your mercy, we may be always free from sin and safe from all disturbance.

Through the same our Lord Jesus Christ, Your Son, Who lives and reigns with You in the unity of the Holy Spirit, God, world without end.
S. Amen.
P. May the peace ✠ of the Lord be ✠ always with ✠ you.
S. And with your spirit.

The Priest puts a small particle into the chalice, saying:

May this mingling and consecration of the Body and Blood of our Lord Jesus Christ help us who receive it to life everlasting. Amen.

LAMB of God, You Who take away the sins of the world, have mercy on us.
Lamb of God, You Who take away the sins of the world, have mercy on us.
Lamb of God, You Who take away the sins of the world, grant us peace.

PRAYERS BEFORE HOLY COMMUNION

Then inclining toward the altar, he says:

O LORD Jesus Christ, Who said to Your Apostles: "Peace I leave with you, My peace I give to you," regard not my sins but the faith of Your Church, and deign to give her peace and unity according to Your Will: Who live and reign, God, world without end. Amen.

O LORD Jesus Christ, Son of the living God, Who, by the will of the Father, with the co-operation of the Holy Spirit, have by Your death given life to the world, deliver me by this Your Most Sacred Body and Blood from all my sins and from every evil. Make me always cling to Your commandments, and never permit me to be separated from You. Who with the same God the Father and the Holy Spirit, live and reign, God, world without end. Amen.

LET not the partaking of Your Body, O Lord Jesus Christ, which I, though unworthy, presume to receive, turn to my judgment and condemnation; but through Your goodness, may it become a safeguard and an effective remedy, both of soul and body. Who live and reign with God the Father, in the unity of the Holy Spirit, God, world without end. Amen.

COMMUNION OF THE PRIEST

I WILL take the Bread of heaven, and call upon the name of the Lord.

Lord, I am not worthy that You should come under my roof; but only say the word, and my soul will be healed. (3 *times.*)

Making the Sign of the Cross with the Host, he says:

MAY the Blood of our Lord Jesus Christ preserve my soul to life everlasting. Amen.

What return shall I make to the Lord for all He has given me? I will take the Chalice of salvation, and I will call upon the name of the Lord. Praising will I call upon the Lord and I shall be saved from my enemies.

Making the Sign of the Cross with the chalice, he says:

MAY the Blood of our Lord Jesus Christ preserve my soul to life everlasting. Amen.

The Priest reverently consumes the Precious Blood.

COMMUNION OF THE FAITHFUL

The Server and people say the "Confiteor."

P. May almighty God have mercy on you, forgive you your sins, and bring you to life everlasting. *S.* Amen.

P. May the almighty and merciful Lord grant you pardon, ✠ absolution and remission of your sins. *S.* Amen.

Holding up a Sacred Host, the Priest says:

Behold the Lamb of God, behold Him Who takes away the sins of the world.

Lord, I am not worthy that You should come under my roof; but only say the word, and my soul will be healed. (3 *times.*)

The Priest says to each communicant:

May the Body of our Lord Jesus Christ preserve your soul to life everlasting. Amen.

The Priest purifies the chalice with wine, saying:

WHAT has passed our lips as food, O Lord, may we possess in purity of heart, that what is given to us in time, be our healing for eternity.

He purifies his fingers with wine and water, saying:

MAY Your Body, O Lord, which I have eaten, and Your Blood which I have drunk, cleave to my very soul, and grant that no trace of sin be found in me, whom these pure and holy mysteries have renewed. Who live and reign, world without end. Amen.

THE COMMUNION • Bar. 5, 5; 4, 36

ARISE, O Jerusalem, and stand on high; and behold the joy that comes to you from your God.

The Priest, turning to the people, says:

P. The Lord be with you. *S.* And with your spirit.
P. Let us pray.

THE POSTCOMMUNION

FILLED with the food of this spiritual nourishment, we suppliantly entreat You, O Lord, that by participation in this mystery You would teach us to despise earthly things, and to love those of heaven. Through our Lord Jesus Christ, Your Son, Who lives and reigns with You in the unity of the Holy Spirit, God, world without end. *S.* Amen.

FINAL PRAYERS

The Priest turns again to the people, and says:

P. The Lord be with you. *S.* And with your spirit.
P. Let us bless the Lord. *S.* Thanks be to God.

MAY the tribute of my worship be pleasing to You, Most Holy Trinity, and grant that the sacrifice which I, all unworthy, have offered in the presence of Your Majesty, may be acceptable to You, and through Your mercy obtain forgiveness for me and all for whom I have offered it. Through Christ our Lord. Amen.

THE LAST BLESSING

He kisses the altar, and facing the people, says:

MAY almighty God bless you: ✠ the Father, and the Son, and the Holy Spirit. *S.* Amen.

The Last Gospel and Prayers after Low Mass are conveniently placed inside the back cover.

"I am the voice of one crying in the desert."

THIRD SUNDAY OF ADVENT

On this *Gaudete* (Rejoice) Sunday, we are invited to spiritual joy, for "the Lord is near"; but we are also warned like the Pharisees to whom St. John the Baptist said: "In the midst of you there has stood One Whom you do not know." (PURPLE OR ROSE VESTMENTS)

PRAYERS AT THE FOOT OF THE ALTAR

IN THE name of the Father, ✠ and of the Son, and of the Holy Spirit. Amen.

Priest. I will go in to the altar of God.

Server. The God of my gladness and joy.

Psalm 42

DO ME justice, O God, and fight my fight against a faithless people; from the deceitful and impious man rescue me.

S. For You, O God, are my strength. Why do You keep me so far away? Why must I go about in mourning, with the enemy oppressing me?

P. Send forth Your light and Your fidelity; they shall lead me on and bring me to Your holy mountain, to Your dwelling-place.

S. Then will I go in to the altar of God, the God of my gladness and joy.
P. Then will I give You thanks upon the harp, O God, my God. Why are you so downcast, O my soul? Why do you sigh within me?
S. Hope in God! For I shall again be thanking Him in the presence of my Savior and my God.
P. Glory be to the Father, and to the Son, and to the Holy Spirit.
S. As it was in the beginning, is now, and ever shall be, world without end. Amen.
P. I will go in to the altar of God.
S. The God of my gladness and joy.
P. Our help ✠ is in the name of the Lord.
S. Who made heaven and earth.
P. I confess to almighty God, etc.
S. May almighty God have mercy on you, forgive you your sins, and bring you to life everlasting.
P. Amen.

The Server, bowing, says the "Confiteor."

I CONFESS to almighty God, to Blessed Mary, ever Virgin, to Blessed Michael the Archangel, to Blessed John the Baptist, to the Holy Apostles Peter and Paul, and to all the Saints, and to you, Father, that I have sinned exceedingly in thought, word and deed, *through my fault, through my fault, through my most grievous fault.* Therefore I beseech Blessed Mary, ever Virgin, Blessed Michael the Archangel, Blessed John the Baptist, the Holy Apostles Peter and Paul, and all the Saints, and you, Father, to pray to the Lord our God for me.
P. May almighty God have mercy on you, forgive you your sins, and bring you to life everlasting.
S. Amen.

MAY the almighty and merciful Lord grant us pardon, ✠ absolution, and remission of our sins. *S.* Amen.
P. Will You not, O God, give us life?
S. And shall not Your people rejoice in You?
P. Show us, O Lord, Your kindness.
S. And grant us Your salvation.
P. O Lord, hear my prayer.
S. And let my cry come to You.
P. The Lord be with you.
S. And with your spirit. *P.* Let us pray.

Going up to the altar, the Priest prays silently:

TAKE away from us our sins, O Lord, we beseech You, that we may enter with pure minds into the Holy of Holies. Through Christ our Lord. Amen.

WE BESEECH You, O Lord, by the merits of Your Saints (*he kisses the altar*) whose relics lie here, and of all the Saints: deign in Your mercy to pardon me all my sins. Amen.

THE INTROIT • Phil. 4, 4-6

At the right side of the altar, the Priest says:

REJOICE in the Lord always: again I say, rejoice. Let your moderation be known to all men: for the Lord is near. Have no anxiety, but in everything, by prayer let your petitions be made known to God. *Ps. 84.* You have favored, O Lord, Your land; You have restored the well-being of Jacob. Glory be to the Father, and to the Son, and to the Holy Spirit. As it was in the beginning, is now, and ever shall be, world without end. Amen. — Rejoice in the Lord always: again I say, rejoice. Let your moderation be known to all men: for the

Lord is near. Have no anxiety, but in everything, by prayer let your petitions be made known to God.

THE KYRIE

P. Lord, have mercy. *S*. Lord, have mercy. *P*. Lord, have mercy. *S*. Christ, have mercy. *P*. Christ, have mercy. *S*. Christ, have mercy. *P*. Lord, have mercy. *S*. Lord, have mercy. *P*. Lord, have mercy.

The Priest kisses the altar and turns to the people, saying:

P. The Lord be with you. *S*. And with your spirit. *P*. Let us pray.

THE PRAYER

Going to the right (Epistle) side, he says:

INCLINE Your ear to our prayers, we beseech You, O Lord, and brighten the darkness of our minds by the grace of Your visitation. Who live and reign with God the Father, in the unity of the Holy Spirit, God, world without end. *S*. Amen.

THE EPISTLE • Phil. 4, 4-7

BRETHREN: Rejoice in the Lord always; again I say, rejoice. Let your moderation be known to all men. The Lord is near. Have no anxiety, but in every prayer and supplication with thanksgiving let your petitions be made known to God. And may the peace of God which surpasses all understanding guard your hearts and your minds in Christ Jesus, our Lord. *S*. Thanks be to God.

THE GRADUAL • Ps. 79, 2. 3. 2

FROM Your throne, O Lord, upon the Cherubim, rouse Your power, and come. ℣. O Shepherd of Israel, hearken, O Guide of the flock of Joseph!

Alleluia, alleluia. ℣. Rouse, O Lord, Your power, and come to save us. Alleluia.

PRAYER BEFORE THE GOSPEL

Bowing down at the center of the altar, he says:

CLEANSE my heart and my lips, O almighty God, Who cleansed the lips of the Prophet Isaias with a burning coal. In Your gracious mercy deign so to purify me that I may worthily proclaim Your holy Gospel. Through Christ our Lord. Amen.

Lord, grant Your blessing. The Lord be in my heart and on my lips, that I may worthily and fittingly proclaim His holy Gospel. Amen.

THE GOSPEL • John 1, 19-28

Going to the left (Gospel) side of the altar, he says:

P. The Lord be with you. *S.* And with your spirit.
P. ✠ The continuation of the holy Gospel according to Saint John. *S.* Glory be to You, O Lord.

AT THAT time, the Jews sent to John from Jerusalem priests and Levites to ask him, "Who are you?" And he acknowledged and did not deny; and he acknowledged, "I am not the Christ." And they asked him, "What then? Are you Elias?" And he said, "I am not." "Are you the Prophet?" And he answered, "No." They therefore said to him, "Who are you? that we may give an answer to those who sent us. What have you to say of yourself?" He said, "I am the voice of one crying in the desert, 'Make straight the way of the Lord,' as said Isaias the prophet." And they who had been sent were from among the Pharisees. And they asked him, and said to him, "Why, then, do you baptize, if you are not the Christ, nor Elias, nor the Prophet?" John said to them in answer, "I baptize with water; but in the midst of you there has stood One Whom you do not know. He it is Who is to come after me, Who has been set above me, the strap of Whose sandal I am not worthy to loose." These things took place at Bethany, beyond the Jordan, where John was baptizing. S. Praise be to You, O Christ.

P. By the words of the Gospel, may our sins be taken away.

THE NICENE CREED

At the center of the altar, he says:

I BELIEVE in one God, the Father almighty, Maker of heaven and earth, and of all things visible and invisible. And in one Lord Jesus Christ, the Only-begotten Son of God. Born of the Father before all ages. God of God; Light of Light; true God of true God. Begotten not made; of one being with the Father; by Whom all things were made. Who for us men, and for our salvation, came down from heaven. (*Here all genuflect.*) And was made Flesh by the Holy Spirit of the Virgin Mary: AND WAS MADE MAN. He was also crucified for us, suffered under Pontius Pilate and was buried. And on the third day He rose again according to the Scriptures. And ascending into heaven, He sits at the right hand of the Father. And He shall come again in glory to judge the living and the dead; and of His kingdom there shall be no end. And I believe in the Holy Spirit, Lord and Giver of life, Who proceeds from the Father and the Son. Who together with the Father and the Son is no less adored, and glorified: Who spoke by the Prophets. And I believe in One, Holy, Catholic and Apostolic Church. I confess one Baptism for the remission of sins. And I look for the resurrection of the dead. ✠ And the life of the world to come. Amen.

THE OFFERTORY

The Priest turns to the people and says:

P. The Lord be with you. *S.* And with your spirit.
P. Let us pray.

THE OFFERTORY VERSE • Ps. 84, 2

YOU have favored, O Lord, Your land; You have restored the well-being of Jacob. You have forgiven the guilt of Your people.

The Priest now uncovers the chalice, places the host on the paten and offering it up, says:

ACCEPT, O holy Father, almighty and eternal God, this spotless host, which I, Your unworthy servant, offer to You, my living and true God, to atone for my numberless sins, offenses, and negligences; on behalf of all here present and likewise for all faithful Christians living and dead, that it may profit me and them as a means of salvation to life everlasting. Amen.

He pours wine and water into the chalice, blessing the water before it is poured.

O GOD, Who established the nature of man in wondrous dignity, and still more admirably restored it, grant that through the mystery of this water and wine, we may be made partakers of His Divinity, Who has condescended to become partaker of our humanity, Jesus Christ, Your Son, our Lord. Who lives and reigns with You in the unity of the Holy Spirit, God, world without end. Amen.

Offering up the wine, the Priest says:

WE OFFER You, O Lord, the chalice of salvation, humbly begging of Your mercy that it may arise before Your Divine Majesty, with a pleasing fragrance, for our salvation and for that of the whole world. Amen.

Bowing down, the Priest says:

IN A humble spirit and with a contrite heart, may we be accepted by You, O Lord, and may our sacrifice so be offered in Your sight this day as to please You, O Lord God.

Raising his eyes and blessing the offering, he says:

COME, O Sanctifier, almighty and eternal God, and bless ✠ this sacrifice prepared for the glory of Your holy name.

WASHING THE FINGERS

I WASH my hands in innocence, and I go around Your altar, O Lord, giving voice to my thanks, and recounting all Your wondrous deeds. O Lord, I love the house in which You dwell, the tenting-place of Your glory. Gather not my soul with those of sinners, nor with men of blood my life. On their hands are crimes, and their right hands are full of bribes. But I walk in integrity; redeem me, and have pity on me. My foot stands on level ground; in the assemblies I will bless You, O Lord. Glory be to the Father, and to the Son, and to the Holy Spirit. As it was in the beginning, is now, and ever shall be, world without end. Amen.

ACCEPT, Most Holy Trinity, this offering which we are making to You in remembrance of the Passion, Resurrection, and Ascension of Jesus Christ, our Lord; and in honor of Blessed Mary, ever Virgin, Blessed John the Baptist, the Holy Apostles Peter and Paul, and of these, and of all the Saints; that it may add to their honor and aid our salvation; and may they deign to intercede in heaven for us who honor their memory here on earth. Through the same Christ our Lord. Amen.

The Priest turns toward the people and says:

Pray, brethren, that my sacrifice and yours may become acceptable to God the Father almighty.

S. May the Lord accept this sacrifice from your hands to the praise and glory of His name, for our advantage, and that of all His holy Church.
P. Amen.

THE SECRET

MAY the sacrifice of our devotion ever be offered up to You, O Lord, and both carry out the institution of this sacred mystery, and in us, wonderfully work Your salvation. Through our Lord Jesus Christ, Your Son, Who lives and reigns with You in the unity of the Holy Spirit, God.
P. World without end. S. Amen.

PREFACE—CANON

P. The Lord be with you. S. And with your spirit.
P. Lift up your hearts.
S. We have lifted them up to the Lord.
P. Let us give thanks to the Lord, our God.
S. It is fitting and just.

IT IS fitting indeed and just, right and helpful to salvation, for us always and everywhere to give thanks to You, O holy Lord, Father almighty, everlasting God, Who with Your Only-begotten Son and the Holy Spirit are one God, one Lord; not in the unity of a single person, but in the trinity of a single nature. For that which we believe on Your revelation concerning Your glory, that same we believe of Your Son, that same of the Holy Spirit, without difference or discrimination. So that in confessing the true and everlasting Godhead, we shall adore distinction in Persons, oneness in being, and equality in Majesty. This the Angels and Archangels, the Cherubim, too, and the Seraphim do praise; day by day they cease not to cry out as with one voice, saying (*the bell is rung* 3 *times*):

HOLY, HOLY, HOLY, Lord God of Hosts. Heaven and earth are filled with Your glory. Hosanna in the highest. ✠ Blessed is He Who comes in the name of the Lord. Hosanna in the highest.

THE CANON OF THE MASS

THEREFORE, most gracious Father, we humbly beg of You and entreat You through Jesus Christ Your Son, our Lord, (*he kisses the altar*) to deem acceptable and bless these ✠ gifts, these ✠ offerings, these ✠ holy and unspotted oblations which, in the first place, we offer You for Your Holy Catholic Church, that You would deign to give her peace and protection, to unite and guard her throughout the world, together with Your servant N., our Pope, and N., our Bishop; and all true believers who cherish the Catholic and Apostolic Faith.

Commemoration of the Living

REMEMBER, O Lord, Your servants and handmaids, N. *and* N., (*name them*) and all here present, whose faith and devotion are known to You, on whose behalf we offer to You, or who themselves offer to You, this sacrifice of praise for themselves, families and friends, for the good of their souls, for their hope of salvation and deliverance from all harm, and who offer their homage to You, eternal, living and true God.

Commemoration of the Saints

IN THE unity of holy fellowship we observe the memory, first of all, of the glorious and ever Virgin Mary, Mother of our Lord and God Jesus Christ; next, that of Your Blessed Apostles and Martyrs, Peter and Paul, Andrew, James, John, Thomas, James, Philip, Bartholomew, Matthew, Simon and Thaddeus; of Linus, Cletus, Clement, Sixtus, Cornelius, Cyprian, Lawrence, Chrysogonus, John and Paul, Cosmas and Damian, and of all Your Saints, by whose merits and prayers grant that we may be always fortified by the help of Your protection. Through the same Christ our Lord. Amen.

Spreading his hands over the oblation, he says:

GRACIOUSLY accept, then, we beseech You, O Lord, this service of our worship and that of all Your household. Provide that our days be spent in Your peace, save us from everlasting damnation, and cause us to be numbered in the flock You have chosen. Through Christ our Lord. Amen.

O GOD, deign to bless ✠ what we offer, and make it approved, ✠ effective, ✠ right, and wholly pleasing in every way, that it may become for our good, the Body ✠ and Blood ✠ of Your dearly beloved Son, Jesus Christ our Lord.

CONSECRATION—ELEVATION

WHO, the day before He suffered, took bread into His holy and venerable hands, and having raised His eyes to heaven, to You, O God, His almighty Father, giving thanks to You, He blessed it, ✠ broke it, and gave it to His disciples, saying: All of you take and eat of this:

FOR THIS IS MY BODY.

IN LIKE manner, when the supper was done, taking also this goodly chalice into His holy and venerable hands, again giving thanks to You, He blessed ✠ it, and gave it to His disciples, saying: All of you take and drink of this:

FOR THIS IS THE CHALICE OF MY BLOOD OF THE NEW AND ETERNAL COVENANT: THE MYSTERY OF FAITH: WHICH SHALL BE SHED FOR YOU AND FOR MANY UNTO THE FORGIVENESS OF SINS.

After replacing the chalice on the corporal, he says:

As often as you shall do these things, in memory of Me shall you do them.

Offering of the Victim

MINDFUL, therefore, O Lord, not only of the blessed Passion of the same Christ, Your Son, our Lord, but also of His Resurrection from the dead, and finally His glorious Ascension into heav-

en, we, Your ministers, as also Your holy people, offer to Your supreme Majesty, of the gifts bestowed upon us, the pure ✠ Victim, the holy ✠ Victim, the all-perfect ✠ Victim: the holy ✠ Bread of life eternal and the Chalice ✠ of unending salvation.

AND this deign to regard with gracious and kindly attention and hold acceptable, as You deigned to accept the offerings of Abel, Your just servant, and the sacrifice of Abraham our patriarch, and that which Your chief priest Melchisedec offered to You, a holy sacrifice and a spotless victim.

MOST humbly we implore You, almighty God, bid these offerings to be brought by the hands of Your holy angel to Your altar above; before the face of Your Divine Majesty; that those of us who, by sharing in the Sacrifice of this altar, shall receive the Most Sacred ✠ Body and ✠ Blood of Your Son, may be filled with every grace and heavenly blessing. Through the same Christ our Lord. Amen.

Commemoration of the Dead

REMEMBER also, O Lord, Your servants and handmaids, N. and N., who have gone before us with the sign of faith, and rest in the sleep of peace. (*Here pray for the dead.*) To these, O Lord, and to all who rest in Christ, we beseech You to grant of Your goodness, a place of comfort, light and peace. Through the same Christ our Lord. Amen.

TO US sinners also, Your servants, trusting in the greatness of Your mercy, deign to grant some part and fellowship with Your Holy Apostles and

Martyrs: with John, Stephen, Matthias, Barnabas, Ignatius, Alexander, Marcellinus, Peter, Felicitas, Perpetua, Agatha, Lucy, Agnes, Cecilia, Anastasia, and all Your Saints; into whose company, we implore You to admit us, not weighing our merits, but freely granting us pardon. Through Christ our Lord.

THROUGH Whom, O Lord, You always create, ✠ sanctify, ✠ fill with life, ✠ bless, and bestow upon us all good things.

The Minor Elevation

THROUGH ✠ Him, and with ✠ Him, and in ✠ Him, is to You, God the Father ✠ almighty, in the unity of the Holy ✠ Spirit, all honor and glory, world without end. S. Amen.

THE COMMUNION AND THANKSGIVING

Let us pray. Prompted by saving precepts, and taught by Your divine teaching, we dare to say:

OUR FATHER, Who art in heaven, hallowed be Thy name: Thy kingdom come: Thy will be done on earth as it is in heaven. Give us this day our daily bread; and forgive us our trespasses, as we forgive those who trespass against us. And lead us not into temptation: S. But deliver us from evil. *P.* Amen.

DELIVER us, we beseech You, O Lord, from all evils, past, present, and to come; and by the intercession of the Blessed and glorious Mary, ever Virgin, Mother of God, together with Your Blessed Apostles Peter and Paul, and Andrew, and all the Saints, grant of Your goodness, peace in our

days, that aided by the riches of Your mercy, we may be always free from sin and safe from all disturbance.

Through the same our Lord Jesus Christ, Your Son, Who lives and reigns with You in the unity of the Holy Spirit, God, world without end.

S. Amen.

P. May the peace ✠ of the Lord be ✠ always with ✠ you.

S. And with your spirit.

The Priest puts a small particle into the chalice, saying:

May this mingling and consecration of the Body and Blood of our Lord Jesus Christ help us who receive it to life everlasting. Amen.

LAMB of God, You Who take away the sins of the world, have mercy on us.

Lamb of God, You Who take away the sins of the world, have mercy on us.

Lamb of God, You Who take away the sins of the world, grant us peace.

PRAYERS BEFORE HOLY COMMUNION

Then inclining toward the altar, he says:

O LORD Jesus Christ, Who said to Your Apostles: "Peace I leave with you, My peace I give to you," regard not my sins but the faith of Your Church, and deign to give her peace and unity according to Your Will: Who live and reign, God, world without end. Amen.

O LORD Jesus Christ, Son of the living God, Who, by the will of the Father, with the co-

operation of the Holy Spirit, have by Your death given life to the world, deliver me by this Your Most Sacred Body and Blood from all my sins and from every evil. Make me always cling to Your commandments, and never permit me to be separated from You. Who with the same God the Father and the Holy Spirit, live and reign, God, world without end. Amen.

LET not the partaking of Your Body, O Lord Jesus Christ, which I, though unworthy, presume to receive, turn to my judgment and condemnation; but through Your goodness, may it become a safeguard and an effective remedy, both of soul and body. Who live and reign with God the Father, in the unity of the Holy Spirit, God, world without end. Amen.

COMMUNION OF THE PRIEST

I WILL take the Bread of heaven, and call upon the name of the Lord.

Lord, I am not worthy that You should come under my roof; but only say the word, and my soul will be healed. (3 *times.*)

Making the Sign of the Cross with the Host, he says:

MAY the Body of our Lord Jesus Christ preserve my soul to life everlasting. Amen.

What return shall I make to the Lord for all He has given me? I will take the Chalice of salvation, and I will call upon the name of the Lord. Praising will I call upon the Lord and I shall be saved from my enemies.

Making the Sign of the Cross with the chalice, he says:

MAY the Blood of our Lord Jesus Christ preserve my soul to life everlasting. Amen.

The Priest reverently consumes the Precious Blood.

COMMUNION OF THE FAITHFUL

The Server and people say the "Confiteor."

P. May almighty God have mercy on you, forgive you your sins, and bring you to life everlasting. S. Amen.

P. May the almighty and merciful Lord grant you pardon, ✠ absolution and remission of your sins. S. Amen.

Holding up a Sacred Host, the Priest says:

Behold the Lamb of God, behold Him Who takes away the sins of the world.

Lord, I am not worthy that You should come under my roof; but only say the word, and my soul will be healed. (3 *times*.)

The Priest says to each communicant:

May the Body of our Lord Jesus Christ preserve your soul to life everlasting. Amen.

The Priest purifies the chalice with wine, saying:

WHAT has passed our lips as food, O Lord, may we possess in purity of heart, that what is given to us in time, be our healing for eternity.

He purifies his fingers with wine and water, saying:

MAY Your Body, O Lord, which I have eaten, and Your Blood which I have drunk, cleave to my very soul, and grant that no trace of sin be found in me, whom these pure and holy mysteries have renewed. Who live and reign, world without end. Amen.

THE COMMUNION • Isa. 35, 4

SAY to the faint-hearted, "Take courage, and fear not; behold, our God will come and will save us."

The Priest, turning to the people, says:

P. The Lord be with you. *S.* And with your spirit.
P. Let us pray.

THE POSTCOMMUNION

WE ENTREAT Your mercy, O Lord, that these divine subsidies, having cleansed us from our vices, may prepare us for the coming festivities. Through our Lord Jesus Christ, Your Son, Who lives and reigns with You in the unity of the Holy Spirit, God, world without end. *S.* Amen.

FINAL PRAYERS

The Priest turns again to the people, and says:

P. The Lord be with you. *S.* And with your spirit.
P. Let us bless the Lord. *S.* Thanks be to God.

MAY the tribute of my worship be pleasing to You, Most Holy Trinity, and grant that the sacrifice which I, all unworthy, have offered in the presence of Your Majesty, may be acceptable to You, and through Your mercy obtain forgiveness for me and all for whom I have offered it. Through Christ our Lord. Amen.

THE LAST BLESSING

He kisses the altar, and facing the people, says:

MAY almighty God bless you: ✠ the Father, and the Son, and the Holy Spirit. *S.* Amen.

The Last Gospel and Prayers after Low Mass are conveniently placed inside the back cover.

John the Baptist preached a baptism of repentance.

FOURTH SUNDAY OF ADVENT

Only with an intense desire for the coming of Jesus Christ can we begin to merit His spiritual gifts. The Catholic Liturgy reminds us, during these four weeks, of the time during which the world was without Jesus. Since we can go to God only through this Mediator, we implore Him to come soon. (PURPLE VESTMENTS)

PRAYERS AT THE FOOT OF THE ALTAR

IN THE name of the Father, ✠ and of the Son, and of the Holy Spirit. Amen.

Priest. I will go in to the altar of God.

Server. The God of my gladness and joy.

Psalm 42

DO ME justice, O God, and fight my fight against a faithless people; from the deceitful and impious man rescue me.

S. For You, O God, are my strength. Why do You keep me so far away? Why must I go about in mourning, with the enemy oppressing me?

P. Send forth Your light and Your fidelity; they shall lead me on and bring me to Your holy mountain, to Your dwelling-place.

S. Then will I go in to the altar of God, the God of my gladness and joy.
P. Then will I give You thanks upon the harp, O God, my God. Why are you so downcast, O my soul? Why do you sigh within me?
S. Hope in God! For I shall again be thanking Him in the presence of my Savior and my God.
P. Glory be to the Father, and to the Son, and to the Holy Spirit.
S. As it was in the beginning, is now, and ever shall be, world without end. Amen.
P. I will go in to the altar of God.
S. The God of my gladness and joy.
P. Our help ✠ is in the name of the Lord.
S. Who made heaven and earth.
P. I confess to almighty God, etc.
S. May almighty God have mercy on you, forgive you your sins, and bring you to life everlasting.
P. Amen.

The Server, bowing, says the "Confiteor."

I CONFESS to almighty God, to Blessed Mary, ever Virgin, to Blessed Michael the Archangel, to Blessed John the Baptist, to the Holy Apostles Peter and Paul, and to all the Saints, and to you, Father, that I have sinned exceedingly in thought, word and deed, *through my fault, through my fault, through my most grievous fault.* Therefore I beseech Blessed Mary, ever Virgin, Blessed Michael the Archangel, Blessed John the Baptist, the Holy Apostles Peter and Paul, and all the Saints, and you, Father, to pray to the Lord our God for me.
P. May almighty God have mercy on you, forgive

you your sins, and bring you to life everlasting. *S.* Amen.

MAY the almighty and merciful Lord grant us pardon, ✠ absolution, and remission of our sins. *S.* Amen.

P. Will You not, O God, give us life?
S. And shall not Your people rejoice in You?
P. Show us, O Lord, Your kindness.
S. And grant us Your salvation.
P. O Lord, hear my prayer.
S. And let my cry come to You.
P. The Lord be with you.
S. And with your spirit. *P.* Let us pray.

Going up to the altar, the Priest prays silently:

TAKE away from us our sins, O Lord, we beseech You, that we may enter with pure minds into the Holy of Holies. Through Christ our Lord. Amen.

WE BESEECH You, O Lord, by the merits of Your Saints (*he kisses the altar*) whose relics lie here, and of all the Saints: deign in Your mercy to pardon me all my sins. Amen.

THE INTROIT • Isa. 45, 8

At the right side of the altar, the Priest says:

DROP down dew, you heavens, from above, and let the clouds rain the just: let the earth be opened, and bud forth a Savior. *Ps.* 18. The heavens declare the glory of God, and the firmament proclaims His handiwork. Glory be to the Father, and to the Son, and to the Holy Spirit. As it was in the beginning, is now, and ever shall be, world without end. Amen. — Drop down dew, you heavens, from above, and let the clouds rain the just: let the earth be opened, and bud forth a Savior.

THE KYRIE

P. Lord, have mercy. *S.* Lord, have mercy. *P.* Lord, have mercy. *S.* Christ, have mercy. *P.* Christ, have mercy. *S.* Christ, have mercy. *P.* Lord, have mercy. *S.* Lord, have mercy. *P.* Lord, have mercy.

The Priest kisses the altar and turns to the people, saying:

P. The Lord be with you. *S.* And with your spirit. *P.* Let us pray.

THE PRAYER

Going to the right (Epistle) side, he says:

STIR up Your power, we beseech You, O Lord, and come, and succor us with great might, that, by the help of Your grace, what is hindered by our sins, may be hastened by the bounty of Your mercy. Who live and reign with God the Father, in the unity of the Holy Spirit, God, world without end. *S.* Amen.

THE EPISTLE • 1 Cor. 4, 1-5

BRETHREN: Let a man so account us, as servants of Christ and stewards of the mysteries of God. Now here it is required in stewards that a man be found trustworthy. But with me it is a very small matter to be judged by you or by man's tribunal. Nay I do not even judge my own self. For I have nothing on my conscience, yet I am not thereby justified; but he who judges me is the Lord. Therefore, pass no judgment before the time, until the Lord comes, Who will both bring to light the things hidden in darkness and make manifest the counsels of hearts; and then everyone will have his praise from God. *S.* Thanks be to God.

THE GRADUAL • Ps. 144, 18. 21

THE Lord is near to all who call upon Him, to all who call upon Him in truth. ℣. May my mouth speak the praise of the Lord, and may all flesh bless His holy name.

Alleluia, alleluia. ℣. Come, O Lord, and delay not; forgive the sins of Your people Israel. Alleluia.

PRAYER BEFORE THE GOSPEL

Bowing down at the center of the altar, he says:

CLEANSE my heart and my lips, O almighty God, Who cleansed the lips of the Prophet Isaias with a burning coal. In Your gracious mercy deign so to purify me that I may worthily proclaim Your holy Gospel. Through Christ our Lord. Amen.

Lord, grant Your blessing. The Lord be in my heart and on my lips, that I may worthily and fittingly proclaim His holy Gospel. Amen.

THE GOSPEL • Luke 3, 1-6

Going to the left (Gospel) side of the altar, he says:

P. The Lord be with you. S. And with your spirit.

P. ✠ The continuation of the holy Gospel according to Saint Luke. S. Glory be to You, O Lord.

NOW in the fifteenth year of the reign of Tiberius Caesar, when Pontius Pilate was procurator of Judea, and Herod tetrarch of Galilee, and Philip his brother tetrarch of the district of Iturea and Trachonitis, and Lysanias tetrarch of Abilene, during the high priesthood of Annas and Caiphas, the word of God came to John, the son of Zachary, in the desert. And he went into all the region about the Jordan, preaching a baptism of repentance for the forgiveness of sins, as it is written in the book of the words of Isaias the prophet, "The voice of one crying in the desert, 'Make ready the way of the Lord, make straight His paths. Every valley shall be filled, and every mountain and hill shall be brought low, and the crooked ways shall be made straight, and the rough ways smooth; and all mankind shall see the salvation of God.'" S. Praise be to You, O Christ.

P. By the words of the Gospel, may our sins be taken away.

THE NICENE CREED

At the center of the altar, he says:

I BELIEVE in one God, the Father almighty, Maker of heaven and earth, and of all things visible and invisible. And in one Lord Jesus Christ, the Only-begotten Son of God. Born of the Father before all ages. God of God; Light of Light; true God of true God. Begotten not made; of one being with the Father; by Whom all things were made. Who for us men, and for our salvation, came down from heaven. (*Here all genuflect.*) And was made Flesh by the Holy Spirit of the Virgin Mary: AND WAS MADE MAN. He was also crucified for us, suffered under Pontius Pilate and was buried. And on the third day He rose again according to the Scriptures. And ascending into heaven, He sits at the right hand of the Father. And He shall come again in glory to judge the living and the dead; and of His kingdom there shall be no end. And I believe in the Holy Spirit, Lord and Giver of life, Who proceeds from the Father and the Son. Who together with the Father and the Son is no less adored, and glorified: Who spoke by

the Prophets. And I believe in One, Holy, Catholic and Apostolic Church. I confess one Baptism for the remission of sins. And I look for the resurrection of the dead. ✠ And the life of the world to come. Amen.

THE OFFERTORY

The Priest turns to the people and says:

P. The Lord be with you. S. And with your spirit.
P. Let us pray.

THE OFFERTORY VERSE • Luke 1, 28. 42

HAIL, Mary, full of grace, the Lord is with you; blessed are you among women, and blessed is the fruit of your womb.

The Priest now uncovers the chalice, places the host on the paten and offering it up, says:

ACCEPT, O holy Father, almighty and eternal God, this spotless host, which I, Your unworthy servant, offer to You, my living and true God, to atone for my numberless sins, offenses, and negligences; on behalf of all here present and likewise for all faithful Christians living and dead, that it may profit me and them as a means of salvation to life everlasting. Amen.

He pours wine and water into the chalice, blessing the water before it is poured.

O GOD, Who established the nature of man in wondrous dignity, and still more admirably restored it, grant that through the mystery of this water and wine, we may be made partakers of His Divinity, Who has condescended to become partaker of our humanity, Jesus Christ, Your Son, our

Lord. Who lives and reigns with You in the unity of the Holy Spirit, God, world without end. Amen.

Offering up the wine, the Priest says:

WE OFFER You, O Lord, the chalice of salvation, humbly begging of Your mercy that it may arise before Your Divine Majesty, with a pleasing fragrance, for our salvation and for that of the whole world. Amen.

Bowing down, the Priest says:

IN A humble spirit and with a contrite heart, may we be accepted by You, O Lord, and may our sacrifice so be offered in Your sight this day as to please You, O Lord God.

Raising his eyes and blessing the offering, he says:

COME, O Sanctifier, almighty and eternal God, and bless ✠ this sacrifice prepared for the glory of Your holy name.

WASHING THE FINGERS

I WASH my hands in innocence, and I go around Your altar, O Lord, giving voice to my thanks, and recounting all Your wondrous deeds. O Lord, I love the house in which You dwell, the tenting-place of Your glory. Gather not my soul with those of sinners, nor with men of blood my life. On their hands are crimes, and their right hands are full of bribes. But I walk in integrity; redeem me, and have pity on me. My foot stands on level ground; in the assemblies I will bless You, O Lord. Glory be to the Father, and to the Son, and to the Holy Spirit. As it was in the beginning, is now, and ever shall be, world without end. Amen.

ACCEPT, Most Holy Trinity, this offering which we are making to You in remembrance of the Passion, Resurrection, and Ascension of Jesus Christ, our Lord; and in honor of Blessed Mary, ever Virgin, Blessed John the Baptist, the Holy Apostles Peter and Paul, and of these, and of all the Saints; that it may add to their honor and aid our salvation; and may they deign to intercede in heaven for us who honor their memory here on earth. Through the same Christ our Lord. Amen.

The Priest turns toward the people and says:

Pray, brethren, that my sacrifice and yours may become acceptable to God the Father almighty.
S. May the Lord accept this sacrifice from your hands to the praise and glory of His name, for our advantage, and that of all His holy Church.
P. Amen.

THE SECRET

LOOK favorably on these sacrifices, we beseech You, O Lord, that they may profit us both for our devotion and our salvation. Through our Lord Jesus Christ, Your Son, Who lives and reigns with You in the unity of the Holy Spirit, God.
P. World without end. S. Amen.

PREFACE—CANON

P. The Lord be with you. S. And with your spirit.
P. Lift up your hearts.
S. We have lifted them up to the Lord.
P. Let us give thanks to the Lord, our God.
S. It is fitting and just.

IT IS fitting indeed and just, right and helpful to salvation, for us always and everywhere to give thanks to You, O holy Lord, Father almighty, everlasting God, Who with Your Only-begotten Son and the Holy Spirit are one God, one Lord; not in the unity of a single person, but in the trinity of a single nature. For that which we believe on Your revelation concerning Your glory, that same we believe of Your Son, that same of the Holy Spirit, without difference or discrimination. So that in confessing the true and everlasting Godhead, we shall adore distinction in Persons, oneness in being, and equality in Majesty. This the Angels and Archangels, the Cherubim, too, and the Seraphim do praise; day by day they cease not to cry out as with one voice, saying (*the bell is rung* 3 *times*):

HOLY, HOLY, HOLY, Lord God of Hosts. Heaven and earth are filled with Your glory. Hosanna in the highest. ✠ Blessed is He Who comes in the name of the Lord. Hosanna in the highest.

THE CANON OF THE MASS

THEREFORE, most gracious Father, we humbly beg of You and entreat You through Jesus Christ Your Son, our Lord, (*he kisses the altar*) to deem acceptable and bless these ✠ gifts, these ✠ offerings, these ✠ holy and unspotted oblations which, in the first place, we offer You for Your Holy Catholic Church, that You would deign to give her peace and protection, to unite and guard her throughout the world, together with Your serv-

ant N., our Pope, and N., our Bishop; and all true believers who cherish the Catholic and Apostolic Faith.

Commemoration of the Living

REMEMBER, O Lord, Your servants and handmaids, *N. and N.*, (*name them*) and all here present, whose faith and devotion are known to You, on whose behalf we offer to You, or who themselves offer to You, this sacrifice of praise for themselves, families and friends, for the good of their souls, for their hope of salvation and deliverance from all harm, and who offer their homage to You, eternal, living and true God.

Commemoration of the Saints

IN THE unity of holy fellowship we observe the memory, first of all, of the glorious and ever Virgin Mary, Mother of our Lord and God Jesus Christ; next, that of Your Blessed Apostles and Martyrs, Peter and Paul, Andrew, James, John, Thomas, James, Philip, Bartholomew, Matthew, Simon and Thaddeus; of Linus, Cletus, Clement, Sixtus, Cornelius, Cyprian, Lawrence, Chrysogonus, John and Paul, Cosmas and Damian, and of all Your Saints, by whose merits and prayers grant that we may be always fortified by the help of Your protection. Through the same Christ our Lord. Amen.

Spreading his hands over the oblation, he says:

GRACIOUSLY accept, then, we beseech You, O Lord, this service of our worship and that of all Your household. Provide that our days be spent in Your peace, save us from everlasting damnation, and cause us to be numbered in the flock You have chosen. Through Christ our Lord. Amen.

O GOD, deign to bless ✠ what we offer, and make it approved, ✠ effective, ✠ right, and wholly pleasing in every way, that it may become for our good, the Body ✠ and Blood ✠ of Your dearly beloved Son, Jesus Christ our Lord.

CONSECRATION—ELEVATION

WHO, the day before He suffered, took bread into His holy and venerable hands, and having raised His eyes to heaven, to You, O God, His almighty Father, giving thanks to You, He blessed it, ✠ broke it, and gave it to His disciples, saying: All of you take and eat of this:

FOR THIS IS MY BODY.

IN LIKE manner, when the supper was done, taking also this goodly chalice into His holy and venerable hands, again giving thanks to You, He blessed ✠ it, and gave it to His disciples, saying: All of you take and drink of this:

FOR THIS IS THE CHALICE OF MY BLOOD OF THE NEW AND ETERNAL COVENANT: THE MYSTERY OF FAITH: WHICH SHALL BE SHED FOR YOU AND FOR MANY UNTO THE FORGIVENESS OF SINS.

After replacing the chalice on the corporal, he says:

As often as you shall do these things, in memory of Me shall you do them.

Offering of the Victim

MINDFUL, therefore, O Lord, not only of the blessed Passion of the same Christ, Your Son, our Lord, but also of His Resurrection from the dead, and finally His glorious Ascension into heav-

en, we, Your ministers, as also Your holy people, offer to Your supreme Majesty, of the gifts bestowed upon us, the pure ✠ Victim, the holy ✠ Victim, the all-perfect ✠ Victim: the holy ✠ Bread of life eternal and the Chalice ✠ of unending salvation.

AND this deign to regard with gracious and kindly attention and hold acceptable, as You deigned to accept the offerings of Abel, Your just servant, and the sacrifice of Abraham our patriarch, and that which Your chief priest Melchisedec offered to You, a holy sacrifice and a spotless victim.

MOST humbly we implore You, almighty God, bid these offerings to be brought by the hands of Your holy angel to Your altar above; before the face of Your Divine Majesty; that those of us who, by sharing in the Sacrifice of this altar, shall receive the Most Sacred ✠ Body and ✠ Blood of Your Son, may be filled with every grace and heavenly blessing. Through the same Christ our Lord. Amen.

Commemoration of the Dead

REMEMBER also, O Lord, Your servants and handmaids, N. and N., who have gone before us with the sign of faith, and rest in the sleep of peace. (*Here pray for the dead.*) To these, O Lord, and to all who rest in Christ, we beseech You to grant of Your goodness, a place of comfort, light and peace. Through the same Christ our Lord. Amen.

TO US sinners also, Your servants, trusting in the greatness of Your mercy, deign to grant some part and fellowship with Your Holy Apostles and

Martyrs: with John, Stephen, Matthias, Barnabas, Ignatius, Alexander, Marcellinus, Peter, Felicitas, Perpetua, Agatha, Lucy, Agnes, Cecilia, Anastasia, and all Your Saints; into whose company, we implore You to admit us, not weighing our merits, but freely granting us pardon. Through Christ our Lord.

THROUGH Whom, O Lord, You always create, ✠ sanctify, ✠ fill with life, ✠ bless, and bestow upon us all good things.

The Minor Elevation

THROUGH ✠ Him, and with ✠ Him, and in ✠ Him, is to You, God the Father ✠ almighty, in the unity of the Holy ✠ Spirit, all honor and glory, world without end. S. Amen.

THE COMMUNION AND THANKSGIVING

Let us pray. Prompted by saving precepts, and taught by Your divine teaching, we dare to say:

OUR FATHER, Who art in heaven, hallowed be Thy name: Thy kingdom come: Thy will be done on earth as it is in heaven. Give us this day our daily bread; and forgive us our trespasses, as we forgive those who trespass against us. And lead us not into temptation: S. But deliver us from evil. *P.* Amen.

DELIVER us, we beseech You, O Lord, from all evils, past, present, and to come; and by the intercession of the Blessed and glorious Mary, ever Virgin, Mother of God, together with Your Blessed Apostles Peter and Paul, and Andrew, and all the Saints, grant of Your goodness, peace in our

days, that aided by the riches of Your mercy, we may be always free from sin and safe from all disturbance.
Through the same our Lord Jesus Christ, Your Son, Who lives and reigns with You in the unity of the Holy Spirit, God, world without end.
S. Amen.
P. May the peace ✠ of the Lord be ✠ always with ✠ you.
S. And with your spirit.

The Priest puts a small particle into the chalice, saying:

May this mingling and consecration of the Body and Blood of our Lord Jesus Christ help us who receive it to life everlasting. Amen.

LAMB of God, You Who take away the sins of the world, have mercy on us.

Lamb of God, You Who take away the sins of the world, have mercy on us.
Lamb of God, You Who take away the sins of the world, grant us peace.

PRAYERS BEFORE HOLY COMMUNION

Then inclining toward the altar, he says:

O LORD Jesus Christ, Who said to Your Apostles: "Peace I leave with you, My peace I give to you," regard not my sins but the faith of Your Church, and deign to give her peace and unity according to Your Will: Who live and reign, God, world without end. Amen.

O LORD Jesus Christ, Son of the living God, Who, by the will of the Father, with the co-

operation of the Holy Spirit, have by Your death given life to the world, deliver me by this Your Most Sacred Body and Blood from all my sins and from every evil. Make me always cling to Your commandments, and never permit me to be separated from You. Who with the same God the Father and the Holy Spirit, live and reign, God, world without end. Amen.

LET not the partaking of Your Body, O Lord Jesus Christ, which I, though unworthy, presume to receive, turn to my judgment and condemnation; but through Your goodness, may it become a safeguard and an effective remedy, both of soul and body. Who live and reign with God the Father, in the unity of the Holy Spirit, God, world without end. Amen.

COMMUNION OF THE PRIEST

I WILL take the Bread of heaven, and call upon the name of the Lord.

Lord, I am not worthy that You should come under my roof; but only say the word, and my soul will be healed. (3 *times.*)

Making the Sign of the Cross with the Host, he says:

MAY the Body of our Lord Jesus Christ preserve my soul to life everlasting. Amen.

What return shall I make to the Lord for all He has given me? I will take the Chalice of salvation, and I will call upon the name of the Lord. Praising will I call upon the Lord and I shall be saved from my enemies.

Making the Sign of the Cross with the chalice, he says:

MAY the Blood of our Lord Jesus Christ preserve my soul to life everlasting. Amen.

The Priest reverently consumes the Precious Blood.

COMMUNION OF THE FAITHFUL

The Server and people say the "Confiteor."

P. May almighty God have mercy on you, forgive you your sins, and bring you to life everlasting. S. Amen.

P. May the almighty and merciful Lord grant you pardon, ✠ absolution and remission of your sins. S. Amen.

Holding up a Sacred Host, the Priest says:

Behold the Lamb of God, behold Him Who takes away the sins of the world.

Lord, I am not worthy that You should come under my roof; but only say the word, and my soul will be healed. (3 *times.*)

The Priest says to each communicant:

May the Body of our Lord Jesus Christ preserve your soul to life everlasting. Amen.

The Priest purifies the chalice with wine, saying:

WHAT has passed our lips as food, O Lord, may we possess in purity of heart, that what is given to us in time, be our healing for eternity.

He purifies his fingers with wine and water, saying:

MAY Your Body, O Lord, which I have eaten, and Your Blood which I have drunk, cleave to my very soul, and grant that no trace of sin be found in me, whom these pure and holy mysteries have renewed. Who live and reign, world without end. Amen.

THE COMMUNION • Isa. 7, 14

BEHOLD, a virgin shall conceive, and bring forth a son, and His name shall be called Emmanuel.

The Priest, turning to the people, says:

P. The Lord be with you. *S.* And with your spirit.
P. Let us pray.

THE POSTCOMMUNION

HAVING received Your sacred gifts, we beseech You, O Lord, that our assistance at these mysteries may result in an increase of our salvation. Through our Lord Jesus Christ, Your Son, Who lives and reigns with You in the unity of the Holy Spirit, God, world without end. *S.* Amen.

FINAL PRAYERS

The Priest turns again to the people, and says:

P. The Lord be with you. *S.* And with your spirit.
P. Let us bless the Lord. *S.* Thanks be to God.

MAY the tribute of my worship be pleasing to You, Most Holy Trinity, and grant that the sacrifice which I, all unworthy, have offered in the presence of Your Majesty, may be acceptable to You, and through Your mercy obtain forgiveness for me and all for whom I have offered it. Through Christ our Lord. Amen.

THE LAST BLESSING

He kisses the altar, and facing the people, says:

MAY almighty God bless you: ✠ the Father, and the Son, and the Holy Spirit. *S.* Amen.

The Last Gospel and Prayers after Low Mass are conveniently placed inside the back cover.

"A Child Is Born to Us, and a Son Is Given to Us, Whose Government Is upon His Shoulder."

Isaias 9, 6.

CHRISTMAS DAY

Today the Church celebrates the Birth of the Word of God according to the flesh. In relatively recent times the three Masses on Christmas have symbolized respectively Christ's human birth from a Virgin, His spiritual birth in our souls and His eternal birth from the Father. (WHITE VESTMENTS)

PRAYERS AT THE FOOT OF THE ALTAR

IN THE name of the Father, ✠ and of the Son, and of the Holy Spirit. Amen.

Priest. I will go in to the altar of God.
Server. The God of my gladness and joy.

Psalm 42

DO ME justice, O God, and fight my fight against a faithless people; from the deceitful and impious man rescue me.

S. For You, O God, are my strength. Why do You keep me so far away? Why must I go about in mourning, with the enemy oppressing me?

P. Send forth Your light and Your fidelity; they shall lead me on and bring me to Your holy mountain, to Your dwelling-place.

S. Then will I go in to the altar of God, the God of my gladness and joy.

P. Then will I give You thanks upon the harp, O God, my God. Why are you so downcast, O my soul? Why do you sigh within me?

S. Hope in God! For I shall again be thanking Him in the presence of my Savior and my God.

P. Glory be to the Father, and to the Son, and to the Holy Spirit.

S. As it was in the beginning, is now, and ever shall be, world without end. Amen.

P. I will go in to the altar of God.
S. The God of my gladness and joy.
P. Our help ✠ is in the name of the Lord.
S. Who made heaven and earth.
P. I confess to almighty God, etc.
S. May almighty God have mercy on you, forgive you your sins, and bring you to life everlasting.
P. Amen.

The Server, bowing, says the "Confiteor."

I CONFESS to almighty God, to Blessed Mary, ever Virgin, to Blessed Michael the Archangel, to Blessed John the Baptist, to the Holy Apostles Peter and Paul, and to all the Saints, and to you, Father, that I have sinned exceedingly in thought, word and deed, *through my fault, through my fault, through my most grievous fault.* Therefore I beseech Blessed Mary, ever Virgin, Blessed Michael the Archangel, Blessed John the Baptist, the Holy Apostles Peter and Paul, and all the Saints, and you, Father, to pray to the Lord our God for me.
P. May almighty God have mercy on you, forgive you your sins, and bring you to life everlasting.
S. Amen.

MAY the almighty and merciful Lord grant us pardon, ✠ absolution, and remission of our sins. S. Amen.
P. Will You not, O God, give us life?
S. And shall not Your people rejoice in You?
P. Show us, O Lord, Your kindness.
S. And grant us Your salvation.
P. O Lord, hear my prayer.
S. And let my cry come to You.

P. The Lord be with you.
S. And with your spirit. *P*. Let us pray.

Going up to the altar, the Priest prays silently:

TAKE away from us our sins, O Lord, we beseech You, that we may enter with pure minds into the Holy of Holies. Through Christ our Lord. Amen.

WE BESEECH You, O Lord, by the merits of Your Saints (*he kisses the altar*) whose relics lie here, and of all the Saints: deign in Your mercy to pardon me all my sins. Amen.

THE INTROIT

Introit, 1st Mass at Midnight. *Ps.* 2, 7. 1. The Lord said to Me, "You are My Son; this day I have begotten You." *Ps.* Why do the nations rage and the people utter folly? Glory be to the Father, and to the Son, and to the Holy Spirit. As it was in the beginning, is now, and ever shall be, world without end. Amen — The Lord said to Me, "You are My Son; this day I have begotten You."

Introit, 2nd Mass at Dawn. *Isa.* 9, 2. 6. A light shall shine upon us this day: for the Lord is born to us: and He shall be called Wonderful, God, the Prince of Peace, the Father of the world to come: of Whose reign there shall be no end. *Ps.* 92. The Lord is King, in splendor robed; robed is the Lord and girt about with strength. Glory be to the Father, and to the Son, and to the Holy Spirit. As it was in the beginning, is now, and ever shall be, world without end. Amen. — A light shall shine upon us this day: for the Lord is born to us: and He shall be called Wonderful, God, the Prince of

Peace, the Father of the world to come: of Whose reign there shall be no end.

Introit, 3rd Mass During the Day. *Isa.* 9, 6. A Child is born to us, and a Son is given to us: Whose government is upon His shoulder: and His name shall be called the Angel of great counsel. *Ps.* 97. Sing to the Lord a new song, for He has done wondrous deeds. Glory be to the Father, and to the Son, and to the Holy Spirit. As it was in the beginning, is now, and ever shall be, world without end. Amen. — A Child is born to us, and a Son is given to us: Whose government is upon His shoulder: and His name shall be called the Angel of great counsel.

THE KYRIE

P. Lord, have mercy. *S.* Lord, have mercy. *P.* Lord, have mercy. *S.* Christ, have mercy. *P.* Christ, have mercy. *S.* Christ, have mercy. *P.* Lord, have mercy. *S.* Lord, have mercy. *P.* Lord, have mercy.

THE GLORIA

GLORY to God in the highest. And on earth peace to men of good will. We praise You. We bless You. We adore You. We glorify You. We give You thanks for Your great glory. O Lord God, heavenly King, God the Father almighty. O Lord Jesus Christ, the Only-begotten Son. O Lord God, Lamb of God, Son of the Father: You Who take away the sins of the world, have mercy on us. You Who take away the sins of the world, receive our prayer. You Who sit at the right hand of the Father, have mercy on us. For You alone are holy. You alone are the Lord. You alone, O Jesus Christ, are most high. Together with the Holy Spirit ✠ in the glory of God the Father. Amen.

The Priest kisses the altar and turns to the people, saying:

P. The Lord be with you. *S.* And with your spirit. *P.* Let us pray.

Going to the right (Epistle) side, he says:

Prayer, 1st Mass at Midnight. O God, You have illumined this most holy night with the brightness of the True Light; grant, we beseech You, that we, who have known the mystery of His light on earth, may also attain to the full enjoyment of His joys in heaven. Who with You lives, etc. *S.* Amen.

Epistle, 1st Mass at Midnight. *Titus 2, 11-15.* Beloved: The grace of God our Savior has appeared to all men, instructing us, in order that, rejecting ungodliness and worldly lusts, we may live temperately and justly and piously in this world; looking for the blessed hope and glorious coming of our great God and Savior, Jesus Christ, Who gave Himself for us that He might redeem us from all iniquity and cleanse for Himself an acceptable people, pursuing good works. Thus speak, and exhort, in Christ Jesus our Lord. *S.* Thanks be to God.

Gradual, 1st Mass at Midnight. *Ps. 109, 3. 1.* Yours is princely power in the day of Your birth, in holy splendor; before the daystar, I have begotten You. ℣. The Lord said to my Lord, "Sit at My right hand, till I make Your enemies Your footstool." Alleluia, alleluia. ℣. *Ps. 2, 7.* The Lord said to Me, "You are My Son; this day I have begotten You." Alleluia.

Prayer, 2nd Mass at Dawn. Grant us, we beseech You, almighty God, that we on whom the new light of Your Incarnate Word is poured, may show forth in our works that brightness, which now illuminates our minds by faith. Through the same our Lord Jesus Christ, Your Son, Who lives and reigns with You in the unity of the Holy Spirit, God, world without end. S. Amen.

Epistle, 2nd Mass at Dawn. *Titus* 3, 4-7. Dearly beloved: When the goodness and kindness of God our Savior appeared, then not by reason of good works that we did ourselves, but according to His mercy, He saved us through the bath of regeneration and renewal by the Holy Spirit; Whom He has abundantly poured out upon us through Jesus Christ our Savior, in order that, justified by His grace, we may be heirs in the hope of life everlasting, in Christ Jesus our Lord. S. Thanks be to God.

Gradual, 2nd Mass at Dawn. *Ps.* 117, 26. 27. 23. Blessed is He Who comes in the name of the Lord; the Lord is God, and He has given us light. ℣. By the Lord has this been done; it is wonderful in our eyes. Alleluia, alleluia. ℣. *Ps.* 92, 1. The Lord is King, in splendor robed; robed is the Lord and girt about with strength. Alleluia.

Prayer, 3rd Mass During the Day. Grant, we beseech You, almighty God, that the new birth of Your Only-begotten Son as man may set us free, who are held by the old bondage under the yoke of sin. Through the same our Lord Jesus Christ, Your Son, Who lives and reigns with You in the unity of the Holy Spirit, God, world without end. S. Amen.

Epistle, 3rd Mass During the Day. *Heb.* 1, 1-12. God, Who at sundry times and in divers manners spoke in times past to the fathers by the prophets, last of all in these days has spoken to us by His Son, Whom He appointed heir of all things, by

Whom also He made the world; Who, being the brightness of His glory and the image of His substance, and upholding all things by the word of His power, has effected man's purgation from sin and taken His seat at the right hand of the Majesty on high, having become so much superior to the angels as He has inherited a more excellent name than they. For to which of the angels has He ever said, "You are My Son, I this day have begotten You?" and again, "I will be to Him a Father, and He shall be to Me a Son?" And again, when He brings the firstborn into the world, He says, "And let all the angels of God adore Him." And of the angels indeed He says, "He makes His angels spirits, and His ministers a flame of fire." But of the Son, "Your throne, O God, is forever and ever, and a sceptre of equity is the sceptre of Your kingdom. You have loved justice and hated iniquity; therefore God, Your God, has anointed You with the oil of gladness above Your fellows." And, "You in the beginning, O Lord, did found the earth, and the heavens are works of Your hands. They shall perish, but You shall continue; and they shall all grow old as does a garment, and as a vesture shall You change them, and they shall be changed. But You are the same, and Your years shall not fail." S. Thanks be to God.

Gradual, 3rd Mass During the Day. *Ps.* 97, 3. 4. 2. All the ends of the earth have seen the salvation by our God. Sing joyfully to God, all you lands. ℣. The Lord has made His salvation known: in the sight of the nations He has revealed His justice.

Alleluia, alleluia. ℣. A sanctified day has shone upon us; come, you nations, and adore the Lord:

for this day a great light has descended upon the earth. Alleluia.

PRAYER BEFORE THE GOSPEL

Bowing down at the center of the altar, he says:

CLEANSE my heart and my lips, O almighty God, Who cleansed the lips of the Prophet Isaias with a burning coal. In Your gracious mercy deign so to purify me that I may worthily proclaim Your holy Gospel. Through Christ our Lord. Amen. Lord, grant Your blessing. The Lord be in my heart and on my lips, that I may worthily and fittingly proclaim His holy Gospel. Amen.

THE GOSPEL

Going to the left (Gospel) side of the altar, he says:

P. The Lord be with you. S. And with your spirit.

P. ✠ The continuation of the holy Gospel according to Saint Luke (John). S. Glory be to You, O Lord.

Gospel, 1st Mass at Midnight. *Luke 2, 1-14.* At that time, there went forth a decree from Caesar Augustus that a census of the whole world should be taken. This first census took place while Cyrinus was governor of Syria. And all were going, each to his own town, to register. And Joseph also went from Galilee out of the town of Nazareth into Judea to the town of David, which is called Bethlehem — because he was of the house and family of David — to register, together with Mary his espoused wife, who was with child. And it came to pass while they were there, that the days for her to be delivered were fulfilled. And she brought forth her firstborn Son, and wrapped Him in swaddling clothes, and laid Him in a manger, because there was no room for them in the inn. And there were shepherds in the same district living in the fields and keeping watch over their flock by night. And behold, an angel of the Lord stood by them and the glory of God shone round about them, and they feared exceedingly. And the angel said to them, "Do not be afraid, for behold, I bring you good news of great joy which shall be to all the people; for today in the town of David a Savior has been born to you, Who is Christ the Lord. And this shall be a sign to you: you will find an Infant wrapped in swaddling clothes and lying in a manger." And suddenly there was with the angel a multitude of the heavenly host praising God and saying, "Glory to God in the highest, and on earth peace among men of good will." *S.* Praise be to You, O Christ. *P.* By the words of the Gospel, may our sins be taken away.

Gospel, 2nd Mass at Dawn. *Luke 2, 15-20.* At that time, the shepherds were saying to one another, "Let us go over to Bethlehem and see this thing that has come to pass, which the Lord has made known to us." So they went with haste, and they found Mary and Joseph, and the Babe lying in the manger. And when they had seen, they understood what had been told them concerning this Child. And all who heard marvelled at the things told them by the shepherds. But Mary kept in mind all these things, pondering them in her heart. And the shepherds returned, glorifying and praising God for all that they had heard and seen, even as it was spoken to them. *S.* Praise be to You, O Christ. *P.* By the words of the Gospel, may our sins be taken away.

Gospel, 3rd Mass During the Day. *John 1, 1-14.* In the beginning was the Word, and the Word was with God; and the Word was God. He was in the beginning with God. All things were made through Him, and without Him was made nothing that has been made. In Him was life, and the life was the light of men. And the light shines in the darkness; and the darkness grasped it not. There was a man, one sent from God, whose name was John. This man came as a witness, to bear witness concerning the light, that all might believe through him. He was not himself the light, but was to bear witness to the light. It was the true light that enlightens every man who comes into the world. He was in the world, and the world was made through Him, and the world knew Him not. He came unto His own, and His own received Him not. But to as many as received Him He gave the power of becoming sons of God; to those who believe in His name: who were born not of blood, nor of the will of the flesh, nor of the will of man, but of God. And the Word was made flesh, and dwelt among us. And we saw His glory — glory as of the Only-begotten of the Father — full of grace and of truth. S. Praise be to You, O Christ. *P.* By the words of the Gospel, may our sins be taken away.

THE NICENE CREED

I BELIEVE in one God, the Father almighty, Maker of heaven and earth, and of all things visible and invisible. And in one Lord Jesus Christ, the Only-begotten Son of God. Born of the Father before all ages. God of God; Light of Light; true God of true God. Begotten not made; of one being with the Father; by Whom all things were

made. Who for us men, and for our salvation, came down from heaven. (*Here all genuflect.*) And was made Flesh by the Holy Spirit of the Virgin Mary: AND WAS MADE MAN. He was also crucified for us, suffered under Pontius Pilate and was buried. And on the third day He rose again according to the Scriptures. And ascending into heaven, He sits at the right hand of the Father. And He shall come again in glory to judge the living and the dead; and of His kingdom there shall be no end. And I believe in the Holy Spirit, Lord and Giver of life, Who proceeds from the Father and the Son. Who together with the Father and the Son is no less adored, and glorified: Who spoke by the Prophets. And I believe in One, Holy, Catholic and Apostolic Church. I confess one Baptism for the remission of sins. And I look for the resurrection of the dead. ✠ And the life of the world to come. Amen.

THE OFFERTORY

The Priest turns to the people and says:

P. The Lord be with you. S. And with your spirit.
P. Let us pray.

THE OFFERTORY VERSE

Offertory, 1st Mass at Midnight. *Ps. 95, 11. 13.* Let the heavens be glad and the earth rejoice before the Lord, for He comes.

Offertory, 2nd Mass at Dawn. *Ps. 92, 1-2.* God has made the world firm, not to be moved. Your throne, O God, stands firm from of old; from everlasting You are.

Offertory, 3rd Mass During the Day. *Ps.* 88, 12. 15. Yours are the heavens, and Yours is the earth; the world and its fullness You have founded. Justice and judgment are the foundation of Your throne.

The Priest now uncovers the chalice, places the host on the paten and offering it up, says:

ACCEPT, O holy Father, almighty and eternal God, this spotless host, which I, Your unworthy servant, offer to You, my living and true God, to atone for my numberless sins, offenses, and negligences; on behalf of all here present and likewise for all faithful Christians living and dead, that it may profit me and them as a means of salvation to life everlasting. Amen.

He pours wine and water into the chalice, blessing the water before it is poured.

O GOD, Who established the nature of man in wondrous dignity, and still more admirably restored it, grant that through the mystery of this water and wine, we may be made partakers of His Divinity, Who has condescended to become partaker of our humanity, Jesus Christ, Your Son, our Lord. Who lives and reigns with You in the unity of the Holy Spirit, God, world without end. Amen.

WE OFFER You, O Lord, the chalice of salvation, humbly begging of Your mercy that it may arise before Your Divine Majesty, with a pleasing fragrance, for our salvation and for that of the whole world. Amen.

IN A humble spirit and with a contrite heart, may we be accepted by You, O Lord, and may our sacrifice so be offered in Your sight this day as to please You, O Lord God.

Raising his eyes and blessing the offering, he says:

COME, O Sanctifier, almighty and eternal God, and bless ✠ this sacrifice prepared for the glory of Your holy name.

WASHING THE FINGERS

I WASH my hands in innocence, and I go around Your altar, O Lord, giving voice to my thanks, and recounting all Your wondrous deeds. O Lord, I love the house in which You dwell, the tenting-place of Your glory. Gather not my soul with those of sinners, nor with men of blood my life. On their hands are crimes, and their right hands are full of bribes. But I walk in integrity; redeem me, and have pity on me. My foot stands on level ground; in the assemblies I will bless You, O Lord. Glory be to the Father, and to the Son, and to the Holy Spirit. As it was in the beginning, is now, and ever shall be, world without end. Amen.

ACCEPT, Most Holy Trinity, this offering which we are making to You in remembrance of the Passion, Resurrection, and Ascension of Jesus Christ, our Lord; and in honor of Blessed Mary, ever Virgin, Blessed John the Baptist, the Holy Apostles Peter and Paul, and of these, and of all the Saints; that it may add to their honor and aid our salvation; and may they deign to intercede in heaven for us who honor their memory here on earth. Through the same Christ our Lord. Amen.

The Priest turns toward the people and says:

Pray, brethren, that my sacrifice and yours may become acceptable to God the Father almighty.

S. May the Lord accept this sacrifice from your hands to the praise and glory of His name, for our advantage, and that of all His holy Church.
P. Amen.

THE SECRET

Secret, 1st Mass at Midnight. May the offering of this day's festival be pleasing to You, O Lord, that by Your bountiful grace, we may, through this sacred intercourse, be found conformed to Him, in Whom our substance is united to You. Who with You lives and reigns, etc.
P. World without end. S. Amen.

Secret, 2nd Mass at Dawn. May our gifts, we beseech You, O Lord, prove worthy of the rites of this day's Nativity, and ever shed peace upon us: that, as He Who was begotten as man, shone forth also as God, so may these earthly creatures bestow on us that which is divine. Through the same our Lord Jesus Christ, Your Son, Who lives, etc.
P. World without end. *S.* Amen.

Secret, 3rd Mass During the Day. Sanctify, O Lord, the gifts offered to You, by the new birth of Your Only-begotten Son, and purify us from the stains of our sins. Through the same our Lord Jesus Christ, Your Son, Who lives, etc.
P. World without end. *S.* Amen.

PREFACE—CANON

P. The Lord be with you. *S.* And with your spirit.
P. Lift up your hearts.
S. We have lifted them up to the Lord.
P. Let us give thanks to the Lord, our God.
S. It is fitting and just.

IT IS fitting indeed and just, right and helpful to salvation, for us always and everywhere to give thanks to You, O holy Lord, Father almighty, everlasting God. Because by the mystery of the Word made flesh the new light of Your glory has shone upon the eyes of our mind: that while we acknowledge Him to be God seen by men, we may be drawn by Him to the love of things unseen. And therefore with Angels and Archangels, with Thrones and Dominations, and with the whole host of the heavenly army, we sing a hymn to Your glory, saying again and again (*the bell is rung* 3 *times*):

HOLY, HOLY, HOLY, Lord God of Hosts. Heaven and earth are filled with Your glory. Hosanna in the highest. ✠ Blessed is He Who comes in the name of the Lord. Hosanna in the highest.

THE CANON OF THE MASS

THEREFORE, most gracious Father, we humbly beg of You and entreat You through Jesus Christ Your Son, our Lord, (*he kisses the altar*) to deem acceptable and bless these ✠ gifts, these ✠ offerings, these ✠ holy and unspotted oblations which, in the first place, we offer You for Your Holy Catholic Church, that You would deign to give her peace and protection, to unite and guard her throughout the world, together with Your servant *N.*, our Pope, and *N.*, our Bishop; and all true believers who cherish the Catholic and Apostolic Faith.

Commemoration of the Living

REMEMBER, O Lord, Your servants and handmaids, *N. and N.*, (*name them*) and all here present, whose faith and devotion are known to You, on whose behalf we offer to You, or who themselves offer to You, this sacrifice of praise for themselves, families and friends, for the good of their souls, for their hope of salvation and deliverance from all harm, and who offer their homage to You, eternal, living and true God.

Commemoration of the Saints

IN THE unity of holy fellowship, and keeping this most holy day, (night) on which the spotless virginity of Blessed Mary brought forth a Savior to this world, we also observe the memory, first of all, of the glorious and ever Virgin Mary, Mother of our Lord and God Jesus Christ; next, that of Your Blessed Apostles and Martyrs, Peter and Paul, Andrew, James, John, Thomas, James, Philip, Bartholomew, Matthew, Simon and Thaddeus; of Linus, Cletus, Clement, Sixtus, Cornelius, Cyprian, Lawrence, Chrysogonus, John and Paul, Cosmas and Damian, and of all Your Saints, by whose merits and prayers grant that we may be always fortified by the help of Your protection. Through the same Christ our Lord. Amen.

Spreading his hands over the oblation, he says:

GRACIOUSLY accept, then, we beseech You, O Lord, this service of our worship and that of all Your household. Provide that our days be spent in Your peace, save us from everlasting damnation, and cause us to be numbered in the flock You have chosen. Through Christ our Lord. Amen.

O GOD, deign to bless ✠ what we offer, and make it approved, ✠ effective, ✠ right, and wholly pleasing in every way, that it may become for our good, the Body ✠ and Blood ✠ of Your dearly beloved Son, Jesus Christ our Lord.

CONSECRATION—ELEVATION

WHO, the day before He suffered, took bread into His holy and venerable hands, and having raised His eyes to heaven, to You, O God, His almighty Father, giving thanks to You, He blessed it, ✠ broke it, and gave it to His disciples, saying: All of you take and eat of this:

FOR THIS IS MY BODY.

IN LIKE manner, when the supper was done, taking also this goodly chalice into His holy and venerable hands, again giving thanks to You, He blessed ✠ it, and gave it to His disciples, saying: All of you take and drink of this:

FOR THIS IS THE CHALICE OF MY BLOOD OF THE NEW AND ETERNAL COVENANT: THE MYSTERY OF FAITH: WHICH SHALL BE SHED FOR YOU AND FOR MANY UNTO THE FORGIVENESS OF SINS.

As often as you shall do these things, in memory of Me shall you do them.

Offering of the Victim

MINDFUL, therefore, O Lord, not only of the blessed Passion of the same Christ, Your Son, our Lord, but also of His Resurrection from the dead, and finally His glorious Ascension into heaven, we, Your ministers, as also Your holy people, offer to Your supreme Majesty, of the gifts bestowed upon us, the pure ✠ Victim, the holy ✠ Victim, the all-perfect ✠ Victim: the holy ✠ Bread of life eternal and the Chalice ✠ of unending salvation.

AND this deign to regard with gracious and kindly attention and hold acceptable, as You deigned to accept the offerings of Abel, Your just servant, and the sacrifice of Abraham our patriarch, and that which Your chief priest Melchisedec offered to You, a holy sacrifice and a spotless victim.

MOST humbly we implore You, almighty God, bid these offerings to be brought by the hands of Your holy angel to Your altar above; before the face of Your Divine Majesty; that those of us who, by sharing in the Sacrifice of this altar, shall receive the Most Sacred ✠ Body and ✠ Blood of Your Son, may be filled with every grace and heavenly blessing. Through the same Christ our Lord. Amen.

Commemoration of the Dead

REMEMBER also, O Lord, Your servants and handmaids, *N.* and *N.*, who have gone before us with the sign of faith, and rest in the sleep of peace. (*Here pray for the dead.*) To these, O Lord, and to all who rest in Christ, we beseech You to grant of Your goodness, a place of comfort, light and peace. Through the same Christ our Lord. Amen.

TO US sinners also, Your servants, trusting in the greatness of Your mercy, deign to grant some part and fellowship with Your Holy Apostles and Martyrs: with John, Stephen, Matthias, Barnabas, Ignatius, Alexander, Marcellinus, Peter, Felicitas, Perpetua, Agatha, Lucy, Agnes, Cecilia, Anastasia, and all Your Saints; into whose company, we implore You to admit us, not weighing our merits, but freely granting us pardon. Through Christ our Lord.

THROUGH Whom, O Lord, You always create, ✠ sanctify, ✠ fill with life, ✠ bless, and bestow upon us all good things.

The Minor Elevation

THROUGH ✠ Him, and with ✠ Him, and in ✠ Him, is to You, God the Father ✠ almighty, in the unity of the Holy ✠ Spirit, all honor and glory, world without end. S. Amen.

THE COMMUNION AND THANKSGIVING

Let us pray. Prompted by saving precepts, and taught by Your divine teaching, we dare to say:

OUR FATHER, Who art in heaven, hallowed be Thy name: Thy kingdom come: Thy will be done on earth as it is in heaven. Give us this day our daily bread; and forgive us our trespasses, as we forgive those who trespass against us. And lead us not into temptation: S. But deliver us from evil. P. Amen.

DELIVER us, we beseech You, O Lord, from all evils, past, present, and to come; and by the intercession of the Blessed and glorious Mary, ever Virgin, Mother of God, together with Your Blessed Apostles Peter and Paul, and Andrew, and all the Saints, grant of Your goodness, peace in our days, that aided by the riches of Your mercy, we may be always free from sin and safe from all disturbance. Through the same our Lord Jesus Christ, Your Son, Who lives and reigns with You in the unity of the Holy Spirit, God, world without end. S. Amen.

P. May the peace ✠ of the Lord be ✠ always with ✠ you. S. And with your spirit.

The Priest puts a small particle into the chalice, saying:

May this mingling and consecration of the Body and Blood of our Lord Jesus Christ help us who receive it to life everlasting. Amen.

LAMB of God, You Who take away the sins of the world, have mercy on us.

Lamb of God, You Who take away the sins of the world, have mercy on us.

Lamb of God, You Who take away the sins of the world, grant us peace.

PRAYERS BEFORE HOLY COMMUNION

O LORD Jesus Christ, Who said to Your Apostles: "Peace I leave with you, My peace I give to you," regard not my sins but the faith of Your Church, and deign to give her peace and unity according to Your Will: Who live and reign, God, world without end. Amen.

O LORD Jesus Christ, Son of the living God, Who, by the will of the Father, with the cooperation of the Holy Spirit, have by Your death given life to the world, deliver me by this Your Most Sacred Body and Blood from all my sins and from every evil. Make me always cling to Your commandments, and never permit me to be separated from You. Who with the same God the Father and the Holy Spirit, live and reign, God, world without end. Amen.

LET not the partaking of Your Body, O Lord Jesus Christ, which I, though unworthy, presume to receive, turn to my judgment and condem-

nation; but through Your goodness, may it become a safeguard and an effective remedy, both of soul and body. Who live and reign with God the Father, in the unity of the Holy Spirit, God, world without end. Amen.

COMMUNION OF THE PRIEST

I WILL take the Bread of heaven, and call upon the name of the Lord.

Lord, I am not worthy that You should come under my roof; but only say the word, and my soul will be healed. (3 *times.*)

Making the Sign of the Cross with the chalice, he says:

MAY the Body of our Lord Jesus Christ preserve my soul to life everlasting. Amen.

What return shall I make to the Lord for all He has given me? I will take the Chalice of salvation, and I will call upon the name of the Lord. Praising will I call upon the Lord and I shall be saved from my enemies.

Making the Sign of the Cross with the Host, he says:

MAY the Blood of our Lord Jesus Christ preserve my soul to life everlasting. Amen.

The Priest reverently consumes the Precious Blood.

COMMUNION OF THE FAITHFUL

The Server and people say the "Confiteor."

P. May almighty God have mercy on you, forgive you your sins, and bring you to life everlasting. S. Amen.

P. May the almighty and merciful Lord grant you pardon, ✠ absolution and remission of your sins. S. Amen.

Holding up a Sacred Host, the Priest says:

Behold the Lamb of God, behold Him Who takes away the sins of the world.

Lord, I am not worthy that You should come under my roof; but only say the word, and my soul will be healed. (3 *times.*)

The Priest says to each communicant:

May the Body of our Lord Jesus Christ preserve your soul to life everlasting. Amen.

The Priest purifies the chalice with wine, saying:

WHAT has passed our lips as food, O Lord, may we possess in purity of heart, that what is given to us in time, be our healing for eternity.

He purifies his fingers with wine and water, saying:

MAY Your Body, O Lord, which I have eaten, and Your Blood which I have drunk, cleave to my very soul, and grant that no trace of sin be found in me, whom these pure and holy mysteries have renewed. Who live and reign, world without end. Amen.

THE COMMUNION

Communion, 1st Mass at Midnight. *Ps.* 109, 3. In holy splendor, before the daystar I have begotten You.

Communion, 2nd Mass at Dawn. *Zach.* 9, 9. Rejoice greatly, O daughter of Sion, shout for joy, O daughter of Jerusalem: behold your King comes, holy, the Savior of the world.

Communion, 3rd Mass During the Day. *Ps.* 97, 3. All the ends of the earth have seen the salvation by our God.

The Priest, turning to the people, says:

P. The Lord be with you. *S.* And with your spirit.
P. Let us pray.

THE POSTCOMMUNION

Postcommunion, 1st Mass at Midnight. Grant, we beseech You, O Lord our God, that we, who rejoice in celebrating these mysteries of the Nativity of our Lord Jesus Christ, may by a fitting conversation become worthy to attain to His fellowship. Who with You lives and reigns, etc. *S.* Amen.

Postcommunion, 2nd Mass at Dawn. May the new life of this sacrament, O Lord, always restore us, especially on the Nativity of Him Whose wondrous Birth has overcome the old nature of our manhood. Through the same our Lord Jesus Christ, Your Son, Who lives and reigns, etc. *S.* Amen.

Postcommunion, 3rd Mass During the Day. Grant, we beseech You, almighty God, that as the Savior of the world, born on this day, is the Author of our divine regeneration, so He may also be for us the Giver of immortality. Who with You lives and reigns, etc. *S.* Amen.

FINAL PRAYERS

P. The Lord be with you. *S.* And with your spirit.
P. Go, you are dismissed. *S.* Thanks be to God.

MAY the tribute of my worship be pleasing to You, Most Holy Trinity, and grant that the sacrifice which I, all unworthy, have offered in the presence of Your Majesty, may be acceptable to You, and through Your mercy obtain forgiveness for me and all for whom I have offered it. Through Christ our Lord. Amen.

THE LAST BLESSING

MAY almighty God bless you: ✠ the Father, and the Son, and the Holy Spirit. S. Amen. P. The Lord be with you. S. And with your spirit.

The Last Gospel and Prayers after Low Mass are conveniently placed inside the back cover.

Last Gospel, 3rd Mass During the Day. *Matt.* 2, 1-12. When Jesus was born in Bethlehem of Judea, in the days of King Herod, behold, Magi came from the East to Jerusalem, saying, "Where is He that is born King of the Jews? For we have seen His star in the East and have come to worship Him." But when King Herod heard this, he was troubled, and so was all Jerusalem with him. And gathering together all the chief priests and Scribes of the people, he inquired of them where the Christ was to be born. And they said to him, "In Bethlehem of Judea; for thus it is written by the prophet, 'And you, Bethlehem, of the land of Juda, are by no means least among the princes of Juda; for from you shall come forth a leader who shall rule my people Israel.'" Then Herod summoned the Magi secretly, and carefully ascertained from them the time when the star had appeared to them. And sending them to Bethlehem, he said, "Go and make careful inquiry concerning the Child, and when you have found Him, bring me word, that I too may go and worship Him." Now they, having heard the king, went their way. And behold, the star that they had seen in the East went before them, until it came and stood over the place where the Child was. And when they saw the star they rejoiced exceedingly. And entering the house, they found the Child with Mary His mother, and falling down they worshipped Him. (*Here genuflect.*) And opening their treasures they offered Him gifts of gold, frankincense and myrrh. And being warned in a dream not to return to Herod, they went back to their own country by another way. S. Thanks be to God.

See inside back cover for Prayers after Low Mass.

Simeon said, "Behold, this Child is destined for the fall and for the rise of many in Israel."

SUNDAY WITHIN THE OCTAVE OF CHRISTMAS

In the Mass of this Sunday, which is like an echo of the Nativity, we read in the Gospel how Jesus grew in wisdom and grace. We must imitate this Divine Model Whose Youth is summed up in His voluntary subjection to His creatures (WHITE VESTMENTS)

PRAYERS AT THE FOOT OF THE ALTAR

IN THE name of the Father, ✠ and of the Son, and of the Holy Spirit. Amen.

Priest. I will go in to the altar of God.

Server. The God of my gladness and joy.

Psalm 42

DO ME justice, O God, and fight my fight against a faithless people; from the deceitful and impious man rescue me.

S. For You, O God, are my strength. Why do You keep me so far away? Why must I go about in mourning, with the enemy oppressing me?

P. Send forth Your light and Your fidelity; they

shall lead me on and bring me to Your holy mountain, to Your dwelling-place.
S. Then will I go in to the altar of God, the God of my gladness and joy.
P. Then will I give You thanks upon the harp, O God, my God. Why are you so downcast, O my soul? Why do you sigh within me?
S. Hope in God! For I shall again be thanking Him in the presence of my Savior and my God.
P. Glory be to the Father, and to the Son, and to the Holy Spirit.
S. As it was in the beginning, is now, and ever shall be, world without end. Amen.
P. I will go in to the altar of God.
S. The God of my gladness and joy.
P. Our help ✠ is in the name of the Lord.
S. Who made heaven and earth.
P. I confess to almighty God, etc.
S. May almighty God have mercy on you, forgive you your sins, and bring you to life everlasting.
P. Amen.

The Server, bowing, says the "Confiteor."

I CONFESS to almighty God, to Blessed Mary, ever Virgin, to Blessed Michael the Archangel, to Blessed John the Baptist, to the Holy Apostles Peter and Paul, and to all the Saints, and to you, Father, that I have sinned exceedingly in thought, word and deed, *through my fault, through my fault, through my most grievous fault.* Therefore I beseech Blessed Mary, ever Virgin, Blessed Michael the Archangel, Blessed John the Baptist, the Holy Apostles Peter and Paul, and all the Saints, and you, Father, to pray to the Lord our God for me.
P. May almighty God have mercy on you, forgive

you your sins, and bring you to life everlasting.
S. Amen.

MAY the almighty and merciful Lord grant us pardon, ✠ absolution, and remission of our sins. *S.* Amen.

P. Will You not, O God, give us life?
S. And shall not Your people rejoice in You?
P. Show us, O Lord, Your kindness.
S. And grant us Your salvation.
P. O Lord, hear my prayer.
S. And let my cry come to You.
P. The Lord be with you.
S. And with your spirit. *P.* Let us pray.

Going up to the altar, the Priest prays silently:

TAKE away from us our sins, O Lord, we beseech You, that we may enter with pure minds into the Holy of Holies. Through Christ our Lord. Amen.

WE BESEECH You, O Lord, by the merits of Your Saints (*he kisses the altar*) whose relics lie here, and of all the Saints: deign in Your mercy to pardon me all my sins. Amen.

THE INTROIT • Wis. 18, 14. 15

At the right side of the altar, the Priest says:

WHEN a profound stillness compassed everything and the night in its swift course was half spent, Your all-powerful Word, O Lord, bounded from heaven's royal throne. *Ps.* 92. The Lord is King, in splendor robed; robed is the Lord and girt about with strength. Glory be to the Father, and to the Son, and to the Holy Spirit. As it was in the beginning, is now, and ever shall be, world without end. Amen. — When a profound stillness compassed everything and the night in its swift course was half spent, Your all-powerful Word, O Lord, bounded from heaven's royal throne.

THE KYRIE

P. Lord, have mercy. *S.* Lord, have mercy. *P.* Lord, have mercy. *S.* Christ, have mercy. *P.* Christ, have mercy. *S.* Christ, have mercy. *P.* Lord, have mercy. *S.* Lord, have mercy. *P.* Lord, have mercy.

THE GLORIA

GLORY to God in the highest. And on earth peace to men of good will. We praise You. We bless You. We adore You. We glorify You. We give You thanks for Your great glory. O Lord God, heavenly King, God the Father almighty. O Lord Jesus Christ, the Only-begotten Son. O Lord God, Lamb of God, Son of the Father: You Who take away the sins of the world, have mercy on us. You Who take away the sins of the world, receive our prayer. You Who sit at the right hand of the Father, have mercy on us. For You alone are holy. You alone are the Lord. You alone, O Jesus Christ, are most high. Together with the Holy Spirit ✠ in the glory of God the Father. Amen.

The Priest kisses the altar and turns to the people, saying:

P. The Lord be with you. *S.* And with your spirit.
P. Let us pray.

THE PRAYER

Going to the right (Epistle) side, he says:

ALMIGHTY and everlasting God, direct our actions according to Your good pleasure; that we may deserve to abound in good works, in the name of Your beloved Son. Who with You lives and reigns in the unity of the Holy Spirit, God, world without end. *S.* Amen.

THE EPISTLE • Gal. 4, 1-7

BRETHREN: As long as the heir is a child, he differs in no way from a slave, though he is the master of all; but he is under guardians and stewards until the time set by his father. So we too, when we were children, were enslaved under the elements of the world. But when the fullness of time came, God sent His Son, born of a woman, born under the Law, that He might redeem those who were under the Law, that we might receive the adoption of sons. And because you are sons, God has sent the Spirit of His Son into our hearts, crying, "Abba, Father." So that He is no longer a slave, but a son; and if a son, an heir also through God. *S.* Thanks be to God.

THE GRADUAL • Ps. 44, 3. 2

FAIRER in beauty are You than the sons of men; grace is poured out upon Your lips. ℣. My heart overflows with a goodly theme; as I sing my ode to the King, my tongue is nimble as the pen of a skillful scribe.

Alleluia, alleluia. ℣. *Ps.* 92, *1.* The Lord is King, in splendor robed; robed is the Lord and girt about with strength. Alleluia.

PRAYER BEFORE THE GOSPEL

Bowing down at the center of the altar, he says:

CLEANSE my heart and my lips, O almighty God, Who cleansed the lips of the Prophet Isaias with a burning coal. In Your gracious mercy

deign so to purify me that I may worthily proclaim Your holy Gospel. Through Christ our Lord. Amen.

Lord, grant Your blessing. The Lord be in my heart and on my lips, that I may worthily and fittingly proclaim His holy Gospel. Amen.

THE GOSPEL • Luke 2, 33-40

Going to the left (Gospel) side of the altar, he says:

P. The Lord be with you. *S.* And with your spirit.
P. ✠ The continuation of the holy Gospel according to Saint Luke. *S.* Glory be to You, O Lord.

AT THAT time, Joseph and Mary, the mother of Jesus, were marvelling at the things spoken concerning Him. And Simeon blessed them, and said to Mary His mother, "Behold, this Child is destined for the fall and for the rise of many in Israel, and for a sign that shall be contradicted. And your own soul a sword shall pierce, that the thoughts of many hearts may be revealed." There was also Anna, a prophetess, daughter of Phanuel, of the tribe of Aser. She was of a great age, having lived with her husband seven years from her maidenhood, and by herself as a widow for eighty-four years. She never left the temple, with fastings and prayers worshipping night and day. And coming up at that very hour, she began to give praise to the Lord, and spoke of Him to all who were awaiting the redemption of Jerusalem. And when they had fulfilled all things as prescribed in the Law of the Lord, they returned to Galilee, into their own town of Nazareth. And the Child grew and became strong. He was full of wisdom and the grace of God was upon Him. *S.* Praise be to You, O Christ.

P. By the words of the Gospel, may our sins be taken away.

THE NICENE CREED

At the center of the altar, he says:

I BELIEVE in one God, the Father almighty, Maker of heaven and earth, and of all things visible and invisible. And in one Lord Jesus Christ, the Only-begotten Son of God. Born of the Father before all ages. God of God; Light of Light; true God of true God. Begotten not made; of one being with the Father; by Whom all things were made. Who for us men, and for our salvation, came down from heaven. (*Here all genuflect.*) And was made Flesh by the Holy Spirit of the Virgin Mary: AND WAS MADE MAN. He was also crucified for us, suffered under Pontius Pilate and was buried. And on the third day He rose again according to the Scriptures. And ascending into heaven, He sits at the right hand of the Father. And He shall come again in glory to judge the living and the dead; and of His kingdom there shall be no end. And I believe in the Holy Spirit, Lord and Giver of life, Who proceeds from the Father and the Son. Who together with the Father and the Son is no less adored, and glorified: Who spoke by the Prophets. And I believe in One, Holy, Catholic and Apostolic Church. I confess one Baptism for the remission of sins. And I look for the resurrection of the dead. ✠ And the life of the world to come. Amen.

THE OFFERTORY

The Priest turns to the people and says:

P. The Lord be with you. *S.* And with your spirit.
P. Let us pray.

THE OFFERTORY VERSE • Ps. 92, 1. 2

GOD has made the world firm, not to be moved. Your throne, O God, stands firm from of old; from everlasting You are.

The Priest now uncovers the chalice, places the host on the paten and offering it up, says:

ACCEPT, O holy Father, almighty and eternal God, this spotless host, which I, Your unworthy servant, offer to You, my living and true God, to atone for my numberless sins, offenses, and negligences; on behalf of all here present and likewise for all faithful Christians living and dead, that it may profit me and them as a means of salvation to life everlasting. Amen.

He pours wine and water into the chalice, blessing the water before it is poured.

O GOD, Who established the nature of man in wondrous dignity, and still more admirably restored it, grant that through the mystery of this water and wine, we may be made partakers of His Divinity, Who has condescended to become partaker of our humanity, Jesus Christ, Your Son, our Lord. Who lives and reigns with You in the unity of the Holy Spirit, God, world without end. Amen.

Offering up the wine, the Priest says:

WE OFFER You, O Lord, the chalice of salvation, humbly begging of Your mercy that it may arise before Your Divine Majesty, with a pleasing fragrance, for our salvation and for that of the whole world. Amen.

Bowing down, the Priest says:

IN A humble spirit and with a contrite heart, may we be accepted by You, O Lord, and may our

sacrifice so be offered in Your sight this day as to please You, O Lord God.

Raising his eyes and blessing the offering, he says:

COME, O Sanctifier, almighty and eternal God, and bless ✠ this sacrifice prepared for the glory of Your holy name.

WASHING THE FINGERS

I WASH my hands in innocence, and I go around Your altar, O Lord, giving voice to my thanks, and recounting all Your wondrous deeds. O Lord, I love the house in which You dwell, the tenting-place of Your glory. Gather not my soul with those of sinners, nor with men of blood my life. On their hands are crimes, and their right hands are full of bribes. But I walk in integrity; redeem me, and have pity on me. My foot stands on level ground; in the assemblies I will bless You, O Lord. Glory be to the Father, and to the Son, and to the Holy Spirit. As it was in the beginning, is now, and ever shall be, world without end. Amen.

ACCEPT, Most Holy Trinity, this offering which we are making to You in remembrance of the Passion, Resurrection, and Ascension of Jesus Christ, our Lord; and in honor of Blessed Mary, ever Virgin, Blessed John the Baptist, the Holy Apostles Peter and Paul, and of these, and of all the Saints; that it may add to their honor and aid our salvation; and may they deign to intercede in heaven for us who honor their memory here on earth. Through the same Christ our Lord. Amen.

The Priest turns toward the people and says:

Pray, brethren, that my sacrifice and yours may become acceptable to God the Father almighty.

S. May the Lord accept this sacrifice from your hands to the praise and glory of His name, for our advantage, and that of all His holy Church.

P. Amen.

THE SECRET

GRANT, we beseech You, almighty God, that the offering made in the sight of Your Majesty may obtain for us the grace of a holy devotion, and the reward of a blessed eternity. Through our Lord Jesus Christ, Your Son, Who lives and reigns with You in the unity of the Holy Spirit, God.

P. World without end. S. Amen.

PREFACE—CANON

P. The Lord be with you. S. And with your spirit.

P. Lift up your hearts.

S. We have lifted them up to the Lord.

P. Let us give thanks to the Lord, our God.

S. It is fitting and just.

IT IS fitting indeed and just, right and helpful to salvation, for us always and everywhere to give thanks to You, O holy Lord, Father almighty, everlasting God. Because by the mystery of the Word made flesh the new light of Your glory has shone upon the eyes of our mind: that while we acknowledge Him to be God seen by men, we may be drawn by Him to the love of things unseen. And therefore with Angels and Archangels, with Thrones and Dominations, and with the whole host of the heavenly army, we sing a hymn to Your glory, saying again and again (*the bell is rung* 3 *times*):

HOLY, HOLY, HOLY, Lord God of Hosts. Heaven and earth are filled with Your glory.

Hosanna in the highest. ✠ Blessed is He Who comes in the name of the Lord. Hosanna in the highest.

THE CANON OF THE MASS

THEREFORE, most gracious Father, we humbly beg of You and entreat You through Jesus Christ Your Son, our Lord, (*he kisses the altar*) to deem acceptable and bless these ✠ gifts, these ✠ offerings, these ✠ holy and unspotted oblations which, in the first place, we offer You for Your Holy Catholic Church, that You would deign to give her peace and protection, to unite and guard her throughout the world, together with Your servant N., our Pope, and N., our Bishop; and all true believers who cherish the Catholic and Apostolic Faith.

Commemoration of the Living

REMEMBER, O Lord, Your servants and handmaids, N. and N., (*name them*) and all here present, whose faith and devotion are known to You, on whose behalf we offer to You, or who themselves offer to You, this sacrifice of praise for themselves, families and friends, for the good of their souls, for their hope of salvation and deliverance from all harm, and who offer their homage to You, eternal, living and true God.

Commemoration of the Saints

IN THE unity of holy fellowship, and keeping this most holy day, on which the spotless virginity of Blessed Mary brought forth a Savior to this world, we also observe the memory, first of all, of the glorious and ever Virgin Mary, Mother of our Lord and God Jesus Christ; next, that of Your

Blessed Apostles and Martyrs, Peter and Paul, Andrew, James, John, Thomas, James, Philip, Bartholomew, Matthew, Simon and Thaddeus; of Linus, Cletus, Clement, Sixtus, Cornelius, Cyprian, Lawrence, Chrysogonus, John and Paul, Cosmas and Damian, and of all Your Saints, by whose merits and prayers grant that we may be always fortified by the help of Your protection. Through the same Christ our Lord. Amen.

Spreading his hands over the oblation, he says:

GRACIOUSLY accept, then, we beseech You, O Lord, this service of our worship and that of all Your household. Provide that our days be spent in Your peace, save us from everlasting damnation, and cause us to be numbered in the flock You have chosen. Through Christ our Lord. Amen.

O GOD, deign to bless ✠ what we offer, and make it approved, ✠ effective, ✠ right, and wholly pleasing in every way, that it may become for our good, the Body ✠ and Blood ✠ of Your dearly beloved Son, Jesus Christ our Lord.

CONSECRATION—ELEVATION

WHO, the day before He suffered, took bread into His holy and venerable hands, and having raised His eyes to heaven, to You, O God, His almighty Father, giving thanks to You, He blessed it, ✠ broke it, and gave it to His disciples, saying: All of you take and eat of this:

FOR THIS IS MY BODY.

IN LIKE manner, when the supper was done, taking also this goodly chalice into His holy and venerable hands, again giving thanks to You, He

blessed ✠ it, and gave it to His disciples, saying: All of you take and drink of this:

FOR THIS IS THE CHALICE OF MY BLOOD OF THE NEW AND ETERNAL COVENANT: THE MYSTERY OF FAITH: WHICH SHALL BE SHED FOR YOU AND FOR MANY UNTO THE FORGIVENESS OF SINS.

After replacing the chalice on the corporal, he says:

As often as you shall do these things, in memory of Me shall you do them.

Offering of the Victim

MINDFUL, therefore, O Lord, not only of the blessed Passion of the same Christ, Your Son, our Lord, but also of His Resurrection from the dead, and finally His glorious Ascension into heaven, we, Your ministers, as also Your holy people, offer to Your supreme Majesty, of the gifts bestowed upon us, the pure ✠ Victim, the holy ✠ Victim, the all-perfect ✠ Victim: the holy ✠ Bread of life eternal and the Chalice ✠ of unending salvation.

AND this deign to regard with gracious and kindly attention and hold acceptable, as You deigned to accept the offerings of Abel, Your just servant, and the sacrifice of Abraham our patriarch, and that which Your chief priest Melchisedec offered to You, a holy sacrifice and a spotless victim.

MOST humbly we implore You, almighty God, bid these offerings to be brought by the hands of Your holy angel to Your altar above; before the face of Your Divine Majesty; that those of us who, by sharing in the Sacrifice of this altar, shall receive the Most Sacred ✠ Body and ✠ Blood of Your

Son, may be filled with every grace and heavenly blessing. Through the same Christ our Lord. Amen.

Commemoration of the Dead

REMEMBER also, O Lord, Your servants and handmaids, N. and N., who have gone before us with the sign of faith, and rest in the sleep of peace. (*Here pray for the dead.*) To these, O Lord, and to all who rest in Christ, we beseech You to grant of Your goodness, a place of comfort, light and peace. Through the same Christ our Lord. Amen.

TO US sinners also, Your servants, trusting in the greatness of Your mercy, deign to grant some part and fellowship with Your Holy Apostles and Martyrs: with John, Stephen, Matthias, Barnabas, Ignatius, Alexander, Marcellinus, Peter, Felicitas, Perpetua, Agatha, Lucy, Agnes, Cecilia, Anastasia, and all Your Saints; into whose company, we implore You to admit us, not weighing our merits, but freely granting us pardon. Through Christ our Lord.

THROUGH Whom, O Lord, You always create, ✠ sanctify, ✠ fill with life, ✠ bless, and bestow upon us all good things.

The Minor Elevation

THROUGH ✠ Him, and with ✠ Him, and in ✠ Him, is to You, God the Father ✠ almighty, in the unity of the Holy ✠ Spirit, all honor and glory, world without end. S. Amen.

THE COMMUNION AND THANKSGIVING

Let us pray. Prompted by saving precepts, and taught by Your divine teaching, we dare to say:

OUR FATHER, Who art in heaven, hallowed be Thy name: Thy kingdom come: Thy will be done on earth as it is in heaven. Give us this day our daily bread; and forgive us our trespasses, as we forgive those who trespass against us. And lead us not into temptation: S. But deliver us from evil. *P.* Amen.

DELIVER us, we beseech You, O Lord, from all evils, past, present, and to come; and by the intercession of the Blessed and glorious Mary, ever Virgin, Mother of God, together with Your Blessed Apostles Peter and Paul, and Andrew, and all the Saints, grant of Your goodness, peace in our days, that aided by the riches of Your mercy, we may be always free from sin and safe from all disturbance.

Through the same our Lord Jesus Christ, Your Son, Who lives and reigns with You in the unity of the Holy Spirit, God, world without end.

S. Amen.

P. May the peace ✠ of the Lord be ✠ always with ✠ you.

S. And with your spirit.

The Priest puts a small particle into the chalice, saying:

May this mingling and consecration of the Body and Blood of our Lord Jesus Christ help us who receive it to life everlasting. Amen.

LAMB of God, You Who take away the sins of the world, have mercy on us.

Lamb of God, You Who take away the sins of the world, have mercy on us.

Lamb of God, You Who take away the sins of the world, grant us peace.

PRAYERS BEFORE HOLY COMMUNION

Then inclining toward the altar, he says:

O LORD Jesus Christ, Who said to Your Apostles: "Peace I leave with you, My peace I give to you," regard not my sins but the faith of Your Church, and deign to give her peace and unity according to Your Will: Who live and reign, God, world without end. Amen.

O LORD Jesus Christ, Son of the living God, Who, by the will of the Father, with the cooperation of the Holy Spirit, have by Your death given life to the world, deliver me by this Your Most Sacred Body and Blood from all my sins and from every evil. Make me always cling to Your commandments, and never permit me to be separated from You. Who with the same God the Father and the Holy Spirit, live and reign, God, world without end. Amen.

LET not the partaking of Your Body, O Lord Jesus Christ, which I, though unworthy, presume to receive, turn to my judgment and condemnation; but through Your goodness, may it become a safeguard and an effective remedy, both of soul and body. Who live and reign with God the Father, in the unity of the Holy Spirit, God, world without end. Amen.

COMMUNION OF THE PRIEST

I WILL take the Bread of heaven, and call upon the name of the Lord.

Lord, I am not worthy that You should come under my roof; but only say the word, and my soul will be healed. (3 *times.*)

MAY the Body of our Lord Jesus Christ preserve my soul to life everlasting. Amen. What return shall I make to the Lord for all He has given me? I will take the Chalice of salvation, and I will call upon the name of the Lord. Praising will I call upon the Lord and I shall be saved from my enemies.

Making the Sign of the Cross with the chalice, he says:

MAY the Blood of our Lord Jesus Christ preserve my soul to life everlasting. Amen.

The Priest reverently consumes the Precious Blood.

COMMUNION OF THE FAITHFUL

The Server and people say the "Confiteor."

P. May almighty God have mercy on you, forgive you your sins, and bring you to life everlasting. S. Amen.

P. May the almighty and merciful Lord grant you pardon, ✠ absolution and remission of your sins. S. Amen.

Holding up a Sacred Host, the Priest says:

Behold the Lamb of God, behold Him Who takes away the sins of the world.

Lord, I am not worthy that You should come under my roof; but only say the word, and my soul will be healed. (3 *times.*)

The Priest says to each communicant:

May the Body of our Lord Jesus Christ preserve your soul to life everlasting. Amen.

The Priest purifies the chalice with wine, saying:

WHAT has passed our lips as food, O Lord, may we possess in purity of heart, that what is given to us in time, be our healing for eternity.

He purifies his fingers with wine and water, saying:

MAY Your Body, O Lord, which I have eaten, and Your Blood which I have drunk, cleave to my very soul, and grant that no trace of sin be found in me, whom these pure and holy mysteries have renewed. Who live and reign, world without end. Amen.

THE COMMUNION • Matt. 2, 20

TAKE the Child and His mother, and go into the land of Israel, for those who sought the Child's life are dead.

P. The Lord be with you. *S.* And with your spirit.
P. Let us pray.

THE POSTCOMMUNION

O LORD, by the working of this mystery, may our vices be purged away and our just desires fulfilled. Through our Lord Jesus Christ, Your Son, Who lives and reigns with You, etc. *S.* Amen.

FINAL PRAYERS

P. The Lord be with you. *S.* And with your spirit.
P. Go, you are dismissed. *S.* Thanks be to God.

MAY the tribute of my worship be pleasing to You, Most Holy Trinity, and grant that the sacrifice which I, all unworthy, have offered in the presence of Your Majesty, may be acceptable to You, and through Your mercy obtain forgiveness for me and all for whom I have offered it. Through Christ our Lord. Amen.

THE LAST BLESSING

MAY almighty God bless you: ✠ the Father, and the Son, and the Holy Spirit. *S.* Amen.

The Last Gospel and Prayers after Low Mass are conveniently placed inside the back cover.

"His Name was called Jesus . . ."

CIRCUMCISION OF OUR LORD

On this, the eighth day after Christmas, the Church commemorates the Circumcision of our Redeemer, and also honors Mary's divine Maternity. The sinless Son of Man sheds for us the first drops of His Blood, and submits to a Mosaic Law. (WHITE VESTMENTS)

PRAYERS AT THE FOOT OF THE ALTAR

IN THE name of the Father, ✠ and of the Son, and of the Holy Spirit. Amen.

Priest. I will go in to the altar of God.

Server. The God of my gladness and joy.

Psalm 42

DO ME justice, O God, and fight my fight against a faithless people; from the deceitful and impious man rescue me.

S. For You, O God, are my strength. Why do You keep me so far away? Why must I go about in mourning, with the enemy oppressing me?

P. Send forth Your light and Your fidelity; they shall lead me on and bring me to Your holy mountain, to Your dwelling-place.

S. Then will I go in to the altar of God, the God of my gladness and joy.
P. Then will I give You thanks upon the harp, O God, my God. Why are you so downcast, O my soul? Why do you sigh within me?
S. Hope in God! For I shall again be thanking Him in the presence of my Savior and my God.
P. Glory be to the Father, and to the Son, and to the Holy Spirit.
S. As it was in the beginning, is now, and ever shall be, world without end. Amen.
P. I will go in to the altar of God.
S. The God of my gladness and joy.
P. Our help ✠ is in the name of the Lord.
S. Who made heaven and earth.
P. I confess to almighty God, etc.
S. May almighty God have mercy on you, forgive you your sins, and bring you to life everlasting.
P. Amen.

The Server, bowing, says the "Confiteor."

I CONFESS to almighty God, to Blessed Mary, ever Virgin, to Blessed Michael the Archangel, to Blessed John the Baptist, to the Holy Apostles Peter and Paul, and to all the Saints, and to you, Father, that I have sinned exceedingly in thought, word and deed, *through my fault, through my fault, through my most grievous fault.* Therefore I beseech Blessed Mary, ever Virgin, Blessed Michael the Archangel, Blessed John the Baptist, the Holy Apostles Peter and Paul, and all the Saints, and you, Father, to pray to the Lord our God for me.
P. May almighty God have mercy on you, forgive you your sins, and bring you to life everlasting.
S. Amen.

MAY the almighty and merciful Lord grant us pardon, ✠ absolution, and remission of our sins. *S.* Amen.
P. Will You not, O God, give us life?
S. And shall not Your people rejoice in You?
P. Show us, O Lord, Your kindness.
S. And grant us Your salvation.
P. O Lord, hear my prayer.
S. And let my cry come to You.
P. The Lord be with you.
S. And with your spirit. *P.* Let us pray.

Going up to the altar, the Priest prays silently:

TAKE away from us our sins, O Lord, we beseech You, that we may enter with pure minds into the Holy of Holies. Through Christ our Lord. Amen.

WE BESEECH You, O Lord, by the merits of Your Saints (*he kisses the altar*) whose relics lie here, and of all the Saints: deign in Your mercy to pardon me all my sins. Amen.

THE INTROIT • Isa. 9, 6

At the right side of the altar, the Priest says:

A CHILD is born to us, and a Son is given to us; Whose government is upon His shoulder; and His name shall be called the Angel of great counsel. *Ps.* 97. Sing to the Lord a new song, for He has done wondrous deeds. Glory be to the Father, and to the Son, and to the Holy Spirit. As it was in the beginning, is now, and ever shall be, world without end. Amen. — A Child is born to us, and a Son is given to us; Whose government is upon His shoulder; and His name shall be called the Angel of great counsel.

THE KYRIE

P. Lord, have mercy. *S.* Lord, have mercy. *P.* Lord, have mercy. *S.* Christ, have mercy. *P.* Christ, have mercy. *S.* Christ, have mercy. *P.* Lord, have mercy. *S.* Lord, have mercy. *P.* Lord, have mercy.

THE GLORIA

GLORY to God in the highest. And on earth peace to men of good will. We praise You. We bless You. We adore You. We glorify You. We give You thanks for Your great glory. O Lord God, heavenly King, God the Father almighty. O Lord Jesus Christ, the Only-begotten Son. O Lord God, Lamb of God, Son of the Father: You Who take away the sins of the world, have mercy on us. You Who take away the sins of the world, receive our prayer. You Who sit at the right hand of the Father, have mercy on us. For You alone are holy. You alone are the Lord. You alone, O Jesus Christ, are most high. Together with the Holy Spirit ✠ in the glory of God the Father. Amen.

The Priest kisses the altar and turns to the people, saying:

P. The Lord be with you. *S.* And with your spirit.

P. Let us pray.

THE PRAYER

Going to the right (Epistle) side, he says:

O GOD, by the fruitful virginity of Blessed Mary, You bestowed upon the human race the rewards of eternal salvation; grant, we beseech You, that we may feel the power of her intercession, through whom we have been made worthy to receive the Author of Life, Jesus Christ Your Son our Lord. Who with You lives and reigns in the unity of the Holy Spirit, God, world without end. S. Amen.

THE EPISTLE • Titus 2, 11-15

BELOVED: The grace of God our Savior has appeared to all men, instructing us, in order that, rejecting ungodliness and worldly lusts, we may live temperately and justly and piously in this world; looking for the blessed hope and glorious coming of our great God and Savior, Jesus Christ, Who gave Himself for us that He might redeem us from all iniquity and cleanse for Himself an acceptable people, pursuing good works. Thus speak, and exhort, in Christ Jesus our Lord. S. Thanks be to God.

THE GRADUAL • Ps. 97, 3. 4. 2

ALL the ends of the earth have seen the salvation by our God. Sing joyfully to God, all you lands. ℣. The Lord has made His salvation known: in the sight of the nations He has revealed His justice.

Alleluia, alleluia. ℣. *Heb. 1, 1. 2.* God, Who in diverse ways spoke in times past to the fathers by the prophets, last of all, in these days, has spoken to us by His Son. Alleluia.

PRAYER BEFORE THE GOSPEL

Bowing down at the center of the altar, he says:

CLEANSE my heart and my lips, O almighty God, Who cleansed the lips of the Prophet Isaias with a burning coal. In Your gracious mercy deign so to purify me that I may worthily proclaim Your holy Gospel. Through Christ our Lord. Amen.

Lord, grant Your blessing. The Lord be in my heart

and on my lips, that I may worthily and fittingly proclaim His holy Gospel. Amen.

THE GOSPEL • Luke 2, 21

Going to the left (Gospel) side of the altar, he says:

P. The Lord be with you. *S.* And with your spirit.
P. ✠ The continuation of the holy Gospel according to Saint Luke. *S.* Glory be to You, O Lord.

AT THAT time, when eight days were fulfilled for the circumcision of the Child, His name was called Jesus, the name given Him by the angel before He was conceived in the womb. *S.* Praise be to You, O Christ.

P. By the words of the Gospel, may our sins be taken away.

THE NICENE CREED

At the center of the altar, he says:

I BELIEVE in one God, the Father almighty, Maker of heaven and earth, and of all things visible and invisible. And in one Lord Jesus Christ, the Only-begotten Son of God. Born of the Father before all ages. God of God; Light of Light; true God of true God. Begotten not made; of one being with the Father; by Whom all things were made. Who for us men, and for our salvation, came down from heaven. (*Here all genuflect.*) And was made Flesh by the Holy Spirit of the Virgin Mary: AND WAS MADE MAN. He was also crucified for us, suffered under Pontius Pilate and was buried. And on the third day He rose again according to the Scriptures. And ascending into heaven, He sits at the right hand of the Father. And He shall come again in glory to judge the living and the dead; and of His kingdom there shall be no end. And I believe in the Holy Spirit, Lord and Giver of life, Who proceeds from the Father and the Son. Who together with the Father and the Son is no less adored, and glorified: Who spoke by the Prophets. And I believe in One, Holy, Catholic and Apostolic Church. I confess one Baptism for the remission of sins. And I look for the resurrection of the dead. ✠ And the life of the world to come. Amen.

THE OFFERTORY

The Priest turns to the people and says:

P. The Lord be with you. *S.* And with your spirit.
P. Let us pray.

THE OFFERTORY VERSE • Ps. 88, 12. 15

YOURS are the heavens, and Yours is the earth; the world and its fullness You have founded. Justice and judgment are the foundation of Your throne.

The Priest now uncovers the chalice, places the host on the paten and offering it up, says:

ACCEPT, O holy Father, almighty and eternal God, this spotless host, which I, Your unworthy servant, offer to You, my living and true God, to atone for my numberless sins, offenses, and negligences; on behalf of all here present and likewise for all faithful Christians living and dead, that it may profit me and them as a means of salvation to life everlasting. Amen.

He pours wine and water into the chalice, blessing the water before it is poured.

O GOD, Who established the nature of man in wondrous dignity, and still more admirably restored it, grant that through the mystery of this water and wine, we may be made partakers of His Divinity, Who has condescended to become partaker of our humanity, Jesus Christ, Your Son, our Lord. Who lives and reigns with You in the unity of the Holy Spirit, God, world without end. Amen.

Offering up the wine, the Priest says:

WE OFFER You, O Lord, the chalice of salvation, humbly begging of Your mercy that it may arise before Your Divine Majesty, with a pleasing fragrance, for our salvation and for that of the whole world. Amen.

Bowing down, the Priest says:

IN A humble spirit and with a contrite heart, may we be accepted by You, O Lord, and may our sacrifice so be offered in Your sight this day as to please You, O Lord God.

Raising his eyes and blessing the offering, he says:

COME, O Sanctifier, almighty and eternal God, and bless ✠ this sacrifice prepared for the glory of Your holy name.

WASHING THE FINGERS

I WASH my hands in innocence, and I go around Your altar, O Lord, giving voice to my thanks, and recounting all Your wondrous deeds. O Lord, I love the house in which You dwell, the tenting-place of Your glory. Gather not my soul with those of sinners, nor with men of blood my life. On their hands are crimes, and their right hands are full of bribes. But I walk in integrity; redeem me, and have pity on me. My foot stands on level ground; in the assemblies I will bless You, O Lord. Glory be to the Father, and to the Son, and to the Holy

Spirit. As it was in the beginning, is now, and ever shall be, world without end. Amen.

ACCEPT, Most Holy Trinity, this offering which we are making to You in remembrance of the Passion, Resurrection, and Ascension of Jesus Christ, our Lord; and in honor of Blessed Mary, ever Virgin, Blessed John the Baptist, the Holy Apostles Peter and Paul, and of these, and of all the Saints; that it may add to their honor and aid our salvation; and may they deign to intercede in heaven for us who honor their memory here on earth. Through the same Christ our Lord. Amen.

The Priest turns toward the people and says:

Pray, brethren, that my sacrifice and yours may become acceptable to God the Father almighty.

S. May the Lord accept this sacrifice from your hands to the praise and glory of His name, for our advantage, and that of all His holy Church.

P. Amen.

THE SECRET

RECEIVE, we beseech You, O Lord, our offerings and prayers; and, through these heavenly mysteries, both cleanse us, and mercifully grant what we ask. Through our Lord Jesus Christ, Your Son, Who lives and reigns with You in the unity of the Holy Spirit, God.

P. World without end. *S.* Amen.

PREFACE—CANON

P. The Lord be with you. *S.* And with your spirit.

P. Lift up your hearts.

S. We have lifted them up to the Lord.

P. Let us give thanks to the Lord, our God.
S. It is fitting and just.

IT IS fitting indeed and just, right and helpful to salvation, for us always and everywhere to give thanks to You, O holy Lord, Father almighty, everlasting God. Because by the mystery of the Word made flesh the new light of Your glory has shone upon the eyes of our mind: that while we acknowledge Him to be God seen by men, we may be drawn by Him to the love of things unseen. And therefore with Angels and Archangels, with Thrones and Dominations, and with the whole host of the heavenly army, we sing a hymn to Your glory, saying again and again (*the bell is rung 3 times*):

HOLY, HOLY, HOLY, Lord God of Hosts. Heaven and earth are filled with Your glory. Hosanna in the highest. ✠ Blessed is He Who comes in the name of the Lord. Hosanna in the highest.

THE CANON OF THE MASS

THEREFORE, most gracious Father, we humbly beg of You and entreat You through Jesus Christ Your Son, our Lord, (*he kisses the altar*) to deem acceptable and bless these ✠ gifts, these ✠ offerings, these ✠ holy and unspotted oblations which, in the first place, we offer You for Your Holy Catholic Church, that You would deign to give her peace and protection, to unite and guard her throughout the world, together with Your servant N., our Pope, and N., our Bishop; and all true believers who cherish the Catholic and Apostolic Faith.

Commemoration of the Living

REMEMBER, O Lord, Your servants and handmaids, N. and N., (*name them*) and all here present, whose faith and devotion are known to You, on whose behalf we offer to You, or who themselves offer to You, this sacrifice of praise for themselves, families and friends, for the good of their souls, for their hope of salvation and deliverance from all harm, and who offer their homage to You, eternal, living and true God.

Commemoration of the Saints

IN THE unity of holy fellowship, and keeping this most holy day, on which the spotless virginity of Blessed Mary brought forth a Savior to this world, we also observe the memory, first of all, of the glorious and ever Virgin Mary, Mother of our Lord and God Jesus Christ; next, that of Your Blessed Apostles and Martyrs, Peter and Paul, Andrew, James, John, Thomas, James, Philip, Bartholomew, Matthew, Simon and Thaddeus; of Linus, Cletus, Clement, Sixtus, Cornelius, Cyprian, Lawrence, Chrysogonus, John and Paul, Cosmas and Damian, and of all Your Saints, by whose merits and prayers grant that we may be always fortified by the help of Your protection. Through the same Christ our Lord. Amen.

Spreading his hands over the oblation, he says:

GRACIOUSLY accept, then, we beseech You, O Lord, this service of our worship and that of all Your household. Provide that our days be spent in Your peace, save us from everlasting damnation, and cause us to be numbered in the flock You have chosen. Through Christ our Lord. Amen.

O GOD, deign to bless ✠ what we offer, and make it approved, ✠ effective, ✠ right, and wholly pleasing in every way, that it may become for our good, the Body ✠ and Blood ✠ of Your dearly beloved Son, Jesus Christ our Lord.

CONSECRATION—ELEVATION

WHO, the day before He suffered, took bread into His holy and venerable hands, and having raised His eyes to heaven, to You, O God, His almighty Father, giving thanks to You, He blessed it, ✠ broke it, and gave it to His disciples, saying: All of you take and eat of this:

FOR THIS IS MY BODY.

IN LIKE manner, when the supper was done, taking also this goodly chalice into His holy and venerable hands, again giving thanks to You, He blessed ✠ it, and gave it to His disciples, saying: All of you take and drink of this:

FOR THIS IS THE CHALICE OF MY BLOOD OF THE NEW AND ETERNAL COVENANT: THE MYSTERY OF FAITH: WHICH SHALL BE SHED FOR YOU AND FOR MANY UNTO THE FORGIVENESS OF SINS.

After replacing the chalice on the corporal, he says:

As often as you shall do these things, in memory of Me shall you do them.

Offering of the Victim

MINDFUL, therefore, O Lord, not only of the blessed Passion of the same Christ, Your Son, our Lord, but also of His Resurrection from the dead, and finally His glorious Ascension into heav-

en, we, Your ministers, as also Your holy people, offer to Your supreme Majesty, of the gifts bestowed upon us, the pure ✠ Victim, the holy ✠ Victim, the all-perfect ✠ Victim: the holy ✠ Bread of life eternal and the Chalice ✠ of unending salvation.

AND this deign to regard with gracious and kindly attention and hold acceptable, as You deigned to accept the offerings of Abel, Your just servant, and the sacrifice of Abraham our patriarch, and that which Your chief priest Melchisedec offered to You, a holy sacrifice and a spotless victim.

MOST humbly we implore You, almighty God, bid these offerings to be brought by the hands of Your holy angel to Your altar above; before the face of Your Divine Majesty; that those of us who, by sharing in the Sacrifice of this altar, shall receive the Most Sacred ✠ Body and ✠ Blood of Your Son, may be filled with every grace and heavenly blessing. Through the same Christ our Lord. Amen.

Commemoration of the Dead

REMEMBER also, O Lord, Your servants and handmaids, N. and N., who have gone before us with the sign of faith, and rest in the sleep of peace. (*Here pray for the dead.*) To these, O Lord, and to all who rest in Christ, we beseech You to grant of Your goodness, a place of comfort, light and peace. Through the same Christ our Lord. Amen.

TO US sinners also, Your servants, trusting in the greatness of Your mercy, deign to grant some part and fellowship with Your Holy Apostles and Martyrs: with John, Stephen, Matthias, Barnabas,

Ignatius, Alexander, Marcellinus, Peter, Felicitas, Perpetua, Agatha, Lucy, Agnes, Cecilia, Anastasia, and all Your Saints; into whose company, we implore You to admit us, not weighing our merits, but freely granting us pardon. Through Christ our Lord.

THROUGH Whom, O Lord, You always create, ✠ sanctify, ✠ fill with life, ✠ bless, and bestow upon us all good things.

The Minor Elevation

THROUGH ✠ Him, and with ✠ Him, and in ✠ Him, is to You, God the Father ✠ almighty, in the unity of the Holy ✠ Spirit, all honor and glory, world without end. S. Amen.

THE COMMUNION AND THANKSGIVING

Let us pray. Prompted by saving precepts, and taught by Your divine teaching, we dare to say:

OUR FATHER, Who art in heaven, hallowed be Thy name: Thy kingdom come: Thy will be done on earth as it is in heaven. Give us this day our daily bread; and forgive us our trespasses, as we forgive those who trespass against us. And lead us not into temptation: S. But deliver us from evil. *P*. Amen.

DELIVER us, we beseech You, O Lord, from all evils, past, present, and to come; and by the intercession of the Blessed and glorious Mary, ever Virgin, Mother of God, together with Your Blessed Apostles Peter and Paul, and Andrew, and all the Saints, grant of Your goodness, peace in our days, that aided by the riches of Your mercy, we

may be always free from sin and safe from all disturbance.

Through the same our Lord Jesus Christ, Your Son, Who lives and reigns with You in the unity of the Holy Spirit, God, world without end.

S. Amen.

P. May the peace ✠ of the Lord be ✠ always with ✠ you.

S. And with your spirit.

The Priest puts a small particle into the chalice, saying:

May this mingling and consecration of the Body and Blood of our Lord Jesus Christ help us who receive it to life everlasting. Amen.

LAMB of God, You Who take away the sins of the world, have mercy on us.

Lamb of God, You Who take away the sins of the world, have mercy on us.

Lamb of God, You Who take away the sins of the world, grant us peace.

PRAYERS BEFORE HOLY COMMUNION

Then inclining toward the altar, he says:

O LORD Jesus Christ, Who said to Your Apostles: "Peace I leave with you, My peace I give to you," regard not my sins but the faith of Your Church, and deign to give her peace and unity according to Your Will: Who live and reign, God, world without end. Amen.

O LORD Jesus Christ, Son of the living God, Who, by the will of the Father, with the cooperation of the Holy Spirit, have by Your death given life to the world, deliver me by this Your

Most Sacred Body and Blood from all my sins and from every evil. Make me always cling to Your commandments, and never permit me to be separated from You, Who with the same God the Father and the Holy Spirit, live and reign, God, world without end. Amen.

LET not the partaking of Your Body, O Lord Jesus Christ, which I, though unworthy, presume to receive, turn to my judgment and condemnation; but through Your goodness, may it become a safeguard and an effective remedy, both of soul and body. Who live and reign with God the Father, in the unity of the Holy Spirit, God, world without end. Amen.

COMMUNION OF THE PRIEST

I WILL take the Bread of heaven, and call upon the name of the Lord.

Lord, I am not worthy that You should come under my roof; but only say the word, and my soul will be healed. (3 *times.*)

Making the Sign of the Cross with the Host, he says:

MAY the Body of our Lord Jesus Christ preserve my soul to life everlasting. Amen.

What return shall I make to the Lord for all He has given me? I will take the Chalice of salvation, and I will call upon the name of the Lord. Praising will I call upon the Lord and I shall be saved from my enemies.

Making the Sign of the Cross with the chalice, he says:

MAY the Blood of our Lord Jesus Christ preserve my soul to life everlasting. Amen.

The Priest reverently consumes the Precious Blood.

COMMUNION OF THE FAITHFUL

The Server and people say the "Confiteor."

P. May almighty God have mercy on you, forgive you your sins, and bring you to life everlasting. S. Amen.

P. May the almighty and merciful Lord grant you pardon, ✠ absolution and remission of your sins. S. Amen.

Holding up a Sacred Host, the Priest says:

Behold the Lamb of God, behold Him Who takes away the sins of the world.

Lord, I am not worthy that You should come under my roof; but only say the word, and my soul will be healed. (3 *times.*)

The Priest says to each communicant:

May the Body of our Lord Jesus Christ preserve your soul to life everlasting. Amen.

The Priest purifies the chalice with wine, saying:

WHAT has passed our lips as food, O Lord, may we possess in purity of heart, that what is given to us in time, be our healing for eternity.

He purifies his fingers with wine and water, saying:

MAY Your Body, O Lord, which I have eaten, and Your Blood which I have drunk, cleave to my very soul, and grant that no trace of sin be found in me, whom these pure and holy mysteries have renewed. Who live and reign, world without end. Amen.

THE COMMUNION • Ps. 97, 3

ALL the ends of the earth have seen the salvation by our God.

The Priest, turning to the people, says:

P. The Lord be with you. S. And with your spirit.
P. Let us pray.

THE POSTCOMMUNION

MAY this Communion, O Lord, cleanse us from guilt, and, through the intercession of Blessed Mary the Virgin-Mother of God, make us share in the heavenly remedy. Through the same our Lord Jesus Christ, Your Son, Who lives and reigns with You in the unity of the Holy Spirit, God, world without end. S. Amen.

FINAL PRAYERS

The Priest turns again to the people, and says:

P. The Lord be with you. S. And with your spirit.
P. Go, you are dismissed. S. Thanks be to God.

MAY the tribute of my worship be pleasing to You, Most Holy Trinity, and grant that the sacrifice which I, all unworthy, have offered in the presence of Your Majesty, may be acceptable to You, and through Your mercy obtain forgiveness for me and all for whom I have offered it. Through Christ our Lord. Amen.

THE LAST BLESSING

He kisses the altar, and facing the people, says:

MAY almighty God bless you: ✠ the Father, and the Son, and the Holy Spirit. S. Amen.

The Last Gospel and Prayers after Low Mass are conveniently placed inside the back cover.

"His Name was called Jesus, the Name given Him by the angel."

HOLY NAME OF JESUS

SUNDAY BETWEEN THE CIRCUMCISION AND THE EPIPHANY, OR JAN. 2

If no Sunday occurs between the Circumcision and Epiphany, this Feast is celebrated on January 2.

The Church invites us to celebrate in a solemn feast, the Holy Name of Jesus. This Most Holy Name should be on our lips during our lives and especially at the moment of our death. (WHITE VESTMENTS)

PRAYERS AT THE FOOT OF THE ALTAR

IN THE name of the Father, ✠ and of the Son, and of the Holy Spirit. Amen.

Priest. I will go in to the altar of God.

Server. The God of my gladness and joy.

Psalm 42

DO ME justice, O God, and fight my fight against a faithless people; from the deceitful and impious man rescue me.

S. For You, O God, are my strength. Why do You keep me so far away? Why must I go about in mourning, with the enemy oppressing me?

P. Send forth Your light and Your fidelity; they shall lead me on and bring me to Your holy mountain, to Your dwelling-place.
S. Then will I go in to the altar of God, the God of my gladness and joy.
P. Then will I give You thanks upon the harp, O God, my God. Why are you so downcast, O my soul? Why do you sigh within me?
S. Hope in God! For I shall again be thanking Him in the presence of my Savior and my God.
P. Glory be to the Father, and to the Son, and to the Holy Spirit.
S. As it was in the beginning, is now, and ever shall be, world without end. Amen.
P. I will go in to the altar of God.
S. The God of my gladness and joy.
P. Our help ✠ is in the name of the Lord.
S. Who made heaven and earth.
P. I confess to almighty God, etc.
S. May almighty God have mercy on you, forgive you your sins, and bring you to life everlasting.
P. Amen.

The Server, bowing, says the "Confiteor."

I CONFESS to almighty God, to Blessed Mary, ever Virgin, to Blessed Michael the Archangel, to Blessed John the Baptist, to the Holy Apostles Peter and Paul, and to all the Saints, and to you, Father, that I have sinned exceedingly in thought, word and deed, *through my fault, through my fault, through my most grievous fault.* Therefore I beseech Blessed Mary, ever Virgin, Blessed Michael the Archangel, Blessed John the Baptist, the Holy Apostles Peter and Paul, and all the Saints, and you, Father, to pray to the Lord our God for me.

P. May almighty God have mercy on you, forgive you your sins, and bring you to life everlasting.
S. Amen.

MAY the almighty and merciful Lord grant us pardon, ✠ absolution, and remission of our sins. *S.* Amen.
P. Will You not, O God, give us life?
S. And shall not Your people rejoice in You?
P. Show us, O Lord, Your kindness.
S. And grant us Your salvation.
P. O Lord, hear my prayer.
S. And let my cry come to You.
P. The Lord be with you.
S. And with your spirit. *P.* Let us pray.

Going up to the altar, the Priest prays silently:

TAKE away from us our sins, O Lord, we beseech You, that we may enter with pure minds into the Holy of Holies. Through Christ our Lord. Amen.

WE BESEECH You, O Lord, by the merits of Your Saints (*he kisses the altar*) whose relics lie here, and of all the Saints: deign in Your mercy to pardon me all my sins. Amen.

THE INTROIT • Phil. 2, 10-11

At the right side of the altar, the Priest says:

AT THE Name of Jesus every knee should bend of those in heaven, on earth, and under the earth, and every tongue should confess that the Lord Jesus Christ is in the glory of God the Father. *Ps.* 8. O Lord, our Lord, how glorious is Your Name over all the earth! Glory be to the Father, and to the Son, and to the Holy Spirit. As it was in the beginning, is now, and ever shall be, world without end. Amen. — At the Name of Jesus every knee should bend of those in heaven, on earth, and under the earth, and every tongue should confess that the Lord Jesus Christ is in the glory of God the Father.

THE KYRIE

P. Lord, have mercy. *S.* Lord, have mercy. *P.* Lord, have mercy. *S.* Christ, have mercy. *P.* Christ, have mercy. *S.* Christ, have mercy. *P.* Lord, have mercy. *S.* Lord, have mercy. *P.* Lord, have mercy.

THE GLORIA

GLORY to God in the highest. And on earth peace to men of good will. We praise You. We bless You. We adore You. We glorify You. We give You thanks for Your great glory. O Lord God, heavenly King, God the Father almighty. O Lord Jesus Christ, the Only-begotten Son. O Lord God, Lamb of God, Son of the Father: You Who take away the sins of the world, have mercy on us. You Who take away the sins of the world, receive our prayer. You Who sit at the right hand of the Father, have mercy on us. For You alone are holy. You alone are the Lord. You alone, O Jesus Christ, are most high. Together with the Holy Spirit ✠ in the glory of God the Father. Amen.

The Priest kisses the altar and turns to the people, saying:

P. The Lord be with you. *S.* And with your spirit. P. Let us pray.

THE PRAYER

Going to the right (Epistle) side, he says:

O GOD, You have established Your Only-begotten Son as the Savior of mankind, and commanded that He should be called Jesus; mercifully grant that we who venerate His holy Name on earth, may also be filled with the enjoyment of the vision of Him in heaven. Through the same our Lord Jesus Christ, Your Son, Who lives and reigns with You in the unity of the Holy Spirit, God, world without end. *S.* Amen.

THE EPISTLE • Acts 4, 8-12

IN THOSE days, Peter, filled with the Holy Spirit, said, "Rulers of the people and elders, if we are on trial today about a good work done to a cripple, as to how this man has been cured, be it known to all of you and to all the people of Israel that in the Name of Jesus Christ of Nazareth, Whom you crucified, Whom God has raised from the dead, even in this Name does he stand here before you, sound. This is 'The stone that was rejected by you, the builders, which has become the cornerstone.' Neither is their salvation in any other. For there is no other name under heaven given to men by which we must be saved." S. Thanks be to God.

THE GRADUAL • Ps. 105, 47

SAVE us, O Lord, our God, and gather us from among the nations, that we may give thanks to Your holy Name and glory in praising You. ℣. *Isa.* 63. You, O Lord, are our Father and our Redeemer, from everlasting is Your Name.

Alleluia, alleluia. ℣. *Ps. 144, 21.* May my mouth speak the praise of the Lord, and may all flesh bless His holy Name. Alleluia.

PRAYER BEFORE THE GOSPEL

Bowing down at the center of the altar, he says:

CLEANSE my heart and my lips, O almighty God, Who cleansed the lips of the Prophet Isaias with a burning coal. In Your gracious mercy deign so to purify me that I may worthily proclaim Your holy Gospel. Through Christ our Lord. Amen. Lord, grant Your blessing. The Lord be in my heart and on my lips, that I may worthily and fittingly proclaim His holy Gospel. Amen.

THE GOSPEL • Luke 2, 21

Going to the left (Gospel) side of the altar, he says:

P. The Lord be with you. *S.* And with your spirit.
P. ✠ The continuation of the holy Gospel according to Saint Luke. *S.* Glory be to You, O Lord.

AT THAT time, when eight days were fulfilled for the circumcision of the Child, His Name was called Jesus, the Name given Him by the angel before He was conceived in the womb. *S.* Praise be to You, O Christ.

P. By the words of the Gospel, may our sins be taken away.

THE NICENE CREED

At the center of the altar, he says:

I BELIEVE in one God, the Father almighty, Maker of heaven and earth, and of all things visible and invisible. And in one Lord Jesus Christ, the Only-begotten Son of God. Born of the Father before all ages. God of God; Light of Light; true God of true God. Begotten not made; of one being with the Father; by Whom all things were made. Who for us men, and for our salvation, came down from heaven. (*Here all genuflect.*) And was made Flesh by the Holy Spirit of the Virgin Mary: AND WAS MADE MAN. He was also crucified for us, suffered under Pontius Pilate and was buried. And on the third day He rose again according to the Scriptures. And ascending into heaven, He sits at the right hand of the Father. And He shall come again in glory to judge the living and the dead; and of His kingdom there shall be no end. And I believe in the Holy Spirit, Lord and Giver of life, Who proceeds from the Father and the Son. Who together with the Father and the Son is no less adored, and glorified: Who spoke by the Prophets. And I believe in One, Holy, Catholic and Apostolic Church. I confess one Baptism for the remission of sins. And I look for the resurrection of the dead. ✠ And the life of the world to come. Amen.

THE OFFERTORY

The Priest turns to the people and says:

P. The Lord be with you. S. And with your spirit.
P. Let us pray.

THE OFFERTORY VERSE • Ps. 85, 12. 5

I WILL give thanks to You, O Lord my God, with all my heart, and I will glorify Your Name forever. For You, O Lord, are good and forgiving, abounding in kindness to all who call upon You. Alleluia.

The Priest now uncovers the chalice, places the host on the paten and offering it up, says:

ACCEPT, O holy Father, almighty and eternal God, this spotless host, which I, Your unworthy servant, offer to You, my living and true God, to atone for my numberless sins, offenses, and negligences; on behalf of all here present and like-

wise for all faithful Christians living and dead, that it may profit me and them as a means of salvation to life everlasting. Amen.

He pours wine and water into the chalice, blessing the water before it is poured.

O GOD, Who established the nature of man in wondrous dignity, and still more admirably restored it, grant that through the mystery of this water and wine, we may be made partakers of His Divinity, Who has condescended to become partaker of our humanity, Jesus Christ, Your Son, our Lord. Who lives and reigns with You in the unity of the Holy Spirit, God, world without end. Amen.

Offering up the wine, the Priest says:

WE OFFER You, O Lord, the chalice of salvation, humbly begging of Your mercy that it may arise before Your Divine Majesty, with a pleasing fragrance, for our salvation and for that of the whole world. Amen.

Bowing down, the Priest says:

IN A humble spirit and with a contrite heart, may we be accepted by You, O Lord, and may our sacrifice so be offered in Your sight this day as to please You, O Lord God.

Raising his eyes and blessing the offering, he says:

COME, O Sanctifier, almighty and eternal God, and bless ✠ this sacrifice prepared for the glory of Your holy name.

WASHING THE FINGERS

I WASH my hands in innocence, and I go around Your altar, O Lord, giving voice to my thanks, and recounting all Your wondrous deeds. O Lord, I love the house in which You dwell, the tenting-place of Your glory. Gather not my soul with those of sinners, nor with men of blood my life. On their hands are crimes, and their right hands are full of bribes. But I walk in integrity; redeem me, and have pity on me. My foot stands on level ground; in the assemblies I will bless You, O Lord. Glory be to the Father, and to the Son, and to the Holy Spirit. As it was in the beginning, is now, and ever shall be, world without end. Amen.

ACCEPT, Most Holy Trinity, this offering which we are making to You in remembrance of the Passion, Resurrection, and Ascension of Jesus Christ, our Lord; and in honor of Blessed Mary, ever Virgin, Blessed John the Baptist, the Holy Apostles Peter and Paul, and of these, and of all the Saints; that it may add to their honor and aid our salvation; and may they deign to intercede in heaven for us who honor their memory here on earth. Through the same Christ our Lord. Amen.

The Priest turns toward the people and says:

Pray, brethren, that my sacrifice and yours may become acceptable to God the Father almighty.

S. May the Lord accept this sacrifice from your hands to the praise and glory of His name, for our advantage, and that of all His holy Church.

P. Amen.

THE SECRET

MAY Your blessing, most merciful God, by which every creature lives, sanctify, we beseech You, this our sacrifice, which we offer to You, to the glory of the Name of Your Son, our Lord Jesus Christ, that it may please Your Majesty as an act of praise, and profit us to salvation. Through the same our Lord Jesus Christ, Your Son,

Who lives and reigns with You in the unity of the Holy Spirit, God.
P. World without end. *S*. Amen.

PREFACE—CANON

P. The Lord be with you. *S*. And with your spirit.
P. Lift up your hearts.
S. We have lifted them up to the Lord.
P. Let us give thanks to the Lord, our God.
S. It is fitting and just.

IT IS fitting indeed and just, right and helpful to salvation, for us always and everywhere to give thanks to You, O holy Lord, Father almighty, everlasting God. Because by the mystery of the Word made flesh the new light of Your glory has shone upon the eyes of our mind: that while we acknowledge Him to be God seen by men, we may be drawn by Him to the love of things unseen. And therefore with Angels and Archangels, with Thrones and Dominations, and with the whole host of the heavenly army, we sing a hymn to Your glory, saying again and again (*the bell is rung* 3 *times*):

HOLY, HOLY, HOLY, Lord God of Hosts. Heaven and earth are filled with Your glory. Hosanna in the highest. ✠ Blessed is He Who comes in the name of the Lord. Hosanna in the highest.

THE CANON OF THE MASS

THEREFORE, most gracious Father, we humbly beg of You and entreat You through Jesus Christ Your Son, our Lord, (*he kisses the altar*) to deem acceptable and bless these ✠ gifts, these ✠ offerings, these ✠ holy and unspotted oblations

which, in the first place, we offer You for Your Holy Catholic Church, that You would deign to give her peace and protection, to unite and guard her throughout the world, together with Your servant N., our Pope, and N., our Bishop; and all true believers who cherish the Catholic and Apostolic Faith.

Commemoration of the Living

REMEMBER, O Lord, Your servants and handmaids, N. and N., (*name them*) and all here present, whose faith and devotion are known to You, on whose behalf we offer to You, or who themselves offer to You, this sacrifice of praise for themselves, families and friends, for the good of their souls, for their hope of salvation and deliverance from all harm, and who offer their homage to You, eternal, living and true God.

Commemoration of the Saints

IN THE unity of holy fellowship we observe the memory, first of all, of the glorious and ever Virgin Mary, Mother of our Lord and God Jesus Christ; next, that of Your Blessed Apostles and Martyrs, Peter and Paul, Andrew, James, John, Thomas, James, Philip, Bartholomew, Matthew, Simon and Thaddeus; of Linus, Cletus, Clement, Sixtus, Cornelius, Cyprian, Lawrence, Chrysogonus, John and Paul, Cosmas and Damian, and of all Your Saints, by whose merits and prayers grant that we may be always fortified by the help of Your protection. Through the same Christ our Lord. Amen.

Spreading his hands over the oblation, he says:

GRACIOUSLY accept, then, we beseech You, O Lord, this service of our worship and that

of all Your household. Provide that our days be spent in Your peace, save us from everlasting damnation, and cause us to be numbered in the flock You have chosen. Through Christ our Lord. Amen.

O GOD, deign to bless ✠ what we offer, and make it approved, ✠ effective, ✠ right, and wholly pleasing in every way, that it may become for our good, the Body ✠ and Blood ✠ of Your dearly beloved Son, Jesus Christ our Lord.

CONSECRATION—ELEVATION

WHO, the day before He suffered, took bread into His holy and venerable hands, and having raised His eyes to heaven, to You, O God, His almighty Father, giving thanks to You, He blessed it, ✠ broke it, and gave it to His disciples, saying: All of you take and eat of this:

FOR THIS IS MY BODY.

IN LIKE manner, when the supper was done, taking also this goodly chalice into His holy and venerable hands, again giving thanks to You, He blessed ✠ it, and gave it to His disciples, saying: All of you take and drink of this:

FOR THIS IS THE CHALICE OF MY BLOOD OF THE NEW AND ETERNAL COVENANT: THE MYSTERY OF FAITH: WHICH SHALL BE SHED FOR YOU AND FOR MANY UNTO THE FORGIVENESS OF SINS.

After replacing the chalice on the corporal, he says:

As often as you shall do these things, in memory of Me shall you do them.

Offering of the Victim

MINDFUL, therefore, O Lord, not only of the blessed Passion of the same Christ, Your Son, our Lord, but also of His Resurrection from the dead, and finally His glorious Ascension into heaven, we, Your ministers, as also Your holy people, offer to Your supreme Majesty, of the gifts bestowed upon us, the pure ✠ Victim, the holy ✠ Victim, the all-perfect ✠ Victim: the holy ✠ Bread of life eternal and the Chalice ✠ of unending salvation.

AND this deign to regard with gracious and kindly attention and hold acceptable, as You deigned to accept the offerings of Abel, Your just servant, and the sacrifice of Abraham our patriarch, and that which Your chief priest Melchisedec offered to You, a holy sacrifice and a spotless victim.

MOST humbly we implore You, almighty God, bid these offerings to be brought by the hands of Your holy angel to Your altar above; before the face of Your Divine Majesty; that those of us who, by sharing in the Sacrifice of this altar, shall receive the Most Sacred ✠ Body and ✠ Blood of Your Son, may be filled with every grace and heavenly blessing. Through the same Christ our Lord. Amen.

Commemoration of the Dead

REMEMBER also, O Lord, Your servants and handmaids, *N.* and *N.*, who have gone before us with the sign of faith, and rest in the sleep of peace. (*Here pray for the dead.*) To these, O Lord, and to all who rest in Christ, we beseech You to grant of Your goodness, a place of comfort, light

and peace. Through the same Christ our Lord. Amen.

TO US sinners also, Your servants, trusting in the greatness of Your mercy, deign to grant some part and fellowship with Your Holy Apostles and Martyrs: with John, Stephen, Matthias, Barnabas, Ignatius, Alexander, Marcellinus, Peter, Felicitas, Perpetua, Agatha, Lucy, Agnes, Cecilia, Anastasia, and all Your Saints; into whose company, we implore You to admit us, not weighing our merits, but freely granting us pardon. Through Christ our Lord.

THROUGH Whom, O Lord, You always create, ✠ sanctify, ✠ fill with life, ✠ bless, and bestow upon us all good things.

The Minor Elevation

THROUGH ✠ Him, and with ✠ Him, and in ✠ Him, is to You, God the Father ✠ almighty, in the unity of the Holy ✠ Spirit, all honor and glory, world without end. S. Amen.

THE COMMUNION AND THANKSGIVING

Let us pray. Prompted by saving precepts, and taught by Your divine teaching, we dare to say:

OUR FATHER, Who art in heaven, hallowed be Thy name: Thy kingdom come: Thy will be done on earth as it is in heaven. Give us this day our daily bread; and forgive us our trespasses, as we forgive those who trespass against us. And lead us not into temptation: S. But deliver us from evil. *P.* Amen.

DELIVER us, we beseech You, O Lord, from all evils, past, present, and to come; and by

the intercession of the Blessed and glorious Mary, ever Virgin, Mother of God, together with Your Blessed Apostles Peter and Paul, and Andrew, and all the Saints, grant of Your goodness, peace in our days, that aided by the riches of Your mercy, we may be always free from sin and safe from all disturbance.

Through the same our Lord Jesus Christ, Your Son, Who lives and reigns with You in the unity of the Holy Spirit, God, world without end. S. Amen.

P. May the peace ✠ of the Lord be ✠ always with ✠ you.

S. And with your spirit.

The Priest puts a small particle into the chalice, saying:

May this mingling and consecration of the Body and Blood of our Lord Jesus Christ help us who receive it to life everlasting. Amen.

LAMB of God, You Who take away the sins of the world, have mercy on us.

Lamb of God, You Who take away the sins of the world, have mercy on us.

Lamb of God, You Who take away the sins of the world, grant us peace.

PRAYERS BEFORE HOLY COMMUNION

O LORD Jesus Christ, Who said to Your Apostles: "Peace I leave with you, My peace I give to you," regard not my sins but the faith of Your Church, and deign to give her peace and unity according to Your Will: Who live and reign, God, world without end. Amen.

O LORD Jesus Christ, Son of the living God, Who, by the will of the Father, with the cooperation of the Holy Spirit, have by Your death given life to the world, deliver me by this Your Most Sacred Body and Blood from all my sins and from every evil. Make me always cling to Your commandments, and never permit me to be separated from You. Who with the same God the Father and the Holy Spirit, live and reign, God, world without end. Amen.

LET not the partaking of Your Body, O Lord Jesus Christ, which I, though unworthy, presume to receive, turn to my judgment and condemnation; but through Your goodness, may it become a safeguard and an effective remedy, both of soul and body. Who live and reign with God the Father, in the unity of the Holy Spirit, God, world without end. Amen.

COMMUNION OF THE PRIEST

I WILL take the Bread of heaven, and call upon the name of the Lord.

Lord, I am not worthy that You should come under my roof; but only say the word, and my soul will be healed. (3 *times.*)

Making the Sign of the Cross with the Host, he says:

MAY the Body of our Lord Jesus Christ preserve my soul to life everlasting. Amen.

What return shall I make to the Lord for all He has given me? I will take the Chalice of salvation, and I will call upon the name of the Lord. Praising will I call upon the Lord and I shall be saved from my enemies.

Making the Sign of the Cross with the chalice, he says:

MAY the Blood of our Lord Jesus Christ preserve my soul to life everlasting. Amen.

The Priest reverently consumes the Precious Blood.

COMMUNION OF THE FAITHFUL

The Server and people say the "Confiteor."

P. May almighty God have mercy on you, forgive you your sins, and bring you to life everlasting. *S.* Amen.

P. May the almighty and merciful Lord grant you pardon, ✠ absolution and remission of your sins. *S.* Amen.

Holding up a Sacred Host, the Priest says:

Behold the Lamb of God, behold Him Who takes away the sins of the world.

Lord, I am not worthy that You should come under my roof; but only say the word, and my soul will be healed. (3 *times.*)

The Priest says to each communicant:

May the Body of our Lord Jesus Christ preserve your soul to life everlasting. Amen.

The Priest purifies the chalice with wine, saying:

WHAT has passed our lips as food, O Lord, may we possess in purity of heart, that what is given to us in time, be our healing for eternity.

He purifies his fingers with wine and water, saying:

MAY Your Body, O Lord, which I have eaten, and Your Blood which I have drunk, cleave to my very soul, and grant that no trace of sin be found in me, whom these pure and holy mysteries have renewed. Who live and reign, world without end. Amen.

THE COMMUNION • Ps. 85, 9-10

ALL the nations You have made shall come and worship You, O Lord, and glorify Your Name. For You are great, and do wondrous deeds; You alone are God. Alleluia.

The Priest, turning to the people, says:

P. The Lord be with you. *S.* And with your spirit.
P. Let us pray.

THE POSTCOMMUNION

O ALMIGHTY and eternal God, You have created and redeemed us; graciously regard our prayers, and vouchsafe to accept with a benign and favorable countenance the sacrifice of the Saving Victim which we have offered to Your Majesty, in honor of the Name of Your Son, our Lord Jesus Christ: that, through the infusion of Your grace into us, we may rejoice over our names having been written under the glorious Name of Jesus, as a pledge of eternal predestination. Through the same our Lord Jesus Christ, Your Son, Who lives and reigns with You in the unity of the Holy Spirit, God, world without end. *S.* Amen.

FINAL PRAYERS

P. The Lord be with you. *S.* And with your spirit.
P. Go, you are dismissed. *S.* Thanks be to God.

MAY the tribute of my worship be pleasing to You, Most Holy Trinity, and grant that the sacrifice which I, all unworthy, have offered in the presence of Your Majesty, may be acceptable to You, and through Your mercy obtain forgiveness for me and all for whom I have offered it. Through Christ our Lord. Amen.

THE LAST BLESSING

He kisses the altar, and facing the people, says:

MAY almighty God bless you: ✠ the Father, and the Son, and the Holy Spirit. *S.* Amen.

The Last Gospel and Prayers after Low Mass are conveniently placed inside the back cover.

The three Kings find the Child Jesus.

THE EPIPHANY OF OUR LORD

The word *Epiphany* means *manifestation.* The Church in the Mass commemorates a triple manifestation of Christ: to the Magi, that is, to the Gentiles; in His Baptism, when the Voice from heaven declared: "This is My Beloved Son"; and in His first public miracle at Cana. (WHITE VESTMENTS)

PRAYERS AT THE FOOT OF THE ALTAR

IN THE name of the Father, ✠ and of the Son and of the Holy Spirit. Amen.

Priest. I will go in to the altar of God.

Server. The God of my gladness and joy.

Psalm 42

DO ME justice, O God, and fight my fight against a faithless people; from the deceitful and impious man rescue me.

S. For You, O God, are my strength. Why do You keep me so far away? Why must I go about in mourning, with the enemy oppressing me?

P. Send forth Your light and Your fidelity; they shall lead me on and bring me to Your holy mountain, to Your dwelling-place.

S. Then will I go in to the altar of God, the God of my gladness and joy.
P. Then will I give You thanks upon the harp, O God, my God. Why are you so downcast, O my soul? Why do you sigh within me?
S. Hope in God! For I shall again be thanking Him in the presence of my Savior and my God.
P. Glory be to the Father, and to the Son, and to the Holy Spirit.
S. As it was in the beginning, is now, and ever shall be, world without end. Amen.
P. I will go in to the altar of God.
S. The God of my gladness and joy.
P. Our help ✠ is in the name of the Lord.
S. Who made heaven and earth.
P. I confess to almighty God, etc.
S. May almighty God have mercy on you, forgive you your sins, and bring you to life everlasting.
P. Amen.

The Server, bowing, says the "Confiteor."

I CONFESS to almighty God, to Blessed Mary, ever Virgin, to Blessed Michael the Archangel, to Blessed John the Baptist, to the Holy Apostles Peter and Paul, and to all the Saints, and to you, Father, that I have sinned exceedingly in thought, word and deed, *through my fault, through my fault, through my most grievous fault.* Therefore I beseech Blessed Mary, ever Virgin, Blessed Michael the Archangel, Blessed John the Baptist, the Holy Apostles Peter and Paul, and all the Saints, and you, Father, to pray to the Lord our God for me.
P. May almighty God have mercy on you, forgive you your sins, and bring you to life everlasting.
S. Amen.

MAY the almighty and merciful Lord grant us pardon, ✠ absolution, and remission of our sins. *S.* Amen.

P. Will You not, O God, give us life?

S. And shall not Your people rejoice in You?

P. Show us, O Lord, Your kindness.

S. And grant us Your salvation.

P. O Lord, hear my prayer.

S. And let my cry come to You.

P. The Lord be with you.

S. And with your spirit. *P.* Let us pray.

Going up to the altar, the Priest prays silently:

TAKE away from us our sins, O Lord, we beseech You, that we may enter with pure minds into the Holy of Holies. Through Christ our Lord. Amen.

WE BESEECH You, O Lord, by the merits of Your Saints (*he kisses the altar*) whose relics lie here, and of all the Saints: deign in Your mercy to pardon me all my sins. Amen.

THE INTROIT • Mal. 3, 1; 1 Par. 29, 12

At the right side of the altar, the Priest says:

BEHOLD the Lord the Ruler is come; and the kingdom is in His hand, and power, and dominion. *Ps. 71.* O God, with Your judgment endow the king, and with Your justice, the king's son. Glory be to the Father, and to the Son, and to the Holy Spirit. As it was in the beginning, is now, and ever shall be, world without end. Amen. — Behold the Lord the Ruler is come; and the kingdom is in His hand, and power, and dominion.

THE KYRIE

P. Lord, have mercy. *S.* Lord, have mercy. *P.* Lord, have mercy. *S.* Christ, have mercy. *P.* Christ, have mercy. *S.* Christ, have mercy. *P.* Lord, have mercy. *S.* Lord, have mercy. *P.* Lord, have mercy.

THE GLORIA

GLORY to God in the highest. And on earth peace to men of good will. We praise You. We bless You. We adore You. We glorify You. We give You thanks for Your great glory. O Lord God, heavenly King, God the Father almighty. O Lord Jesus Christ, the Only-begotten Son. O Lord God, Lamb of God, Son of the Father: You Who take away the sins of the world, have mercy on us. You Who take away the sins of the world, receive our prayer. You Who sit at the right hand of the Father, have mercy on us. For You alone are holy. You alone are the Lord. You alone, O Jesus Christ, are most high. Together with the Holy Spirit ✠ in the glory of God the Father. Amen.

The Priest kisses the altar and turns to the people, saying:

P. The Lord be with you. *S.* And with your spirit. *P.* Let us pray.

THE PRAYER

Going to the right (Epistle) side, he says:

O GOD, on this day, by the guiding star, You revealed Your Only-begotten Son to the Gentiles; mercifully grant, that we who now know You by faith, may be led on even to look upon the beauty of Your Majesty. Through the same our

Lord Jesus Christ, Your Son, Who lives and reigns with You in the unity of the Holy Spirit, God, world without end. S. Amen.

THE EPISTLE • Isa. 60, 1-6

ARISE, be enlightened, O Jerusalem; for your light is come, and the glory of the Lord is risen upon you. For behold, darkness shall cover the earth, and a mist the people; but the Lord shall arise upon you, and His glory shall be seen upon you. And the Gentiles shall walk in your light, and kings in the brightness of your rising. Lift up your eyes round about, and see; all these are gathered together: they are come to you; your sons shall come from afar, and your daughters shall rise up at your side. Then shall you see, and abound; and your heart shall wonder and be enlarged, when the multitude of the sea shall be converted to you, the strength of the Gentiles shall come to you. The multitude of camels shall cover you, the dromedaries of Madian and Epha; all they from Saba shall come, bringing gold and frankincense, and showing forth praise to the Lord. S. Thanks be to God.

THE GRADUAL • Isa. 60, 6. 1

ALL they from Saba shall come, bringing gold and frankincense, and showing forth praise to the Lord. ℣. Arise, and be enlightened, O Jerusalem, for the glory of the Lord is risen upon you.

Alleluia, alleluia. ℣. *Matt.* 2, 2. We have seen His star in the East: and have come with gifts to worship the Lord. Alleluia.

PRAYER BEFORE THE GOSPEL

Bowing down at the center of the altar, he says:

CLEANSE my heart and my lips, O almighty God, Who cleansed the lips of the Prophet Isaias with a burning coal. In Your gracious mercy deign so to purify me that I may worthily proclaim Your holy Gospel. Through Christ our Lord. Amen.

Lord, grant Your blessing. The Lord be in my heart and on my lips, that I may worthily and fittingly proclaim His holy Gospel. Amen.

THE GOSPEL • Matt. 2, 1-12

Going to the left (Gospel) side of the altar, he says:

P. The Lord be with you. *S.* And with your spirit.

P. ✠ The continuation of the holy Gospel according to Saint Matthew. *S.* Glory be to You, O Lord.

WHEN Jesus was born in Bethlehem of Judea, in the days of King Herod, behold, Magi came from the East to Jerusalem, saying, "Where is He that is born King of the Jews? For we have seen His star in the East and have come to worship Him." But when King Herod heard this, he was troubled, and so was all Jerusalem with him. And gathering together all the chief priests and Scribes of the people, he inquired of them where the Christ was to be born. And they said to him, "In Bethlehem of Judea; for thus it is written by the prophet, 'And you, Bethlehem, of the land of Juda, are by no means least among the princes of Juda; for from you shall come forth a leader who shall rule my people Israel.' " Then Herod summoned the Magi secretly, and carefully ascertained from them the time when the star had appeared to them. And sending them to Bethlehem, he said, "Go and make careful inquiry concerning the Child, and when you have found Him, bring me word, that I too may go and worship Him." Now they, having heard the king, went their way. And behold, the star that they had seen in the East went before them, until it came and stood over the place where the Child was. And when they saw the star they rejoiced exceedingly. And entering the house, they found the Child with Mary His mother, and falling down they worshipped Him. (*Here genuflect.*) And opening their treasures they offered Him gifts of gold, frankincense and myrrh. And being warned in a dream not to return to Herod, they went back to their own country by another way. *S.* Praise be to You, O Christ.

P. By the words of the Gospel, may our sins be taken away.

THE NICENE CREED

At the center of the altar, he says:

I BELIEVE in one God, the Father almighty, Maker of heaven and earth, and of all things visible and invisible. And in one Lord Jesus Christ, the Only-begotten Son of God. Born of the Father before all ages. God of God; Light of Light; true God of true God. Begotten not made; of one being with the Father; by Whom all things were made. Who for us men, and for our salvation, came down from heaven. (*Here all genuflect.*) And was made Flesh by the Holy Spirit of the Virgin Mary: AND WAS MADE MAN. He was also crucified for us, suffered under Pontius Pilate and was buried. And on the third day He rose again according to the Scriptures. And ascending into heaven, He sits at the right hand of the Father. And He shall come again in glory to judge the living and the dead; and of His kingdom there shall be no end. And I believe in the Holy Spirit, Lord and Giver of life, Who proceeds from the Father and the Son. Who together with the Father and the Son is no less adored, and glorified: Who spoke by the Prophets. And I believe in One, Holy, Catholic and Apostolic Church. I confess one Baptism for the remission of sins. And I look for the resurrection of the dead. ✠ And the life of the world to come. Amen.

THE OFFERTORY

The Priest turns to the people and says:

P. The Lord be with you. *S.* And with your spirit.
P. Let us pray.

THE OFFERTORY VERSE • Ps. 71, 10-11

THE kings of Tharsis and the Isles shall offer gifts; the kings of Arabia and Saba shall bring tribute. All kings shall pay Him homage, all nations shall serve Him.

The Priest now uncovers the chalice, places the host on the paten and offering it up, says:

ACCEPT, O holy Father, almighty and eternal God, this spotless host, which I, Your unworthy servant, offer to You, my living and true God, to atone for my numberless sins, offenses, and negligences; on behalf of all here present and likewise for all faithful Christians living and dead, that it may profit me and them as a means of salvation to life everlasting. Amen.

He pours wine and water into the chalice, blessing the water before it is poured.

O GOD, Who established the nature of man in wondrous dignity, and still more admirably restored it, grant that through the mystery of this water and wine, we may be made partakers of His Divinity, Who has condescended to become partaker of our humanity, Jesus Christ, Your Son, our Lord. Who lives and reigns with You in the unity of the Holy Spirit, God, world without end. Amen.

Offering up the wine, the Priest says:

WE OFFER You, O Lord, the chalice of salvation, humbly begging of Your mercy that it may arise before Your Divine Majesty, with a pleasing fragrance, for our salvation and for that of the whole world. Amen.

Bowing down, the Priest says:

IN A humble spirit and with a contrite heart, may we be accepted by You, O Lord, and may our sacrifice so be offered in Your sight this day as to please You, O Lord God.

Raising his eyes and blessing the offering, he says:

COME, O Sanctifier, almighty and eternal God, and bless ✠ this sacrifice prepared for the glory of Your holy name.

WASHING THE FINGERS

I WASH my hands in innocence, and I go around Your altar, O Lord, giving voice to my thanks, and recounting all Your wondrous deeds. O Lord, I love the house in which You dwell, the tenting-place of Your glory. Gather not my soul with those of sinners, nor with men of blood my life. On their hands are crimes, and their right hands are full of bribes. But I walk in integrity; redeem me, and have pity on me. My foot stands on level ground; in the assemblies I will bless You, O Lord. Glory be to the Father, and to the Son, and to the Holy Spirit. As it was in the beginning, is now, and ever shall be, world without end. Amen.

ACCEPT, Most Holy Trinity, this offering which we are making to You in remembrance of the Passion, Resurrection, and Ascension of Jesus Christ, our Lord; and in honor of Blessed Mary, ever Virgin, Blessed John the Baptist, the Holy Apostles Peter and Paul, and of these, and of all the Saints; that it may add to their honor and aid our salvation; and may they deign to intercede in heaven for us who honor their memory here on earth. Through the same Christ our Lord. Amen.

The Priest turns toward the people and says:

Pray, brethren, that my sacrifice and yours may become acceptable to God the Father almighty.

S. May the Lord accept this sacrifice from your hands to the praise and glory of His name, for our advantage, and that of all His holy Church.

P. Amen.

THE SECRET

GRACIOUSLY regard, we beseech You, O Lord, the offerings of Your Church, in which gold, frankincense, and myrrh are no longer laid before You, but He is sacrificed and received, Who by those gifts was signified, Jesus Christ Your Son our Lord. Who with You lives and reigns in the unity of the Holy Spirit, God.

P. World without end. *S.* Amen.

PREFACE—CANON

P. The Lord be with you. *S.* And with your spirit.

P. Lift up your hearts.

S. We have lifted them up to the Lord.

P. Let us give thanks to the Lord, our God.

S. It is fitting and just.

IT IS fitting indeed and just, right and helpful to salvation, for us always and everywhere to give thanks to You, O holy Lord, Father almighty, everlasting God; for when Your Only-begotten Son showed Himself in the substance of our mortal nature, He restored us by the new light of His own immortality. And therefore with Angels and Archangels, with Thrones and Dominations, and with the whole host of the heavenly army we sing a hymn to Your glory, saying again and again (*the bell is rung* 3 *times*):

HOLY, HOLY, HOLY, Lord God of Hosts. Heaven and earth are filled with Your glory. Hosanna in the highest. ✠ Blessed is He Who comes in the name of the Lord. Hosanna in the highest.

THE CANON OF THE MASS

THEREFORE, most gracious Father, we humbly beg of You and entreat You through Jesus Christ Your Son, our Lord, (*he kisses the altar*) to deem acceptable and bless these ✠ gifts, these ✠ offerings, these ✠ holy and unspotted oblations which, in the first place, we offer You for Your Holy Catholic Church, that You would deign to give her peace and protection, to unite and guard her throughout the world, together with Your servant N., our Pope, and N., our Bishop; and all true believers who cherish the Catholic and Apostolic Faith.

Commemoration of the Living

REMEMBER, O Lord, Your servants and handmaids, N. and N., (*name them*) and all here present, whose faith and devotion are known to You, on whose behalf we offer to You, or who themselves offer to You, this sacrifice of praise for themselves, families and friends, for the good of their souls, for their hope of salvation and deliverance from all harm, and who offer their homage to You, eternal, living and true God.

Commemoration of the Saints

IN THE unity of holy fellowship, and keeping this most holy day on which Your Only-begotten Son Who is co-eternal with You in Your glory, showed himself in true flesh and with a visible body like us, we also observe the memory, first of all, of the glorious and ever Virgin Mary, Mother of our Lord and God Jesus Christ; next, that of Your Blessed Apostles and Martyrs, Peter and Paul, Andrew, James, John, Thomas, James, Philip, Bartholomew, Matthew, Simon and Thaddeus; of Linus, Cletus, Clement, Sixtus, Cornelius, Cyprian, Lawrence, Chrysogonus, John and Paul, Cosmas and Damian, and of all Your Saints, by whose merits and prayers grant that we may be always fortified by the help of Your protection. Through the same Christ our Lord. Amen.

Spreading his hands over the oblation, he says:

GRACIOUSLY accept, then, we beseech You, O Lord, this service of our worship and that of all Your household. Provide that our days be spent in Your peace, save us from everlasting damnation, and cause us to be numbered in the flock You have chosen. Through Christ our Lord. Amen.

O GOD, deign to bless ✠ what we offer, and make it approved, ✠ effective, ✠ right, and wholly pleasing in every way, that it may become for our good, the Body ✠ and Blood ✠ of Your dearly beloved Son, Jesus Christ our Lord.

CONSECRATION—ELEVATION

WHO, the day before He suffered, took bread into His holy and venerable hands, and having raised His eyes to heaven, to You, O God, His almighty Father, giving thanks to You, He blessed it, ✠ broke it, and gave it to His disciples, saying: All of you take and eat of this:

FOR THIS IS MY BODY.

IN LIKE manner, when the supper was done, taking also this goodly chalice into His holy and venerable hands, again giving thanks to You, He blessed ✠ it, and gave it to His disciples, saying: All of you take and drink of this:

FOR THIS IS THE CHALICE OF MY BLOOD OF THE NEW AND ETERNAL COVENANT: THE MYSTERY OF FAITH: WHICH SHALL BE SHED FOR YOU AND FOR MANY UNTO THE FORGIVENESS OF SINS.

After replacing the chalice on the corporal, he says:

As often as you shall do these things, in memory of Me shall you do them.

Offering of the Victim

MINDFUL, therefore, O Lord, not only of the blessed Passion of the same Christ, Your Son,

our Lord, but also of His Resurrection from the dead, and finally His glorious Ascension into heaven, we, Your ministers, as also Your holy people, offer to Your supreme Majesty, of the gifts bestowed upon us, the pure ✠ Victim, the holy ✠ Victim, the all-perfect ✠ Victim: the holy ✠ Bread of life eternal and the Chalice ✠ of unending salvation.

AND this deign to regard with gracious and kindly attention and hold acceptable, as You deigned to accept the offerings of Abel, Your just servant, and the sacrifice of Abraham our patriarch, and that which Your chief priest Melchisedec offered to You, a holy sacrifice and a spotless victim.

MOST humbly we implore You, almighty God, bid these offerings to be brought by the hands of Your holy angel to Your altar above; before the face of Your Divine Majesty; that those of us who, by sharing in the Sacrifice of this altar, shall receive the Most Sacred ✠ Body and ✠ Blood of Your Son, may be filled with every grace and heavenly blessing. Through the same Christ our Lord. Amen.

Commemoration of the Dead

REMEMBER also, O Lord, Your servants and handmaids, N. and N., who have gone before us with the sign of faith, and rest in the sleep of peace. (*Here pray for the dead.*) To these, O Lord, and to all who rest in Christ, we beseech You to grant of Your goodness, a place of comfort, light and peace. Through the same Christ our Lord. Amen.

TO US sinners also, Your servants, trusting in the greatness of Your mercy, deign to grant some part and fellowship with Your Holy Apostles and Martyrs: with John, Stephen, Matthias, Barnabas, Ignatius, Alexander, Marcellinus, Peter, Felicitas, Perpetua, Agatha, Lucy, Agnes, Cecilia, Anastasia, and all Your Saints; into whose company, we implore You to admit us, not weighing our merits, but freely granting us pardon. Through Christ our Lord.

THROUGH Whom, O Lord, You always create, ✠ sanctify, ✠ fill with life, ✠ bless, and bestow upon us all good things.

The Minor Elevation

THROUGH ✠ Him, and with ✠ Him, and in ✠ Him, is to You, God the Father ✠ almighty, in the unity of the Holy ✠ Spirit, all honor and glory, world without end. S. Amen.

THE COMMUNION AND THANKSGIVING

Let us pray. Prompted by saving precepts, and taught by Your divine teaching, we dare to say:

OUR FATHER, Who art in heaven, hallowed be Thy name: Thy kingdom come: Thy will be done on earth as it is in heaven. Give us this day our daily bread; and forgive us our trespasses, as we forgive those who trespass against us. And lead us not into temptation: S. But deliver us from evil. *P.* Amen.

DELIVER us, we beseech You, O Lord, from all evils, past, present, and to come; and by the intercession of the Blessed and glorious Mary, ever Virgin, Mother of God, together with Your Blessed Apostles Peter and Paul, and Andrew, and all the Saints, grant of Your goodness, peace in our days, that aided by the riches of Your mercy, we may be always free from sin and safe from all disturbance.

Through the same our Lord Jesus Christ, Your Son, Who lives and reigns with You in the unity of the Holy Spirit, God, world without end.

S. Amen.

P. May the peace ✠ of the Lord be ✠ always with ✠ you.

S. And with your spirit.

The Priest puts a small particle into the chalice, saying:

May this mingling and consecration of the Body and Blood of our Lord Jesus Christ help us who receive it to life everlasting. Amen.

LAMB of God, You Who take away the sins of the world, have mercy on us.

Lamb of God, You Who take away the sins of the world, have mercy on us.

Lamb of God, You Who take away the sins of the world, grant us peace.

PRAYERS BEFORE HOLY COMMUNION

Then inclining toward the altar, he says:

O LORD Jesus Christ, Who said to Your Apostles: "Peace I leave with you, My peace I give to you," regard not my sins but the faith of Your Church, and deign to give her peace and unity according to Your Will: Who live and reign, God, world without end. Amen.

O LORD Jesus Christ, Son of the living God, Who, by the will of the Father, with the cooperation of the Holy Spirit, have by Your death given life to the world, deliver me by this Your Most Sacred Body and Blood from all my sins and from every evil. Make me always cling to Your commandments, and never permit me to be separated from You. Who with the same God the Father and the Holy Spirit, live and reign, God, world without end. Amen.

LET not the partaking of Your Body, O Lord Jesus Christ, which I, though unworthy, presume to receive, turn to my judgment and condemnation; but through Your goodness, may it become a safeguard and an effective remedy, both of soul and body. Who live and reign with God the Father, in the unity of the Holy Spirit, God, world without end. Amen.

COMMUNION OF THE PRIEST

I WILL take the Bread of heaven, and call upon the name of the Lord.

Lord, I am not worthy that You should come under my roof; but only say the word, and my soul will be healed. (3 *times.*)

Making the Sign of the Cross with the Host, he says:

MAY the Body of our Lord Jesus Christ preserve my soul to life everlasting. Amen.

What return shall I make to the Lord for all He has given me? I will take the Chalice of salvation, and I will call upon the name of the Lord. Praising will I call upon the Lord and I shall be saved from my enemies.

Making the Sign of the Cross with the chalice, he says:

MAY the Blood of our Lord Jesus Christ preserve my soul to life everlasting. Amen.

The Priest reverently consumes the Precious Blood.

COMMUNION OF THE FAITHFUL

The Server and people say the "Confiteor."

P. May almighty God have mercy on you, forgive you your sins, and bring you to life everlasting. S. Amen.

P. May the almighty and merciful Lord grant you pardon, ✠ absolution and remission of your sins. S. Amen.

Holding up a Sacred Host, the Priest says:

Behold the Lamb of God, behold Him Who takes away the sins of the world.

Lord, I am not worthy that You should come under my roof; but only say the word, and my soul will be healed. (3 *times.*)

The Priest says to each communicant:

May the Body of our Lord Jesus Christ preserve your soul to life everlasting. Amen.

The Priest purifies the chalice with wine, saying:

WHAT has passed our lips as food, O Lord, may we possess in purity of heart, that what is given to us in time, be our healing for eternity.

He purifies his fingers with wine and water, saying:

MAY Your Body, O Lord, which I have eaten, and Your Blood which I have drunk, cleave to my very soul, and grant that no trace of sin be found in me, whom these pure and holy mysteries have renewed. Who live and reign, world without end. Amen.

THE COMMUNION • Matt. 2, 2

WE HAVE seen His star in the East; and have come with gifts to worship the Lord.

The Priest, turning to the people, says:

P. The Lord be with you. *S.* And with your spirit.
P. Let us pray.

THE POSTCOMMUNION

GRANT, we beseech You, almighty God, that we may attain by the understanding of a purified mind what we have celebrated in a solemn office. Through our Lord Jesus Christ, Your Son, Who lives and reigns with You in the unity of the Holy Spirit, God, world without end. *S.* Amen.

FINAL PRAYERS

The Priest turns again to the people, and says:

P. The Lord be with you. *S.* And with your spirit.
P. Go, you are dismissed. *S.* Thanks be to God.

MAY the tribute of my worship be pleasing to You, Most Holy Trinity, and grant that the sacrifice which I, all unworthy, have offered in the presence of Your Majesty, may be acceptable to You, and through Your mercy obtain forgiveness for me and all for whom I have offered it. Through Christ our Lord. Amen.

THE LAST BLESSING

He kisses the altar, and facing the people, says:

MAY almighty God bless you: ✠ the Father, and the Son, and the Holy Spirit.

S. Amen.

The Last Gospel and Prayers after Low Mass are conveniently placed inside the back cover.

Jesus went with them to Nazareth and was subject to them.

FEAST OF THE HOLY FAMILY

FIRST SUNDAY AFTER THE EPIPHANY

The Church proposes for our imitation the virtues of Jesus, Mary and Joseph in their hidden and humble life at Nazareth, especially the subjection of the Son of God, throughout His earthly life, by obedience to Mary and Joseph. (WHITE VESTMENTS)

PRAYERS AT THE FOOT OF THE ALTAR

IN THE name of the Father, ✠ and of the Son, and of the Holy Spirit. Amen.

Priest. I will go in to the altar of God.

Server. The God of my gladness and joy.

Psalm 42

DO ME justice, O God, and fight my fight against a faithless people; from the deceitful and impious man rescue me.

S. For You, O God, are my strength. Why do You keep me so far away? Why must I go about in mourning, with the enemy oppressing me?

P. Send forth Your light and Your fidelity; they shall lead me on and bring me to Your holy mountain, to Your dwelling-place.

S. Then will I go in to the altar of God, the God of my gladness and joy.
P. Then will I give You thanks upon the harp, O God, my God. Why are you so downcast, O my soul? Why do you sigh within me?
S. Hope in God! For I shall again be thanking Him in the presence of my Savior and my God.
P. Glory be to the Father, and to the Son, and to the Holy Spirit.
S. As it was in the beginning, is now, and ever shall be world without end. Amen.
P. I will go in to the altar of God.
S. The God of my gladness and joy.
P. Our help ✠ is in the name of the Lord.
S. Who made heaven and earth.
P. I confess to almighty God, etc.
S. May almighty God have mercy on you, forgive you your sins, and bring you to life everlasting.
P. Amen.

The Server, bowing, says the "Confiteor."

I CONFESS to almighty God, to Blessed Mary, ever Virgin, to Blessed Michael the Archangel, to Blessed John the Baptist, to the Holy Apostles Peter and Paul, and to all the Saints, and to you, Father, that I have sinned exceedingly in thought, word and deed, *through my fault, through my fault, through my most grievous fault.* Therefore I beseech Blessed Mary, ever Virgin, Blessed Michael the Archangel, Blessed John the Baptist, the Holy Apostles Peter and Paul, and all the Saints, and you, Father, to pray to the Lord our God for me.
P. May almighty God have mercy on you, forgive you your sins, and bring you to life everlasting.
S. Amen.

MAY the almighty and merciful Lord grant us pardon, ✠ absolution, and remission of our sins. *S.* Amen.

P. Will You not, O God, give us life?
S. And shall not Your people rejoice in You?
P. Show us, O Lord, Your kindness.
S. And grant us Your salvation.
P. O Lord, hear my prayer.
S. And let my cry come to You.
P. The Lord be with you.
S. And with your spirit. *P.* Let us pray.

Going up to the altar, the Priest prays silently:

TAKE away from us our sins, O Lord, we beseech You, that we may enter with pure minds into the Holy of Holies. Through Christ our Lord. Amen.

WE BESEECH You, O Lord, by the merits of Your Saints (*he kisses the altar*) whose relics lie here, and of all the Saints: deign in Your mercy to pardon me all my sins. Amen.

THE INTROIT • Prov. 23, 24. 25

At the right side of the altar, the Priest says:

THE father of the Just will exult with glee; let Your father and mother have joy; let her who bore You exult. *Ps.* 83. How lovely is Your dwelling place, O Lord of Hosts! My soul yearns and pines for the courts of the Lord. Glory be to the Father, and to the Son, and to the Holy Spirit. As it was in the beginning, is now, and ever shall be, word without end. Amen. — The father of the Just will exult with glee; let Your father and mother have joy; let her who bore You exult.

THE KYRIE

P. Lord, have mercy. *S.* Lord, have mercy. *P.* Lord, have mercy. *S.* Christ, have mercy. *P.* Christ, have mercy. *S.* Christ, have mercy. *P.* Lord, have mercy. *S.* Lord, have mercy. *P.* Lord, have mercy.

THE GLORIA

GLORY to God in the highest. And on earth peace to men of good will. We praise You. We bless You. We adore You. We glorify You. We give You thanks for Your great glory. O Lord God, heavenly King, God the Father almighty. O Lord Jesus Christ, the Only-begotten Son. O Lord God, Lamb of God, Son of the Father: You Who take away the sins of the world, have mercy on us. You Who take away the sins of the world, receive our prayer. You Who sit at the right hand of the Father, have mercy on us. For You alone are holy. You alone are the Lord. You alone, O Jesus Christ, are most high. Together with the Holy Spirit ✠ in the glory of God the Father. Amen.

The Priest kisses the altar and turns to the people, saying:

P. The Lord be with you. *S.* And with your spirit. *P.* Let us pray.

THE PRAYER

Going to the right (Epistle) side, he says:

O LORD Jesus Christ, by subjecting Yourself to Mary and Joseph, You consecrated family life with wonderful virtues; grant that, by their joint assistance, we may fashion our lives after the example of Your Holy Family, and obtain everlasting fellowship with it. Who live and reign with God the Father, in the unity of the Holy Spirit, God, world without end. S. Amen.

THE EPISTLE • Col. 3, 12-17

BRETHREN: Put on, as God's chosen ones, holy and beloved, a heart of mercy, kindness, humility, meekness, patience. Bear with one another and forgive one another, if anyone has a grievance against any other; even as the Lord has forgiven you, so also do you forgive. But above all these things have charity, which is the bond of perfection. And may the peace of Christ reign in your hearts; unto that peace, indeed, you were called in one body. Show yourselves thankful. Let the word of Christ dwell in you abundantly: in all wisdom teach and admonish one another by psalms, hymns and spiritual songs, singing in your hearts to God by His grace. Whatever you do in word or in work, do all in the name of the Lord Jesus Christ, giving thanks to God the Father through Him. S. Thanks be to God.

THE GRADUAL • Ps. 26, 4

ONE thing I ask of the Lord; this I seek: to dwell in the house of the Lord all the days of my life. ℣. *Ps.* 83. Happy they who dwell in Your house, O Lord! continually they praise You.

Alleluia, alleluia. ℣. *Isa.* 45, 15. Truly You are a hidden God, the God of Israel, the Savior. Alleluia.

PRAYER BEFORE THE GOSPEL

Bowing down at the center of the altar, he says:

CLEANSE my heart and my lips, O almighty God, Who cleansed the lips of the Prophet Isaias with a burning coal. In Your gracious mercy deign so to purify me that I may worthily proclaim Your holy Gospel. Through Christ our Lord. Amen.

Lord, grant Your blessing. The Lord be in my heart and on my lips, that I may worthily and fittingly proclaim His holy Gospel. Amen.

THE GOSPEL • Luke 2, 42-52

Going to the left (Gospel) side of the altar, he says:

P. The Lord be with you. *S.* And with your spirit.
P. ✠ The continuation of the holy Gospel according to Saint Luke. *S.* Glory be to You, O Lord.

WHEN Jesus was twelve years old, they went up to Jerusalem according to the custom of the feast. And after they had fulfilled the days, when they were returning, the Boy Jesus remained in Jerusalem, and His parents did not know it. But thinking that He was in the caravan, they had come a day's journey before it occurred to them to look for Him among their relatives and acquaintances. And not finding Him, they returned to Jerusalem in search of Him. And it came to pass after three days, that they found Him in the temple, sitting in the midst of the teachers, listening to them and asking them questions. And all who were listening to Him were amazed at His understanding and His answers. And when they saw Him, they were astonished. And His mother said to Him, "Son, why have You done so to us? Behold, in sorrow Your father and I have been seeking You." And He said to them, "How is it that you sought Me? Did you not know that I must be about My Father's business?" And they did not understand the word that He spoke to them. And He went down with them and came to Nazareth, and was subject to them; and His mother kept all these things carefully in her heart. And Jesus advanced in wisdom and age and grace before God and men. S. Praise be to You, O Christ.

P. By the words of the Gospel, may our sins be taken away.

THE NICENE CREED

At the center of the altar, he says:

I BELIEVE in one God, the Father almighty, Maker of heaven and earth, and of all things visible and invisible. And in one Lord Jesus Christ, the Only-begotten Son of God. Born of the Father before all ages. God of God; Light of Light; true God of true God. Begotten not made; of one being with the Father; by Whom all things were made. Who for us men, and for our salvation, came down from heaven. (*Here all genuflect.*) And was made Flesh by the Holy Spirit of the Virgin Mary: AND WAS MADE MAN. He was also crucified for us, suffered under Pontius Pilate and was buried. And on the third day He rose again according to the Scriptures. And ascending into heaven, He sits at the right hand of the Father. And He shall come again in glory to judge the living and the dead; and of His kingdom there shall be no end. And I believe in the Holy Spirit, Lord and Giver of life, Who proceeds from the Father and the Son. Who together with the Father and the Son is no less adored, and glorified: Who spoke by the Prophets. And I believe in One, Holy, Catholic and Apostolic Church. I confess one Baptism for the remission of sins. And I look for the resurrection of the dead. ✠ And the life of the world to come. Amen.

THE OFFERTORY

The Priest turns to the people and says:

P. The Lord be with you. *S.* And with your spirit.
P. Let us pray.

THE OFFERTORY VERSE • Luke 2, 22

THE parents of Jesus took Him up to Jerusalem, to present Him to the Lord.

The Priest now uncovers the chalice, places the host on the paten and offering it up, says:

ACCEPT, O holy Father, almighty and eternal God, this spotless host, which I, Your unworthy servant, offer to You, my living and true God, to atone for my numberless sins, offenses, and negligences; on behalf of all here present and likewise for all faithful Christians living and dead, that it may profit me and them as a means of salvation to life everlasting. Amen.

He pours wine and water into the chalice, blessing the water before it is poured.

O GOD, Who established the nature of man in wondrous dignity, and still more admirably restored it, grant that through the mystery of this water and wine, we may be made partakers of His Divinity, Who has condescended to become partaker of our humanity, Jesus Christ, Your Son, our Lord. Who lives and reigns with You in the unity of the Holy Spirit, God, world without end. Amen.

Offering up the wine, the Priest says:

WE OFFER You, O Lord, the chalice of salvation, humbly begging of Your mercy that it may arise before Your Divine Majesty, with a pleasing fragrance, for our salvation and for that of the whole world. Amen.

Bowing down, the Priest says:

IN A humble spirit and with a contrite heart, may we be accepted by You, O Lord, and may our sacrifice so be offered in Your sight this day as to please You, O Lord God.

Raising his eyes and blessing the offering, he says:

COME, O Sanctifier, almighty and eternal God, and bless ✠ this sacrifice prepared for the glory of Your holy name.

WASHING THE FINGERS

I WASH my hands in innocence, and I go around Your altar, O Lord, giving voice to my thanks, and recounting all Your wondrous deeds. O Lord, I love the house in which You dwell, the tenting-place of Your glory. Gather not my soul with those of sinners, nor with men of blood my life. On their hands are crimes, and their right hands are full of bribes. But I walk in integrity; redeem me, and have pity on me. My foot stands on level ground; in the assemblies I will bless You, O Lord. Glory be to the Father, and to the Son, and to the Holy Spirit. As it was in the beginning, is now, and ever shall be, world without end. Amen.

ACCEPT, Most Holy Trinity, this offering which we are making to You in remembrance of the Passion, Resurrection, and Ascension of Jesus Christ, our Lord; and in honor of Blessed Mary, ever Virgin, Blessed John the Baptist, the Holy Apostles Peter and Paul, and of these, and of all the Saints; that it may add to their honor and aid our salvation; and may they deign to intercede in heaven for us who honor their memory here on earth. Through the same Christ our Lord. Amen.

The Priest turns toward the people and says:

Pray, brethren, that my sacrifice and yours may become acceptable to God the Father almighty.

S. May the Lord accept this sacrifice from your hands to the praise and glory of His name, for our advantage, and that of all His holy Church.

P. Amen.

THE SECRET

WE OFFER You, O Lord, the sacrifice of reconciliation, humbly entreating that, by the intercession of the Virgin-Mother of God and Saint Joseph, You may firmly establish our families in Your peace and grace. Through the same our Lord Jesus Christ, Your Son, Who lives and reigns with You in the unity of the Holy Spirit, God.

P. World without end. *S.* Amen.

PREFACE—CANON

P. The Lord be with you. *S.* And with your spirit.

P. Lift up your hearts.

S. We have lifted them up to the Lord.

P. Let us give thanks to the Lord, our God.

S. It is fitting and just.

IT IS fitting indeed and just, right and helpful to salvation, for us always and everywhere to give thanks to You, O holy Lord, Father almighty, everlasting God; for when Your Only-begotten Son showed Himself in the substance of our mortal nature, He restored us by the new light of His own immortality. And therefore with Angels and Archangels, with Thrones and Dominations, and with the whole host of the heavenly army we sing a hymn to Your glory, saying again and again (*the bell is rung 3 times*):

HOLY, HOLY, HOLY, Lord God of Hosts. Heaven and earth are filled with Your glory. Hosanna in the highest. ✠ Blessed is He Who comes in the name of the Lord. Hosanna in the highest.

THE CANON OF THE MASS

THEREFORE, most gracious Father, we humbly beg of You and entreat You through Jesus Christ Your Son, our Lord, (*he kisses the altar*) to deem acceptable and bless these ✠ gifts, these ✠ offerings, these ✠ holy and unspotted oblations which, in the first place, we offer You for Your Holy Catholic Church, that You would deign to give her peace and protection, to unite and guard her throughout the world, together with Your servant N., our Pope, and N., our Bishop; and all true believers who cherish the Catholic and Apostolic Faith.

Commemoration of the Living

REMEMBER, O Lord, Your servants and handmaids, N. and N., (*name them*) and all here present, whose faith and devotion are known to You, on whose behalf we offer to You, or who themselves offer to You, this sacrifice of praise for themselves, families and friends, for the good of their souls, for their hope of salvation and deliverance from all harm, and who offer their homage to You, eternal, living and true God.

Commemoration of the Saints

IN THE unity of holy fellowship we observe the memory, first of all, of the glorious and ever Virgin Mary, Mother of our Lord and God Jesus

Christ; next, that of Your Blessed Apostles and Martyrs, Peter and Paul, Andrew, James, John, Thomas, James, Philip, Bartholomew, Matthew, Simon and Thaddeus; of Linus, Cletus, Clement, Sixtus, Cornelius, Cyprian, Lawrence, Chrysogonus, John and Paul, Cosmas and Damian, and of all Your Saints, by whose merits and prayers grant that we may be always fortified by the help of Your protection. Through the same Christ our Lord. Amen.

Spreading his hands over the oblation, he says:

GRACIOUSLY accept, then, we beseech You, O Lord, this service of our worship and that of all Your household. Provide that our days be spent in Your peace, save us from everlasting damnation, and cause us to be numbered in the flock You have chosen. Through Christ our Lord. Amen.

O GOD, deign to bless ✠ what we offer, and make it approved, ✠ effective, ✠ right, and wholly pleasing in every way, that it may become for our good, the Body ✠ and Blood ✠ of Your dearly beloved Son, Jesus Christ our Lord.

CONSECRATION—ELEVATION

WHO, the day before He suffered, took bread into His holy and venerable hands, and having raised His eyes to heaven, to You, O God, His almighty Father, giving thanks to You, He blessed it, ✠ broke it, and gave it to His disciples, saying: All of you take and eat of this:

FOR THIS IS MY BODY.

IN LIKE manner, when the supper was done, taking also this goodly chalice into His holy and venerable hands, again giving thanks to You, He

OUR FATHER, Who art in heaven, hallowed be Thy name: Thy kingdom come: Thy will be done on earth as it is in heaven. Give us this day our daily bread; and forgive us our trespasses, as we forgive those who trespass against us. And lead us not into temptation: S. But deliver us from evil. *P.* Amen.

DELIVER us, we beseech You, O Lord, from all evils, past, present, and to come; and by the intercession of the Blessed and glorious Mary, ever Virgin, Mother of God, together with Your Blessed Apostles Peter and Paul, and Andrew, and all the Saints, grant of Your goodness, peace in our days, that aided by the riches of Your mercy, we may be always free from sin and safe from all disturbance.
Through the same our Lord Jesus Christ, Your Son, Who lives and reigns with You in the unity of the Holy Spirit, God, world without end.
S. Amen.
P. May the peace ✠ of the Lord be ✠ always with ✠ you.
S. And with your spirit.

The Priest puts a small particle into the chalice, saying:
May this mingling and consecration of the Body and Blood of our Lord Jesus Christ help us who receive it to life everlasting. Amen.

LAMB of God, You Who take away the sins of the world, have mercy on us.
Lamb of God, You Who take away the sins of the world, have mercy on us.
Lamb of God, You Who take away the sins of the world, grant us peace.

PRAYERS BEFORE HOLY COMMUNION

O LORD Jesus Christ, Who said to Your Apostles: "Peace I leave with you, My peace I give to you," regard not my sins but the faith of Your Church, and deign to give her peace and unity according to Your Will: Who live and reign, God, world without end. Amen.

O LORD Jesus Christ, Son of the living God, Who, by the will of the Father, with the cooperation of the Holy Spirit, have by Your death given life to the world, deliver me by this Your Most Sacred Body and Blood from all my sins and from every evil. Make me always cling to Your commandments, and never permit me to be separated from You, Who with the same God the Father and the Holy Spirit, live and reign, God, world without end. Amen.

LET not the partaking of Your Body, O Lord Jesus Christ, which I, though unworthy, presume to receive, turn to my judgment and condemnation; but through Your goodness, may it become a safeguard and an effective remedy, both of soul and body. Who live and reign with God the Father, in the unity of the Holy Spirit, God, world without end. Amen.

COMMUNION OF THE PRIEST

I WILL take the Bread of heaven, and call upon the name of the Lord.

Lord, I am not worthy that You should come under my roof; but only say the word, and my soul will be healed. (3 *times.*)

MAY the Body of our Lord Jesus Christ preserve my soul to life everlasting. Amen.

What return shall I make to the Lord for all He has given me? I will take the Chalice of salvation, and I will call upon the name of the Lord. Praising will I call upon the Lord and I shall be saved from my enemies.

Making the Sign of the Cross with the chalice, he says:

MAY the Blood of our Lord Jesus Christ preserve my soul to life everlasting. Amen.

The Priest reverently consumes the Precious Blood.

COMMUNION OF THE FAITHFUL

The Server and people say the "Confiteor."

P. May almighty God have mercy on you, forgive you your sins, and bring you to life everlasting. S. Amen.

P. May the almighty and merciful Lord grant you pardon, ✠ absolution and remission of your sins. S. Amen.

Holding up a Sacred Host, the Priest says:

Behold the Lamb of God, behold Him Who takes away the sins of the world.

Lord, I am not worthy that You should come under my roof; but only say the word, and my soul will be healed. (3 *times.*)

The Priest says to each communicant:

May the Body of our Lord Jesus Christ preserve your soul to life everlasting. Amen.

The Priest purifies the chalice with wine, saying:

WHAT has passed our lips as food, O Lord, may we possess in purity of heart, that what is given to us in time, be our healing for eternity.

MAY Your Body, O Lord, which I have eaten, and Your Blood which I have drunk, cleave to my very soul, and grant that no trace of sin be

found in me, whom these pure and holy mysteries have renewed. Who live and reign, world without end. Amen.

THE COMMUNION • Luke 2, 51

JESUS went down with them, and came to Nazareth and was subject to them.

P. The Lord be with you. *S.* And with your spirit.
P. Let us pray.

THE POSTCOMMUNION

O LORD Jesus, cause those whom You refresh with the heavenly sacrament, to imitate continually the example of Your Holy Family, that being welcomed at the hour of death by the glorious Virgin-Mother with Saint Joseph, we may be found worthy to be received by You into Your everlasting dwellings. Who live etc. *S.* Amen.

FINAL PRAYERS

P. The Lord be with you. *S.* And with your spirit.
P. Go, you are dismissed. *S.* Thanks be to God.

MAY the tribute of my worship be pleasing to You, Most Holy Trinity, and grant that the sacrifice which I, all unworthy, have offered in the presence of Your Majesty, may be acceptable to You, and through Your mercy obtain forgiveness for me and all for whom I have offered it. Through Christ our Lord. Amen.

THE LAST BLESSING

MAY almighty God bless you: ✠ the Father, and the Son, and the Holy Spirit. *S.* Amen.

The Last Gospel and Prayers after Low Mass are conveniently placed inside the back cover.

Mary said to Jesus, "They have no wine."

SECOND SUNDAY AFTER EPIPHANY

Our Lord at the wedding feast in Cana of Galilee, brings before our eyes the miracle of changing water into wine prompted by Mary, His mother. This miracle establishes her as our Mediatrix. (GREEN VESTMENTS)

PRAYERS AT THE FOOT OF THE ALTAR

IN THE name of the Father, ✠ and of the Son, and of the Holy Spirit. Amen.

Priest. I will go in to the altar of God.

Server. The God of my gladness and joy.

Psalm 42

DO ME justice, O God, and fight my fight against a faithless people; from the deceitful and impious man rescue me.

S. For You, O God, are my strength. Why do You keep me so far away? Why must I go about in mourning, with the enemy oppressing me?

P. Send forth Your light and Your fidelity; they shall lead me on and bring me to Your holy mountain, to Your dwelling-place.

S. Then will I go in to the altar of God, the God of my gladness and joy.
P. Then will I give You thanks upon the harp, O God, my God. Why are you so downcast, O my soul? Why do you sigh within me?
S. Hope in God! For I shall again be thanking Him in the presence of my Savior and my God.
P. Glory be to the Father, and to the Son, and to the Holy Spirit.
S. As it was in the beginning, is now, and ever shall be, world without end. Amen.
P. I will go in to the altar of God.
S. The God of my gladness and joy.
P. Our help ✠ is in the name of the Lord.
S. Who made heaven and earth.
P. I confess to almighty God, etc.
S. May almighty God have mercy on you, forgive you your sins, and bring you to life everlasting.
P. Amen.

The Server, bowing, says the "Confiteor."

I CONFESS to almighty God, to Blessed Mary, ever Virgin, to Blessed Michael the Archangel, to Blessed John the Baptist, to the Holy Apostles Peter and Paul, and to all the Saints, and to you, Father, that I have sinned exceedingly in thought, word and deed, *through my fault, through my fault, through my most grievous fault.* Therefore I beseech Blessed Mary, ever Virgin, Blessed Michael the Archangel, Blessed John the Baptist, the Holy Apostles Peter and Paul, and all the Saints, and you, Father, to pray to the Lord our God for me.
P. May almighty God have mercy on you, forgive you your sins, and bring you to life everlasting.
S. Amen.

MAY the almighty and merciful Lord grant us pardon, ✠ absolution, and remission of our sins. *S.* Amen.

P. Will You not, O God, give us life?
S. And shall not Your people rejoice in You?
P. Show us, O Lord, Your kindness.
S. And grant us Your salvation.
P. O Lord, hear my prayer.
S. And let my cry come to You.
P. The Lord be with you.
S. And with your spirit. *P.* Let us pray.

Going up to the altar, the Priest prays silently:

TAKE away from us our sins, O Lord, we beseech You, that we may enter with pure minds into the Holy of Holies. Through Christ our Lord. Amen.

WE BESEECH You, O Lord, by the merits of Your Saints (*he kisses the altar*) whose relics lie here, and of all the Saints: deign in Your mercy to pardon me all my sins. Amen.

THE INTROIT • Ps. 65, 4. 1. 2

At the right side of the altar, the Priest says:

LET all on earth worship You, O God, and sing praise to You, sing praise to Your name, Most High. *Ps.* Shout joyfully to God, all you on earth, sing praise to the glory of His name; proclaim His glorious praise. Glory be to the Father, and to the Son, and to the Holy Spirit. As it was in the beginning, is now, and ever shall be, world without end. Amen. — Let all on earth worship You, O God, and sing praise to You, sing praise to Your name, Most High.

THE KYRIE

P. Lord, have mercy. *S*. Lord, have mercy. *P*. Lord, have mercy. *S*. Christ, have mercy. *P*. Christ, have mercy. *S*. Christ, have mercy. *P*. Lord, have mercy. *S*. Lord, have mercy. *P*. Lord, have mercy.

THE GLORIA

GLORY to God in the highest. And on earth peace to men of good will. We praise You. We bless You. We adore You. We glorify You. We give You thanks for Your great glory. O Lord God, heavenly King, God the Father almighty. O Lord Jesus Christ, the Only-begotten Son. O Lord God, Lamb of God, Son of the Father: You Who take away the sins of the world, have mercy on us. You Who take away the sins of the world, receive our prayer. You Who sit at the right hand of the Father, have mercy on us. For You alone are holy. You alone are the Lord. You alone, O Jesus Christ, are most high. Together with the Holy Spirit ✠ in the glory of God the Father. Amen.

The Priest kisses the altar and turns to the people, saying:

P. The Lord be with you. *S*. And with your spirit.
P. Let us pray.

THE PRAYER

Going to the right (Epistle) side, he says:

ALMIGHTY and eternal God, You govern all things in heaven and on earth; in Your mercy hear the supplication of Your people, and grant Your peace in our times. Through our Lord Jesus Christ, Your Son, Who lives and reigns with You in the unity of the Holy Spirit, God, world without end. *S*. Amen.

THE EPISTLE • Rom. 12, 6-16

BRETHREN: We have gifts differing according to the grace that has been given us, such as prophecy to be used according to the proportion of faith; or ministry, in ministering; or he who teaches, in teaching; he who exhorts, in exhorting; he who gives, in simplicity; he who presides, with carefulness; he who shows mercy, with cheerfulness. Let love be without pretense. Hate what is evil, hold to what is good. Love one another with fraternal charity, anticipating one another with honor. Be not slothful in zeal; be fervent in spirit, serving the Lord, rejoicing in hope. Be patient in tribulation, persevering in prayer. Share the needs of the saints, practicing hospitality. Bless those who persecute you; bless and do not curse. Rejoice with those who rejoice; weep with those who weep. Be of one mind toward one another. Do not set your mind on high things but condescend to the lowly. S. Thanks be to God.

THE GRADUAL • Ps. 106, 20-21

THE Lord sent forth His word to heal them and to snatch them from destruction. ℣. Let them give thanks to the Lord for His kindness and His wondrous deeds to the children of men.

Alleluia, alleluia. ℣. *Ps.* 148, 2. Praise the Lord, all you His angels, praise Him, all you His hosts. Alleluia.

PRAYER BEFORE THE GOSPEL

Bowing down at the center of the altar, he says:

CLEANSE my heart and my lips, O almighty God, Who cleansed the lips of the Prophet Isaias with a burning coal. In Your gracious mercy deign so to purify me that I may worthily proclaim

Your holy Gospel. Through Christ our Lord. Amen. Lord, grant Your blessing. The Lord be in my heart and on my lips, that I may worthily and fittingly proclaim His holy Gospel. Amen.

THE GOSPEL • John 2, 1-11

Going to the left (Gospel) side of the altar, he says:

P. The Lord be with you. *S.* And with your spirit.
P. ✠ The continuation of the holy Gospel according to Saint John. *S.* Glory be to You, O Lord.

AT THAT time, a marriage took place at Cana of Galilee, and the mother of Jesus was there. Now Jesus too was invited to the marriage, and also His disciples. And the wine having run short, the mother of Jesus said to Him, "They have no wine." And Jesus said to her, "What would you have Me do, woman? My hour has not yet come." His mother said to the attendants, "Do whatever He tells you." Now six stone water-jars were placed there, after the Jewish manner of purification, each holding two or three measures. Jesus said to them, "Fill the jars with water." And they filled them to the brim. And Jesus said to them, "Draw out now, and take to the chief steward." And they took it to him. Now when the chief steward had tasted the water after it had become wine, not knowing whence it was (though the attendants who had drawn the water knew), the chief steward called the bridegroom, and said to him, "Every man at first sets forth the good wine, and when they have drunk freely, then that which is poorer. But you have kept the good wine until now." This first of His signs Jesus worked at Cana of Galilee; and He manifested His glory, and His disciples believed in Him. *S.* Praise be to You, O Christ.

P. By the words of the Gospel, may our sins be taken away.

THE NICENE CREED

At the center of the altar, he says:

I BELIEVE in one God, the Father almighty, Maker of heaven and earth, and of all things visible and invisible. And in one Lord Jesus Christ, the Only-begotten Son of God. Born of the Father before all ages. God of God; Light of Light; true God of true God. Begotten not made; of one being with the Father; by Whom all things were made. Who for us men, and for our salvation, came down from heaven. (*Here all genuflect.*) And was made Flesh by the Holy Spirit of the Virgin Mary: AND WAS MADE MAN. He was also crucified for us, suffered under Pontius Pilate and was buried. And on the third day He rose again according to the Scriptures. And ascending into heaven, He sits at the right hand of the Father. And He shall come again in glory to judge the living and the dead; and of His kingdom there shall be no end. And I believe in the Holy Spirit, Lord and Giver of life, Who proceeds from the Father and the Son. Who together with the Father and the Son is no less adored, and glorified: Who spoke by the Prophets. And I believe in One, Holy, Catholic and Apostolic Church. I confess one Baptism for the remission of sins. And I look for the resurrection of the dead. ✠ And the life of the world to come. Amen.

THE OFFERTORY

The Priest turns to the people and says:

P. The Lord be with you. S. And with your spirit.

P. Let us pray.

THE OFFERTORY VERSE • Ps. 65, 1-2. 16

SHOUT joyfully to God, all you on earth, sing praise to the glory of His name. Hear now, all you who fear God, while I declare what the Lord has done for me. Alleluia.

The Priest now uncovers the chalice, places the host on the paten and offering it up, says:

ACCEPT, O holy Father, almighty and eternal God, this spotless host, which I, Your unworthy servant, offer to You, my living and true God, to atone for my numberless sins, offenses, and negligences; on behalf of all here present and likewise for all faithful Christians living and dead, that it may profit me and them as a means of salvation to life everlasting. Amen.

He pours wine and water into the chalice, blessing the water before it is poured.

O GOD, Who established the nature of man in wondrous dignity, and still more admirably restored it, grant that through the mystery of this water and wine, we may be made partakers of His Divinity, Who has condescended to become partaker of our humanity, Jesus Christ, Your Son, our Lord. Who lives and reigns with You in the unity of the Holy Spirit, God, world without end. Amen.

Offering up the wine, the Priest says:

WE OFFER You, O Lord, the chalice of salvation, humbly begging of Your mercy that it may arise before Your Divine Majesty, with a pleasing fragrance, for our salvation and for that of the whole world. Amen.

Bowing down, the Priest says:

IN A humble spirit and with a contrite heart, may we be accepted by You, O Lord, and may our

sacrifice so be offered in Your sight this day as to please You, O Lord God.

Raising his eyes and blessing the offering, he says:

COME, O Sanctifier, almighty and eternal God, and bless ✠ this sacrifice prepared for the glory of Your holy name.

WASHING THE FINGERS

I WASH my hands in innocence, and I go around Your altar, O Lord, giving voice to my thanks, and recounting all Your wondrous deeds. O Lord, I love the house in which You dwell, the tenting-place of Your glory. Gather not my soul with those of sinners, nor with men of blood my life. On their hands are crimes, and their right hands are full of bribes. But I walk in integrity; redeem me, and have pity on me. My foot stands on level ground; in the assemblies I will bless You, O Lord. Glory be to the Father, and to the Son, and to the Holy Spirit. As it was in the beginning, is now, and ever shall be, world without end. Amen.

ACCEPT, Most Holy Trinity, this offering which we are making to You in remembrance of the Passion, Resurrection, and Ascension of Jesus Christ, our Lord; and in honor of Blessed Mary, ever Virgin, Blessed John the Baptist, the Holy Apostles Peter and Paul, and of these, and of all the Saints; that it may add to their honor and aid our salvation; and may they deign to intercede in heaven for us who honor their memory here on earth. Through the same Christ our Lord. Amen.

The Priest turns toward the people and says:

Pray, brethren, that my sacrifice and yours may become acceptable to God the Father almighty.

S. May the Lord accept this sacrifice from your hands to the praise and glory of His name, for our advantage, and that of all His holy Church.
P. Amen.

THE SECRET

SANCTIFY, O Lord, the gifts we offer, and purify us from the stains of our sins. Through our Lord Jesus Christ, Your Son, Who lives and reigns with You in the unity of the Holy Spirit, God.
P. World without end. *S*. Amen.

PREFACE—CANON

P. The Lord be with you. *S*. And with your spirit.
P. Lift up your hearts.
S. We have lifted them up to the Lord.
P. Let us give thanks to the Lord, our God.
S. It is fitting and just.

IT IS fitting indeed and just, right and helpful to salvation, for us always and everywhere to give thanks to You, O holy Lord, Father almighty, everlasting God, Who with Your Only-begotten Son and the Holy Spirit are one God, one Lord; not in the unity of a single person, but in the trinity of a single nature. For that which we believe on Your revelation concerning Your glory, that same we believe of Your Son, that same of the Holy Spirit, without difference or discrimination. So that in confessing the true and everlasting Godhead, we shall adore distinction in Persons, oneness in being, and equality in Majesty. This the Angels and Archangels, the Cherubim, too, and the Seraphim do praise; day by day they cease not to cry out as with one voice, saying (*the bell is rung* 3 *times*):

HOLY, HOLY, HOLY, Lord God of Hosts. Heaven and earth are filled with Your glory. Hosanna in the highest. ✠ Blessed is He Who comes in the name of the Lord. Hosanna in the highest.

THE CANON OF THE MASS

THEREFORE, most gracious Father, we humbly beg of You and entreat You through Jesus Christ Your Son, our Lord, (*he kisses the altar*) to deem acceptable and bless these ✠ gifts, these ✠ offerings, these ✠ holy and unspotted oblations which, in the first place, we offer You for Your Holy Catholic Church, that You would deign to give her peace and protection, to unite and guard her throughout the world, together with Your servant N., our Pope, and N., our Bishop; and all true believers who cherish the Catholic and Apostolic Faith.

Commemoration of the Living

REMEMBER, O Lord, Your servants and handmaids, N. and N., (*name them*) and all here present, whose faith and devotion are known to You, on whose behalf we offer to You, or who themselves offer to You, this sacrifice of praise for themselves, families and friends, for the good of their souls, for their hope of salvation and deliverance from all harm, and who offer their homage to You, eternal, living and true God.

Commemoration of the Saints

IN THE unity of holy fellowship we observe the memory, first of all, of the glorious and ever Virgin Mary, Mother of our Lord and God Jesus Christ; next, that of Your Blessed Apostles and

Martyrs, Peter and Paul, Andrew, James, John, Thomas, James, Philip, Bartholomew, Matthew, Simon and Thaddeus; of Linus, Cletus, Clement, Sixtus, Cornelius, Cyprian, Lawrence, Chrysogonus, John and Paul, Cosmas and Damian, and of all Your Saints, by whose merits and prayers grant that we may be always fortified by the help of Your protection. Through the same Christ our Lord. Amen.

Spreading his hands over the oblation, he says:

GRACIOUSLY accept, then, we beseech You, O Lord, this service of our worship and that of all Your household. Provide that our days be spent in Your peace, save us from everlasting damnation, and cause us to be numbered in the flock You have chosen. Through Christ our Lord. Amen.

O GOD, deign to bless ✠ what we offer, and make it approved, ✠ effective, ✠ right, and wholly pleasing in every way, that it may become for our good, the Body ✠ and Blood ✠ of Your dearly beloved Son, Jesus Christ our Lord.

CONSECRATION—ELEVATION

WHO, the day before He suffered, took bread into His holy and venerable hands, and having raised His eyes to heaven, to You, O God, His almighty Father, giving thanks to You, He blessed it, ✠ broke it, and gave it to His disciples, saying: All of you take and eat of this:

FOR THIS IS MY BODY.

IN LIKE manner, when the supper was done, taking also this goodly chalice into His holy and venerable hands, again giving thanks to You, He blessed ✠ it, and gave it to His disciples, saying: All of you take and drink of this:

FOR THIS IS THE CHALICE OF MY BLOOD OF THE NEW AND ETERNAL COVENANT: THE MYSTERY OF FAITH: WHICH SHALL BE SHED FOR YOU AND FOR MANY UNTO THE FORGIVENESS OF SINS.

After replacing the chalice on the corporal, he says:

As often as you shall do these things, in memory of Me shall you do them.

Offering of the Victim

MINDFUL, therefore, O Lord, not only of the blessed Passion of the same Christ, Your Son, our Lord, but also of His Resurrection from the dead, and finally His glorious Ascension into heaven, we, Your ministers, as also Your holy people, offer to Your supreme Majesty, of the gifts bestowed upon us, the pure ✠ Victim, the holy ✠ Victim, the all-perfect ✠ Victim: the holy ✠ Bread of life eternal and the Chalice ✠ of unending salvation.

AND this deign to regard with gracious and kindly attention and hold acceptable, as You deigned to accept the offerings of Abel, Your just servant, and the sacrifice of Abraham our patriarch, and that which Your chief priest Melchisedec offered to You, a holy sacrifice and a spotless victim.

MOST humbly we implore You, almighty God, bid these offerings to be brought by the hands of Your holy angel to Your altar above; before the face of Your Divine Majesty; that those of us who, by sharing in the Sacrifice of this altar, shall receive the Most Sacred ✠ Body and ✠ Blood of Your Son, may be filled with every grace and heavenly blessing. Through the same Christ our Lord. Amen.

Commemoration of the Dead

REMEMBER also, O Lord, Your servants and handmaids, N. and N., who have gone before us with the sign of faith, and rest in the sleep of peace. (*Here pray for the dead.*) To these, O Lord, and to all who rest in Christ, we beseech You to grant of Your goodness, a place of comfort, light and peace. Through the same Christ our Lord. Amen.

TO US sinners also, Your servants, trusting in the greatness of Your mercy, deign to grant some part and fellowship with Your Holy Apostles and Martyrs: with John, Stephen, Matthias, Barnabas, Ignatius, Alexander, Marcellinus, Peter, Felicitas, Perpetua, Agatha, Lucy, Agnes, Cecilia, Anastasia, and all Your Saints; into whose company, we implore You to admit us, not weighing our merits, but freely granting us pardon. Through Christ our Lord.

THROUGH Whom, O Lord, You always create, ✠ sanctify, ✠ fill with life, ✠ bless, and bestow upon us all good things.

The Minor Elevation

THROUGH ✠ Him, and with ✠ Him, and in ✠ Him, is to You, God the Father ✠ almighty, in the unity of the Holy ✠ Spirit, all honor and glory, world without end. S. Amen.

THE COMMUNION AND THANKSGIVING

Let us pray. Prompted by saving precepts, and taught by Your divine teaching, we dare to say:

OUR FATHER, Who art in heaven, hallowed be Thy name: Thy kingdom come: Thy will be done on earth as it is in heaven. Give us this day

our daily bread; and forgive us our trespasses, as we forgive those who trespass against us. And lead us not into temptation: S. But deliver us from evil. *P.* Amen.

DELIVER us, we beseech You, O Lord, from all evils, past, present, and to come; and by the intercession of the Blessed and glorious Mary, ever Virgin, Mother of God, together with Your Blessed Apostles Peter and Paul, and Andrew, and all the Saints, grant of Your goodness, peace in our days, that aided by the riches of Your mercy, we may be always free from sin and safe from all disturbance.

Through the same our Lord Jesus Christ, Your Son, Who lives and reigns with You in the unity of the Holy Spirit, God, world without end. S. Amen.

P. May the peace ✠ of the Lord be ✠ always with ✠ you.

S. And with your spirit.

The Priest puts a small particle into the chalice, saying:

May this mingling and consecration of the Body and Blood of our Lord Jesus Christ help us who receive it to life everlasting. Amen.

LAMB of God, You Who take away the sins of the world, have mercy on us.

Lamb of God, You Who take away the sins of the world, have mercy on us.

Lamb of God, You Who take away the sins of the world, grant us peace.

PRAYERS BEFORE HOLY COMMUNION

Then inclining toward the altar, he says:

O LORD Jesus Christ, Who said to Your Apostles: "Peace I leave with you, My peace I give

to you," regard not my sins but the faith of Your Church, and deign to give her peace and unity according to Your Will: Who live and reign, God, world without end. Amen.

O LORD Jesus Christ, Son of the living God, Who, by the will of the Father, with the co-operation of the Holy Spirit, have by Your death given life to the world, deliver me by this Your Most Sacred Body and Blood from all my sins and from every evil. Make me always cling to Your commandments, and never permit me to be separated from You. Who with the same God the Father and the Holy Spirit, live and reign, God, world without end. Amen.

LET not the partaking of Your Body, O Lord Jesus Christ, which I, though unworthy, presume to receive, turn to my judgment and condemnation; but through Your goodness, may it become a safeguard and an effective remedy, both of soul and body. Who live and reign with God the Father, in the unity of the Holy Spirit, God, world without end. Amen.

COMMUNION OF THE PRIEST

I WILL take the Bread of heaven, and call upon the name of the Lord.

Lord, I am not worthy that You should come under my roof; but only say the word, and my soul will be healed. (3 *times.*)

Making the Sign of the Cross with the Host, he says:

MAY the Body of our Lord Jesus Christ preserve my soul to life everlasting. Amen.

What return shall I make to the Lord for all He has given me? I will take the Chalice of salvation,

and I will call upon the name of the Lord. Praising will I call upon the Lord and I shall be saved from my enemies.

Making the Sign of the Cross with the chalice, he says:

MAY the Blood of our Lord Jesus Christ preserve my soul to life everlasting. Amen.

The Priest reverently consumes the Precious Blood.

COMMUNION OF THE FAITHFUL

The Server and people say the "Confiteor."

P. May almighty God have mercy on you, forgive you your sins, and bring you to life everlasting. *S.* Amen.

P. May the almighty and merciful Lord grant you pardon, ✠ absolution and remission of your sins. *S.* Amen.

Holding up a Sacred Host, the Priest says:

Behold the Lamb of God, behold Him Who takes away the sins of the world.

Lord, I am not worthy that You should come under my roof; but only say the word, and my soul will be healed. (3 *times.*)

The Priest says to each communicant:

May the Body of our Lord Jesus Christ preserve your soul to life everlasting. Amen.

The Priest purifies the chalice with wine, saying:

WHAT has passed our lips as food, O Lord, may we possess in purity of heart, that what is given to us in time, be our healing for eternity.

He purifies his fingers with wine and water, saying:

MAY Your Body, O Lord, which I have eaten, and Your Blood which I have drunk, cleave to my very soul, and grant that no trace of sin be found in me, whom these pure and holy mysteries have renewed. Who live and reign, world without end. Amen.

THE COMMUNION • John 2, 7. 8. 9, 10-11

THE Lord said, "Fill the jars with water and take to the chief steward." When the chief steward had tasted the water after it had become wine, he said to the bridegroom, "You have kept the good wine until now." This first miracle Jesus worked in the presence of His disciples.

P. The Lord be with you. S. And with your spirit.

P. Let us pray.

THE POSTCOMMUNION

MAY the working of Your power, we beg of You, O Lord, be increased in us, that, being nourished by divine sacraments, we may by Your grace be prepared to obtain that which they promise. Through our Lord Jesus Christ, Your Son, Who lives and reigns, etc. S. Amen.

FINAL PRAYERS

P. The Lord be with you. S. And with your spirit

P. Go, you are dismissed. S. Thanks be to God.

MAY the tribute of my worship be pleasing to You, Most Holy Trinity, and grant that the sacrifice which I, all unworthy, have offered in the presence of Your Majesty, may be acceptable to You, and through Your mercy obtain forgiveness for me and all for whom I have offered it. Through Christ our Lord. Amen.

THE LAST BLESSING

MAY almighty God bless you: ✠ the Father and the Son, and the Holy Spirit. S. Amen

The Last Gospel and Prayers after Low Mass are conveniently placed inside the back cover.

"Lord . . . only say the word, and my servant will be healed."

THIRD SUNDAY AFTER EPIPHANY

The Centurion asked only one word of Jesus so that his servant could be cured; similarly only one word is sufficient from our Redeemer to cure the leprosy of mortal sin. (GREEN VESTMENTS)

PRAYERS AT THE FOOT OF THE ALTAR

IN THE name of the Father, ✠ and of the Son, and of the Holy Spirit. Amen.

Priest. I will go in to the altar of God.

Server. The God of my gladness and joy.

Psalm 42

DO ME justice, O God, and fight my fight against a faithless people; from the deceitful and impious man rescue me.

S. For You, O God, are my strength. Why do You keep me so far away? Why must I go about in mourning, with the enemy oppressing me?

P. Send forth Your light and Your fidelity; they shall lead me on and bring me to Your holy mountain, to Your dwelling-place.

S. Then will I go in to the altar of God, the God of my gladness and joy.
P. Then will I give You thanks upon the harp, O God, my God. Why are you so downcast, O my soul? Why do you sigh within me?
S. Hope in God! For I shall again be thanking Him in the presence of my Savior and my God.
P. Glory be to the Father, and to the Son, and to the Holy Spirit.
S. As it was in the beginning, is now, and ever shall be, world without end. Amen.
P. I will go in to the altar of God.
S. The God of my gladness and joy.
P. Our help ✠ is in the name of the Lord.
S. Who made heaven and earth.
P. I confess to almighty God, etc.
S. May almighty God have mercy on you, forgive you your sins, and bring you to life everlasting.
P. Amen.

The Server, bowing, says the "Confiteor."

I CONFESS to almighty God, to Blessed Mary, ever Virgin, to Blessed Michael the Archangel, to Blessed John the Baptist, to the Holy Apostles Peter and Paul, and to all the Saints, and to you, Father, that I have sinned exceedingly in thought, word and deed, *through my fault, through my fault, through my most grievous fault.* Therefore I beseech Blessed Mary, ever Virgin, Blessed Michael the Archangel, Blessed John the Baptist, the Holy Apostles Peter and Paul, and all the Saints, and you, Father, to pray to the Lord our God for me.
P. May almighty God have mercy on you, forgive you your sins, and bring you to life everlasting.
S. Amen.

MAY the almighty and merciful Lord grant us pardon, ✠ absolution, and remission of our sins. S. Amen.
P. Will You not, O God, give us life?
S. And shall not Your people rejoice in You?
P. Show us, O Lord, Your kindness.
S. And grant us Your salvation.
P. O Lord, hear my prayer.
S. And let my cry come to You.
P. The Lord be with you.
S. And with your spirit. *P.* Let us pray.

Going up to the altar, the Priest prays silently:

TAKE away from us our sins, O Lord, we beseech You, that we may enter with pure minds into the Holy of Holies. Through Christ our Lord. Amen.

WE BESEECH You, O Lord, by the merits of Your Saints (*he kisses the altar*) whose relics lie here, and of all the Saints: deign in Your mercy to pardon me all my sins. Amen.

THE INTROIT • Ps. 96, 7. 8. 1

At the right side of the altar, the Priest says:

ADORE God, all you His angels: Sion hears and is glad, and the cities of Juda rejoice. *Ps.* The Lord is King; let the earth rejoice; let the many isles be glad. Glory be to the Father, and to the Son, and to the Holy Spirit. As it was in the beginning, is now, and ever shall be, world without end. Amen — Adore God, all you His angels: Sion hears and is glad, and the cities of Juda rejoice.

THE KYRIE

P. Lord, have mercy. *S.* Lord, have mercy. *P.* Lord, have mercy. S. Christ, have mercy. *P.* Christ, have

mercy. *S.* Christ, have mercy. *P.* Lord, have mercy. *S.* Lord, have mercy. *P.* Lord, have mercy.

THE GLORIA

GLORY to God in the highest. And on earth peace to men of good will. We praise You. We bless You. We adore You. We glorify You. We give You thanks for Your great glory. O Lord God, heavenly King, God the Father almighty. O Lord Jesus Christ, the Only-begotten Son. O Lord God, Lamb of God, Son of the Father: You Who take away the sins of the world, have mercy on us. You Who take away the sins of the world, receive our prayer. You Who sit at the right hand of the Father, have mercy on us. For You alone are holy. You alone are the Lord. You alone, O Jesus Christ, are most high. Together with the Holy Spirit ✠ in the glory of God the Father. Amen.

The Priest kisses the altar and turns to the people, saying:

P. The Lord be with you. *S.* And with your spirit. *P.* Let us pray.

THE PRAYER

Going to the right (Epistle) side, he says:

ALMIGHTY and everlasting God, graciously look upon our infirmity, and, for our protection, stretch forth the right hand of Your Majesty. Through our Lord Jesus Christ, Your Son, Who lives and reigns with You in the unity of the Holy Spirit, God, world without end. *S.* Amen.

THE EPISTLE • Rom. 12, 16-21

BRETHREN: Be not wise in your own conceits. To no man render evil for evil, but provide good things not only in the sight of God, but also in the sight of all men. If it be possible, as far as in you lies, be at peace with all men. Do not avenge yourselves, beloved, but give place to the wrath, for it is written, "Vengeance is Mine: I will repay, says the Lord." But, "If your enemy is hungry, give him food; if he is thirsty, give him drink; for by so doing you will heap coals of fire upon his head." Be not overcome by evil, but overcome evil with good. S. Thanks be to God.

THE GRADUAL • Ps. 101, 16. 17

THE nations shall revere Your name, O Lord, and all the kings of the earth Your glory. ℣. For the Lord has rebuilt Sion, and He shall appear in His glory.

Alleluia, alleuia. ℣. *Ps. 96, 1.* The Lord is King; let the earth rejoice; let the many isles be glad. Alleluia.

PRAYER BEFORE THE GOSPEL

Bowing down at the center of the altar, he says:

CLEANSE my heart and my lips, O almighty God, Who cleansed the lips of the Prophet Isaias with a burning coal. In Your gracious mercy deign so to purify me that I may worthily proclaim Your holy Gospel. Through Christ our Lord. Amen.

Lord, grant Your blessing. The Lord be in my heart and on my lips, that I may worthily and fittingly proclaim His holy Gospel. Amen.

THE GOSPEL • Matt. 8, 1-13

Going to the left (Gospel) side of the altar, he says:

P. The Lord be with you. S. And with your spirit.
P. ✠ The continuation of the holy Gospel according to Saint Matthew. S. Glory be to You, O Lord.

AT THAT time, when Jesus had come down from the mountain, great crowds followed

Him. And behold, a leper came up and worshipped Him, saying, "Lord, if You will, You can make me clean." And stretching forth His hand Jesus touched him, saying, "I will; be made clean." And immediately his leprosy was cleansed. And Jesus said to him, "See that you tell no one; but go, show yourself to the priest, and offer the gift that Moses commanded, for a witness to them." Now when He had entered Capharnaum, there came to Him a centurion who entreated Him, saying, "Lord, my servant is lying sick in the house, paralyzed, and is grievously afflicted." Jesus said to him, "I will come and cure him." But in answer the centurion said, "Lord, I am not worthy that You should come under my roof; but only say the word, and my servant will be healed. For I too am a man subject to authority, and have soldiers subject to me; and I say to one, 'Go,' and he goes; and to another, 'Come,' and he comes; and to my servant, 'Do this,' and he does it." And when Jesus heard this, He marvelled, and said to those who were following Him, "Amen I say to you, I have not found such great faith in Israel. And I tell you that many will come from the east and from the west, and will feast with Abraham and Isaac and Jacob in the kingdom of heaven, but the children of the kingdom will be put forth into the darkness outside; there will be the weeping, and the gnashing of teeth." Then Jesus said to the centurion, "Go your way; as you have believed, so be it done to you." And the servant was healed in that hour. S. Praise be to You, O Christ.

P. By the words of the Gospel, may our sins be taken away.

THE NICENE CREED

At the center of the altar, he says:

I BELIEVE in one God, the Father almighty, Maker of heaven and earth, and of all things visible and invisible. And in one Lord Jesus Christ, the Only-begotten Son of God. Born of the Father before all ages. God of God; Light of Light; true God of true God. Begotten not made; of one being with the Father; by Whom all things were made. Who for us men, and for our salvation, came down from heaven. (*Here all genuflect.*) And was made Flesh by the Holy Spirit of the Virgin Mary: AND WAS MADE MAN. He was also crucified for us, suffered under Pontius Pilate and was buried. And on the third day He rose again according to the Scriptures. And ascending into heaven, He sits at the right hand of the Father. And He shall come again in glory to judge the living and the dead; and of His kingdom there shall be no end. And I believe in the Holy Spirit, Lord and Giver of life, Who proceeds from the Father and the Son. Who together with the Father and the Son is no less adored, and glorified: Who spoke by the Prophets. And I believe in One, Holy, Catholic and Apostolic Church. I confess one Baptism for the remission of sins. And I look for the resurrection of the dead. ✠ And the life of the world to come. Amen.

THE OFFERTORY

The Priest turns to the people and says:

P. The Lord be with you. *S.* And with your spirit.
P. Let us pray.

THE OFFERTORY VERSE • Ps. 117, 16. 17

THE right hand of the Lord has struck with power: the right hand of the Lord has exalted me; I shall not die, but live, and declare the works of the Lord.

The Priest now uncovers the chalice, places the host on the paten and offering it up, says:

ACCEPT, O holy Father, almighty and eternal God, this spotless host, which I, Your unworthy servant, offer to You, my living and true God, to atone for my numberless sins, offenses, and negligences; on behalf of all here present and likewise for all faithful Christians living and dead, that it may profit me and them as a means of salvation to life everlasting. Amen.

He pours wine and water into the chalice, blessing the water before it is poured.

O GOD, Who established the nature of man in wondrous dignity, and still more admirably restored it, grant that through the mystery of this water and wine, we may be made partakers of His Divinity, Who has condescended to become partaker of our humanity, Jesus Christ, Your Son, our Lord. Who lives and reigns with You in the unity of the Holy Spirit, God, world without end. Amen.

Offering up the wine, the Priest says:

WE OFFER You, O Lord, the chalice of salvation, humbly begging of Your mercy that it may arise before Your Divine Majesty, with a pleasing fragrance, for our salvation and for that of the whole world. Amen.

Bowing down, the Priest says:

IN A humble spirit and with a contrite heart, may we be accepted by You, O Lord, and may our

sacrifice so be offered in Your sight this day as to please You, O Lord God.

Raising his eyes and blessing the offering, he says:

COME, O Sanctifier, almighty and eternal God, and bless ✠ this sacrifice prepared for the glory of Your holy name.

WASHING THE FINGERS

I WASH my hands in innocence, and I go around Your altar, O Lord, giving voice to my thanks, and recounting all Your wondrous deeds. O Lord, I love the house in which You dwell, the tenting-place of Your glory. Gather not my soul with those of sinners, nor with men of blood my life. On their hands are crimes, and their right hands are full of bribes. But I walk in integrity; redeem me, and have pity on me. My foot stands on level ground; in the assemblies I will bless You, O Lord. Glory be to the Father, and to the Son, and to the Holy Spirit. As it was in the beginning, is now, and ever shall be, world without end. Amen.

ACCEPT, Most Holy Trinity, this offering which we are making to You in remembrance of the Passion, Resurrection, and Ascension of Jesus Christ, our Lord; and in honor of Blessed Mary, ever Virgin, Blessed John the Baptist, the Holy Apostles Peter and Paul, and of these, and of all the Saints; that it may add to their honor and aid our salvation; and may they deign to intercede in heaven for us who honor their memory here on earth. Through the same Christ our Lord. Amen.

The Priest turns toward the people and says:

Pray, brethren, that my sacrifice and yours may become acceptable to God the Father almighty.

S. May the Lord accept this sacrifice from your hands to the praise and glory of His name, for our advantage, and that of all His holy Church.
P. Amen.

THE SECRET

MAY this offering, we beseech You, O Lord, cleanse away our sins, and sanctify the bodies and minds of Your servants for the celebration of this sacrifice. Through our Lord Jesus Christ, Your Son, Who lives and reigns with You in the unity of the Holy Spirit, God.
P. World without end. *S.* Amen.

PREFACE—CANON

P. The Lord be with you. *S.* And with your spirit.
P. Lift up your hearts.
S. We have lifted them up to the Lord.
P. Let us give thanks to the Lord, our God.
S. It is fitting and just.

IT IS fitting indeed and just, right and helpful to salvation, for us always and everywhere to give thanks to You, O holy Lord, Father almighty, everlasting God, Who with Your Only-begotten Son and the Holy Spirit are one God, one Lord; not in the unity of a single person, but in the trinity of a single nature. For that which we believe on Your revelation concerning Your glory, that same we believe of Your Son, that same of the Holy Spirit, without difference or discrimination. So that in confessing the true and everlasting Godhead, we shall adore distinction in Persons, oneness in being, and equality in Majesty. This the Angels and Archangels, the Cherubim, too, and the Seraphim do praise; day by day they cease not to cry out as with one voice, saying (*the bell is rung 3 times*):

HOLY, HOLY, HOLY, Lord God of Hosts. Heaven and earth are filled with Your glory. Hosanna in the highest. ✠ Blessed is He Who comes in the name of the Lord. Hosanna in the highest.

THE CANON OF THE MASS

THEREFORE, most gracious Father, we humbly beg of You and entreat You through Jesus Christ Your Son, our Lord, (*he kisses the altar*) to deem acceptable and bless these ✠ gifts, these ✠ offerings, these ✠ holy and unspotted oblations which, in the first place, we offer You for Your Holy Catholic Church, that You would deign to give her peace and protection, to unite and guard her throughout the world, together with Your servant N., our Pope, and N., our Bishop; and all true believers who cherish the Catholic and Apostolic Faith.

Commemoration of the Living

REMEMBER, O Lord, Your servants and handmaids, N. and N., (*name them*) and all here present, whose faith and devotion are known to You, on whose behalf we offer to You, or who themselves offer to You, this sacrifice of praise for themselves, families and friends, for the good of their souls, for their hope of salvation and deliverance from all harm, and who offer their homage to You, eternal, living and true God.

Commemoration of the Saints

IN THE unity of holy fellowship we observe the memory, first of all, of the glorious and ever Virgin Mary, Mother of our Lord and God Jesus Christ; next, that of Your Blessed Apostles and

Martyrs, Peter and Paul, Andrew, James, John, Thomas, James, Philip, Bartholomew, Matthew, Simon and Thaddeus; of Linus, Cletus, Clement, Sixtus, Cornelius, Cyprian, Lawrence, Chrysogonus, John and Paul, Cosmas and Damian, and of all Your Saints, by whose merits and prayers grant that we may be always fortified by the help of Your protection. Through the same Christ our Lord. Amen.

Spreading his hands over the oblation, he says:

GRACIOUSLY accept, then, we beseech You, O Lord, this service of our worship and that of all Your household. Provide that our days be spent in Your peace, save us from everlasting damnation, and cause us to be numbered in the flock You have chosen. Through Christ our Lord. Amen.

O GOD, deign to bless ✠ what we offer, and make it approved, ✠ effective, ✠ right, and wholly pleasing in every way, that it may become for our good, the Body ✠ and Blood ✠ of Your dearly beloved Son, Jesus Christ our Lord.

CONSECRATION—ELEVATION

WHO, the day before He suffered, took bread into His holy and venerable hands, and having raised His eyes to heaven, to You, O God, His almighty Father, giving thanks to You, He blessed it, ✠ broke it, and gave it to His disciples, saying: All of you take and eat of this:

FOR THIS IS MY BODY.

IN LIKE manner, when the supper was done, taking also this goodly chalice into His holy and venerable hands, again giving thanks to You, He blessed ✠ it, and gave it to His disciples, saying: All of you take and drink of this:

FOR THIS IS THE CHALICE OF MY BLOOD OF THE NEW AND ETERNAL COVENANT: THE MYSTERY OF FAITH: WHICH SHALL BE SHED FOR YOU AND FOR MANY UNTO THE FORGIVENESS OF SINS.

After replacing the chalice on the corporal, he says:

As often as you shall do these things, in memory of Me shall you do them.

Offering of the Victim

MINDFUL, therefore, O Lord, not only of the blessed Passion of the same Christ, Your Son, our Lord, but also of His Resurrection from the dead, and finally His glorious Ascension into heaven, we, Your ministers, as also Your holy people, offer to Your supreme Majesty, of the gifts bestowed upon us, the pure ✠ Victim, the holy ✠ Victim, the all-perfect ✠ Victim: the holy ✠ Bread of life eternal and the Chalice ✠ of unending salvation.

AND this deign to regard with gracious and kindly attention and hold acceptable, as You deigned to accept the offerings of Abel, Your just servant, and the sacrifice of Abraham our patriarch, and that which Your chief priest Melchisedec offered to You, a holy sacrifice and a spotless victim.

MOST humbly we implore You, almighty God, bid these offerings to be brought by the hands of Your holy angel to Your altar above; before the face of Your Divine Majesty; that those of us who, by sharing in the Sacrifice of this altar, shall receive the Most Sacred ✠ Body and ✠ Blood of Your Son, may be filled with every grace and heavenly blessing. Through the same Christ our Lord. Amen.

Commemoration of the Dead

REMEMBER also, O Lord, Your servants and handmaids, *N.* and *N.*, who have gone before us with the sign of faith, and rest in the sleep of peace. (*Here pray for the dead.*) To these, O Lord, and to all who rest in Christ, we beseech You to grant of Your goodness, a place of comfort, light and peace. Through the same Christ our Lord. Amen.

TO US sinners also, Your servants, trusting in the greatness of Your mercy, deign to grant some part and fellowship with Your Holy Apostles and Martyrs: with John, Stephen, Matthias, Barnabas, Ignatius, Alexander, Marcellinus, Peter, Felicitas, Perpetua, Agatha, Lucy, Agnes, Cecilia, Anastasia, and all Your Saints; into whose company, we implore You to admit us, not weighing our merits, but freely granting us pardon. Through Christ our Lord.

THROUGH Whom, O Lord, You always create, ✠ sanctify, ✠ fill with life, ✠ bless, and bestow upon us all good things.

The Minor Elevation

THROUGH ✠ Him, and with ✠ Him, and in ✠ Him, is to You, God the Father ✠ almighty, in the unity of the Holy ✠ Spirit, all honor and glory, world without end. *S.* Amen.

THE COMMUNION AND THANKSGIVING

Let us pray. Prompted by saving precepts, and taught by Your divine teaching, we dare to say:

OUR FATHER, Who art in heaven, hallowed be Thy name: Thy kingdom come: Thy will be done on earth as it is in heaven. Give us this day our daily bread; and forgive us our trespasses, as we forgive those who trespass against us. And lead us not into temptation: S. But deliver us from evil. *P.* Amen.

DELIVER us, we beseech You, O Lord, from all evils, past, present, and to come; and by the intercession of the Blessed and glorious Mary, ever Virgin, Mother of God, together with Your Blessed Apostles Peter and Paul, and Andrew, and all the Saints, grant of Your goodness, peace in our days, that aided by the riches of Your mercy, we may be always free from sin and safe from all disturbance.
Through the same our Lord Jesus Christ, Your Son, Who lives and reigns with You in the unity of the Holy Spirit, God, world without end.
S. Amen.
P. May the peace ✠ of the Lord be ✠ always with ✠ you.
S. And with your spirit.

The Priest puts a small particle into the chalice, saying:
May this mingling and consecration of the Body and Blood of our Lord Jesus Christ help us who receive it to life everlasting. Amen.

LAMB of God, You Who take away the sins of the world, have mercy on us.
Lamb of God, You Who take away the sins of the world, have mercy on us.
Lamb of God, You Who take away the sins of the world, grant us peace.

PRAYERS BEFORE HOLY COMMUNION

Then inclining toward the altar, he says:

O LORD Jesus Christ, Who said to Your Apostles: "Peace I leave with you, My peace I give to you," regard not my sins but the faith of Your Church, and deign to give her peace and unity according to Your Will: Who live and reign, God, world without end. Amen.

O LORD Jesus Christ, Son of the living God, Who, by the will of the Father, with the cooperation of the Holy Spirit, have by Your death given life to the world, deliver me by this Your Most Sacred Body and Blood from all my sins and from every evil. Make me always cling to Your commandments, and never permit me to be separated from You. Who with the same God the Father and the Holy Spirit, live and reign, God, world without end. Amen.

LET not the partaking of Your Body, O Lord Jesus Christ, which I, though unworthy, presume to receive, turn to my judgment and condemnation; but through Your goodness, may it become a safeguard and an effective remedy, both of soul and body. Who live and reign with God the Father, in the unity of the Holy Spirit, God, world without end. Amen.

COMMUNION OF THE PRIEST

I WILL take the Bread of heaven, and call upon the name of the Lord.

Lord, I am not worthy that You should come under my roof; but only say the word, and my soul will be healed. (3 *times.*)

MAY the Body of our Lord Jesus Christ preserve my soul to life everlasting. Amen.
What return shall I make to the Lord for all He has given me? I will take the Chalice of salvation, and I will call upon the name of the Lord. Praising will I call upon the Lord and I shall be saved from my enemies.

MAY the Blood of our Lord Jesus Christ preserve my soul to life everlasting. Amen.

The Priest reverently consumes the Precious Blood.

COMMUNION OF THE FAITHFUL

The Server and people say the "Confiteor."

P. May almighty God have mercy on you, forgive you your sins, and bring you to life everlasting. *S.* Amen.

P. May the almighty and merciful Lord grant you pardon, ✠ absolution and remission of your sins. S. Amen.

Holding up a Sacred Host, the Priest says:

Behold the Lamb of God, behold Him Who takes away the sins of the world.

Lord, I am not worthy that You should come under my roof; but only say the word, and my soul will be healed. (3 *times.*)

The Priest says to each communicant:

May the Body of our Lord Jesus Christ preserve your soul to life everlasting. Amen.

The Priest purifies the chalice with wine, saying:

WHAT has passed our lips as food, O Lord, may we possess in purity of heart, that what is given to us in time, be our healing for eternity.

He purifies his fingers with wine and water, saying:

MAY Your Body, O Lord, which I have eaten, and Your Blood which I have drunk, cleave to my very soul, and grant that no trace of sin be found in me, whom these pure and holy mysteries have renewed. Who live and reign, world without end. Amen.

THE COMMUNION • Luke 4, 22

ALL marvelled at the words that came from the mouth of God.

The Priest, turning to the people, says:

P. The Lord be with you. *S.* And with your spirit.
P. Let us pray.

THE POSTCOMMUNION

WE, O Lord, to whom You grant the use of mysteries so great, beseech You to render us truly fitted to obtain their effect. Through our Lord Jesus Christ, Your Son, Who lives and reigns with You in the unity of the Holy Spirit, God, world without end. *S.* Amen.

FINAL PRAYERS

P. The Lord be with you. *S.* And with your spirit.
P. Go, you are dismissed. *S.* Thanks be to God.

MAY the tribute of my worship be pleasing to You, Most Holy Trinity, and grant that the sacrifice which I, all unworthy, have offered in the presence of Your Majesty, may be acceptable to You, and through Your mercy obtain forgiveness for me and all for whom I have offered it. Through Christ our Lord. Amen.

THE LAST BLESSING

MAY almighty God bless you: ✠ the Father, and the Son, and the Holy Spirit. *S.* Amen.

The Last Gospel and Prayers after Low Mass are conveniently placed inside the back cover.

The Last Gospel and Prayers after Low Mass are conveniently placed inside the back cover.

"Why are you fearful, O you of little faith."

FOURTH SUNDAY AFTER EPIPHANY

OR

ADDITIONAL MASS AFTER PENTECOST

The Gospel in today's Mass describes how the Apostles implored Jesus to save them from the fury of the sea and the violence of the winds. By commanding the ungovernable forces in nature, our Lord manifests His Divinity. (GREEN VESTMENTS)

When this Mass is used as an Additional Mass after Pentecost, as indicated by the Liturgical Calendar, substitute the Introit, Gradual, Offertory and Communion as indicated below.

PRAYERS AT THE FOOT OF THE ALTAR

IN THE name of the Father, ✠ and of the Son, and of the Holy Spirit. Amen.

Priest. I will go in to the altar of God.

Server. The God of my gladness and joy.

Psalm 42

DO ME justice, O God, and fight my fight against a faithless people; from the deceitful and impious man rescue me.

S. For You, O God, are my strength. Why do You keep me so far away? Why must I go about in mourning, with the enemy oppressing me?
P. Send forth Your light and Your fidelity; they shall lead me on and bring me to Your holy mountain, to Your dwelling-place.
S. Then will I go in to the altar of God, the God of my gladness and joy.
P. Then will I give You thanks upon the harp, O God, my God. Why are you so downcast, O my soul? Why do you sigh within me?
S. Hope in God! For I shall again be thanking Him in the presence of my Savior and my God.
P. Glory be to the Father, and to the Son, and to the Holy Spirit.
S. As it was in the beginning, is now, and ever shall be, world without end. Amen.
P. I will go in to the altar of God.
S. The God of my gladness and joy.
P. Our help ✠ is in the name of the Lord.
S. Who made heaven and earth.
P. I confess to almighty God, etc.
S. May almighty God have mercy on you, forgive you your sins, and bring you to life everlasting.
P. Amen.

The Server, bowing, says the "Confiteor."

I CONFESS to almighty God, to Blessed Mary, ever Virgin, to Blessed Michael the Archangel, to Blessed John the Baptist, to the Holy Apostles Peter and Paul, and to all the Saints, and to you, Father, that I have sinned exceedingly in thought, word and deed, *through my fault, through my fault, through my most grievous fault.* Therefore I be-

seech Blessed Mary, ever Virgin, Blessed Michael the Archangel, Blessed John the Baptist, the Holy Apostles Peter and Paul, and all the Saints, and you, Father, to pray to the Lord our God for me.
P. May almighty God have mercy on you, forgive you your sins, and bring you to life everlasting.
S. Amen.

MAY the almighty and merciful Lord grant us pardon, ✠ absolution, and remission of our sins. *S.* Amen.
P. Will You not, O God, give us life?
S. And shall not Your people rejoice in You?
P. Show us, O Lord, Your kindness.
S. And grant us Your salvation.
P. O Lord, hear my prayer.
S. And let my cry come to You.
P. The Lord be with you.
S. And with your spirit. *P.* Let us pray.

Going up to the altar, the Priest prays silently:

TAKE away from us our sins, O Lord, we beseech You, that we may enter with pure minds into the Holy of Holies. Through Christ our Lord. Amen.

WE BESEECH You, O Lord, by the merits of Your Saints (*he kisses the altar*) whose relics lie here, and of all the Saints: deign in Your mercy to pardon me all my sins. Amen.

THE INTROIT • Ps. 96, 7. 8. 1

At the right side of the altar, the Priest says:

ADORE God, all you His angels: Sion hears and is glad, and the cities of Juda rejoice. *Ps.* The

Lord is King; let the earth rejoice; let the many isles be glad. Glory be to the Father, and to the Son, and to the Holy Spirit. As it was in the beginning, is now, and ever shall be, world without end. Amen. — Adore God, all you His angels: Sion hears and is glad, and the cities of Juda rejoice.

Introit (Jer. 29) for Additional Mass after Pentecost

THE Lord says: "I think thoughts of peace, and not of affliction. You shall call upon Me, and I will hear you; and I will bring back your captivity from all places." *Ps. 84.* You have favored, O Lord, Your land; You have restored the well-being of Jacob. Glory be to the Father, and to the Son, and to the Holy Spirit. As it was in the beginning, is now, and ever shall be, world without end. Amen. — The Lord says: "I think thoughts of peace, and not of affliction. You shall call upon Me, and I will hear you; and I will bring back your captivity from all places."

THE KYRIE

P. Lord, have mercy. *S.* Lord, have mercy. *P.* Lord, have mercy. *S.* Christ, have mercy. *P.* Christ, have mercy. *S.* Christ, have mercy. *P.* Lord, have mercy. *S.* Lord, have mercy. *P.* Lord, have mercy.

THE GLORIA

GLORY to God in the highest. And on earth peace to men of good will. We praise You. We bless You. We adore You. We glorify You. We give You thanks for Your great glory. O Lord God, heavenly King, God the Father almighty. O Lord Jesus Christ, the Only-begotten Son. O Lord God, Lamb of God, Son of the Father: You Who take away the sins of the world, have mercy on us. You Who take away the sins of the world, receive our prayer. You Who sit at the right hand of the Father, have mercy on us. For You alone are holy. You alone are the Lord. You alone, O Jesus Christ, are most high. Together with the Holy Spirit ✠ in the glory of God the Father. Amen.

The Priest kisses the altar and turns to the people, saying:

P. The Lord be with you. S. And with your spirit.

P. Let us pray.

THE PRAYER

Going to the right (Epistle) side, he says:

O GOD, You know that, placed as we are amid such great dangers, we cannot by reason of our human frailty stand; grant us health of mind and of body, that, by Your help, we may overcome the things which we suffer for our sins. Through our Lord Jesus Christ, Your Son, Who lives and reigns with You in the unity of the Holy Spirit, God, world without end. *S.* Amen.

THE EPISTLE • Rom. 13, 8-10

BRETHREN: Owe no man anything except to love one another; for he who loves his neighbor has fulfilled the Law. For "You shall not commit adultery. You shall not kill. You shall not steal. You shall not bear false witness. You shall not covet"; and if there is any other commandment, it is summed up in this saying, "You shall love your neighbor as yourself." Love does no evil to a neighbor. Love therefore is the fulfillment of the Law. *S.* Thanks be to God.

THE GRADUAL • Ps. 101, 16. 17

THE nations shall revere Your name, O Lord, and all the kings of the earth Your glory. ℣. For the Lord has rebuilt Sion, and He shall appear in His glory.

Alleluia, alleluia. ℣. *Ps. 96, 1.* The Lord is King; let the earth rejoice; let the many isles be glad. Alleluia.

Gradual (Ps. 43) for Additional Mass after Pentecost

YOU saved us, O Lord, from our foes, and those who hated us You put to shame. ℣. In God we gloried day by day; Your name we praised always.

Alleluia, alleluia. ℣. *Ps. 129, 1. 2.* Out of the depths I cry to You, O Lord; Lord, hear my prayer. Alleluia.

PRAYER BEFORE THE GOSPEL

CLEANSE my heart and my lips, O almighty God, Who cleansed the lips of the Prophet Isaias with a burning coal. In Your gracious mercy deign so to purify me that I may worthily proclaim Your holy Gospel. Through Christ our Lord. Amen.

Lord, grant Your blessing. The Lord be in my heart and on my lips, that I may worthily and fittingly proclaim His holy Gospel. Amen.

THE GOSPEL • Matt. 8, 23-27

Going to the left (Gospel) side of the altar, he says:

P. The Lord be with you. *S.* And with your spirit.

P. ✠ The continuation of the holy Gospel according to Saint Matthew. *S.* Glory be to You, O Lord.

AT THAT time, Jesus got into a boat, and His disciples followed Him. And behold, there arose a great storm on the sea, so that the boat was covered by the waves; but He was asleep. So they came and woke Him, saying, "Lord save us! we are perishing!" But He said to them, "Why are you fearful, O you of little faith?" Then He arose and rebuked the wind and the sea, and there came a great calm. And the men marvelled, saying, "What manner of Man is this, that even the wind and the sea obey Him?" *S.* Praise be to You, O Christ.

P. By the words of the Gospel, may our sins be taken away.

THE NICENE CREED

At the center of the altar, he says:

I BELIEVE in one God, the Father almighty, Maker of heaven and earth, and of all things visible and invisible. And in one Lord Jesus Christ, the Only-begotten Son of God. Born of the Father before all ages. God of God; Light of Light; true God of true God. Begotten not made; of one being with the Father; by Whom all things were made. Who for us men, and for our salvation, came down from heaven. (*Here all genuflect.*) And was made Flesh by the Holy Spirit of the Virgin Mary: AND WAS MADE MAN. He was also crucified for us, suffered under Pontius Pilate and was buried. And on the third day He rose again according to the Scriptures. And ascending into heaven, He sits at the right hand of the Father. And He shall come again in glory to judge the living and the dead; and of His kingdom there shall be no end. And I believe in the Holy Spirit, Lord and Giver of life, Who proceeds from the Father and the Son. Who together with the Father and the Son is no less adored, and glorified: Who spoke by

the Prophets. And I believe in One, Holy, Catholic and Apostolic Church. I confess one Baptism for the remission of sins. And I look for the resurrection of the dead. ✠ And the life of the world to come. Amen.

THE OFFERTORY

The Priest turns to the people and says:

P. The Lord be with you. *S.* And with your spirit.
P. Let us pray.

THE OFFERTORY VERSE • Ps. 117, 16. 17

THE right hand of the Lord has struck with power: the right hand of the Lord has exalted me; I shall not die, but live, and declare the works of the Lord.

Offertory (Ps. 129) for Additional Mass after Pentecost

OUT of the depths I cry to You, O Lord; Lord, hear my prayer! Out of the depths I cry to You, O Lord.

The Priest now uncovers the chalice, places the host on the paten and offering it up, says:

ACCEPT, O holy Father, almighty and eternal God, this spotless host, which I, Your unworthy servant, offer to You, my living and true God, to atone for my numberless sins, offenses, and negligences; on behalf of all here present and likewise for all faithful Christians living and dead, that it may profit me and them as a means of salvation to life everlasting. Amen.

He pours wine and water into the chalice, blessing the water before it is poured.

O GOD, Who established the nature of man in wondrous dignity, and still more admirably restored it, grant that through the mystery of this water and wine, we may be made partakers of His Divinity, Who has condescended to become partaker of our humanity, Jesus Christ, Your Son, our Lord. Who lives and reigns with You in the unity of the Holy Spirit, God, world without end. Amen.

Offering up the wine, the Priest says:

WE OFFER You, O Lord, the chalice of salvation, humbly begging of Your mercy that it may arise before Your Divine Majesty, with a pleasing fragrance, for our salvation and for that of the whole world. Amen.

Bowing down, the Priest says:

IN A humble spirit and with a contrite heart, may we be accepted by You, O Lord, and may our sacrifice so be offered in Your sight this day as to please You, O Lord God.

Raising his eyes and blessing the offering, he says:

COME, O Sanctifier, almighty and eternal God, and bless ✠ this sacrifice prepared for the glory of Your holy name.

WASHING THE FINGERS

I WASH my hands in innocence, and I go around Your altar, O Lord, giving voice to my thanks, and recounting all Your wondrous deeds. O Lord, I love the house in which You dwell, the tenting-place of Your glory. Gather not my soul with those of sinners, nor with men of blood my life. On their hands are crimes, and their right hands are full of bribes. But I walk in integrity; redeem me, and have pity on me. My foot stands on level ground; in the assemblies I will bless You, O Lord. Glory be to the Father, and to the Son, and to the Holy Spirit. As it was in the beginning, is now, and ever shall be, world without end. Amen.

ACCEPT, Most Holy Trinity, this offering which we are making to You in remembrance of the Passion, Resurrection, and Ascension of Jesus Christ, our Lord; and in honor of Blessed Mary, ever Virgin, Blessed John the Baptist, the Holy Apostles Peter and Paul, and of these, and of all the Saints; that it may add to their honor and aid our salvation; and may they deign to intercede in heaven for us who honor their memory here on earth. Through the same Christ our Lord. Amen.

The Priest turns toward the people and says:

Pray, brethren, that my sacrifice and yours may become acceptable to God the Father almighty.

S. May the Lord accept this sacrifice from your hands to the praise and glory of His name, for our advantage, and that of all His holy Church.

P. Amen.

THE SECRET

GRANT, we beseech You, almighty God, that the offering of the gift of this sacrifice, may ever purify and protect our frailty from all evil. Through our Lord Jesus Christ, Your Son, Who lives and reigns with You in the unity of the Holy Spirit, God.

P. World without end. *S.* Amen.

PREFACE—CANON

P. The Lord be with you. *S.* And with your spirit.

P. Lift up your hearts.

S. We have lifted them up to the Lord.

P. Let us give thanks to the Lord, our God.
S. It is fitting and just.

IT IS fitting indeed and just, right and helpful to salvation, for us always and everywhere to give thanks to You, O holy Lord, Father almighty, everlasting God, Who with Your Only-begotten Son and the Holy Spirit are one God, one Lord; not in the unity of a single person, but in the trinity of a single nature. For that which we believe on Your revelation concerning Your glory, that same we believe of Your Son, that same of the Holy Spirit, without difference or discrimination. So that in confessing the true and everlasting Godhead, we shall adore distinction in Persons, oneness in being, and equality in Majesty. This the Angels and Archangels, the Cherubim, too, and the Seraphim do praise; day by day they cease not to cry out as with one voice, saying (*the bell is rung 3 times*):

HOLY, HOLY, HOLY, Lord God of Hosts. Heaven and earth are filled with Your glory. Hosanna in the highest. ✠ Blessed is He Who comes in the name of the Lord. Hosanna in the highest.

THE CANON OF THE MASS

THEREFORE, most gracious Father, we humbly beg of You and entreat You through Jesus Christ Your Son, our Lord, (*he kisses the altar*) to deem acceptable and bless these ✠ gifts, these ✠ offerings, these ✠ holy and unspotted oblations which, in the first place, we offer You for Your Holy Catholic Church, that You would deign to give her peace and protection, to unite and guard her throughout the world, together with Your serv-

ant *N.*, our Pope, and *N.*, our Bishop; and all true believers who cherish the Catholic and Apostolic Faith.

Commemoration of the Living

REMEMBER, O Lord, Your servants and handmaids, *N.* and *N.*, (*name them*) and all here present, whose faith and devotion are known to You, on whose behalf we offer to You, or who themselves offer to You, this sacrifice of praise for themselves, families and friends, for the good of their souls, for their hope of salvation and deliverance from all harm, and who offer their homage to You, eternal, living and true God.

Commemoration of the Saints

IN THE unity of holy fellowship we observe the memory, first of all, of the glorious and ever Virgin Mary, Mother of our Lord and God Jesus Christ; next, that of Your Blessed Apostles and Martyrs, Peter and Paul, Andrew, James, John, Thomas, James, Philip, Bartholomew, Matthew, Simon and Thaddeus; of Linus, Cletus, Clement, Sixtus, Cornelius, Cyprian, Lawrence, Chrysogonus, John and Paul, Cosmas and Damian, and of all Your Saints, by whose merits and prayers grant that we may be always fortified by the help of Your protection. Through the same Christ our Lord. Amen.

Spreading his hands over the oblation, he says:

GRACIOUSLY accept, then, we beseech You, O Lord, this service of our worship and that of all Your household. Provide that our days be spent in Your peace, save us from everlasting damnation, and cause us to be numbered in the flock You have chosen. Through Christ our Lord. Amen.

O GOD, deign to bless ✠ what we offer, and make it approved, ✠ effective, ✠ right, and wholly pleasing in every way, that it may become for our good, the Body ✠ and Blood ✠ of Your dearly beloved Son, Jesus Christ our Lord.

CONSECRATION—ELEVATION

WHO, the day before He suffered, took bread into His holy and venerable hands, and having raised His eyes to heaven, to You, O God, His almighty Father, giving thanks to You, He blessed it, ✠ broke it, and gave it to His disciples, saying: All of you take and eat of this:

FOR THIS IS MY BODY.

IN LIKE manner, when the supper was done, taking also this goodly chalice into His holy and venerable hands, again giving thanks to You, He blessed ✠ it, and gave it to His disciples, saying: All of you take and drink of this:

FOR THIS IS THE CHALICE OF MY BLOOD OF THE NEW AND ETERNAL COVENANT: THE MYSTERY OF FAITH: WHICH SHALL BE SHED FOR YOU AND FOR MANY UNTO THE FORGIVENESS OF SINS.

After replacing the chalice on the corporal, he says:

As often as you shall do these things, in memory of Me shall you do them.

Offering of the Victim

MINDFUL, therefore, O Lord, not only of the blessed Passion of the same Christ, Your Son, our Lord, but also of His Resurrection from the dead, and finally His glorious Ascension into heaven, we, Your ministers, as also Your holy people, offer to Your supreme Majesty, of the gifts be-

stowed upon us, the pure ✠ Victim, the holy ✠ Victim, the all-perfect ✠ Victim: the holy ✠ Bread of life eternal and the Chalice ✠ of unending salvation.

AND this deign to regard with gracious and kindly attention and hold acceptable, as You deigned to accept the offerings of Abel, Your just servant, and the sacrifice of Abraham our patriarch, and that which Your chief priest Melchisedec offered to You, a holy sacrifice and a spotless victim.

MOST humbly we implore You, almighty God, bid these offerings to be brought by the hands of Your holy angel to Your altar above; before the face of Your Divine Majesty; that those of us who, by sharing in the Sacrifice of this altar, shall receive the Most Sacred ✠ Body and ✠ Blood of Your Son, may be filled with every grace and heavenly blessing. Through the same Christ our Lord. Amen.

Commemoration of the Dead

REMEMBER also, O Lord, Your servants and handmaids, N. and N., who have gone before us with the sign of faith, and rest in the sleep of peace. (*Here pray for the dead.*) To these, O Lord, and to all who rest in Christ, we beseech You to grant of Your goodness, a place of comfort, light and peace. Through the same Christ our Lord. Amen.

TO US sinners also, Your servants, trusting in the greatness of Your mercy, deign to grant some part and fellowship with Your Holy Apostles and Martyrs: with John, Stephen, Matthias, Barnabas, Ignatius, Alexander, Marcellinus, Peter, Felicitas, Perpetua, Agatha, Lucy, Agnes, Cecilia, Anastasia, and all Your Saints; into whose company, we implore You to admit us, not weighing our merits, but freely granting us pardon. Through Christ our Lord.

THROUGH Whom, O Lord, You always create, ✠ sanctify, ✠ fill with life, ✠ bless, and bestow upon us all good things.

The Minor Elevation

THROUGH ✠ Him, and with ✠ Him, and in ✠ Him, is to You, God the Father ✠ almighty, in the unity of the Holy ✠ Spirit, all honor and glory, world without end. S. Amen.

THE COMMUNION AND THANKSGIVING

Let us pray. Prompted by saving precepts, and taught by Your divine teaching, we dare to say:

OUR FATHER, Who art in heaven, hallowed be Thy name: Thy kingdom come: Thy will be done on earth as it is in heaven. Give us this day our daily bread; and forgive us our trespasses, as we forgive those who trespass against us. And lead us not into temptation: S. But deliver us from evil. *P*. Amen.

DELIVER us, we beseech You, O Lord, from all evils, past, present, and to come; and by the intercession of the Blessed and glorious Mary, ever Virgin, Mother of God, together with Your Blessed Apostles Peter and Paul, and Andrew, and all the Saints, grant of Your goodness, peace in our days, that aided by the riches of Your mercy, we may be always free from sin and safe from all disturbance.
Through the same our Lord Jesus Christ, Your Son,

Who lives and reigns with You in the unity of the Holy Spirit, God, world without end.

S. Amen.

P. May the peace ✠ of the Lord be ✠ always with ✠ you.

S. And with your spirit.

The Priest puts a small particle into the chalice, saying:

May this mingling and consecration of the Body and Blood of our Lord Jesus Christ help us who receive it to life everlasting. Amen.

LAMB of God, You Who take away the sins of the world, have mercy on us.

Lamb of God, You Who take away the sins of the world, have mercy on us.

Lamb of God, You Who take away the sins of the world, grant us peace.

PRAYERS BEFORE HOLY COMMUNION

Then inclining toward the altar, he says:

O LORD Jesus Christ, Who said to Your Apostles: "Peace I leave with you, My peace I give to you," regard not my sins but the faith of Your Church, and deign to give her peace and unity according to Your Will: Who live and reign, God, world without end. Amen.

O LORD Jesus Christ, Son of the living God, Who, by the will of the Father, with the cooperation of the Holy Spirit, have by Your death given life to the world, deliver me by this Your Most Sacred Body and Blood from all my sins and from every evil. Make me always cling to Your commandments, and never permit me to be separated from You. Who with the same God the Father and the Holy Spirit, live and reign, God, world without end. Amen.

LET not the partaking of Your Body, O Lord Jesus Christ, which I, though unworthy, presume to receive, turn to my judgment and condemnation; but through Your goodness, may it become a safeguard and an effective remedy, both of soul and body. Who live and reign with God the Father, in the unity of the Holy Spirit, God, world without end. Amen.

COMMUNION OF THE PRIEST

I WILL take the Bread of heaven, and call upon the name of the Lord.

Lord, I am not worthy that You should come under my roof; but only say the word, and my soul will be healed. (3 *times.*)

Making the Sign of the Cross with the Host, he says:

MAY the Body of our Lord Jesus Christ preserve my soul to life everlasting. Amen.

What return shall I make to the Lord for all He has given me? I will take the Chalice of salvation, and I will call upon the name of the Lord. Praising will I call upon the Lord and I shall be saved from my enemies.

Making the Sign of the Cross with the chalice, he says:

MAY the Blood of our Lord Jesus Christ preserve my soul to life everlasting. Amen.

The Priest reverently consumes the Precious Blood.

COMMUNION OF THE FAITHFUL

The Server and people say the "Confiteor."

P. May almighty God have mercy on you, forgive you your sins, and bring you to life everlasting. **S.** Amen.

P. May the almighty and merciful Lord grant you pardon, ✠ absolution and remission of your sins.
S. Amen.

Holding up a Sacred Host, the Priest says:

Behold the Lamb of God, behold Him Who takes away the sins of the world.
Lord, I am not worthy that You should come under my roof; but only say the word, and my soul will be healed. (3 *times.*)

The Priest says to each communicant:

May the Body of our Lord Jesus Christ preserve your soul to life everlasting. Amen.

The Priest purifies the chalice with wine, saying:

WHAT has passed our lips as food, O Lord, may we possess in purity of heart, that what is given to us in time, be our healing for eternity.

He purifies his fingers with wine and water, saying:

MAY Your Body, O Lord, which I have eaten, and Your Blood which I have drunk, cleave to my very soul, and grant that no trace of sin be found in me, whom these pure and holy mysteries have renewed. Who live and reign, world without end. Amen.

THE COMMUNION • Luke 4, 22.

ALL marvelled at the words that came from the mouth of God.

Communion (Mark 11) for Additional Mass after Pent.

AMEN I say to you, all things whatever you ask for in prayer, believe that you shall receive, and it shall be done to you.

The Priest, turning to the people, says:

P. The Lord be with you. S. And with your spirit.
P. Let us pray.

THE POSTCOMMUNION

MAY Your gifts, O God, detach us from earthly pleasures, and ever fill us with heavenly refreshment. Through our Lord Jesus Christ, Your Son, Who lives and reigns with You in the unity of the Holy Spirit, God, world without end. S. Amen.

FINAL PRAYERS

The Priest turns again to the people, and says:

P. The Lord be with you. S. And with your spirit.
P. Go, you are dismissed. S. Thanks be to God.

MAY the tribute of my worship be pleasing to You, Most Holy Trinity, and grant that the sacrifice which I, all unworthy, have offered in the presence of Your Majesty, may be acceptable to You, and through Your mercy obtain forgiveness for me and all for whom I have offered it. Through Christ our Lord. Amen.

THE LAST BLESSING

He kisses the altar, and facing the people, says:

MAY almighty God bless you: ✠ the Father, and the Son, and the Holy Spirit.
S. Amen.

The Last Gospel and Prayers after Low Mass are conveniently placed inside the back cover.

"His enemy came and sowed weeds among the wheat."

FIFTH SUNDAY AFTER EPIPHANY

OR

ADDITIONAL MASS AFTER PENTECOST

God is the Creator of the world, and what He has made is good. How then do we account for the evil in the world? Because man has free will, he can misuse God's gifts and transgress His Commandments and do evil. (GREEN VESTMENTS)

When this Mass is used as an Additional Mass after Pentecost, as indicated by the Liturgical Calendar, substitute the Introit, Gradual, Offertory and Communion as indicated below.

PRAYERS AT THE FOOT OF THE ALTAR

IN THE name of the Father, ✠ and of the Son, and of the Holy Spirit. Amen.

Priest. I will go in to the altar of God.

Server. The God of my gladness and joy.

Psalm 42

DO ME justice, O God, and fight my fight against a faithless people; from the deceitful and impious man rescue me.

S. For You, O God, are my strength. Why do You keep me so far away? Why must I go about in mourning, with the enemy oppressing me?
P. Send forth Your light and Your fidelity; they shall lead me on and bring me to Your holy mountain, to Your dwelling-place.
S. Then will I go in to the altar of God, the God of my gladness and joy.
P. Then will I give You thanks upon the harp, O God, my God. Why are you so downcast, O my soul? Why do you sigh within me?
S. Hope in God! For I shall again be thanking Him in the presence of my Savior and my God.
P. Glory be to the Father, and to the Son, and to the Holy Spirit.
S. As it was in the beginning, is now, and ever shall be, world without end. Amen.
P. I will go in to the altar of God.
S. The God of my gladness and joy.
P. Our help ✠ is in the name of the Lord.
S. Who made heaven and earth.
P. I confess to almighty God, etc.
S. May almighty God have mercy on you, forgive you your sins, and bring you to life everlasting.
P. Amen.

The Server, bowing, says the "Confiteor."

I CONFESS to almighty God, to Blessed Mary, ever Virgin, to Blessed Michael the Archangel, to Blessed John the Baptist, to the Holy Apostles Peter and Paul, and to all the Saints, and to you, Father, that I have sinned exceedingly in thought, word and deed, *through my fault, through my fault, through my most grievous fault.* Therefore I beseech Blessed Mary, ever Virgin, Blessed Michael

the Archangel, Blessed John the Baptist, the Holy Apostles Peter and Paul, and all the Saints, and you, Father, to pray to the Lord our God for me.
P. May almighty God have mercy on you, forgive you your sins, and bring you to life everlasting.
S. Amen.

MAY the almighty and merciful Lord grant us pardon, ✠ absolution, and remission of our sins. *S.* Amen.
P. Will You not, O God, give us life?
S. And shall not Your people rejoice in You?
P. Show us, O Lord, Your kindness.
S. And grant us Your salvation.
P. O Lord, hear my prayer.
S. And let my cry come to You.
P. The Lord be with you.
S. And with your spirit. *P.* Let us pray.

Going up to the altar, the Priest prays silently:

TAKE away from us our sins, O Lord, we beseech You, that we may enter with pure minds into the Holy of Holies. Through Christ our Lord. Amen.

WE BESEECH You, O Lord, by the merits of Your Saints (*he kisses the altar*) whose relics lie here, and of all the Saints: deign in Your mercy to pardon me all my sins. Amen.

THE INTROIT • Ps. 96, 7. 8. 1

At the right side of the altar, the Priest says:

ADORE God, all you His angels: Sion hears and is glad, and the cities of Juda rejoice. *Ps.* The Lord is King; let the earth rejoice; let the many isles be glad. Glory be to the Father, and to the

Son, and to the Holy Spirit. As it was in the beginning, is now, and ever shall be, world without end. Amen. — Adore God, all you His angels: Sion hears and is glad, and the cities of Juda rejoice.

Introit (Jer. 29) for Additional Mass after Pentecost

THE Lord says: "I think thoughts of peace, and not of affliction. You shall call upon Me, and I will hear you; and I will bring back your captivity from all places." *Ps. 84.* You have favored, O Lord, Your land; You have restored the well-being of Jacob. Glory be to the Father, and to the Son, and to the Holy Spirit. As it was in the beginning, is now, and ever shall be, world without end. Amen. — The Lord says: "I think thoughts of peace, and not of affliction. You shall call upon Me, and I will hear you; and I will bring back your captivity from all places."

THE KYRIE

P. Lord, have mercy. *S.* Lord, have mercy. *P.* Lord, have mercy. *S.* Christ, have mercy. *P.* Christ, have mercy. *S.* Christ, have mercy. *P.* Lord, have mercy. *S.* Lord, have mercy. *P.* Lord, have mercy.

THE GLORIA

GLORY to God in the highest. And on earth peace to men of good will. We praise You. We bless You. We adore You. We glorify You. We give You thanks for Your great glory. O Lord God, heavenly King, God the Father almighty. O Lord Jesus Christ, the Only-begotten Son. O Lord God, Lamb of God, Son of the Father: You Who take away the sins of the world, have mercy on us. You Who take away the sins of the world, receive our prayer. You Who sit at the right hand of the Father, have mercy on us. For You alone are holy.

You alone are the Lord. You alone, O Jesus Christ, are most high. Together with the Holy Spirit ✠ in the glory of God the Father. Amen.

The Priest kisses the altar and turns to the people, saying:

P. The Lord be with you. *S.* And with your spirit.
P. Let us pray.

THE PRAYER

Going to the right (Epistle) side, he says:

WE BESEECH You, O Lord, in Your unceasing goodness, guard Your family; that we who lean only upon the hope of Your heavenly grace, may always be defended by Your protection. Through our Lord Jesus Christ, Your Son, Who lives and reigns with You in the unity of the Holy Spirit, God, world without end. *S.* Amen.

THE EPISTLE • Col. 3, 12-17

BRETHREN: Put on, as God's chosen ones, holy and beloved, a heart of mercy, kindness, humility, meekness, patience. Bear with one another and forgive one another, if anyone has a grievance against any other; even as the Lord has forgiven you, so also do you forgive. But above all these things have charity, which is the bond of perfection. And may the peace of Christ reign in your hearts; unto that peace, indeed, you were called in one body. Show yourselves thankful. Let the word of Christ dwell in you abundantly: in all wisdom teach and admonish one another by psalms, hymns and spiritual songs, singing in your hearts to God by His grace. Whatever you do in word or in work, do all in the name of the Lord Jesus Christ, giving thanks to God the Father through Jesus Christ our Lord. *S.* Thanks be to God.

THE GRADUAL • Ps. 101, 16-17

THE nations shall revere Your name, O Lord, and all the kings of the earth Your glory. ℣. For the Lord has rebuilt Sion, and He shall appear in His glory.

Alleluia, alleluia. ℣. *Ps. 96, 1.* The Lord is King; let the earth rejoice; let the many isles be glad. Alleluia.

Gradual (Ps. 43) for Additional Mass after Pentecost

YOU saved us, O Lord, from our foes, and those who hated us You put to shame. ℣. In God we gloried day by day; Your name we praised always.

Alleluia, alleluia. ℣. *Ps. 129, 1. 2.* Out of the depths I cry to You, O Lord; Lord, hear my prayer. Alleluia.

PRAYER BEFORE THE GOSPEL

Bowing down at the center of the altar, he says:

CLEANSE my heart and my lips, O almighty God, Who cleansed the lips of the Prophet Isaias with a burning coal. In Your gracious mercy deign so to purify me that I may worthily proclaim Your holy Gospel. Through Christ our Lord. Amen. Lord, grant Your blessing. The Lord be in my heart and on my lips, that I may worthily and fittingly proclaim His holy Gospel. Amen.

THE GOSPEL • Matt. 13, 24-30

Going to the left (Gospel) side of the altar, he says:

P. The Lord be with you. S. And with your spirit.
P. ✠ The continuation of the holy Gospel according to Saint Matthew. S. Glory be to You, O Lord.

AT THAT time, Jesus spoke this parable to the crowds: "The kingdom of heaven is like a man who sowed good seed in his field; but while men were asleep, his enemy came and sowed weeds among the wheat, and went away. And when the blade sprang up and brought forth fruit, then the weeds appeared as well. And the servants of the householder came and said to him, 'Sir, did you not sow good seed in your field? How then does it have weeds?' He said to them, 'An enemy has done this.' And the servants said to him, 'Will you have us go and gather them up?' 'No,' he said, 'lest in gathering the weeds you root up the wheat along with them. Let both grow together until the harvest; and at harvest time I will say to the reapers: Gather up the weeds first, and bind them in bundles to burn; but gather the wheat into my barn.'" *S.* Praise be to You, O Christ.

P. By the words of the Gospel, may our sins be taken away.

THE NICENE CREED

At the center of the altar, he says:

I BELIEVE in one God, the Father almighty, Maker of heaven and earth, and of all things visible and invisible. And in one Lord Jesus Christ, the Only-begotten Son of God. Born of the Father before all ages. God of God; Light of Light; true God of true God. Begotten not made; of one being with the Father; by Whom all things were made. Who for us men, and for our salvation, came down from heaven. (*Here all genuflect.*) And was made Flesh by the Holy Spirit of the Virgin Mary: AND WAS MADE MAN. He was also crucified for us, suffered under Pontius Pilate and was buried. And on the third day He rose again according to the Scriptures. And ascending into heaven, He sits at the right hand of the Father. And He shall come again in glory to judge the living and the dead; and of His kingdom there shall be no end. And I believe in the Holy Spirit, Lord and Giver of life, Who proceeds from the Father and the Son. Who together with the Father and the Son is no less adored, and glorified: Who spoke by the Prophets. And I believe in One, Holy, Catholic and Apostolic Church. I confess one Baptism for the remission of sins. And I look for the resurrection of the dead. ✠ And the life of the world to come. Amen.

THE OFFERTORY

The Priest turns to the people and says:

P. The Lord be with you. *S.* And with your spirit.

P. Let us pray.

THE OFFERTORY VERSE • Ps. 117, 16. 17

THE right hand of the Lord has struck with power: the right hand of the Lord has exalted me; I shall not die, but live, and declare the works of the Lord.

Offertory (Ps. 129) for Additional Mass after Pentecost

OUT of the depths I cry to You, O Lord; Lord, hear my prayer! Out of the depths I cry to You, O Lord.

The Priest now uncovers the chalice, places the host on the paten and offering it up, says:

ACCEPT, O holy Father, almighty and eternal God, this spotless host, which I, Your unworthy servant, offer to You, my living and true God, to atone for my numberless sins, offenses, and negligences; on behalf of all here present and like-

wise for all faithful Christians living and dead, that it may profit me and them as a means of salvation to life everlasting. Amen.

He pours wine and water into the chalice, blessing the water before it is poured.

O GOD, Who established the nature of man in wondrous dignity, and still more admirably restored it, grant that through the mystery of this water and wine, we may be made partakers of His Divinity, Who has condescended to become partaker of our humanity, Jesus Christ, Your Son, our Lord. Who lives and reigns with You in the unity of the Holy Spirit, God, world without end. Amen.

Offering up the wine, the Priest says:

WE OFFER You, O Lord, the chalice of salvation, humbly begging of Your mercy that it may arise before Your Divine Majesty, with a pleasing fragrance, for our salvation and for that of the whole world. Amen.

Bowing down, the Priest says:

IN A humble spirit and with a contrite heart, may we be accepted by You, O Lord, and may our sacrifice so be offered in Your sight this day as to please You, O Lord God.

Raising his eyes and blessing the offering, he says:

COME, O Sanctifier, almighty and eternal God, and bless ✠ this sacrifice prepared for the glory of Your holy name.

WASHING THE FINGERS

I WASH my hands in innocence, and I go around Your altar, O Lord, giving voice to my thanks, and recounting all Your wondrous deeds. O Lord, I love the house in which You dwell, the tenting-place of Your glory. Gather not my soul with those of sinners, nor with men of blood my life. On their hands are crimes, and their right hands are full of bribes. But I walk in integrity; redeem me, and have pity on me. My foot stands on level ground; in the assemblies I will bless You, O Lord. Glory be to the Father, and to the Son, and to the Holy Spirit. As it was in the beginning, is now, and ever shall be, world without end. Amen.

ACCEPT, Most Holy Trinity, this offering which we are making to You in remembrance of the Passion, Resurrection, and Ascension of Jesus Christ, our Lord; and in honor of Blessed Mary, ever Virgin, Blessed John the Baptist, the Holy Apostles Peter and Paul, and of these, and of all the Saints; that it may add to their honor and aid our salvation; and may they deign to intercede in heaven for us who honor their memory here on earth. Through the same Christ our Lord. Amen.

The Priest turns toward the people and says:

Pray, brethren, that my sacrifice and yours may become acceptable to God the Father almighty.

S. May the Lord accept this sacrifice from your hands to the praise and glory of His name, for our advantage, and that of all His holy Church.

P. Amen.

THE SECRET

WE OFFER You, O Lord, sacrifices of propitiation; that, taking compassion on us, You may both absolve us from our sins, and guide our inconstant hearts. Through our Lord Jesus Christ, Your Son, Who lives and reigns with You in the unity of the Holy Spirit, God.

P. World without end. S. Amen.

PREFACE—CANON

P. The Lord be with you. *S.* And with your spirit.
P. Lift up your hearts.
S. We have lifted them up to the Lord.
P. Let us give thanks to the Lord, our God.
S. It is fitting and just.

IT IS fitting indeed and just, right and helpful to salvation, for us always and everywhere to give thanks to You, O holy Lord, Father almighty, everlasting God, Who with Your Only-begotten Son and the Holy Spirit are one God, one Lord; not in the unity of a single person, but in the trinity of a single nature. For that which we believe on Your revelation concerning Your glory, that same we believe of Your Son, that same of the Holy Spirit, without difference or discrimination. So that in confessing the true and everlasting Godhead, we shall adore distinction in Persons, oneness in being, and equality in Majesty. This the Angels and Archangels, the Cherubim, too, and the Seraphim do praise; day by day they cease not to cry out as with one voice, saying (*the bell is rung* 3 *times*):

HOLY, HOLY, HOLY, Lord God of Hosts. Heaven and earth are filled with Your glory. Hosanna in the highest. ✠ Blessed is He Who comes in the name of the Lord. Hosanna in the highest.

THE CANON OF THE MASS

THEREFORE, most gracious Father, we humbly beg of You and entreat You through Jesus Christ Your Son, our Lord, (*he kisses the altar*) to deem acceptable and bless these ✠ gifts, these ✠ offerings, these ✠ holy and unspotted oblations

which, in the first place, we offer You for Your Holy Catholic Church, that You would deign to give her peace and protection, to unite and guard her throughout the world, together with Your servant N., our Pope, and N., our Bishop; and all true believers who cherish the Catholic and Apostolic Faith.

Commemoration of the Living

REMEMBER, O Lord, Your servants and handmaids, N. and N., (*name them*) and all here present, whose faith and devotion are known to You, on whose behalf we offer to You, or who themselves offer to You, this sacrifice of praise for themselves, families and friends, for the good of their souls, for their hope of salvation and deliverance from all harm, and who offer their homage to You, eternal, living and true God.

Commemoration of the Saints

IN THE unity of holy fellowship we observe the memory, first of all, of the glorious and ever Virgin Mary, Mother of our Lord and God Jesus Christ; next, that of Your Blessed Apostles and Martyrs, Peter and Paul, Andrew, James, John, Thomas, James, Philip, Bartholomew, Matthew, Simon and Thaddeus; of Linus, Cletus, Clement, Sixtus, Cornelius, Cyprian, Lawrence, Chrysogonus, John and Paul, Cosmas and Damian, and of all Your Saints, by whose merits and prayers grant that we may be always fortified by the help of Your protection. Through the same Christ our Lord. Amen.

Spreading his hands over the oblation, he says:

GRACIOUSLY accept, then, we beseech You, O Lord, this service of our worship and that of all Your household. Provide that our days be

spent in Your peace, save us from everlasting damnation, and cause us to be numbered in the flock You have chosen. Through Christ our Lord. Amen.

O GOD, deign to bless ✠ what we offer, and make it approved, ✠ effective, ✠ right, and wholly pleasing in every way, that it may become for our good, the Body ✠ and Blood ✠ of Your dearly beloved Son, Jesus Christ our Lord.

CONSECRATION—ELEVATION

WHO, the day before He suffered, took bread into His holy and venerable hands, and having raised His eyes to heaven, to You, O God, His almighty Father, giving thanks to You, He blessed it, ✠ broke it, and gave it to His disciples, saying: All of you take and eat of this:

FOR THIS IS MY BODY.

IN LIKE manner, when the supper was done, taking also this goodly chalice into His holy and venerable hands, again giving thanks to You, He blessed ✠ it, and gave it to His disciples, saying: All of you take and drink of this:

FOR THIS IS THE CHALICE OF MY BLOOD OF THE NEW AND ETERNAL COVENANT: THE MYSTERY OF FAITH: WHICH SHALL BE SHED FOR YOU AND FOR MANY UNTO THE FORGIVENESS OF SINS.

After replacing the chalice on the corporal, he says:

As often as you shall do these things, in memory of Me shall you do them.

Offering of the Victim

MINDFUL, therefore, O Lord, not only of the blessed Passion of the same Christ, Your Son,

our Lord, but also of His Resurrection from the dead, and finally His glorious Ascension into heaven, we, Your ministers, as also Your holy people, offer to Your supreme Majesty, of the gifts bestowed upon us, the pure ✠ Victim, the holy ✠ Victim, the all-perfect ✠ Victim: the holy ✠ Bread of life eternal and the Chalice ✠ of unending salvation.

AND this deign to regard with gracious and kindly attention and hold acceptable, as You deigned to accept the offerings of Abel, Your just servant, and the sacrifice of Abraham our patriarch, and that which Your chief priest Melchisedec offered to You, a holy sacrifice and a spotless victim.

MOST humbly we implore You, almighty God, bid these offerings to be brought by the hands of Your holy angel to Your altar above; before the face of Your Divine Majesty; that those of us who, by sharing in the Sacrifice of this altar, shall receive the Most Sacred ✠ Body and ✠ Blood of Your Son, may be filled with every grace and heavenly blessing. Through the same Christ our Lord. Amen.

Commemoration of the Dead

REMEMBER also, O Lord, Your servants and handmaids, N. and N., who have gone before us with the sign of faith, and rest in the sleep of peace. (*Here pray for the dead.*) To these, O Lord, and to all who rest in Christ, we beseech You to grant of Your goodness, a place of comfort, light and peace. Through the same Christ our Lord. Amen.

TO US sinners also, Your servants, trusting in the greatness of Your mercy, deign to grant some

part and fellowship with Your Holy Apostles and Martyrs: with John, Stephen, Matthias, Barnabas, Ignatius, Alexander, Marcellinus, Peter, Felicitas, Perpetua, Agatha, Lucy, Agnes, Cecilia, Anastasia, and all Your Saints; into whose company, we implore You to admit us, not weighing our merits, but freely granting us pardon. Through Christ our Lord.

THROUGH Whom, O Lord, You always create, ✠ sanctify, ✠ fill with life, ✠ bless, and bestow upon us all good things.

The Minor Elevation

THROUGH ✠ Him, and with ✠ Him, and in ✠ Him, is to You, God the Father ✠ almighty, in the unity of the Holy ✠ Spirit, all honor and glory, world without end. *S.* Amen.

THE COMMUNION AND THANKSGIVING

Let us pray. Prompted by saving precepts, and taught by Your divine teaching, we dare to say:

OUR FATHER, Who art in heaven, hallowed be Thy name: Thy kingdom come: Thy will be done on earth as it is in heaven. Give us this day our daily bread; and forgive us our trespasses, as we forgive those who trespass against us. And lead us not into temptation: *S.* But deliver us from evil. *P.* Amen.

DELIVER us, we beseech You, O Lord, from all evils, past, present, and to come; and by the intercession of the Blessed and glorious Mary, ever Virgin, Mother of God, together with Your Blessed Apostles Peter and Paul, and Andrew, and all the Saints, grant of Your goodness, peace in our

days, that aided by the riches of Your mercy, we may be always free from sin and safe from all disturbance.

Through the same our Lord Jesus Christ, Your Son, Who lives and reigns with You in the unity of the Holy Spirit, God, world without end. S. Amen.

P. May the peace ✠ of the Lord be ✠ always with ✠ you.

S. And with your spirit.

The Priest puts a small particle into the chalice, saying:

May this mingling and consecration of the Body and Blood of our Lord Jesus Christ help us who receive it to life everlasting. Amen.

LAMB of God, You Who take away the sins of the world, have mercy on us.

Lamb of God, You Who take away the sins of the world, have mercy on us.

Lamb of God, You Who take away the sins of the world, grant us peace.

PRAYERS BEFORE HOLY COMMUNION

Then inclining toward the altar, he says:

O LORD Jesus Christ, Who said to Your Apostles: "Peace I leave with you, My peace I give to you," regard not my sins but the faith of Your Church, and deign to give her peace and unity according to Your Will: Who live and reign, God, world without end. Amen.

O LORD Jesus Christ, Son of the living God, Who, by the will of the Father, with the cooperation of the Holy Spirit, have by Your death given life to the world, deliver me by this Your

Most Sacred Body and Blood from all my sins and from every evil. Make me always cling to Your commandments, and never permit me to be separated from You. Who with the same God the Father and the Holy Spirit, live and reign, God, world without end. Amen.

LET not the partaking of Your Body, O Lord Jesus Christ, which I, though unworthy, presume to receive, turn to my judgment and condemnation; but through Your goodness, may it become a safeguard and an effective remedy, both of soul and body. Who live and reign with God the Father, in the unity of the Holy Spirit, God, world without end. Amen.

COMMUNION OF THE PRIEST

I WILL take the Bread of heaven, and call upon the name of the Lord.

Lord, I am not worthy that You should come under my roof; but only say the word, and my soul will be healed. (3 *times.*)

Making the Sign of the Cross with the Host, he says:

MAY the Body of our Lord Jesus Christ preserve my soul to life everlasting. Amen.

What return shall I make to the Lord for all He has given me? I will take the Chalice of salvation, and I will call upon the name of the Lord. Praising will I call upon the Lord and I shall be saved from my enemies.

Making the Sign of the Cross with the chalice, he says:

MAY the Blood of our Lord Jesus Christ preserve my soul to life everlasting. Amen.

The Priest reverently consumes the Precious Blood.

COMMUNION OF THE FAITHFUL

The Server and people say the "Confiteor."

P. May almighty God have mercy on you, forgive you your sins, and bring you to life everlasting. *S.* Amen.

P. May the almighty and merciful Lord grant you pardon, ✠ absolution and remission of your sins.

S. Amen.

Holding up a Sacred Host, the Priest says:

Behold the Lamb of God, behold Him Who takes away the sins of the world.
Lord, I am not worthy that You should come under my roof; but only say the word, and my soul will be healed. (3 *times.*)

The Priest says to each communicant:

May the Body of our Lord Jesus Christ preserve your soul to life everlasting. Amen.

The Priest purifies the chalice with wine, saying:

WHAT has passed our lips as food, O Lord, may we possess in purity of heart, that what is given to us in time, be our healing for eternity.

He purifies his fingers with wine and water, saying:

MAY Your Body, O Lord, which I have eaten, and Your Blood which I have drunk, cleave to my very soul, and grant that no trace of sin be found in me, whom these pure and holy mysteries have renewed. Who live and reign, world without end. Amen.

THE COMMUNION • Luke 4, 22

ALL marvelled at the words that came from the mouth of God.

Communion (Mark 11) for Additional Mass after Pent.

AMEN I say to you, all things whatever you ask for in prayer, believe that you shall receive, and it shall be done to you.

The Priest, turning to the people, says:

P. The Lord be with you. *S.* And with your spirit.
P. Let us pray.

THE POSTCOMMUNION

WE BESEECH You, almighty God, that we may obtain the effect of that salvation, whose pledge we have received in these mysteries. Through our Lord Jesus Christ, Your Son, Who lives and reigns with You in the unity of the Holy Spirit, God, world without end. *S.* Amen.

FINAL PRAYERS

The Priest turns again to the people, and says:

P. The Lord be with you. *S.* And with your spirit.
P. Go, you are dismissed. *S.* Thanks be to God.

MAY the tribute of my worship be pleasing to You, Most Holy Trinity, and grant that the sacrifice which I, all unworthy, have offered in the presence of Your Majesty, may be acceptable to You, and through Your mercy obtain forgiveness for me and all for whom I have offered it. Through Christ our Lord. Amen.

THE LAST BLESSING

He kisses the altar, and facing the people, says:

MAY almighty God bless you: ✠ the Father, and the Son, and the Holy Spirit.

S. Amen.

The Last Gospel and Prayers after Low Mass are conveniently placed inside the back cover.

The kingdom of heaven is like leaven buried in three measures of flour.

SIXTH SUNDAY AFTER EPIPHANY

OR

ADDITIONAL MASS AFTER PENTECOST

The admirable parables of the mustard seed and the leaven serve to demonstrate to us the immense influence of the Church, which Christ uses to spread His saving Doctrine to all nations. (GREEN VESTMENTS)

When this Mass is used as an Additional Mass after Pentecost, as indicated by the Liturgical Calendar, substitute the Introit, Gradual, Offertory and Communion as indicated below.

PRAYERS AT THE FOOT OF THE ALTAR

IN THE name of the Father, ✠ and of the Son, and of the Holy Spirit. Amen.

Priest. I will go in to the altar of God.

Server. The God of my gladness and joy.

Psalm 42

DO ME justice, O God, and fight my fight against a faithless people; from the deceitful and impious man rescue me.

S. For You, O God, are my strength. Why do You keep me so far away? Why must I go about in mourning, with the enemy oppressing me?
P. Send forth Your light and Your fidelity; they shall lead me on and bring me to Your holy mountain, to Your dwelling-place.
S. Then will I go in to the altar of God, the God of my gladness and joy.
P. Then will I give You thanks upon the harp, O God, my God. Why are you so downcast, O my soul? Why do you sigh within me?
S. Hope in God! For I shall again be thanking Him in the presence of my Savior and my God.
P. Glory be to the Father, and to the Son, and to the Holy Spirit.
S. As it was in the beginning, is now, and ever shall be, world without end. Amen.
P. I will go in to the altar of God.
S. The God of my gladness and joy.
P. Our help ✠ is in the name of the Lord.
S. Who made heaven and earth.
P. I confess to almighty God, etc.
S. May almighty God have mercy on you, forgive you your sins, and bring you to life everlasting.
P. Amen.

The Server, bowing, says the "Confiteor."

I CONFESS to almighty God, to Blessed Mary, ever Virgin, to Blessed Michael the Archangel, to Blessed John the Baptist, to the Holy Apostles Peter and Paul, and to all the Saints, and to you, Father, that I have sinned exceedingly in thought, word and deed, *through my fault, through my fault, through my most grievous fault.* Therefore I be-

seech Blessed Mary, ever Virgin, Blessed Michael the Archangel, Blessed John the Baptist, the Holy Apostles Peter and Paul, and all the Saints, and you, Father, to pray to the Lord our God for me.
P. May almighty God have mercy on you, forgive you your sins, and bring you to life everlasting.
S. Amen.

MAY the almighty and merciful Lord grant us pardon, ✠ absolution, and remission of our sins. *S.* Amen.
P. Will You not, O God, give us life?
S. And shall not Your people rejoice in You?
P. Show us, O Lord, Your kindness.
S. And grant us Your salvation.
P. O Lord, hear my prayer.
S. And let my cry come to You.
P. The Lord be with you.
S. And with your spirit. *P.* Let us pray.

Going up to the altar, the Priest prays silently:

TAKE away from us our sins, O Lord, we beseech You, that we may enter with pure minds into the Holy of Holies. Through Christ our Lord. Amen.

WE BESEECH You, O Lord, by the merits of Your Saints (*he kisses the altar*) whose relics lie here, and of all the Saints: deign in Your mercy to pardon me all my sins. Amen.

THE INTROIT • Ps. 96, 7. 8. 1

At the right side of the altar, the Priest says:

ADORE God, all you His angels: Sion hears and is glad, and the cities of Juda rejoice. *Ps.* The

Lord is King; let the earth rejoice; let the many isles be glad. Glory be to the Father, and to the Son, and to the Holy Spirit. As it was in the beginning, is now, and ever shall be, world without end. Amen. — Adore God, all you His angels: Sion hears and is glad, and the cities of Juda rejoice.

Introit (Jer. 29) for Additional Mass after Pentecost

THE Lord says: "I think thoughts of peace, and not of affliction. You shall call upon Me, and I will hear you; and I will bring back your captivity from all places." *Ps. 84.* You have favored, O Lord, Your land; You have restored the well-being of Jacob. Glory be to the Father, and to the Son, and to the Holy Spirit. As it was in the beginning, is now, and ever shall be, world without end. Amen. — The Lord says: "I think thoughts of peace, and not of affliction. You shall call upon Me, and I will hear you; and I will bring back your captivity from all places."

THE KYRIE

P. Lord, have mercy. *S.* Lord, have mercy. ***P.*** Lord, have mercy. *S.* Christ, have mercy. ***P.*** Christ, have mercy. *S.* Christ, have mercy. ***P.*** Lord, have mercy. *S.* Lord, have mercy. ***P.*** Lord, have mercy.

THE GLORIA

GLORY to God in the highest. And on earth peace to men of good will. We praise You. We bless You. We adore You. We glorify You. We give You thanks for Your great glory. O Lord God, heavenly King, God the Father almighty. O Lord Jesus Christ, the Only-begotten Son. O Lord God, Lamb of God, Son of the Father: You Who take away the sins of the world, have mercy on us. You Who take away the sins of the world, receive our prayer. You Who sit at the right hand of the Father, have mercy on us. For You alone are holy. You alone are the Lord. You alone, O Jesus Christ, are most high. Together with the Holy Spirit ✠ in the glory of God the Father. Amen.

The Priest kisses the altar and turns to the people, saying:

P. The Lord be with you. *S.* And with your spirit.
P. Let us pray.

THE PRAYER

Going to the right (Epistle) side, he says:

GRANT, we beseech You, almighty God, that, ever fixing our thoughts on such things that are reasonable, we may, both in word and in work, do that which is pleasing to You. Through our Lord Jesus Christ, Your Son, Who lives and reigns with You in the unity of the Holy Spirit, God, world without end. *S.* Amen.

THE EPISTLE • 1 Thess. 1, 2-10

BRETHREN: We give thanks to God always for you all, continually making a remembrance of you in our prayers; being mindful before God our Father of your work of faith, and labor, and charity, and your enduring hope in our Lord Jesus Christ. We know, brethren, beloved of God, how you were chosen. For our gospel was not delivered to you in word only, but in power also, and in the Holy Spirit, and in much fullness, as indeed you know what manner of men we have been among you for your sakes. And you became imitators of us and of the Lord, receiving the word in great tribulation, with joy of the Holy Spirit, so that you became a pattern to all the believers in Macedonia and in Achaia. For from you the word of the Lord has been spread abroad, not only in Macedonia and Achaia, but in every place your faith in God has gone forth, so that we need say nothing further. For they themselves report concerning us how we entered among you, and how you turned to God from idols, to serve the living and true God, and to await from heaven Jesus, His Son, Whom He raised from the dead, Who has delivered us from the wrath to come. *S.* Thanks be to God.

THE GRADUAL • Ps. 101, 16-17

THE nations shall revere Your name, O Lord, and all the kings of the earth Your glory. ℣. For the Lord has rebuilt Sion, and He shall appear in His glory. Alleluia, alleluia. ℣. *Ps.* 96, 1. The Lord is King; let the earth rejoice; let the many isles be glad. Alleluia.

Gradual (Ps. 43) for Additional Mass after Pentecost

YOU saved us, O Lord, from our foes, and those who hated us You put to shame. ℣. In God we gloried day by day; Your name we praised always.

Alleluia, alleluia. ℣. *Ps. 129, 1. 2.* Out of the depths I cry to You, O Lord; Lord, hear my prayer. Alleluia.

PRAYER BEFORE THE GOSPEL

Bowing down at the center of the altar, he says:

CLEANSE my heart and my lips, O almighty God, Who cleansed the lips of the Prophet Isaias with a burning coal. In Your gracious mercy deign so to purify me that I may worthily proclaim Your holy Gospel. Through Christ our Lord. Amen. Lord, grant Your blessing. The Lord be in my heart and on my lips, that I may worthily and fittingly proclaim His holy Gospel. Amen.

THE GOSPEL • Matt. 13, 31-35

P. The Lord be with you. *S.* And with your spirit.
P. ✠ The continuation of the holy Gospel according to Saint Matthew. *S.* Glory be to You, O Lord.

AT THAT time, Jesus spoke this parable to the crowds: "The kingdom of heaven is like a grain of mustard seed, which a man took and sowed in his field. This indeed is the smallest of all the seeds; but when it grows up it is larger than any herb and becomes a tree, so that the birds of the air come and dwell in its branches." He told them another parable: "The kingdom of heaven is like leaven, which a woman took and buried in three measures of flour, until all of it was leavened." All these things Jesus spoke to the crowds in parables, and without parables He did not speak to them; that what was spoken by the prophet might be fulfilled, "I will open My mouth in parables, I will utter things hidden since the foundation of the world." *S.* Praise be to You, O Christ.

P. By the words of the Gospel, may our sins be taken away.

THE NICENE CREED

At the center of the altar, he says:

I BELIEVE in one God, the Father almighty, Maker of heaven and earth, and of all things visible and invisible. And in one Lord Jesus Christ, the Only-begotten Son of God. Born of the Father before all ages. God of God; Light of Light; true God of true God. Begotten not made; of one being with the Father; by Whom all things were made. Who for us men, and for our salvation, came down from heaven. (*Here all genuflect.*) And was made Flesh by the Holy Spirit of the Virgin Mary: AND WAS MADE MAN. He was also crucified for us, suffered under Pontius Pilate and was buried. And on the third day He rose again according to the Scriptures. And ascending into heaven, He sits at the right hand of the Father. And He shall come again in glory to judge the living and the dead; and of His kingdom there shall be no end. And I believe in the Holy Spirit, Lord and Giver of life, Who proceeds from the Father and the Son. Who together with the Father and the Son is no less adored, and glorified: Who spoke by the Prophets. And I believe in One, Holy, Catholic and Apostolic Church. I confess one Baptism for the remission of sins. And I look for the resurrection of the dead. ✠ And the life of the world to come. Amen.

THE OFFERTORY

P. The Lord be with you. *S.* And with your spirit.
P. Let us pray.

THE OFFERTORY VERSE • Ps. 117, 16. 17

THE right hand of the Lord has struck with power: the right hand of the Lord has exalted me; I shall not die, but live, and declare the works of the Lord.

Offertory (Ps. 129) for Additional Mass after Pentecost

OUT of the depths I cry to You, O Lord; Lord, hear my prayer! Out of the depths I cry to You, O Lord.

The Priest offering the host on the paten, says:

ACCEPT, O holy Father, almighty and eternal God, this spotless host, which I, Your unworthy servant, offer to You, my living and true

God, to atone for my numberless sins, offenses, and negligences; on behalf of all here present and likewise for all faithful Christians living and dead, that it may profit me and them as a means of salvation to life everlasting. Amen.

He pours wine and water into the chalice, blessing the water before it is poured.

O GOD, Who established the nature of man in wondrous dignity, and still more admirably restored it, grant that through the mystery of this water and wine, we may be made partakers of His Divinity, Who has condescended to become partaker of our humanity, Jesus Christ, Your Son, our Lord. Who lives and reigns with You in the unity of the Holy Spirit, God, world without end. Amen.

Offering up the wine, the Priest says:

WE OFFER You, O Lord, the chalice of salvation, humbly begging of Your mercy that it may arise before Your Divine Majesty, with a pleasing fragrance, for our salvation and for that of the whole world. Amen.

IN A humble spirit and with a contrite heart, may we be accepted by You, O Lord, and may our sacrifice so be offered in Your sight this day as to please You, O Lord God.

Raising his eyes and blessing the offering, he says:

COME, O Sanctifier, almighty and eternal God, and bless ✠ this sacrifice prepared for the glory of Your holy name.

WASHING THE FINGERS

I WASH my hands in innocence, and I go around Your altar, O Lord, giving voice to my thanks, and recounting all Your wondrous deeds. O Lord,

I love the house in which You dwell, the tenting-place of Your glory. Gather not my soul with those of sinners, nor with men of blood my life. On their hands are crimes, and their right hands are full of bribes. But I walk in integrity; redeem me, and have pity on me. My foot stands on level ground; in the assemblies I will bless You, O Lord. Glory be to the Father, and to the Son, and to the Holy Spirit. As it was in the beginning, is now, and ever shall be, world without end. Amen.

ACCEPT, Most Holy Trinity, this offering which we are making to You in remembrance of the Passion, Resurrection, and Ascension of Jesus Christ, our Lord; and in honor of Blessed Mary, ever Virgin, Blessed John the Baptist, the Holy Apostles Peter and Paul, and of these, and of all the Saints; that it may add to their honor and aid our salvation; and may they deign to intercede in heaven for us who honor their memory here on earth. Through the same Christ our Lord. Amen.

The Priest turns toward the people and says:

Pray, brethren, that my sacrifice and yours may become acceptable to God the Father almighty.

S. May the Lord accept this sacrifice from your hands to the praise and glory of His name, for our advantage, and that of all His holy Church.

P. Amen.

THE SECRET

MAY this offering, O God, we beseech You cleanse and renew, govern and protect us. Through our Lord Jesus Christ, Your Son, Who lives and reigns with You in the unity of the Holy Spirit, God.

P. World without end. S. Amen.

PREFACE—CANON

P. The Lord be with you. *S.* And with your spirit.
P. Lift up your hearts.
S. We have lifted them up to the Lord.
P. Let us give thanks to the Lord, our God.
S. It is fitting and just.

IT IS fitting indeed and just, right and helpful to salvation, for us always and everywhere to give thanks to You, O holy Lord, Father almighty, everlasting God, Who with Your Only-begotten Son and the Holy Spirit are one God, one Lord; not in the unity of a single person, but in the trinity of a single nature. For that which we believe on Your revelation concerning Your glory, that same we believe of Your Son, that same of the Holy Spirit, without difference or discrimination. So that in confessing the true and everlasting Godhead, we shall adore distinction in Persons, oneness in being, and equality in Majesty. This the Angels and Archangels, the Cherubim, too, and the Seraphim do praise; day by day they cease not to cry out as with one voice, saying (*the bell is rung 3 times*):

HOLY, HOLY, HOLY, Lord God of Hosts. Heaven and earth are filled with Your glory. Hosanna in the highest. ✠ Blessed is He Who comes in the name of the Lord. Hosanna in the highest.

THE CANON OF THE MASS

THEREFORE, most gracious Father, we humbly beg of You and entreat You through Jesus Christ Your Son, our Lord, (*he kisses the altar*) to deem acceptable and bless these ✠ gifts, these ✠

offerings, these ✠ holy and unspotted oblations which, in the first place, we offer You for Your Holy Catholic Church, that You would deign to give her peace and protection, to unite and guard her throughout the world, together with Your servant N., our Pope, and N., our Bishop; and all true believers who cherish the Catholic and Apostolic Faith.

Commemoration of the Living

REMEMBER, O Lord, Your servants and handmaids, N. and N., (*name them*) and all here present, whose faith and devotion are known to You, on whose behalf we offer to You, or who themselves offer to You, this sacrifice of praise for themselves, families and friends, for the good of their souls, for their hope of salvation and deliverance from all harm, and who offer their homage to You, eternal, living and true God.

Commemoration of the Saints

IN THE unity of holy fellowship we observe the memory, first of all, of the glorious and ever Virgin Mary, Mother of our Lord and God Jesus Christ; next, that of Your Blessed Apostles and Martyrs, Peter and Paul, Andrew, James, John, Thomas, James, Philip, Bartholomew, Matthew, Simon and Thaddeus; of Linus, Cletus, Clement, Sixtus, Cornelius, Cyprian, Lawrence, Chrysogonus, John and Paul, Cosmas and Damian, and of all Your Saints, by whose merits and prayers grant that we may be always fortified by the help of Your protection. Through the same Christ our Lord. Amen.

Spreading his hands over the oblation, he says:

GRACIOUSLY accept, then, we beseech You, O Lord, this service of our worship and that of all Your household. Provide that our days be spent in Your peace, save us from everlasting damnation, and cause us to be numbered in the flock You have chosen. Through Christ our Lord. Amen.

O GOD, deign to bless ✠ what we offer, and make it approved, ✠ effective, ✠ right, and wholly pleasing in every way, that it may become for our good, the Body ✠ and Blood ✠ of Your dearly beloved Son, Jesus Christ our Lord.

CONSECRATION—ELEVATION

WHO, the day before He suffered, took bread into His holy and venerable hands, and having raised His eyes to heaven, to You, O God, His almighty Father, giving thanks to You, He blessed it, ✠ broke it, and gave it to His disciples, saying: All of you take and eat of this:

FOR THIS IS MY BODY.

IN LIKE manner, when the supper was done, taking also this goodly chalice into His holy and venerable hands, again giving thanks to You, He blessed ✠ it, and gave it to His disciples, saying: All of you take and drink of this:

FOR THIS IS THE CHALICE OF MY BLOOD OF THE NEW AND ETERNAL COVENANT: THE MYSTERY OF FAITH: WHICH SHALL BE SHED FOR YOU AND FOR MANY UNTO THE FORGIVENESS OF SINS.

After replacing the chalice on the corporal, he says:

As often as you shall do these things, in memory of Me shall you do them.

Offering of the Victim

MINDFUL, therefore, O Lord, not only of the blessed Passion of the same Christ, Your Son, our Lord, but also of His Resurrection from the dead, and finally His glorious Ascension into heaven, we, Your ministers, as also Your holy people, offer to Your supreme Majesty, of the gifts bestowed upon us, the pure ✠ Victim, the holy ✠ Victim, the all-perfect ✠ Victim: the holy ✠ Bread of life eternal and the Chalice ✠ of unending salvation.

AND this deign to regard with gracious and kindly attention and hold acceptable, as You deigned to accept the offerings of Abel, Your just servant, and the sacrifice of Abraham our patriarch, and that which Your chief priest Melchisedec offered to You, a holy sacrifice and a spotless victim.

MOST humbly we implore You, almighty God, bid these offerings to be brought by the hands of Your holy angel to Your altar above; before the face of Your Divine Majesty; that those of us who, by sharing in the Sacrifice of this altar, shall receive the Most Sacred ✠ Body and ✠ Blood of Your Son, may be filled with every grace and heavenly blessing. Through the same Christ our Lord. Amen.

Commemoration of the Dead

REMEMBER also, O Lord, Your servants and handmaids, *N.* and *N.*, who have gone before us with the sign of faith, and rest in the sleep of peace. (*Here pray for the dead.*) To these, O Lord, and to all who rest in Christ, we beseech You to grant of Your goodness, a place of comfort, light

and peace. Through the same Christ our Lord. Amen.

TO US sinners also, Your servants, trusting in the greatness of Your mercy, deign to grant some part and fellowship with Your Holy Apostles and Martyrs: with John, Stephen, Matthias, Barnabas, Ignatius, Alexander, Marcellinus, Peter, Felicitas, Perpetua, Agatha, Lucy, Agnes, Cecilia, Anastasia, and all Your Saints; into whose company, we implore You to admit us, not weighing our merits, but freely granting us pardon. Through Christ our Lord.

THROUGH Whom, O Lord, You always create, ✠ sanctify, ✠ fill with life, ✠ bless, and bestow upon us all good things.

The Minor Elevation

THROUGH ✠ Him, and with ✠ Him, and in ✠ Him, is to You, God the Father ✠ almighty, in the unity of the Holy ✠ Spirit, all honor and glory, world without end. S. Amen.

THE COMMUNION AND THANKSGIVING

Let us pray. Prompted by saving precepts, and taught by Your divine teaching, we dare to say:

OUR FATHER, Who art in heaven, hallowed be Thy name: Thy kingdom come: Thy will be done on earth as it is in heaven. Give us this day our daily bread; and forgive us our trespasses, as we forgive those who trespass against us. And lead us not into temptation: S. But deliver us from evil. *P.* Amen.

DELIVER us, we beseech You, O Lord, from all evils, past, present, and to come; and by

the intercession of the Blessed and glorious Mary, ever Virgin, Mother of God, together with Your Blessed Apostles Peter and Paul, and Andrew, and all the Saints, grant of Your goodness, peace in our days, that aided by the riches of Your mercy, we may be always free from sin and safe from all disturbance.

Through the same our Lord Jesus Christ, Your Son, Who lives and reigns with You in the unity of the Holy Spirit, God, world without end.

P. May the peace ✠ of the Lord be ✠ always with ✠ you.

S. And with your spirit.

The Priest puts a small particle into the chalice, saying:

May this mingling and consecration of the Body and Blood of our Lord Jesus Christ help us who receive it to life everlasting. Amen.

LAMB of God, You Who take away the sins of the world, have mercy on us.

Lamb of God, You Who take away the sins of the world, have mercy on us.

Lamb of God, You Who take away the sins of the world, grant us peace.

PRAYERS BEFORE HOLY COMMUNION

O LORD Jesus Christ, Who said to Your Apostles: "Peace I leave with you, My peace I give to you," regard not my sins but the faith of Your Church, and deign to give her peace and unity according to Your Will: Who live and reign, God, world without end. Amen.

O LORD Jesus Christ, Son of the living God, Who, by the will of the Father, with the co-

operation of the Holy Spirit, have by Your death given life to the world, deliver me by this Your Most Sacred Body and Blood from all my sins and from every evil. Make me always cling to Your commandments, and never permit me to be separated from You. Who with the same God the Father and the Holy Spirit, live and reign, God, world without end. Amen.

LET not the partaking of Your Body, O Lord Jesus Christ, which I, though unworthy, presume to receive, turn to my judgment and condemnation; but through Your goodness, may it become a safeguard and an effective remedy, both of soul and body. Who live and reign with God the Father, in the unity of the Holy Spirit, God, world without end. Amen.

COMMUNION OF THE PRIEST

I WILL take the Bread of heaven, and call upon the name of the Lord.

Lord, I am not worthy that You should come under my roof; but only say the word, and my soul will be healed. (3 *times.*)

Making the Sign of the Cross with the Host, he says:

MAY the Body of our Lord Jesus Christ preserve my soul to life everlasting. Amen.

What return shall I make to the Lord for all He has given me? I will take the Chalice of salvation, and I will call upon the name of the Lord. Praising will I call upon the Lord and I shall be saved from my enemies.

Making the Sign of the Cross with the chalice, he says:

MAY the Blood of our Lord Jesus Christ preserve my soul to life everlasting. Amen.

The Priest reverently consumes the Precious Blood.

COMMUNION OF THE FAITHFUL

The Server and people say the "Confiteor."

P. May almighty God have mercy on you, forgive you your sins, and bring you to life everlasting. *S.* Amen.

P. May the almighty and merciful Lord grant you pardon, ✠ absolution and remission of your sins.

S. Amen.

Holding up a Sacred Host, the Priest says:

Behold the Lamb of God, behold Him Who takes away the sins of the world.

Lord, I am not worthy that You should come under my roof; but only say the word, and my soul will be healed. (3 *times.*)

The Priest says to each communicant:

May the Body of our Lord Jesus Christ preserve your soul to life everlasting. Amen.

The Priest purifies the chalice with wine, saying:

WHAT has passed our lips as food, O Lord, may we possess in purity of heart, that what is given to us in time, be our healing for eternity.

He purifies his fingers with wine and water, saying:

MAY Your Body, O Lord, which I have eaten, and Your Blood which I have drunk, cleave to my very soul, and grant that no trace of sin be found in me, whom these pure and holy mysteries have renewed. Who live and reign, world without end. Amen.

THE COMMUNION · Luke 4, 22

ALL marvelled at the words that came from the mouth of God.

Communion (Mark 11) for Additional Mass after Pent.

AMEN I say to you, all things whatever you ask for in prayer, believe that you shall receive, and it shall be done to you.

The Priest, turning to the people, says:

P. The Lord be with you. *S.* And with your spirit.
P. Let us pray.

THE POSTCOMMUNION

BEING fed, O Lord, with heavenly delights, we beseech You, that we may ever seek after those things by which we truly live. Through our Lord Jesus Christ, Your Son, Who lives, etc. *S.* Amen.

FINAL PRAYERS

The Priest turns again to the people, and says:

P. The Lord be with you. *S.* And with your spirit.
P. Go, you are dismissed. *S.* Thanks be to God.

MAY the tribute of my worship be pleasing to You, Most Holy Trinity, and grant that the sacrifice which I, all unworthy, have offered in the presence of Your Majesty, may be acceptable to You, and through Your mercy obtain forgiveness for me and all for whom I have offered it. Through Christ our Lord. Amen.

THE LAST BLESSING

He kisses the altar, and facing the people, says:

MAY almighty God bless you: ✠ the Father, and the Son, and the Holy Spirit. *S.* Amen.

The Last Gospel and Prayers after Low Mass are conveniently placed inside the back cover.

"The last shall be first, and the first last."

SEPTUAGESIMA SUNDAY

When viewed in the light of Adam's fall, the Mass celebrated today contains a solemn note of sorrow. God holds out a great reward to us, but we must work to receive it. Unfortunately, we are by nature more inclined to endure hardships for the goods of this life than for the Kingdom of God. (PURPLE VESTMENTS)

PRAYERS AT THE FOOT OF THE ALTAR

IN THE name of the Father, ✠ and of the Son, and of the Holy Spirit. Amen.

Priest. I will go in to the altar of God.

Server. The God of my gladness and joy.

Psalm 42

DO ME justice, O God, and fight my fight against a faithless people; from the deceitful and impious man rescue me.

S. For You, O God, are my strength. Why do You keep me so far away? Why must I go about in mourning, with the enemy oppressing me?

P. Send forth Your light and Your fidelity; they shall lead me on and bring me to Your holy mountain, to Your dwelling-place.

S. Then will I go in to the altar of God, the God of my gladness and joy.
P. Then will I give You thanks upon the harp, O God, my God. Why are you so downcast, O my soul? Why do you sigh within me?
S. Hope in God! For I shall again be thanking Him in the presence of my Savior and my God.
P. Glory be to the Father, and to the Son, and to the Holy Spirit.
S. As it was in the beginning, is now, and ever shall be, world without end. Amen.
P. I will go in to the altar of God.
S. The God of my gladness and joy.
P. Our help ✠ is in the name of the Lord.
S. Who made heaven and earth.
P. I confess to almighty God, etc.
S. May almighty God have mercy on you, forgive you your sins, and bring you to life everlasting.
P. Amen.

The Server, bowing, says the "Confiteor."

I CONFESS to almighty God, to Blessed Mary, ever Virgin, to Blessed Michael the Archangel, to Blessed John the Baptist, to the Holy Apostles Peter and Paul, and to all the Saints, and to you, Father, that I have sinned exceedingly in thought, word and deed, *through my fault, through my fault, through my most grievous fault.* Therefore I beseech Blessed Mary, ever Virgin, Blessed Michael the Archangel, Blessed John the Baptist, the Holy Apostles Peter and Paul, and all the Saints, and you, Father, to pray to the Lord our God for me.
P. May almighty God have mercy on you, forgive you your sins, and bring you to life everlasting.
S. Amen.

MAY the almighty and merciful Lord grant us pardon, ✠ absolution, and remission of our sins. *S.* Amen.
P. Will You not, O God, give us life?
S. And shall not Your people rejoice in You?
P. Show us, O Lord, Your kindness.
S. And grant us Your salvation.
P. O Lord, hear my prayer.
S. And let my cry come to You.
P. The Lord be with you.
S. And with your spirit. *P.* Let us pray.

Going up to the altar, the Priest prays silently:

TAKE away from us our sins, O Lord, we beseech You, that we may enter with pure minds into the Holy of Holies. Through Christ our Lord. Amen.

WE BESEECH You, O Lord, by the merits of Your Saints (*he kisses the altar*) whose relics lie here, and of all the Saints: deign in Your mercy to pardon me all my sins. Amen.

THE INTROIT • Ps. 17, 5-7. 2-3

At the right side of the altar, the Priest says:

THE terrors of death surged round about me, the cords of the nether world enmeshed me. In my distress I called upon the Lord; from His holy temple He heard my voice. *Ps.* I love You, O Lord, my strength, O Lord, my rock, my fortress, my deliverer. Glory be to the Father, and to the Son, and to the Holy Spirit. As it was in the beginning, is now, and ever shall be, world without end. Amen. — The terrors of death surged round about me, the cords of the nether world enmeshed me. In my distress I called upon the Lord; from His holy temple He heard my voice.

THE KYRIE

P. Lord, have mercy. *S.* Lord, have mercy. *P.* Lord, have mercy. *S.* Christ, have mercy. *P.* Christ, have mercy. *S.* Christ, have mercy. *P.* Lord, have mercy. *S.* Lord, have mercy. *P.* Lord, have mercy.

The Priest kisses the altar and turns to the people, saying:

P. The Lord be with you. *S.* And with your spirit. *P.* Let us pray.

THE PRAYER

Going to the right (Epistle) side, he says:

GRACIOUSLY hear the prayers of Your people, we beseech You, O Lord, that we, who are justly punished for our sins, may be mercifully delivered for the glory of Your name. Through our Lord Jesus Christ, Your Son, Who lives and reigns with You in the unity of the Holy Spirit, God, world without end. *S.* Amen.

THE EPISTLE • 1 Cor. 9, 24 – 10, 5

BRETHREN: Do you not know that those who run in a race, all indeed run, but one receives the prize? So run as to obtain it. And everyone in a contest abstains from all things — and they indeed to receive a perishable crown, but we an imperishable. I, therefore, so run as not without a purpose; I so fight as not beating the air; but I chastise my body and bring it into subjection, lest perhaps after preaching to others I myself should be rejected. For I would not have you ignorant, brethren, that our fathers were all under the cloud, and all passed through the sea, and all were baptized in Moses, in the cloud and in the sea. And all ate the same spiritual food, and all drank the same spiritual drink (for they drank from the spiritual rock which followed them, and the rock was Christ). Yet with most of them God was not well pleased. *S.* Thanks be to God.

THE GRADUAL • Ps. 9, 10. 11. 19. 20

A STRONGHOLD in times of distress; they trust in You who cherish You; for You forsake not those who seek You, O Lord. ℣. For the needy shall not always be forgotten; nor shall the hope of the afflicted forever perish; rise, O Lord, let not man prevail.

THE TRACT • Ps. 129, 1-4

OUT of the depths I cry to You, O Lord; Lord, hear my voice! ℣. Let Your ears be attentive to the prayer of Your servant. ℣. If You, O Lord, mark iniquities, Lord, who can stand it? ℣. But with You is forgiveness, and by reason of Your law I have waited for You, O Lord.

PRAYER BEFORE THE GOSPEL

Bowing down at the center of the altar, he says:

CLEANSE my heart and my lips, O almighty God, Who cleansed the lips of the Prophet Isaias with a burning coal. In Your gracious mercy deign so to purify me that I may worthily proclaim Your holy Gospel. Through Christ our Lord. Amen.

Lord, grant Your blessing. The Lord be in my heart and on my lips, that I may worthily and fittingly proclaim His holy Gospel. Amen.

THE GOSPEL • Matt. 20, 1-16

Going to the left (Gospel) side of the altar, he says:

P. The Lord be with you. *S.* And with your spirit.
P. ✠ The continuation of the holy Gospel according to Saint Matthew. *S.* Glory be to You, O Lord.

AT THAT time, Jesus spoke to His disciples this parable: "The kingdom of heaven is like a householder who went out early in the morning to hire laborers for his vineyard. And having agreed with the laborers for a denarius a day, he sent them into his vineyard. And about the third hour, he went out and saw others standing in the market place idle; and he said to them, 'Go you also into the vineyard, and I will give you whatever is just.' So they went. And again he went out about the sixth, and about the ninth hour, and did as before. But about the eleventh hour he went out and found others standing about and he said to them, 'Why do you stand here all day idle?' They said to him, 'Because no man has hired us.' He said to them, 'Go you also into the vineyard.' But when evening had come, the owner of the vineyard said to his steward, 'Call the laborers, and pay them their wages, beginning from the last even to the first.' Now when they of the eleventh hour came, they received each a denarius. And when the first in their turn came, they thought that they would receive more; but they also received each his denarius. And on receiving it, they began to murmur against the householder, saying, 'These last have worked a single hour, and you have put them on a level with us, who have borne the burden of the day's heat.' But answering one of them, he said, 'Friend, I do you no injustice; did you not agree with me for a denarius? Take what is yours and go; I choose to give to this last even as to you. Have I not a right to do what I choose? Or are you envious because I am generous?' Even so the last shall be first, and the first last; for many are called, but few are chosen." *S*. Praise be to You, O Christ.

P. By the words of the Gospel, may our sins be taken away.

THE NICENE CREED

At the center of the altar, he says:

I BELIEVE in one God, the Father almighty, Maker of heaven and earth, and of all things visible and invisible. And in one Lord Jesus Christ, the Only-begotten Son of God. Born of the Father before all ages. God of God; Light of Light; true God of true God. Begotten not made; of one being with the Father; by Whom all things were made. Who for us men, and for our salvation, came down from heaven. (*Here all genuflect.*) And was made Flesh by the Holy Spirit of the Virgin Mary: AND WAS MADE MAN. He was also crucified for us, suffered under Pontius Pilate and was buried. And on the third day He rose again according to the Scriptures. And ascending into heaven, He sits at the right hand of the Father. And He shall come again in glory to judge the living and the dead; and of His kingdom there shall be no end. And I believe in the Holy Spirit, Lord and Giver of life, Who proceeds from the Father and the Son. Who together with the Father and the Son is no less adored, and glorified: Who spoke by the Prophets. And I believe in One, Holy, Catholic and Apostolic Church. I confess one Baptism for the remission of sins. And I look for the resurrection of the dead. ✠ And the life of the world to come. Amen.

THE OFFERTORY

The Priest turns to the people and says:

P. The Lord be with you. *S*. And with your spirit.

P. Let us pray.

THE OFFERTORY VERSE • Ps. 91, 2

IT IS good to give thanks to the Lord, and to sing praise to Your name, Most High.

The Priest now uncovers the chalice, places the host on the paten and offering it up, says:

ACCEPT, O holy Father, almighty and eternal God, this spotless host, which I, Your unworthy servant, offer to You, my living and true God, to atone for my numberless sins, offenses, and negligences; on behalf of all here present and likewise for all faithful Christians living and dead, that it may profit me and them as a means of salvation to life everlasting. Amen.

He pours wine and water into the chalice, blessing the water before it is poured.

O GOD, Who established the nature of man in wondrous dignity, and still more admirably restored it, grant that through the mystery of this water and wine, we may be made partakers of His Divinity, Who has condescended to become partaker of our humanity, Jesus Christ, Your Son, our Lord. Who lives and reigns with You in the unity of the Holy Spirit, God, world without end. Amen.

Offering up the wine, the Priest says:

WE OFFER You, O Lord, the chalice of salvation, humbly begging of Your mercy that it may arise before Your Divine Majesty, with a pleasing fragrance, for our salvation and for that of the whole world. Amen.

Bowing down, the Priest says:

IN A humble spirit and with a contrite heart, may we be accepted by You, O Lord, and may our sacrifice so be offered in Your sight this day as to please You, O Lord God.

Raising his eyes and blessing the offering, he says:

COME, O Sanctifier, almighty and eternal God, and bless ✠ this sacrifice prepared for the glory of Your holy name.

WASHING THE FINGERS

I WASH my hands in innocence, and I go around Your altar, O Lord, giving voice to my thanks, and recounting all Your wondrous deeds. O Lord, I love the house in which You dwell, the tenting-place of Your glory. Gather not my soul with those of sinners, nor with men of blood my life. On their hands are crimes, and their right hands are full of bribes. But I walk in integrity; redeem me, and have pity on me. My foot stands on level ground; in the assemblies I will bless You, O Lord. Glory be to the Father, and to the Son, and to the Holy Spirit. As it was in the beginning, is now, and ever shall be, world without end. Amen.

ACCEPT, Most Holy Trinity, this offering which we are making to You in remembrance of the Passion, Resurrection, and Ascension of Jesus Christ, our Lord; and in honor of Blessed Mary, ever Virgin, Blessed John the Baptist, the Holy Apostles Peter and Paul, and of these, and of all the Saints; that it may add to their honor and aid our salvation; and may they deign to intercede in heaven for us who honor their memory here on earth. Through the same Christ our Lord. Amen.

The Priest turns toward the people and says:

Pray, brethren, that my sacrifice and yours may become acceptable to God the Father almighty.

S. May the Lord accept this sacrifice from your

hands to the praise and glory of His name, for our advantage, and that of all His holy Church.
P. Amen.

THE SECRET

RECEIVE, we beseech You, O Lord, our offerings and prayers; and, through these heavenly mysteries, both cleanse us, and also mercifully grant what we ask. Through our Lord Jesus Christ, Your Son, Who lives and reigns with You in the unity of the Holy Spirit, God.
P. World without end. *S.* Amen.

PREFACE—CANON

P. The Lord be with you. *S.* And with your spirit.
P. Lift up your hearts.
S. We have lifted them up to the Lord.
P. Let us give thanks to the Lord, our God.
S. It is fitting and just.

IT IS fitting indeed and just, right and helpful to salvation, for us always and everywhere to give thanks to You, O holy Lord, Father almighty, everlasting God, Who with Your Only-begotten Son and the Holy Spirit are one God, one Lord; not in the unity of a single person, but in the trinity of a single nature. For that which we believe on Your revelation concerning Your glory, that same we believe of Your Son, that same of the Holy Spirit, without difference or discrimination. So that in confessing the true and everlasting Godhead, we shall adore distinction in Persons, oneness in being, and equality in Majesty. This the Angels and Archangels, the Cherubim, too, and the Seraphim do praise; day by day they cease not to cry out as with one voice, saying (*the bell is rung 3 times*):

HOLY, HOLY, HOLY, Lord God of Hosts. Heaven and earth are filled with Your glory. Hosanna in the highest. ✠ Blessed is He Who comes in the name of the Lord. Hosanna in the highest.

THE CANON OF THE MASS

THEREFORE, most gracious Father, we humbly beg of You and entreat You through Jesus Christ Your Son, our Lord, (*he kisses the altar*) to deem acceptable and bless these ✠ gifts, these ✠ offerings, these ✠ holy and unspotted oblations which, in the first place, we offer You for Your Holy Catholic Church, that You would deign to give her peace and protection, to unite and guard her throughout the world, together with Your servant N., our Pope, and N., our Bishop; and all true believers who cherish the Catholic and Apostolic Faith.

Commemoration of the Living

REMEMBER, O Lord, Your servants and handmaids, N. and N., (*name them*) and all here present, whose faith and devotion are known to You, on whose behalf we offer to You, or who themselves offer to You, this sacrifice of praise for themselves, families and friends, for the good of their souls, for their hope of salvation and deliverance from all harm, and who offer their homage to You, eternal, living and true God.

Commemoration of the Saints

IN THE unity of holy fellowship we observe the memory, first of all, of the glorious and ever Virgin Mary, Mother of our Lord and God Jesus Christ; next, that of Your Blessed Apostles and

Martyrs, Peter and Paul, Andrew, James, John, Thomas, James, Philip, Bartholomew, Matthew, Simon and Thaddeus; of Linus, Cletus, Clement, Sixtus, Cornelius, Cyprian, Lawrence, Chrysogonus, John and Paul, Cosmas and Damian, and of all Your Saints, by whose merits and prayers grant that we may be always fortified by the help of Your protection. Through the same Christ our Lord. Amen.

Spreading his hands over the oblation, he says:

GRACIOUSLY accept, then, we beseech You, O Lord, this service of our worship and that of all Your household. Provide that our days be spent in Your peace, save us from everlasting damnation, and cause us to be numbered in the flock You have chosen. Through Christ our Lord. Amen.

O GOD, deign to bless ✠ what we offer, and make it approved, ✠ effective, ✠ right, and wholly pleasing in every way, that it may become for our good, the Body ✠ and Blood ✠ of Your dearly beloved Son, Jesus Christ our Lord.

CONSECRATION—ELEVATION

WHO, the day before He suffered, took bread into His holy and venerable hands, and having raised His eyes to heaven, to You, O God, His almighty Father, giving thanks to You, He blessed it, ✠ broke it, and gave it to His disciples, saying: All of you take and eat of this:

FOR THIS IS MY BODY.

IN LIKE manner, when the supper was done, taking also this goodly chalice into His holy and venerable hands, again giving thanks to You, He

blessed ✠ it, and gave it to His disciples, saying: All of you take and drink of this:

FOR THIS IS THE CHALICE OF MY BLOOD OF THE NEW AND ETERNAL COVENANT: THE MYSTERY OF FAITH: WHICH SHALL BE SHED FOR YOU AND FOR MANY UNTO THE FORGIVENESS OF SINS.

After replacing the chalice on the corporal, he says:

As often as you shall do these things, in memory of Me shall you do them.

Offering of the Victim

MINDFUL, therefore, O Lord, not only of the blessed Passion of the same Christ, Your Son, our Lord, but also of His Resurrection from the dead, and finally His glorious Ascension into heaven, we, Your ministers, as also Your holy people, offer to Your supreme Majesty, of the gifts bestowed upon us, the pure ✠ Victim, the holy ✠ Victim, the all-perfect ✠ Victim: the holy ✠ Bread of life eternal and the Chalice ✠ of unending salvation.

AND this deign to regard with gracious and kindly attention and hold acceptable, as You deigned to accept the offerings of Abel, Your just servant, and the sacrifice of Abraham our patriarch, and that which Your chief priest Melchisedec offered to You, a holy sacrifice and a spotless victim.

MOST humbly we implore You, almighty God, bid these offerings to be brought by the hands of Your holy angel to Your altar above; before the face of Your Divine Majesty; that those of us who, by sharing in the Sacrifice of this altar, shall receive the Most Sacred ✠ Body and ✠ Blood of Your

Son, may be filled with every grace and heavenly blessing. Through the same Christ our Lord. Amen.

Commemoration of the Dead

REMEMBER also, O Lord, Your servants and handmaids, *N.* and *N.*, who have gone before us with the sign of faith, and rest in the sleep of peace. (*Here pray for the dead.*) To these, O Lord, and to all who rest in Christ, we beseech You to grant of Your goodness, a place of comfort, light and peace. Through the same Christ our Lord. Amen.

TO US sinners also, Your servants, trusting in the greatness of Your mercy, deign to grant some part and fellowship with Your Holy Apostles and Martyrs: with John, Stephen, Matthias, Barnabas, Ignatius, Alexander, Marcellinus, Peter, Felicitas, Perpetua, Agatha, Lucy, Agnes, Cecilia, Anastasia, and all Your Saints; into whose company, we implore You to admit us, not weighing our merits, but freely granting us pardon. Through Christ our Lord.

THROUGH Whom, O Lord, You always create, ✠ sanctify, ✠ fill with life, ✠ bless, and bestow upon us all good things.

The Minor Elevation

THROUGH ✠ Him, and with ✠ Him, and in ✠ Him, is to You, God the Father ✠ almighty, in the unity of the Holy ✠ Spirit, all honor and glory, world without end. *S.* Amen.

THE COMMUNION AND THANKSGIVING

Let us pray. Prompted by saving precepts, and taught by Your divine teaching, we dare to say:

OUR FATHER, Who art in heaven, hallowed be Thy name: Thy kingdom come: Thy will be done on earth as it is in heaven. Give us this day our daily bread; and forgive us our trespasses, as we forgive those who trespass against us. And lead us not into temptation: *S.* But deliver us from evil. *P.* Amen.

DELIVER us, we beseech You, O Lord, from all evils, past, present, and to come; and by the intercession of the Blessed and glorious Mary, ever Virgin, Mother of God, together with Your Blessed Apostles Peter and Paul, and Andrew, and all the Saints, grant of Your goodness, peace in our days, that aided by the riches of Your mercy, we may be always free from sin and safe from all disturbance.

Through the same our Lord Jesus Christ, Your Son, Who lives and reigns with You in the unity of the Holy Spirit, God, world without end. *S.* Amen.

P. May the peace ✠ of the Lord be ✠ always with ✠ you.

S. And with your spirit.

The Priest puts a small particle into the chalice, saying:

May this mingling and consecration of the Body and Blood of our Lord Jesus Christ help us who receive it to life everlasting. Amen.

LAMB of God, You Who take away the sins of the world, have mercy on us.

Lamb of God, You Who take away the sins of the world, have mercy on us.

Lamb of God, You Who take away the sins of the world, grant us peace.

PRAYERS BEFORE HOLY COMMUNION

Then inclining toward the altar, he says:

O LORD Jesus Christ, Who said to Your Apostles: "Peace I leave with you, My peace I give to you," regard not my sins but the faith of Your Church, and deign to give her peace and unity according to Your Will: Who live and reign, God, world without end. Amen.

O LORD Jesus Christ, Son of the living God, Who, by the will of the Father, with the cooperation of the Holy Spirit, have by Your death given life to the world, deliver me by this Your Most Sacred Body and Blood from all my sins and from every evil. Make me always cling to Your commandments, and never permit me to be separated from You. Who with the same God the Father and the Holy Spirit, live and reign, God, world without end. Amen.

LET not the partaking of Your Body, O Lord Jesus Christ, which I, though unworthy, presume to receive, turn to my judgment and condemnation; but through Your goodness, may it become a safeguard and an effective remedy, both of soul and body. Who live and reign with God the Father, in the unity of the Holy Spirit, God, world without end. Amen.

COMMUNION OF THE PRIEST

I WILL take the Bread of heaven, and call upon the name of the Lord.

Lord, I am not worthy that You should come under my roof; but only say the word, and my soul will be healed. (3 *times.*)

Making the Sign of the Cross with the Host, he says:

MAY the Body of our Lord Jesus Christ preserve my soul to life everlasting. Amen. What return shall I make to the Lord for all He has given me? I will take the Chalice of salvation, and I will call upon the name of the Lord. Praising will I call upon the Lord and I shall be saved from my enemies.

Making the Sign of the Cross with the chalice, he says:

MAY the Blood of our Lord Jesus Christ preserve my soul to life everlasting. Amen.

The Priest reverently consumes the Precious Blood.

COMMUNION OF THE FAITHFUL

The Server and people say the "Confiteor."

P. May almighty God have mercy on you, forgive you your sins, and bring you to life everlasting. **S.** Amen.

P. May the almighty and merciful Lord grant you pardon, ✠ absolution and remission of your sins. **S.** Amen.

Holding up a Sacred Host, the Priest says:

Behold the Lamb of God, behold Him Who takes away the sins of the world.

Lord, I am not worthy that You should come under my roof; but only say the word, and my soul will be healed. (3 *times.*)

The Priest says to each communicant:

May the Body of our Lord Jesus Christ preserve your soul to life everlasting. Amen.

The Priest purifies the chalice with wine, saying:

WHAT has passed our lips as food, O Lord, may we possess in purity of heart, that what is given to us in time, be our healing for eternity.

MAY Your Body, O Lord, which I have eaten, and Your Blood which I have drunk, cleave to my very soul, and grant that no trace of sin be found in me, whom these pure and holy mysteries have renewed. Who live and reign, world without end. Amen.

THE COMMUNION • Ps. 30, 17. 18

LET Your face shine upon Your servant; save me in Your kindness. O Lord, let me not be put to shame, for I call upon You.

P. The Lord be with you. *S.* And with your spirit.
P. Let us pray.

THE POSTCOMMUNION

MAY Your faithful people, O God, be strengthened by Your gifts; that, by receiving them, they may the more desire them, and by desiring them they may receive them forever. Through our Lord Jesus Christ, Your Son, etc. *S.* Amen.

FINAL PRAYERS

P. The Lord be with you. *S.* And with your spirit.
P. Let us bless the Lord. *S.* Thanks be to God.

MAY the tribute of my worship be pleasing to You, Most Holy Trinity, and grant that the sacrifice which I, all unworthy, have offered in the presence of Your Majesty, may be acceptable to You, and through Your mercy obtain forgiveness for me and all for whom I have offered it. Through Christ our Lord. Amen.

THE LAST BLESSING

MAY almighty God bless you: ✠ the Father, and the Son, and the Holy Spirit. *S.* Amen.

The Last Gospel and Prayers after Low Mass are conveniently placed inside the back cover.

"The sower went out to sow his seed."

SEXAGESIMA SUNDAY

Distrusting our own powers we should always have perfect confidence in God's grace which will be "sufficient" for us if we humbly ask for it. May then the seed of God's Word find "a right and good heart" in us to receive it, that we may bear much fruit in patience. (PURPLE VESTMENTS)

PRAYERS AT THE FOOT OF THE ALTAR

IN THE name of the Father, ✠ and of the Son, and of the Holy Spirit. Amen.

Priest. I will go in to the altar of God.

Server. The God of my gladness and joy.

Psalm 42

DO ME justice, O God, and fight my fight against a faithless people; from the deceitful and impious man rescue me.

S. For You, O God, are my strength. Why do You keep me so far away? Why must I go about in mourning, with the enemy oppressing me?

P. Send forth Your light and Your fidelity; they shall lead me on and bring me to Your holy mountain, to Your dwelling-place.

S. Then will I go in to the altar of God, the God of my gladness and joy.
P. Then will I give You thanks upon the harp, O God, my God. Why are you so downcast, O my soul? Why do you sigh within me?
S. Hope in God! For I shall again be thanking Him in the presence of my Savior and my God.
P. Glory be to the Father, and to the Son, and to the Holy Spirit.
S. As it was in the beginning, is now, and ever shall be, world without end. Amen.
P. I will go in to the altar of God.
S. The God of my gladness and joy.
P. Our help ✠ is in the name of the Lord.
S. Who made heaven and earth.
P. I confess to almighty God, etc.
S. May almighty God have mercy on you, forgive you your sins, and bring you to life everlasting.
P. Amen.

The Server, bowing, says the "Confiteor."

I CONFESS to almighty God, to Blessed Mary, ever Virgin, to Blessed Michael the Archangel, to Blessed John the Baptist, to the Holy Apostles Peter and Paul, and to all the Saints, and to you, Father, that I have sinned exceedingly in thought, word and deed, *through my fault, through my fault, through my most grievous fault*. Therefore I beseech Blessed Mary, ever Virgin, Blessed Michael the Archangel, Blessed John the Baptist, the Holy Apostles Peter and Paul, and all the Saints, and you, Father, to pray to the Lord our God for me.
P. May almighty God have mercy on you, forgive you your sins, and bring you to life everlasting.
S. Amen.

MAY the almighty and merciful Lord grant us pardon, ✠ absolution, and remission of our sins. *S.* Amen.

P. Will You not, O God, give us life?
S. And shall not Your people rejoice in You?
P. Show us, O Lord, Your kindness.
S. And grant us Your salvation.
P. O Lord, hear my prayer.
S. And let my cry come to You.
P. The Lord be with you.
S. And with your spirit. *P.* Let us pray.

Going up to the altar, the Priest prays silently:

TAKE away from us our sins, O Lord, we beseech You, that we may enter with pure minds into the Holy of Holies. Through Christ our Lord. Amen.

WE BESEECH You, O Lord, by the merits of Your Saints (*he kisses the altar*) whose relics lie here, and of all the Saints: deign in Your mercy to pardon me all my sins. Amen.

THE INTROIT • Ps. 43, 23-26. 2

At the right side of the altar, the Priest says:

AWAKE! Why are You asleep, O Lord? Arise! Cast us not off forever! Why do You hide Your face, forgetting our oppression? Our bodies are pressed to the earth. Arise, O Lord, help us, and deliver us. *Ps.* O God, our ears have heard, our fathers have declared to us. Glory be to the Father, and to the Son, and to the Holy Spirit. As it was in the beginning, is now, and ever shall be, world without end. Amen. — Awake! Why are You asleep, O Lord? Arise! Cast us not off forever! Why do You hide Your face, forgetting our oppression?

Our bodies are pressed to the earth. Arise, O Lord, help us, and deliver us.

THE KYRIE

P. Lord, have mercy. *S.* Lord, have mercy. *P.* Lord, have mercy. *S.* Christ, have mercy. *P.* Christ, have mercy. *S.* Christ, have mercy. *P.* Lord, have mercy. *S.* Lord, have mercy. *P.* Lord, have mercy.

The Priest kisses the altar and turns to the people, saying:

P. The Lord be with you. *S.* And with your spirit. *P.* Let us pray.

THE PRAYER

Going to the right (Epistle) side, he says:

O GOD, You see that we do not trust in anything which we ourselves can do; mercifully grant, that by the protection of the teacher of the Gentiles, we may be defended against all adversities. Through our Lord Jesus Christ, Your Son, Who lives and reigns with You in the unity of the Holy Spirit, God, world without end. *S.* Amen.

THE EPISTLE • 2 Cor. 11, 19 – 12, 9

BRETHREN: You gladly put up with fools, because you are wise yourselves! For you suffer it if a man enslaves you, if a man devours you, if a man takes from you, if a man is arrogant, if a man slaps your face! I speak to my own shame, as though we had been weak. But wherein any man is bold — I am speaking foolishly — I also am bold. Are they Hebrews? So am I! Are they Israelites? So am I! Are they offspring of Abraham? So am I! Are they ministers of Christ? I — to speak as a fool — am more: in many more labors, in prisons more frequently, in lashes above measure, often exposed to death. From the Jews five times I received forty lashes less one. Thrice I was scourged, once I was stoned, thrice I suffered shipwreck, a night and a day I was adrift on the sea; in journeyings often, in perils from floods, in perils from robbers, in perils from my own nation, in perils from the Gentiles, in perils in the city, in perils in the wilderness, in perils in the sea, in perils from false brethren; in labor and hardships, in many sleepless nights, in hunger and thirst, in fastings often, in cold and nakedness. Besides those outer things, there is my daily pressing anxiety, the care of all the churches! Who is weak, and I am not weak? Who is made to stumble, and I am not inflamed? If I must boast, I will boast of the things that concern my weakness. The God and Father of the Lord Jesus, Who is blessed forevermore, knows that I do not lie. In Damascus the governor under King Aretas was guarding the city of the Damascenes in order to arrest me, but I was lowered in a basket through a window in the wall, and escaped his hands. If I must boast — it is not indeed expedient to do so — but I will come to visions and revelations of the Lord. I know a man in Christ who fourteen years ago — whether in the body I do not know, or out of the body I do not know, God knows — such a one was caught up to the third heaven. And I know such a man — whether in the body or out of the body I do not know, God knows — that he was caught up into paradise and heard secret words that man may not repeat. Of such a man I will boast; but of myself I will glory in nothing save in my infirmities. For if I do wish to boast, I shall not be foolish; for I shall be speaking the truth. But I forbear, lest any man should reckon me beyond what he sees in me or hears from me. And lest the greatness of the revelations should puff me up, there was given me a thorn for the flesh, a messenger of Satan, to buffet me. Concerning this I thrice besought the Lord that it might leave me. And He has said to me, "My grace is sufficient for you, for strength is made perfect in weakness." Gladly therefore I will glory in my infirmities, that the strength of Christ may dwell in me. S. Thanks be to God.

THE GRADUAL • Ps. 82, 19, 14

LET the nations know that God is Your name; You alone are the Most High over all the earth. ℣. O my God, make them like leaves in a whirlwind, like chaff before the wind.

THE TRACT • Ps. 59, 4. 6

YOU have rocked the country, O Lord, and split it open. ℣. Repair the cracks in it, for it is tottering. ℣. That they may flee out of bowshot; that Your loved ones may escape.

PRAYER BEFORE THE GOSPEL

Bowing down at the center of the altar, he says:

CLEANSE my heart and my lips, O almighty God, Who cleansed the lips of the Prophet Isaias with a burning coal. In Your gracious mercy deign so to purify me that I may worthily proclaim Your holy Gospel. Through Christ our Lord. Amen.

Lord, grant Your blessing. The Lord be in my heart and on my lips, that I may worthily and fittingly proclaim His holy Gospel. Amen.

THE GOSPEL • Luke 8, 4-15

Going to the left (Gospel) side of the altar, he says:

P. The Lord be with you. S. And with your spirit.

P. ✠ The continuation of the holy Gospel according to Saint Luke. S. Glory be to You, O Lord.

AT THAT time, when a very great crowd was gathering together and men from every town were resorting to Jesus, He said in a parable: "The sower went out to sow his seed. And as he sowed, some seed fell by the wayside and was trodden under foot, and the birds of the air ate it up. And other seed fell upon the rock, and as soon as it had sprung up it withered away, because it had no moisture. And other seed fell among thorns, and the thorns sprang up with it and choked it. And other seed fell upon good ground, and sprang up and yielded fruit a hundredfold." As He said these things He cried out, "He who has ears to hear, let him hear!" But His disciples then began to ask Him what this parable meant. He said to them, "To you it is given to know the mystery of the kingdom of God, but to the rest in parables, that 'Seeing they may not see, and hearing they may not understand.' Now the parable is this: the seed is the word of God. And those by the wayside are they who have heard; then the devil comes and takes away the word from their heart, that they may not believe and be saved. Now those upon the rock are they who, when they have heard, receive the word with joy; and these have no root, but believe for a while, and in time of temptation fall away. And that which fell among the thorns, these are they who have heard, and as they go their way are choked by the cares and riches and pleasures of life, and their fruit does not ripen. But that upon good ground, these are they who, with a right and good heart, having heard the word, hold it fast, and bear fruit in patience." *S.* Praise be to You, O Christ.

P. By the words of the Gospel, may our sins be taken away.

THE NICENE CREED

At the center of the altar, he says:

I BELIEVE in one God, the Father almighty, Maker of heaven and earth, and of all things visible and invisible. And in one Lord Jesus Christ, the Only-begotten Son of God. Born of the Father before all ages. God of God; Light of Light; true God of true God. Begotten not made; of one being with the Father; by Whom all things were made. Who for us men, and for our salvation, came down from heaven. (*Here all genuflect.*) And was made Flesh by the Holy Spirit of the Virgin Mary: AND WAS MADE MAN. He was also crucified for us, suffered under Pontius Pilate and was buried. And on the third day He rose again according to the Scriptures. And ascending into heaven, He sits at the right hand of the Father. And He shall come again in glory to judge the living and the dead; and of His kingdom there shall be no end. And I believe in the Holy Spirit, Lord and Giver of life, Who proceeds from the Father and the Son. Who together with the Father and the Son is no less adored, and glorified: Who spoke by the Prophets. And I believe in One, Holy, Catholic and Apostolic Church. I confess one Baptism for the remission of sins. And I look for the resurrection of the dead. ✠ And the life of the world to come. Amen.

THE OFFERTORY

The Priest turns to the people and says:

P. The Lord be with you. S. And with your spirit.
P. Let us pray.

THE OFFERTORY VERSE • Ps. 16, 5. 6. 7

MAKE my steps steadfast in Your paths, that my feet may not falter. Incline Your ear to me; hear my word. Show Your wondrous kindness, O Lord, Savior of those who trust in You.

The Priest now uncovers the chalice, places the host on the paten and offering it up, says:

ACCEPT, O holy Father, almighty and eternal God, this spotless host, which I, Your unworthy servant, offer to You, my living and true God, to atone for my numberless sins, offenses, and negligences; on behalf of all here present and likewise for all faithful Christians living and dead, that it may profit me and them as a means of salvation to life everlasting. Amen.

He pours wine and water into the chalice, blessing the water before it is poured.

O GOD, Who established the nature of man in wondrous dignity, and still more admirably restored it, grant that through the mystery of this water and wine, we may be made partakers of His Divinity, Who has condescended to become partaker of our humanity, Jesus Christ, Your Son, our Lord. Who lives and reigns with You in the unity of the Holy Spirit, God, world without end. Amen.

Offering up the wine, the Priest says:

WE OFFER You, O Lord, the chalice of salvation, humbly begging of Your mercy that it may arise before Your Divine Majesty, with a pleasing fragrance, for our salvation and for that of the whole world. Amen.

Bowing down, the Priest says:

IN A humble spirit and with a contrite heart, may we be accepted by You, O Lord, and may our sacrifice so be offered in Your sight this day as to please You, O Lord God.

Raising his eyes and blessing the offering, he says:

COME, O Sanctifier, almighty and eternal God, and bless ✠ this sacrifice prepared for the glory of Your holy name.

WASHING THE FINGERS

I WASH my hands in innocence, and I go around Your altar, O Lord, giving voice to my thanks, and recounting all Your wondrous deeds. O Lord, I love the house in which You dwell, the tenting-place of Your glory. Gather not my soul with those of sinners, nor with men of blood my life. On their hands are crimes, and their right hands are full of bribes. But I walk in integrity; redeem me, and have pity on me. My foot stands on level ground; in the assemblies I will bless You, O Lord. Glory be to the Father, and to the Son, and to the Holy Spirit. As it was in the beginning, is now, and ever shall be, world without end. Amen.

ACCEPT, Most Holy Trinity, this offering which we are making to You in remembrance of the Passion, Resurrection, and Ascension of Jesus Christ, our Lord; and in honor of Blessed Mary, ever Virgin, Blessed John the Baptist, the Holy Apostles Peter and Paul, and of these, and of all the Saints; that it may add to their honor and aid our salvation; and may they deign to intercede in heaven for us who honor their memory here on earth. Through the same Christ our Lord. Amen.

The Priest turns toward the people and says:

Pray, brethren, that my sacrifice and yours may become acceptable to God the Father almighty.

S. May the Lord accept this sacrifice from your hands to the praise and glory of His name, for our advantage, and that of all His holy Church.

P. Amen.

THE SECRET

MAY the sacrifice we offer You, O Lord, give us life always and defend us. Through our Lord Jesus Christ, Your Son, Who lives and reigns with You in the unity of the Holy Spirit, God.

P. World without end. *S.* Amen.

PREFACE—CANON

P. The Lord be with you. *S.* And with your spirit.

P. Lift up your hearts.

S. We have lifted them up to the Lord.

P. Let us give thanks to the Lord, our God.

S. It is fitting and just.

IT IS fitting indeed and just, right and helpful to salvation, for us always and everywhere to give thanks to You, O holy Lord, Father almighty, everlasting God, Who with Your Only-begotten Son and the Holy Spirit are one God, one Lord; not in the unity of a single person, but in the trinity of a single nature. For that which we believe on Your revelation concerning Your glory, that same we believe of Your Son, that same of the Holy Spirit, without difference or discrimination. So that in confessing the true and everlasting Godhead, we shall adore distinction in Persons, oneness in being, and equality in Majesty. This the Angels and Archangels, the Cherubim, too, and the Seraphim do

praise; day by day they cease not to cry out as with one voice, saying (*the bell is rung 3 times*):

HOLY, HOLY, HOLY, Lord God of Hosts. Heaven and earth are filled with Your glory. Hosanna in the highest. ✠ Blessed is He Who comes in the name of the Lord. Hosanna in the highest.

THE CANON OF THE MASS

THEREFORE, most gracious Father, we humbly beg of You and entreat You through Jesus Christ Your Son, our Lord, (*he kisses the altar*) to deem acceptable and bless these ✠ gifts, these ✠ offerings, these ✠ holy and unspotted oblations which, in the first place, we offer You for Your Holy Catholic Church, that You would deign to give her peace and protection, to unite and guard her throughout the world, together with Your servant N., our Pope, and N., our Bishop; and all true believers who cherish the Catholic and Apostolic Faith.

Commemoration of the Living

REMEMBER, O Lord, Your servants and handmaids, N. and N., (*name them*) and all here present, whose faith and devotion are known to You, on whose behalf we offer to You, or who themselves offer to You, this sacrifice of praise for themselves, families and friends, for the good of their souls, for their hope of salvation and deliverance from all harm, and who offer their homage to You, eternal, living and true God.

Commemoration of the Saints

IN THE unity of holy fellowship we observe the memory, first of all, of the glorious and ever

Virgin Mary, Mother of our Lord and God Jesus Christ; next, that of Your Blessed Apostles and Martyrs, Peter and Paul, Andrew, James, John, Thomas, James, Philip, Bartholomew, Matthew, Simon and Thaddeus; of Linus, Cletus, Clement, Sixtus, Cornelius, Cyprian, Lawrence, Chrysogonus, John and Paul, Cosmas and Damian, and of all Your Saints, by whose merits and prayers grant that we may be always fortified by the help of Your protection. Through the same Christ our Lord. Amen.

Spreading his hands over the oblation, he says:

GRACIOUSLY accept, then, we beseech You, O Lord, this service of our worship and that of all Your household. Provide that our days be spent in Your peace, save us from everlasting damnation, and cause us to be numbered in the flock You have chosen. Through Christ our Lord. Amen.

O GOD, deign to bless ✠ what we offer, and make it approved, ✠ effective, ✠ right, and wholly pleasing in every way, that it may become for our good, the Body ✠ and Blood ✠ of Your dearly beloved Son, Jesus Christ our Lord.

CONSECRATION—ELEVATION

WHO, the day before He suffered, took bread into His holy and venerable hands, and having raised His eyes to heaven, to You, O God, His almighty Father, giving thanks to You, He blessed it, ✠ broke it, and gave it to His disciples, saying: All of you take and eat of this:

FOR THIS IS MY BODY.

IN LIKE manner, when the supper was done, taking also this goodly chalice into His holy and venerable hands, again giving thanks to You, He

blessed ✠ it, and gave it to His disciples, saying: All of you take and drink of this:

FOR THIS IS THE CHALICE OF MY BLOOD OF THE NEW AND ETERNAL COVENANT: THE MYSTERY OF FAITH: WHICH SHALL BE SHED FOR YOU AND FOR MANY UNTO THE FORGIVENESS OF SINS.

After replacing the chalice on the corporal, he says:

As often as you shall do these things, in memory of Me shall you do them.

Offering of the Victim

MINDFUL, therefore, O Lord, not only of the blessed Passion of the same Christ, Your Son, our Lord, but also of His Resurrection from the dead, and finally His glorious Ascension into heaven, we, Your ministers, as also Your holy people, offer to Your supreme Majesty, of the gifts bestowed upon us, the pure ✠ Victim, the holy ✠ Victim, the all-perfect ✠ Victim: the holy ✠ Bread of life eternal and the Chalice ✠ of unending salvation.

AND this deign to regard with gracious and kindly attention and hold acceptable, as You deigned to accept the offerings of Abel, Your just servant, and the sacrifice of Abraham our patriarch, and that which Your chief priest Melchisedec offered to You, a holy sacrifice and a spotless victim.

MOST humbly we implore You, almighty God, bid these offerings to be brought by the hands of Your holy angel to Your altar above; before the face of Your Divine Majesty; that those of us who, by sharing in the Sacrifice of this altar, shall receive the Most Sacred ✠ Body and ✠ Blood of Your

Son, may be filled with every grace and heavenly blessing. Through the same Christ our Lord. Amen.

Commemoration of the Dead

REMEMBER also, O Lord, Your servants and handmaids, *N.* and *N.*, who have gone before us with the sign of faith, and rest in the sleep of peace. (*Here pray for the dead.*) To these, O Lord, and to all who rest in Christ, we beseech You to grant of Your goodness, a place of comfort, light and peace. Through the same Christ our Lord. Amen.

TO US sinners also, Your servants, trusting in the greatness of Your mercy, deign to grant some part and fellowship with Your Holy Apostles and Martyrs: with John, Stephen, Matthias, Barnabas, Ignatius, Alexander, Marcellinus, Peter, Felicitas, Perpetua, Agatha, Lucy, Agnes, Cecilia, Anastasia, and all Your Saints; into whose company, we implore You to admit us, not weighing our merits, but freely granting us pardon. Through Christ our Lord.

THROUGH Whom, O Lord, You always create, ✠ sanctify, ✠ fill with life, ✠ bless, and bestow upon us all good things.

The Minor Elevation

THROUGH ✠ Him, and with ✠ Him, and in ✠ Him, is to You, God the Father ✠ almighty, in the unity of the Holy ✠ Spirit, all honor and glory, world without end. *S.* Amen.

THE COMMUNION AND THANKSGIVING

Let us pray. Prompted by saving precepts, and taught by Your divine teaching, we dare to say:

OUR FATHER, Who art in heaven, hallowed be Thy name: Thy kingdom come: Thy will be done on earth as it is in heaven. Give us this day our daily bread; and forgive us our trespasses, as we forgive those who trespass against us. And lead us not into temptation: S. But deliver us from evil. *P*. Amen.

DELIVER us, we beseech You, O Lord, from all evils, past, present, and to come; and by the intercession of the Blessed and glorious Mary, ever Virgin, Mother of God, together with Your Blessed Apostles Peter and Paul, and Andrew, and all the Saints, grant of Your goodness, peace in our days, that aided by the riches of Your mercy, we may be always free from sin and safe from all disturbance.

Through the same our Lord Jesus Christ, Your Son, Who lives and reigns with You in the unity of the Holy Spirit, God, world without end.

S. Amen.

P. May the peace ✠ of the Lord be ✠ always with ✠ you.

S. And with your spirit.

The Priest puts a small particle into the chalice, saying:

May this mingling and consecration of the Body and Blood of our Lord Jesus Christ help us who receive it to life everlasting. Amen.

LAMB of God, You Who take away the sins of the world, have mercy on us.

Lamb of God, You Who take away the sins of the world, have mercy on us.

Lamb of God, You Who take away the sins of the world, grant us peace.

PRAYERS BEFORE HOLY COMMUNION

Then inclining toward the altar, he says:

O LORD Jesus Christ, Who said to Your Apostles: "Peace I leave with you, My peace I give to you," regard not my sins but the faith of Your Church, and deign to give her peace and unity according to Your Will: Who live and reign, God, world without end. Amen.

O LORD Jesus Christ, Son of the living God, Who, by the will of the Father, with the co-operation of the Holy Spirit, have by Your death given life to the world, deliver me by this Your Most Sacred Body and Blood from all my sins and from every evil. Make me always cling to Your commandments, and never permit me to be separated from You. Who with the same God the Father and the Holy Spirit, live and reign, God, world without end. Amen.

LET not the partaking of Your Body, O Lord Jesus Christ, which I, though unworthy, presume to receive, turn to my judgment and condemnation; but through Your goodness, may it become a safeguard and an effective remedy, both of soul and body. Who live and reign with God the Father, in the unity of the Holy Spirit, God, world without end. Amen.

COMMUNION OF THE PRIEST

I WILL take the Bread of heaven, and call upon the name of the Lord.

Lord, I am not worthy that You should come under my roof; but only say the word, and my soul will be healed. (3 *times.*)

MAY the Body of our Lord Jesus Christ preserve my soul to life everlasting. Amen.

What return shall I make to the Lord for all He has given me? I will take the Chalice of salvation, and I will call upon the name of the Lord. Praising will I call upon the Lord and I shall be saved from my enemies.

Making the Sign of the Cross with the chalice, he says:

MAY the Blood of our Lord Jesus Christ preserve my soul to life everlasting. Amen.

The Priest reverently consumes the Precious Blood.

COMMUNION OF THE FAITHFUL

The Server and people say the "Confiteor."

P. May almighty God have mercy on you, forgive you your sins, and bring you to life everlasting. *S.* Amen.

P. May the almighty and merciful Lord grant you pardon, ✠ absolution and remission of your sins. *S.* Amen.

Behold the Lamb of God, behold Him Who takes away the sins of the world.

Lord, I am not worthy that You should come under my roof; but only say the word, and my soul will be healed. (3 *times.*)

The Priest says to each communicant:

May the Body of our Lord Jesus Christ preserve your soul to life everlasting. Amen.

The Priest purifies the chalice with wine, saying:

WHAT has passed our lips as food, O Lord, may we possess in purity of heart, that what is given to us in time, be our healing for eternity.

MAY Your Body, O Lord, which I have eaten, and Your Blood which I have drunk, cleave to my very soul, and grant that no trace of sin be found in me, whom these pure and holy mysteries have renewed. Who live and reign, world without end. Amen.

THE COMMUNION • Ps. 42, 4

I WILL go in to the altar of God, the God of my gladness and joy.

The Priest, turning to the people, says:

P. The Lord be with you. *S.* And with your spirit.
P. Let us pray.

THE POSTCOMMUNION

WE HUMBLY beseech You, almighty God, to grant that those whom You refresh with Your sacraments, may serve You worthily by a life well pleasing to You. Through our Lord Jesus Christ, Your Son, Who lives and reigns, etc. *S.* Amen.

FINAL PRAYERS

The Priest turns again to the people, and says:

P. The Lord be with you. *S.* And with your spirit.
P. Let us bless the Lord. *S.* Thanks be to God.

MAY the tribute of my worship be pleasing to You, Most Holy Trinity, and grant that the sacrifice which I, all unworthy, have offered in the presence of Your Majesty, may be acceptable to You, and through Your mercy obtain forgiveness for me and all for whom I have offered it. Through Christ our Lord. Amen.

THE LAST BLESSING

MAY almighty God bless you: ✠ the Father, and the Son, and the Holy Spirit. *S.* Amen.

The Last Gospel and Prayers after Low Mass are conveniently placed inside the back cover.

✠

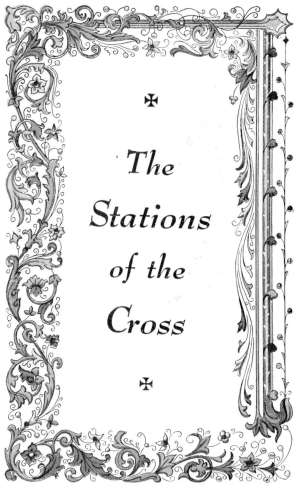

The Stations of the Cross

✠

(T-720)

THE WAY OF THE CROSS

THE Way of the Cross is a devotion in which we accompany, in spirit, our Blessed Lord in His sorrowful journey to Calvary, and devoutly meditate on His sufferings and death.

INDULGENCES

Those who devoutly make the Stations of the Cross, may gain a plenary indulgence. An added plenary indulgence with the reception of Holy Communion on the same day, or within a month after having made the Stations of the Cross 10 times. An indulgence of 10 years for each Station if the entire Way of the Cross is unavoidably interrupted.

Those who are lawfully hindered from making the Stations of the Cross, may gain the same indulgences if they hold a Crucifix, blessed for this purpose, in their hand, and piously recite twenty times Our Father, Hail Mary, *and* Glory be, *one for each Station, five for the five Sacred Wounds of our Lord, and one for the intention of the Holy Father. If prevented from doing this, an indulgence of 10 years for each recitation of* Our Father, Hail Mary, *and* Glory be.

The sick may gain the same indulgences if they devoutly kiss or fix their gaze upon a Crucifix, blessed for this very purpose, held before them, and recite, if possible, a short prayer or ejaculation in memory of the Passion and Death of our Lord, Jesus Christ. (No. 194.)

All that is required to gain the indulgences is to go from Station to Station and meditate on the Passion. No vocal prayers are necessary. However, the meditations printed below each Station may be helpful.

FIRST STATION

JESUS IS CONDEMNED TO DEATH

O Jesus, You desired to die for me that I may receive the supernatural life, sanctifying grace, and become a child of God. How precious must be that life. Teach me to appreciate it more and more.

EIGHTH STATION

JESUS SPEAKS TO THE WOMEN

O Jesus, You told the women of Jerusalem to weep rather over themselves. Make me weep over my sins which caused Your sufferings and the loss of my friendship with You.

NINTH STATION

JESUS FALLS A THIRD TIME

O Jesus, I see You bowed to the earth, enduring the pains of extreme exhaustion. Grant that I never yield to despair but come to You for help in hardship and spiritual distress.

TENTH STATION

JESUS IS STRIPPED OF HIS GARMENTS

O Jesus, You permitted Yourself to be stripped of Your garments. Grant that I may sacrifice all my attachments rather than to imperil the divine life of my soul.

ELEVENTH STATION

JESUS IS NAILED TO THE CROSS

O Jesus, how could I complain to be nailed to God's commandments which are given for my salvation, when I see You nailed to the Cross. Strengthen my faith and increase my love for You.

TWELFTH STATION

JESUS DIES ON THE CROSS

O Jesus, dying on the Cross, You preached love and forgiveness. May I be thankful that You have made me a child of God. Help me to forgive all those who have injured me.

THIRTEENTH STATION

JESUS IS TAKEN FROM THE CROSS

O Jesus, a sword of grief pierced Your Mother's heart when You were lying lifeless in her arms. Grant me through her intercession to lead the life of a loyal child of Mary.

FOURTEENTH STATION

JESUS IS LAID IN THE SEPULCHRE

O Jesus, Your enemies triumphed when they sealed Your tomb. But Your eternal triumph began on Easter morning. Strengthen my good will to live for You until the divine life of my soul will be manifested in the bliss of heaven.

"Jesus, Son of David, have mercy on me!"

QUINQUAGESIMA SUNDAY

The Gospel of this Sunday affords us a good occasion to ask the Master to give us the power of sight, to lift up our eyes from the transitory, and catch a glimpse of eternal happiness. (PURPLE VESTMENTS)

PRAYERS AT THE FOOT OF THE ALTAR

IN THE name of the Father, ✠ and of the Son, and of the Holy Spirit. Amen.

Priest. I will go in to the altar of God.

Server. The God of my gladness and joy.

Psalm 42

DO ME justice, O God, and fight my fight against a faithless people; from the deceitful and impious man rescue me.

S. For You, O God, are my strength. Why do You keep me so far away? Why must I go about in mourning, with the enemy oppressing me?

P. Send forth Your light and Your fidelity; they shall lead me on and bring me to Your holy mountain, to Your dwelling-place.

720-12

S. Then will I go in to the altar of God, the God of my gladness and joy.
P. Then will I give You thanks upon the harp, O God, my God. Why are you so downcast, O my soul? Why do you sigh within me?
S. Hope in God! For I shall again be thanking Him in the presence of my Savior and my God.
P. Glory be to the Father, and to the Son, and to the Holy Spirit.
S. As it was in the beginning, is now, and ever shall be, world without end. Amen.
P. I will go in to the altar of God.
S. The God of my gladness and joy.
P. Our help ✠ is in the name of the Lord.
S. Who made heaven and earth.
P. I confess to almighty God, etc.
S. May almighty God have mercy on you, forgive you your sins, and bring you to life everlasting.
P. Amen.

The Server, bowing, says the "Confiteor."

I CONFESS to almighty God, to Blessed Mary, ever Virgin, to Blessed Michael the Archangel, to Blessed John the Baptist, to the Holy Apostles Peter and Paul, and to all the Saints, and to you, Father, that I have sinned exceedingly in thought, word and deed, *through my fault, through my fault, through my most grievous fault*. Therefore I beseech Blessed Mary, ever Virgin, Blessed Michael the Archangel, Blessed John the Baptist, the Holy Apostles Peter and Paul, and all the Saints, and you, Father, to pray to the Lord our God for me.
P. May almighty God have mercy on you, forgive you your sins, and bring you to life everlasting.
S. Amen.

MAY the almighty and merciful Lord grant us pardon, ✠ absolution, and remission of our sins. *S.* Amen.
P. Will You not, O God, give us life?
S. And shall not Your people rejoice in You?
P. Show us, O Lord, Your kindness.
S. And grant us Your salvation.
P. O Lord, hear my prayer.
S. And let my cry come to You.
P. The Lord be with you.
S. And with your spirit. *P.* Let us pray.

Going up to the altar, the Priest prays silently:

TAKE away from us our sins, O Lord, we beseech You, that we may enter with pure minds into the Holy of Holies. Through Christ our Lord. Amen.

WE BESEECH You, O Lord, by the merits of Your Saints (*he kisses the altar*) whose relics lie here, and of all the Saints: deign in Your mercy to pardon me all my sins. Amen.

THE INTROIT • Ps. 30, 3. 4. 2

At the right side of the altar, the Priest says:

BE MY rock of refuge, O God, a stronghold to give me safety. You are my rock and my fortress; for Your name's sake You will lead and guide me. *Ps.* In You, O Lord, I take refuge; let me never be put to shame. In Your justice rescue me and deliver me. Glory be to the Father, and to the Son, and to the Holy Spirit. As it was in the beginning, is now, and ever shall be, world without end. Amen. — Be my rock of refuge, O God, a stronghold to give me safety. You are my rock and my fortress; for Your name's sake You will lead and guide me.

THE KYRIE

P. Lord, have mercy. *S*. Lord, have mercy. *P*. Lord, have mercy. *S*. Christ, have mercy. *P*. Christ, have mercy. *S*. Christ, have mercy. *P*. Lord, have mercy. *S*. Lord, have mercy. *P*. Lord, have mercy.

The Priest kisses the altar and turns to the people, saying:

P. The Lord be with you. *S*. And with your spirit. *P*. Let us pray.

THE PRAYER

Going to the right (Epistle) side, he says:

WE BESEECH You, O Lord, graciously hear our prayers; and having freed us from the bonds of our sins, guard us from all adversity. Through our Lord Jesus Christ, Your Son, Who lives and reigns with You in the unity of the Holy Spirit, God, world without end. *S*. Amen.

THE EPISTLE • 1 Cor. 13, 1-13

BRETHREN: If I should speak with the tongues of men and of angels, but do not have charity, I have become as sounding brass or a tinkling cymbal. And if I have prophecy and know all mysteries and all knowledge, and if I have all faith so as to remove mountains, yet do not have charity, I am nothing. And if I distribute all my goods to feed the poor, and if I deliver my body to be burned, yet do not have charity, it profits me nothing. Charity is patient, is kind; charity does not envy, is not pretentious, is not puffed up, is not ambitious, is not self-seeking, is not provoked; thinks no evil, does not rejoice over wickedness, but rejoices with the truth; bears with all things, believes all things, hopes all things, endures all things. Charity never fails, whereas prophecies will disappear, and tongues will cease, and knowledge will be destroyed. For we know in part and we prophesy in part; but when that which is perfect has come, that which is imperfect will be done away with. When I was a child, I spoke as a child, I felt as a child, I thought as a child. Now that I have become a man, I have put away the things of a child. We see now through a mirror in an obscure manner, but then face to face. Now I know in part, but then I shall know even as I have been known. So there abide faith, hope and charity, these three; but the greatest of these is charity. S. Thanks be to God.

THE GRADUAL • Ps. 76, 15. 16

YOU are the God Who alone works wonders; among the peoples You have made known Your power. ℣. With Your strong arm You delivered Your people, the sons of Israel and Joseph.

THE TRACT • Ps. 99, 1-2

SING joyfully to God, all you lands; serve the Lord with gladness. ℣. Come before Him with joyful song; know that the Lord is God. ℣. He made us, His we are; His people, the flock He tends.

PRAYER BEFORE THE GOSPEL

Bowing down at the center of the altar, he says:

CLEANSE my heart and my lips, O almighty God, Who cleansed the lips of the Prophet Isaias with a burning coal. In Your gracious mercy deign so to purify me that I may worthily proclaim Your holy Gospel. Through Christ our Lord. Amen.

Lord, grant Your blessing. The Lord be in my heart and on my lips, that I may worthily and fittingly proclaim His holy Gospel. Amen.

THE GOSPEL • Luke 18, 31-43

Going to the left (Gospel) side of the altar, he says:

P. The Lord be with you. *S.* And with your spirit.

P. ✠ The continuation of the holy Gospel according to Saint Luke. *S.* Glory be to You, O Lord.

AT THAT time, Jesus taking to Himself the Twelve said to them, "Behold, we are going up to Jerusalem, and all things that have been written by the prophets concerning the Son of Man will be accomplished. For He will be delivered to the Gentiles, and will be mocked and scourged and spit upon; and after they have scourged Him, they will put Him to death; and on the third day He will rise again." And they understood none of these things and this saying was hidden from them, neither did they get to know the things that were being said. Now it came to pass as He drew near to Jericho, that a certain blind man was sitting by the wayside, begging; but hearing a crowd passing by, he inquired what this might be. And they told him that Jesus of Nazareth was passing by. And he cried out, saying, "Jesus, Son of David, have mercy on me!" And they who went in front angrily tried to silence him. But he cried out all the louder, "Son of David, have mercy on me!" Then Jesus stopped and commanded that he should be brought to Him. And when he drew near, He asked him, saying, "What would you have Me do for you?" And he said, "Lord, that I may see." And Jesus said to him, "Receive your sight, your faith has saved you." And at once he received his sight, and followed Him, glorifying God. And all the people upon seeing it gave praise to God. *S.* Praise be to You, O Christ.

P. By the words of the Gospel, may our sins be taken away.

THE NICENE CREED

At the center of the altar, he says:

I BELIEVE in one God, the Father almighty, Maker of heaven and earth, and of all things visible and invisible. And in one Lord Jesus Christ, the Only-begotten Son of God. Born of the Father before all ages. God of God; Light of Light; true God of true God. Begotten not made; of one being with the Father; by Whom all things were made. Who for us men, and for our salvation, came down from heaven. (*Here all genuflect.*) And was made Flesh by the Holy Spirit of the Virgin Mary: AND WAS MADE MAN. He was also crucified for us, suffered under Pontius Pilate and was buried. And on the third day He rose again according to the Scriptures. And ascending into heaven, He sits at the right hand of the Father. And He shall come again in glory to judge the living and the dead; and of His kingdom there shall be no end. And I believe in the Holy Spirit, Lord and Giver of life, Who proceeds from the Father and the Son. Who together with the Father and the Son is no less adored, and glorified: Who spoke by the Prophets. And I believe in One, Holy, Catholic and Apostolic Church. I confess one Baptism for the remission of sins. And I look for the resurrection of the dead. ✠ And the life of the world to come. Amen.

THE OFFERTORY

The Priest turns to the people and says:

P. The Lord be with you. *S.* And with your spirit.
P. Let us pray.

THE OFFERTORY VERSE • Ps. 118, 12-13

BLESSED are You, O Lord; teach me Your statutes. With my lips I declare all the ordinances of Your mouth.

The Priest now uncovers the chalice, places the host on the paten and offering it up, says:

ACCEPT, O holy Father, almighty and eternal God, this spotless host, which I, Your unworthy servant, offer to You, my living and true God, to atone for my numberless sins, offenses, and negligences; on behalf of all here present and likewise for all faithful Christians living and dead, that it may profit me and them as a means of salvation to life everlasting. Amen.

He pours wine and water into the chalice, blessing the water before it is poured.

O GOD, Who established the nature of man in wondrous dignity, and still more admirably restored it, grant that through the mystery of this water and wine, we may be made partakers of His Divinity, Who has condescended to become partaker of our humanity, Jesus Christ, Your Son, our Lord. Who lives and reigns with You in the unity of the Holy Spirit, God, world without end. Amen.

Offering up the wine, the Priest says:

WE OFFER You, O Lord, the chalice of salvation, humbly begging of Your mercy that it may arise before Your Divine Majesty, with a pleasing fragrance, for our salvation and for that of the whole world. Amen.

Bowing down, the Priest says:

IN A humble spirit and with a contrite heart, may we be accepted by You, O Lord, and may our

sacrifice so be offered in Your sight this day as to please You, O Lord God.

Raising his eyes and blessing the offering, he says:

COME, O Sanctifier, almighty and eternal God, and bless ✠ this sacrifice prepared for the glory of Your holy name.

WASHING THE FINGERS

I WASH my hands in innocence, and I go around Your altar, O Lord, giving voice to my thanks, and recounting all Your wondrous deeds. O Lord, I love the house in which You dwell, the tenting-place of Your glory. Gather not my soul with those of sinners, nor with men of blood my life. On their hands are crimes, and their right hands are full of bribes. But I walk in integrity; redeem me, and have pity on me. My foot stands on level ground; in the assemblies I will bless You, O Lord. Glory be to the Father, and to the Son, and to the Holy Spirit. As it was in the beginning, is now, and ever shall be, world without end. Amen.

ACCEPT, Most Holy Trinity, this offering which we are making to You in remembrance of the Passion, Resurrection, and Ascension of Jesus Christ, our Lord; and in honor of Blessed Mary, ever Virgin, Blessed John the Baptist, the Holy Apostles Peter and Paul, and of these, and of all the Saints; that it may add to their honor and aid our salvation; and may they deign to intercede in heaven for us who honor their memory here on earth. Through the same Christ our Lord. Amen.

The Priest turns toward the people and says:

Pray, brethren, that my sacrifice and yours may become acceptable to God the Father almighty.

S. May the Lord accept this sacrifice from your hands to the praise and glory of His name, for our advantage, and that of all His holy Church.
P. Amen.

THE SECRET

MAY this offering, we beseech You, O Lord, cleanse away our sins, and sanctify the bodies and minds of Your servants for the celebration of this sacrifice. Through our Lord Jesus Christ, Your Son, Who lives and reigns with You in the unity of the Holy Spirit, God.
P. World without end. *S.* Amen.

PREFACE—CANON

P. The Lord be with you. *S.* And with your spirit.
P. Lift up your hearts.
S. We have lifted them up to the Lord.
P. Let us give thanks to the Lord, our God.
S. It is fitting and just.

IT IS fitting indeed and just, right and helpful to salvation, for us always and everywhere to give thanks to You, O holy Lord, Father almighty, everlasting God, Who with Your Only-begotten Son and the Holy Spirit are one God, one Lord; not in the unity of a single person, but in the trinity of a single nature. For that which we believe on Your revelation concerning Your glory, that same we believe of Your Son, that same of the Holy Spirit, without difference or discrimination. So that in confessing the true and everlasting Godhead, we shall adore distinction in Persons, oneness in being, and equality in Majesty. This the Angels and Archangels, the Cherubim, too, and the Seraphim do praise; day by day they cease not to cry out as with one voice, saying (*the bell is rung* 3 *times*):

HOLY, HOLY, HOLY, Lord God of Hosts. Heaven and earth are filled with Your glory. Hosanna in the highest. ✠ Blessed is He Who comes in the name of the Lord. Hosanna in the highest.

THE CANON OF THE MASS

THEREFORE, most gracious Father, we humbly beg of You and entreat You through Jesus Christ Your Son, our Lord, (*he kisses the altar*) to deem acceptable and bless these ✠ gifts, these ✠ offerings, these ✠ holy and unspotted oblations which, in the first place, we offer You for Your Holy Catholic Church, that You would deign to give her peace and protection, to unite and guard her throughout the world, together with Your servant N., our Pope, and N., our Bishop; and all true believers who cherish the Catholic and Apostolic Faith.

Commemoration of the Living

REMEMBER, O Lord, Your servants and handmaids, N. and N., (*name them*) and all here present, whose faith and devotion are known to You, on whose behalf we offer to You, or who themselves offer to You, this sacrifice of praise for themselves, families and friends, for the good of their souls, for their hope of salvation and deliverance from all harm, and who offer their homage to You, eternal, living and true God.

Commemoration of the Saints

IN THE unity of holy fellowship we observe the memory, first of all, of the glorious and ever Virgin Mary, Mother of our Lord and God Jesus Christ; next, that of Your Blessed Apostles and

Martyrs, Peter and Paul, Andrew, James, John, Thomas, James, Philip, Bartholomew, Matthew, Simon and Thaddeus; of Linus, Cletus, Clement, Sixtus, Cornelius, Cyprian, Lawrence, Chrysogonus, John and Paul, Cosmas and Damian, and of all Your Saints, by whose merits and prayers grant that we may be always fortified by the help of Your protection. Through the same Christ our Lord. Amen.

Spreading his hands over the oblation, he says:

GRACIOUSLY accept, then, we beseech You, O Lord, this service of our worship and that of all Your household. Provide that our days be spent in Your peace, save us from everlasting damnation, and cause us to be numbered in the flock You have chosen. Through Christ our Lord. Amen.

O GOD, deign to bless ✠ what we offer, and make it approved, ✠ effective, ✠ right, and wholly pleasing in every way, that it may become for our good, the Body ✠ and Blood ✠ of Your dearly beloved Son, Jesus Christ our Lord.

CONSECRATION—ELEVATION

WHO, the day before He suffered, took bread into His holy and venerable hands, and having raised His eyes to heaven, to You, O God, His almighty Father, giving thanks to You, He blessed it, ✠ broke it, and gave it to His disciples, saying: All of you take and eat of this:

FOR THIS IS MY BODY.

IN LIKE manner, when the supper was done, taking also this goodly chalice into His holy and venerable hands, again giving thanks to You, He blessed ✠ it, and gave it to His disciples, saying: All of you take and drink of this:

FOR THIS IS THE CHALICE OF MY BLOOD OF THE NEW AND ETERNAL COVENANT: THE MYSTERY OF FAITH: WHICH SHALL BE SHED FOR YOU AND FOR MANY UNTO THE FORGIVENESS OF SINS.

After replacing the chalice on the corporal, he says:

As often as you shall do these things, in memory of Me shall you do them.

Offering of the Victim

MINDFUL, therefore, O Lord, not only of the blessed Passion of the same Christ, Your Son, our Lord, but also of His Resurrection from the dead, and finally His glorious Ascension into heaven, we, Your ministers, as also Your holy people, offer to Your supreme Majesty, of the gifts bestowed upon us, the pure ✠ Victim, the holy ✠ Victim, the all-perfect ✠ Victim: the holy ✠ Bread of life eternal and the Chalice ✠ of unending salvation.

AND this deign to regard with gracious and kindly attention and hold acceptable, as You deigned to accept the offerings of Abel, Your just servant, and the sacrifice of Abraham our patriarch, and that which Your chief priest Melchisedec offered to You, a holy sacrifice and a spotless victim.

MOST humbly we implore You, almighty God, bid these offerings to be brought by the hands of Your holy angel to Your altar above; before the face of Your Divine Majesty; that those of us who, by sharing in the Sacrifice of this altar, shall receive the Most Sacred ✠ Body and ✠ Blood of Your Son, may be filled with every grace and heavenly blessing. Through the same Christ our Lord. Amen.

Commemoration of the Dead

REMEMBER also, O Lord, Your servants and handmaids, *N.* and *N.*, who have gone before us with the sign of faith, and rest in the sleep of peace. (*Here pray for the dead.*) To these, O Lord, and to all who rest in Christ, we beseech You to grant of Your goodness, a place of comfort, light and peace. Through the same Christ our Lord. Amen.

TO US sinners also, Your servants, trusting in the greatness of Your mercy, deign to grant some part and fellowship with Your Holy Apostles and Martyrs: with John, Stephen, Matthias, Barnabas, Ignatius, Alexander, Marcellinus, Peter, Felicitas, Perpetua, Agatha, Lucy, Agnes, Cecilia, Anastasia, and all Your Saints; into whose company, we implore You to admit us, not weighing our merits, but freely granting us pardon. Through Christ our Lord.

THROUGH Whom, O Lord, You always create, ✠ sanctify, ✠ fill with life, ✠ bless, and bestow upon us all good things.

The Minor Elevation

THROUGH ✠ Him, and with ✠ Him, and in ✠ Him, is to You, God the Father ✠ almighty, in the unity of the Holy ✠ Spirit, all honor and glory, world without end. *S.* Amen.

THE COMMUNION AND THANKSGIVING

Let us pray. Prompted by saving precepts, and taught by Your divine teaching, we dare to say:

OUR FATHER, Who art in heaven, hallowed be Thy name: Thy kingdom come: Thy will be

done on earth as it is in heaven. Give us this day our daily bread; and forgive us our trespasses, as we forgive those who trespass against us. And lead us not into temptation: *S*. But deliver us from evil. *P*. Amen.

DELIVER us, we beseech You, O Lord, from all evils, past, present, and to come; and by the intercession of the Blessed and glorious Mary, ever Virgin, Mother of God, together with Your Blessed Apostles Peter and Paul, and Andrew, and all the Saints, grant of Your goodness, peace in our days, that aided by the riches of Your mercy, we may be always free from sin and safe from all disturbance.

Through the same our Lord Jesus Christ, Your Son, Who lives and reigns with You in the unity of the Holy Spirit, God, world without end. *S*. Amen.
P. May the peace ✠ of the Lord be ✠ always with ✠ you. *S*. And with your spirit.

The Priest puts a small particle into the chalice, saying:

May this mingling and consecration of the Body and Blood of our Lord Jesus Christ help us who receive it to life everlasting. Amen.

LAMB of God, You Who take away the sins of the world, have mercy on us.
Lamb of God, You Who take away the sins of the world, have mercy on us.
Lamb of God, You Who take away the sins of the world, grant us peace.

PRAYERS BEFORE HOLY COMMUNION

Then inclining toward the altar, he says:

O LORD Jesus Christ, Who said to Your Apostles: "Peace I leave with you, My peace I give

to you," regard not my sins but the faith of Your Church, and deign to give her peace and unity according to Your Will: Who live and reign, God, world without end. Amen.

O LORD Jesus Christ, Son of the living God, Who, by the will of the Father, with the co-operation of the Holy Spirit, have by Your death given life to the world, deliver me by this Your Most Sacred Body and Blood from all my sins and from every evil. Make me always cling to Your commandments, and never permit me to be separated from You. Who with the same God the Father and the Holy Spirit, live and reign, God, world without end. Amen.

LET not the partaking of Your Body, O Lord Jesus Christ, which I, though unworthy, presume to receive, turn to my judgment and condemnation; but through Your goodness, may it become a safeguard and an effective remedy, both of soul and body. Who live and reign with God the Father, in the unity of the Holy Spirit, God, world without end. Amen.

COMMUNION OF THE PRIEST

I WILL take the Bread of heaven, and call upon the name of the Lord.

Lord, I am not worthy that You should come under my roof; but only say the word, and my soul will be healed. (3 *times.*)

Making the Sign of the Cross with the Host, he says:

MAY the Body of our Lord Jesus Christ preserve my soul to life everlasting. Amen.

What return shall I make to the Lord for all He has given me? I will take the Chalice of salvation,

and I will call upon the name of the Lord. Praising will I call upon the Lord and I shall be saved from my enemies.

Making the Sign of the Cross with the chalice, he says:

MAY the Blood of our Lord Jesus Christ preserve my soul to life everlasting. Amen.

The Priest reverently consumes the Precious Blood.

COMMUNION OF THE FAITHFUL

The Server and people say the "Confiteor."

P. May almighty God have mercy on you, forgive you your sins, and bring you to life everlasting. *S.* Amen.

P. May the almighty and merciful Lord grant you pardon, ✠ absolution and remission of your sins. *S.* Amen.

Holding up a Sacred Host, the Priest says:

Behold the Lamb of God, behold Him Who takes away the sins of the world.

Lord, I am not worthy that You should come under my roof; but only say the word, and my soul will be healed. (3 *times.*)

The Priest says to each communicant:

May the Body of our Lord Jesus Christ preserve your soul to life everlasting. Amen.

The Priest purifies the chalice with wine, saying:

WHAT has passed our lips as food, O Lord, may we possess in purity of heart, that what is given to us in time, be our healing for eternity.

He purifies his fingers with wine and water, saying:

MAY Your Body, O Lord, which I have eaten, and Your Blood which I have drunk, cleave to my very soul, and grant that no trace of sin be

found in me, whom these pure and holy mysteries have renewed. Who live and reign, world without end. Amen.

THE COMMUNION • Ps. 77, 29-30

THEY ate and were wholly surfeited; the Lord had brought them what they craved: they were not defrauded of that which they craved.

The Priest, turning to the people, says:

P. The Lord be with you. *S.* And with your spirit.
P. Let us pray.

THE POSTCOMMUNION

WE BESEECH You, almighty God, that we who have received celestial food, may be defended by it against all adversities. Through our Lord Jesus Christ, Your Son, Who lives and reigns with You, etc. *S.* Amen.

FINAL PRAYERS

P. The Lord be with you. *S.* And with your spirit.
P. Let us bless the Lord. *S.* Thanks be to God.

MAY the tribute of my worship be pleasing to You, Most Holy Trinity, and grant that the sacrifice which I, all unworthy, have offered in the presence of Your Majesty, may be acceptable to You, and through Your mercy obtain forgiveness for me and all for whom I have offered it. Through Christ our Lord. Amen.

THE LAST BLESSING

MAY almighty God bless you: ✠ the Father, and the Son, and the Holy Spirit. *S.* Amen.

The Last Gospel and Prayers after Low Mass are conveniently placed inside the back cover.

"The Lord your God shall you worship."

FIRST SUNDAY IN LENT

As Christ Himself was tempted by Satan, so are we. Our strength to resist lies in fasting, in guarding and controlling our senses, in almsgiving, in prayers, and in uniting ourselves with Christ in Holy Mass and Communion. (PURPLE VESTMENTS)

PRAYERS AT THE FOOT OF THE ALTAR

IN THE name of the Father, ✠ and of the Son, and of the Holy Spirit. Amen.

Priest. I will go in to the altar of God.

Server. The God of my gladness and joy.

Psalm 42

DO ME justice, O God, and fight my fight against a faithless people; from the deceitful and impious man rescue me.

S. For You, O God, are my strength. Why do You keep me so far away? Why must I go about in mourning, with the enemy oppressing me?

P. Send forth Your light and Your fidelity; they shall lead me on and bring me to Your holy mountain, to Your dwelling-place.

S. Then will I go in to the altar of God, the God of my gladness and joy.
P. Then will I give You thanks upon the harp, O God, my God. Why are you so downcast, O my soul? Why do you sigh within me?
S. Hope in God! For I shall again be thanking Him in the presence of my Savior and my God.
P. Glory be to the Father, and to the Son, and to the Holy Spirit.
S. As it was in the beginning, is now, and ever shall be, world without end. Amen.
P. I will go in to the altar of God.
S. The God of my gladness and joy.
P. Our help ✠ is in the name of the Lord.
S. Who made heaven and earth.
P. I confess to almighty God, etc.
S. May almighty God have mercy on you, forgive you your sins, and bring you to life everlasting.
P. Amen.

The Server, bowing, says the "Confiteor."

I CONFESS to almighty God, to Blessed Mary, ever Virgin, to Blessed Michael the Archangel, to Blessed John the Baptist, to the Holy Apostles Peter and Paul, and to all the Saints, and to you, Father, that I have sinned exceedingly in thought, word and deed, *through my fault, through my fault, through my most grievous fault.* Therefore I beseech Blessed Mary, ever Virgin, Blessed Michael the Archangel, Blessed John the Baptist, the Holy Apostles Peter and Paul, and all the Saints, and you, Father, to pray to the Lord our God for me.
P. May almighty God have mercy on you, forgive you your sins, and bring you to life everlasting.
S. Amen.

MAY the almighty and merciful Lord grant us pardon, ✠ absolution, and remission of our sins. *S.* Amen.

P. Will You not, O God, give us life?
S. And shall not Your people rejoice in You?
P. Show us, O Lord, Your kindness.
S. And grant us Your salvation.
P. O Lord, hear my prayer.
S. And let my cry come to You.
P. The Lord be with you.
S. And with your spirit. *P.* Let us pray.

Going up to the altar, the Priest prays silently:

TAKE away from us our sins, O Lord, we beseech You, that we may enter with pure minds into the Holy of Holies. Through Christ our Lord. Amen.

WE BESEECH You, O Lord, by the merits of Your Saints (*he kisses the altar*) whose relics lie here, and of all the Saints: deign in Your mercy to pardon me all my sins. Amen.

THE INTROIT • Ps. 90, 15. 16. 1

At the right side of the altar, the Priest says:

HE SHALL call upon me, and I will answer him; I will deliver him and glorify him; with length of days I will gratify him. *Ps.* You who dwell in the shelter of the Most High, shall abide in the shadow of the almighty. Glory be to the Father, and to the Son, and to the Holy Spirit. As it was in the beginning, is now, and ever shall be, world without end. Amen. — He shall call upon Me, and I will answer him; I will deliver him and glorify him; with length of days I will gratify him.

THE KYRIE

P. Lord, have mercy. *S.* Lord, have mercy. *P.* Lord, have mercy. *S.* Christ, have mercy. *P.* Christ, have mercy. *S.* Christ, have mercy. *P.* Lord, have mercy. *S.* Lord, have mercy. *P.* Lord, have mercy.

The Priest kisses the altar and turns to the people, saying:

P. The Lord be with you. *S.* And with your spirit. *P.* Let us pray.

THE PRAYER

Going to the right (Epistle) side, he says:

O GOD, You purify Your Church by the yearly observance of Lent; grant to Your family that what we endeavor to obtain from You by abstinence, we may secure by good works. Through our Lord Jesus Christ, Your Son, Who lives and reigns with You in the unity of the Holy Spirit, God, world without end. *S.* Amen.

THE EPISTLE · 2 Cor. 6, 1-10

BRETHREN: We entreat you not to receive the grace of God in vain. For He says, "In an acceptable time I have heard you, and in the day of salvation I have helped you." Behold, now is the acceptable time; behold, now is the day of salvation! We give no offense to anyone, that our ministry may not be blamed. On the contrary, let us conduct ourselves in all circumstances as God's ministers, in much patience; in tribulations, in hardships, in distresses; in stripes, in imprisonments, in tumults; in labors, in sleepless nights, in fastings; in innocence, in knowledge, in long-sufferings; in kindness, in the Holy Spirit, in unaffected love; in the word of truth, in the power of God; with the armor of justice on the right hand and on the left; in honor and dishonor, in evil report and good report; as deceivers and yet truthful, as unknown and yet well known, as dying, and behold, we live, as chastised but not killed, as sorrowful yet always rejoicing, as poor yet enriching many, as having nothing yet possessing all things. S. Thanks be to God.

THE GRADUAL • Ps. 90, 11-12

TO HIS angels God has given command about you, that they guard you in all your ways. ℣. Upon their hands they shall bear you up, lest you dash your foot against a stone.

THE TRACT • Ps. 90, 1-7. 11-16

YOU who dwell in the shelter of the Most High, shall abide in the shadow of the almighty. ℣. Say to the Lord, "My refuge and my fortress, my God, in Whom I trust." ℣. For He will rescue you from the snare of the fowler, from the destroying pestilence. ℣. With His pinions He will cover you, and under His wings you shall take refuge. ℣. His faithfulness is a buckler and a shield; you shall not fear the terror of the night. ℣. Nor the arrow that flies by day; nor the pestilence that roams in darkness; nor the devastating plague at noon. ℣. Though a thousand fall at your side, ten thousand at your right side, near you it shall not come. ℣. For to His angels He has given command about you, that they may guard you in all your ways. ℣. Upon their hands they shall bear you up, lest you dash your foot against a stone. ℣. You shall tread upon the asp and the viper; you shall trample down the lion and the dragon. ℣. Because he clings to Me, I will deliver him; I will set him on high because he acknowledges My name. ℣. He shall call upon Me, and I will answer him; I will be with him in distress. ℣. I will deliver him and glorify him; with length of days I will gratify him and will show him My salvation.

PRAYER BEFORE THE GOSPEL

Bowing down at the center of the altar, he says:

CLEANSE my heart and my lips, O almighty God, Who cleansed the lips of the Prophet Isaias with a burning coal. In Your gracious mercy deign so to purify me that I may worthily proclaim Your holy Gospel. Through Christ our Lord. Amen.

Lord, grant Your blessing. The Lord be in my heart and on my lips, that I may worthily and fittingly proclaim His holy Gospel. Amen.

THE GOSPEL • Matt. 4, 1-11

Going to the left (Gospel) side of the altar, he says:

P. The Lord be with you. *S*. And with your spirit.

P. ✠ The continuation of the holy Gospel according to Saint Matthew. *S*. Glory be to You, O Lord.

AT THAT time, Jesus was led into the desert by the Spirit, to be tempted by the devil. And after fasting forty days and forty nights, He was hungry. And the tempter came and said to Him, "If You are the Son of God, command that these stones become loaves of bread." But He answered and said, "It is written, 'Not by bread alone does man live, but by every word that comes forth from the mouth of God.'" Then the devil took Him into the holy city and set Him on the pinnacle of the temple, and said to Him, "If You are the Son of God, throw Yourself down; for it is written, 'He has given his angels charge concerning You; and upon their hands they shall bear You up, lest You dash Your foot against a stone.'" Jesus said to him,

"It is written further, 'You shall not tempt the Lord your God.'" Again, the devil took Him to a very high mountain, and showed Him all the kingdoms of the world and the glory of them. And he said to Him, "All these things will I give You, if You will fall down and worship me." Then Jesus said to him, "Begone, Satan, for it is written, 'The Lord your God shall you worship and Him only shall you serve.'" Then the devil left Him; and behold, angels came and ministered to Him. *S.* Praise be to You, O Christ.

P. By the words of the Gospel, may our sins be taken away.

THE NICENE CREED

At the center of the altar, he says:

I BELIEVE in one God, the Father almighty, Maker of heaven and earth, and of all things visible and invisible. And in one Lord Jesus Christ, the Only-begotten Son of God. Born of the Father before all ages. God of God; Light of Light; true God of true God. Begotten not made; of one being with the Father; by Whom all things were made. Who for us men, and for our salvation, came down from heaven. (*Here all genuflect.*) And was made Flesh by the Holy Spirit of the Virgin Mary: AND WAS MADE MAN. He was also crucified for us, suffered under Pontius Pilate and was buried. And on the third day He rose again according to the Scriptures. And ascending into heaven, He sits at the right hand of the Father. And He shall come again in glory to judge the living and the dead; and of His kingdom there shall be no end. And I believe in the Holy Spirit, Lord and Giver of life, Who proceeds from the Father and the Son. Who together with the Father and the

Son is no less adored, and glorified: Who spoke by the Prophets. And I believe in One, Holy, Catholic and Apostolic Church. I confess one Baptism for the remission of sins. And I look for the resurrection of the dead. ✠ And the life of the world to come. Amen.

THE OFFERTORY

The Priest turns to the people and says:

P. The Lord be with you. *S.* And with your spirit.
P. Let us pray.

THE OFFERTORY VERSE • Ps. 90, 4. 5

WITH His pinions the Lord will cover you, and under His wings you shall take refuge; His faithfulness is a buckler and a shield.

The Priest now uncovers the chalice, places the host on the paten and offering it up, says:

ACCEPT, O holy Father, almighty and eternal God, this spotless host, which I, Your unworthy servant, offer to You, my living and true God, to atone for my numberless sins, offenses, and negligences; on behalf of all here present and likewise for all faithful Christians living and dead, that it may profit me and them as a means of salvation to life everlasting. Amen.

He pours wine and water into the chalice, blessing the water before it is poured.

O GOD, Who established the nature of man in wondrous dignity, and still more admirably restored it, grant that through the mystery of this water and wine, we may be made partakers of His Divinity, Who has condescended to become partaker of our humanity, Jesus Christ, Your Son, our Lord. Who lives and reigns with You in the unity of the Holy Spirit, God, world without end. Amen.

Offering up the wine, the Priest says:

WE OFFER You, O Lord, the chalice of salvation, humbly begging of Your mercy that it may arise before Your Divine Majesty, with a pleasing fragrance, for our salvation and for that of the whole world. Amen.

Bowing down, the Priest says:

IN A humble spirit and with a contrite heart, may we be accepted by You, O Lord, and may our sacrifice so be offered in Your sight this day as to please You, O Lord God.

Raising his eyes and blessing the offering, he says:

COME, O Sanctifier, almighty and eternal God, and bless ✠ this sacrifice prepared for the glory of Your holy name.

WASHING THE FINGERS

I WASH my hands in innocence, and I go around Your altar, O Lord, giving voice to my thanks, and recounting all Your wondrous deeds. O Lord, I love the house in which You dwell, the tenting-place of Your glory. Gather not my soul with those of sinners, nor with men of blood my life. On their hands are crimes, and their right hands are full of bribes. But I walk in integrity; redeem me, and have pity on me. My foot stands on level ground; in the assemblies I will bless You, O Lord. Glory be to the Father, and to the Son, and to the Holy Spirit. As it was in the beginning, is now, and ever shall be, world without end. Amen.

ACCEPT, Most Holy Trinity, this offering which we are making to You in remembrance of the Passion, Resurrection, and Ascension of Jesus Christ, our Lord; and in honor of Blessed Mary, ever Virgin, Blessed John the Baptist, the Holy Apostles Peter and Paul, and of these, and of all the Saints; that it may add to their honor and aid our salvation; and may they deign to intercede in heaven for us who honor their memory here on earth. Through the same Christ our Lord. Amen.

The Priest turns toward the people and says:

Pray, brethren, that my sacrifice and yours may become acceptable to God the Father almighty.
S. May the Lord accept this sacrifice from your hands to the praise and glory of His name, for our advantage, and that of all His holy Church.
P. Amen.

THE SECRET

WE SOLEMNLY offer up this sacrifice at the beginning of Lent, and beseech You, O Lord, that with the restriction of bodily food, we may also refrain from harmful pleasures. Through our Lord Jesus Christ, Your Son, Who lives and reigns with You in the unity of the Holy Spirit, God.
P. World without end. *S.* Amen.

PREFACE—CANON

P. The Lord be with you. *S.* And with your spirit.
P. Lift up your hearts.
S. We have lifted them up to the Lord.
P. Let us give thanks to the Lord, our God.
S. It is fitting and just.

IT IS fitting indeed and just, right and helpful to salvation, for us always and everywhere to give thanks to You, O holy Lord, Father almighty, everlasting God, Who by this bodily fast extinguish our vices, elevate our understanding, bestow on us virtue and its reward, through Christ our Lord. Through Whom the Angels praise Your Majesty, the Dominations adore it, the Powers are in awe. The heavens and the heavenly hosts, and the blessed Seraphim, join together in celebrating their joy. With these, we pray You, join our own voices also, while we say with lowly praise (*the bell is rung 3 times*):

HOLY, HOLY, HOLY, Lord God of Hosts. Heaven and earth are filled with Your glory. Hosanna in the highest. ✠ Blessed is He Who comes in the name of the Lord. Hosanna in the highest.

THE CANON OF THE MASS

THEREFORE, most gracious Father, we humbly beg of You and entreat You through Jesus Christ Your Son, our Lord, (*he kisses the altar*) to deem acceptable and bless these ✠ gifts, these ✠ offerings, these ✠ holy and unspotted oblations which, in the first place, we offer You for Your Holy Catholic Church, that You would deign to give her peace and protection, to unite and guard her throughout the world, together with Your servant N., our Pope, and N., our Bishop; and all true believers who cherish the Catholic and Apostolic Faith.

Commemoration of the Living

REMEMBER, O Lord, Your servants and handmaids, N. and N., (*name them*) and all here present, whose faith and devotion are known to You, on whose behalf we offer to You, or who themselves offer to You, this sacrifice of praise for themselves, families and friends, for the good of their souls, for their hope of salvation and deliverance from all harm, and who offer their homage to You, eternal, living and true God.

Commemoration of the Saints

IN THE unity of holy fellowship we observe the memory, first of all, of the glorious and ever Virgin Mary, Mother of our Lord and God Jesus Christ; next, that of Your Blessed Apostles and Martyrs, Peter and Paul, Andrew, James, John, Thomas, James, Philip, Bartholomew, Matthew, Simon and Thaddeus; of Linus, Cletus, Clement, Sixtus, Cornelius, Cyprian, Lawrence, Chrysogonus, John and Paul, Cosmas and Damian, and of all Your Saints, by whose merits and prayers grant that we may be always fortified by the help of Your protection. Through the same Christ our Lord. Amen.

Spreading his hands over the oblation, he says:

GRACIOUSLY accept, then, we beseech You, O Lord, this service of our worship and that of all Your household. Provide that our days be spent in Your peace, save us from everlasting damnation, and cause us to be numbered in the flock You have chosen. Through Christ our Lord. Amen.

O GOD, deign to bless ✠ what we offer, and make it approved, ✠ effective, ✠ right, and wholly pleasing in every way, that it may become for our good, the Body ✠ and Blood ✠ of Your dearly beloved Son, Jesus Christ our Lord.

CONSECRATION—ELEVATION

WHO, the day before He suffered, took bread into His holy and venerable hands, and having raised His eyes to heaven, to You, O God, His almighty Father, giving thanks to You, He blessed it, ✠ broke it, and gave it to His disciples, saying: All of you take and eat of this:

FOR THIS IS MY BODY.

IN LIKE manner, when the supper was done, taking also this goodly chalice into His holy and venerable hands, again giving thanks to You, He blessed ✠ it, and gave it to His disciples, saying: All of you take and drink of this:

FOR THIS IS THE CHALICE OF MY BLOOD OF THE NEW AND ETERNAL COVENANT: THE MYSTERY OF FAITH: WHICH SHALL BE SHED FOR YOU AND FOR MANY UNTO THE FORGIVENESS OF SINS.

After replacing the chalice on the corporal, he says:

As often as you shall do these things, in memory of Me shall you do them.

Offering of the Victim

MINDFUL, therefore, O Lord, not only of the blessed Passion of the same Christ, Your Son, our Lord, but also of His Resurrection from the dead, and finally His glorious Ascension into heaven, we, Your ministers, as also Your holy people, offer to Your supreme Majesty, of the gifts bestowed upon us, the pure ✠ Victim, the holy ✠ Victim, the all-perfect ✠ Victim: the holy ✠ Bread of life eternal and the Chalice ✠ of unending salvation.

AND this deign to regard with gracious and kindly attention and hold acceptable, as You deigned to accept the offerings of Abel, Your just servant, and the sacrifice of Abraham our patriarch, and that which Your chief priest Melchisedec offered to You, a holy sacrifice and a spotless victim.

MOST humbly we implore You, almighty God, bid these offerings to be brought by the hands of Your holy angel to Your altar above; before the face of Your Divine Majesty; that those of us who, by sharing in the Sacrifice of this altar, shall receive the Most Sacred ✠ Body and ✠ Blood of Your Son, may be filled with every grace and heavenly blessing. Through the same Christ our Lord. Amen.

Commemoration of the Dead

REMEMBER also, O Lord, Your servants and handmaids, N. and N., who have gone before us with the sign of faith, and rest in the sleep of peace. (*Here pray for the dead.*) To these, O Lord, and to all who rest in Christ, we beseech You to grant of Your goodness, a place of comfort, light and peace. Through the same Christ our Lord. Amen.

TO US sinners also, Your servants, trusting in the greatness of Your mercy, deign to grant some part and fellowship with Your Holy Apostles and Martyrs: with John, Stephen, Matthias, Barnabas, Ignatius, Alexander, Marcellinus, Peter, Felicitas, Perpetua, Agatha, Lucy, Agnes, Cecilia, Anastasia, and all Your Saints; into whose company, we implore You to admit us, not weighing our merits, but freely granting us pardon. Through Christ our Lord.

THROUGH Whom, O Lord, You always create, ✠ sanctify, ✠ fill with life, ✠ bless, and bestow upon us all good things.

The Minor Elevation

THROUGH ✠ Him, and with ✠ Him, and in ✠ Him, is to You, God the Father ✠ almighty, in the unity of the Holy ✠ Spirit, all honor and glory, world without end. S. Amen.

THE COMMUNION AND THANKSGIVING

Let us pray. Prompted by saving precepts, and taught by Your divine teaching, we dare to say:

OUR FATHER, Who art in heaven, hallowed be Thy name: Thy kingdom come: Thy will be done on earth as it is in heaven. Give us this day our daily bread; and forgive us our trespasses, as we forgive those who trespass against us. And lead us not into temptation: S. But deliver us from evil. *P.* Amen.

DELIVER us, we beseech You, O Lord, from all evils, past, present, and to come; and by the intercession of the Blessed and glorious Mary, ever Virgin, Mother of God, together with Your Blessed Apostles Peter and Paul, and Andrew, and all the Saints, grant of Your goodness, peace in our days, that aided by the riches of Your mercy, we may be always free from sin and safe from all disturbance.

Through the same our Lord Jesus Christ, Your Son, Who lives and reigns with You in the unity of the Holy Spirit, God, world without end. *S.* Amen.

P. May the peace ✠ of the Lord be ✠ always with ✠ you.

S. And with your spirit.

The Priest puts a small particle into the chalice, saying:

May this mingling and consecration of the Body and Blood of our Lord Jesus Christ help us who receive it to life everlasting. Amen.

LAMB of God, You Who take away the sins of the world, have mercy on us.

Lamb of God, You Who take away the sins of the world, have mercy on us.

Lamb of God, You Who take away the sins of the world, grant us peace.

PRAYERS BEFORE HOLY COMMUNION

Then inclining toward the altar, he says:

O LORD Jesus Christ, Who said to Your Apostles: "Peace I leave with you, My peace I give to you," regard not my sins but the faith of Your Church, and deign to give her peace and unity according to Your Will: Who live and reign, God, world without end. Amen.

O LORD Jesus Christ, Son of the living God, Who, by the will of the Father, with the cooperation of the Holy Spirit, have by Your death given life to the world, deliver me by this Your Most Sacred Body and Blood from all my sins and from every evil. Make me always cling to Your commandments, and never permit me to be separated from You. Who with the same God the Father and the Holy Spirit, live and reign, God, world without end. Amen.

LET not the partaking of Your Body, O Lord Jesus Christ, which I, though unworthy, presume to receive, turn to my judgment and condemnation; but through Your goodness, may it become a safeguard and an effective remedy, both of soul and body. Who live and reign with God the Father, in the unity of the Holy Spirit, God, world without end. Amen.

COMMUNION OF THE PRIEST

I WILL take the Bread of heaven, and call upon the name of the Lord.

Lord, I am not worthy that You should come under my roof; but only say the word, and my soul will be healed. (3 *times.*)

Making the Sign of the Cross with the Host, he says:

MAY the Body of our Lord Jesus Christ preserve my soul to life everlasting. Amen.
What return shall I make to the Lord for all He has given me? I will take the Chalice of salvation, and I will call upon the name of the Lord. Praising will I call upon the Lord and I shall be saved from my enemies.

MAY the Blood of our Lord Jesus Christ preserve my soul to life everlasting. Amen.

The Priest reverently consumes the Precious Blood.

COMMUNION OF THE FAITHFUL

The Server and people say the "Confiteor."

P. May almighty God have mercy on you, forgive you your sins, and bring you to life everlasting. S. Amen.
P. May the almighty and merciful Lord grant you pardon, ✠ absolution and remission of your sins. S. Amen.

Holding up a Sacred Host, the Priest says:

Behold the Lamb of God, behold Him Who takes away the sins of the world.
Lord, I am not worthy that You should come under my roof; but only say the word, and my soul will be healed. (3 *times.*)

The Priest says to each communicant:

May the Body of our Lord Jesus Christ preserve your soul to life everlasting. Amen.

The Priest purifies the chalice with wine, saying:

WHAT has passed our lips as food, O Lord, may we possess in purity of heart, that what is given to us in time, be our healing for eternity.

He purifies his fingers with wine and water, saying:

MAY Your Body, O Lord, which I have eaten, and Your Blood which I have drunk, cleave to my very soul, and grant that no trace of sin be found in me, whom these pure and holy mysteries have renewed. Who live and reign, world without end. Amen.

THE COMMUNION • Ps. 90, 4. 5

WITH His pinions the Lord will cover you, and under His wings you shall take refuge; His faithfulness is a buckler and a shield.

P. The Lord be with you. *S*. And with your spirit.
P. Let us pray.

THE POSTCOMMUNION

MAY the holy reception of Your sacrament, O Lord, revive us, and, cleansing us from our former life, enable us to enjoy a closer union with that saving mystery. Through our Lord Jesus Christ, Your Son, Who lives and reigns, etc. *S*. Amen.

FINAL PRAYERS

P. The Lord be with you. *S*. And with your spirit.
P. Let us bless the Lord. *S*. Thanks be to God.

MAY the tribute of my worship be pleasing to You, Most Holy Trinity, and grant that the sacrifice which I, all unworthy, have offered in the presence of Your Majesty, may be acceptable to You, and through Your mercy obtain forgiveness for me and all for whom I have offered it. Through Christ our Lord. Amen.

THE LAST BLESSING

MAY almighty God bless you: ✠ the Father, and the Son, and the Holy Spirit. *S*. Amen.

The Last Gospel and Prayers after Low Mass are conveniently placed inside the back cover.

Moses and Elias appeared talking together with Him.

SECOND SUNDAY IN LENT

The Transfiguration of our Lord gives us an idea of the beauty of a soul in the state of sanctifying grace. "This is the will of God, your sanctification." It must be our firm determination to preserve the divine life of our soul, at any price. (PURPLE VESTMENTS)

PRAYERS AT THE FOOT OF THE ALTAR

IN THE name of the Father, ✠ and of the Son, and of the Holy Spirit. Amen.

Priest. I will go in to the altar of God.

Server. The God of my gladness and joy.

Psalm 42

DO ME justice, O God, and fight my fight against a faithless people; from the deceitful and impious man rescue me.

S. For You, O God, are my strength. Why do You keep me so far away? Why must I go about in mourning, with the enemy oppressing me?

P. Send forth Your light and Your fidelity; they shall lead me on and bring me to Your holy mountain, to Your dwelling-place.

S. Then will I go in to the altar of God, the God of my gladness and joy.
P. Then will I give You thanks upon the harp, O God, my God. Why are you so downcast, O my soul? Why do you sigh within me?
S. Hope in God! For I shall again be thanking Him in the presence of my Savior and my God.
P. Glory be to the Father, and to the Son, and to the Holy Spirit.
S. As it was in the beginning, is now, and ever shall be, world without end. Amen.
P. I will go in to the altar of God.
S. The God of my gladness and joy.
P. Our help ✠ is in the name of the Lord.
S. Who made heaven and earth.
P. I confess to almighty God, etc.
S. May almighty God have mercy on you, forgive you your sins, and bring you to life everlasting.
P. Amen.

The Server, bowing, says the "Confiteor."

I CONFESS to almighty God, to Blessed Mary, ever Virgin, to Blessed Michael the Archangel, to Blessed John the Baptist, to the Holy Apostles Peter and Paul, and to all the Saints, and to you, Father, that I have sinned exceedingly in thought, word and deed, *through my fault, through my fault, through my most grievous fault.* Therefore I beseech Blessed Mary, ever Virgin, Blessed Michael the Archangel, Blessed John the Baptist, the Holy Apostles Peter and Paul, and all the Saints, and you, Father, to pray to the Lord our God for me.
P. May almighty God have mercy on you, forgive you your sins, and bring you to life everlasting.
S. Amen.

MAY the almighty and merciful Lord grant us pardon, ✠ absolution, and remission of our sins. *S.* Amen.

P. Will You not, O God, give us life?
S. And shall not Your people rejoice in You?
P. Show us, O Lord, Your kindness.
S. And grant us Your salvation.
P. O Lord, hear my prayer.
S. And let my cry come to You.
P. The Lord be with you.
S. And with your spirit. *P.* Let us pray.

Going up to the altar, the Priest prays silently:

TAKE away from us our sins, O Lord, we beseech You, that we may enter with pure minds into the Holy of Holies. Through Christ our Lord. Amen.

WE BESEECH You, O Lord, by the merits of Your Saints (*he kisses the altar*) whose relics lie here, and of all the Saints: deign in Your mercy to pardon me all my sins. Amen.

THE INTROIT • Ps. 24, 6. 3. 22. 1-2

At the right side of the altar, the Priest says:

REMEMBER that Your compassion, O Lord, and Your kindness are from of old; let not our enemies exult over us; deliver us, O God of Israel, from all our tribulations. *Ps.* To You I lift up my soul, O Lord; in You, O my God, I trust; let me not be put to shame. Glory be to the Father, and to the Son, and to the Holy Spirit. As it was in the beginning, is now, and ever shall be, world without end. Amen. — Remember that Your compassion, O Lord, and Your kindness are from of old; let not our enemies exult over us; deliver us, O God of Israel, from all our tribulations.

THE KYRIE

P. Lord, have mercy. *S*. Lord, have mercy. *P*. Lord, have mercy. *S*. Christ, have mercy. *P*. Christ, have mercy. *S*. Christ, have mercy. *P*. Lord, have mercy. *S*. Lord, have mercy. *P*. Lord, have mercy.

The Priest kisses the altar and turns to the people, saying:

P. The Lord be with you. *S*. And with your spirit. *P*. Let us pray.

THE PRAYER

Going to the right (Epistle) side, he says:

O GOD, You see that we are destitute of all strength; protect us both inwardly and outwardly; that in body we may be defended from all adversities, and in mind cleansed from evil thoughts. Through our Lord Jesus Christ, Your Son, Who lives and reigns with You in the unity of the Holy Spirit, God, world without end. *S*. Amen.

THE EPISTLE • 1 Thess. 4, 1-7

BRETHREN: Even as you have learned from us how you ought to walk and to please God — as indeed you are walking — we beseech and exhort you in the Lord Jesus to make even greater progress. For you know what precepts I have given to you by the Lord Jesus. For this is the will of God, your sanctification; that you abstain from immorality; that every one of you learn how to possess his vessel in holiness and honor, not in the passion of lust like the Gentiles who do not know God; that no one transgress and overreach his brother in the matter, because the Lord is the avenger of all these things, as we have told you before and have testified. For God has not called us unto uncleanness, but unto holiness, in Christ Jesus our Lord. *S.* Thanks be to God.

THE GRADUAL • Ps. 24, 17. 18

RELIEVE the troubles of my heart and bring me out of my distress, O Lord. ℣. Put an end to my affliction and my suffering, and take away all my sins.

THE TRACT • Ps. 105, 1-4

GIVE thanks to the Lord, for He is good, for His kindness endures forever. ℣. Who can tell the mighty deeds of the Lord, or proclaim all His praises? ℣. Happy are they who observe what is right, who do always what is just. ℣. Remember us, O Lord, as You favor Your people; visit us with Your saving help.

PRAYER BEFORE THE GOSPEL

Bowing down at the center of the altar, he says:

CLEANSE my heart and my lips, O almighty God, Who cleansed the lips of the Prophet Isaias with a burning coal. In Your gracious mercy deign so to purify me that I may worthily proclaim Your holy Gospel. Through Christ our Lord. Amen. Lord, grant Your blessing. The Lord be in my heart and on my lips, that I may worthily and fittingly proclaim His holy Gospel. Amen.

THE GOSPEL • Matt. 17, 1-9

Going to the left (Gospel) side of the altar, he says:

P. The Lord be with you. *S.* And with your spirit.
P. ✠ The continuation of the holy Gospel according to Saint Matthew. *S.* Glory be to You, O Lord.

AT THAT time, Jesus took Peter, James and his brother John, and led them up a high mountain by themselves, and was transfigured before them. And His face shone as the sun, and His garments became white as snow. And behold, there appeared to them Moses and Elias talking together with Him. Then Peter addressed Jesus, saying, "Lord, it is good for us to be here. If You will, let us set up three tents here, one for You, one for Moses, and one for Elias." As he was still speaking, behold, a bright cloud overshadowed them, and behold, a voice out of the cloud said, "This is My beloved Son, in Whom I am well pleased; hear Him." And on hearing it the disciples fell on their faces and were exceedingly afraid. And Jesus came near and touched them, and said to them, "Arise, and do not be afraid." But lifting up their eyes, they saw no one but Jesus only. And as they were coming down from the mountain, Jesus cautioned them, saying, "Tell the vision to no one, till the Son of Man has risen from the dead." S. Praise be to You, O Christ.

P. By the words of the Gospel, may our sins be taken away.

THE NICENE CREED

At the center of the altar, he says:

I BELIEVE in one God, the Father almighty, Maker of heaven and earth, and of all things visible and invisible. And in one Lord Jesus Christ, the Only-begotten Son of God. Born of the Father before all ages. God of God; Light of Light; true God of true God. Begotten not made; of one being with the Father; by Whom all things were made. Who for us men, and for our salvation, came down from heaven. (*Here all genuflect.*) And was made Flesh by the Holy Spirit of the Virgin Mary: AND WAS MADE MAN. He was also crucified for us, suffered under Pontius Pilate and was buried. And on the third day He rose again according to the Scriptures. And ascending into heaven, He sits at the right hand of the Father. And He shall come again in glory to judge the living and the dead; and of His kingdom there shall be no end. And I believe in the Holy Spirit, Lord and Giver of life, Who proceeds from the Father and the Son. Who together with the Father and the Son is no less adored, and glorified: Who spoke by the Prophets. And I believe in One, Holy, Catholic and Apostolic Church. I confess one Baptism for the remission of sins. And I look for the resurrection of the dead. ✠ And the life of the world to come. Amen.

THE OFFERTORY

The Priest turns to the people and says:

P. The Lord be with you. *S.* And with your spirit.
P. Let us pray.

THE OFFERTORY VERSE • Ps. 118, 47. 48

I WILL delight in Your commands, which I love exceedingly; and I will lift up my hands to Your commands, which I love.

The Priest now uncovers the chalice, places the host on the paten and offering it up, says:

ACCEPT, O holy Father, almighty and eternal God, this spotless host, which I, Your unworthy servant, offer to You, my living and true God, to atone for my numberless sins, offenses, and negligences; on behalf of all here present and like-

wise for all faithful Christians living and dead, that it may profit me and them as a means of salvation to life everlasting. Amen.

He pours wine and water into the chalice, blessing the water before it is poured.

O GOD, Who established the nature of man in wondrous dignity, and still more admirably restored it, grant that through the mystery of this water and wine, we may be made partakers of His Divinity, Who has condescended to become partaker of our humanity, Jesus Christ, Your Son, our Lord. Who lives and reigns with You in the unity of the Holy Spirit, God, world without end. Amen.

Offering up the wine, the Priest says:

WE OFFER You, O Lord, the chalice of salvation, humbly begging of Your mercy that it may arise before Your Divine Majesty, with a pleasing fragrance, for our salvation and for that of the whole world. Amen.

Bowing down, the Priest says:

IN A humble spirit and with a contrite heart, may we be accepted by You, O Lord, and may our sacrifice so be offered in Your sight this day as to please You, O Lord God.

Raising his eyes and blessing the offering, he says:

COME, O Sanctifier, almighty and eternal God, and bless ✠ this sacrifice prepared for the glory of Your holy name.

WASHING THE FINGERS

I WASH my hands in innocence, and I go around Your altar, O Lord, giving voice to my thanks, and recounting all Your wondrous deeds. O Lord,

I love the house in which You dwell, the tenting-place of Your glory. Gather not my soul with those of sinners, nor with men of blood my life. On their hands are crimes, and their right hands are full of bribes. But I walk in integrity; redeem me, and have pity on me. My foot stands on level ground; in the assemblies I will bless You, O Lord. Glory be to the Father, and to the Son, and to the Holy Spirit. As it was in the beginning, is now, and ever shall be, world without end. Amen.

ACCEPT, Most Holy Trinity, this offering which we are making to You in remembrance of the Passion, Resurrection, and Ascension of Jesus Christ, our Lord; and in honor of Blessed Mary, ever Virgin, Blessed John the Baptist, the Holy Apostles Peter and Paul, and of these, and of all the Saints; that it may add to their honor and aid our salvation; and may they deign to intercede in heaven for us who honor their memory here on earth. Through the same Christ our Lord. Amen.

The Priest turns toward the people and says:

Pray, brethren, that my sacrifice and yours may become acceptable to God the Father almighty.

S. May the Lord accept this sacrifice from your hands to the praise and glory of His name, for our advantage, and that of all His holy Church.

P. Amen.

THE SECRET

O LORD, we beseech You, look favorably upon these present sacrifices, that they may profit us both for our devotion and our salvation. Through our Lord Jesus Christ, Your Son, Who lives and reigns with You in the unity of the Holy Spirit, God.

P. World without end. *S.* Amen.

PREFACE—CANON

P. The Lord be with you. *S.* And with your spirit.

P. Lift up your hearts.

S. We have lifted them up to the Lord.

P. Let us give thanks to the Lord, our God.

S. It is fitting and just.

IT IS fitting indeed and just, right and helpful to salvation, for us always and everywhere to give thanks to You, O holy Lord, Father almighty, everlasting God, Who by this bodily fast extinguish our vices, elevate our understanding, bestow on us virtue and its reward, through Christ our Lord. Through Whom the Angels praise Your Majesty, the Dominations adore it, the Powers are in awe. The heavens and the heavenly hosts, and the blessed Seraphim, join together in celebrating their joy. With these, we pray You, join our own voices also, while we say with lowly praise (*the bell is rung 3 times*):

HOLY, HOLY, HOLY, Lord God of Hosts. Heaven and earth are filled with Your glory. Hosanna in the highest. ✠ Blessed is He Who comes in the name of the Lord. Hosanna in the highest.

THE CANON OF THE MASS

THEREFORE, most gracious Father, we humbly beg of You and entreat You through Jesus Christ Your Son, our Lord, (*he kisses the altar*) to deem acceptable and bless these ✠ gifts, these ✠ offerings, these ✠ holy and unspotted oblations which, in the first place, we offer You for Your Holy Catholic Church, that You would deign to give her peace and protection, to unite and guard her throughout the world, together with Your servant *N.*, our Pope, and *N.*, our Bishop; and all true believers who cherish the Catholic and Apostolic Faith.

Commemoration of the Living

REMEMBER, O Lord, Your servants and handmaids, *N.* and *N.*, (*name them*) and all here present, whose faith and devotion are known to You, on whose behalf we offer to You, or who themselves offer to You, this sacrifice of praise for themselves, families and friends, for the good of their souls, for their hope of salvation and deliverance from all harm, and who offer their homage to You, eternal, living and true God.

Commemoration of the Saints

IN THE unity of holy fellowship we observe the memory, first of all, of the glorious and ever Virgin Mary, Mother of our Lord and God Jesus Christ; next, that of Your Blessed Apostles and Martyrs, Peter and Paul, Andrew, James, John, Thomas, James, Philip, Bartholomew, Matthew, Simon and Thaddeus; of Linus, Cletus, Clement, Sixtus, Cornelius, Cyprian, Lawrence, Chrysogonus, John and Paul, Cosmas and Damian, and of all Your Saints, by whose merits and prayers grant that we may be always fortified by the help of Your protection. Through the same Christ our Lord. Amen.

Spreading his hands over the oblation, he says:

GRACIOUSLY accept, then, we beseech You, O Lord, this service of our worship and that of all Your household. Provide that our days be spent in Your peace, save us from everlasting damnation, and cause us to be numbered in the flock You have chosen. Through Christ our Lord. Amen.

O GOD, deign to bless ✠ what we offer, and make it approved, ✠ effective, ✠ right, and wholly pleasing in every way, that it may become for our good, the Body ✠ and Blood ✠ of Your dearly beloved Son, Jesus Christ our Lord.

CONSECRATION—ELEVATION

WHO, the day before He suffered, took bread into His holy and venerable hands, and having raised His eyes to heaven, to You, O God, His almighty Father, giving thanks to You, He blessed it, ✠ broke it, and gave it to His disciples, saying: All of you take and eat of this:

FOR THIS IS MY BODY.

IN LIKE manner, when the supper was done, taking also this goodly chalice into His holy and venerable hands, again giving thanks to You, He blessed ✠ it, and gave it to His disciples, saying: All of you take and drink of this:

FOR THIS IS THE CHALICE OF MY BLOOD OF THE NEW AND ETERNAL COVENANT: THE MYSTERY OF FAITH: WHICH SHALL BE SHED FOR YOU AND FOR MANY UNTO THE FORGIVENESS OF SINS.

After replacing the chalice on the corporal, he says:

As often as you shall do these things, in memory of Me shall you do them.

Offering of the Victim

MINDFUL, therefore, O Lord, not only of the blessed Passion of the same Christ, Your Son, our Lord, but also of His Resurrection from the dead, and finally His glorious Ascension into heaven, we, Your ministers, as also Your holy people, offer to Your supreme Majesty, of the gifts bestowed upon us, the pure ✠ Victim, the holy ✠ Victim, the all-perfect ✠ Victim: the holy ✠ Bread of life eternal and the Chalice ✠ of unending salvation.

AND this deign to regard with gracious and kindly attention and hold acceptable, as You deigned to accept the offerings of Abel, Your just servant, and the sacrifice of Abraham our patriarch, and that which Your chief priest Melchisedec offered to You, a holy sacrifice and a spotless victim.

MOST humbly we implore You, almighty God, bid these offerings to be brought by the hands of Your holy angel to Your altar above; before the face of Your Divine Majesty; that those of us who, by sharing in the Sacrifice of this altar, shall receive the Most Sacred ✠ Body and ✠ Blood of Your Son, may be filled with every grace and heavenly blessing. Through the same Christ our Lord. Amen.

Commemoration of the Dead

REMEMBER also, O Lord, Your servants and handmaids, *N.* and *N.*, who have gone before us with the sign of faith, and rest in the sleep of peace. (*Here pray for the dead.*) To these, O Lord, and to all who rest in Christ, we beseech You to grant of Your goodness, a place of comfort, light

and peace. Through the same Christ our Lord. Amen.

TO US sinners also, Your servants, trusting in the greatness of Your mercy, deign to grant some part and fellowship with Your Holy Apostles and Martyrs: with John, Stephen, Matthias, Barnabas, Ignatius, Alexander, Marcellinus, Peter, Felicitas, Perpetua, Agatha, Lucy, Agnes, Cecilia, Anastasia, and all Your Saints; into whose company, we implore You to admit us, not weighing our merits, but freely granting us pardon. Through Christ our Lord.

THROUGH Whom, O Lord, You always create, ✠ sanctify, ✠ fill with life, ✠ bless, and bestow upon us all good things.

The Minor Elevation

THROUGH ✠ Him, and with ✠ Him, and in ✠ Him, is to You, God the Father ✠ almighty, in the unity of the Holy ✠ Spirit, all honor and glory, world without end. S. Amen.

THE COMMUNION AND THANKSGIVING

Let us pray. Prompted by saving precepts, and taught by Your divine teaching, we dare to say:

OUR FATHER, Who art in heaven, hallowed be Thy name: Thy kingdom come: Thy will be done on earth as it is in heaven. Give us this day our daily bread; and forgive us our trespasses, as we forgive those who trespass against us. And lead us not into temptation: S. But deliver us from evil. *P.* Amen.

DELIVER us, we beseech You, O Lord, from all evils, past, present, and to come; and by the intercession of the Blessed and glorious Mary, ever Virgin, Mother of God, together with Your Blessed Apostles Peter and Paul, and Andrew, and all the Saints, grant of Your goodness, peace in our days, that aided by the riches of Your mercy, we may be always free from sin and safe from all disturbance.
Through the same our Lord Jesus Christ, Your Son, Who lives and reigns with You in the unity of the Holy Spirit, God, world without end.
S. Amen.
P. May the peace ✠ of the Lord be ✠ always with ✠ you.
S. And with your spirit.

The Priest puts a small particle into the chalice, saying:

May this mingling and consecration of the Body and Blood of our Lord Jesus Christ help us who receive it to life everlasting. Amen.

LAMB of God, You Who take away the sins of the world, have mercy on us.
Lamb of God, You Who take away the sins of the world, have mercy on us.
Lamb of God, You Who take away the sins of the world, grant us peace.

PRAYERS BEFORE HOLY COMMUNION

Then inclining toward the altar, he says:

O LORD Jesus Christ, Who said to Your Apostles: "Peace I leave with you, My peace I give to you," regard not my sins but the faith of Your Church, and deign to give her peace and unity

according to Your Will: Who live and reign, God, world without end. Amen.

O LORD Jesus Christ, Son of the living God, Who, by the will of the Father, with the co-operation of the Holy Spirit, have by Your death given life to the world, deliver me by this Your Most Sacred Body and Blood from all my sins and from every evil. Make me always cling to Your commandments, and never permit me to be separated from You. Who with the same God the Father and the Holy Spirit, live and reign, God, world without end. Amen.

LET not the partaking of Your Body, O Lord Jesus Christ, which I, though unworthy, presume to receive, turn to my judgment and condemnation; but through Your goodness, may it become a safeguard and an effective remedy, both of soul and body. Who live and reign with God the Father, in the unity of the Holy Spirit, God, world without end. Amen.

COMMUNION OF THE PRIEST

I WILL take the Bread of heaven, and call upon the name of the Lord.

Lord, I am not worthy that You should come under my roof; but only say the word, and my soul will be healed. (3 *times.*)

Making the Sign of the Cross with the Host, he says:

MAY the Body of our Lord Jesus Christ preserve my soul to life everlasting. Amen.

What return shall I make to the Lord for all He has given me? I will take the Chalice of salvation, and I will call upon the name of the Lord. Prais-

ing will I call upon the Lord and I shall be saved from my enemies.

Making the Sign of the Cross with the chalice, he says:

MAY the Blood of our Lord Jesus Christ preserve my soul to life everlasting. Amen.

The Priest reverently consumes the Precious Blood.

COMMUNION OF THE FAITHFUL

The Server and people say the "Confiteor."

P. May almighty God have mercy on you, forgive you your sins, and bring you to life everlasting. *S.* Amen.

P. May the almighty and merciful Lord grant you pardon, ✠ absolution and remission of your sins. *S.* Amen.

Holding up a Sacred Host, the Priest says:

Behold the Lamb of God, behold Him Who takes away the sins of the world.

Lord, I am not worthy that You should come under my roof; but only say the word, and my soul will be healed. (3 *times.*)

The Priest says to each communicant:

May the Body of our Lord Jesus Christ preserve your soul to life everlasting. Amen.

The Priest purifies the chalice with wine, saying:

WHAT has passed our lips as food, O Lord, may we possess in purity of heart, that what is given to us in time, be our healing for eternity.

He purifies his fingers with wine and water, saying:

MAY Your Body, O Lord, which I have eaten, and Your Blood which I have drunk, cleave to my very soul, and grant that no trace of sin be found in me, whom these pure and holy mysteries

have renewed. Who live and reign, world without end. Amen.

THE COMMUNION • Ps. 5, 2-4

ATTEND to my sighing; heed my call for help, my King and my God! To You I pray, O Lord.

The Priest, turning to the people, says:

P. The Lord be with you. *S.* And with your spirit.
P. Let us pray.

THE POSTCOMMUNION

WE HUMBLY beseech You, almighty God, to grant that those whom You refresh with Your sacraments, may serve You worthily by a life well pleasing to You. Through our Lord Jesus Christ, Your Son, Who lives and reigns with You in the unity of the Holy Spirit, God, world without end. S. Amen.

FINAL PRAYERS

The Priest turns again to the people, and says:

P. The Lord be with you. *S.* And with your spirit.
P. Let us bless the Lord. *S.* Thanks be to God.

MAY the tribute of my worship be pleasing to You, Most Holy Trinity, and grant that the sacrifice which I, all unworthy, have offered in the presence of Your Majesty, may be acceptable to You, and through Your mercy obtain forgiveness for me and all for whom I have offered it. Through Christ our Lord. Amen.

THE LAST BLESSING

MAY almighty God bless you: ✠ the Father, and the Son, and the Holy Spirit. *S.* Amen.

The Last Gospel and Prayers after Low Mass are conveniently placed inside the back cover.

"If I cast out devils by Beelzebub, by whom do your children cast them out?"

THIRD SUNDAY IN LENT

"He who is not with Me, is against Me." We cannot be neutral in our relation to God. If we do not serve Him, we will become slaves to our own pride and selfishness. "Blessed are they who hear the word of God, and keep it." (PURPLE VESTMENTS)

PRAYERS AT THE FOOT OF THE ALTAR

IN THE name of the Father, ✠ and of the Son, and of the Holy Spirit. Amen.

Priest. I will go in to the altar of God.

Server. The God of my gladness and joy.

Psalm 42

DO ME justice, O God, and fight my fight against a faithless people; from the deceitful and impious man rescue me.

S. For You, O God, are my strength. Why do You keep me so far away? Why must I go about in mourning, with the enemy oppressing me?

P. Send forth Your light and Your fidelity; they shall lead me on and bring me to Your holy mountain, to Your dwelling-place.

S. Then will I go in to the altar of God, the God of my gladness and joy.
P. Then will I give You thanks upon the harp, O God, my God. Why are you so downcast, O my soul? Why do you sigh within me?
S. Hope in God! For I shall again be thanking Him in the presence of my Savior and my God.
P. Glory be to the Father, and to the Son, and to the Holy Spirit.
S. As it was in the beginning, is now, and ever shall be, world without end. Amen.
P. I will go in to the altar of God.
S. The God of my gladness and joy.
P. Our help ✠ is in the name of the Lord.
S. Who made heaven and earth.
P. I confess to almighty God, etc.
S. May almighty God have mercy on you, forgive you your sins, and bring you to life everlasting.
P. Amen.

The Server, bowing, says the "Confiteor."

I CONFESS to almighty God, to Blessed Mary, ever Virgin, to Blessed Michael the Archangel, to Blessed John the Baptist, to the Holy Apostles Peter and Paul, and to all the Saints, and to you, Father, that I have sinned exceedingly in thought, word and deed, *through my fault, through my fault, through my most grievous fault.* Therefore I beseech Blessed Mary, ever Virgin, Blessed Michael the Archangel, Blessed John the Baptist, the Holy Apostles Peter and Paul, and all the Saints, and you, Father, to pray to the Lord our God for me.
P. May almighty God have mercy on you, forgive you your sins, and bring you to life everlasting.
S. Amen.

MAY the almighty and merciful Lord grant us pardon, ✠ absolution, and remission of our sins. *S.* Amen.

P. Will You not, O God, give us life?
S. And shall not Your people rejoice in You?
P. Show us, O Lord, Your kindness.
S. And grant us Your salvation.
P. O Lord, hear my prayer.
S. And let my cry come to You.
P. The Lord be with you.
S. And with your spirit. *P.* Let us pray.

Going up to the altar, the Priest prays silently:

TAKE away from us our sins, O Lord, we beseech You, that we may enter with pure minds into the Holy of Holies. Through Christ our Lord. Amen.

WE BESEECH You, O Lord, by the merits of Your Saints (*he kisses the altar*) whose relics lie here, and of all the Saints: deign in Your mercy to pardon me all my sins. Amen.

THE INTROIT • Ps. 24, 15-16. 1. 2

At the right side of the altar, the Priest says:

MY EYES are ever toward the Lord, for He will free my feet from the snare. Look toward me, and have pity on me, for I am alone and afflicted. *Ps.* To You I lift up my soul, O Lord. In You, O my God, I trust; let me not be put to shame. Glory be to the Father, and to the Son, and to the Holy Spirit. As it was in the beginning, is now, and ever shall be, world without end. Amen. — My eyes are ever toward the Lord, for He will free my feet from the snare. Look toward me, and have pity on me, for I am alone and afflicted.

THE KYRIE

P. Lord, have mercy. *S*. Lord, have mercy. *P*. Lord, have mercy. *S*. Christ, have mercy. *P*. Christ, have mercy. *S*. Christ, have mercy. *P*. Lord, have mercy. *S*. Lord, have mercy. *P*. Lord, have mercy.

The Priest kisses the altar and turns to the people, saying:

P. The Lord be with you. *S*. And with your spirit. *P*. Let us pray.

THE PRAYER

Going to the right (Epistle) side, he says:

WE BESEECH You, almighty God, to regard the desires of those who humble themselves, and, for our defense, stretch forth the right hand of Your Majesty. Through our Lord Jesus Christ, Your Son, Who lives and reigns with You in the unity of the Holy Spirit, God, world without end. *S*. Amen.

THE EPISTLE • Eph. 5, 1-9

BRETHREN: Be imitators of God, as very dear children and walk in love, as Christ also loved us and delivered Himself up for us an offering and a sacrifice to God to ascend in fragrant odor. But immorality and every uncleanness or covetousness, let it not even be named among you, as becomes saints; or obscenity or foolish talk or scurrility, which are out of place; but rather thanksgiving. For know this and understand, that no fornicator, or unclean person, or covetous one (for that is idolatry) has any inheritance in the kingdom of Christ and God. Let no one lead you astray with empty words; for because of these things the wrath of God comes upon the children of disobedience. Do not, then, become partakers with them. For you were once darkness, but now you are light in the Lord. Walk, then, as children of light, for the fruit of the light is in all goodness and justice and truth. *S.* Thanks be to God.

THE GRADUAL • Ps. 9, 20. 4

RISE, O Lord, let not man prevail; let the nations be judged in Your presence. ℣. Because my enemies are turned back, overthrown and destroyed before You.

THE TRACT • Ps. 122, 1-3

TO YOU I lift up my eyes, Who are enthroned in heaven. ℣. Behold, as the eyes of servants are on the hands of their masters. ℣. As the eyes of a maid are on the hands of her mistress, so are our eyes on the Lord our God, till He have pity on us. ℣. Have pity on us, O Lord, have pity on us.

PRAYER BEFORE THE GOSPEL

Bowing down at the center of the altar, he says:

CLEANSE my heart and my lips, O almighty God, Who cleansed the lips of the Prophet Isaias with a burning coal. In Your gracious mercy deign so to purify me that I may worthily proclaim Your holy Gospel. Through Christ our Lord. Amen. Lord, grant Your blessing. The Lord be in my heart and on my lips, that I may worthily and fittingly proclaim His holy Gospel. Amen.

THE GOSPEL • Luke 11, 14-28

Going to the left (Gospel) side of the altar, he says:

P. The Lord be with you. *S.* And with your spirit.
P. ✠ The continuation of the holy Gospel according to Saint Luke. *S.* Glory be to You, O Lord.

AT THAT time, Jesus was casting out a devil, and the same was dumb; and when He had cast out the devil, the dumb man spoke. And the crowds marvelled. But some of them said, "By Beelzebub, the prince of devils, He casts out devils." And others, to test Him, demanded from Him a sign from heaven. But He, seeing their thoughts, said to them: "Every kingdom divided against itself is brought to desolation, and house will fall upon house. If, then, Satan also is divided against himself, how shall his kingdom stand? because you say that I cast out devils by Beelzebub. Now, if I cast out devils by Beelzebub, by whom do your children cast them out? Therefore they shall be your judges. But if I cast out devils by the finger of God, then the kingdom of God has come upon you. When the strong man, fully armed, guards his courtyard, his property is undisturbed. But if a stronger than he attacks and overcomes him, he will take away all his weapons that he relied upon, and will divide his spoils. He who is not with Me is against Me; and he who does not gather with Me scatters. When the unclean spirit has gone out of a man, he roams through waterless places in search of rest; and finding none, he says, 'I will return to my house which I left.' And when he has come to it, he finds the place swept. Then he goes and takes seven other spirits more evil than himself, and they enter in and dwell there; and the last state of that man becomes worse than the first." Now it came to pass as He was saying these things, that a certain woman from the crowd lifted up her voice and said to Him, "Blessed is the womb that bore You, and the breasts that nursed You." But He said, "Rather, blessed are they who hear the word of God and keep it." S. Praise be to You, O Christ.

P. By the words of the Gospel, may our sins be taken away.

THE NICENE CREED

At the center of the altar, he says:

I BELIEVE in one God, the Father almighty, Maker of heaven and earth, and of all things visible and invisible. And in one Lord Jesus Christ, the Only-begotten Son of God. Born of the Father before all ages. God of God; Light of Light; true God of true God. Begotten not made; of one being with the Father; by Whom all things were made. Who for us men, and for our salvation, came down from heaven. (*Here all genuflect.*) And was made Flesh by the Holy Spirit of the Virgin Mary: AND WAS MADE MAN. He was also crucified for us, suffered under Pontius Pilate and was buried. And on the third day He rose again according to the Scriptures. And ascending into heaven, He sits at the right hand of the Father. And He shall come again in glory to judge the living and the dead; and of His kingdom there shall be no end. And I believe in the Holy Spirit, Lord and Giver of life, Who proceeds from the Father and the Son. Who together with the Father and the Son is no less adored, and glorified: Who spoke by the Prophets. And I believe in One, Holy, Catholic and Apostolic Church. I confess one Baptism for the remission of sins. And I look for the resurrection of the dead. ✠ And the life of the world to come. Amen.

THE OFFERTORY

The Priest turns to the people and says:

P. The Lord be with you. *S.* And with your spirit.
P. Let us pray.

THE OFFERTORY VERSE • Ps. 18, 9-12

THE precepts of the Lord are right, rejoicing the heart, and His ordinances are sweeter than syrup or honey from the comb; therefore Your servant is careful of them.

The Priest now uncovers the chalice, places the host on the paten and offering it up, says:

ACCEPT, O holy Father, almighty and eternal God, this spotless host, which I, Your unworthy servant, offer to You, my living and true God, to atone for my numberless sins, offenses, and negligences; on behalf of all here present and likewise for all faithful Christians living and dead, that it may profit me and them as a means of salvation to life everlasting. Amen.

He pours wine and water into the chalice, blessing the water before it is poured.

O GOD, Who established the nature of man in wondrous dignity, and still more admirably restored it, grant that through the mystery of this water and wine, we may be made partakers of His Divinity, Who has condescended to become partaker of our humanity, Jesus Christ, Your Son, our Lord. Who lives and reigns with You in the unity of the Holy Spirit, God, world without end. Amen.

Offering up the wine, the Priest says:

WE OFFER You, O Lord, the chalice of salvation, humbly begging of Your mercy that it may arise before Your Divine Majesty, with a pleasing fragrance, for our salvation and for that of the whole world. Amen.

Bowing down, the Priest says:

IN A humble spirit and with a contrite heart, may we be accepted by You, O Lord, and may our

sacrifice so be offered in Your sight this day as to please You, O Lord God.

Raising his eyes and blessing the offering, he says:

COME, O Sanctifier, almighty and eternal God, and bless ✠ this sacrifice prepared for the glory of Your holy name.

WASHING THE FINGERS

I WASH my hands in innocence, and I go around Your altar, O Lord, giving voice to my thanks, and recounting all Your wondrous deeds. O Lord, I love the house in which You dwell, the tenting-place of Your glory. Gather not my soul with those of sinners, nor with men of blood my life. On their hands are crimes, and their right hands are full of bribes. But I walk in integrity; redeem me, and have pity on me. My foot stands on level ground; in the assemblies I will bless You, O Lord. Glory be to the Father, and to the Son, and to the Holy Spirit. As it was in the beginning, is now, and ever shall be, world without end. Amen.

ACCEPT, Most Holy Trinity, this offering which we are making to You in remembrance of the Passion, Resurrection, and Ascension of Jesus Christ, our Lord; and in honor of Blessed Mary, ever Virgin, Blessed John the Baptist, the Holy Apostles Peter and Paul, and of these, and of all the Saints; that it may add to their honor and aid our salvation; and may they deign to intercede in heaven for us who honor their memory here on earth. Through the same Christ our Lord. Amen.

The Priest turns toward the people and says:

Pray, brethren, that my sacrifice and yours may become acceptable to God the Father almighty.

S. May the Lord accept this sacrifice from your hands to the praise and glory of His name, for our advantage, and that of all His holy Church.
P. Amen.

THE SECRET

MAY this offering, we beseech You, O Lord, cleanse away our sins, and sanctify the bodies and minds of Your servants for the celebration of this sacrifice. Through our Lord Jesus Christ, etc.
P. World without end. *S.* Amen.

PREFACE—CANON

P. The Lord be with you. *S.* And with your spirit.
P. Lift up your hearts.
S. We have lifted them up to the Lord.
P. Let us give thanks to the Lord, our God.
S. It is fitting and just.

IT IS fitting indeed and just, right and helpful to salvation, for us always and everywhere to give thanks to You, O holy Lord, Father almighty, everlasting God, Who by this bodily fast extinguish our vices, elevate our understanding, bestow on us virtue and its reward, through Christ our Lord. Through Whom the Angels praise Your Majesty, the Dominations adore it, the Powers are in awe. The heavens and the heavenly hosts, and the blessed Seraphim, join together in celebrating their joy. With these, we pray You, join our own voices also, while we say with lowly praise (*the bell is rung* 3 *times*):

HOLY, HOLY, HOLY, Lord God of Hosts. Heaven and earth are filled with Your glory. Hosanna in the highest. ✠ Blessed is He Who comes in the name of the Lord. Hosanna in the highest.

THE CANON OF THE MASS

THEREFORE, most gracious Father, we humbly beg of You and entreat You through Jesus Christ Your Son, our Lord, (*he kisses the altar*) to deem acceptable and bless these ✠ gifts, these ✠ offerings, these ✠ holy and unspotted oblations which, in the first place, we offer You for Your Holy Catholic Church, that You would deign to give her peace and protection, to unite and guard her throughout the world, together with Your servant *N.*, our Pope, and *N.*, our Bishop; and all true believers who cherish the Catholic and Apostolic Faith.

Commemoration of the Living

REMEMBER, O Lord, Your servants and handmaids, *N.* and *N.*, (*name them*) and all here present, whose faith and devotion are known to You, on whose behalf we offer to You, or who themselves offer to You, this sacrifice of praise for themselves, families and friends, for the good of their souls, for their hope of salvation and deliverance from all harm, and who offer their homage to You, eternal, living and true God.

Commemoration of the Saints

IN THE unity of holy fellowship we observe the memory, first of all, of the glorious and ever Virgin Mary, Mother of our Lord and God Jesus Christ; next, that of Your Blessed Apostles and Martyrs, Peter and Paul, Andrew, James, John, Thomas, James, Philip, Bartholomew, Matthew, Simon and Thaddeus; of Linus, Cletus, Clement, Sixtus, Cornelius, Cyprian, Lawrence, Chrysogonus, John and Paul, Cosmas and Damian, and of all

Your Saints, by whose merits and prayers grant that we may be always fortified by the help of Your protection. Through the same Christ our Lord. Amen.

Spreading his hands over the oblation, he says:

GRACIOUSLY accept, then, we beseech You, O Lord, this service of our worship and that of all Your household. Provide that our days be spent in Your peace, save us from everlasting damnation, and cause us to be numbered in the flock You have chosen. Through Christ our Lord. Amen.

O GOD, deign to bless ✠ what we offer, and make it approved, ✠ effective, ✠ right, and wholly pleasing in every way, that it may become for our good, the Body ✠ and Blood ✠ of Your dearly beloved Son, Jesus Christ our Lord.

CONSECRATION—ELEVATION

WHO, the day before He suffered, took bread into His holy and venerable hands, and having raised His eyes to heaven, to You, O God, His almighty Father, giving thanks to You, He blessed it, ✠ broke it, and gave it to His disciples, saying: All of you take and eat of this:

FOR THIS IS MY BODY.

IN LIKE manner, when the supper was done, taking also this goodly chalice into His holy and venerable hands, again giving thanks to You, He blessed ✠ it, and gave it to His disciples, saying: All of you take and drink of this:

FOR THIS IS THE CHALICE OF MY BLOOD OF THE NEW AND ETERNAL COVENANT: THE MYSTERY OF FAITH: WHICH SHALL BE SHED FOR YOU AND FOR MANY UNTO THE FORGIVENESS OF SINS.

After replacing the chalice on the corporal, he says:

As often as you shall do these things, in memory of Me shall you do them.

Offering of the Victim

MINDFUL, therefore, O Lord, not only of the blessed Passion of the same Christ, Your Son, our Lord, but also of His Resurrection from the dead, and finally His glorious Ascension into heaven, we, Your ministers, as also Your holy people, offer to Your supreme Majesty, of the gifts bestowed upon us, the pure ✠ Victim, the holy ✠ Victim, the all-perfect ✠ Victim: the holy ✠ Bread of life eternal and the Chalice ✠ of unending salvation.

AND this deign to regard with gracious and kindly attention and hold acceptable, as You deigned to accept the offerings of Abel, Your just servant, and the sacrifice of Abraham our patriarch, and that which Your chief priest Melchisedec offered to You, a holy sacrifice and a spotless victim.

MOST humbly we implore You, almighty God, bid these offerings to be brought by the hands of Your holy angel to Your altar above; before the face of Your Divine Majesty; that those of us who, by sharing in the Sacrifice of this altar, shall receive the Most Sacred ✠ Body and ✠ Blood of Your Son, may be filled with every grace and heavenly blessing. Through the same Christ our Lord. Amen.

Commemoration of the Dead

REMEMBER also, O Lord, Your servants and handmaids, N. and N., who have gone before us with the sign of faith, and rest in the sleep of

peace. (*Here pray for the dead.*) To these, O Lord, and to all who rest in Christ, we beseech You to grant of Your goodness, a place of comfort, light and peace. Through the same Christ our Lord. Amen.

TO US sinners also, Your servants, trusting in the greatness of Your mercy, deign to grant some part and fellowship with Your Holy Apostles and Martyrs: with John, Stephen, Matthias, Barnabas, Ignatius, Alexander, Marcellinus, Peter, Felicitas, Perpetua, Agatha, Lucy, Agnes, Cecilia, Anastasia, and all Your Saints; into whose company, we implore You to admit us, not weighing our merits, but freely granting us pardon. Through Christ our Lord.

THROUGH Whom, O Lord, You always create, ✠ sanctify, ✠ fill with life, ✠ bless, and bestow upon us all good things.

The Minor Elevation

THROUGH ✠ Him, and with ✠ Him, and in ✠ Him, is to You, God the Father ✠ almighty, in the unity of the Holy ✠ Spirit, all honor and glory, world without end. S. Amen.

THE COMMUNION AND THANKSGIVING

Let us pray. Prompted by saving precepts, and taught by Your divine teaching, we dare to say:

OUR FATHER, Who art in heaven, hallowed be Thy name: Thy kingdom come: Thy will be done on earth as it is in heaven. Give us this day our daily bread; and forgive us our trespasses, as we forgive those who trespass against us. And lead us

not into temptation: *S.* But deliver us from evil.
P. Amen.

DELIVER us, we beseech You, O Lord, from all evils, past, present, and to come; and by the intercession of the Blessed and glorious Mary, ever Virgin, Mother of God, together with Your Blessed Apostles Peter and Paul, and Andrew, and all the Saints, grant of Your goodness, peace in our days, that aided by the riches of Your mercy, we may be always free from sin and safe from all disturbance.

Through the same our Lord Jesus Christ, Your Son, Who lives and reigns with You in the unity of the Holy Spirit, God, world without end. *S.* Amen.
P. May the peace ✠ of the Lord be ✠ always with ✠ you.
S. And with your spirit.

The Priest puts a small particle into the chalice, saying:

May this mingling and consecration of the Body and Blood of our Lord Jesus Christ help us who receive it to life everlasting. Amen.

LAMB of God, You Who take away the sins of the world, have mercy on us.
Lamb of God, You Who take away the sins of the world, have mercy on us.
Lamb of God, You Who take away the sins of the world, grant us peace.

PRAYERS BEFORE HOLY COMMUNION

Then inclining toward the altar, he says:

O LORD Jesus Christ, Who said to Your Apostles: "Peace I leave with you, My peace I give to you," regard not my sins but the faith of Your

Church, and deign to give her peace and unity according to Your Will: Who live and reign, God, world without end. Amen.

O LORD Jesus Christ, Son of the living God, Who, by the will of the Father, with the co-operation of the Holy Spirit, have by Your death given life to the world, deliver me by this Your Most Sacred Body and Blood from all my sins and from every evil. Make me always cling to Your commandments, and never permit me to be separated from You. Who with the same God the Father and the Holy Spirit, live and reign, God, world without end. Amen.

LET not the partaking of Your Body, O Lord Jesus Christ, which I, though unworthy, presume to receive, turn to my judgment and condemnation; but through Your goodness, may it become a safeguard and an effective remedy, both of soul and body. Who live and reign with God the Father, in the unity of the Holy Spirit, God, world without end. Amen.

COMMUNION OF THE PRIEST

I WILL take the Bread of heaven, and call upon the name of the Lord.

Lord, I am not worthy that You should come under my roof; but only say the word, and my soul will be healed (3 *times.*)

Making the Sign of the Cross with the Host, he says:

MAY the Body of our Lord Jesus Christ preserve my soul to life everlasting. Amen.

What return shall I make to the Lord for all He has given me? I will take the Chalice of salvation, and I will call upon the name of the Lord. Prais-

ing will I call upon the Lord and I shall be saved from my enemies.

Making the Sign of the Cross with the chalice, he says:

MAY the Blood of our Lord Jesus Christ preserve my soul to life everlasting. Amen.

The Priest reverently consumes the Precious Blood.

COMMUNION OF THE FAITHFUL

The Server and people say the "Confiteor."

P. May almighty God have mercy on you, forgive you your sins, and bring you to life everlasting. S. Amen.

P. May the almighty and merciful Lord grant you pardon, ✠ absolution and remission of your sins. S. Amen.

Holding up a Sacred Host, the Priest says:

Behold the Lamb of God, behold Him Who takes away the sins of the world.

Lord, I am not worthy that You should come under my roof; but only say the word, and my soul will be healed. (3 *times.*)

The Priest says to each communicant:

May the Body of our Lord Jesus Christ preserve your soul to life everlasting. Amen.

The Priest purifies the chalice with wine, saying:

WHAT has passed our lips as food, O Lord, may we possess in purity of heart, that what is given to us in time, be our healing for eternity.

He purifies his fingers with wine and water, saying:

MAY Your Body, O Lord, which I have eaten, and Your Blood which I have drunk, cleave to my very soul, and grant that no trace of sin be found in me, whom these pure and holy mysteries have renewed. Who live and reign, world without end. Amen.

THE COMMUNION • Ps. 83, 4. 5

THE sparrow finds a home, and the swallow a nest in which she puts her young — Your altars, O Lord of Hosts, my King and my God! Happy they who dwell in Your house! continually they praise You.

The Priest, turning to the people, says:

P. The Lord be with you. *S.* And with your spirit.
P. Let us pray.

THE POSTCOMMUNION

MERCIFULLY absolve us, we beseech You, O Lord, from all guilt and danger, whom You grant to be partakers of so great a mystery. Through our Lord Jesus Christ, Your Son, Who lives and reigns with You in the unity of the Holy Spirit, God, world without end. *S.* Amen.

FINAL PRAYERS

The Priest turns again to the people, and says:

P. The Lord be with you. *S.* And with your spirit.
P. Let us bless the Lord. *S.* Thanks be to God.

MAY the tribute of my worship be pleasing to You, Most Holy Trinity, and grant that the sacrifice which I, all unworthy, have offered in the presence of Your Majesty, may be acceptable to You, and through Your mercy obtain forgiveness for me and all for whom I have offered it. Through Christ our Lord. Amen.

THE LAST BLESSING

MAY almighty God bless you: ✠ the Father, and the Son, and the Holy Spirit. *S.* Amen.

The Last Gospel and Prayers after Low Mass are conveniently placed inside the back cover.

When He had given thanks, He distributed the loaves and fishes.

FOURTH SUNDAY IN LENT

Laetare (Rejoice) *Sunday* offers us a rest in the midst of the Lenten observance. We are to rise again soon with Jesus through confession and Easter Communion. (PURPLE OR ROSE VESTMENTS)

PRAYERS AT THE FOOT OF THE ALTAR

IN THE name of the Father, ✠ and of the Son, and of the Holy Spirit. Amen.

Priest. I will go in to the altar of God.

Server. The God of my gladness and joy.

Psalm 42

DO ME justice, O God, and fight my fight against a faithless people; from the deceitful and impious man rescue me.

S. For You, O God, are my strength. Why do You keep me so far away? Why must I go about in mourning, with the enemy oppressing me?

P. Send forth Your light and Your fidelity; they shall lead me on and bring me to Your holy mountain, to Your dwelling-place.

S. Then will I go in to the altar of God, the God of my gladness and joy.
P. Then will I give You thanks upon the harp, O God, my God. Why are you so downcast, O my soul? Why do you sigh within me?
S. Hope in God! For I shall again be thanking Him in the presence of my Savior and my God.
P. Glory be to the Father, and to the Son, and to the Holy Spirit.
S. As it was in the beginning, is now, and ever shall be, world without end. Amen.
P. I will go in to the altar of God.
S. The God of my gladness and joy.
P. Our help ✠ is in the name of the Lord.
S. Who made heaven and earth.
P. I confess to almighty God, etc.
S. May almighty God have mercy on you, forgive you your sins, and bring you to life everlasting.
P. Amen.

The Server, bowing, says the "Confiteor."

I CONFESS to almighty God, to Blessed Mary, ever Virgin, to Blessed Michael the Archangel, to Blessed John the Baptist, to the Holy Apostles Peter and Paul, and to all the Saints, and to you, Father, that I have sinned exceedingly in thought, word and deed, *through my fault, through my fault, through my most grievous fault.* Therefore I beseech Blessed Mary, ever Virgin, Blessed Michael the Archangel, Blessed John the Baptist, the Holy Apostles Peter and Paul, and all the Saints, and you, Father, to pray to the Lord our God for me.
P. May almighty God have mercy on you, forgive you your sins, and bring you to life everlasting.
S. Amen.

MAY the almighty and merciful Lord grant us pardon, ✠ absolution, and remission of our sins. *S.* Amen.

P. Will You not, O God, give us life?
S. And shall not Your people rejoice in You?
P. Show us, O Lord, Your kindness.
S. And grant us Your salvation.
P. O Lord, hear my prayer.
S. And let my cry come to You.
P. The Lord be with you.
S. And with your spirit. *P.* Let us pray.

Going up to the altar, the Priest prays silently:

TAKE away from us our sins, O Lord, we beseech You, that we may enter with pure minds into the Holy of Holies. Through Christ our Lord. Amen.

WE BESEECH You, O Lord, by the merits of Your Saints (*he kisses the altar*) whose relics lie here, and of all the Saints: deign in Your mercy to pardon me all my sins. Amen.

THE INTROIT • Isa. 66, 10. 11

At the right side of the altar, the Priest says:

REJOICE, O Jerusalem, and come together all you who love her: rejoice with joy, you who have been in sorrow: that you may exult, and be filled from the breasts of your consolation. *Ps. 121.* I rejoiced because they said to me, "We will go up to the house of the Lord." Glory be to the Father, and to the Son, and to the Holy Spirit. As it was in the beginning, is now, and ever shall be, world without end. Amen. — Rejoice, O Jerusalem, and come together all you who love her: rejoice with joy, you who have been in sorrow: that you may exult, and be filled from the breasts of your consolation.

THE KYRIE

P. Lord, have mercy. *S*. Lord, have mercy. *P*. Lord, have mercy. *S*. Christ, have mercy. *P*. Christ, have mercy. *S*. Christ, have mercy. *P*. Lord, have mercy. *S*. Lord, have mercy. *P*. Lord, have mercy.

The Priest kisses the altar and turns to the people, saying:

P. The Lord be with you. *S*. And with your spirit. *P*. Let us pray.

THE PRAYER

Going to the right (Epistle) side, he says:

GRANT, we beseech You, almighty God, that we who justly suffer for our deeds, may be relieved by the comfort of Your grace. Through our Lord Jesus Christ, Your Son, Who lives and reigns with You in the unity of the Holy Spirit, God, world without end. *S*. Amen.

THE EPISTLE • Gal. 4, 22-31

BRETHREN: It is written that Abraham had two sons, the one by a slave-girl and the other by a free woman. And the son of the slave-girl was born according to the flesh, but the son of the free woman in virtue of the promise. This is said by way of allegory. For these are the two covenants: one indeed from Mount Sinai bringing forth children unto bondage, which is Agar. For Sinai is a mountain in Arabia, which corresponds to the present Jerusalem, and is in slavery with her children. But that Jerusalem which is above is free, which is our mother. For it is written, "Rejoice, O barren one, that do not bear; break forth and cry, you that do not travail; for many are the children of the desolate, more than of her that has a husband."

Now we, brethren, are the children of promise, as Isaac was. But as then he who was born according to the flesh, persecuted him who was born according to the spirit, so also it is now. But what does the Scripture say? "Cast out the slave-girl and her son, for the son of the slave-girl shall not be heir with the son of the free woman." Therefore, brethren, we are not children of a slave-girl, but of the free woman — in virtue of the freedom wherewith Christ has made us free. S. Thanks be to God.

THE GRADUAL • Ps. 121, 1. 7

I REJOICED because they said to me, "We will go up to the house of the Lord." ℣. May peace be within your walls, prosperity in your buildings.

THE TRACT • Ps. 124, 1. 2

THEY who trust in the Lord are like Mount Sion, which is immovable; which forever stands. ℣. Mountains are round about Jerusalem; so the Lord is round about His people, both now and forever.

PRAYER BEFORE THE GOSPEL

Bowing down at the center of the altar, he says:

CLEANSE my heart and my lips, O almighty God, Who cleansed the lips of the Prophet Isaias with a burning coal. In Your gracious mercy deign so to purify me that I may worthily proclaim Your holy Gospel. Through Christ our Lord. Amen. Lord, grant Your blessing. The Lord be in my heart and on my lips, that I may worthily and fittingly proclaim His holy Gospel. Amen.

THE GOSPEL • John 6, 1-15

Going to the left (Gospel) side of the altar, he says:

P. The Lord be with you. S. And with your spirit.

P. ✠ The continuation of the holy Gospel according to Saint John. *S.* Glory be to You, O Lord.

AT THAT time, Jesus went away to the other side of the sea of Galilee, which is that of Tiberias. And there followed Him a great crowd, because they witnessed the signs He worked on those who were sick. Jesus therefore went up the mountain, and sat there with His disciples. Now the Passover, the feast of the Jews, was near. When, therefore, Jesus had lifted up His eyes and seen that a very great crowd had come to Him, He said to Philip, "Whence shall we buy bread that these may eat?" But He said this to try him, for He Himself knew what He would do. Philip answered Him, "Two hundred denarii worth of bread is not enough for them, that each one may receive a little." One of His disciples, Andrew, the brother of Simon Peter, said to Him, "There is a young boy here who has five barley loaves and two fishes; but what are these among so many?" Jesus then said, "Make the people recline." Now there was much grass in the place. The men therefore reclined, in number about five thousand. Jesus then took the loaves, and when He had given thanks, distributed them to those reclining; and likewise the fishes, as much as they wished. But when they were filled, He said to His disciples, "Gather the fragments that are left over, lest they be wasted." They therefore gathered them up; and they filled twelve baskets with the fragments of the five barley loaves left over by those who had eaten. When the people, therefore, had seen the sign which Jesus had worked, they said, "This is indeed the Prophet who is to come into the world." So when Jesus perceived that they would come to take Him by force and make Him king, He fled again to the mountain, Himself alone. *S.* Praise be to You, O Christ.

P. By the words of the Gospel, may our sins be taken away.

THE NICENE CREED

At the center of the altar, he says:

I BELIEVE in one God, the Father almighty, Maker of heaven and earth, and of all things visible and invisible. And in one Lord Jesus Christ, the Only-begotten Son of God. Born of the Father before all ages. God of God; Light of Light; true God of true God. Begotten not made; of one being with the Father; by Whom all things were made. Who for us men, and for our salvation, came down from heaven. (*Here all genuflect.*) And was made Flesh by the Holy Spirit of the Virgin Mary: AND WAS MADE MAN. He was also crucified for us, suffered under Pontius Pilate and was buried. And on the third day He rose again according to the Scriptures. And ascending into heaven, He sits at the right hand of the Father. And He shall come again in glory to judge the living and the dead; and of His kingdom there shall be no end. And I believe in the Holy Spirit, Lord and Giver of life, Who proceeds from the Father and the Son. Who together with the Father and the Son is no less adored, and glorified: Who spoke by the Prophets. And I believe in One, Holy, Catholic and Apostolic Church. I confess one Baptism for the remission of sins. And I look for the resurrection of the dead. ✠ And the life of the world to come. Amen.

THE OFFERTORY

The Priest turns to the people and says:

P. The Lord be with you. S. And with your spirit.
P. Let us pray.

THE OFFERTORY VERSE • Ps. 134, 3. 6

PRAISE the Lord, for He is good; sing praise to His name, for He is sweet; all that He wills He does in heaven and on earth.

The Priest now uncovers the chalice, places the host on the paten and offering it up, says:

ACCEPT, O holy Father, almighty and eternal God, this spotless host, which I, Your unworthy servant, offer to You, my living and true God, to atone for my numberless sins, offenses, and negligences; on behalf of all here present and likewise for all faithful Christians living and dead, that it may profit me and them as a means of salvation to life everlasting. Amen.

He pours wine and water into the chalice, blessing the water before it is poured.

O GOD, Who established the nature of man in wondrous dignity, and still more admirably restored it, grant that through the mystery of this water and wine, we may be made partakers of His Divinity, Who has condescended to become partaker of our humanity, Jesus Christ, Your Son, our Lord. Who lives and reigns with You in the unity of the Holy Spirit, God, world without end. Amen.

Offering up the wine, the Priest says:

WE OFFER You, O Lord, the chalice of salvation, humbly begging of Your mercy that it may arise before Your Divine Majesty, with a pleasing fragrance, for our salvation and for that of the whole world. Amen.

Bowing down, the Priest says:

IN A humble spirit and with a contrite heart, may we be accepted by You, O Lord, and may our sacrifice so be offered in Your sight this day as to please You, O Lord God.

Raising his eyes and blessing the offering, he says:

COME, O Sanctifier, almighty and eternal God, and bless ✠ this sacrifice prepared for the glory of Your holy name.

WASHING THE FINGERS

I WASH my hands in innocence, and I go around Your altar, O Lord, giving voice to my thanks, and recounting all Your wondrous deeds. O Lord, I love the house in which You dwell, the tenting-place of Your glory. Gather not my soul with those of sinners, nor with men of blood my life. On their hands are crimes, and their right hands are full of bribes. But I walk in integrity; redeem me, and have pity on me. My foot stands on level ground; in the assemblies I will bless You, O Lord. Glory be to the Father, and to the Son, and to the Holy Spirit. As it was in the beginning, is now, and ever shall be, world without end. Amen.

ACCEPT, Most Holy Trinity, this offering which we are making to You in remembrance of the Passion, Resurrection, and Ascension of Jesus Christ, our Lord; and in honor of Blessed Mary, ever Virgin, Blessed John the Baptist, the Holy Apostles Peter and Paul, and of these, and of all the Saints; that it may add to their honor and aid our salvation; and may they deign to intercede in heaven for us who honor their memory here on earth. Through the same Christ our Lord. Amen.

The Priest turns toward the people and says:

Pray, brethren, that my sacrifice and yours may become acceptable to God the Father almighty.

S. May the Lord accept this sacrifice from your hands to the praise and glory of His name, for our advantage, and that of all His holy Church.

P. Amen.

THE SECRET

LOOK favorably on these sacrifices, we beseech You, O Lord, that they may profit us both for our devotion and our salvation. Through our Lord Jesus Christ, Your Son, Who lives and reigns with with You in the unity of the Holy Spirit, God.

P. World without end. *S.* Amen.

PREFACE—CANON

P. The Lord be with you. *S.* And with your spirit.

P. Lift up your hearts.

S. We have lifted them up to the Lord.

P. Let us give thanks to the Lord, our God.

S. It is fitting and just.

IT IS fitting indeed and just, right and helpful to salvation, for us always and everywhere to give thanks to You, O holy Lord, Father almighty, everlasting God, Who by this bodily fast extinguish our vices, elevate our understanding, bestow on us virtue and its reward, through Christ our Lord. Through Whom the Angels praise Your Majesty, the Dominations adore it, the Powers are in awe. The heavens and the heavenly hosts, and the blessed Seraphim, join together in celebrating their joy. With these, we pray You, join our own voices also, while we say with lowly praise (*the bell is rung 3 times*):

HOLY, HOLY, HOLY, Lord God of Hosts. Heaven and earth are filled with Your glory. Hosanna in the highest. ✠ Blessed is He Who comes in the name of the Lord. Hosanna in the highest.

THE CANON OF THE MASS

THEREFORE, most gracious Father, we humbly beg of You and entreat You through Jesus Christ Your Son, our Lord, (*he kisses the altar*) to deem acceptable and bless these ✠ gifts, these ✠ offerings, these ✠ holy and unspotted oblations which, in the first place, we offer You for Your Holy Catholic Church, that You would deign to give her peace and protection, to unite and guard her throughout the world, together with Your servant *N.*, our Pope, and *N.*, our Bishop; and all true believers who cherish the Catholic and Apostolic Faith.

Commemoration of the Living

REMEMBER, O Lord, Your servants and handmaids, *N.* and *N.*, (*name them*) and all here present, whose faith and devotion are known to You, on whose behalf we offer to You, or who themselves offer to You, this sacrifice of praise for themselves, families and friends, for the good of their souls, for their hope of salvation and deliverance from all harm, and who offer their homage to You, eternal, living and true God.

Commemoration of the Saints

IN THE unity of holy fellowship we observe the memory, first of all, of the glorious and ever Virgin Mary, Mother of our Lord and God Jesus Christ; next, that of Your Blessed Apostles and

Martyrs, Peter and Paul, Andrew, James, John, Thomas, James, Philip, Bartholomew, Matthew, Simon and Thaddeus; of Linus, Cletus, Clement, Sixtus, Cornelius, Cyprian, Lawrence, Chrysogonus, John and Paul, Cosmas and Damian, and of all Your Saints, by whose merits and prayers grant that we may be always fortified by the help of Your protection. Through the same Christ our Lord. Amen.

Spreading his hands over the oblation, he says:

GRACIOUSLY accept, then, we beseech You, O Lord, this service of our worship and that of all Your household. Provide that our days be spent in Your peace, save us from everlasting damnation, and cause us to be numbered in the flock You have chosen. Through Christ our Lord. Amen.

O GOD, deign to bless ✠ what we offer, and make it approved, ✠ effective, ✠ right, and wholly pleasing in every way, that it may become for our good, the Body ✠ and Blood ✠ of Your dearly beloved Son, Jesus Christ our Lord.

CONSECRATION—ELEVATION

WHO, the day before He suffered, took bread into His holy and venerable hands, and having raised His eyes to heaven, to You, O God, His almighty Father, giving thanks to You, He blessed it, ✠ broke it, and gave it to His disciples, saying: All of you take and eat of this:

FOR THIS IS MY BODY.

IN LIKE manner, when the supper was done, taking also this goodly chalice into His holy and venerable hands, again giving thanks to You, He blessed ✠ it, and gave it to His disciples, saying: All of you take and drink of this:

FOR THIS IS THE CHALICE OF MY BLOOD OF THE NEW AND ETERNAL COVENANT: THE MYSTERY OF FAITH: WHICH SHALL BE SHED FOR YOU AND FOR MANY UNTO THE FORGIVENESS OF SINS.

After replacing the chalice on the corporal, he says:

As often as you shall do these things, in memory of Me shall you do them.

Offering of the Victim

MINDFUL, therefore, O Lord, not only of the blessed Passion of the same Christ, Your Son, our Lord, but also of His Resurrection from the dead, and finally His glorious Ascension into heaven, we, Your ministers, as also Your holy people, offer to Your supreme Majesty, of the gifts bestowed upon us, the pure ✠ Victim, the holy ✠ Victim, the all-perfect ✠ Victim: the holy ✠ Bread of life eternal and the Chalice ✠ of unending salvation.

AND this deign to regard with gracious and kindly attention and hold acceptable, as You deigned to accept the offerings of Abel, Your just servant, and the sacrifice of Abraham our patriarch, and that which Your chief priest Melchisedec offered to You, a holy sacrifice and a spotless victim.

MOST humbly we implore You, almighty God, bid these offerings to be brought by the hands of Your holy angel to Your altar above; before the face of Your Divine Majesty; that those of us who, by sharing in the Sacrifice of this altar, shall receive the Most Sacred ✠ Body and ✠ Blood of Your Son, may be filled with every grace and heavenly blessing. Through the same Christ our Lord. Amen.

Commemoration of the Dead

REMEMBER also, O Lord, Your servants and handmaids, *N.* and *N.*, who have gone before us with the sign of faith, and rest in the sleep of peace. (*Here pray for the dead.*) To these, O Lord, and to all who rest in Christ, we beseech You to grant of Your goodness, a place of comfort, light and peace. Through the same Christ our Lord. Amen.

TO US sinners also, Your servants, trusting in the greatness of Your mercy, deign to grant some part and fellowship with Your Holy Apostles and Martyrs: with John, Stephen, Matthias, Barnabas, Ignatius, Alexander, Marcellinus, Peter, Felicitas, Perpetua, Agatha, Lucy, Agnes, Cecilia, Anastasia, and all Your Saints; into whose company, we implore You to admit us, not weighing our merits, but freely granting us pardon. Through Christ our Lord.

THROUGH Whom, O Lord, You always create, ✠ sanctify, ✠ fill with life, ✠ bless, and bestow upon us all good things.

The Minor Elevation

THROUGH ✠ Him, and with ✠ Him, and in ✠ Him, is to You, God the Father ✠ almighty, in the unity of the Holy ✠ Spirit, all honor and glory, world without end. *S.* Amen.

THE COMMUNION AND THANKSGIVING

Let us pray. Prompted by saving precepts, and taught by Your divine teaching, we dare to say:

OUR FATHER, Who art in heaven, hallowed be Thy name: Thy kingdom come: Thy will be

done on earth as it is in heaven. Give us this day our daily bread; and forgive us our trespasses, as we forgive those who trespass against us. And lead us not into temptation: *S.* But deliver us from evil. *P.* Amen.

DELIVER us, we beseech You, O Lord, from all evils, past, present, and to come; and by the intercession of the Blessed and glorious Mary, ever Virgin, Mother of God, together with Your Blessed Apostles Peter and Paul, and Andrew, and all the Saints, grant of Your goodness, peace in our days, that aided by the riches of Your mercy, we may be always free from sin and safe from all disturbance.

Through the same our Lord Jesus Christ, Your Son, Who lives and reigns with You in the unity of the Holy Spirit, God, world without end. *S.* Amen.

P. May the peace ✠ of the Lord be ✠ always with ✠ you. *S.* And with your spirit.

The Priest puts a small particle into the chalice, saying:

May this mingling and consecration of the Body and Blood of our Lord Jesus Christ help us who receive it to life everlasting. Amen.

LAMB of God, You Who take away the sins of the world, have mercy on us.

Lamb of God, You Who take away the sins of the world, have mercy on us.

Lamb of God, You Who take away the sins of the world, grant us peace.

PRAYERS BEFORE HOLY COMMUNION

Then inclining toward the altar, he says:

O LORD Jesus Christ, Who said to Your Apostles: "Peace I leave with you, My peace I give

to you," regard not my sins but the faith of Your Church, and deign to give her peace and unity according to Your Will: Who live and reign, God, world without end. Amen.

O LORD Jesus Christ, Son of the living God, Who, by the will of the Father, with the cooperation of the Holy Spirit, have by Your death given life to the world, deliver me by this Your Most Sacred Body and Blood from all my sins and from every evil. Make me always cling to Your commandments, and never permit me to be separated from You. Who with the same God the Father and the Holy Spirit, live and reign, God, world without end. Amen.

LET not the partaking of Your Body, O Lord Jesus Christ, which I, though unworthy, presume to receive, turn to my judgment and condemnation; but through Your goodness, may it become a safeguard and an effective remedy, both of soul and body. Who live and reign with God the Father, in the unity of the Holy Spirit, God, world without end. Amen.

COMMUNION OF THE PRIEST

I WILL take the Bread of heaven, and call upon the name of the Lord.

Lord, I am not worthy that You should come under my roof; but only say the word, and my soul will be healed. (3 *times.*)

Making the Sign of the Cross with the Host, he says:

MAY the Body of our Lord Jesus Christ preserve my soul to life everlasting. Amen.

What return shall I make to the Lord for all He has given me? I will take the Chalice of salvation,

and I will call upon the name of the Lord. Praising will I call upon the Lord and I shall be saved from my enemies.

Making the Sign of the Cross with the chalice, he says:

MAY the Blood of our Lord Jesus Christ preserve my soul to life everlasting. Amen.

The Priest reverently consumes the Precious Blood.

COMMUNION OF THE FAITHFUL

The Server and people say the "Confiteor."

P. May almighty God have mercy on you, forgive you your sins, and bring you to life everlasting. S. Amen.

P. May the almighty and merciful Lord grant you pardon, ✠ absolution and remission of your sins. S. Amen.

Holding up a Sacred Host, the Priest says:

Behold the Lamb of God, behold Him Who takes away the sins of the world.

Lord, I am not worthy that You should come under my roof; but only say the word, and my soul will be healed. (3 *times.*)

The Priest says to each communicant:

May the Body of our Lord Jesus Christ preserve your soul to life everlasting. Amen.

The Priest purifies the chalice with wine, saying:

WHAT has passed our lips as food, O Lord, may we possess in purity of heart, that what is given to us in time, be our healing for eternity.

He purifies his fingers with wine and water, saying:

MAY Your Body, O Lord, which I have eaten, and Your Blood which I have drunk, cleave to my very soul, and grant that no trace of sin be

found in me, whom these pure and holy mysteries have renewed. Who live and reign, world without end. Amen.

THE COMMUNION • Ps. 121, 3. 4

JERUSALEM, built as a city, with compact unity: to it the tribes go up, the tribes of the Lord, to give thanks to Your name, O Lord.

P. The Lord be with you. *S.* And with your spirit.
P. Let us pray.

THE POSTCOMMUNION

GRANT, we beseech You, O merciful God, that we may use with sincere veneration, and always receive with faithful minds, Your holy mysteries with which we are continually fed. Through our Lord Jesus Christ, Your Son, Who lives, etc. *S.* Amen.

FINAL PRAYERS

The Priest turns again to the people, and says:

P. The Lord be with you. *S.* And with your spirit.
P. Let us bless the Lord. *S.* Thanks be to God.

MAY the tribute of my worship be pleasing to You, Most Holy Trinity, and grant that the sacrifice which I, all unworthy, have offered in the presence of Your Majesty, may be acceptable to You, and through Your mercy obtain forgiveness for me and all for whom I have offered it. Through Christ our Lord. Amen.

THE LAST BLESSING

He kisses the altar, and facing the people, says:

MAY almighty God bless you: ✠ the Father, and the Son, and the Holy Spirit. *S.* Amen.

The Last Gospel and Prayers after Low Mass are conveniently placed inside the back cover.

"Jesus hid Himself, and went out from the temple."

PASSION SUNDAY

The Mass of Passion Sunday is full of the thought of the Passion of Jesus and of the infidelity of the Jews, whose place in the Kingdom of God was taken by those who were baptized, that is to say, by the Christians. (PURPLE VESTMENTS)

PRAYERS AT THE FOOT OF THE ALTAR

IN THE name of the Father, ✠ and of the Son, and of the Holy Spirit. Amen.

Priest. I will go in to the altar of God.

Server. The God of my gladness and joy.

P. Our help ✠ is in the name of the Lord.

S. Who made heaven and earth.

P. I confess to almighty God, etc.

S. May almighty God have mercy on you, forgive you your sins, and bring you to life everlasting.

P. Amen.

The Server, bowing, says the "Confiteor."

I CONFESS to almighty God, to Blessed Mary, ever Virgin, to Blessed Michael the Archangel, to Blessed John the Baptist, to the Holy Apostles Peter and Paul, and to all the Saints, and to you, Father, that I have sinned exceedingly in thought,

word and deed, *through my fault, through my fault, through my most grievous fault.* Therefore I beseech Blessed Mary, ever Virgin, Blessed Michael the Archangel, Blessed John the Baptist, the Holy Apostles Peter and Paul, and all the Saints, and you, Father, to pray to the Lord our God for me.
P. May almighty God have mercy on you, forgive you your sins, and bring you to life everlasting.
S. Amen.

MAY the almighty and merciful Lord grant us pardon, ✠ absolution, and remission of our sins. *S.* Amen.

P. Will You not, O God, give us life?
S. And shall not Your people rejoice in You?
P. Show us, O Lord, Your kindness.
S. And grant us Your salvation.
P. O Lord, hear my prayer.
S. And let my cry come to You.
P. The Lord be with you.
S. And with your spirit. *P.* Let us pray.

Going up to the altar, the Priest prays silently:

TAKE away from us our sins, O Lord, we beseech You, that we may enter with pure minds into the Holy of Holies. Through Christ our Lord. Amen.

WE BESEECH You, O Lord, by the merits of Your Saints (*he kisses the altar*) whose relics lie here, and of all the Saints: deign in Your mercy to pardon me all my sins. Amen.

THE INTROIT • Ps. 42, 1. 2. 3

At the right side of the altar, the Priest says:

DO ME justice, O God, and fight my fight against a faithless people; from the deceitful and impious man rescue me. For You are my God and my strength. *Ps.* Send forth Your light and Your fidelity; they shall lead me on and bring me to Your holy mountain, to Your dwelling-place. — Do me justice, O God, and fight my fight against a faithless people; from the deceitful and impious man rescue me. For You are my God and my strength.

THE KYRIE

P. Lord, have mercy. *S.* Lord, have mercy. *P.* Lord, have mercy. *S.* Christ, have mercy. *P.* Christ, have mercy. *S.* Christ, have mercy. *P.* Lord, have mercy. *S.* Lord, have mercy. *P.* Lord, have mercy.

The Priest turns to the people, saying:

P. The Lord be with you. *S.* And with your spirit.
P. Let us pray.

THE PRAYER

Going to the right (Epistle) side, he says:

WE BESEECH You, almighty God, mercifully look upon Your family, that by Your bounty it may be governed in body, and by Your protection, guarded in spirit. Through our Lord Jesus Christ, Your Son, Who lives and reigns with You in the unity of the Holy Spirit, God, world without end. *S.* Amen.

THE EPISTLE • Heb. 9, 11-15

BRETHREN: When Christ appeared as High Priest of the good things to come, He entered once for all through the greater and more perfect tabernacle, not made by hands (that is, not of this creation), nor again by virtue of blood of goats and calves, but by virtue of His own Blood, into the Holies, having obtained eternal redemption. For if the blood of goats and bulls and the sprinkled ashes of a heifer sanctify the unclean unto the cleansing of the flesh, how much more will the Blood of Christ, Who through the Holy Spirit offered Himself unblemished unto God, cleanse your conscience from dead works to serve the living God? And this is why He is mediator of a new covenant, that whereas a death has taken place for redemption from the transgressions committed under the former covenant, they who have been called may receive eternal inheritance according to the promise, in Christ Jesus our Lord. S. Thanks be to God.

THE GRADUAL • Ps. 142, 9. 10

RESCUE me from my enemies, O Lord; teach me to do Your will. ℣. *Ps. 17, 48. 49.* O Lord, my deliverer from the angry nations, truly above my adversaries You exalt me and from the violent man You have rescued me.

THE TRACT • Ps. 128, 1-4

MUCH have they oppressed me from my youth. ℣. Let Israel say: Much have they oppressed me from my youth. ℣. Yet they have not prevailed against me; upon my back the plowers plowed. ℣. Long did they make their furrows. But the just Lord has severed the cords of the wicked.

PRAYER BEFORE THE GOSPEL

Bowing down at the center of the altar, he says:

CLEANSE my heart and my lips, O almighty God, Who cleansed the lips of the Prophet Isaias with a burning coal. In Your gracious mercy deign so to purify me that I may worthily proclaim Your holy Gospel. Through Christ our Lord. Amen. Lord, grant Your blessing. The Lord be in my heart

and on my lips, that I may worthily and fittingly proclaim His holy Gospel. Amen.

THE GOSPEL • John 8, 46-59

Going to the left (Gospel) side of the altar, he says:

P. The Lord be with you. *S.* And with your spirit.
P. ✠ The continuation of the holy Gospel according to Saint John. *S.* Glory be to You, O Lord.

AT THAT time, Jesus said to the crowds of the Jews: "Which of you can convict Me of sin? If I speak the truth, why do you not believe Me? He who is of God hears the words of God. The reason why you do not hear is that you are not of God." The Jews therefore in answer said to Him, "Are we not right in saying that You are a Samaritan, and have a devil?" Jesus answered, "I have not a devil, but I honor My Father, and you dishonor Me. Yet, I do not seek My own glory; there is One Who seeks and Who judges. Amen, amen, I say to you, if anyone keep My word, he will never see death." The Jews therefore said, "Now we know that You have a devil. Abraham is dead, and the prophets, and You say, 'If anyone keep My word he will never taste death.' Are You greater than our father Abraham, who is dead? And the prophets are dead. Whom do You make Yourself?" Jesus answered, "If I glorify Myself, My glory is nothing. It is My Father Who glorifies Me, of Whom you say that He is your God. And you do not know Him, but I know Him. And if I say that I do not know Him, I shall be like you, a liar. But I know Him, and I keep His word. Abraham your father rejoiced that he was to see My day. He saw it and was glad." The Jews therefore said to Him, "You are not yet fifty years old, and have You seen Abraham?" Jesus said to them, "Amen, amen, I say to you, before Abraham came to be, I am." They therefore took up stones to cast at Him; but Jesus hid Himself, and went out from the temple. S. Praise be to You, O Christ.

P. By the words of the Gospel, may our sins be taken away.

THE NICENE CREED

At the center of the altar, he says:

I BELIEVE in one God, the Father almighty, Maker of heaven and earth, and of all things visible and invisible. And in one Lord Jesus Christ, the Only-begotten Son of God. Born of the Father before all ages. God of God; Light of Light; true God of true God. Begotten not made; of one being with the Father; by Whom all things were made. Who for us men, and for our salvation, came down from heaven. (*Here all genuflect.*) And was made Flesh by the Holy Spirit of the Virgin Mary: AND WAS MADE MAN. He was also crucified for us, suffered under Pontius Pilate and was buried. And on the third day He rose again according to the Scriptures. And ascending into heaven, He sits at the right hand of the Father. And He shall come again in glory to judge the living and the dead; and of His kingdom there shall be no end. And I believe in the Holy Spirit, Lord and Giver of life, Who proceeds from the Father and the Son. Who together with the Father and the Son is no less adored, and glorified: Who spoke by the Prophets. And I believe in One, Holy, Catholic and Apostolic Church. I confess one Baptism for the remission of sins. And I look for the resurrec-

tion of the dead. ✠ And the life of the world to come. Amen.

THE OFFERTORY

The Priest turns to the people and says:

P. The Lord be with you. S. And with your spirit.
P. Let us pray.

THE OFFERTORY VERSE • Ps. 118, 17. 107

I PRAISE You, O Lord, with all my heart; be good to Your servant, that I may live and keep Your words. O Lord, give me life according to Your word.

The Priest now uncovers the chalice, places the host on the paten and offering it up, says:

ACCEPT, O holy Father, almighty and eternal God, this spotless host, which I, Your unworthy servant, offer to You, my living and true God, to atone for my numberless sins, offenses, and negligences; on behalf of all here present and likewise for all faithful Christians living and dead, that it may profit me and them as a means of salvation to life everlasting. Amen.

He pours wine and water into the chalice, blessing the water before it is poured.

O GOD, Who established the nature of man in wondrous dignity, and still more admirably restored it, grant that through the mystery of this water and wine, we may be made partakers of His Divinity, Who has condescended to become partaker of our humanity, Jesus Christ, Your Son, our Lord. Who lives and reigns with You in the unity of the Holy Spirit, God, world without end. Amen.

Offering up the wine, the Priest says:

WE OFFER You, O Lord, the chalice of salvation, humbly begging of Your mercy that

it may arise before Your Divine Majesty, with a pleasing fragrance, for our salvation and for that of the whole world. Amen.

Bowing down, the Priest says:

IN A humble spirit and with a contrite heart, may we be accepted by You, O Lord, and may our sacrifice so be offered in Your sight this day as to please You, O Lord God.

Raising his eyes and blessing the offering, he says:

COME, O Sanctifier, almighty and eternal God, and bless ✠ this sacrifice prepared for the glory of Your holy name.

WASHING THE FINGERS

I WASH my hands in innocence, and I go around Your altar, O Lord, giving voice to my thanks, and recounting all Your wondrous deeds. O Lord, I love the house in which You dwell, the tenting-place of Your glory. Gather not my soul with those of sinners, nor with men of blood my life. On their hands are crimes, and their right hands are full of bribes. But I walk in integrity; redeem me, and have pity on me. My foot stands on level ground; in the assemblies I will bless You, O Lord.

ACCEPT, Most Holy Trinity, this offering which we are making to You in remembrance of the Passion, Resurrection, and Ascension of Jesus Christ, our Lord; and in honor of Blessed Mary, ever Virgin, Blessed John the Baptist, the Holy Apostles Peter and Paul, and of these, and of all the Saints; that it may add to their honor and aid our salvation; and may they deign to intercede in heaven for us who honor their memory here on earth. Through the same Christ our Lord. Amen.

The Priest turns toward the people and says:
Pray, brethren, that my sacrifice and yours may become acceptable to God the Father almighty.
S. May the Lord accept this sacrifice from your hands to the praise and glory of His name, for our advantage, and that of all His holy Church.
P. Amen.

THE SECRET

MAY these gifts, we beseech You, O Lord, both loosen the bonds of our wickedness, and obtain for us the gifts of Your mercy. Through our Lord Jesus Christ, Your Son, Who lives and reigns with You in the unity of the Holy Spirit, God.
P. World without end. *S.* Amen.

PREFACE—CANON

P. The Lord be with you. *S.* And with your spirit.
P. Lift up your hearts.
S. We have lifted them up to the Lord.
P. Let us give thanks to the Lord, our God.
S. It is fitting and just.

IT IS fitting indeed and just, right and helpful to salvation, for us always and everywhere to give thanks to You, O holy Lord, Father almighty and everlasting God; Who set the salvation of mankind upon the tree of the Cross, so that whence came death, thence also life might rise again, and he that overcame by the tree, by the tree also might be overcome: through Christ our Lord. Through Whom the Angels praise Your Majesty, the Dominations worship it, and the Powers are in awe. The heavens and the heavenly hosts, and the blessed Seraphim join together in celebrating their joy. With these, we pray You, join our own voices also, while we say with lowly praise (*the bell is rung 3 times*):

HOLY, HOLY, HOLY, Lord God of Hosts. Heaven and earth are filled with Your glory. Hosanna in the highest. ✠ Blessed is He Who comes in the name of the Lord. Hosanna in the highest.

THE CANON OF THE MASS

THEREFORE, most gracious Father, we humbly beg of You and entreat You through Jesus Christ Your Son, our Lord, (*he kisses the altar*) to deem acceptable and bless these ✠ gifts, these ✠ offerings, these ✠ holy and unspotted oblations which, in the first place, we offer You for Your Holy Catholic Church, that You would deign to give her peace and protection, to unite and guard her throughout the world, together with Your servant N., our Pope, and N., our Bishop; and all true believers who cherish the Catholic and Apostolic Faith.

Commemoration of the Living

REMEMBER, O Lord, Your servants and handmaids, N. and N., (*name them*) and all here present, whose faith and devotion are known to You, on whose behalf we offer to You, or who themselves offer to You, this sacrifice of praise for themselves, families and friends, for the good of their souls, for their hope of salvation and deliverance from all harm, and who offer their homage to You, eternal, living and true God.

Commemoration of the Saints

IN THE unity of holy fellowship we observe the memory, first of all, of the glorious and ever Virgin Mary, Mother of our Lord and God Jesus Christ; next, that of Your Blessed Apostles and

Martyrs, Peter and Paul, Andrew, James, John, Thomas, James, Philip, Bartholomew, Matthew, Simon and Thaddeus; of Linus, Cletus, Clement, Sixtus, Cornelius, Cyprian, Lawrence, Chrysogonus, John and Paul, Cosmas and Damian, and of all Your Saints, by whose merits and prayers grant that we may be always fortified by the help of Your protection. Through the same Christ our Lord. Amen.

Spreading his hands over the oblation, he says:

GRACIOUSLY accept, then, we beseech You, O Lord, this service of our worship and that of all Your household. Provide that our days be spent in Your peace, save us from everlasting damnation, and cause us to be numbered in the flock You have chosen. Through Christ our Lord. Amen.

O GOD, deign to bless ✠ what we offer, and make it approved, ✠ effective, ✠ right, and wholly pleasing in every way, that it may become for our good, the Body ✠ and Blood ✠ of Your dearly beloved Son, Jesus Christ our Lord.

CONSECRATION—ELEVATION

WHO, the day before He suffered, took bread into His holy and venerable hands, and having raised His eyes to heaven, to You, O God, His almighty Father, giving thanks to You, He blessed it, ✠ broke it, and gave it to His disciples, saying: All of you take and eat of this:

FOR THIS IS MY BODY.

IN LIKE manner, when the supper was done, taking also this goodly chalice into His holy and venerable hands, again giving thanks to You, He blessed ✠ it, and gave it to His disciples, saying: All of you take and drink of this:

FOR THIS IS THE CHALICE OF MY BLOOD OF THE NEW AND ETERNAL COVENANT: THE MYSTERY OF FAITH: WHICH SHALL BE SHED FOR YOU AND FOR MANY UNTO THE FORGIVENESS OF SINS.

After replacing the chalice on the corporal, he says:

As often as you shall do these things, in memory of Me shall you do them.

Offering of the Victim

MINDFUL, therefore, O Lord, not only of the blessed Passion of the same Christ, Your Son, our Lord, but also of His Resurrection from the dead, and finally His glorious Ascension into heaven, we, Your ministers, as also Your holy people, offer to Your supreme Majesty, of the gifts bestowed upon us, the pure ✠ Victim, the holy ✠ Victim, the all-perfect ✠ Victim: the holy ✠ Bread of life eternal and the Chalice ✠ of unending salvation.

AND this deign to regard with gracious and kindly attention and hold acceptable, as You deigned to accept the offerings of Abel, Your just servant, and the sacrifice of Abraham our patriarch, and that which Your chief priest Melchisedec offered to You, a holy sacrifice and a spotless victim.

MOST humbly we implore You, almighty God, bid these offerings to be brought by the hands of Your holy angel to Your altar above; before the face of Your Divine Majesty; that those of us who, by sharing in the Sacrifice of this altar, shall receive the Most Sacred ✠ Body and ✠ Blood of Your Son, may be filled with every grace and heavenly blessing. Through the same Christ our Lord. Amen.

Commemoration of the Dead

REMEMBER also, O Lord, Your servants and handmaids, N. and N., who have gone before us with the sign of faith, and rest in the sleep of peace. (*Here pray for the dead.*) To these, O Lord, and to all who rest in Christ, we beseech You to grant of Your goodness, a place of comfort, light and peace. Through the same Christ our Lord. Amen.

TO US sinners also, Your servants, trusting in the greatness of Your mercy, deign to grant some part and fellowship with Your Holy Apostles and Martyrs: with John, Stephen, Matthias, Barnabas, Ignatius, Alexander, Marcellinus, Peter, Felicitas, Perpetua, Agatha, Lucy, Agnes, Cecilia, Anastasia, and all Your Saints; into whose company, we implore You to admit us, not weighing our merits, but freely granting us pardon. Through Christ our Lord.

THROUGH Whom, O Lord, You always create, ✠ sanctify, ✠ fill with life, ✠ bless, and bestow upon us all good things.

The Minor Elevation

THROUGH ✠ Him, and with ✠ Him, and in ✠ Him, is to You, God the Father ✠ almighty, in the unity of the Holy ✠ Spirit, all honor and glory, world without end. S. Amen.

THE COMMUNION AND THANKSGIVING

Let us pray. Prompted by saving precepts, and taught by Your divine teaching, we dare to say:

OUR FATHER, Who art in heaven, hallowed be Thy name: Thy kingdom come: Thy will be done on earth as it is in heaven. Give us this day

our daily bread; and forgive us our trespasses, as we forgive those who trespass against us. And lead us not into temptation: S. But deliver us from evil. *P*. Amen.

DELIVER us, we beseech You, O Lord, from all evils, past, present, and to come; and by the intercession of the Blessed and glorious Mary, ever Virgin, Mother of God, together with Your Blessed Apostles Peter and Paul, and Andrew, and all the Saints, grant of Your goodness, peace in our days, that aided by the riches of Your mercy, we may be always free from sin and safe from all disturbance.

Through the same our Lord Jesus Christ, Your Son, Who lives and reigns with You in the unity of the Holy Spirit, God, world without end. S. Amen.

P. May the peace ✠ of the Lord be ✠ always with ✠ you.

S. And with your spirit.

The Priest puts a small particle into the chalice, saying:

May this mingling and consecration of the Body and Blood of our Lord Jesus Christ help us who receive it to life everlasting. Amen.

LAMB of God, You Who take away the sins of the world, have mercy on us.

Lamb of God, You Who take away the sins of the world, have mercy on us.

Lamb of God, You Who take away the sins of the world, grant us peace.

PRAYERS BEFORE HOLY COMMUNION

Then inclining toward the altar, he says:

O LORD Jesus Christ, Who said to Your Apostles: "Peace I leave with you, My peace I give

to you," regard not my sins but the faith of Your Church, and deign to give her peace and unity according to Your Will: Who live and reign, God, world without end. Amen.

O LORD Jesus Christ, Son of the living God, Who, by the will of the Father, with the co-operation of the Holy Spirit, have by Your death given life to the world, deliver me by this Your Most Sacred Body and Blood from all my sins and from every evil. Make me always cling to Your commandments, and never permit me to be separated from You. Who with the same God the Father and the Holy Spirit, live and reign, God, world without end. Amen.

LET not the partaking of Your Body, O Lord Jesus Christ, which I, though unworthy, presume to receive, turn to my judgment and condemnation; but through Your goodness, may it become a safeguard and an effective remedy, both of soul and body. Who live and reign with God the Father, in the unity of the Holy Spirit, God, world without end. Amen.

COMMUNION OF THE PRIEST

I WILL take the Bread of heaven, and call upon the name of the Lord.

Lord, I am not worthy that You should come under my roof; but only say the word, and my soul will be healed. (3 *times.*)

Making the Sign of the Cross with the Host, he says:

MAY the Body of our Lord Jesus Christ preserve my soul to life everlasting. Amen.

What return shall I make to the Lord for all He has given me? I will take the Chalice of salvation,

and I will call upon the name of the Lord. Praising will I call upon the Lord and I shall be saved from my enemies.

Making the Sign of the Cross with the chalice, he says:

MAY the Blood of our Lord Jesus Christ preserve my soul to life everlasting. Amen.

The Priest reverently consumes the Precious Blood.

COMMUNION OF THE FAITHFUL

The Server and people say the "Confiteor."

P. May almighty God have mercy on you, forgive you your sins, and bring you to life everlasting. S. Amen.

P. May the almighty and merciful Lord grant you pardon, ✠ absolution and remission of your sins. S. Amen.

Holding up a Sacred Host, the Priest says:

Behold the Lamb of God, behold Him Who takes away the sins of the world.

Lord, I am not worthy that You should come under my roof; but only say the word, and my soul will be healed. (3 *times.*)

The Priest says to each communicant:

May the Body of our Lord Jesus Christ preserve your soul to life everlasting. Amen.

The Priest purifies the chalice with wine, saying:

WHAT has passed our lips as food, O Lord, may we possess in purity of heart, that what is given to us in time, be our healing for eternity.

He purifies his fingers with wine and water, saying:

MAY Your Body, O Lord, which I have eaten, and Your Blood which I have drunk, cleave to my very soul, and grant that no trace of sin be

found in me, whom these pure and holy mysteries have renewed. Who live and reign, world without end. Amen.

THE COMMUNION • 1 Cor. 11, 24. 25

"THIS is My Body which shall be given up for you: this is the cup of the new testament in My Blood," says the Lord; "do this as often as you receive it, in remembrance of Me."

The Priest, turning to the people, says:

P. The Lord be with you. *S.* And with your spirit.
P. Let us pray.

THE POSTCOMMUNION

BE PRESENT with us, O Lord our God, and support with unceasing help, those whom You have refreshed with Your mysteries. Through our Lord Jesus Christ, Your Son, Who lives and reigns with You, etc. *S.* Amen.

FINAL PRAYERS

P. The Lord be with you. *S.* And with your spirit.
P. Let us bless the Lord. *S.* Thanks be to God.

MAY the tribute of my worship be pleasing to You, Most Holy Trinity, and grant that the sacrifice which I, all unworthy, have offered in the presence of Your Majesty, may be acceptable to You, and through Your mercy obtain forgiveness for me and all for whom I have offered it. Through Christ our Lord. Amen.

THE LAST BLESSING

MAY almighty God bless you: ✠ the Father, and the Son, and the Holy Spirit. *S.* Amen.

The Last Gospel and Prayers after Low Mass are conveniently placed inside the back cover.

"Hosanna to the Son of David! Blessed Is He Who Comes in the Name of the Lord."

Matthew 21, 9.

PALM SUNDAY

This Sunday commemorates Christ's triumphal entrance into Jerusalem. For this reason the Church blesses palms to remind us of the multitude which accompanied Him carrying branches and strewing them in His way, while they chanted: "Hosanna to the Son of David! Blessed is He Who comes in the name of the Lord!" (PURPLE VESTMENTS)

PRAYERS AT THE FOOT OF THE ALTAR

IN THE name of the Father, ✠ and of the Son, and of the Holy Spirit. Amen.

Priest. I will go in to the altar of God.

Server. The God of my gladness and joy.

P. Our help ✠ is in the name of the Lord.

S. Who made heaven and earth.

P. I confess to almighty God, etc.

S. May almighty God have mercy on you, forgive you your sins, and bring you to life everlasting.

P. Amen.

The Server, bowing, says the "Confiteor."

I CONFESS to almighty God, to Blessed Mary, ever Virgin, to Blessed Michael the Archangel, to Blessed John the Baptist, to the Holy Apostles Peter and Paul, and to all the Saints, and to you, Father, that I have sinned exceedingly in thought, word and deed, *through my fault, through my fault, through my most grievous fault.* Therefore I beseech Blessed Mary, ever Virgin, Blessed Michael the Archangel, Blessed John the Baptist, the Holy Apostles Peter and Paul, and all the Saints, and you, Father, to pray to the Lord our God for me.

P. May almighty God have mercy on you, forgive you your sins, and bring you to life everlasting.

S. Amen.

MAY the almighty and merciful Lord grant us pardon, ✠ absolution, and remission of our sins. *S.* Amen.

P. Will You not, O God, give us life?

S. And shall not Your people rejoice in You?

P. Show us, O Lord, Your kindness.

S. And grant us Your salvation.

P. O Lord, hear my prayer.

S. And let my cry come to You.

P. The Lord be with you.

S. And with your spirit. *P.* Let us pray.

Going up to the altar, the Priest prays silently:

TAKE away from us our sins, O Lord, we beseech You, that we may enter with pure minds into the Holy of Holies. Through Christ our Lord. Amen.

WE BESEECH You, O Lord, by the merits of Your Saints (*he kisses the altar*) whose relics lie here, and of all the Saints: deign in Your mercy to pardon me all my sins. Amen.

THE INTROIT • Ps. 21, 20. 22. 2

At the right side of the altar, the Priest says:

O LORD, be not far from me; O my help, hasten to aid me. Save me from the lion's mouth; from the horns of the wild bulls, my wretched life. *Ps.* My God, my God, look upon me, why have You forsaken me? Far from my salvation, are the words of my sins. — O Lord, be not far from me; O my help, hasten to aid me. Save me from the lion's mouth; from the horns of the wild bulls, my wretched life.

THE KYRIE

P. Lord, have mercy. *S*. Lord, have mercy. *P*. Lord, have mercy. *S*. Christ, have mercy. *P*. Christ, have mercy. *S*. Christ, have mercy. *P*. Lord, have mercy. *S*. Lord, have mercy. *P*. Lord, have mercy.

The Priest kisses the altar and turns to the people, saying:

P. The Lord be with you. S. And with your spirit. *P*. Let us pray.

THE PRAYER

Going to the right (Epistle) side, he says:

ALMIGHTY and everlasting God, Who willed that our Savior should take upon Himself our flesh, and suffer on the Cross, that all mankind might have His example of humility for their imitation: grant that we may merit both to keep in mind the lesson of His patience, and to be made partakers of His Resurrection. Through the same our Lord Jesus Christ, Your Son, Who lives and reigns with You in the unity of the Holy Spirit, God, world without end. S. Amen.

THE EPISTLE • Phil. 2, 5-11

BRETHREN: Have this mind in you which was also in Christ Jesus, Who though He was by nature God, did not consider being equal to God a thing to be clung to, but emptied Himself, taking the nature of a slave and being made like unto men. And appearing in the form of man, He humbled Himself, becoming obedient to death, even to death on a cross. Therefore God has exalted Him and has bestowed upon Him the name that is above every name, (*here all genuflect*) so that at the name of Jesus every knee should bend of those in heaven, on earth and under the earth, and every tongue should confess that the Lord Jesus Christ is in the glory of God the Father. S. Thanks be to God.

THE GRADUAL • Ps. 72, 24. 1-3

YOU have hold of my right hand; with Your counsel You guide me; and in the end You will receive me in glory. ℣. How good God is to Israel, to those who are clean of heart! But, as for me, I almost lost my balance; my feet all but slipped, because I was envious of sinners when I saw them prosper though they were wicked.

THE TRACT • Ps. 21, 2-32

MY GOD, my God, look upon me: why have You forsaken me? ℣. Far from my salvation, are the words of my sins. ℣. O my God, I cry out by day and You answer not; by night, and there is no relief. ℣. But You are enthroned in the holy place, O glory of Israel! ℣. In You our fathers trusted; they trusted and You delivered them. ℣. To You they cried, and they escaped; in You they trusted, and they were not put to shame. ℣. But I am a worm, not a man; the scorn of men, despised by the people. ℣. All who see me, scoff at me; they mock me with parted lips, they wag their heads. ℣. "He relied on the Lord; let Him deliver him, let Him rescue him, if he loves Him." ℣. But they look on and gloat over me; they divide my garments among them, and for my vesture they cast lots. ℣. Save me from the lion's mouth; from the horns of the wild bulls, my wretched life. ℣. You who fear the Lord, praise Him: all you descendants of Jacob, give glory to Him. ℣. There shall be declared to the Lord a generation to come: and the heavens shall show forth His justice. ℣. To a people that shall be born, which the Lord has made.

PRAYER BEFORE THE GOSPEL

Bowing down at the center of the altar, he says:

CLEANSE my heart and my lips, O almighty God, Who cleansed the lips of the Prophet Isaias with a burning coal. In Your gracious mercy deign so to purify me that I may worthily proclaim Your holy Gospel. Through Christ our Lord. Amen.

Lord, grant Your blessing. The Lord be in my heart and on my lips, that I may worthily and fittingly proclaim His holy Gospel. Amen.

PASSION OF OUR LORD JESUS CHRIST

Saint Matthew 26, 36-75; 27, 1-60

AT THAT time, Jesus came with His disciples to a country place called Gethsemani, and He said to His disciples, "Sit down here, while I go over yonder and pray." And He took with Him Peter and the two sons of Zebedee, and He began to be saddened and exceedingly troubled. Then He said to them, "My soul is sad, even unto death. Wait here and watch with Me." And going forward a little, He fell prostrate and prayed, saying, "Father, if it is possible, let this cup pass away from Me; yet not as I will, but as You will." Then He came to the disciples and found them sleeping. And He said to Peter, "Could you not, then, watch one hour with Me? Watch and pray, that you may not enter into temptation. The spirit indeed is willing, but the flesh is weak." Again a second time He went away and prayed, saying, "My Father, if this cup cannot pass away unless I drink it, Your will be done." And He came again and found them sleeping, for their eyes were heavy. And leaving them He went back again, and prayed a third time, saying the same words over. Then He came to His disciples, and said to them, "Sleep on now, and take your rest! Behold, the hour is at hand when the Son of Man will be betrayed into the hands of sinners. Rise, let us go. Behold, he who betrays Me is at hand."

And while He was yet speaking, behold Judas, one of the Twelve, came and with him a great crowd with swords and clubs, from the chief priests and elders of the people. Now His betrayer had given them a sign, saying, "Whomever I kiss, that is He; lay hold of Him." And he went straight up to Jesus and said, "Hail, Rabbi!" and kissed Him. And Jesus said to him, "Friend, for what purpose have you come?" Then they came forward and set hands on Jesus and took Him. And behold, one of those who were with Jesus, reached out his hand, drew his sword, and struck the servant of the high priest, cutting off his ear. Then Jesus said to him, "Put back your sword into its place; for all those who take the sword will perish by the sword. Or do you suppose that I cannot entreat My Father, and He will even now furnish Me with more than twelve legions of angels? How then are the Scriptures to be fulfilled, that thus it must take place?"

In that hour Jesus said to the crowds, "As against a robber you have come out, with swords and clubs, to seize Me. I sat daily with you in the temple teaching, and you did not lay hands on Me." Now all this was done that the Scriptures of the prophets might be fulfilled. Then all the disciples left Him and fled.

Now those who had taken Jesus led Him away to Caiphas the high priest, where the Scribes and the elders had gathered together. But Peter was following Him at a distance, even to the courtyard of the high priest, and he went in and sat with the attendants to see the end. Now the chief priests and all the Sanhedrin were seeking false witness against Jesus, that they might put Him to death, but they found none, though many false witnesses came forward. But last of all two false witnesses came forward, and said, "This man said, 'I am able to destroy the temple of God, and to rebuild it after three days.'" Then the high priest, standing up, said to Him, "Do You make no answer to the things that these men prefer against You?" But Jesus kept silence. And the high priest said to Him, "I adjure You by the living God that You tell us whether You are the Christ, the Son of God." Jesus said to him, "You have said it. Nevertheless, I say to you, hereafter you shall see the Son of Man sitting at the right hand of the Power and coming upon the clouds of heaven." Then the high priest tore his garments, saying, "He has blasphemed; what further need have we of witnesses? Behold, now you have heard the blasphemy. What do you think?" And they answered and said, "He is liable to death."

Then they spat in His face and buffeted Him; while others struck His face with the palms of their hands, saying, "Prophesy to us, O Christ! who is it that struck You?" Now Peter was sitting outside in the courtyard; and a maidservant came up to him and said, "You also were with Jesus the Galilean." But he denied it before them all, saying, "I do not know what you are saying." And when he had gone out to the gateway, another maid saw him, and said to those who were there, "This man also was with Jesus of Nazareth." And again he denied it with an oath, "I do not know the Man!" And after a little while the bystanders came up and said to Peter, "Surely you also are one of them, for even your speech betrays you." Then he began to curse and to swear that he did not know the Man. And at that moment a cock crowed. And Peter remembered the word that Jesus had said, "Before a cock crows, you will deny Me three times." And he went out and wept bitterly.

Now when morning came all the chief priests and the elders of the people took counsel together against Jesus in order to put Him to death. And they bound Him and led Him away, and delivered Him to Pontius Pilate the procurator. Then Judas, who betrayed Him, when he saw that He was condemned, repented and brought back the thirty pieces of silver to the chief priests and the elders, saying, "I have sinned in betraying innocent blood." But they said, "What is that to us? See to it yourself." And he flung the pieces of silver into the temple, and withdrew; and went away and hanged himself with a halter. And the chief priests took the pieces of silver, and said, "It is not lawful to put them into the treasury, seeing that it is the price of blood." And after they had consulted together, they bought with them the potter's field, as a burial place for strangers. For this reason that field has been called even to this day, Haceldama, that is, the Field of Blood. Then what was spoken through Jeremias the prophet was fulfilled, "And they took the thirty pieces of silver, the price of Him Who was priced, upon Whom the children of Israel set a price; and they gave them for the potter's field, as the Lord directed me."

Now Jesus stood before the procurator, and the procurator asked Him, saying, "Are You the King of the Jews?" Jesus said to him, "You say it." And when He was accused by the chief priests and the elders, He made no answer. Then Pilate said to Him, "Do You not hear how many things they prefer against You?" But He did not answer him a single word, so that the procurator wondered exceedingly. Now at festival time the procurator used to release to the crowd a prisoner, whomever they would. Now he had at that time a notorious prisoner called Barabbas. Therefore, when they had gathered together, Pilate said, "Whom do you wish that I release to you? Barabbas, or Jesus Who is called Christ?" For he knew that they had delivered Him up out of envy. Now, as he was sitting on the judgment-seat, his wife sent to him, saying, "Have nothing to do with that just Man, for I have suffered many things in a dream today because of Him." But the chief priests and the elders persuaded the crowds to ask for Barabbas and to destroy Jesus. But the procurator addressed them, and said to them, "Which of the two do you wish that I release to you?" And they said, "Barabbas." Pilate said to them, "What then am I to do with Jesus Who is called Christ?" They all said, "Let Him be crucified!" The procurator said to them, "Why, what evil has He done?" But they kept crying out the more, saying, "Let Him be crucified!" Now Pilate, seeing that he was doing no good, but rather that a riot was breaking out, took water and washed his hands in sight of the crowd, saying, "I am innocent of the blood of this just Man; see to it yourselves." And all the people answered and said, "His Blood be on us and on our children." Then he released to them Barabbas; but Jesus he scourged and delivered to them to be crucified.

Then the soldiers of the procurator took Jesus into the prætorium, and gathered together about Him the whole cohort. And they stripped Him and put on Him a scarlet cloak; and plaiting a crown of thorns, they put it upon His head, and a reed into His right hand; and bending the knee before Him they mocked Him, saying, "Hail, King of the Jews!" And they spat on Him, and took the reed and kept striking Him on the head. And when they had mocked Him, they took the cloak off Him and put His own garments on Him, and led Him away to crucify Him.

Now as they went out, they found a man of Cyrene named Simon; him they forced to take up His Cross. And they came to the place called Golgotha, that is, the Place of the Skull. And they gave Him wine to drink mixed with gall; but when He had tasted it, He would not drink. And after they had crucified Him, they divided His garments, casting lots, [to fulfill what was spoken through the prophet, "They divided My garments among them, and upon My vesture they cast lots."] And sitting down they kept watch over Him. And they put above His head the charge against Him, written, "This is Jesus, the King of the Jews."

Then two robbers were crucified with Him, one on His right hand and one on His left. Now the passers-by were jeering at Him, shaking their heads, and saying, "You Who would destroy the temple, and in three days build it up again, save Yourself!

If You are the Son of God, come down from the Cross!" In like manner, the chief priests with the Scribes and the elders, mocking, said, "He saved others, Himself He cannot save! If He is the King of Israel, let Him come down now from the Cross, and we will believe Him. He trusted in God; let Him deliver Him now, if He wants Him; for He said, 'I am the Son of God.'" And the robbers also, who were crucified with Him, reproached Him in the same way.

Now from the sixth hour there was darkness over the whole land until the ninth hour. But about the ninth hour Jesus cried out with a loud voice, saying, "Eli, Eli, lamma sabacthani," that is, "My God, My God, why have You forsaken Me?" And some of the bystanders on hearing this said, "This Man is calling Elias." And immediately one of them ran and, taking a sponge, soaked it in common wine, put it on a reed and offered it to Him to drink. But the rest said, "Wait, let us see whether Elias is coming to save Him." But Jesus again cried out with a loud voice, and gave up His spirit. (*Here all kneel and pause a few moments.*)

And behold, the curtain of the temple was torn in two from top to bottom; and the earth quaked, and the rocks were rent, and the tombs were opened, and many bodies of the saints who had fallen asleep arose; and coming forth out of the tombs after His Resurrection, they came into the Holy City, and appeared to many. Now when the centurion, and those who were with him keeping guard over Jesus, saw the earthquake and the things that were happening, they were very much afraid, and they said, "Truly He was the Son of God." And many women were there, looking on from a distance, who had followed Jesus from Galilee, ministering to Him. Among them were Mary Magdalene, and Mary the mother of James and Joseph, and the mother of the sons of Zebedee.

Now when it was evening, there came a certain rich man of Arimathea, Joseph by name, who was himself a disciple of Jesus. He went to Pilate and asked for the Body of Jesus. Then Pilate ordered the Body to be given up. And Joseph taking the Body, wrapped it in a clean linen cloth, and laid it in his new tomb, which he had hewn out in the rock. Then he rolled a large stone to the entrance of the tomb, and departed. *S.* Praise be to You, O Christ.

Those who celebrate a second or third Mass today are not bound to repeat the reading of the Lord's Passion; in place of it the following Gospel is read in the usual manner:

THE GOSPEL • Matt. 27, 45-52

Going to the left (Gospel) side of the altar, he says:

P. The Lord be with you. *S.* And with your spirit.
P. ✠ The continuation of the holy Gospel according to Saint Matthew. *S.* Glory be to You, O Lord.

AFTER they had crucified Jesus, from the sixth hour there was darkness over the whole land until the ninth hour. But about the ninth hour Jesus cried out with a loud voice, saying, "Eli, Eli, lamma sabacthani," that is, "My God, My God, why have You forsaken Me?" And some of the bystanders on hearing this said, "This Man is calling Elias." And immediately one of them ran and, taking a sponge, soaked it in common wine, put it on a reed and offered it to Him to drink. But the rest said, "Wait, let us see whether Elias is coming to save Him." But Jesus again cried out with a loud voice, and gave up His spirit. (*Here all kneel and pause a few moments.*) And behold, the curtain of the temple was torn in two from top to bottom; and the earth quaked, and the rocks were rent, and the tombs were opened, and many bodies of the saints who had fallen asleep arose. *S.* Praise be to You, O Christ.

P. By the words of the Gospel, may our sins be taken away.

THE NICENE CREED

At the center of the altar, he says:

I BELIEVE in one God, the Father almighty, Maker of heaven and earth, and of all things visible and invisible. And in one Lord Jesus Christ, the Only-begotten Son of God. Born of the Father before all ages. God of God; Light of Light; true God of true God. Begotten not made; of one being with the Father; by Whom all things were made. Who for us men, and for our salvation, came down from heaven. (*Here all genuflect.*) And was made Flesh by the Holy Spirit of the Virgin Mary: AND WAS MADE MAN. He was also crucified for us, suffered under Pontius Pilate and was buried. And on the third day He rose again according to the Scriptures. And ascending into heaven, He sits at the right hand of the Father. And He shall come again in glory to judge the living and the dead; and of His kingdom there shall be no end. And I believe in the Holy Spirit, Lord and Giver of life, Who proceeds from the Father and the Son. Who together with the Father and the Son is no less adored, and glorified: Who spoke by

the Prophets. And I believe in One, Holy, Catholic and Apostolic Church. I confess one Baptism for the remission of sins. And I look for the resurrection of the dead. ✠ And the life of the world to come. Amen.

THE OFFERTORY

The Priest turns to the people and says:

P. The Lord be with you. *S.* And with your spirit.
P. Let us pray.

THE OFFERTORY VERSE • Ps. 68, 21-22

INSULT has broken my heart, and I am weak; I looked for sympathy, but there was none; for comforters, and I found none. Rather they put gall in my food and in my thirst they gave me vinegar to drink.

The Priest now uncovers the chalice, places the host on the paten and offering it up, says:

ACCEPT, O holy Father, almighty and eternal God, this spotless host, which I, Your unworthy servant, offer to You, my living and true God, to atone for my numberless sins, offenses, and negligences; on behalf of all here present and likewise for all faithful Christians living and dead, that it may profit me and them as a means of salvation to life everlasting. Amen.

He pours wine and water into the chalice, blessing the water before it is poured.

O GOD, Who established the nature of man in wondrous dignity, and still more admirably restored it, grant that through the mystery of this water and wine, we may be made partakers of His Divinity, Who has condescended to become partaker of our humanity, Jesus Christ, Your Son, our

Lord. Who lives and reigns with You in the unity of the Holy Spirit, God, world without end. Amen.

Offering up the wine, the Priest says:

WE OFFER You, O Lord, the chalice of salvation, humbly begging of Your mercy that it may arise before Your Divine Majesty, with a pleasing fragrance, for our salvation and for that of the whole world. Amen.

Bowing down, the Priest says:

IN A humble spirit and with a contrite heart, may we be accepted by You, O Lord, and may our sacrifice so be offered in Your sight this day as to please You, O Lord God.

Raising his eyes and blessing the offering, he says:

COME, O Sanctifier, almighty and eternal God, and bless ✠ this sacrifice prepared for the glory of Your holy name.

WASHING THE FINGERS

I WASH my hands in innocence, and I go around Your altar, O Lord, giving voice to my thanks, and recounting all Your wondrous deeds. O Lord, I love the house in which You dwell, the tenting-place of Your glory. Gather not my soul with those of sinners, nor with men of blood my life. On their hands are crimes, and their right hands are full of bribes. But I walk in integrity; redeem me, and have pity on me. My foot stands on level ground; in the assemblies I will bless You, O Lord.

ACCEPT, Most Holy Trinity, this offering which we are making to You in remembrance of the Passion, Resurrection, and Ascension of Jesus Christ, our Lord; and in honor of Blessed Mary, ever Virgin, Blessed John the Baptist, the Holy

Apostles Peter and Paul, and of these, and of all the Saints; that it may add to their honor and aid our salvation; and may they deign to intercede in heaven for us who honor their memory here on earth. Through the same Christ our Lord. Amen.

The Priest turns toward the people and says:

Pray, brethren, that my sacrifice and yours may become acceptable to God the Father almighty.

S. May the Lord accept this sacrifice from your hands to the praise and glory of His name, for our advantage, and that of all His holy Church.

P. Amen.

THE SECRET

GRANT, we beseech You, O Lord, that the gift now offered in the sight of Your Majesty, may obtain for us both the grace of devotion, and the reward of a blessed eternity. Through our Lord Jesus Christ, Your Son, Who lives and reigns with You in the unity of the Holy Spirit, God.

P. World without end. *S.* Amen.

PREFACE—CANON

P. The Lord be with you. *S.* And with your spirit.

P. Lift up your hearts.

S. We have lifted them up to the Lord.

P. Let us give thanks to the Lord, our God.

S. It is fitting and just.

IT IS fitting indeed and just, right and helpful to salvation, for us always and everywhere to give thanks to You, O holy Lord, Father almighty and everlasting God; Who set the salvation of mankind upon the tree of the Cross, so that whence came death, thence also life might rise again, and he that overcame by the tree, by the tree also might be overcome: through Christ our Lord. Through Whom the Angels praise Your Majesty, the Dominations worship it, and the Powers are in awe. The heavens and the heavenly hosts, and the blessed Seraphim join together in celebrating their joy. With these, we pray You, join our own voices also, while we say with lowly praise (*the bell is rung 3 times*):

HOLY, HOLY, HOLY, Lord God of Hosts. Heaven and earth are filled with Your glory. Hosanna in the highest. ✠ Blessed is He Who comes in the name of the Lord. Hosanna in the highest.

THE CANON OF THE MASS

THEREFORE, most gracious Father, we humbly beg of You and entreat You through Jesus Christ Your Son, our Lord, (*he kisses the altar*) to deem acceptable and bless these ✠ gifts, these ✠ offerings, these ✠ holy and unspotted oblations which, in the first place, we offer You for Your Holy Catholic Church, that You would deign to give her peace and protection, to unite and guard her throughout the world, together with Your servant N., our Pope, and N., our Bishop; and all true believers who cherish the Catholic and Apostolic Faith.

Commemoration of the Living

REMEMBER, O Lord, Your servants and handmaids, N. and N., (*name them*) and all here present, whose faith and devotion are known to You, on whose behalf we offer to You, or who themselves offer to You, this sacrifice of praise for themselves, families and friends, for the good of their souls, for their hope of salvation and deliverance from all harm, and who offer their homage to You, eternal, living and true God.

Commemoration of the Saints

IN THE unity of holy fellowship we observe the memory, first of all, of the glorious and ever Virgin Mary, Mother of our Lord and God Jesus Christ; next, that of Your Blessed Apostles and Martyrs, Peter and Paul, Andrew, James, John, Thomas, James, Philip, Bartholomew, Matthew, Simon and Thaddeus; of Linus, Cletus, Clement, Sixtus, Cornelius, Cyprian, Lawrence, Chrysogonus, John and Paul, Cosmas and Damian, and of all Your Saints, by whose merits and prayers grant that we may be always fortified by the help of Your protection. Through the same Christ our Lord. Amen.

Spreading his hands over the oblation, he says:

GRACIOUSLY accept, then, we beseech You, O Lord, this service of our worship and that of all Your household. Provide that our days be spent in Your peace, save us from everlasting damnation, and cause us to be numbered in the flock You have chosen. Through Christ our Lord. Amen.

O GOD, deign to bless ✠ what we offer, and make it approved, ✠ effective, ✠ right, and wholly pleasing in every way, that it may become for our good, the Body ✠ and Blood ✠ of Your dearly beloved Son, Jesus Christ our Lord.

CONSECRATION—ELEVATION

WHO, the day before He suffered, took bread into His holy and venerable hands, and having raised His eyes to heaven, to You, O God, His almighty Father, giving thanks to You, He blessed it, ✠ broke it, and gave it to His disciples, saying: All of you take and eat of this:

FOR THIS IS MY BODY.

IN LIKE manner, when the supper was done, taking also this goodly chalice into His holy and venerable hands, again giving thanks to You, He blessed ✠ it, and gave it to His disciples, saying: All of you take and drink of this:

FOR THIS IS THE CHALICE OF MY BLOOD OF THE NEW AND ETERNAL COVENANT: THE MYSTERY OF FAITH: WHICH SHALL BE SHED FOR YOU AND FOR MANY UNTO THE FORGIVENESS OF SINS.

After replacing the chalice on the corporal, he says:

As often as you shall do these things, in memory of Me shall you do them.

Offering of the Victim

MINDFUL, therefore, O Lord, not only of the blessed Passion of the same Christ, Your Son, our Lord, but also of His Resurrection from the dead, and finally His glorious Ascension into heaven, we, Your ministers, as also Your holy people, offer to Your supreme Majesty, of the gifts bestowed upon us, the pure ✠ Victim, the holy ✠ Victim, the all-perfect ✠ Victim: the holy ✠ Bread of life eternal and the Chalice ✠ of unending salvation.

AND this deign to regard with gracious and kindly attention and hold acceptable, as You deigned to accept the offerings of Abel, Your just servant, and the sacrifice of Abraham our patriarch, and that which Your chief priest Melchisedec offered to You, a holy sacrifice and a spotless victim.

MOST humbly we implore You, almighty God, bid these offerings to be brought by the hands of Your holy angel to Your altar above; before the face of Your Divine Majesty; that those of us who, by sharing in the Sacrifice of this altar, shall receive the Most Sacred ✠ Body and ✠ Blood of Your Son, may be filled with every grace and heavenly blessing. Through the same Christ our Lord. Amen.

Commemoration of the Dead

REMEMBER also, O Lord, Your servants and handmaids, N. and N., who have gone before us with the sign of faith, and rest in the sleep of peace. (*Here pray for the dead.*) To these, O Lord, and to all who rest in Christ, we beseech You to grant of Your goodness, a place of comfort, light and peace. Through the same Christ our Lord. Amen.

TO US sinners also, Your servants, trusting in the greatness of Your mercy, deign to grant some part and fellowship with Your Holy Apostles and Martyrs: with John, Stephen, Matthias, Barnabas, Ignatius, Alexander, Marcellinus, Peter, Felicitas, Perpetua, Agatha, Lucy, Agnes, Cecilia, Anastasia, and all Your Saints; into whose company, we implore You to admit us, not weighing our merits, but freely granting us pardon. Through Christ our Lord.

THROUGH Whom, O Lord, You always create, ✠ sanctify, ✠ fill with life, ✠ bless, and bestow upon us all good things.

The Minor Elevation

THROUGH ✠ Him, and with ✠ Him, and in ✠ Him, is to You, God the Father ✠ almighty, in the unity of the Holy ✠ Spirit, all honor and glory, world without end. S. Amen.

THE COMMUNION AND THANKSGIVING

Let us pray. Prompted by saving precepts, and taught by Your divine teaching, we dare to say:

OUR FATHER, Who art in heaven, hallowed be Thy name: Thy kingdom come: Thy will be done on earth as it is in heaven. Give us this day our daily bread; and forgive us our trespasses, as we forgive those who trespass against us. And lead us not into temptation: S. But deliver us from evil. *P*. Amen.

DELIVER us, we beseech You, O Lord, from all evils, past, present, and to come; and by the intercession of the Blessed and glorious Mary, ever Virgin, Mother of God, together with Your Blessed Apostles Peter and Paul, and Andrew, and all the Saints, grant of Your goodness, peace in our days, that aided by the riches of Your mercy, we may be always free from sin and safe from all disturbance.

Through the same our Lord Jesus Christ, Your Son, Who lives and reigns with You in the unity of the Holy Spirit, God, world without end.

S. Amen.

P. May the peace ✠ of the Lord be ✠ always with ✠ you.

S. And with your spirit.

The Priest puts a small particle into the chalice, saying:

May this mingling and consecration of the Body and Blood of our Lord Jesus Christ help us who receive it to life everlasting. Amen.

720-16

LAMB of God, You Who take away the sins of the world, have mercy on us.

Lamb of God, You Who take away the sins of the world, have mercy on us.

Lamb of God, You Who take away the sins of the world, grant us peace.

PRAYERS BEFORE HOLY COMMUNION

Then inclining toward the altar, he says:

O LORD Jesus Christ, Who said to Your Apostles: "Peace I leave with you, My peace I give to you," regard not my sins but the faith of Your Church, and deign to give her peace and unity according to Your Will: Who live and reign, God, world without end. Amen.

O LORD Jesus Christ, Son of the living God, Who, by the will of the Father, with the cooperation of the Holy Spirit, have by Your death given life to the world, deliver me by this Your Most Sacred Body and Blood from all my sins and from every evil. Make me always cling to Your commandments, and never permit me to be separated from You. Who with the same God the Father and the Holy Spirit, live and reign, God, world without end. Amen.

LET not the partaking of Your Body, O Lord Jesus Christ, which I, though unworthy, presume to receive, turn to my judgment and condemnation; but through Your goodness, may it become a safeguard and an effective remedy, both of soul and body. Who live and reign with God the Father, in the unity of the Holy Spirit, God, world without end. Amen.

COMMUNION OF THE PRIEST

I WILL take the Bread of heaven, and call upon the name of the Lord.

Lord, I am not worthy that You should come under my roof; but only say the word, and my soul will be healed. (3 *times.*)

Making the Sign of the Cross with the Host, he says:

MAY the Body of our Lord Jesus Christ preserve my soul to life everlasting. Amen.

What return shall I make to the Lord for all He has given me? I will take the Chalice of salvation, and I will call upon the name of the Lord. Praising will I call upon the Lord and I shall be saved from my enemies.

Making the Sign of the Cross with the chalice, he says:

MAY the Blood of our Lord Jesus Christ preserve my soul to life everlasting. Amen.

The Priest reverently consumes the Precious Blood.

COMMUNION OF THE FAITHFUL

The Server and people say the "Confiteor."

P. May almighty God have mercy on you, forgive you your sins, and bring you to life everlasting. *S.* Amen.

P. May the almighty and merciful Lord grant you pardon, ✠ absolution and remission of your sins. S. Amen.

Holding up a Sacred Host, the Priest says:

Behold the Lamb of God, behold Him Who takes away the sins of the world.

Lord, I am not worthy that You should come under my roof; but only say the word, and my soul will be healed. (3 *times.*)

The Priest says to each communicant:

May the Body of our Lord Jesus Christ preserve your soul to life everlasting. Amen.

The Priest purifies the chalice with wine, saying:

WHAT has passed our lips as food, O Lord, may we possess in purity of heart, that what is given to us in time, be our healing for eternity.

He purifies his fingers with wine and water, saying:

MAY Your Body, O Lord, which I have eaten, and Your Blood which I have drunk, cleave to my very soul, and grant that no trace of sin be found in me, whom these pure and holy mysteries have renewed. Who live and reign, world without end. Amen.

THE COMMUNION • Matt. 26, 42

FATHER, if this cup cannot pass away, unless I drink it, Your will be done.

The Priest, turning to the people, says:

P. The Lord be with you. *S.* And with your spirit.
P. Let us pray.

THE POSTCOMMUNION

O LORD, by the working of this mystery, may our vices be purged away and our just desires fulfilled. Through our Lord Jesus Christ, Your Son, Who lives and reigns with You in the unity of the Holy Spirit, God, world without end. *S.* Amen.

FINAL PRAYERS

P. The Lord be with you. *S.* And with your spirit.
P. Let us bless the Lord. *S.* Thanks be to God.

MAY the tribute of my worship be pleasing to You, Most Holy Trinity, and grant that the sacrifice which I, all unworthy, have offered in the presence of Your Majesty, may be acceptable to You, and through Your mercy obtain forgiveness for me and all for whom I have offered it. Through Christ our Lord. Amen.

THE LAST BLESSING

MAY almighty God bless you: ✠ the Father, and the Son, and the Holy Spirit.
S. Amen.

In Masses without the blessing of Palm branches, the following Gospel is read at the end.

P. The Lord be with you. *S.* And with your spirit.
P. ✠ The continuation of the holy Gospel according to Saint Matthew. *S.* Glory be to You, O Lord.

AT THAT time, when Jesus drew near to Jerusalem, and came to Bethphage, on the Mount of Olives, He sent two disciples, saying to them, "Go into the village opposite you, and immediately you will find an ass tied, and a colt with her; loose them and bring them to Me. And if anyone say anything to you, you shall say that the Lord has need of them, and immediately he will send them." Now this was done that what was spoken through the prophet might be fulfilled, "Tell the daughter of Sion: Behold, your King comes to you, meek and seated upon an ass, and upon a colt, the foal of a beast of burden." So the disciples went and did as Jesus had directed them. And they brought the ass and the colt, laid their cloaks on them, and made Him sit thereon. And most of the crowd spread their cloaks upon the road, while others were cutting branches from the trees, and strewing them on the road. And the crowds that went before Him, and those that followed, kept crying out, saying, "Hosanna to the Son of David! Blessed is He Who comes in the name of the Lord!" S. Thanks be to God.

The Prayers after Low Mass are conveniently placed inside the back cover.

"Do not Be Terrified. You Are Looking for Jesus of Nazareth, Who Was Crucified. He Has Risen, He Is not Here." Mark 16, 6.

EASTER SUNDAY

The Resurrection of Christ is a historical fact. By it our Lord fulfilled His promise that He would rise on the third day and thus proved His Divinity, giving a sure foundation to our faith. When His enemies believed that they had destroyed Him, His real triumph began. To die to sin and to live with Christ is our way to victory and resurrection.

Alleluia, or "Praise the Lord," is an expression of joy and hope for the eternal happiness which our Lord obtained for us by His glorious Resurrection. The Church sings Alleluia today, and often during Paschal Time, because Christ is risen from the grave.

(WHITE VESTMENTS)

PRAYERS AT THE FOOT OF THE ALTAR

IN THE name of the Father, ✠ and of the Son, and of the Holy Spirit. Amen.

Priest. I will go in to the altar of God.

Server. The God of my gladness and joy.

Psalm 42

DO ME justice, O God, and fight my fight against a faithless people; from the deceitful and impious man rescue me.

S. For You, O God, are my strength. Why do You keep me so far away? Why must I go about in mourning, with the enemy oppressing me?

P. Send forth Your light and Your fidelity; they shall lead me on and bring me to Your holy mountain, to Your dwelling-place.

S. Then will I go in to the altar of God, the God of my gladness and joy.
P. Then will I give You thanks upon the harp, O God, my God. Why are you so downcast, O my soul? Why do you sigh within me?
S. Hope in God! For I shall again be thanking Him in the presence of my Savior and my God.
P. Glory be to the Father, and to the Son, and to the Holy Spirit.
S. As it was in the beginning, is now, and ever shall be, world without end. Amen.
P. I will go in to the altar of God.
S. The God of my gladness and joy.
P. Our help ✠ is in the name of the Lord.
S. Who made heaven and earth.
P. I confess to almighty God, etc.
S. May almighty God have mercy on you, forgive you your sins, and bring you to life everlasting.
P. Amen.

The Server, bowing, says the "Confiteor."

I CONFESS to almighty God, to Blessed Mary, ever Virgin, to Blessed Michael the Archangel, to Blessed John the Baptist, to the Holy Apostles Peter and Paul, and to all the Saints, and to you, Father, that I have sinned exceedingly in thought, word and deed, *through my fault, through my fault, through my most grievous fault.* Therefore I beseech Blessed Mary, ever Virgin, Blessed Michael the Archangel, Blessed John the Baptist, the Holy Apostles Peter and Paul, and all the Saints, and you, Father, to pray to the Lord our God for me.
P. May almighty God have mercy on you, forgive you your sins, and bring you to life everlasting.
S. Amen.

MAY the almighty and merciful Lord grant us pardon, ✠ absolution, and remission of our sins. *S.* Amen.

P. Will You not, O God, give us life?
S. And shall not Your people rejoice in You?
P. Show us, O Lord, Your kindness.
S. And grant us Your salvation.
P. O Lord, hear my prayer.
S. And let my cry come to You.
P. The Lord be with you.
S. And with your spirit. *P.* Let us pray.

Going up to the altar, the Priest prays silently:

TAKE away from us our sins, O Lord, we beseech You, that we may enter with pure minds into the Holy of Holies. Through Christ our Lord. Amen.

WE BESEECH You, O Lord, by the merits of Your Saints (*he kisses the altar*) whose relics lie here, and of all the Saints: deign in Your mercy to pardon me all my sins. Amen.

THE INTROIT • Ps. 138, 18. 5. 6. 1-2

At the right side of the altar, the Priest says:

I AROSE, and am still with You, alleluia; You rest Your hand upon Me, alleluia; Your knowledge is too wonderful, alleluia, alleluia. *Ps.* O Lord, You have probed Me and You know Me; You know when I sit and when I stand. Glory be to the Father, and to the Son, and to the Holy Spirit. As it was in the beginning, is now, and ever shall be, world without end. Amen. — I arose, and am still with You, alleluia; You rest Your hand upon Me, alleluia; Your knowledge is too wonderful, alleluia, alleluia.

THE KYRIE

P. Lord, have mercy. *S.* Lord, have mercy. *P.* Lord, have mercy. *S.* Christ, have mercy. *P.* Christ, have mercy. *S.* Christ, have mercy. *P.* Lord, have mercy. *S.* Lord, have mercy. *P.* Lord, have mercy.

THE GLORIA

GLORY to God in the highest. And on earth peace to men of good will. We praise You. We bless You. We adore You. We glorify You. We give You thanks for Your great glory. O Lord God, heavenly King, God the Father almighty. O Lord Jesus Christ, the Only-begotten Son. O Lord God, Lamb of God, Son of the Father: You Who take away the sins of the world, have mercy on us. You Who take away the sins of the world, receive our prayer. You Who sit at the right hand of the Father, have mercy on us. For You alone are holy. You alone are the Lord. You alone, O Jesus Christ, are most high. Together with the Holy Spirit ✠ in the glory of God the Father. Amen.

The Priest kisses the altar and turns to the people, saying:

P. The Lord be with you. *S.* And with your spirit. *P.* Let us pray.

THE PRAYER

Going to the right (Epistle) side, he says:

O GOD, Who on this day, through Your Only-begotten Son, overcame death, and opened to us the gate of everlasting life: as, by Your anticipating grace, You breathe good desires into our hearts, so also, by Your gracious help, bring them to good effect. Through the same our Lord Jesus Christ, Your Son, Who lives and reigns with You in the unity of the Holy Spirit, God, world without end. S. Amen.

THE EPISTLE • 1 Cor. 5, 7-8

BRETHREN: Purge out the old leaven, that you may be a new dough, as you really are without leaven. For Christ, our Passover, has been sacrificed. Therefore let us keep festival, not with the old leaven, nor with the leaven of malice and wickedness, but with the unleavened bread of sincerity and truth. S. Thanks be to God.

THE GRADUAL • Ps. 117, 24. 1

THIS is the day the Lord has made; let us be glad and rejoice in it. ℣. Give thanks to the Lord, for He is good, for His mercy endures forever.

Alleluia, alleluia. ℣. *1 Cor. 5,* 7. Christ, our Passover, has been sacrificed.

THE SEQUENCE

O CHRISTIANS, to the Paschal Victim bring:
Of praise the sacrificial Offering.
For the sheep the Lamb His Blood did shed:
The sinless Christ in the sinners' stead:
With God the guilty reconciling.
The Life with Death did fiercely strive:
Through dying the Leader now reigns alive.

O Mary, what did your wond'ring eyes adore?
"I saw the tomb of One Who dies no more!
The glorious risen Lord was shown to me:
The napkin, linen cloths there lying:
I heard the angels testifying.
Yes, Christ is ris'n and you shall see
Your Hope and mine in Galilee!"

We know that Christ rose from the grave:
O conqu'ring King, us sinners save.
Amen. Alleluia.

PRAYER BEFORE THE GOSPEL

Bowing down at the center of the altar, he says:

CLEANSE my heart and my lips, O almighty God, Who cleansed the lips of the Prophet Isaias with a burning coal. In Your gracious mercy deign so to purify me that I may worthily proclaim Your holy Gospel. Through Christ our Lord. Amen.

Lord, grant Your blessing. The Lord be in my heart and on my lips, that I may worthily and fittingly proclaim His holy Gospel. Amen.

THE GOSPEL • Mark 16, 1-7

Going to the left (Gospel) side of the altar, he says:

P. The Lord be with you. *S.* And with your spirit.
P. ✠ The continuation of the holy Gospel according to Saint Mark. *S.* Glory be to You, O Lord.

AT THAT time, Mary Magdalene, Mary the mother of James, and Salome, bought spices, that they might go and anoint Jesus. And very early on the first day of the week, they came to the tomb, when the sun had just risen. And they were saying to one another, "Who will roll the stone back from the entrance of the tomb for us?" And looking up they saw that the stone had been rolled back, for it was very large. But on entering the tomb, they saw a young man sitting at the right side, clothed in a white robe, and they were amazed. He said to them, "Do not be terrified. You are looking for Jesus of Nazareth, Who was crucified. He has risen, He is not here. Behold the place where they laid Him. But go, tell His disciples and Peter that He goes before you into Galilee; there you shall see Him, as He told you." S. Praise be to You, O Christ.

P. By the words of the Gospel, may our sins be taken away.

THE NICENE CREED

At the center of the altar, he says:

I BELIEVE in one God, the Father almighty, Maker of heaven and earth, and of all things visible and invisible. And in one Lord Jesus Christ, the Only-begotten Son of God. Born of the Father before all ages. God of God; Light of Light; true God of true God. Begotten not made; of one being with the Father; by Whom all things were made. Who for us men, and for our salvation, came down from heaven. (*Here all genuflect.*) And was made Flesh by the Holy Spirit of the Virgin Mary: AND WAS MADE MAN. He was also crucified for us, suffered under Pontius Pilate and was buried. And on the third day He rose again according to the Scriptures. And ascending into heaven, He sits at the right hand of the Father. And He shall come again in glory to judge the living and the dead; and of His kingdom there shall be no end. And I believe in the Holy Spirit, Lord and Giver of life, Who proceeds from the Father and the Son. Who together with the Father and the Son is no less adored, and glorified: Who spoke by the Prophets. And I believe in One, Holy, Catholic and Apostolic Church. I confess one Baptism for the remission of sins. And I look for the resurrection of the dead. ✠ And the life of the world to come. Amen.

THE OFFERTORY

The Priest turns to the people and says:

P. The Lord be with you. *S.* And with your spirit.
P. Let us pray.

THE OFFERTORY VERSE • Ps. 75, 9. 10

THE earth feared and was silent when God arose for judgment. Alleluia.

The Priest now uncovers the chalice, places the host on the paten and offering it up, says:

ACCEPT, O holy Father, almighty and eternal God, this spotless host, which I, Your unworthy servant, offer to You, my living and true God, to atone for my numberless sins, offenses, and negligences; on behalf of all here present and likewise for all faithful Christians living and dead, that it may profit me and them as a means of salvation to life everlasting. Amen.

He pours wine and water into the chalice, blessing the water before it is poured.

O GOD, Who established the nature of man in wondrous dignity, and still more admirably restored it, grant that through the mystery of this water and wine, we may be made partakers of His Divinity, Who has condescended to become partaker of our humanity, Jesus Christ, Your Son, our Lord. Who lives and reigns with You in the unity of the Holy Spirit, God, world without end. Amen.

Offering up the wine, the Priest says:

WE OFFER You, O Lord, the chalice of salvation, humbly begging of Your mercy that it may arise before Your Divine Majesty, with a pleasing fragrance, for our salvation and for that of the whole world. Amen.

Bowing down, the Priest says:

IN A humble spirit and with a contrite heart, may we be accepted by You, O Lord, and may our sacrifice so be offered in Your sight this day as to please You, O Lord God.

Raising his eyes and blessing the offering, he says:

COME, O Sanctifier, almighty and eternal God, and bless ✠ this sacrifice prepared for the glory of Your holy name.

WASHING THE FINGERS

I WASH my hands in innocence, and I go around Your altar, O Lord, giving voice to my thanks, and recounting all Your wondrous deeds. O Lord, I love the house in which You dwell, the tenting-place of Your glory. Gather not my soul with those of sinners, nor with men of blood my life. On their hands are crimes, and their right hands are full of bribes. But I walk in integrity; redeem me, and have pity on me. My foot stands on level ground; in the assemblies I will bless You, O Lord. Glory be to the Father, and to the Son, and to the Holy Spirit. As it was in the beginning, is now, and ever shall be, world without end. Amen.

ACCEPT, Most Holy Trinity, this offering which we are making to You in remembrance of the Passion, Resurrection, and Ascension of Jesus Christ, our Lord; and in honor of Blessed Mary, ever Virgin, Blessed John the Baptist, the Holy Apostles Peter and Paul, and of these, and of all the Saints; that it may add to their honor and aid our salvation; and may they deign to intercede in heaven for us who honor their memory here on earth. Through the same Christ our Lord. Amen.

The Priest turns toward the people and says:

Pray, brethren, that my sacrifice and yours may become acceptable to God the Father almighty.

S. May the Lord accept this sacrifice from your hands to the praise and glory of His name, for our advantage, and that of all His holy Church.

P. Amen.

THE SECRET

ACCEPT, we beseech You, O Lord, the prayers of Your people together with the sacrifice they offer, that what has been begun by these Easter mysteries, may by Your working profit us to everlasting salvation. Through our Lord Jesus Christ, Your Son, Who lives and reigns with You in the unity of the Holy Spirit, God.

P. World without end. *S.* Amen.

PREFACE—CANON

P. The Lord be with you. *S.* And with your spirit.

P. Lift up your hearts.

S. We have lifted them up to the Lord.

P. Let us give thanks to the Lord, our God.

S. It is fitting and just.

IT IS fitting indeed and just, right and helpful to salvation for us always to praise You, O Lord, but more gloriously on this day above others when Christ our Passover was sacrificed. For He is the true Lamb Who has taken away the sins of the world: Who by dying has destroyed our death; and by rising again has restored us to life. And therefore with Angels and Archangels, with Thrones and Dominations, and with the whole host of the heavenly army, we sing a hymn to Your glory, saying again and again (*the bell is rung* 3 *times*):

HOLY, HOLY, HOLY, Lord God of Hosts. Heaven and earth are filled with Your glory. Hosanna in the highest. ✠ Blessed is He Who comes in the name of the Lord. Hosanna in the highest.

THE CANON OF THE MASS

THEREFORE, most gracious Father, we humbly beg of You and entreat You through Jesus Christ Your Son, our Lord, (*he kisses the altar*) to deem acceptable and bless these ✠ gifts, these ✠ offerings, these ✠ holy and unspotted oblations which, in the first place, we offer You for Your Holy Catholic Church, that You would deign to give her peace and protection, to unite and guard her throughout the world, together with Your servant N., our Pope, and N., our Bishop; and all true believers who cherish the Catholic and Apostolic Faith.

Commemoration of the Living

REMEMBER, O Lord, Your servants and handmaids, N. and N., (*name them*) and all here present, whose faith and devotion are known to You, on whose behalf we offer to You, or who themselves offer to You, this sacrifice of praise for themselves, families and friends, for the good of their souls, for their hope of salvation and deliverance from all harm, and who offer their homage to You, eternal, living and true God.

Commemoration of the Saints

IN THE unity of holy fellowship, and keeping the most holy day of the Resurrection of our Lord Jesus Christ according to the flesh, we also observe the memory, first of all, of the glorious and ever Virgin Mary, Mother of our Lord and God Jesus Christ; next, that of Your Blessed Apostles and Martyrs, Peter and Paul, Andrew, James, John, Thomas, James, Philip, Bartholomew, Matthew, Simon and Thaddeus; of Linus, Cletus, Clement, Sixtus, Cornelius, Cyprian, Lawrence, Chrysogonus, John and Paul, Cosmas and Damian, and of all Your Saints, by whose merits and prayers grant that we may be always fortified by the help of Your protection. Through the same Christ our Lord. Amen.

Spreading his hands over the oblation, he says:

GRACIOUSLY accept, then, we beseech You, O Lord, this service of our worship, and that of all Your household, which we make to You in behalf of those whom You have vouchsafed to bring to a new birth by water and the Holy Spirit, giving them remission of all their sins. Provide that our days be spent in Your peace, save us from everlasting damnation, and cause us to be numbered in the flock You have chosen. Through Christ our Lord. Amen.

O GOD, deign to bless ✠ what we offer, and make it approved, ✠ effective, ✠ right, and wholly pleasing in every way, that it may become for our good, the Body ✠ and Blood ✠ of Your dearly beloved Son, Jesus Christ our Lord.

CONSECRATION—ELEVATION

WHO, the day before He suffered, took bread into His holy and venerable hands, and having raised His eyes to heaven, to You, O God, His almighty Father, giving thanks to You, He blessed it, ✠ broke it, and gave it to His disciples, saying: All of you take and eat of this:

FOR THIS IS MY BODY.

IN LIKE manner, when the supper was done, taking also this goodly chalice into His holy and venerable hands, again giving thanks to You, He blessed ✠ it, and gave it to His disciples, saying: All of you take and drink of this:

FOR THIS IS THE CHALICE OF MY BLOOD OF THE NEW AND ETERNAL COVENANT: THE MYSTERY OF FAITH: WHICH SHALL BE SHED FOR YOU AND FOR MANY UNTO THE FORGIVENESS OF SINS.

After replacing the chalice on the corporal, he says:

As often as you shall do these things, in memory of Me shall you do them.

Offering of the Victim

MINDFUL, therefore, O Lord, not only of the blessed Passion of the same Christ, Your Son, our Lord, but also of His Resurrection from the dead, and finally His glorious Ascension into heaven, we, Your ministers, as also Your holy people, offer to Your supreme Majesty, of the gifts bestowed upon us, the pure ✠ Victim, the holy ✠ Victim, the all-perfect ✠ Victim: the holy ✠ Bread of life eternal and the Chalice ✠ of unending salvation.

AND this deign to regard with gracious and kindly attention and hold acceptable, as You deigned to accept the offerings of Abel, Your just servant, and the sacrifice of Abraham our patriarch, and that which Your chief priest Melchisedec offered to You, a holy sacrifice and a spotless victim.

MOST humbly we implore You, almighty God, bid these offerings to be brought by the hands of Your holy angel to Your altar above; before the face of Your Divine Majesty; that those of us who, by sharing in the Sacrifice of this altar shall, receive the Most Sacred ✠ Body and ✠ Blood of Your Son, may be filled with every grace and heavenly blessing. Through the same Christ our Lord. Amen.

Commemoration of the Dead

REMEMBER also, O Lord, Your servants and handmaids, N. and N., who have gone before us with the sign of faith, and rest in the sleep of peace. (*Here pray for the dead.*) To these, O Lord, and to all who rest in Christ, we beseech You to grant of Your goodness, a place of comfort, light and peace. Through the same Christ our Lord. Amen.

TO US sinners also, Your servants, trusting in the greatness of Your mercy, deign to grant some part and fellowship with Your Holy Apostles and Martyrs: with John, Stephen, Matthias, Barnabas, Ignatius, Alexander, Marcellinus, Peter, Felicitas, Perpetua, Agatha, Lucy, Agnes, Cecilia, Anastasia, and all Your Saints; into whose company, we implore You to admit us, not weighing our merits, but freely granting us pardon. Through Christ our Lord.

THROUGH Whom, O Lord, You always create, ✠ sanctify, ✠ fill with life, ✠ bless, and bestow upon us all good things.

The Minor Elevation

THROUGH ✠ Him, and with ✠ Him, and in ✠ Him, is to You, God the Father ✠ almighty, in the unity of the Holy ✠ Spirit, all honor and glory, world without end. S. Amen.

THE COMMUNION AND THANKSGIVING

Let us pray. Prompted by saving precepts, and taught by Your divine teaching, we dare to say:

OUR FATHER, Who art in heaven, hallowed be Thy name: Thy kingdom come: Thy will be done on earth as it is in heaven. Give us this day our daily bread; and forgive us our trespasses, as we forgive those who trespass against us. And lead us not into temptation: S. But deliver us from evil. *P.* Amen.

DELIVER us, we beseech You, O Lord, from all evils, past, present, and to come; and by the intercession of the Blessed and glorious Mary, ever Virgin, Mother of God, together with Your Blessed Apostles Peter and Paul, and Andrew, and all the Saints, grant of Your goodness, peace in our days, that aided by the riches of Your mercy, we may be always free from sin and safe from all disturbance.

Through the same our Lord Jesus Christ, Your Son, Who lives and reigns with You in the unity of the Holy Spirit, God, world without end.

S. Amen.

P. May the peace ✠ of the Lord be ✠ always with ✠ you.

S. And with your spirit.

The Priest puts a small particle into the chalice, saying:

May this mingling and consecration of the Body and Blood of our Lord Jesus Christ help us who receive it to life everlasting. Amen.

LAMB of God, You Who take away the sins of the world, have mercy on us.
Lamb of God, You Who take away the sins of the world, have mercy on us.
Lamb of God, You Who take away the sins of the world, grant us peace.

PRAYERS BEFORE HOLY COMMUNION

Then inclining toward the altar, he says:

O LORD Jesus Christ, Who said to Your Apostles: "Peace I leave with you, My peace I give to you," regard not my sins but the faith of Your Church, and deign to give her peace and unity according to Your Will: Who live and reign, God world without end. Amen.

O LORD Jesus Christ, Son of the living God, Who, by the will of the Father, with the cooperation of the Holy Spirit, have by Your death given life to the world, deliver me by this Your Most Sacred Body and Blood from all my sins and from every evil. Make me always cling to Your commandments, and never permit me to be separated from You. Who with the same God the Father and the Holy Spirit, live and reign, God, world without end. Amen.

LET not the partaking of Your Body, O Lord Jesus Christ, which I, though unworthy, presume to receive, turn to my judgment and condem-

nation; but through Your goodness, may it become a safeguard and an effective remedy, both of soul and body. Who live and reign with God the Father, in the unity of the Holy Spirit, God, world without end. Amen.

COMMUNION OF THE PRIEST

I WILL take the Bread of heaven, and call upon the name of the Lord.

Lord, I am not worthy that You should come under my roof; but only say the word, and my soul will be healed. (3 *times.*)

Making the Sign of the Cross with the Host, he says:

MAY the Body of our Lord Jesus Christ preserve my soul to life everlasting. Amen.

What return shall I make to the Lord for all He has given me? I will take the Chalice of salvation, and I will call upon the name of the Lord. Praising will I call upon the Lord and I shall be saved from my enemies.

Making the Sign of the Cross with the chalice, he says:

MAY the Blood of our Lord Jesus Christ preserve my soul to life everlasting. Amen.

The Priest reverently consumes the Precious Blood.

COMMUNION OF THE FAITHFUL

The Server and people say the "Confiteor."

P. May almighty God have mercy on you, forgive you your sins, and bring you to life everlasting. S. Amen.

P. May the almighty and merciful Lord grant you pardon, ✠ absolution and remission of your sins. S. Amen.

Holding up a Sacred Host, the Priest says:

Behold the Lamb of God, behold Him Who takes away the sins of the world.

Lord, I am not worthy that You should come under my roof; but only say the word, and my soul will be healed. (3 *times.*)

The Priest says to each communicant:

May the Body of our Lord Jesus Christ preserve your soul to life everlasting. Amen.

The Priest purifies the chalice with wine, saying:

WHAT has passed our lips as food, O Lord, may we possess in purity of heart, that what is given to us in time, be our healing for eternity.

He purifies his fingers with wine and water, saying:

MAY Your Body, O Lord, which I have eaten, and Your Blood which I have drunk, cleave to my very soul, and grant that no trace of sin be found in me, whom these pure and holy mysteries have renewed. Who live and reign, world without end. Amen.

THE COMMUNION • 1 Cor. 5, 7. 8

CHRIST, our Passover, has been sacrificed, alleluia: therefore let us keep festival with the unleavened bread of sincerity and truth, alleluia, alleluia, alleluia.

The Priest, turning to the people, says:

P. The Lord be with you. *S.* And with your spirit.
P. Let us pray.

THE POSTCOMMUNION

POUR forth upon us, O Lord, the Spirit of Your love, that those whom You have filled with the

Easter sacraments may, by Your goodness, be of one mind. Through our Lord Jesus Christ, Your Son, Who lives and reigns with You in the unity of the Holy Spirit, God, world without end. S. Amen.

FINAL PRAYERS

The Priest turns again to the people, and says:

P. The Lord be with you. *S*. And with your spirit.

P. Go, you are dismissed, alleluia, alleluia.

S. Thanks be to God, alleluia, alleluia.

MAY the tribute of my worship be pleasing to You, Most Holy Trinity, and grant that the sacrifice which I, all unworthy, have offered in the presence of Your Majesty, may be acceptable to You, and through Your mercy obtain forgiveness for me and all for whom I have offered it. Through Christ our Lord. Amen.

THE LAST BLESSING

He kisses the altar, and facing the people, says:

MAY almighty God bless you: ✠ the Father, and the Son, and the Holy Spirit.

S. Amen.

The Last Gospel and Prayers after Low Mass are conveniently placed inside the back cover.

Thomas said to Him, "My Lord and my God!"

FIRST SUNDAY AFTER EASTER

ALSO CALLED LOW SUNDAY

This Sunday is called *"in albis"* because those who had been baptized at Easter had put aside their white garments. It is also named *"Quasimodo"* from the first words of the Introit, and *"Low Sunday"* in contrast to Easter, prototype of all Sundays. (WHITE VESTMENTS)

PRAYERS AT THE FOOT OF THE ALTAR

IN THE name of the Father, ✠ and of the Son, and of the Holy Spirit. Amen.

Priest. I will go in to the altar of God.

Server. The God of my gladness and joy.

Psalm 42

DO ME justice, O God, and fight my fight against a faithless people; from the deceitful and impious man rescue me.

S. For You, O God, are my strength. Why do You keep me so far away? Why must I go about in mourning, with the enemy oppressing me?

P. Send forth Your light and Your fidelity; they shall lead me on and bring me to Your holy mountain, to Your dwelling-place.

S. Then will I go in to the altar of God, the God of my gladness and joy.
P. Then will I give You thanks upon the harp, O God, my God. Why are you so downcast, O my soul? Why do you sigh within me?
S. Hope in God! For I shall again be thanking Him in the presence of my Savior and my God.
P. Glory be to the Father, and to the Son, and to the Holy Spirit.
S. As it was in the beginning, is now, and ever shall be, world without end. Amen.
P. I will go in to the altar of God.
S. The God of my gladness and joy.
P. Our help ✠ is in the name of the Lord.
S. Who made heaven and earth.
P. I confess to almighty God, etc.
S. May almighty God have mercy on you, forgive you your sins, and bring you to life everlasting.
P. Amen.

The Server, bowing, says the "Confiteor."

I CONFESS to almighty God, to Blessed Mary, ever Virgin, to Blessed Michael the Archangel, to Blessed John the Baptist, to the Holy Apostles Peter and Paul, and to all the Saints, and to you, Father, that I have sinned exceedingly in thought, word and deed, *through my fault, through my fault, through my most grievous fault.* Therefore I beseech Blessed Mary, ever Virgin, Blessed Michael the Archangel, Blessed John the Baptist, the Holy Apostles Peter and Paul, and all the Saints, and you, Father, to pray to the Lord our God for me.
P. May almighty God have mercy on you, forgive you your sins, and bring you to life everlasting.
S. Amen.

MAY the almighty and merciful Lord grant us pardon, ✠ absolution, and remission of our sins. *S.* Amen.
P. Will You not, O God, give us life?
S. And shall not Your people rejoice in You?
P. Show us, O Lord, Your kindness.
S. And grant us Your salvation.
P. O Lord, hear my prayer.
S. And let my cry come to You.
P. The Lord be with you.
S. And with your spirit. *P.* Let us pray.

Going up to the altar, the Priest prays silently:

TAKE away from us our sins, O Lord, we beseech You, that we may enter with pure minds into the Holy of Holies. Through Christ our Lord. Amen.

WE BESEECH You, O Lord, by the merits of Your Saints (*he kisses the altar*) whose relics lie here, and of all the Saints: deign in Your mercy to pardon me all my sins. Amen.

THE INTROIT • 1 Pet. 2, 2

At the right side of the altar, the Priest says:

CRAVE as newborn babes, alleluia: pure spiritual milk: alleluia, alleluia, alleluia. *Ps. 80.* Sing joyfully to God our strength; acclaim the God of Jacob. Glory be to the Father, and to the Son, and to the Holy Spirit. As it was in the beginning, is now, and ever shall be, world without end. Amen. — Crave as newborn babes, alleluia: pure spiritual milk: alleluia, alleluia, alleluia.

THE KYRIE

P. Lord, have mercy. *S.* Lord, have mercy. *P.* Lord, have mercy. *S.* Christ, have mercy. *P.* Christ, have

mercy. *S.* Christ, have mercy. *P.* Lord, have mercy. *S.* Lord, have mercy. *P.* Lord, have mercy.

THE GLORIA

GLORY to God in the highest. And on earth peace to men of good will. We praise You. We bless You. We adore You. We glorify You. We give You thanks for Your great glory. O Lord God, heavenly King, God the Father almighty. O Lord Jesus Christ, the Only-begotten Son. O Lord God, Lamb of God, Son of the Father: You Who take away the sins of the world, have mercy on us. You Who take away the sins of the world, receive our prayer. You Who sit at the right hand of the Father, have mercy on us. For You alone are holy. You alone are the Lord. You alone, O Jesus Christ, are most high. Together with the Holy Spirit ✠ in the glory of God the Father. Amen.

The Priest kisses the altar and turns to the people, saying:

P. The Lord be with you. *S.* And with your spirit. *P.* Let us pray.

THE PRAYER

Going to the right (Epistle) side, he says:

GRANT, we beseech You, almighty God, that we who have been celebrating the Paschal festivities, may, through Your bounty, ever retain their effect, both in life and in conversation. Through our Lord Jesus Christ, Your Son, Who lives and reigns with You in the unity of the Holy Spirit, God, world without end. *S.* Amen.

THE EPISTLE • 1 John 5, 4-10

BELOVED: All that is born of God overcomes the world; and this is the victory that overcomes the world, our faith. Who is there that overcomes the world if not he who believes that Jesus is the Son of God? This is He Who came in water and in blood, Jesus Christ; not in the water only, but in the water and in the blood. And it is the Spirit that bears witness that Christ is the truth. For there are three that bear witness in heaven: the Father, the Word and the Holy Spirit: and these three are one. And there are three that bear witness on earth: the Spirit, and the water, and the blood; and these three are one. If we receive the testimony of men, the testimony of God is greater; for this is the testimony of God which is greater, that He has borne witness concerning His Son. He who believes in the Son of God has the testimony of God in himself. *S.* Thanks be to God.

Alleluia, alleluia. ℣. *Matt.* 28, 7. "On the day of My Resurrection," says the Lord, "I will go before you into Galilee." Alleluia. ℣. *John* 20, 26. After eight days, the doors being closed, Jesus stood in the midst of His disciples, and said, "Peace be to you!" Alleluia.

PRAYER BEFORE THE GOSPEL

Bowing down at the center of the altar, he says:

CLEANSE my heart and my lips, O almighty God, Who cleansed the lips of the Prophet Isaias with a burning coal. In Your gracious mercy deign so to purify me that I may worthily proclaim Your holy Gospel. Through Christ our Lord. Amen. Lord, grant Your blessing. The Lord be in my heart and on my lips, that I may worthily and fittingly proclaim His holy Gospel. Amen.

THE GOSPEL • John 20, 19-31

Going to the left (Gospel) side of the altar, he says:

P. The Lord be with you. *S.* And with your spirit.

P. ✠ The continuation of the holy Gospel according to Saint John. S. Glory be to You, O Lord.

AT THAT time, when it was late that same day, the first of the week, though the doors where the disciples gathered had been closed for fear of the Jews, Jesus came and stood in the midst and said to them, "Peace be to you!" And when He had said this, He showed them His hands and His side. The disciples therefore rejoiced at the sight of the Lord. He therefore said to them again, "Peace be to you! As the Father has sent Me, I also send you." When He had said this, He breathed upon them, and said to them, "Receive the Holy Spirit; whose sins you shall forgive, they are forgiven them; and whose sins you shall retain, they are retained." Now Thomas, one of the Twelve, called the Twin, was not with them when Jesus came. The other disciples therefore said to him, "We have seen the Lord." But he said to them, "Unless I see in His hands the print of the nails, and put my finger into the place of the nails, and put my hand into His side, I will not believe." And after eight days, His disciples were again inside, and Thomas with them. Jesus came, the doors being closed, and stood in their midst, and said, "Peace be to you!" Then He said to Thomas, "Bring here your finger, and see My hands; and bring here your hand, and put it into My side; and be not unbelieving, but believing." Thomas answered and said to Him, "My Lord and my God!" Jesus said to him, "Because you have seen Me, Thomas, you have believed. Blessed are they who have not seen, and yet have believed." Many other signs also Jesus worked in the sight of His disciples, which are not written in this book.

But these are written that you may believe that Jesus is the Christ, the Son of God, and that believing you may have life in His name. *S.* Praise be to You, O Christ.

P. By the words of the Gospel, may our sins be taken away.

THE NICENE CREED

At the center of the altar, he says:

I BELIEVE in one God, the Father almighty, Maker of heaven and earth, and of all things visible and invisible. And in one Lord Jesus Christ, the Only-begotten Son of God. Born of the Father before all ages. God of God; Light of Light; true God of true God. Begotten not made; of one being with the Father; by Whom all things were made. Who for us men, and for our salvation, came down from heaven. (*Here all genuflect.*) And was made Flesh by the Holy Spirit of the Virgin Mary: AND WAS MADE MAN. He was also crucified for us, suffered under Pontius Pilate and was buried. And on the third day He rose again according to the Scriptures. And ascending into heaven, He sits at the right hand of the Father. And He shall come again in glory to judge the living and the dead; and of His kingdom there shall be no end. And I believe in the Holy Spirit, Lord and Giver of life, Who proceeds from the Father and the Son. Who together with the Father and the Son is no less adored, and glorified: Who spoke by the Prophets. And I believe in One, Holy, Catholic and Apostolic Church. I confess one Baptism for the remission of sins. And I look for the resurrection of the dead. ✠ And the life of the world to come. Amen.

THE OFFERTORY

The Priest turns to the people and says:

P. The Lord be with you. *S.* And with your spirit.
P. Let us pray.

THE OFFERTORY VERSE • Matt. 28, 2. 5. 6

AN ANGEL of the Lord came down from heaven, and said to the women, "He Whom you seek has risen even as He said." Alleluia.

The Priest now uncovers the chalice, places the host on the paten and offering it up, says:

ACCEPT, O holy Father, almighty and eternal God, this spotless host, which I, Your unworthy servant, offer to You, my living and true God, to atone for my numberless sins, offenses, and negligences; on behalf of all here present and likewise for all faithful Christians living and dead, that it may profit me and them as a means of salvation to life everlasting. Amen.

He pours wine and water into the chalice, blessing the water before it is poured.

O GOD, Who established the nature of man in wondrous dignity, and still more admirably restored it, grant that through the mystery of this water and wine, we may be made partakers of His Divinity, Who has condescended to become partaker of our humanity, Jesus Christ, Your Son, our Lord. Who lives and reigns with You in the unity of the Holy Spirit, God, world without end. Amen.

Offering up the wine, the Priest says:

WE OFFER You, O Lord, the chalice of salvation, humbly begging of Your mercy that it may arise before Your Divine Majesty, with a pleasing fragrance, for our salvation and for that of the whole world. Amen.

720-17

Bowing down, the Priest says:

IN A humble spirit and with a contrite heart, may we be accepted by You, O Lord, and may our sacrifice so be offered in Your sight this day as to please You, O Lord God.

Raising his eyes and blessing the offering, he says:

COME, O Sanctifier, almighty and eternal God, and bless ✠ this sacrifice prepared for the glory of Your holy name.

WASHING THE FINGERS

I WASH my hands in innocence, and I go around Your altar, O Lord, giving voice to my thanks, and recounting all Your wondrous deeds. O Lord, I love the house in which You dwell, the tenting-place of Your glory. Gather not my soul with those of sinners, nor with men of blood my life. On their hands are crimes, and their right hands are full of bribes. But I walk in integrity; redeem me, and have pity on me. My foot stands on level ground; in the assemblies I will bless You, O Lord. Glory be to the Father, and to the Son, and to the Holy Spirit. As it was in the beginning, is now, and ever shall be, world without end. Amen.

ACCEPT, Most Holy Trinity, this offering which we are making to You in remembrance of the Passion, Resurrection, and Ascension of Jesus Christ, our Lord; and in honor of Blessed Mary, ever Virgin, Blessed John the Baptist, the Holy Apostles Peter and Paul, and of these, and of all the Saints; that it may add to their honor and aid our salvation; and may they deign to intercede in heaven for us who honor their memory here on earth. Through the same Christ our Lord. Amen.

The Priest turns toward the people and says:
Pray, brethren, that my sacrifice and yours may become acceptable to God the Father almighty.
S. May the Lord accept this sacrifice from your hands to the praise and glory of His name, for our advantage, and that of all His holy Church.
P. Amen.

THE SECRET

RECEIVE, we beseech You, O Lord, the offerings of Your exulting Church; and to her, to whom You have given cause for so great a joy, grant the fruit of perpetual gladness. Through our Lord Jesus Christ, Your Son, Who lives and reigns with You in the unity of the Holy Spirit, God.
P. World without end. *S*. Amen.

PREFACE—CANON

P. The Lord be with you. *S*. And with your spirit.
P. Lift up your hearts.
S. We have lifted them up to the Lord.
P. Let us give thanks to the Lord, our God.
S. It is fitting and just.

IT IS fitting indeed and just, right and helpful to salvation for us always to praise You, O Lord, but more gloriously at this time above others when Christ our Passover was sacrificed. For He is the true Lamb Who has taken away the sins of the world: Who by dying has destroyed our death; and by rising again has restored us to life. And therefore with Angels and Archangels, with Thrones and Dominations, and with the whole host of the heavenly army, we sing a hymn to Your glory, saying again and again (*the bell is rung 3 times*):

HOLY, HOLY, HOLY, Lord God of Hosts. Heaven and earth are filled with Your glory.

Hosanna in the highest. ✠ Blessed is He Who comes in the name of the Lord. Hosanna in the highest.

THE CANON OF THE MASS

THEREFORE, most gracious Father, we humbly beg of You and entreat You through Jesus Christ Your Son, our Lord, (*he kisses the altar*) to deem acceptable and bless these ✠ gifts, these ✠ offerings, these ✠ holy and unspotted oblations which, in the first place, we offer You for Your Holy Catholic Church, that You would deign to give her peace and protection, to unite and guard her throughout the world, together with Your servant N., our Pope, and N., our Bishop; and all true believers who cherish the Catholic and Apostolic Faith.

Commemoration of the Living

REMEMBER, O Lord, Your servants and handmaids, N. and N., (*name them*) and all here present, whose faith and devotion are known to You, on whose behalf we offer to You, or who themselves offer to You, this sacrifice of praise for themselves, families and friends, for the good of their souls, for their hope of salvation and deliverance from all harm, and who offer their homage to You, eternal, living and true God.

Commemoration of the Saints

IN THE unity of holy fellowship we observe the memory, first of all, of the glorious and ever Virgin Mary, Mother of our Lord and God Jesus Christ; next, that of Your Blessed Apostles and Martyrs, Peter and Paul, Andrew, James, John, Thomas, James, Philip, Bartholomew, Matthew, Simon and Thaddeus; of Linus, Cletus, Clement, Sixtus, Cornelius, Cyprian, Lawrence, Chrysogonus,

John and Paul, Cosmas and Damian, and of all Your Saints, by whose merits and prayers grant that we may be always fortified by the help of Your protection. Through the same Christ our Lord. Amen.

Spreading his hands over the oblation, he says:

GRACIOUSLY accept, then, we beseech You, O Lord, this service of our worship and that of all Your household. Provide that our days be spent in Your peace, save us from everlasting damnation, and cause us to be numbered in the flock You have chosen. Through Christ our Lord. Amen.

O GOD, deign to bless ✠ what we offer, and make it approved, ✠ effective, ✠ right, and wholly pleasing in every way, that it may become for our good, the Body ✠ and Blood ✠ of Your dearly beloved Son, Jesus Christ our Lord.

CONSECRATION—ELEVATION

WHO, the day before He suffered, took bread into His holy and venerable hands, and having raised His eyes to heaven, to You, O God, His almighty Father, giving thanks to You, He blessed it, ✠ broke it, and gave it to His disciples, saying: All of you take and eat of this:

FOR THIS IS MY BODY.

IN LIKE manner, when the supper was done, taking also this goodly chalice into His holy and venerable hands, again giving thanks to You, He blessed ✠ it, and gave it to His disciples, saying: All of you take and drink of this:

FOR THIS IS THE CHALICE OF MY BLOOD OF THE NEW AND ETERNAL COVENANT: THE MYSTERY OF FAITH: WHICH SHALL BE SHED FOR YOU AND FOR MANY UNTO THE FORGIVENESS OF SINS.

After replacing the chalice on the corporal, he says:

As often as you shall do these things, in memory of Me shall you do them.

Offering of the Victim

MINDFUL, therefore, O Lord, not only of the blessed Passion of the same Christ, Your Son, our Lord, but also of His Resurrection from the dead, and finally His glorious Ascension into heaven, we, Your ministers, as also Your holy people, offer to Your supreme Majesty, of the gifts bestowed upon us, the pure ✠ Victim, the holy ✠ Victim, the all-perfect ✠ Victim: the holy ✠ Bread of life eternal and the Chalice ✠ of unending salvation.

AND this deign to regard with gracious and kindly attention and hold acceptable, as You deigned to accept the offerings of Abel, Your just servant, and the sacrifice of Abraham our patriarch, and that which Your chief priest Melchisedec offered to You, a holy sacrifice and a spotless victim.

MOST humbly we implore You, almighty God, bid these offerings to be brought by the hands of Your holy angel to Your altar above; before the face of Your Divine Majesty; that those of us who, by sharing in the Sacrifice of this altar, shall receive the Most Sacred ✠ Body and ✠ Blood of Your Son, may be filled with every grace and heavenly blessing. Through the same Christ our Lord. Amen.

Commemoration of the Dead

REMEMBER also, O Lord, Your servants and handmaids, N. and N., who have gone before us with the sign of faith, and rest in the sleep of peace. (*Here pray for the dead.*) To these, O Lord,

and to all who rest in Christ, we beseech You to grant of Your goodness, a place of comfort, light and peace. Through the same Christ our Lord. Amen.

TO US sinners also, Your servants, trusting in the greatness of Your mercy, deign to grant some part and fellowship with Your Holy Apostles and Martyrs: with John, Stephen, Matthias, Barnabas, Ignatius, Alexander, Marcellinus, Peter, Felicitas, Perpetua, Agatha, Lucy, Agnes, Cecilia, Anastasia, and all Your Saints; into whose company, we implore You to admit us, not weighing our merits, but freely granting us pardon. Through Christ our Lord.

THROUGH Whom, O Lord, You always create, ✠ sanctify, ✠ fill with life, ✠ bless, and bestow upon us all good things.

The Minor Elevation

THROUGH ✠ Him, and with ✠ Him, and in ✠ Him, is to You, God the Father ✠ almighty, in the unity of the Holy ✠ Spirit, all honor and glory, world without end. S. Amen.

THE COMMUNION AND THANKSGIVING

Let us pray. Prompted by saving precepts, and taught by Your divine teaching, we dare to say:

OUR FATHER, Who art in heaven, hallowed be Thy name: Thy kingdom come: Thy will be done on earth as it is in heaven. Give us this day our daily bread; and forgive us our trespasses as we forgive those who trespass against us. And lead us not into temptation: S. But deliver us from evil. P. Amen.

DELIVER us, we beseech You, O Lord, from all evils, past, present, and to come; and by the intercession of the Blessed and glorious Mary, ever Virgin, Mother of God, together with Your Blessed Apostles Peter and Paul, and Andrew, and all the Saints, grant of Your goodness, peace in our days, that aided by the riches of Your mercy, we may be always free from sin and safe from all disturbance.

Through the same our Lord Jesus Christ, Your Son, Who lives and reigns with You in the unity of the Holy Spirit, God, world without end.

S. Amen.

P. May the peace ✠ of the Lord be ✠ always with ✠ you.

S. And with your spirit.

The Priest puts a small particle into the chalice, saying:

May this mingling and consecration of the Body and Blood of our Lord Jesus Christ help us who receive it to life everlasting. Amen.

LAMB of God, You Who take away the sins of the world, have mercy on us.

Lamb of God, You Who take away the sins of the world, have mercy on us.

Lamb of God, You Who take away the sins of the world, grant us peace.

PRAYERS BEFORE HOLY COMMUNION

Then inclining toward the altar, he says:

O LORD Jesus Christ, Who said to Your Apostles: "Peace I leave with you, My peace I give to you," regard not my sins but the faith of Your Church, and deign to give her peace and unity

according to Your Will: Who live and reign God world without end. Amen.

O LORD Jesus Christ, Son of the living God, Who, by the will of the Father, with the co-operation of the Holy Spirit, have by Your death given life to the world, deliver me by this Your Most Sacred Body and Blood from all my sins and from every evil. Make me always cling to Your commandments, and never permit me to be separated from You. Who with the same God the Father and the Holy Spirit, live and reign, God, world without end. Amen.

LET not the partaking of Your Body, O Lord Jesus Christ, which I, though unworthy, presume to receive, turn to my judgment and condemnation; but through Your goodness, may it become a safeguard and an effective remedy, both of soul and body. Who live and reign with God the Father, in the unity of the Holy Spirit, God, world without end. Amen.

COMMUNION OF THE PRIEST

I WILL take the Bread of heaven, and call upon the name of the Lord.

Lord, I am not worthy that You should come under my roof; but only say the word, and my soul will be healed. (3 *times.*)

Making the Sign of the Cross with the Host, he says:

MAY the Body of our Lord Jesus Christ preserve my soul to life everlasting. Amen.

What return shall I make to the Lord for all He has given me? I will take the Chalice of salvation, and I will call upon the name of the Lord. Prais-

ing will I call upon the Lord and I shall be saved from my enemies.

Making the Sign of the Cross with the chalice, he says:

MAY the Blood of our Lord Jesus Christ preserve my soul to life everlasting. Amen.

The Priest reverently consumes the Precious Blood.

COMMUNION OF THE FAITHFUL

The Server and people say the "Confiteor."

P. May almighty God have mercy on you, forgive you your sins, and bring you to life everlasting. **S.** Amen.

P. May the almighty and merciful Lord grant you pardon, ✠ absolution and remission of your sins. **S.** Amen.

Holding up a Sacred Host, the Priest says:

Behold the Lamb of God, behold Him Who takes away the sins of the world.

Lord, I am not worthy that You should come under my roof; but only say the word, and my soul will be healed. (3 *times.*)

The Priest says to each communicant:

May the Body of our Lord Jesus Christ preserve your soul to life everlasting. Amen.

The Priest purifies the chalice with wine, saying:

WHAT has passed our lips as food, O Lord, may we possess in purity of heart, that what is given to us in time, be our healing for eternity.

He purifies his fingers with wine and water, saying:

MAY Your Body, O Lord, which I have eaten, and Your Blood which I have drunk, cleave to my very soul, and grant that no trace of sin be found in me, whom these pure and holy mysteries

have renewed. Who live and reign, world without end. Amen.

THE COMMUNION • John 20, 27

PUT in your hand, and know the place of the nails, alleluia: and be not unbelieving, but believing: alleluia, alleluia.

The Priest, turning to the people, says:

P. The Lord be with you. *S.* And with your spirit.
P. Let us pray.

THE POSTCOMMUNION

WE BESEECH You, O Lord our God, that the most holy rites, which You have given us for a safeguard for this new life, may become our remedy both now and for time to come. Through our Lord Jesus Christ, Your Son, Who lives and reigns with You in the unity of the Holy Spirit, God, world without end. *S.* Amen.

FINAL PRAYERS

P. The Lord be with you. *S.* And with your spirit.
P. Go, you are dismissed. *S.* Thanks be to God.

MAY the tribute of my worship be pleasing to You, Most Holy Trinity, and grant that the sacrifice which I, all unworthy, have offered in the presence of Your Majesty, may be acceptable to You, and through Your mercy obtain forgiveness for me and all for whom I have offered it. Through Christ our Lord. Amen.

THE LAST BLESSING

MAY almighty God bless you: ✠ the Father, and the Son, and the Holy Spirit. *S.* Amen.

The Last Gospel and Prayers after Low Mass are conveniently placed inside the back cover.

"There shall be one fold and one Shepherd."

SECOND SUNDAY AFTER EASTER

This Sunday is often called *Good Shepherd Sunday*: the Gospel tells us of the Good Shepherd. Jesus is indeed the Good Shepherd of our souls. He came to give His life for us. We must help to bring the "sheep going astray" back to Christ, that there may be "one fold and one Shepherd." (WHITE VESTMENTS)

PRAYERS AT THE FOOT OF THE ALTAR

IN THE name of the Father, ✠ and of the Son, and of the Holy Spirit. Amen.

Priest. I will go in to the altar of God.

Server. The God of my gladness and joy.

Psalm 42

DO ME justice, O God, and fight my fight against a faithless people; from the deceitful and impious man rescue me.

S. For You, O God, are my strength. Why do You keep me so far away? Why must I go about in mourning, with the enemy oppressing me?

P. Send forth Your light and Your fidelity; they shall lead me on and bring me to Your holy mountain, to Your dwelling-place.

S. Then will I go in to the altar of God, the God of my gladness and joy.
P. Then will I give You thanks upon the harp, O God, my God. Why are you so downcast, O my soul? Why do you sigh within me?
S. Hope in God! For I shall again be thanking Him in the presence of my Savior and my God.
P. Glory be to the Father, and to the Son, and to the Holy Spirit.
S. As it was in the beginning, is now, and ever shall be, world without end. Amen.
P. I will go in to the altar of God.
S. The God of my gladness and joy.
P. Our help ✠ is in the name of the Lord.
S. Who made heaven and earth.
P. I confess to almighty God, etc.
S. May almighty God have mercy on you, forgive you your sins, and bring you to life everlasting.
P. Amen.

The Server, bowing, says the "Confiteor."

I CONFESS to almighty God, to Blessed Mary, ever Virgin, to Blessed Michael the Archangel, to Blessed John the Baptist, to the Holy Apostles Peter and Paul, and to all the Saints, and to you, Father, that I have sinned exceedingly in thought, word and deed, *through my fault, through my fault, through my most grievous fault.* Therefore I beseech Blessed Mary, ever Virgin, Blessed Michael the Archangel, Blessed John the Baptist, the Holy Apostles Peter and Paul, and all the Saints, and you, Father, to pray to the Lord our God for me.
P. May almighty God have mercy on you, forgive you your sins, and bring you to life everlasting.
S. Amen.

MAY the almighty and merciful Lord grant us pardon, ✠ absolution, and remission of our sins. S. Amen.

P. Will You not, O God, give us life?
S. And shall not Your people rejoice in You?
P. Show us, O Lord, Your kindness.
S. And grant us Your salvation.
P. O Lord, hear my prayer.
S. And let my cry come to You.
P. The Lord be with you.
S. And with your spirit. *P*. Let us pray.

Going up to the altar, the Priest prays silently:

TAKE away from us our sins, O Lord, we beseech You, that we may enter with pure minds into the Holy of Holies. Through Christ our Lord. Amen.

WE BESEECH You, O Lord, by the merits of Your Saints (*he kisses the altar*) whose relics lie here, and of all the Saints: deign in Your mercy to pardon me all my sins. Amen.

THE INTROIT • Ps. 32, 5, 6. 1

At the right side of the altar, the Priest says:

OF THE kindness of the Lord the earth is full, alleluia; by the word of the Lord the heavens were made, alleluia, alleluia. *Ps.* Exult, you just, in the Lord; praise from the upright is fitting. Glory be to the Father, and to the Son, and to the Holy Spirit. As it was in the beginning, is now, and ever shall be, world without end. Amen. — Of the kindness of the Lord the earth is full, alleluia; by the word of the Lord the heavens were made, alleluia, alleluia.

THE KYRIE

P. Lord, have mercy. *S*. Lord, have mercy. *P*. Lord, have mercy. *S*. Christ, have mercy. *P*. Christ, have mercy. *S*. Christ, have mercy. *P*. Lord, have mercy. *S*. Lord, have mercy. *P*. Lord, have mercy.

THE GLORIA

GLORY to God in the highest. And on earth peace to men of good will. We praise You. We bless You. We adore You. We glorify You. We give You thanks for Your great glory. O Lord God, heavenly King, God the Father almighty. O Lord Jesus Christ, the Only-begotten Son. O Lord God, Lamb of God, Son of the Father: You Who take away the sins of the world, have mercy on us. You Who take away the sins of the world, receive our prayer. You Who sit at the right hand of the Father, have mercy on us. For You alone are holy. You alone are the Lord. You alone, O Jesus Christ, are most high. Together with the Holy Spirit ✠ in the glory of God the Father. Amen.

The Priest kisses the altar and turns to the people, saying:

P. The Lord be with you. *S*. And with your spirit. *P*. Let us pray.

THE PRAYER

Going to the right (Epistle) side, he says:

O GOD, Who by the humility of Your Son have raised up a fallen world, grant everlasting joy to Your faithful people; that those whom You have rescued from the perils of endless death, You may cause to enjoy endless happiness. Through the same our Lord Jesus Christ, Your Son, Who lives and reigns with You in the unity of the Holy Spirit, God, world without end. S. Amen.

THE EPISTLE • 1 Pet. 2, 21-25

BELOVED: Christ has suffered for you, leaving you an example that you may follow in His steps: "Who did no sin, neither was deceit found in His mouth." Who, when He was reviled, did not revile; when He suffered, did not threaten, but yielded Himself to him who judged Him unjustly; Who Himself bore our sins in His body upon the tree, that we, having died to sin, might live to justice; and by His stripes you were healed. For you were as sheep going astray, but now you have returned to the shepherd and guardian of your souls. S. Thanks be to God.

Alleluia, alleluia. ℣. *Luke 24, 35.* The disciples recognized the Lord Jesus in the breaking of the bread. Alleluia. ℣. *John 10, 14.* I am the Good Shepherd: and I know My sheep, and Mine know Me. Alleluia.

PRAYER BEFORE THE GOSPEL

Bowing down at the center of the altar, he says:

CLEANSE my heart and my lips, O almighty God, Who cleansed the lips of the Prophet Isaias with a burning coal. In Your gracious mercy deign so to purify me that I may worthily proclaim Your holy Gospel. Through Christ our Lord. Amen.

Lord, grant Your blessing. The Lord be in my heart and on my lips, that I may worthily and fittingly proclaim His holy Gospel. Amen.

THE GOSPEL • John 10, 11-16

Going to the left (Gospel) side of the altar, he says:

P. The Lord be with you. S. And with your spirit.
P. ✠ The continuation of the holy Gospel according to Saint John. S. Glory be to You, O Lord.

AT THAT time, Jesus said to the Pharisees: "I am the Good Shepherd. The good shepherd lays down his life for his sheep. But the hireling, who is not a shepherd, whose own the sheep are not, sees the wolf coming and leaves the sheep and flees. And the wolf snatches and scatters the sheep; but the hireling flees because he is a hireling, and has no concern for the sheep. I am the Good Shepherd, and I know Mine and Mine know Me, even as the Father knows Me and I know the Father; and I lay down My life for My sheep. And other sheep I have that are not of this fold. Them also I must bring, and they shall hear My voice, and there shall be one fold and one Shepherd." *S.* Praise be to You, O Christ.

P. By the words of the Gospel, may our sins be taken away.

THE NICENE CREED

At the center of the altar, he says:

I BELIEVE in one God, the Father almighty, Maker of heaven and earth, and of all things visible and invisible. And in one Lord Jesus Christ, the Only-begotten Son of God. Born of the Father before all ages. God of God; Light of Light; true God of true God. Begotten not made; of one being with the Father; by Whom all things were made. Who for us men, and for our salvation, came down from heaven. (*Here all genuflect.*) And was made Flesh by the Holy Spirit of the Virgin Mary: AND WAS MADE MAN. He was also crucified for us, suffered under Pontius Pilate and was buried. And on the third day He rose again according to the Scriptures. And ascending into heaven, He sits at the right hand of the Father. And He shall come again in glory to judge the living and the dead; and of His kingdom there shall be no end. And I believe in the Holy Spirit, Lord and Giver of life, Who proceeds from the Father and the Son. Who together with the Father and the Son is no less adored, and glorified: Who spoke by the Prophets. And I believe in One, Holy, Catholic and Apostolic Church. I confess one Baptism for the remission of sins. And I look for the resurrection of the dead. ✠ And the life of the world to come. Amen.

THE OFFERTORY

The Priest turns to the people and says:

P. The Lord be with you. S. And with your spirit.
P. Let us pray.

THE OFFERTORY VERSE • Ps. 62, 2. 5

O GOD, my God, to You do I watch at break of day, and in Your name I will lift up my hands, alleluia.

The Priest now uncovers the chalice, places the host on the paten and offering it up, says:

ACCEPT, O holy Father, almighty and eternal God, this spotless host, which I, Your unworthy servant, offer to You, my living and true God, to atone for my numberless sins, offenses, and negligences; on behalf of all here present and likewise for all faithful Christians living and dead, that it may profit me and them as a means of salvation to life everlasting. Amen.

He pours wine and water into the chalice, blessing the water before it is poured.

O GOD, Who established the nature of man in wondrous dignity, and still more admirably restored it, grant that through the mystery of this water and wine, we may be made partakers of His

Divinity, Who has condescended to become partaker of our humanity, Jesus Christ, Your Son, our Lord. Who lives and reigns with You in the unity of the Holy Spirit, God, world without end. Amen.

Offering up the wine, the Priest says:

WE OFFER You, O Lord, the chalice of salvation, humbly begging of Your mercy that it may arise before Your Divine Majesty, with a pleasing fragrance, for our salvation and for that of the whole world. Amen.

Bowing down, the Priest says:

IN A humble spirit and with a contrite heart, may we be accepted by You, O Lord, and may our sacrifice so be offered in Your sight this day as to please You, O Lord God.

Raising his eyes and blessing the offering, he says:

COME, O Sanctifier, almighty and eternal God, and bless ✠ this sacrifice prepared for the glory of Your holy name.

WASHING THE FINGERS

I WASH my hands in innocence, and I go around Your altar, O Lord, giving voice to my thanks, and recounting all Your wondrous deeds. O Lord, I love the house in which You dwell, the tenting-place of Your glory. Gather not my soul with those of sinners, nor with men of blood my life. On their hands are crimes, and their right hands are full of bribes. But I walk in integrity; redeem me, and have pity on me. My foot stands on level ground; in the assemblies I will bless You, O Lord. Glory be to the Father, and to the Son, and to the Holy Spirit. As it was in the beginning, is now, and ever shall be, world without end. Amen.

ACCEPT, Most Holy Trinity, this offering which we are making to You in remembrance of the Passion, Resurrection, and Ascension of Jesus Christ, our Lord; and in honor of Blessed Mary, ever Virgin, Blessed John the Baptist, the Holy Apostles Peter and Paul, and of these, and of all the Saints; that it may add to their honor and aid our salvation; and may they deign to intercede in heaven for us who honor their memory here on earth. Through the same Christ our Lord. Amen.

The Priest turns toward the people and says:

Pray, brethren, that my sacrifice and yours may become acceptable to God the Father almighty.

S. May the Lord accept this sacrifice from your hands to the praise and glory of His name, for our advantage, and that of all His holy Church.

P. Amen.

THE SECRET

MAY this sacred oblation, O Lord, ever confer upon us Your salutary blessing, that what is performed in mystery, may by virtue thereof be fulfilled. Through our Lord Jesus Christ, Your Son, Who lives and reigns with You in the unity of the Holy Spirit, God.

P. World without end. *S.* Amen.

PREFACE—CANON

P. The Lord be with you. *S.* And with your spirit.

P. Lift up your hearts.

S. We have lifted them up to the Lord.

P. Let us give thanks to the Lord, our God.

S. It is fitting and just.

IT IS fitting indeed and just, right and helpful to salvation for us always to praise You, O Lord, but more gloriously at this time above others when

Christ our Passover was sacrificed. For He is the true Lamb Who has taken away the sins of the world: Who by dying has destroyed our death; and by rising again has restored us to life. And therefore with Angels and Archangels, with Thrones and Dominations, and with the whole host of the heavenly army, we sing a hymn to Your glory, saying again and again (*the bell is rung 3 times*):

HOLY, HOLY, HOLY, Lord God of Hosts. Heaven and earth are filled with Your glory. Hosanna in the highest. ✠ Blessed is He Who comes in the name of the Lord. Hosanna in the highest.

THE CANON OF THE MASS

THEREFORE, most gracious Father, we humbly beg of You and entreat You through Jesus Christ Your Son, our Lord, (*he kisses the altar*) to deem acceptable and bless these ✠ gifts, these ✠ offerings, these ✠ holy and unspotted oblations which, in the first place, we offer You for Your Holy Catholic Church, that You would deign to give her peace and protection, to unite and guard her throughout the world, together with Your servant N., our Pope, and N., our Bishop; and all true believers who cherish the Catholic and Apostolic Faith.

Commemoration of the Living

REMEMBER, O Lord, Your servants and handmaids, N. and N., (*name them*) and all here present, whose faith and devotion are known to You, on whose behalf we offer to You, or who themselves offer to You, this sacrifice of praise for themselves, families and friends, for the good of their souls, for their hope of salvation and deliverance from all harm, and who offer their homage to You, eternal, living and true God.

Commemoration of the Saints

IN THE unity of holy fellowship we observe the memory, first of all, of the glorious and ever Virgin Mary, Mother of our Lord and God Jesus Christ; next, that of Your Blessed Apostles and Martyrs, Peter and Paul, Andrew, James, John, Thomas, James, Philip, Bartholomew, Matthew, Simon and Thaddeus; of Linus, Cletus, Clement, Sixtus, Cornelius, Cyprian, Lawrence, Chrysogonus, John and Paul, Cosmas and Damian, and of all Your Saints, by whose merits and prayers grant that we may be always fortified by the help of Your protection. Through the same Christ our Lord. Amen.

Spreading his hands over the oblation, he says:

GRACIOUSLY accept, then, we beseech You, O Lord, this service of our worship and that of all Your household. Provide that our days be spent in Your peace, save us from everlasting damnation, and cause us to be numbered in the flock You have chosen. Through Christ our Lord. Amen.

O GOD, deign to bless ✠ what we offer, and make it approved, ✠ effective, ✠ right, and wholly pleasing in every way, that it may become for our good, the Body ✠ and Blood ✠ of Your dearly beloved Son, Jesus Christ our Lord.

CONSECRATION—ELEVATION

WHO, the day before He suffered, took bread into His holy and venerable hands, and having raised His eyes to heaven, to You, O God, His almighty Father, giving thanks to You, He blessed it, ✠ broke it, and gave it to His disciples, saying: All of you take and eat of this:

FOR THIS IS MY BODY.

IN LIKE manner, when the supper was done, taking also this goodly chalice into His holy and venerable hands, again giving thanks to You, He blessed ✠ it, and gave it to His disciples, saying: All of you take and drink of this:

FOR THIS IS THE CHALICE OF MY BLOOD OF THE NEW AND ETERNAL COVENANT: THE MYSTERY OF FAITH: WHICH SHALL BE SHED FOR YOU AND FOR MANY UNTO THE FORGIVENESS OF SINS.

After replacing the chalice on the corporal, he says:

As often as you shall do these things, in memory of Me shall you do them.

Offering of the Victim

MINDFUL, therefore, O Lord, not only of the blessed Passion of the same Christ, Your Son, our Lord, but also of His Resurrection from the dead, and finally His glorious Ascension into heaven, we, Your ministers, as also Your holy people, offer to Your supreme Majesty, of the gifts bestowed upon us, the pure ✠ Victim, the holy ✠ Victim, the all-perfect ✠ Victim: the holy ✠ Bread of life eternal and the Chalice ✠ of unending salvation.

AND this deign to regard with gracious and kindly attention and hold acceptable, as You deigned to accept the offerings of Abel, Your just servant, and the sacrifice of Abraham our patriarch, and that which Your chief priest Melchisedec offered to You, a holy sacrifice and a spotless victim.

MOST humbly we implore You, almighty God, bid these offerings to be brought by the hands of Your holy angel to Your altar above; before the face of Your Divine Majesty; that those of us who, by sharing in the Sacrifice of this altar shall, receive the Most Sacred ✠ Body and ✠ Blood of Your Son, may be filled with every grace and heavenly blessing. Through the same Christ our Lord. Amen.

Commemoration of the Dead

REMEMBER also, O Lord, Your servants and handmaids, N. and N., who have gone before us with the sign of faith, and rest in the sleep of peace. (*Here pray for the dead.*) To these, O Lord, and to all who rest in Christ, we beseech You to grant of Your goodness, a place of comfort, light and peace. Through the same Christ our Lord. Amen.

TO US sinners also, Your servants, trusting in the greatness of Your mercy, deign to grant some part and fellowship with Your Holy Apostles and Martyrs: with John, Stephen, Matthias, Barnabas, Ignatius, Alexander, Marcellinus, Peter, Felicitas, Perpetua, Agatha, Lucy, Agnes, Cecilia, Anastasia; and all Your Saints; into whose company, we implore You to admit us, not weighing our merits, but freely granting us pardon. Through Christ our Lord.

THROUGH Whom, O Lord, You always create, ✠ sanctify, ✠ fill with life, ✠ bless, and bestow upon us all good things.

The Minor Elevation

THROUGH ✠ Him, and with ✠ Him, and in ✠ Him, is to You, God the Father ✠ almighty, in the unity of the Holy ✠ Spirit, all honor and glory, world without end. S. Amen.

THE COMMUNION AND THANKSGIVING

Let us pray. Prompted by saving precepts, and taught by Your divine teaching, we dare to say:

OUR FATHER, Who art in heaven, hallowed be Thy name: Thy kingdom come: Thy will be done on earth as it is in heaven. Give us this day our daily bread; and forgive us our trespasses, as we forgive those who trespass against us. And lead us not into temptation: S. But deliver us from evil. *P.* Amen.

DELIVER us, we beseech You, O Lord, from all evils, past, present, and to come; and by the intercession of the Blessed and glorious Mary, ever Virgin, Mother of God, together with Your Blessed Apostles Peter and Paul, and Andrew, and all the Saints, grant of Your goodness, peace in our days, that aided by the riches of Your mercy, we may be always free from sin and safe from all disturbance.

Through the same our Lord Jesus Christ, Your Son, Who lives and reigns with You in the unity of the Holy Spirit, God, world without end.

S. Amen.

P. May the peace ✠ of the Lord be ✠ always with ✠ you.

S. And with your spirit.

The Priest puts a small particle into the chalice, saying:

May this mingling and consecration of the Body and Blood of our Lord Jesus Christ help us who receive it to life everlasting. Amen.

LAMB of God, You Who take away the sins of the world, have mercy on us.

Lamb of God, You Who take away the sins of the world, have mercy on us.

Lamb of God, You Who take away the sins of the world, grant us peace.

PRAYERS BEFORE HOLY COMMUNION

Then inclining toward the altar, he says:

O LORD Jesus Christ, Who said to Your Apostles: "Peace I leave with you, My peace I give to you," regard not my sins but the faith of Your Church, and deign to give her peace and unity according to Your Will: Who live and reign God world without end. Amen.

O LORD Jesus Christ, Son of the living God, Who, by the will of the Father, with the co-operation of the Holy Spirit, have by Your death given life to the world, deliver me by this Your Most Sacred Body and Blood from all my sins and from every evil. Make me always cling to Your commandments, and never permit me to be separated from You. Who with the same God the Father and the Holy Spirit, live and reign, God, world without end. Amen.

LET not the partaking of Your Body, O Lord Jesus Christ, which I, though unworthy, presume to receive, turn to my judgment and condem-

nation; but through Your goodness, may it become a safeguard and an effective remedy, both of soul and body. Who live and reign with God the Father, in the unity of the Holy Spirit, God, world without end. Amen.

COMMUNION OF THE PRIEST

I WILL take the Bread of heaven, and call upon the name of the Lord.

Lord, I am not worthy that You should come under my roof; but only say the word, and my soul will be healed. (3 *times.*)

Making the Sign of the Cross with the Host, he says:

MAY the Body of our Lord Jesus Christ preserve my soul to life everlasting. Amen.

What return shall I make to the Lord for all He has given me? I will take the Chalice of salvation, and I will call upon the name of the Lord. Praising will I call upon the Lord and I shall be saved from my enemies.

Making the Sign of the Cross with the chalice, he says:

MAY the Blood of our Lord Jesus Christ preserve my soul to life everlasting. Amen.

The Priest reverently consumes the Precious Blood.

COMMUNION OF THE FAITHFUL

The Server and people say the "Confiteor."

P. May almighty God have mercy on you, forgive you your sins, and bring you to life everlasting. **S.** Amen.

P. May the almighty and merciful Lord grant you pardon, ✠ absolution and remission of your sins. **S.** Amen.

Holding up a Sacred Host, the Priest says:

Behold the Lamb of God, behold Him Who takes away the sins of the world.

Lord, I am not worthy that You should come under my roof; but only say the word, and my soul will be healed. (3 *times.*)

The Priest says to each communicant:

May the Body of our Lord Jesus Christ preserve your soul to life everlasting. Amen.

The Priest purifies the chalice with wine, saying:

WHAT has passed our lips as food, O Lord, may we possess in purity of heart, that what is given to us in time, be our healing for eternity.

He purifies his fingers with wine and water, saying:

MAY Your Body, O Lord, which I have eaten, and Your Blood which I have drunk, cleave to my very soul, and grant that no trace of sin be found in me, whom these pure and holy mysteries have renewed. Who live and reign, world without end. Amen.

THE COMMUNION • John 10, 14

I AM the Good Shepherd, alleluia: and I know My sheep, and Mine know Me: alleluia, alleluia.

The Priest, turning to the people, says:

P. The Lord be with you. S. And with your spirit.
P. Let us pray.

THE POSTCOMMUNION

GRANT, we beseech You, almighty God, that obtaining the grace of Your new life, we may ever glory in Your gift. Through our Lord Jesus

Christ, Your Son, Who lives and reigns with You in the unity of the Holy Spirit, God, world without end. S. Amen.

FINAL PRAYERS

The Priest turns again to the people, and says:

P. The Lord be with you. S. And with your spirit.

P. Go, you are dismissed. S. Thanks be to God.

MAY the tribute of my worship be pleasing to You, Most Holy Trinity, and grant that the sacrifice which I, all unworthy, have offered in the presence of Your Majesty, may be acceptable to You, and through Your mercy obtain forgiveness for me and all for whom I have offered it. Through Christ our Lord. Amen.

THE LAST BLESSING

He kisses the altar, and facing the people, says:

MAY almighty God bless you: ✠ the Father, and the Son, and the Holy Spirit.

S. Amen.

The Last Gospel and Prayers after Low Mass are conveniently placed inside the back cover.

"A little while and you shall see Me no longer . . ."

THIRD SUNDAY AFTER EASTER

All those who resolve to live up to their Christian principles will meet with opposition and persecution. But our life on earth is only "a little while," and our "sorrow shall be turned into joy." (WHITE VESTMENTS)

PRAYERS AT THE FOOT OF THE ALTAR

IN THE name of the Father, ✠ and of the Son, and of the Holy Spirit. Amen.

Priest. I will go in to the altar of God.

Server. The God of my gladness and joy.

Psalm 42

DO ME justice, O God, and fight my fight against a faithless people; from the deceitful and impious man rescue me.

S. For You, O God, are my strength. Why do You keep me so far away? Why must I go about in mourning, with the enemy oppressing me?

P. Send forth Your light and Your fidelity; they shall lead me on and bring me to Your holy mountain, to Your dwelling-place.

S. Then will I go in to the altar of God, the God of my gladness and joy.
P. Then will I give You thanks upon the harp, O God, my God. Why are you so downcast, O my soul? Why do you sigh within me?
S. Hope in God! For I shall again be thanking Him in the presence of my Savior and my God.
P. Glory be to the Father, and to the Son, and to the Holy Spirit.
S. As it was in the beginning, is now, and ever shall be, world without end. Amen.
P. I will go in to the altar of God.
S. The God of my gladness and joy.
P. Our help ✠ is in the name of the Lord.
S. Who made heaven and earth.
P. I confess to almighty God, etc.
S. May almighty God have mercy on you, forgive you your sins, and bring you to life everlasting.
P. Amen.

The Server, bowing, says the "Confiteor."

I CONFESS to almighty God, to Blessed Mary, ever Virgin, to Blessed Michael the Archangel, to Blessed John the Baptist, to the Holy Apostles Peter and Paul, and to all the Saints, and to you, Father, that I have sinned exceedingly in thought, word and deed, *through my fault, through my fault, through my most grievous fault.* Therefore I beseech Blessed Mary, ever Virgin, Blessed Michael the Archangel, Blessed John the Baptist, the Holy Apostles Peter and Paul, and all the Saints, and you, Father, to pray to the Lord our God for me.
P. May almighty God have mercy on you, forgive you your sins, and bring you to life everlasting.
S. Amen.

MAY the almighty and merciful Lord grant us pardon, ✠ absolution, and remission of our sins. S. Amen.

P. Will You not, O God, give us life?
S. And shall not Your people rejoice in You?
P. Show us, O Lord, Your kindness.
S. And grant us Your salvation.
P. O Lord, hear my prayer.
S. And let my cry come to You.
P. The Lord be with you.
S. And with your spirit. *P.* Let us pray.

Going up to the altar, the Priest prays silently:

TAKE away from us our sins, O Lord, we beseech You, that we may enter with pure minds into the Holy of Holies. Through Christ our Lord. Amen.

WE BESEECH You, O Lord, by the merits of Your Saints (*he kisses the altar*) whose relics lie here, and of all the Saints: deign in Your mercy to pardon me all my sins. Amen.

THE INTROIT • Ps. 65, 1. 2. 3

At the right side of the altar, the Priest says:

SHOUT joyfully to God, all you on earth, alleluia; sing praise to the glory of His name, alleluia; proclaim His glorious praise, alleluia, alleluia, alleluia. *Ps.* Say to God, "How tremendous are Your deeds, O Lord! For Your great strength Your enemies fawn upon You." Glory be to the Father, and to the Son, and to the Holy Spirit. As it was in the beginning, is now, and ever shall be, world without end. Amen. — Shout joyfully to God, all you on earth, alleluia; sing praise to the glory of

His name, alleluia; proclaim His glorious praise, alleluia, alleluia, alleluia.

THE KYRIE

P. Lord, have mercy. *S.* Lord, have mercy. *P.* Lord, have mercy. *S.* Christ, have mercy. *P.* Christ, have mercy. *S.* Christ, have mercy. *P.* Lord, have mercy. *S.* Lord, have mercy. *P.* Lord, have mercy.

THE GLORIA

GLORY to God in the highest. And on earth peace to men of good will. We praise You. We bless You. We adore You. We glorify You. We give You thanks for Your great glory. O Lord God, heavenly King, God the Father almighty. O Lord Jesus Christ, the Only-begotten Son. O Lord God, Lamb of God, Son of the Father: You Who take away the sins of the world, have mercy on us. You Who take away the sins of the world, receive our prayer. You Who sit at the right hand of the Father, have mercy on us. For You alone are holy. You alone are the Lord. You alone, O Jesus Christ, are most high. Together with the Holy Spirit ✠ in the glory of God the Father. Amen.

The Priest kisses the altar and turns to the people, saying:

P. The Lord be with you. *S.* And with your spirit. *P.* Let us pray.

THE PRAYER

Going to the right (Epistle) side, he says:

O GOD, to those who go astray, You display the light of Your truth that they may return into the way of righteousness; grant to all those who profess themselves Christians, both to avoid the things which are contrary to that name, and to follow those which are agreeable thereto. Through our Lord Jesus Christ, Your Son, Who lives and reigns with You in the unity of the Holy Spirit, God, world without end. *S.* Amen.

THE EPISTLE • 1 Pet. 2, 11-19

BELOVED: I exhort you as strangers and pilgrims to abstain from carnal desires which war against the soul. Behave yourselves honorably among the pagans; that, whereas they slander you as evildoers, they may, through observing you, by reason of your good works glorify God in the day of visitation. Be subject therefore to every human creature for God's sake, whether to the king as supreme, or to governors as sent through him for vengeance on evildoers and for the praise of the good. For such is the will of God, that by doing good you should put to silence the ignorance of foolish men. Live as freemen, yet not using your freedom as a cloak for malice but as servants of God. Honor all men; love the brotherhood; fear God; honor the king. Servants, be subject to your masters in all fear, not only to the good and moderate, but also to the severe. This is indeed a grace, in Christ Jesus our Lord. *S.* Thanks be to God.

Alleluia, alleluia. ℣. *Ps. 110,* 9. The Lord has sent deliverance to His people. Alleluia. ℣. *Luke 24, 46.* It behooved Christ to suffer and to rise again from the dead, and so to enter into His glory. Alleluia.

PRAYER BEFORE THE GOSPEL

Bowing down at the center of the altar, he says:

CLEANSE my heart and my lips, O almighty God, Who cleansed the lips of the Prophet Isaias with a burning coal. In Your gracious mercy deign so to purify me that I may worthily proclaim

Your holy Gospel. Through Christ our Lord. Amen. Lord, grant Your blessing. The Lord be in my heart and on my lips, that I may worthily and fittingly proclaim His holy Gospel. Amen.

THE GOSPEL • John 16, 16-22

Going to the left (Gospel) side of the altar, he says:

P. The Lord be with you. *S.* And with your spirit.

P. ✠ The continuation of the holy Gospel according to Saint John. *S.* Glory be to You, O Lord.

AT THAT time, Jesus said to His disciples, "A little while and you shall see Me no longer; and again a little while and you shall see Me, because I go to the Father." Some of His disciples therefore said to one another, "What is this He says to us, 'A little while and you shall not see Me, and again a little while and you shall see Me'; and, 'I go to the Father'?" They kept saying therefore, "What is this 'little while' of which He speaks? We do not know what He is saying." But Jesus knew that they wanted to ask Him, and He said to them, "You inquire about this among yourselves because I said, 'A little while and you shall not see Me, and again a little while and you shall see Me.' Amen, amen, I say to you, that you shall weep and lament, but the world shall rejoice; and you shall be sorrowful, but your sorrow shall be turned into joy. A woman about to give birth has sorrow, because her hour has come. But when she has brought forth the child, she no longer remembers the anguish for her joy that a man is born into the world. And you therefore have sorrow now; but I will see you again, and your heart shall rejoice, and your joy no one shall take from you." *S.* Praise be to You, O Christ.

P. By the words of the Gospel, may our sins be taken away.

THE NICENE CREED

At the center of the altar, he says:

I BELIEVE in one God the Father almighty, Maker of heaven and earth, and of all things visible and invisible. And in one Lord Jesus Christ, the Only-begotten Son of God. Born of the Father before all ages. God of God; Light of Light; true God of true God. Begotten not made; of one being with the Father; by Whom all things were made. Who for us men, and for our salvation, came down from heaven. (*Here all genuflect.*) And was made Flesh by the Holy Spirit of the Virgin Mary: AND WAS MADE MAN. He was also crucified for us, suffered under Pontius Pilate and was buried. And on the third day He rose again according to the Scriptures. And ascending into heaven, He sits at the right hand of the Father. And He shall come again in glory to judge the living and the dead; and of His kingdom there shall be no end. And I believe in the Holy Spirit, Lord and Giver of life, Who proceeds from the Father and the Son. Who together with the Father and the Son is no less adored, and glorified: Who spoke by the Prophets. And I believe in One, Holy, Catholic and Apostolic Church. I confess one Baptism for the remission of sins. And I look for the resurrection of the dead. ✠ And the life of the world to come. Amen.

THE OFFERTORY

The Priest turns to the people and says:

P. The Lord be with you. *S.* And with your spirit.
P. Let us pray.

THE OFFERTORY VERSE • Ps. 145, 2

PRAISE the Lord, O my soul; I will praise the Lord all my life; I will sing praise to my God while I live. Alleluia.

The Priest now uncovers the chalice, places the host on the paten and offering it up, says:

ACCEPT, O holy Father, almighty and eternal God, this spotless host, which I, Your unworthy servant, offer to You, my living and true God, to atone for my numberless sins, offenses, and negligences; on behalf of all here present and likewise for all faithful Christians living and dead, that it may profit me and them as a means of salvation to life everlasting. Amen.

He pours wine and water into the chalice, blessing the water before it is poured.

O GOD, Who established the nature of man in wondrous dignity, and still more admirably restored it, grant that through the mystery of this water and wine, we may be made partakers of His Divinity, Who has condescended to become partaker of our humanity, Jesus Christ, Your Son, our Lord. Who lives and reigns with You in the unity of the Holy Spirit, God, world without end. Amen.

Offering up the wine, the Priest says:

WE OFFER You, O Lord, the chalice of salvation, humbly begging of Your mercy that it may arise before Your Divine Majesty, with a pleasing fragrance, for our salvation and for that of the whole world. Amen.

Bowing down, the Priest says:

IN A humble spirit and with a contrite heart, may we be accepted by You, O Lord, and may our sacrifice so be offered in Your sight this day as to please You, O Lord God.

Raising his eyes and blessing the offering, he says:

COME, O Sanctifier, almighty and eternal God, and bless ✠ this sacrifice prepared for the glory of Your holy name.

WASHING THE FINGERS

I WASH my hands in innocence, and I go around Your altar, O Lord, giving voice to my thanks, and recounting all Your wondrous deeds. O Lord, I love the house in which You dwell, the tenting-place of Your glory. Gather not my soul with those of sinners, nor with men of blood my life. On their hands are crimes, and their right hands are full of bribes. But I walk in integrity; redeem me, and have pity on me. My foot stands on level ground; in the assemblies I will bless You, O Lord. Glory be to the Father, and to the Son, and to the Holy Spirit. As it was in the beginning, is now, and ever shall be, world without end. Amen.

ACCEPT, Most Holy Trinity, this offering which we are making to You in remembrance of the Passion, Resurrection, and Ascension of Jesus Christ, our Lord; and in honor of Blessed Mary, ever Virgin, Blessed John the Baptist, the Holy Apostles Peter and Paul, and of these, and of all the Saints; that it may add to their honor and aid our salvation; and may they deign to intercede in heaven for us who honor their memory here on earth. Through the same Christ our Lord. Amen.

The Priest turns toward the people and says:

Pray, brethren, that my sacrifice and yours may become acceptable to God the Father almighty.

S. May the Lord accept this sacrifice from your hands to the praise and glory of His name, for our

advantage, and that of all His holy Church.
P. Amen.

THE SECRET

THROUGH these mysteries may grace be given us, O Lord, that moderating our earthly desires, we may learn to love the things of heaven. Through our Lord Jesus Christ, Your Son, Who lives and reigns with You in the unity of the Holy Spirit, God.
P. World without end. *S.* Amen.

PREFACE–CANON

P. The Lord be with you. *S.* And with your spirit.
P. Lift up your hearts.
S. We have lifted them up to the Lord.
P. Let us give thanks to the Lord, our God.
S. It is fitting and just.

IT IS fitting indeed and just, right and helpful to salvation for us always to praise You, O Lord, but more gloriously at this time above others when Christ our Passover was sacrificed. For He is the true Lamb Who has taken away the sins of the world: Who by dying has destroyed our death; and by rising again has restored us to life. And therefore with Angels and Archangels, with Thrones and Dominations, and with the whole host of the heavenly army, we sing a hymn to Your glory, saying again and again (*the bell is rung* 3 *times*):

HOLY, HOLY, HOLY, Lord God of Hosts. Heaven and earth are filled with Your glory. Hosanna in the highest. ✠ Blessed is He Who comes in the name of the Lord. Hosanna in the highest.

THE CANON OF THE MASS

THEREFORE, most gracious Father, we humbly beg of You and entreat You through Jesus Christ Your Son, our Lord, (*he kisses the altar*) to deem acceptable and bless these ✠ gifts, these ✠ offerings, these ✠ holy and unspotted oblations which, in the first place, we offer You for Your Holy Catholic Church, that You would deign to give her peace and protection, to unite and guard her throughout the world, together with Your servant N., our Pope, and N., our Bishop; and all true believers who cherish the Catholic and Apostolic Faith.

Commemoration of the Living

REMEMBER, O Lord, Your servants and handmaids, N. and N., (*name them*) and all here present, whose faith and devotion are known to You, on whose behalf we offer to You, or who themselves offer to You, this sacrifice of praise for themselves, families and friends, for the good of their souls, for their hope of salvation and deliverance from all harm, and who offer their homage to You, eternal, living and true God.

Commemoration of the Saints

IN THE unity of holy fellowship we observe the memory, first of all, of the glorious and ever Virgin Mary, Mother of our Lord and God Jesus Christ; next, that of Your Blessed Apostles and Martyrs, Peter and Paul, Andrew, James, John, Thomas, James, Philip, Bartholomew, Matthew, Simon and Thaddeus; of Linus, Cletus, Clement, Sixtus, Cornelius, Cyprian, Lawrence, Chrysogonus, John and Paul, Cosmas and Damian, and of all

Your Saints, by whose merits and prayers grant that we may be always fortified by the help of Your protection. Through the same Christ our Lord. Amen.

Spreading his hands over the oblation, he says:

GRACIOUSLY accept, then, we beseech You, O Lord, this service of our worship and that of all Your household. Provide that our days be spent in Your peace, save us from everlasting damnation, and cause us to be numbered in the flock You have chosen. Through Christ our Lord. Amen.

O GOD, deign to bless ✠ what we offer, and make it approved, ✠ effective, ✠ right, and wholly pleasing in every way, that it may become for our good, the Body ✠ and Blood ✠ of Your dearly beloved Son, Jesus Christ our Lord.

CONSECRATION—ELEVATION

WHO the day before He suffered, took bread into His holy and venerable hands, and having raised His eyes to heaven, to You, O God, His almighty Father, giving thanks to You, He blessed it, ✠ broke it, and gave it to His disciples, saying: All of you take and eat of this:

FOR THIS IS MY BODY.

IN LIKE manner, when the supper was done, taking also this goodly chalice into His holy and venerable hands, again giving thanks to You, He blessed ✠ it, and gave it to His disciples, saying: All of you take and drink of this:

FOR THIS IS THE CHALICE OF MY BLOOD OF THE NEW AND ETERNAL COVENANT: THE MYSTERY OF FAITH: WHICH SHALL BE SHED FOR YOU AND FOR MANY UNTO THE FORGIVENESS OF SINS.

After replacing the chalice on the corporal, he says:

As often as you shall do these things, in memory of Me shall you do them.

Offering of the Victim

MINDFUL, therefore, O Lord, not only of the blessed Passion of the same Christ, Your Son, our Lord, but also of His Resurrection from the dead, and finally His glorious Ascension into heaven, we, Your ministers, as also Your holy people, offer to Your supreme Majesty, of the gifts bestowed upon us, the pure ✠ Victim, the holy ✠ Victim, the all-perfect ✠ Victim: the holy ✠ Bread of life eternal and the Chalice ✠ of unending salvation.

AND this deign to regard with gracious and kindly attention and hold acceptable, as You deigned to accept the offerings of Abel, Your just servant, and the sacrifice of Abraham our patriarch, and that which Your chief priest Melchisedec offered to You, a holy sacrifice and a spotless victim.

MOST humbly we implore You, almighty God, bid these offerings to be brought by the hands of Your holy angel to Your altar above; before the face of Your Divine Majesty; that those of us who, by sharing in the Sacrifice of this altar shall, receive the Most Sacred ✠ Body and ✠ Blood of Your Son, may be filled with every grace and heavenly blessing. Through the same Christ our Lord. Amen.

Commemoration of the Dead

REMEMBER also, O Lord, Your servants and handmaids, N. and N., who have gone before us with the sign of faith, and rest in the sleep of peace. (*Here pray for the dead.*) To these, O Lord,

and to all who rest in Christ, we beseech You to grant of Your goodness, a place of comfort, light and peace. Through the same Christ our Lord. Amen.

TO US sinners also, Your servants, trusting in the greatness of Your mercy, deign to grant some part and fellowship with Your Holy Apostles and Martyrs: with John, Stephen, Matthias, Barnabas, Ignatius, Alexander, Marcellinus, Peter, Felicitas, Perpetua, Agatha, Lucy, Agnes, Cecilia, Anastasia; and all Your Saints; into whose company, we implore You to admit us, not weighing our merits, but freely granting us pardon. Through Christ our Lord.

THROUGH Whom, O Lord, You always create, ✠ sanctify, ✠ fill with life, ✠ bless, and bestow upon us all good things.

The Minor Elevation

THROUGH ✠ Him, and with ✠ Him, and in ✠ Him, is to You, God the Father ✠ almighty, in the unity of the Holy ✠ Spirit, all honor and glory, world without end. S. Amen.

THE COMMUNION AND THANKSGIVING

Let us pray. Prompted by saving precepts, and taught by Your divine teaching, we dare to say:

OUR FATHER, Who art in heaven, hallowed be Thy name: Thy kingdom come: Thy will be done on earth as it is in heaven. Give us this day our daily bread; and forgive us our trespasses, as we forgive those who trespass against us. And lead us not into temptation: S. But deliver us from evil. P. Amen.

DELIVER us, we beseech You, O Lord, from all evils, past, present, and to come; and by the intercession of the Blessed and glorious Mary, ever Virgin, Mother of God, together with Your Blessed Apostles Peter and Paul, and Andrew, and all the Saints, grant of Your goodness, peace in our days, that aided by the riches of Your mercy, we may be always free from sin and safe from all disturbance.

Through the same our Lord Jesus Christ, Your Son, Who lives and reigns with You in the unity of the Holy Spirit, God, world without end. *S.* Amen.

P. May the peace ✠ of the Lord be ✠ always with ✠ you. *S.* And with your spirit.

The Priest puts a small particle into the chalice, saying:

May this mingling and consecration of the Body and Blood of our Lord Jesus Christ help us who receive it to life everlasting. Amen.

LAMB of God, You Who take away the sins of the world, have mercy on us.

Lamb of God, You Who take away the sins of the world, have mercy on us.

Lamb of God, You Who take away the sins of the world, grant us peace.

PRAYERS BEFORE HOLY COMMUNION

Then inclining toward the altar, he says:

O LORD Jesus Christ, Who said to Your Apostles: "Peace I leave with you, My peace I give to you," regard not my sins but the faith of Your Church, and deign to give her peace and unity according to Your Will: Who live and reign, God world without end. Amen.

O LORD Jesus Christ, Son of the living God, Who, by the will of the Father, with the co-operation of the Holy Spirit, have by Your death given life to the world, deliver me by this Your Most Sacred Body and Blood from all my sins and from every evil. Make me always cling to Your commandments, and never permit me to be separated from You. Who with the same God the Father and the Holy Spirit, live and reign, God, world without end. Amen.

LET not the partaking of Your Body, O Lord Jesus Christ, which I, though unworthy, presume to receive, turn to my judgment and condemnation; but through Your goodness, may it become a safeguard and an effective remedy, both of soul and body. Who live and reign with God the Father, in the unity of the Holy Spirit, God, world without end. Amen.

COMMUNION OF THE PRIEST

I WILL take the Bread of heaven, and call upon the name of the Lord.

Lord, I am not worthy that You should come under my roof; but only say the word, and my soul will be healed. (3 *times.*)

Making the Sign of the Cross with the Host, he says:

MAY the Body of our Lord Jesus Christ preserve my soul to life everlasting. Amen.

What return shall I make to the Lord for all He has given me? I will take the Chalice of salvation, and I will call upon the name of the Lord. Praising will I call upon the Lord and I shall be saved from my enemies.

Making the Sign of the Cross with the chalice, he says:

MAY the Blood of our Lord Jesus Christ preserve my soul to life everlasting. Amen.

The Priest reverently consumes the Precious Blood.

COMMUNION OF THE FAITHFUL

The Server and people say the "Confiteor."

P. May almighty God have mercy on you, forgive you your sins, and bring you to life everlasting. S. Amen.

P. May the almighty and merciful Lord grant you pardon, ✠ absolution and remission of your sins. S. Amen.

Holding up a Sacred Host, the Priest says:

Behold the Lamb of God, behold Him Who takes away the sins of the world.

Lord, I am not worthy that You should come under my roof; but only say the word, and my soul will be healed. (3 *times.*)

The Priest says to each communicant:

May the Body of our Lord Jesus Christ preserve your soul to life everlasting. Amen.

The Priest purifies the chalice with wine, saying:

WHAT has passed our lips as food, O Lord, may we possess in purity of heart, that what is given to us in time, be our healing for eternity.

He purifies his fingers with wine and water, saying:

MAY Your Body, O Lord, which I have eaten, and Your Blood which I have drunk, cleave to my very soul, and grant that no trace of sin be found in me, whom these pure and holy mysteries have renewed. Who live and reign, world without end. Amen.

THE COMMUNION • John 16, 16

A LITTLE while, and you shall not see Me, alleluia: and again a little while, and you shall see Me: because I go to the Father, alleluia, alleluia.

The Priest, turning to the people, says:

P. The Lord be with you. S. And with your spirit.
P. Let us pray.

THE POSTCOMMUNION

MAY the sacrament which we have received, we beseech You, O Lord, both strengthen us with spiritual food, and uphold us with bodily succor. Through our Lord Jesus Christ, Your Son, Who lives and reigns with You in the unity of the Holy Spirit, God, world without end. S. Amen.

FINAL PRAYERS

The Priest turns again to the people, and says:

P. The Lord be with you. S. And with your spirit.
P. Go, you are dismissed. S. Thanks be to God.

MAY the tribute of my worship be pleasing to You, Most Holy Trinity, and grant that the sacrifice which I, all unworthy, have offered in the presence of Your Majesty, may be acceptable to You, and through Your mercy obtain forgiveness for me and all for whom I have offered it. Through Christ our Lord. Amen.

THE LAST BLESSING

He kisses the altar, and facing the people, says:

MAY almighty God bless you: ✠ the Father, and the Son, and the Holy Spirit.

S. Amen.

The Last Gospel and Prayers after Low Mass are conveniently placed inside the back cover.

"When He, the Spirit of Truth, has come . . ."

FOURTH SUNDAY AFTER EASTER

The Holy Spirit promised by Christ to His Church continues "to convict the world of sin, and of justice, and of judgment." Only those people who follow this teaching can secure true peace. (WHITE VESTMENTS)

PRAYERS AT THE FOOT OF THE ALTAR

IN THE name of the Father, ✠ and of the Son, and of the Holy Spirit. Amen.

Priest. I will go in to the altar of God.

Server. The God of my gladness and joy.

Psalm 42

DO ME justice, O God, and fight my fight against a faithless people; from the deceitful and impious man rescue me.

S. For You, O God, are my strength. Why do You keep me so far away? Why must I go about in mourning, with the enemy oppressing me?

P. Send forth Your light and Your fidelity; they shall lead me on and bring me to Your holy mountain, to Your dwelling-place.

S. Then will I go in to the altar of God, the God of my gladness and joy.
P. Then will I give You thanks upon the harp, O God, my God. Why are you so downcast, O my soul? Why do you sigh within me?
S. Hope in God! For I shall again be thanking Him in the presence of my Savior and my God.
P. Glory be to the Father, and to the Son, and to the Holy Spirit.
S. As it was in the beginning, is now, and ever shall be, world without end. Amen.
P. I will go in to the altar of God.
S. The God of my gladness and joy.
P. Our help ✠ is in the name of the Lord.
S. Who made heaven and earth.
P. I confess to almighty God, etc.
S. May almighty God have mercy on you, forgive you your sins, and bring you to life everlasting.
P. Amen.

The Server, bowing, says the "Confiteor."

I CONFESS to almighty God, to Blessed Mary, ever Virgin, to Blessed Michael the Archangel, to Blessed John the Baptist, to the Holy Apostles Peter and Paul, and to all the Saints, and to you, Father, that I have sinned exceedingly in thought, word and deed, *through my fault, through my fault, through my most grievous fault.* Therefore I beseech Blessed Mary, ever Virgin, Blessed Michael the Archangel, Blessed John the Baptist, the Holy Apostles Peter and Paul, and all the Saints, and you, Father, to pray to the Lord our God for me.
P. May almighty God have mercy on you, forgive you your sins, and bring you to life everlasting.
S. Amen.

MAY the almighty and merciful Lord grant us pardon, ✠ absolution, and remission of our sins. S. Amen.

P. Will You not, O God, give us life?
S. And shall not Your people rejoice in You?
P. Show us, O Lord, Your kindness.
S. And grant us Your salvation.
P. O Lord, hear my prayer.
S. And let my cry come to You.
P. The Lord be with you.
S. And with your spirit. *P.* Let us pray.

Going up to the altar, the Priest prays silently:

TAKE away from us our sins, O Lord, we beseech You, that we may enter with pure minds into the Holy of Holies. Through Christ our Lord. Amen.

WE BESEECH You, O Lord, by the merits of Your Saints (*he kisses the altar*) whose relics lie here, and of all the Saints: deign in Your mercy to pardon me all my sins. Amen.

THE INTROIT • Ps. 97, 1. 2. 1

At the right side of the altar, the Priest says:

SING to the Lord a new song, alleluia; for the Lord has done wondrous deeds, alleluia; in the sight of the nations He has revealed His justice: alleluia, alleluia, alleluia. *Ps.* His right hand has won victory for Him, His holy arm. Glory be to the Father, and to the Son, and to the Holy Spirit. As it was in the beginning, is now, and ever shall be, world without end. Amen. — Sing to the Lord a new song, alleluia; for the Lord has done wondrous deeds, alleluia; in the sight of the nations He has revealed His justice: alleluia, alleluia, alleluia.

THE KYRIE

P. Lord, have mercy. *S.* Lord, have mercy. *P.* Lord, have mercy. *S.* Christ, have mercy. *P.* Christ, have mercy. *S.* Christ, have mercy. *P.* Lord, have mercy. *S.* Lord, have mercy. *P.* Lord, have mercy.

THE GLORIA

GLORY to God in the highest. And on earth peace to men of good will. We praise You. We bless You. We adore You. We glorify You. We give You thanks for Your great glory. O Lord God, heavenly King, God the Father almighty. O Lord Jesus Christ, the Only-begotten Son. O Lord God, Lamb of God, Son of the Father: You Who take away the sins of the world, have mercy on us. You Who take away the sins of the world, receive our prayer. You Who sit at the right hand of the Father, have mercy on us. For You alone are holy. You alone are the Lord. You alone, O Jesus Christ, are most high. Together with the Holy Spirit ✠ in the glory of God the Father. Amen.

The Priest kisses the altar and turns to the people, saying:

P. The Lord be with you. *S.* And with your spirit. *P.* Let us pray.

THE PRAYER

Going to the right (Epistle) side, he says:

O GOD, You make the minds of the faithful to be of one will; grant to Your people to love that which You command, and to desire that which You promise; that amidst the changes of this world, our hearts may be fixed where there are true joys. Through our Lord Jesus Christ, Your Son, Who lives and reigns with You in the unity of the Holy Spirit, God, world without end. *S.* Amen.

THE EPISTLE • James 1, 17-21

BELOVED: Every good gift and every perfect gift is from above, coming down from the Father of Lights, with Whom there is no change, nor shadow of alteration. Of His own will He has begotten us by the word of truth, that we might be, as it were, the first-fruits of His creatures. You know this, my beloved brethren. But let every man be swift to hear, slow to speak, and slow to wrath. For the wrath of man does not work the justice of God. Therefore, casting aside all uncleanness and abundance of malice, with meekness receive the ingrafted word, which is able to save your souls. *S.* Thanks be to God.

Alleluia, alleluia. ℣. *Ps. 117, 16.* The right hand of the Lord has struck with power; the right hand of the Lord has exalted me. Alleluia. ℣. *Rom. 6, 9.* Christ, having risen from the dead, dies now no more; death shall no more have dominion over Him. Alleluia.

PRAYER BEFORE THE GOSPEL

Bowing down at the center of the altar, he says:

CLEANSE my heart and my lips, O almighty God, Who cleansed the lips of the Prophet Isaias with a burning coal. In Your gracious mercy deign so to purify me that I may worthily proclaim Your holy Gospel. Through Christ our Lord. Amen.

Lord, grant Your blessing. The Lord be in my heart and on my lips, that I may worthily and fittingly proclaim His holy Gospel. Amen.

THE GOSPEL • John 16, 5-14

Going to the left (Gospel) side of the altar, he says:

P. The Lord be with you. *S.* And with your spirit.
P. ✠ The continuation of the holy Gospel according to Saint John. *S.* Glory be to You, O Lord.

AT THAT time, Jesus said to His disciples: "I am going to Him Who sent Me, and no one of you asks Me, 'Where are You going?' But because I have spoken to you these things, sorrow has filled your heart. But I speak the truth to you; it is expedient for you that I depart. For if I do not go, the Advocate will not come to you; but if I go, I will send Him to you. And when He has come He will convict the world of sin, and of justice, and of judgment: of sin, because they do not believe in Me; of justice, because I go to the Father, and you will see Me no more; and of judgment, because the prince of this world has already been judged. Many things yet I have to say to you, but you cannot bear them now. But when He, the Spirit of truth, has come, He will teach you all the truth. For He will not speak on His own authority, but whatever He will hear He will speak, and the things that are to come He will declare to you. He will glorify Me, because He will receive of what is Mine and declare it to you." *S.* Praise be to You, O Christ.

P. By the words of the Gospel, may our sins be taken away.

THE NICENE CREED

At the center of the altar, he says:

I BELIEVE in one God, the Father almighty, Maker of heaven and earth, and of all things visible and invisible. And in one Lord Jesus Christ, the Only-begotten Son of God. Born of the Father before all ages. God of God; Light of Light; true God of true God. Begotten not made; of one being with the Father; by Whom all things were made. Who for us men, and for our salvation, came down from heaven. (*Here all genuflect.*) And was made Flesh by the Holy Spirit of the Virgin Mary: AND WAS MADE MAN. He was also crucified for us, suffered under Pontius Pilate and was buried. And on the third day He rose again according to the Scriptures. And ascending into heaven, He sits at the right hand of the Father. And He shall come again in glory to judge the living and the dead; and of His kingdom there shall be no end. And I believe in the Holy Spirit, Lord and Giver of life, Who proceeds from the Father and the Son. Who together with the Father and the Son is no less adored, and glorified: Who spoke by the Prophets. And I believe in One, Holy, Catholic and Apostolic Church. I confess one Baptism for the remission of sins. And I look for the resurrection of the dead. ✠ And the life of the world to come. Amen.

THE OFFERTORY

The Priest turns to the people and says:

P. The Lord be with you. S. And with your spirit.
P. Let us pray.

THE OFFERTORY VERSE • Ps. 65, 1. 2. 16

SHOUT joyfully to God, all you on earth, sing praise to the glory of His name; hear now, all you who fear God, while I declare what the Lord has done for me. Alleluia.

The Priest now uncovers the chalice, places the host on the paten and offering it up, says:

ACCEPT, O holy Father, almighty and eternal God, this spotless host, which I, Your unworthy servant, offer to You, my living and true God, to atone for my numberless sins, offenses, and negligences; on behalf of all here present and likewise for all faithful Christians living and dead, that it may profit me and them as a means of salvation to life everlasting. Amen.

He pours wine and water into the chalice, blessing the water before it is poured.

O GOD, Who established the nature of man in wondrous dignity, and still more admirably restored it, grant that through the mystery of this water and wine, we may be made partakers of His Divinity, Who has condescended to become partaker of our humanity, Jesus Christ, Your Son, our Lord. Who lives and reigns with You in the unity of the Holy Spirit, God, world without end. Amen.

Offering up the wine, the Priest says:

WE OFFER You, O Lord, the chalice of salvation, humbly begging of Your mercy that it may arise before Your Divine Majesty, with a pleasing fragrance, for our salvation and for that of the whole world. Amen.

Bowing down, the Priest says:

IN A humble spirit and with a contrite heart, may we be accepted by You, O Lord, and may our sacrifice so be offered in Your sight this day as to please You, O Lord God.

Raising his eyes and blessing the offering, he says:

COME, O Sanctifier, almighty and eternal God, and bless ✠ this sacrifice prepared for the glory of Your holy name.

WASHING THE FINGERS

I WASH my hands in innocence, and I go around Your altar, O Lord, giving voice to my thanks, and recounting all Your wondrous deeds. O Lord, I love the house in which You dwell, the tenting-place of Your glory. Gather not my soul with those of sinners, nor with men of blood my life. On their hands are crimes, and their right hands are full of bribes. But I walk in integrity; redeem me, and have pity on me. My foot stands on level ground; in the assemblies I will bless You, O Lord. Glory be to the Father, and to the Son, and to the Holy Spirit. As it was in the beginning, is now, and ever shall be, world without end. Amen.

ACCEPT, Most Holy Trinity, this offering which we are making to You in remembrance of the Passion, Resurrection, and Ascension of Jesus Christ, our Lord; and in honor of Blessed Mary, ever Virgin, Blessed John the Baptist, the Holy Apostles Peter and Paul, and of these, and of all the Saints; that it may add to their honor and aid our salvation; and may they deign to intercede in heaven for us who honor their memory here on earth. Through the same Christ our Lord. Amen.

The Priest turns toward the people and says:

Pray, brethren, that my sacrifice and yours may become acceptable to God the Father almighty.

S. May the Lord accept this sacrifice from your hands to the praise and glory of His name, for our advantage, and that of all His holy Church.

P. Amen.

THE SECRET

O GOD, by the adorable Communion of this sacrifice You make us partakers in the one

Supreme Godhead; grant, we beseech You, that even as we recognize Your truth, so we may attain to it by a worthy life. Through our Lord Jesus Christ, Your Son, Who lives and reigns with You in the unity of the Holy Spirit, God.
P. World without end. *S.* Amen.

PREFACE—CANON

P. The Lord be with you. *S.* And with your spirit.
P. Lift up your hearts.
S. We have lifted them up to the Lord.
P. Let us give thanks to the Lord, our God.
S. It is fitting and just.

IT IS fitting indeed and just, right and helpful to salvation for us always to praise You, O Lord, but more gloriously at this time above others when Christ our Passover was sacrificed. For He is the true Lamb Who has taken away the sins of the world: Who by dying has destroyed our death; and by rising again has restored us to life. And therefore with Angels and Archangels, with Thrones and Dominations, and with the whole host of the heavenly army, we sing a hymn to Your glory, saying again and again (*the bell is rung 3 times*):

HOLY, HOLY, HOLY, Lord God of Hosts. Heaven and earth are filled with Your glory. Hosanna in the highest. ✠ Blessed is He Who comes in the name of the Lord. Hosanna in the highest.

THE CANON OF THE MASS

THEREFORE, most gracious Father, we humbly beg of You and entreat You through Jesus Christ Your Son, our Lord, (*he kisses the altar*) to deem acceptable and bless these ✠ gifts, these ✠ offerings, these ✠ holy and unspotted oblations which, in the first place, we offer You for Your Holy Catholic Church, that You would deign to give her peace and protection, to unite and guard her throughout the world, together with Your servant N., our Pope, and N., our Bishop; and all true believers who cherish the Catholic and Apostolic Faith.

Commemoration of the Living

REMEMBER, O Lord, Your servants and handmaids, N. and N., (*name them*) and all here present, whose faith and devotion are known to You, on whose behalf we offer to You, or who themselves offer to You, this sacrifice of praise for themselves, families and friends, for the good of their souls, for their hope of salvation and deliverance from all harm, and who offer their homage to You, eternal, living and true God.

Commemoration of the Saints

IN THE unity of holy fellowship we observe the memory, first of all, of the glorious and ever Virgin Mary, Mother of our Lord and God Jesus Christ; next, that of Your Blessed Apostles and Martyrs, Peter and Paul, Andrew, James, John, Thomas, James, Philip, Bartholomew, Matthew, Simon and Thaddeus; of Linus, Cletus, Clement, Sixtus, Cornelius, Cyprian, Lawrence, Chrysogonus, John and Paul, Cosmas and Damian, and of all Your Saints, by whose merits and prayers grant that we may be always fortified by the help of Your protection. Through the same Christ our Lord. Amen.

Spreading his hands over the oblation, he says:

GRACIOUSLY accept, then, we beseech You, O Lord, this service of our worship and that of all Your household. Provide that our days be spent in Your peace, save us from everlasting damnation, and cause us to be numbered in the flock You have chosen. Through Christ our Lord. Amen.

O GOD, deign to bless ✠ what we offer, and make it approved, ✠ effective, ✠ right, and wholly pleasing in every way, that it may become for our good, the Body ✠ and Blood ✠ of Your dearly beloved Son, Jesus Christ our Lord.

CONSECRATION—ELEVATION

WHO, the day before He suffered, took bread into His holy and venerable hands, and having raised His eyes to heaven, to You, O God, His almighty Father, giving thanks to You, He blessed it, ✠ broke it, and gave it to His disciples, saying: All of you take and eat of this:

FOR THIS IS MY BODY.

IN LIKE manner, when the supper was done, taking also this goodly chalice into His holy and venerable hands, again giving thanks to You, He blessed ✠ it, and gave it to His disciples, saying: All of you take and drink of this:

FOR THIS IS THE CHALICE OF MY BLOOD OF THE NEW AND ETERNAL COVENANT: THE MYSTERY OF FAITH: WHICH SHALL BE SHED FOR YOU AND FOR MANY UNTO THE FORGIVENESS OF SINS.

After replacing the chalice on the corporal, he says:

As often as you shall do these things, in memory of Me shall you do them.

Offering of the Victim

MINDFUL, therefore, O Lord, not only of the blessed Passion of the same Christ, Your Son, our Lord, but also of His Resurrection from the dead, and finally His glorious Ascension into heaven, we, Your ministers, as also Your holy people, offer to Your supreme Majesty, of the gifts bestowed upon us, the pure ✠ Victim, the holy ✠ Victim, the all-perfect ✠ Victim: the holy ✠ Bread of life eternal and the Chalice ✠ of unending salvation.

AND this deign to regard with gracious and kindly attention and hold acceptable, as You deigned to accept the offerings of Abel, Your just servant, and the sacrifice of Abraham our patriarch, and that which Your chief priest Melchisedec offered to You, a holy sacrifice and a spotless victim.

MOST humbly we implore You, almighty God, bid these offerings to be brought by the hands of Your holy angel to Your altar above; before the face of Your Divine Majesty; that those of us who, by sharing in the Sacrifice of this altar, shall receive the Most Sacred ✠ Body and ✠ Blood of Your Son, may be filled with every grace and heavenly blessing. Through the same Christ our Lord. Amen.

Commemoration of the Dead

REMEMBER also, O Lord, Your servants and handmaids, *N.* and *N.*, who have gone before us with the sign of faith, and rest in the sleep of peace. (*Here pray for the dead.*) To these, O Lord, and to all who rest in Christ, we beseech You to grant of Your goodness, a place of comfort, light

and peace. Through the same Christ our Lord. Amen.

TO US sinners also, Your servants, trusting in the greatness of Your mercy, deign to grant some part and fellowship with Your Holy Apostles and Martyrs: with John, Stephen, Matthias, Barnabas, Ignatius, Alexander, Marcellinus, Peter, Felicitas, Perpetua, Agatha, Lucy, Agnes, Cecilia, Anastasia; and all Your Saints; into whose company, we implore You to admit us, not weighing our merits, but freely granting us pardon. Through Christ our Lord.

THROUGH Whom, O Lord, You always create, ✠ sanctify, ✠ fill with life, ✠ bless, and bestow upon us all good things.

The Minor Elevation

THROUGH ✠ Him, and with ✠ Him, and in ✠ Him, is to You, God the Father ✠ almighty, in the unity of the Holy ✠ Spirit, all honor and glory, world without end. *S.* Amen.

THE COMMUNION AND THANKSGIVING

Let us pray. Prompted by saving precepts, and taught by Your divine teaching, we dare to say:

OUR FATHER, Who art in heaven, hallowed be Thy name: Thy kingdom come: Thy will be done on earth as it is in heaven. Give us this day our daily bread; and forgive us our trespasses, as we forgive those who trespass against us. And lead us not into temptation: S. But deliver us from evil. *P.* Amen.

DELIVER us, we beseech You, O Lord, from all evils, past, present, and to come; and by

the intercession of the Blessed and glorious Mary, ever Virgin, Mother of God, together with Your Blessed Apostles Peter and Paul, and Andrew, and all the Saints, grant of Your goodness, peace in our days, that aided by the riches of Your mercy, we may be always free from sin and safe from all disturbance.

Through the same our Lord Jesus Christ, Your Son, Who lives and reigns with You in the unity of the Holy Spirit, God, world without end.

S. Amen.

P. May the peace ✠ of the Lord be ✠ always with ✠ you.

S. And with your spirit.

The Priest puts a small particle into the chalice, saying:

May this mingling and consecration of the Body and Blood of our Lord Jesus Christ help us who receive it to life everlasting. Amen.

LAMB of God, You Who take away the sins of the world, have mercy on us.

Lamb of God, You Who take away the sins of the world, have mercy on us.

Lamb of God, You Who take away the sins of the world, grant us peace.

PRAYERS BEFORE HOLY COMMUNION

Then inclining toward the altar, he says:

O LORD Jesus Christ, Who said to Your Apostles: "Peace I leave with you, My peace I give to you," regard not my sins but the faith of Your Church, and deign to give her peace and unity according to Your Will: Who live and reign, God, world without end. Amen.

O LORD Jesus Christ, Son of the living God, Who, by the will of the Father, with the cooperation of the Holy Spirit, have by Your death given life to the world, deliver me by this Your Most Sacred Body and Blood from all my sins and from every evil. Make me always cling to Your commandments, and never permit me to be separated from You. Who with the same God the Father and the Holy Spirit, live and reign, God, world without end. Amen.

LET not the partaking of Your Body, O Lord Jesus Christ, which I, though unworthy, presume to receive, turn to my judgment and condemnation; but through Your goodness, may it become a safeguard and an effective remedy, both of soul and body. Who live and reign with God the Father, in the unity of the Holy Spirit, God, world without end. Amen.

COMMUNION OF THE PRIEST

I WILL take the Bread of heaven, and call upon the name of the Lord.

Lord, I am not worthy that You should come under my roof; but only say the word, and my soul will be healed. (3 *times.*)

Making the Sign of the Cross with the Host, he says:

MAY the Body of our Lord Jesus Christ preserve my soul to life everlasting. Amen.

What return shall I make to the Lord for all He has given me? I will take the Chalice of salvation, and I will call upon the name of the Lord. Praising will I call upon the Lord and I shall be saved from my enemies.

Making the Sign of the Cross with the chalice, he says:

MAY the Blood of our Lord Jesus Christ preserve my soul to life everlasting. Amen.

The Priest reverently consumes the Precious Blood.

COMMUNION OF THE FAITHFUL

The Server and people say the "Confiteor."

P. May almighty God have mercy on you, forgive you your sins, and bring you to life everlasting. S. Amen.

P. May the almighty and merciful Lord grant you pardon, ✠ absolution and remission of your sins. S. Amen.

Holding up a Sacred Host, the Priest says:

Behold the Lamb of God, behold Him Who takes away the sins of the world.

Lord, I am not worthy that You should come under my roof; but only say the word, and my soul will be healed. (3 *times.*)

The Priest says to each communicant:

May the Body of our Lord Jesus Christ preserve your soul to life everlasting. Amen.

The Priest purifies the chalice with wine, saying:

WHAT has passed our lips as food, O Lord, may we possess in purity of heart, that what is given to us in time, be our healing for eternity.

He purifies his fingers with wine and water, saying:

MAY Your Body, O Lord, which I have eaten, and Your Blood which I have drunk, cleave to my very soul, and grant that no trace of sin be found in me, whom these pure and holy mysteries have renewed. Who live and reign, world without end. Amen.

THE COMMUNION • John 16, 8

WHEN the Paraclete has come, the Spirit of truth, He will convict the word of sin, and of justice, and of judgment, alleluia, alleluia.

The Priest, turning to the people, says:

P. The Lord be with you. *S.* And with your spirit.
P. Let us pray.

THE POSTCOMMUNION

BE WITH us, O Lord, our God: that by these mysteries which we have faithfully received, we may both be purified from vice, and delivered from all dangers. Through our Lord Jesus Christ, Your Son, Who lives and reigns with You in the unity of the Holy Spirit, God, world without end. *S.* Amen.

FINAL PRAYERS

The Priest turns again to the people, and says:

P. The Lord be with you. *S.* And with your spirit.
P. Go, you are dismissed. *S.* Thanks be to God.

MAY the tribute of my worship be pleasing to You, Most Holy Trinity, and grant that the sacrifice which I, all unworthy, have offered in the presence of Your Majesty, may be acceptable to You, and through Your mercy obtain forgiveness for me and all for whom I have offered it. Through Christ our Lord. Amen.

THE LAST BLESSING

MAY almighty God bless you: ✠ the Father, and the Son, and the Holy Spirit. *S.* Amen.

The Last Gospel and Prayers after Low Mass are conveniently placed inside the back cover.

720-19

"Ask, and you shall receive, that your joy may be full."

FIFTH SUNDAY AFTER EASTER

This Sunday before the Rogation Days teaches us to have confidence in prayer that is made in Christ's name, in and with His Spirit. We ought to pray above all that God's Kingdom will come on earth, that Christ may be served and loved by all. (WHITE VESTMENTS)

PRAYERS AT THE FOOT OF THE ALTAR

IN THE name of the Father, ✠ and of the Son, and of the Holy Spirit. Amen.

Priest. I will go in to the altar of God.

Server. The God of my gladness and joy.

Psalm 42

DO ME justice, O God, and fight my fight against a faithless people; from the deceitful and impious man rescue me.

S. For You, O God, are my strength. Why do You keep me so far away? Why must I go about in mourning, with the enemy oppressing me?

P. Send forth Your light and Your fidelity; they shall lead me on and bring me to Your holy mountain, to Your dwelling-place.

S. Then will I go in to the altar of God, the God of my gladness and joy.
P. Then will I give You thanks upon the harp, O God, my God. Why are you so downcast, O my soul? Why do you sigh within me?
S. Hope in God! For I shall again be thanking Him in the presence of my Savior and my God.
P. Glory be to the Father, and to the Son, and to the Holy Spirit.
S. As it was in the beginning, is now, and ever shall be, world without end. Amen.
P. I will go in to the altar of God.
S. The God of my gladness and joy.
P. Our help ✠ is in the name of the Lord.
S. Who made heaven and earth.
P. I confess to almighty God, etc.
S. May almighty God have mercy on you, forgive you your sins, and bring you to life everlasting.
P. Amen.

The Server, bowing, says the "Confiteor."

I CONFESS to almighty God, to Blessed Mary, ever Virgin, to Blessed Michael the Archangel, to Blessed John the Baptist, to the Holy Apostles Peter and Paul, and to all the Saints, and to you, Father, that I have sinned exceedingly in thought, word and deed, *through my fault, through my fault, through my most grievous fault*. Therefore I beseech Blessed Mary, ever Virgin, Blessed Michael the Archangel, Blessed John the Baptist, the Holy Apostles Peter and Paul, and all the Saints, and you, Father, to pray to the Lord our God for me.
P. May almighty God have mercy on you, forgive you your sins, and bring you to life everlasting.
S. Amen.

MAY the almighty and merciful Lord grant us pardon, ✠ absolution, and remission of our sins. *S.* Amen.

P. Will You not, O God, give us life?
S. And shall not Your people rejoice in You?
P. Show us, O Lord, Your kindness.
S. And grant us Your salvation.
P. O Lord, hear my prayer.
S. And let my cry come to You.
P. The Lord be with you.
S. And with your spirit. *P.* Let us pray.

Going up to the altar, the Priest prays silently:

TAKE away from us our sins, O Lord, we beseech You, that we may enter with pure minds into the Holy of Holies. Through Christ our Lord. Amen.

WE BESEECH You, O Lord, by the merits of Your Saints (*he kisses the altar*) whose relics lie here, and of all the Saints: deign in Your mercy to pardon me all my sins. Amen.

THE INTROIT • Isa. 48, 20

At the right side of the altar, the Priest says:

DECLARE the word of joy, and let it be heard, alleluia: declare it even to the ends of the earth; the Lord has delivered His people: alleluia, alleluia. *Ps. 65.* Shout joyfully to God, all you on earth, sing praise to the glory of His name; proclaim His glorious praise. Glory be to the Father, and to the Son, and to the Holy Spirit. As it was in the beginning, is now, and ever shall be, world without end. Amen. — Declare the word of joy, and let it be heard, alleluia: declare it even to the ends of the earth; the Lord has delivered His people: alleluia, alleluia.

THE KYRIE

P. Lord, have mercy. *S*. Lord, have mercy. *P*. Lord, have mercy. *S*. Christ, have mercy. *P*. Christ, have mercy. *S*. Christ, have mercy. *P*. Lord, have mercy. *S*. Lord, have mercy. *P*. Lord, have mercy.

THE GLORIA

GLORY to God in the highest. And on earth peace to men of good will. We praise You. We bless You. We adore You. We glorify You. We give You thanks for Your great glory. O Lord God, heavenly King, God the Father almighty. O Lord Jesus Christ, the Only-begotten Son. O Lord God, Lamb of God, Son of the Father: You Who take away the sins of the world, have mercy on us. You Who take away the sins of the world, receive our prayer. You Who sit at the right hand of the Father, have mercy on us. For You alone are holy. You alone are the Lord. You alone, O Jesus Christ, are most high. Together with the Holy Spirit ✠ in the glory of God the Father. Amen.

The Priest kisses the altar and turns to the people, saying:

P. The Lord be with you. *S*. And with your spirit. *P*. Let us pray.

THE PRAYER

Going to the right (Epistle) side, he says:

O GOD, from Whom all good things proceed, grant to Your suppliants, that by Your inspiration we may think those things that are right, and under Your guidance perform them. Through our Lord Jesus Christ, Your Son, Who lives and reigns with You in the unity of the Holy Spirit, God, world without end. S. Amen.

THE EPISTLE • James 1, 22-27

BELOVED: Be doers of the word, and not hearers only, deceiving yourselves. For if anyone is a hearer of the word, and not a doer, he is like a man looking at his natural face in a mirror: for he looks at himself and goes away, and presently he forgets what kind of man he is. But he who has looked carefully into the perfect law of liberty and has remained in it, not becoming a forgetful hearer but a doer of the word, shall be blessed in his deed. And if anyone thinks himself to be religious, not restraining his tongue but deceiving his own heart, that man's religion is vain. Religion pure and undefiled before God the Father is this: to give aid to orphans and widows in their tribulation, and to keep oneself unspotted from this world. S. Thanks be to God.

Alleluia, alleluia. ℣. Christ is risen, and has shone upon us, whom He redeemed with His Blood. Alleluia. ℣. *John 16, 28.* I came forth from the Father, and have come into the world. Again I leave the world, and go to the Father. Alleluia.

PRAYER BEFORE THE GOSPEL

Bowing down at the center of the altar, he says:

CLEANSE my heart and my lips, O almighty God, Who cleansed the lips of the Prophet Isaias with a burning coal. In Your gracious mercy deign so to purify me that I may worthily proclaim Your holy Gospel. Through Christ our Lord. Amen.

Lord, grant Your blessing. The Lord be in my heart

and on my lips, that I may worthily and fittingly proclaim His holy Gospel. Amen.

THE GOSPEL • John 16, 23-30

Going to the left (Gospel) side of the altar, he says:

P. The Lord be with you. *S.* And with your spirit.
P. ✠ The continuation of the holy Gospel according to Saint John. *S.* Glory be to You, O Lord.

AT THAT time, Jesus said to His disciples: "Amen, amen, I say to you, if you ask the Father anything in My name, He will give it to you. Hitherto you have not asked anything in My name. Ask, and you shall receive, that your joy may be full. These things I have spoken to you in parables. The hour is coming when I will no longer speak to you in parables, but will speak to you plainly of the Father. In that day you shall ask in My name; and I do not say to you that I will ask the Father for you, for the Father Himself loves you because you have loved Me, and have believed that I came forth from God. I came forth from the Father and have come into the world. Again I leave the world and go to the Father." His disciples said to Him, "Behold, now You speak plainly, and utter no parable. Now we know that You know all things, and do not need that anyone should question You. For this reason we believe that You came forth from God." *S.* Praise be to You, O Christ.

P. By the words of the Gospel, may our sins be taken away.

THE NICENE CREED

At the center of the altar, he says:

I BELIEVE in one God, the Father almighty, Maker of heaven and earth, and of all things

visible and invisible. And in one Lord Jesus Christ, the Only-begotten Son of God. Born of the Father before all ages. God of God; Light of Light; true God of true God. Begotten not made; of one being with the Father; by Whom all things were made. Who for us men, and for our salvation, came down from heaven. (*Here all genuflect.*) And was made Flesh by the Holy Spirit of the Virgin Mary: AND WAS MADE MAN. He was also crucified for us, suffered under Pontius Pilate and was buried. And on the third day He rose again according to the Scriptures. And ascending into heaven, He sits at the right hand of the Father. And He shall come again in glory to judge the living and the dead; and of His kingdom there shall be no end. And I believe in the Holy Spirit, Lord and Giver of life, Who proceeds from the Father and the Son. Who together with the Father and the Son is no less adored, and glorified: Who spoke by the Prophets. And I believe in One, Holy, Catholic and Apostolic Church. I confess one Baptism for the remission of sins. And I look for the resurrection of the dead. ✠ And the life of the world to come. Amen.

THE OFFERTORY

The Priest turns to the people and says:

P. The Lord be with you. *S.* And with your spirit.
P. Let us pray.

THE OFFERTORY VERSE • Ps. 65, 8. 9. 20

BLESS the Lord our God, you peoples, loudly sound His praise; He has given life to my soul, and has not let my feet slip. Blessed be the Lord, Who refused me not my prayer, or His kindness. Alleluia.

The Priest now uncovers the chalice, places the host on the paten and offering it up, says:

ACCEPT, O holy Father, almighty and eternal God, this spotless host, which I, Your unworthy servant, offer to You, my living and true God, to atone for my numberless sins, offenses, and negligences; on behalf of all here present and likewise for all faithful Christians living and dead, that it may profit me and them as a means of salvation to life everlasting. Amen.

He pours wine and water into the chalice, blessing the water before it is poured.

O GOD, Who established the nature of man in wondrous dignity, and still more admirably restored it, grant that through the mystery of this water and wine, we may be made partakers of His Divinity, Who has condescended to become partaker of our humanity, Jesus Christ, Your Son, our Lord. Who lives and reigns with You in the unity of the Holy Spirit, God, world without end. Amen.

Offering up the wine, the Priest says:

WE OFFER You, O Lord, the chalice of salvation, humbly begging of Your mercy that it may arise before Your Divine Majesty, with a pleasing fragrance, for our salvation and for that of the whole world. Amen.

Bowing down, the Priest says:

IN A humble spirit and with a contrite heart, may we be accepted by You, O Lord, and may our sacrifice so be offered in Your sight this day as to please You, O Lord God.

Raising his eyes and blessing the offering, he says:

COME, O Sanctifier, almighty and eternal God, and bless ✠ this sacrifice prepared for the glory of Your holy name.

WASHING THE FINGERS

I WASH my hands in innocence, and I go around Your altar, O Lord, giving voice to my thanks, and recounting all Your wondrous deeds. O Lord, I love the house in which You dwell, the tenting-place of Your glory. Gather not my soul with those of sinners, nor with men of blood my life. On their hands are crimes, and their right hands are full of bribes. But I walk in integrity; redeem me, and have pity on me. My foot stands on level ground; in the assemblies I will bless You, O Lord. Glory be to the Father, and to the Son, and to the Holy Spirit. As it was in the beginning, is now, and ever shall be, world without end. Amen.

ACCEPT, Most Holy Trinity, this offering which we are making to You in remembrance of the Passion, Resurrection, and Ascension of Jesus Christ, our Lord; and in honor of Blessed Mary, ever Virgin, Blessed John the Baptist, the Holy Apostles Peter and Paul, and of these, and of all the Saints; that it may add to their honor and aid our salvation; and may they deign to intercede in heaven for us who honor their memory here on earth. Through the same Christ our Lord. Amen.

The Priest turns toward the people and says:

Pray, brethren, that my sacrifice and yours may become acceptable to God the Father almighty.

S. May the Lord accept this sacrifice from your hands to the praise and glory of His name, for our

advantage, and that of all His holy Church.
P. Amen.

THE SECRET

ACCEPT, we beseech You, O Lord, the prayers of the faithful with the offerings of these sacrifices, that by these services of pious devotion we may pass to heavenly glory. Through our Lord Jesus Christ, Your Son, Who lives and reigns with You in the unity of the Holy Spirit, God.
P. World without end. *S.* Amen.

PREFACE—CANON

P. The Lord be with you. *S.* And with your spirit.
P. Lift up your hearts.
S. We have lifted them up to the Lord.
P. Let us give thanks to the Lord, our God.
S. It is fitting and just.

IT IS fitting indeed and just, right and helpful to salvation for us always to praise You, O Lord, but more gloriously at this time above others when Christ our Passover was sacrificed. For He is the true Lamb Who has taken away the sins of the world: Who by dying has destroyed our death; and by rising again has restored us to life. And therefore with Angels and Archangels, with Thrones and Dominations, and with the whole host of the heavenly army, we sing a hymn to Your glory, saying again and again (*the bell is rung 3 times*):

HOLY, HOLY, HOLY, Lord God of Hosts. Heaven and earth are filled with Your glory. Hosanna in the highest. ✠ Blessed is He Who comes in the name of the Lord. Hosanna in the highest.

THE CANON OF THE MASS

THEREFORE, most gracious Father, we humbly beg of You and entreat You through Jesus Christ Your Son, our Lord, (*he kisses the altar*) to deem acceptable and bless these ✠ gifts, these ✠ offerings, these ✠ holy and unspotted oblations which, in the first place, we offer You for Your Holy Catholic Church, that You would deign to give her peace and protection, to unite and guard her throughout the world, together with Your servant N., our Pope, and N., our Bishop; and all true believers who cherish the Catholic and Apostolic Faith.

Commemoration of the Living

REMEMBER, O Lord, Your servants and handmaids, N. and N., (*name them*) and all here present, whose faith and devotion are known to You, on whose behalf we offer to You, or who themselves offer to You, this sacrifice of praise for themselves, families and friends, for the good of their souls, for their hope of salvation and deliverance from all harm, and who offer their homage to You, eternal, living and true God.

Commemoration of the Saints

IN THE unity of holy fellowship we observe the memory, first of all, of the glorious and ever Virgin Mary, Mother of our Lord and God Jesus Christ; next, that of Your Blessed Apostles and Martyrs, Peter and Paul, Andrew, James, John, Thomas, James, Philip, Bartholomew, Matthew, Simon and Thaddeus; of Linus, Cletus, Clement, Sixtus, Cornelius, Cyprian, Lawrence, Chrysogonus, John and Paul, Cosmas and Damian, and of all

Your Saints, by whose merits and prayers grant that we may be always fortified by the help of Your protection. Through the same Christ our Lord. Amen.

Spreading his hands over the oblation, he says:

GRACIOUSLY accept, then, we beseech You, O Lord, this service of our worship and that of all Your household. Provide that our days be spent in Your peace, save us from everlasting damnation, and cause us to be numbered in the flock You have chosen. Through Christ our Lord. Amen.

O GOD, deign to bless ✠ what we offer, and make it approved, ✠ effective, ✠ right, and wholly pleasing in every way, that it may become for our good, the Body ✠ and Blood ✠ of Your dearly beloved Son, Jesus Christ our Lord.

CONSECRATION—ELEVATION

WHO, the day before He suffered, took bread into His holy and venerable hands, and having raised His eyes to heaven, to You, O God, His almighty Father, giving thanks to You, He blessed it, ✠ broke it, and gave it to His disciples, saying: All of you take and eat of this:

FOR THIS IS MY BODY.

IN LIKE manner, when the supper was done, taking also this goodly chalice into His holy and venerable hands, again giving thanks to You, He blessed ✠ it, and gave it to His disciples, saying: All of you take and drink of this:

FOR THIS IS THE CHALICE OF MY BLOOD OF THE NEW AND ETERNAL COVENANT: THE MYSTERY OF FAITH: WHICH SHALL BE SHED FOR YOU AND FOR MANY UNTO THE FORGIVENESS OF SINS.

After replacing the chalice on the corporal, he says:

As often as you shall do these things, in memory of Me shall you do them.

Offering of the Victim

MINDFUL, therefore, O Lord, not only of the blessed Passion of the same Christ, Your Son, our Lord, but also of His Resurrection from the dead, and finally His glorious Ascension into heaven, we, Your ministers, as also Your holy people, offer to Your supreme Majesty, of the gifts bestowed upon us, the pure ✠ Victim, the holy ✠ Victim, the all-perfect ✠ Victim: the holy ✠ Bread of life eternal and the Chalice ✠ of unending salvation.

AND this deign to regard with gracious and kindly attention and hold acceptable, as You deigned to accept the offerings of Abel, Your just servant, and the sacrifice of Abraham our patriarch, and that which Your chief priest Melchisedec offered to You, a holy sacrifice and a spotless victim.

MOST humbly we implore You, almighty God, bid these offerings to be brought by the hands of Your holy angel to Your altar above; before the face of Your Divine Majesty; that those of us who, by sharing in the Sacrifice of this altar, shall receive the Most Sacred ✠ Body and ✠ Blood of Your Son, may be filled with every grace and heavenly blessing. Through the same Christ our Lord. Amen.

Commemoration of the Dead

REMEMBER also, O Lord, Your servants and handmaids, N. and N., who have gone before us with the sign of faith, and rest in the sleep of

peace. (*Here pray for the dead.*) To these, O Lord, and to all who rest in Christ, we beseech You to grant of Your goodness, a place of comfort, light and peace. Through the same Christ our Lord. Amen.

TO US sinners also, Your servants, trusting in the greatness of Your mercy, deign to grant some part and fellowship with Your Holy Apostles and Martyrs: with John, Stephen, Matthias, Barnabas, Ignatius, Alexander, Marcellinus, Peter, Felicitas, Perpetua, Agatha, Lucy, Agnes, Cecilia, Anastasia; and all Your Saints; into whose company, we implore You to admit us, not weighing our merits, but freely granting us pardon. Through Christ our Lord.

THROUGH Whom, O Lord, You always create, ✠ sanctify, ✠ fill with life, ✠ bless, and bestow upon us all good things.

The Minor Elevation

THROUGH ✠ Him, and with ✠ Him, and in ✠ Him, is to You, God the Father ✠ almighty, in the unity of the Holy ✠ Spirit, all honor and glory, world without end. S. Amen.

THE COMMUNION AND THANKSGIVING

Let us pray. Prompted by saving precepts, and taught by Your divine teaching, we dare to say:

OUR FATHER, Who art in heaven, hallowed be Thy name: Thy kingdom come: Thy will be done on earth as it is in heaven. Give us this day our daily bread; and forgive us our trespasses, as we forgive those who trespass against us. And lead us not into temptation: S. But deliver us from evil. *P.* Amen.

DELIVER us, we beseech You, O Lord, from all evils, past, present, and to come; and by the intercession of the Blessed and glorious Mary, ever Virgin, Mother of God, together with Your Blessed Apostles Peter and Paul, and Andrew, and all the Saints, grant of Your goodness, peace in our days, that aided by the riches of Your mercy, we may be always free from sin and safe from all disturbance.

Through the same our Lord Jesus Christ, Your Son, Who lives and reigns with You in the unity of the Holy Spirit, God, world without end.
S. Amen.
P. May the peace ✠ of the Lord be ✠ always with ✠ you.
S. And with your spirit.

The Priest puts a small particle into the chalice, saying:

May this mingling and consecration of the Body and Blood of our Lord Jesus Christ help us who receive it to life everlasting. Amen.

LAMB of God, You Who take away the sins of the world, have mercy on us.

Lamb of God, You Who take away the sins of the world, have mercy on us.

Lamb of God, You Who take away the sins of the world, grant us peace.

PRAYERS BEFORE HOLY COMMUNION

Then inclining toward the altar, he says:

O LORD Jesus Christ, Who said to Your Apostles: "Peace I leave with you, My peace I give to you," regard not my sins but the faith of Your Church, and deign to give her peace and unity

according to Your Will: Who live and reign, God, world without end. Amen.

O LORD Jesus Christ, Son of the living God, Who, by the will of the Father, with the co-operation of the Holy Spirit, have by Your death given life to the world, deliver me by this Your Most Sacred Body and Blood from all my sins and from every evil. Make me always cling to Your commandments, and never permit me to be separated from You. Who with the same God the Father and the Holy Spirit, live and reign, God, world without end. Amen.

LET not the partaking of Your Body, O Lord Jesus Christ, which I, though unworthy, presume to receive, turn to my judgment and condemnation; but through Your goodness, may it become a safeguard and an effective remedy, both of soul and body. Who live and reign with God the Father, in the unity of the Holy Spirit, God, world without end. Amen.

COMMUNION OF THE PRIEST

I WILL take the Bread of heaven, and call upon the name of the Lord.

Lord, I am not worthy that You should come under my roof; but only say the word, and my soul will be healed. (3 *times.*)

Making the Sign of the Cross with the chalice, he says:

MAY the Body of our Lord Jesus Christ preserve my soul to life everlasting. Amen.

What return shall I make to the Lord for all He has given me? I will take the Chalice of salvation, and I will call upon the name of the Lord. Prais-

ing will I call upon the Lord and I shall be saved from my enemies.

Making the Sign of the Cross with the Host, he says:

MAY the Blood of our Lord Jesus Christ preserve my soul to life everlasting. Amen.

The Priest reverently consumes the Precious Blood.

COMMUNION OF THE FAITHFUL

The Server and people say the "Confiteor."

P. May almighty God have mercy on you, forgive you your sins, and bring you to life everlasting. S. Amen.

P. May the almighty and merciful Lord grant you pardon, ✠ absolution and remission of your sins. S. Amen.

Holding up a Sacred Host, the Priest says:

Behold the Lamb of God, behold Him Who takes away the sins of the world.

Lord, I am not worthy that You should come under my roof; but only say the word, and my soul will be healed. (3 *times.*)

The Priest says to each communicant:

May the Body of our Lord Jesus Christ preserve your soul to life everlasting. Amen.

The Priest purifies the chalice with wine, saying:

WHAT has passed our lips as food, O Lord, may we possess in purity of heart, that what is given to us in time, be our healing for eternity.

He purifies his fingers with wine and water, saying:

MAY Your Body, O Lord, which I have eaten, and Your Blood which I have drunk, cleave to my very soul, and grant that no trace of sin be found in me, whom these pure and holy mysteries

have renewed. Who live and reign, world without end. Amen.

THE COMMUNION • Ps. 95, 2

SING to the Lord, alleluia; sing to the Lord; bless His name; announce His salvation, day after day, alleluia, alleluia.

The Priest, turning to the people, says:

P. The Lord be with you. *S.* And with your spirit.
P. Let us pray.

THE POSTCOMMUNION

O LORD, grant us who have been satisfied with the strength of the heavenly table, both to desire those things which are right and to obtain what we desire. Through our Lord Jesus Christ, Your Son, Who lives and reigns with You in the unity of the Holy Spirit, God, world without end. S. Amen.

FINAL PRAYERS

P. The Lord be with you. *S.* And with your spirit.
P. Go, you are dismissed. *S.* Thanks be to God.

MAY the tribute of my worship be pleasing to You, Most Holy Trinity, and grant that the sacrifice which I, all unworthy, have offered in the presence of Your Majesty, may be acceptable to You, and through Your mercy obtain forgiveness for me and all for whom I have offered it. Through Christ our Lord. Amen.

THE LAST BLESSING

MAY almighty God bless you: ✠ the Father, and the Son, and the Holy Spirit. S. Amen.

The Last Gospel and Prayers after Low Mass are conveniently placed inside the back cover.

"So then the Lord Jesus . . . was taken up into heaven."

ASCENSION DAY

Our Lord ascended into heaven to prepare a place for us. His apostles were sent to teach all nations what He had commanded them. We must now cleanse our hearts from sin, and store up good deeds. These will speak for us before God. (WHITE VESTMENTS)

PRAYERS AT THE FOOT OF THE ALTAR

IN THE name of the Father, ✠ and of the Son, and of the Holy Spirit. Amen.

Priest. I will go in to the altar of God.

Server. The God of my gladness and joy.

Psalm 42

DO ME justice, O God, and fight my fight against a faithless people; from the deceitful and impious man rescue me.

S. For You, O God, are my strength. Why do You keep me so far away? Why must I go about in mourning, with the enemy oppressing me?

P. Send forth Your light and Your fidelity; they shall lead me on and bring me to Your holy mountain, to Your dwelling-place.

S. Then will I go in to the altar of God, the God of my gladness and joy.
P. Then will I give You thanks upon the harp, O God, my God. Why are you so downcast, O my soul? Why do you sigh within me?
S. Hope in God! For I shall again be thanking Him in the presence of my Savior and my God.
P. Glory be to the Father, and to the Son, and to the Holy Spirit.
S. As it was in the beginning, is now, and ever shall be, world without end. Amen.
P. I will go in to the altar of God.
S. The God of my gladness and joy.
S. Who made heaven and earth.
P. I confess to almighty God, etc.
S. May almighty God have mercy on you, forgive you your sins, and bring you to life everlasting.
P. Amen.

The Server, bowing, says the "Confiteor."

I CONFESS to almighty God, to Blessed Mary, ever Virgin, to Blessed Michael the Archangel, to Blessed John the Baptist, to the Holy Apostles Peter and Paul, and to all the Saints, and to you, Father, that I have sinned exceedingly in thought, word and deed, *through my fault, through my fault, through my most grievous fault.* Therefore I beseech Blessed Mary, ever Virgin, Blessed Michael the Archangel, Blessed John the Baptist, the Holy Apostles Peter and Paul, and all the Saints, and you, Father, to pray to the Lord our God for me.
P. May almighty God have mercy on you, forgive you your sins, and bring you to life everlasting.
S. Amen.

MAY the almighty and merciful Lord grant us pardon, ✠ absolution, and remission of our sins. *S.* Amen.

P. Will You not, O God, give us life?
S. And shall not Your people rejoice in You?
P. Show us, O Lord, Your kindness.
S. And grant us Your salvation.
P. O Lord, hear my prayer.
S. And let my cry come to You.
P. The Lord be with you.
S. And with your spirit. *P.* Let us pray.

Going up to the altar, the Priest prays silently:

TAKE away from us our sins, O Lord, we beseech You, that we may enter with pure minds into the Holy of Holies. Through Christ our Lord Amen.

WE BESEECH You, O Lord, by the merits of Your Saints (*he kisses the altar*) whose relics lie here, and of all the Saints: deign in Your mercy to pardon me all my sins. Amen.

THE INTROIT • Acts 1, 11

At the right side of the altar, the Priest says:

MEN of Galilee, why do you stand looking up to heaven? Alleluia. He shall come in the same way as you have seen Him going up to heaven: alleluia, alleluia, alleluia. *Ps. 46.* All you peoples, clap your hands, shout to God with cries of gladness. Glory be to the Father, and to the Son, and to the Holy Spirit. As it was in the beginning, is now, and ever shall be, world without end. Amen. — Men of Galilee, why do you stand looking up to heaven? Alleluia. He shall come in the same way as you have seen Him going up to heaven: alleluia, alleluia, alleluia.

THE KYRIE

P. Lord, have mercy. *S*. Lord, have mercy. *P*. Lord, have mercy. *S*. Christ, have mercy. *P*. Christ, have mercy. *S*. Christ, have mercy. *P*. Lord, have mercy. *S*. Lord, have mercy. *P*. Lord, have mercy.

THE GLORIA

GLORY to God in the highest. And on earth peace to men of good will. We praise You. We bless You. We adore You. We glorify You. We give You thanks for Your great glory. O Lord God, heavenly King, God the Father almighty. O Lord Jesus Christ, the Only-begotten Son. O Lord God, Lamb of God, Son of the Father: You Who take away the sins of the world, have mercy on us. You Who take away the sins of the world, receive our prayer. You Who sit at the right hand of the Father, have mercy on us. For You alone are holy. You alone are the Lord. You alone, O Jesus Christ, are most high. Together with the Holy Spirit ✠ in the glory of God the Father. Amen.

The Priest kisses the altar and turns to the people, saying:

P. The Lord be with you. *S*. And with your spirit. *P*. Let us pray.

THE PRAYER

Going to the right (Epistle) side, he says:

GRANT, we beseech You, almighty God, that we who believe Your Only-begotten Son, our Redeemer, to have this day ascended into heaven, may ourselves also in mind dwell amid heavenly things. Through the same our Lord Jesus Christ, Your Son, Who lives and reigns with You in the unity of the Holy Spirit, God, world without end. S. Amen.

THE EPISTLE • Acts 1, 1-11

IN THE former book, O Theophilus, I spoke of all that Jesus did and taught from the beginning until the day on which He was taken up, after He had given commandments through the Holy Spirit to the apostles whom He had chosen. To them also He showed Himself alive after His Passion by many proofs, during forty days appearing to them and speaking of the kingdom of God. And while eating with them, He charged them not to depart from Jerusalem, but to wait for the promise of the Father, "of which you have heard," said He, "by My mouth; for John indeed baptized with water, but you shall be baptized with the Holy Spirit not many days hence." They therefore who had come together began to ask Him, saying, "Lord, will You at this time restore the kingdom to Israel?" But He said to them, "It is not for you to know the times or dates which the Father has fixed by His own authority; but you shall receive power when the Holy Spirit comes upon you, and you shall be witnesses for Me in Jerusalem and in all Judea and Samaria and even to the very ends of the earth." And when He had said this, He was lifted up before their eyes, and a cloud took Him out of their sight. And while they were gazing up to heaven as He went, behold, two men stood by them in white garments, and said to them, "Men of Galilee, why do you stand looking up to heaven? This Jesus Who has been taken up from you into heaven, shall come in the same way as you have seen Him going up to heaven." S. Thanks be to God.

Alleluia, alleluia. ℣. *Ps. 46, 6.* God mounts His throne amid shouts of joy; the Lord, amid trumpet blasts. Alleluia. ℣. *Ps. 67, 18. 19.* The Lord advances from Sinai to the sanctuary; ascending on high, He has led captivity captive. Alleluia.

PRAYER BEFORE THE GOSPEL

Bowing down at the center of the altar, he says:

CLEANSE my heart and my lips, O almighty God, Who cleansed the lips of the Prophet Isaias with a burning coal. In Your gracious mercy deign so to purify me that I may worthily proclaim Your holy Gospel. Through Christ our Lord. Amen.

Lord, grant Your blessing. The Lord be in my heart and on my lips, that I may worthily and fittingly proclaim His holy Gospel. Amen.

THE GOSPEL • Mark 16, 14-20

Going to the left (Gospel) side of the altar, he says:

P. The Lord be with you. S. And with your spirit.
P. ✠ The continuation of the holy Gospel according to Saint Mark. S. Glory be to You, O Lord.

AT THAT time, Jesus appeared to the eleven disciples as they were at table; and He upbraided them for their lack of faith and hardness of heart, in that they had not believed those who had seen Him after He had risen. And He said to them, "Go into the whole world and preach the Gospel to every creature. He who believes and is baptized shall be saved, but he who does not believe shall be condemned. And these signs shall attend those who believe: in My name they shall cast out devils; they shall speak in new tongues; they shall take up serpents; and if they drink any deadly thing, it shall not hurt them; they shall lay hands upon the sick and they shall get well." So then the Lord Jesus, after He had spoken to them, was taken up into heaven, and sits at the right hand of God. But they went forth and preached everywhere, while the Lord worked with them and confirmed the preaching by the signs that followed.

S. Praise be to You, O Christ.

P. By the words of the Gospel, may our sins be taken away.

THE NICENE CREED

At the center of the altar, he says:

I BELIEVE in one God, the Father almighty, Maker of heaven and earth, and of all things visible and invisible. And in one Lord Jesus Christ, the Only-begotten Son of God. Born of the Father before all ages. God of God; Light of Light; true God of true God. Begotten not made; of one being with the Father; by Whom all things were made. Who for us men, and for our salvation, came down from heaven. (*Here all genuflect.*) And was made Flesh by the Holy Spirit of the Virgin Mary: AND WAS MADE MAN. He was also crucified for us, suffered under Pontius Pilate and was buried. And on the third day He rose again according to the Scriptures. And ascending into heaven, He sits at the right hand of the Father. And He shall come again in glory to judge the living and the dead; and of His kingdom there shall be no end. And I believe in the Holy Spirit, Lord and Giver of life, Who proceeds from the Father and the Son. Who together with the Father and the Son is no less adored, and glorified: Who spoke by the Prophets. And I believe in One, Holy, Catholic and Apostolic Church. I confess one Baptism for the remission of sins. And I look for the resurrec-

tion of the dead. ✠ And the life of the world to come. Amen.

THE OFFERTORY

The Priest turns to the people and says:

P. The Lord be with you. S. And with your spirit.
P. Let us pray.

THE OFFERTORY VERSE · Ps. 46, 6

GOD mounts His throne amid shouts of joy; the Lord, amid trumpet blasts. Alleluia.

The Priest now uncovers the chalice, places the host on the paten and offering it up, says:

ACCEPT, O holy Father, almighty and eternal God, this spotless host, which I, Your unworthy servant, offer to You, my living and true God, to atone for my numberless sins, offenses, and negligences; on behalf of all here present and likewise for all faithful Christians living and dead, that it may profit me and them as a means of salvation to life everlasting. Amen.

He pours wine and water into the chalice, blessing the water before it is poured.

O GOD, Who established the nature of man in wondrous dignity, and still more admirably restored it, grant that through the mystery of this water and wine, we may be made partakers of His Divinity, Who has condescended to become partaker of our humanity, Jesus Christ, Your Son, our Lord. Who lives and reigns with You in the unity of the Holy Spirit, God, world without end. Amen.

Offering up the wine, the Priest says:

WE OFFER You, O Lord, the chalice of salvation, humbly begging of Your mercy that it may arise before Your Divine Majesty, with a pleasing fragrance, for our salvation and for that of the whole world. Amen.

Bowing down, the Priest says:

IN A humble spirit and with a contrite heart, may we be accepted by You, O Lord, and may our sacrifice so be offered in Your sight this day as to please You, O Lord God.

Raising his eyes and blessing the offering, he says:

COME, O Sanctifier, almighty and eternal God, and bless ✠ this sacrifice prepared for the glory of Your holy name.

WASHING THE FINGERS

I WASH my hands in innocence, and I go around Your altar, O Lord, giving voice to my thanks, and recounting all Your wondrous deeds. O Lord, I love the house in which You dwell, the tenting-place of Your glory. Gather not my soul with those of sinners, nor with men of blood my life. On their hands are crimes, and their right hands are full of bribes. But I walk in integrity; redeem me, and have pity on me. My foot stands on level ground; in the assemblies I will bless You, O Lord. Glory be to the Father, and to the Son, and to the Holy Spirit. As it was in the beginning, is now, and ever shall be, world without end. Amen.

ACCEPT, Most Holy Trinity, this offering which we are making to You in remembrance of the Passion, Resurrection, and Ascension of Jesus Christ, our Lord; and in honor of Blessed Mary, ever Virgin, Blessed John the Baptist, the Holy Apostles Peter and Paul, and of these, and of all the Saints; that it may add to their honor and aid our salvation; and may they deign to intercede in heaven for us who honor their memory here on earth. Through the same Christ our Lord. Amen.

The Priest turns toward the people and says:

Pray, brethren, that my sacrifice and yours may become acceptable to God the Father almighty.

S. May the Lord accept this sacrifice from your hands to the praise and glory of His name, for our advantage, and that of all His holy Church.

P. Amen.

THE SECRET

RECEIVE, O Lord, the gifts which we lay before You in honor of the glorious Ascension of Your Son, and mercifully grant that we may be delivered from present dangers, and arrive at everlasting life. Through the same our Lord Jesus Christ, Your Son, Who lives and reigns with You in the unity of the Holy Spirit, God.

P. World without end. *S.* Amen.

PREFACE—CANON

P. The Lord be with you. *S.* And with your spirit.

P. Lift up your hearts.

S. We have lifted them up to the Lord.

P. Let us give thanks to the Lord, our God.

S. It is fitting and just.

IT IS fitting indeed and just, right and helpful to salvation, for us always and everywhere to give thanks to You, O holy Lord, Father almighty, everlasting God; through Christ our Lord. Who, after His Resurrection, appeared openly to all His disciples, and, while they looked on, was taken up into heaven, that He might grant us to be sharers in His own divinity. And therefore, with Angels and Archangels, with Thrones and Dominations, and with the whole host of the heavenly army, we sing a hymn to Your glory, saying again and again (*the bell is rung 3 times*):

HOLY, HOLY, HOLY, Lord God of Hosts. Heaven and earth are filled with Your glory. Hosanna in the highest. ✠ Blessed is He Who comes in the name of the Lord. Hosanna in the highest.

THE CANON OF THE MASS

THEREFORE, most gracious Father, we humbly beg of You and entreat You through Jesus Christ Your Son, our Lord, (*he kisses the altar*) to deem acceptable and bless these ✠ gifts, these ✠ offerings, these ✠ holy and unspotted oblations which, in the first place, we offer You for Your Holy Catholic Church, that You would deign to give her peace and protection, to unite and guard her throughout the world, together with Your servant N., our Pope, and N., our Bishop; and all true believers who cherish the Catholic and Apostolic Faith.

Commemoration of the Living

REMEMBER, O Lord, Your servants and handmaids, N. and N., (*name them*) and all here present, whose faith and devotion are known to You, on whose behalf we offer to You, or who themselves offer to You, this sacrifice of praise for themselves, families and friends, for the good of their souls, for their hope of salvation and deliverance from all harm, and who offer their homage to You, eternal, living and true God.

Commemoration of the Saints

IN THE unity of holy fellowship, and keeping this most holy day on which Your Only-begotten Son, our Lord set at the right hand of Your glory the substance of our frail human nature, which He had taken to Himself, we also observe the memory, first of all, of the glorious and ever Virgin Mary, Mother of our Lord and God Jesus Christ; next, that of Your Blessed Apostles and Martyrs, Peter and Paul, Andrew, James, John, Thomas, James, Philip, Bartholomew, Matthew, Simon and Thaddeus; of Linus, Cletus, Clement, Sixtus, Cornelius, Cyprian, Lawrence, Chrysogonus, John and Paul, Cosmas and Damian, and of all Your Saints, by whose merits and prayers grant that we may be always fortified by the help of Your protection. Through the same Christ our Lord. Amen.

Spreading his hands over the oblation, he says:

GRACIOUSLY accept, then, we beseech You, O Lord, this service of our worship and that of all Your household. Provide that our days be spent in Your peace, save us from everlasting damnation, and cause us to be numbered in the flock You have chosen. Through Christ our Lord. Amen.

O GOD, deign to bless ✠ what we offer, and make it approved, ✠ effective, ✠ right, and wholly pleasing in every way, that it may become for our good, the Body ✠ and Blood ✠ of Your dearly beloved Son, Jesus Christ our Lord.

CONSECRATION—ELEVATION

WHO, the day before He suffered, took bread into His holy and venerable hands, and having raised His eyes to heaven, to You, O God, His almighty Father, giving thanks to You, He blessed it, ✠ broke it, and gave it to His disciples, saying: All of you take and eat of this:

FOR THIS IS MY BODY.

IN LIKE manner, when the supper was done, taking also this goodly chalice into His holy and

venerable hands, again giving thanks to You, He blessed ✠ it, and gave it to His disciples, saying: All of you take and drink of this:

FOR THIS IS THE CHALICE OF MY BLOOD OF THE NEW AND ETERNAL COVENANT: THE MYSTERY OF FAITH: WHICH SHALL BE SHED FOR YOU AND FOR MANY UNTO THE FORGIVENESS OF SINS.

After replacing the chalice on the corporal, he says:

As often as you shall do these things, in memory of Me shall you do them.

Offering of the Victim

MINDFUL, therefore, O Lord, not only of the blessed Passion of the same Christ, Your Son, our Lord, but also of His Resurrection from the dead, and finally His glorious Ascension into heaven, we, Your ministers, as also Your holy people, offer to Your supreme Majesty, of the gifts bestowed upon us, the pure ✠ Victim, the holy ✠ Victim, the all-perfect ✠ Victim: the holy ✠ Bread of life eternal and the Chalice ✠ of unending salvation.

AND this deign to regard with gracious and kindly attention and hold acceptable, as You deigned to accept the offerings of Abel, Your just servant, and the sacrifice of Abraham our patriarch, and that which Your chief priest Melchisedec offered to You, a holy sacrifice and a spotless victim.

MOST humbly we implore You, almighty God, bid these offerings to be brought by the hands of Your holy angel to Your altar above; before the face of Your Divine Majesty; that those of us who, by sharing in the Sacrifice of this altar, shall receive the Most Sacred ✠ Body and ✠ Blood of Your

Son, may be filled with every grace and heavenly blessing. Through the same Christ our Lord. Amen.

Commemoration of the Dead

REMEMBER also, O Lord, Your servants and handmaids, N. and N., who have gone before us with the sign of faith, and rest in the sleep of peace. (*Here pray for the dead.*) To these, O Lord, and to all who rest in Christ, we beseech You to grant of Your goodness, a place of comfort, light and peace. Through the same Christ our Lord. Amen.

TO US sinners also, Your servants, trusting in the greatness of Your mercy, deign to grant some part and fellowship with Your Holy Apostles and Martyrs: with John, Stephen, Matthias, Barnabas, Ignatius, Alexander, Marcellinus, Peter, Felicitas, Perpetua, Agatha, Lucy, Agnes, Cecilia, Anastasia; and all Your Saints; into whose company, we implore You to admit us, not weighing our merits, but freely granting us pardon. Through Christ our Lord.

THROUGH Whom, O Lord, You always create, ✠ sanctify, ✠ fill with life, ✠ bless, and bestow upon us all good things.

The Minor Elevation

THROUGH ✠ Him, and with ✠ Him, and in ✠ Him, is to You, God the Father ✠ almighty, in the unity of the Holy ✠ Spirit, all honor and glory, world without end. S. Amen.

THE COMMUNION AND THANKSGIVING

Let us pray. Prompted by saving precepts, and taught by Your divine teaching, we dare to say:

OUR FATHER, Who art in heaven, hallowed be Thy name: Thy kingdom come: Thy will be done on earth as it is in heaven. Give us this day our daily bread; and forgive us our trespasses, as we forgive those who trespass against us. And lead us not into temptation: *S*. But deliver us from evil. *P*. Amen.

DELIVER us, we beseech You, O Lord, from all evils, past, present, and to come; and by the intercession of the Blessed and glorious Mary, ever Virgin, Mother of God, together with Your Blessed Apostles Peter and Paul, and Andrew, and all the Saints, grant of Your goodness, peace in our days, that aided by the riches of Your mercy, we may be always free from sin and safe from all disturbance.

Through the same our Lord Jesus Christ, Your Son, Who lives and reigns with You in the unity of the Holy Spirit, God, world without end. *S*. Amen.

P. May the peace ✠ of the Lord be ✠ always with ✠ you.

S. And with your spirit.

The Priest puts a small particle into the chalice, saying:

May this mingling and consecration of the Body and Blood of our Lord Jesus Christ help us who receive it to life everlasting. Amen.

LAMB of God, You Who take away the sins of the world, have mercy on us.

Lamb of God, You Who take away the sins of the world, have mercy on us.

Lamb of God, You Who take away the sins of the world, grant us peace.

PRAYERS BEFORE HOLY COMMUNION

Then inclining toward the altar, he says:

O LORD Jesus Christ, Who said to Your Apostles: "Peace I leave with you, My peace I give to you," regard not my sins but the faith of Your Church, and deign to give her peace and unity according to Your Will: Who live and reign, God, world without end. Amen.

O LORD Jesus Christ, Son of the living God, Who, by the will of the Father, with the cooperation of the Holy Spirit, have by Your death given life to the world, deliver me by this Your Most Sacred Body and Blood from all my sins and from every evil. Make me always cling to Your commandments, and never permit me to be separated from You. Who with the same God the Father and the Holy Spirit, live and reign, God, world without end. Amen.

LET not the partaking of Your Body, O Lord Jesus Christ, which I, though unworthy, presume to receive, turn to my judgment and condemnation; but through Your goodness, may it become a safeguard and an effective remedy, both of soul and body. Who live and reign with God the Father, in the unity of the Holy Spirit, God, world without end. Amen.

COMMUNION OF THE PRIEST

I WILL take the Bread of heaven, and call upon the name of the Lord.

Lord, I am not worthy that You should come under my roof; but only say the word, and my soul will be healed. (3 *times.*)

Making the Sign of the Cross with the Host, he says:

MAY the Body of our Lord Jesus Christ preserve my soul to life everlasting. Amen.

What return shall I make to the Lord for all He has given me? I will take the Chalice of salvation, and I will call upon the name of the Lord. Praising will I call upon the Lord and I shall be saved from my enemies.

Making the Sign of the Cross with the chalice, he says:

MAY the Blood of our Lord Jesus Christ preserve my soul to life everlasting. Amen.

The Priest reverently consumes the Precious Blood.

COMMUNION OF THE FAITHFUL

The Server and people say the "Confiteor."

P. May almighty God have mercy on you, forgive you your sins, and bring you to life everlasting. *S.* Amen.

P. May the almighty and merciful Lord grant you pardon, ✠ absolution and remission of your sins. *S.* Amen.

Holding up a Sacred Host, the Priest says:

Behold the Lamb of God, behold Him Who takes away the sins of the world.

Lord, I am not worthy that You should come under my roof; but only say the word, and my soul will be healed. (3 *times.*)

The Priest says to each communicant:

May the Body of our Lord Jesus Christ preserve your soul to life everlasting. Amen.

The Priest purifies the chalice with wine, saying:

WHAT has passed our lips as food, O Lord, may we possess in purity of heart, that what is given to us in time, be our healing for eternity.

MAY Your Body, O Lord, which I have eaten, and Your Blood which I have drunk, cleave to my very soul, and grant that no trace of sin be found in me, whom these pure and holy mysteries have renewed. Who live and reign, world without end. Amen.

THE COMMUNION • Ps. 67, 33. 34

CHANT praise to the Lord, Who rides on the heights of the heavens to the East. Alleluia.

The Priest, turning to the people, says:

P. The Lord be with you. *S.* And with your spirit.
P. Let us pray.

THE POSTCOMMUNION

GRANT, we beseech You, almighty and merciful God, that what we have received in visible mysteries we may obtain by an invisible effect. Through our Lord Jesus Christ, Your Son, Who lives and reigns, etc. *S.* Amen.

FINAL PRAYERS

P. The Lord be with you. *S.* And with your spirit.
P. Go, you are dismissed. *S.* Thanks be to God.

MAY the tribute of my worship be pleasing to You, Most Holy Trinity, and grant that the sacrifice which I, all unworthy, have offered in the presence of Your Majesty, may be acceptable to You, and through Your mercy obtain forgiveness for me and all for whom I have offered it. Through Christ our Lord. Amen.

THE LAST BLESSING

MAY almighty God bless you: ✠ the Father, and the Son, and the Holy Spirit. *S.* Amen.

The Last Gospel and Prayers after Low Mass are conveniently placed inside the back cover.

"He will bear witness concerning Me."

SUNDAY AFTER THE ASCENSION

Fervent prayers are being said during this week in preparation for Pentecost. To make these prayers more acceptable to God, "have a constant mutual charity among yourselves; for charity covers a multitude of sins." (WHITE VESTMENTS)

PRAYERS AT THE FOOT OF THE ALTAR

IN THE name of the Father, ✠ and of the Son, and of the Holy Spirit. Amen.

Priest. I will go in to the altar of God.

Server. The God of my gladness and joy.

Psalm 42

DO ME justice, O God, and fight my fight against a faithless people; from the deceitful and impious man rescue me.

S. For You, O God, are my strength. Why do You keep me so far away? Why must I go about in mourning, with the enemy oppressing me?

P. Send forth Your light and Your fidelity; they shall lead me on and bring me to Your holy mountain, to Your dwelling-place.

S. Then will I go in to the altar of God, the God of my gladness and joy.
P. Then will I give You thanks upon the harp, O God, my God. Why are you so downcast, O my soul? Why do you sigh within me?
S. Hope in God! For I shall again be thanking Him in the presence of my Savior and my God.
P. Glory be to the Father, and to the Son, and to the Holy Spirit.
S. As it was in the beginning, is now, and ever shall be, world without end. Amen.
P. I will go in to the altar of God.
S. The God of my gladness and joy.
P. Our help ✠ is in the name of the Lord.
S. Who made heaven and earth.
P. I confess to almighty God, etc.
S. May almighty God have mercy on you, forgive you your sins, and bring you to life everlasting.
P. Amen.

The Server, bowing, says the "Confiteor."

I CONFESS to almighty God, to Blessed Mary, ever Virgin, to Blessed Michael the Archangel, to Blessed John the Baptist, to the Holy Apostles Peter and Paul, and to all the Saints, and to you, Father, that I have sinned exceedingly in thought, word and deed, *through my fault, through my fault, through my most grievous fault.* Therefore I beseech Blessed Mary, ever Virgin, Blessed Michael the Archangel, Blessed John the Baptist, the Holy Apostles Peter and Paul, and all the Saints, and you, Father, to pray to the Lord our God for me.
P. May almighty God have mercy on you, forgive you your sins, and bring you to life everlasting.
S. Amen.

MAY the almighty and merciful Lord grant us pardon, ✠ absolution, and remission of our sins. S. Amen.
P. Will You not, O God, give us life?
S. And shall not Your people rejoice in You?
P. Show us, O Lord, Your kindness.
S. And grant us Your salvation.
P. O Lord, hear my prayer.
S. And let my cry come to You.
P. The Lord be with you.
S. And with your spirit. *P*. Let us pray.

Going up to the altar, the Priest prays silently:

TAKE away from us our sins, O Lord, we beseech You, that we may enter with pure minds into the Holy of Holies. Through Christ our Lord. Amen.

WE BESEECH You, O Lord, by the merits of Your Saints (*he kisses the altar*) whose relics lie here, and of all the Saints: deign in Your mercy to pardon me all my sins. Amen.

THE INTROIT • Ps. 26, 7. 8. 9. 1

At the right side of the altar, the Priest says:

HEAR, O Lord, the sound of my call, alleluia; to You my heart speaks; Your glance I seek; Your presence, O Lord, I seek. Hide not Your face from me, alleluia, alleluia, *Ps.* The Lord is my light and my salvation; whom should I fear? Glory be to the Father, and to the Son, and to the Holy Spirit. As it was in the beginning, is now, and ever shall be, world without end. Amen. — Hear, O Lord, the sound of my call, alleluia; to You my heart speaks; Your glance I seek; Your presence,

O Lord, I seek. Hide not Your face from me, alleluia, alleluia.

THE KYRIE

P. Lord, have mercy. *S*. Lord, have mercy. *P*. Lord, have mercy. *S*. Christ, have mercy. *P*. Christ, have mercy. *S*. Christ, have mercy. *P*. Lord, have mercy. *S*. Lord, have mercy. *P*. Lord, have mercy.

THE GLORIA

GLORY to God in the highest. And on earth peace to men of good will. We praise You. We bless You. We adore You. We glorify You. We give You thanks for Your great glory. O Lord God, heavenly King, God the Father almighty. O Lord Jesus Christ, the Only-begotten Son. O Lord God, Lamb of God, Son of the Father: You Who take away the sins of the world, have mercy on us. You Who take away the sins of the world, receive our prayer. You Who sit at the right hand of the Father, have mercy on us. For You alone are holy. You alone are the Lord. You alone, O Jesus Christ, are most high. Together with the Holy Spirit ✠ in the glory of God the Father. Amen.

The Priest kisses the altar and turns to the people, saying:

P. The Lord be with you. *S*. And with your spirit. *P*. Let us pray.

THE PRAYER

Going to the right (Epistle) side, he says:

ALMIGHTY and everlasting God, grant us both ever to have a will devoted to You, and to serve Your Majesty with a sincere heart. Through our Lord Jesus Christ, Your Son, Who lives and reigns with You in the unity of the Holy Spirit, God, world without end. *S*. Amen.

THE EPISTLE • 1 Pet. 4, 7-11

BELOVED: Be prudent and watchful in prayers. But above all things have a constant mutual charity among yourselves; for charity covers a multitude of sins. Be hospitable to one another without murmuring. According to the gift that each has received, administer it to one another as good stewards of the manifold grace of God. If anyone speaks, let it be as with words of God. If anyone ministers, let it be as from the strength that God furnishes; that in all things God may be honored through Jesus Christ our Lord. S. Thanks be to God.

Alleluia, alleluia. ℣. *Ps. 46,* 9. The Lord reigns over all the nations, God sits upon His holy throne. Alleluia. ℣. *John 14, 18.* I will not leave you orphans; I go away and I come to you, and your heart shall rejoice. Alleluia.

PRAYER BEFORE THE GOSPEL

Bowing down at the center of the altar, he says:

CLEANSE my heart and my lips, O almighty God, Who cleansed the lips of the Prophet Isaias with a burning coal. In Your gracious mercy deign so to purify me that I may worthily proclaim Your holy Gospel. Through Christ our Lord. Amen.

Lord, grant Your blessing. The Lord be in my heart and on my lips, that I may worthily and fittingly proclaim His holy Gospel. Amen.

THE GOSPEL • John 15, 26. 27; 16, 1-4

Going to the left (Gospel) side of the altar, he says:

P. The Lord be with you. S. And with your spirit.

P. ✠ The continuation of the holy Gospel according to Saint John. S. Glory be to You, O Lord.

AT THAT time, Jesus said to His disciples: "When the Advocate has come, Whom I will send you from the Father, the Spirit of truth Who proceeds from the Father, He will bear witness concerning Me. And you also bear witness, because from the beginning you are with Me. These things I have spoken to you that you may not be scandalized. They will expel you from the synagogues. Yes, the hour is coming for everyone who kills you to think he is offering worship to God. And these things they will do because they have not known the Father nor Me. But these things I have spoken to you, that when the time for them has come you may remember that I told you." S. Praise be to You, O Christ.

P. By the words of the Gospel, may our sins be taken away.

THE NICENE CREED

At the center of the altar, he says:

I BELIEVE in one God, the Father almighty, Maker of heaven and earth, and of all things visible and invisible. And in one Lord Jesus Christ, the Only-begotten Son of God. Born of the Father before all ages. God of God; Light of Light; true God of true God. Begotten not made; of one being with the Father; by Whom all things were made. Who for us men, and for our salvation, came down from heaven. (*Here all genuflect.*) And was made Flesh by the Holy Spirit of the Virgin Mary: AND WAS MADE MAN. He was also crucified for us, suffered under Pontius Pilate and was buried. And on the third day He rose again according to the Scriptures. And ascending into heaven, He sits at the right hand of the Father. And He shall come again in glory to judge the living and the dead; and of His kingdom there shall be no end. And I believe in the Holy Spirit, Lord and Giver of life, Who proceeds from the Father and the Son. Who together with the Father and the Son is no less adored, and glorified: Who spoke by the Prophets. And I believe in One, Holy, Catholic and Apostolic Church. I confess one Baptism for the remission of sins. And I look for the resurrection of the dead. ✠ And the life of the world to come. Amen.

THE OFFERTORY

The Priest turns to the people and says:

P. The Lord be with you. *S.* And with your spirit.
P. Let us pray.

THE OFFERTORY VERSE • Ps. 46, 6

GOD mounts His throne amid shouts of joy; the Lord, amid trumpet blasts. Alleluia.

The Priest now uncovers the chalice, places the host on the paten and offering it up, says:

ACCEPT, O holy Father, almighty and eternal God, this spotless host, which I, Your unworthy servant, offer to You, my living and true God, to atone for my numberless sins, offenses, and negligences; on behalf of all here present and likewise for all faithful Christians living and dead, that it may profit me and them as a means of salvation to life everlasting. Amen.

He pours wine and water into the chalice, blessing the water before it is poured.

O GOD, Who established the nature of man in wondrous dignity, and still more admirably restored it, grant that through the mystery of this water and wine, we may be made partakers of His

Divinity, Who has condescended to become partaker of our humanity, Jesus Christ, Your Son, our Lord. Who lives and reigns with You in the unity of the Holy Spirit, God, world without end. Amen.

Offering up the wine, the Priest says:

WE OFFER You, O Lord, the chalice of salvation, humbly begging of Your mercy that it may arise before Your Divine Majesty, with a pleasing fragrance, for our salvation and for that of the whole world. Amen.

Bowing down, the Priest says:

IN A humble spirit and with a contrite heart, may we be accepted by You, O Lord, and may our sacrifice so be offered in Your sight this day as to please You, O Lord God.

Raising his eyes and blessing the offering, he says:

COME, O Sanctifier, almighty and eternal God, and bless ✠ this sacrifice prepared for the glory of Your holy name.

WASHING THE FINGERS

I WASH my hands in innocence, and I go around Your altar, O Lord, giving voice to my thanks, and recounting all Your wondrous deeds. O Lord, I love the house in which You dwell, the tenting-place of Your glory. Gather not my soul with those of sinners, nor with men of blood my life. On their hands are crimes, and their right hands are full of bribes. But I walk in integrity; redeem me, and have pity on me. My foot stands on level ground; in the assemblies I will bless You, O Lord. Glory be to the Father, and to the Son, and to the Holy Spirit. As it was in the beginning, is now, and ever shall be, world without end. Amen.

ACCEPT, Most Holy Trinity, this offering which we are making to You in remembrance of the Passion, Resurrection, and Ascension of Jesus Christ, our Lord; and in honor of Blessed Mary, ever Virgin, Blessed John the Baptist, the Holy Apostles Peter and Paul, and of these, and of all the Saints; that it may add to their honor and aid our salvation; and may they deign to intercede in heaven for us who honor their memory here on earth. Through the same Christ our Lord. Amen.

The Priest turns toward the people and says:

Pray, brethren, that my sacrifice and yours may become acceptable to God the Father almighty.
S. May the Lord accept this sacrifice from your hands to the praise and glory of His name, for our advantage, and that of all His holy Church.
P. Amen.

THE SECRET

MAY this spotless sacrifice purify us, O Lord, and infuse into our minds the vigor of heavenly grace. Through our Lord Jesus Christ, Your Son, Who lives and reigns with You in the unity of the Holy Spirit, God.
P. World without end. S. Amen.

PREFACE—CANON

P. The Lord be with you. S. And with your spirit.
P. Lift up your hearts.
S. We have lifted them up to the Lord.
P. Let us give thanks to the Lord, our God.
S. It is fitting and just.

IT IS fitting indeed and just, right and helpful to salvation, for us always and everywhere to give thanks to You, O holy Lord, Father almighty, everlasting God; through Christ our Lord. Who, after His Resurrection, appeared openly to all His disciples, and, while they looked on, was taken up into heaven, that He might grant us to be sharers in His own divinity. And therefore, with Angels and Archangels, with Thrones and Dominations, and with the whole host of the heavenly army, we sing a hymn to Your glory, saying again and again (*the bell is rung* 3 *times*):

HOLY, HOLY, HOLY, Lord God of Hosts. Heaven and earth are filled with Your glory. Hosanna in the highest. ✠ Blessed is He Who comes in the name of the Lord. Hosanna in the highest.

THE CANON OF THE MASS

THEREFORE, most gracious Father, we humbly beg of You and entreat You through Jesus Christ Your Son, our Lord, (*he kisses the altar*) to deem acceptable and bless these ✠ gifts, these ✠ offerings, these ✠ holy and unspotted oblations which, in the first place, we offer You for Your Holy Catholic Church, that You would deign to give her peace and protection, to unite and guard her throughout the world, together with Your servant N., our Pope, and N., our Bishop; and all true believers who cherish the Catholic and Apostolic Faith.

Commemoration of the Living

REMEMBER, O Lord, Your servants and handmaids, N. and N., (*name them*) and all here present, whose faith and devotion are known to You, on whose behalf we offer to You, or who themselves offer to You, this sacrifice of praise for themselves, families and friends, for the good of their souls, for their hope of salvation and deliverance from all harm, and who offer their homage to You, eternal, living and true God.

Commemoration of the Saints

IN THE unity of holy fellowship we observe the memory, first of all, of the glorious and ever Virgin Mary, Mother of our Lord and God Jesus Christ; next, that of Your Blessed Apostles and Martyrs, Peter and Paul, Andrew, James, John, Thomas, James, Philip, Bartholomew, Matthew, Simon and Thaddeus; of Linus, Cletus, Clement, Sixtus, Cornelius, Cyprian, Lawrence, Chrysogonus, John and Paul, Cosmas and Damian, and of all Your Saints, by whose merits and prayers grant that we may be always fortified by the help of Your protection. Through the same Christ our Lord. Amen.

Spreading his hands over the oblation, he says:

GRACIOUSLY accept, then, we beseech You, O Lord, this service of our worship and that of all Your household. Provide that our days be spent in Your peace, save us from everlasting damnation, and cause us to be numbered in the flock You have chosen. Through Christ our Lord. Amen.

O GOD, deign to bless ✠ what we offer, and make it approved, ✠ effective, ✠ right, and wholly pleasing in every way, that it may become for our good, the Body ✠ and Blood ✠ of Your dearly beloved Son, Jesus Christ our Lord.

CONSECRATION—ELEVATION

WHO, the day before He suffered, took bread into His holy and venerable hands, and having raised His eyes to heaven, to You, O God, His almighty Father, giving thanks to You, He blessed it, ✠ broke it, and gave it to His disciples, saying: All of you take and eat of this:

FOR THIS IS MY BODY.

IN LIKE manner, when the supper was done, taking also this goodly chalice into His holy and venerable hands, again giving thanks to You, He blessed ✠ it, and gave it to His disciples, saying: All of you take and drink of this:

FOR THIS IS THE CHALICE OF MY BLOOD OF THE NEW AND ETERNAL COVENANT: THE MYSTERY OF FAITH: WHICH SHALL BE SHED FOR YOU AND FOR MANY UNTO THE FORGIVENESS OF SINS.

After replacing the chalice on the corporal, he says:

As often as you shall do these things, in memory of Me shall you do them.

Offering of the Victim

MINDFUL, therefore, O Lord, not only of the blessed Passion of the same Christ, Your Son, our Lord, but also of His Resurrection from the dead, and finally His glorious Ascension into heaven, we, Your ministers, as also Your holy people, offer to Your supreme Majesty, of the gifts bestowed upon us, the pure ✠ Victim, the holy ✠ Victim, the all-perfect ✠ Victim: the holy ✠ Bread of life eternal and the Chalice ✠ of unending salvation.

AND this deign to regard with gracious and kindly attention and hold acceptable, as You deigned to accept the offerings of Abel, Your just servant, and the sacrifice of Abraham our patriarch, and that which Your chief priest Melchisedec offered to You, a holy sacrifice and a spotless victim.

MOST humbly we implore You, almighty God, bid these offerings to be brought by the hands of Your holy angel to Your altar above; before the face of Your Divine Majesty; that those of us who, by sharing in the Sacrifice of this altar, shall receive the Most Sacred ✠ Body and ✠ Blood of Your Son, may be filled with every grace and heavenly blessing. Through the same Christ our Lord. Amen.

Commemoration of the Dead

REMEMBER also, O Lord, Your servants and handmaids, N. and N., who have gone before us with the sign of faith, and rest in the sleep of peace. (*Here pray for the dead.*) To these, O Lord, and to all who rest in Christ, we beseech You to grant of Your goodness, a place of comfort, light and peace. Through the same Christ our Lord. Amen.

TO US sinners also, Your servants, trusting in the greatness of Your mercy, deign to grant some part and fellowship with Your Holy Apostles and Martyrs: with John, Stephen, Matthias, Barnabas, Ignatius, Alexander, Marcellinus, Peter, Felicitas, Perpetua, Agatha, Lucy, Agnes, Cecilia, Anastasia, and all Your Saints; into whose company, we implore You to admit us, not weighing our merits, but freely granting us pardon. Through Christ our Lord.

THROUGH Whom, O Lord, You always create, ✠ sanctify, ✠ fill with life, ✠ bless, and bestow upon us all good things.

The Minor Elevation

THROUGH ✠ Him, and with ✠ Him, and in ✠ Him, is to You, God the Father ✠ almighty, in the unity of the Holy ✠ Spirit, all honor and glory, world without end. S. Amen.

THE COMMUNION AND THANKSGIVING

Let us pray. Prompted by saving precepts, and taught by Your divine teaching, we dare to say:

OUR FATHER, Who art in heaven, hallowed be Thy name: Thy kingdom come: Thy will be done on earth as it is in heaven. Give us this day our daily bread; and forgive us our trespasses, as we forgive those who trespass against us. And lead us not into temptation: S. But deliver us from evil. *P.* Amen.

DELIVER us, we beseech You, O Lord, from all evils, past, present, and to come; and by the intercession of the Blessed and glorious Mary, ever Virgin, Mother of God, together with Your Blessed Apostles Peter and Paul, and Andrew, and all the Saints, grant of Your goodness, peace in our days, that aided by the riches of Your mercy, we may be always free from sin and safe from all disturbance.

Through the same our Lord Jesus Christ, Your Son, Who lives and reigns with You in the unity of the Holy Spirit, God, world without end.

S. Amen.

P. May the peace ✠ of the Lord be ✠ always with ✠ you.

S. And with your spirit.

The Priest puts a small particle into the chalice, saying:

May this mingling and consecration of the Body and Blood of our Lord Jesus Christ help us who receive it to life everlasting. Amen.

LAMB of God, You Who take away the sins of the world, have mercy on us.

Lamb of God, You Who take away the sins of the world, have mercy on us.

Lamb of God, You Who take away the sins of the world, grant us peace.

PRAYERS BEFORE HOLY COMMUNION

Then inclining toward the altar, he says:

O LORD Jesus Christ, Who said to Your Apostles: "Peace I leave with you, My peace I give to you," regard not my sins but the faith of Your Church, and deign to give her peace and unity according to Your Will: Who live and reign, God, world without end. Amen.

O LORD Jesus Christ, Son of the living God, Who, by the will of the Father, with the co-operation of the Holy Spirit, have by Your death given life to the world, deliver me by this Your Most Sacred Body and Blood from all my sins and from every evil. Make me always cling to Your commandments, and never permit me to be separated from You. Who with the same God the Father and the Holy Spirit, live and reign, God, world without end. Amen.

LET not the partaking of Your Body, O Lord Jesus Christ, which I, though unworthy, presume to receive, turn to my judgment and condem-

nation; but through Your goodness, may it become a safeguard and an effective remedy, both of soul and body. Who live and reign with God the Father, in the unity of the Holy Spirit, God, world without end. Amen.

COMMUNION OF THE PRIEST

I WILL take the Bread of heaven, and call upon the name of the Lord.

Lord, I am not worthy that You should come under my roof; but only say the word, and my soul will be healed. (3 *times.*)

Making the Sign of the Cross with the Host, he says:

MAY the Body of our Lord Jesus Christ preserve my soul to life everlasting. Amen.

What return shall I make to the Lord for all He has given me? I will take the Chalice of salvation, and I will call upon the name of the Lord. Praising will I call upon the Lord and I shall be saved from my enemies.

Making the Sign of the Cross with the chalice, he says:

MAY the Blood of our Lord Jesus Christ preserve my soul to life everlasting. Amen.

The Priest reverently consumes the Precious Blood.

COMMUNION OF THE FAITHFUL

The Server and people say the "Confiteor."

P. May almighty God have mercy on you, forgive you your sins, and bring you to life everlasting. **S.** Amen.

P. May the almighty and merciful Lord grant you pardon, ✠ absolution and remission of your sins. **S.** Amen.

Holding up a Sacred Host, the Priest says:

Behold the Lamb of God, behold Him Who takes away the sins of the world.

Lord, I am not worthy that You should come under my roof; but only say the word, and my soul will be healed. (*3 times.*)

The Priest says to each communicant:

May the Body of our Lord Jesus Christ preserve your soul to life everlasting. Amen.

The Priest purifies the chalice with wine, saying:

WHAT has passed our lips as food, O Lord, may we possess in purity of heart, that what is given to us in time, be our healing for eternity.

He purifies his fingers with wine and water, saying:

MAY Your Body, O Lord, which I have eaten, and Your Blood which I have drunk, cleave to my very soul, and grant that no trace of sin be found in me, whom these pure and holy mysteries have renewed. Who live and reign, world without end. Amen.

THE COMMUNION • John 17, 12. 13. 15

FATHER, while I was with them, I kept them whom You have given Me, alleluia; but now I am coming to You: I do not pray that You take them out of the world, but that You keep them from evil, alleluia, alleluia.

The Priest, turning to the people, says:

P. The Lord be with you. S. And with your spirit.
P. Let us pray.

THE POSTCOMMUNION

BEING replenished with the sacred gifts, grant us, we beseech You, O Lord, always to continue in thanksgiving. Through our Lord Jesus Christ, Your Son, Who lives and reigns with You in the unity of the Holy Spirit, God, world without end. S. Amen.

FINAL PRAYERS

The Priest turns again to the people, and says:

P. The Lord be with you. S. And with your spirit.
P. Go, you are dismissed. S. Thanks be to God.

MAY the tribute of my worship be pleasing to You, Most Holy Trinity, and grant that the sacrifice which I, all unworthy, have offered in the presence of Your Majesty, may be acceptable to You, and through Your mercy obtain forgiveness for me and all for whom I have offered it. Through Christ our Lord. Amen.

THE LAST BLESSING

He kisses the altar, and facing the people, says:

MAY almighty God bless you: ✠ the Father, and the Son, and the Holy Spirit.

S. Amen.

The Last Gospel and Prayers after Low Mass are conveniently placed inside the back cover.

"And there Appeared to Them Parted Tongues as of Fire, Which Settled upon Each of Them."
Acts 2, 3.

PENTECOST SUNDAY

Jesus had frequently promised His disciples that He would send them another Advocate and Consoler. The marvelous events which accompanied His arrival were signs of the far greater effects of grace He produces in the souls which receive Him. (RED VESTMENTS)

PRAYERS AT THE FOOT OF THE ALTAR

IN THE name of the Father, ✠ and of the Son, and of the Holy Spirit. Amen.

Priest. I will go in to the altar of God.

Server. The God of my gladness and joy.

Psalm 42

DO ME justice, O God, and fight my fight against a faithless people; from the deceitful and impious man rescue me.

S. For You, O God, are my strength. Why do You keep me so far away? Why must I go about in mourning, with the enemy oppressing me?

P. Send forth Your light and Your fidelity; they shall lead me on and bring me to Your holy mountain, to Your dwelling-place.

S. Then will I go in to the altar of God, the God of my gladness and joy.

P. Then will I give You thanks upon the harp, O God, my God. Why are you so downcast, O my soul? Why do you sigh within me?

S. Hope in God! For I shall again be thanking Him in the presence of my Savior and my God.

P. Glory be to the Father, and to the Son, and to the Holy Spirit.

S. As it was in the beginning, is now, and ever shall be, world without end. Amen.
P. I will go in to the altar of God.
S. The God of my gladness and joy.
P. Our help ✠ is in the name of the Lord.
S. Who made heaven and earth.
P. I confess to almighty God, etc.
S. May almighty God have mercy on you, forgive you your sins, and bring you to life everlasting.
P. Amen.

The Server, bowing, says the "Confiteor."

I CONFESS to almighty God, to Blessed Mary, ever Virgin, to Blessed Michael the Archangel, to Blessed John the Baptist, to the Holy Apostles Peter and Paul, and to all the Saints, and to you, Father, that I have sinned exceedingly in thought, word and deed, *through my fault, through my fault, through my most grievous fault.* Therefore I beseech Blessed Mary, ever Virgin, Blessed Michael the Archangel, Blessed John the Baptist, the Holy Apostles Peter and Paul, and all the Saints, and you, Father, to pray to the Lord our God for me.
P. May almighty God have mercy on you, forgive you your sins, and bring you to life everlasting.
S. Amen.

MAY the almighty and merciful Lord grant us pardon, ✠ absolution, and remission of our sins. *S.* Amen.
P. Will You not, O God, give us life?
S. And shall not Your people rejoice in You?
P. Show us, O Lord, Your kindness.
S. And grant us Your salvation.

P. O Lord, hear my prayer.
S. And let my cry come to You.
P. The Lord be with you.
S. And with your spirit. *P.* Let us pray.

Going up to the altar, the Priest prays silently:

TAKE away from us our sins, O Lord, we beseech You, that we may enter with pure minds into the Holy of Holies. Through Christ our Lord. Amen.

WE BESEECH You, O Lord, by the merits of Your Saints (*he kisses the altar*) whose relics lie here, and of all the Saints: deign in Your mercy to pardon me all my sins. Amen.

THE INTROIT • Wis. 1, 7

At the right side of the altar, the Priest says:

THE Spirit of the Lord fills the world, alleluia, is all-embracing, and knows man's utterance, alleluia, alleluia, alleluia. *Ps. 67.* God arises; His enemies are scattered, and those who hate Him flee before Him. Glory be to the Father, and to the Son, and to the Holy Spirit. As it was in the beginning, is now, and ever shall be, world without end. Amen. — The Spirit of the Lord fills the world, alleluia, is all-embracing, and knows man's utterance, alleluia, alleluia, alleluia.

THE KYRIE

P. Lord, have mercy. S. Lord, have mercy. *P.* Lord, have mercy. S. Christ, have mercy. *P.* Christ, have mercy. S. Christ, have mercy. *P.* Lord, have mercy. S. Lord, have mercy. *P.* Lord, have mercy.

THE GLORIA

GLORY to God in the highest. And on earth peace to men of good will. We praise You. We bless You. We adore You. We glorify You. We give You thanks for Your great glory. O Lord God, heavenly King, God the Father almighty. O Lord Jesus Christ, the Only-begotten Son. O Lord God, Lamb of God, Son of the Father: You Who take away the sins of the world, have mercy on us. You Who take away the sins of the world, receive our prayer. You Who sit at the right hand of the Father, have mercy on us. For You alone are holy. You alone are the Lord. You alone, O Jesus Christ, are most high. Together with the Holy Spirit ✠ in the glory of God the Father. Amen.

The Priest kisses the altar and turns to the people, saying:

P. The Lord be with you. *S.* And with your spirit.
P. Let us pray.

THE PRAYER

Going to the right (Epistle) side, he says:

O GOD, Who on this day by the light of the Holy Spirit taught the hearts of the faithful, grant us by the same Spirit to relish what is right, and always to rejoice in His comfort. Through our Lord Jesus Christ, Your Son, Who lives and reigns with You in the unity of the same Holy Spirit, God, world without end. *S.* Amen.

THE EPISTLE • Acts 2, 1-11

WHEN the days of Pentecost were drawing to a close, they were all together in one place. And suddenly there came a sound from heaven, as of a violent wind blowing, and it filled the whole house where they were sitting. And there appeared to them parted tongues as of fire, which settled upon each of them. And they were all filled with the Holy Spirit and began to speak in foreign tongues, even as the Holy Spirit prompted them to speak. Now there were staying at Jerusalem devout Jews, from every nation under heaven. And when this sound was heard, the multitude gathered and were bewildered in mind, because each heard them speaking in his own language. But they were all amazed and marvelled, saying, "Behold, are not all these that are speaking Galileans? And how have we heard each his own language in which he was born? Parthians and Medes and Elamites, and inhabitants of Mesopotamia, Judea, and Cappadocia, Pontus and Asia, Phrygia and Pamphilia, Egypt and the parts of Libya about Cyrene, and visitors from Rome, Jews also and proselytes, Cretans and Arabians, we have heard them speaking in our own languages of the wonderful works of God." S. Thanks be to God.

Alleluia, alleluia. ℣. *Ps. 103, 30.* Send forth Your Spirit, and they shall be created; and You shall renew the face of the earth. Alleluia. (*Here all kneel.*) Come, O Holy Spirit, fill the hearts of Your faithful; and kindle in them the fire of Your love.

THE SEQUENCE

COME, O Holy Spirit, come!
From Your bright and blissful Home
Rays of healing light impart.

Come, Father of the poor,
Source of gifts that will endure
Light of ev'ry human heart.

You of all consolers best,
Of the soul most kindly Guest,
Quick'ning courage do bestow.

In hard labor You are rest,
In the heat You refresh best,
And solace give in our woe.

O most blessed Light divine,
Let Your radiance in us shine,
And our inmost being fill.

Nothing good by man is thought,
Nothing right by him is wrought,
When he spurns Your gracious Will.

Cleanse our souls from sinful stain,
Lave our dryness with Your rain,
Heal our wounds and mend our way.

Bend the stubborn heart and will,
Melt the frozen, warm the chill,
Guide the steps that go astray.

On the faithful who in You,
Trust with childlike piety,
Deign Your sevenfold gift to send.

Give them virtue's rich increase,
Saving grace to die in peace,
Give them joys that never end. Amen. Alleluia.

PRAYER BEFORE THE GOSPEL

Bowing down at the center of the altar, he says:

CLEANSE my heart and my lips, O almighty God, Who cleansed the lips of the Prophet Isaias with a burning coal. In Your gracious mercy deign so to purify me that I may worthily proclaim Your holy Gospel. Through Christ our Lord. Amen.

Lord, grant Your blessing. The Lord be in my heart and on my lips, that I may worthily and fittingly proclaim His holy Gospel. Amen.

THE GOSPEL • John 14, 23-31

Going to the left (Gospel) side of the altar, he says:

P. The Lord be with you. *S.* And with your spirit.
P. ✠ The continuation of the holy Gospel according to Saint John. *S.* Glory be to You, O Lord.

AT THAT time, Jesus said to His disciples: "If anyone love Me, he will keep My word, and My Father will love him, and We will come to him and make Our abode with him. He who does not love Me, does not keep My words. And the word that you have heard is not Mine, but the Father's Who sent Me. These things I have spoken to you while yet dwelling with you. But the Advocate, the Holy Spirit, Whom the Father will send in My name, He will teach you all things, and bring to your mind whatever I have said to you. Peace I leave with you, My peace I give to you; not as the world gives do I give to you. Do not let your heart be troubled, or be afraid. You have heard Me say to you, 'I go away and I am coming to you.' If you loved Me, you would indeed rejoice that I am going to the Father, for the Father is greater than I. And now I have told you before it comes to pass, that when it has come to pass you may believe. I will no longer speak much with you, for the Prince of the world is coming, and in Me He has nothing. But He comes that the world may know that I love the Father, and that I do as the Father has commanded Me." *S.* Praise be to You, O Christ.

P. By the words of the Gospel, may our sins be taken away.

THE NICENE CREED

At the center of the altar, he says:

I BELIEVE in one God, the Father almighty, Maker of heaven and earth, and of all things visible and invisible. And in one Lord Jesus Christ, the Only-begotten Son of God. Born of the Father before all ages. God of God; Light of Light; true God of true God. Begotten not made; of one being with the Father; by Whom all things were made. Who for us men, and for our salvation, came down from heaven. (*Here all genuflect.*) And was made Flesh by the Holy Spirit of the Virgin Mary: AND WAS MADE MAN. He was also crucified for us, suffered under Pontius Pilate and was buried. And on the third day He rose again according to the Scriptures. And ascending into heaven, He sits at the right hand of the Father. And He shall come again in glory to judge the living and the dead; and of His kingdom there shall be no end. And I believe in the Holy Spirit, Lord and Giver of life, Who proceeds from the Father and the Son. Who together with the Father and the Son is no less adored, and glorified: Who spoke by the Prophets. And I believe in One, Holy, Catholic and Apostolic Church. I confess one Baptism for the remission of sins. And I look for the resurrection of the dead. ✠ And the life of the world to come. Amen.

THE OFFERTORY

The Priest turns to the people and says:

P. The Lord be with you. *S.* And with your spirit.
P. Let us pray.

THE OFFERTORY VERSE • Ps. 67, 29. 30

CONFIRM, O God, what You have wrought in us; from Your temple, which is in Jerusalem, kings shall offer gifts to You, alleluia.

The Priest now uncovers the chalice, places the host on the paten and offering it up, says:

ACCEPT, O holy Father, almighty and eternal God, this spotless host, which I, Your unworthy servant, offer to You, my living and true God, to atone for my numberless sins, offenses, and negligences; on behalf of all here present and likewise for all faithful Christians living and dead, that it may profit me and them as a means of salvation to life everlasting. Amen.

He pours wine and water into the chalice, blessing the water before it is poured.

O GOD, Who established the nature of man in wondrous dignity, and still more admirably restored it, grant that through the mystery of this water and wine, we may be made partakers of His Divinity, Who has condescended to become partaker of our humanity, Jesus Christ, Your Son, our Lord. Who lives and reigns with You in the unity of the Holy Spirit, God, world without end. Amen.

Offering up the wine, the Priest says:

WE OFFER You, O Lord, the chalice of salvation, humbly begging of Your mercy that it may arise before Your Divine Majesty, with a pleasing fragrance, for our salvation and for that of the whole world. Amen.

Bowing down, the Priest says:

IN A humble spirit and with a contrite heart, may we be accepted by You, O Lord, and may our

sacrifice so be offered in Your sight this day as to please You, O Lord God.

Raising his eyes and blessing the offering, he says:

COME, O Sanctifier, almighty and eternal God, and bless ✠ this sacrifice prepared for the glory of Your holy name.

WASHING THE FINGERS

I WASH my hands in innocence, and I go around Your altar, O Lord, giving voice to my thanks, and recounting all Your wondrous deeds. O Lord, I love the house in which You dwell, the tenting-place of Your glory. Gather not my soul with those of sinners, nor with men of blood my life. On their hands are crimes, and their right hands are full of bribes. But I walk in integrity; redeem me, and have pity on me. My foot stands on level ground; in the assemblies I will bless You, O Lord. Glory be to the Father, and to the Son, and to the Holy Spirit. As it was in the beginning, is now, and ever shall be, world without end. Amen.

ACCEPT, Most Holy Trinity, this offering which we are making to You in remembrance of the Passion, Resurrection, and Ascension of Jesus Christ, our Lord; and in honor of Blessed Mary, ever Virgin, Blessed John the Baptist, the Holy Apostles Peter and Paul, and of these, and of all the Saints; that it may add to their honor and aid our salvation; and may they deign to intercede in heaven for us who honor their memory here on earth. Through the same Christ our Lord. Amen.

The Priest turns toward the people and says:

Pray, brethren, that my sacrifice and yours may become acceptable to God the Father almighty.

S. May the Lord accept this sacrifice from your hands to the praise and glory of His name, for our advantage, and that of all His holy Church.
P. Amen.

THE SECRET

SANCTIFY, we beseech You, O Lord, the gifts we offer, and purify our hearts by the light of the Holy Spirit. Through our Lord Jesus Christ, Your Son, Who lives and reigns with You in the unity of the same Holy Spirit, God.
P. World without end. S. Amen.

PREFACE—CANON

P. The Lord be with you. S. And with your spirit.
P. Lift up your hearts.
S. We have lifted them up to the Lord.
P. Let us give thanks to the Lord, our God.
S. It is fitting and just.

IT IS fitting indeed and just, right and helpful to salvation, for us always and everywhere to give thanks to You, O holy Lord, Father almighty, everlasting God: through Christ our Lord. Who ascending above all the heavens, and sitting at Your right hand, on this day sent forth the Holy Spirit, as He had promised, on the children of adoption. Wherefore does the whole world rejoice with exceeding great joy; and the hosts above and the angelic powers also join in singing a hymn to Your glory, saying again and again (*the bell is rung 3 times*):

HOLY, HOLY, HOLY, Lord God of Hosts. Heaven and earth are filled with Your glory. Hosanna in the highest. ✠ Blessed is He Who comes in the name of the Lord. Hosanna in the highest.

THE CANON OF THE MASS

THEREFORE, most gracious Father, we humbly beg of You and entreat You through Jesus Christ Your Son, our Lord, (*he kisses the altar*) to deem acceptable and bless these ✠ gifts, these ✠ offerings, these ✠ holy and unspotted oblations which, in the first place, we offer You for Your Holy Catholic Church, that You would deign to give her peace and protection, to unite and guard her throughout the world, together with Your servant N., our Pope, and N., our Bishop; and all true believers who cherish the Catholic and Apostolic Faith.

Commemoration of the Living

REMEMBER, O Lord, Your servants and handmaids, N. and N., (*name them*) and all here present, whose faith and devotion are known to You, on whose behalf we offer to You, or who themselves offer to You, this sacrifice of praise for themselves, families and friends, for the good of their souls, for their hope of salvation and deliverance from all harm, and who offer their homage to You, eternal, living and true God.

Commemoration of the Saints

IN THE unity of holy fellowship, and keeping the most holy day of Pentecost, whereon the Holy Spirit appeared to the Apostles in countless tongues, we also observe the memory, first of all, of the glorious and ever Virgin Mary, Mother of our Lord and God Jesus Christ; next, that of Your Blessed Apostles and Martyrs, Peter and Paul, Andrew, James, John, Thomas, James, Philip, Bartholomew, Matthew, Simon and Thaddeus; of Linus, Cletus, Clement, Sixtus, Cornelius, Cyprian;

Lawrence, Chrysogonus, John and Paul, Cosmas and Damian, and of all Your Saints, by whose merits and prayers grant that we may be always fortified by the help of Your protection. Through the same Christ our Lord. Amen.

Spreading his hands over the oblation, he says:

GRACIOUSLY accept, then, we beseech You, O Lord, this service of our worship, and that of all Your household, which we make to You in behalf of those whom You have vouchsafed to bring to a new birth by water and the Holy Spirit, giving them remission of all their sins. Provide that our days be spent in Your peace, save us from everlasting damnation, and cause us to be numbered in the flock You have chosen. Through Christ our Lord. Amen.

O GOD, deign to bless ✠ what we offer, and make it approved, ✠ effective, ✠ right, and wholly pleasing in every way, that it may become for our good, the Body ✠ and Blood ✠ of Your dearly beloved Son, Jesus Christ our Lord.

CONSECRATION—ELEVATION

WHO, the day before He suffered, took bread into His holy and venerable hands, and having raised His eyes to heaven, to You, O God, His almighty Father, giving thanks to You, He blessed it, ✠ broke it, and gave it to His disciples, saying: All of you take and eat of this:

FOR THIS IS MY BODY.

IN LIKE manner, when the supper was done, taking also this goodly chalice into His holy and venerable hands, again giving thanks to You, He blessed ✠ it, and gave it to His disciples, saying: All of you take and drink of this:

FOR THIS IS THE CHALICE OF MY BLOOD OF THE NEW AND ETERNAL COVENANT: THE MYSTERY OF FAITH: WHICH SHALL BE SHED FOR YOU AND FOR MANY UNTO THE FORGIVENESS OF SINS.

After replacing the chalice on the corporal, he says:

As often as you shall do these things, in memory of Me shall you do them.

Offering of the Victim

MINDFUL, therefore, O Lord, not only of the blessed Passion of the same Christ, Your Son, our Lord, but also of His Resurrection from the dead, and finally His glorious Ascension into heaven, we, Your ministers, as also Your holy people, offer to Your supreme Majesty, of the gifts bestowed upon us, the pure ✠ Victim, the holy ✠ Victim, the all-perfect ✠ Victim: the holy ✠ Bread of life eternal and the Chalice ✠ of unending salvation.

AND this deign to regard with gracious and kindly attention and hold acceptable, as You deigned to accept the offerings of Abel, Your just servant, and the sacrifice of Abraham our patriarch, and that which Your chief priest Melchisedec offered to You, a holy sacrifice and a spotless victim.

MOST humbly we implore You, almighty God, bid these offerings to be brought by the hands of Your holy angel to Your altar above; before the face of Your Divine Majesty; that those of us who, by sharing in the Sacrifice of this altar, shall receive the Most Sacred ✠ Body and ✠ Blood of Your Son, may be filled with every grace and heavenly blessing. Through the same Christ our Lord. Amen.

Commemoration of the Dead

REMEMBER also, O Lord, Your servants and handmaids, N. and N., who have gone before us with the sign of faith, and rest in the sleep of peace. (*Here pray for the dead.*) To these, O Lord, and to all who rest in Christ, we beseech You to grant of Your goodness, a place of comfort, light and peace. Through the same Christ our Lord. Amen.

TO US sinners also, Your servants, trusting in the greatness of Your mercy, deign to grant some part and fellowship with Your Holy Apostles and Martyrs: with John, Stephen, Matthias, Barnabas, Ignatius, Alexander, Marcellinus, Peter, Felicitas, Perpetua, Agatha, Lucy, Agnes, Cecilia, Anastasia, and all Your Saints; into whose company, we implore You to admit us, not weighing our merits, but freely granting us pardon. Through Christ our Lord.

THROUGH Whom, O Lord, You always create, ✠ sanctify, ✠ fill with life, ✠ bless, and bestow upon us all good things.

The Minor Elevation

THROUGH ✠ Him, and with ✠ Him, and in ✠ Him, is to You, God the Father ✠ almighty, in the unity of the Holy ✠ Spirit, all honor and glory, world without end. S. Amen.

THE COMMUNION AND THANKSGIVING

Let us pray. Prompted by saving precepts, and taught by Your divine teaching, we dare to say:

OUR FATHER, Who art in heaven, hallowed be Thy name: Thy kingdom come: Thy will be done on earth as it is in heaven. Give us this day

our daily bread; and forgive us our trespasses, as we forgive those who trespass against us. And lead us not into temptation: S. But deliver us from evil. *P*. Amen.

DELIVER us, we beseech You, O Lord, from all evils, past, present, and to come; and by the intercession of the Blessed and glorious Mary, ever Virgin, Mother of God, together with Your Blessed Apostles Peter and Paul, and Andrew, and all the Saints, grant of Your goodness, peace in our days, that aided by the riches of Your mercy, we may be always free from sin and safe from all disturbance.

Through the same our Lord Jesus Christ, Your Son, Who lives and reigns with You in the unity of the Holy Spirit, God, world without end. S. Amen.

P. May the peace ✠ of the Lord be ✠ always with ✠ you. S. And with your spirit.

The Priest puts a small particle into the chalice, saying:

May this mingling and consecration of the Body and Blood of our Lord Jesus Christ help us who receive it to life everlasting. Amen.

LAMB of God, You Who take away the sins of the world, have mercy on us.

Lamb of God, You Who take away the sins of the world, have mercy on us.

Lamb of God, You Who take away the sins of the world, grant us peace.

PRAYERS BEFORE HOLY COMMUNION

Then inclining toward the altar, he says:

O LORD Jesus Christ, Who said to Your Apostles: "Peace I leave with you, My peace I give

to you," regard not my sins but the faith of Your Church, and deign to give her peace and unity according to Your Will: Who live and reign, God, world without end. Amen.

O LORD Jesus Christ, Son of the living God, Who, by the will of the Father, with the co-operation of the Holy Spirit, have by Your death given life to the world, deliver me by this Your Most Sacred Body and Blood from all my sins and from every evil. Make me always cling to Your commandments, and never permit me to be separated from You. Who with the same God the Father and the Holy Spirit, live and reign, God, world without end. Amen.

LET not the partaking of Your Body, O Lord Jesus Christ, which I, though unworthy, presume to receive, turn to my judgment and condemnation; but through Your goodness, may it become a safeguard and an effective remedy, both of soul and body. Who live and reign with God the Father, in the unity of the Holy Spirit, God, world without end. Amen.

COMMUNION OF THE PRIEST

I WILL take the Bread of heaven, and call upon the name of the Lord.

Lord, I am not worthy that You should come under my roof; but only say the word, and my soul will be healed. (3 *times.*)

Making the Sign of the Cross with the Host, he says:

MAY the Body of our Lord Jesus Christ preserve my soul to life everlasting. Amen.

What return shall I make to the Lord for all He has given me? I will take the Chalice of salvation,

and I will call upon the name of the Lord. Praising will I call upon the Lord and I shall be saved from my enemies.

Making the Sign of the Cross with the chalice, he says:

MAY the Blood of our Lord Jesus Christ preserve my soul to life everlasting. Amen.

The Priest reverently consumes the Precious Blood.

COMMUNION OF THE FAITHFUL

The Server and people say the "Confiteor."

P. May almighty God have mercy on you, forgive you your sins, and bring you to life everlasting. S. Amen.

P. May the almighty and merciful Lord grant you pardon, ✠ absolution and remission of your sins. S. Amen.

Holding up a Sacred Host, the Priest says:

Behold the Lamb of God, behold Him Who takes away the sins of the world.

Lord, I am not worthy that You should come under my roof; but only say the word, and my soul will be healed. (3 *times.*)

The Priest says to each communicant:

May the Body of our Lord Jesus Christ preserve your soul to life everlasting. Amen.

The Priest purifies the chalice with wine, saying:

WHAT has passed our lips as food, O Lord, may we possess in purity of heart, that what is given to us in time, be our healing for eternity.

He purifies his fingers with wine and water, saying:

MAY Your Body, O Lord, which I have eaten, and Your Blood which I have drunk, cleave to my very soul, and grant that no trace of sin be found in me, whom these pure and holy mysteries

have renewed. Who live and reign, world without end. Amen.

THE COMMUNION • Acts 2, 2. 4

SUDDENLY there came a sound from heaven, as of a violent wind blowing, where they were sitting, alleluia: and they were all filled with the Holy Spirit, speaking of the wonderful works of God, alleluia, alleluia.

The Priest, turning to the people, says:

P. The Lord be with you. *S*. And with your spirit.
P. Let us pray.

THE POSTCOMMUNION

MAY the infusion of the Holy Spirit cleanse our hearts, O Lord, and render them fertile by the inward sprinkling of His heavenly dew. Through our Lord Jesus Christ, Your Son, Who lives and reigns with You, etc. *S*. Amen.

FINAL PRAYERS

P. The Lord be with you. *S*. And with your spirit.
P. Go, you are dismissed. *S*. Thanks be to God.

MAY the tribute of my worship be pleasing to You, Most Holy Trinity, and grant that the sacrifice which I, all unworthy, have offered in the presence of Your Majesty, may be acceptable to You, and through Your mercy obtain forgiveness for me and all for whom I have offered it. Through Christ our Lord. Amen.

THE LAST BLESSING

MAY almighty God bless you: ✠ the Father, and the Son, and the Holy Spirit. *S*. Amen.

The Last Gospel and Prayers after Low Mass are conveniently placed inside the back cover.

"Blessed be the Holy Trinity and undivided Unity."

TRINITY SUNDAY

Today the Church honors the Supreme Majesty of One God in Three Divine Persons. Our intellect is too limited to comprehend the inner essence and life of the Infinite God. Our contemplation of this Mystery is an occasion for humble adoration and a petition for an increase of faith. (WHITE VESTMENTS)

PRAYERS AT THE FOOT OF THE ALTAR

IN THE name of the Father, ✠ and of the Son, and of the Holy Spirit. Amen.

Priest. I will go in to the altar of God.

Server. The God of my gladness and joy.

Psalm 42

DO ME justice, O God, and fight my fight against a faithless people; from the deceitful and impious man rescue me.

S. For You, O God, are my strength. Why do You keep me so far away? Why must I go about in mourning, with the enemy oppressing me?

P. Send forth Your light and Your fidelity; they shall lead me on and bring me to Your holy mountain, to Your dwelling-place.

S. Then will I go in to the altar of God, the God of my gladness and joy.

P. Then will I give You thanks upon the harp, O God, my God. Why are you so downcast, O my soul? Why do you sigh within me?

S. Hope in God! For I shall again be thanking Him in the presence of my Savior and my God.

P. Glory be to the Father, and to the Son, and to the Holy Spirit.

S. As it was in the beginning, is now, and ever shall be, world without end. Amen.

P. I will go in to the altar of God.

S. The God of my gladness and joy.

P. Our help ✠ is in the name of the Lord.

S. Who made heaven and earth.

P. I confess to almighty God, etc.

S. May almighty God have mercy on you, forgive you your sins, and bring you to life everlasting.

P. Amen.

The Server, bowing, says the "Confiteor."

I CONFESS to almighty God, to Blessed Mary, ever Virgin, to Blessed Michael the Archangel, to Blessed John the Baptist, to the Holy Apostles Peter and Paul, and to all the Saints, and to you, Father, that I have sinned exceedingly in thought, word and deed, *through my fault, through my fault, through my most grievous fault.* Therefore I beseech Blessed Mary, ever Virgin, Blessed Michael the Archangel, Blessed John the Baptist, the Holy Apostles Peter and Paul, and all the Saints, and you, Father, to pray to the Lord our God for me.

P. May almighty God have mercy on you, forgive

you your sins, and bring you to life everlasting.
S. Amen.

MAY the almighty and merciful Lord grant us pardon, ✠ absolution, and remission of our sins. S. Amen.

P. Will You not, O God, give us life?
S. And shall not Your people rejoice in You?
P. Show us, O Lord, Your kindness.
S. And grant us Your salvation.
P. O Lord, hear my prayer.
S. And let my cry come to You.
P. The Lord be with you.
S. And with your spirit. *P.* Let us pray.

Going up to the altar, the Priest prays silently:

TAKE away from us our sins, O Lord, we beseech You, that we may enter with pure minds into the Holy of Holies. Through Christ our Lord. Amen.

WE BESEECH You, O Lord, by the merits of Your Saints (*he kisses the altar*) whose relics lie here, and of all the Saints: deign in Your mercy to pardon me all my sins. Amen.

THE INTROIT • Tob. 12, 6

At the right side of the altar, the Priest says:

BLESSED be the Holy Trinity and undivided Unity: we will give glory to Him, because He has shown His mercy to us. *Ps.* 8. O Lord, our Lord, how glorious is Your name over all the earth! Glory be to the Father, and to the Son, and to the Holy Spirit. As it was in the beginning, is now, and ever shall be, world without end. Amen. — Blessed be the Holy Trinity and undivided Unity: we will give glory to Him, because He has shown His mercy to us.

THE KYRIE

P. Lord, have mercy. *S.* Lord, have mercy. *P.* Lord, have mercy. *S.* Christ, have mercy. *P.* Christ, have mercy. *S.* Christ, have mercy. *P.* Lord, have mercy. *S.* Lord, have mercy. *P.* Lord, have mercy.

THE GLORIA

GLORY to God in the highest. And on earth peace to men of good will. We praise You. We bless You. We adore You. We glorify You. We give You thanks for Your great glory. O Lord God, heavenly King, God the Father almighty. O Lord Jesus Christ, the Only-begotten Son. O Lord God, Lamb of God, Son of the Father: You Who take away the sins of the world, have mercy on us. You Who take away the sins of the world, receive our prayer. You Who sit at the right hand of the Father, have mercy on us. For You alone are holy. You alone are the Lord. You alone, O Jesus Christ, are most high. Together with the Holy Spirit ✠ in the glory of God the Father. Amen.

The Priest kisses the altar and turns to the people, saying:

P. The Lord be with you. *S.* And with your spirit. *P.* Let us pray.

THE PRAYER

Going to the right (Epistle) side, he says:

ALMIGHTY and everlasting God, You have given Your servants in the confession of the true faith, to acknowledge the glory of the Eternal Trinity, and to adore the unity in the power of Your Majesty; grant, that by steadfastness in this faith we may ever be defended from all adversities. Through our Lord Jesus Christ, Your Son, Who lives and reigns with You in the unity of the Holy Spirit, God, world without end. S. Amen.

THE EPISTLE • Rom. 11, 33-36

OH, THE depth of the riches of the wisdom and of the knowledge of God! How incomprehensible are His judgments and how unsearchable His ways! For "Who has known the mind of the Lord, or who has been His counsellor? Or who has first given to Him, that recompense should be made him?" For from Him and through Him and unto Him are all things. To Him be the glory forever, amen. S. Thanks be to God.

THE GRADUAL • Dan. 3, 55. 56

BLESSED are You, O Lord, Who look into the depths from Your throne upon the Cherubim. ℣. Blessed are You, O Lord, in the firmament of heaven, and praiseworthy forever.

Alleluia, alleluia. ℣. *Dan.* 3, 52. Blessed are You, O Lord, the God of our fathers, and praiseworthy forever. Alleluia.

PRAYER BEFORE THE GOSPEL

Bowing down at the center of the altar, he says:

CLEANSE my heart and my lips, O almighty God, Who cleansed the lips of the Prophet Isaias with a burning coal. In Your gracious mercy deign so to purify me that I may worthily proclaim Your holy Gospel. Through Christ our Lord. Amen.

Lord, grant Your blessing. The Lord be in my heart and on my lips, that I may worthily and fittingly proclaim His holy Gospel. Amen.

THE GOSPEL • Matt. 28, 18-20

Going to the left (Gospel) side of the altar, he says:

P. The Lord be with you. S. And with your spirit.

P. ✠ The continuation of the holy Gospel according to Saint Matthew. *S.* Glory be to You, O Lord.

AT THAT time, Jesus said to His disciples: "All power in heaven and on earth has been given to Me. Go, therefore, and make disciples of all nations, baptizing them in the name of the Father, and of the Son, and of the Holy Spirit, teaching them to observe all that I have commanded you; and behold, I am with you all days, even unto the consummation of the word." *S.* Praise be to You, O Christ.

P. By the words of the Gospel, may our sins be taken away.

THE NICENE CREED

At the center of the altar, he says:

I BELIEVE in one God, the Father almighty, Maker of heaven and earth, and of all things visible and invisible. And in one Lord Jesus Christ, the Only-begotten Son of God. Born of the Father before all ages. God of God; Light of Light; true God of true God. Begotten not made; of one being with the Father; by Whom all things were made. Who for us men, and for our salvation, came down from heaven. (*Here all genuflect.*) And was made Flesh by the Holy Spirit of the Virgin Mary: AND WAS MADE MAN. He was also crucified for us, suffered under Pontius Pilate and was buried. And on the third day He rose again according to the Scriptures. And ascending into heaven, He sits at the right hand of the Father. And He shall come again in glory to judge the living and the dead; and of His kingdom there shall be no end. And I believe in the Holy Spirit, Lord and Giver of life, Who proceeds from the Father and the Son. Who together with the Father and the Son is no less adored, and glorified: Who spoke by the Prophets. And I believe in One, Holy, Catholic and Apostolic Church. I confess one Baptism for the remission of sins. And I look for the resurrection of the dead. ✠ And the life of the world to come. Amen.

THE OFFERTORY

The Priest turns to the people and says:

P. The Lord be with you. *S.* And with your spirit.
P. Let us pray.

THE OFFERTORY VERSE • Tob. 12, 6

BLESSED be God the Father, and the Only-begotten Son of God, and also the Holy Spirit: because He has shown His mercy to us.

The Priest now uncovers the chalice, places the host on the paten and offering it up, says:

ACCEPT, O holy Father, almighty and eternal God, this spotless host, which I, Your unworthy servant, offer to You, my living and true God, to atone for my numberless sins, offenses, and negligences; on behalf of all here present and likewise for all faithful Christians living and dead, that it may profit me and them as a means of salvation to life everlasting. Amen.

He pours wine and water into the chalice, blessing the water before it is poured.

O GOD, Who established the nature of man in wondrous dignity, and still more admirably restored it, grant that through the mystery of this water and wine, we may be made partakers of His Divinity, Who has condescended to become partaker of our humanity, Jesus Christ, Your Son, our

Lord. Who lives and reigns with You in the unity of the Holy Spirit, God, world without end. Amen.

Offering up the wine, the Priest says:

WE OFFER You, O Lord, the chalice of salvation, humbly begging of Your mercy that it may arise before Your Divine Majesty, with a pleasing fragrance, for our salvation and for that of the whole world. Amen.

Bowing down, the Priest says:

IN A humble spirit and with a contrite heart, may we be accepted by You, O Lord, and may our sacrifice so be offered in Your sight this day as to please You, O Lord God.

Raising his eyes and blessing the offering, he says:

COME, O Sanctifier, almighty and eternal God, and bless ✠ this sacrifice prepared for the glory of Your holy name.

WASHING THE FINGERS

I WASH my hands in innocence, and I go around Your altar, O Lord, giving voice to my thanks, and recounting all Your wondrous deeds. O Lord, I love the house in which You dwell, the tenting-place of Your glory. Gather not my soul with those of sinners, nor with men of blood my life. On their hands are crimes, and their right hands are full of bribes. But I walk in integrity; redeem me, and have pity on me. My foot stands on level ground; in the assemblies I will bless You, O Lord. Glory be to the Father, and to the Son, and to the Holy Spirit. As it was in the beginning, is now, and ever shall be, world without end. Amen.

ACCEPT, Most Holy Trinity, this offering which we are making to You in remembrance of the Passion, Resurrection, and Ascension of Jesus Christ, our Lord; and in honor of Blessed Mary, ever Virgin, Blessed John the Baptist, the Holy Apostles Peter and Paul, and of these, and of all the Saints; that it may add to their honor and aid our salvation; and may they deign to intercede in heaven for us who honor their memory here on earth. Through the same Christ our Lord. Amen.

The Priest turns toward the people and says:

Pray, brethren, that my sacrifice and yours may become acceptable to God the Father almighty.

S. May the Lord accept this sacrifice from your hands to the praise and glory of His name, for our advantage, and that of all His holy Church.
P. Amen.

THE SECRET

SANCTIFY the victim of this offering, we beseech You, O Lord, our God, by the invocation of Your holy name; and through the same render us an everlasting offering to You. Through our Lord Jesus Christ, Your Son, Who lives and reigns with You in the unity of the Holy Spirit, God.
P. World without end. *S.* Amen.

PREFACE—CANON

P. The Lord be with you. *S.* And with your spirit.
P. Lift up your hearts.
S. We have lifted them up to the Lord.
P. Let us give thanks to the Lord, our God.
S. It is fitting and just.

IT IS fitting indeed and just, right and helpful to salvation, for us always and everywhere to give thanks to You, O holy Lord, Father almighty, everlasting God, Who with Your Only-begotten Son and the Holy Spirit are one God, one Lord; not in the unity of a single person, but in the trinity of a single nature. For that which we believe on Your revelation concerning Your glory, that same we believe of Your Son, that same of the Holy Spirit, without difference or discrimination. So that in confessing the true and everlasting Godhead, we shall adore distinction in Persons, oneness in being, and equality in Majesty. This the Angels and Archangels, the Cherubim, too, and the Seraphim do praise; day by day they cease not to cry out as with one voice, saying (*the bell is rung* 3 *times*):

HOLY, HOLY, HOLY, Lord God of Hosts. Heaven and earth are filled with Your glory. Hosanna in the highest. ✠ Blessed is He Who comes in the name of the Lord. Hosanna in the highest.

THE CANON OF THE MASS

THEREFORE, most gracious Father, we humbly beg of You and entreat You through Jesus Christ Your Son, our Lord, (*he kisses the altar*) to deem acceptable and bless these ✠ gifts, these ✠ offerings, these ✠ holy and unspotted oblations which, in the first place, we offer You for Your Holy Catholic Church, that You would deign to give her peace and protection, to unite and guard her throughout the world, together with Your servant N., our Pope, and N., our Bishop; and all true believers who cherish the Catholic and Apostolic Faith.

Commemoration of the Living

REMEMBER, O Lord, Your servants and handmaids, N. and N., (*name them*) and all here present, whose faith and devotion are known to You, on whose behalf we offer to You, or who themselves offer to You, this sacrifice of praise for themselves, families and friends, for the good of their souls, for their hope of salvation and deliverance from all harm, and who offer their homage to You, eternal, living and true God.

Commemoration of the Saints

IN THE unity of holy fellowship we observe the memory, first of all, of the glorious and ever Virgin Mary, Mother of our Lord and God Jesus Christ; next, that of Your Blessed Apostles and Martyrs, Peter and Paul, Andrew, James, John, Thomas, James, Philip, Bartholomew, Matthew, Simon and Thaddeus; of Linus, Cletus, Clement, Sixtus, Cornelius, Cyprian, Lawrence, Chrysogonus, John and Paul, Cosmas and Damian, and of all Your Saints, by whose merits and prayers grant that we may be always fortified by the help of Your protection. Through the same Christ our Lord. Amen.

Spreading his hands over the oblation, he says:

GRACIOUSLY accept, then, we beseech You, O Lord, this service of our worship and that of all Your household. Provide that our days be spent in Your peace, save us from everlasting damnation, and cause us to be numbered in the flock You have chosen. Through Christ our Lord. Amen.

O GOD, deign to bless ✠ what we offer, and make it approved, ✠ effective, ✠ right, and

wholly pleasing in every way, that it may become for our good, the Body ✠ and Blood ✠ of Your dearly beloved Son, Jesus Christ our Lord.

CONSECRATION—ELEVATION

WHO, the day before He suffered, took bread into His holy and venerable hands, and having raised His eyes to heaven, to You, O God, His almighty Father, giving thanks to You, He blessed it, ✠ broke it, and gave it to His disciples, saying: All of you take and eat of this:

FOR THIS IS MY BODY.

IN LIKE manner, when the supper was done, taking also this goodly chalice into His holy and venerable hands, again giving thanks to You, He blessed ✠ it, and gave it to His disciples, saying: All of you take and drink of this:

FOR THIS IS THE CHALICE OF MY BLOOD OF THE NEW AND ETERNAL COVENANT: THE MYSTERY OF FAITH: WHICH SHALL BE SHED FOR YOU AND FOR MANY UNTO THE FORGIVENESS OF SINS.

After replacing the chalice on the corporal, he says:

As often as you shall do these things, in memory of Me shall you do them.

Offering of the Victim

MINDFUL, therefore, O Lord, not only of the blessed Passion of the same Christ, Your Son, our Lord, but also of His Resurrection from the dead, and finally His glorious Ascension into heaven, we, Your ministers, as also Your holy people, offer to Your supreme Majesty, of the gifts be-

stowed upon us, the pure ✠ Victim, the holy ✠ Victim, the all-perfect ✠ Victim: the holy ✠ Bread of life eternal and the Chalice ✠ of unending salvation.

AND this deign to regard with gracious and kindly attention and hold acceptable, as You deigned to accept the offerings of Abel, Your just servant, and the sacrifice of Abraham our patriarch, and that which Your chief priest Melchisedec offered to You, a holy sacrifice and a spotless victim.

MOST humbly we implore You, almighty God, bid these offerings to be brought by the hands of Your holy angel to Your altar above; before the face of Your Divine Majesty; that those of us who, by sharing in the Sacrifice of this altar, shall receive the Most Sacred ✠ Body and ✠ Blood of Your Son, may be filled with every grace and heavenly blessing. Through the same Christ our Lord. Amen.

Commemoration of the Dead

REMEMBER also, O Lord, Your servants and handmaids, *N.* and *N.*, who have gone before us with the sign of faith, and rest in the sleep of peace. (*Here pray for the dead.*) To these, O Lord, and to all who rest in Christ, we beseech You to grant of Your goodness, a place of comfort, light and peace. Through the same Christ our Lord. Amen.

TO US sinners also, Your servants, trusting in the greatness of Your mercy, deign to grant some part and fellowship with Your Holy Apostles and Martyrs: with John, Stephen, Matthias, Barnabas, Ignatius, Alexander, Marcellinus, Peter, Felicitas,

Perpetua, Agatha, Lucy, Agnes, Cecilia, Anastasia, and all Your Saints; into whose company, we implore You to admit us, not weighing our merits, but freely granting us pardon. Through Christ our Lord.

THROUGH Whom, O Lord, You always create, ✠ sanctify, ✠ fill with life, ✠ bless, and bestow upon us all good things.

The Minor Elevation

THROUGH ✠ Him, and with ✠ Him, and in ✠ Him, is to You, God the Father ✠ almighty, in the unity of the Holy ✠ Spirit, all honor and glory, world without end. S. Amen.

THE COMMUNION AND THANKSGIVING

Let us pray. Prompted by saving precepts, and taught by Your divine teaching, we dare to say:

OUR FATHER, Who art in heaven, hallowed be Thy name: Thy kingdom come: Thy will be done on earth as it is in heaven. Give us this day our daily bread; and forgive us our trespasses, as we forgive those who trespass against us. And lead us not into temptation: S. But deliver us from evil. *P.* Amen.

DELIVER us, we beseech You, O Lord, from all evils, past, present, and to come; and by the intercession of the Blessed and glorious Mary, ever Virgin, Mother of God, together with Your Blessed Apostles Peter and Paul, and Andrew, and all the Saints, grant of Your goodness, peace in our days, that aided by the riches of Your mercy, we

may be always free from sin and safe from all disturbance.

Through the same our Lord Jesus Christ, Your Son, Who lives and reigns with You in the unity of the Holy Spirit, God, world without end

S. Amen.

P. May the peace ✠ of the Lord be ✠ always with ✠ you.

S. And with your spirit.

The Priest puts a small particle into the chalice, saying:

May this mingling and consecration of the Body and Blood of our Lord Jesus Christ help us who receive it to life everlasting. Amen.

LAMB of God, You Who take away the sins of the world, have mercy on us.

Lamb of God, You Who take away the sins of the world, have mercy on us.

Lamb of God, You Who take away the sins of the world, grant us peace.

PRAYERS BEFORE HOLY COMMUNION

Then inclining toward the altar, he says:

O LORD Jesus Christ, Who said to Your Apostles: "Peace I leave with you, My peace I give to you," regard not my sins but the faith of Your Church, and deign to give her peace and unity according to Your Will: Who live and reign, God, world without end. Amen.

O LORD Jesus Christ, Son of the living God, Who, by the will of the Father, with the cooperation of the Holy Spirit, have by Your death given life to the world, deliver me by this Your

Most Sacred Body and Blood from all my sins and from every evil. Make me always cling to Your commandments, and never permit me to be separated from You. Who with the same God the Father and the Holy Spirit, live and reign, God, world without end. Amen.

LET not the partaking of Your Body, O Lord Jesus Christ, which I, though unworthy, presume to receive, turn to my judgment and condemnation; but through Your goodness, may it become a safeguard and an effective remedy, both of soul and body. Who live and reign with God the Father, in the unity of the Holy Spirit, God, world without end. Amen.

COMMUNION OF THE PRIEST

I WILL take the Bread of heaven, and call upon the name of the Lord.

Lord, I am not worthy that You should come under my roof; but only say the word, and my soul will be healed. (3 *times.*)

Making the Sign of the Cross with the Host, he says:

MAY the Body of our Lord Jesus Christ preserve my soul to life everlasting. Amen.

What return shall I make to the Lord for all He has given me? I will take the Chalice of salvation, and I will call upon the name of the Lord. Praising will I call upon the Lord and I shall be saved from my enemies.

Making the Sign of the Cross with the chalice, he says:

MAY the Blood of our Lord Jesus Christ preserve my soul to life everlasting. Amen.

The Priest reverently consumes the Precious Blood.

COMMUNION OF THE FAITHFUL

The Server and people say the "Confiteor."

P. May almighty God have mercy on you, forgive you your sins, and bring you to life everlasting. *S.* Amen.

P. May the almighty and merciful Lord grant you pardon, ✠ absolution and remission of your sins. *S.* Amen.

Holding up a Sacred Host, the Priest says:

Behold the Lamb of God, behold Him Who takes away the sins of the world.

Lord, I am not worthy that You should come under my roof; but only say the word, and my soul will be healed. (3 *times.*)

The Priest says to each communicant:

May the Body of our Lord Jesus Christ preserve your soul to life everlasting. Amen.

The Priest purifies the chalice with wine, saying:

WHAT has passed our lips as food, O Lord, may we possess in purity of heart, that what is given to us in time, be our healing for eternity.

He purifies his fingers with wine and water, saying:

MAY Your Body, O Lord, which I have eaten, and Your Blood which I have drunk, cleave to my very soul, and grant that no trace of sin be found in me, whom these pure and holy mysteries have renewed. Who live and reign, world without end. Amen.

THE COMMUNION • Tob. 12, 6

WE BLESS the God of heaven, and before all living we will praise Him; because He has shown His mercy to us.

The Priest, turning to the people, says:

P. The Lord be with you. S. And with your spirit.
P. Let us pray.

THE POSTCOMMUNION

MAY the reception of this sacrament, O Lord, our God, as also the confession of our faith in the holy and everlasting Trinity, and of its undivided Unity, profit us for the health of body and soul. Through our Lord Jesus Christ, Your Son, Who lives and reigns with You in the unity of the Holy Spirit, God, world without end. S. Amen.

FINAL PRAYERS

The Priest turns again to the people, and says:

P. The Lord be with you. S. And with your spirit.
P. Go, you are dismissed. S. Thanks be to God.

MAY the tribute of my worship be pleasing to You, Most Holy Trinity, and grant that the sacrifice which I, all unworthy, have offered in the presence of Your Majesty, may be acceptable to You, and through Your mercy obtain forgiveness for me and all for whom I have offered it. Through Christ our Lord. Amen.

THE LAST BLESSING

He kisses the altar, and facing the people, says:

MAY almighty God bless you: ✠ the Father, and the Son, and the Holy Spirit.

S. Amen.

The Last Gospel and Prayers after Low Mass are conveniently placed inside the back cover.

"Hail! Bread of Angels, broken, for us pilgrims food . . ."

FEAST OF CORPUS CHRISTI

THURSDAY AFTER TRINITY SUNDAY

Since Holy Thursday is so near Good Friday, the joy over the institution of the Holy Eucharist is not sufficiently expressed on Holy Thursday. Wherever possible, public homage and adoration are paid to Jesus in the Blessed Sacrament with a colorful procession around the church on this Feast. (WHITE VESTMENTS)

PRAYERS AT THE FOOT OF THE ALTAR

IN THE name of the Father, ✠ and of the Son, and of the Holy Spirit. Amen.

Priest. I will go in to the altar of God.

Server. The God of my gladness and joy.

Psalm 42

DO ME justice, O God, and fight my fight against a faithless people; from the deceitful and impious man rescue me.

S. For You, O God, are my strength. Why do You keep me so far away? Why must I go about in mourning, with the enemy oppressing me?

P. Send forth Your light and Your fidelity; they shall lead me on and bring me to Your holy mountain, to Your dwelling-place.

S. Then will I go in to the altar of God, the God of my gladness and joy.
P. Then will I give You thanks upon the harp, O God, my God. Why are you so downcast, O my soul? Why do you sigh within me?
S. Hope in God! For I shall again be thanking Him in the presence of my Savior and my God.
P. Glory be to the Father, and to the Son, and to the Holy Spirit.
S. As it was in the beginning, is now, and ever shall be, world without end. Amen.
P. I will go in to the altar of God.
S. The God of my gladness and joy.
P. Our help ✠ is in the name of the Lord.
S. Who made heaven and earth.
P. I confess to almighty God, etc.
S. May almighty God have mercy on you, forgive you your sins, and bring you to life everlasting.
P. Amen.

The Server, bowing, says the "Confiteor."

I CONFESS to almighty God, to Blessed Mary, ever Virgin, to Blessed Michael the Archangel, to Blessed John the Baptist, to the Holy Apostles Peter and Paul, and to all the Saints, and to you, Father, that I have sinned exceedingly in thought, word and deed, *through my fault, through my fault, through my most grievous fault.* Therefore I beseech Blessed Mary, ever Virgin, Blessed Michael the Archangel, Blessed John the Baptist, the Holy Apostles Peter and Paul, and all the Saints, and you, Father, to pray to the Lord our God for me.
P. May almighty God have mercy on you, forgive you your sins, and bring you to life everlasting.
S. Amen.

MAY the almighty and merciful Lord grant us pardon, ✠ absolution, and remission of our sins. *S.* Amen.

P. Will You not, O God, give us life?
S. And shall not Your people rejoice in You?
P. Show us, O Lord, Your kindness.
S. And grant us Your salvation.
P. O Lord, hear my prayer.
S. And let my cry come to You.
P. The Lord be with you.
S. And with your spirit. *P.* Let us pray.

Going up to the altar, the Priest prays silently:

TAKE away from us our sins, O Lord, we beseech You, that we may enter with pure minds into the Holy of Holies. Through Christ our Lord. Amen.

WE BESEECH You, O Lord, by the merits of Your Saints (*he kisses the altar*) whose relics lie here, and of all the Saints: deign in Your mercy to pardon me all my sins. Amen.

THE INTROIT • Ps. 80, 17. 2

At the right side of the altar, the Priest says:

HE FED them with the best of wheat, alleluia; and filled them with honey from the rock, alleluia, alleluia, alleluia. *Ps.* Sing joyfully to God our strength; acclaim the God of Jacob. Glory be to the Father, and to the Son, and to the Holy Spirit. As it was in the beginning, is now, and ever shall be, world without end. Amen. — He fed them with the best of wheat, alleluia; and filled them with honey from the rock, alleluia, alleluia, alleluia.

THE KYRIE

P. Lord, have mercy. *S.* Lord, have mercy. *P.* Lord,

have mercy. *S.* Christ, have mercy. *P.* Christ, have mercy. *S.* Christ, have mercy. *P.* Lord, have mercy. *S.* Lord, have mercy. *P.* Lord, have mercy.

THE GLORIA

GLORY to God in the highest. And on earth peace to men of good will. We praise You. We bless You. We adore You. We glorify You. We give You thanks for Your great glory. O Lord God, heavenly King, God the Father almighty. O Lord Jesus Christ, the Only-begotten Son. O Lord God, Lamb of God, Son of the Father: You Who take away the sins of the world, have mercy on us. You Who take away the sins of the world, receive our prayer. You Who sit at the right hand of the Father, have mercy on us. For You alone are holy. You alone are the Lord. You alone, O Jesus Christ, are most high. Together with the Holy Spirit ✠ in the glory of God the Father. Amen.

The Priest kisses the altar and turns to the people, saying:

P. The Lord be with you. *S.* And with your spirit. *P.* Let us pray.

THE PRAYER

Going to the right (Epistle) side, he says:

O GOD, under a marvelous sacrament You have left us the memorial of Your Passion; grant us, we beseech You, so to venerate the sacred mysteries of Your Body and Blood, that we may ever perceive within us the fruit of Your Redemption. Who live and reign with God the Father, in the unity of the Holy Spirit, God, world without end. *S.* Amen.

THE EPISTLE • 1 Cor. 11, 23-29

BRETHREN: I myself have received from the Lord (what I also delivered to you), that the

Lord Jesus, on the night in which He was betrayed, took bread, and giving thanks broke, and said, "Take and eat. This is My Body which shall be given up for you; do this in remembrance of Me." In like manner also the cup, after He had supped, saying, "This cup is the new covenant in My Blood; do this as often as you drink it, in remembrance of Me. For as often as you shall eat this Bread and drink the cup, you proclaim the death of the Lord, until He comes." Therefore whoever eats this Bread or drinks the cup of the Lord unworthily, will be guilty of the Body and the Blood of the Lord. But let a man prove himself, and so let him eat of that Bread and drink of the cup; for he who eats and drinks unworthily, without distinguishing the Body, eats and drinks judgment to himself. S. Thanks be to God.

THE GRADUAL • Ps. 144, 15-16

THE eyes of all look hopefully to You, O Lord; and You give them their food in due season. ℣. You open Your hand; and satisfy the desire of every living thing.

Alleluia, alleluia. *John 6, 56-57.* My Flesh is food indeed, and My Blood is drink indeed. He who eats My Flesh, and drinks My Blood, abides in Me and I in him.

At Low Mass apart from the Feast Day, if the Sequence is omitted, Alleluia is said here.

THE SEQUENCE

(Extract)

SION, to Your Savior sing,
To Your Shepherd and Your King!
Let the air with praises ring!

Words a nature's course derange,
That in Flesh the bread may change
And the wine in Christ's own Blood.

Does it pass your comprehending?
Faith, the law of light transcending
Leaps to things not understood.

Here beneath these signs are hidden
Priceless things, to sense forbidden;
Signs, not things, are all we see.

Flesh from bread, and Blood from wine,
Yet is Christ in either sign,
All entire confessed to be.

And whoe'er of Him partakes,
Severs not, nor rends, nor breaks:
All entire, their Lord receive.

Whether one or thousand eat,
All receive the selfsame meat,
Nor do less for others leave.

Both the wicked and the good
Eat of this celestial Food:
But with ends how opposite!

With this most substantial Bread,
Unto life or death they're fed,
In a difference infinite.

Nor a single doubt retain,
When they break the Host in twain,
But that each part remain
What was in the whole before;

For the outward sign alone
May some change have undergone,
While the Signified stays one,
And the same forevermore.

Hail! Bread of Angels, broken,
For us pilgrims food, and token
Of the promise by Christ spoken,
Children's meat, to dogs denied!

Jesus, Shepherd mild and meek,
Shield the poor, support the weak,
Pity all who pardon seek,
And who place all trust in You,
Fill them with Your Charity!

Source of all we have or know,
Feed and lead us here below.
Grant that with Your Saints above,
Sitting at the feast of love
We may see You face to face. Amen. Alleluia.

PRAYER BEFORE THE GOSPEL

Bowing down at the center of the altar, he says:

CLEANSE my heart and my lips, O almighty God, Who cleansed the lips of the Prophet Isaias with a burning coal. In Your gracious mercy deign so to purify me that I may worthily proclaim Your holy Gospel. Through Christ our Lord. Amen.

Lord, grant Your blessing. The Lord be in my heart and on my lips, that I may worthily and fittingly proclaim His holy Gospel. Amen.

THE GOSPEL • John 6, 56-59

Going to the left (Gospel) side of the altar, he says:

P. The Lord be with you. *S.* And with your spirit.
P. ✠ The continuation of the holy Gospel according to Saint John. *S.* Glory be to You, O Lord.

AT THAT time, Jesus said to the crowds of the Jews: "My Flesh is food indeed, and My Blood is drink indeed. He who eats My Flesh, and drinks

My Blood, abides in Me and I in him. As the living Father has sent Me, and as I live because of the Father, so he who eats Me, he also shall live because of Me. This is the Bread that has come down from heaven; not as your fathers ate the manna, and died. He who eats this Bread shall live forever." S. Praise be to You, O Christ.

P. By the words of the Gospel, may our sins be taken away.

THE NICENE CREED

At the center of the altar, he says:

I BELIEVE in one God, the Father almighty, Maker of heaven and earth, and of all things visible and invisible. And in one Lord Jesus Christ, the Only-begotten Son of God. Born of the Father before all ages. God of God; Light of Light; true God of true God. Begotten not made; of one being with the Father; by Whom all things were made. Who for us men, and for our salvation, came down from heaven. (*Here all genuflect.*) And was made Flesh by the Holy Spirit of the Virgin Mary: AND WAS MADE MAN. He was also crucified for us, suffered under Pontius Pilate and was buried. And on the third day He rose again according to the Scriptures. And ascending into heaven, He sits at the right hand of the Father. And He shall come again in glory to judge the living and the dead; and of His kingdom there shall be no end. And I believe in the Holy Spirit, Lord and Giver of life, Who proceeds from the Father and the Son. Who together with the Father and the Son is no less adored, and glorified: Who spoke by the Prophets. And I believe in One, Holy, Catholic and Apostolic Church. I confess one Baptism for the remission of sins. And I look for the resurrec-

tion of the dead. ✠ And the life of the world to come. Amen.

THE OFFERTORY

The Priest turns to the people and says:

P. The Lord be with you. *S.* And with your spirit. *P.* Let us pray.

THE OFFERTORY VERSE • Lev. 21, 6

THE priests of the Lord offer incense and loaves to God, and therefore they shall be sacred to their God and shall not profane His name. Alleluia.

The Priest now uncovers the chalice, places the host on the paten and offering it up, says:

ACCEPT, O holy Father, almighty and eternal God, this spotless host, which I, Your unworthy servant, offer to You, my living and true God, to atone for my numberless sins, offenses, and negligences; on behalf of all here present and likewise for all faithful Christians living and dead, that it may profit me and them as a means of salvation to life everlasting. Amen.

He pours wine and water into the chalice, blessing the water before it is poured.

O GOD, Who established the nature of man in wondrous dignity, and still more admirably restored it, grant that through the mystery of this water and wine, we may be made partakers of His Divinity, Who has condescended to become partaker of our humanity, Jesus Christ, Your Son, our Lord. Who lives and reigns with You in the unity of the Holy Spirit, God, world without end. Amen.

Offering up the wine, the Priest says:

WE OFFER You, O Lord, the chalice of salvation, humbly begging of Your mercy that

it may arise before Your Divine Majesty, with a pleasing fragrance, for our salvation and for that of the whole world. Amen.

Bowing down, the Priest says:

IN A humble spirit and with a contrite heart, may we be accepted by You, O Lord, and may our sacrifice so be offered in Your sight this day as to please You, O Lord God.

Raising his eyes and blessing the offering, he says:

COME, O Sanctifier, almighty and eternal God, and bless ✠ this sacrifice prepared for the glory of Your holy name.

WASHING THE FINGERS

I WASH my hands in innocence, and I go around Your altar, O Lord, giving voice to my thanks, and recounting all Your wondrous deeds. O Lord, I love the house in which You dwell, the tenting-place of Your glory. Gather not my soul with those of sinners, nor with men of blood my life. On their hands are crimes, and their right hands are full of bribes. But I walk in integrity; redeem me, and have pity on me. My foot stands on level ground; in the assemblies I will bless You, O Lord. Glory be to the Father, and to the Son, and to the Holy Spirit. As it was in the beginning, is now, and ever shall be, world without end. Amen.

ACCEPT, Most Holy Trinity, this offering which we are making to You in remembrance of the Passion, Resurrection, and Ascension of Jesus Christ, our Lord; and in honor of Blessed Mary, ever Virgin, Blessed John the Baptist, the Holy Apostles Peter and Paul, and of these, and of all the Saints; that it may add to their honor and aid our salvation; and may they deign to intercede in heaven for us who honor their memory here on earth. Through the same Christ our Lord. Amen.

The Priest turns toward the people and says:

Pray, brethren, that my sacrifice and yours may become acceptable to God the Father almighty.

S. May the Lord accept this sacrifice from your hands to the praise and glory of His name, for our advantage, and that of all His holy Church.

P. Amen.

THE SECRET

WE BESEECH You, O Lord, graciously grant to Your Church the gifts of unity and peace, which, in the gifts offered, are mystically signified. Through our Lord Jesus Christ, Your Son, Who lives and reigns with You in the unity of the Holy Spirit, God.

P. World without end. *S.* Amen.

PREFACE—CANON

P. The Lord be with you. *S.* And with your spirit.

P. Lift up your hearts.

S. We have lifted them up to the Lord.

P. Let us give thanks to the Lord, our God.

S. It is fitting and just.

IT IS fitting indeed and just, right and helpful to salvation, for us always and everywhere to give thanks to You, O holy Lord, Father almighty, everlasting God, through Christ our Lord. Through Him the Angels praise Your Majesty, the Dominations adore it, the Powers are in awe. The Heavens and the heavenly hosts, and the blessed Seraphim, join together in celebrating their joy. With these, we pray You, join our own voices also, while we say with lowly praise (*the bell is rung 3 times*):

HOLY, HOLY, HOLY, Lord God of Hosts. Heaven and earth are filled with Your glory. Hosanna in the highest. ✠ Blessed is He Who comes in the name of the Lord. Hosanna in the highest.

THE CANON OF THE MASS

THEREFORE, most gracious Father, we humbly beg of You and entreat You through Jesus Christ Your Son, our Lord, (*he kisses the altar*) to deem acceptable and bless these ✠ gifts, these ✠ offerings, these ✠ holy and unspotted oblations which, in the first place, we offer You for Your Holy Catholic Church, that You would deign to give her peace and protection, to unite and guard her throughout the world, together with Your servant N., our Pope, and N., our Bishop; and all true believers who cherish the Catholic and Apostolic Faith.

Commemoration of the Living

REMEMBER, O Lord, Your servants and handmaids, N. and N., (*name them*) and all here present, whose faith and devotion are known to You, on whose behalf we offer to You, or who themselves offer to You, this sacrifice of praise for themselves, families and friends, for the good of their souls, for their hope of salvation and deliverance from all harm, and who offer their homage to You, eternal, living and true God.

Commemoration of the Saints

IN THE unity of holy fellowship we observe the memory, first of all, of the glorious and ever Virgin Mary, Mother of our Lord and God Jesus Christ; next, that of Your Blessed Apostles and Martyrs, Peter and Paul, Andrew, James, John,

Thomas, James, Philip, Bartholomew, Matthew, Simon and Thaddeus; of Linus, Cletus, Clement, Sixtus, Cornelius, Cyprian, Lawrence, Chrysogonus, John and Paul, Cosmas and Damian, and of all Your Saints, by whose merits and prayers grant that we may be always fortified by the help of Your protection. Through the same Christ our Lord. Amen.

Spreading his hands over the oblation, he says:

GRACIOUSLY accept, then, we beseech You, O Lord, this service of our worship and that of all Your household. Provide that our days be spent in Your peace, save us from everlasting damnation, and cause us to be numbered in the flock You have chosen. Through Christ our Lord. Amen.

O GOD, deign to bless ✠ what we offer, and make it approved, ✠ effective, ✠ right, and wholly pleasing in every way, that it may become for our good, the Body ✠ and Blood ✠ of Your dearly beloved Son, Jesus Christ our Lord.

CONSECRATION—ELEVATION

WHO, the day before He suffered, took bread into His holy and venerable hands, and having raised His eyes to heaven, to You, O God, His almighty Father, giving thanks to You, He blessed it, ✠ broke it, and gave it to His disciples, saying: All of you take and eat of this:

FOR THIS IS MY BODY.

IN LIKE manner, when the supper was done, taking also this goodly chalice into His holy and venerable hands, again giving thanks to You, He blessed ✠ it, and gave it to His disciples, saying: All of you take and drink of this:

FOR THIS IS THE CHALICE OF MY BLOOD OF THE NEW AND ETERNAL COVENANT: THE MYSTERY OF FAITH: WHICH SHALL BE SHED FOR YOU AND FOR MANY UNTO THE FORGIVENESS OF SINS.

After replacing the chalice on the corporal, he says:

As often as you shall do these things, in memory of Me shall you do them.

Offering of the Victim

MINDFUL, therefore, O Lord, not only of the blessed Passion of the same Christ, Your Son, our Lord, but also of His Resurrection from the dead, and finally His glorious Ascension into heaven, we, Your ministers, as also Your holy people, offer to Your supreme Majesty, of the gifts bestowed upon us, the pure ✠ Victim, the holy ✠ Victim, the all-perfect ✠ Victim: the holy ✠ Bread of life eternal and the Chalice ✠ of unending salvation.

AND this deign to regard with gracious and kindly attention and hold acceptable, as You deigned to accept the offerings of Abel, Your just servant, and the sacrifice of Abraham our patriarch, and that which Your chief priest Melchisedec offered to You, a holy sacrifice and a spotless victim.

MOST humbly we implore You, almighty God, bid these offerings to be brought by the hands of Your holy angel to Your altar above; before the face of Your Divine Majesty; that those of us who, by sharing in the Sacrifice of this altar, shall receive the Most Sacred ✠ Body and ✠ Blood of Your Son, may be filled with every grace and heavenly blessing. Through the same Christ our Lord. Amen.

Commemoration of the Dead

REMEMBER also, O Lord, Your servants and handmaids, N. and N., who have gone before us with the sign of faith, and rest in the sleep of peace. (*Here pray for the dead.*) To these, O Lord, and to all who rest in Christ, we beseech You to grant of Your goodness, a place of comfort, light and peace. Through the same Christ our Lord. Amen.

TO US sinners also, Your servants, trusting in the greatness of Your mercy, deign to grant some part and fellowship with Your Holy Apostles and Martyrs: with John, Stephen, Matthias, Barnabas, Ignatius, Alexander, Marcellinus, Peter, Felicitas, Perpetua, Agatha, Lucy, Agnes, Cecilia, Anastasia, and all Your Saints; into whose company, we implore You to admit us, not weighing our merits, but freely granting us pardon. Through Christ our Lord.

THROUGH Whom, O Lord, You always create, ✠ sanctify, ✠ fill with life, ✠ bless, and bestow upon us all good things.

The Minor Elevation

THROUGH ✠ Him, and with ✠ Him, and in ✠ Him, is to You, God the Father ✠ almighty, in the unity of the Holy ✠ Spirit, all honor and glory, world without end. S. Amen.

THE COMMUNION AND THANKSGIVING

Let us pray. Prompted by saving precepts, and taught by Your divine teaching, we dare to say:

OUR FATHER, Who art in heaven, hallowed be Thy name: Thy kingdom come: Thy will be done on earth as it is in heaven. Give us this day

our daily bread; and forgive us our trespasses, as we forgive those who trespass against us. And lead us not into temptation: *S.* But deliver us from evil. *P.* Amen.

DELIVER us, we beseech You, O Lord, from all evils, past, present, and to come; and by the intercession of the Blessed and glorious Mary, ever Virgin, Mother of God, together with Your Blessed Apostles Peter and Paul, and Andrew, and all the Saints, grant of Your goodness, peace in our days, that aided by the riches of Your mercy, we may be always free from sin and safe from all disturbance.

Through the same our Lord Jesus Christ, Your Son, Who lives and reigns with You in the unity of the Holy Spirit, God, world without end. *S.* Amen.

P. May the peace ✠ of the Lord be ✠ always with ✠ you. *S.* And with your spirit.

The Priest puts a small particle into the chalice, saying:

May this mingling and consecration of the Body and Blood of our Lord Jesus Christ help us who receive it to life everlasting. Amen.

LAMB of God, You Who take away the sins of the world, have mercy on us.

Lamb of God, You Who take away the sins of the world, have mercy on us.

Lamb of God, You Who take away the sins of the world, grant us peace.

PRAYERS BEFORE HOLY COMMUNION

Then inclining toward the altar, he says:

O LORD Jesus Christ, Who said to Your Apostles: "Peace I leave with you, My peace I give

to you," regard not my sins but the faith of Your Church, and deign to give her peace and unity according to Your Will: Who live and reign, God, world without end. Amen.

O LORD Jesus Christ, Son of the living God, Who, by the will of the Father, with the co-operation of the Holy Spirit, have by Your death given life to the world, deliver me by this Your Most Sacred Body and Blood from all my sins and from every evil. Make me always cling to Your commandments, and never permit me to be separated from You. Who with the same God the Father and the Holy Spirit, live and reign, God, world without end. Amen.

LET not the partaking of Your Body, O Lord Jesus Christ, which I, though unworthy, presume to receive, turn to my judgment and condemnation; but through Your goodness, may it become a safeguard and an effective remedy, both of soul and body. Who live and reign with God the Father, in the unity of the Holy Spirit, God, world without end. Amen.

COMMUNION OF THE PRIEST

I WILL take the Bread of heaven, and call upon the name of the Lord.

Lord, I am not worthy that You should come under my roof; but only say the word, and my soul will be healed. (3 *times.*)

Making the Sign of the Cross with the Host, he says:

MAY the Body of our Lord Jesus Christ preserve my soul to life everlasting. Amen.

What return shall I make to the Lord for all He has given me? I will take the Chalice of salvation,

and I will call upon the name of the Lord. Praising will I call upon the Lord and I shall be saved from my enemies.

Making the Sign of the Cross with the chalice, he says:

MAY the Blood of our Lord Jesus Christ preserve my soul to life everlasting. Amen.

The Priest reverently consumes the Precious Blood.

COMMUNION OF THE FAITHFUL

The Server and people say the "Confiteor."

P. May almighty God have mercy on you, forgive you your sins, and bring you to life everlasting. S. Amen.

P. May the almighty and merciful Lord grant you pardon, ✠ absolution and remission of your sins. S. Amen.

Holding up a Sacred Host, the Priest says:

Behold the Lamb of God, behold Him Who takes away the sins of the world.

Lord, I am not worthy that You should come under my roof; but only say the word, and my soul will be healed. (3 *times.*)

The Priest says to each communicant:

May the Body of our Lord Jesus Christ preserve your soul to life everlasting. Amen.

The Priest purifies the chalice with wine, saying:

WHAT has passed our lips as food, O Lord, may we possess in purity of heart, that what is given to us in time, be our healing for eternity.

He purifies his fingers with wine and water, saying:

MAY Your Body, O Lord, which I have eaten, and Your Blood which I have drunk, cleave to my very soul, and grant that no trace of sin be found in me, whom these pure and holy mysteries

have renewed. Who live and reign, world without end. Amen.

THE COMMUNION • 1 Cor. 11, 26-27

AS OFTEN as you shall eat this Bread and drink the cup, you proclaim the death of the Lord, until He comes. Therefore whoever eats this Bread or drinks the cup of the Lord unworthily, will be guilty of the Body and Blood of the Lord, alleluia.

The Priest, turning to the people, says:

P. The Lord be with you. S. And with your spirit.
P. Let us pray.

THE POSTCOMMUNION

GRANT us, we beseech You, O Lord, to be filled with the eternal enjoyment of Your Divinity, which is prefigured by the reception of Your precious Body and Blood in this life. Who live and reign with God the Father, etc. S. Amen.

FINAL PRAYERS

P. The Lord be with you. S. And with your spirit.
P. Go, you are dismissed. S. Thanks be to God.

MAY the tribute of my worship be pleasing to You, Most Holy Trinity, and grant that the sacrifice which I, all unworthy, have offered in the presence of Your Majesty, may be acceptable to You, and through Your mercy obtain forgiveness for me and all for whom I have offered it. Through Christ our Lord. Amen.

THE LAST BLESSING

MAY almighty God bless you: ✠ the Father, and the Son, and the Holy Spirit. S. Amen.

The Last Gospel and Prayers after Low Mass are conveniently placed inside the back cover.

"Bring in here the poor, and the crippled . . ."

SECOND SUNDAY AFTER PENTECOST

The Communion-Banquet is offered not only to Saints but to the poor, the weak, the blind and lame in their religious life provided they sincerely desire to be cured. But if they are dead by sin, they must first rise again by a good Confession. (GREEN VESTMENTS)

PRAYERS AT THE FOOT OF THE ALTAR

IN THE name of the Father, ✠ and of the Son, and of the Holy Spirit. Amen.

Priest. I will go in to the altar of God.

Server. The God of my gladness and joy.

Psalm 42

DO ME justice, O God, and fight my fight against a faithless people; from the deceitful and impious man rescue me.

S. For You, O God, are my strength. Why do You keep me so far away? Why must I go about in mourning, with the enemy oppressing me?

P. Send forth Your light and Your fidelity; they shall lead me on and bring me to Your holy mountain, to Your dwelling-place.

S. Then will I go in to the altar of God, the God of my gladness and joy.
P. Then will I give You thanks upon the harp, O God, my God. Why are you so downcast, O my soul? Why do you sigh within me?
S. Hope in God! For I shall again be thanking Him in the presence of my Savior and my God.
P. Glory be to the Father, and to the Son, and to the Holy Spirit.
S. As it was in the beginning, is now, and ever shall be, world without end. Amen.
P. I will go in to the altar of God.
S. The God of my gladness and joy.
P. Our help ✠ is in the name of the Lord.
S. Who made heaven and earth.
P. I confess to almighty God, etc.
S. May almighty God have mercy on you, forgive you your sins, and bring you to life everlasting.
P. Amen.

The Server, bowing, says the "Confiteor."

I CONFESS to almighty God, to Blessed Mary, ever Virgin, to Blessed Michael the Archangel, to Blessed John the Baptist, to the Holy Apostles Peter and Paul, and to all the Saints, and to you, Father, that I have sinned exceedingly in thought, word and deed, *through my fault, through my fault, through my most grievous fault.* Therefore I beseech Blessed Mary, ever Virgin, Blessed Michael the Archangel, Blessed John the Baptist, the Holy Apostles Peter and Paul, and all the Saints, and you, Father, to pray to the Lord our God for me.
P. May almighty God have mercy on you, forgive you your sins, and bring you to life everlasting.
S. Amen.

MAY the almighty and merciful Lord grant us pardon, ✠ absolution, and remission of our sins. *S.* Amen.

P. Will You not, O God, give us life?
S. And shall not Your people rejoice in You?
P. Show us, O Lord, Your kindness.
S. And grant us Your salvation.
P. O Lord, hear my prayer.
S. And let my cry come to You.
P. The Lord be with you.
S. And with your spirit. *P.* Let us pray.

Going up to the altar, the Priest prays silently:

TAKE away from us our sins, O Lord, we beseech You, that we may enter with pure minds into the Holy of Holies. Through Christ our Lord. Amen.

WE BESEECH You, O Lord, by the merits of Your Saints (*he kisses the altar*) whose relics lie here, and of all the Saints: deign in Your mercy to pardon me all my sins. Amen.

THE INTROIT • Ps. 17, 19. 20. 2. 3

At the right side of the altar, the Priest says:

THE Lord came to my support. He set me free in the open, and rescued me, because He loves me. *Ps.* I love You, O Lord, my strength, O Lord, my rock, my fortress, my deliverer. Glory be to the Father, and to the Son, and to the Holy Spirit. As it was in the beginning, is now, and ever shall be, world without end. Amen. — The Lord came to my support. He set me free in the open, and rescued me, because He loves me.

THE KYRIE

P. Lord, have mercy. *S.* Lord, have mercy. *P.* Lord,

have mercy. *S.* Christ, have mercy. *P.* Christ, have mercy. *S.* Christ, have mercy. *P.* Lord, have mercy. *S.* Lord, have mercy. *P.* Lord, have mercy.

THE GLORIA

GLORY to God in the highest. And on earth peace to men of good will. We praise You. We bless You. We adore You. We glorify You. We give You thanks for Your great glory. O Lord God, heavenly King, God the Father almighty. O Lord Jesus Christ, the Only-begotten Son. O Lord God, Lamb of God, Son of the Father: You Who take away the sins of the world, have mercy on us. You Who take away the sins of the world, receive our prayer. You Who sit at the right hand of the Father, have mercy on us. For You alone are holy. You alone are the Lord. You alone, O Jesus Christ, are most high. Together with the Holy Spirit ✠ in the glory of God the Father. Amen.

The Priest kisses the altar and turns to the people, saying:

P. The Lord be with you. *S.* And with your spirit. *P.* Let us pray.

THE PRAYER

Going to the right (Epistle) side, he says:

GRANT, O Lord, that we may have a constant fear and love of Your holy name; for You never cease to direct and govern by Your grace those whom You solidly establish in Your love. Through our Lord Jesus Christ, Your Son, Who lives and reigns with You in the unity of the Holy Spirit, God, world without end. *S.* Amen.

THE EPISTLE • 1 John 3, 13-18

BELOVED: Do not be surprised if the world hates you. We know that we have passed from death to life, because we love the brethren. He who does not love abides in death. Everyone who hates his brother is a murderer. And you know that no murderer has eternal life abiding in him. In this we have come to know His love, that He laid down His life for us; and we likewise ought to lay down our life for the brethren. He who has the goods of this world and sees his brother in need and closes his heart to him, how does the love of God abide in him? My dear children, let us not love in word, neither with the tongue, but in deed and in truth. S. Thanks be to God.

THE GRADUAL • Ps. 119, 1-2

IN MY distress I called to the Lord, and He answered me. ℣. O Lord, deliver me from lying lips, from treacherous tongue.

Alleluia, alleluia. ℣. *Ps.* 7, 2. O Lord my God, in You I take refuge; save me from all my pursuers and rescue me. Alleluia.

PRAYER BEFORE THE GOSPEL

Bowing down at the center of the altar, he says:

CLEANSE my heart and my lips, O almighty God, Who cleansed the lips of the Prophet Isaias with a burning coal. In Your gracious mercy deign so to purify me that I may worthily proclaim Your holy Gospel. Through Christ our Lord. Amen. Lord, grant Your blessing. The Lord be in my heart and on my lips, that I may worthily and fittingly proclaim His holy Gospel. Amen.

THE GOSPEL • Luke 14, 16-24

Going to the left (Gospel) side of the altar, he says:

P. The Lord be with you. S. And with your spirit.
P. ✠ The continuation of the holy Gospel according to Saint Luke. S. Glory be to You, O Lord.

AT THAT time, Jesus spoke to the Pharisees this parable: "A certain man gave a great supper, and he invited many. And he sent his servant at supper time to tell those invited to come, for everything is now ready. And they all with one accord began to excuse themselves. The first said to him, 'I have bought a farm, and I must go out and see it; I pray you hold me excused.' And another said, 'I have bought five yoke of oxen, and I am on my way to try them; I pray you hold me excused.' And another said, 'I have married a wife, and therefore I cannot come.' And the servant returned, and reported these things to his master. Then the master of the house was angry and said to his servant, 'Go out quickly into the streets and lanes of the city, and bring in here the poor, and the crippled, and the blind, and the lame.' And the servant said, 'Sir, your order has been carried out, and still there is room.' Then the master said to the servant, 'Go out into the highways and hedges, and make them come in, so that my house may be filled. For I tell you that none of those who were invited shall taste of my supper.'" S. Praise be to You, O Christ.

P. By the words of the Gospel, may our sins be taken away.

THE NICENE CREED

At the center of the altar, he says:

I BELIEVE in one God, the Father almighty, Maker of heaven and earth, and of all things visible and invisible. And in one Lord Jesus Christ, the Only-begotten Son of God. Born of the Father before all ages. God of God; Light of Light; true God of true God. Begotten not made; of one being with the Father; by Whom all things were

made. Who for us men, and for our salvation, came down from heaven. (*Here all genuflect.*) And was made Flesh by the Holy Spirit of the Virgin Mary: AND WAS MADE MAN. He was also crucified for us, suffered under Pontius Pilate and was buried. And on the third day He rose again according to the Scriptures. And ascending into heaven, He sits at the right hand of the Father. And He shall come again in glory to judge the living and the dead; and of His kingdom there shall be no end. And I believe in the Holy Spirit, Lord and Giver of life, Who proceeds from the Father and the Son. Who together with the Father and the Son is no less adored, and glorified: Who spoke by the Prophets. And I believe in One, Holy, Catholic and Apostolic Church. I confess one Baptism for the remission of sins. And I look for the resurrection of the dead. ✠ And the life of the world to come. Amen.

THE OFFERTORY

The Priest turns to the people and says:

P. The Lord be with you. S. And with your spirit.
P. Let us pray.

THE OFFERTORY VERSE • Ps. 6, 5

RETURN, O Lord, save my life; rescue me because of Your kindness.

The Priest now uncovers the chalice, places the host on the paten and offering it up, says:

ACCEPT, O holy Father, almighty and eternal God, this spotless host, which I, Your unworthy servant, offer to You, my living and true God, to atone for my numberless sins, offenses, and negligences; on behalf of all here present and likewise for all faithful Christians living and dead,

that it may profit me and them as a means of salvation to life everlasting. Amen.

He pours wine and water into the chalice, blessing the water before it is poured.

O GOD, Who established the nature of man in wondrous dignity, and still more admirably restored it, grant that through the mystery of this water and wine, we may be made partakers of His Divinity, Who has condescended to become partaker of our humanity, Jesus Christ, Your Son, our Lord. Who lives and reigns with You in the unity of the Holy Spirit, God, world without end. Amen.

Offering up the wine, the Priest says:

WE OFFER You, O Lord, the chalice of salvation, humbly begging of Your mercy that it may arise before Your Divine Majesty, with a pleasing fragrance, for our salvation and for that of the whole world. Amen.

Bowing down, the Priest says:

IN A humble spirit and with a contrite heart, may we be accepted by You, O Lord, and may our sacrifice so be offered in Your sight this day as to please You, O Lord God.

Raising his eyes and blessing the offering, he says:

COME, O Sanctifier, almighty and eternal God, and bless ✠ this sacrifice prepared for the glory of Your holy name.

WASHING THE FINGERS

I WASH my hands in innocence, and I go around Your altar, O Lord, giving voice to my thanks, and recounting all Your wondrous deeds. O Lord, I love the house in which You dwell, the tenting-place of Your glory. Gather not my soul with those of sinners, nor with men of blood my life. On their hands are crimes, and their right hands are full of bribes. But I walk in integrity; redeem me, and have pity on me. My foot stands on level ground; in the assemblies I will bless You, O Lord. Glory be to the Father, and to the Son, and to the Holy Spirit. As it was in the beginning, is now, and ever shall be, world without end. Amen.

ACCEPT, Most Holy Trinity, this offering which we are making to You in remembrance of the Passion, Resurrection, and Ascension of Jesus Christ, our Lord; and in honor of Blessed Mary, ever Virgin, Blessed John the Baptist, the Holy Apostles Peter and Paul, and of these, and of all the Saints; that it may add to their honor and aid our salvation; and may they deign to intercede in heaven for us who honor their memory here on earth. Through the same Christ our Lord. Amen.

The Priest turns toward the people and says:

Pray, brethren, that my sacrifice and yours may become acceptable to God the Father almighty.

S. May the Lord accept this sacrifice from your hands to the praise and glory of His name, for our advantage, and that of all His holy Church.

P. Amen.

THE SECRET

MAY the offering about to be dedicated to Your name purify us, O Lord, so that from day to day it may carry us on to the reality of heavenly life. Through our Lord Jesus Christ, Your Son, Who lives and reigns with You in the unity of the Holy Spirit, God.

P. World without end. *S.* Amen.

PREFACE—CANON

P. The Lord be with you. *S.* And with your spirit.
P. Lift up your hearts.
S. We have lifted them up to the Lord.
P. Let us give thanks to the Lord, our God.
S. It is fitting and just.

IT IS fitting indeed and just, right and helpful to salvation, for us always and everywhere to give thanks to You, O holy Lord, Father almighty, everlasting God, Who with Your Only-begotten Son and the Holy Spirit are one God, one Lord; not in the unity of a single person, but in the trinity of a single nature. For that which we believe on Your revelation concerning Your glory, that same we believe of Your Son, that same of the Holy Spirit, without difference or discrimination. So that in confessing the true and everlasting Godhead, we shall adore distinction in Persons, oneness in being, and equality in Majesty. This the Angels and Archangels, the Cherubim, too, and the Seraphim do praise; day by day they cease not to cry out as with one voice, saying (*the bell is rung* 3 *times*):

HOLY, HOLY, HOLY, Lord God of Hosts. Heaven and earth are filled with Your glory. Hosanna in the highest. ✠ Blessed is He Who comes in the name of the Lord. Hosanna in the highest.

THE CANON OF THE MASS

THEREFORE, most gracious Father, we humbly beg of You and entreat You through Jesus Christ Your Son, our Lord, (*he kisses the altar*) to deem acceptable and bless these ✠ gifts, these ✠

offerings, these ✠ holy and unspotted oblations which, in the first place, we offer You for Your Holy Catholic Church, that You would deign to give her peace and protection, to unite and guard her throughout the world, together with Your servant *N.*, our Pope, and *N.*, our Bishop; and all true believers who cherish the Catholic and Apostolic Faith.

Commemoration of the Living

REMEMBER, O Lord, Your servants and handmaids, N. and N., (*name them*) and all here present, whose faith and devotion are known to You, on whose behalf we offer to You, or who themselves offer to You, this sacrifice of praise for themselves, families and friends, for the good of their souls, for their hope of salvation and deliverance from all harm, and who offer their homage to You, eternal, living and true God.

Commemoration of the Saints

IN THE unity of holy fellowship we observe the memory, first of all, of the glorious and ever Virgin Mary, Mother of our Lord and God Jesus Christ; next, that of Your Blessed Apostles and Martyrs, Peter and Paul, Andrew, James, John, Thomas, James, Philip, Bartholomew, Matthew, Simon and Thaddeus; of Linus, Cletus, Clement, Sixtus, Cornelius, Cyprian, Lawrence, Chrysogonus, John and Paul, Cosmas and Damian, and of all Your Saints, by whose merits and prayers grant that we may be always fortified by the help of Your protection. Through the same Christ our Lord. Amen.

Spreading his hands over the oblation, he says:

GRACIOUSLY accept, then, we beseech You, O Lord, this service of our worship and that of all Your household. Provide that our days be

spent in Your peace, save us from everlasting damnation, and cause us to be numbered in the flock You have chosen. Through Christ our Lord. Amen.

O GOD, deign to bless ✠ what we offer, and make it approved, ✠ effective, ✠ right, and wholly pleasing in every way, that it may become for our good, the Body ✠ and Blood ✠ of Your dearly beloved Son, Jesus Christ our Lord.

CONSECRATION—ELEVATION

WHO, the day before He suffered, took bread into His holy and venerable hands, and having raised His eyes to heaven, to You, O God, His almighty Father, giving thanks to You, He blessed it, ✠ broke it, and gave it to His disciples, saying: All of you take and eat of this:

FOR THIS IS MY BODY.

IN LIKE manner, when the supper was done, taking also this goodly chalice into His holy and venerable hands, again giving thanks to You, He blessed ✠ it, and gave it to His disciples, saying: All of you take and drink of this:

FOR THIS IS THE CHALICE OF MY BLOOD OF THE NEW AND ETERNAL COVENANT: THE MYSTERY OF FAITH: WHICH SHALL BE SHED FOR YOU AND FOR MANY UNTO THE FORGIVENESS OF SINS.

After replacing the chalice on the corporal, he says:

As often as you shall do these things, in memory of Me shall you do them.

Offering of the Victim

MINDFUL, therefore, O Lord, not only of the blessed Passion of the same Christ, Your Son, our Lord, but also of His Resurrection from the dead, and finally His glorious Ascension into heaven, we, Your ministers, as also Your holy people, offer to Your supreme Majesty, of the gifts bestowed upon us, the pure ✠ Victim, the holy ✠ Victim, the all-perfect ✠ Victim: the holy ✠ Bread of life eternal and the Chalice ✠ of unending salvation.

AND this deign to regard with gracious and kindly attention and hold acceptable, as You deigned to accept the offerings of Abel, Your just servant, and the sacrifice of Abraham our patriarch, and that which Your chief priest Melchisedec offered to You, a holy sacrifice and a spotless victim.

MOST humbly we implore You, almighty God, bid these offerings to be brought by the hands of Your holy angel to Your altar above; before the face of Your Divine Majesty; that those of us who, by sharing in the Sacrifice of this altar, shall receive the Most Sacred ✠ Body and ✠ Blood of Your Son, may be filled with every grace and heavenly blessing. Through the same Christ our Lord. Amen.

Commemoration of the Dead

REMEMBER also, O Lord, Your servants and handmaids, N., and N., who have gone before us with the sign of faith, and rest in the sleep of peace. (*Here pray for the dead.*) To these, O Lord, and to all who rest in Christ, we beseech You to grant of Your goodness, a place of comfort, light and peace. Through the same Christ our Lord. Amen.

TO US sinners also, Your servants, trusting in the greatness of Your mercy, deign to grant some

part and fellowship with Your Holy Apostles and Martyrs: with John, Stephen, Matthias, Barnabas, Ignatius, Alexander, Marcellinus, Peter, Felicitas, Perpetua, Agatha, Lucy, Agnes, Cecilia, Anastasia, and all Your Saints; into whose company, we implore You to admit us, not weighing our merits, but freely granting us pardon. Through Christ our Lord.

THROUGH Whom, O Lord, You always create, ✠ sanctify, ✠ fill with life, ✠ bless, and bestow upon us all good things.

The Minor Elevation

THROUGH ✠ Him, and with ✠ Him, and in ✠ Him, is to You, God the Father ✠ almighty, in the unity of the Holy ✠ Spirit, all honor and glory, world without end. S. Amen.

THE COMMUNION AND THANKSGIVING

Let us pray. Prompted by saving precepts, and taught by Your divine teaching, we dare to say:

OUR FATHER, Who art in heaven, hallowed be Thy name: Thy kingdom come: Thy will be done on earth as it is in heaven. Give us this day our daily bread; and forgive us our trespasses, as we forgive those who trespass against us. And lead us not into temptation: S. But deliver us from evil. *P.* Amen.

DELIVER us, we beseech You, O Lord, from all evils, past, present, and to come; and by the intercession of the Blessed and glorious Mary, ever Virgin, Mother of God, together with Your Blessed Apostles Peter and Paul, and Andrew, and all the Saints, grant of Your goodness, peace in our

days, that aided by the riches of Your mercy, we may be always free from sin and safe from all disturbance.

Through the same our Lord Jesus Christ, Your Son, Who lives and reigns with You in the unity of the Holy Spirit, God, world without end.

S. Amen.

P. May the peace ✠ of the Lord be ✠ always with ✠ you.

S. And with your spirit.

The Priest puts a small particle into the chalice, saying:

May this mingling and consecration of the Body and Blood of our Lord Jesus Christ help us who receive it to life everlasting. Amen.

LAMB of God, You Who take away the sins of the world, have mercy on us.

Lamb of God, You Who take away the sins of the world, have mercy on us.

Lamb of God, You Who take away the sins of the world, grant us peace.

PRAYERS BEFORE HOLY COMMUNION

Then inclining toward the altar, he says:

O LORD Jesus Christ, Who said to Your Apostles: "Peace I leave with you, My peace I give to you," regard not my sins but the faith of Your Church, and deign to give her peace and unity according to Your Will: Who live and reign, God, world without end. Amen.

O LORD Jesus Christ, Son of the living God, Who, by the will of the Father, with the cooperation of the Holy Spirit, have by Your death given life to the world, deliver me by this Your

Most Sacred Body and Blood from all my sins and from every evil. Make me always cling to Your commandments, and never permit me to be separated from You. Who with the same God the Father and the Holy Spirit, live and reign, God, world without end. Amen.

LET not the partaking of Your Body, O Lord Jesus Christ, which I, though unworthy, presume to receive, turn to my judgment and condemnation; but through Your goodness, may it become a safeguard and an effective remedy, both of soul and body. Who live and reign with God the Father, in the unity of the Holy Spirit, God, world without end. Amen.

COMMUNION OF THE PRIEST

I WILL take the Bread of heaven, and call upon the name of the Lord.

Lord, I am not worthy that You should come under my roof; but only say the word, and my soul will be healed. (3 *times.*)

Making the Sign of the Cross with the Host, he says:

MAY the Body of our Lord Jesus Christ preserve my soul to life everlasting. Amen.

What return shall I make to the Lord for all He has given me? I will take the Chalice of salvation, and I will call upon the name of the Lord. Praising will I call upon the Lord and I shall be saved from my enemies.

Making the Sign of the Cross with the chalice, he says:

MAY the Blood of our Lord Jesus Christ preserve my soul to life everlasting. Amen.

The Priest reverently consumes the Precious Blood.

COMMUNION OF THE FAITHFUL

The Server and people say the "Confiteor."

P. May almighty God have mercy on you, forgive you your sins, and bring you to life everlasting. S. Amen.

P. May the almighty and merciful Lord grant you pardon, ✠ absolution and remission of your sins. S. Amen.

Holding up a Sacred Host, the Priest says:

Behold the Lamb of God, behold Him Who takes away the sins of the world.

Lord, I am not worthy that You should come under my roof; but only say the word, and my soul will be healed. (3 *times.*)

The Priest says to each communicant:

May the Body of our Lord Jesus Christ preserve your soul to life everlasting. Amen.

The Priest purifies the chalice with wine, saying:

WHAT has passed our lips as food, O Lord, may we possess in purity of heart, that what is given to us in time, be our healing for eternity.

He purifies his fingers with wine and water, saying:

MAY Your Body, O Lord, which I have eaten, and Your Blood which I have drunk, cleave to my very soul, and grant that no trace of sin be found in me, whom these pure and holy mysteries have renewed. Who live and reign, world without end. Amen.

THE COMMUNION • Ps. 12, 6

I WILL sing to the Lord, "He has been good to me"; and I will sing to the name of the Lord the Most High.

The Priest, turning to the people, says:

P. The Lord be with you. S. And with your spirit.
P. Let us pray.

THE POSTCOMMUNION

HAVING received Your sacred gifts, we beseech You, O Lord, that our assistance at these mysteries may result in an increase of our salvation. Through our Lord Jesus Christ, Your Son, Who lives and reigns with You in the unity of the Holy Spirit, God, world without end. S. Amen.

FINAL PRAYERS

The Priest turns again to the people, and says:

P. The Lord be with you. S. And with your spirit.
P. Go, you are dismissed. S. Thanks be to God.

MAY the tribute of my worship be pleasing to You, Most Holy Trinity, and grant that the sacrifice which I, all unworthy, have offered in the presence of Your Majesty, may be acceptable to You, and through Your mercy obtain forgiveness for me and all for whom I have offered it. Through Christ our Lord. Amen.

THE LAST BLESSING

He kisses the altar, and facing the people, says:

MAY almighty God bless you: ✠ the Father, and the Son, and the Holy Spirit.
S. Amen.

The Last Gospel and Prayers after Low Mass are conveniently placed inside the back cover.

"One of the soldiers opened His side with a lance."

FEAST OF THE SACRED HEART

THIRD FRIDAY AFTER PENTECOST

The Feast of the Sacred Heart of Jesus is a reminder of all that we owe to the love of our Divine Redeemer. It is an appeal to our gratitude and it should prompt us to offer to the Divine Heart satisfaction and reparation for the numerous offenses of which we and others have been guilty. (WHITE VESTMENTS)

This Mass may be said on the First Friday of each month.

PRAYERS AT THE FOOT OF THE ALTAR

IN THE name of the Father, ✠ and of the Son, and of the Holy Spirit. Amen.

Priest. I will go in to the altar of God.

Server. The God of my gladness and joy.

Psalm 42

DO ME justice, O God, and fight my fight against a faithless people; from the deceitful and impious man rescue me.

S. For You, O God, are my strength. Why do You keep me so far away? Why must I go about in mourning, with the enemy oppressing me?

P. Send forth Your light and Your fidelity; they shall lead me on and bring me to Your holy mountain, to Your dwelling-place.

S. Then will I go in to the altar of God, the God of my gladness and joy.

P. Then will I give You thanks upon the harp, O God, my God. Why are you so downcast, O my soul? Why do you sigh within me?

S. Hope in God! For I shall again be thanking Him in the presence of my Savior and my God.

P. Glory be to the Father, and to the Son, and to the Holy Spirit.

S. As it was in the beginning, is now, and ever shall be, world without end. Amen.

P. I will go in to the altar of God.

S. The God of my gladness and joy.

P. Our help ✠ is in the name of the Lord.

S. Who made heaven and earth.

P. I confess to almighty God, etc.

S. May almighty God have mercy on you, forgive you your sins, and bring you to life everlasting.

P. Amen.

The Server, bowing, says the "Confiteor."

I CONFESS to almighty God, to Blessed Mary, ever Virgin, to Blessed Michael the Archangel, to Blessed John the Baptist, to the Holy Apostles Peter and Paul, and to all the Saints, and to you, Father, that I have sinned exceedingly in thought, word and deed, *through my fault, through my fault, through my most grievous fault.* Therefore I beseech Blessed Mary, ever Virgin, Blessed Michael the Archangel, Blessed John the Baptist, the Holy

Apostles Peter and Paul, and all the Saints, and you, Father, to pray to the Lord our God for me.
P. May almighty God have mercy on you, forgive you your sins, and bring you to life everlasting.
S. Amen.

MAY the almighty and merciful Lord grant us pardon, ✠ absolution, and remission of our sins. S. Amen.
P. Will You not, O God, give us life?
S. And shall not Your people rejoice in You?
P. Show us, O Lord, Your kindness.
S. And grant us Your salvation.
P. O Lord, hear my prayer.
S. And let my cry come to You.
P. The Lord be with you.
S. And with your spirit. *P.* Let us pray.

Going up to the altar, the Priest prays silently:

TAKE away from us our sins, O Lord, we beseech You, that we may enter with pure minds into the Holy of Holies. Through Christ our Lord. Amen.

WE BESEECH You, O Lord, by the merits of Your Saints (*he kisses the altar*) whose relics lie here, and of all the Saints: deign in Your mercy to pardon me all my sins. Amen.

THE INTROIT • Ps. 32, 11. 19. 1

At the right side of the altar, the Priest says:

THE thoughts of His Heart are to all generations: to deliver them from death and preserve them in spite of famine. (*P.T.* Alleluia, alleluia.) *Ps.* Exult, you just, in the Lord; praise from the upright is fitting. Glory be to the Father, and to the Son, and to the Holy Spirit. As it was in the beginning, is now, and ever shall be, world without end. Amen. — The thoughts of His Heart are to all generations: to deliver them from death and preserve them in spite of famine. (*P.T.* Alleluia, alleluia.)

THE KYRIE

P. Lord, have mercy. *S.* Lord, have mercy. *P.* Lord, have mercy. *S.* Christ, have mercy. *P.* Christ, have mercy. *S.* Christ, have mercy. *P.* Lord, have mercy. *S.* Lord, have mercy. *P.* Lord, have mercy.

THE GLORIA

GLORY to God in the highest. And on earth peace to men of good will. We praise You. We bless You. We adore You. We glorify You. We give You thanks for Your great glory. O Lord God, heavenly King, God the Father almighty. O Lord Jesus Christ, the Only-begotten Son. O Lord God, Lamb of God, Son of the Father: You Who take away the sins of the world, have mercy on us. You Who take away the sins of the world, receive our prayer. You Who sit at the right hand of the Father, have mercy on us. For You alone are holy. You alone are the Lord. You alone, O Jesus Christ, are most high. Together with the Holy Spirit ✠ in the glory of God the Father. Amen.

The Priest kisses the altar and turns to the people, saying:

P. The Lord be with you. *S.* And with your spirit. *P.* Let us pray.

THE PRAYER

Going to the right (Epistle) side, he says:

O GOD, You mercifully deign to bestow on us in the Heart of Your Son, wounded by our sins, an infinite treasure of love; grant, we beseech You, that rendering It the devout homage of our affection, we may also make a worthy reparation for our sins. Through the same our Lord Jesus Christ, Your Son, Who lives and reigns with You in the unity of the Holy Spirit, God, world without end. S. Amen.

THE EPISTLE • Eph. 3, 8-12. 14-19

BRETHREN: To me, the very least of all saints, there was given this grace, to announce among the Gentiles the good tidings of the unfathomable riches of Christ, and to enlighten all men as to what is the dispensation of the mystery which has been hidden from eternity in God, Who created all things; in order that through the Church there be made known to the Principalities and the Powers in the heavens the manifold wisdom of God according to the eternal purpose which He accomplished in Christ Jesus our Lord. In Him we have assurance and confident access through faith in Him. For this reason I bend my knees to the Father of our Lord Jesus Christ, from Whom all fatherhood in heaven and on earth receives its name, that He may grant you from His glorious riches to be strengthened with power through His Spirit unto the progress of the inner man; and to have Christ dwelling through faith in your hearts: so that, being rooted and grounded in love, you may be able to comprehend with all the saints what is the breadth and length and height and depth, and to know Christ's love which surpasses knowledge, in order that you may be filled unto all the fullness of God. S. Thanks be to God.

THE GRADUAL • Ps. 24, 8-9

GOOD and upright is the Lord; thus He shows sinners the way. ℣. He guides the humble to justice; He teaches the humble His way.

Alleluia, alleluia. ℣. *Matt. 11*, 29. Take My yoke upon you, and learn from Me, for I am meek, and humble of heart: and you will find rest for your souls. Alleluia.

After Septuagesima, omit Alleluia and versicle, and say:

THE TRACT • Ps. 102, 8-10

GRACIOUS and merciful is the Lord, slow to anger and abounding in kindness. ℣. He will not always chide, nor does He keep His wrath forever. ℣. Not according to our sins does He deal with us, nor does He requite us according to our crimes.

During Paschaltime, omit Gradual and Tract, and say:

Alleluia, alleluia. ℣. *Matt. 11*, 29. Take My yoke upon you and learn from Me, for I am meek and humble of heart: and you will find rest for your souls. Alleluia. ℣. *Matt. 11*, 28. Come to me, all you who labor and are burdened, and I will give you rest. Alleluia.

PRAYER BEFORE THE GOSPEL

Bowing down at the center of the altar, he says:

CLEANSE my heart and my lips, O almighty God, Who cleansed the lips of the Prophet Isaias with a burning coal. In Your gracious mercy deign so to purify me that I may worthily proclaim Your holy Gospel. Through Christ our Lord. Amen.

Lord, grant Your blessing. The Lord be in my heart and on my lips, that I may worthily and fittingly proclaim His holy Gospel. Amen.

THE GOSPEL • John 19, 31-37

Going to the left (Gospel) side of the altar, he says:

P. The Lord be with you. S. And with your spirit.
P. ✠ The continuation of the holy Gospel according to Saint John. S. Glory be to You, O Lord.

AT THAT time, the Jews, since it was the Preparation Day, in order that the bodies might not remain upon the cross on the Sabbath (for that Sabbath was a solemn day), besought Pilate that their legs might be broken, and that they might be taken away. The soldiers therefore came and broke the legs of the first, and of the other, who had been crucified with Him. But when they came to Jesus, and saw that He was already dead, they did not break His legs; but one of the soldiers opened His side with a lance, and immediately there came out blood and water. And he who saw it has borne witness, and his witness is true; and he knows that he tells the truth, that you also may believe. For these things came to pass that the Scripture might be fulfilled, "Not a bone of Him shall you break." And again another Scripture says, "They shall look upon Him Whom they have pierced." S. Praise be to You, O Christ.

P. By the words of the Gospel, may our sins be taken away.

Omit Creed on First Fridays except in sung Masses.

THE NICENE CREED

At the center of the altar, he says:

I BELIEVE in one God, the Father almighty, Maker of heaven and earth, and of all things visible and invisible. And in one Lord Jesus Christ, the Only-begotten Son of God. Born of the Father before all ages. God of God; Light of Light; true God of true God. Begotten not made; of one being with the Father; by Whom all things were made. Who for us men, and for our salvation, came down from heaven. (*Here all genuflect.*) And was made Flesh by the Holy Spirit of the Virgin Mary: AND WAS MADE MAN. He was also crucified for us, suffered under Pontius Pilate and was buried. And on the third day He rose again according to the Scriptures. And ascending into heaven, He sits at the right hand of the Father. And He shall come again in glory to judge the living and the dead; and of His kingdom there shall be no end. And I believe in the Holy Spirit, Lord and Giver of life, Who proceeds from the Father and the Son. Who together with the Father and the Son is no less adored, and glorified: Who spoke by the Prophets. And I believe in One, Holy, Catholic and Apostolic Church. I confess one Baptism for the remission of sins. And I look for the resurrection of the dead. ✠ And the life of the world to come. Amen.

THE OFFERTORY

The Priest turns to the people and says:

P. The Lord be with you. *S.* And with your spirit.
P. Let us pray.

THE OFFERTORY VERSE • Ps. 68, 21

MY HEART expected reproach and misery; I looked for sympathy, but there was none; and for comforters, and I found none.

During Paschaltime, the Offertory Verse is as follows:

THE OFFERTORY VERSE • Ps. 39, 7-9

HOLOCAUSTS or sin-offerings You sought not; then said I: "Behold I come; in the written scroll it is prescribed for Me; to do Your will, O My God, is My delight, and Your law is within My Heart." Alleluia.

The Priest now uncovers the chalice, places the host on the paten and offering it up, says:

ACCEPT, O holy Father, almighty and eternal God, this spotless host, which I, Your unworthy servant, offer to You, my living and true God, to atone for my numberless sins, offenses, and negligences; on behalf of all here present and likewise for all faithful Christians living and dead, that it may profit me and them as a means of salvation to life everlasting. Amen.

He pours wine and water into the chalice, blessing the water before it is poured.

O GOD, Who established the nature of man in wondrous dignity, and still more admirably restored it, grant that through the mystery of this water and wine, we may be made partakers of His Divinity, Who has condescended to become partaker of our humanity, Jesus Christ, Your Son, our Lord. Who lives and reigns with You in the unity of the Holy Spirit, God, world without end. Amen.

Offering up the wine, the Priest says:

WE OFFER You, O Lord, the chalice of salvation, humbly begging of Your mercy that it may arise before Your Divine Majesty, with a pleasing fragrance, for our salvation and for that of the whole world. Amen.

Bowing down, the Priest says:

IN A humble spirit and with a contrite heart, may we be accepted by You, O Lord, and may our sacrifice so be offered in Your sight this day as to please You, O Lord God.

Raising his eyes and blessing the offering, he says:

COME, O Sanctifier, almighty and eternal God, and bless ✠ this sacrifice prepared for the glory of Your holy name.

WASHING THE FINGERS

I WASH my hands in innocence, and I go around Your altar, O Lord, giving voice to my thanks, and recounting all Your wondrous deeds. O Lord, I love the house in which You dwell, the tenting-place of Your glory. Gather not my soul with those of sinners, nor with men of blood my life. On their hands are crimes, and their right hands are full of bribes. But I walk in integrity; redeem me, and have pity on me. My foot stands on level ground; in the assemblies I will bless You, O Lord. Glory be to the Father, and to the Son, and to the Holy Spirit. As it was in the beginning, is now, and ever shall be, world without end. Amen.

ACCEPT, Most Holy Trinity, this offering which we are making to You in remembrance of the Passion, Resurrection, and Ascension of Jesus Christ, our Lord; and in honor of Blessed Mary, ever Virgin, Blessed John the Baptist, the Holy Apostles Peter and Paul, and of these, and of all the Saints; that it may add to their honor and aid our salvation; and may they deign to intercede in heaven for us who honor their memory here on earth. Through the same Christ our Lord. Amen.

The Priest turns toward the people and says:

Pray, brethren, that my sacrifice and yours may become acceptable to God the Father almighty.

S. May the Lord accept this sacrifice from your hands to the praise and glory of His name, for our advantage, and that of all His holy Church.
P. Amen.

THE SECRET

REGARD, we beseech You, O Lord, the ineffable charity of the Heart of Your beloved Son, that what we offer may be an acceptable gift and an atonement for our sins. Through the same our Lord Jesus Christ, Your Son, Who lives and reigns with You in the unity of the Holy Spirit, God.
P. World without end. *S.* Amen.

PREFACE—CANON

P. The Lord be with you. *S.* And with your spirit.
P. Lift up your hearts.
S. We have lifted them up to the Lord.
P. Let us give thanks to the Lord, our God.
S. It is fitting and just.

IT IS fitting indeed and just, right and helpful to salvation, always and everywhere to give thanks to You, O holy Lord, Father almighty, everlasting God, Who willed that Your Only-begotten Son should be pierced by the soldier's lance as He hung upon the Cross; that the Heart thus opened, the sanctuary of divine bounty, should pour out on us an abundance of mercy and grace, and as It never ceases to burn with love for us, It may be for the devout a haven of rest, and for the penitent an ever-open refuge of salvation. And therefore, with Angels and Archangels, with Thrones and Dominations, and with the whole host of the heavenly army, we sing a hymn to Your glory, saying again and again (*the bell is rung 3 times*):

HOLY, HOLY, HOLY, Lord God of Hosts. Heaven and earth are filled with Your glory. Hosanna in the highest. ✠ Blessed is He Who comes in the name of the Lord. Hosanna in the highest.

THE CANON OF THE MASS

THEREFORE, most gracious Father, we humbly beg of You and entreat You through Jesus Christ Your Son, our Lord, (*he kisses the altar*) to deem acceptable and bless these ✠ gifts, these ✠ offerings, these ✠ holy and unspotted oblations which, in the first place, we offer You for Your Holy Catholic Church, that You would deign to give her peace and protection, to unite and guard her throughout the world, together with Your servant *N.*, our Pope, and *N.*, our Bishop; and all true believers who cherish the Catholic and Apostolic Faith.

Commemoration of the Living

REMEMBER, O Lord, Your servants and handmaids, N. and N., (*name them*) and all here present, whose faith and devotion are known to You, on whose behalf we offer to You, or who themselves offer to You, this sacrifice of praise for themselves, families and friends, for the good of their souls, for their hope of salvation and deliverance from all harm, and who offer their homage to You, eternal, living and true God.

Commemoration of the Saints

IN THE unity of holy fellowship we observe the memory, first of all, of the glorious and ever Virgin Mary, Mother of our Lord and God Jesus Christ; next, that of Your Blessed Apostles and

Martyrs, Peter and Paul, Andrew, James, John, Thomas, James, Philip, Bartholomew, Matthew, Simon and Thaddeus; of Linus, Cletus, Clement, Sixtus, Cornelius, Cyprian, Lawrence, Chrysogonus, John and Paul, Cosmas and Damian, and of all Your Saints, by whose merits and prayers grant that we may be always fortified by the help of Your protection. Through the same Christ our Lord. Amen.

Spreading his hands over the oblation, he says:

GRACIOUSLY accept, then, we beseech You, O Lord, this service of our worship and that of all Your household. Provide that our days be spent in Your peace, save us from everlasting damnation, and cause us to be numbered in the flock You have chosen. Through Christ our Lord. Amen.

O GOD, deign to bless ✠ what we offer, and make it approved, ✠ effective, ✠ right, and wholly pleasing in every way, that it may become for our good, the Body ✠ and Blood ✠ of Your dearly beloved Son, Jesus Christ our Lord.

CONSECRATION—ELEVATION

WHO, the day before He suffered, took bread into His holy and venerable hands, and having raised His eyes to heaven, to You, O God, His almighty Father, giving thanks to You, He blessed it, ✠ broke it, and gave it to His disciples, saying: All of you take and eat of this:

FOR THIS IS MY BODY.

IN LIKE manner, when the supper was done, taking also this goodly chalice into His holy and venerable hands, again giving thanks to You, He blessed ✠ it, and gave it to His disciples, saying: All of you take and drink of this:

FOR THIS IS THE CHALICE OF MY BLOOD OF THE NEW AND ETERNAL COVENANT: THE MYSTERY OF FAITH: WHICH SHALL BE SHED FOR YOU AND FOR MANY UNTO THE FORGIVENESS OF SINS.

After replacing the chalice on the corporal, he says:

As often as you shall do these things, in memory of Me shall you do them.

Offering of the Victim

MINDFUL, therefore, O Lord, not only of the blessed Passion of the same Christ, Your Son, our Lord, but also of His Resurrection from the dead, and finally His glorious Ascension into heaven, we, Your ministers, as also Your holy people, offer to Your supreme Majesty, of the gifts bestowed upon us, the pure ✠ Victim, the holy ✠ Victim, the all-perfect ✠ Victim: the holy ✠ Bread of life eternal and the Chalice ✠ of unending salvation.

AND this deign to regard with gracious and kindly attention and hold acceptable, as You deigned to accept the offerings of Abel, Your just servant, and the sacrifice of Abraham our patriarch, and that which Your chief priest Melchisedec offered to You, a holy sacrifice and a spotless victim.

MOST humbly we implore You, almighty God, bid these offerings to be brought by the hands of Your holy angel to Your altar above; before the face of Your Divine Majesty; that those of us who, by sharing in the Sacrifice of this altar, shall receive the Most Sacred ✠ Body and ✠ Blood of Your Son, may be filled with every grace and heavenly blessing. Through the same Christ our Lord. Amen.

Commemoration of the Dead

REMEMBER also, O Lord, Your servants and handmaids, N. and N., who have gone before us with the sign of faith, and rest in the sleep of peace. (*Here pray for the dead.*) To these, O Lord, and to all who rest in Christ, we beseech You to grant of Your goodness, a place of comfort, light and peace. Through the same Christ our Lord. Amen.

TO US sinners also, Your servants, trusting in the greatness of Your mercy, deign to grant some part and fellowship with Your Holy Apostles and Martyrs: with John, Stephen, Matthias, Barnabas, Ignatius, Alexander, Marcellinus, Peter, Felicitas, Perpetua, Agatha, Lucy, Agnes, Cecilia, Anastasia, and all Your Saints; into whose company, we implore You to admit us, not weighing our merits, but freely granting us pardon. Through Christ our Lord.

THROUGH Whom, O Lord, You always create, ✠ sanctify, ✠ fill with life, ✠ bless, and bestow upon us all good things.

The Minor Elevation

THROUGH ✠ Him, and with ✠ Him, and in ✠ Him, is to You, God the Father ✠ almighty, in the unity of the Holy ✠ Spirit, all honor and glory, world without end. S. Amen.

THE COMMUNION AND THANKSGIVING

Let us pray. Prompted by saving precepts, and taught by Your divine teaching, we dare to say:

OUR FATHER, Who art in heaven, hallowed be Thy name: Thy kingdom come: Thy will be done on earth as it is in heaven. Give us this day

our daily bread; and forgive us our trespasses, as we forgive those who trespass against us. And lead us not into temptation: *S.* But deliver us from evil. *P.* Amen.

DELIVER us, we beseech You, O Lord, from all evils, past, present, and to come; and by the intercession of the Blessed and glorious Mary, ever Virgin, Mother of God, together with Your Blessed Apostles Peter and Paul, and Andrew, and all the Saints, grant of Your goodness, peace in our days, that aided by the riches of Your mercy, we may be always free from sin and safe from all disturbance.

Through the same our Lord Jesus Christ, Your Son, Who lives and reigns with You in the unity of the Holy Spirit, God, world without end. *S.* Amen.

P. May the peace ✠ of the Lord be ✠ always with ✠ you. *S.* And with your spirit.

The Priest puts a small particle into the chalice, saying:

May this mingling and consecration of the Body and Blood of our Lord Jesus Christ help us who receive it to life everlasting. Amen.

LAMB of God, You Who take away the sins of the world, have mercy on us.

Lamb of God, You Who take away the sins of the world, have mercy on us.

Lamb of God, You Who take away the sins of the world, grant us peace.

PRAYERS BEFORE HOLY COMMUNION

Then inclining toward the altar, he says:

O LORD Jesus Christ, Who said to Your Apostles: "Peace I leave with you, My peace I give to you," regard not my sins but the faith of Your

Church, and deign to give her peace and unity according to Your Will: Who live and reign, God, world without end. Amen.

O LORD Jesus Christ, Son of the living God, Who, by the will of the Father, with the co-operation of the Holy Spirit, have by Your death given life to the world, deliver me by this Your Most Sacred Body and Blood from all my sins and from every evil. Make me always cling to Your commandments, and never permit me to be separated from You. Who with the same God the Father and the Holy Spirit, live and reign, God, world without end. Amen.

LET not the partaking of Your Body, O Lord Jesus Christ, which I, though unworthy, presume to receive, turn to my judgment and condemnation; but through Your goodness, may it become a safeguard and an effective remedy, both of soul and body. Who live and reign with God the Father, in the unity of the Holy Spirit, God, world without end. Amen.

COMMUNION OF THE PRIEST

I WILL take the Bread of heaven, and call upon the name of the Lord.

Lord, I am not worthy that You should come under my roof; but only say the word, and my soul will be healed. (3 *times.*)

Making the Sign of the Cross with the Host, he says:

MAY the Body of our Lord Jesus Christ preserve my soul to life everlasting. Amen.

What return shall I make to the Lord for all He has given me? I will take the Chalice of salvation, and I will call upon the name of the Lord. Prais-

ing will I call upon the Lord and I shall be saved from my enemies.

Making the Sign of the Cross with the chalice, he says:

MAY the Blood of our Lord Jesus Christ preserve my soul to life everlasting. Amen.

The Priest reverently consumes the Precious Blood.

COMMUNION OF THE FAITHFUL

The Server and people say the "Confiteor."

P. May almighty God have mercy on you, forgive you your sins, and bring you to life everlasting. S. Amen.

P. May the almighty and merciful Lord grant you pardon, ✠ absolution and remission of your sins. S. Amen.

Holding up a Sacred Host, the Priest says:

Behold the Lamb of God, behold Him Who takes away the sins of the world.

Lord, I am not worthy that You should come under my roof; but only say the word, and my soul will be healed. (3 *times.*)

The Priest says to each communicant:

May the Body of our Lord Jesus Christ preserve your soul to life everlasting. Amen.

The Priest purifies the chalice with wine, saying:

WHAT has passed our lips as food, O Lord, may we possess in purity of heart, that what is given to us in time, be our healing for eternity.

He purifies his fingers with wine and water, saying:

MAY Your Body, O Lord, which I have eaten, and Your Blood which I have drunk, cleave to my very soul, and grant that no trace of sin be found in me, whom these pure and holy mysteries have renewed. Who live and reign, world without end. Amen.

THE COMMUNION • John 19, 34

ONE of the soldiers opened His side with a lance, and immediately there came out blood and water.

During Paschaltime, the Communion is as follows:

THE COMMUNION • John 7, 37

IF ANYONE thirst, let him come to Me and drink, alleluia, alleluia.

The Priest, turning to the people, says:

P. The Lord be with you. *S.* And with your spirit.
P. Let us pray.

THE POSTCOMMUNION

MAY Your holy mysteries, O Lord Jesus, impart to us a divine fervor, whereby, having known the sweetness of Your most tender Heart, we may learn to despise what is earthly and to love what is heavenly. Who live and reign with God the Father, in the unity of the Holy Spirit, God, world without end. *S.* Amen.

FINAL PRAYERS

P. The Lord be with you. *S.* And with your spirit.
P. Go, you are dismissed. *S.* Thanks be to God.

MAY the tribute of my worship be pleasing to You, Most Holy Trinity, and grant that the sacrifice which I, all unworthy, have offered in the presence of Your Majesty, may be acceptable to You, and through Your mercy obtain forgiveness for me and all for whom I have offered it. Through Christ our Lord. Amen.

THE LAST BLESSING

MAY almighty God bless you: ✠ the Father, and the Son, and the Holy Spirit. *S.* Amen.

The Last Gospel is placed inside the back cover. Prayers after Low Mass are omitted on First Fridays.

"Rejoice . . . I have found my sheep that was lost."

THIRD SUNDAY AFTER PENTECOST

Two parables in today's Gospel speak of the joy of regaining what had been lost, as a symbol of the joy in heaven at the conversion of one sinner. Christ came to seek straying souls. He lived, suffered, and died to regain what was lost. (GREEN VESTMENTS)

PRAYERS AT THE FOOT OF THE ALTAR

IN THE name of the Father, ✠ and of the Son, and of the Holy Spirit. Amen.

Priest. I will go in to the altar of God.

Server. The God of my gladness and joy.

Psalm 42

DO ME justice, O God, and fight my fight against a faithless people; from the deceitful and impious man rescue me.

S. For You, O God, are my strength. Why do You keep me so far away? Why must I go about in mourning, with the enemy oppressing me?

P. Send forth Your light and Your fidelity; they shall lead me on and bring me to Your holy mountain, to Your dwelling-place.

S. Then will I go in to the altar of God, the God of my gladness and joy.
P. Then will I give You thanks upon the harp, O God, my God. Why are you so downcast, O my soul? Why do you sigh within me?
S. Hope in God! For I shall again be thanking Him in the presence of my Savior and my God.
P. Glory be to the Father, and to the Son, and to the Holy Spirit.
S. As it was in the beginning, is now, and ever shall be, world without end. Amen.
P. I will go in to the altar of God.
S. The God of my gladness and joy.
P. Our help ✠ is in the name of the Lord.
S. Who made heaven and earth.
P. I confess to almighty God, etc.
S. May almighty God have mercy on you, forgive you your sins, and bring you to life everlasting.
P. Amen.

The Server, bowing, says the "Confiteor."

I CONFESS to almighty God, to Blessed Mary, ever Virgin, to Blessed Michael the Archangel, to Blessed John the Baptist, to the Holy Apostles Peter and Paul, and to all the Saints, and to you, Father, that I have sinned exceedingly in thought, word and deed, *through my fault, through my fault, through my most grievous fault.* Therefore I beseech Blessed Mary, ever Virgin, Blessed Michael the Archangel, Blessed John the Baptist, the Holy Apostles Peter and Paul, and all the Saints, and you, Father, to pray to the Lord our God for me.
P. May almighty God have mercy on you, forgive you your sins, and bring you to life everlasting.
S. Amen.

MAY the almighty and merciful Lord grant us pardon, ✠ absolution, and remission of our sins. *S.* Amen.

P. Will You not, O God, give us life?
S. And shall not Your people rejoice in You?
P. Show us, O Lord, Your kindness.
S. And grant us Your salvation.
P. O Lord, hear my prayer.
S. And let my cry come to You.
P. The Lord be with you.
S. And with your spirit. *P.* Let us pray.

Going up to the altar, the Priest prays silently:

TAKE away from us our sins, O Lord, we beseech You, that we may enter with pure minds into the Holy of Holies. Through Christ our Lord. Amen.

WE BESEECH You, O Lord, by the merits of Your Saints (*he kisses the altar*) whose relics lie here, and of all the Saints: deign in Your mercy to pardon me all my sins. Amen.

THE INTROIT • Ps. 24, 16. 18. 1. 2

At the right side of the altar, the Priest says:

LOOK toward me, and have pity on me, O Lord, for I am alone and afflicted. Put an end to my affliction and my suffering, and take away all my sins, O my God. *Ps.* To You, I lift up my soul, O Lord. In You, O my God, I trust; let me not be put to shame. Glory be to the Father, and to the Son, and to the Holy Spirit. As it was in the beginning, is now, and ever shall be, world without end. Amen. — Look toward me, and have pity on me, O Lord, for I am alone and afflicted. Put an end to my affliction and my suffering, and take away all my sins, O my God.

THE KYRIE

P. Lord, have mercy. *S.* Lord, have mercy. *P.* Lord, have mercy. *S.* Christ, have mercy. *P.* Christ, have mercy. *S.* Christ, have mercy. *P.* Lord, have mercy. *S.* Lord, have mercy. *P.* Lord, have mercy.

THE GLORIA

GLORY to God in the highest. And on earth peace to men of good will. We praise You. We bless You. We adore You. We glorify You. We give You thanks for Your great glory. O Lord God, heavenly King, God the Father almighty. O Lord Jesus Christ, the Only-begotten Son. O Lord God, Lamb of God, Son of the Father: You Who take away the sins of the world, have mercy on us. You Who take away the sins of the world, receive our prayer. You Who sit at the right hand of the Father, have mercy on us. For You alone are holy. You alone are the Lord. You alone, O Jesus Christ, are most high. Together with the Holy Spirit ✠ in the glory of God the Father. Amen.

The Priest kisses the altar and turns to the people, saying:

P. The Lord be with you. *S.* And with your spirit. *P.* Let us pray.

THE PRAYER

Going to the right (Epistle) side, he says:

O GOD, the Protector of those who hope in You, without Whom nothing is strong, nothing holy: multiply upon us Your mercy, that with You as our ruler and guide, we may so pass through temporal things, as not to lose those which are eternal. Through our Lord Jesus Christ, Your Son, Who lives and reigns with You in the unity of the Holy Spirit, God, world without end. *S.* Amen.

THE EPISTLE • 1 Pet. 5, 6-11

BELOVED: Humble yourselves under the mighty hand of God, that He may exalt you in the time of visitation; cast all your anxiety upon Him, because He cares for you. Be sober, be watchful! For your adversary the devil, as a roaring lion, goes about seeking someone to devour. Resist him, steadfast in the Faith, knowing that the same suffering befalls your brethren all over the world. But the God of all grace, Who has called us unto His eternal glory in Christ Jesus, will Himself, after we have suffered a little while, perfect, strengthen and establish us. To Him is the glory and the dominion forever and ever. Amen. S. Thanks be to God.

THE GRADUAL • Ps. 54, 23. 17. 19

CAST your care upon the Lord, and He will support you. ℣. When I called upon the Lord, He heard my voice from those who war against me.

Alleluia, alleluia. ℣. *Ps.* 7, 12. A just judge is God, strong and patient; is He angry every day? Alleluia.

PRAYER BEFORE THE GOSPEL

Bowing down at the center of the altar, he says:

CLEANSE my heart and my lips, O almighty God, Who cleansed the lips of the Prophet Isaias with a burning coal. In Your gracious mercy deign so to purify me that I may worthily proclaim Your holy Gospel. Through Christ our Lord. Amen.

Lord, grant Your blessing. The Lord be in my heart and on my lips, that I may worthily and fittingly proclaim His holy Gospel. Amen.

THE GOSPEL • Luke 15, 1-10

Going to the left (Gospel) side of the altar, he says:

P. The Lord be with you. S. And with your spirit.

P. ✠ The continuation of the holy Gospel according to Saint Luke. *S.* Glory be to You, O Lord.

AT THAT time, the publicans and sinners were drawing near to Jesus to listen to Him. And the Pharisees and the Scribes murmured, saying, "This Man welcomes sinners and eats with them." But He spoke to them this parable, saying, "What man of you having a hundred sheep, and losing one of them, does not leave the ninety-nine in the desert, and go after that which is lost, until he finds it? And when he has found it, he lays it upon his shoulders rejoicing. And on coming home he calls together his friends and neighbors, saying to them, 'Rejoice with me, because I have found my sheep that was lost.' I say to you that, even so, there will be joy in heaven over one sinner who repents, more than over ninety-nine just who have no need of repentance. Or what woman, having ten drachmas, if she loses one drachma, does not light a lamp and sweep the house and search carefully until she finds it? And when she has found it, she calls together her friends and neighbors, saying, 'Rejoice with me, for I have found the drachma that I had lost.' Even so, I say to you, there will be joy among the angels of God over one sinner who repents." *S.* Praise be to You, O Christ.

P. By the words of the Gospel, may our sins be taken away.

THE NICENE CREED

At the center of the altar, he says:

I BELIEVE in one God, the Father almighty, Maker of heaven and earth, and of all things visible and invisible. And in one Lord Jesus Christ, the Only-begotten Son of God. Born of the Father before all ages. God of God; Light of Light; true

God of true God. Begotten not made; of one being with the Father; by Whom all things were made. Who for us men, and for our salvation, came down from heaven. (*Here all genuflect.*) And was made Flesh by the Holy Spirit of the Virgin Mary: AND WAS MADE MAN. He was also crucified for us, suffered under Pontius Pilate and was buried. And on the third day He rose again according to the Scriptures. And ascending into heaven, He sits at the right hand of the Father. And He shall come again in glory to judge the living and the dead; and of His kingdom there shall be no end. And I believe in the Holy Spirit, Lord and Giver of life, Who proceeds from the Father and the Son. Who together with the Father and the Son is no less adored, and glorified: Who spoke by the Prophets. And I believe in One, Holy, Catholic and Apostolic Church. I confess one Baptism for the remission of sins. And I look for the resurrection of the dead. ✠ And the life of the world to come. Amen.

THE OFFERTORY

The Priest turns to the people and says:

P. The Lord be with you. *S.* And with your spirit.
P. Let us pray.

THE OFFERTORY VERSE • Ps. 9, 11. 12. 13

THEY trust in You who cherish Your name, O Lord, for You forsake not those who seek You. Sing praise to the Lord enthroned in Sion, for He has not forgotten the cry of the afflicted.

The Priest now uncovers the chalice, places the host on the paten and offering it up, says:

ACCEPT, O holy Father, almighty and eternal God, this spotless host, which I, Your unworthy servant, offer to You, my living and true

God, to atone for my numberless sins, offenses, and negligences; on behalf of all here present and likewise for all faithful Christians living and dead, that it may profit me and them as a means of salvation to life everlasting. Amen.

He pours wine and water into the chalice, blessing the water before it is poured.

O GOD, Who established the nature of man in wondrous dignity, and still more admirably restored it, grant that through the mystery of this water and wine, we may be made partakers of His Divinity, Who has condescended to become partaker of our humanity, Jesus Christ, Your Son, our Lord. Who lives and reigns with You in the unity of the Holy Spirit, God, world without end. Amen.

Offering up the wine, the Priest says:

WE OFFER You, O Lord, the chalice of salvation, humbly begging of Your mercy that it may arise before Your Divine Majesty, with a pleasing fragrance, for our salvation and for that of the whole world. Amen.

Bowing down, the Priest says:

IN A humble spirit and with a contrite heart, may we be accepted by You, O Lord, and may our sacrifice so be offered in Your sight this day as to please You, O Lord God.

Raising his eyes and blessing the offering, he says:

COME, O Sanctifier, almighty and eternal God, and bless ✠ this sacrifice prepared for the glory of Your holy name.

WASHING THE FINGERS

I WASH my hands in innocence, and I go around Your altar, O Lord, giving voice to my thanks,

and recounting all Your wondrous deeds. O Lord, I love the house in which You dwell, the tenting-place of Your glory. Gather not my soul with those of sinners, nor with men of blood my life. On their hands are crimes, and their right hands are full of bribes. But I walk in integrity; redeem me, and have pity on me. My foot stands on level ground; in the assemblies I will bless You, O Lord. Glory be to the Father, and to the Son, and to the Holy Spirit. As it was in the beginning, is now, and ever shall be, world without end. Amen.

ACCEPT, Most Holy Trinity, this offering which we are making to You in remembrance of the Passion, Resurrection, and Ascension of Jesus Christ, our Lord; and in honor of Blessed Mary, ever Virgin, Blessed John the Baptist, the Holy Apostles Peter and Paul, and of these, and of all the Saints; that it may add to their honor and aid our salvation; and may they deign to intercede in heaven for us who honor their memory here on earth. Through the same Christ our Lord. Amen.

The Priest turns toward the people and says:

Pray, brethren, that my sacrifice and yours may become acceptable to God the Father almighty.

S. May the Lord accept this sacrifice from your hands to the praise and glory of His name, for our advantage, and that of all His holy Church.

P. Amen.

THE SECRET

REGARD with favor, O Lord, the gifts of Your suppliant Church, and grant that they may avail to the salvation of the faithful who partake of them. Through our Lord Jesus Christ, Your Son,

Who lives and reigns with You in the unity of the Holy Spirit, God.
P. World without end. *S.* Amen.

PREFACE—CANON

P. The Lord be with you. *S.* And with your spirit.
P. Lift up your hearts.
S. We have lifted them up to the Lord.
P. Let us give thanks to the Lord, our God.
S. It is fitting and just.

IT IS fitting indeed and just, right and helpful to salvation, for us always and everywhere to give thanks to You, O holy Lord, Father almighty, everlasting God, Who with Your Only-begotten Son and the Holy Spirit are one God, one Lord; not in the unity of a single person, but in the trinity of a single nature. For that which we believe on Your revelation concerning Your glory, that same we believe of Your Son, that same of the Holy Spirit, without difference or discrimination. So that in confessing the true and everlasting Godhead, we shall adore distinction in Persons, oneness in being, and equality in Majesty. This the Angels and Archangels, the Cherubim, too, and the Seraphim do praise; day by day they cease not to cry out as with one voice, saying (*the bell is rung 3 times*):

HOLY, HOLY, HOLY, Lord God of Hosts. Heaven and earth are filled with Your glory. Hosanna in the highest. ✠ Blessed is He Who comes in the name of the Lord. Hosanna in the highest.

THE CANON OF THE MASS

THEREFORE, most gracious Father, we humbly beg of You and entreat You through Jesus

Christ Your Son, our Lord, (*he kisses the altar*) to deem acceptable and bless these ✠ gifts, these ✠ offerings, these ✠ holy and unspotted oblations which, in the first place, we offer You for Your Holy Catholic Church, that You would deign to give her peace and protection, to unite and guard her throughout the world, together with Your servant N., our Pope, and N., our Bishop; and all true believers who cherish the Catholic and Apostolic Faith.

Commemoration of the Living

REMEMBER, O Lord, Your servants and handmaids, N. and N., (*name them*) and all here present, whose faith and devotion are known to You, on whose behalf we offer to You, or who themselves offer to You, this sacrifice of praise for themselves, families and friends, for the good of their souls, for their hope of salvation and deliverance from all harm, and who offer their homage to You, eternal, living and true God.

Commemoration of the Saints

IN THE unity of holy fellowship we observe the memory, first of all, of the glorious and ever Virgin Mary, Mother of our Lord and God Jesus Christ; next, that of Your Blessed Apostles and Martyrs, Peter and Paul, Andrew, James, John, Thomas, James, Philip, Bartholomew, Matthew, Simon and Thaddeus; of Linus, Cletus, Clement, Sixtus, Cornelius, Cyprian, Lawrence, Chrysogonus, John and Paul, Cosmas and Damian, and of all Your Saints, by whose merits and prayers grant that we may be always fortified by the help of Your protection. Through the same Christ our Lord. Amen.

Spreading his hands over the oblation, he says:

GRACIOUSLY accept, then, we beseech You, O Lord, this service of our worship and that of all Your household. Provide that our days be spent in Your peace, save us from everlasting damnation, and cause us to be numbered in the flock You have chosen. Through Christ our Lord. Amen.

O GOD, deign to bless ✠ what we offer, and make it approved, ✠ effective, ✠ right, and wholly pleasing in every way, that it may become for our good, the Body ✠ and Blood ✠ of Your dearly beloved Son, Jesus Christ our Lord.

CONSECRATION—ELEVATION

WHO, the day before He suffered, took bread into His holy and venerable hands, and having raised His eyes to heaven, to You, O God, His almighty Father, giving thanks to You, He blessed it, ✠ broke it, and gave it to His disciples, saying: All of you take and eat of this:

FOR THIS IS MY BODY.

IN LIKE manner, when the supper was done, taking also this goodly chalice into His holy and venerable hands, again giving thanks to You, He blessed ✠ it, and gave it to His disciples, saying: All of you take and drink of this:

FOR THIS IS THE CHALICE OF MY BLOOD OF THE NEW AND ETERNAL COVENANT: THE MYSTERY OF FAITH: WHICH SHALL BE SHED FOR YOU AND FOR MANY UNTO THE FORGIVENESS OF SINS.

After replacing the chalice on the corporal, he says:

As often as you shall do these things, in memory of Me shall you do them.

Offering of the Victim

MINDFUL, therefore, O Lord, not only of the blessed Passion of the same Christ, Your Son, our Lord, but also of His Resurrection from the dead, and finally His glorious Ascension into heaven, we, Your ministers, as also Your holy people, offer to Your supreme Majesty, of the gifts bestowed upon us, the pure ✠ Victim, the holy ✠ Victim, the all-perfect ✠ Victim: the holy ✠ Bread of life eternal and the Chalice ✠ of unending salvation.

AND this deign to regard with gracious and kindly attention and hold acceptable, as You deigned to accept the offerings of Abel, Your just servant, and the sacrifice of Abraham our patriarch, and that which Your chief priest Melchisedec offered to You, a holy sacrifice and a spotless victim.

MOST humbly we implore You, almighty God, bid these offerings to be brought by the hands of Your holy angel to Your altar above; before the face of Your Divine Majesty; that those of us who, by sharing in the Sacrifice of this altar, shall receive the Most Sacred ✠ Body and ✠ Blood of Your Son, may be filled with every grace and heavenly blessing. Through the same Christ our Lord. Amen.

Commemoration of the Dead

REMEMBER also, O Lord, Your servants and handmaids, N. and N., who have gone before us with the sign of faith, and rest in the sleep of peace. (*Here pray for the dead.*) To these, O Lord, and to all who rest in Christ, we beseech You to grant of Your goodness, a place of comfort, light

and peace. Through the same Christ our Lord. Amen.

TO US sinners also, Your servants, trusting in the greatness of Your mercy, deign to grant some part and fellowship with Your Holy Apostles and Martyrs: with John, Stephen, Matthias, Barnabas, Ignatius, Alexander, Marcellinus, Peter, Felicitas, Perpetua, Agatha, Lucy, Agnes, Cecilia, Anastasia; and all Your Saints; into whose company, we implore You to admit us, not weighing our merits, but freely granting us pardon. Through Christ our Lord.

THROUGH Whom, O Lord, You always create, ✠ sanctify, ✠ fill with life, ✠ bless, and bestow upon us all good things.

The Minor Elevation

THROUGH ✠ Him, and with ✠ Him, and in ✠ Him, is to You, God the Father ✠ almighty, in the unity of the Holy ✠ Spirit, all honor and glory, world without end. S. Amen.

THE COMMUNION AND THANKSGIVING

Let us pray. Prompted by saving precepts, and taught by Your divine teaching, we dare to say:

OUR FATHER, Who art in heaven, hallowed be Thy name: Thy kingdom come: Thy will be done on earth as it is in heaven. Give us this day our daily bread; and forgive us our trespasses, as we forgive those who trespass against us. And lead us not into temptation: S. But deliver us from evil. *P.* Amen.

DELIVER us, we beseech You, O Lord, from all evils, past, present, and to come; and by

the intercession of the Blessed and glorious Mary, ever Virgin, Mother of God, together with Your Blessed Apostles Peter and Paul, and Andrew, and all the Saints, grant of Your goodness, peace in our days, that aided by the riches of Your mercy, we may be always free from sin and safe from all disturbance.

Through the same our Lord Jesus Christ, Your Son, Who lives and reigns with You in the unity of the Holy Spirit, God, world without end.

S. Amen.

P. May the peace ✠ of the Lord be ✠ always with ✠ you.

S. And with your spirit.

The Priest puts a small particle into the chalice, saying:

May this mingling and consecration of the Body and Blood of our Lord Jesus Christ help us who receive it to life everlasting. Amen.

LAMB of God, You Who take away the sins of the world, have mercy on us.

Lamb of God, You Who take away the sins of the world, have mercy on us.

Lamb of God, You Who take away the sins of the world, grant us peace.

PRAYERS BEFORE HOLY COMMUNION

Then inclining toward the altar, he says:

O LORD Jesus Christ, Who said to Your Apostles: "Peace I leave with you, My peace I give to you," regard not my sins but the faith of Your Church, and deign to give her peace and unity according to Your Will: Who live and reign, God, world without end. Amen.

O LORD Jesus Christ, Son of the living God, Who, by the will of the Father, with the co-operation of the Holy Spirit, have by Your death given life to the world, deliver me by this Your Most Sacred Body and Blood from all my sins and from every evil. Make me always cling to Your commandments, and never permit me to be separated from You. Who with the same God the Father and the Holy Spirit, live and reign, God, world without end. Amen.

LET not the partaking of Your Body, O Lord Jesus Christ, which I, though unworthy, presume to receive, turn to my judgment and condemnation; but through Your goodness, may it become a safeguard and an effective remedy, both of soul and body. Who live and reign with God the Father, in the unity of the Holy Spirit, God, world without end. Amen.

COMMUNION OF THE PRIEST

I WILL take the Bread of heaven, and call upon the name of the Lord.

Lord, I am not worthy that You should come under my roof; but only say the word, and my soul will be healed. (3 *times*.)

Making the Sign of the Cross with the Host, he says:

MAY the Body of our Lord Jesus Christ preserve my soul to life everlasting. Amen.

What return shall I make to the Lord for all He has given me? I will take the Chalice of salvation, and I will call upon the name of the Lord. Praising will I call upon the Lord and I shall be saved from my enemies.

Making the Sign of the Cross with the chalice, he says:

MAY the Blood of our Lord Jesus Christ preserve my soul to life everlasting. Amen.

The Priest reverently consumes the Precious Blood.

COMMUNION OF THE FAITHFUL

The Server and people say the "Confiteor."

P. May almighty God have mercy on you, forgive you your sins, and bring you to life everlasting. *S.* Amen.

P. May the almighty and merciful Lord grant you pardon, ✠ absolution and remission of your sins. *S.* Amen.

Holding up a Sacred Host, the Priest says:

Behold the Lamb of God, behold Him Who takes away the sins of the world.

Lord, I am not worthy that You should come under my roof; but only say the word, and my soul will be healed. (3 *times.*)

The Priest says to each communicant:

May the Body of our Lord Jesus Christ preserve your soul to life everlasting. Amen.

The Priest purifies the chalice with wine, saying:

WHAT has passed our lips as food, O Lord, may we possess in purity of heart, that what is given to us in time, be our healing for eternity.

He purifies his fingers with wine and water, saying:

MAY Your Body, O Lord, which I have eaten, and Your Blood which I have drunk, cleave to my very soul, and grant that no trace of sin be found in me, whom these pure and holy mysteries have renewed. Who live and reign, world without end. Amen.

THE COMMUNION • Luke 15, 10

I SAY to you: there is joy among the angels of God over one sinner who repents.

The Priest, turning to the people, says:

P. The Lord be with you. *S.* And with your spirit.
P. Let us pray.

THE POSTCOMMUNION

MAY Your sacrament which we have received quicken us, O Lord; and having cleansed us from sin, prepare us for Your everlasting mercy. Through our Lord Jesus Christ, Your Son, Who lives and reigns with You in the unity of the Holy Spirit, God, world without end. *S.* Amen.

FINAL PRAYERS

The Priest turns again to the people, and says:

P. The Lord be with you. *S.* And with your spirit.
P. Go, you are dismissed. *S.* Thanks be to God.

MAY the tribute of my worship be pleasing to You, Most Holy Trinity, and grant that the sacrifice which I, all unworthy, have offered in the presence of Your Majesty, may be acceptable to You, and through Your mercy obtain forgiveness for me and all for whom I have offered it. Through Christ our Lord. Amen.

THE LAST BLESSING

He kisses the altar, and facing the people, says:

MAY almighty God bless you: ✠ the Father, and the Son, and the Holy Spirit. *S.* Amen.

The Last Gospel and Prayers after Low Mass are conveniently placed inside the back cover.

"They enclosed a great number of fishes . . ."

FOURTH SUNDAY AFTER PENTECOST

This Sunday brings to our minds the miraculous draught of fishes, at the suggestion of the Master. Let us cast our nets following the Lord's suggestions. We shall always be spiritually successful if we try to follow God's will and plan. (GREEN VESTMENTS)

PRAYERS AT THE FOOT OF THE ALTAR

IN THE name of the Father, ✠ and of the Son, and of the Holy Spirit. Amen.

Priest. I will go in to the altar of God.

Server. The God of my gladness and joy.

Psalm 42

DO ME justice, O God, and fight my fight against a faithless people; from the deceitful and impious man rescue me.

S. For You, O God, are my strength. Why do You keep me so far away? Why must I go about in mourning, with the enemy oppressing me?

P. Send forth Your light and Your fidelity; they shall lead me on and bring me to Your holy mountain, to Your dwelling-place.

S. Then will I go in to the altar of God, the God of my gladness and joy.
P. Then will I give You thanks upon the harp, O God, my God. Why are you so downcast, O my soul? Why do you sigh within me?
S. Hope in God! For I shall again be thanking Him in the presence of my Savior and my God.
P. Glory be to the Father, and to the Son, and to the Holy Spirit.
S. As it was in the beginning, is now, and ever shall be, world without end. Amen.
P. I will go in to the altar of God.
S. The God of my gladness and joy.
P. Our help ✠ is in the name of the Lord.
S. Who made heaven and earth.
P. I confess to almighty God, etc.
S. May almighty God have mercy on you, forgive you your sins, and bring you to life everlasting.
P. Amen.

The Server, bowing, says the "Confiteor."

I CONFESS to almighty God, to Blessed Mary, ever Virgin, to Blessed Michael the Archangel, to Blessed John the Baptist, to the Holy Apostles Peter and Paul, and to all the Saints, and to you, Father, that I have sinned exceedingly in thought, word and deed, *through my fault, through my fault, through my most grievous fault.* Therefore I beseech Blessed Mary, ever Virgin, Blessed Michael the Archangel, Blessed John the Baptist, the Holy Apostles Peter and Paul, and all the Saints, and you, Father, to pray to the Lord our God for me.
P. May almighty God have mercy on you, forgive you your sins, and bring you to life everlasting.
S. Amen.

MAY the almighty and merciful Lord grant us pardon, ✠ absolution, and remission of our sins. S. Amen.

P. Will You not, O God, give us life?
S. And shall not Your people rejoice in You?
P. Show us, O Lord, Your kindness.
S. And grant us Your salvation.
P. O Lord, hear my prayer.
S. And let my cry come to You.
P. The Lord be with you.
S. And with your spirit. *P.* Let us pray.

Going up to the altar, the Priest prays silently:

TAKE away from us our sins, O Lord, we beseech You, that we may enter with pure minds into the Holy of Holies. Through Christ our Lord. Amen.

WE BESEECH You, O Lord, by the merits of Your Saints (*he kisses the altar*) whose relics lie here, and of all the Saints: deign in Your mercy to pardon me all my sins. Amen.

THE INTROIT • Ps. 26, 1. 2. 3

At the right side of the altar, the Priest says:

THE Lord is my light and my salvation; whom should I fear? The Lord is my life's refuge; of whom should I be afraid? My enemies that trouble me, themselves stumble and fall. *Ps.* Though an army encamp against me, my heart will not fear. Glory be to the Father, and to the Son, and to the Holy Spirit. As it was in the beginning, is now, and ever shall be, world without end. Amen. — The Lord is my light and my salvation; whom should I fear? The Lord is my life's refuge; of whom should I be afraid? My enemies that trouble me, themselves stumble and fall.

THE KYRIE

P. Lord, have mercy. *S.* Lord, have mercy. *P.* Lord, have mercy. *S.* Christ, have mercy. *P.* Christ, have mercy. *S.* Christ, have mercy. *P.* Lord, have mercy. *S.* Lord, have mercy. *P.* Lord, have mercy.

THE GLORIA

GLORY to God in the highest. And on earth peace to men of good will. We praise You. We bless You. We adore You. We glorify You. We give You thanks for Your great glory. O Lord God, heavenly King, God the Father almighty. O Lord Jesus Christ, the Only-begotten Son. O Lord God, Lamb of God, Son of the Father: You Who take away the sins of the world, have mercy on us. You Who take away the sins of the world, receive our prayer. You Who sit at the right hand of the Father have mercy on us. For You alone are holy. You alone are the Lord. You alone, O Jesus Christ, are most high. Together with the Holy Spirit ✠ in the glory of God the Father. Amen.

The Priest kisses the altar and turns to the people, saying:

P. The Lord be with you. *S.* And with your spirit. *P.* Let us pray.

THE PRAYER

Going to the right (Epistle) side, he says:

GRANT, we beseech You, O Lord, that the course of the world may, by Your governance, be peaceably ordered for us, and that Your Church may rejoice in quiet devotion. Through our Lord Jesus Christ, Your Son, Who lives and reigns with

You in the unity of the Holy Spirit, God, world without end. *S.* Amen.

THE EPISTLE • Rom. 8, 18-23

BRETHREN: I reckon that the sufferings of the present time are not worthy to be compared with the glory to come that will be revealed in us. For the eager longing of creation awaits the revelation of the sons of God. For creation was made subject to vanity — not by its own will but by reason of Him Who made it subject — in hope, because creation itself also will be delivered from its slavery to corruption into the freedom of the glory of the sons of God. For we know that all creation groans and travails in pain until now. And not only it, but we ourselves also who have the first-fruits of the Spirit — we ourselves groan within ourselves, waiting for the adoption as sons of God, the redemption of our body, in Christ Jesus our Lord. *S.* Thanks be to God.

THE GRADUAL • Ps. 78, 9. 10

PARDON our sins, O Lord; why should the nations say, "Where is their God?" ℣. Help us, O God our Savior; because of the glory of Your name, O Lord, deliver us.

Alleluia, alleluia. ℣. *Ps. 9, 5. 10.* O God, seated on Your throne, judging justly: be a stronghold for the oppressed in times of distress. Alleluia.

PRAYER BEFORE THE GOSPEL

Bowing down at the center of the altar, he says:

CLEANSE my heart and my lips, O almighty God, Who cleansed the lips of the Prophet Isaias with a burning coal. In Your gracious mercy

deign so to purify me that I may worthily proclaim Your holy Gospel. Through Christ our Lord. Amen.

Lord, grant Your blessing. The Lord be in my heart and on my lips, that I may worthily and fittingly proclaim His holy Gospel. Amen.

THE GOSPEL • Luke 5, 1-11

Going to the left (Gospel) side of the altar, he says:

P. The Lord be with you. *S.* And with your spirit.
P. ✠ The continuation of the holy Gospel according to Saint Luke. *S.* Glory be to You, O Lord.

AT THAT time, while the crowds were pressing upon Jesus to hear the word of God, He was standing by Lake Genesareth. And He saw two boats moored by the lake, but the fishermen had left them and were washing their nets. And getting into one of the boats, the one that was Simon's, He asked him to put out a little from the land. And sitting down, He began to teach the crowds from the boat. But when He had ceased speaking, He said to Simon, "Put out into the deep, and lower your nets for a catch." And Simon answered and said to Him, "Master, the whole night through we have toiled and have taken nothing; but at Your word I will lower the net." And when they had done so, they enclosed a great number of fishes, but their net was breaking. And they beckoned to their comrades in the other boat to come and help them. And they came and filled both the boats, so that they began to sink. But when Simon Peter saw this, he fell down at Jesus' knees, saying, "Depart from me, for I am a sinful man, O Lord." For he and all who were with him were amazed at the catch of fish they had made; and so were also James and John, the sons of Zebedee, who were partners with Simon. And Jesus said to Simon, "Do not be afraid; henceforth you shall catch men." And when they had brought their boats to land, they left all and followed Him. S. Praise be to You, O Christ.

P. By the words of the Gospel, may our sins be taken away.

THE NICENE CREED

At the center of the altar, he says:

I BELIEVE in one God, the Father almighty, Maker of heaven and earth, and of all things visible and invisible. And in one Lord Jesus Christ, the Only-begotten Son of God. Born of the Father before all ages. God of God; Light of Light; true God of true God. Begotten not made; of one being with the Father; by Whom all things were made. Who for us men, and for our salvation, came down from heaven. (*Here all genuflect.*) And was made Flesh by the Holy Spirit of the Virgin Mary: AND WAS MADE MAN. He was also crucified for us, suffered under Pontius Pilate and was buried. And on the third day He rose again according to the Scriptures. And ascending into heaven, He sits at the right hand of the Father. And He shall come again in glory to judge the living and the dead; and of His kingdom there shall be no end. And I believe in the Holy Spirit, Lord and Giver of life, Who proceeds from the Father and the Son. Who together with the Father and the Son is no less adored, and glorified: Who spoke by the Prophets. And I believe in One, Holy, Catholic and Apostolic Church. I confess one Baptism for the remission of sins. And I look for the resurrection of the dead. ✠ And the life of the world to come. Amen.

THE OFFERTORY

The Priest turns to the people and says:

P. The Lord be with you. **S.** And with your spirit.
P. Let us pray.

THE OFFERTORY VERSE • Ps. 12, 4. 5

GIVE light to my eyes that I may never sleep in death, lest my enemy say, "I have overcome him."

The Priest now uncovers the chalice, places the host on the paten and offering it up, says:

ACCEPT, O holy Father, almighty and eternal God, this spotless host, which I, Your unworthy servant, offer to You, my living and true God, to atone for my numberless sins, offenses, and negligences; on behalf of all here present and likewise for all faithful Christians living and dead, that it may profit me and them as a means of salvation to life everlasting. Amen.

He pours wine and water into the chalice, blessing the water before it is poured.

O GOD, Who established the nature of man in wondrous dignity, and still more admirably restored it, grant that through the mystery of this water and wine, we may be made partakers of His Divinity, Who has condescended to become partaker of our humanity, Jesus Christ, Your Son, our Lord. Who lives and reigns with You in the unity of the Holy Spirit, God, world without end. Amen.

Offering up the wine, the Priest says:

WE OFFER You, O Lord, the chalice of salvation, humbly begging of Your mercy that it may arise before Your Divine Majesty, with a pleasing fragrance, for our salvation and for that of the whole world. Amen.

Bowing down, the Priest says:

IN A humble spirit and with a contrite heart, may we be accepted by You, O Lord, and may our sacrifice so be offered in Your sight this day as to please You, O Lord God.

Raising his eyes and blessing the offering, he says:

COME, O Sanctifier, almighty and eternal God, and bless ✠ this sacrifice prepared for the glory of Your holy name.

WASHING THE FINGERS

I WASH my hands in innocence, and I go around Your altar, O Lord, giving voice to my thanks, and recounting all Your wondrous deeds. O Lord, I love the house in which You dwell, the tenting-place of Your glory. Gather not my soul with those of sinners, nor with men of blood my life. On their hands are crimes, and their right hands are full of bribes. But I walk in integrity; redeem me, and have pity on me. My foot stands on level ground; in the assemblies I will bless You, O Lord. Glory be to the Father, and to the Son, and to the Holy Spirit. As it was in the beginning, is now, and ever shall be, world without end. Amen.

ACCEPT, Most Holy Trinity, this offering which we are making to You in remembrance of the Passion, Resurrection, and Ascension of Jesus Christ, our Lord; and in honor of Blessed Mary, ever Virgin, Blessed John the Baptist, the Holy Apostles Peter and Paul, and of these, and of all the Saints; that it may add to their honor and aid our salvation; and may they deign to intercede in heaven for us who honor their memory here on earth. Through the same Christ our Lord. Amen.

The Priest turns toward the people and says:

Pray, brethren, that my sacrifice and yours may become acceptable to God the Father almighty.

S. May the Lord accept this sacrifice from your hands to the praise and glory of His name, for our advantage, and that of all His holy Church.
P. Amen.

THE SECRET

BE APPEASED, we beseech You, O Lord, by the acceptance of our offerings, and graciously compel our wills, even though rebellious, to turn to You. Through our Lord Jesus Christ, Your Son, Who lives and reigns with You in the unity of the Holy Spirit, God.
P. World without end. *S.* Amen.

PREFACE—CANON

P. The Lord be with you. *S.* And with your spirit.
P. Lift up your hearts.
S. We have lifted them up to the Lord.
P. Let us give thanks to the Lord, our God.
S. It is fitting and just.

IT IS fitting indeed and just, right and helpful to salvation, for us always and everywhere to give thanks to You, O holy Lord, Father almighty, everlasting God, Who with Your Only-begotten Son and the Holy Spirit are one God, one Lord; not in the unity of a single person, but in the trinity of a single nature. For that which we believe on Your revelation concerning Your glory, that same we believe of Your Son, that same of the Holy Spirit, without difference or discrimination. So that in confessing the true and everlasting Godhead, we shall adore distinction in Persons, oneness in being, and equality in Majesty. This the Angels and Archangels, the Cherubim, too, and the Seraphim do praise; day by day they cease not to cry out as with one voice, saying (*the bell is rung 3 times*):

HOLY, HOLY, HOLY, Lord God of Hosts. Heaven and earth are filled with Your glory. Hosanna in the highest. ✠ Blessed is He Who comes in the name of the Lord. Hosanna in the highest.

THE CANON OF THE MASS

THEREFORE, most gracious Father, we humbly beg of You and entreat You through Jesus Christ Your Son, our Lord, (*he kisses the altar*) to deem acceptable and bless these ✠ gifts, these ✠ offerings, these ✠ holy and unspotted oblations which, in the first place, we offer You for Your Holy Catholic Church, that You would deign to give her peace and protection, to unite and guard her throughout the world, together with Your servant N., our Pope, and N., our Bishop; and all true believers who cherish the Catholic and Apostolic Faith.

Commemoration of the Living

REMEMBER, O Lord, Your servants and handmaids, N. and N., (*name them*) and all here present, whose faith and devotion are known to You, on whose behalf we offer to You, or who themselves offer to You, this sacrifice of praise for themselves, families and friends, for the good of their souls, for their hope of salvation and deliverance from all harm, and who offer their homage to You, eternal, living and true God.

Commemoration of the Saints

IN THE unity of holy fellowship we observe the memory, first of all, of the glorious and ever Virgin Mary, Mother of our Lord and God Jesus Christ; next, that of Your Blessed Apostles and Martyrs, Peter and Paul, Andrew, James, John, Thomas, James, Philip, Bartholomew, Matthew, Simon and Thaddeus; of Linus, Cletus, Clement, Sixtus, Cornelius, Cyprian, Lawrence, Chrysogonus, John and Paul, Cosmas and Damian, and of all Your Saints, by whose merits and prayers grant that we may be always fortified by the help of Your protection. Through the same Christ our Lord. Amen.

Spreading his hands over the oblation, he says:

GRACIOUSLY accept, then, we beseech You, O Lord, this service of our worship and that of all Your household. Provide that our days be spent in Your peace, save us from everlasting damnation, and cause us to be numbered in the flock You have chosen. Through Christ our Lord. Amen.

O GOD, deign to bless ✠ what we offer, and make it approved, ✠ effective, ✠ right, and wholly pleasing in every way, that it may become for our good, the Body ✠ and Blood ✠ of Your dearly beloved Son, Jesus Christ our Lord.

CONSECRATION—ELEVATION

WHO, the day before He suffered, took bread into His holy and venerable hands, and having raised His eyes to heaven, to You, O God, His almighty Father, giving thanks to You, He blessed it, ✠ broke it, and gave it to His disciples, saying: All of you take and eat of this:

FOR THIS IS MY BODY.

IN LIKE manner, when the supper was done, taking also this goodly chalice into His holy and venerable hands, again giving thanks to You, He blessed ✠ it, and gave it to His disciples, saying: All of you take and drink of this:

FOR THIS IS THE CHALICE OF MY BLOOD OF THE NEW AND ETERNAL COVENANT: THE MYSTERY OF FAITH: WHICH SHALL BE SHED FOR YOU AND FOR MANY UNTO THE FORGIVENESS OF SINS.

After replacing the chalice on the corporal, he says:

As often as you shall do these things, in memory of Me shall you do them.

Offering of the Victim

MINDFUL, therefore, O Lord, not only of the blessed Passion of the same Christ, Your Son, our Lord, but also of His Resurrection from the dead, and finally His glorious Ascension into heaven, we, Your ministers, as also Your holy people, offer to Your supreme Majesty, of the gifts bestowed upon us, the pure ✠ Victim, the holy ✠ Victim, the all-perfect ✠ Victim: the holy ✠ Bread of life eternal and the Chalice ✠ of unending salvation.

AND this deign to regard with gracious and kindly attention and hold acceptable, as You deigned to accept the offerings of Abel, Your just servant, and the sacrifice of Abraham our patriarch, and that which Your chief priest Melchisedec offered to You, a holy sacrifice and a spotless victim.

MOST humbly we implore You, almighty God, bid these offerings to be brought by the hands of Your holy angel to Your altar above; before the face of Your Divine Majesty; that those of us who, by sharing in the Sacrifice of this altar, shall receive the Most Sacred ✠ Body and ✠ Blood of Your Son, may be filled with every grace and heavenly blessing. Through the same Christ our Lord. Amen.

Commemoration of the Dead

REMEMBER also, O Lord, Your servants and handmaids, N. and N., who have gone before us with the sign of faith, and rest in the sleep of peace. (*Here pray for the dead.*) To these, O Lord, and to all who rest in Christ, we beseech You to grant of Your goodness, a place of comfort, light and peace. Through the same Christ our Lord. Amen.

TO US sinners also, Your servants, trusting in the greatness of Your mercy, deign to grant some part and fellowship with Your Holy Apostles and Martyrs: with John, Stephen, Matthias, Barnabas, Ignatius, Alexander, Marcellinus, Peter, Felicitas, Perpetua, Agatha, Lucy, Agnes, Cecilia, Anastasia, and all Your Saints; into whose company, we implore You to admit us, not weighing our merits, but freely granting us pardon. Through Christ our Lord.

THROUGH Whom, O Lord, You always create, ✠ sanctify, ✠ fill with life, ✠ bless, and bestow upon us all good things.

The Minor Elevation

THROUGH ✠ Him, and with ✠ Him, and in ✠ Him, is to You, God the Father ✠ almighty, in the unity of the Holy ✠ Spirit, all honor and glory, world without end. S. Amen.

THE COMMUNION AND THANKSGIVING

Let us pray. Prompted by saving precepts, and taught by Your divine teaching, we dare to say:

OUR FATHER, Who art in heaven, hallowed be Thy name: Thy kingdom come: Thy will be done on earth as it is in heaven. Give us this day our daily bread; and forgive us our trespasses, as we forgive those who trespass against us. And lead us not into temptation: S. But deliver us from evil.
P. Amen.

DELIVER us, we beseech You, O Lord, from all evils, past, present, and to come; and by the intercession of the Blessed and glorious Mary, ever Virgin, Mother of God, together with Your Blessed Apostles Peter and Paul, and Andrew, and all the Saints, grant of Your goodness, peace in our days, that aided by the riches of Your mercy, we may be always free from sin and safe from all disturbance.

Through the same our Lord Jesus Christ, Your Son, Who lives and reigns with You in the unity of the Holy Spirit, God, world without end.

S. Amen.

P. May the peace ✠ of the Lord be ✠ always with ✠ you.

S. And with your spirit.

The Priest puts a small particle into the chalice, saying:

May this mingling and consecration of the Body and Blood of our Lord Jesus Christ help us who receive it to life everlasting. Amen.

LAMB of God, You Who take away the sins of the world, have mercy on us.

Lamb of God, You Who take away the sins of the world, have mercy on us.

Lamb of God, You Who take away the sins of the world, grant us peace.

PRAYERS BEFORE HOLY COMMUNION

Then inclining toward the altar, he says:

O LORD Jesus Christ, Who said to Your Apostles: "Peace I leave with you, My peace I give to you," regard not my sins but the faith of Your Church, and deign to give her peace and unity according to Your Will: Who live and reign, God, world without end. Amen.

O LORD Jesus Christ, Son of the living God, Who, by the will of the Father, with the cooperation of the Holy Spirit, have by Your death given life to the world, deliver me by this Your Most Sacred Body and Blood from all my sins and from every evil. Make me always cling to Your commandments, and never permit me to be separated from You. Who with the same God the Father and the Holy Spirit, live and reign, God, world without end. Amen.

LET not the partaking of Your Body, O Lord Jesus Christ, which I, though unworthy, presume to receive, turn to my judgment and condemnation; but through Your goodness, may it become a safeguard and an effective remedy, both of soul and body. Who live and reign with God the Father, in the unity of the Holy Spirit, God, world without end. Amen.

COMMUNION OF THE PRIEST

I WILL take the Bread of heaven, and call upon the name of the Lord.

Lord, I am not worthy that You should come under my roof; but only say the word, and my soul will be healed. (3 *times.*)

Making the Sign of the Cross with the Host, he says:

MAY the Body of our Lord Jesus Christ preserve my soul to life everlasting. Amen.

What return shall I make to the Lord for all He has given me? I will take the Chalice of salvation, and I will call upon the name of the Lord. Praising will I call upon the Lord and I shall be saved from my enemies.

Making the Sign of the Cross with the chalice, he says:

MAY the Blood of our Lord Jesus Christ preserve my soul to life everlasting. Amen.

The Priest reverently consumes the Precious Blood.

COMMUNION OF THE FAITHFUL

The Server and people say the "Confiteor."

P. May almighty God have mercy on you, forgive you your sins, and bring you to life everlasting. S. Amen.

P. May the almighty and merciful Lord grant you pardon, ✠ absolution and remission of your sins. S. Amen.

Holding up a Sacred Host, the Priest says:

Behold the Lamb of God, behold Him Who takes away the sins of the world.

Lord, I am not worthy that You should come under my roof; but only say the word, and my soul will be healed. (3 *times.*)

The Priest says to each communicant:

May the Body of our Lord Jesus Christ preserve your soul to life everlasting. Amen.

The Priest purifies the chalice with wine, saying:

WHAT has passed our lips as food, O Lord, may we possess in purity of heart, that what is given to us in time, be our healing for eternity.

He purifies his fingers with wine and water, saying:

MAY Your Body, O Lord, which I have eaten, and Your Blood which I have drunk, cleave to my very soul, and grant that no trace of sin be found in me, whom these pure and holy mysteries have renewed. Who live and reign, world without end. Amen.

THE COMMUNION • Ps. 17, 3

O LORD, my rock, my fortress, my deliverer: my God, my rock of refuge!

The Priest, turning to the people, says:

P. The Lord be with you. S. And with your spirit.
P. Let us pray.

THE POSTCOMMUNION

MAY the mysteries which we have received purify us, we beseech You, O Lord, and may we be defended by their power. Through our Lord Jesus Christ, Your Son, Who lives and reigns with You in the unity of the Holy Spirit, God, world without end. S. Amen.

FINAL PRAYERS

The Priest turns again to the people, and says:

P. The Lord be with you. S. And with your spirit.
P. Go, you are dismissed. S. Thanks be to God.

MAY the tribute of my worship be pleasing to You, Most Holy Trinity, and grant that the sacrifice which I, all unworthy, have offered in the presence of Your Majesty, may be acceptable to You, and through Your mercy obtain forgiveness for me and all for whom I have offered it. Through Christ our Lord. Amen.

THE LAST BLESSING

He kisses the altar, and facing the people, says:

MAY almighty God bless you: ✠ the Father, and the Son, and the Holy Spirit.

S. Amen.

The Last Gospel and Prayers after Low Mass are conveniently placed inside the back cover.

"Go first to be reconciled with your brother . . ."

FIFTH SUNDAY AFTER PENTECOST

One heart and one mind with Christ and through Him with our neighbor, such is the Christian ideal. Hence, our Lord demands that we seek reconciliation with an offended person before making our offering at the altar. (GREEN VESTMENTS)

PRAYERS AT THE FOOT OF THE ALTAR

IN THE name of the Father, ✠ and of the Son, and of the Holy Spirit. Amen.

Priest. I will go in to the altar of God.

Server. The God of my gladness and joy.

Psalm 42

DO ME justice, O God, and fight my fight against a faithless people; from the deceitful and impious man rescue me.

S. For You, O God, are my strength. Why do You keep me so far away? Why must I go about in mourning, with the enemy oppressing me?

P. Send forth Your light and Your fidelity; they shall lead me on and bring me to Your holy mountain, to Your dwelling-place.

S. Then will I go in to the altar of God, the God of my gladness and joy.

P. Then will I give You thanks upon the harp, O God, my God. Why are you so downcast, O my soul? Why do you sigh within me?

S. Hope in God! For I shall again be thanking Him in the presence of my Savior and my God.

P. Glory be to the Father, and to the Son, and to the Holy Spirit.

S. As it was in the beginning, is now, and ever shall be, world without end. Amen.

P. I will go in to the altar of God.

S. The God of my gladness and joy.

P. Our help ✠ is in the name of the Lord.

S. Who made heaven and earth.

P. I confess to almighty God, etc.

S. May almighty God have mercy on you, forgive you your sins, and bring you to life everlasting.

P. Amen.

The Server, bowing, says the "Confiteor."

I CONFESS to almighty God, to Blessed Mary, ever Virgin, to Blessed Michael the Archangel, to Blessed John the Baptist, to the Holy Apostles Peter and Paul, and to all the Saints, and to you, Father, that I have sinned exceedingly in thought, word and deed, *through my fault, through my fault, through my most grievous fault.* Therefore I beseech Blessed Mary, ever Virgin, Blessed Michael the Archangel, Blessed John the Baptist, the Holy Apostles Peter and Paul, and all the Saints, and you, Father, to pray to the Lord our God for me.

P. May almighty God have mercy on you, forgive you your sins, and bring you to life everlasting.
S. Amen.

MAY the almighty and merciful Lord grant us pardon, ✠ absolution, and remission of our sins. *S*. Amen.
P. Will You not, O God, give us life?
S. And shall not Your people rejoice in You?
P. Show us, O Lord, Your kindness.
S. And grant us Your salvation.
P. O Lord, hear my prayer.
S. And let my cry come to You.
P. The Lord be with you.
S. And with your spirit. *P*. Let us pray.

Going up to the altar, the Priest prays silently:

TAKE away from us our sins, O Lord, we beseech You, that we may enter with pure minds into the Holy of Holies. Through Christ our Lord. Amen.

WE BESEECH You, O Lord, by the merits of Your Saints (*he kisses the altar*) whose relics lie here, and of all the Saints: deign in Your mercy to pardon me all my sins. Amen.

THE INTROIT • Ps. 26, 7. 9. 1

At the right side of the altar, the Priest says:

HEAR, O Lord, the sound of my call; be my helper: forsake me not: depise me not, O God my Savior. *Ps*. The Lord is my light and my salvation; whom should I fear? Glory be to the Father, and to the Son, and to the Holy Spirit. As it was in the beginning, is now, and ever shall be, world without end. Amen. — Hear, O Lord, the sound of my call; be my helper: forsake me not: despise me not, O God my Savior.

THE KYRIE

P. Lord, have mercy. *S.* Lord, have mercy. *P.* Lord, have mercy. *S.* Christ, have mercy. *P.* Christ, have mercy. *S.* Christ, have mercy. *P.* Lord, have mercy. *S.* Lord, have mercy. *P.* Lord, have mercy.

THE GLORIA

GLORY to God in the highest. And on earth peace to men of good will. We praise You. We bless You. We adore You. We glorify You. We give You thanks for Your great glory. O Lord God, heavenly King, God the Father almighty. O Lord Jesus Christ, the Only-begotten Son. O Lord God, Lamb of God, Son of the Father: You Who take away the sins of the world, have mercy on us. You Who take away the sins of the world, receive our prayer. You Who sit at the right hand of the Father, have mercy on us. For You alone are holy. You alone are the Lord. You alone, O Jesus Christ, are most high. Together with the Holy Spirit ✠ in the glory of God the Father. Amen.

The Priest kisses the altar and turns to the people, saying:

P. The Lord be with you. *S.* And with your spirit. *P.* Let us pray.

THE PRAYER

Going to the right (Epistle) side, he says:

O GOD, You have prepared invisible good things for those who love You; pour into our hearts an ardent love of You, that loving You in all things, and above all things, we may obtain Your promises, which exceed all that we can desire. Through our Lord Jesus Christ, Your Son, Who lives and reigns with You in the unity of the Holy Spirit, God, world without end. S. Amen.

THE EPISTLE • 1 Pet. 3, 8-15

BELOVED: Be all like-minded in prayer, compassionate, lovers of the brethren, merciful, reserved, humble; not rendering evil for evil, or abuse for abuse, but contrariwise, blessing; for unto this were you called that you might inherit a blessing. For, "He who would love life, and see good days, let him refrain his tongue from evil, and his lips that they speak no deceit. Let him turn away from evil and do good, let him seek after peace and pursue it. For the eyes of the Lord are upon the just, and His ears unto their prayers; but the face of the Lord is against those who do evil." And who is there to harm you, if you are zealous for what is good? But even if you suffer anything for justice' sake, blessed are you. So have no fear of their fear and do not be troubled. But hallow the Lord Christ in your hearts. S. Thanks be to God.

THE GRADUAL • Ps. 83, 10. 9

BEHOLD, O God, our Protector, and look on Your servants. ℣. O Lord God of Hosts, hear the prayers of Your servants.

Alleluia, alleluia. ℣. *Ps. 20, 1.* O Lord, in Your strength the king is glad; in Your victory how greatly he rejoices! Alleluia.

PRAYER BEFORE THE GOSPEL

Bowing down at the center of the altar, he says:

CLEANSE my heart and my lips, O almighty God, Who cleansed the lips of the Prophet

Isaias with a burning coal. In Your gracious mercy deign so to purify me that I may worthily proclaim Your holy Gospel. Through Christ our Lord. Amen.

Lord, grant Your blessing. The Lord be in my heart and on my lips, that I may worthily and fittingly proclaim His holy Gospel. Amen.

THE GOSPEL • Matt. 5, 20-24

Going to the left (Gospel) side of the altar, he says:

P. The Lord be with you. *S.* And with your spirit.
P. ✠ The continuation of the holy Gospel according to Saint Matthew. *S.* Glory be to You, O Lord.

AT THAT time, Jesus said to His disciples: "Unless your justice exceeds that of the Scribes and Pharisees, you shall not enter the kingdom of heaven. You have heard that it was said to the ancients, 'You shall not kill'; and that whoever shall kill shall be liable to judgment. But I say to you that everyone who is angry with his brother shall be liable to judgment; and whoever says to his brother, 'Raca,' shall be liable to the Sanhedrin; and whoever says, 'You fool!', shall be liable to the fire of Gehenna. Therefore, if you are offering your gift at the altar, and there remember that your brother has anything against you, leave your gift before the altar and go first to be reconciled to your brother; and then come and offer your gift."
S. Praise be to You, O Christ.

P. By the words of the Gospel, may our sins be taken away.

THE NICENE CREED

At the center of the altar, he says:

I BELIEVE in one God, the Father almighty, Maker of heaven and earth, and of all things

visible and invisible. And in one Lord Jesus Christ, the Only-begotten Son of God. Born of the Father before all ages. God of God; Light of Light; true God of true God. Begotten not made; of one being with the Father; by Whom all things were made. Who for us men, and for our salvation, came down from heaven. (*Here all genuflect.*) And was made Flesh by the Holy Spirit of the Virgin Mary: AND WAS MADE MAN. He was also crucified for us, suffered under Pontius Pilate and was buried. And on the third day He rose again according to the Scriptures. And ascending into heaven, He sits at the right hand of the Father. And He shall come again in glory to judge the living and the dead; and of His kingdom there shall be no end. And I believe in the Holy Spirit, Lord and Giver of life, Who proceeds from the Father and the Son. Who together with the Father and the Son is no less adored, and glorified: Who spoke by the Prophets. And I believe in One, Holy, Catholic and Apostolic Church. I confess one Baptism for the remission of sins. And I look for the resurrection of the dead. ✠ And the life of the world to come. Amen.

THE OFFERTORY

The Priest turns to the people and says:

P. The Lord be with you. *S.* And with your spirit.

P. Let us pray.

THE OFFERTORY VERSE • Ps. 15, 7. 8

I BLESS the Lord Who counsels me; I set God ever before me; with Him at my right hand I shall not be disturbed.

The Priest now uncovers the chalice, places the host on the paten and offering it up, says:

ACCEPT, O holy Father, almighty and eternal God, this spotless host, which I, Your unworthy servant, offer to You, my living and true God, to atone for my numberless sins, offenses, and negligences; on behalf of all here present and likewise for all faithful Christians living and dead, that it may profit me and them as a means of salvation to life everlasting. Amen.

He pours wine and water into the chalice, blessing the water before it is poured.

O GOD, Who established the nature of man in wondrous dignity, and still more admirably restored it, grant that through the mystery of this water and wine, we may be made partakers of His Divinity, Who has condescended to become partaker of our humanity, Jesus Christ, Your Son, our Lord. Who lives and reigns with You in the unity of the Holy Spirit, God, world without end. Amen.

Offering up the wine, the Priest says:

WE OFFER You, O Lord, the chalice of salvation, humbly begging of Your mercy that it may arise before Your Divine Majesty, with a pleasing fragrance, for our salvation and for that of the whole world. Amen.

Bowing down, the Priest says:

IN A humble spirit and with a contrite heart, may we be accepted by You, O Lord, and may our sacrifice so be offered in Your sight this day as to please You, O Lord God.

Raising his eyes and blessing the offering, he says:

COME, O Sanctifier, almighty and eternal God, and bless ✠ this sacrifice prepared for the glory of Your holy name.

WASHING THE FINGERS

I WASH my hands in innocence, and I go around Your altar, O Lord, giving voice to my thanks, and recounting all Your wondrous deeds. O Lord, I love the house in which You dwell, the tenting-place of Your glory. Gather not my soul with those of sinners, nor with men of blood my life. On their hands are crimes, and their right hands are full of bribes. But I walk in integrity; redeem me, and have pity on me. My foot stands on level ground; in the assemblies I will bless You, O Lord. Glory be to the Father, and to the Son, and to the Holy Spirit. As it was in the beginning, is now, and ever shall be, world without end. Amen.

ACCEPT, Most Holy Trinity, this offering which we are making to You in remembrance of the Passion, Resurrection, and Ascension of Jesus Christ, our Lord; and in honor of Blessed Mary, ever Virgin, Blessed John the Baptist, the Holy Apostles Peter and Paul, and of these, and of all the Saints; that it may add to their honor and aid our salvation; and may they deign to intercede in heaven for us who honor their memory here on earth. Through the same Christ our Lord. Amen.

The Priest turns toward the people and says:

Pray, brethren, that my sacrifice and yours may become acceptable to God the Father almighty.

S. May the Lord accept this sacrifice from your hands to the praise and glory of His name, for our advantage, and that of all His holy Church.

P. Amen.

THE SECRET

BE PROPITIOUS to our supplications, O Lord, and graciously receive these oblations of Your servants and handmaids, that what each one offered to the glory of Your name, may profit all to salvation. Through our Lord Jesus Christ, Your Son, Who lives and reigns with You in the unity of the Holy Spirit, God.

P. World without end. *S.* Amen.

PREFACE—CANON

P. The Lord be with you. *S.* And with your spirit.
P. Lift up your hearts.
S. We have lifted them up to the Lord.
P. Let us give thanks to the Lord, our God.
S. It is fitting and just.

IT IS fitting indeed and just, right and helpful to salvation, for us always and everywhere to give thanks to You, O holy Lord, Father almighty, everlasting God, Who with Your Only-begotten Son and the Holy Spirit are one God, one Lord; not in the unity of a single person, but in the trinity of a single nature. For that which we believe on Your revelation concerning Your glory, that same we believe of Your Son, that same of the Holy Spirit, without difference or discrimination. So that in confessing the true and everlasting Godhead, we shall adore distinction in Persons, oneness in being, and equality in Majesty. This the Angels and Archangels, the Cherubim, too, and the Seraphim do praise; day by day they cease not to cry out as with one voice, saying (*the bell is rung 3 times*):

HOLY, HOLY, HOLY, Lord God of Hosts. Heaven and earth are filled with Your glory. Hosanna in the highest. ✠ Blessed is He Who comes in the name of the Lord. Hosanna in the highest.

THE CANON OF THE MASS

THEREFORE, most gracious Father, we humbly beg of You and entreat You through Jesus Christ Your Son, our Lord, (*he kisses the altar*) to deem acceptable and bless these ✠ gifts, these ✠ offerings, these ✠ holy and unspotted oblations which, in the first place, we offer You for Your Holy Catholic Church, that You would deign to give her peace and protection, to unite and guard her throughout the world, together with Your servant N., our Pope, and N., our Bishop; and all true believers who cherish the Catholic and Apostolic Faith.

Commemoration of the Living

REMEMBER, O Lord, Your servants and handmaids, N. and N., (*name them*) and all here present, whose faith and devotion are known to You, on whose behalf we offer to You, or who themselves offer to You, this sacrifice of praise for themselves, families and friends, for the good of their souls, for their hope of salvation and deliverance from all harm, and who offer their homage to You, eternal, living and true God.

Commemoration of the Saints

IN THE unity of holy fellowship we observe the memory, first of all, of the glorious and ever Virgin Mary, Mother of our Lord and God Jesus Christ; next, that of Your Blessed Apostles and Martyrs, Peter and Paul, Andrew, James, John, Thomas, James, Philip, Bartholomew, Matthew, Simon and Thaddeus; of Linus, Cletus, Clement, Sixtus, Cornelius, Cyprian, Lawrence, Chrysogonus, John and Paul, Cosmas and Damian, and of all Your Saints, by whose merits and prayers grant that

we may be always fortified by the help of Your protection. Through the same Christ our Lord. Amen.

Spreading his hands over the oblation, he says:

GRACIOUSLY accept, then, we beseech You, O Lord, this service of our worship and that of all Your household. Provide that our days be spent in Your peace, save us from everlasting damnation, and cause us to be numbered in the flock You have chosen. Through Christ our Lord. Amen.

O GOD, deign to bless ✠ what we offer, and make it approved, ✠ effective, ✠ right, and wholly pleasing in every way, that it may become for our good, the Body ✠ and Blood ✠ of Your dearly beloved Son, Jesus Christ our Lord.

CONSECRATION—ELEVATION

WHO, the day before He suffered, took bread into His holy and venerable hands, and having raised His eyes to heaven, to You, O God, His almighty Father, giving thanks to You, He blessed it, ✠ broke it, and gave it to His disciples, saying: All of you take and eat of this:

FOR THIS IS MY BODY.

IN LIKE manner, when the supper was done, taking also this goodly chalice into His holy and venerable hands, again giving thanks to You, He blessed ✠ it, and gave it to His disciples, saying: All of you take and drink of this:

FOR THIS IS THE CHALICE OF MY BLOOD OF THE NEW AND ETERNAL COVENANT: THE MYSTERY OF FAITH: WHICH SHALL BE SHED FOR YOU AND FOR MANY UNTO THE FORGIVENESS OF SINS.

After replacing the chalice on the corporal, he says:

As often as you shall do these things, in memory of Me shall you do them.

Offering of the Victim

MINDFUL, therefore, O Lord, not only of the blessed Passion of the same Christ, Your Son, our Lord, but also of His Resurrection from the dead, and finally His glorious Ascension into heaven, we, Your ministers, as also Your holy people, offer to Your supreme Majesty, of the gifts bestowed upon us, the pure ✠ Victim, the holy ✠ Victim, the all-perfect ✠ Victim: the holy ✠ Bread of life eternal and the Chalice ✠ of unending salvation.

AND this deign to regard with gracious and kindly attention and hold acceptable, as You deigned to accept the offerings of Abel, Your just servant, and the sacrifice of Abraham our patriarch, and that which Your chief priest Melchisedec offered to You, a holy sacrifice and a spotless victim.

MOST humbly we implore You, almighty God, bid these offerings to be brought by the hands of Your holy angel to Your altar above; before the face of Your Divine Majesty; that those of us who, by sharing in the Sacrifice of this altar, shall receive the Most Sacred ✠ Body and ✠ Blood of Your Son, may be filled with every grace and heavenly blessing. Through the same Christ our Lord. Amen.

Commemoration of the Dead

REMEMBER also, O Lord, Your servants and handmaids, N. and N., who have gone before us with the sign of faith, and rest in the sleep of peace. (*Here pray for the dead.*) To these, O Lord,

and to all who rest in Christ, we beseech You to grant of Your goodness, a place of comfort, light and peace. Through the same Christ our Lord. Amen.

TO US sinners also, Your servants, trusting in the greatness of Your mercy, deign to grant some part and fellowship with Your Holy Apostles and Martyrs: with John, Stephen, Matthias, Barnabas, Ignatius, Alexander, Marcellinus, Peter, Felicitas, Perpetua, Agatha, Lucy, Agnes, Cecilia, Anastasia, and all Your Saints; into whose company, we implore You to admit us, not weighing our merits, but freely granting us pardon. Through Christ our Lord.

THROUGH Whom, O Lord, You always create, ✠ sanctify, ✠ fill with life, ✠ bless, and bestow upon us all good things.

The Minor Elevation

THROUGH ✠ Him, and with ✠ Him, and in ✠ Him, is to You, God the Father ✠ almighty, in the unity of the Holy ✠ Spirit, all honor and glory, world without end. S. Amen.

THE COMMUNION AND THANKSGIVING

Let us pray. Prompted by saving precepts, and taught by Your divine teaching, we dare to say:

OUR FATHER, Who art in heaven, hallowed be Thy name: Thy kingdom come: Thy will be done on earth as it is in heaven. Give us this day our daily bread; and forgive us our trespasses, as we forgive those who trespass against us. And lead us not into temptation: S. But deliver us from evil. **P.** Amen.

DELIVER us, we beseech You, O Lord, from all evils, past, present, and to come; and by the intercession of the Blessed and glorious Mary, ever Virgin, Mother of God, together with Your Blessed Apostles Peter and Paul, and Andrew, and all the Saints, grant of Your goodness, peace in our days, that aided by the riches of Your mercy, we may be always free from sin and safe from all disturbance.

Through the same our Lord Jesus Christ, Your Son, Who lives and reigns with You in the unity of the Holy Spirit, God, world without end. S. Amen.

P. May the peace ✠ of the Lord be ✠ always with ✠ you. S. And with your spirit.

The Priest puts a small particle into the chalice, saying:

May this mingling and consecration of the Body and Blood of our Lord Jesus Christ help us who receive it to life everlasting. Amen.

LAMB of God, You Who take away the sins of the world, have mercy on us.

Lamb of God, You Who take away the sins of the world, have mercy on us.

Lamb of God, You Who take away the sins of the world, grant us peace.

PRAYERS BEFORE HOLY COMMUNION

Then inclining toward the altar, he says:

O LORD Jesus Christ, Who said to Your Apostles: "Peace I leave with you, My peace I give to you," regard not my sins but the faith of Your Church, and deign to give her peace and unity according to Your Will: Who live and reign, God, world without end. Amen.

O LORD Jesus Christ, Son of the living God, Who, by the will of the Father, with the co-operation of the Holy Spirit, have by Your death given life to the world, deliver me by this Your Most Sacred Body and Blood from all my sins and from every evil. Make me always cling to Your commandments, and never permit me to be separated from You. Who with the same God the Father and the Holy Spirit, live and reign, God, world without end. Amen.

LET not the partaking of Your Body, O Lord Jesus Christ, which I, though unworthy, presume to receive, turn to my judgment and condemnation; but through Your goodness, may it become a safeguard and an effective remedy, both of soul and body. Who live and reign with God the Father, in the unity of the Holy Spirit, God, world without end. Amen.

COMMUNION OF THE PRIEST

I WILL take the Bread of heaven, and call upon the name of the Lord.

Lord, I am not worthy that You should come under my roof; but only say the word, and my soul will be healed. (3 *times.*)

Making the Sign of the Cross with the Host, he says:

MAY the Body of our Lord Jesus Christ preserve my soul to life everlasting. Amen.

What return shall I make to the Lord for all He has given me? I will take the Chalice of salvation, and I will call upon the name of the Lord. Praising will I call upon the Lord and I shall be saved from my enemies.

Making the Sign of the Cross with the chalice, he says:

MAY the Blood of our Lord Jesus Christ preserve my soul to life everlasting. Amen.

The Priest reverently consumes the Precious Blood.

COMMUNION OF THE FAITHFUL

The Server and people say the "Confiteor."

P. May almighty God have mercy on you, forgive you your sins, and bring you to life everlasting. **S.** Amen.

P. May the almighty and merciful Lord grant you pardon, ✠ absolution and remission of your sins. **S.** Amen.

Holding up a Sacred Host, the Priest says:

Behold the Lamb of God, behold Him Who takes away the sins of the world.

Lord, I am not worthy that You should come under my roof; but only say the word, and my soul will be healed. (3 *times.*)

The Priest says to each communicant:

May the Body of our Lord Jesus Christ preserve your soul to life everlasting. Amen.

The Priest purifies the chalice with wine, saying:

WHAT has passed our lips as food, O Lord, may we possess in purity of heart, that what is given to us in time, be our healing for eternity.

He purifies his fingers with wine and water, saying:

MAY Your Body, O Lord, which I have eaten, and Your Blood which I have drunk, cleave to my very soul, and grant that no trace of sin be found in me, whom these pure and holy mysteries have renewed. Who live and reign, world without end. Amen.

THE COMMUNION • Ps. 26, 4

ONE thing I ask of the Lord; this I seek: to dwell in the house of the Lord all the days of my life.

The Priest, turning to the people, says:

P. The Lord be with you. *S*. And with your spirit.
P. Let us pray.

THE POSTCOMMUNION

GRANT, we beseech You, O Lord, that we, whom You have fed with Your heavenly Gift, may both be cleansed from our hidden sins, and delivered from the snares of our enemies. Through our Lord Jesus Christ, Your Son, Who lives and reigns with You in the unity of the Holy Spirit, God, world without end. *S*. Amen.

FINAL PRAYERS

P. The Lord be with you. *S*. And with your spirit.
P. Go, you are dismissed. *S*. Thanks be to God.

MAY the tribute of my worship be pleasing to You, Most Holy Trinity, and grant that the sacrifice which I, all unworthy, have offered in the presence of Your Majesty, may be acceptable to You, and through Your mercy obtain forgiveness for me and all for whom I have offered it. Through Christ our Lord. Amen.

THE LAST BLESSING

MAY almighty God bless you: ✠ the Father, and the Son, and the Holy Spirit. *S*. Amen.

The Last Gospel and Prayers after Low Mass are conveniently placed inside the back cover.

The Miracle of the Loaves and Fishes.

SIXTH SUNDAY AFTER PENTECOST

Easter time has passed, but its spirit should never pass. Christ died once and now lives His glorious unending life. We also should remain dead to sin and continue to live together with Christ the new life of holiness. (GREEN VESTMENTS)

PRAYERS AT THE FOOT OF THE ALTAR

IN THE name of the Father, ✠ and of the Son, and of the Holy Spirit. Amen.

Priest. I will go in to the altar of God.

Server. The God of my gladness and joy.

Psalm 42

DO ME justice, O God, and fight my fight against a faithless people; from the deceitful and impious man rescue me.

S. For You, O God, are my strength. Why do You keep me so far away? Why must I go about in mourning, with the enemy oppressing me?

P. Send forth Your light and Your fidelity; they shall lead me on and bring me to Your holy mountain, to Your dwelling-place.

S. Then will I go in to the altar of God, the God of my gladness and joy.
P. Then will I give You thanks upon the harp, O God, my God. Why are you so downcast, O my soul? Why do you sigh within me?
S. Hope in God! For I shall again be thanking Him in the presence of my Savior and my God.
P. Glory be to the Father, and to the Son, and to the Holy Spirit.
S. As it was in the beginning, is now, and ever shall be, world without end. Amen.
P. I will go in to the altar of God.
S. The God of my gladness and joy.
P. Our help ✠ is in the name of the Lord.
S. Who made heaven and earth.
P. I confess to almighty God, etc.
S. May almighty God have mercy on you, forgive you your sins, and bring you to life everlasting.
P. Amen.

The Server, bowing, says the "Confiteor."

I CONFESS to almighty God, to Blessed Mary, ever Virgin, to Blessed Michael the Archangel, to Blessed John the Baptist, to the Holy Apostles Peter and Paul, and to all the Saints, and to you, Father, that I have sinned exceedingly in thought, word and deed, *through my fault, through my fault, through my most grievous fault.* Therefore I beseech Blessed Mary, ever Virgin, Blessed Michael the Archangel, Blessed John the Baptist, the Holy Apostles Peter and Paul, and all the Saints, and you, Father, to pray to the Lord our God for me.
P. May almighty God have mercy on you, forgive you your sins, and bring you to life everlasting.
S. Amen.

MAY the almighty and merciful Lord grant us pardon, ✠ absolution, and remission of our sins. *S.* Amen.

P. **Will You not, O God, give us life?**
S. **And shall not Your people rejoice in You?**
P. **Show us, O Lord, Your kindness.**
S. **And grant us Your salvation.**
P. **O Lord, hear my prayer.**
S. **And let my cry come to You.**
P. **The Lord be with you.**
S. **And with your spirit.** ***P.*** **Let us pray.**

Going up to the altar, the Priest prays silently:

TAKE away from us our sins, O Lord, we beseech You, that we may enter with pure minds into the Holy of Holies. Through Christ our Lord. Amen.

WE BESEECH You, O Lord, by the merits of Your Saints (*he kisses the altar*) whose relics lie here, and of all the Saints: deign in Your mercy to pardon me all my sins. Amen.

THE INTROIT • Ps. 27, 8. 9. 1

At the right side of the altar, the Priest says:

THE Lord is the strength of His people, the saving refuge of His anointed. Save Your people, O Lord, and bless Your inheritance; and rule them forever! *Ps.* To You, O Lord, I call; O my God, be not deaf to me, lest, if You heed me not, I become one of those going down into the pit. Glory be to the Father, and to the Son, and to the Holy Spirit. As it was in the beginning, is now, and ever shall be, world without end. Amen. — The Lord is the strength of His people, the saving refuge of His anointed. Save Your people, O Lord, and bless Your inheritance; and rule over them forever!

THE KYRIE

P. Lord, have mercy. *S.* Lord, have mercy. *P.* Lord, have mercy. *S.* Christ, have mercy. *P.* Christ, have mercy. *S.* Christ, have mercy. *P.* Lord, have mercy. *S.* Lord, have mercy. *P.* Lord, have mercy.

THE GLORIA

GLORY to God in the highest. And on earth peace to men of good will. We praise You. We bless You. We adore You. We glorify You. We give You thanks for Your great glory. O Lord God, heavenly King, God the Father almighty. O Lord Jesus Christ, the Only-begotten Son. O Lord God, Lamb of God, Son of the Father: You Who take away the sins of the world, have mercy on us. You Who take away the sins of the world, receive our prayer. You Who sit at the right hand of the Father, have mercy on us. For You alone are holy. You alone are the Lord. You alone, O Jesus Christ, are most high. Together with the Holy Spirit ✠ in the glory of God the Father. Amen.

The Priest kisses the altar and turns to the people, saying:

P. The Lord be with you. *S.* And with your spirit.
P. Let us pray.

THE PRAYER

Going to the right (Epistle) side, he says:

O GOD of power, to Whom belongs all that is perfect, engraft in our hearts the love of Your name, and grant us an increase of religion; that what in us is good, You may nourish, and, in Your loving-kindness, preserve in us what You have nourished. Through our Lord Jesus Christ, Your Son, Who lives and reigns with You in the unity of the Holy Spirit, God, world without end. S. Amen.

THE EPISTLE • Rom. 6, 3-11

BRETHREN: All we who have been baptized into Christ Jesus have been baptized into His death. For we were buried with Him by means of Baptism into death, in order that, just as Christ has arisen from the dead through the glory of the Father, so we also may walk in newness of life. For if we have been united with Him in the likeness of His death, we shall be so in the likeness of His Resurrection also. For we know that our old self has been crucified with Him, in order that the body of sin may be destroyed, that we may no longer be slaves to sin; for he who is dead is acquitted of sin. But if we have died with Christ, we believe that we shall also live together with Christ; for we know that Christ, having risen from the dead, dies now no more, death shall no longer have dominion over Him. For the death that He died, He died to sin once for all, but the life that He lives, He lives unto God. Thus do you consider yourselves also as dead to sin, but alive to God in Christ Jesus our Lord. S. Thanks be to God.

THE GRADUAL • Ps. 89, 13. 1.

RETURN, O Lord! How long? Have pity on Your servants! ℣. O Lord, You have been our refuge through all generations.

Alleluia, alleluia. ℣. *Ps. 30,* 2. 3. In You, O Lord, I take refuge; let me never be put to shame. In Your justice rescue me and release me, incline Your ear to me, make haste to deliver me! Alleluia.

PRAYER BEFORE THE GOSPEL

Bowing down at the center of the altar, he says:

CLEANSE my heart and my lips, O almighty God, Who cleansed the lips of the Prophet Isaias with a burning coal. In Your gracious mercy deign so to purify me that I may worthily proclaim Your holy Gospel. Through Christ our Lord. Amen.

Lord, grant Your blessing. The Lord be in my heart and on my lips, that I may worthily and fittingly proclaim His holy Gospel. Amen.

THE GOSPEL • Mark 8, 1-9

Going to the left (Gospel) side of the altar, he says:

P. The Lord be with you. *S.* And with your spirit.

P. ✠ The continuation of the holy Gospel according to Saint Mark. *S.* Glory be to You, O Lord.

AT THAT time, when there was a great crowd with Jesus, and they had nothing to eat, He called His disciples together and said to them, "I have compassion on the crowd, for behold, they have now been with Me three days, and have nothing to eat; and if I send them away to their homes fasting, they will faint on the way, for some of them have come from a distance." And His disciples answered Him, "How will anyone be able to satisfy these with bread, here in a desert?" And He asked them, "How many loaves have you?" And they said, "Seven." And He bade the crowd recline on the ground. Then taking the seven loaves, He gave thanks, broke them and gave them to His disciples to distribute; and they set them before the crowd. And they had a few little fishes; and He blessed them, and ordered them to be distributed. And they ate and were satisfied; and they took up what was left of the fragments, seven baskets. Now those who had eaten were about four thousand. And He dismissed them. S. Praise be to You, O Christ.

P. By the words of the Gospel, may our sins be taken away.

THE NICENE CREED

At the center of the altar, he says:

I BELIEVE in one God, the Father almighty, Maker of heaven and earth, and of all things visible and invisible. And in one Lord Jesus Christ, the Only-begotten Son of God. Born of the Father before all ages. God of God; Light of Light; true God of true God. Begotten not made; of one being with the Father; by Whom all things were made. Who for us men, and for our salvation, came down from heaven. (*Here all genuflect.*) And was made Flesh by the Holy Spirit of the Virgin Mary: AND WAS MADE MAN. He was also crucified for us, suffered under Pontius Pilate and was buried. And on the third day He rose again according to the Scriptures. And ascending into heaven, He sits at the right hand of the Father. And He shall come again in glory to judge the living and the dead; and of His kingdom there shall be no end. And I believe in the Holy Spirit, Lord and Giver of life, Who proceeds from the Father and the Son. Who together with the Father and the Son is no less adored, and glorified: Who spoke by the Prophets. And I believe in One, Holy, Catholic and Apostolic Church. I confess one Baptism for the remission of sins. And I look for the resurrection of the dead. ✠ And the life of the world to come. Amen.

THE OFFERTORY

The Priest turns to the people and says:

P. The Lord be with you. *S.* And with your spirit.
P. Let us pray.

THE OFFERTORY VERSE • Ps. 16, 5. 6. 7

MAKE my steps steadfast in Your paths, that my feet may not falter. Incline Your ear to me; hear my word. Show Your wondrous kindness, O Lord, O Savior of those who trust in You.

The Priest now uncovers the chalice, places the host on the paten and offering it up, says:

ACCEPT, O holy Father, almighty and eternal God, this spotless host, which I, Your unworthy servant, offer to You, my living and true God, to atone for my numberless sins, offenses, and negligences; on behalf of all here present and likewise for all faithful Christians living and dead, that it may profit me and them as a means of salvation to life everlasting. Amen.

He pours wine and water into the chalice, blessing the water before it is poured.

O GOD, Who established the nature of man in wondrous dignity, and still more admirably restored it, grant that through the mystery of this water and wine, we may be made partakers of His Divinity, Who has condescended to become partaker of our humanity, Jesus Christ, Your Son, our Lord. Who lives and reigns with You in the unity of the Holy Spirit, God, world without end. Amen.

Offering up the wine, the Priest says:

WE OFFER You, O Lord, the chalice of salvation, humbly begging of Your mercy that

it may arise before Your Divine Majesty, with a pleasing fragrance, for our salvation and for that of the whole world. Amen.

Bowing down, the Priest says:

IN A humble spirit and with a contrite heart, may we be accepted by You, O Lord, and may our sacrifice so be offered in Your sight this day as to please You, O Lord God.

Raising his eyes and blessing the offering, he says:

COME, O Sanctifier, almighty and eternal God, and bless ✠ this sacrifice prepared for the glory of Your holy name.

WASHING THE FINGERS

I WASH my hands in innocence, and I go around Your altar, O Lord, giving voice to my thanks, and recounting all Your wondrous deeds. O Lord, I love the house in which You dwell, the tenting-place of Your glory. Gather not my soul with those of sinners, nor with men of blood my life. On their hands are crimes, and their right hands are full of bribes. But I walk in integrity; redeem me, and have pity on me. My foot stands on level ground; in the assemblies I will bless You, O Lord. Glory be to the Father, and to the Son, and to the Holy Spirit. As it was in the beginning, is now, and ever shall be, world without end. Amen.

ACCEPT, Most Holy Trinity, this offering which we are making to You in remembrance of the Passion, Resurrection, and Ascension of Jesus Christ, our Lord; and in honor of Blessed Mary, ever Virgin, Blessed John the Baptist, the Holy Apostles Peter and Paul, and of these, and of all the Saints; that it may add to their honor and aid our salvation; and may they deign to intercede in heaven for us who honor their memory here on earth. Through the same Christ our Lord. Amen.

The Priest turns toward the people and says:

Pray, brethren, that my sacrifice and yours may become acceptable to God the Father almighty.
S. May the Lord accept this sacrifice from your hands to the praise and glory of His name, for our advantage, and that of all His holy Church.
P. Amen.

THE SECRET

BE PROPITIOUS, O Lord, to our supplications, and graciously receive these oblations of Your people; and that the prayer of none be in vain nor the petition of any without effect, grant that what we ask with faith, we may efficaciously obtain. Through our Lord Jesus Christ, Your Son, Who lives and reigns with You in the unity of the Holy Spirit, God.
P. World without end. S. Amen.

PREFACE—CANON

P. The Lord be with you. S. And with your spirit.
P. Lift up your hearts.
S. We have lifted them up to the Lord.
P. Let us give thanks to the Lord, our God.
S. It is fitting and just.

IT IS fitting indeed and just, right and helpful to salvation, for us always and everywhere to give thanks to You, O holy Lord, Father almighty, everlasting God, Who with Your Only-begotten Son and the Holy Spirit are one God, one Lord; not in the unity of a single person, but in the trinity of a single nature. For that which we believe on Your revelation concerning Your glory, that same we believe of Your Son, that same of the Holy Spirit, without difference or discrimination. So that in confessing the true and everlasting Godhead, we shall adore distinction in Persons, oneness in being, and equality in Majesty. This the Angels and Archangels, the Cherubim, too, and the Seraphim do praise; day by day they cease not to cry out as with one voice, saying (*the bell is rung* 3 *times*):

HOLY, HOLY, HOLY, Lord God of Hosts. Heaven and earth are filled with Your glory. Hosanna in the highest. ✠ Blessed is He Who comes in the name of the Lord. Hosanna in the highest.

THE CANON OF THE MASS

THEREFORE, most gracious Father, we humbly beg of You and entreat You through Jesus Christ Your Son, our Lord, (*he kisses the altar*) to deem acceptable and bless these ✠ gifts, these ✠ offerings, these ✠ holy and unspotted oblations which, in the first place, we offer You for Your Holy Catholic Church, that You would deign to give her peace and protection, to unite and guard her throughout the world, together with Your servant N., our Pope, and N., our Bishop; and all true believers who cherish the Catholic and Apostolic Faith.

Commemoration of the Living

REMEMBER, O Lord, Your servants and handmaids, N. and N., (*name them*) and all here present, whose faith and devotion are known to You, on whose behalf we offer to You, or who themselves offer to You, this sacrifice of praise for themselves, families and friends, for the good of their souls, for their hope of salvation and deliverance from all harm, and who offer their homage to You, eternal, living and true God.

Commemoration of the Saints

IN THE unity of holy fellowship we observe the memory, first of all, of the glorious and ever Virgin Mary, Mother of our Lord and God Jesus Christ; next, that of Your Blessed Apostles and Martyrs, Peter and Paul, Andrew, James, John, Thomas, James, Philip, Bartholomew, Matthew, Simon and Thaddeus; of Linus, Cletus, Clement, Sixtus, Cornelius, Cyprian, Lawrence, Chrysogonus, John and Paul, Cosmas and Damian, and of all Your Saints, by whose merits and prayers grant that we may be always fortified by the help of Your protection. Through the same Christ our Lord. Amen.

Spreading his hands over the oblation, he says:

GRACIOUSLY accept, then, we beseech You, O Lord, this service of our worship and that of all Your household. Provide that our days be spent in Your peace, save us from everlasting damnation, and cause us to be numbered in the flock You have chosen. Through Christ our Lord. Amen.

O GOD, deign to bless ✠ what we offer, and make it approved, ✠ effective, ✠ right, and wholly pleasing in every way, that it may become for our good, the Body ✠ and Blood ✠ of Your dearly beloved Son, Jesus Christ our Lord.

CONSECRATION—ELEVATION

WHO, the day before He suffered, took bread into His holy and venerable hands, and having raised His eyes to heaven, to You, O God, His almighty Father, giving thanks to You, He blessed it, ✠ broke it, and gave it to His disciples, saying: All of you take and eat of this:

FOR THIS IS MY BODY.

IN LIKE manner, when the supper was done, taking also this goodly chalice into His holy and venerable hands, again giving thanks to You, He blessed ✠ it, and gave it to His disciples, saying: All of you take and drink of this:

FOR THIS IS THE CHALICE OF MY BLOOD OF THE NEW AND ETERNAL COVENANT: THE MYSTERY OF FAITH: WHICH SHALL BE SHED FOR YOU AND FOR MANY UNTO THE FORGIVENESS OF SINS.

After replacing the chalice on the corporal, he says:

As often as you shall do these things, in memory of Me shall you do them.

Offering of the Victim

MINDFUL, therefore, O Lord, not only of the blessed Passion of the same Christ, Your Son, our Lord, but also of His Resurrection from the dead, and finally His glorious Ascension into heaven, we, Your ministers, as also Your holy people, offer to Your supreme Majesty, of the gifts bestowed upon us, the pure ✠ Victim, the holy ✠ Victim, the all-perfect ✠ Victim: the holy ✠ Bread of life eternal and the Chalice ✠ of unending salvation.

AND this deign to regard with gracious and kindly attention and hold acceptable, as You deigned to accept the offerings of Abel, Your just servant, and the sacrifice of Abraham our patriarch, and that which Your chief priest Melchisedec offered to You, a holy sacrifice and a spotless victim.

MOST humbly we implore You, almighty God, bid these offerings to be brought by the hands of Your holy angel to Your altar above; before the face of Your Divine Majesty; that those of us who, by sharing in the Sacrifice of this altar, shall receive the Most Sacred ✠ Body and ✠ Blood of Your Son, may be filled with every grace and heavenly blessing. Through the same Christ our Lord. Amen.

Commemoration of the Dead

REMEMBER also, O Lord, Your servants and handmaids, *N.* and *N.*, who have gone before us with the sign of faith, and rest in the sleep of peace. (*Here pray for the dead.*) To these, O Lord, and to all who rest in Christ, we beseech You to grant of Your goodness, a place of comfort, light and peace. Through the same Christ our Lord. Amen.

TO US sinners also, Your servants, trusting in the greatness of Your mercy, deign to grant some part and fellowship with Your Holy Apostles and Martyrs: with John, Stephen, Matthias, Barnabas, Ignatius, Alexander, Marcellinus, Peter, Felicitas, Perpetua, Agatha, Lucy, Agnes, Cecilia, Anastasia, and all Your Saints; into whose company, we implore You to admit us, not weighing our merits, but freely granting us pardon. Through Christ our Lord.

THROUGH Whom, O Lord, You always create, ✠ sanctify, ✠ fill with life, ✠ bless, and bestow upon us all good things.

The Minor Elevation

THROUGH ✠ Him, and with ✠ Him, and in ✠ Him, is to You, God the Father ✠ almighty, in the unity of the Holy ✠ Spirit, all honor and glory, world without end. S. Amen.

THE COMMUNION AND THANKSGIVING

Let us pray. Prompted by saving precepts, and taught by Your divine teaching, we dare to say:

OUR FATHER, Who art in heaven, hallowed be Thy name: Thy kingdom come: Thy will be done on earth as it is in heaven. Give us this day our daily bread; and forgive us our trespasses, as we forgive those who trespass against us. And lead us not into temptation: S. But deliver us from evil. *P.* Amen.

DELIVER us, we beseech You, O Lord, from all evils, past, present, and to come; and by the intercession of the Blessed and glorious Mary, ever Virgin, Mother of God, together with Your Blessed Apostles Peter and Paul, and Andrew, and all the Saints, grant of Your goodness, peace in our days, that aided by the riches of Your mercy, we may be always free from sin and safe from all disturbance.

Through the same our Lord Jesus Christ, Your Son, Who lives and reigns with You in the unity of the Holy Spirit, God, world without end.

S. Amen.

P. May the peace ✠ of the Lord be ✠ always with ✠ you.

S. And with your spirit.

The Priest puts a small particle into the chalice, saying:

May this mingling and consecration of the Body and Blood of our Lord Jesus Christ help us who receive it to life everlasting. Amen.

LAMB of God, You Who take away the sins of the world, have mercy on us.
Lamb of God, You Who take away the sins of the world, have mercy on us.
Lamb of God, You Who take away the sins of the world, grant us peace.

PRAYERS BEFORE HOLY COMMUNION

Then inclining toward the altar, he says:

O LORD Jesus Christ, Who said to Your Apostles: "Peace I leave with you, My peace I give to you," regard not my sins but the faith of Your Church, and deign to give her peace and unity according to Your Will: Who live and reign, God, world without end. Amen.

O LORD Jesus Christ, Son of the living God, Who, by the will of the Father, with the cooperation of the Holy Spirit, have by Your death given life to the world, deliver me by this Your Most Sacred Body and Blood from all my sins and from every evil. Make me always cling to Your commandments, and never permit me to be separated from You. Who with the same God the Father and the Holy Spirit, live and reign, God, world without end. Amen.

LET not the partaking of Your Body, O Lord Jesus Christ, which I, though unworthy, presume to receive, turn to my judgment and condem-

nation; but through Your goodness, may it become a safeguard and an effective remedy, both of soul and body. Who live and reign with God the Father, in the unity of the Holy Spirit, God, world without end. Amen.

COMMUNION OF THE PRIEST

I WILL take the Bread of heaven, and call upon the name of the Lord.

Lord, I am not worthy that You should come under my roof; but only say the word, and my soul will be healed. (3 *times.*)

Making the Sign of the Cross with the Host, he says:

MAY the Body of our Lord Jesus Christ preserve my soul to life everlasting. Amen.

What return shall I make to the Lord for all He has given me? I will take the Chalice of salvation, and I will call upon the name of the Lord. Praising will I call upon the Lord and I shall be saved from my enemies.

Making the Sign of the Cross with the chalice, he says:

MAY the Blood of our Lord Jesus Christ preserve my soul to life everlasting. Amen.

The Priest reverently consumes the Precious Blood.

COMMUNION OF THE FAITHFUL

The Server and people say the "Confiteor."

P. May almighty God have mercy on you, forgive you your sins, and bring you to life everlasting. **S.** Amen.

P. May the almighty and merciful Lord grant you pardon, ✠ absolution and remission of your sins. **S.** Amen.

Holding up a Sacred Host, the Priest says:

Behold the Lamb of God, behold Him Who takes away the sins of the world.
Lord, I am not worthy that You should come under my roof; but only say the word, and my soul will be healed. (3 *times.*)

The Priest says to each communicant:

May the Body of our Lord Jesus Christ preserve your soul to life everlasting. Amen.

The Priest purifies the chalice with wine, saying:

WHAT has passed our lips as food, O Lord, may we possess in purity of heart, that what is given to us in time, be our healing for eternity.

He purifies his fingers with wine and water, saying:

MAY Your Body, O Lord, which I have eaten, and Your Blood which I have drunk, cleave to my very soul, and grant that no trace of sin be found in me, whom these pure and holy mysteries have renewed. Who live and reign, world without end. Amen.

THE COMMUNION • Ps. 26, 6

I WILL go round, and offer in His tent, sacrifices with shouts of gladness; I will sing and chant praise to the Lord.

The Priest, turning to the people, says:

P. The Lord be with you. *S.* And with your spirit.
P. Let us pray.

THE POSTCOMMUNION

WE HAVE been filled with Your gifts, O Lord, and beseech You to grant that we may both be cleansed by their virtue, and strengthened by their help. Through our Lord Jesus Christ, Your Son, Who lives and reigns with You in the unity of the Holy Spirit, God, world without end. S. Amen.

FINAL PRAYERS

The Priest turns again to the people, and says:

P. The Lord be with you. S. And with your spirit.
P. Go, you are dismissed. **S.** Thanks be to God.

MAY the tribute of my worship be pleasing to You, Most Holy Trinity, and grant that the sacrifice which I, all unworthy, have offered in the presence of Your Majesty, may be acceptable to You, and through Your mercy obtain forgiveness for me and all for whom I have offered it. Through Christ our Lord. Amen.

THE LAST BLESSING

He kisses the altar, and facing the people, says:

MAY almighty God bless you: ✠ the Father, and the Son, and the Holy Spirit.

S. Amen.

The Last Gospel and Prayers after Low Mass are conveniently placed inside the back cover.

"By their fruits you will know them."

SEVENTH SUNDAY AFTER PENTECOST

The gift of God is life everlasting. But to deserve it, we must, as good trees, bring forth good fruit. Pious words are not sufficient, we must yield the substantial fruit of good deeds. (GREEN VESTMENTS)

PRAYERS AT THE FOOT OF THE ALTAR

IN THE name of the Father, ✠ and of the Son, and of the Holy Spirit. Amen.

Priest. I will go in to the altar of God.

Server. The God of my gladness and joy.

Psalm 42

DO ME justice, O God, and fight my fight against a faithless people; from the deceitful and impious man rescue me.

S. For You, O God, are my strength. Why do You keep me so far away? Why must I go about in mourning, with the enemy oppressing me?

P. Send forth Your light and Your fidelity; they shall lead me on and bring me to Your holy mountain, to Your dwelling-place.

S. Then will I go in to the altar of God, the God of my gladness and joy.
P. Then will I give You thanks upon the harp, O God, my God. Why are you so downcast, O my soul? Why do you sigh within me?
S. Hope in God! For I shall again be thanking Him in the presence of my Savior and my God.
P. Glory be to the Father, and to the Son, and to the Holy Spirit.
S. As it was in the beginning, is now, and ever shall be, world without end. Amen.
P. I will go in to the altar of God.
S. The God of my gladness and joy.
P. Our help ✠ is in the name of the Lord.
S. Who made heaven and earth.
P. I confess to almighty God, etc.
S. May almighty God have mercy on you, forgive you your sins, and bring you to life everlasting.
P. Amen.

The Server, bowing, says the "Confiteor."

I CONFESS to almighty God, to Blessed Mary, ever Virgin, to Blessed Michael the Archangel, to Blessed John the Baptist, to the Holy Apostles Peter and Paul, and to all the Saints, and to you, Father, that I have sinned exceedingly in thought, word and deed, *through my fault, through my fault, through my most grievous fault.* Therefore I beseech Blessed Mary, ever Virgin, Blessed Michael the Archangel, Blessed John the Baptist, the Holy Apostles Peter and Paul, and all the Saints, and you, Father, to pray to the Lord our God for me.
P. May almighty God have mercy on you, forgive you your sins, and bring you to life everlasting.
S. Amen.

MAY the almighty and merciful Lord grant us pardon, ✠ absolution, and remission of our sins. S. Amen.

P. Will You not, O God, give us life?

S. And shall not Your people rejoice in You?

P. Show us, O Lord, Your kindness.

S. And grant us Your salvation.

P. O Lord, hear my prayer.

S. And let my cry come to You.

P. The Lord be with you.

S. And with your spirit. *P.* Let us pray.

Going up to the altar, the Priest prays silently:

TAKE away from us our sins, O Lord, we beseech You, that we may enter with pure minds into the Holy of Holies. Through Christ our Lord. Amen.

WE BESEECH You, O Lord, by the merits of Your Saints (*he kisses the altar*) whose relics lie here, and of all the Saints: deign in Your mercy to pardon me all my sins. Amen.

THE INTROIT • Ps. 46, 2. 3

At the right side of the altar, the Priest says:

ALL you peoples, clap your hands, shout to God with cries of gladness. *Ps.* For the Lord, the Most High, the awesome, is the great King over all the earth. Glory be to the Father, and to the Son, and to the Holy Spirit. As it was in the beginning, is now, and ever shall be, world without end. Amen. — All you peoples, clap your hands, shout to God with cries of gladness.

THE KYRIE

P. Lord, have mercy. *S.* Lord, have mercy. *P.* Lord, have mercy. S. Christ, have mercy. *P.* Christ, have

mercy. *S.* Christ, have mercy. *P.* Lord, have mercy. *S.* Lord, have mercy. *P.* Lord, have mercy.

THE GLORIA

GLORY to God in the highest. And on earth peace to men of good will. We praise You. We bless You. We adore You. We glorify You. We give You thanks for Your great glory. O Lord God, heavenly King, God the Father almighty. O Lord Jesus Christ, the Only-begotten Son. O Lord God, Lamb of God, Son of the Father: You Who take away the sins of the world, have mercy on us. You Who take away the sins of the world, receive our prayer. You Who sit at the right hand of the Father, have mercy on us. For You alone are holy. You alone are the Lord. You alone, O Jesus Christ, are most high. Together with the Holy Spirit ✠ in the glory of God the Father. Amen.

The Priest kisses the altar and turns to the people, saying:

P. The Lord be with you. *S.* And with your spirit. *P.* Let us pray.

THE PRAYER

Going to the right (Epistle) side, he says:

O GOD, Whose providence never fails in what it ordains, we humbly beseech You to put away from us all things harmful, and to give all things profitable to us. Through our Lord Jesus Christ, Your Son, Who lives and reigns with You in the unity of the Holy Spirit, God, world without end. *S.* Amen.

THE EPISTLE • Rom. 6, 19-23

BRETHREN: I speak in a human way because of the weakness of your flesh; for as you yielded your members as slaves of uncleanness and

iniquity unto iniquity, so now yield your members as slaves of justice unto sanctification. For when you were the slaves of sin, you were free as regards justice. But what fruit had you then from those things of which you are now ashamed? For the end of these things is death. But now set free from sin and become slaves to God, you have your fruit unto sanctification, and as your end, life everlasting. For the wages of sin is death, but the gift of God is life everlasting in Christ Jesus our Lord.
S. Thanks be to God.

THE GRADUAL • Ps. 33, 12. 6

COME, children, hear me; I will teach you the fear of the Lord. ℣. Look to Him that you may be radiant with joy, and your faces may not blush with shame.

Alleluia, alleluia. ℣. *Ps. 46*, 2. All you peoples, clap your hands, shout to God with cries of gladness. Alleluia.

PRAYER BEFORE THE GOSPEL

Bowing down at the center of the altar, he says:

CLEANSE my heart and my lips, O almighty God, Who cleansed the lips of the Prophet Isaias with a burning coal. In Your gracious mercy deign so to purify me that I may worthily proclaim Your holy Gospel. Through Christ our Lord. Amen.

Lord, grant Your blessing. The Lord be in my heart and on my lips, that I may worthily and fittingly proclaim His holy Gospel. Amen.

THE GOSPEL • Matt. 7, 15-21

Going to the left (Gospel) side of the altar, he says:

P. The Lord be with you. S. And with your spirit.

P. ✠ The continuation of the holy Gospel according to Saint Matthew. S. Glory be to You, O Lord.

AT THAT time, Jesus said to His disciples: "Beware of false prophets, who come to you in sheep's clothing, but inwardly are ravenous wolves. By their fruits you will know them. Do men gather grapes from thorns, or figs from thistles? Even so, every good tree bears good fruit, but the bad tree bears bad fruit. A good tree cannot bear bad fruit, nor can a bad tree bear good fruit. Every tree that does not bear good fruit is cut down and thrown into the fire. Therefore, by their fruits you will know them. Not everyone who says to Me, 'Lord, Lord,' shall enter the kingdom of heaven; but he who does the will of My Father in heaven shall enter the kingdom of heaven." S. Praise be to You, O Christ.

P. By the words of the Gospel, may our sins be taken away.

THE NICENE CREED

At the center of the altar, he says:

I BELIEVE in one God, the Father almighty, Maker of heaven and earth, and of all things visible and invisible. And in one Lord Jesus Christ, the Only-begotten Son of God. Born of the Father before all ages. God of God; Light of Light; true God of true God. Begotten not made; of one being with the Father; by Whom all things were made. Who for us men, and for our salvation, came down from heaven. (*Here all genuflect.*) And was made Flesh by the Holy Spirit of the Virgin Mary: AND WAS MADE MAN. He was also crucified for us, suffered under Pontius Pilate and was buried.

And on the third day He rose again according to the Scriptures. And ascending into heaven, He sits at the right hand of the Father. And He shall come again in glory to judge the living and the dead; and of His kingdom there shall be no end. And I believe in the Holy Spirit, Lord and Giver of life, Who proceeds from the Father and the Son. Who together with the Father and the Son is no less adored, and glorified: Who spoke by the Prophets. And I believe in One, Holy, Catholic and Apostolic Church. I confess one Baptism for the remission of sins. And I look for the resurrection of the dead. ✠ And the life of the world to come. Amen.

THE OFFERTORY

The Priest turns to the people and says:

P. The Lord be with you. *S.* And with your spirit.
P. Let us pray.

THE OFFERTORY VERSE • Dan. 3, 40

AS IN holocausts of rams and bullocks, and as in thousands of fat lambs, so let our sacrifice be made in Your sight this day, that it may please You: for there is no confusion to those who trust in You, O Lord.

The Priest now uncovers the chalice, places the host on the paten and offering it up, says:

ACCEPT, O holy Father, almighty and eternal God, this spotless host, which I, Your unworthy servant, offer to You, my living and true God, to atone for my numberless sins, offenses, and negligences; on behalf of all here present and likewise for all faithful Christians living and dead, that it may profit me and them as a means of salvation to life everlasting. Amen.

He pours wine and water into the chalice, blessing the water before it is poured.

O GOD, Who established the nature of man in wondrous dignity, and still more admirably restored it, grant that through the mystery of this water and wine, we may be made partakers of His Divinity, Who has condescended to become partaker of our humanity, Jesus Christ, Your Son, our Lord. Who lives and reigns with You in the unity of the Holy Spirit, God, world without end. Amen.

Offering up the wine, the Priest says:

WE OFFER You, O Lord, the chalice of salvation, humbly begging of Your mercy that it may arise before Your Divine Majesty, with a pleasing fragrance, for our salvation and for that of the whole world. Amen.

Bowing down, the Priest says:

IN A humble spirit and with a contrite heart, may we be accepted by You, O Lord, and may our sacrifice so be offered in Your sight this day as to please You, O Lord God.

Raising his eyes and blessing the offering, he says:

COME, O Sanctifier, almighty and eternal God, and bless ✠ this sacrifice prepared for the glory of Your holy name.

WASHING THE FINGERS

I WASH my hands in innocence, and I go around Your altar, O Lord, giving voice to my thanks, and recounting all Your wondrous deeds. O Lord, I love the house in which You dwell, the tenting-place of Your glory. Gather not my soul with those of sinners, nor with men of blood my life. On their hands are crimes, and their right hands are full of bribes. But I walk in integrity; redeem me, and have pity on me. My foot stands on level ground; in the assemblies I will bless You, O Lord. Glory be to the Father, and to the Son, and to the Holy Spirit. As it was in the beginning, is now, and ever shall be, world without end. Amen.

ACCEPT, Most Holy Trinity, this offering which we are making to You in remembrance of the Passion, Resurrection, and Ascension of Jesus Christ, our Lord; and in honor of Blessed Mary, ever Virgin, Blessed John the Baptist, the Holy Apostles Peter and Paul, and of these, and of all the Saints; that it may add to their honor and aid our salvation; and may they deign to intercede in heaven for us who honor their memory here on earth. Through the same Christ our Lord. Amen.

The Priest turns toward the people and says:

Pray, brethren, that my sacrifice and yours may become acceptable to God the Father almighty.

S. May the Lord accept this sacrifice from your hands to the praise and glory of His name, for our advantage, and that of all His holy Church.

P. Amen.

THE SECRET

O GOD, Who, in the one perfect sacrifice, have ratified the variety of victims prescribed by the law, receive this sacrifice from Your devoted servants, and sanctify it with a blessing like that wherewith You blessed the gifts of Abel: that what is offered individually to the honor of Your Majesty, may profit for the salvation of all. Through our Lord Jesus Christ, Your Son, Who lives and reigns with You in the unity of the Holy Spirit, God.

P. World without end. S. Amen.

PREFACE—CANON

P. The Lord be with you. S. And with your spirit.
P. Lift up your hearts.
S. We have lifted them up to the Lord.
P. Let us give thanks to the Lord, our God.
S. It is fitting and just.

IT IS fitting indeed and just, right and helpful to salvation, for us always and everywhere to give thanks to You, O holy Lord, Father almighty, everlasting God, Who with Your Only-begotten Son and the Holy Spirit are one God, one Lord; not in the unity of a single person, but in the trinity of a single nature. For that which we believe on Your revelation concerning Your glory, that same we believe of Your Son, that same of the Holy Spirit, without difference or discrimination. So that in confessing the true and everlasting Godhead, we shall adore distinction in Persons, oneness in being, and equality in Majesty. This the Angels and Archangels, the Cherubim, too, and the Seraphim do praise; day by day they cease not to cry out as with one voice, saying (*the bell is rung* 3 *times*):

HOLY, HOLY, HOLY, Lord God of Hosts. Heaven and earth are filled with Your glory. Hosanna in the highest. ✠ Blessed is He Who comes in the name of the Lord. Hosanna in the highest.

THE CANON OF THE MASS

THEREFORE, most gracious Father, we humbly beg of You and entreat You through Jesus Christ Your Son, our Lord, (*he kisses the altar*) to deem acceptable and bless these ✠ gifts, these ✠

offerings, these ✠ holy and unspotted oblations which, in the first place, we offer You for Your Holy Catholic Church, that You would deign to give her peace and protection, to unite and guard her throughout the world, together with Your servant N., our Pope, and N., our Bishop; and all true believers who cherish the Catholic and Apostolic Faith.

Commemoration of the Living

REMEMBER, O Lord, Your servants and handmaids, N. and N., (*name them*) and all here present, whose faith and devotion are known to You, on whose behalf we offer to You, or who themselves offer to You, this sacrifice of praise for themselves, families and friends, for the good of their souls, for their hope of salvation and deliverance from all harm, and who offer their homage to You, eternal, living and true God.

Commemoration of the Saints

IN THE unity of holy fellowship we observe the memory, first of all, of the glorious and ever Virgin Mary, Mother of our Lord and God Jesus Christ; next, that of Your Blessed Apostles and Martyrs, Peter and Paul, Andrew, James, John, Thomas, James, Philip, Bartholomew, Matthew, Simon and Thaddeus; of Linus, Cletus, Clement, Sixtus, Cornelius, Cyprian, Lawrence, Chrysogonus, John and Paul, Cosmas and Damian, and of all Your Saints, by whose merits and prayers grant that we may be always fortified by the help of Your protection. Through the same Christ our Lord. Amen.

Spreading his hands over the oblation, he says:

GRACIOUSLY accept, then, we beseech You, O Lord, this service of our worship and that

of all Your household. Provide that our
spent in Your peace, save us from everlast
nation, and cause us to be numbered in the
You have chosen. Through Christ our Lord. Amen.

O GOD, deign to bless ✠ what we offer, and make it approved, ✠ effective, ✠ right, and wholly pleasing in every way, that it may become for our good, the Body ✠ and Blood ✠ of Your dearly beloved Son, Jesus Christ our Lord.

CONSECRATION—ELEVATION

WHO, the day before He suffered, took bread into His holy and venerable hands, and having raised His eyes to heaven, to You, O God, His almighty Father, giving thanks to You, He blessed it, ✠ broke it, and gave it to His disciples, saying: All of you take and eat of this:

FOR THIS IS MY BODY.

IN LIKE manner, when the supper was done, taking also this goodly chalice into His holy and venerable hands, again giving thanks to You, He blessed ✠ it, and gave it to His disciples, saying: All of you take and drink of this:

FOR THIS IS THE CHALICE OF MY BLOOD OF THE NEW AND ETERNAL COVENANT: THE MYSTERY OF FAITH: WHICH SHALL BE SHED FOR YOU AND FOR MANY UNTO THE FORGIVENESS OF SINS.

After replacing the chalice on the corporal, he says:

As often as you shall do these things, in memory of Me shall you do them.

Offering of the Victim

MINDFUL, therefore, O Lord, not only of the blessed Passion of the same Christ, Your Son,

our Lord, but also of His Resurrection from the dead, and finally His glorious Ascension into heaven, we, Your ministers, as also Your holy people, offer to Your supreme Majesty, of the gifts bestowed upon us, the pure ✠ Victim, the holy ✠ Victim, the all-perfect ✠ Victim: the holy ✠ Bread of life eternal and the Chalice ✠ of unending salvation.

AND this deign to regard with gracious and kindly attention and hold acceptable, as You deigned to accept the offerings of Abel, Your just servant, and the sacrifice of Abraham our patriarch, and that which Your chief priest Melchisedec offered to You, a holy sacrifice and a spotless victim.

MOST humbly we implore You, almighty God, bid these offerings to be brought by the hands of Your holy angel to Your altar above; before the face of Your Divine Majesty; that those of us who, by sharing in the Sacrifice of this altar, shall receive the Most Sacred ✠ Body and ✠ Blood of Your Son, may be filled with every grace and heavenly blessing. Through the same Christ our Lord. Amen.

Commemoration of the Dead

REMEMBER also, O Lord, Your servants and handmaids, N. and N., who have gone before us with the sign of faith, and rest in the sleep of peace. (*Here pray for the dead.*) To these, O Lord, and to all who rest in Christ, we beseech You to grant of Your goodness, a place of comfort, light and peace. Through the same Christ our Lord. Amen.

TO US sinners also, Your servants, trusting in the greatness of Your mercy, deign to grant some

part and fellowship with Your Holy Apostles and Martyrs: with John, Stephen, Matthias, Barnabas, Ignatius, Alexander, Marcellinus, Peter, Felicitas, Perpetua, Agatha, Lucy, Agnes, Cecilia, Anastasia, and all Your Saints; into whose company, we implore You to admit us, not weighing our merits, but freely granting us pardon. Through Christ our Lord.

THROUGH Whom, O Lord, You always create, ✠ sanctify, ✠ fill with life, ✠ bless, and bestow upon us all good things.

The Minor Elevation

THROUGH ✠ Him, and with ✠ Him, and in ✠ Him, is to You, God the Father ✠ almighty, in the unity of the Holy ✠ Spirit, all honor and glory, world without end. S. Amen.

THE COMMUNION AND THANKSGIVING

Let us pray. Prompted by saving precepts, and taught by Your divine teaching, we dare to say:

OUR FATHER, Who art in heaven, hallowed be Thy name: Thy kingdom come: Thy will be done on earth as it is in heaven. Give us this day our daily bread; and forgive us our trespasses, as we forgive those who trespass against us. And lead us not into temptation: S. But deliver us from evil. *P.* Amen.

DELIVER us, we beseech You, O Lord, from all evils, past, present, and to come; and by the intercession of the Blessed and glorious Mary, ever Virgin, Mother of God, together with Your Blessed Apostles Peter and Paul, and Andrew, and all the Saints, grant of Your goodness, peace in our days, that aided by the riches of Your mercy, we may be always free from sin and safe from all disturbance.

Through the same our Lord Jesus Christ, Your Son, Who lives and reigns with You in the unity of the Holy Spirit, God, world without end.

S. Amen.

P. May the peace ✠ of the Lord be ✠ always with ✠ you.

S. And with your spirit.

The Priest puts a small particle into the chalice, saying:

May this mingling and consecration of the Body and Blood of our Lord Jesus Christ help us who receive it to life everlasting. Amen.

LAMB of God, You Who take away the sins of the world, have mercy on us.

Lamb of God, You Who take away the sins of the world, have mercy on us.

Lamb of God, You Who take away the sins of the world, grant us peace.

PRAYERS BEFORE HOLY COMMUNION

Then inclining toward the altar, he says:

O LORD Jesus Christ, Who said to Your Apostles: "Peace I leave with you, My peace I give to you," regard not my sins but the faith of Your Church, and deign to give her peace and unity according to Your Will: Who live and reign, God, world without end. Amen.

O LORD Jesus Christ, Son of the living God, Who, by the will of the Father, with the co-

operation of the Holy Spirit, have by Your death given life to the world, deliver me by this Your Most Sacred Body and Blood from all my sins and from every evil. Make me always cling to Your commandments, and never permit me to be separated from You. Who with the same God the Father and the Holy Spirit, live and reign, God, world without end. Amen.

LET not the partaking of Your Body, O Lord Jesus Christ, which I, though unworthy, presume to receive, turn to my judgment and condemnation; but through Your goodness, may it become a safeguard and an effective remedy, both of soul and body. Who live and reign with God the Father, in the unity of the Holy Spirit, God, world without end. Amen.

COMMUNION OF THE PRIEST

I WILL take the Bread of heaven, and call upon the name of the Lord.

Lord, I am not worthy that You should come under my roof; but only say the word, and my soul will be healed. (3 *times.*)

Making the Sign of the Cross with the Host, he says:

MAY the Body of our Lord Jesus Christ preserve my soul to life everlasting. Amen.

What return shall I make to the Lord for all He has given me? I will take the Chalice of salvation, and I will call upon the name of the Lord. Praising will I call upon the Lord and I shall be saved from my enemies.

Making the Sign of the Cross with the chalice, he says:

MAY the Blood of our Lord Jesus Christ preserve my soul to life everlasting. Amen.

The Priest reverently consumes the Precious Blood.

COMMUNION OF THE FAITHFUL

The Server and people say the "Confiteor."

P. May almighty God have mercy on you, forgive you your sins, and bring you to life everlasting. *S.* Amen.

P. May the almighty and merciful Lord grant you pardon, ✠ absolution and remission of your sins. *S.* Amen.

Holding up a Sacred Host, the Priest says:

Behold the Lamb of God, behold Him Who takes away the sins of the world.

Lord, I am not worthy that You should come under my roof; but only say the word, and my soul will be healed. (3 *times.*)

The Priest says to each communicant:

May the Body of our Lord Jesus Christ preserve your soul to life everlasting. Amen.

The Priest purifies the chalice with wine, saying:

WHAT has passed our lips as food, O Lord, may we possess in purity of heart, that what is given to us in time, be our healing for eternity.

He purifies his fingers with wine and water, saying:

MAY Your Body, O Lord, which I have eaten, and Your Blood which I have drunk, cleave to my very soul, and grant that no trace of sin be found in me, whom these pure and holy mysteries have renewed. Who live and reign, world without end. Amen.

THE COMMUNION • Ps. 30, 3

INCLINE Your ear to me, make haste to deliver me.

The Priest, turning to the people, says:

P. The Lord be with you. S. And with your spirit.
P. Let us pray.

THE POSTCOMMUNION

MAY Your health-giving operation, O Lord, both mercifully free us from our evil inclinations, and lead us to do that which is right. Through our Lord Jesus Christ, Your Son, Who lives and reigns with You in the unity of the Holy Spirit, God, world without end. S. Amen.

FINAL PRAYERS

The Priest turns again to the people, and says:

P. The Lord be with you. S. And with your spirit.
P. Go, you are dismissed. S. Thanks be to God.

MAY the tribute of my worship be pleasing to You, Most Holy Trinity, and grant that the sacrifice which I, all unworthy, have offered in the presence of Your Majesty, may be acceptable to You, and through Your mercy obtain forgiveness for me and all for whom I have offered it. Through Christ our Lord. Amen.

THE LAST BLESSING

He kisses the altar, and facing the people, says:

MAY almighty God bless you: ✠ the Father, and the Son, and the Holy Spirit. S. Amen.

The Last Gospel and Prayers after Low Mass are conveniently placed inside the back cover.

"Take your bond . . . and write fifty."

EIGHTH SUNDAY AFTER PENTECOST

The parable of the steward shows the cleverness of "the children of this world." "The children of the light," on the other hand, let earthly means of sanctification go by unused. Let us use worldly goods to gain a happy eternity. (GREEN VESTMENTS)

PRAYERS AT THE FOOT OF THE ALTAR

IN THE name of the Father, ✠ and of the Son, and of the Holy Spirit. Amen.

Priest. I will go in to the altar of God.

Server. The God of my gladness and joy.

Psalm 42

DO ME justice, O God, and fight my fight against a faithless people; from the deceitful and impious man rescue me.

S. For You, O God, are my strength. Why do You keep me so far away? Why must I go about in mourning, with the enemy oppressing me?

P. Send forth Your light and Your fidelity; they shall lead me on and bring me to Your holy mountain, to Your dwelling-place.

S. Then will I go in to the altar of God, the God of my gladness and joy.
P. Then will I give You thanks upon the harp, O God, my God. Why are you so downcast, O my soul? Why do you sigh within me?
S. Hope in God! For I shall again be thanking Him in the presence of my Savior and my God.
P. Glory be to the Father, and to the Son, and to the Holy Spirit.
S. As it was in the beginning, is now, and ever shall be, world without end. Amen.
P. I will go in to the altar of God.
S. The God of my gladness and joy.
P. Our help ✠ is in the name of the Lord.
S. Who made heaven and earth.
P. I confess to almighty God, etc.
S. May almighty God have mercy on you, forgive you your sins, and bring you to life everlasting.
P. Amen.

The Server, bowing, says the "Confiteor."

I CONFESS to almighty God, to Blessed Mary, ever Virgin, to Blessed Michael the Archangel, to Blessed John the Baptist, to the Holy Apostles Peter and Paul, and to all the Saints, and to you, Father, that I have sinned exceedingly in thought, word and deed, *through my fault, through my fault, through my most grievous fault.* Therefore I beseech Blessed Mary, ever Virgin, Blessed Michael the Archangel, Blessed John the Baptist, the Holy Apostles Peter and Paul, and all the Saints, and you, Father, to pray to the Lord our God for me.
P. May almighty God have mercy on you, forgive you your sins, and bring you to life everlasting.
S. Amen.

MAY the almighty and merciful Lord grant us pardon, ✠ absolution, and remission of our sins. *S.* Amen.

P. Will You not, O God, give us life?
S. And shall not Your people rejoice in You?
P. Show us, O Lord, Your kindness.
S. And grant us Your salvation.
P. O Lord, hear my prayer.
S. And let my cry come to You.
P. The Lord be with you.
S. And with your spirit. *P.* Let us pray.

Going up to the altar, the Priest prays silently:

TAKE away from us our sins, O Lord, we beseech You, that we may enter with pure minds into the Holy of Holies. Through Christ our Lord. Amen.

WE BESEECH You, O Lord, by the merits of Your Saints (*he kisses the altar*) whose relics lie here, and of all the Saints: deign in Your mercy to pardon me all my sins. Amen.

THE INTROIT • Ps. 47, 10. 11. 2

At the right side of the altar, the Priest says:

O GOD, we ponder Your kindness within Your temple. As Your name, O God, so also Your praise reaches to the ends of the earth. Of justice Your right hand is full. *Ps.* Great is the Lord and wholly to be praised in the city of our God, His holy mountain. Glory be to the Father, and to the Son, and to the Holy Spirit. As it was in the beginning, is now, and ever shall be, world without end. Amen. — O God, we ponder Your kindness within Your temple. As Your name, O God, so also Your praise reaches to the ends of the earth. Of justice Your right hand is full.

THE KYRIE

P. Lord, have mercy. *S.* Lord, have mercy. *P.* Lord, have mercy. *S.* Christ, have mercy. *P.* Christ, have mercy. *S.* Christ, have mercy. *P.* Lord, have mercy. *S.* Lord, have mercy. *P.* Lord, have mercy.

THE GLORIA

GLORY to God in the highest. And on earth peace to men of good will. We praise You. We bless You. We adore You. We glorify You. We give You thanks for Your great glory. O Lord God, heavenly King, God the Father almighty. O Lord Jesus Christ, the Only-begotten Son. O Lord God, Lamb of God, Son of the Father: You Who take away the sins of the world, have mercy on us. You Who take away the sins of the world, receive our prayer. You Who sit at the right hand of the Father, have mercy on us. For You alone are holy. You alone are the Lord. You alone, O Jesus Christ, are most high. Together with the Holy Spirit ✠ in the glory of God the Father. Amen.

The Priest kisses the altar and turns to the people, saying:

P. The Lord be with you. *S.* And with your spirit. *P.* Let us pray.

THE PRAYER

Going to the right (Epistle) side, he says:

GRACIOUSLY impart to us, we beseech You, O Lord, the spirit at all times to think and to do the things that are right; that we, who cannot subsist without You, may be enabled to live according to Your will. Through our Lord Jesus Christ, Your Son, Who lives and reigns with You in the unity of the Holy Spirit, God, world without end. *S.* Amen.

THE EPISTLE • Rom. 8, 12-17

BRETHREN: We are debtors, not to the flesh, that we should live according to the flesh, for if you live according to the flesh you will die; but if by the spirit you put to death the deeds of the flesh, you will live. For whoever are led by the Spirit of God, they are the sons of God. Now you have not received a spirit of bondage so as to be again in fear, but you have received a spirit of adoption as sons, by virtue of which we cry, "Abba! Father!" The Spirit Himself gives testimony to our spirit that we are sons of God. But if we are sons, we are heirs also: heirs indeed of God and joint heirs with Christ. S. Thanks be to God.

THE GRADUAL • Ps. 30, 3

BE MY rock of refuge, O God, a stronghold to give me safety. ℣. *Ps. 70, 1.* In You, O God, I take refuge; O Lord, let me never be put to shame.

Alleluia, alleluia. ℣. *Ps. 47,* 2. Great is the Lord and wholly to be praised in the city of our God, His holy mountain. Alleluia.

PRAYER BEFORE THE GOSPEL

Bowing down at the center of the altar, he says:

CLEANSE my heart and my lips, O almighty God, Who cleansed the lips of the Prophet Isaias with a burning coal. In Your gracious mercy deign so to purify me that I may worthily proclaim Your holy Gospel. Through Christ our Lord. Amen.

Lord, grant Your blessing. The Lord be in my heart and on my lips, that I may worthily and fittingly proclaim His holy Gospel. Amen.

THE GOSPEL • Luke 16, 1-9

Going to the left (Gospel) side of the altar, he says:

P. The Lord be with you. *S.* And with your spirit. *P.* ✠ The continuation of the holy Gospel according to Saint Luke. *S.* Glory be to You, O Lord.

AT THAT time, Jesus spoke to His disciples this parable: "There was a certain rich man who had a steward, who was reported to him as squandering his possessions. And he called him and said to him, 'What is this that I hear of you? Make an accounting of your stewardship, for you can be steward no longer.' And the steward said within himself, 'What shall I do, seeing that my master is taking away the stewardship from me? To dig I am not able; to beg I am ashamed. I know what I shall do, that when I am removed from my stewardship they may receive me into their houses.' And he summoned each of his master's debtors and said to the first, 'How much do you owe my master?' And he said, 'A hundred jars of oil.' He said to him, 'Take your bond and sit down at once and write fifty.' Then he said to another, 'How much do you owe?' He said, 'A hundred kors of wheat.' He said to him, 'Take your bond and write eighty.' And the master commended the unjust steward, in that he had acted prudently; for the children of this world, in relation to their own generation, are more prudent than the children of the light. And I say to you, make friends for yourselves with the mammon of wickedness, so that when you fail they may receive you into the everlasting dwellings." *S.* Praise be to You, O Christ.

P. By the words of the Gospel, may our sins be taken away.

THE NICENE CREED

At the center of the altar, he says:

I BELIEVE in one God, the Father almighty, Maker of heaven and earth, and of all things visible and invisible. And in one Lord Jesus Christ, the Only-begotten Son of God. Born of the Father before all ages. God of God; Light of Light; true God of true God. Begotten not made; of one being with the Father; by Whom all things were made. Who for us men, and for our salvation, came down from heaven. (*Here all genuflect.*) And was made Flesh by the Holy Spirit of the Virgin Mary: AND WAS MADE MAN. He was also crucified for us, suffered under Pontius Pilate and was buried. And on the third day He rose again according to the Scriptures. And ascending into heaven, He sits at the right hand of the Father. And He shall come again in glory to judge the living and the dead; and of His kingdom there shall be no end. And I believe in the Holy Spirit, Lord and Giver of life, Who proceeds from the Father and the Son. Who together with the Father and the Son is no less adored, and glorified: Who spoke by the Prophets. And I believe in One, Holy, Catholic and Apostolic Church. I confess one Baptism for the remission of sins. And I look for the resurrection of the dead. ✠ And the life of the world to come. Amen.

THE OFFERTORY

The Priest turns to the people and says:

P. The Lord be with you. *S.* And with your spirit.
P. Let us pray.

THE OFFERTORY VERSE • Ps. 17, 28. 32

LOWLY people You save, O Lord, but haughty eyes You bring low; for who is God except You, O Lord?

The Priest now uncovers the chalice, places the host on the paten and offering it up, says:

ACCEPT, O holy Father, almighty and eternal God, this spotless host, which I, Your unworthy servant, offer to You, my living and true God, to atone for my numberless sins, offenses, and negligences; on behalf of all here present and likewise for all faithful Christians living and dead, that it may profit me and them as a means of salvation to life everlasting. Amen.

He pours wine and water into the chalice, blessing the water before it is poured.

O GOD, Who established the nature of man in wondrous dignity, and still more admirably restored it, grant that through the mystery of this water and wine, we may be made partakers of His Divinity, Who has condescended to become partaker of our humanity, Jesus Christ, Your Son, our Lord. Who lives and reigns with You in the unity of the Holy Spirit, God, world without end. Amen.

Offering up the wine, the Priest says:

WE OFFER You, O Lord, the chalice of salvation, humbly begging of Your mercy that it may arise before Your Divine Majesty, with a pleasing fragrance, for our salvation and for that of the whole world. Amen.

Bowing down, the Priest says:

IN A humble spirit and with a contrite heart, may we be accepted by You, O Lord, and may our

sacrifice so be offered in Your sight this day as to please You, O Lord God.

Raising his eyes and blessing the offering, he says:

COME, O Sanctifier, almighty and eternal God, and bless ✠ this sacrifice prepared for the glory of Your holy name.

WASHING THE FINGERS

I WASH my hands in innocence, and I go around Your altar, O Lord, giving voice to my thanks, and recounting all Your wondrous deeds. O Lord, I love the house in which You dwell, the tenting-place of Your glory. Gather not my soul with those of sinners, nor with men of blood my life. On their hands are crimes, and their right hands are full of bribes. But I walk in integrity; redeem me, and have pity on me. My foot stands on level ground; in the assemblies I will bless You, O Lord. Glory be to the Father, and to the Son, and to the Holy Spirit. As it was in the beginning, is now, and ever shall be, world without end. Amen.

ACCEPT, Most Holy Trinity, this offering which we are making to You in remembrance of the Passion, Resurrection, and Ascension of Jesus Christ, our Lord; and in honor of Blessed Mary, ever Virgin, Blessed John the Baptist, the Holy Apostles Peter and Paul, and of these, and of all the Saints; that it may add to their honor and aid our salvation; and may they deign to intercede in heaven for us who honor their memory here on earth. Through the same Christ our Lord. Amen.

The Priest turns toward the people and says:

Pray, brethren, that my sacrifice and yours may become acceptable to God the Father almighty.

S. May the Lord accept this sacrifice from your hands to the praise and glory of His name, for our advantage, and that of all His holy Church.
P. Amen.

THE SECRET

ACCEPT, we beseech You, O Lord, the gifts which, of Your bounty, we bring to You: that, by the working of the power of Your grace, these most sacred mysteries may both sanctify us during the course of this life, and bring us to everlasting joys. Through our Lord Jesus Christ, Your Son, Who lives and reigns with You in the unity of the Holy Spirit, God.
P. World without end. *S.* Amen.

PREFACE—CANON

P. The Lord be with you. *S.* And with your spirit.
P. Lift up your hearts.
S. We have lifted them up to the Lord.
P. Let us give thanks to the Lord, our God.
S. It is fitting and just.

IT IS fitting indeed and just, right and helpful to salvation, for us always and everywhere to give thanks to You, O holy Lord, Father almighty, everlasting God, Who with Your Only-begotten Son and the Holy Spirit are one God, one Lord; not in the unity of a single person, but in the trinity of a single nature. For that which we believe on Your revelation concerning Your glory, that same we believe of Your Son, that same of the Holy Spirit, without difference or discrimination. So that in confessing the true and everlasting Godhead, we shall adore distinction in Persons, oneness in being, and equality in Majesty. This the Angels and Archangels, the Cherubim, too, and the Seraphim do

praise; day by day they cease not to cry out as with one voice, saying (*the bell is rung 3 times*):

HOLY, HOLY, HOLY, Lord God of Hosts. Heaven and earth are filled with Your glory. Hosanna in the highest. ✠ Blessed is He Who comes in the name of the Lord. Hosanna in the highest.

THE CANON OF THE MASS

THEREFORE, most gracious Father, we humbly beg of You and entreat You through Jesus Christ Your Son, our Lord, (*he kisses the altar*) to deem acceptable and bless these ✠ gifts, these ✠ offerings, these ✠ holy and unspotted oblations which, in the first place, we offer You for Your Holy Catholic Church, that You would deign to give her peace and protection, to unite and guard her throughout the world, together with Your servant N., our Pope, and N., our Bishop; and all true believers who cherish the Catholic and Apostolic Faith.

Commemoration of the Living

REMEMBER, O Lord, Your servants and handmaids, N. and N., (*name them*) and all here present, whose faith and devotion are known to You, on whose behalf we offer to You, or who themselves offer to You, this sacrifice of praise for themselves, families and friends, for the good of their souls, for their hope of salvation and deliverance from all harm, and who offer their homage to You, eternal, living and true God.

Commemoration of the Saints

IN THE unity of holy fellowship we observe the memory, first of all, of the glorious and ever

Virgin Mary, Mother of our Lord and God Jesus Christ; next, that of Your Blessed Apostles and Martyrs, Peter and Paul, Andrew, James, John, Thomas, James, Philip, Bartholomew, Matthew, Simon and Thaddeus; of Linus, Cletus, Clement, Sixtus, Cornelius, Cyprian, Lawrence, Chrysogonus, John and Paul, Cosmas and Damian, and of all Your Saints, by whose merits and prayers grant that we may be always fortified by the help of Your protection. Through the same Christ our Lord. Amen.

Spreading his hands over the oblation, he says:

GRACIOUSLY accept, then, we beseech You, O Lord, this service of our worship and that of all Your household. Provide that our days be spent in Your peace, save us from everlasting damnation, and cause us to be numbered in the flock You have chosen. Through Christ our Lord. Amen.

O GOD, deign to bless ✠ what we offer, and make it approved, ✠ effective, ✠ right, and wholly pleasing in every way, that it may become for our good, the Body ✠ and Blood ✠ of Your dearly beloved Son, Jesus Christ our Lord.

CONSECRATION—ELEVATION

WHO, the day before He suffered, took bread into His holy and venerable hands, and having raised His eyes to heaven, to You, O God, His almighty Father, giving thanks to You, He blessed it, ✠ broke it, and gave it to His disciples, saying: All of you take and eat of this:

FOR THIS IS MY BODY.

IN LIKE manner, when the supper was done, taking also this goodly chalice into His holy and venerable hands, again giving thanks to You, He

blessed ✠ it, and gave it to His disciples, saying: All of you take and drink of this:

FOR THIS IS THE CHALICE OF MY BLOOD OF THE NEW AND ETERNAL COVENANT: THE MYSTERY OF FAITH: WHICH SHALL BE SHED FOR YOU AND FOR MANY UNTO THE FORGIVENESS OF SINS.

As often as you shall do these things, in memory of Me shall you do them.

Offering of the Victim

MINDFUL, therefore, O Lord, not only of the blessed Passion of the same Christ, Your Son, our Lord, but also of His Resurrection from the dead, and finally His glorious Ascension into heaven, we, Your ministers, as also Your holy people, offer to Your supreme Majesty, of the gifts bestowed upon us, the pure ✠ Victim, the holy ✠ Victim, the all-perfect ✠ Victim: the holy ✠ Bread of life eternal and the Chalice ✠ of unending salvation.

AND this deign to regard with gracious and kindly attention and hold acceptable, as You deigned to accept the offerings of Abel, Your just servant, and the sacrifice of Abraham our patriarch, and that which Your chief priest Melchisedec offered to You, a holy sacrifice and a spotless victim.

MOST humbly we implore You, almighty God, bid these offerings to be brought by the hands of Your holy angel to Your altar above; before the face of Your Divine Majesty; that those of us who, by sharing in the Sacrifice of this altar, shall receive the Most Sacred ✠ Body and ✠ Blood of Your Son, may be filled with every grace and heavenly blessing. Through the same Christ our Lord. Amen.

Commemoration of the Dead

REMEMBER also, O Lord, Your servants and handmaids, N. and N., who have gone before us with the sign of faith, and rest in the sleep of peace. (*Here pray for the dead.*) To these, O Lord, and to all who rest in Christ, we beseech You to grant of Your goodness, a place of comfort, light and peace. Through the same Christ our Lord. Amen.

TO US sinners also, Your servants, trusting in the greatness of Your mercy, deign to grant some part and fellowship with Your Holy Apostles and Martyrs: with John, Stephen, Matthias, Barnabas, Ignatius, Alexander, Marcellinus, Peter, Felicitas, Perpetua, Agatha, Lucy, Agnes, Cecilia, Anastasia, and all Your Saints; into whose company, we implore You to admit us, not weighing our merits, but freely granting us pardon. Through Christ our Lord.

THROUGH Whom, O Lord, You always create, ✠ sanctify, ✠ fill with life, ✠ bless, and bestow upon us all good things.

The Minor Elevation

THROUGH ✠ Him, and with ✠ Him, and in ✠ Him, is to You, God the Father ✠ almighty, in the unity of the Holy ✠ Spirit, all honor and glory, world without end. S. Amen.

THE COMMUNION AND THANKSGIVING

Let us pray. Prompted by saving precepts, and taught by Your divine teaching, we dare to say:

OUR FATHER, Who art in heaven, hallowed be Thy name: Thy kingdom come: Thy will be

done on earth as it is in heaven. Give us this day our daily bread; and forgive us our trespasses, as we forgive those who trespass against us. And lead us not into temptation: *S.* But deliver us from evil. *P.* Amen.

DELIVER us, we beseech You, O Lord, from all evils, past, present, and to come; and by the intercession of the Blessed and glorious Mary, ever Virgin, Mother of God, together with Your Blessed Apostles Peter and Paul, and Andrew, and all the Saints, grant of Your goodness, peace in our days, that aided by the riches of Your mercy, we may be always free from sin and safe from all disturbance.

Through the same our Lord Jesus Christ, Your Son, Who lives and reigns with You in the unity of the Holy Spirit, God, world without end. *S.* Amen.

P. May the peace ✠ of the Lord be ✠ always with ✠ you. *S.* And with your spirit.

The Priest puts a small particle into the chalice, saying:

May this mingling and consecration of the Body and Blood of our Lord Jesus Christ help us who receive it to life everlasting. Amen.

LAMB of God, You Who take away the sins of the world, have mercy on us.

Lamb of God, You Who take away the sins of the world, have mercy on us.

Lamb of God, You Who take away the sins of the world, grant us peace.

PRAYERS BEFORE HOLY COMMUNION

Then inclining toward the altar, he says:

O LORD Jesus Christ, Who said to Your Apostles: "Peace I leave with you, My peace I give

to you," regard not my sins but the faith of Your Church, and deign to give her peace and unity according to Your Will: Who live and reign, God, world without end. Amen.

O LORD Jesus Christ, Son of the living God, Who, by the will of the Father, with the co-operation of the Holy Spirit, have by Your death given life to the world, deliver me by this Your Most Sacred Body and Blood from all my sins and from every evil. Make me always cling to Your commandments, and never permit me to be separated from You. Who with the same God the Father and the Holy Spirit, live and reign, God, world without end. Amen.

LET not the partaking of Your Body, O Lord Jesus Christ, which I, though unworthy, presume to receive, turn to my judgment and condemnation; but through Your goodness, may it become a safeguard and an effective remedy, both of soul and body. Who live and reign with God the Father, in the unity of the Holy Spirit, God, world without end. Amen.

COMMUNION OF THE PRIEST

I WILL take the Bread of heaven, and call upon the name of the Lord.

Lord, I am not worthy that You should come under my roof; but only say the word, and my soul will be healed. (3 *times.*)

Making the Sign of the Cross with the Host, he says:

MAY the Body of our Lord Jesus Christ preserve my soul to life everlasting. Amen.

What return shall I make to the Lord for all He has given me? I will take the Chalice of salvation,

and I will call upon the name of the Lord. Praising will I call upon the Lord and I shall be saved from my enemies.

Making the Sign of the Cross with the chalice, he says:

MAY the Blood of our Lord Jesus Christ preserve my soul to life everlasting. Amen.

The Priest reverently consumes the Precious Blood.

COMMUNION OF THE FAITHFUL

The Server and people say the "Confiteor."

P. May almighty God have mercy on you, forgive you your sins, and bring you to life everlasting. *S.* Amen.

P. May the almighty and merciful Lord grant you pardon, ✠ absolution and remission of your sins. *S.* Amen.

Holding up a Sacred Host, the Priest says:

Behold the Lamb of God, behold Him Who takes away the sins of the world.

Lord, I am not worthy that You should come under my roof; but only say the word, and my soul will be healed. (3 *times.*)

The Priest says to each communicant:

May the Body of our Lord Jesus Christ preserve your soul to life everlasting. Amen.

The Priest purifies the chalice with wine, saying:

WHAT has passed our lips as food, O Lord, may we possess in purity of heart, that what is given to us in time, be our healing for eternity.

He purifies his fingers with wine and water, saying:

MAY Your Body, O Lord, which I have eaten, and Your Blood which I have drunk, cleave to my very soul, and grant that no trace of sin be

found in me, whom these pure and holy mysteries have renewed. Who live and reign, world without end. Amen.

THE COMMUNION • Ps. 33, 9

TASTE and see how good the Lord is; happy the man who takes refuge in Him.

The Priest, turning to the people, says:

P. The Lord be with you. *S*. And with your spirit.
P. Let us pray.

THE POSTCOMMUNION

MAY this heavenly mystery, O Lord, renew us in mind and body, that we may feel the effect of that which we celebrate. Through our Lord Jesus Christ, Your Son, Who lives and reigns with You in the unity of the Holy Spirit, God, world without end. *S*. Amen.

FINAL PRAYERS

P. The Lord be with you. *S*. And with your spirit.
P. Go, you are dismissed. *S*. Thanks be to God.

MAY the tribute of my worship be pleasing to You, Most Holy Trinity, and grant that the sacrifice which I, all unworthy, have offered in the presence of Your Majesty, may be acceptable to You, and through Your mercy obtain forgiveness for me and all for whom I have offered it. Through Christ our Lord. Amen.

THE LAST BLESSING

MAY almighty God bless you: ✠ the Father, and the Son, and the Holy Spirit. *S*. Amen.

The Last Gospel and Prayers after Low Mass are conveniently placed inside the back cover.

When Jesus drew near to Jerusalem, He wept over it.

NINTH SUNDAY AFTER PENTECOST

The history of the Old and New Testaments proves that God rewards and punishes even here on earth. Jerusalem rejected the Savior and it was destroyed. No temptation is so strong that we cannot conquer it with the grace of God. (GREEN VESTMENTS)

PRAYERS AT THE FOOT OF THE ALTAR

IN THE name of the Father, ✠ and of the Son, and of the Holy Spirit. Amen.

Priest. I will go in to the altar of God.

Server. The God of my gladness and joy.

Psalm 42

DO ME justice, O God, and fight my fight against a faithless people; from the deceitful and impious man rescue me.

S. For You, O God, are my strength. Why do You keep me so far away? Why must I go about in mourning, with the enemy oppressing me?

P. Send forth Your light and Your fidelity; they shall lead me on and bring me to Your holy mountain, to Your dwelling-place.

S. Then will I go in to the altar of God, the God of my gladness and joy.
P. Then will I give You thanks upon the harp, O God, my God. Why are you so downcast, O my soul? Why do you sigh within me?
S. Hope in God! For I shall again be thanking Him in the presence of my Savior and my God.
P. Glory be to the Father, and to the Son, and to the Holy Spirit.
S. As it was in the beginning, is now, and ever shall be, world without end. Amen.
P. I will go in to the altar of God.
S. The God of my gladness and joy.
P. Our help ✠ is in the name of the Lord.
S. Who made heaven and earth.
P. I confess to almighty God, etc.
S. May almighty God have mercy on you, forgive you your sins, and bring you to life everlasting.
P. Amen.

The Server, bowing, says the "Confiteor."

I CONFESS to almighty God, to Blessed Mary, ever Virgin, to Blessed Michael the Archangel, to Blessed John the Baptist, to the Holy Apostles Peter and Paul, and to all the Saints, and to you, Father, that I have sinned exceedingly in thought, word and deed, *through my fault, through my fault, through my most grievous fault*. Therefore I beseech Blessed Mary, ever Virgin, Blessed Michael the Archangel, Blessed John the Baptist, the Holy Apostles Peter and Paul, and all the Saints, and you, Father, to pray to the Lord our God for me.
P. May almighty God have mercy on you, forgive you your sins, and bring you to life everlasting.
S. Amen.

MAY the almighty and merciful Lord grant us pardon, ✠ absolution, and remission of our sins. *S.* Amen.

P. Will You not, O God, give us life?

S. And shall not Your people rejoice in You?

P. Show us, O Lord, Your kindness.

S. And grant us Your salvation.

P. O Lord, hear my prayer.

S. And let my cry come to You.

P. The Lord be with you.

S. And with your spirit. *P.* Let us pray.

Going up to the altar, the Priest prays silently:

TAKE away from us our sins, O Lord, we beseech You, that we may enter with pure minds into the Holy of Holies. Through Christ our Lord. Amen.

WE BESEECH You, O Lord, by the merits of Your Saints (*he kisses the altar*) whose relics lie here, and of all the Saints: deign in Your mercy to pardon me all my sins. Amen.

THE INTROIT • Ps. 53, 6. 7. 3

At the right side of the altar, the Priest says:

BEHOLD, God is my helper, the Lord sustains my life. Turn back the evil upon my foes; in Your faithfulness destroy them, O Lord, my protector. *Ps.* O God, by Your name save me, and by Your might deliver me. Glory be to the Father, and to the Son, and to the Holy Spirit. As it was in the beginning, is now, and ever shall be, world without end. Amen. — Behold, God is my helper, the Lord sustains my life. Turn back the evil upon my foes; in Your faithfulness destroy them, O Lord, my protector.

THE KYRIE

P. Lord, have mercy. *S*. Lord, have mercy. *P*. Lord, have mercy. *S*. Christ, have mercy. *P*. Christ, have mercy. *S*. Christ, have mercy. *P*. Lord, have mercy. *S*. Lord, have mercy. *P*. Lord, have mercy.

THE GLORIA

GLORY to God in the highest. And on earth peace to men of good will. We praise You. We bless You. We adore You. We glorify You. We give You thanks for Your great glory. O Lord God, heavenly King, God the Father almighty. O Lord Jesus Christ, the Only-begotten Son. O Lord God, Lamb of God, Son of the Father: You Who take away the sins of the world, have mercy on us. You Who take away the sins of the world, receive our prayer. You Who sit at the right hand of the Father, have mercy on us. For You alone are holy. You alone are the Lord. You alone, O Jesus Christ, are most high. Together with the Holy Spirit ✠ in the glory of God the Father. Amen.

The Priest kisses the altar and turns to the people, saying:

P. The Lord be with you. *S*. And with your spirit. *P*. Let us pray.

THE PRAYER

Going to the right (Epistle) side, he says:

LET the ears of Your mercy, O Lord, be open to the prayers of Your suppliants; and that You may grant them what they desire, make them ask the things that are pleasing to You. Through our Lord Jesus Christ, Your Son, Who lives and reigns with You in the unity of the Holy Spirit, God, world without end. *S*. Amen.

THE EPISTLE • 1 Cor. 10, 6-13

BRETHREN: We should not lust after evil things even as they lusted. And do not become idolaters, even as some of them were, as it is written, "The people sat down to eat and drink, and rose up to play." Neither let us commit fornication, even as some of them committed fornication, and there fell in one day twenty-three thousand. Neither let us tempt Christ, as some of them tempted, and perished by the serpents. Neither murmur, as some of them murmured, and perished at the hands of the destroyer. Now all these things happened to them as a type, and they were written for our correction, upon whom the final age of the world has come. Therefore let him who thinks he stands take heed lest he fall. May no temptation take hold of you but such as man is equal to. God is faithful and will not permit you to be tempted beyond your strength, but with the temptation will also give you a way out that you may be able to bear it. *S.* Thanks be to God.

THE GRADUAL • Ps. 8, 2

O LORD, our Lord, how glorious is Your name over all the earth! ℣. You have elevated Your Majesty above the heavens.

Alleluia, alleluia. ℣. *Ps.* 58, 2. Rescue me from my enemies, O my God; from my adversaries defend me. Alleluia.

PRAYER BEFORE THE GOSPEL

Bowing down at the center of the altar, he says:

CLEANSE my heart and my lips, O almighty God, Who cleansed the lips of the Prophet Isaias with a burning coal. In Your gracious mercy

deign so to purify me that I may worthily proclaim Your holy Gospel. Through Christ our Lord. Amen.

Lord, grant Your blessing. The Lord be in my heart and on my lips, that I may worthily and fittingly proclaim His holy Gospel. Amen.

THE GOSPEL • Luke 19, 41-47

Going to the left (Gospel) side of the altar, he says:

P. The Lord be with you. S. And with your spirit.
P. ✠ The continuation of the holy Gospel according to Saint Luke. S. Glory be to You, O Lord.

AT THAT time, when Jesus drew near to Jerusalem and saw the city, He wept over it, saying, "If you had known, in this your day, even you, the things that are for your peace! But now they are hidden from your eyes. For days will come upon you when your enemies will throw up a rampart about you, and surround you and shut you in on every side, and will dash you to the ground and your children within you, and will not leave in you one stone upon another, because you have not known the time of your visitation." And He entered the temple, and began to cast out those who were selling and buying in it, saying to them, "It is written, 'My house is a house of prayer,' but you have made it a den of thieves." And He was teaching daily in the temple. S. Praise be to You, O Christ.

P. By the words of the Gospel, may our sins be taken away.

THE NICENE CREED

At the center of the altar, he says:

I BELIEVE in one God, the Father almighty, Maker of heaven and earth, and of all things

visible and invisible. And in one Lord Jesus Christ, the Only-begotten Son of God. Born of the Father before all ages. God of God; Light of Light; true God of true God. Begotten not made; of one being with the Father; by Whom all things were made. Who for us men, and for our salvation, came down from heaven. (*Here all genuflect.*) And was made Flesh by the Holy Spirit of the Virgin Mary: AND WAS MADE MAN. He was also crucified for us, suffered under Pontius Pilate and was buried. And on the third day He rose again according to the Scriptures. And ascending into heaven, He sits at the right hand of the Father. And He shall come again in glory to judge the living and the dead; and of His kingdom there shall be no end. And I believe in the Holy Spirit, Lord and Giver of life, Who proceeds from the Father and the Son. Who together with the Father and the Son is no less adored, and glorified: Who spoke by the Prophets. And I believe in One, Holy, Catholic and Apostolic Church. I confess one Baptism for the remission of sins. And I look for the resurrection of the dead. ✠ And the life of the world to come. Amen.

THE OFFERTORY

The Priest turns to the people and says:

P. The Lord be with you. *S.* And with your spirit.
P. Let us pray.

THE OFFERTORY VERSE • Ps. 18, 9. 10. 11. 12

THE precepts of the Lord are right, rejoicing the heart, and His ordinances sweeter than syrup or honey from the comb; therefore Your servant is careful of them.

The Priest now uncovers the chalice, places the host on the paten and offering it up, says:

ACCEPT, O holy Father, almighty and eternal God, this spotless host, which I, Your unworthy servant, offer to You, my living and true God, to atone for my numberless sins, offenses, and negligences; on behalf of all here present and likewise for all faithful Christians living and dead, that it may profit me and them as a means of salvation to life everlasting. Amen.

He pours wine and water into the chalice, blessing the water before it is poured.

O GOD, Who established the nature of man in wondrous dignity, and still more admirably restored it, grant that through the mystery of this water and wine, we may be made partakers of His Divinity, Who has condescended to become partaker of our humanity, Jesus Christ, Your Son, our Lord. Who lives and reigns with You in the unity of the Holy Spirit, God, world without end. Amen.

Offering up the wine, the Priest says:

WE OFFER You, O Lord, the chalice of salvation, humbly begging of Your mercy that it may arise before Your Divine Majesty, with a pleasing fragrance, for our salvation and for that of the whole world. Amen.

Bowing down, the Priest says:

IN A humble spirit and with a contrite heart, may we be accepted by You, O Lord, and may our sacrifice so be offered in Your sight this day as to please You, O Lord God.

Raising his eyes and blessing the offering, he says:

COME, O Sanctifier, almighty and eternal God, and bless ✠ this sacrifice prepared for the glory of Your holy name.

WASHING THE FINGERS

I WASH my hands in innocence, and I go around Your altar, O Lord, giving voice to my thanks, and recounting all Your wondrous deeds. O Lord, I love the house in which You dwell, the tenting-place of Your glory. Gather not my soul with those of sinners, nor with men of blood my life. On their hands are crimes, and their right hands are full of bribes. But I walk in integrity; redeem me, and have pity on me. My foot stands on level ground; in the assemblies I will bless You, O Lord. Glory be to the Father, and to the Son, and to the Holy Spirit. As it was in the beginning, is now, and ever shall be, world without end. Amen.

ACCEPT, Most Holy Trinity, this offering which we are making to You in remembrance of the Passion, Resurrection, and Ascension of Jesus Christ, our Lord; and in honor of Blessed Mary, ever Virgin, Blessed John the Baptist, the Holy Apostles Peter and Paul, and of these, and of all the Saints; that it may add to their honor and aid our salvation; and may they deign to intercede in heaven for us who honor their memory here on earth. Through the same Christ our Lord. Amen.

The Priest turns toward the people and says:

Pray, brethren, that my sacrifice and yours may become acceptable to God the Father almighty.
S. May the Lord accept this sacrifice from your hands to the praise and glory of His name, for our advantage, and that of all His holy Church.
P. Amen.

THE SECRET

GRANT us, we beseech You, O Lord, worthily to frequent these mysteries; since as often as

the remembrance of this Victim is celebrated, so often is the work of our redemption carried on. Through our Lord Jesus Christ, Your Son, Who lives and reigns with You in the unity of the Holy Spirit, God.
P. World without end. *S.* Amen.

PREFACE—CANON

P. The Lord be with you. *S.* And with your spirit.
P. Lift up your hearts.
S. We have lifted them up to the Lord.
P. Let us give thanks to the Lord, our God.
S. It is fitting and just.

IT IS fitting indeed and just, right and helpful to salvation, for us always and everywhere to give thanks to You, O holy Lord, Father almighty, everlasting God, Who with Your Only-begotten Son and the Holy Spirit are one God, one Lord; not in the unity of a single person, but in the trinity of a single nature. For that which we believe on Your revelation concerning Your glory, that same we believe of Your Son, that same of the Holy Spirit, without difference or discrimination. So that in confessing the true and everlasting Godhead, we shall adore distinction in Persons, oneness in being, and equality in Majesty. This the Angels and Archangels, the Cherubim, too, and the Seraphim do praise; day by day they cease not to cry out as with one voice, saying (*the bell is rung 3 times*):

HOLY, HOLY, HOLY, Lord God of Hosts. Heaven and earth are filled with Your glory. Hosanna in the highest. ✠ Blessed is He Who comes in the name of the Lord. Hosanna in the highest.

THE CANON OF THE MASS

THEREFORE, most gracious Father, we humbly beg of You and entreat You through Jesus Christ Your Son, our Lord, (*he kisses the altar*) to deem acceptable and bless these ✠ gifts, these ✠ offerings, these ✠ holy and unspotted oblations which, in the first place, we offer You for Your Holy Catholic Church, that You would deign to give her peace and protection, to unite and guard her throughout the world, together with Your servant *N.*, our Pope, and *N.*, our Bishop; and all true believers who cherish the Catholic and Apostolic Faith.

Commemoration of the Living

REMEMBER, O Lord, Your servants and handmaids, *N.* and *N.*, (*name them*) and all here present, whose faith and devotion are known to You, on whose behalf we offer to You, or who themselves offer to You, this sacrifice of praise for themselves, families and friends, for the good of their souls, for their hope of salvation and deliverance from all harm, and who offer their homage to You, eternal, living and true God.

Commemoration of the Saints

IN THE unity of holy fellowship we observe the memory, first of all, of the glorious and ever Virgin Mary, Mother of our Lord and God Jesus Christ; next, that of Your Blessed Apostles and Martyrs, Peter and Paul, Andrew, James, John, Thomas, James, Philip, Bartholomew, Matthew, Simon and Thaddeus; of Linus, Cletus, Clement, Sixtus, Cornelius, Cyprian, Lawrence, Chrysogonus, John and Paul, Cosmas and Damian, and of all Your Saints, by whose merits and prayers grant that

we may be always fortified by the help of Your protection. Through the same Christ our Lord. Amen.

Spreading his hands over the oblation, he says:

GRACIOUSLY accept, then, we beseech You, O Lord, this service of our worship and that of all Your household. Provide that our days be spent in Your peace, save us from everlasting damnation, and cause us to be numbered in the flock You have chosen. Through Christ our Lord. Amen.

O GOD, deign to bless ✠ what we offer, and make it approved, ✠ effective, ✠ right, and wholly pleasing in every way, that it may become for our good, the Body ✠ and Blood ✠ of Your dearly beloved Son, Jesus Christ our Lord.

CONSECRATION—ELEVATION

WHO, the day before He suffered, took bread into His holy and venerable hands, and having raised His eyes to heaven, to You, O God, His almighty Father, giving thanks to You, He blessed it, ✠ broke it, and gave it to His disciples, saying: All of you take and eat of this:

FOR THIS IS MY BODY.

IN LIKE manner, when the supper was done, taking also this goodly chalice into His holy and venerable hands, again giving thanks to You, He blessed ✠ it, and gave it to His disciples, saying: All of you take and drink of this:

FOR THIS IS THE CHALICE OF MY BLOOD OF THE NEW AND ETERNAL COVENANT: THE MYSTERY OF FAITH: WHICH SHALL BE SHED FOR YOU AND FOR MANY UNTO THE FORGIVENESS OF SINS.

After replacing the chalice on the corporal, he says:

As often as you shall do these things, in memory of Me shall you do them.

Offering of the Victim

MINDFUL, therefore, O Lord, not only of the blessed Passion of the same Christ, Your Son, our Lord, but also of His Resurrection from the dead, and finally His glorious Ascension into heaven, we, Your ministers, as also Your holy people, offer to Your supreme Majesty, of the gifts bestowed upon us, the pure ✠ Victim, the holy ✠ Victim, the all-perfect ✠ Victim: the holy ✠ Bread of life eternal and the Chalice ✠ of unending salvation.

AND this deign to regard with gracious and kindly attention and hold acceptable, as You deigned to accept the offerings of Abel, Your just servant, and the sacrifice of Abraham our patriarch, and that which Your chief priest Melchisedec offered to You, a holy sacrifice and a spotless victim.

MOST humbly we implore You, almighty God, bid these offerings to be brought by the hands of Your holy angel to Your altar above; before the face of Your Divine Majesty; that those of us who, by sharing in the Sacrifice of this altar, shall receive the Most Sacred ✠ Body and ✠ Blood of Your Son, may be filled with every grace and heavenly blessing. Through the same Christ our Lord. Amen.

Commemoration of the Dead

REMEMBER also, O Lord, Your servants and handmaids, N. and N., who have gone before us with the sign of faith, and rest in the sleep of peace. (*Here pray for the dead.*) To these, O Lord,

and to all who rest in Christ, we beseech You to grant of Your goodness, a place of comfort, light and peace. Through the same Christ our Lord. Amen.

TO US sinners also, Your servants, trusting in the greatness of Your mercy, deign to grant some part and fellowship with Your Holy Apostles and Martyrs: with John, Stephen, Matthias, Barnabas, Ignatius, Alexander, Marcellinus, Peter, Felicitas, Perpetua, Agatha, Lucy, Agnes, Cecilia, Anastasia, and all Your Saints; into whose company, we implore You to admit us, not weighing our merits, but freely granting us pardon. Through Christ our Lord.

THROUGH Whom, O Lord, You always create, ✠ sanctify, ✠ fill with life, ✠ bless, and bestow upon us all good things.

The Minor Elevation

THROUGH ✠ Him, and with ✠ Him, and in ✠ Him, is to You, God the Father ✠ almighty, in the unity of the Holy ✠ Spirit, all honor and glory, world without end. S. Amen.

THE COMMUNION AND THANKSGIVING

Let us pray. Prompted by saving precepts, and taught by Your divine teaching, we dare to say:

OUR FATHER, Who art in heaven, hallowed be Thy name: Thy kingdom come: Thy will be done on earth as it is in heaven. Give us this day our daily bread; and forgive us our trespasses, as we forgive those who trespass against us. And lead us not into temptation: S. But deliver us from evil. *P.* Amen.

DELIVER us, we beseech You, O Lord, from all evils, past, present, and to come; and by the intercession of the Blessed and glorious Mary, ever Virgin, Mother of God, together with Your Blessed Apostles Peter and Paul, and Andrew, and all the Saints, grant of Your goodness, peace in our days, that aided by the riches of Your mercy, we may be always free from sin and safe from all disturbance.

Through the same our Lord Jesus Christ, Your Son, Who lives and reigns with You in the unity of the Holy Spirit, God, world without end. *S.* Amen.

P. May the peace ✠ of the Lord be ✠ always with ✠ you. *S.* And with your spirit.

The Priest puts a small particle into the chalice, saying:

May this mingling and consecration of the Body and Blood of our Lord Jesus Christ help us who receive it to life everlasting. Amen.

LAMB of God, You Who take away the sins of the world, have mercy on us.

Lamb of God, You Who take away the sins of the world, have mercy on us.

Lamb of God, You Who take away the sins of the world, grant us peace.

PRAYERS BEFORE HOLY COMMUNION

Then inclining toward the altar, he says:

O LORD Jesus Christ, Who said to Your Apostles: "Peace I leave with you, My peace I give to you," regard not my sins but the faith of Your Church, and deign to give her peace and unity according to Your Will: Who live and reign, God, world without end. Amen.

O LORD Jesus Christ, Son of the living God, Who, by the will of the Father, with the cooperation of the Holy Spirit, have by Your death given life to the world, deliver me by this Your Most Sacred Body and Blood from all my sins and from every evil. Make me always cling to Your commandments, and never permit me to be separated from You. Who with the same God the Father and the Holy Spirit, live and reign, God, world without end. Amen.

LET not the partaking of Your Body, O Lord Jesus Christ, which I, though unworthy, presume to receive, turn to my judgment and condemnation; but through Your goodness, may it become a safeguard and an effective remedy, both of soul and body. Who live and reign with God the Father, in the unity of the Holy Spirit, God, world without end. Amen.

COMMUNION OF THE PRIEST

I WILL take the Bread of heaven, and call upon the name of the Lord.

Lord, I am not worthy that You should come under my roof; but only say the word, and my soul will be healed. (3 *times.*)

Making the Sign of the Cross with the Host, he says:

MAY the Body of our Lord Jesus Christ preserve my soul to life everlasting. Amen.

What return shall I make to the Lord for all He has given me? I will take the Chalice of salvation, and I will call upon the name of the Lord. Praising will I call upon the Lord and I shall be saved from my enemies.

Making the Sign of the Cross with the chalice, he says:

MAY the Blood of our Lord Jesus Christ preserve my soul to life everlasting. Amen.

The Priest reverently consumes the Precious Blood.

COMMUNION OF THE FAITHFUL

The Server and people say the "Confiteor."

P. May almighty God have mercy on you, forgive you your sins, and bring you to life everlasting. S. Amen.

P. May the almighty and merciful Lord grant you pardon, ✠ absolution and remission of your sins. S. Amen.

Holding up a Sacred Host, the Priest says:

Behold the Lamb of God, behold Him Who takes away the sins of the world.

Lord, I am not worthy that You should come under my roof; but only say the word, and my soul will be healed. (3 *times.*)

The Priest says to each communicant:

May the Body of our Lord Jesus Christ preserve your soul to life everlasting. Amen.

The Priest purifies the chalice with wine, saying:

WHAT has passed our lips as food, O Lord, may we possess in purity of heart, that what is given to us in time, be our healing for eternity.

He purifies his fingers with wine and water, saying:

MAY Your Body, O Lord, which I have eaten, and Your Blood which I have drunk, cleave to my very soul, and grant that no trace of sin be found in me, whom these pure and holy mysteries have renewed. Who live and reign, world without end. Amen.

THE COMMUNION • John 6, 57

"HE WHO eats My Flesh, and drinks My Blood, abides in Me, and I in him," says the Lord.

The Priest, turning to the people, says:

P. The Lord be with you. *S.* And with your spirit.
P. Let us pray.

THE POSTCOMMUNION

MAY the communion of Your sacrament, we beseech You, O Lord, both purify us, and grant us unity in Your service. Through our Lord Jesus Christ, Your Son, Who lives and reigns with You in the unity of the Holy Spirit, God, world without end. S. Amen.

FINAL PRAYERS

The Priest turns again to the people, and says:

P. The Lord be with you. *S.* And with your spirit.
P. Go, you are dismissed. *S.* Thanks be to God.

MAY the tribute of my worship be pleasing to You, Most Holy Trinity, and grant that the sacrifice which I, all unworthy, have offered in the presence of Your Majesty, may be acceptable to You, and through Your mercy obtain forgiveness for me and all for whom I have offered it. Through Christ our Lord. Amen.

THE LAST BLESSING

He kisses the altar, and facing the people, says:

MAY almighty God bless you: ✠ the Father, and the Son, and the Holy Spirit. *S.* Amen.

The Last Gospel and Prayers after Low Mass are conveniently placed inside the back cover.

"I thank You that I am not like the rest of men."

TENTH SUNDAY AFTER PENTECOST

God reveals Himself to the humble and despises arrogance and pride. We may be aware of our capabilities and accomplishments, but we must remember that "all these things are the work of one and the same Spirit." (GREEN VESTMENTS)

PRAYERS AT THE FOOT OF THE ALTAR

IN THE name of the Father, ✠ and of the Son, and of the Holy Spirit. Amen.

Priest. I will go in to the altar of God.

Server. The God of my gladness and joy.

Psalm 42

DO ME justice, O God, and fight my fight against a faithless people; from the deceitful and impious man rescue me.

S. For You, O God, are my strength. Why do You keep me so far away? Why must I go about in mourning, with the enemy oppressing me?

P. Send forth Your light and Your fidelity; they shall lead me on and bring me to Your holy mountain, to Your dwelling-place.

S. Then will I go in to the altar of God, the God of my gladness and joy.
P. Then will I give You thanks upon the harp, O God, my God. Why are you so downcast, O my soul? Why do you sigh within me?
S. Hope in God! For I shall again be thanking Him in the presence of my Savior and my God.
P. Glory be to the Father, and to the Son, and to the Holy Spirit.
S. As it was in the beginning, is now, and ever shall be, world without end. Amen.
P. I will go in to the altar of God.
S. The God of my gladness and joy.
P. Our help ✠ is in the name of the Lord.
S. Who made heaven and earth.
P. I confess to almighty God, etc.
S. May almighty God have mercy on you, forgive you your sins, and bring you to life everlasting.
P. Amen.

The Server, bowing, says the "Confiteor."

I CONFESS to almighty God, to Blessed Mary, ever Virgin, to Blessed Michael the Archangel, to Blessed John the Baptist, to the Holy Apostles Peter and Paul, and to all the Saints, and to you, Father, that I have sinned exceedingly in thought, word and deed, *through my fault, through my fault, through my most grievous fault.* Therefore I beseech Blessed Mary, ever Virgin, Blessed Michael the Archangel, Blessed John the Baptist, the Holy Apostles Peter and Paul, and all the Saints, and you, Father, to pray to the Lord our God for me.
P. May almighty God have mercy on you, forgive you your sins, and bring you to life everlasting.
S. Amen.

MAY the almighty and merciful Lord grant us pardon, ✠ absolution, and remission of our sins. *S.* Amen.

P. Will You not, O God, give us life?
S. And shall not Your people rejoice in You?
P. Show us, O Lord, Your kindness.
S. And grant us Your salvation.
P. O Lord, hear my prayer.
S. And let my cry come to You.
P. The Lord be with you.
S. And with your spirit. *P.* Let us pray.

Going up to the altar, the Priest prays silently:

TAKE away from us our sins, O Lord, we beseech You, that we may enter with pure minds into the Holy of Holies. Through Christ our Lord. Amen.

WE BESEECH You, O Lord, by the merits of Your Saints (*he kisses the altar*) whose relics lie here, and of all the Saints: deign in Your mercy to pardon me all my sins. Amen.

THE INTROIT • Ps. 54, 17. 18. 20. 23. 2. 3

At the right side of the altar, the Priest says:

WHEN I called upon the Lord, He heard my voice, from those who war against me; and He humbled them, Who is before all ages, and remains forever: cast your care upon the Lord, and He will support you. *Ps.* Hearken, O God, to my prayer; turn not away from my pleading; give heed to me, and answer me. Glory be to the Father, and to the Son, and to the Holy Spirit. As it was in the beginning, is now, and ever shall be, world without end. Amen. — When I called upon the Lord, He heard my voice, from those who war against me;

and He humbled them, Who is before all ages, and remains forever: cast your care upon the Lord, and He will support you.

THE KYRIE

P. Lord, have mercy. *S.* Lord, have mercy. *P.* Lord, have mercy. *S.* Christ, have mercy. *P.* Christ, have mercy. *S.* Christ, have mercy. *P.* Lord, have mercy. *S.* Lord, have mercy. *P.* Lord, have mercy.

THE GLORIA

GLORY to God in the highest. And on earth peace to men of good will. We praise You. We bless You. We adore You. We glorify You. We give You thanks for Your great glory. O Lord God, heavenly King, God the Father almighty. O Lord Jesus Christ, the Only-begotten Son. O Lord God, Lamb of God, Son of the Father: You Who take away the sins of the world, have mercy on us. You Who take away the sins of the world, receive our prayer. You Who sit at the right hand of the Father, have mercy on us. For You alone are holy. You alone are the Lord. You alone, O Jesus Christ, are most high. Together with the Holy Spirit ✠ in the glory of God the Father. Amen.

The Priest kisses the altar and turns to the people, saying:

P. The Lord be with you. *S.* And with your spirit. *P.* Let us pray.

THE PRAYER

Going to the right (Epistle) side, he says:

O GOD, You manifest Your almighty power most of all in sparing and showing mercy; multiply upon us Your mercy, that we, running to Your promises, may be made partakers of Your heavenly goods. Through our Lord Jesus Christ,

Your Son, Who lives and reigns with You in the unity of the Holy Spirit, God, world without end. S. Amen.

THE EPISTLE • 1 Cor. 12, 2-11

BRETHREN: You know that when you were Gentiles, you went to dumb idols according as you were led. Wherefore I give you to understand that no one speaking in the Spirit of God says "Anathema" to Jesus. And no one can say "Jesus is Lord," except in the Holy Spirit. Now there are varieties of gifts, but the same Spirit; and there are varieties of ministries, but the same Lord; and there are varieties of workings, but the same God, Who works all things in all. Now the manifestation of the Spirit is given to everyone for profit. To one through the Spirit is given the utterance of wisdom; and to another the utterance of knowledge, according to the same Spirit; to another faith, in the same Spirit; to another the gift of healing, in the one Spirit; to another the working of miracles; to another prophecy; to another the distinguishing of spirits; to another various kinds of tongues; to another interpretation of tongues. But all these things are the work of one and the same Spirit, Who allots to everyone according as He will. S. Thanks be to God.

THE GRADUAL • Ps. 16, 8. 2

KEEP me, O Lord, as the apple of Your eye; hide me in the shadow of Your wings. ℣. From You let judgment come; Your eyes behold what is right.

Alleluia, alleluia. ℣. *Ps. 64*, 2. To You we owe our hymn of praise, O God, in Sion; to You must vows be fulfilled in Jerusalem. Alleluia.

PRAYER BEFORE THE GOSPEL

Bowing down at the center of the altar, he says:

CLEANSE my heart and my lips, O almighty God, Who cleansed the lips of the Prophet Isaias with a burning coal. In Your gracious mercy deign so to purify me that I may worthily proclaim Your holy Gospel. Through Christ our Lord. Amen.

Lord, grant Your blessing. The Lord be in my heart and on my lips, that I may worthily and fittingly proclaim His holy Gospel. Amen.

THE GOSPEL • Luke 18, 9-14

Going to the left (Gospel) side of the altar, he says:

P. The Lord be with you. *S.* And with your spirit.

P. ✠ The continuation of the holy Gospel according to Saint Luke. *S.* Glory be to You, O Lord.

AT THAT time, Jesus spoke this parable to some who trusted in themselves as being just and despised others. "Two men went up to the temple to pray, the one a Pharisee and the other a publican. The Pharisee stood and began to pray thus within himself: 'O God, I thank You that I am not like the rest of men, robbers, dishonest, adulterers, or even like this publican. I fast twice a week; I pay tithes of all that I possess.' But the publican, standing afar off, would not so much as lift up his eyes to heaven, but kept striking his breast, saying, 'O God, be merciful to me the sinner!' I tell you, this man went back to his home justified rather than the other; for everyone who exalts himself shall be humbled, and he who humbles himself shall be exalted." *S.* Praise be to You, O Christ.

P. By the words of the Gospel, may our sins be taken away.

THE NICENE CREED

At the center of the altar, he says:

I BELIEVE in one God, the Father almighty, Maker of heaven and earth, and of all things visible and invisible. And in one Lord Jesus Christ, the Only-begotten Son of God. Born of the Father before all ages. God of God; Light of Light; true God of true God. Begotten not made; of one being with the Father; by Whom all things were made. Who for us men, and for our salvation, came down from heaven. (*Here all genuflect.*) And was made Flesh by the Holy Spirit of the Virgin Mary: AND WAS MADE MAN. He was also crucified for us, suffered under Pontius Pilate and was buried. And on the third day He rose again according to the Scriptures. And ascending into heaven, He sits at the right hand of the Father. And He shall come again in glory to judge the living and the dead; and of His kingdom there shall be no end. And I believe in the Holy Spirit, Lord and Giver of life, Who proceeds from the Father and the Son. Who together with the Father and the Son is no less adored, and glorified: Who spoke by the Prophets. And I believe in One, Holy, Catholic and Apostolic Church. I confess one Baptism for the remission of sins. And I look for the resurrection of the dead. ✠ And the life of the world to come. Amen.

THE OFFERTORY

The Priest turns to the people and says:

P. The Lord be with you. *S.* And with your spirit.

P. Let us pray.

THE OFFERTORY VERSE • Ps. 24, 1-3

TO YOU I lift up my soul, O Lord. In You, O my God, I trust; let me not be put to shame, let not my enemies exult over me. No one who waits for You shall be put to shame.

The Priest now uncovers the chalice, places the host on the paten and offering it up, says:

ACCEPT, O holy Father, almighty and eternal God, this spotless host, which I, Your unworthy servant, offer to You, my living and true God, to atone for my numberless sins, offenses, and negligences; on behalf of all here present and likewise for all faithful Christians living and dead, that it may profit me and them as a means of salvation to life everlasting. Amen.

He pours wine and water into the chalice, blessing the water before it is poured.

O GOD, Who established the nature of man in wondrous dignity, and still more admirably restored it, grant that through the mystery of this water and wine, we may be made partakers of His Divinity, Who has condescended to become partaker of our humanity, Jesus Christ, Your Son, our Lord. Who lives and reigns with You in the unity of the Holy Spirit, God, world without end. Amen.

Offering up the wine, the Priest says:

WE OFFER You, O Lord, the chalice of salvation, humbly begging of Your mercy that it may arise before Your Divine Majesty, with a pleasing fragrance, for our salvation and for that of the whole world. Amen.

Bowing down, the Priest says:

IN A humble spirit and with a contrite heart, may we be accepted by You, O Lord, and may our

sacrifice so be offered in Your sight this day as to please You, O Lord God.

Raising his eyes and blessing the offering, he says:

COME, O Sanctifier, almighty and eternal God, and bless ✠ this sacrifice prepared for the glory of Your holy name.

WASHING THE FINGERS

I WASH my hands in innocence, and I go around Your altar, O Lord, giving voice to my thanks, and recounting all Your wondrous deeds. O Lord, I love the house in which You dwell, the tenting-place of Your glory. Gather not my soul with those of sinners, nor with men of blood my life. On their hands are crimes, and their right hands are full of bribes. But I walk in integrity; redeem me, and have pity on me. My foot stands on level ground; in the assemblies I will bless You, O Lord. Glory be to the Father, and to the Son, and to the Holy Spirit. As it was in the beginning, is now, and ever shall be, world without end. Amen.

ACCEPT, Most Holy Trinity, this offering which we are making to You in remembrance of the Passion, Resurrection, and Ascension of Jesus Christ, our Lord; and in honor of Blessed Mary, ever Virgin, Blessed John the Baptist, the Holy Apostles Peter and Paul, and of these, and of all the Saints; that it may add to their honor and aid our salvation; and may they deign to intercede in heaven for us who honor their memory here on earth. Through the same Christ our Lord. Amen.

The Priest turns toward the people and says:

Pray, brethren, that my sacrifice and yours may become acceptable to God the Father almighty.

S. May the Lord accept this sacrifice from your hands to the praise and glory of His name, for our advantage, and that of all His holy Church.
P. Amen.

THE SECRET

MAY this sacrifice become dedicated to You, O Lord: a sacrifice which, it has pleased You, should in such a manner be offered to the honor of Your name, and at the same time become our remedy. Through our Lord Jesus Christ, Your Son, Who lives and reigns with You in the unity of the Holy Spirit, God.
P. World without end. *S.* Amen.

PREFACE—CANON

P. The Lord be with you. *S.* And with your spirit.
P. Lift up your hearts.
S. We have lifted them up to the Lord.
P. Let us give thanks to the Lord, our God.
S. It is fitting and just.

IT IS fitting indeed and just, right and helpful to salvation, for us always and everywhere to give thanks to You, O holy Lord, Father almighty, everlasting God, Who with Your Only-begotten Son and the Holy Spirit are one God, one Lord; not in the unity of a single person, but in the trinity of a single nature. For that which we believe on Your revelation concerning Your glory, that same we believe of Your Son, that same of the Holy Spirit, without difference or discrimination. So that in confessing the true and everlasting Godhead, we shall adore distinction in Persons, oneness in being, and equality in Majesty. This the Angels and Archangels, the Cherubim, too, and the Seraphim do

praise; day by day they cease not to cry out as with one voice, saying (*the bell is rung 3 times*):

HOLY, HOLY, HOLY, Lord God of Hosts. Heaven and earth are filled with Your glory. Hosanna in the highest. ✠ Blessed is He Who comes in the name of the Lord. Hosanna in the highest.

THE CANON OF THE MASS

THEREFORE, most gracious Father, we humbly beg of You and entreat You through Jesus Christ Your Son, our Lord, (*he kisses the altar*) to deem acceptable and bless these ✠ gifts, these ✠ offerings, these ✠ holy and unspotted oblations which, in the first place, we offer You for Your Holy Catholic Church, that You would deign to give her peace and protection, to unite and guard her throughout the world, together with Your servant N., our Pope, and N., our Bishop; and all true believers who cherish the Catholic and Apostolic Faith.

Commemoration of the Living

REMEMBER, O Lord, Your servants and handmaids, N. and N., (*name them*) and all here present, whose faith and devotion are known to You, on whose behalf we offer to You, or who themselves offer to You, this sacrifice of praise for themselves, families and friends, for the good of their souls, for their hope of salvation and deliverance from all harm, and who offer their homage to You, eternal, living and true God.

Commemoration of the Saints

IN THE unity of holy fellowship we observe the memory, first of all, of the glorious and ever Virgin Mary, Mother of our Lord and God Jesus

Christ; next, that of Your Blessed Apostles and Martyrs, Peter and Paul, Andrew, James, John, Thomas, James, Philip, Bartholomew, Matthew, Simon and Thaddeus; of Linus, Cletus, Clement, Sixtus, Cornelius, Cyprian, Lawrence, Chrysogonus, John and Paul, Cosmas and Damian, and of all Your Saints, by whose merits and prayers grant that we may be always fortified by the help of Your protection. Through the same Christ our Lord. Amen.

Spreading his hands over the oblation, he says:

GRACIOUSLY accept, then, we beseech You, O Lord, this service of our worship and that of all Your household. Provide that our days be spent in Your peace, save us from everlasting damnation, and cause us to be numbered in the flock You have chosen. Through Christ our Lord. Amen.

O GOD, deign to bless ✠ what we offer, and make it approved, ✠ effective, ✠ right, and wholly pleasing in every way, that it may become for our good, the Body ✠ and Blood ✠ of Your dearly beloved Son, Jesus Christ our Lord.

CONSECRATION—ELEVATION

WHO, the day before He suffered, took bread into His holy and venerable hands, and having raised His eyes to heaven, to You, O God, His almighty Father, giving thanks to You, He blessed it, ✠ broke it, and gave it to His disciples, saying: All of you take and eat of this:

FOR THIS IS MY BODY.

IN LIKE manner, when the supper was done, taking also this goodly chalice into His holy and venerable hands, again giving thanks to You, He blessed ✠ it, and gave it to His disciples, saying: All of you take and drink of this:

FOR THIS IS THE CHALICE OF MY BLOOD OF THE NEW AND ETERNAL COVENANT: THE MYSTERY OF FAITH: WHICH SHALL BE SHED FOR YOU AND FOR MANY UNTO THE FORGIVENESS OF SINS.

After replacing the chalice on the corporal, he says:

As often as you shall do these things, in memory of Me shall you do them.

Offering of the Victim

MINDFUL, therefore, O Lord, not only of the blessed Passion of the same Christ, Your Son, our Lord, but also of His Resurrection from the dead, and finally His glorious Ascension into heaven, we, Your ministers, as also Your holy people, offer to Your supreme Majesty, of the gifts bestowed upon us, the pure ✠ Victim, the holy ✠ Victim, the all-perfect ✠ Victim: the holy ✠ Bread of life eternal and the Chalice ✠ of unending salvation.

AND this deign to regard with gracious and kindly attention and hold acceptable, as You deigned to accept the offerings of Abel, Your just servant, and the sacrifice of Abraham our patriarch, and that which Your chief priest Melchisedec offered to You, a holy sacrifice and a spotless victim.

MOST humbly we implore You, almighty God, bid these offerings to be brought by the hands of Your holy angel to Your altar above; before the face of Your Divine Majesty; that those of us who, by sharing in the Sacrifice of this altar, shall receive the Most Sacred ✠ Body and ✠ Blood of Your Son, may be filled with every grace and heavenly blessing. Through the same Christ our Lord. Amen.

Commemoration of the Dead

REMEMBER also, O Lord, Your servants and handmaids, N. and N., who have gone before us with the sign of faith, and rest in the sleep of peace. (*Here pray for the dead.*) To these, O Lord, and to all who rest in Christ, we beseech You to grant of Your goodness, a place of comfort, light and peace. Through the same Christ our Lord. Amen.

TO US sinners also, Your servants, trusting in the greatness of Your mercy, deign to grant some part and fellowship with Your Holy Apostles and Martyrs: with John, Stephen, Matthias, Barnabas, Ignatius, Alexander, Marcellinus, Peter, Felicitas, Perpetua, Agatha, Lucy, Agnes, Cecilia, Anastasia, and all Your Saints; into whose company, we implore You to admit us, not weighing our merits, but freely granting us pardon. Through Christ our Lord.

THROUGH Whom, O Lord, You always create, ✠ sanctify, ✠ fill with life, ✠ bless, and bestow upon us all good things.

The Minor Elevation

THROUGH ✠ Him, and with ✠ Him, and in ✠ Him, is to You, God the Father ✠ almighty, in the unity of the Holy ✠ Spirit, all honor and glory, world without end. S. Amen.

THE COMMUNION AND THANKSGIVING

Let us pray. Prompted by saving precepts, and taught by Your divine teaching, we dare to say:

OUR FATHER, Who art in heaven, hallowed be Thy name: Thy kingdom come: Thy will be done on earth as it is in heaven. Give us this day

our daily bread; and forgive us our trespasses, as we forgive those who trespass against us. And lead us not into temptation: S. But deliver us from evil. *P*. Amen.

DELIVER us, we beseech You, O Lord, from all evils, past, present, and to come; and by the intercession of the Blessed and glorious Mary, ever Virgin, Mother of God, together with Your Blessed Apostles Peter and Paul, and Andrew, and all the Saints, grant of Your goodness, peace in our days, that aided by the riches of Your mercy, we may be always free from sin and safe from all disturbance.

Through the same our Lord Jesus Christ, Your Son, Who lives and reigns with You in the unity of the Holy Spirit, God, world without end. S. Amen.

P. May the peace ✠ of the Lord be ✠ always with ✠ you. S. And with your spirit.

The Priest puts a small particle into the chalice, saying:

May this mingling and consecration of the Body and Blood of our Lord Jesus Christ help us who receive it to life everlasting. Amen.

LAMB of God, You Who take away the sins of the world, have mercy on us.

Lamb of God, You Who take away the sins of the world, have mercy on us.

Lamb of God, You Who take away the sins of the world, grant us peace.

PRAYERS BEFORE HOLY COMMUNION

Then inclining toward the altar, he says:

O LORD Jesus Christ, Who said to Your Apostles: "Peace I leave with you, My peace I give to you," regard not my sins but the faith of Your

Church, and deign to give her peace and unity according to Your Will: Who live and reign, God, world without end. Amen.

O LORD Jesus Christ, Son of the living God, Who, by the will of the Father, with the co-operation of the Holy Spirit, have by Your death given life to the world, deliver me by this Your Most Sacred Body and Blood from all my sins and from every evil. Make me always cling to Your commandments, and never permit me to be separated from You. Who with the same God the Father and the Holy Spirit, live and reign, God, world without end. Amen.

LET not the partaking of Your Body, O Lord Jesus Christ, which I, though unworthy, presume to receive, turn to my judgment and condemnation; but through Your goodness, may it become a safeguard and an effective remedy, both of soul and body. Who live and reign with God the Father, in the unity of the Holy Spirit, God, world without end. Amen.

COMMUNION OF THE PRIEST

I WILL take the Bread of heaven, and call upon the name of the Lord.

Lord, I am not worthy that You should come under my roof; but only say the word, and my soul will be healed. (3 *times.*)

Making the Sign of the Cross with the Host, he says:

MAY the Body of our Lord Jesus Christ preserve my soul to life everlasting. Amen.

What return shall I make to the Lord for all He has given me? I will take the Chalice of salvation, and I will call upon the name of the Lord. Prais-

ing will I call upon the Lord and I shall be saved from my enemies.

Making the Sign of the Cross with the chalice, he says:

MAY the Blood of our Lord Jesus Christ preserve my soul to life everlasting. Amen.

The Priest reverently consumes the Precious Blood.

COMMUNION OF THE FAITHFUL

The Server and people say the "Confiteor."

P. May almighty God have mercy on you, forgive you your sins, and bring you to life everlasting. S. Amen.

P. May the almighty and merciful Lord grant you pardon, ✠ absolution and remission of your sins. S. Amen.

Holding up a Sacred Host, the Priest says:

Behold the Lamb of God, behold Him Who takes away the sins of the world.

Lord, I am not worthy that You should come under my roof; but only say the word, and my soul will be healed. (3 *times.*)

The Priest says to each communicant:

May the Body of our Lord Jesus Christ preserve your soul to life everlasting. Amen.

The Priest purifies the chalice with wine, saying:

WHAT has passed our lips as food, O Lord, may we possess in purity of heart, that what is given to us in time, be our healing for eternity.

He purifies his fingers with wine and water, saying:

MAY Your Body, O Lord, which I have eaten, and Your Blood which I have drunk, cleave to my very soul, and grant that no trace of sin be found in me, whom these pure and holy mysteries have renewed. Who live and reign, world without end. Amen.

THE COMMUNION • Ps. 50, 21

YOU shall be pleased with due sacrifices, burnt offerings and holocausts on Your altar, O Lord.

The Priest, turning to the people, says:

P. The Lord be with you. *S.* And with your spirit.
P. Let us pray.

THE POSTCOMMUNION

WE BESEECH You, O Lord our God, that in Your goodness You would not deprive of Your aid those whom You do not cease to refresh with Your divine sacraments. Through our Lord Jesus Christ, Your Son, Who lives and reigns with You in the unity of the Holy Spirit, God, world without end. *S.* Amen.

FINAL PRAYERS

The Priest turns again to the people, and says:

P. The Lord be with you. *S.* And with your spirit.
P. Go, you are dismissed. *S.* Thanks be to God.

MAY the tribute of my worship be pleasing to You, Most Holy Trinity, and grant that the sacrifice which I, all unworthy, have offered in the presence of Your Majesty, may be acceptable to You, and through Your mercy obtain forgiveness for me and all for whom I have offered it. Through Christ our Lord. Amen.

THE LAST BLESSING

He kisses the altar, and facing the people, says:

MAY almighty God bless you: ✠ the Father, and the Son, and the Holy Spirit. *S.* Amen.

The Last Gospel and Prayers after Low Mass are conveniently placed inside the back cover.

"Ephpheta," that is, "Be opened."

ELEVENTH SUNDAY AFTER PENTECOST

St. Paul at first persecuted the Church of Christ. But he was later converted and then "he began to speak correctly." Like St. Paul we should draw our inspiration from Christ and rely constantly on His graces. (GREEN VESTMENTS)

PRAYERS AT THE FOOT OF THE ALTAR

IN THE name of the Father, ✠ and of the Son, and of the Holy Spirit. Amen.

Priest. I will go in to the altar of God.

Server. The God of my gladness and joy.

Psalm 42

DO ME justice, O God, and fight my fight against a faithless people; from the deceitful and impious man rescue me.

S. For You, O God, are my strength. Why do You keep me so far away? Why must I go about in mourning, with the enemy oppressing me?

P. Send forth Your light and Your fidelity; they shall lead me on and bring me to Your holy mountain, to Your dwelling-place.

S. Then will I go in to the altar of God, the God of my gladness and joy.
P. Then will I give You thanks upon the harp, O God, my God. Why are you so downcast, O my soul? Why do you sigh within me?
S. Hope in God! For I shall again be thanking Him in the presence of my Savior and my God.
P. Glory be to the Father, and to the Son, and to the Holy Spirit.
S. As it was in the beginning, is now, and ever shall be, world without end. Amen.
P. I will go in to the altar of God.
S. The God of my gladness and joy.
P. Our help ✠ is in the name of the Lord.
S. Who made heaven and earth.
P. I confess to almighty God, etc.
S. May almighty God have mercy on you, forgive you your sins, and bring you to life everlasting.
P. Amen.

The Server, bowing, says the "Confiteor."

I CONFESS to almighty God, to Blessed Mary, ever Virgin, to Blessed Michael the Archangel, to Blessed John the Baptist, to the Holy Apostles Peter and Paul, and to all the Saints, and to you, Father, that I have sinned exceedingly in thought, word and deed, *through my fault, through my fault, through my most grievous fault.* Therefore I beseech Blessed Mary, ever Virgin, Blessed Michael the Archangel, Blessed John the Baptist, the Holy Apostles Peter and Paul, and all the Saints, and you, Father, to pray to the Lord our God for me.
P. May almighty God have mercy on you, forgive you your sins, and bring you to life everlasting.
S. Amen.

MAY the almighty and merciful Lord grant us pardon, ✠ absolution, and remission of our sins. *S*. Amen.

P. Will You not, O God, give us life?
S. And shall not Your people rejoice in You?
P. Show us, O Lord, Your kindness.
S. And grant us Your salvation.
P. O Lord, hear my prayer.
S. And let my cry come to You.
P. The Lord be with you.
S. And with your spirit. *P*. Let us pray.

Going up to the altar, the Priest prays silently:

TAKE away from us our sins, O Lord, we beseech You, that we may enter with pure minds into the Holy of Holies. Through Christ our Lord. Amen.

WE BESEECH You, O Lord, by the merits of Your Saints (*he kisses the altar*) whose relics lie here, and of all the Saints: deign in Your mercy to pardon me all my sins. Amen.

THE INTROIT • Ps. 67, 6. 7. 36. 2

At the right side of the altar, the Priest says:

GOD is in His holy dwelling, God Who makes men of one mind to dwell in a house; He shall give power and strength to His people. *Ps.* God arises; His enemies are scattered, and those who hate Him flee before Him. Glory be to the Father, and to the Son, and to the Holy Spirit. As it was in the beginning, is now, and ever shall be, world without end. Amen. — God is in His holy dwelling, God Who makes men of one mind to dwell in a house; He shall give power and strength to His people.

THE KYRIE

P. Lord, have mercy. *S.* Lord, have mercy. *P.* Lord, have mercy. *S.* Christ, have mercy. *P.* Christ, have mercy. *S.* Christ, have mercy. *P.* Lord, have mercy. *S.* Lord, have mercy. *P.* Lord, have mercy.

THE GLORIA

GLORY to God in the highest. And on earth peace to men of good will. We praise You. We bless You. We adore You. We glorify You. We give You thanks for Your great glory. O Lord God, heavenly King, God the Father almighty. O Lord Jesus Christ, the Only-begotten Son. O Lord God, Lamb of God, Son of the Father: You Who take away the sins of the world, have mercy on us. You Who take away the sins of the world, receive our prayer. You Who sit at the right hand of the Father, have mercy on us. For You alone are holy. You alone are the Lord. You alone, O Jesus Christ, are most high. Together with the Holy Spirit ✠ in the glory of God the Father. Amen.

The Priest kisses the altar and turns to the people, saying:

P. The Lord be with you. *S.* And with your spirit.
P. Let us pray.

THE PRAYER

Going to the right (Epistle) side, he says:

ALMIGHTY and everlasting God, in the abundance of Your loving-kindness, You exceed both the merits and the desires of Your suppliants; pour forth Your mercy upon us, that You may forgive what our consciences fear and grant what we do not presume to ask. Through our Lord Jesus Christ, Your Son, Who lives and reigns with

You in the unity of the Holy Spirit, God, world without end. S. Amen.

THE EPISTLE • 1 Cor. 15, 1-10

BRETHREN: I recall to your minds the gospel that I preached to you, which also you received, wherein also you stand, through which also you are being saved, if you hold it fast, as I preached it to you — unless you have believed to no purpose. For I delivered to you first of all, what I also received, that Christ died for our sins according to the Scriptures, and that He was buried, and that He rose again the third day, according to the Scriptures, and that He appeared to Cephas, and after that to the Eleven. Then He was seen by more than five hundred brethren at one time, many of whom are with us still, but some have fallen asleep. After that He was seen by James, then by all the apostles. And last of all, as by one born out of due time, He was seen also by me. For I am the least of the apostles, and am not worthy to be called an apostle, because I persecuted the Church of God. But by the grace of God I am what I am, and His grace in me has not been fruitless. S. Thanks be to God.

THE GRADUAL • Ps. 27, 7. 1

IN GOD my heart trusts, and I find help; then my heart exults, and with my song I give Him thanks. ℣. To You, O Lord, I call; O my God, be not deaf to me; depart not from me.

Alleluia, alleluia. ℣. *Ps.* 80, 2. 3. Sing joyfully to God our strength; acclaim the God of Jacob. Take up a pleasant psalm with the harp. Alleluia.

PRAYER BEFORE THE GOSPEL

Bowing down at the center of the altar, he says:

CLEANSE my heart and my lips, O almighty God, Who cleansed the lips of the Prophet Isaias with a burning coal. In Your gracious mercy deign so to purify me that I may worthily proclaim Your holy Gospel. Through Christ our Lord. Amen. Lord, grant Your blessing. The Lord be in my heart and on my lips, that I may worthily and fittingly proclaim His holy Gospel. Amen.

THE GOSPEL • Mark 7, 31-37

Going to the left (Gospel) side of the altar, he says:

P. The Lord be with you. *S.* And with your spirit.
P. ✠ The continuation of the holy Gospel according to Saint Mark. *S.* Glory be to You, O Lord.

AT THAT time, Jesus departing from the district of Tyre came by way of Sidon to the sea of Galilee, through the midst of the district of Decapolis. And they brought to Him one deaf and dumb, and entreated Him to lay His hand upon him. And taking him aside from the crowd, He put His fingers into the man's ears, and spitting, He touched his tongue. And looking up to heaven, He sighed, and said to him, "Ephpheta," that is, "Be opened." And his ears were at once opened, and the bond of his tongue was loosed, and he began to speak correctly. And He charged them to tell no one. But the more He charged them, so much the more did they continue to publish it. And so much the more did they wonder, saying, "He has done all things well. He has made both the deaf to hear and the dumb to speak." S. Praise be to You, O Christ.

P. By the words of the Gospel, may our sins be taken away.

THE NICENE CREED

At the center of the altar, he says:

I BELIEVE in one God, the Father almighty, Maker of heaven and earth, and of all things visible and invisible. And in one Lord Jesus Christ, the Only-begotten Son of God. Born of the Father before all ages. God of God; Light of Light; true God of true God. Begotten not made; of one being with the Father; by Whom all things were made. Who for us men, and for our salvation, came down from heaven. (*Here all genuflect.*) And was made Flesh by the Holy Spirit of the Virgin Mary: AND WAS MADE MAN. He was also crucified for us, suffered under Pontius Pilate and was buried. And on the third day He rose again according to the Scriptures. And ascending into heaven, He sits at the right hand of the Father. And He shall come again in glory to judge the living and the dead; and of His kingdom there shall be no end. And I believe in the Holy Spirit, Lord and Giver of life, Who proceeds from the Father and the Son. Who together with the Father and the Son is no less adored, and glorified: Who spoke by the Prophets. And I believe in One, Holy, Catholic and Apostolic Church. I confess one Baptism for the remission of sins. And I look for the resurrection of the dead. ✠ And the life of the world to come. Amen.

THE OFFERTORY

The Priest turns to the people and says:

P. The Lord be with you. S. And with your spirit.

P. Let us pray.

THE OFFERTORY VERSE • Ps. 29, 2-3

I WILL extol You, O Lord, for You drew me clear and did not let my enemies rejoice over me; O Lord, I cried out to You and You healed me.

The Priest now uncovers the chalice, places the host on the paten and offering it up, says:

ACCEPT, O holy Father, almighty and eternal God, this spotless host, which I, Your unworthy servant, offer to You, my living and true God, to atone for my numberless sins, offenses, and negligences; on behalf of all here present and likewise for all faithful Christians living and dead, that it may profit me and them as a means of salvation to life everlasting. Amen.

He pours wine and water into the chalice, blessing the water before it is poured.

O GOD, Who established the nature of man in wondrous dignity, and still more admirably restored it, grant that through the mystery of this water and wine, we may be made partakers of His Divinity, Who has condescended to become partaker of our humanity, Jesus Christ, Your Son, our Lord. Who lives and reigns with You in the unity of the Holy Spirit, God, world without end. Amen.

Offering up the wine, the Priest says:

WE OFFER You, O Lord, the chalice of salvation, humbly begging of Your mercy that it may arise before Your Divine Majesty, with a pleasing fragrance, for our salvation and for that of the whole world. Amen.

Bowing down, the Priest says:

IN A humble spirit and with a contrite heart, may we be accepted by You, O Lord, and may our

sacrifice so be offered in Your sight this day as to please You, O Lord God.

Raising his eyes and blessing the offering, he says:

COME, O Sanctifier, almighty and eternal God, and bless ✠ this sacrifice prepared for the glory of Your holy name.

WASHING THE FINGERS

I WASH my hands in innocence, and I go around Your altar, O Lord, giving voice to my thanks, and recounting all Your wondrous deeds. O Lord, I love the house in which You dwell, the tenting-place of Your glory. Gather not my soul with those of sinners, nor with men of blood my life. On their hands are crimes, and their right hands are full of bribes. But I walk in integrity; redeem me, and have pity on me. My foot stands on level ground; in the assemblies I will bless You, O Lord. Glory be to the Father, and to the Son, and to the Holy Spirit. As it was in the beginning, is now, and ever shall be, world without end. Amen.

ACCEPT, Most Holy Trinity, this offering which we are making to You in remembrance of the Passion, Resurrection, and Ascension of Jesus Christ, our Lord; and in honor of Blessed Mary, ever Virgin, Blessed John the Baptist, the Holy Apostles Peter and Paul, and of these, and of all the Saints; that it may add to their honor and aid our salvation; and may they deign to intercede in heaven for us who honor their memory here on earth. Through the same Christ our Lord. Amen.

The Priest turns toward the people and says:

Pray, brethren, that my sacrifice and yours may become acceptable to God the Father almighty.

S. May the Lord accept this sacrifice from your hands to the praise and glory of His name, for our advantage, and that of all His holy Church.
P. Amen.

THE SECRET

MERCIFULLY regard our service, we beseech You, O Lord, that the gift which we offer may be acceptable to You, and be the support of our frailty. Through our Lord Jesus Christ, Your Son, Who lives and reigns with You in the unity of the Holy Spirit, God.
P. World without end. S. Amen.

PREFACE—CANON

P. The Lord be with you. S. And with your spirit.
P. Lift up your hearts.
S. We have lifted them up to the Lord.
P. Let us give thanks to the Lord, our God.
S. It is fitting and just.

IT IS fitting indeed and just, right and helpful to salvation, for us always and everywhere to give thanks to You, O holy Lord, Father almighty, everlasting God, Who with Your Only-begotten Son and the Holy Spirit are one God, one Lord; not in the unity of a single person, but in the trinity of a single nature. For that which we believe on Your revelation concerning Your glory, that same we believe of Your Son, that same of the Holy Spirit, without difference or discrimination. So that in confessing the true and everlasting Godhead, we shall adore distinction in Persons, oneness in being, and equality in Majesty. This the Angels and Archangels, the Cherubim, too, and the Seraphim do praise; day by day they cease not to cry out as with one voice, saying (*the bell is rung* 3 *times*):

HOLY, HOLY, HOLY, Lord God of Hosts. Heaven and earth are filled with Your glory. Hosanna in the highest. ✠ Blessed is He Who comes in the name of the Lord. Hosanna in the highest.

THE CANON OF THE MASS

THEREFORE, most gracious Father, we humbly beg of You and entreat You through Jesus Christ Your Son, our Lord, (*he kisses the altar*) to deem acceptable and bless these ✠ gifts, these ✠ offerings, these ✠ holy and unspotted oblations which, in the first place, we offer You for Your Holy Catholic Church, that You would deign to give her peace and protection, to unite and guard her throughout the world, together with Your servant N., our Pope, and N., our Bishop; and all true believers who cherish the Catholic and Apostolic Faith.

Commemoration of the Living

REMEMBER, O Lord, Your servants and handmaids, N. and N., (*name them*) and all here present, whose faith and devotion are known to You, on whose behalf we offer to You, or who themselves offer to You, this sacrifice of praise for themselves, families and friends, for the good of their souls, for their hope of salvation and deliverance from all harm, and who offer their homage to You, eternal, living and true God.

Commemoration of the Saints

IN THE unity of holy fellowship we observe the memory, first of all, of the glorious and ever Virgin Mary, Mother of our Lord and God Jesus Christ; next, that of Your Blessed Apostles and Martyrs, Peter and Paul, Andrew, James, John,

Thomas, James, Philip, Bartholomew, Matthew, Simon and Thaddeus; of Linus, Cletus, Clement, Sixtus, Cornelius, Cyprian, Lawrence, Chrysogonus, John and Paul, Cosmas and Damian, and of all Your Saints, by whose merits and prayers grant that we may be always fortified by the help of Your protection. Through the same Christ our Lord. Amen.

Spreading his hands over the oblation, he says:

GRACIOUSLY accept, then, we beseech You, O Lord, this service of our worship and that of all Your household. Provide that our days be spent in Your peace, save us from everlasting damnation, and cause us to be numbered in the flock You have chosen. Through Christ our Lord. Amen.

O GOD, deign to bless ✠ what we offer, and make it approved, ✠ effective, ✠ right, and wholly pleasing in every way, that it may become for our good, the Body ✠ and Blood ✠ of Your dearly beloved Son, Jesus Christ our Lord.

CONSECRATION—ELEVATION

WHO, the day before He suffered, took bread into His holy and venerable hands, and having raised His eyes to heaven, to You, O God, His almighty Father, giving thanks to You, He blessed it, ✠ broke it, and gave it to His disciples, saying: All of you take and eat of this:

FOR THIS IS MY BODY.

IN LIKE manner, when the supper was done, taking also this goodly chalice into His holy and venerable hands, again giving thanks to You, He blessed ✠ it, and gave it to His disciples, saying: All of you take and drink of this:

FOR THIS IS THE CHALICE OF MY BLOOD OF THE NEW AND ETERNAL COVENANT: THE MYSTERY OF FAITH: WHICH SHALL BE SHED FOR YOU AND FOR MANY UNTO THE FORGIVENESS OF SINS.

After replacing the chalice on the corporal, he says:

As often as you shall do these things, in memory of Me shall you do them.

Offering of the Victim

MINDFUL, therefore, O Lord, not only of the blessed Passion of the same Christ, Your Son, our Lord, but also of His Resurrection from the dead, and finally His glorious Ascension into heaven, we, Your ministers, as also Your holy people, offer to Your supreme Majesty, of the gifts bestowed upon us, the pure ✠ Victim, the holy ✠ Victim, the all-perfect ✠ Victim: the holy ✠ Bread of life eternal and the Chalice ✠ of unending salvation.

AND this deign to regard with gracious and kindly attention and hold acceptable, as You deigned to accept the offerings of Abel, Your just servant, and the sacrifice of Abraham our patriarch, and that which Your chief priest Melchisedec offered to You, a holy sacrifice and a spotless victim.

MOST humbly we implore You, almighty God, bid these offerings to be brought by the hands of Your holy angel to Your altar above; before the face of Your Divine Majesty; that those of us who, by sharing in the Sacrifice of this altar, shall receive the Most Sacred ✠ Body and ✠ Blood of Your Son, may be filled with every grace and heavenly blessing. Through the same Christ our Lord. Amen.

Commemoration of the Dead

REMEMBER also, O Lord, Your servants and handmaids, N. and N., who have gone before us with the sign of faith, and rest in the sleep of peace. (*Here pray for the dead.*) To these, O Lord, and to all who rest in Christ, we beseech You to grant of Your goodness, a place of comfort, light and peace. Through the same Christ our Lord. Amen.

TO US sinners also, Your servants, trusting in the greatness of Your mercy, deign to grant some part and fellowship with Your Holy Apostles and Martyrs: with John, Stephen, Matthias, Barnabas, Ignatius, Alexander, Marcellinus, Peter, Felicitas, Perpetua, Agatha, Lucy, Agnes, Cecilia, Anastasia, and all Your Saints; into whose company, we implore You to admit us, not weighing our merits, but freely granting us pardon. Through Christ our Lord.

THROUGH Whom, O Lord, You always create, ✠ sanctify, ✠ fill with life, ✠ bless, and bestow upon us all good things.

The Minor Elevation

THROUGH ✠ Him, and with ✠ Him, and in ✠ Him, is to You, God the Father ✠ almighty, in the unity of the Holy ✠ Spirit, all honor and glory, world without end. S. Amen.

THE COMMUNION AND THANKSGIVING

Let us pray. Prompted by saving precepts, and taught by Your divine teaching, we dare to say:

OUR FATHER, Who art in heaven, hallowed be Thy name: Thy kingdom come: Thy will be done on earth as it is in heaven. Give us this day

our daily bread; and forgive us our trespasses, as we forgive those who trespass against us. And lead us not into temptation: S. But deliver us from evil. *P.* Amen.

DELIVER us, we beseech You, O Lord, from all evils, past, present, and to come; and by the intercession of the Blessed and glorious Mary, ever Virgin, Mother of God, together with Your Blessed Apostles Peter and Paul, and Andrew, and all the Saints, grant of Your goodness, peace in our days, that aided by the riches of Your mercy, we may be always free from sin and safe from all disturbance.

Through the same our Lord Jesus Christ, Your Son, Who lives and reigns with You in the unity of the Holy Spirit, God, world without end. S. Amen.

P. May the peace ✠ of the Lord be ✠ always with ✠ you. *S.* And with your spirit.

The Priest puts a small particle into the chalice, saying:

May this mingling and consecration of the Body and Blood of our Lord Jesus Christ help us who receive it to life everlasting. Amen.

LAMB of God, You Who take away the sins of the world, have mercy on us.

Lamb of God, You Who take away the sins of the world, have mercy on us.

Lamb of God, You Who take away the sins of the world, grant us peace.

PRAYERS BEFORE HOLY COMMUNION

Then inclining toward the altar, he says:

O LORD Jesus Christ, Who said to Your Apostles: "Peace I leave with you, My peace I give

to you," regard not my sins but the faith of Your Church, and deign to give her peace and unity according to Your Will: Who live and reign, God, world without end. Amen.

O LORD Jesus Christ, Son of the living God, Who, by the will of the Father, with the co-operation of the Holy Spirit, have by Your death given life to the world, deliver me by this Your Most Sacred Body and Blood from all my sins and from every evil. Make me always cling to Your commandments, and never permit me to be separated from You. Who with the same God the Father and the Holy Spirit, live and reign, God, world without end. Amen.

LET not the partaking of Your Body, O Lord Jesus Christ, which I, though unworthy, presume to receive, turn to my judgment and condemnation; but through Your goodness, may it become a safeguard and an effective remedy, both of soul and body. Who live and reign with God the Father, in the unity of the Holy Spirit, God, world without end. Amen.

COMMUNION OF THE PRIEST

I WILL take the Bread of heaven, and call upon the name of the Lord.

Lord, I am not worthy that You should come under my roof; but only say the word, and my soul will be healed. (3 *times.*)

Making the Sign of the Cross with the Host, he says:

MAY the Body of our Lord Jesus Christ preserve my soul to life everlasting. Amen.

What return shall I make to the Lord for all He has given me? I will take the Chalice of salvation,

and I will call upon the name of the Lord. Praising will I call upon the Lord and I shall be saved from my enemies.

Making the Sign of the Cross with the chalice, he says:

MAY the Blood of our Lord Jesus Christ preserve my soul to life everlasting. Amen.

The Priest reverently consumes the Precious Blood.

COMMUNION OF THE FAITHFUL

The Server and people say the "Confiteor."

P. May almighty God have mercy on you, forgive you your sins, and bring you to life everlasting. S. Amen.

P. May the almighty and merciful Lord grant you pardon, ✠ absolution and remission of your sins. S. Amen.

Holding up a Sacred Host, the Priest says:

Behold the Lamb of God, behold Him Who takes away the sins of the world.

Lord, I am not worthy that You should come under my roof; but only say the word, and my soul will be healed. (3 *times.*)

The Priest says to each communicant:

May the Body of our Lord Jesus Christ preserve your soul to life everlasting. Amen.

The Priest purifies the chalice with wine, saying:

WHAT has passed our lips as food, O Lord, may we possess in purity of heart, that what is given to us in time, be our healing for eternity.

He purifies his fingers with wine and water, saying:

MAY Your Body, O Lord, which I have eaten, and Your Blood which I have drunk, cleave to my very soul, and grant that no trace of sin be found in me, whom these pure and holy mysteries

have renewed. Who live and reign, world without end. Amen.

THE COMMUNION • Prov. 3, 9-10

HONOR the Lord with your wealth, with first fruits of all your produce. Then will your barns be filled with grain, with new wine your vats will overflow.

The Priest, turning to the people, says:

P. The Lord be with you. S. And with your spirit.
P. Let us pray.

THE POSTCOMMUNION

BY THE reception of Your sacrament, we beseech You, O Lord, may we feel a support of mind and body, that, saved in both, we may glory in the fullness of the heavenly remedy. Through our Lord Jesus Christ, Your Son, Who lives and reigns with You in the unity of the Holy Spirit, God, world without end. S. Amen.

FINAL PRAYERS

P. The Lord be with you. S. And with your spirit.
P. Go, you are dismissed. S. Thanks be to God.

MAY the tribute of my worship be pleasing to You, Most Holy Trinity, and grant that the sacrifice which I, all unworthy, have offered in the presence of Your Majesty, may be acceptable to You, and through Your mercy obtain forgiveness for me and all for whom I have offered it. Through Christ our Lord. Amen.

THE LAST BLESSING

MAY almighty God bless you: ✠ the Father, and the Son, and the Holy Spirit. S. Amen.

The Last Gospel and Prayers after Low Mass are conveniently placed inside the back cover.

The Good Samaritan bound up his wounds.

TWELFTH SUNDAY AFTER PENTECOST

"Blessed are the eyes that see what you see." At Mass, we see with the eyes of faith Christ present in the Consecrated Host. Personally and actively to participate in the Mass makes us love God more and more; it increases the spirit of sacrifice and kindness in dealing with others. (GREEN VESTMENTS)

PRAYERS AT THE FOOT OF THE ALTAR

IN THE name of the Father, ✠ and of the Son, and of the Holy Spirit. Amen.

Priest. I will go in to the altar of God.

Server. The God of my gladness and joy.

Psalm 42

DO ME justice, O God, and fight my fight against a faithless people; from the deceitful and impious man rescue me.

S. For You, O God, are my strength. Why do You keep me so far away? Why must I go about in mourning, with the enemy oppressing me?

P. Send forth Your light and Your fidelity; they shall lead me on and bring me to Your holy mountain, to Your dwelling-place.

S. Then will I go in to the altar of God, the God of my gladness and joy.
P. Then will I give You thanks upon the harp, O God, my God. Why are you so downcast, O my soul? Why do you sigh within me?
S. Hope in God! For I shall again be thanking Him in the presence of my Savior and my God.
P. Glory be to the Father, and to the Son, and to the Holy Spirit.
S. As it was in the beginning, is now, and ever shall be, world without end. Amen.
P. I will go in to the altar of God.
S. The God of my gladness and joy.
P. Our help ✠ is in the name of the Lord.
S. Who made heaven and earth.
P. I confess to almighty God, etc.
S. May almighty God have mercy on you, forgive you your sins, and bring you to life everlasting.
P. Amen.

The Server, bowing, says the "Confiteor."

I CONFESS to almighty God, to Blessed Mary, ever Virgin, to Blessed Michael the Archangel, to Blessed John the Baptist, to the Holy Apostles Peter and Paul, and to all the Saints, and to you, Father, that I have sinned exceedingly in thought, word and deed, *through my fault, through my fault, through my most grievous fault*. Therefore I beseech Blessed Mary, ever Virgin, Blessed Michael the Archangel, Blessed John the Baptist, the Holy Apostles Peter and Paul, and all the Saints, and you, Father, to pray to the Lord our God for me.
P. May almighty God have mercy on you, forgive you your sins, and bring you to life everlasting.
S. Amen.

MAY the almighty and merciful Lord grant us pardon, ✠ absolution, and remission of our sins. S. Amen.

P. Will You not, O God, give us life?
S. And shall not Your people rejoice in You?
P. Show us, O Lord, Your kindness.
S. And grant us Your salvation.
P. O Lord, hear my prayer.
S. And let my cry come to You.
P. The Lord be with you.
S. And with your spirit. *P.* Let us pray.

Going up to the altar, the Priest prays silently:

TAKE away from us our sins, O Lord, we beseech You, that we may enter with pure minds into the Holy of Holies. Through Christ our Lord. Amen.

WE BESEECH You, O Lord, by the merits of Your Saints (*he kisses the altar*) whose relics lie here, and of all the Saints: deign in Your mercy to pardon me all my sins. Amen.

THE INTROIT • Ps. 69, 2-3. 4

At the right side of the altar, the Priest says:

DEIGN, O God, to rescue me; O Lord, make haste to help me. Let them be put to shame and confounded who seek my life. *Ps.* Let them be turned back in disgrace, who desire my ruin. Glory be to the Father, and to the Son, and to the Holy Spirit. As it was in the beginning, is now, and ever shall be, world without end. Amen. — Deign, O God, to rescue me; O Lord, make haste to help me. Let them be put to shame and confounded who seek my life.

THE KYRIE

P. Lord, have mercy. *S.* Lord, have mercy. *P.* Lord, have mercy. *S.* Christ, have mercy. *P.* Christ, have mercy. *S.* Christ, have mercy. *P.* Lord, have mercy. *S.* Lord, have mercy. *P.* Lord, have mercy.

THE GLORIA

GLORY to God in the highest. And on earth peace to men of good will. We praise You. We bless You. We adore You. We glorify You. We give You thanks for Your great glory. O Lord God, heavenly King, God the Father almighty. O Lord Jesus Christ, the Only-begotten Son. O Lord God, Lamb of God, Son of the Father: You Who take away the sins of the world, have mercy on us. You Who take away the sins of the world, receive our prayer. You Who sit at the right hand of the Father, have mercy on us. For You alone are holy. You alone are the Lord. You alone, O Jesus Christ, are most high. Together with the Holy Spirit ✠ in the glory of God the Father. Amen.

The Priest kisses the altar and turns to the people, saying:

P. The Lord be with you. *S.* And with your spirit. *P.* Let us pray.

THE PRAYER

Going to the right (Epistle) side, he says:

ALMIGHTY and merciful God, of Whose gift it comes that Your faithful people do You worthy and laudable service, grant, we beseech You, that we may run without stumbling to the attainment of Your promises. Through our Lord Jesus Christ, Your Son, Who lives and reigns with You in the unity of the Holy Spirit, God, world without end. *S.* Amen.

THE EPISTLE • 2 Cor. 3, 4-9

BRETHREN: Such is the assurance I have through Christ toward God. Not that we are sufficient of ourselves to think anything, as from ourselves, but our sufficiency is from God. He also it is Who has made us fit ministers of the new covenant, not of the letter but of the spirit; for the letter kills, but the spirit gives life. Now if the ministration of death, which was engraved in letters upon stones, was inaugurated in such glory that the children of Israel could not look steadfastly upon the face of Moses on account of the transient glory that shone upon it, shall not the ministration of the spirit be still more glorious? For if there is glory in the ministration that condemned, much more does the ministration that justifies abound in glory. S. Thanks be to God.

THE GRADUAL • Ps. 33, 2. 3

I WILL bless the Lord at all times; His praise shall be ever in my mouth. ℣. Let my soul glory in the Lord; the lowly will hear and be glad.

Alleluia, alleluia. ℣. *Ps.* 87, 2. O Lord, the God of my salvation, by day I cry out, at night I clamor in Your presence. Alleluia.

PRAYER BEFORE THE GOSPEL

Bowing down at the center of the altar, he says:

CLEANSE my heart and my lips, O almighty God, Who cleansed the lips of the Prophet Isaias with a burning coal. In Your gracious mercy deign so to purify me that I may worthily proclaim Your holy Gospel. Through Christ our Lord. Amen.

Lord, grant Your blessing. The Lord be in my heart and on my lips, that I may worthily and fittingly proclaim His holy Gospel. Amen.

THE GOSPEL • Luke 10, 23-37

Going to the left (Gospel) side of the altar, he says:

P. The Lord be with you. S. And with your spirit.
P. ✠ The continuation of the holy Gospel according to Saint Luke. S. Glory be to You, O Lord.

AT THAT time, Jesus said to His disciples: "Blessed are the eyes that see what you see! For I say to you, many prophets and kings have desired to see what you see, and they have not seen it; and to hear what you hear, and they have not heard it." And behold, a certain lawyer got up to test Him, saying, "Master, what must I do to gain eternal life?" But He said to him, "What is written in the Law? How do you read?" He answered and said, "You shall love the Lord your God with your whole heart, and with your whole soul, and with your whole strength, and with your whole mind; and your neighbor as yourself." And He said to him, "You have answered rightly; do this and you shall live." But he, wishing to justify himself, said to Jesus, "And who is my neighbor?" Jesus answered and said, "A certain man was going down from Jerusalem to Jericho, and he fell in with robbers, who after both stripping him and beating him went their way, leaving him half-dead. But, as it happened, a certain priest was going down the same way; and when he saw him, he passed by. And likewise a Levite also, when he was near the place and saw him, passed by. But a certain Samaritan as he journeyed came upon him, and seeing him, was moved with compassion. And he went up to him and bound up his wounds, pouring on oil and wine. And setting him on his own beast, he brought him to an inn and took care of him.

And the next day he took out two denarii and gave them to the innkeeper and said, 'Take care of him; and whatever more you spend, I, on my way back, will repay you.' Which of these three, in your opinion, proved himself neighbor to him who fell among the robbers?" And he said, "He who took pity on him." And Jesus said to him, "Go and do also in like manner." S. Praise be to You, O Christ.

P. By the words of the Gospel, may our sins be taken away.

THE NICENE CREED

At the center of the altar, he says:

I BELIEVE in one God, the Father almighty, Maker of heaven and earth, and of all things visible and invisible. And in one Lord Jesus Christ, the Only-begotten Son of God. Born of the Father before all ages. God of God; Light of Light; true God of true God. Begotten not made; of one being with the Father; by Whom all things were made. Who for us men, and for our salvation, came down from heaven. (*Here all genuflect.*) And was made Flesh by the Holy Spirit of the Virgin Mary: AND WAS MADE MAN. He was also crucified for us, suffered under Pontius Pilate and was buried. And on the third day He rose again according to the Scriptures. And ascending into heaven, He sits at the right hand of the Father. And He shall come again in glory to judge the living and the dead; and of His kingdom there shall be no end. And I believe in the Holy Spirit, Lord and Giver of life, Who proceeds from the Father and the Son. Who together with the Father and the Son is no less adored, and glorified: Who spoke by the Prophets. And I believe in One, Holy, Catholic and Apostolic Church. I confess one Baptism for the remission of sins. And I look for the resurrection of the dead. ✠ And the life of the world to come. Amen.

THE OFFERTORY

The Priest turns to the people and says:

P. The Lord be with you. *S.* And with your spirit.
P. Let us pray.

THE OFFERTORY VERSE • Ex. 32, 11. 13. 14

MOSES prayed in the sight of the Lord his God, and said, "Why, O Lord, is Your indignation enkindled against Your people? Let the anger of Your mind cease; remember Abraham, Isaac, and Jacob, to whom You swore to give a land flowing with milk and honey." And the Lord was appeased from doing the evil which He had spoken of doing against His people.

The Priest now uncovers the chalice, places the host on the paten and offering it up, says:

ACCEPT, O holy Father, almighty and eternal God, this spotless host, which I, Your unworthy servant, offer to You, my living and true God, to atone for my numberless sins, offenses, and negligences; on behalf of all here present and likewise for all faithful Christians living and dead, that it may profit me and them as a means of salvation to life everlasting. Amen.

He pours wine and water into the chalice, blessing the water before it is poured.

O GOD, Who established the nature of man in wondrous dignity, and still more admirably restored it, grant that through the mystery of this water and wine, we may be made partakers of His Divinity, Who has condescended to become partaker of our humanity, Jesus Christ, Your Son, our

Lord. Who lives and reigns with You in the unity of the Holy Spirit, God, world without end. Amen.

Offering up the wine, the Priest says:

WE OFFER You, O Lord, the chalice of salvation, humbly begging of Your mercy that it may arise before Your Divine Majesty, with a pleasing fragrance, for our salvation and for that of the whole world. Amen.

Bowing down, the Priest says:

IN A humble spirit and with a contrite heart, may we be accepted by You, O Lord, and may our sacrifice so be offered in Your sight this day as to please You, O Lord God.

Raising his eyes and blessing the offering, he says:

COME, O Sanctifier, almighty and eternal God, and bless ✠ this sacrifice prepared for the glory of Your holy name.

WASHING THE FINGERS

I WASH my hands in innocence, and I go around Your altar, O Lord, giving voice to my thanks, and recounting all Your wondrous deeds. O Lord, I love the house in which You dwell, the tenting-place of Your glory. Gather not my soul with those of sinners, nor with men of blood my life. On their hands are crimes, and their right hands are full of bribes. But I walk in integrity; redeem me, and have pity on me. My foot stands on level ground; in the assemblies I will bless You, O Lord. Glory be to the Father, and to the Son, and to the Holy Spirit. As it was in the beginning, is now, and ever shall be, world without end. Amen.

ACCEPT, Most Holy Trinity, this offering which we are making to You in remembrance of the Passion, Resurrection, and Ascension of Jesus Christ, our Lord; and in honor of Blessed Mary, ever Virgin, Blessed John the Baptist, the Holy Apostles Peter and Paul, and of these, and of all the Saints; that it may add to their honor and aid our salvation; and may they deign to intercede in heaven for us who honor their memory here on earth. Through the same Christ our Lord. Amen.

The Priest turns toward the people and says:

Pray, brethren, that my sacrifice and yours may become acceptable to God the Father almighty.

S. May the Lord accept this sacrifice from your hands to the praise and glory of His name, for our advantage, and that of all His holy Church.

P. Amen.

THE SECRET

MERCIFULLY look down, we beseech You, O Lord, upon the sacrifices which we present on Your sacred altar; that while procuring pardon for us, they may render honor to Your name. Through our Lord Jesus Christ, Your Son, Who lives and reigns with You in the unity of the Holy Spirit, God.

P. World without end. *S.* Amen.

PREFACE—CANON

P. The Lord be with you. *S.* And with your spirit.
P. Lift up your hearts.
S. We have lifted them up to the Lord.
P. Let us give thanks to the Lord, our God.
S. It is fitting and just.

IT IS fitting indeed and just, right and helpful to salvation, for us always and everywhere to give thanks to You, O holy Lord, Father almighty, everlasting God, Who with Your Only-begotten Son and the Holy Spirit are one God, one Lord; not in the unity of a single person, but in the trinity of a single nature. For that which we believe on Your revelation concerning Your glory, that same we believe of Your Son, that same of the Holy Spirit, without difference or discrimination. So that in confessing the true and everlasting Godhead, we shall adore distinction in Persons, oneness in being, and equality in Majesty. This the Angels and Archangels, the Cherubim, too, and the Seraphim do praise; day by day they cease not to cry out as with one voice, saying (*the bell is rung* 3 *times*):

HOLY, HOLY, HOLY, Lord God of Hosts. Heaven and earth are filled with Your glory. Hosanna in the highest. ✠ Blessed is He Who comes in the name of the Lord. Hosanna in the highest.

THE CANON OF THE MASS

THEREFORE, most gracious Father, we humbly beg of You and entreat You through Jesus Christ Your Son, our Lord, (*he kisses the altar*) to deem acceptable and bless these ✠ gifts, these ✠ offerings, these ✠ holy and unspotted oblations which, in the first place, we offer You for Your Holy Catholic Church, that You would deign to give her peace and protection, to unite and guard her throughout the world, together with Your servant N., our Pope, and N., our Bishop; and all true believers who cherish the Catholic and Apostolic Faith.

Commemoration of the Living

REMEMBER, O Lord, Your servants and handmaids, N. and N., (*name them*) and all here present, whose faith and devotion are known to You, on whose behalf we offer to You, or who themselves offer to You, this sacrifice of praise for themselves, families and friends, for the good of their souls, for their hope of salvation and deliverance from all harm, and who offer their homage to You, eternal, living and true God.

Commemoration of the Saints

IN THE unity of holy fellowship we observe the memory, first of all, of the glorious and ever Virgin Mary, Mother of our Lord and God Jesus Christ; next, that of Your Blessed Apostles and Martyrs, Peter and Paul, Andrew, James, John, Thomas, James, Philip, Bartholomew, Matthew, Simon and Thaddeus; of Linus, Cletus, Clement, Sixtus, Cornelius, Cyprian, Lawrence, Chrysogonus, John and Paul, Cosmas and Damian, and of all Your Saints, by whose merits and prayers grant that we may be always fortified by the help of Your protection. Through the same Christ our Lord. Amen.

Spreading his hands over the oblation, he says:

GRACIOUSLY accept, then, we beseech You, O Lord, this service of our worship and that of all Your household. Provide that our days be spent in Your peace, save us from everlasting damnation, and cause us to be numbered in the flock You have chosen. Through Christ our Lord. Amen.

O GOD, deign to bless ✠ what we offer, and make it approved, ✠ effective, ✠ right, and wholly pleasing in every way, that it may become for our good, the Body ✠ and Blood ✠ of Your dearly beloved Son, Jesus Christ our Lord.

CONSECRATION—ELEVATION

WHO, the day before He suffered, took bread into His holy and venerable hands, and having raised His eyes to heaven, to You, O God, His almighty Father, giving thanks to You, He blessed it, ✠ broke it, and gave it to His disciples, saying: All of you take and eat of this:

FOR THIS IS MY BODY.

IN LIKE manner, when the supper was done, taking also this goodly chalice into His holy and venerable hands, again giving thanks to You, He blessed ✠ it, and gave it to His disciples, saying: All of you take and drink of this:

FOR THIS IS THE CHALICE OF MY BLOOD OF THE NEW AND ETERNAL COVENANT: THE MYSTERY OF FAITH: WHICH SHALL BE SHED FOR YOU AND FOR MANY UNTO THE FORGIVENESS OF SINS.

After replacing the chalice on the corporal, he says:

As often as you shall do these things, in memory of Me shall you do them.

Offering of the Victim

MINDFUL, therefore, O Lord, not only of the blessed Passion of the same Christ, Your Son, our Lord, but also of His Resurrection from the dead, and finally His glorious Ascension into heaven, we, Your ministers, as also Your holy people, offer to Your supreme Majesty, of the gifts bestowed upon us, the pure ✠ Victim, the holy ✠ Victim, the all-perfect ✠ Victim: the holy ✠ Bread of life eternal and the Chalice ✠ of unending salvation.

AND this deign to regard with gracious and kindly attention and hold acceptable, as You deigned to accept the offerings of Abel, Your just servant, and the sacrifice of Abraham our patriarch, and that which Your chief priest Melchisedec offered to You, a holy sacrifice and a spotless victim.

MOST humbly we implore You, almighty God, bid these offerings to be brought by the hands of Your holy angel to Your altar above; before the face of Your Divine Majesty; that those of us who, by sharing in the Sacrifice of this altar, shall receive the Most Sacred ✠ Body and ✠ Blood of Your Son, may be filled with every grace and heavenly blessing. Through the same Christ our Lord. Amen.

Commemoration of the Dead

REMEMBER also, O Lord, Your servants and handmaids, N. and N., who have gone before us with the sign of faith, and rest in the sleep of peace. (*Here pray for the dead.*) To these, O Lord, and to all who rest in Christ, we beseech You to grant of Your goodness, a place of comfort, light and peace. Through the same Christ our Lord. Amen.

TO US sinners also, Your servants, trusting in the greatness of Your mercy, deign to grant some part and fellowship with Your Holy Apostles and Martyrs: with John, Stephen, Matthias, Barnabas, Ignatius, Alexander, Marcellinus, Peter, Felicitas, Perpetua, Agatha, Lucy, Agnes, Cecilia, Anastasia, and all Your Saints; into whose company, we implore You to admit us, not weighing our merits, but freely granting us pardon. Through Christ our Lord.

THROUGH Whom, O Lord, You always create, ✠ sanctify, ✠ fill with life, ✠ bless, and bestow upon us all good things.

The Minor Elevation

THROUGH ✠ Him, and with ✠ Him, and in ✠ Him, is to You, God the Father ✠ almighty, in the unity of the Holy ✠ Spirit, all honor and glory, world without end. S. Amen.

THE COMMUNION AND THANKSGIVING

Let us pray. Prompted by saving precepts, and taught by Your divine teaching, we dare to say:

OUR FATHER, Who art in heaven, hallowed be Thy name: Thy kingdom come: Thy will be done on earth as it is in heaven. Give us this day our daily bread; and forgive us our trespasses, as we forgive those who trespass against us. And lead us not into temptation: S. But deliver us from evil. *P.* Amen.

DELIVER us, we beseech You, O Lord, from all evils, past, present, and to come; and by the intercession of the Blessed and glorious Mary, ever Virgin, Mother of God, together with Your Blessed Apostles Peter and Paul, and Andrew, and all the Saints, grant of Your goodness, peace in our days, that aided by the riches of Your mercy, we may be always free from sin and safe from all disturbance.

Through the same our Lord Jesus Christ, Your Son, Who lives and reigns with You in the unity of the Holy Spirit, God, world without end.

S. Amen.

P. May the peace ✠ of the Lord be ✠ always with ✠ you.
S. And with your spirit.

The Priest puts a small particle into the chalice, saying:

May this mingling and consecration of the Body and Blood of our Lord Jesus Christ help us who receive it to life everlasting. Amen.

LAMB of God, You Who take away the sins of the world, have mercy on us.
Lamb of God, You Who take away the sins of the world, have mercy on us.
Lamb of God, You Who take away the sins of the world, grant us peace.

PRAYERS BEFORE HOLY COMMUNION

Then inclining toward the altar, he says:

O LORD Jesus Christ, Who said to Your Apostles: "Peace I leave with you, My peace I give to you," regard not my sins but the faith of Your Church, and deign to give her peace and unity according to Your Will: Who live and reign, God, world without end. Amen.

O LORD Jesus Christ, Son of the living God, Who, by the will of the Father, with the cooperation of the Holy Spirit, have by Your death given life to the world, deliver me by this Your Most Sacred Body and Blood from all my sins and from every evil. Make me always cling to Your commandments, and never permit me to be separated from You. Who with the same God the Father and the Holy Spirit, live and reign, God, world without end. Amen.

LET not the partaking of Your Body, O Lord Jesus Christ, which I, though unworthy, presume to receive, turn to my judgment and condemnation; but through Your goodness, may it become a safeguard and an effective remedy, both of soul and body. Who live and reign with God the Father, in the unity of the Holy Spirit, God, world without end. Amen.

COMMUNION OF THE PRIEST

I WILL take the Bread of heaven, and call upon the name of the Lord.

Lord, I am not worthy that You should come under my roof; but only say the word, and my soul will be healed. (3 *times.*)

Making the Sign of the Cross with the Host, he says:

MAY the Body of our Lord Jesus Christ preserve my soul to life everlasting. Amen.

What return shall I make to the Lord for all He has given me? I will take the Chalice of salvation, and I will call upon the name of the Lord. Praising will I call upon the Lord and I shall be saved from my enemies.

Making the Sign of the Cross with the chalice, he says:

MAY the Blood of our Lord Jesus Christ preserve my soul to life everlasting. Amen.

The Priest reverently consumes the Precious Blood.

COMMUNION OF THE FAITHFUL

The Server and people say the "Confiteor."

P. May almighty God have mercy on you, forgive you your sins, and bring you to life everlasting. **S.** Amen.

P. May the almighty and merciful Lord grant you pardon, ✠ absolution and remission of your sins. S. Amen.

Holding up a Sacred Host, the Priest says:

Behold the Lamb of God, behold Him Who takes away the sins of the world.

Lord, I am not worthy that You should come under my roof; but only say the word, and my soul will be healed. (3 *times.*)

The Priest says to each communicant:

May the Body of our Lord Jesus Christ preserve your soul to life everlasting. Amen.

The Priest purifies the chalice with wine, saying:

WHAT has passed our lips as food, O Lord, may we possess in purity of heart, that what is given to us in time, be our healing for eternity.

He purifies his fingers with wine and water, saying:

MAY Your Body, O Lord, which I have eaten, and Your Blood which I have drunk, cleave to my very soul, and grant that no trace of sin be found in me, whom these pure and holy mysteries have renewed. Who live and reign, world without end. Amen.

THE COMMUNION • Ps. 103, 13. 14. 15

THE earth is replete with the fruit of Your works, O Lord; You produce bread from the earth, and wine to gladden men's hearts, so that their faces gleam with oil, and bread fortifies the hearts of men.

The Priest, turning to the people, says:

P. The Lord be with you. S. And with your spirit.

P. Let us pray.

THE POSTCOMMUNION

MAY the holy participation of this mystery give life to us, we beseech You, O Lord, and afford us both expiation and protection. Through our Lord Jesus Christ, Your Son, Who lives and reigns with You in the unity of the Holy Spirit, God, world without end. S. Amen.

FINAL PRAYERS

The Priest turns again to the people, and says:

P. The Lord be with you. *S.* And with your spirit.
P. Go, you are dismissed. *S.* Thanks be to God.

MAY the tribute of my worship be pleasing to You, Most Holy Trinity, and grant that the sacrifice which I, all unworthy, have offered in the presence of Your Majesty, may be acceptable to You, and through Your mercy obtain forgiveness for me and all for whom I have offered it. Through Christ our Lord. Amen.

THE LAST BLESSING

He kisses the altar, and facing the people, says:

MAY almighty God bless you: ✠ the Father, and the Son, and the Holy Spirit.
S. Amen.

The Last Gospel and Prayers after Low Mass are conveniently placed inside the back cover.

"Arise . . . for your faith has saved you."

THIRTEENTH SUNDAY AFTER PENTECOST

Ten men afflicted with leprosy cried out: "Jesus, Master, have pity on us!" And the Divine power of God restored freshness to their flesh. However, as often happens, only one of the ten returned to give thanks to the Master. (GREEN VESTMENTS)

PRAYERS AT THE FOOT OF THE ALTAR

IN THE name of the Father, ✠ and of the Son, and of the Holy Spirit. Amen.

Priest. I will go in to the altar of God.

Server. The God of my gladness and joy.

Psalm 42

DO ME justice, O God, and fight my fight against a faithless people; from the deceitful and impious man rescue me.

S. For You, O God, are my strength. Why do You keep me so far away? Why must I go about in mourning, with the enemy oppressing me?

P. Send forth Your light and Your fidelity; they shall lead me on and bring me to Your holy mountain, to Your dwelling-place.

S. Then will I go in to the altar of God, the God of my gladness and joy.
P. Then will I give You thanks upon the harp, O God, my God. Why are you so downcast, O my soul? Why do you sigh within me?
S. Hope in God! For I shall again be thanking Him in the presence of my Savior and my God.
P. Glory be to the Father, and to the Son, and to the Holy Spirit.
S. As it was in the beginning, is now, and ever shall be, world without end. Amen.
P. I will go in to the altar of God.
S. The God of my gladness and joy.
P. Our help ✠ is in the name of the Lord.
S. Who made heaven and earth.
P. I confess to almighty God, etc.
S. May almighty God have mercy on you, forgive you your sins, and bring you to life everlasting.
P. Amen.

The Server, bowing, says the "Confiteor."

I CONFESS to almighty God, to Blessed Mary, ever Virgin, to Blessed Michael the Archangel, to Blessed John the Baptist, to the Holy Apostles Peter and Paul, and to all the Saints, and to you, Father, that I have sinned exceedingly in thought, word and deed, *through my fault, through my fault, through my most grievous fault.* Therefore I beseech Blessed Mary, ever Virgin, Blessed Michael the Archangel, Blessed John the Baptist, the Holy Apostles Peter and Paul, and all the Saints, and you, Father, to pray to the Lord our God for me.
P. May almighty God have mercy on you, forgive you your sins, and bring you to life everlasting.
S. Amen.

MAY the almighty and merciful Lord grant us pardon, ✠ absolution, and remission of our sins. S. Amen.

P. Will You not, O God, give us life?

S. And shall not Your people rejoice in You?

P. Show us, O Lord, Your kindness.

S. And grant us Your salvation.

P. O Lord, hear my prayer.

S. And let my cry come to You.

P. The Lord be with you.

S. And with your spirit. *P*. Let us pray.

Going up to the altar, the Priest prays silently:

TAKE away from us our sins, O Lord, we beseech You, that we may enter with pure minds into the Holy of Holies. Through Christ our Lord. Amen.

WE BESEECH You, O Lord, by the merits of Your Saints (*he kisses the altar*) whose relics lie here, and of all the Saints: deign in Your mercy to pardon me all my sins. Amen.

THE INTROIT • Ps. 73, 20. 19. 23. 1

At the right side of the altar, the Priest says:

LOOK to Your covenant, O Lord, forsake not forever the lives of Your afflicted ones. Arise, O God; defend Your cause; be not unmindful of the voices of those who ask You. *Ps.* Why, O God, have You cast us off forever? Why does Your anger smolder against the sheep of Your pasture? Glory be to the Father, and to the Son, and to the Holy Spirit. As it was in the beginning, is now, and ever shall be, world without end. Amen. — Look to

Your covenant, O Lord, forsake not forever the lives of Your afflicted ones. Arise, O God; defend Your cause; be not unmindful of the voices of those who ask You.

THE KYRIE

P. Lord, have mercy. *S.* Lord, have mercy. *P.* Lord, have mercy. *S.* Christ, have mercy. *P.* Christ, have mercy. *S.* Christ, have mercy. *P.* Lord, have mercy. *S.* Lord, have mercy. *P.* Lord, have mercy.

THE GLORIA

GLORY to God in the highest. And on earth peace to men of good will. We praise You. We bless You. We adore You. We glorify You. We give You thanks for Your great glory. O Lord God, heavenly King, God the Father almighty. O Lord Jesus Christ, the Only-begotten Son. O Lord God, Lamb of God, Son of the Father: You Who take away the sins of the world, have mercy on us. You Who take away the sins of the world, receive our prayer. You Who sit at the right hand of the Father, have mercy on us. For You alone are holy. You alone are the Lord. You alone, O Jesus Christ, are most high. Together with the Holy Spirit ✠ in the glory of God the Father. Amen.

The Priest kisses the altar and turns to the people, saying:

P. The Lord be with you. *S.* And with your spirit. *P.* Let us pray.

THE PRAYER

Going to the right (Epistle) side, he says:

ALMIGHTY and everlasting God, give us an increase of Faith, Hope and Charity; and that we may deserve to obtain that which You promise, make us love that which You command. Through our Lord Jesus Christ, Your Son, Who lives and reigns with You in the unity of the Holy Spirit, God, world without end. S. Amen.

THE EPISTLE • Gal. 3, 16-22

BRETHREN: The promises were made to Abraham and to his offspring. He does not say, "And to his offsprings," as of many; but as of one, "And to your offspring," who is Christ. Now I mean this: The Law which was made four hundred and thirty years later does not annul the covenant which was ratified by God, so as to make the promise void. For if the right to inherit be from the Law, it is no longer from a promise. But God gave it to Abraham by promise. What then was the Law? It was enacted on account of transgressions, being delivered by angels through a mediator, until the offspring should come to whom the promise was made. Now there is no intermediary where there is only one; but God is one. Is the Law then contrary to the promises of God? By no means. For if a law had been given that could give life, justice would truly be from the Law. But the Scripture shut up all things under sin, that by the faith of Jesus Christ the promise might be given to those who believe. S. Thanks be to God.

THE GRADUAL • Ps. 73, 20. 19. 22

LOOK to Your covenant, O Lord, be not unmindful of the lives of Your afflicted ones. ℣. Arise, O Lord; defend Your cause; remember the reproach of Your servants.

Alleluia, alleluia. ℣. *Ps. 89, 1.* O Lord, You have been our refuge through all generations. Alleluia.

PRAYER BEFORE THE GOSPEL

Bowing down at the center of the altar, he says:

CLEANSE my heart and my lips, O almighty God, Who cleansed the lips of the Prophet Isaias with a burning coal. In Your gracious mercy deign so to purify me that I may worthily proclaim Your holy Gospel. Through Christ our Lord. Amen.

Lord, grant Your blessing. The Lord be in my heart and on my lips, that I may worthily and fittingly proclaim His holy Gospel. Amen.

THE GOSPEL • Luke 17, 11-19

Going to the left (Gospel) side of the altar, he says:

P. The Lord be with you. S. And with your spirit.
P. ✠ The continuation of the holy Gospel according to Saint Luke. S. Glory be to You, O Lord.

AT THAT time, as Jesus was going to Jerusalem, He was passing between Samaria and Galilee. And as He was entering a certain village, there met Him ten lepers, who stood afar off and lifted up their voice, saying, "Jesus, Master, have pity on us." And when He saw them He said, "Go, show yourselves to the priests." And it came to pass as they were on their way, that they were made clean. But one of them, seeing that he was made clean, returned, with a loud voice glorifying God, and he fell on his face at His feet, giving thanks; and he was a Samaritan. But Jesus answered and said, "Were not the ten made clean? But where are the nine? Has no one been found to return and give glory to God except this foreigner?" And He said to him, "Arise, go your way, for your faith has saved you." S. Praise be to You, O Christ.

P. By the words of the Gospel, may our sins be taken away.

THE NICENE CREED

At the center of the altar, he says:

I BELIEVE in one God, the Father almighty, Maker of heaven and earth, and of all things visible and invisible. And in one Lord Jesus Christ, the Only-begotten Son of God. Born of the Father before all ages. God of God; Light of Light; true God of true God. Begotten not made; of one being with the Father; by Whom all things were made. Who for us men, and for our salvation, came down from heaven. (*Here all genuflect.*) And was made Flesh by the Holy Spirit of the Virgin Mary: AND WAS MADE MAN. He was also crucified for us, suffered under Pontius Pilate and was buried. And on the third day He rose again according to the Scriptures. And ascending into heaven, He sits at the right hand of the Father. And He shall come again in glory to judge the living and the dead; and of His kingdom there shall be no end. And I believe in the Holy Spirit, Lord and Giver of life, Who proceeds from the Father and the Son. Who together with the Father and the Son is no less adored, and glorified: Who spoke by the Prophets. And I believe in One, Holy, Catholic and Apostolic Church. I confess one Baptism for the remission of sins. And I look for the resurrection of the dead. ✠ And the life of the world to come. Amen.

THE OFFERTORY

The Priest turns to the people and says:

P. The Lord be with you. *S.* And with your spirit.
P. Let us pray.

THE OFFERTORY VERSE • Ps. 30, 15. 16

MY TRUST is in You, O Lord; I say, "You are my God." In Your hands is my destiny.

The Priest now uncovers the chalice, places the host on the paten and offering it up, says:

ACCEPT, O holy Father, almighty and eternal God, this spotless host, which I, Your unworthy servant, offer to You, my living and true God, to atone for my numberless sins, offenses, and negligences; on behalf of all here present and likewise for all faithful Christians living and dead, that it may profit me and them as a means of salvation to life everlasting. Amen.

He pours wine and water into the chalice, blessing the water before it is poured.

O GOD, Who established the nature of man in wondrous dignity, and still more admirably restored it, grant that through the mystery of this water and wine, we may be made partakers of His Divinity, Who has condescended to become partaker of our humanity, Jesus Christ, Your Son, our Lord. Who lives and reigns with You in the unity of the Holy Spirit, God, world without end. Amen.

Offering up the wine, the Priest says:

WE OFFER You, O Lord, the chalice of salvation, humbly begging of Your mercy that it may arise before Your Divine Majesty, with a pleasing fragrance, for our salvation and for that of the whole world. Amen.

Bowing down, the Priest says:

IN A humble spirit and with a contrite heart, may we be accepted by You, O Lord, and may our sacrifice so be offered in Your sight this day as to please You, O Lord God.

Raising his eyes and blessing the offering, he says:

COME, O Sanctifier, almighty and eternal God, and bless ✠ this sacrifice prepared for the glory of Your holy name.

WASHING THE FINGERS

I WASH my hands in innocence, and I go around Your altar, O Lord, giving voice to my thanks, and recounting all Your wondrous deeds. O Lord, I love the house in which You dwell, the tenting-place of Your glory. Gather not my soul with those of sinners, nor with men of blood my life. On their hands are crimes, and their right hands are full of bribes. But I walk in integrity; redeem me, and have pity on me. My foot stands on level ground; in the assemblies I will bless You, O Lord. Glory be to the Father, and to the Son, and to the Holy Spirit. As it was in the beginning, is now, and ever shall be, world without end. Amen.

ACCEPT, Most Holy Trinity, this offering which we are making to You in remembrance of the Passion, Resurrection, and Ascension of Jesus Christ, our Lord; and in honor of Blessed Mary, ever Virgin, Blessed John the Baptist, the Holy Apostles Peter and Paul, and of these, and of all the Saints; that it may add to their honor and aid our salvation; and may they deign to intercede in heaven for us who honor their memory here on earth. Through the same Christ our Lord. Amen.

The Priest turns toward the people and says:

Pray, brethren, that my sacrifice and yours may become acceptable to God the Father almighty.

S. May the Lord accept this sacrifice from your

hands to the praise and glory of His name, for our advantage, and that of all His holy Church.
P. Amen.

THE SECRET

BE MERCIFUL, O Lord, to Your people: and favorable to their offerings, that, appeased by this oblation, You may bestow upon us pardon, and grant what we ask. Through our Lord Jesus Christ, Your Son, Who lives and reigns with You in the unity of the Holy Spirit, God.
P. World without end. *S.* Amen.

PREFACE—CANON

P. The Lord be with you. *S.* And with your spirit.
P. Lift up your hearts.
S. We have lifted them up to the Lord.
P. Let us give thanks to the Lord, our God.
S. It is fitting and just.

IT IS fitting indeed and just, right and helpful to salvation, for us always and everywhere to give thanks to You, O holy Lord, Father almighty, everlasting God, Who with Your Only-begotten Son and the Holy Spirit are one God, one Lord; not in the unity of a single person, but in the trinity of a single nature. For that which we believe on Your revelation concerning Your glory, that same we believe of Your Son, that same of the Holy Spirit, without difference or discrimination. So that in confessing the true and everlasting Godhead, we shall adore distinction in Persons, oneness in being, and equality in Majesty. This the Angels and Archangels, the Cherubim, too, and the Seraphim do praise; day by day they cease not to cry out as with one voice, saying (*the bell is rung* 3 *times*):

HOLY, HOLY, HOLY, Lord God of Hosts. Heaven and earth are filled with Your glory. Hosanna in the highest. ✠ Blessed is He Who comes in the name of the Lord. Hosanna in the highest.

THE CANON OF THE MASS

THEREFORE, most gracious Father, we humbly beg of You and entreat You through Jesus Christ Your Son, our Lord, (*he kisses the altar*) to deem acceptable and bless these ✠ gifts, these ✠ offerings, these ✠ holy and unspotted oblations which, in the first place, we offer You for Your Holy Catholic Church, that You would deign to give her peace and protection, to unite and guard her throughout the world, together with Your servant *N.*, our Pope, and *N.*, our Bishop; and all true believers who cherish the Catholic and Apostolic Faith.

Commemoration of the Living

REMEMBER, O Lord, Your servants and handmaids, *N.* and *N.*, (*name them*) and all here present, whose faith and devotion are known to You, on whose behalf we offer to You, or who themselves offer to You, this sacrifice of praise for themselves, families and friends, for the good of their souls, for their hope of salvation and deliverance from all harm, and who offer their homage to You, eternal, living and true God.

Commemoration of the Saints

IN THE unity of holy fellowship we observe the memory, first of all, of the glorious and ever Virgin Mary, Mother of our Lord and God Jesus Christ; next, that of Your Blessed Apostles and

Martyrs, Peter and Paul, Andrew, James, John, Thomas, James, Philip, Bartholomew, Matthew, Simon and Thaddeus; of Linus, Cletus, Clement, Sixtus, Cornelius, Cyprian, Lawrence, Chrysogonus, John and Paul, Cosmas and Damian, and of all Your Saints, by whose merits and prayers grant that we may be always fortified by the help of Your protection. Through the same Christ our Lord. Amen.

Spreading his hands over the oblation, he says:

GRACIOUSLY accept, then, we beseech You, O Lord, this service of our worship and that of all Your household. Provide that our days be spent in Your peace, save us from everlasting damnation, and cause us to be numbered in the flock You have chosen. Through Christ our Lord. Amen.

O GOD, deign to bless ✠ what we offer, and make it approved, ✠ effective, ✠ right, and wholly pleasing in every way, that it may become for our good, the Body ✠ and Blood ✠ of Your dearly beloved Son, Jesus Christ our Lord.

CONSECRATION—ELEVATION

WHO, the day before He suffered, took bread into His holy and venerable hands, and having raised His eyes to heaven, to You, O God, His almighty Father, giving thanks to You, He blessed it, ✠ broke it, and gave it to His disciples, saying: All of you take and eat of this:

FOR THIS IS MY BODY.

IN LIKE manner, when the supper was done, taking also this goodly chalice into His holy and venerable hands, again giving thanks to You, He blessed ✠ it, and gave it to His disciples, saying: All of you take and drink of this:

FOR THIS IS THE CHALICE OF MY BLOOD OF THE NEW AND ETERNAL COVENANT: THE MYSTERY OF FAITH: WHICH SHALL BE SHED FOR YOU AND FOR MANY UNTO THE FORGIVENESS OF SINS.

After replacing the chalice on the corporal, he says:

As often as you shall do these things, in memory of Me shall you do them.

Offering of the Victim

MINDFUL, therefore, O Lord, not only of the blessed Passion of the same Christ, Your Son, our Lord, but also of His Resurrection from the dead, and finally His glorious Ascension into heaven, we, Your ministers, as also Your holy people, offer to Your supreme Majesty, of the gifts bestowed upon us, the pure ✠ Victim, the holy ✠ Victim, the all-perfect ✠ Victim: the holy ✠ Bread of life eternal and the Chalice ✠ of unending salvation.

AND this deign to regard with gracious and kindly attention and hold acceptable, as You deigned to accept the offerings of Abel, Your just servant, and the sacrifice of Abraham our patriarch, and that which Your chief priest Melchisedec offered to You, a holy sacrifice and a spotless victim.

MOST humbly we implore You, almighty God, bid these offerings to be brought by the hands of Your holy angel to Your altar above; before the face of Your Divine Majesty; that those of us who, by sharing in the Sacrifice of this altar, shall receive the Most Sacred ✠ Body and ✠ Blood of Your Son may be filled with every grace and heavenly blessing. Through the same Christ our Lord. Amen.

Commemoration of the Dead

REMEMBER also, O Lord, Your servants and handmaids, N. and N., who have gone before us with the sign of faith, and rest in the sleep of peace. (*Here pray for the dead.*) To these, O Lord, and to all who rest in Christ, we beseech You to grant of Your goodness, a place of comfort, light and peace. Through the same Christ our Lord. Amen.

TO US sinners also, Your servants, trusting in the greatness of Your mercy, deign to grant some part and fellowship with Your Holy Apostles and Martyrs: with John, Stephen, Matthias, Barnabas, Ignatius, Alexander, Marcellinus, Peter, Felicitas, Perpetua, Agatha, Lucy, Agnes, Cecilia, Anastasia, and all Your Saints; into whose company, we implore You to admit us, not weighing our merits, but freely granting us pardon. Through Christ our Lord.

THROUGH Whom, O Lord, You always create, ✠ sanctify, ✠ fill with life, ✠ bless, and bestow upon us all good things.

The Minor Elevation

THROUGH ✠ Him, and with ✠ Him, and in ✠ Him, is to You, God the Father ✠ almighty, in the unity of the Holy ✠ Spirit, all honor and glory, world without end. S. Amen.

THE COMMUNION AND THANKSGIVING

Let us pray. Prompted by saving precepts, and taught by Your divine teaching, we dare to say:

OUR FATHER, Who art in heaven, hallowed be Thy name: Thy kingdom come: Thy will be

done on earth as it is in heaven. Give us this day our daily bread; and forgive us our trespasses, as we forgive those who trespass against us. And lead us not into temptation: S. But deliver us from evil. *P*. Amen.

DELIVER us, we beseech You, O Lord, from all evils, past, present, and to come; and by the intercession of the Blessed and glorious Mary, ever Virgin, Mother of God, together with Your Blessed Apostles Peter and Paul, and Andrew, and all the Saints, grant of Your goodness, peace in our days, that aided by the riches of Your mercy, we may be always free from sin and safe from all disturbance.

Through the same our Lord Jesus Christ, Your Son, Who lives and reigns with You in the unity of the Holy Spirit, God, world without end. *S*. Amen.

P. May the peace ✠ of the Lord be ✠ always with ✠ you. *S*. And with your spirit.

The Priest puts a small particle into the chalice, saying:

May this mingling and consecration of the Body and Blood of our Lord Jesus Christ help us who receive it to life everlasting. Amen.

LAMB of God, You Who take away the sins of the world, have mercy on us.

Lamb of God, You Who take away the sins of the world, have mercy on us.

Lamb of God, You Who take away the sins of the world, grant us peace.

PRAYERS BEFORE HOLY COMMUNION

Then inclining toward the altar, he says:

O LORD Jesus Christ, Who said to Your Apostles: "Peace I leave with you, My peace I give

to you," regard not my sins but the faith of Your Church, and deign to give her peace and unity according to Your Will: Who live and reign, God, world without end. Amen.

O LORD Jesus Christ, Son of the living God, Who, by the will of the Father, with the co-operation of the Holy Spirit, have by Your death given life to the world, deliver me by this Your Most Sacred Body and Blood from all my sins and from every evil. Make me always cling to Your commandments, and never permit me to be separated from You. Who with the same God the Father and the Holy Spirit, live and reign, God, world without end. Amen.

LET not the partaking of Your Body, O Lord Jesus Christ, which I, though unworthy, presume to receive, turn to my judgment and condemnation; but through Your goodness, may it become a safeguard and an effective remedy, both of soul and body. Who live and reign with God the Father, in the unity of the Holy Spirit, God, world without end. Amen.

COMMUNION OF THE PRIEST

I WILL take the Bread of heaven, and call upon the name of the Lord.

Lord, I am not worthy that You should come under my roof; but only say the word, and my soul will be healed. (3 *times.*)

Making the Sign of the Cross with the Host, he says:

MAY the Body of our Lord Jesus Christ preserve my soul to life everlasting. Amen.

What return shall I make to the Lord for all He has given me? I will take the Chalice of salvation,

and I will call upon the name of the Lord. Praising will I call upon the Lord and I shall be saved from my enemies.

Making the Sign of the Cross with the chalice, he says:

MAY the Blood of our Lord Jesus Christ preserve my soul to life everlasting. Amen.

The Priest reverently consumes the Precious Blood.

COMMUNION OF THE FAITHFUL

The Server and people say the "Confiteor."

P. May almighty God have mercy on you, forgive you your sins, and bring you to life everlasting. *S.* Amen.

P. May the almighty and merciful Lord grant you pardon, ✠ absolution and remission of your sins. *S.* Amen.

Holding up a Sacred Host, the Priest says:

Behold the Lamb of God, behold Him Who takes away the sins of the world.

Lord, I am not worthy that You should come under my roof; but only say the word, and my soul will be healed. (3 *times.*)

The Priest says to each communicant:

May the Body of our Lord Jesus Christ preserve your soul to life everlasting. Amen.

The Priest purifies the chalice with wine, saying:

WHAT has passed our lips as food, O Lord, may we possess in purity of heart, that what is given to us in time, be our healing for eternity.

He purifies his fingers with wine and water, saying:

MAY Your Body, O Lord, which I have eaten, and Your Blood which I have drunk, cleave to my very soul, and grant that no trace of sin be found in me, whom these pure and holy mysteries

have renewed. Who live and reign, world without end. Amen.

THE COMMUNION • Wis. 16, 20

YOU have given us, O Lord, bread from heaven, endowed with all delights and the sweetness of every taste.

The Priest, turning to the people, says:

P. The Lord be with you. *S.* And with your spirit.
P. Let us pray.

THE POSTCOMMUNION

WE WHO have partaken of Your heavenly sacraments beseech You, O Lord, that we may profit to the increase of everlasting redemption. Through our Lord Jesus Christ, Your Son, Who lives and reigns with You in the unity of the Holy Spirit, God, world without end. *S.* Amen.

FINAL PRAYERS

The Priest turns again to the people, and says:

P. The Lord be with you. *S.* And with your spirit.
P. Go, you are dismissed. *S.* Thanks be to God.

MAY the tribute of my worship be pleasing to You, Most Holy Trinity, and grant that the sacrifice which I, all unworthy, have offered in the presence of Your Majesty, may be acceptable to You, and through Your mercy obtain forgiveness for me and all for whom I have offered it. Through Christ our Lord. Amen.

THE LAST BLESSING

MAY almighty God bless you: ✠ the Father, and the Son, and the Holy Spirit. *S.* Amen.

The Last Gospel and Prayers after Low Mass are conveniently placed inside the back cover.

"Seek first the kingdom of God and His justice . . ."

FOURTEENTH SUNDAY AFTER PENTECOST

God's providence takes care of the birds of the air and the lilies of the field. But we "of little faith" attend more to our temporal interests than our religious duties. Seeking the supernatural first, we may be sure of God's help in our daily affairs. (GREEN VESTMENTS)

PRAYERS AT THE FOOT OF THE ALTAR

IN THE name of the Father, ✠ and of the Son, and of the Holy Spirit. Amen.

Priest. I will go in to the altar of God.

Server. The God of my gladness and joy.

Psalm 42

DO Me justice, O God, and fight my fight against a faithless people; from the deceitful and impious man rescue me.

S. For You, O God, are my strength. Why do You keep me so far away? Why must I go about in mourning, with the enemy oppressing me?

P. Send forth Your light and Your fidelity; they shall lead me on and bring me to Your holy mountain, to Your dwelling-place.

S. Then will I go in to the altar of God, the God of my gladness and joy.
P. Then will I give You thanks upon the harp, O God, my God. Why are you so downcast, O my soul? Why do you sigh within me?
S. Hope in God! For I shall again be thanking Him in the presence of my Savior and my God.
P. Glory be to the Father, and to the Son, and to the Holy Spirit.
S. As it was in the beginning, is now, and ever shall be, world without end. Amen.
P. I will go in to the altar of God.
S. The God of my gladness and joy.
P. Our help ✠ is in the name of the Lord.
S. Who made heaven and earth.
P. I confess to almighty God, etc.
S. May almighty God have mercy on you, forgive you your sins, and bring you to life everlasting.
P. Amen.

The Server, bowing, says the "Confiteor."

I CONFESS to almighty God, to Blessed Mary, ever Virgin, to Blessed Michael the Archangel, to Blessed John the Baptist, to the Holy Apostles Peter and Paul, and to all the Saints, and to you, Father, that I have sinned exceedingly in thought, word and deed, *through my fault, through my fault, through my most grievous fault.* Therefore I beseech Blessed Mary, ever Virgin, Blessed Michael the Archangel, Blessed John the Baptist, the Holy Apostles Peter and Paul, and all the Saints, and you, Father, to pray to the Lord our God for me.
P. May almighty God have mercy on you, forgive you your sins, and bring you to life everlasting.
S. Amen.

MAY the almighty and merciful Lord grant us pardon, ✠ absolution, and remission of our sins. *S.* Amen.

P. Will You not, O God, give us life?
S. And shall not Your people rejoice in You?
P. Show us, O Lord, Your kindness.
S. And grant us Your salvation.
P. O Lord, hear my prayer.
S. And let my cry come to You.
P. The Lord be with you.
S. And with your spirit. *P.* Let us pray.

Going up to the altar, the Priest prays silently:

TAKE away from us our sins, O Lord, we beseech You, that we may enter with pure minds into the Holy of Holies. Through Christ our Lord. Amen.

WE BESEECH You, O Lord, by the merits of Your Saints (*he kisses the altar*) whose relics lie here, and of all the Saints: deign in Your mercy to pardon me all my sins. Amen.

THE INTROIT • Ps. 83, 10. 11. 2. 3

At the right side of the altar, the Priest says:

BEHOLD, O God, our Protector, and look upon the face of Your anointed. Better is one day in Your courts than a thousand elsewhere. *Ps.* How lovely is Your dwelling place, O Lord of Hosts! My soul yearns and pines for the courts of the Lord. Glory be to the Father, and to the Son, and to the Holy Spirit. As it was in the beginning, is now, and ever shall be, world without end. Amen. — Behold, O God, our Protector, and look upon the face of Your anointed. Better is one day in Your courts than a thousand elsewhere.

THE KYRIE

P. Lord, have mercy. *S*. Lord, have mercy. *P*. Lord, have mercy. *S*. Christ, have mercy. *P*. Christ, have mercy. *S*. Christ, have mercy. *P*. Lord, have mercy. *S*. Lord, have mercy. *P*. Lord, have mercy.

THE GLORIA

GLORY to God in the highest. And on earth peace to men of good will. We praise You. We bless You. We adore You. We glorify You. We give You thanks for Your great glory. O Lord God, heavenly King, God the Father almighty. O Lord Jesus Christ, the Only-begotten Son. O Lord God, Lamb of God, Son of the Father: You Who take away the sins of the world, have mercy on us. You Who take away the sins of the world, receive our prayer. You Who sit at the right and of the Father, have mercy on us. For You alone are holy. You alone are the Lord. You alone, O Jesus Christ, are most high. Together with the Holy Spirit ✠ in the glory of God the Father. Amen.

The Priest kisses the altar and turns to the people, saying:

P. The Lord be with you. *S*. And with your spirit. *P*. Let us pray.

THE PRAYER

Going to the right (Epistle) side, he says:

PROTECT, we beseech You, O Lord, Your Church with Your perpetual mercy, and because without You human frailty goes astray, may we be ever withheld by Your grace from what is hurtful, and directed to what is profitable. Through our Lord Jesus Christ, Your Son, Who lives and reigns with You in the unity of the Holy Spirit, God, world without end. S. Amen.

THE EPISTLE • Gal. 5, 16-24

BRETHREN: Walk in the Spirit, and you will not fulfill the lusts of the flesh. For the flesh lusts against the spirit, and the spirit against the flesh; for these are opposed to each other, so that you do not do what you would. But if you are led by the Spirit, you are not under the Law. Now the works of the flesh are manifest, which are immorality, uncleanness, licentiousness, idolatry, witchcrafts, enmities, contentions, jealousies, anger, quarrels, factions, parties, envies, murders, drunkenness, carousings, and suchlike. And concerning these I warn you, as I have warned you, that they who do such things will not attain the kingdom of God. But the fruit of the Spirit is: charity, joy, peace, patience, kindness, goodness, long-suffering, mildness, faith, modesty, continency, chastity. Against such things there is no law. And they who belong to Christ have crucified their flesh with its passions and desires. S. Thanks be to God.

THE GRADUAL • Ps. 117, 8. 9

IT IS better to take refuge in the Lord than to trust in man. ℣. It is better to take refuge in the Lord than to trust in princes.

Alleluia, alleluia. ℣. *Ps. 94, 1.* Come, let us sing joyfully to the Lord; let us acclaim the God of our salvation. Alleluia.

PRAYER BEFORE THE GOSPEL

Bowing down at the center of the altar, he says:

CLEANSE my heart and my lips, O almighty God, Who cleansed the lips of the Prophet Isaias with a burning coal. In Your gracious mercy

deign so to purify me that I may worthily proclaim Your holy Gospel. Through Christ our Lord. Amen.

Lord, grant Your blessing. The Lord be in my heart and on my lips, that I may worthily and fittingly proclaim His holy Gospel. Amen.

THE GOSPEL • Matt. 6, 24-33

Going to the left (Gospel) side of the altar, he says:

P. The Lord be with you. *S.* And with your spirit.

P. ✠ The continuation of the holy Gospel according to Saint Matthew. *S.* Glory be to You, O Lord.

AT THAT time, Jesus said to His disciples: "No man can serve two masters; for either he will hate the one and love the other, or else he will stand by the one and despise the other. You cannot serve God and mammon. Therefore I say to you, do not be anxious for your life, what you shall eat; nor yet for your body, what you shall put on. Is not the life a greater thing than the food, and the body than the clothing? Look at the birds of the air: they do not sow, or reap, or gather into barns; yet your heavenly Father feeds them. Are not you of much more value than they? But which of you by being anxious about it can add to his stature a single cubit? And as for clothing, why are you anxious? Consider how the lilies of the field grow; they neither toil nor spin, yet I say to you that not even Solomon in all his glory was arrayed like one of these. But if God so clothes the grass of the field, which flourishes today but tomorrow is thrown into the oven, how much more you, O you of little faith! Therefore do not be anxious, saying, 'What shall we eat?' or, 'What shall we drink?' or, 'What are we to put on?' (for after all these things the Gentiles seek); for your Father knows that you need all these things. But seek first the kingdom of God and His justice, and all these things shall be given you besides." S. Praise be to You, O Christ.

P. By the words of the Gospel, may our sins be taken away.

THE NICENE CREED

At the center of the altar, he says:

I BELIEVE in one God, the Father almighty, Maker of heaven and earth, and of all things visible and invisible. And in one Lord Jesus Christ, the Only-begotten Son of God. Born of the Father before all ages. God of God; Light of Light; true God of true God. Begotten not made; of one being with the Father; by Whom all things were made. Who for us men, and for our salvation, came down from heaven. (*Here all genuflect.*) And was made Flesh by the Holy Spirit of the Virgin Mary: AND WAS MADE MAN. He was also crucified for us, suffered under Pontius Pilate and was buried. And on the third day He rose again according to the Scriptures. And ascending into heaven, He sits at the right hand of the Father. And He shall come again in glory to judge the living and the dead; and of His kingdom there shall be no end. And I believe in the Holy Spirit, Lord and Giver of life, Who proceeds from the Father and the Son. Who together with the Father and the Son is no less adored, and glorified: Who spoke by the Prophets. And I believe in One, Holy, Catholic and Apostolic Church. I confess one Baptism for the remission of sins. And I look for the resurrection of the dead. ✠ And the life of the world to come. Amen.

THE OFFERTORY

The Priest turns to the people and says:

P. The Lord be with you. S. And with your spirit.
P. Let us pray.

THE OFFERTORY VERSE • Ps. 33, 8. 9

THE Angel of the Lord encamps around those who fear Him, and delivers them. Taste and see how good the Lord is.

The Priest now uncovers the chalice, places the host on the paten and offering it up, says:

ACCEPT, O holy Father, almighty and eternal God, this spotless host, which I, Your unworthy servant, offer to You, my living and true God, to atone for my numberless sins, offenses, and negligences; on behalf of all here present and likewise for all faithful Christians living and dead, that it may profit me and them as a means of salvation to life everlasting. Amen.

He pours wine and water into the chalice, blessing the water before it is poured.

O GOD, Who established the nature of man in wondrous dignity, and still more admirably restored it, grant that through the mystery of this water and wine, we may be made partakers of His Divinity, Who has condescended to become partaker of our humanity, Jesus Christ, Your Son, our Lord. Who lives and reigns with You in the unity of the Holy Spirit, God, world without end. Amen.

Offering up the wine, the Priest says:

WE OFFER You, O Lord, the chalice of salvation, humbly begging of Your mercy that it may arise before Your Divine Majesty, with a pleasing fragrance, for our salvation and for that of the whole world. Amen.

Bowing down, the Priest says:

IN A humble spirit and with a contrite heart, may we be accepted by You, O Lord, and may our sacrifice so be offered in Your sight this day as to please You, O Lord God.

Raising his eyes and blessing the offering, he says:

COME, O Sanctifier, almighty and eternal God, and bless ✠ this sacrifice prepared for the glory of Your holy name.

WASHING THE FINGERS

I WASH my hands in innocence, and I go around Your altar, O Lord, giving voice to my thanks, and recounting all Your wondrous deeds. O Lord, I love the house in which You dwell, the tenting-place of Your glory. Gather not my soul with those of sinners, nor with men of blood my life. On their hands are crimes, and their right hands are full of bribes. But I walk in integrity; redeem me, and have pity on me. My foot stands on level ground; in the assemblies I will bless You, O Lord. Glory be to the Father, and to the Son, and to the Holy Spirit. As it was in the beginning, is now, and ever shall be, world without end. Amen.

ACCEPT, Most Holy Trinity, this offering which we are making to You in remembrance of the Passion, Resurrection, and Ascension of Jesus Christ, our Lord; and in honor of Blessed Mary, ever Virgin, Blessed John the Baptist, the Holy Apostles Peter and Paul, and of these, and of all the Saints; that it may add to their honor and aid our salvation; and may they deign to intercede in heaven for us who honor their memory here on earth. Through the same Christ our Lord. Amen.

The Priest turns toward the people and says:

Pray, brethren, that my sacrifice and yours may become acceptable to God the Father almighty.

S. May the Lord accept this sacrifice from your hands to the praise and glory of His name, for our advantage, and that of all His holy Church.

P. Amen.

THE SECRET

GRANT, we beseech You, O Lord, that this salutary offering may both cleanse us from our offenses, and propitiate Your power. Through our Lord Jesus Christ, Your Son, Who lives and reigns with You in the unity of the Holy Spirit, God.
P. World without end. *S.* Amen.

PREFACE—CANON

P. The Lord be with you. *S.* And with your spirit.
P. Lift up your hearts.
S. We have lifted them up to the Lord.
P. Let us give thanks to the Lord, our God.
S. It is fitting and just.

IT IS fitting indeed and just, right and helpful to salvation, for us always and everywhere to give thanks to You, O holy Lord, Father almighty, everlasting God, Who with Your Only-begotten Son and the Holy Spirit are one God, one Lord; not in the unity of a single person, but in the trinity of a single nature. For that which we believe on Your revelation concerning Your glory, that same we believe of Your Son, that same of the Holy Spirit, without difference or discrimination. So that in confessing the true and everlasting Godhead, we shall adore distinction in Persons, oneness in being, and equality in Majesty. This the Angels and Archangels, the Cherubim, too, and the Seraphim do

praise; day by day they cease not to cry out as with one voice, saying (*the bell is rung 3 times*):

HOLY, HOLY, HOLY, Lord God of Hosts. Heaven and earth are filled with Your glory. Hosanna in the highest. ✠ Blessed is He Who comes in the name of the Lord. Hosanna in the highest.

THE CANON OF THE MASS

THEREFORE, most gracious Father, we humbly beg of You and entreat You through Jesus Christ Your Son, our Lord, (*he kisses the altar*) to deem acceptable and bless these ✠ gifts, these ✠ offerings, these ✠ holy and unspotted oblations which, in the first place, we offer You for Your Holy Catholic Church, that You would deign to give her peace and protection, to unite and guard her throughout the world, together with Your servant N., our Pope, and N., our Bishop; and all true believers who cherish the Catholic and Apostolic Faith.

Commemoration of the Living

REMEMBER, O Lord, Your servants and handmaids, N. and N., (*name them*) and all here present, whose faith and devotion are known to You, on whose behalf we offer to You, or who themselves offer to You, this sacrifice of praise for themselves, families and friends, for the good of their souls, for their hope of salvation and deliverance from all harm, and who offer their homage to You, eternal, living and true God.

Commemoration of the Saints

IN THE unity of holy fellowship we observe the memory, first of all, of the glorious and ever

Virgin Mary, Mother of our Lord and God Jesus Christ; next, that of Your Blessed Apostles and Martyrs, Peter and Paul, Andrew, James, John, Thomas, James, Philip, Bartholomew, Matthew, Simon and Thaddeus; of Linus, Cletus, Clement, Sixtus, Cornelius, Cyprian, Lawrence, Chrysogonus, John and Paul, Cosmas and Damian, and of all Your Saints, by whose merits and prayers grant that we may be always fortified by the help of Your protection. Through the same Christ our Lord. Amen.

Spreading his hands over the oblation, he says:

GRACIOUSLY accept, then, we beseech You, O Lord, this service of our worship and that of all Your household. Provide that our days be spent in Your peace, save us from everlasting damnation, and cause us to be numbered in the flock You have chosen. Through Christ our Lord. Amen.

O GOD, deign to bless ✠ what we offer, and make it approved, ✠ effective, ✠ right, and wholly pleasing in every way, that it may become for our good, the Body ✠ and Blood ✠ of Your dearly beloved Son, Jesus Christ our Lord.

CONSECRATION—ELEVATION

WHO, the day before He suffered, took bread into His holy and venerable hands, and having raised His eyes to heaven, to You, O God, His almighty Father, giving thanks to You, He blessed it, ✠ broke it, and gave it to His disciples, saying: All of you take and eat of this:

FOR THIS IS MY BODY.

IN LIKE manner, when the supper was done, taking also this goodly chalice into His holy and venerable hands, again giving thanks to You, He

blessed ✠ it, and gave it to His disciples, saying: All of you take and drink of this:

FOR THIS IS THE CHALICE OF MY BLOOD OF THE NEW AND ETERNAL COVENANT: THE MYSTERY OF FAITH: WHICH SHALL BE SHED FOR YOU AND FOR MANY UNTO THE FORGIVENESS OF SINS.

After replacing the chalice on the corporal, he says:

As often as you shall do these things, in memory of Me shall you do them.

Offering of the Victim

MINDFUL, therefore, O Lord, not only of the blessed Passion of the same Christ, Your Son, our Lord, but also of His Resurrection from the dead, and finally His glorious Ascension into heaven, we, Your ministers, as also Your holy people, offer to Your supreme Majesty, of the gifts bestowed upon us, the pure ✠ Victim, the holy ✠ Victim, the all-perfect ✠ Victim: the holy ✠ Bread of life eternal and the Chalice ✠ of unending salvation.

AND this deign to regard with gracious and kindly attention and hold acceptable, as You deigned to accept the offerings of Abel, Your just servant, and the sacrifice of Abraham our patriarch, and that which Your chief priest Melchisedec offered to You, a holy sacrifice and a spotless victim.

MOST humbly we implore You, almighty God, bid these offerings to be brought by the hands of Your holy angel to Your altar above; before the face of Your Divine Majesty; that those of us who, by sharing in the Sacrifice of this altar, shall receive the Most Sacred ✠ Body and ✠ Blood of Your

Son, may be filled with every grace and heavenly blessing. Through the same Christ our Lord. Amen.

Commemoration of the Dead

REMEMBER also, O Lord, Your servants and handmaids, N. and N., who have gone before us with the sign of faith, and rest in the sleep of peace. (*Here pray for the dead.*) To these, O Lord, and to all who rest in Christ, we beseech You to grant of Your goodness, a place of comfort, light and peace. Through the same Christ our Lord. Amen.

TO US sinners also, Your servants, trusting in the greatness of Your mercy, deign to grant some part and fellowship with Your Holy Apostles and Martyrs: with John, Stephen, Matthias, Barnabas, Ignatius, Alexander, Marcellinus, Peter, Felicitas, Perpetua, Agatha, Lucy, Agnes, Cecilia, Anastasia, and all Your Saints; into whose company, we implore You to admit us, not weighing our merits, but freely granting us pardon. Through Christ our Lord.

THROUGH Whom, O Lord, You always create, ✠ sanctify, ✠ fill with life, ✠ bless, and bestow upon us all good things.

The Minor Elevation

THROUGH ✠ Him, and with ✠ Him, and in ✠ Him, is to You, God the Father ✠ almighty, in the unity of the Holy ✠ Spirit, all honor and glory, world without end. S. Amen.

THE COMMUNION AND THANKSGIVING

Let us pray. Prompted by saving precepts, and taught by Your divine teaching, we dare to say:

OUR FATHER, Who art in heaven, hallowed be Thy name: Thy kingdom come: Thy will be done on earth as it is in heaven. Give us this day our daily bread; and forgive us our trespasses, as we forgive those who trespass against us. And lead us not into temptation: *S.* But deliver us from evil. *P.* Amen.

DELIVER us, we beseech You, O Lord, from all evils, past, present, and to come; and by the intercession of the Blessed and glorious Mary, ever Virgin, Mother of God, together with Your Blessed Apostles Peter and Paul, and Andrew, and all the Saints, grant of Your goodness, peace in our days, that aided by the riches of Your mercy, we may be always free from sin and safe from all disturbance.
Through the same our Lord Jesus Christ, Your Son, Who lives and reigns with You in the unity of the Holy Spirit, God, world without end.
S. Amen.
P. May the peace ✠ of the Lord be ✠ always with ✠ you.
S. And with your spirit.

The Priest puts a small particle into the chalice, saying:

May this mingling and consecration of the Body and Blood of our Lord Jesus Christ help us who receive it to life everlasting. Amen.

LAMB of God, You Who take away the sins of the world, have mercy on us.
Lamb of God, You Who take away the sins of the world, have mercy on us.
Lamb of God, You Who take away the sins of the world, grant us peace.

PRAYERS BEFORE HOLY COMMUNION

Then inclining toward the altar, he says:

O LORD Jesus Christ, Who said to Your Apostles: "Peace I leave with you, My peace I give to you," regard not my sins but the faith of Your Church, and deign to give her peace and unity according to Your Will: Who live and reign, God, world without end. Amen.

O LORD Jesus Christ, Son of the living God, Who, by the will of the Father, with the cooperation of the Holy Spirit, have by Your death given life to the world, deliver me by this Your Most Sacred Body and Blood from all my sins and from every evil. Make me always cling to Your commandments, and never permit me to be separated from You. Who with the same God the Father and the Holy Spirit, live and reign, God, world without end. Amen.

LET not the partaking of Your Body, O Lord Jesus Christ, which I, though unworthy, presume to receive, turn to my judgment and condemnation; but through Your goodness, may it become a safeguard and an effective remedy, both of soul and body. Who live and reign with God the Father, in the unity of the Holy Spirit, God, world without end. Amen.

COMMUNION OF THE PRIEST

I WILL take the Bread of heaven, and call upon the name of the Lord.

Lord, I am not worthy that You should come under my roof; but only say the word, and my soul will be healed. (3 *times.*)

Making the Sign of the Cross with the Host, he says:

MAY the Body of our Lord Jesus Christ preserve my soul to life everlasting. Amen.

What return shall I make to the Lord for all He has given me? I will take the Chalice of salvation, and I will call upon the name of the Lord. Praising will I call upon the Lord and I shall be saved from my enemies.

Making the Sign of the Cross with the chalice, he says:

MAY the Blood of our Lord Jesus Christ preserve my soul to life everlasting. Amen.

The Priest reverently consumes the Precious Blood.

COMMUNION OF THE FAITHFUL

The Server and people say the "Confiteor."

P. May almighty God have mercy on you, forgive you your sins, and bring you to life everlasting. *S.* Amen.

P. May the almighty and merciful Lord grant you pardon, ✠ absolution and remission of your sins. *S.* Amen.

Holding up a Sacred Host, the Priest says:

Behold the Lamb of God, behold Him Who takes away the sins of the world.

Lord, I am not worthy that You should come under my roof; but only say the word, and my soul will be healed. (3 *times.*)

The Priest says to each communicant:

May the Body of our Lord Jesus Christ preserve your soul to life everlasting. Amen.

The Priest purifies the chalice with wine, saying:

WHAT has passed our lips as food, O Lord, may we possess in purity of heart, that what is given to us in time, be our healing for eternity.

He purifies his fingers with wine and water, saying:

MAY Your Body, O Lord, which I have eaten, and Your Blood which I have drunk, cleave to my very soul, and grant that no trace of sin be found in me, whom these pure and holy mysteries have renewed. Who live and reign, world without end. Amen.

THE COMMUNION • Matt. 6, 33

"SEEK first the kingdom of God; and all things shall be given you besides," says the Lord.

The Priest, turning to the people, says:

P. The Lord be with you. *S.* And with your spirit.
P. Let us pray.

THE POSTCOMMUNION

MAY Your sacraments, O God, ever purify and protect us; and lead us to the attainment of eternal salvation. Through our Lord Jesus Christ, Your Son, Who lives and reigns, etc. *S.* Amen.

FINAL PRAYERS

P. The Lord be with you. *S.* And with your spirit.
P. Go, you are dismissed. *S.* Thanks be to God.

MAY the tribute of my worship be pleasing to You, Most Holy Trinity, and grant that the sacrifice which I, all unworthy, have offered in the presence of Your Majesty, may be acceptable to You, and through Your mercy obtain forgiveness for me and all for whom I have offered it. Through Christ our Lord. Amen.

THE LAST BLESSING

MAY almighty God bless you: ✠ the Father, and the Son, and the Holy Spirit. *S.* Amen.

The Last Gospel and Prayers after Low Mass are conveniently placed inside the back cover.

"And he who was dead sat up and began to speak."

FIFTEENTH SUNDAY AFTER PENTECOST

Today's Gospel shows us Christ's compassion for a widowed mother whose dead son was being carried out for burial. It prefigures another mother, the Church, who weeps unceasingly over the spiritual death of so many of her children. (GREEN VESTMENTS)

PRAYERS AT THE FOOT OF THE ALTAR

IN THE name of the Father, ✠ and of the Son, and of the Holy Spirit. Amen.

Priest. I will go in to the altar of God.

Server. The God of my gladness and joy.

Psalm 42

DO ME justice, O God, and fight my fight against a faithless people; from the deceitful and impious man rescue me.

S. For You, O God, are my strength. Why do You keep me so far away? Why must I go about in mourning, with the enemy oppressing me?

P. Send forth Your light and Your fidelity; they shall lead me on and bring me to Your holy mountain, to Your dwelling-place.

S. Then will I go in to the altar of God, the God of my gladness and joy.
P. Then will I give You thanks upon the harp, O God, my God. Why are you so downcast, O my soul? Why do you sigh within me?
S. Hope in God! For I shall again be thanking Him in the presence of my Savior and my God.
P. Glory be to the Father, and to the Son, and to the Holy Spirit.

S. As it was in the beginning, is now, and ever shall be, world without end. Amen.
P. I will go in to the altar of God.
S. The God of my gladness and joy.
P. Our help ✠ is in the name of the Lord.
S. Who made heaven and earth.
P. I confess to almighty God, etc.
S. May almighty God have mercy on you, forgive you your sins, and bring you to life everlasting.
P. Amen.

The Server, bowing, says the "Confiteor."

I CONFESS to almighty God, to Blessed Mary, ever Virgin, to Blessed Michael the Archangel, to Blessed John the Baptist, to the Holy Apostles Peter and Paul, and to all the Saints, and to you, Father, that I have sinned exceedingly in thought, word and deed, *through my fault, through my fault, through my most grievous fault.* Therefore I beseech Blessed Mary, ever Virgin, Blessed Michael the Archangel, Blessed John the Baptist, the Holy Apostles Peter and Paul, and all the Saints, and you, Father, to pray to the Lord our God for me.
P. May almighty God have mercy on you, forgive you your sins, and bring you to life everlasting.
S. Amen.

MAY the almighty and merciful Lord grant us pardon, ✠ absolution, and remission of our sins. *S.* Amen.

P. Will You not, O God, give us life?
S. And shall not Your people rejoice in You?
P. Show us, O Lord, Your kindness.
S. And grant us Your salvation.
P. O Lord, hear my prayer.
S. And let my cry come to You.
P. The Lord be with you.
S. And with your spirit. *P.* Let us pray.

Going up to the altar, the Priest prays silently:

TAKE away from us our sins, O Lord, we beseech You, that we may enter with pure minds into the Holy of Holies. Through Christ our Lord. Amen.

WE BESEECH You, O Lord, by the merits of Your Saints (*he kisses the altar*) whose relics lie here, and of all the Saints: deign in Your mercy to pardon me all my sins. Amen.

THE INTROIT • Ps. 85, 1. 2. 3. 4

At the right side of the altar, the Priest says:

INCLINE Your ear, O Lord; answer me; save Your servant, O my God, who trusts in You. Have pity on me, O Lord, for to You I call all the day. *Ps.* Gladden the soul of Your servant, for to You, O Lord, I lift up my soul. Glory be to the Father, and to the Son, and to the Holy Spirit. As it was in the beginning, is now, and ever shall be, world without end. Amen. — Incline Your ear, O Lord; answer me; save Your servant, O my God, who trusts in You. Have pity on me, O Lord, for to You I call all the day.

THE KYRIE

P. Lord, have mercy. *S*. Lord, have mercy. *P*. Lord, have mercy. *S*. Christ, have mercy. *P*. Christ, have mercy. *S*. Christ, have mercy. *P*. Lord, have mercy. *S*. Lord, have mercy. *P*. Lord, have mercy.

THE GLORIA

GLORY to God in the highest. And on earth peace to men of good will. We praise You. We bless You. We adore You. We glorify You. We give You thanks for Your great glory. O Lord God, heavenly King, God the Father almighty. O Lord Jesus Christ, the Only-begotten Son. O Lord God, Lamb of God, Son of the Father: You Who take away the sins of the world, have mercy on us. You Who take away the sins of the world, receive our prayer. You Who sit at the right hand of the Father, have mercy on us. For You alone are holy. You alone are the Lord. You alone, O Jesus Christ, are most high. Together with the Holy Spirit ✠ in the glory of God the Father. Amen.

The Priest kisses the altar and turns to the people, saying:

P. The Lord be with you. *S*. And with your spirit. *P*. Let us pray.

THE PRAYER

Going to the right (Epistle) side, he says:

MAY Your continual pity, O Lord, cleanse and defend Your Church; and, because without You she cannot endure in safety, may she ever be governed by Your bounty. Through our Lord Jesus Christ, Your Son, Who lives and reigns with You in the unity of the Holy Spirit, God, world without end. S. Amen.

THE EPISTLE • Gal. 5, 25-26; 6, 1-10

BRETHREN: If we live by the Spirit, by the Spirit let us also walk. Let us not become desirous of vainglory, provoking one another, envying one another. Brethren, even if a person is caught doing something wrong, you who are spiritual instruct such a one in a spirit of meekness, considering yourself, lest you also be tempted. Bear one another's burdens, and so you will fulfill the law of Christ. For if anyone thinks himself to be something, whereas he is nothing, he deceives himself. But let everyone test his own work, and so he will have glory in himself only, and not in comparison with another. For each one will bear his own burden. And let him who is instructed in the word share all good things with his teacher. Be not deceived, God is not mocked. For what a man sows, that he will also reap. For he who sows in the flesh, from the flesh also will reap corruption. But he who sows in the spirit, from the spirit will reap life everlasting. And in doing good let us not grow tired; for in due time we shall reap if we do not relax. Therefore, while we have time, let us do good to all men, but especially to those who are of the household of faith. S. Thanks be to God.

THE GRADUAL • Ps. 91, 2. 3.

IT IS good to give thanks to the Lord, to sing to Your name, Most High. ℣. To proclaim Your kindness at dawn and Your faithfulness throughout the night.

Alleluia, alleluia. ℣. *Ps.* 94, 3. For the Lord is

a great God, and a great King over all the earth. Alleluia.

PRAYER BEFORE THE GOSPEL

Bowing down at the center of the altar, he says:

CLEANSE my heart and my lips, O almighty God, Who cleansed the lips of the Prophet Isaias with a burning coal. In Your gracious mercy deign so to purify me that I may worthily proclaim Your holy Gospel. Through Christ our Lord. Amen.

Lord, grant Your blessing. The Lord be in my heart and on my lips, that I may worthily and fittingly proclaim His holy Gospel. Amen.

THE GOSPEL • Luke 7, 11-16

Going to the left (Gospel) side of the altar, he says:

P. The Lord be with you. S. And with your spirit.
P. ✠ The continuation of the holy Gospel according to Saint Luke. S. Glory be to You, O Lord.

AT THAT time, Jesus went to a town called Naim; and His disciples and a large crowd went with Him. And as He drew near the gate of the town, behold, a dead man was being carried out, the only son of his mother, and she was a widow; and a large gathering from the town was with her. And the Lord, seeing her, had compassion on her, and said to her, "Do not weep." And He went up and touched the stretcher; and the bearers stood still. And He said, "Young man, I say to you, arise." And he who was dead, sat up, and began to speak. And He gave him to his mother. But fear seized upon all, and they began to glorify God, saying, "A great prophet has risen among us," and "God has visited His people." S. Praise be to You, O Christ.

P. By the words of the Gospel, may our sins be taken away.

THE NICENE CREED

At the center of the altar, he says:

I BELIEVE in one God, the Father almighty, Maker of heaven and earth, and of all things visible and invisible. And in one Lord Jesus Christ, the Only-begotten Son of God. Born of the Father before all ages. God of God; Light of Light; true God of true God. Begotten not made; of one being with the Father; by Whom all things were made. Who for us men, and for our salvation, came down from heaven. (*Here all genuflect.*) And was made Flesh by the Holy Spirit of the Virgin Mary: AND WAS MADE MAN. He was also crucified for us, suffered under Pontius Pilate and was buried. And on the third day He rose again according to the Scriptures. And ascending into heaven, He sits at the right hand of the Father. And He shall come again in glory to judge the living and the dead; and of His kingdom there shall be no end. And I believe in the Holy Spirit, Lord and Giver of life, Who proceeds from the Father and the Son. Who together with the Father and the Son is no less adored, and glorified: Who spoke by the Prophets. And I believe in One, Holy, Catholic and Apostolic Church. I confess one Baptism for the remission of sins. And I look for the resurrection of the dead. ✠ And the life of the world to come. Amen.

THE OFFERTORY

The Priest turns to the people and says:

P. The Lord be with you. S. And with your spirit.
P. Let us pray.

THE OFFERTORY VERSE • Ps. 39, 2. 3. 4

I HAVE waited, waited for the Lord, and He stooped toward me, and heard my cry. And He put a new song into my mouth, a hymn to our God.

The Priest now uncovers the chalice, places the host on the paten and offering it up, says:

ACCEPT, O holy Father, almighty and eternal God, this spotless host, which I, Your unworthy servant, offer to You, my living and true God, to atone for my numberless sins, offenses, and negligences; on behalf of all here present and likewise for all faithful Christians living and dead, that it may profit me and them as a means of salvation to life everlasting. Amen.

He pours wine and water into the chalice, blessing the water before it is poured.

O GOD, Who established the nature of man in wondrous dignity, and still more admirably restored it, grant that through the mystery of this water and wine, we may be made partakers of His Divinity, Who has condescended to become partaker of our humanity, Jesus Christ, Your Son, our Lord. Who lives and reigns with You in the unity of the Holy Spirit, God, world without end. Amen.

Offering up the wine, the Priest says:

WE OFFER You, O Lord, the chalice of salvation, humbly begging of Your mercy that it may arise before Your Divine Majesty, with a pleasing fragrance, for our salvation and for that of the whole world. Amen.

Bowing down, the Priest says:

IN A humble spirit and with a contrite heart, may we be accepted by You, O Lord, and may our

sacrifice so be offered in Your sight this day as to please You, O Lord God.

Raising his eyes and blessing the offering, he says:

COME, O Sanctifier, almighty and eternal God, and bless ✠ this sacrifice prepared for the glory of Your holy name.

WASHING THE FINGERS

I WASH my hands in innocence, and I go around Your altar, O Lord, giving voice to my thanks, and recounting all Your wondrous deeds. O Lord, I love the house in which You dwell, the tenting-place of Your glory. Gather not my soul with those of sinners, nor with men of blood my life. On their hands are crimes, and their right hands are full of bribes. But I walk in integrity; redeem me, and have pity on me. My foot stands on level ground; in the assemblies I will bless You, O Lord. Glory be to the Father, and to the Son, and to the Holy Spirit. As it was in the beginning, is now, and ever shall be, world without end. Amen.

ACCEPT, Most Holy Trinity, this offering which we are making to You in remembrance of the Passion, Resurrection, and Ascension of Jesus Christ, our Lord; and in honor of Blessed Mary, ever Virgin, Blessed John the Baptist, the Holy Apostles Peter and Paul, and of these, and of all the Saints; that it may add to their honor and aid our salvation; and may they deign to intercede in heaven for us who honor their memory here on earth. Through the same Christ our Lord. Amen.

The Priest turns toward the people and says:

Pray, brethren, that my sacrifice and yours may become acceptable to God the Father almighty.

S. May the Lord accept this sacrifice from your hands to the praise and glory of His name, for our advantage, and that of all His holy Church.
P. Amen.

THE SECRET

MAY Your sacraments guard us, O Lord, and ever protect us against the assaults of the devil. Through our Lord Jesus Christ, Your Son, Who lives and reigns with You in the unity of the Holy Spirit, God.
P. World without end. *S.* Amen.

PREFACE—CANON

P. The Lord be with you. *S.* And with your spirit.
P. Lift up your hearts.
S. We have lifted them up to the Lord.
P. Let us give thanks to the Lord, our God.
S. It is fitting and just.

IT IS fitting indeed and just, right and helpful to salvation, for us always and everywhere to give thanks to You, O holy Lord, Father almighty, everlasting God, Who with Your Only-begotten Son and the Holy Spirit are one God, one Lord; not in the unity of a single person, but in the trinity of a single nature. For that which we believe on Your revelation concerning Your glory, that same we believe of Your Son, that same of the Holy Spirit, without difference or discrimination. So that in confessing the true and everlasting Godhead, we shall adore distinction in Persons, oneness in being, and equality in Majesty. This the Angels and Archangels, the Cherubim, too, and the Seraphim do praise; day by day they cease not to cry out as with one voice, saying (*the bell is rung* 3 *times*):

HOLY, HOLY, HOLY, Lord God of Hosts. Heaven and earth are filled with Your glory. Hosanna in the highest. ✠ Blessed is He Who comes in the name of the Lord. Hosanna in the highest.

THE CANON OF THE MASS

THEREFORE, most gracious Father, we humbly beg of You and entreat You through Jesus Christ Your Son, our Lord, (*he kisses the altar*) to deem acceptable and bless these ✠ gifts, these ✠ offerings, these ✠ holy and unspotted oblations which, in the first place, we offer You for Your Holy Catholic Church, that You would deign to give her peace and protection, to unite and guard her throughout the world, together with Your servant N., our Pope, and N., our Bishop; and all true believers who cherish the Catholic and Apostolic Faith.

Commemoration of the Living

REMEMBER, O Lord, Your servants and handmaids, N. and N., (*name them*) and all here present, whose faith and devotion are known to You, on whose behalf we offer to You, or who themselves offer to You, this sacrifice of praise for themselves, families and friends, for the good of their souls, for their hope of salvation and deliverance from all harm, and who offer their homage to You, eternal, living and true God.

Commemoration of the Saints

IN THE unity of holy fellowship we observe the memory, first of all, of the glorious and ever Virgin Mary, Mother of our Lord and God Jesus Christ; next, that of Your Blessed Apostles and Martyrs, Peter and Paul, Andrew, James, John,

Thomas, James, Philip, Bartholomew, Matthew, Simon and Thaddeus; of Linus, Cletus, Clement, Sixtus, Cornelius, Cyprian, Lawrence, Chrysogonus, John and Paul, Cosmas and Damian, and of all Your Saints, by whose merits and prayers grant that we may be always fortified by the help of Your protection. Through the same Christ our Lord. Amen.

Spreading his hands over the oblation, he says:

GRACIOUSLY accept, then, we beseech You, O Lord, this service of our worship and that of all Your household. Provide that our days be spent in Your peace, save us from everlasting damnation, and cause us to be numbered in the flock You have chosen. Through Christ our Lord. Amen.

O GOD, deign to bless ✠ what we offer, and make it approved, ✠ effective, ✠ right, and wholly pleasing in every way, that it may become for our good, the Body ✠ and Blood ✠ of Your dearly beloved Son, Jesus Christ our Lord.

CONSECRATION—ELEVATION

WHO, the day before He suffered, took bread into His holy and venerable hands, and having raised His eyes to heaven, to You, O God, His almighty Father, giving thanks to You, He blessed it, ✠ broke it, and gave it to His disciples, saying: All of you take and eat of this:

FOR THIS IS MY BODY.

IN LIKE manner, when the supper was done, taking also this goodly chalice into His holy and venerable hands, again giving thanks to You, He blessed ✠ it, and gave it to His disciples, saying: All of you take and drink of this:

FOR THIS IS THE CHALICE OF MY BLOOD OF THE NEW AND ETERNAL COVENANT: THE MYSTERY OF FAITH: WHICH SHALL BE SHED FOR YOU AND FOR MANY UNTO THE FORGIVENESS OF SINS.

After replacing the chalice on the corporal, he says:

As often as you shall do these things, in memory of Me shall you do them.

Offering of the Victim

MINDFUL, therefore, O Lord, not only of the blessed Passion of the same Christ, Your Son, our Lord, but also of His Resurrection from the dead, and finally His glorious Ascension into heaven, we, Your ministers, as also Your holy people, offer to Your supreme Majesty, of the gifts bestowed upon us, the pure ✠ Victim, the holy ✠ Victim, the all-perfect ✠ Victim: the holy ✠ Bread of life eternal and the Chalice ✠ of unending salvation.

AND this deign to regard with gracious and kindly attention and hold acceptable, as You deigned to accept the offerings of Abel, Your just servant, and the sacrifice of Abraham our patriarch, and that which Your chief priest Melchisedec offered to You, a holy sacrifice and a spotless victim.

MOST humbly we implore You, almighty God, bid these offerings to be brought by the hands of Your holy angel to Your altar above; before the face of Your Divine Majesty; that those of us who, by sharing in the Sacrifice of this altar, shall receive the Most Sacred ✠ Body and ✠ Blood of Your Son, may be filled with every grace and heavenly blessing. Through the same Christ our Lord. Amen.

Commemoration of the Dead

REMEMBER also, O Lord, Your servants and handmaids, N. and N., who have gone before us with the sign of faith, and rest in the sleep of peace. (*Here pray for the dead.*) To these, O Lord, and to all who rest in Christ, we beseech You to grant of Your goodness, a place of comfort, light and peace. Through the same Christ our Lord. Amen.

TO US sinners also, Your servants, trusting in the greatness of Your mercy, deign to grant some part and fellowship with Your Holy Apostles and Martyrs: with John, Stephen, Matthias, Barnabas, Ignatius, Alexander, Marcellinus, Peter, Felicitas, Perpetua, Agatha, Lucy, Agnes, Cecilia, Anastasia, and all Your Saints; into whose company, we implore You to admit us, not weighing our merits, but freely granting us pardon. Through Christ our Lord.

THROUGH Whom, O Lord, You always create, ✠ sanctify, ✠ fill with life, ✠ bless, and bestow upon us all good things.

The Minor Elevation

THROUGH ✠ Him, and with ✠ Him, and in ✠ Him, is to You, God the Father ✠ almighty, in the unity of the Holy ✠ Spirit, all honor and glory, world without end. S. Amen.

THE COMMUNION AND THANKSGIVING

Let us pray. Prompted by saving precepts, and taught by Your divine teaching, we dare to say:

OUR FATHER, Who art in heaven, hallowed be Thy name: Thy kingdom come: Thy will be

done on earth as it is in heaven. Give us this day our daily bread; and forgive us our trespasses, as we forgive those who trespass against us. And lead us not into temptation: *S.* But deliver us from evil. *P.* Amen.

DELIVER us, we beseech You, O Lord, from all evils, past, present, and to come; and by the intercession of the Blessed and glorious Mary, ever Virgin, Mother of God, together with Your Blessed Apostles Peter and Paul, and Andrew, and all the Saints, grant of Your goodness, peace in our days, that aided by the riches of Your mercy, we may be always free from sin and safe from all disturbance.

Through the same our Lord Jesus Christ, Your Son, Who lives and reigns with You in the unity of the Holy Spirit, God, world without end. *S.* Amen.

P. May the peace ✠ of the Lord be ✠ always with ✠ you. *S.* And with your spirit.

The Priest puts a small particle into the chalice, saying:

May this mingling and consecration of the Body and Blood of our Lord Jesus Christ help us who receive it to life everlasting. Amen.

LAMB of God, You Who take away the sins of the world, have mercy on us.

Lamb of God, You Who take away the sins of the world, have mercy on us.

Lamb of God, You Who take away the sins of the world, grant us peace.

PRAYERS BEFORE HOLY COMMUNION

Then inclining toward the altar, he says:

O LORD Jesus Christ, Who said to Your Apostles: "Peace I leave with you, My peace I give

to you," regard not my sins but the faith of Your Church, and deign to give her peace and unity according to Your Will: Who live and reign, God, world without end. Amen.

O LORD Jesus Christ, Son of the living God, Who, by the will of the Father, with the cooperation of the Holy Spirit, have by Your death given life to the world, deliver me by this Your Most Sacred Body and Blood from all my sins and from every evil. Make me always cling to Your commandments, and never permit me to be separated from You. Who with the same God the Father and the Holy Spirit, live and reign, God, world without end. Amen.

LET not the partaking of Your Body, O Lord Jesus Christ, which I, though unworthy, presume to receive, turn to my judgment and condemnation; but through Your goodness, may it become a safeguard and an effective remedy, both of soul and body. Who live and reign with God the Father, in the unity of the Holy Spirit, God, world without end. Amen.

COMMUNION OF THE PRIEST

I WILL take the Bread of heaven, and call upon the name of the Lord.

Lord, I am not worthy that You should come under my roof; but only say the word, and my soul will be healed. (3 *times.*)

Making the Sign of the Cross with the Host, he says:

MAY the Body of our Lord Jesus Christ preserve my soul to life everlasting. Amen.

What return shall I make to the Lord for all He has given me? I will take the Chalice of salvation,

and I will call upon the name of the Lord. Praising will I call upon the Lord and I shall be saved from my enemies.

Making the Sign of the Cross with the chalice, he says:

MAY the Blood of our Lord Jesus Christ preserve my soul to life everlasting. Amen.

The Priest reverently consumes the Precious Blood.

COMMUNION OF THE FAITHFUL

The Server and people say the "Confiteor."

P. May almighty God have mercy on you, forgive you your sins, and bring you to life everlasting. *S.* Amen.

P. May the almighty and merciful Lord grant you pardon, ✠ absolution and remission of your sins. *S.* Amen.

Holding up a Sacred Host, the Priest says:

Behold the Lamb of God, behold Him Who takes away the sins of the world.

Lord, I am not worthy that You should come under my roof; but only say the word, and my soul will be healed. (3 *times.*)

The Priest says to each communicant:

May the Body of our Lord Jesus Christ preserve your soul to life everlasting. Amen.

The Priest purifies the chalice with wine, saying:

WHAT has passed our lips as food, O Lord, may we possess in purity of heart, that what is given to us in time, be our healing for eternity.

He purifies his fingers with wine and water, saying:

MAY Your Body, O Lord, which I have eaten, and Your Blood which I have drunk, cleave to my very soul, and grant that no trace of sin be found in me, whom these pure and holy mysteries

have renewed. Who live and reign, world without end. Amen.

THE COMMUNION • John 6, 52

THE bread that I will give is My Flesh for the life of the world.

The Priest, turning to the people, says:

P. The Lord be with you. *S.* And with your spirit.
P. Let us pray.

THE POSTCOMMUNION

MAY the working of this heavenly Gift, we beseech You, O Lord, possess our minds and bodies: that its effect, and not our own inclinations, have precedence within us. Through our Lord Jesus Christ, Your Son, Who lives and reigns with You in the unity of the Holy Spirit, God, world without end. *S.* Amen.

FINAL PRAYERS

The Priest turns again to the people, and says:

P. The Lord be with you. *S.* And with your spirit.
P. Go, you are dismissed. *S.* Thanks be to God.

MAY the tribute of my worship be pleasing to You, Most Holy Trinity, and grant that the sacrifice which I, all unworthy, have offered in the presence of Your Majesty, may be acceptable to You, and through Your mercy obtain forgiveness for me and all for whom I have offered it. Through Christ our Lord. Amen.

THE LAST BLESSING

MAY almighty God bless you: ✠ the Father, and the Son, and the Holy Spirit. *S.* Amen.

The Last Gospel and Prayers after Low Mass are conveniently placed inside the back cover.

"Everyone who exalts himself shall be humbled."

SIXTEENTH SUNDAY AFTER PENTECOST

The supernatural life which we receive in Baptism is like a seed that must be developed. "Rooted and grounded in love," we pray that God may increase our faith and hope, and that His grace may stir up in us a zeal for good works. (GREEN VESTMENTS)

PRAYERS AT THE FOOT OF THE ALTAR

IN THE name of the Father, ✠ and of the Son, and of the Holy Spirit. Amen.

Priest. I will go in to the altar of God.

Server. The God of my gladness and joy.

Psalm 42

DO ME justice, O God, and fight my fight against a faithless people; from the deceitful and impious man rescue me.

S. For You, O God, are my strength. Why do You keep me so far away? Why must I go about in mourning, with the enemy oppressing me?

P. Send forth Your light and Your fidelity; they shall lead me on and bring me to Your holy mountain, to Your dwelling-place.

S. Then will I go in to the altar of God, the God of my gladness and joy.
P. Then will I give You thanks upon the harp, O God, my God. Why are you so downcast, O my soul? Why do you sigh within me?
S. Hope in God! For I shall again be thanking Him in the presence of my Savior and my God.
P. Glory be to the Father, and to the Son, and to the Holy Spirit.
S. As it was in the beginning, is now, and ever shall be, world without end. Amen.
P. I will go in to the altar of God.
S. The God of my gladness and joy.
P. Our help ✠ is in the name of the Lord.
S. Who made heaven and earth.
P. I confess to almighty God, etc.
S. May almighty God have mercy on you, forgive you your sins, and bring you to life everlasting.
P. Amen.

The Server, bowing, says the "Confiteor."

I CONFESS to almighty God, to Blessed Mary, ever Virgin, to Blessed Michael the Archangel, to Blessed John the Baptist, to the Holy Apostles Peter and Paul, and to all the Saints, and to you, Father, that I have sinned exceedingly in thought, word and deed, *through my fault, through my fault, through my most grievous fault.* Therefore I beseech Blessed Mary, ever Virgin, Blessed Michael the Archangel, Blessed John the Baptist, the Holy Apostles Peter and Paul, and all the Saints, and you, Father, to pray to the Lord our God for me.
P. May almighty God have mercy on you, forgive you your sins, and bring you to life everlasting.
S. Amen.

MAY the almighty and merciful Lord grant us pardon, ✠ absolution, and remission of our sins. *S.* Amen.

P. Will You not, O God, give us life?

S. And shall not Your people rejoice in You?

P. Show us, O Lord, Your kindness.

S. And grant us Your salvation.

P. O Lord, hear my prayer.

S. And let my cry come to You.

P. The Lord be with you.

S. And with your spirit. *P.* Let us pray.

Going up to the altar, the Priest prays silently:

TAKE away from us our sins, O Lord, we beseech You, that we may enter with pure minds into the Holy of Holies. Through Christ our Lord. Amen.

WE BESEECH You, O Lord, by the merits of Your Saints (*he kisses the altar*) whose relics lie here, and of all the Saints: deign in Your mercy to pardon me all my sins. Amen.

THE INTROIT • Ps. 85, 3. 5. 1

At the right side of the altar, the Priest says:

HAVE pity on me, O Lord, for to You I call all the day; for You, O Lord, are good and forgiving, abounding in kindness to all who call upon You. *Ps.* Incline Your ear, O Lord; answer me, for I am afflicted and poor. Glory be to the Father, and to the Son, and to the Holy Spirit. As it was in the beginning, is now, and ever shall be, world without end. Amen. — Have pity on me, O Lord, for to You I call all the day; for You, O Lord, are good and forgiving, abounding in kindness to all who call upon You.

THE KYRIE

P. Lord, have mercy. S. Lord, have mercy. P. Lord, have mercy. S. Christ, have mercy. P. Christ, have mercy. S. Christ, have mercy. P. Lord, have mercy. S. Lord, have mercy. P. Lord, have mercy.

THE GLORIA

GLORY to God in the highest. And on earth peace to men of good will. We praise You. We bless You. We adore You. We glorify You. We give You thanks for Your great glory. O Lord God, heavenly King, God the Father almighty. O Lord Jesus Christ, the Only-begotten Son. O Lord God, Lamb of God, Son of the Father: You Who take away the sins of the world, have mercy on us. You Who take away the sins of the world, receive our prayer. You Who sit at the right hand of the Father, have mercy on us. For You alone are holy. You alone are the Lord. You alone, O Jesus Christ, are most high. Together with the Holy Spirit ✠ in the glory of God the Father. Amen.

The Priest kisses the altar and turns to the people, saying:

P. The Lord be with you. S. And with your spirit.
P. Let us pray.

THE PRAYER

Going to the right (Epistle) side, he says:

LET Your grace, we beseech You, O Lord, always go before us and follow us, and make us continually intent upon good works. Through our Lord Jesus Christ, Your Son, Who lives and reigns with You in the unity of the Holy Spirit, God, world without end. S. Amen.

THE EPISTLE • Eph. 3, 13-21

BRETHREN: I pray you not to be disheartened at my tribulations for you, for they are your glory. For this reason I bend my knees to the Father of our Lord Jesus Christ, from Whom all fatherhood in heaven and on earth receives its name, that He may grant you from His glorious riches to be strengthened with power through His Spirit unto the progress of the inner man; and to have Christ dwelling through faith in your hearts: so that, being rooted and grounded in love, you may be able to comprehend with all the saints what is the breadth and length and height and depth, and to know Christ's love which surpasses knowledge, in order that you may be filled unto all the fullness of God. Now, to Him Who is able to accomplish all things in a measure far beyond what we ask or conceive, in keeping with the power that is at work in us — to Him be glory in the Church and in Christ Jesus down through all the ages of time without end. Amen. S. Thanks be to God.

THE GRADUAL • Ps. 101, 16-17

THE nations shall revere Your name, O Lord, and all the kings of the earth Your glory. ℣. For the Lord has rebuilt Sion, and He shall appear in His glory.

Alleluia, alleluia. ℣. *Ps. 97, 1.* Sing to the Lord a new song, for the Lord has done wondrous deeds. Alleluia.

PRAYER BEFORE THE GOSPEL

Bowing down at the center of the altar, he says:

CLEANSE my heart and my lips, O almighty God, Who cleansed the lips of the Prophet

Isaias with a burning coal. In Your gracious mercy deign so to purify me that I may worthily proclaim Your holy Gospel. Through Christ our Lord. Amen. Lord, grant Your blessing. The Lord be in my heart and on my lips, that I may worthily and fittingly proclaim His holy Gospel. Amen.

THE GOSPEL • Luke 14, 1-11

Going to the left (Gospel) side of the altar, he says:

P. The Lord be with you. *S.* And with your spirit.
P. ✠ The continuation of the holy Gospel according to Saint Luke. *S.* Glory be to You, O Lord.

AT THAT time, when Jesus entered the house of one of the rulers of the Pharisees on the Sabbath to take food, they watched Him. And behold, there was a certain man before Him who had the dropsy. And Jesus asked the lawyers and Pharisees, saying, "Is it lawful to cure on the Sabbath?" But they remained silent. And He took and healed him and let him go. Then addressing them, He said, "Which of you shall have an ass or an ox fall into a pit, and will not immediately draw him up on the Sabbath?" And they could give Him no answer to these things. But He also spoke a parable to those invited, observing how they were choosing the first places at table, and He said to them, "When you are invited to a wedding feast, do not recline in the first place, lest perhaps one more distinguished than you have been invited by him, and he who invited you and him come and say to you, 'Make room for this man'; and then you begin with shame to take the last place. But when you are invited, go and recline in the last place; that when he who invited you comes in, he may say to you, 'Friend, go up higher!' Then you will be honored in the presence of all who are at table with you. For everyone who exalts himself shall be humbled, and he who humbles himself shall be exalted." S. Praise be to You, O Christ.

P. By the words of the Gospel, may our sins be taken away.

THE NICENE CREED

At the center of the altar, he says:

I BELIEVE in one God, the Father almighty, Maker of heaven and earth, and of all things visible and invisible. And in one Lord Jesus Christ, the Only-begotten Son of God. Born of the Father before all ages. God of God; Light of Light; true God of true God. Begotten not made; of one being with the Father; by Whom all things were made. Who for us men, and for our salvation, came down from heaven. (*Here all genuflect.*) And was made Flesh by the Holy Spirit of the Virgin Mary: AND WAS MADE MAN. He was also crucified for us, suffered under Pontius Pilate and was buried. And on the third day He rose again according to the Scriptures. And ascending into heaven, He sits at the right hand of the Father. And He shall come again in glory to judge the living and the dead; and of His kingdom there shall be no end. And I believe in the Holy Spirit, Lord and Giver of life, Who proceeds from the Father and the Son. Who together with the Father and the Son is no less adored, and glorified: Who spoke by the Prophets. And I believe in One, Holy, Catholic and Apostolic Church. I confess one Baptism for the remission of sins. And I look for the resurrection of the dead. ✠ And the life of the world to come. Amen.

THE OFFERTORY

The Priest turns to the people and says:

P. The Lord be with you. *S.* And with your spirit.
P. Let us pray.

THE OFFERTORY VERSE • Ps. 39, 14. 15

DEIGN, O Lord, to rescue me; let all be put to shame and confusion who seek to snatch away my life. Deign, O Lord, to rescue me.

The Priest now uncovers the chalice, places the host on the paten and offering it up, says:

ACCEPT, O holy Father, almighty and eternal God, this spotless host, which I, Your unworthy servant, offer to You, my living and true God, to atone for my numberless sins, offenses, and negligences; on behalf of all here present and likewise for all faithful Christians living and dead, that it may profit me and them as a means of salvation to life everlasting. Amen.

He pours wine and water into the chalice, blessing the water before it is poured.

O GOD, Who established the nature of man in wondrous dignity, and still more admirably restored it, grant that through the mystery of this water and wine, we may be made partakers of His Divinity, Who has condescended to become partaker of our humanity, Jesus Christ, Your Son, our Lord. Who lives and reigns with You in the unity of the Holy Spirit, God, world without end. Amen.

Offering up the wine, the Priest says:

WE OFFER You, O Lord, the chalice of salvation, humbly begging of Your mercy that it may arise before Your Divine Majesty, with a pleasing fragrance, for our salvation and for that of the whole world. Amen.

Bowing down, the Priest says:

IN A humble spirit and with a contrite heart, may we be accepted by You, O Lord, and may our sacrifice so be offered in Your sight this day as to please You, O Lord God.

Raising his eyes and blessing the offering, he says:

COME, O Sanctifier, almighty and eternal God, and bless ✠ this sacrifice prepared for the glory of Your holy name.

WASHING THE FINGERS

I WASH my hands in innocence, and I go around Your altar, O Lord, giving voice to my thanks, and recounting all Your wondrous deeds. O Lord, I love the house in which You dwell, the tenting-place of Your glory. Gather not my soul with those of sinners, nor with men of blood my life. On their hands are crimes, and their right hands are full of bribes. But I walk in integrity; redeem me, and have pity on me. My foot stands on level ground; in the assemblies I will bless You, O Lord. Glory be to the Father, and to the Son, and to the Holy Spirit. As it was in the beginning, is now, and ever shall be, world without end. Amen.

ACCEPT, Most Holy Trinity, this offering which we are making to You in remembrance of the Passion, Resurrection, and Ascension of Jesus Christ, our Lord; and in honor of Blessed Mary, ever Virgin, Blessed John the Baptist, the Holy Apostles Peter and Paul, and of these, and of all the Saints; that it may add to their honor and aid our salvation; and may they deign to intercede in heaven for us who honor their memory here on earth. Through the same Christ our Lord. Amen.

The Priest turns toward the people and says:

Pray, brethren, that my sacrifice and yours may become acceptable to God the Father almighty.

S. May the Lord accept this sacrifice from your hands to the praise and glory of His name, for our advantage, and that of all His holy Church.

P. Amen.

THE SECRET

CLEANSE us, we beseech You, O Lord, through the effect of this sacrifice; and taking pity on us, grant that we may become worthy partakers of it. Through our Lord Jesus Christ, Your Son, Who lives and reigns with You in the unity of the Holy Spirit, God.

P. World without end. *S.* Amen.

PREFACE—CANON

P. The Lord be with you. *S.* And with your spirit.

P. Lift up your hearts.

S. We have lifted them up to the Lord.

P. Let us give thanks to the Lord, our God.

S. It is fitting and just.

IT IS fitting indeed and just, right and helpful to salvation, for us always and everywhere to give thanks to You, O holy Lord, Father almighty, everlasting God, Who with Your Only-begotten Son and the Holy Spirit are one God, one Lord; not in the unity of a single person, but in the trinity of a single nature. For that which we believe on Your revelation concerning Your glory, that same we believe of Your Son, that same of the Holy Spirit, without difference or discrimination. So that in confessing the true and everlasting Godhead, we shall adore distinction in Persons, oneness in being, and equality in Majesty. This the Angels and Archangels, the Cherubim, too, and the Seraphim do praise; day by day they cease not to cry out as with one voice, saying (*the bell is rung 3 times*):

HOLY, HOLY, HOLY, Lord God of Hosts. Heaven and earth are filled with Your glory. Hosanna in the highest. ✠ Blessed is He Who comes in the name of the Lord. Hosanna in the highest.

THE CANON OF THE MASS

THEREFORE, most gracious Father, we humbly beg of You and entreat You through Jesus Christ Your Son, our Lord, (*he kisses the altar*) to deem acceptable and bless these ✠ gifts, these ✠ offerings, these ✠ holy and unspotted oblations which, in the first place, we offer You for Your Holy Catholic Church, that You would deign to give her peace and protection, to unite and guard her throughout the world, together with Your servant N., our Pope, and N., our Bishop; and all true believers who cherish the Catholic and Apostolic Faith.

Commemoration of the Living

REMEMBER, O Lord, Your servants and handmaids, N. and N., (*name them*) and all here present, whose faith and devotion are known to You, on whose behalf we offer to You, or who themselves offer to You, this sacrifice of praise for themselves, families and friends, for the good of their souls, for their hope of salvation and deliverance from all harm, and who offer their homage to You, eternal, living and true God.

Commemoration of the Saints

IN THE unity of holy fellowship we observe the memory, first of all, of the glorious and ever

Virgin Mary, Mother of our Lord and God Jesus Christ; next, that of Your Blessed Apostles and Martyrs, Peter and Paul, Andrew, James, John, Thomas, James, Philip, Bartholomew, Matthew, Simon and Thaddeus; of Linus, Cletus, Clement, Sixtus, Cornelius, Cyprian, Lawrence, Chrysogonus, John and Paul, Cosmas and Damian, and of all Your Saints, by whose merits and prayers grant that we may be always fortified by the help of Your protection. Through the same Christ our Lord. Amen.

Spreading his hands over the oblation, he says:

GRACIOUSLY accept, then, we beseech You, O Lord, this service of our worship and that of all Your household. Provide that our days be spent in Your peace, save us from everlasting damnation, and cause us to be numbered in the flock You have chosen. Through Christ our Lord. Amen.

O GOD, deign to bless ✠ what we offer, and make it approved, ✠ effective, ✠ right, and wholly pleasing in every way; that it may become for our good, the Body ✠ and Blood ✠ of Your dearly beloved Son, Jesus Christ our Lord.

CONSECRATION—ELEVATION

WHO, the day before He suffered, took bread into His holy and venerable hands, and having raised His eyes to heaven, to You, O God, His almighty Father, giving thanks to You, He blessed it, ✠ broke it, and gave it to His disciples, saying: All of you take and eat of this:

FOR THIS IS MY BODY.

IN LIKE manner, when the supper was done, taking also this goodly chalice into His holy and venerable hands, again giving thanks to You, He

blessed ✠ it, and gave it to His disciples, saying: All of you take and drink of this:

FOR THIS IS THE CHALICE OF MY BLOOD OF THE NEW AND ETERNAL COVENANT: THE MYSTERY OF FAITH: WHICH SHALL BE SHED FOR YOU AND FOR MANY UNTO THE FORGIVENESS OF SINS.

After replacing the chalice on the corporal, he says:

As often as you shall do these things, in memory of Me shall you do them.

Offering of the Victim

MINDFUL, therefore, O Lord, not only of the blessed Passion of the same Christ, Your Son, our Lord, but also of His Resurrection from the dead, and finally His glorious Ascension into heaven, we, Your ministers, as also Your holy people, offer to Your supreme Majesty, of the gifts bestowed upon us, the pure ✠ Victim, the holy ✠ Victim, the all-perfect ✠ Victim: the holy ✠ Bread of life eternal and the Chalice ✠ of unending salvation.

AND this deign to regard with gracious and kindly attention and hold acceptable, as You deigned to accept the offerings of Abel, Your just servant, and the sacrifice of Abraham our patriarch, and that which Your chief priest Melchisedec offered to You, a holy sacrifice and a spotless victim.

MOST humbly we implore You, almighty God, bid these offerings to be brought by the hands of Your holy angel to Your altar above; before the face of Your Divine Majesty; that those of us who, by sharing in the Sacrifice of this altar, shall receive the Most Sacred ✠ Body and ✠ Blood of Your Son, may be filled with every grace and heavenly blessing. Through the same Christ our Lord. Amen.

Commemoration of the Dead

REMEMBER also, O Lord, Your servants and handmaids, N. and N., who have gone before us with the sign of faith, and rest in the sleep of peace. (*Here pray for the dead.*) To these, O Lord, and to all who rest in Christ, we beseech You to grant of Your goodness, a place of comfort, light and peace. Through the same Christ our Lord. Amen.

TO US sinners also, Your servants, trusting in the greatness of Your mercy, deign to grant some part and fellowship with Your Holy Apostles and Martyrs: with John, Stephen, Matthias, Barnabas, Ignatius, Alexander, Marcellinus, Peter, Felicitas, Perpetua, Agatha, Lucy, Agnes, Cecilia, Anastasia, and all Your Saints; into whose company, we implore You to admit us, not weighing our merits, but freely granting us pardon. Through Christ our Lord.

THROUGH Whom, O Lord, You always create, ✠ sanctify, ✠ fill with life, ✠ bless, and bestow upon us all good things.

The Minor Elevation

THROUGH ✠ Him, and with ✠ Him, and in ✠ Him, is to You, God the Father ✠ almighty, in the unity of the Holy ✠ Spirit, all honor and glory, world without end. S. Amen.

THE COMMUNION AND THANKSGIVING

Let us pray. Prompted by saving precepts, and taught by Your divine teaching, we dare to say:

OUR FATHER, Who art in heaven, hallowed be Thy name: Thy kingdom come: Thy will be

done on earth as it is in heaven. Give us this day our daily bread; and forgive us our trespasses, as we forgive those who trespass against us. And lead us not into temptation: *S.* But deliver us from evil. *P.* Amen.

DELIVER us, we beseech You, O Lord, from all evils, past, present, and to come; and by the intercession of the Blessed and glorious Mary, ever Virgin, Mother of God, together with Your Blessed Apostles Peter and Paul, and Andrew, and all the Saints, grant of Your goodness, peace in our days, that aided by the riches of Your mercy, we may be always free from sin and safe from all disturbance.

Through the same our Lord Jesus Christ, Your Son, Who lives and reigns with You in the unity of the Holy Spirit, God, world without end. *S.* Amen.

P. May the peace ✠ of the Lord be ✠ always with ✠ you. *S.* And with your spirit.

The Priest puts a small particle into the chalice, saying:

May this mingling and consecration of the Body and Blood of our Lord Jesus Christ help us who receive it to life everlasting. Amen.

LAMB of God, You Who take away the sins of the world, have mercy on us.

Lamb of God, You Who take away the sins of the world, have mercy on us.

Lamb of God, You Who take away the sins of the world, grant us peace.

PRAYERS BEFORE HOLY COMMUNION

Then inclining toward the altar, he says:

O LORD Jesus Christ, Who said to Your Apostles: "Peace I leave with you, My peace I give

to you," regard not my sins but the faith of Your Church, and deign to give her peace and unity according to Your Will: Who live and reign, God, world without end. Amen.

O LORD Jesus Christ, Son of the living God, Who, by the will of the Father, with the co-operation of the Holy Spirit, have by Your death given life to the world, deliver me by this Your Most Sacred Body and Blood from all my sins and from every evil. Make me always cling to Your commandments, and never permit me to be separated from You. Who with the same God the Father and the Holy Spirit, live and reign, God, world without end. Amen.

LET not the partaking of Your Body, O Lord Jesus Christ, which I, though unworthy, presume to receive, turn to my judgment and condemnation; but through Your goodness, may it become a safeguard and an effective remedy, both of soul and body. Who live and reign with God the Father, in the unity of the Holy Spirit, God, world without end. Amen.

COMMUNION OF THE PRIEST

I WILL take the Bread of heaven, and call upon the name of the Lord.

Lord, I am not worthy that You should come under my roof; but only say the word, and my soul will be healed. (3 *times.*)

Making the Sign of the Cross with the Host, he says:

MAY the Body of our Lord Jesus Christ preserve my soul to life everlasting. Amen.

What return shall I make to the Lord for all He has given me? I will take the Chalice of salvation,

and I will call upon the name of the Lord. Praising will I call upon the Lord and I shall be saved from my enemies.

Making the Sign of the Cross with the chalice, he says:

MAY the Blood of our Lord Jesus Christ preserve my soul to life everlasting. Amen.

The Priest reverently consumes the Precious Blood.

COMMUNION OF THE FAITHFUL

The Server and people say the "Confiteor."

P. May almighty God have mercy on you, forgive you your sins, and bring you to life everlasting. **S.** Amen.

P. May the almighty and merciful Lord grant you pardon, ✠ absolution and remission of your sins. **S.** Amen.

Holding up a Sacred Host, the Priest says:

Behold the Lamb of God, behold Him Who takes away the sins of the world.

Lord, I am not worthy that You should come under my roof; but only say the word, and my soul will be healed. (3 *times.*)

The Priest says to each communicant:

May the Body of our Lord Jesus Christ preserve your soul to life everlasting. Amen.

The Priest purifies the chalice with wine, saying:

WHAT has passed our lips as food, O Lord, may we possess in purity of heart, that what is given to us in time, be our healing for eternity.

He purifies his fingers with wine and water, saying:

MAY Your Body, O Lord, which I have eaten, and Your Blood which I have drunk, cleave to my very soul, and grant that no trace of sin be found in me, whom these pure and holy mysteries

have renewed. Who live and reign, world without end. Amen.

THE COMMUNION • Ps. 70, 16. 17. 18

O LORD, I will tell of Your singular justice; O God, You have taught me from my youth; and now that I am old and gray, O God, forsake me not.

The Priest, turning to the people, says:

P. The Lord be with you. *S.* And with your spirit.
P. Let us pray.

THE POSTCOMMUNION

GRACIOUSLY purify our minds, we beseech You, O Lord, and renew them with these heavenly sacraments, so that our bodies may likewise receive help both for the present and the future. Through our Lord Jesus Christ, Your Son, Who lives and reigns with You in the unity of the Holy Spirit, God, world without end. *S.* Amen.

FINAL PRAYERS

P. The Lord be with you. *S.* And with your spirit.
P. Go, you are dismissed. *S.* Thanks be to God.

MAY the tribute of my worship be pleasing to You, Most Holy Trinity, and grant that the sacrifice which I, all unworthy, have offered in the presence of Your Majesty, may be acceptable to You, and through Your mercy obtain forgiveness for me and all for whom I have offered it. Through Christ our Lord. Amen.

THE LAST BLESSING

MAY almighty God bless you: ✠ the Father, and the Son, and the Holy Spirit. *S.* Amen.

The Last Gospel and Prayers after Low Mass are conveniently placed inside the back cover.

"You shall love your neighbor as yourself!"

SEVENTEENTH SUNDAY AFTER PENTECOST

Jesus Christ recommends the love of neighbor as most necessary by reason of the selfishness of mankind. Let us be Christian in our relations with our neighbor, loving not merely in words but by deeds corresponding to them. (GREEN VESTMENTS)

PRAYERS AT THE FOOT OF THE ALTAR

IN THE name of the Father, ✠ and of the Son, and of the Holy Spirit. Amen.

Priest. I will go in to the altar of God.

Server. The God of my gladness and joy.

Psalm 42

DO ME justice, O God, and fight my fight against a faithless people; from the deceitful and impious man rescue me.

S. For You, O God, are my strength. Why do You keep me so far away? Why must I go about in mourning, with the enemy oppressing me?

P. Send forth Your light and Your fidelity; they shall lead me on and bring me to Your holy mountain, to Your dwelling-place.
S. Then will I go in to the altar of God, the God of my gladness and joy.
P. Then will I give You thanks upon the harp, O God, my God. Why are you so downcast, O my soul? Why do you sigh within me?
S. Hope in God! For I shall again be thanking Him in the presence of my Savior and my God.
P. Glory be to the Father, and to the Son, and to the Holy Spirit.
S. As it was in the beginning, is now, and ever shall be, world without end. Amen.
P. I will go in to the altar of God.
S. The God of my gladness and joy.
P. Our help ✠ is in the name of the Lord.
S. Who made heaven and earth.
P. I confess to almighty God, etc.
S. May almighty God have mercy on you, forgive you your sins, and bring you to life everlasting.
P. Amen.

The Server, bowing, says the "Confiteor."

I CONFESS to almighty God, to Blessed Mary, ever Virgin, to Blessed Michael the Archangel, to Blessed John the Baptist, to the Holy Apostles Peter and Paul, and to all the Saints, and to you, Father, that I have sinned exceedingly in thought, word and deed, *through my fault, through my fault, through my most grievous fault.* Therefore I beseech Blessed Mary, ever Virgin, Blessed Michael the Archangel, Blessed John the Baptist, the Holy Apostles Peter and Paul, and all the Saints, and you, Father, to pray to the Lord our God for me. *P.* May almighty God have mercy on you, forgive you your sins, and bring you to life everlasting. *S.* Amen.

MAY the almighty and merciful Lord grant us pardon, ✠ absolution, and remission of our sins. *S.* Amen.

P. Will You not, O God, give us life?
S. And shall not Your people rejoice in You?
P. Show us, O Lord, Your kindness.
S. And grant us Your salvation.
P. O Lord, hear my prayer.
S. And let my cry come to You.
P. The Lord be with you.
S. And with your spirit. *P.* Let us pray.

Going up to the altar, the Priest prays silently:

TAKE away from us our sins, O Lord, we beseech You, that we may enter with pure minds into the Holy of Holies. Through Christ our Lord. Amen.

WE BESEECH You, O Lord, by the merits of Your Saints (*he kisses the altar*) whose relics lie here, and of all the Saints: deign in Your mercy to pardon me all my sins. Amen.

THE INTROIT • Ps. 118, 137. 124. 1

At the right side of the altar, the Priest says:

YOU are just, O Lord, and Your ordinance is right. Deal with Your servant according to Your kindness. *Ps.* Happy are they whose way is blameless, who walk in the law of the Lord. Glory be to the Father, and to the Son, and to the Holy Spirit. As it was in the beginning, is now, and ever shall be, world without end. Amen. — You are just, O Lord, and Your ordinance is right. Deal with Your servant according to Your kindness.

THE KYRIE

P. Lord, have mercy. *S.* Lord, have mercy. *P.* Lord, have mercy. *S.* Christ, have mercy. *P.* Christ, have mercy. *S.* Christ, have mercy. *P.* Lord, have mercy. *S.* Lord, have mercy. *P.* Lord, have mercy.

THE GLORIA

GLORY to God in the highest. And on earth peace to men of good will. We praise You. We bless You. We adore You. We glorify You. We give You thanks for Your great glory. O Lord God, heavenly King, God the Father almighty. O Lord Jesus Christ, the Only-begotten Son. O Lord God, Lamb of God, Son of the Father: You Who take away the sins of the world, have mercy on us. You Who take away the sins of the world, receive our prayer. You Who sit at the right hand of the Father, have mercy on us. For You alone are holy. You alone are the Lord. You alone, O Jesus Christ, are most high. Together with the Holy Spirit ✠ in the glory of God the Father. Amen.

The Priest kisses the altar and turns to the people, saying:

P. The Lord be with you. *S.* And with your spirit. *P.* Let us pray.

THE PRAYER

Going to the right (Epistle) side, he says:

GRANT to Your people, we beseech You, O Lord, to avoid every contamination of the devil, and, with pure minds, to follow You, the only God. Through our Lord Jesus Christ, Your Son,

Who lives and reigns with You in the unity of the Holy Spirit, God, world without end. S. Amen.

THE EPISTLE • Eph. 4, 1-6

BRETHREN: I, the prisoner in the Lord, exhort you to walk in a manner worthy of the calling with which you were called, with all humility and meekness, with patience, bearing with one another in love, careful to preserve the unity of the Spirit in the bond of peace: one body and one Spirit, even as you were called in one hope of your calling; one Lord, one faith, one Baptism, one God and Father of all, Who is above all, and throughout all, and in us all, Who is blessed forever and ever. Amen. S. Thanks be to God.

THE GRADUAL • Ps. 32, 12. 6

HAPPY the nation whose God is the Lord, the people the Lord has chosen for His own inheritance. ℣. By the word of the Lord the heavens were made; by the breath of His mouth all their host.

Alleluia, alleluia. ℣. *Ps. 101,* 2. O Lord, hear my prayer, and let my cry come to You. Alleluia.

PRAYER BEFORE THE GOSPEL

Bowing down at the center of the altar, he says:

CLEANSE my heart and my lips, O almighty God, Who cleansed the lips of the Prophet Isaias with a burning coal. In Your gracious mercy deign so to purify me that I may worthily proclaim Your holy Gospel. Through Christ our Lord. Amen.

Lord, grant Your blessing. The Lord be in my heart and on my lips, that I may worthily and fittingly proclaim His holy Gospel. Amen.

THE GOSPEL • Matt. 22, 34-46

Going to the left (Gospel) side of the altar, he says:

P. The Lord be with you. S. And with your spirit.
P. ✠ The continuation of the holy Gospel according to Saint Matthew. S. Glory be to You, O Lord.

AT THAT time, the Pharisees came to Jesus and one of them, a doctor of the Law, putting Him to the test, asked Him, "Master, which is the greatest commandment in the Law?" Jesus said to him, "'You shall love the Lord your God with your whole heart, and with your whole soul, and with your whole mind.' This is the greatest and first commandment. And the second is like it, 'You shall love your neighbor as yourself.' On these two commandments depend the whole Law and the Prophets." Now while the Pharisees were gathered together, Jesus questioned them, saying, "What do you think of the Christ? Whose son is He?" They said to Him, "David's." He said to them, "How then does David in the Spirit call Him Lord, saying, 'The Lord said to my Lord: Sit at My right hand, till I make Your enemies Your footstool?' If David, therefore, calls Him 'Lord,' how is He his son?" And no one could answer Him a word; neither did anyone dare from that day forth to ask Him any more questions. S. Praise be to You, O Christ.

P. By the words of the Gospel, may our sins be taken away.

THE NICENE CREED

At the center of the altar, he says:

I BELIEVE in one God, the Father almighty, Maker of heaven and earth, and of all things

visible and invisible. And in one Lord Jesus Christ, the Only-begotten Son of God. Born of the Father before all ages. God of God; Light of Light; true God of true God. Begotten not made; of one being with the Father; by Whom all things were made. Who for us men, and for our salvation, came down from heaven. (*Here all genuflect.*) And was made Flesh by the Holy Spirit of the Virgin Mary: AND WAS MADE MAN. He was also crucified for us, suffered under Pontius Pilate and was buried. And on the third day He rose again according to the Scriptures. And ascending into heaven, He sits at the right hand of the Father. And He shall come again in glory to judge the living and the dead; and of His kingdom there shall be no end. And I believe in the Holy Spirit, Lord and Giver of life, Who proceeds from the Father and the Son. Who together with the Father and the Son is no less adored, and glorified: Who spoke by the Prophets. And I believe in One, Holy, Catholic and Apostolic Church. I confess one Baptism for the remission of sins. And I look for the resurrection of the dead. ✠ And the life of the world to come. Amen.

THE OFFERTORY

The Priest turns to the people and says:

P. The Lord be with you. *S*. And with your spirit.
P. Let us pray.

THE OFFERTORY VERSE • Dan. 9, 17. 18. 19

I DANIEL, prayed to my God, saying, "Hear, O Lord, the prayers of Your servants; show Your face upon Your sanctuary, and favorably look down upon this people, upon whom Your name is invoked, O God."

The Priest now uncovers the chalice, places the host on the paten and offering it up, says:

ACCEPT, O holy Father, almighty and eternal God, this spotless host, which I, Your unworthy servant, offer to You, my living and true God, to atone for my numberless sins, offenses, and negligences; on behalf of all here present and likewise for all faithful Christians living and dead, that it may profit me and them as a means of salvation to life everlasting. Amen.

He pours wine and water into the chalice, blessing the water before it is poured.

O GOD, Who established the nature of man in wondrous dignity, and still more admirably restored it, grant that through the mystery of this water and wine, we may be made partakers of His Divinity, Who has condescended to become partaker of our humanity, Jesus Christ, Your Son, our Lord. Who lives and reigns with You in the unity of the Holy Spirit, God, world without end. Amen.

Offering up the wine, the Priest says:

WE OFFER You, O Lord, the chalice of salvation, humbly begging of Your mercy that it may arise before Your Divine Majesty, with a pleasing fragrance, for our salvation and for that of the whole world. Amen.

Bowing down, the Priest says:

IN A humble spirit and with a contrite heart, may we be accepted by You, O Lord, and may our sacrifice so be offered in Your sight this day as to please You, O Lord God.

Raising his eyes and blessing the offering, he says:

COME, O Sanctifier, almighty and eternal God, and bless ✠ this sacrifice prepared for the glory of Your holy name.

WASHING THE FINGERS

I WASH my hands in innocence, and I go around Your altar, O Lord, giving voice to my thanks, and recounting all Your wondrous deeds. O Lord, I love the house in which You dwell, the tenting-place of Your glory. Gather not my soul with those of sinners, nor with men of blood my life. On their hands are crimes, and their right hands are full of bribes. But I walk in integrity; redeem me, and have pity on me. My foot stands on level ground; in the assemblies I will bless You, O Lord. Glory be to the Father, and to the Son, and to the Holy Spirit. As it was in the beginning, is now, and ever shall be, world without end. Amen.

ACCEPT, Most Holy Trinity, this offering which we are making to You in remembrance of the Passion, Resurrection, and Ascension of Jesus Christ, our Lord; and in honor of Blessed Mary, ever Virgin, Blessed John the Baptist, the Holy Apostles Peter and Paul, and of these, and of all the Saints; that it may add to their honor and aid our salvation; and may they deign to intercede in heaven for us who honor their memory here on earth. Through the same Christ our Lord. Amen.

The Priest turns toward the people and says:

Pray, brethren, that my sacrifice and yours may become acceptable to God the Father almighty.

S. May the Lord accept this sacrifice from your hands to the praise and glory of His name, for our advantage, and that of all His holy Church.

P. Amen.

THE SECRET

WE SUPPLIANTLY beseech Your Majesty, O Lord, that the sacred mysteries which we perform, may free us both from past sins and future transgressions. Through our Lord Jesus Christ, Your Son, Who lives and reigns with You in the unity of the Holy Spirit, God.

P. World without end. *S.* Amen.

PREFACE—CANON

P. The Lord be with you. *S.* And with your spirit.
P. Lift up your hearts.
S. We have lifted them up to the Lord.
P. Let us give thanks to the Lord, our God.
S. It is fitting and just.

IT IS fitting indeed and just, right and helpful to salvation, for us always and everywhere to give thanks to You, O holy Lord, Father almighty, everlasting God, Who with Your Only-begotten Son and the Holy Spirit are one God, one Lord; not in the unity of a single person, but in the trinity of a single nature. For that which we believe on Your revelation concerning Your glory, that same we believe of Your Son, that same of the Holy Spirit, without difference or discrimination. So that in confessing the true and everlasting Godhead, we shall adore distinction in Persons, oneness in being, and equality in Majesty. This the Angels and Archangels, the Cherubim, too, and the Seraphim do praise; day by day they cease not to cry out as with one voice, saying (*the bell is rung* 3 *times*):

HOLY, HOLY, HOLY, Lord God of Hosts. Heaven and earth are filled with Your glory. Hosanna in the highest. ✠ Blessed is He Who comes in the name of the Lord. Hosanna in the highest.

THE CANON OF THE MASS

THEREFORE, most gracious Father, we humbly beg of You and entreat You through Jesus Christ Your Son, our Lord, (*he kisses the altar*) to deem acceptable and bless these ✠ gifts, these ✠ offerings, these ✠ holy and unspotted oblations which, in the first place, we offer You for Your Holy Catholic Church, that You would deign to give her peace and protection, to unite and guard her throughout the world, together with Your servant N., our Pope, and N., our Bishop; and all true believers who cherish the Catholic and Apostolic Faith.

Commemoration of the Living

REMEMBER, O Lord, Your servants and handmaids, N. and N., (*name them*) and all here present, whose faith and devotion are known to You, on whose behalf we offer to You, or who themselves offer to You, this sacrifice of praise for themselves, families and friends, for the good of their souls, for their hope of salvation and deliverance from all harm, and who offer their homage to You, eternal, living and true God.

Commemoration of the Saints

IN THE unity of holy fellowship we observe the memory, first of all, of the glorious and ever Virgin Mary, Mother of our Lord and God Jesus Christ; next, that of Your Blessed Apostles and Martyrs, Peter and Paul, Andrew, James, John, Thomas, James, Philip, Bartholomew, Matthew, Simon and Thaddeus; of Linus, Cletus, Clement, Sixtus, Cornelius, Cyprian, Lawrence, Chrysogonus, John and Paul, Cosmas and Damian, and of all Your Saints, by whose merits and prayers grant that

we may be always fortified by the help of Your protection. Through the same Christ our Lord. Amen.

Spreading his hands over the oblation, he says:

GRACIOUSLY accept, then, we beseech You, O Lord, this service of our worship and that of all Your household. Provide that our days be spent in Your peace, save us from everlasting damnation, and cause us to be numbered in the flock You have chosen. Through Christ our Lord. Amen.

O GOD, deign to bless ✠ what we offer, and make it approved, ✠ effective, ✠ right, and wholly pleasing in every way, that it may become for our good, the Body ✠ and Blood ✠ of Your dearly beloved Son, Jesus Christ our Lord.

CONSECRATION—ELEVATION

WHO, the day before He suffered, took bread into His holy and venerable hands, and having raised His eyes to heaven, to You, O God, His almighty Father, giving thanks to You, He blessed it, ✠ broke it, and gave it to His disciples, saying: All of you take and eat of this:

FOR THIS IS MY BODY.

IN LIKE manner, when the supper was done, taking also this goodly chalice into His holy and venerable hands, again giving thanks to You, He blessed ✠ it, and gave it to His disciples, saying: All of you take and drink of this:

FOR THIS IS THE CHALICE OF MY BLOOD OF THE NEW AND ETERNAL COVENANT: THE MYSTERY OF FAITH: WHICH SHALL BE SHED FOR YOU AND FOR MANY UNTO THE FORGIVENESS OF SINS.

✠

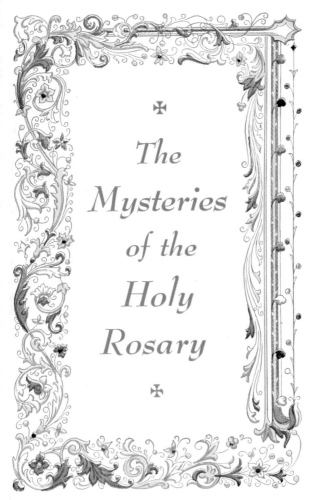

The Mysteries of the Holy Rosary

✠

(T-729)

FIRST JOYFUL MYSTERY

THE ANNUNCIATION

Lord Jesus, I *offer* You this first decade in honor of Your Incarnation in Mary's womb, and I *ask* of You, through this Mystery and through her intercession, a deep *humility*. Amen.

Our Father. Hail Mary, ten times. Glory be.

SECOND JOYFUL MYSTERY

THE VISITATION

Lord Jesus, I *offer* You this second decade in honor of the Visitation of Your holy Mother to her cousin St. Elizabeth and the sanctification of St. John the Baptist, and I *ask* of You, through this Mystery and through the intercession of Your holy Mother, *charity toward my neighbor*. Amen.

Our Father. Hail Mary, ten times. Glory be.

THIRD JOYFUL MYSTERY

THE NATIVITY

Lord Jesus, I *offer* You this third decade in honor of Your Nativity in the stable of Bethlehem, and I *ask* of You, through this Mystery and through the intercession of Your holy Mother, *detachment from things of the world, contempt of riches and love of poverty.* Amen.

Our Father. Hail Mary, ten times. Glory be.

FOURTH JOYFUL MYSTERY

THE PRESENTATION IN THE TEMPLE

Lord Jesus, I *offer* You this fourth decade in honor of Your Presentation in the Temple and the Purification of Mary, and I *ask* of You, through this Mystery and through the intercession of Your holy Mother, *purity of body and soul.* Amen.

Our Father. Hail Mary, ten times. Glory be.

FIFTH JOYFUL MYSTERY

THE FINDING OF JESUS IN THE TEMPLE

Lord Jesus, I *offer* You this fifth decade in honor of Mary's finding You in the Temple, and I *ask* of You, through this Mystery and through her intercession, *the gift of true wisdom.* Amen.

Our Father. Hail Mary, ten times. Glory be. Hail, Holy Queen.

FIRST SORROWFUL MYSTERY

THE AGONY IN THE GARDEN

Lord Jesus, I *offer* You this first decade in honor of Your agony in the Garden of Olives, and I *ask* of You, through this Mystery and through the intercession of Your holy Mother, *contrition for my sins.* Amen.

Our Father. Hail Mary, ten times. Glory be.

SECOND SORROWFUL MYSTERY

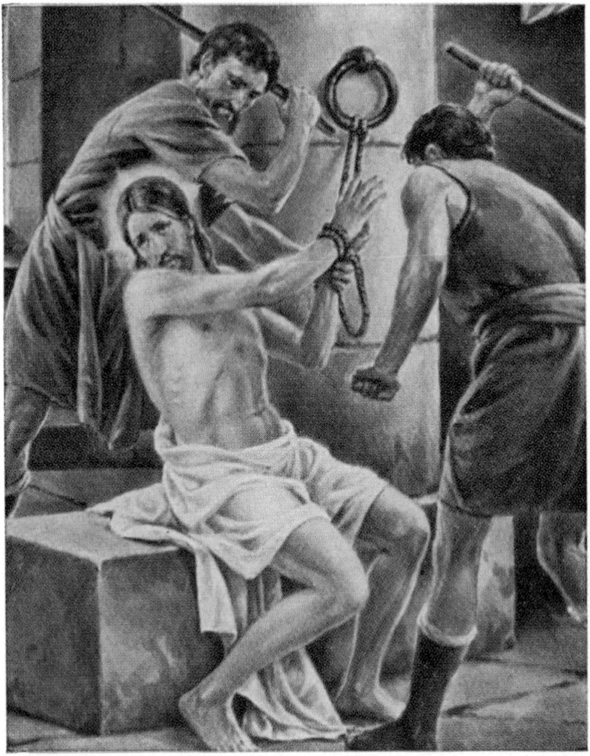

THE SCOURGING

Lord Jesus, I *offer* You this second decade in honor of Your bloody scourging, and I *ask* of You, through this Mystery and through the intercession of Your holy Mother, *the grace of mortifying my senses.* Amen.

Our Father. Hail Mary, ten times. Glory be.

THIRD SORROWFUL MYSTERY

THE CROWNING WITH THORNS

Lord Jesus, I *offer* You this third decade in honor of Your crowning with thorns, and I *ask* of You, through this Mystery and through the intercession of Your holy Mother, *contempt of the world.* Amen.

Our Father. Hail Mary, ten times. Glory be.

FOURTH SORROWFUL MYSTERY

THE CARRYING OF THE CROSS

Lord Jesus, I *offer* You this fourth decade in honor of Your carrying of the Cross, and I *ask* of You, through this Mystery and through the intercession of Your holy Mother, *patience in bearing my crosses.* Amen.

Our Father. Hail Mary, ten times. Glory be.

FIFTH SORROWFUL MYSTERY

THE CRUCIFIXION

Lord Jesus, I *offer* You this fifth decade in honor of Your Crucifixion and death on Calvary, and I *ask* of You, through this Mystery and through the intercession of Your holy Mother, *the conversion of sinners and the relief of the souls in Purgatory*. Amen.

Our Father. Hail Mary, ten times. Glory be. Hail, Holy Queen.

FIRST GLORIOUS MYSTERY

THE RESURRECTION

Lord Jesus, I *offer* You this first decade in honor of Your glorious Resurrection, and I *ask* of You, through this Mystery and through the intercession of Your holy Mother, *love of God and fervor in Your service.* Amen.

Our Father. Hail Mary, ten times. Glory be.

SECOND GLORIOUS MYSTERY

THE ASCENSION

Lord Jesus, I *offer* You this second decade in honor of Your triumphant Ascension, and I *ask* of You, through this Mystery and through the intercession of Your holy Mother, *an ardent desire for heaven, my true home.* Amen.

Our Father. Hail Mary, ten times. Glory be.

THIRD GLORIOUS MYSTERY

THE DESCENT OF THE HOLY GHOST

Lord Jesus, I *offer* You this third decade in honor of the Mystery of Pentecost, and I *ask* of You, through this Mystery and through the intercession of Your holy Mother, *the coming of the Holy Ghost in my soul.* Amen.

Our Father. Hail Mary, ten times. Glory be.

FOURTH GLORIOUS MYSTERY

THE ASSUMPTION

Lord Jesus, I *offer* You this fourth decade in honor of the resurrection and triumphant Assumption of Your holy Mother into Heaven, and I *ask* of You, through this Mystery and through her intercession, *a tender devotion to so good a Mother.* Amen.

Our Father. Hail Mary, ten times. Glory be.

FIFTH GLORIOUS MYSTERY

THE CORONATION OF THE BLESSED VIRGIN

Lord Jesus, I *offer* You this fifth decade in honor of the Coronation of Your holy Mother, and I *ask* of You, through this Mystery and through her intercession, *perseverance in grace and a crown of glory hereafter.* Amen.

Our Father. Hail Mary, ten times. Glory be. Hail, Holy Queen.

After replacing the chalice on the corporal, he says:

As often as you shall do these things, in memory of Me shall you do them.

Offering of the Victim

MINDFUL, therefore, O Lord, not only of the blessed Passion of the same Christ, Your Son, our Lord, but also of His Resurrection from the dead, and finally His glorious Ascension into heaven, we, Your ministers, as also Your holy people, offer to Your supreme Majesty, of the gifts bestowed upon us, the pure ✠ Victim, the holy ✠ Victim, the all-perfect ✠ Victim: the holy ✠ Bread of life eternal and the Chalice ✠ of unending salvation.

AND this deign to regard with gracious and kindly attention and hold acceptable, as You deigned to accept the offerings of Abel, Your just servant, and the sacrifice of Abraham our patriarch, and that which Your chief priest Melchisedec offered to You, a holy sacrifice and a spotless victim.

MOST humbly we implore You, almighty God, bid these offerings to be brought by the hands of Your holy angel to Your altar above; before the face of Your Divine Majesty; that those of us who, by sharing in the Sacrifice of this altar, shall receive the Most Sacred ✠ Body and ✠ Blood of Your Son, may be filled with every grace and heavenly blessing. Through the same Christ our Lord. Amen.

Commemoration of the Dead

REMEMBER also, O Lord, Your servants and handmaids, N. and N., who have gone before us with the sign of faith, and rest in the sleep of

peace. (*Here pray for the dead.*) To these, O Lord, and to all who rest in Christ, we beseech You to grant of Your goodness, a place of comfort, light and peace. Through the same Christ our Lord. Amen.

TO US sinners also, Your servants, trusting in the greatness of Your mercy, deign to grant some part and fellowship with Your Holy Apostles and Martyrs: with John, Stephen, Matthias, Barnabas, Ignatius, Alexander, Marcellinus, Peter, Felicitas, Perpetua, Agatha, Lucy, Agnes, Cecilia, Anastasia, and all Your Saints; into whose company, we implore You to admit us, not weighing our merits, but freely granting us pardon. Through Christ our Lord.

THROUGH Whom, O Lord, You always create, ✠ sanctify, ✠ fill with life, ✠ bless, and bestow upon us all good things.

The Minor Elevation

THROUGH ✠ Him, and with ✠ Him, and in ✠ Him, is to You, God the Father ✠ almighty, in the unity of the Holy ✠ Spirit, all honor and glory, world without end. S. Amen.

THE COMMUNION AND THANKSGIVING

Let us pray. Prompted by saving precepts, and taught by Your divine teaching, we dare to say:

OUR FATHER, Who art in heaven, hallowed be Thy name: Thy kingdom come: Thy will be done on earth as it is in heaven. Give us this day our daily bread; and forgive us our trespasses, as we forgive those who trespass against us. And lead us

not into temptation: S. But deliver us from evil. *P.* Amen.

DELIVER us, we beseech You, O Lord, from all evils, past, present, and to come; and by the intercession of the Blessed and glorious Mary, ever Virgin, Mother of God, together with Your Blessed Apostles Peter and Paul, and Andrew, and all the Saints, grant of Your goodness, peace in our days, that aided by the riches of Your mercy, we may be always free from sin and safe from all disturbance.

Through the same our Lord Jesus Christ, Your Son, Who lives and reigns with You in the unity of the Holy Spirit, God, world without end. *S.* Amen.

P. May the peace ✠ of the Lord be ✠ always with ✠ you. *S.* And with your spirit.

The Priest puts a small particle into the chalice, saying:

May this mingling and consecration of the Body and Blood of our Lord Jesus Christ help us who receive it to life everlasting. Amen.

LAMB of God, You Who take away the sins of the world, have mercy on us.

Lamb of God, You Who take away the sins of the world, have mercy on us.

Lamb of God, You Who take away the sins of the world, grant us peace.

PRAYERS BEFORE HOLY COMMUNION

Then inclining toward the altar, he says:

O LORD Jesus Christ, Who said to Your Apostles: "Peace I leave with you, My peace I give to you," regard not my sins but the faith of Your Church, and deign to give her peace and unity

according to Your Will: Who live and reign, God, world without end. Amen.

O LORD Jesus Christ, Son of the living God, Who, by the will of the Father, with the co-operation of the Holy Spirit, have by Your death given life to the world, deliver me by this Your Most Sacred Body and Blood from all my sins and from every evil. Make me always cling to Your commandments, and never permit me to be separated from You. Who with the same God the Father and the Holy Spirit, live and reign, God, world without end. Amen.

LET not the partaking of Your Body, O Lord Jesus Christ, which I, though unworthy, presume to receive, turn to my judgment and condemnation; but through Your goodness, may it become a safeguard and an effective remedy, both of soul and body. Who live and reign with God the Father, in the unity of the Holy Spirit, God, world without end. Amen.

COMMUNION OF THE PRIEST

I WILL take the Bread of heaven, and call upon the name of the Lord.

Lord, I am not worthy that You should come under my roof; but only say the word, and my soul will be healed. (3 *times.*)

Making the Sign of the Cross with the Host, he says:

MAY the Body of our Lord Jesus Christ preserve my soul to life everlasting. Amen.

What return shall I make to the Lord for all He has given me? I will take the Chalice of salvation, and I will call upon the name of the Lord. Prais-

ing will I call upon the Lord and I shall be saved from my enemies.

Making the Sign of the Cross with the chalice, he says:

MAY the Blood of our Lord Jesus Christ preserve my soul to life everlasting. Amen.

The Priest reverently consumes the Precious Blood.

COMMUNION OF THE FAITHFUL

The Server and people say the "Confiteor."

P. May almighty God have mercy on you, forgive you your sins, and bring you to life everlasting. S. Amen.

P. May the almighty and merciful Lord grant you pardon, ✠ absolution and remission of your sins. S. Amen.

Holding up a Sacred Host, the Priest says:

Behold the Lamb of God, behold Him Who takes away the sins of the world.

Lord, I am not worthy that You should come under my roof; but only say the word, and my soul will be healed. (3 *times.*)

The Priest says to each communicant:

May the Body of our Lord Jesus Christ preserve your soul to life everlasting. Amen.

The Priest purifies the chalice with wine, saying:

WHAT has passed our lips as food, O Lord, may we possess in purity of heart, that what is given to us in time, be our healing for eternity.

He purifies his fingers with wine and water, saying:

MAY Your Body, O Lord, which I have eaten, and Your Blood which I have drunk, cleave to my very soul, and grant that no trace of sin be found in me, whom these pure and holy mysteries

have renewed. Who live and reign, world without end. Amen.

THE COMMUNION • Ps. 75, 12-13

MAKE vows to the Lord, your God, and fulfill them; let all round about Him bring gifts to the terrible Lord Who checks the pride of princes, Who is terrible to the kings of the earth.

The Priest, turning to the people, says:

P. The Lord be with you. *S.* And with your spirit.
P. Let us pray.

THE POSTCOMMUNION

O ALMIGHTY God, may our vices be cured by Your sanctifying graces, and may everlasting remedies be bestowed upon us. Through our Lord Jesus Christ, Your Son, Who lives and reigns with You in the unity of the Holy Spirit, God, world without end. *S.* Amen.

FINAL PRAYERS

P. The Lord be with you. *S.* And with your spirit.
P. Go, you are dismissed. *S.* Thanks be to God.

MAY the tribute of my worship be pleasing to You, Most Holy Trinity, and grant that the sacrifice which I, all unworthy, have offered in the presence of Your Majesty, may be acceptable to You, and through Your mercy obtain forgiveness for me and all for whom I have offered it. Through Christ our Lord. Amen.

THE LAST BLESSING

MAY almighty God bless you: ✠ the Father, and the Son, and the Holy Spirit. *S.* Amen.

The Last Gospel and Prayers after Low Mass are conveniently placed inside the back cover.

"Arise, take up your pallet and go to your house."

EIGHTEENTH SUNDAY AFTER PENTECOST

"Your sins are forgiven you." We also hear similar words, "I absolve you from your sins," when after due preparation, we humbly confess our sins. Let us be grateful to God for the Sacrament of Penance and use it frequently. (GREEN VESTMENTS)

PRAYERS AT THE FOOT OF THE ALTAR

IN THE name of the Father, ✠ and of the Son, and of the Holy Spirit. Amen.

Priest. I will go in to the altar of God.

Server. The God of my gladness and joy.

Psalm 42

DO ME justice, O God, and fight my fight against a faithless people; from the deceitful and impious man rescue me.

S. For You, O God, are my strength. Why do You keep me so far away? Why must I go about in mourning, with the enemy oppressing me?

P. Send forth Your light and Your fidelity; they shall lead me on and bring me to Your holy mountain, to Your dwelling-place.
S. Then will I go in to the altar of God, the God of my gladness and joy.
P. Then will I give You thanks upon the harp, O God, my God. Why are you so downcast, O my soul? Why do you sigh within me?
S. Hope in God! For I shall again be thanking Him in the presence of my Savior and my God.
P. Glory be to the Father, and to the Son, and to the Holy Spirit.
S. As it was in the beginning, is now, and ever shall be, world without end. Amen.
P. I will go in to the altar of God.
S. The God of my gladness and joy.
P. Our help ✠ is in the name of the Lord.
S. Who made heaven and earth.
P. I confess to almighty God, etc.
S. May almighty God have mercy on you, forgive you your sins, and bring you to life everlasting.
P. Amen.

The Server, bowing, says the "Confiteor."

I CONFESS to almighty God, to Blessed Mary, ever Virgin, to Blessed Michael the Archangel, to Blessed John the Baptist, to the Holy Apostles Peter and Paul, and to all the Saints, and to you, Father, that I have sinned exceedingly in thought, word and deed, *through my fault, through my fault, through my most grievous fault.* Therefore I beseech Blessed Mary, ever Virgin, Blessed Michael the Archangel, Blessed John the Baptist, the Holy Apostles Peter and Paul, and all the Saints, and you, Father, to pray to the Lord our God for me.

P. May almighty God have mercy on
you your sins, and bring you to life ev
S. Amen.

MAY the almighty and merciful Lord gr
pardon, ✠ absolution, and remission of
sins. *S.* Amen.

P. Will You not, O God, give us life?
S. And shall not Your people rejoice in You?
P. Show us, O Lord, Your kindness.
S. And grant us Your salvation.
P. O Lord, hear my prayer.
S. And let my cry come to You.
P. The Lord be with you.
S. And with your spirit. *P.* Let us pray.

Going up to the altar, the Priest prays silently:

TAKE away from us our sins, O Lord, we beseech You, that we may enter with pure minds into the Holy of Holies. Through Christ our Lord. Amen.

WE BESEECH You, O Lord, by the merits of Your Saints (*he kisses the altar*) whose relics lie here, and of all the Saints: deign in Your mercy to pardon me all my sins. Amen.

THE INTROIT • Ecclus. 36, 18

At the right side of the altar, the Priest says:

GIVE peace, O Lord, to those who have hoped in You, and let Your Prophets be proved true. Hear the prayers of Your servant, and of Your people Israel. *Ps. 121.* I rejoiced because they said to me, "We will go up to the house of the Lord." Glory be to the Father, and to the Son, and to the Holy Spirit. As it was in the beginning, is now, and er shall be, world without end. Amen. — Give eace, O Lord, to those who have hoped in You, nd let Your Prophets be proved true. Hear the prayers of Your servant, and of Your people Israel.

THE KYRIE

P. Lord, have mercy. *S.* Lord, have mercy. *P.* Lord, have mercy. *S.* Christ, have mercy. *P.* Christ, have mercy. *S.* Christ, have mercy. *P.* Lord, have mercy. *S.* Lord, have mercy. *P.* Lord, have mercy.

THE GLORIA

GLORY to God in the highest. And on earth peace to men of good will. We praise You. We bless You. We adore You. We glorify You. We give You thanks for Your great glory. O Lord God, heavenly King, God the Father almighty. O Lord Jesus Christ, the Only-begotten Son. O Lord God, Lamb of God, Son of the Father: You Who take away the sins of the world, have mercy on us. You Who take away the sins of the world, receive our prayer. You Who sit at the right hand of the Father, have mercy on us. For You alone are holy. You alone are the Lord. You alone, O Jesus Christ, are most high. Together with the Holy Spirit ✠ in the glory of God the Father. Amen.

The Priest kisses the altar and turns to the people, saying:

P. The Lord be with you. S. And with your spirit. *P.* Let us pray.

THE PRAYER

Going to the right (Epistle) side, he says:

MAY the working of Your mercy direct our hearts, we beseech You, O Lord; for without You, we are not able to please You. Through our

Lord Jesus Christ, Your Son, Who lives and reigns with You in the unity of the Holy Spirit, God, world without end. S. Amen.

THE EPISTLE • 1 Cor. 1, 4-8

BRETHREN: I give thanks to my God always concerning you for the grace of God which was given you in Christ Jesus, because in everything you have been enriched in Him, in all utterance and in all knowledge; even as the witness to the Christ has been made so firm in you that you lack no grace, while awaiting the appearance of our Lord Jesus Christ, Who will also keep you secure unto the end, unimpeachable in the day of the coming of our Lord Jesus Christ. S. Thanks be to God.

THE GRADUAL • Ps. 121, 1. 7

I REJOICED because they said to me, "We will go up to the house of the Lord." ℣. May peace be within your walls, prosperity in your buildings.

Alleluia, alleluia. ℣. *Ps. 101, 16.* The nations shall revere Your name, O Lord, and all the kings of the earth Your glory. Alleluia.

PRAYER BEFORE THE GOSPEL

Bowing down at the center of the altar, he says:

CLEANSE my heart and my lips, O almighty God, Who cleansed the lips of the Prophet Isaias with a burning coal. In Your gracious mercy deign so to purify me that I may worthily proclaim Your holy Gospel. Through Christ our Lord. Amen.

Lord, grant Your blessing. The Lord be in my heart and on my lips, that I may worthily and fittingly proclaim His holy Gospel. Amen.

THE GOSPEL • Matt. 9, 1-8

Going to the left (Gospel) side of the altar, he says:

P. The Lord be with you. *S.* And with your spirit.

P. ✠ The continuation of the holy Gospel according to Saint Matthew. *S.* Glory be to You, O Lord.

AT THAT time, Jesus, getting into a boat, crossed over and came to His own town. And behold, they brought to Him a paralytic lying on a pallet. And Jesus, seeing their faith, said to the paralytic, "Take courage, son; your sins are forgiven you." And behold, some of the Scribes said within themselves, "This man blasphemes." And Jesus, knowing their thoughts, said, "Why do you harbor evil thoughts in your hearts? For which is easier, to say, 'Your sins are forgiven you,' or to say, 'Arise, and walk'? But that you may know that the Son of Man has power on earth to forgive sins," — then He said to the paralytic — "Arise, take up your pallet and go to your house." And he arose, and went away to his house. But when the crowds saw it, they were struck with fear, and glorified God Who had given such power to men. *S.* Praise be to You, O Christ.

P. By the words of the Gospel, may our sins be taken away.

THE NICENE CREED

At the center of the altar, he says:

I BELIEVE in one God, the Father almighty, Maker of heaven and earth, and of all things visible and invisible. And in one Lord Jesus Christ, the Only-begotten Son of God. Born of the Father before all ages. God of God; Light of Light; true God of true God. Begotten not made; of one being with the Father; by Whom all things were

made. Who for us men, and for our salvation, came down from heaven. (*Here all genuflect.*) And was made Flesh by the Holy Spirit of the Virgin Mary: AND WAS MADE MAN. He was also crucified for us, suffered under Pontius Pilate and was buried. And on the third day He rose again according to the Scriptures. And ascending into heaven, He sits at the right hand of the Father. And He shall come again in glory to judge the living and the dead; and of His kingdom there shall be no end. And I believe in the Holy Spirit, Lord and Giver of life, Who proceeds from the Father and the Son. Who together with the Father and the Son is no less adored, and glorified: Who spoke by the Prophets. And I believe in One, Holy, Catholic and Apostolic Church. I confess one Baptism for the remission of sins. And I look for the resurrection of the dead. ✠ And the life of the world to come. Amen.

THE OFFERTORY

The Priest turns to the people and says:

P. The Lord be with you. *S.* And with your spirit.
P. Let us pray.

THE OFFERTORY VERSE • Ex. 24, 4. 5

MOSES consecrated an altar to the Lord, offering upon it holocausts, and sacrificing victims: he made an evening sacrifice to the Lord God for an odor of sweetness, in the sight of the Israelites.

The Priest now uncovers the chalice, places the host on the paten and offering it up, says:

ACCEPT, O holy Father, almighty and eternal God, this spotless host, which I, Your unworthy servant, offer to You, my living and true God, to atone for my numberless sins, offenses, and negligences; on behalf of all here present and likewise for all faithful Christians living and dead, that it may profit me and them as a means of salvation to life everlasting. Amen.

He pours wine and water into the chalice, blessing the water before it is poured.

O GOD, Who established the nature of man in wondrous dignity, and still more admirably restored it, grant that through the mystery of this water and wine, we may be made partakers of His Divinity, Who has condescended to become partaker of our humanity, Jesus Christ, Your Son, our Lord. Who lives and reigns with You in the unity of the Holy Spirit, God, world without end. Amen.

Offering up the wine, the Priest says:

WE OFFER You, O Lord, the chalice of salvation, humbly begging of Your mercy that it may arise before Your Divine Majesty, with a pleasing fragrance, for our salvation and for that of the whole world. Amen.

Bowing down, the Priest says:

IN A humble spirit and with a contrite heart, may we be accepted by You, O Lord, and may our sacrifice so be offered in Your sight this day as to please You, O Lord God.

Raising his eyes and blessing the offering, he says:

COME, O Sanctifier, almighty and eternal God, and bless ✠ this sacrifice prepared for the glory of Your holy name.

WASHING THE FINGERS

I WASH my hands in innocence, and I go around Your altar, O Lord, giving voice to my thanks, and recounting all Your wondrous deeds. O Lord,

I love the house in which You dwell, the tenting-place of Your glory. Gather not my soul with those of sinners, nor with men of blood my life. On their hands are crimes, and their right hands are full of bribes. But I walk in integrity; redeem me, and have pity on me. My foot stands on level ground; in the assemblies I will bless You, O Lord. Glory be to the Father, and to the Son, and to the Holy Spirit. As it was in the beginning, is now, and ever shall be, world without end. Amen.

ACCEPT, Most Holy Trinity, this offering which we are making to You in remembrance of the Passion, Resurrection, and Ascension of Jesus Christ, our Lord; and in honor of Blessed Mary, ever Virgin, Blessed John the Baptist, the Holy Apostles Peter and Paul, and of these, and of all the Saints; that it may add to their honor and aid our salvation; and may they deign to intercede in heaven for us who honor their memory here on earth. Through the same Christ our Lord. Amen.

The Priest turns toward the people and says:

Pray, brethren, that my sacrifice and yours may become acceptable to God the Father almighty.

S. May the Lord accept this sacrifice from your hands to the praise and glory of His name, for our advantage, and that of all His holy Church.

P. Amen.

THE SECRET

O GOD, by the adorable Communion of this sacrifice You make us partakers of the one Supreme Godhead; grant, we beseech You, that even as we recognize Your truth, so we may attain to it by a worthy life. Through our Lord Jesus

Christ, Your Son, Who lives and reigns with You in the unity of the Holy Spirit, God.
P. World without end. *S.* Amen.

PREFACE–CANON

P. The Lord be with you. *S.* And with your spirit.
P. Lift up your hearts.
S. We have lifted them up to the Lord.
P. Let us give thanks to the Lord, our God.
S. It is fitting and just.

IT IS fitting indeed and just, right and helpful to salvation, for us always and everywhere to give thanks to You, O holy Lord, Father almighty, everlasting God, Who with Your Only-begotten Son and the Holy Spirit are one God, one Lord; not in the unity of a single person, but in the trinity of a single nature. For that which we believe on Your revelation concerning Your glory, that same we believe of Your Son, that same of the Holy Spirit, without difference or discrimination. So that in confessing the true and everlasting Godhead, we shall adore distinction in Persons, oneness in being, and equality in Majesty. This the Angels and Archangels, the Cherubim, too, and the Seraphim do praise; day by day they cease not to cry out as with one voice, saying (*the bell is rung 3 times*):

HOLY, HOLY, HOLY, Lord God of Hosts. Heaven and earth are filled with Your glory. Hosanna in the highest. ✠ Blessed is He Who comes in the name of the Lord. Hosanna in the highest.

THE CANON OF THE MASS

THEREFORE, most gracious Father, we humbly beg of You and entreat You through Jesus Christ Your Son, our Lord, (*he kisses the altar*) to deem acceptable and bless these ✠ gifts, these ✠ offerings, these ✠ holy and unspotted oblations which, in the first place, we offer You for Your Holy Catholic Church, that You would deign to give her peace and protection, to unite and guard her throughout the world, together with Your servant N., our Pope, and N., our Bishop; and all true believers who cherish the Catholic and Apostolic Faith.

REMEMBER, O Lord, Your servants and handmaids, N. and N., (*name them*) and all here present, whose faith and devotion are known to You, on whose behalf we offer to You, or who themselves offer to You, this sacrifice of praise for themselves, families and friends, for the good of their souls, for their hope of salvation and deliverance from all harm, and who offer their homage to You, eternal, living and true God.

Commemoration of the Saints

IN THE unity of holy fellowship we observe the memory, first of all, of the glorious and ever Virgin Mary, Mother of our Lord and God Jesus Christ; next, that of Your Blessed Apostles and Martyrs, Peter and Paul, Andrew, James, John, Thomas, James, Philip, Bartholomew, Matthew, Simon and Thaddeus; of Linus, Cletus, Clement, Sixtus, Cornelius, Cyprian, Lawrence, Chrysogonus, John and Paul, Cosmas and Damian, and of all Your Saints, by whose merits and prayers grant that

we may be always fortified by the help of Your protection. Through the same Christ our Lord. Amen.

Spreading his hands over the oblation, he says:

GRACIOUSLY accept, then, we beseech You, O Lord, this service of our worship and that of all Your household. Provide that our days be spent in Your peace, save us from everlasting damnation, and cause us to be numbered in the flock You have chosen. Through Christ our Lord. Amen.

O GOD, deign to bless ✠ what we offer, and make it approved, ✠ effective, ✠ right, and wholly pleasing in every way, that it may become for our good, the Body ✠ and Blood ✠ of Your dearly beloved Son, Jesus Christ our Lord.

CONSECRATION—ELEVATION

WHO, the day before He suffered, took bread into His holy and venerable hands, and having raised His eyes to heaven, to You, O God, His almighty Father, giving thanks to You, He blessed it, ✠ broke it, and gave it to His disciples, saying: All of you take and eat of this:

FOR THIS IS MY BODY.

IN LIKE manner, when the supper was done, taking also this goodly chalice into His holy and venerable hands, again giving thanks to You, He blessed ✠ it, and gave it to His disciples, saying: All of you take and drink of this:

FOR THIS IS THE CHALICE OF MY BLOOD OF THE NEW AND ETERNAL COVENANT: THE MYSTERY OF FAITH: WHICH SHALL BE SHED FOR YOU AND FOR MANY UNTO THE FORGIVENESS OF SINS.

After replacing the chalice on the corporal, he says:

As often as you shall do these things, in memory of Me shall you do them.

Offering of the Victim

MINDFUL, therefore, O Lord, not only of the blessed Passion of the same Christ, Your Son, our Lord, but also of His Resurrection from the dead, and finally His glorious Ascension into heaven, we, Your ministers, as also Your holy people, offer to Your supreme Majesty, of the gifts bestowed upon us, the pure ✠ Victim, the holy ✠ Victim, the all-perfect ✠ Victim: the holy ✠ Bread of life eternal and the Chalice ✠ of unending salvation.

AND this deign to regard with gracious and kindly attention and hold acceptable, as You deigned to accept the offerings of Abel, Your just servant, and the sacrifice of Abraham our patriarch, and that which Your chief priest Melchisedec offered to You, a holy sacrifice and a spotless victim.

MOST humbly we implore You, almighty God, bid these offerings to be brought by the hands of Your holy angel to Your altar above; before the face of Your Divine Majesty; that those of us who, by sharing in the Sacrifice of this altar, shall receive the Most Sacred ✠ Body and ✠ Blood of Your Son, may be filled with every grace and heavenly blessing. Through the same Christ our Lord. Amen.

Commemoration of the Dead

REMEMBER also, O Lord, Your servants and handmaids, N. and N., who have gone before us with the sign of faith, and rest in the sleep of peace. (*Here pray for the dead.*) To these, O Lord,

and to all who rest in Christ, we beseech You to grant of Your goodness, a place of comfort, light and peace. Through the same Christ our Lord. Amen.

TO US sinners also, Your servants, trusting in the greatness of Your mercy, deign to grant some part and fellowship with Your Holy Apostles and Martyrs: with John, Stephen, Matthias, Barnabas, Ignatius, Alexander, Marcellinus, Peter, Felicitas, Perpetua, Agatha, Lucy, Agnes, Cecilia, Anastasia, and all Your Saints; into whose company, we implore You to admit us, not weighing our merits, but freely granting us pardon. Through Christ our Lord.

THROUGH Whom, O Lord, You always create, ✠ sanctify, ✠ fill with life, ✠ bless, and bestow upon us all good things.

The Minor Elevation

THROUGH ✠ Him, and with ✠ Him, and in ✠ Him, is to You, God the Father ✠ almighty, in the unity of the Holy ✠ Spirit, all honor and glory, world without end. S. Amen.

THE COMMUNION AND THANKSGIVING

Let us pray. Prompted by saving precepts, and taught by Your divine teaching, we dare to say:

OUR FATHER, Who art in heaven, hallowed be Thy name: Thy kingdom come: Thy will be done on earth as it is in heaven. Give us this day our daily bread; and forgive us our trespasses, as we forgive those who trespass against us. And lead us not into temptation: S. But deliver us from evil. *P.* Amen.

DELIVER us, we beseech You, O Lord, from all evils, past, present, and to come; and by the intercession of the Blessed and glorious Mary, ever Virgin, Mother of God, together with Your Blessed Apostles Peter and Paul, and Andrew, and all the Saints, grant of Your goodness, peace in our days, that aided by the riches of Your mercy, we may be always free from sin and safe from all disturbance.

Through the same our Lord Jesus Christ, Your Son, Who lives and reigns with You in the unity of the Holy Spirit, God, world without end.

S. Amen.

P. May the peace ✠ of the Lord be ✠ always with ✠ you.

S. And with your spirit.

The Priest puts a small particle into the chalice, saying:

May this mingling and consecration of the Body and Blood of our Lord Jesus Christ help us who receive it to life everlasting. Amen.

LAMB of God, You Who take away the sins of the world, have mercy on us.

Lamb of God, You Who take away the sins of the world, have mercy on us.

Lamb of God, You Who take away the sins of the world, grant us peace.

PRAYERS BEFORE HOLY COMMUNION

Then inclining toward the altar, he says:

O LORD Jesus Christ, Who said to Your Apostles: "Peace I leave with you, My peace I give to you," regard not my sins but the faith of Your Church, and deign to give her peace and unity

according to Your Will: Who live and reign, God, world without end. Amen.

O LORD Jesus Christ, Son of the living God, Who, by the will of the Father, with the cooperation of the Holy Spirit, have by Your death given life to the world, deliver me by this Your Most Sacred Body and Blood from all my sins and from every evil. Make me always cling to Your commandments, and never permit me to be separated from You. Who with the same God the Father and the Holy Spirit, live and reign, God, world without end. Amen.

LET not the partaking of Your Body, O Lord Jesus Christ, which I, though unworthy, presume to receive, turn to my judgment and condemnation; but through Your goodness, may it become a safeguard and an effective remedy, both of soul and body. Who live and reign with God the Father, in the unity of the Holy Spirit, God, world without end. Amen.

COMMUNION OF THE PRIEST

I WILL take the Bread of heaven, and call upon the name of the Lord.

Lord, I am not worthy that You should come under my roof; but only say the word, and my soul will be healed. (3 *times.*)

Making the Sign of the Cross with the Host, he says:

MAY the Body of our Lord Jesus Christ preserve my soul to life everlasting. Amen.

What return shall I make to the Lord for all He has given me? I will take the Chalice of salvation, and I will call upon the name of the Lord. Prais-

ing will I call upon the Lord and I shall be saved from my enemies.

Making the Sign of the Cross with the chalice, he says:

MAY the Blood of our Lord Jesus Christ preserve my soul to life everlasting. Amen.

The Priest reverently consumes the Precious Blood.

COMMUNION OF THE FAITHFUL

The Server and people say the "Confiteor."

P. May almighty God have mercy on you, forgive you your sins, and bring you to life everlasting. *S.* Amen.

P. May the almighty and merciful Lord grant you pardon, ✠ absolution and remission of your sins. *S.* Amen.

Holding up a Sacred Host, the Priest says:

Behold the Lamb of God, behold Him Who takes away the sins of the world.

Lord, I am not worthy that You should come under my roof; but only say the word, and my soul will be healed. (3 *times.*)

The Priest says to each communicant:

May the Body of our Lord Jesus Christ preserve your soul to life everlasting. Amen.

The Priest purifies the chalice with wine, saying:

WHAT has passed our lips as food, O Lord, may we possess in purity of heart, that what is given to us in time, be our healing for eternity.

He purifies his fingers with wine and water, saying:

MAY Your Body, O Lord, which I have eaten, and Your Blood which I have drunk, cleave to my very soul, and grant that no trace of sin be found in me, whom these pure and holy mysteries

have renewed. Who live and reign, world without end. Amen.

THE COMMUNION • Ps. 95, 8. 9

BRING gifts and enter His courts; worship the Lord in His holy court.

The Priest, turning to the people, says:

P. The Lord be with you. S. And with your spirit.
P. Let us pray.

THE POSTCOMMUNION

FED with this sacred Gift, O Lord, we give You thanks, beseeching Your mercy to render us worthy of our participation in it. Through our Lord Jesus Christ, Your Son, Who lives and reigns with You in the unity of the Holy Spirit, God, world without end. S. Amen.

FINAL PRAYERS

The Priest turns again to the people, and says:

P. The Lord be with you. S. And with your spirit.
P. Go, you are dismissed. S. Thanks be to God.

MAY the tribute of my worship be pleasing to You, Most Holy Trinity, and grant that the sacrifice which I, all unworthy, have offered in the presence of Your Majesty, may be acceptable to You, and through Your mercy obtain forgiveness for me and all for whom I have offered it. Through Christ our Lord. Amen.

THE LAST BLESSING

He kisses the altar, and facing the people, says:

MAY almighty God bless you: ✠ the Father, and the Son, and the Holy Spirit. S. Amen.

The Last Gospel and Prayers after Low Mass are conveniently placed inside the back cover.

"For many are called but few are chosen."

NINETEENTH SUNDAY AFTER PENTECOST

Without sanctifying grace (the "wedding garment") we cannot enter the kingdom of heaven. To die in the state of grace is a special gift for which we must pray and which God will certainly not deny us if we ever cleave to His commandments. (GREEN VESTMENTS)

PRAYERS AT THE FOOT OF THE ALTAR

IN THE name of the Father, ✠ and of the Son, and of the Holy Spirit. Amen.

Priest. I will go in to the altar of God.

Server. The God of my gladness and joy.

Psalm 42

DO ME justice, O God, and fight my fight against a faithless people; from the deceitful and impious man rescue me.

S. For You, O God, are my strength. Why do You keep me so far away? Why must I go about in mourning, with the enemy oppressing me?

P. Send forth Your light and Your fidelity; they

shall lead me on and bring me to Your holy mountain, to Your dwelling-place.
S. Then will I go in to the altar of God, the God of my gladness and joy.
P. Then will I give You thanks upon the harp, O God, my God. Why are you so downcast, O my soul? Why do you sigh within me?
S. Hope in God! For I shall again be thanking Him in the presence of my Savior and my God.
P. Glory be to the Father, and to the Son, and to the Holy Spirit.
S. As it was in the beginning, is now, and ever shall be, world without end. Amen.
P. I will go in to the altar of God.
S. The God of my gladness and joy.
P. Our help ✠ is in the name of the Lord.
S. Who made heaven and earth.
P. I confess to almighty God, etc.
S. May almighty God have mercy on you, forgive you your sins, and bring you to life everlasting.
P. Amen.

The Server, bowing, says the "Confiteor."

I CONFESS to almighty God, to Blessed Mary, ever Virgin, to Blessed Michael the Archangel, to Blessed John the Baptist, to the Holy Apostles Peter and Paul, and to all the Saints, and to you, Father, that I have sinned exceedingly in thought, word and deed, *through my fault, through my fault, through my most grievous fault.* Therefore I beseech Blessed Mary, ever Virgin, Blessed Michael the Archangel, Blessed John the Baptist, the Holy Apostles Peter and Paul, and all the Saints, and you, Father, to pray to the Lord our God for me.
P. May almighty God have mercy on you, forgive

you your sins, and bring you to life everlasting.
S. Amen.

MAY the almighty and merciful Lord grant us pardon, ✠ absolution, and remission of our sins. S. Amen.

P. Will You not, O God, give us life?
S. And shall not Your people rejoice in You?
P. Show us, O Lord, Your kindness.
S. And grant us Your salvation.
P. O Lord, hear my prayer.
S. And let my cry come to You.
P. The Lord be with you.
S. And with your spirit. P. Let us pray.

Going up to the altar, the Priest prays silently:

TAKE away from us our sins, O Lord, we beseech You, that we may enter with pure minds into the Holy of Holies. Through Christ our Lord. Amen.

WE BESEECH You, O Lord, by the merits of Your Saints (*he kisses the altar*) whose relics lie here, and of all the Saints: deign in Your mercy to pardon me all my sins. Amen.

THE INTROIT • Ps. 77, 1

At the right side of the altar, the Priest says:

"I AM the salvation of the people," says the Lord; "in whatever tribulation they shall cry to Me, I will hear them; and I will be their Lord forever." *Ps.* Hearken, My people, to My teaching; incline your ears to the words of My mouth. Glory be to the Father, and to the Son, and to the Holy Spirit. As it was in the beginning, is now, and ever shall be, world without end. Amen. — "I am the salvation of the people," says the Lord; "in whatever tribulation they shall cry to Me, I will hear them; and I will be their Lord forever."

THE KYRIE

P. Lord, have mercy. *S.* Lord, have mercy. *P.* Lord, have mercy. *S.* Christ, have mercy. *P.* Christ, have mercy. *S.* Christ, have mercy. *P.* Lord, have mercy. *S.* Lord, have mercy. *P.* Lord, have mercy.

THE GLORIA

GLORY to God in the highest. And on earth peace to men of good will. We praise You. We bless You. We adore You. We glorify You. We give You thanks for Your great glory. O Lord God, heavenly King, God the Father almighty. O Lord Jesus Christ, the Only-begotten Son. O Lord God, Lamb of God, Son of the Father: You Who take away the sins of the world, have mercy on us. You Who take away the sins of the world, receive our prayer. You Who sit at the right hand of the Father, have mercy on us. For You alone are holy. You alone are the Lord. You alone, O Jesus Christ, are most high. Together with the Holy Spirit ✠ in the glory of God the Father. Amen.

The Priest kisses the altar and turns to the people, saying:

P. The Lord be with you. *S.* And with your spirit. *P.* Let us pray.

THE PRAYER

Going to the right (Epistle) side, he says:

ALMIGHTY and merciful God, in Your bounty, graciously defend us from all that is hurtful; that, free in mind and body, we may with ready minds carry out the things that are Yours. Through our Lord Jesus Christ, Your Son, Who lives and reigns with You in the unity of the Holy Spirit, God, world without end. *S.* Amen.

THE EPISTLE • Eph. 4, 23-28

BRETHREN: Be renewed in the spirit of your mind, and put on the new man, which has been created according to God in justice and holiness of truth. Wherefore, put away lying and speak truth each one with his neighbor, because we are members of one another. "Be angry and do not sin"; do not let the sun go down upon your anger; do not give place to the devil. He who was wont to steal, let him steal no longer; but rather let him labor, working with his hands at what is good, that he may have something to share with him who suffers need. *S.* Thanks be to God.

THE GRADUAL • Ps. 140, 2

LET my prayer come like incense before You, O Lord. ℣. The lifting up of my hands like the evening sacrifice.

Alleluia, alleluia. ℣. *Ps. 104, 1.* Give thanks to the Lord, invoke His name; make known among the nations His deeds. Alleluia.

PRAYER BEFORE THE GOSPEL

Bowing down at the center of the altar, he says:

CLEANSE my heart and my lips, O almighty God, Who cleansed the lips of the Prophet Isaias with a burning coal. In Your gracious mercy deign so to purify me that I may worthily proclaim Your holy Gospel. Through Christ our Lord. Amen.

Lord, grant Your blessing. The Lord be in my heart and on my lips, that I may worthily and fittingly proclaim His holy Gospel. Amen.

THE GOSPEL • Matt. 22, 1-14

Going to the left (Gospel) side of the altar, he says:

P. The Lord be with you. *S.* And with your spirit.

P. ✠ The continuation of the holy Gospel according to Saint Matthew. *S.* Glory be to You, O Lord.

AT THAT time, Jesus spoke to the chief priests and the Pharisees in parables, saying, "The kingdom of heaven is like a king who made a marriage feast for his son. And he sent his servants to call in those invited to the marriage feast, but they would not come. Again he sent out other servants, saying, 'Tell those who are invited, behold, I have prepared my dinner; my oxen and fatlings are killed, and everything is ready; come to the marriage feast.' But they made light of it, and went off, one to his farm, and another to his business; and the rest laid hold of his servants, treated them shamefully, and killed them. But when the king heard of it, he was angry; and he sent his armies, destroyed those murderers, and burnt their city. Then he said to his servants, 'The marriage feast indeed is ready, but those who were invited were not worthy; go therefore to the crossroads, and invite to the marriage feast whomever you shall find.' And his servants went out into the roads, and gathered all whom they found, both good and bad; and the marriage feast was filled with guests. Now the king went in to see the guests, and he saw there a man who had not on a wedding garment. And he said to him, 'Friend, how did you come in here without a wedding garment?' But he was speechless. Then the king said to the attendants, 'Bind his hands and feet and cast him forth into the darkness outside, where there will be the weeping, and the gnashing of teeth.' For many are called, but few are chosen." *S.* Praise be to You, O Christ.

P. By the words of the Gospel, may our sins be taken away.

THE NICENE CREED

At the center of the altar, he says:

I BELIEVE in one God, the Father almighty, Maker of heaven and earth, and of all things visible and invisible. And in one Lord Jesus Christ, the Only-begotten Son of God. Born of the Father before all ages. God of God; Light of Light; true God of true God. Begotten not made; of one being with the Father; by Whom all things were made. Who for us men, and for our salvation, came down from heaven. (*Here all genuflect.*) And was made Flesh by the Holy Spirit of the Virgin Mary: AND WAS MADE MAN. He was also crucified for us, suffered under Pontius Pilate and was buried. And on the third day He rose again according to the Scriptures. And ascending into heaven, He sits at the right hand of the Father. And He shall come again in glory to judge the living and the dead; and of His kingdom there shall be no end. And I believe in the Holy Spirit, Lord and Giver of life, Who proceeds from the Father and the Son. Who together with the Father and the Son is no less adored, and glorified: Who spoke by the Prophets. And I believe in One, Holy, Catholic and Apostolic Church. I confess one Baptism for the remission of sins. And I look for the resurrection of the dead. ✠ And the life of the world to come. Amen.

THE OFFERTORY

The Priest turns to the people and says:

P. The Lord be with you. S. And with your spirit.
P. Let us pray.

THE OFFERTORY VERSE • Ps. 137, 7

THOUGH I walk amid distress, You preserve me, O Lord; against the anger of my enemies You raise Your hand; Your right hand saves me.

The Priest now uncovers the chalice, places the host on the paten and offering it up, says:

ACCEPT, O holy Father, almighty and eternal God, this spotless host, which I, Your unworthy servant, offer to You, my living and true God, to atone for my numberless sins, offenses, and negligences; on behalf of all here present and likewise for all faithful Christians living and dead, that it may profit me and them as a means of salvation to life everlasting. Amen.

He pours wine and water into the chalice, blessing the water before it is poured.

O GOD, Who established the nature of man in wondrous dignity, and still more admirably restored it, grant that through the mystery of this water and wine, we may be made partakers of His Divinity, Who has condescended to become partaker of our humanity, Jesus Christ, Your Son, our Lord. Who lives and reigns with You in the unity of the Holy Spirit, God, world without end. Amen.

Offering up the wine, the Priest says:

WE OFFER You, O Lord, the chalice of salvation, humbly begging of Your mercy that it may arise before Your Divine Majesty, with a pleasing fragrance, for our salvation and for that of the whole world. Amen.

Bowing down, the Priest says:

IN A humble spirit and with a contrite heart, may we be accepted by You, O Lord, and may our sacrifice so be offered in Your sight this day as to please You, O Lord God.

Raising his eyes and blessing the offering, he says:

COME, O Sanctifier, almighty and eternal God, and bless ✠ this sacrifice prepared for the glory of Your holy name.

WASHING THE FINGERS

I WASH my hands in innocence, and I go around Your altar, O Lord, giving voice to my thanks, and recounting all Your wondrous deeds. O Lord, I love the house in which You dwell, the tenting-place of Your glory. Gather not my soul with those of sinners, nor with men of blood my life. On their hands are crimes, and their right hands are full of bribes. But I walk in integrity; redeem me, and have pity on me. My foot stands on level ground; in the assemblies I will bless You, O Lord. Glory be to the Father, and to the Son, and to the Holy Spirit. As it was in the beginning, is now, and ever shall be, world without end. Amen.

ACCEPT, Most Holy Trinity, this offering which we are making to You in remembrance of the Passion, Resurrection, and Ascension of Jesus Christ, our Lord; and in honor of Blessed Mary, ever Virgin, Blessed John the Baptist, the Holy Apostles Peter and Paul, and of these, and of all the Saints; that it may add to their honor and aid our salvation; and may they deign to intercede in heaven for us who honor their memory here on earth. Through the same Christ our Lord. Amen.

The Priest turns toward the people and says:

Pray, brethren, that my sacrifice and yours may become acceptable to God the Father almighty.

S. May the Lord accept this sacrifice from your hands to the praise and glory of His name, for our advantage, and that of all His holy Church.

P. Amen.

THE SECRET

GRANT, we beseech You, O Lord, that these gifts which we offer in the sight of Your Majesty, may be salutary to us. Through our Lord Jesus Christ, Your Son, Who lives and reigns with You in the unity of the Holy Spirit, God.

P. World without end. *S.* Amen.

PREFACE—CANON

P. The Lord be with you. *S.* And with your spirit.

P. Lift up your hearts.

S. We have lifted them up to the Lord.

P. Let us give thanks to the Lord, our God.

S. It is fitting and just.

IT IS fitting indeed and just, right and helpful to salvation, for us always and everywhere to give thanks to You, O holy Lord, Father almighty, everlasting God, Who with Your Only-begotten Son and the Holy Spirit are one God, one Lord; not in the unity of a single person, but in the trinity of a single nature. For that which we believe on Your revelation concerning Your glory, that same we believe of Your Son, that same of the Holy Spirit, without difference or discrimination. So that in confessing the true and everlasting Godhead, we shall adore distinction in Persons, oneness in being, and equality in Majesty. This the Angels and Archangels, the Cherubim, too, and the Seraphim do

praise; day by day they cease not to cry out as with one voice, saying (*the bell is rung 3 times*):

HOLY, HOLY, HOLY, Lord God of Hosts. Heaven and earth are filled with Your glory. Hosanna in the highest. ✠ Blessed is He Who comes in the name of the Lord. Hosanna in the highest.

THE CANON OF THE MASS

THEREFORE, most gracious Father, we humbly beg of You and entreat You through Jesus Christ Your Son, our Lord, (*he kisses the altar*) to deem acceptable and bless these ✠ gifts, these ✠ offerings, these ✠ holy and unspotted oblations which, in the first place, we offer You for Your Holy Catholic Church, that You would deign to give her peace and protection, to unite and guard her throughout the world, together with Your servant N., our Pope, and N., our Bishop; and all true believers who cherish the Catholic and Apostolic Faith.

Commemoration of the Living

REMEMBER, O Lord, Your servants and handmaids, N. and N., (*name them*) and all here present, whose faith and devotion are known to You, on whose behalf we offer to You, or who themselves offer to You, this sacrifice of praise for themselves, families and friends, for the good of their souls, for their hope of salvation and deliverance from all harm, and who offer their homage to You, eternal, living and true God.

Commemoration of the Saints

IN THE unity of holy fellowship we observe the memory, first of all, of the glorious and ever Virgin Mary, Mother of our Lord and God Jesus Christ; next, that of Your Blessed Apostles and

Martyrs, Peter and Paul, Andrew, James, John, Thomas, James, Philip, Bartholomew, Matthew, Simon and Thaddeus; of Linus, Cletus, Clement, Sixtus, Cornelius, Cyprian, Lawrence, Chrysogonus, John and Paul, Cosmas and Damian, and of all Your Saints, by whose merits and prayers grant that we may be always fortified by the help of Your protection. Through the same Christ our Lord. Amen.

Spreading his hands over the oblation, he says:

GRACIOUSLY accept, then, we beseech You, O Lord, this service of our worship and that of all Your household. Provide that our days be spent in Your peace, save us from everlasting damnation, and cause us to be numbered in the flock You have chosen. Through Christ our Lord. Amen.

O GOD, deign to bless ✠ what we offer, and make it approved, ✠ effective, ✠ right, and wholly pleasing in every way, that it may become for our good, the Body ✠ and Blood ✠ of Your dearly beloved Son, Jesus Christ our Lord.

CONSECRATION—ELEVATION

WHO, the day before He suffered, took bread into His holy and venerable hands, and having raised His eyes to heaven, to You, O God, His almighty Father, giving thanks to You, He blessed it, ✠ broke it, and gave it to His disciples, saying: All of you take and eat of this:

FOR THIS IS MY BODY.

IN LIKE manner, when the supper was done, taking also this goodly chalice into His holy and venerable hands, again giving thanks to You, He blessed ✠ it, and gave it to His disciples, saying: All of you take and drink of this:

FOR THIS IS THE CHALICE OF MY BLOOD OF THE NEW AND ETERNAL COVENANT: THE MYSTERY OF FAITH: WHICH SHALL BE SHED FOR YOU AND FOR MANY UNTO THE FORGIVENESS OF SINS.

After replacing the chalice on the corporal, he says:

As often as you shall do these things, in memory of Me shall you do them.

Offering of the Victim

MINDFUL, therefore, O Lord, not only of the blessed Passion of the same Christ, Your Son, our Lord, but also of His Resurrection from the dead, and finally His glorious Ascension into heaven, we, Your ministers, as also Your holy people, offer to Your supreme Majesty, of the gifts bestowed upon us, the pure ✠ Victim, the holy ✠ Victim, the all-perfect ✠ Victim: the holy ✠ Bread of life eternal and the Chalice ✠ of unending salvation.

AND this deign to regard with gracious and kindly attention and hold acceptable, as You deigned to accept the offerings of Abel, Your just servant, and the sacrifice of Abraham our patriarch, and that which Your chief priest Melchisedec offered to You, a holy sacrifice and a spotless victim.

MOST humbly we implore You, almighty God, bid these offerings to be brought by the hands of Your holy angel to Your altar above; before the face of Your Divine Majesty; that those of us who, by sharing in the Sacrifice of this altar, shall receive the Most Sacred ✠ Body and ✠ Blood of Your Son, may be filled with every grace and heavenly blessing. Through the same Christ our Lord. Amen.

Commemoration of the Dead

REMEMBER also, O Lord, Your servants and handmaids, N. and N., who have gone before us with the sign of faith, and rest in the sleep of peace. (*Here pray for the dead.*) To these, O Lord, and to all who rest in Christ, we beseech You to grant of Your goodness, a place of comfort, light and peace. Through the same Christ our Lord. Amen.

TO US sinners also, Your servants, trusting in the greatness of Your mercy, deign to grant some part and fellowship with Your Holy Apostles and Martyrs: with John, Stephen, Matthias, Barnabas, Ignatius, Alexander, Marcellinus, Peter, Felicitas, Perpetua, Agatha, Lucy, Agnes, Cecilia, Anastasia, and all Your Saints; into whose company, we implore You to admit us, not weighing our merits, but freely granting us pardon. Through Christ our Lord.

THROUGH Whom, O Lord, You always create, ✠ sanctify, ✠ fill with life, ✠ bless, and bestow upon us all good things.

The Minor Elevation

THROUGH ✠ Him, and with ✠ Him, and in ✠ Him, is to You, God the Father ✠ almighty, in the unity of the Holy ✠ Spirit, all honor and glory, world without end. S. Amen.

THE COMMUNION AND THANKSGIVING

Let us pray. Prompted by saving precepts, and taught by Your divine teaching, we dare to say:

OUR FATHER, Who art in heaven, hallowed be Thy name: Thy kingdom come: Thy will be

done on earth as it is in heaven. Give us this day our daily bread; and forgive us our trespasses, as we forgive those who trespass against us. And lead us not into temptation: S. But deliver us from evil. *P.* Amen.

DELIVER us, we beseech You, O Lord, from all evils, past, present, and to come; and by the intercession of the Blessed and glorious Mary, ever Virgin, Mother of God, together with Your Blessed Apostles Peter and Paul, and Andrew, and all the Saints, grant of Your goodness, peace in our days, that aided by the riches of Your mercy, we may be always free from sin and safe from all disturbance.

Through the same our Lord Jesus Christ, Your Son, Who lives and reigns with You in the unity of the Holy Spirit, God, world without end. S. Amen.

P. May the peace ✠ of the Lord be ✠ always with ✠ you. S. And with your spirit.

The Priest puts a small particle into the chalice, saying:

May this mingling and consecration of the Body and Blood of our Lord Jesus Christ help us who receive it to life everlasting. Amen.

LAMB of God, You Who take away the sins of the world, have mercy on us.

Lamb of God, You Who take away the sins of the world, have mercy on us.

Lamb of God, You Who take away the sins of the world, grant us peace.

PRAYERS BEFORE HOLY COMMUNION

Then inclining toward the altar, he says:

O LORD Jesus Christ, Who said to Your Apostles: "Peace I leave with you, My peace I give

to you," regard not my sins but the faith of Your Church, and deign to give her peace and unity according to Your Will: Who live and reign, God, world without end. Amen.

O LORD Jesus Christ, Son of the living God, Who, by the will of the Father, with the co-operation of the Holy Spirit, have by Your death given life to the world, deliver me by this Your Most Sacred Body and Blood from all my sins and from every evil. Make me always cling to Your commandments, and never permit me to be separated from You. Who with the same God the Father and the Holy Spirit, live and reign, God, world without end. Amen.

LET not the partaking of Your Body, O Lord Jesus Christ, which I, though unworthy, presume to receive, turn to my judgment and condemnation; but through Your goodness, may it become a safeguard and an effective remedy, both of soul and body. Who live and reign with God the Father, in the unity of the Holy Spirit, God, world without end. Amen.

COMMUNION OF THE PRIEST

I WILL take the Bread of heaven, and call upon the name of the Lord.

Lord, I am not worthy that You should come under my roof; but only say the word, and my soul will be healed. (3 *times.*)

Making the Sign of the Cross with the Host, he says:

MAY the Body of our Lord Jesus Christ preserve my soul to life everlasting. Amen.

What return shall I make to the Lord for all He has given me? I will take the Chalice of salvation,

and I will call upon the name of the Lord. Praising will I call upon the Lord and I shall be saved from my enemies.

Making the Sign of the Cross with the chalice, he says:

MAY the Blood of our Lord Jesus Christ preserve my soul to life everlasting. Amen.

The Priest reverently consumes the Precious Blood.

COMMUNION OF THE FAITHFUL

The Server and people say the "Confiteor."

P. May almighty God have mercy on you, forgive you your sins, and bring you to life everlasting. *S.* Amen.

P. May the almighty and merciful Lord grant you pardon, ✠ absolution and remission of your sins. *S.* Amen.

Holding up a Sacred Host, the Priest says:

Behold the Lamb of God, behold Him Who takes away the sins of the world.

Lord, I am not worthy that You should come under my roof; but only say the word, and my soul will be healed. (3 *times.*)

The Priest says to each communicant:

May the Body of our Lord Jesus Christ preserve your soul to life everlasting. Amen.

The Priest purifies the chalice with wine, saying:

WHAT has passed our lips as food, O Lord, may we possess in purity of heart, that what is given to us in time, be our healing for eternity.

He purifies his fingers with wine and water, saying:

MAY Your Body, O Lord, which I have eaten, and Your Blood which I have drunk, cleave to my very soul, and grant that no trace of sin be found in me, whom these pure and holy mysteries

have renewed. Who live and reign, world without end. Amen.

THE COMMUNION • Ps. 118, 4-5

YOU have commanded that Your precepts be diligently kept. Oh, that I might be firm in the ways of keeping Your statutes!

The Priest, turning to the people, says:

P. The Lord be with you. *S.* And with your spirit.
P. Let us pray.

THE POSTCOMMUNION

MAY Your healing power, O Lord, mercifully free us from our perverse inclinations, and make us ever cleave to Your commandments. Through our Lord Jesus Christ, Your Son, Who lives and reigns with You, etc. *S.* Amen.

FINAL PRAYERS

The Priest turns again to the people, and says:

P. The Lord be with you. *S.* And with your spirit.
P. Go, you are dismissed. *S.* Thanks be to God.

MAY the tribute of my worship be pleasing to You, Most Holy Trinity, and grant that the sacrifice which I, all unworthy, have offered in the presence of Your Majesty, may be acceptable to You, and through Your mercy obtain forgiveness for me and all for whom I have offered it. Through Christ our Lord. Amen.

THE LAST BLESSING

He kisses the altar, and facing the people, says:

MAY almighty God bless you: ✠ the Father, and the Son, and the Holy Spirit. *S.* Amen.

The Last Gospel and Prayers after Low Mass are conveniently placed inside the back cover.

His servants met him saying that his son lived.

TWENTIETH SUNDAY AFTER PENTECOST

"The days are evil." Numberless sins, that are committed daily on earth, cry to heaven for punishment. Let us appease God by leading a good Christian life. The Holy Sacraments are the medicine to "cleanse away the vices of our hearts." (GREEN VESTMENTS)

PRAYERS AT THE FOOT OF THE ALTAR

IN THE name of the Father, ✠ and of the Son, and of the Holy Spirit. Amen.

Priest. I will go in to the altar of God.

Server. The God of my gladness and joy.

Psalm 42

DO ME justice, O God, and fight my fight against a faithless people; from the deceitful and impious man rescue me.

S. For You, O God, are my strength. Why do You keep me so far away? Why must I go about in mourning, with the enemy oppressing me?

P. Send forth Your light and Your fidelity; they shall lead me on and bring me to Your holy mountain, to Your dwelling-place.

S. Then will I go in to the altar of God, the God of my gladness and joy.
P. Then will I give You thanks upon the harp, O God, my God. Why are you so downcast, O my soul? Why do you sigh within me?
S. Hope in God! For I shall again be thanking Him in the presence of my Savior and my God.
P. Glory be to the Father, and to the Son, and to the Holy Spirit.
S. As it was in the beginning, is now, and ever shall be, world without end. Amen.
P. I will go in to the altar of God.
S. The God of my gladness and joy.
P. Our help ✠ is in the name of the Lord.
S. Who made heaven and earth.
P. I confess to almighty God, etc.
S. May almighty God have mercy on you, forgive you your sins, and bring you to life everlasting.
P. Amen.

The Server, bowing, says the "Confiteor."

I CONFESS to almighty God, to Blessed Mary, ever Virgin, to Blessed Michael the Archangel, to Blessed John the Baptist, to the Holy Apostles Peter and Paul, and to all the Saints, and to you, Father, that I have sinned exceedingly in thought, word and deed, *through my fault, through my fault, through my most grievous fault.* Therefore I beseech Blessed Mary, ever Virgin, Blessed Michael the Archangel, Blessed John the Baptist, the Holy Apostles Peter and Paul, and all the Saints, and you, Father, to pray to the Lord our God for me.
P. May almighty God have mercy on you, forgive you your sins, and bring you to life everlasting.
S. Amen.

MAY the almighty and merciful Lord grant us pardon, ✠ absolution, and remission of our sins. *S.* Amen.

P. Will You not, O God, give us life?

S. And shall not Your people rejoice in You?

P. Show us, O Lord, Your kindness.

S. And grant us Your salvation.

P. O Lord, hear my prayer.

S. And let my cry come to You.

P. The Lord be with you.

S. And with your spirit. *P.* Let us pray.

Going up to the altar, the Priest prays silently:

TAKE away from us our sins, O Lord, we beseech You, that we may enter with pure minds into the Holy of Holies. Through Christ our Lord. Amen.

WE BESEECH You, O Lord, by the merits of Your Saints (*he kisses the altar*) whose relics lie here, and of all the Saints: deign in Your mercy to pardon me all my sins. Amen.

THE INTROIT • Dan. 3, 31. 29. 35

At the right side of the altar, the Priest says:

ALL that You have done to us, O Lord, You have done in true judgment; because we have sinned against You, and we have not obeyed Your commandments; but give glory to Your name, and deal with us according to the multitude of Your mercy. *Ps. 118.* Happy are they whose way is blameless, who walk in the law of the Lord. Glory be to the Father, and to the Son, and to the Holy Spirit. As it was in the beginning, is now, and ever shall be, world without end. Amen. — All that You have done to us, O Lord, You have done in true judgment; because we have sinned against You, and we have not obeyed Your commandments; but give glory to Your name, and deal with us according to the multitude of Your mercy.

THE KYRIE

P. Lord, have mercy. *S.* Lord, have mercy. *P.* Lord, have mercy. *S.* Christ, have mercy. *P.* Christ, have mercy. *S.* Christ, have mercy. *P.* Lord, have mercy. *S.* Lord, have mercy. *P.* Lord, have mercy.

THE GLORIA

GLORY to God in the highest. And on earth peace to men of good will. We praise You. We bless You. We adore You. We glorify You. We give You thanks for Your great glory. O Lord God, heavenly King, God the Father almighty. O Lord Jesus Christ, the Only-begotten Son. O Lord God, Lamb of God, Son of the Father: You Who take away the sins of the world, have mercy on us. You Who take away the sins of the world, receive our prayer. You Who sit at the right hand of the Father, have mercy on us. For You alone are holy. You alone are the Lord. You alone, O Jesus Christ, are most high. Together with the Holy Spirit ✠ in the glory of God the Father. Amen.

The Priest kisses the altar and turns to the people, saying:

P. The Lord be with you. *S.* And with your spirit. *P.* Let us pray.

THE PRAYER

Going to the right (Epistle) side, he says:

BE APPEASED, O Lord, we beseech You, and grant to Your faithful people pardon and peace; that they may both be cleansed from all their offenses, and serve You with secure minds. Through our Lord Jesus Christ, Your Son, Who lives and reigns with You in the unity of the Holy Spirit, God, world without end. S. Amen.

THE EPISTLE • Eph. 5, 15-21

BRETHREN: See to it that you walk with care: not as unwise but as wise, making the most of your time, because the days are evil. Therefore, do not become foolish, but understand what the will of the Lord is. And do not be drunk with wine, for in that is debauchery; but be filled with the Spirit, speaking to one another in psalms and hymns and spiritual songs, singing and making melody in your hearts to the Lord, giving thanks always for all things in the name of our Lord Jesus Christ to God the Father. Be subject to one another in the fear of Christ. *S.* Thanks be to God.

THE GRADUAL • Ps. 144, 15-16

THE eyes of all look hopefully to You, O Lord, and You give them their food in due season. ℣. You open Your hand and satisfy the desire of every living thing.

Alleluia, alleluia. ℣. *Ps. 107*, 2. My heart is steadfast, O God; my heart is steadfast; I will sing and chant praise to You, my glory. Alleluia.

PRAYER BEFORE THE GOSPEL

Bowing down at the center of the altar, he says:

CLEANSE my heart and my lips, O almighty God, Who cleansed the lips of the Prophet Isaias with a burning coal. In Your gracious mercy deign so to purify me that I may worthily proclaim Your holy Gospel. Through Christ our Lord. Amen. Lord, grant Your blessing. The Lord be in my heart

and on my lips, that I may worthily and fittingly proclaim His holy Gospel. Amen.

THE GOSPEL • John 4, 46-53

Going to the left (Gospel) side of the altar, he says:

P. The Lord be with you. *S.* And with your spirit.
P. ✠ The continuation of the holy Gospel according to Saint John. *S.* Glory be to You, O Lord.

AT THAT time, there was a certain royal official whose son was lying sick at Capharnaum. When he heard that Jesus had come from Judea into Galilee, he went to Him and besought Him to come down and heal his son, for he was at the point of death. Jesus therefore said to him, "Unless you see signs and wonders, you do not believe." The royal official said to Him, "Sir, come down before my child dies." Jesus said to him, "Go your way, your son lives." The man believed the word that Jesus spoke to him, and departed. But even as he was now going down, his servants met him and brought word saying that his son lived. He asked of them therefore the hour in which he had got better. And they told him, "Yesterday, at the seventh hour, the fever left him." The father knew then that it was at that very hour in which Jesus had said to him, "Your son lives." And he himself believed, and his whole household.
S. Praise be to You, O Christ.

P. By the words of the Gospel, may our sins be taken away.

THE NICENE CREED

At the center of the altar, he says:

I BELIEVE in one God, the Father almighty, Maker of heaven and earth, and of all things visible and invisible. And in one Lord Jesus Christ, the Only-begotten Son of God. Born of the Father before all ages. God of God; Light of Light; true God of true God. Begotten not made; of one being with the Father; by Whom all things were made. Who for us men, and for our salvation, came down from heaven. (*Here all genuflect.*) And was made Flesh by the Holy Spirit of the Virgin Mary: AND WAS MADE MAN. He was also crucified for us, suffered under Pontius Pilate and was buried. And on the third day He rose again according to the Scriptures. And ascending into heaven, He sits at the right hand of the Father. And He shall come again in glory to judge the living and the dead; and of His kingdom there shall be no end. And I believe in the Holy Spirit, Lord and Giver of life, Who proceeds from the Father and the Son. Who together with the Father and the Son is no less adored, and glorified: Who spoke by the Prophets. And I believe in One, Holy, Catholic and Apostolic Church. I confess one Baptism for the remission of sins. And I look for the resurrection of the dead. ✠ And the life of the world to come. Amen.

THE OFFERTORY

The Priest turns to the people and says:

P. The Lord be with you. *S.* And with your spirit.
P. Let us pray.

THE OFFERTORY VERSE • Ps. 136, 1

BY THE streams of Babylon we sat and wept when we remembered you, O Sion.

The Priest now uncovers the chalice, places the host on the paten and offering it up, says:

ACCEPT, O holy Father, almighty and eternal God, this spotless host, which I, Your unworthy servant, offer to You, my living and true God, to atone for my numberless sins, offenses, and negligences; on behalf of all here present and likewise for all faithful Christians living and dead, that it may profit me and them as a means of salvation to life everlasting. Amen.

He pours wine and water into the chalice, blessing the water before it is poured.

O GOD, Who established the nature of man in wondrous dignity, and still more admirably restored it, grant that through the mystery of this water and wine, we may be made partakers of His Divinity, Who has condescended to become partaker of our humanity, Jesus Christ, Your Son, our Lord. Who lives and reigns with You in the unity of the Holy Spirit, God, world without end. Amen.

Offering up the wine, the Priest says:

WE OFFER You, O Lord, the chalice of salvation, humbly begging of Your mercy that it may arise before Your Divine Majesty, with a pleasing fragrance, for our salvation and for that of the whole world. Amen.

Bowing down, the Priest says:

IN A humble spirit and with a contrite heart, may we be accepted by You, O Lord, and may our sacrifice so be offered in Your sight this day as to please You, O Lord God.

Raising his eyes and blessing the offering, he says:

COME, O Sanctifier, almighty and eternal God, and bless ✠ this sacrifice prepared for the glory of Your holy name.

WASHING THE FINGERS

I WASH my hands in innocence, and I go around Your altar, O Lord, giving voice to my thanks,

and recounting all Your wondrous deeds. O Lord, I love the house in which You dwell, the tenting-place of Your glory. Gather not my soul with those of sinners, nor with men of blood my life. On their hands are crimes, and their right hands are full of bribes. But I walk in integrity; redeem me, and have pity on me. My foot stands on level ground; in the assemblies I will bless You, O Lord. Glory be to the Father, and to the Son, and to the Holy Spirit. As it was in the beginning, is now, and ever shall be, world without end. Amen.

ACCEPT, Most Holy Trinity, this offering which we are making to You in remembrance of the Passion, Resurrection, and Ascension of Jesus Christ, our Lord; and in honor of Blessed Mary, ever Virgin, Blessed John the Baptist, the Holy Apostles Peter and Paul, and of these, and of all the Saints; that it may add to their honor and aid our salvation; and may they deign to intercede in heaven for us who honor their memory here on earth. Through the same Christ our Lord. Amen.

The Priest turns toward the people and says:

Pray, brethren, that my sacrifice and yours may become acceptable to God the Father almighty.

S. May the Lord accept this sacrifice from your hands to the praise and glory of His name, for our advantage, and that of all His holy Church.

P. Amen.

THE SECRET

MAY these mysteries, we beseech You, O Lord, afford us a heavenly remedy, and cleanse away the vices of our hearts. Through our Lord

Jesus Christ, Your Son, Who lives and reigns with You in the unity of the Holy Spirit, God.
P. World without end. *S.* Amen.

PREFACE—CANON

P. The Lord be with you. *S.* And with your spirit.
P. Lift up your hearts.
S. We have lifted them up to the Lord.
P. Let us give thanks to the Lord, our God.
S. It is fitting and just.

IT IS fitting indeed and just, right and helpful to salvation, for us always and everywhere to give thanks to You, O holy Lord, Father almighty, everlasting God, Who with Your Only-begotten Son and the Holy Spirit are one God, one Lord; not in the unity of a single person, but in the trinity of a single nature. For that which we believe on Your revelation concerning Your glory, that same we believe of Your Son, that same of the Holy Spirit, without difference or discrimination. So that in confessing the true and everlasting Godhead, we shall adore distinction in Persons, oneness in being, and equality in Majesty. This the Angels and Archangels, the Cherubim, too, and the Seraphim do praise; day by day they cease not to cry out as with one voice, saying (*the bell is rung* 3 *times*):

HOLY, HOLY, HOLY, Lord God of Hosts. Heaven and earth are filled with Your glory. Hosanna in the highest. ✠ Blessed is He Who comes in the name of the Lord. Hosanna in the highest.

THE CANON OF THE MASS

THEREFORE, most gracious Father, we humbly beg of You and entreat You through Jesus

Christ Your Son, our Lord, (*he kisses the altar*) to deem acceptable and bless these ✠ gifts, these ✠ offerings, these ✠ holy and unspotted oblations which, in the first place, we offer You for Your Holy Catholic Church, that You would deign to give her peace and protection, to unite and guard her throughout the world, together with Your servant *N.*, our Pope, and *N.*, our Bishop; and all true believers who cherish the Catholic and Apostolic Faith.

Commemoration of the Living

REMEMBER, O Lord, Your servants and handmaids, *N.* and *N.*, (*name them*) and all here present, whose faith and devotion are known to You, on whose behalf we offer to You, or who themselves offer to You, this sacrifice of praise for themselves, families and friends, for the good of their souls, for their hope of salvation and deliverance from all harm, and who offer their homage to You, eternal, living and true God.

Commemoration of the Saints

IN THE unity of holy fellowship we observe the memory, first of all, of the glorious and ever Virgin Mary, Mother of our Lord and God Jesus Christ; next, that of Your Blessed Apostles and Martyrs, Peter and Paul, Andrew, James, John, Thomas, James, Philip, Bartholomew, Matthew, Simon and Thaddeus; of Linus, Cletus, Clement, Sixtus, Cornelius, Cyprian, Lawrence, Chrysogonus, John and Paul, Cosmas and Damian, and of all Your Saints, by whose merits and prayers grant that we may be always fortified by the help of Your protection. Through the same Christ our Lord. Amen.

Spreading his hands over the oblation, he says:

GRACIOUSLY accept, then, we beseech You, O Lord, this service of our worship and that of all Your household. Provide that our days be spent in Your peace, save us from everlasting damnation, and cause us to be numbered in the flock You have chosen. Through Christ our Lord. Amen.

O GOD, deign to bless ✠ what we offer, and make it approved, ✠ effective, ✠ right, and wholly pleasing in every way, that it may become for our good, the Body ✠ and Blood ✠ of Your dearly beloved Son, Jesus Christ our Lord.

CONSECRATION—ELEVATION

WHO, the day before He suffered, took bread into His holy and venerable hands, and having raised His eyes to heaven, to You, O God, His almighty Father, giving thanks to You, He blessed it, ✠ broke it, and gave it to His disciples, saying: All of you take and eat of this:

FOR THIS IS MY BODY.

IN LIKE manner, when the supper was done, taking also this goodly chalice into His holy and venerable hands, again giving thanks to You, He blessed ✠ it, and gave it to His disciples, saying: All of you take and eat of this:

FOR THIS IS THE CHALICE OF MY BLOOD OF THE NEW AND ETERNAL COVENANT: THE MYSTERY OF FAITH: WHICH SHALL BE SHED FOR YOU AND FOR MANY UNTO THE FORGIVENESS OF SINS.

After replacing the chalice on the corporal, he says:

As often as you shall do these things, in memory of Me shall you do them.

Offering of the Victim

MINDFUL, therefore, O Lord, not only of the blessed Passion of the same Christ, Your Son, our Lord, but also of His Resurrection from the dead, and finally His glorious Ascension into heaven, we, Your ministers, as also Your holy people, offer to Your supreme Majesty, of the gifts bestowed upon us, the pure ✠ Victim, the holy ✠ Victim, the all-perfect ✠ Victim: the holy ✠ Bread of life eternal and the Chalice ✠ of unending salvation.

AND this deign to regard with gracious and kindly attention and hold acceptable, as You deigned to accept the offerings of Abel, Your just servant, and the sacrifice of Abraham our patriarch, and that which Your chief priest Melchisedec offered to You, a holy sacrifice and a spotless victim.

MOST humbly we implore You, almighty God, bid these offerings to be brought by the hands of Your holy angel to Your altar above; before the face of Your Divine Majesty; that those of us who, by sharing in the Sacrifice of this altar, shall receive the Most Sacred ✠ Body and ✠ Blood of Your Son, may be filled with every grace and heavenly blessing. Through the same Christ our Lord. Amen.

Commemoration of the Dead

REMEMBER also, O Lord, Your servants and handmaids, N. and N., who have gone before us with the sign of faith, and rest in the sleep of peace. (*Here pray for the dead.*) To these, O Lord,

and to all who rest in Christ, we beseech You to grant of Your goodness, a place of comfort, light and peace. Through the same Christ our Lord. Amen.

TO US sinners also, Your servants, trusting in the greatness of Your mercy, deign to grant some part and fellowship with Your Holy Apostles and Martyrs: with John, Stephen, Matthias, Barnabas, Ignatius, Alexander, Marcellinus, Peter, Felicitas, Perpetua, Agatha, Lucy, Agnes, Cecilia, Anastasia, and all Your Saints; into whose company, we implore You to admit us, not weighing our merits, but freely granting us pardon. Through Christ our Lord.

THROUGH Whom, O Lord, You always create, ✠ sanctify, ✠ fill with life, ✠ bless, and bestow upon us all good things.

The Minor Elevation

THROUGH ✠ Him, and with ✠ Him, and in ✠ Him, is to You, God the Father ✠ almighty, in the unity of the Holy ✠ Spirit, all honor and glory, world without end. S. Amen.

THE COMMUNION AND THANKSGIVING

Let us pray. Prompted by saving precepts, and taught by Your divine teaching, we dare to say:

OUR FATHER, Who art in heaven, hallowed be Thy name: Thy kingdom come: Thy will be done on earth as it is in heaven. Give us this day our daily bread; and forgive us our trespasses, as we forgive those who trespass against us. And lead us not into temptation: S. But deliver us from evil. *P.* Amen.

DELIVER us, we beseech You, O Lord, from all evils, past, present, and to come; and by the intercession of the Blessed and glorious Mary, ever Virgin, Mother of God, together with Your Blessed Apostles Peter and Paul, and Andrew, and all the Saints, grant of Your goodness, peace in our days, that aided by the riches of Your mercy, we may be always free from sin and safe from all disturbance.

Through the same our Lord Jesus Christ, Your Son, Who lives and reigns with You in the unity of the Holy Spirit, God, world without end. S. Amen.

P. May the peace ✠ of the Lord be ✠ always with ✠ you. S. And with your spirit.

The Priest puts a small particle into the chalice, saying:

May this mingling and consecration of the Body and Blood of our Lord Jesus Christ help us who receive it to life everlasting. Amen.

LAMB of God, You Who take away the sins of the world, have mercy on us.

Lamb of God, You Who take away the sins of the world, have mercy on us.

Lamb of God, You Who take away the sins of the world, grant us peace.

PRAYERS BEFORE HOLY COMMUNION

Then inclining toward the altar, he says:

O LORD Jesus Christ, Who said to Your Apostles: "Peace I leave with you, My peace I give to you," regard not my sins but the faith of Your Church, and deign to give her peace and unity according to Your Will: Who live and reign, God, world without end. Amen.

O LORD Jesus Christ, Son of the living God, Who, by the will of the Father, with the cooperation of the Holy Spirit, have by Your death given life to the world, deliver me by this Your Most Sacred Body and Blood from all my sins and from every evil. Make me always cling to Your commandments, and never permit me to be separated from You. Who with the same God the Father and the Holy Spirit, live and reign, God, world without end. Amen.

LET not the partaking of Your Body, O Lord Jesus Christ, which I, though unworthy, presume to receive, turn to my judgment and condemnation; but through Your goodness, may it become a safeguard and an effective remedy, both of soul and body. Who live and reign with God the Father, in the unity of the Holy Spirit, God, world without end. Amen.

COMMUNION OF THE PRIEST

I WILL take the Bread of heaven, and call upon the name of the Lord.

Lord, I am not worthy that You should come under my roof; but only say the word, and my soul will be healed. (3 *times.*)

Making the Sign of the Cross with the Host, he says:

MAY the Body of our Lord Jesus Christ preserve my soul to life everlasting. Amen.

What return shall I make to the Lord for all He has given me? I will take the Chalice of salvation, and I will call upon the name of the Lord. Praising will I call upon the Lord and I shall be saved from my enemies.

Making the Sign of the Cross with the chalice, he says:

MAY the Blood of our Lord Jesus Christ preserve my soul to life everlasting. Amen.

The Priest reverently consumes the Precious Blood.

COMMUNION OF THE FAITHFUL

The Server and people say the "Confiteor."

P. May almighty God have mercy on you, forgive you your sins, and bring you to life everlasting. *S.* Amen.

P. May the almighty and merciful Lord grant you pardon, ✠ absolution and remission of your sins. *S.* Amen.

Holding up a Sacred Host, the Priest says:

Behold the Lamb of God, behold Him Who takes away the sins of the world.

Lord, I am not worthy that You should come under my roof; but only say the word, and my soul will be healed. (3 *times.*)

The Priest says to each communicant:

May the Body of our Lord Jesus Christ preserve your soul to life everlasting. Amen.

The Priest purifies the chalice with wine, saying:

WHAT has passed our lips as food, O Lord, may we possess in purity of heart, that what is given to us in time, be our healing for eternity.

He purifies his fingers with wine and water, saying:

MAY Your Body, O Lord, which I have eaten, and Your Blood which I have drunk, cleave to my very soul, and grant that no trace of sin be found in me, whom these pure and holy mysteries have renewed. Who live and reign, world without end. Amen.

THE COMMUNION • Ps. 118, 49. 50

REMEMBER Your word to Your servant, O Lord, since You have given me hope. This is my comfort in my affliction.

The Priest, turning to the people, says:

P. The Lord be with you. *S.* And with your spirit.
P. Let us pray.

THE POSTCOMMUNION

THAT we may be made worthy of Your sacred gifts, grant us, we beseech You, O Lord, always to observe Your commandments. Through our Lord Jesus Christ, Your Son, Who lives and reigns with You in the unity of the Holy Spirit, God, world without end. *S.* Amen.

FINAL PRAYERS

The Priest turns again to the people, and says:

P. The Lord be with you. *S.* And with your spirit.
P. Go, you are dismissed. *S.* Thanks be to God.

MAY the tribute of my worship be pleasing to You, Most Holy Trinity, and grant that the sacrifice which I, all unworthy, have offered in the presence of Your Majesty, may be acceptable to You, and through Your mercy obtain forgiveness for me and all for whom I have offered it. Through Christ our Lord. Amen.

THE LAST BLESSING

He kisses the altar, and facing the people, says:

MAY almighty God bless you: ✠ the Father, and the Son, and the Holy Spirit. *S.* Amen.

The Last Gospel and Prayers after Low Mass are conveniently placed inside the back cover.

"You say it; I am a King."

FEAST OF CHRIST THE KING

LAST SUNDAY IN OCTOBER

Jesus said: "My kingdom is not of this world," but it is in the world. He came to establish a kingdom of truth for our intellect; a kingdom of justice and holiness for our will; a kingdom of love and peace for our heart. If we follow Him, He will lead us into His eternal kingdom. (WHITE VESTMENTS)

PRAYERS AT THE FOOT OF THE ALTAR

IN THE name of the Father, ✠ and of the Son, and of the Holy Spirit. Amen.

Priest. I will go in to the altar of God.

Server. The God of my gladness and joy.

Psalm 42

DO ME justice, O God, and fight my fight against a faithless people; from the deceitful and impious man rescue me.

S. For You, O God, are my strength. Why do You keep me so far away? Why must I go about in mourning, with the enemy oppressing me?

P. Send forth Your light and Your fidelity; they shall lead me on and bring me to Your holy mountain, to Your dwelling-place.

S. Then will I go in to the altar of God, the God of my gladness and joy.
P. Then will I give You thanks upon the harp, O God, my God. Why are you so downcast, O my soul? Why do you sigh within me?
S. Hope in God! For I shall again be thanking Him in the presence of my Savior and my God.
P. Glory be to the Father, and to the Son, and to the Holy Spirit.
S. As it was in the beginning, is now, and ever shall be, world without end. Amen.
P. I will go in to the altar of God.
S. The God of my gladness and joy.
P. Our help ✠ is in the name of the Lord.
S. Who made heaven and earth.
P. I confess to almighty God, etc.
S. May almighty God have mercy on you, forgive you your sins, and bring you to life everlasting.
P. Amen.

The Server, bowing, says the "Confiteor."

I CONFESS to almighty God, to Blessed Mary, ever Virgin, to Blessed Michael the Archangel, to Blessed John the Baptist, to the Holy Apostles Peter and Paul, and to all the Saints, and to you, Father, that I have sinned exceedingly in thought, word and deed, *through my fault, through my fault, through my most grievous fault.* Therefore I beseech Blessed Mary, ever Virgin, Blessed Michael the Archangel, Blessed John the Baptist, the Holy Apostles Peter and Paul, and all the Saints, and you, Father, to pray to the Lord our God for me.
P. May almighty God have mercy on you, forgive you your sins, and bring you to life everlasting.
S. Amen.

MAY the almighty and merciful Lord grant us pardon, ✠ absolution, and remission of our sins. *S.* Amen.
P. Will You not, O God, give us life?
S. And shall not Your people rejoice in You?
P. Show us, O Lord, Your kindness.
S. And grant us Your salvation.
P. O Lord, hear my prayer.
S. And let my cry come to You.
P. The Lord be with you.
S. And with your spirit. *P.* Let us pray.

Going up to the altar, the Priest prays silently:

TAKE away from us our sins, O Lord, we beseech You, that we may enter with pure minds into the Holy of Holies. Through Christ our Lord. Amen.

WE BESEECH You, O Lord, by the merits of Your Saints (*he kisses the altar*) whose relics lie here, and of all the Saints: deign in Your mercy to pardon me all my sins. Amen.

THE INTROIT • Apoc. 5, 12; 1, 6

At the right side of the altar, the Priest says:

WORTHY is the Lamb Who was slain to receive power, and divinity, and wisdom, and strength, and honor. To Him belong glory and dominion forever and ever. (*P.T.* Alleluia, alleluia.) *Ps.* 71. O God, with Your judgment endow the King, and with Your justice, the King's son. Glory be to the Father, and to the Son, and to the Holy Spirit. As it was in the beginning, is now, and ever shall be, world without end. Amen. — Worthy is the Lamb Who was slain to receive power, and divinity, and wisdom, and strength, and honor. To

Him belong glory and dominion forever and ever. (*P.T.* Alleluia, alleluia.)

THE KYRIE

P. Lord, have mercy. *S*. Lord, have mercy. *P*. Lord, have mercy. *S*. Christ, have mercy. *P*. Christ, have mercy. *S*. Christ, have mercy. *P*. Lord, have mercy. *S*. Lord, have mercy. *P*. Lord, have mercy.

THE GLORIA

GLORY to God in the highest. And on earth peace to men of good will. We praise You. We bless You. We adore You. We glorify You. We give You thanks for Your great glory. O Lord God, heavenly King, God the Father almighty. O Lord Jesus Christ, the Only-begotten Son. O Lord God, Lamb of God, Son of the Father: You Who take away the sins of the world, have mercy on us. You Who take away the sins of the world, receive our prayer. You Who sit at the right hand of the Father, have mercy on us. For You alone are holy. You alone are the Lord. You alone, O Jesus Christ, are most high. Together with the Holy Spirit ✠ in the glory of God the Father. Amen.

The Priest kisses the altar and turns to the people, saying:

P. The Lord be with you. *S*. And with your spirit. *P*. Let us pray.

THE PRAYER

Going to the right (Epistle) side, he says:

ALMIGHTY and everlasting God, You have willed to restore all things in Your beloved Son, the King of the whole creation; mercifully grant that all the families of nations that have been disunited by the wound of sin may become subject to His most sweet dominion. Who with You lives and reigns in the unity of the Holy Spirit, God, world without end. S. Amen.

THE EPISTLE • Col. 1, 12-20

BRETHREN: We give thanks to God the Father Who has made us worthy to share the lot of the saints in light. He has rescued us from the power of darkness, and transferred us into the kingdom of His beloved Son, in Whom we have our redemption through His Blood, the remission of sins. He is the image of the invisible God, the firstborn of every creature. For in Him were created all things in the heavens and on the earth, things visible and things invisible, whether Thrones, or Dominations, or Principalities, or Powers. All things have been created through and unto Him, and He is before all creatures, and in Him all things hold together. Again, He is the head of the body, the Church; He, Who is the beginning, the firstborn from the dead, that in all things He may have the first place. For it has pleased [God the Father] that in Him all fullness should dwell, and that through Him He should reconcile to Himself all things, whether on the earth or in the heavens, making peace through the Blood of His Cross, in Christ Jesus our Lord. S. Thanks be to God.

THE GRADUAL • Ps. 71, 8. 11

HE SHALL rule from sea to sea, and from the River to the ends of the earth. ℣. All kings shall pay Him homage, all nations shall serve Him.

Alleluia, alleluia. ℣. *Dan. 7, 14.* His power shall be an everlasting power which shall not be taken away: and His kingdom shall not be destroyed. Alleluia.

After Septuagesima omit Alleluia and versicle, and say:

THE TRACT • Ps. 88, 27. 28. 30

HE SHALL say to Me, "You are My Father, My God, My Rock, My Savior." ℣. And I will make Him the firstborn, highest of the kings of the earth. ℣. I will make His posterity endure forever and His throne as the days of heaven.

During Paschaltime omit Gradual, and say:

Alleluia, alleluia. ℣. *Dan. 7, 14.* His power is an everlasting power that shall not be taken away: and His kingdom shall not be destroyed. Alleluia. ℣. *Apoc. 19, 16.* He has on His garment, and on His thigh a name written, "King of kings, and Lord of lords." Alleluia.

PRAYER BEFORE THE GOSPEL

Bowing down at the center of the altar, he says:

CLEANSE my heart and my lips, O almighty God, Who cleansed the lips of the Prophet Isaias with a burning coal. In Your gracious mercy deign so to purify me that I may worthily proclaim Your holy Gospel. Through Christ our Lord. Amen. Lord, grant Your blessing. The Lord be in my heart and on my lips, that I may worthily and fittingly proclaim His holy Gospel. Amen.

THE GOSPEL • John 18, 33-37

Going to the left (Gospel) side of the altar, he says:

P. The Lord be with you. *S.* And with your spirit.
P. ✠ The continuation of the holy Gospel according to Saint John. *S.* Glory be to You, O Lord.

AT THAT time, Pilate said to Jesus, "Are You the King of the Jews?" Jesus answered, "Do you say this of yourself, or have others told you of

Me?" Pilate answered, "Am I a Jew? Your own people and the chief priests have delivered You to me. What have You done?" Jesus answered, "My kingdom is not of this world. If My kingdom were of this world, My followers would certainly have fought that I might not be delivered to the Jews. But, as it is, My kingdom is not from here." Pilate therefore said to Him, "You are then a King?" Jesus answered, "You say it; I am a King. This is why I was born, and why I have come into the world, to bear witness to the truth. Everyone who is of the truth hears My voice." S. Praise be to You, O Christ.

P. By the words of the Gospel, may our sins be taken away.

THE NICENE CREED

At the center of the altar, he says:

I BELIEVE in one God, the Father almighty, Maker of heaven and earth, and of all things visible and invisible. And in one Lord Jesus Christ, the Only-begotten Son of God. Born of the Father before all ages. God of God; Light of Light; true God of true God. Begotten not made; of one being with the Father; by Whom all things were made. Who for us men, and for our salvation, came down from heaven. (*Here all genuflect.*) And was made Flesh by the Holy Spirit of the Virgin Mary: AND WAS MADE MAN. He was also crucified for us, suffered under Pontius Pilate and was buried. And on the third day He rose again according to the Scriptures. And ascending into heaven, He sits at the right hand of the Father. And He shall come again in glory to judge the living and the dead; and of His kingdom there shall be no end. And I believe in the Holy Spirit, Lord and

Giver of life, Who proceeds from the Father and the Son. Who together with the Father and the Son is no less adored, and glorified: Who spoke by the Prophets. And I believe in One, Holy, Catholic and Apostolic Church. I confess one Baptism for the remission of sins. And I look for the resurrection of the dead. ✠ And the life of the world to come. Amen.

THE OFFERTORY

The Priest turns to the people and says:

P. The Lord be with you. *S.* And with your spirit.
P. Let us pray.

THE OFFERTORY VERSE • Ps. 2, 8

ASK of Me and I will give You the nations for an inheritance and the ends of the earth for Your possession. (*P.T.* Alleluia.)

The Priest now uncovers the chalice, places the host on the paten and offering it up, says:

ACCEPT, O holy Father, almighty and eternal God, this spotless host, which I, Your unworthy servant, offer to You, my living and true God, to atone for my numberless sins, offenses, and negligences; on behalf of all here present and likewise for all faithful Christians living and dead, that it may profit me and them as a means of salvation to life everlasting. Amen.

He pours wine and water into the chalice, blessing the water before it is poured.

O GOD, Who established the nature of man in wondrous dignity, and still more admirably restored it, grant that through the mystery of this water and wine, we may be made partakers of His Divinity, Who has condescended to become par-

taker of our humanity, Jesus Christ, Your Son, our Lord. Who lives and reigns with You in the unity of the Holy Spirit, God, world without end. Amen.

Offering up the wine, the Priest says:

WE OFFER You, O Lord, the chalice of salvation, humbly begging of Your mercy that it may arise before Your Divine Majesty, with a pleasing fragrance, for our salvation and for that of the whole world. Amen.

Bowing down, the Priest says:

IN A humble spirit and with a contrite heart, may we be accepted by You, O Lord, and may our sacrifice so be offered in Your sight this day as to please You, O Lord God.

Raising his eyes and blessing the offering, he says:

COME, O Sanctifier, almighty and eternal God, and bless ✠ this sacrifice prepared for the glory of Your holy name.

WASHING THE FINGERS

I WASH my hands in innocence, and I go around Your altar, O Lord, giving voice to my thanks, and recounting all Your wondrous deeds. O Lord, I love the house in which You dwell, the tenting-place of Your glory. Gather not my soul with those of sinners, nor with men of blood my life. On their hands are crimes, and their right hands are full of bribes. But I walk in integrity; redeem me, and have pity on me. My foot stands on level ground; in the assemblies I will bless You, O Lord. Glory be to the Father, and to the Son, and to the Holy Spirit. As it was in the beginning, is now, and ever shall be, world without end. Amen.

ACCEPT, Most Holy Trinity, this offering which we are making to You in remembrance of the Passion, Resurrection, and Ascension of Jesus Christ, our Lord; and in honor of Blessed Mary, ever Virgin, Blessed John the Baptist, the Holy Apostles Peter and Paul, and of these, and of all the Saints; that it may add to their honor and aid our salvation; and may they deign to intercede in heaven for us who honor their memory here on earth. Through the same Christ our Lord. Amen.

The Priest turns toward the people and says:

Pray, brethren, that my sacrifice and yours may become acceptable to God the Father almighty.
S. May the Lord accept this sacrifice from your hands to the praise and glory of His name, for our advantage, and that of all His holy Church.
P. Amen.

THE SECRET

O LORD, we offer You the Victim of man's reconciliation; grant, we beseech You, that He Whom we immolate by these present sacrifices, may bestow on all nations, the gifts of unity and peace, Jesus Christ, Your Son, our Lord. Who with You lives and reigns in the unity of the Holy Spirit, God.
P. World without end. *S.* Amen.

PREFACE—CANON

P. The Lord be with you. *S.* And with your spirit.
P. Lift up your hearts.
S. We have lifted them up to the Lord.
P. Let us give thanks to the Lord, our God.
S. It is fitting and just.

IT IS fitting indeed and just, right and helpful to salvation, for us always and everywhere to give thanks to You, O holy Lord, Father almighty and everlasting God. Who with the oil of gladness have anointed Your Only-begotten Son, our Lord Jesus Christ, as eternal High Priest and universal King; that offering Himself on the altar of the Cross as an immaculate and peaceful oblation, He might complete the pledges of human redemption; and all creation being made subject to His dominion, He might deliver into the hands of Your infinite Majesty an eternal and universal kingdom: a kingdom of truth and life, a kingdom of holiness and grace, a kingdom of justice, love and peace. And therefore with Angels and Archangels, with Thrones and Dominations, and with the whole host of the heavenly army, we sing a hymn to Your glory, saying again and again (*the bell is rung 3 times*):

HOLY, HOLY, HOLY, Lord God of Hosts. Heaven and earth are filled with Your glory. Hosanna in the highest. ✠ Blessed is He Who comes in the name of the Lord. Hosanna in the highest.

THE CANON OF THE MASS

THEREFORE, most gracious Father, we humbly beg of You and entreat You through Jesus Christ Your Son, our Lord, (*he kisses the altar*) to deem acceptable and bless these ✠ gifts, these ✠ offerings, these ✠ holy and unspotted oblations which, in the first place, we offer You for Your Holy Catholic Church, that You would deign to give her peace and protection, to unite and guard her throughout the world, together with Your serv-

ant N., our Pope, and N., our Bishop; and all true believers who cherish the Catholic and Apostolic Faith.

Commemoration of the Living

REMEMBER, O Lord, Your servants and handmaids, N. and N., (*name them*) and all here present, whose faith and devotion are known to You, on whose behalf we offer to You, or who themselves offer to You, this sacrifice of praise for themselves, families and friends, for the good of their souls, for their hope of salvation and deliverance from all harm, and who offer their homage to You, eternal, living and true God.

Commemoration of the Saints

IN THE unity of holy fellowship we observe the memory, first of all, of the glorious and ever Virgin Mary, Mother of our Lord and God Jesus Christ; next, that of Your Blessed Apostles and Martyrs, Peter and Paul, Andrew, James, John, Thomas, James, Philip, Bartholomew, Matthew, Simon and Thaddeus; of Linus, Cletus, Clement, Sixtus, Cornelius, Cyprian, Lawrence, Chrysogonus, John and Paul, Cosmas and Damian, and of all Your Saints, by whose merits and prayers grant that we may be always fortified by the help of Your protection. Through the same Christ our Lord. Amen.

Spreading his hands over the oblation, he says:

GRACIOUSLY accept, then, we beseech You, O Lord, this service of our worship and that of all Your household. Provide that our days be spent in Your peace, save us from everlasting damnation, and cause us to be numbered in the flock You have chosen. Through Christ our Lord. Amen.

O GOD, deign to bless ✠ what we offer, and make it approved, ✠ effective, ✠ right, and wholly pleasing in every way, that it may become for our good, the Body ✠ and Blood ✠ of Your dearly beloved Son, Jesus Christ our Lord.

CONSECRATION—ELEVATION

WHO, the day before He suffered, took bread into His holy and venerable hands, and having raised His eyes to heaven, to You, O God, His almighty Father, giving thanks to You, He blessed it, ✠ broke it, and gave it to His disciples, saying: All of you take and eat of this:

FOR THIS IS MY BODY.

IN LIKE manner, when the supper was done, taking also this goodly chalice into His holy and venerable hands, again giving thanks to You, He blessed ✠ it, and gave it to His disciples, saying: All of you take and drink of this:

FOR THIS IS THE CHALICE OF MY BLOOD OF THE NEW AND ETERNAL COVENANT: THE MYSTERY OF FAITH: WHICH SHALL BE SHED FOR YOU AND FOR MANY UNTO THE FORGIVENESS OF SINS.

After replacing the chalice on the corporal, he says:

As often as you shall do these things, in memory of Me shall you do them.

Offering of the Victim

MINDFUL, therefore, O Lord, not only of the blessed Passion of the same Christ, Your Son, our Lord, but also of His Resurrection from the dead, and finally His glorious Ascension into heav-

en, we, Your ministers, as also Your holy people, offer to Your supreme Majesty, of the gifts bestowed upon us, the pure ✠ Victim, the holy ✠ Victim, the all-perfect ✠ Victim: the holy ✠ Bread of life eternal and the Chalice ✠ of unending salvation.

AND this deign to regard with gracious and kindly attention and hold acceptable, as You deigned to accept the offerings of Abel, Your just servant, and the sacrifice of Abraham our patriarch, and that which Your chief priest Melchisedec offered to You, a holy sacrifice and a spotless victim.

MOST humbly we implore You, almighty God, bid these offerings to be brought by the hands of Your holy angel to Your altar above; before the face of Your Divine Majesty; that those of us who, by sharing in the Sacrifice of this altar, shall receive the Most Sacred ✠ Body and ✠ Blood of Your Son, may be filled with every grace and heavenly blessing. Through the same Christ our Lord. Amen.

Commemoration of the Dead

REMEMBER also, O Lord, Your servants and handmaids, N. and N., who have gone before us with the sign of faith, and rest in the sleep of peace. (*Here pray for the dead.*) To these, O Lord, and to all who rest in Christ, we beseech You to grant of Your goodness, a place of comfort, light and peace. Through the same Christ our Lord. Amen.

TO US sinners also, Your servants, trusting in the greatness of Your mercy, deign to grant some part and fellowship with Your Holy Apostles and Martyrs: with John, Stephen, Matthias, Barnabas,

Ignatius, Alexander, Marcellinus, Peter, Felicitas, Perpetua, Agatha, Lucy, Agnes, Cecilia, Anastasia, and all Your Saints; into whose company, we implore You to admit us, not weighing our merits, but freely granting us pardon. Through Christ our Lord.

THROUGH Whom, O Lord, You always create, ✠ sanctify, ✠ fill with life, ✠ bless, and bestow upon us all good things.

The Minor Elevation

THROUGH ✠ Him, and with ✠ Him, and in ✠ Him, is to You, God the Father ✠ almighty, in the unity of the Holy ✠ Spirit, all honor and glory, world without end. S. Amen.

THE COMMUNION AND THANKSGIVING

Let us pray. Prompted by saving precepts, and taught by Your divine teaching, we dare to say:

OUR FATHER, Who art in heaven, hallowed be Thy name: Thy kingdom come: Thy will be done on earth as it is in heaven. Give us this day our daily bread; and forgive us our trespasses, as we forgive those who trespass against us. And lead us not into temptation: S. But deliver us from evil. *P.* Amen.

DELIVER us, we beseech You, O Lord, from all evils, past, present, and to come; and by the intercession of the Blessed and glorious Mary, ever Virgin, Mother of God, together with Your Blessed Apostles Peter and Paul, and Andrew, and all the Saints, grant of Your goodness, peace in our days, that aided by the riches of Your mercy, we

may be always free from sin and safe from all disturbance.

Through the same our Lord Jesus Christ, Your Son, Who lives and reigns with You in the unity of the Holy Spirit, God, world without end.

S. Amen.

P. May the peace ✠ of the Lord be ✠ always with ✠ you.

S. And with your spirit.

The Priest puts a small particle into the chalice, saying:

May this mingling and consecration of the Body and Blood of our Lord Jesus Christ help us who receive it to life everlasting. Amen.

LAMB of God, You Who take away the sins of the world, have mercy on us.

Lamb of God, You Who take away the sins of the world, have mercy on us.

Lamb of God, You Who take away the sins of the world, grant us peace.

PRAYERS BEFORE HOLY COMMUNION

Then inclining toward the altar, he says:

O LORD Jesus Christ, Who said to Your Apostles: "Peace I leave with you, My peace I give to you," regard not my sins but the faith of Your Church, and deign to give her peace and unity according to Your Will: Who live and reign, God, world without end. Amen.

O LORD Jesus Christ, Son of the living God, Who, by the will of the Father, with the cooperation of the Holy Spirit, have by Your death given life to the world, deliver me by this Your

Most Sacred Body and Blood from all my sins and from every evil. Make me always cling to Your commandments, and never permit me to be separated from You. Who with the same God the Father and the Holy Spirit, live and reign, God, world without end. Amen.

LET not the partaking of Your Body, O Lord Jesus Christ, which I, though unworthy, presume to receive, turn to my judgment and condemnation; but through Your goodness, may it become a safeguard and an effective remedy, both of soul and body. Who live and reign with God the Father, in the unity of the Holy Spirit, God, world without end. Amen.

COMMUNION OF THE PRIEST

I WILL take the Bread of heaven, and call upon the name of the Lord.

Lord, I am not worthy that You should come under my roof; but only say the word, and my soul will be healed. (3 *times.*)

Making the Sign of the Cross with the Host, he says:

MAY the Body of our Lord Jesus Christ preserve my soul to life everlasting. Amen.

What return shall I make to the Lord for all He has given me? I will take the Chalice of salvation, and I will call upon the name of the Lord. Praising will I call upon the Lord and I shall be saved from my enemies.

Making the Sign of the Cross with the chalice, he says:

MAY the Blood of our Lord Jesus Christ preserve my soul to life everlasting. Amen.

The Priest reverently consumes the Precious Blood.

COMMUNION OF THE FAITHFUL

The Server and people say the "Confiteor."

P. May almighty God have mercy on you, forgive you your sins, and bring you to life everlasting. *S.* Amen.

P. May the almighty and merciful Lord grant you pardon, ✠ absolution and remission of your sins. *S.* Amen.

Holding up a Sacred Host, the Priest says:

Behold the Lamb of God, behold Him Who takes away the sins of the world.

Lord, I am not worthy that You should come under my roof; but only say the word, and my soul will be healed. (3 *times.*)

The Priest says to each communicant:

May the Body of our Lord Jesus Christ preserve your soul to life everlasting. Amen.

The Priest purifies the chalice with wine, saying:

WHAT has passed our lips as food, O Lord, may we possess in purity of heart, that what is given to us in time, be our healing for eternity.

He purifies his fingers with wine and water, saying:

MAY Your Body, O Lord, which I have eaten, and Your Blood which I have drunk, cleave to my very soul, and grant that no trace of sin be found in me, whom these pure and holy mysteries have renewed. Who live and reign, world without end. Amen.

THE COMMUNION • Ps. 28, 10. 11

THE Lord is enthroned as King forever; may the Lord bless His people with peace! (*P.T.* Alleluia.)

The Priest, turning to the people, says:

P. The Lord be with you. *S.* And with your spirit.
P. Let us pray.

THE POSTCOMMUNION

HAVING received the food of immortality, we beseech You, O Lord, that we who glory in our warfare under the banners of Christ our King, may reign with Him forever in His heavenly dwelling place. Who with You lives and reigns in the unity of the Holy Spirit, God, world without end.
S. Amen.

FINAL PRAYERS

The Priest turns again to the people, and says:

P. The Lord be with you. *S.* And with your spirit.
P. Go, you are dismissed. *S.* Thanks be to God.

MAY the tribute of my worship be pleasing to You, Most Holy Trinity, and grant that the sacrifice which I, all unworthy, have offered in the presence of Your Majesty, may be acceptable to You, and through Your mercy obtain forgiveness for me and all for whom I have offered it. Through Christ our Lord. Amen.

THE LAST BLESSING

He kisses the altar, and facing the people, says:

MAY almighty God bless you: ✠ the Father, and the Son, and the Holy Spirit.
S. Amen.

The Last Gospel and Prayers after Low Mass are conveniently placed inside the back cover.

"Forgive your brothers from your hearts."

TWENTY-FIRST SUNDAY AFTER PENTECOST

Those do not forgive who nourish hatred in their hearts, think only of revenge, and never forget an offense. They act like the "wicked servant." "Blessed are the merciful: for they shall obtain mercy" from their heavenly Father. (GREEN VESTMENTS)

PRAYERS AT THE FOOT OF THE ALTAR

IN THE name of the Father, ✠ and of the Son, and of the Holy Spirit. Amen.

Priest. I will go in to the altar of God.

Server. The God of my gladness and joy.

Psalm 42

DO ME justice, O God, and fight my fight against a faithless people; from the deceitful and impious man rescue me.

S. For You, O God, are my strength. Why do You keep me so far away? Why must I go about in mourning, with the enemy oppressing me?

P. Send forth Your light and Your fidelity; they shall lead me on and bring me to Your holy mountain, to Your dwelling-place.

S. Then will I go in to the altar of God, the God of my gladness and joy.
P. Then will I give You thanks upon the harp, O God, my God. Why are you so downcast, O my soul? Why do you sigh within me?
S. Hope in God! For I shall again be thanking Him in the presence of my Savior and my God.
P. Glory be to the Father, and to the Son, and to the Holy Spirit.
S. As it was in the beginning, is now, and ever shall be, world without end. Amen.
P. I will go in to the altar of God.
S. The God of my gladness and joy.
P. Our help ✠ is in the name of the Lord.
S. Who made heaven and earth.
P. I confess to almighty God, etc.
S. May almighty God have mercy on you, forgive you your sins, and bring you to life everlasting.
P. Amen.

The Server, bowing, says the "Confiteor."

I CONFESS to almighty God, to Blessed Mary, ever Virgin, to Blessed Michael the Archangel, to Blessed John the Baptist, to the Holy Apostles Peter and Paul, and to all the Saints, and to you, Father, that I have sinned exceedingly in thought, word and deed, *through my fault, through my fault, through my most grievous fault.* Therefore I beseech Blessed Mary, ever Virgin, Blessed Michael the Archangel, Blessed John the Baptist, the Holy Apostles Peter and Paul, and all the Saints, and you, Father, to pray to the Lord our God for me.
P. May almighty God have mercy on you, forgive you your sins, and bring you to life everlasting.
S. Amen.

MAY the almighty and merciful Lord grant us pardon, ✠ absolution, and remission of our sins. *S.* Amen.

P. Will You not, O God, give us life?
S. And shall not Your people rejoice in You?
P. Show us, O Lord, Your kindness.
S. And grant us Your salvation.
P. O Lord, hear my prayer.
S. And let my cry come to You.
P. The Lord be with you.
S. And with your spirit. *P.* Let us pray.

Going up to the altar, the Priest prays silently:

TAKE away from us our sins, O Lord, we beseech You, that we may enter with pure minds into the Holy of Holies. Through Christ our Lord. Amen.

WE BESEECH You, O Lord, by the merits of Your Saints (*he kisses the altar*) whose relics lie here, and of all the Saints: deign in Your mercy to pardon me all my sins. Amen.

THE INTROIT • Esther 13, 9. 10. 11

At the right side of the altar, the Priest says:

IN YOUR will are all things, O Lord, and there is none that can resist Your will; for You have made all things, heaven and earth, and all things that are under the cope of heaven. You are Lord of all. *Ps. 118.* Happy are they whose way is blameless, who walk in the law of the Lord. Glory be to the Father, and to the Son, and to the Holy Spirit. As it was in the beginning, is now, and ever shall be, world without end. Amen. — In Your will are all things, O Lord, and there is none that can resist Your will; for You have made all things, heaven and earth, and all things that are under the cope of heaven. You are Lord of all.

THE KYRIE

P. Lord, have mercy. *S*. Lord, have mercy. *P*. Lord, have mercy. *S*. Christ, have mercy. *P*. Christ, have mercy. *S*. Christ, have mercy. *P*. Lord, have mercy. *S*. Lord, have mercy. *P*. Lord, have mercy.

THE GLORIA

GLORY to God in the highest. And on earth peace to men of good will. We praise You. We bless You. We adore You. We glorify You. We give You thanks for Your great glory. O Lord God, heavenly King, God the Father almighty. O Lord Jesus Christ, the Only-begotten Son. O Lord God, Lamb of God, Son of the Father: You Who take away the sins of the world, have mercy on us. You Who take away the sins of the world, receive our prayer. You Who sit at the right hand of the Father, have mercy on us. For You alone are holy. You alone are the Lord. You alone, O Jesus Christ, are most high. Together with the Holy Spirit ✠ in the glory of God the Father. Amen.

The Priest kisses the altar and turns to the people, saying:

P. The Lord be with you. *S*. And with your spirit. *P*. Let us pray.

THE PRAYER

Going to the right (Epistle) side, he says:

GUARD Your household, we beseech You, O Lord, with continued goodness; that, through Your protection, it may be free from all adversities, and by good works be devoted to Your name. Through our Lord Jesus Christ, Your Son, Who lives and reigns with You in the unity of the Holy Spirit, God, world without end. S. Amen.

THE EPISTLE • Eph. 6, 10-17

BRETHREN: Be strengthened in the Lord and in the might of His power. Put on the armor of God, that you may be able to stand against the wiles of the devil. For our wrestling is not against flesh and blood, but against the Principalities and the Powers, against the world rulers of this darkness, against the spiritual forces of wickedness on high. Therefore, take up the armor of God, that you may be able to resist in the evil day, and stand in all things perfect. Stand, therefore, having girded your loins with truth, and having put on the breastplate of justice, and having your feet shod with the readiness of the Gospel of peace, in all things taking up the shield of faith, with which you may be able to quench all the fiery darts of the most wicked one. And take unto you the helmet of salvation and the sword of the spirit, that is, the word of God. S. Thanks be to God.

THE GRADUAL • Ps. 89, 1-2

O LORD, You have been our refuge through all generations. ℣. Before the mountains were begotten and the earth and the world were brought forth, from everlasting to everlasting You are God.

Alleluia, alleluia. ℣. *Ps. 113, 1.* When Israel came forth from Egypt, the house of Jacob from a people of alien tongue. Alleluia.

PRAYER BEFORE THE GOSPEL

Bowing down at the center of the altar, he says:

CLEANSE my heart and my lips, O almighty God, Who cleansed the lips of the Prophet

Isaias with a burning coal. In Your gracious mercy deign so to purify me that I may worthily proclaim Your holy Gospel. Through Christ our Lord. Amen.

Lord, grant Your blessing. The Lord be in my heart and on my lips, that I may worthily and fittingly proclaim His holy Gospel. Amen.

THE GOSPEL • Matt. 18, 23-35

Going to the left (Gospel) side of the altar, he says:

P. The Lord be with you. *S.* And with your spirit.
P. ✠ The continuation of the holy Gospel according to Saint Matthew. *S.* Glory be to You, O Lord.

AT THAT time, Jesus spoke to His disciples this parable: "The kingdom of heaven is likened to a king who desired to settle accounts with his servants. And when he had begun the settlement, one was brought to him who owed him ten thousand talents. And as he had no means of paying, his master ordered him to be sold, with his wife and children and all that he had, and payment to be made. But the servant fell down and besought him, saying, 'Have patience with me and I will pay you all!' And moved with compassion, the master of that servant released him, and forgave him the debt. But as that servant went out, he met one of his fellow-servants who owed him a hundred denarii, and he laid hold of him and throttled him, saying, 'Pay what you owe.' His fellow-servant therefore fell down and began to entreat him, saying, 'Have patience with me and I will pay you all.' But he would not; but went away and cast him into prison until he should pay what was due. His fellow-servants therefore, seeing what had happened, were very much saddened, and they went and informed their master of what had happened. Then his master called him, and said to him, 'Wicked servant! I forgave you all the debt, because you entreated me. Should not you also have had pity on your fellow-servant, even as I had pity on you?' And his master, being angry, handed him over to the torturers until he should pay all that was due to him. So also My heavenly Father will do to you, if you do not each forgive your brothers from your hearts." S. Praise be to You, O Christ. *P.* By the words of the Gospel, may our sins be taken away.

THE NICENE CREED

At the center of the altar, he says:

I BELIEVE in one God, the Father almighty, Maker of heaven and earth, and of all things visible and invisible. And in one Lord Jesus Christ, the Only-begotten Son of God. Born of the Father before all ages. God of God; Light of Light; true God of true God. Begotten not made; of one being with the Father; by Whom all things were made. Who for us men, and for our salvation, came down from heaven. (*Here all genuflect.*) And was made Flesh by the Holy Spirit of the Virgin Mary: AND WAS MADE MAN. He was also crucified for us, suffered under Pontius Pilate and was buried. And on the third day He rose again according to the Scriptures. And ascending into heaven, He sits at the right hand of the Father. And He shall come again in glory to judge the living and the dead; and of His kingdom there shall be no end. And I believe in the Holy Spirit, Lord and Giver of life, Who proceeds from the Father and the Son. Who together with the Father and the

Son is no less adored, and glorified: Who spoke by the Prophets. And I believe in One, Holy, Catholic and Apostolic Church. I confess one Baptism for the remission of sins. And I look for the resurrection of the dead. ✠ And the life of the world to come. Amen.

THE OFFERTORY

The Priest turns to the people and says:

P. The Lord be with you. *S.* And with your spirit.
P. Let us pray.

THE OFFERTORY VERSE • Job 1

THERE was a man in the land of Hus, whose name was Job, simple, and upright, and fearing God, whom Satan besought that he might tempt: and power was given him from the Lord over his possessions and his flesh; and he destroyed all his substance and his children, and wounded his flesh also with a grievous ulcer.

The Priest now uncovers the chalice, places the host on the paten and offering it up, says:

ACCEPT, O holy Father, almighty and eternal God, this spotless host, which I, Your unworthy servant, offer to You, my living and true God, to atone for my numberless sins, offenses, and negligences; on behalf of all here present and likewise for all faithful Christians living and dead, that it may profit me and them as a means of salvation to life everlasting. Amen.

He pours wine and water into the chalice, blessing the water before it is poured.

O GOD, Who established the nature of man in wondrous dignity, and still more admirably restored it, grant that through the mystery of this water and wine, we may be made partakers of His Divinity, Who has condescended to become partaker of our humanity, Jesus Christ, Your Son, our Lord. Who lives and reigns with You in the unity of the Holy Spirit, God, world without end. Amen.

Offering up the wine, the Priest says:

WE OFFER You, O Lord, the chalice of salvation, humbly begging of Your mercy that it may arise before Your Divine Majesty, with a pleasing fragrance, for our salvation and for that of the whole world. Amen.

Bowing down, the Priest says:

IN A humble spirit and with a contrite heart, may we be accepted by You, O Lord, and may our sacrifice so be offered in Your sight this day as to please You, O Lord God.

Raising his eyes and blessing the offering, he says:

COME, O Sanctifier, almighty and eternal God, and bless ✠ this sacrifice prepared for the glory of Your holy name.

WASHING THE FINGERS

I WASH my hands in innocence, and I go around Your altar, O Lord, giving voice to my thanks, and recounting all Your wondrous deeds. O Lord, I love the house in which You dwell, the tenting-place of Your glory. Gather not my soul with those of sinners, nor with men of blood my life. On their hands are crimes, and their right hands are full of bribes. But I walk in integrity; redeem me, and have pity on me. My foot stands on level ground; in the assemblies I will bless You, O Lord. Glory be to the Father, and to the Son, and to the Holy

Spirit. As it was in the beginning, is now, and ever shall be, world without end. Amen.

ACCEPT, Most Holy Trinity, this offering which we are making to You in remembrance of the Passion, Resurrection, and Ascension of Jesus Christ, our Lord; and in honor of Blessed Mary, ever Virgin, Blessed John the Baptist, the Holy Apostles Peter and Paul, and of these, and of all the Saints; that it may add to their honor and aid our salvation; and may they deign to intercede in heaven for us who honor their memory here on earth. Through the same Christ our Lord. Amen.

The Priest turns toward the people and says:

Pray, brethren, that my sacrifice and yours may become acceptable to God the Father almighty.

S. May the Lord accept this sacrifice from your hands to the praise and glory of His name, for our advantage, and that of all His holy Church.

P. Amen.

THE SECRET

MERCIFULLY receive, O Lord, this sacrifice, by which You have been pleased to be pacified and to restore salvation to us by Your powerful mercy. Through our Lord Jesus Christ, Your Son, Who lives and reigns with You in the unity of the Holy Spirit, God.

P. World without end. *S.* Amen.

PREFACE—CANON

P. The Lord be with you. *S.* And with your spirit.

P. Lift up your hearts.

S. We have lifted them up to the Lord.

P. Let us give thanks to the Lord, our God.

S. It is fitting and just.

IT IS fitting indeed and just, right and helpful to salvation, for us always and everywhere to give thanks to You, O holy Lord, Father almighty, everlasting God, Who with Your Only-begotten Son and the Holy Spirit are one God, one Lord; not in the unity of a single person, but in the trinity of a single nature. For that which we believe on Your revelation concerning Your glory, that same we believe of Your Son, that same of the Holy Spirit, without difference or discrimination. So that in confessing the true and everlasting Godhead, we shall adore distinction in Persons, oneness in being, and equality in Majesty. This the Angels and Archangels, the Cherubim, too, and the Seraphim do praise; day by day they cease not to cry out as with one voice, saying (*the bell is rung 3 times*):

HOLY, HOLY, HOLY, Lord God of Hosts. Heaven and earth are filled with Your glory. Hosanna in the highest. ✠ Blessed is He Who comes in the name of the Lord. Hosanna in the highest.

THE CANON OF THE MASS

THEREFORE, most gracious Father, we humbly beg of You and entreat You through Jesus Christ Your Son, our Lord, (*he kisses the altar*) to deem acceptable and bless these ✠ gifts, these ✠ offerings, these ✠ holy and unspotted oblations which, in the first place, we offer You for Your Holy Catholic Church, that You would deign to give her peace and protection, to unite and guard her throughout the world, together with Your servant N., our Pope, and N., our Bishop; and all true believers who cherish the Catholic and Apostolic Faith.

Commemoration of the Living

REMEMBER, O Lord, Your servants and handmaids, N. and N., (*name them*) and all here present, whose faith and devotion are known to You, on whose behalf we offer to You, or who themselves offer to You, this sacrifice of praise for themselves, families and friends, for the good of their souls, for their hope of salvation and deliverance from all harm, and who offer their homage to You, eternal, living and true God.

Commemoration of the Saints

IN THE unity of holy fellowship we observe the memory, first of all, of the glorious and ever Virgin Mary, Mother of our Lord and God Jesus Christ; next, that of Your Blessed Apostles and Martyrs, Peter and Paul, Andrew, James, John, Thomas, James, Philip, Bartholomew, Matthew, Simon and Thaddeus; of Linus, Cletus, Clement, Sixtus, Cornelius, Cyprian, Lawrence, Chrysogonus, John and Paul, Cosmas and Damian, and of all Your Saints, by whose merits and prayers grant that we may be always fortified by the help of Your protection. Through the same Christ our Lord. Amen.

Spreading his hands over the oblation, he says:

GRACIOUSLY accept, then, we beseech You, O Lord, this service of our worship and that of all Your household. Provide that our days be spent in Your peace, save us from everlasting damnation, and cause us to be numbered in the flock You have chosen. Through Christ our Lord. Amen.

O GOD, deign to bless ✠ what we offer, and make it approved, ✠ effective, ✠ right, and wholly pleasing in every way, that it may become for our good, the Body ✠ and Blood ✠ of Your dearly beloved Son, Jesus Christ our Lord.

CONSECRATION—ELEVATION

WHO, the day before He suffered, took bread into His holy and venerable hands, and having raised His eyes to heaven, to You, O God, His almighty Father, giving thanks to You, He blessed it, ✠ broke it, and gave it to His disciples, saying: All of you take and eat of this:

FOR THIS IS MY BODY.

IN LIKE manner, when the supper was done, taking also this goodly chalice into His holy and venerable hands, again giving thanks to You, He blessed ✠ it, and gave it to His disciples, saying: All of you take and drink of this:

FOR THIS IS THE CHALICE OF MY BLOOD OF THE NEW AND ETERNAL COVENANT: THE MYSTERY OF FAITH: WHICH SHALL BE SHED FOR YOU AND FOR MANY UNTO THE FORGIVENESS OF SINS.

After replacing the chalice on the corporal, he says:

As often as you shall do these things, in memory of Me shall you do them.

Offering of the Victim

MINDFUL, therefore, O Lord, not only of the blessed Passion of the same Christ, Your Son, our Lord, but also of His Resurrection from the dead, and finally His glorious Ascension into heav-

en, we, Your ministers, as also Your holy people, offer to Your supreme Majesty, of the gifts bestowed upon us, the pure ✠ Victim, the holy ✠ Victim, the all-perfect ✠ Victim: the holy ✠ Bread of life eternal and the Chalice ✠ of unending salvation.

AND this deign to regard with gracious and kindly attention and hold acceptable, as You deigned to accept the offerings of Abel, Your just servant, and the sacrifice of Abraham our patriarch, and that which Your chief priest Melchisedec offered to You, a holy sacrifice and a spotless victim.

MOST humbly we implore You, almighty God, bid these offerings to be brought by the hands of Your holy angel to Your altar above; before the face of Your Divine Majesty; that those of us who, by sharing in the Sacrifice of this altar, shall receive the Most Sacred ✠ Body and ✠ Blood of Your Son, may be filled with every grace and heavenly blessing. Through the same Christ our Lord. Amen.

Commemoration of the Dead

REMEMBER also, O Lord, Your servants and handmaids, N. and N., who have gone before us with the sign of faith, and rest in the sleep of peace. (*Here pray for the dead.*) To these, O Lord, and to all who rest in Christ, we beseech You to grant of Your goodness, a place of comfort, light and peace. Through the same Christ our Lord. Amen.

TO US sinners also, Your servants, trusting in the greatness of Your mercy, deign to grant some part and fellowship with Your Holy Apostles and Martyrs: with John, Stephen, Matthias, Barnabas,

Ignatius, Alexander, Marcellinus, Peter, Felicitas, Perpetua, Agatha, Lucy, Agnes, Cecilia, Anastasia, and all Your Saints; into whose company, we implore You to admit us, not weighing our merits, but freely granting us pardon. Through Christ our Lord.

THROUGH Whom, O Lord, You always create, ✠ sanctify, ✠ fill with life, ✠ bless, and bestow upon us all good things.

The Minor Elevation

THROUGH ✠ Him, and with ✠ Him, and in ✠ Him, is to You, God the Father ✠ almighty, in the unity of the Holy ✠ Spirit, all honor and glory, world without end. *S.* Amen.

THE COMMUNION AND THANKSGIVING

Let us pray. Prompted by saving precepts, and taught by Your divine teaching, we dare to say:

OUR FATHER, Who art in heaven, hallowed be Thy name: Thy kingdom come: Thy will be done on earth as it is in heaven. Give us this day our daily bread; and forgive us our trespasses, as we forgive those who trespass against us. And lead us not into temptation: *S.* But deliver us from evil. *P.* Amen.

DELIVER us, we beseech You, O Lord, from all evils, past, present, and to come; and by the intercession of the Blessed and glorious Mary, ever Virgin, Mother of God, together with Your Blessed Apostles Peter and Paul, and Andrew, and all the Saints, grant of Your goodness, peace in our days, that aided by the riches of Your mercy, we

may be always free from sin and safe from all disturbance.

Through the same our Lord Jesus Christ, Your Son, Who lives and reigns with You in the unity of the Holy Spirit, God, world without end.

S. Amen.

P. May the peace ✠ of the Lord be ✠ always with ✠ you.

S. And with your spirit.

The Priest puts a small particle into the chalice, saying:

May this mingling and consecration of the Body and Blood of our Lord Jesus Christ help us who receive it to life everlasting. Amen.

LAMB of God, You Who take away the sins of the world, have mercy on us.

Lamb of God, You Who take away the sins of the world, have mercy on us.

Lamb of God, You Who take away the sins of the world, grant us peace.

PRAYERS BEFORE HOLY COMMUNION

Then inclining toward the altar, he says:

O LORD Jesus Christ, Who said to Your Apostles: "Peace I leave with you, My peace I give to you," regard not my sins but the faith of Your Church, and deign to give her peace and unity according to Your Will: Who live and reign, God, world without end. Amen.

O LORD Jesus Christ, Son of the living God, Who, by the will of the Father, with the cooperation of the Holy Spirit, have by Your death given life to the world, deliver me by this Your

Most Sacred Body and Blood from all my sins and from every evil. Make me always cling to Your commandments, and never permit me to be separated from You. Who with the same God the Father and the Holy Spirit, live and reign, God, world without end. Amen.

LET not the partaking of Your Body, O Lord Jesus Christ, which I, though unworthy, presume to receive, turn to my judgment and condemnation; but through Your goodness, may it become a safeguard and an effective remedy, both of soul and body. Who live and reign with God the Father, in the unity of the Holy Spirit, God, world without end. Amen.

COMMUNION OF THE PRIEST

I WILL take the Bread of heaven, and call upon the name of the Lord.

Lord, I am not worthy that You should come under my roof; but only say the word, and my soul will be healed. (3 *times.*)

Making the Sign of the Cross with the Host, he says:

MAY the Body of our Lord Jesus Christ preserve my soul to life everlasting. Amen.

What return shall I make to the Lord for all He has given me? I will take the Chalice of salvation, and I will call upon the name of the Lord. Praising will I call upon the Lord and I shall be saved from my enemies.

Making the Sign of the Cross with the chalice, he says:

MAY the Blood of our Lord Jesus Christ preserve my soul to life everlasting. Amen.

The Priest reverently consumes the Precious Blood.

COMMUNION OF THE FAITHFUL

The Server and people say the "Confiteor."

P. May almighty God have mercy on you, forgive you your sins, and bring you to life everlasting. *S.* Amen.

P. May the almighty and merciful Lord grant you pardon, ✠ absolution and remission of your sins. *S.* Amen.

Holding up a Sacred Host, the Priest says:

Behold the Lamb of God, behold Him Who takes away the sins of the world.

Lord, I am not worthy that You should come under my roof; but only say the word, and my soul will be healed. (3 *times.*)

The Priest says to each communicant:

May the Body of our Lord Jesus Christ preserve your soul to life everlasting. Amen.

The Priest purifies the chalice with wine, saying:

WHAT has passed our lips as food, O Lord, may we possess in purity of heart, that what is given to us in time, be our healing for eternity.

He purifies his fingers with wine and water, saying:

MAY Your Body, O Lord, which I have eaten, and Your Blood which I have drunk, cleave to my very soul, and grant that no trace of sin be found in me, whom these pure and holy mysteries have renewed. Who live and reign, world without end. Amen.

THE COMMUNION • Ps. 118, 81. 84. 86

MY SOUL pines for Your salvation; I hope in Your word. When will You do judgment on my persecutors? The wicked persecuted me wrongfully; help me, O Lord my God!

The Priest, turning to the people, says:

P. The Lord be with you. *S.* And with your spirit.

P. Let us pray.

THE POSTCOMMUNION

HAVING received the food of immortality, we beseech You, O Lord, that what has passed our lips, we may cherish in purity of heart. Through our Lord Jesus Christ, Your Son, Who lives and reigns with You in the unity of the Holy Spirit, God, world without end. *S.* Amen.

FINAL PRAYERS

The Priest turns again to the people, and says:

P. The Lord be with you. *S.* And with your spirit.

P. Go, you are dismissed. *S.* Thanks be to God.

MAY the tribute of my worship be pleasing to You, Most Holy Trinity, and grant that the sacrifice which I, all unworthy, have offered in the presence of Your Majesty, may be acceptable to You, and through Your mercy obtain forgiveness for me and all for whom I have offered it. Through Christ our Lord. Amen.

THE LAST BLESSING

He kisses the altar, and facing the people, says:

MAY almighty God bless you: ✠ the Father, and the Son, and the Holy Spirit.

S. Amen.

The Last Gospel and Prayers after Low Mass are conveniently placed inside the back cover.

"Render to Cæsar the things that are Cæsar's . . ."

TWENTY-SECOND SUNDAY AFTER PENTECOST

"Render to Cæsar the things that are Cæsar's and to God the things that are God's." To Civil Authority we must render taxes, honor and obedience in the temporal sphere. But to God we must render the best: adoration, thanksgiving, humble and perfect obedience to His will. (GREEN VESTMENTS)

PRAYERS AT THE FOOT OF THE ALTAR

IN THE name of the Father, ✠ and of the Son, and of the Holy Spirit. Amen.

Priest. I will go in to the altar of God.

Server. The God of my gladness and joy.

Psalm 42

DO ME justice, O God, and fight my fight against a faithless people; from the deceitful and impious man rescue me.

S. For You, O God, are my strength. Why do You keep me so far away? Why must I go about in mourning, with the enemy oppressing me?

P. Send forth Your light and Your fidelity; they shall lead me on and bring me to Your holy mountain, to Your dwelling-place.
S. Then will I go in to the altar of God, the God of my gladness and joy.
P. Then will I give You thanks upon the harp, O God, my God. Why are you so downcast, O my soul? Why do you sigh within me?
S. Hope in God! For I shall again be thanking Him in the presence of my Savior and my God.
P. Glory be to the Father, and to the Son, and to the Holy Spirit.
S. As it was in the beginning, is now, and ever shall be, world without end. Amen.
P. I will go in to the altar of God.
S. The God of my gladness and joy.
P. Our help ✠ is in the name of the Lord.
S. Who made heaven and earth.
P. I confess to almighty God, etc.
S. May almighty God have mercy on you, forgive you your sins, and bring you to life everlasting.
P. Amen.

The Server, bowing, says the "Confiteor."

I CONFESS to almighty God, to Blessed Mary, ever Virgin, to Blessed Michael the Archangel, to Blessed John the Baptist, to the Holy Apostles Peter and Paul, and to all the Saints, and to you, Father, that I have sinned exceedingly in thought, word and deed, *through my fault, through my fault, through my most grievous fault.* Therefore I beseech Blessed Mary, ever Virgin, Blessed Michael the Archangel, Blessed John the Baptist, the Holy

Apostles Peter and Paul, and all the Saints, and you, Father, to pray to the Lord our God for me.
P. May almighty God have mercy on you, forgive you your sins, and bring you to life everlasting.
S. Amen.

MAY the almighty and merciful Lord grant us pardon, ✠ absolution, and remission of our sins. *S.* Amen.
P. Will You not, O God, give us life?
S. And shall not Your people rejoice in You?
P. Show us, O Lord, Your kindness.
S. And grant us Your salvation.
P. O Lord, hear my prayer.
S. And let my cry come to You.
P. The Lord be with you.
S. And with your spirit. *P.* Let us pray.

Going up to the altar, the Priest prays silently:

TAKE away from us our sins, O Lord, we beseech You, that we may enter with pure minds into the Holy of Holies. Through Christ our Lord. Amen.

WE BESEECH You, O Lord, by the merits of Your Saints (*he kisses the altar*) whose relics lie here, and of all the Saints: deign in Your mercy to pardon me all my sins. Amen.

THE INTROIT • Ps. 129, 3. 4. 1. 2

At the right side of the altar, the Priest says:

IF YOU, O Lord, mark iniquities, Lord, who can stand? But with You is forgiveness, O God of Israel. *Ps.* Out of the depths I cry to You, O Lord; Lord, hear my voice! Glory be to the Father, and to the Son, and to the Holy Spirit. As it was in the beginning, is now, and ever shall be, world without end. Amen. — If You, O Lord, mark iniquities, Lord, who can stand? But with You is forgiveness, O God of Israel.

THE KYRIE

P. Lord, have mercy. *S.* Lord, have mercy. *P.* Lord, have mercy. *S.* Christ, have mercy. *P.* Christ, have mercy. *S.* Christ, have mercy. *P.* Lord, have mercy. *S.* Lord, have mercy. *P.* Lord, have mercy.

THE GLORIA

GLORY to God in the highest. And on earth peace to men of good will. We praise You. We bless You. We adore You. We glorify You. We give You thanks for Your great glory. O Lord God, heavenly King, God the Father almighty. O Lord Jesus Christ, the Only-begotten Son. O Lord God, Lamb of God, Son of the Father: You Who take away the sins of the world, have mercy on us. You Who take away the sins of the world, receive our prayer. You Who sit at the right hand of the Father, have mercy on us. For You alone are holy. You alone are the Lord. You alone, O Jesus Christ, are most high. Together with the Holy Spirit ✠ in the glory of God the Father. Amen.

The Priest kisses the altar and turns to the people, saying:

P. The Lord be with you. *S.* And with your spirit. *P.* Let us pray.

THE PRAYER

Going to the right (Epistle) side, he says:

O GOD, our refuge and strength, the author of all piety, give ear to the devout prayers of Your Church; and grant that what we ask with faith, we may obtain effectually. Through our Lord

Jesus Christ, Your Son, Who lives and reigns with You in the unity of the Holy Spirit, God, world without end. *S.* Amen.

THE EPISTLE • Phil. 1, 6-11

BRETHREN: We are confident in the Lord Jesus that He Who has begun a good work in you will bring it to perfection until the day of Christ Jesus. And I have the right to feel so about you all, because I have you in my heart, all of you, alike in my chains and in the defense and confirmation of the Gospel, as sharers in my joy. For God is my witness how I long for you all in the heart of Christ Jesus. And this I pray, that your charity may more and more abound in knowledge and all discernment, so that you may approve the better things, that you may be upright and without offense unto the day of Christ, filled with the fruit of justice, through Jesus Christ, to the glory and praise of God. *S.* Thanks be to God.

THE GRADUAL • Ps. 132, 1-2

BEHOLD how good it is, and how pleasant where brethren dwell as one! ℣. It is as when the precious ointment upon the head runs down over the beard, the beard of Aaron.

Alleluia, alleluia. ℣. *Ps. 113, 11.* Those who fear the Lord trust in the Lord; He is their help and their shield. Alleluia.

PRAYER BEFORE THE GOSPEL

Bowing down at the center of the altar, he says:

CLEANSE my heart and my lips, O almighty God, Who cleansed the lips of the Prophet Isaias with a burning coal. In Your gracious mercy deign so to purify me that I may worthily proclaim

Your holy Gospel. Through Christ our Lord. Amen.

Lord, grant Your blessing. The Lord be in my heart and on my lips, that I may worthily and fittingly proclaim His holy Gospel. Amen.

THE GOSPEL • Matt. 22, 15-21

Going to the left (Gospel) side of the altar, he says:

P. The Lord be with you. *S.* And with your spirit.

P. ✠ The continuation of the holy Gospel according to Saint Matthew. *S.* Glory be to You, O Lord.

AT THAT time, the Pharisees went and took counsel how they might trap Jesus in His talk. And they sent to Him their disciples with the Herodians, saying, "Master, we know that You are truthful, and that You teach the way of God in truth, and that You care naught for any man; for You do not regard the person of men. Tell us, therefore, what do You think: Is it lawful to give tribute to Cæsar, or not?" But Jesus, knowing their wickedness, said, "Why do you test Me, you hypocrites? Show Me the coin of the tribute." So they offered Him a denarius. Then Jesus said to them, "Whose are this image and the inscription?" They said to Him, "Cæsar's." Then He said to them, "Render, therefore, to Cæsar the things that are Cæsar's and to God the things that are God's."

S. Praise be to You, O Christ.

P. By the words of the Gospel, may our sins be taken away.

THE NICENE CREED

At the center of the altar, he says:

I BELIEVE in one God, the Father almighty, Maker of heaven and earth, and of all things visible and invisible. And in one Lord Jesus Christ, the Only-begotten Son of God. Born of the Father before all ages. God of God; Light of Light; true God of true God. Begotten not made; of one being with the Father; by Whom all things were made. Who for us men, and for our salvation, came down from heaven. (*Here all genuflect.*) And was made Flesh by the Holy Spirit of the Virgin Mary: AND WAS MADE MAN. He was also crucified for us, suffered under Pontius Pilate and was buried. And on the third day He rose again according to the Scriptures. And ascending into heaven, He sits at the right hand of the Father. And He shall come again in glory to judge the living and the dead; and of His kingdom there shall be no end. And I believe in the Holy Spirit, Lord and Giver of life, Who proceeds from the Father and the Son. Who together with the Father and the Son is no less adored, and glorified: Who spoke by the Prophets. And I believe in One, Holy, Catholic and Apostolic Church. I confess one Baptism for the remission of sins. And I look for the resurrection of the dead. ✠ And the life of the world to come. Amen.

THE OFFERTORY

The Priest turns to the people and says:

P. The Lord be with you. *S.* And with your spirit. *P.* Let us pray.

THE OFFERTORY VERSE • Esther 14, 12. 13

REMEMBER me, O Lord, You Who rule above all power: and give a well-ordered speech in my mouth, that my words may be pleasing in the sight of the prince.

The Priest now uncovers the chalice, places the host on the paten and offering it up, says:

ACCEPT, O holy Father, almighty and eternal God, this spotless host, which I, Your unworthy servant, offer to You, my living and true God, to atone for my numberless sins, offenses, and negligences; on behalf of all here present and likewise for all faithful Christians living and dead, that it may profit me and them as a means of salvation to life everlasting. Amen.

He pours wine and water into the chalice, blessing the water before it is poured.

O GOD, Who established the nature of man in wondrous dignity, and still more admirably restored it, grant that through the mystery of this water and wine, we may be made partakers of His Divinity, Who has condescended to become partaker of our humanity, Jesus Christ, Your Son, our Lord. Who lives and reigns with You in the unity of the Holy Spirit, God, world without end. Amen.

Offering up the wine, the Priest says:

WE OFFER You, O Lord, the chalice of salvation, humbly begging of Your mercy that it may arise before Your Divine Majesty, with a pleasing fragrance, for our salvation and for that of the whole world. Amen.

Bowing down, the Priest says:

IN A humble spirit and with a contrite heart, may we be accepted by You, O Lord, and may our sacrifice so be offered in Your sight this day as to please You, O Lord God.

Raising his eyes and blessing the offering, he says:

COME, O Sanctifier, almighty and eternal God, and bless ✠ this sacrifice prepared for the glory of Your holy name.

WASHING THE FINGERS

I WASH my hands in innocence, and I go around Your altar, O Lord, giving voice to my thanks,

and recounting all Your wondrous deeds. O Lord, I love the house in which You dwell, the tenting-place of Your glory. Gather not my soul with those of sinners, nor with men of blood my life. On their hands are crimes, and their right hands are full of bribes. But I walk in integrity; redeem me, and have pity on me. My foot stands on level ground; in the assemblies I will bless You, O Lord. Glory be to the Father, and to the Son, and to the Holy Spirit. As it was in the beginning, is now, and ever shall be, world without end. Amen.

ACCEPT, Most Holy Trinity, this offering which we are making to You in remembrance of the Passion, Resurrection, and Ascension of Jesus Christ, our Lord; and in honor of Blessed Mary, ever Virgin, Blessed John the Baptist, the Holy Apostles Peter and Paul, and of these, and of all the Saints; that it may add to their honor and aid our salvation; and may they deign to intercede in heaven for us who honor their memory here on earth. Through the same Christ our Lord. Amen.

The Priest turns toward the people and says:

Pray, brethren, that my sacrifice and yours may become acceptable to God the Father almighty.

S. May the Lord accept this sacrifice from your hands to the praise and glory of His name, for our advantage, and that of all His holy Church.

P. Amen.

THE SECRET

GRANT, O merciful God, that this salutary oblation may forever free us from our faults, and shield us from all adversities. Through our Lord Jesus Christ, Your Son, Who lives and reigns with

You in the unity of the Holy Spirit, God.
P. World without end. *S.* Amen.

PREFACE—CANON

P. The Lord be with you. *S.* And with your spirit.
P. Lift up your hearts.
S. We have lifted them up to the Lord.
P. Let us give thanks to the Lord, our God.
S. It is fitting and just.

IT IS fitting indeed and just, right and helpful to salvation, for us always and everywhere to give thanks to You, O holy Lord, Father almighty, everlasting God, Who with Your Only-begotten Son and the Holy Spirit are one God, one Lord; not in the unity of a single person, but in the trinity of a single nature. For that which we believe on Your revelation concerning Your glory, that same we believe of Your Son, that same of the Holy Spirit, without difference or discrimination. So that in confessing the true and everlasting Godhead, we shall adore distinction in Persons, oneness in being, and equality in Majesty. This the Angels and Archangels, the Cherubim, too, and the Seraphim do praise; day by day they cease not to cry out as with one voice, saying (*the bell is rung 3 times*):

HOLY, HOLY, HOLY, Lord God of Hosts. Heaven and earth are filled with Your glory. Hosanna in the highest. ✠ Blessed is He Who comes in the name of the Lord. Hosanna in the highest.

THE CANON OF THE MASS

THEREFORE, most gracious Father, we humbly beg of You and entreat You through Jesus

Christ Your Son, our Lord, (*he kisses the altar*) to deem acceptable and bless these ✠ gifts, these ✠ offerings, these ✠ holy and unspotted oblations which, in the first place, we offer You for Your Holy Catholic Church, that You would deign to give her peace and protection, to unite and guard her throughout the world, together with Your servant N., our Pope, and N., our Bishop; and all true believers who cherish the Catholic and Apostolic Faith.

Commemoration of the Living

REMEMBER, O Lord, Your servants and handmaids, N. and N., (*name them*) and all here present, whose faith and devotion are known to You, on whose behalf we offer to You, or who themselves offer to You, this sacrifice of praise for themselves, families and friends, for the good of their souls, for their hope of salvation and deliverance from all harm, and who offer their homage to You, eternal, living and true God.

Commemoration of the Saints

IN THE unity of holy fellowship we observe the memory, first of all, of the glorious and ever Virgin Mary, Mother of our Lord and God Jesus Christ; next, that of Your Blessed Apostles and Martyrs, Peter and Paul, Andrew, James, John, Thomas, James, Philip, Bartholomew, Matthew, Simon and Thaddeus; of Linus, Cletus, Clement, Sixtus, Cornelius, Cyprian, Lawrence, Chrysogonus, John and Paul, Cosmas and Damian, and of all Your Saints, by whose merits and prayers grant that we may be always fortified by the help of Your protection. Through the same Christ our Lord. Amen.

Spreading his hands over the oblation, he says:

GRACIOUSLY accept, then, we beseech You, O Lord, this service of our worship and that of all Your household. Provide that our days be spent in Your peace, save us from everlasting damnation, and cause us to be numbered in the flock You have chosen. Through Christ our Lord. Amen.

O GOD, deign to bless ✠ what we offer, and make it approved, ✠ effective, ✠ right, and wholly pleasing in every way, that it may become for our good, the Body ✠ and Blood ✠ of Your dearly beloved Son, Jesus Christ our Lord.

CONSECRATION—ELEVATION

WHO, the day before He suffered, took bread into His holy and venerable hands, and having raised His eyes to heaven, to You, O God, His almighty Father, giving thanks to You, He blessed it, ✠ broke it, and gave it to His disciples, saying: All of you take and eat of this:

FOR THIS IS MY BODY.

IN LIKE manner, when the supper was done, taking also this goodly chalice into His holy and venerable hands, again giving thanks to You, He blessed ✠ it, and gave it to His disciples, saying: All of you take and drink of this:

FOR THIS IS THE CHALICE OF MY BLOOD OF THE NEW AND ETERNAL COVENANT: THE MYSTERY OF FAITH: WHICH SHALL BE SHED FOR YOU AND FOR MANY UNTO THE FORGIVENESS OF SINS.

After replacing the chalice on the corporal, he says:

As often as you shall do these things, in memory of Me shall you do them.

Offering of the Victim

MINDFUL, therefore, O Lord, not only of the blessed Passion of the same Christ, Your Son, our Lord, but also of His Resurrection from the dead, and finally His glorious Ascension into heaven, we, Your ministers, as also Your holy people, offer to Your supreme Majesty, of the gifts bestowed upon us, the pure ✠ Victim, the holy ✠ Victim, the all-perfect ✠ Victim: the holy ✠ Bread of life eternal and the Chalice ✠ of unending salvation.

AND this deign to regard with gracious and kindly attention and hold acceptable, as You deigned to accept the offerings of Abel, Your just servant, and the sacrifice of Abraham our patriarch, and that which Your chief priest Melchisedec offered to You, a holy sacrifice and a spotless victim.

MOST humbly we implore You, almighty God, bid these offerings to be brought by the hands of Your holy angel to Your altar above; before the face of Your Divine Majesty; that those of us who, by sharing in the Sacrifice of this altar, shall receive the Most Sacred ✠ Body and ✠ Blood of Your Son, may be filled with every grace and heavenly blessing. Through the same Christ our Lord. Amen.

Commemoration of the Dead

REMEMBER also, O Lord, Your servants and handmaids, N. and N., who have gone before us with the sign of faith, and rest in the sleep of peace. (*Here pray for the dead.*) To these, O Lord, and to all who rest in Christ, we beseech You to grant of Your goodness, a place of comfort, light

and peace. Through the same Christ our Lord. Amen.

TO US sinners also, Your servants, trusting in the greatness of Your mercy, deign to grant some part and fellowship with Your Holy Apostles and Martyrs: with John, Stephen, Matthias, Barnabas, Ignatius, Alexander, Marcellinus, Peter, Felicitas, Perpetua, Agatha, Lucy, Agnes, Cecilia, Anastasia, and all Your Saints; into whose company, we implore You to admit us, not weighing our merits, but freely granting us pardon. Through Christ our Lord.

THROUGH Whom, O Lord, You always create, ✠ sanctify, ✠ fill with life, ✠ bless, and bestow upon us all good things.

The Minor Elevation

THROUGH ✠ Him, and with ✠ Him, and in ✠ Him, is to You, God the Father ✠ almighty, in the unity of the Holy ✠ Spirit, all honor and glory, world without end. S. Amen.

THE COMMUNION AND THANKSGIVING

Let us pray. Prompted by saving precepts, and taught by Your divine teaching, we dare to say:

OUR FATHER, Who art in heaven, hallowed be Thy name: Thy kingdom come: Thy will be done on earth as it is in heaven. Give us this day our daily bread; and forgive us our trespasses, as we forgive those who trespass against us. And lead us not into temptation: S. But deliver us from evil. *P.* Amen.

DELIVER us, we beseech You, O Lord, from all evils, past, present, and to come; and by

the intercession of the Blessed and glorious Mary, ever Virgin, Mother of God, together with Your Blessed Apostles Peter and Paul, and Andrew, and all the Saints, grant of Your goodness, peace in our days, that aided by the riches of Your mercy, we may be always free from sin and safe from all disturbance.

Through the same our Lord Jesus Christ, Your Son, Who lives and reigns with You in the unity of the Holy Spirit, God, world without end. *S.* Amen.

P. May the peace ✠ of the Lord be ✠ always with ✠ you. *S.* And with your spirit.

The Priest puts a small particle into the chalice, saying:

May this mingling and consecration of the Body and Blood of our Lord Jesus Christ help us who receive it to life everlasting. Amen.

LAMB of God, You Who take away the sins of the world, have mercy on us.

Lamb of God, You Who take away the sins of the world, have mercy on us.

Lamb of God, You Who take away the sins of the world, grant us peace.

PRAYERS BEFORE HOLY COMMUNION

Then inclining toward the altar, he says:

O LORD Jesus Christ, Who said to Your Apostles: "Peace I leave with you, My peace I give to you," regard not my sins but the faith of Your Church, and deign to give her peace and unity according to Your Will: Who live and reign, God, world without end. Amen.

O LORD Jesus Christ, Son of the living God, Who, by the will of the Father, with the cooperation of the Holy Spirit, have by Your death given life to the world, deliver me by this Your Most Sacred Body and Blood from all my sins and from every evil. Make me always cling to Your commandments, and never permit me to be separated from You. Who with the same God the Father and the Holy Spirit, live and reign, God, world without end. Amen.

LET not the partaking of Your Body, O Lord Jesus Christ, which I, though unworthy, presume to receive, turn to my judgment and condemnation; but through Your goodness, may it become a safeguard and an effective remedy, both of soul and body. Who live and reign with God the Father, in the unity of the Holy Spirit, God, world without end. Amen.

COMMUNION OF THE PRIEST

I WILL take the Bread of heaven, and call upon the name of the Lord.

Lord, I am not worthy that You should come under my roof; but only say the word, and my soul will be healed. (3 *times.*)

Making the Sign of the Cross with the Host, he says:

MAY the Body of our Lord Jesus Christ preserve my soul to life everlasting. Amen.

What return shall I make to the Lord for all He has given me? I will take the Chalice of salvation, and I will call upon the name of the Lord. Praising will I call upon the Lord and I shall be saved from my enemies.

Making the Sign of the Cross with the chalice, he says:

MAY the Blood of our Lord Jesus Christ preserve my soul to life everlasting. Amen.

The Priest reverently consumes the Precious Blood.

COMMUNION OF THE FAITHFUL

The Server and people say the "Confiteor."

P. May almighty God have mercy on you, forgive you your sins, and bring you to life everlasting. S. Amen.

P. May the almighty and merciful Lord grant you pardon, ✠ absolution and remission of your sins. S. Amen.

Holding up a Sacred Host, the Priest says:

Behold the Lamb of God, behold Him Who takes away the sins of the world.

Lord, I am not worthy that You should come under my roof; but only say the word, and my soul will be healed. (3 *times.*)

The Priest says to each communicant:

May the Body of our Lord Jesus Christ preserve your soul to life everlasting. Amen.

The Priest purifies the chalice with wine, saying:

WHAT has passed our lips as food, O Lord, may we possess in purity of heart, that what is given to us in time, be our healing for eternity.

He purifies his fingers with wine and water, saying:

MAY Your Body, O Lord, which I have eaten, and Your Blood which I have drunk, cleave to my very soul, and grant that no trace of sin be found in me, whom these pure and holy mysteries have renewed. Who live and reign, world without end. Amen.

THE COMMUNION • Ps. 16, 6

I CALL upon You, for You will answer me, O God; incline Your ear to me; hear my word.

The Priest, turning to the people, says:

P. The Lord be with you. *S.* And with your spirit.
P. Let us pray.

THE POSTCOMMUNION

WE HAVE partaken, O Lord, of the gifts of this sacred mystery, and humbly beseech You, that what You have commanded us to do in remembrance of You may profit us as an aid to our weakness. Who live and reign with God the Father, in the unity of the Holy Spirit, God, world without end. *S.* Amen.

FINAL PRAYERS

The Priest turns again to the people, and says:

P. The Lord be with you. *S.* And with your spirit.
P. Go, you are dismissed. *S.* Thanks be to God.

MAY the tribute of my worship be pleasing to You, Most Holy Trinity, and grant that the sacrifice which I, all unworthy, have offered in the presence of Your Majesty, may be acceptable to You, and through Your mercy obtain forgiveness for me and all for whom I have offered it. Through Christ our Lord. Amen.

THE LAST BLESSING

He kisses the altar, and facing the people, says:

MAY almighty God bless you: ✠ the Father, and the Son, and the Holy Spirit. *S.* Amen.

The Last Gospel and Prayers after Low Mass are conveniently placed inside the back cover.

"He went in and took her by the hand . . ."

TWENTY-THIRD SUNDAY AFTER PENTECOST

The same Jesus Who raised the maid to life again will conform our body "to the Body of His glory." Therefore, let us not walk as "enemies of the Cross" yielding to blind passions, but rather let us consider all in the light of eternity. (GREEN VESTMENTS)

If there are only twenty-three Sundays after Pentecost, the Mass of the "Last Sunday after Pentecost" is said today, page 1095.

PRAYERS AT THE FOOT OF THE ALTAR

IN THE name of the Father, ✠ and of the Son, and of the Holy Spirit. Amen.

Priest. I will go in to the altar of God.

Server. The God of my gladness and joy.

Psalm 42

DO ME justice, O God, and fight my fight against a faithless people; from the deceitful and impious man rescue me.

S. For You, O God, are my strength. Why do You keep me so far away? Why must I go about in mourning, with the enemy oppressing me?

P. Send forth Your light and Your fidelity; they shall lead me on and bring me to Your holy mountain, to Your dwelling-place.
S. Then will I go in to the altar of God, the God of my gladness and joy.
P. Then will I give You thanks upon the harp, O God, my God. Why are you so downcast, O my soul? Why do you sigh within me?
S. Hope in God! For I shall again be thanking Him in the presence of my Savior and my God.
P. Glory be to the Father, and to the Son, and to the Holy Spirit.
S. As it was in the beginning, is now, and ever shall be, world without end. Amen.
P. I will go in to the altar of God.
S. The God of my gladness and joy.
P. Our help ✠ is in the name of the Lord.
S. Who made heaven and earth.
P. I confess to almighty God, etc.
S. May almighty God have mercy on you, forgive you your sins, and bring you to life everlasting.
P. Amen.

The Server, bowing, says the "Confiteor."

I CONFESS to almighty God, to Blessed Mary, ever Virgin, to Blessed Michael the Archangel, to Blessed John the Baptist, to the Holy Apostles Peter and Paul, and to all the Saints, and to you, Father, that I have sinned exceedingly in thought, word and deed, *through my fault, through my fault, through my most grievous fault.* Therefore I beseech Blessed Mary, ever Virgin, Blessed Michael the Archangel, Blessed John the Baptist, the Holy Apostles Peter and Paul, and all the Saints, and you, Father, to pray to the Lord our God for me.

P. May almighty God have mercy on you, forgive you your sins, and bring you to life everlasting.
S. Amen.

MAY the almighty and merciful Lord grant us pardon, ✠ absolution, and remission of our sins. *S.* Amen.
P. Will You not, O God, give us life?
S. And shall not Your people rejoice in You?
P. Show us, O Lord, Your kindness.
S. And grant us Your salvation.
P. O Lord, hear my prayer.
S. And let my cry come to You.
P. The Lord be with you.
S. And with your spirit. *P.* Let us pray.

Going up to the altar, the Priest prays silently:

TAKE away from us our sins, O Lord, we beseech You, that we may enter with pure minds into the Holy of Holies. Through Christ our Lord. Amen.

WE BESEECH You, O Lord, by the merits of Your Saints (*he kisses the altar*) whose relics lie here, and of all the Saints: deign in Your mercy to pardon me all my sins. Amen.

THE INTROIT • Jer. 29, 11. 12. 14

At the right side of the altar, the Priest says:

THE Lord says: "I think thoughts of peace, and not of affliction. You shall call upon Me, and I will hear you; and I will bring back your captivity from all places." *Ps. 84.* You have favored, O Lord, Your land; You have restored the well-being of Jacob. Glory be to the Father, and to the Son, and to the Holy Spirit. As it was in the beginning, is now, and ever shall be, world without end. Amen. — The Lord says: "I think thoughts of peace, and not of affliction. You shall call upon Me, and I will hear you; and I will bring back your captivity from all places."

THE KYRIE

P. Lord, have mercy. *S.* Lord, have mercy. *P.* Lord, have mercy. *S.* Christ, have mercy. *P.* Christ, have mercy. *S.* Christ, have mercy. *P.* Lord, have mercy. *S.* Lord, have mercy. *P.* Lord, have mercy.

THE GLORIA

GLORY to God in the highest. And on earth peace to men of good will. We praise You. We bless You. We adore You. We glorify You. We give You thanks for Your great glory. O Lord God, heavenly King, God the Father almighty. O Lord Jesus Christ, the Only-begotten Son. O Lord God, Lamb of God, Son of the Father: You Who take away the sins of the world, have mercy on us. You Who take away the sins of the world, receive our prayer. You Who sit at the right hand of the Father, have mercy on us. For You alone are holy. You alone are the Lord. You alone, O Jesus Christ, are most high. Together with the Holy Spirit ✠ in the glory of God the Father. Amen.

The Priest kisses the altar and turns to the people, saying:

P. The Lord be with you. *S.* And with your spirit. *P.* Let us pray.

THE PRAYER

Going to the right (Epistle) side, he says:

ABSOLVE Your people from their offenses, we beseech You, O Lord; that through Your bountiful goodness we may be delivered from the bonds of sin, which through our frailty we have contracted. Through our Lord Jesus Christ, Your Son, Who lives and reigns with You in the unity of the Holy Spirit, God, world without end. S. Amen.

THE EPISTLE • Phil. 3, 17-21; 4, 1-3

BRETHREN: Be imitators of me, and mark those who walk after the pattern you have in us. For many walk, of whom I have told you often and now tell you even weeping, that they are enemies of the Cross of Christ. Their end is ruin, their god is the belly, their glory is in their shame, they mind the things of earth. But our citizenship is in heaven from which also we eagerly await a Savior, our Lord Jesus Christ, Who will refashion the body of our lowliness, conforming it to the body of His glory by exerting the power by which He is able also to subject all things to Himself. So then, my brethren, beloved and longed for, my joy and my crown, stand fast thus in the Lord, beloved. I entreat Evodia and I exhort Syntyche to be of one mind in the Lord. And I beseech you also, my loyal comrade, help them, for they have toiled with me in the Gospel, as have Clement and the rest of my fellow-workers whose names are in the book of life. S. Thanks be to God.

THE GRADUAL • Ps. 43, 8-9

YOU saved us, O Lord, from our foes, and those who hated us You put to shame. ℣. In God we gloried day by day; Your name we praised always.

Alleluia, alleluia. ℣. *Ps. 129, 1.* 2. Out of the depths I cry to You, O Lord; Lord hear my prayer! Alleluia.

PRAYER BEFORE THE GOSPEL

Bowing down at the center of the altar, he says:

CLEANSE my heart and my lips, O almighty God, Who cleansed the lips of the Prophet Isaias with a burning coal. In Your gracious mercy deign so to purify me that I may worthily proclaim Your holy Gospel. Through Christ our Lord. Amen.

Lord, grant Your blessing. The Lord be in my heart and on my lips, that I may worthily and fittingly proclaim His holy Gospel. Amen.

THE GOSPEL • Matt. 9, 18-26

Going to the left (Gospel) side of the altar, he says:

P. The Lord be with you. *S.* And with your spirit.

P. ✠ The continuation of the holy Gospel according to Saint Matthew. *S.* Glory be to You, O Lord.

AT THAT time, as Jesus was speaking to the crowds, behold, a ruler came up and worshipped Him, saying, "Lord, my daughter has just now died; but come and lay Your hand upon her, and she will return to life." And Jesus arose and followed him, and so did His disciples. Now a woman who for twelve years had been suffering from hemorrhage, came up behind Him and touched the tassel of His cloak, saying to herself, "If I touch but His cloak I shall be saved." But Jesus, turning and seeing her, said, "Take courage, daughter; your faith has saved you." And the woman was restored to health from that moment. And when Jesus came to the ruler's house, and saw the flute players and the crowd making a din, He said, "Begone, the girl is asleep, not dead." And they laughed Him to scorn. But when the crowd had been put out, He went in and took her by the hand; and the girl arose. And the report of this spread throughout all that district. *S.* Praise be to You, O Christ.

P. By the words of the Gospel, may our sins be taken away.

THE NICENE CREED

At the center of the altar, he says:

I BELIEVE in one God, the Father almighty, Maker of heaven and earth, and of all things visible and invisible. And in one Lord Jesus Christ, the Only-begotten Son of God. Born of the Father before all ages. God of God; Light of Light; true God of true God. Begotten not made; of one being with the Father; by Whom all things were made. Who for us men, and for our salvation, came down from heaven. (*Here all genuflect.*) And was made Flesh by the Holy Spirit of the Virgin Mary: AND WAS MADE MAN. He was also crucified for us, suffered under Pontius Pilate and was buried. And on the third day He rose again according to the Scriptures. And ascending into heaven, He sits at the right hand of the Father. And He shall come again in glory to judge the living and the dead; and of His kingdom there shall be no end. And I believe in the Holy Spirit, Lord and Giver of life, Who proceeds from the Father and the Son. Who together with the Father and the Son is no less adored, and glorified: Who spoke by the Prophets. And I believe in One, Holy, Catholic and Apostolic Church. I confess one Baptism for the remission of sins. And I look for the resurrection of the dead. ✠ And the life of the world to come. Amen.

THE OFFERTORY

The Priest turns to the people and says:

P. The Lord be with you. *S.* And with your spirit.
P. Let us pray.

THE OFFERTORY VERSE • Ps. 129, 1. 2

OUT of the depths I cry to You, O Lord; Lord, hear my prayer! Out of the depths I cry to You, O Lord.

The Priest now uncovers the chalice, places the host on the paten and offering it up, says:

ACCEPT, O holy Father, almighty and eternal God, this spotless host, which I, Your unworthy servant, offer to You, my living and true God, to atone for my numberless sins, offenses, and negligences; on behalf of all here present and likewise for all faithful Christians living and dead, that it may profit me and them as a means of salvation to life everlasting. Amen.

He pours wine and water into the chalice, blessing the water before it is poured.

O GOD, Who established the nature of man in wondrous dignity, and still more admirably restored it, grant that through the mystery of this water and wine, we may be made partakers of His Divinity, Who has condescended to become partaker of our humanity, Jesus Christ, Your Son, our Lord. Who lives and reigns with You in the unity of the Holy Spirit, God, world without end. Amen.

Offering up the wine, the Priest says:

WE OFFER You, O Lord, the chalice of salvation, humbly begging of Your mercy that it may arise before Your Divine Majesty, with a pleasing fragrance, for our salvation and for that of the whole world. Amen.

Bowing down, the Priest says:

IN A humble spirit and with a contrite heart, may we be accepted by You, O Lord, and may our sacrifice so be offered in Your sight this day as to please You, O Lord God.

Raising his eyes and blessing the offering, he says:

COME, O Sanctifier, almighty and eternal God, and bless ✠ this sacrifice prepared for the glory of Your holy name.

WASHING THE FINGERS

I WASH my hands in innocence, and I go around Your altar, O Lord, giving voice to my thanks, and recounting all Your wondrous deeds. O Lord, I love the house in which You dwell, the tenting-place of Your glory. Gather not my soul with those of sinners, nor with men of blood my life. On their hands are crimes, and their right hands are full of bribes. But I walk in integrity; redeem me, and have pity on me. My foot stands on level ground; in the assemblies I will bless You, O Lord. Glory be to the Father, and to the Son, and to the Holy Spirit. As it was in the beginning, is now, and ever shall be, world without end. Amen.

ACCEPT, Most Holy Trinity, this offering which we are making to You in remembrance of the Passion, Resurrection, and Ascension of Jesus Christ, our Lord; and in honor of Blessed Mary, ever Virgin, Blessed John the Baptist, the Holy Apostles Peter and Paul, and of these, and of all the Saints; that it may add to their honor and aid our salvation; and may they deign to intercede in heaven for us who honor their memory here on earth. Through the same Christ our Lord. Amen.

The Priest turns toward the people and says:

Pray, brethren, that my sacrifice and yours may become acceptable to God the Father almighty.

S. May the Lord accept this sacrifice from your hands to the praise and glory of His name, for our advantage, and that of all His holy Church.

P. Amen.

THE SECRET

WE OFFER You, O Lord, this sacrifice of praise as an additional act of homage; that what You granted to us without any merit of ours, You would mercifully accomplish. Through our Lord Jesus Christ, Your Son, Who lives and reigns with You in the unity of the Holy Spirit, God.
P. World without end. *S.* Amen.

PREFACE—CANON

P. The Lord be with you. *S.* And with your spirit.
P. Lift up your hearts.
S. We have lifted them up to the Lord.
P. Let us give thanks to the Lord, our God.
S. It is fitting and just.

IT IS fitting indeed and just, right and helpful to salvation, for us always and everywhere to give thanks to You, O holy Lord, Father almighty, everlasting God, Who with Your Only-begotten Son and the Holy Spirit are one God, one Lord; not in the unity of a single person, but in the trinity of a single nature. For that which we believe on Your revelation concerning Your glory, that same we believe of Your Son, that same of the Holy Spirit, without difference or discrimination. So that in confessing the true and everlasting Godhead, we shall adore distinction in Persons, oneness in being, and equality in Majesty. This the Angels and Archangels, the Cherubim, too, and the Seraphim do praise; day by day they cease not to cry out as with one voice, saying (*the bell is rung 3 times*):

HOLY, HOLY, HOLY, Lord God of Hosts. Heaven and earth are filled with Your glory. Hosanna in the highest. ✠ Blessed is He Who comes in the name of the Lord. Hosanna in the highest.

THE CANON OF THE MASS

THEREFORE, most gracious Father, we humbly beg of You and entreat You through Jesus Christ Your Son, our Lord, (*he kisses the altar*) to deem acceptable and bless these ✠ gifts, these ✠ offerings, these ✠ holy and unspotted oblations which, in the first place, we offer You for Your Holy Catholic Church, that You would deign to give her peace and protection, to unite and guard her throughout the world, together with Your servant N., our Pope, and N., our Bishop; and all true believers who cherish the Catholic and Apostolic Faith.

Commemoration of the Living

REMEMBER, O Lord, Your servants and handmaids, N. and N., (*name them*) and all here present, whose faith and devotion are known to You, on whose behalf we offer to You, or who themselves offer to You, this sacrifice of praise for themselves, families and friends, for the good of their souls, for their hope of salvation and deliverance from all harm, and who offer their homage to You, eternal, living and true God.

Commemoration of the Saints

IN THE unity of holy fellowship we observe the memory, first of all, of the glorious and ever

Virgin Mary, Mother of our Lord and God Jesus Christ; next, that of Your Blessed Apostles and Martyrs, Peter and Paul, Andrew, James, John, Thomas, James, Philip, Bartholomew, Matthew, Simon and Thaddeus; of Linus, Cletus, Clement, Sixtus, Cornelius, Cyprian, Lawrence, Chrysogonus, John and Paul, Cosmas and Damian, and of all Your Saints, by whose merits and prayers grant that we may be always fortified by the help of Your protection. Through the same Christ our Lord. Amen.

Spreading his hands over the oblation, he says:

GRACIOUSLY accept, then, we beseech You, O Lord, this service of our worship and that of all Your household. Provide that our days be spent in Your peace, save us from everlasting damnation, and cause us to be numbered in the flock You have chosen. Through Christ our Lord. Amen.

O GOD, deign to bless ✠ what we offer, and make it approved, ✠ effective, ✠ right, and wholly pleasing in every way, that it may become for our good, the Body ✠ and Blood ✠ of Your dearly beloved Son, Jesus Christ our Lord.

CONSECRATION—ELEVATION

WHO, the day before He suffered, took bread into His holy and venerable hands, and having raised His eyes to heaven, to You, O God, His almighty Father, giving thanks to You, He blessed it, ✠ broke it, and gave it to His disciples, saying: All of you take and eat of this:

FOR THIS IS MY BODY.

IN LIKE manner, when the supper was done, taking also this goodly chalice into His holy and

venerable hands, again giving thanks to You, He blessed ✠ it, and gave it to His disciples, saying: All of you take and drink of this:

FOR THIS IS THE CHALICE OF MY BLOOD OF THE NEW AND ETERNAL COVENANT: THE MYSTERY OF FAITH: WHICH SHALL BE SHED FOR YOU AND FOR MANY UNTO THE FORGIVENESS OF SINS.

After replacing the chalice on the corporal, he says:

As often as you shall do these things, in memory of Me shall you do them.

Offering of the Victim

MINDFUL, therefore, O Lord, not only of the blessed Passion of the same Christ, Your Son, our Lord, but also of His Resurrection from the dead, and finally His glorious Ascension into heaven, we, Your ministers, as also Your holy people, offer to Your supreme Majesty, of the gifts bestowed upon us, the pure ✠ Victim, the holy ✠ Victim, the all-perfect ✠ Victim: the holy ✠ Bread of life eternal and the Chalice ✠ of unending salvation.

AND this deign to regard with gracious and kindly attention and hold acceptable, as You deigned to accept the offerings of Abel, Your just servant, and the sacrifice of Abraham our patriarch, and that which Your chief priest Melchisedec offered to You, a holy sacrifice and a spotless victim.

MOST humbly we implore You, almighty God, bid these offerings to be brought by the hands of Your holy angel to Your altar above; before the face of Your Divine Majesty; that those of us who, by sharing in the Sacrifice of this altar, shall receive the Most Sacred ✠ Body and ✠ Blood of Your Son, may be filled with every grace and heavenly blessing. Through the same Christ our Lord. Amen.

Commemoration of the Dead

REMEMBER also, O Lord, Your servants and handmaids, *N.* and *N.*, who have gone before us with the sign of faith, and rest in the sleep of peace. (*Here pray for the dead*). To these, O Lord, and to all who rest in Christ, we beseech You to grant of Your goodness, a place of comfort, light and peace. Through the same Christ our Lord. Amen.

TO US sinners also, Your servants, trusting in the greatness of Your mercy, deign to grant some part and fellowship with Your Holy Apostles and Martyrs: with John, Stephen, Matthias, Barnabas, Ignatius, Alexander, Marcellinus, Peter, Felicitas, Perpetua, Agatha, Lucy, Agnes, Cecilia, Anastasia, and all Your Saints; into whose company, we implore You to admit us, not weighing our merits, but freely granting us pardon. Through Christ our Lord.

THROUGH Whom, O Lord, You always create, ✠ sanctify, ✠ fill with life, ✠ bless, and bestow upon us all good things.

The Minor Elevation

THROUGH ✠ Him, and with ✠ Him, and in ✠ Him, is to You, God the Father ✠ almighty, in the unity of the Holy ✠ Spirit, all honor and glory, world without end. S. Amen.

THE COMMUNION AND THANKSGIVING

Let us pray. Prompted by saving precepts, and taught by Your divine teaching, we dare to say:

OUR FATHER, Who art in heaven, hallowed be Thy name: Thy kingdom come: Thy will be done on earth as it is in heaven. Give us this day our daily bread; and forgive us our trespasses, as we forgive those who trespass against us. And lead us not into temptation: S. But deliver us from evil. *P.* Amen.

DELIVER us, we beseech You, O Lord, from all evils, past, present, and to come; and by the intercession of the Blessed and glorious Mary, ever Virgin, Mother of God, together with Your Blessed Apostles Peter and Paul, and Andrew, and all the Saints, grant of Your goodness, peace in our days, that aided by the riches of Your mercy, we may be always free from sin and safe from all disturbance.

Through the same our Lord Jesus Christ, Your Son, Who lives and reigns with You in the unity of the Holy Spirit, God, world without end. *S.* Amen.

P. May the peace ✠ of the Lord be ✠ always with ✠ you. *S.* And with your spirit.

The Priest puts a small particle into the chalice, saying:

May this mingling and consecration of the Body and Blood of our Lord Jesus Christ help us who receive it to life everlasting. Amen.

LAMB of God, You Who take away the sins of the world, have mercy on us.

Lamb of God, You Who take away the sins of the world, have mercy on us.

Lamb of God, You Who take away the sins of the world, grant us peace.

PRAYERS BEFORE HOLY COMMUNION

O LORD Jesus Christ, Who said to Your Apostles: "Peace I leave with you, My peace I give to you," regard not my sins but the faith of Your Church, and deign to give her peace and unity according to Your Will: Who live and reign, God, world without end. Amen.

O LORD Jesus Christ, Son of the living God, Who, by the will of the Father, with the co-operation of the Holy Spirit, have by Your death given life to the world, deliver me by this Your Most Sacred Body and Blood from all my sins and from every evil. Make me always cling to Your commandments, and never permit me to be separated from You. Who with the same God the Father and the Holy Spirit, live and reign, God, world without end. Amen.

LET not the partaking of Your Body, O Lord Jesus Christ, which I, though unworthy, presume to receive, turn to my judgment and condemnation; but through Your goodness, may it become a safeguard and an effective remedy, both of soul and body. Who live and reign with God the Father, in the unity of the Holy Spirit, God, world without end. Amen.

COMMUNION OF THE PRIEST

I WILL take the Bread of heaven, and call upon the name of the Lord.

Lord, I am not worthy that You should come under my roof; but only say the word, and my soul will be healed. (3 *times.*)

Making the Sign of the Cross with the Host, he says:

MAY the Body of our Lord Jesus Christ preserve my soul to life everlasting. Amen.

What return shall I make to the Lord for all He has given me? I will take the Chalice of salvation, and I will call upon the name of the Lord. Praising will I call upon the Lord and I shall be saved from my enemies.

Making the Sign of the Cross with the chalice, he says:

MAY the Blood of our Lord Jesus Christ preserve my soul to life everlasting. Amen.

The Priest reverently consumes the Precious Blood.

COMMUNION OF THE FAITHFUL

The Server and people say the "Confiteor."

P. May almighty God have mercy on you, forgive you your sins, and bring you to life everlasting. S. Amen.

P. May the almighty and merciful Lord grant you pardon, ✠ absolution and remission of your sins. S. Amen.

Holding up a Sacred Host, the Priest says:

Behold the Lamb of God, behold Him Who takes away the sins of the world.

Lord, I am not worthy that You should come under my roof; but only say the word, and my soul will be healed. (3 *times.*)

The Priest says to each communicant:

May the Body of our Lord Jesus Christ preserve your soul to life everlasting. Amen.

The Priest purifies the chalice with wine, saying:

WHAT has passed our lips as food, O Lord, may we possess in purity of heart, that what is given to us in time, be our healing for eternity.

MAY Your Body, O Lord, which I have eaten, and Your Blood which I have drunk, cleave to my very soul, and grant that no trace of sin be found in me, whom these pure and holy mysteries have renewed. Who live and reign, world without end. Amen.

THE COMMUNION • Mark 11, 24

AMEN I say to you, all things whatever you ask for in prayer, believe that you shall receive, and it shall be done to you.

P. The Lord be with you. *S.* And with your spirit.
P. Let us pray.

THE POSTCOMMUNION

WE BESEECH You, almighty God, not to allow those to be subject to human dangers, whom You grant to rejoice in the participation of divine mysteries. Through our Lord, etc. *S.* Amen.

FINAL PRAYERS

P. The Lord be with you. *S.* And with your spirit.
P. Go, you are dismissed. *S.* Thanks be to God.

MAY the tribute of my worship be pleasing to You, Most Holy Trinity, and grant that the sacrifice which I, all unworthy, have offered in the presence of Your Majesty, may be acceptable to You, and through Your mercy obtain forgiveness for me and all for whom I have offered it. Through Christ our Lord. Amen.

THE LAST BLESSING

MAY almighty God bless you: ✠ the Father, and the Son, and the Holy Spirit. *S.* Amen.

The Last Gospel and Prayers after Low Mass are conveniently placed inside the back cover.

"And He will send forth His angels with a trumpet."

LAST SUNDAY AFTER PENTECOST

At the end of the ecclesiastical year the Church earnestly reminds us of the judgment that we must pass before the all-knowing God. It is wise to anticipate that judgment in frequent and contrite confession. (GREEN VESTMENTS)

This Mass is always said on the Last Sunday after Pentecost.

PRAYERS AT THE FOOT OF THE ALTAR

IN THE name of the Father, ✠ and of the Son, and of the Holy Spirit. Amen.

Priest. I will go in to the altar of God.

Server. The God of my gladness and joy.

Psalm 42

DO ME justice, O God, and fight my fight against a faithless people; from the deceitful and impious man rescue me.

S. For You, O God, are my strength. Why do You keep me so far away? Why must I go about in mourning, with the enemy oppressing me?

P. Send forth Your light and Your fidelity; they shall lead me on and bring me to Your holy mountain, to Your dwelling-place.
S. Then will I go in to the altar of God, the God of my gladness and joy.
P. Then will I give You thanks upon the harp, O God, my God. Why are you so downcast, O my soul? Why do you sigh within me?
S. Hope in God! For I shall again be thanking Him in the presence of my Savior and my God.
P. Glory be to the Father, and to the Son, and to the Holy Spirit.
S. As it was in the beginning, is now, and ever shall be, world without end. Amen.
P. I will go in to the altar of God.
S. The God of my gladness and joy.
P. Our help ✠ is in the name of the Lord.
S. Who made heaven and earth.
P. I confess to almighty God, etc.
S. May almighty God have mercy on you, forgive you your sins, and bring you to life everlasting.
P. Amen.

The Server, bowing, says the "Confiteor."

I CONFESS to almighty God, to Blessed Mary, ever Virgin, to Blessed Michael the Archangel, to Blessed John the Baptist, to the Holy Apostles Peter and Paul, and to all the Saints, and to you, Father, that I have sinned exceedingly in thought, word and deed, *through my fault, through my fault, through my most grievous fault.* Therefore I beseech Blessed Mary, ever Virgin, Blessed Michael the Archangel, Blessed John the Baptist, the Holy Apostles Peter and Paul, and all the Saints, and you, Father, to pray to the Lord our God for me.

P. May almighty God have mercy on you, forgive you your sins, and bring you to life everlasting.
S. Amen.

MAY the almighty and merciful Lord grant us pardon, ✠ absolution, and remission of our sins. *S.* Amen.

P. Will You not, O God, give us life?
S. And shall not Your people rejoice in You?
P. Show us, O Lord, Your kindness.
S. And grant us Your salvation.
P. O Lord, hear my prayer.
S. And let my cry come to You.
P. The Lord be with you.
S. And with your spirit. *P.* Let us pray.

Going up to the altar, the Priest prays silently:

TAKE away from us our sins, O Lord, we beseech You, that we may enter with pure minds into the Holy of Holies. Through Christ our Lord. Amen.

WE BESEECH You, O Lord, by the merits of Your Saints (*he kisses the altar*) whose relics lie here, and of all the Saints: deign in Your mercy to pardon me all my sins. Amen.

THE INTROIT • Jer. 29, 11. 12. 14

At the right side of the altar, the Priest says:

THE Lord says: "I think thoughts of peace, and not of affliction. You shall call upon Me, and I will hear you; and I will bring back your captivity from all places." *Ps. 84.* You have favored, O Lord, Your land; You have restored the well-being of Jacob. Glory be to the Father, and to the Son, and to the Holy Spirit. As it was in the beginning, is now, and ever shall be, world without end. Amen. — The Lord says: "I think thoughts of peace, and not of affliction. You shall call upon Me, and I will hear you; and I will bring back your captivity from all places."

THE KYRIE

P. Lord, have mercy. *S.* Lord, have mercy. *P.* Lord, have mercy. *S.* Christ, have mercy. *P.* Christ, have mercy. *S.* Christ, have mercy. *P.* Lord, have mercy. *S.* Lord, have mercy. *P.* Lord, have mercy.

THE GLORIA

GLORY to God in the highest. And on earth peace to men of good will. We praise You. We bless You. We adore You. We glorify You. We give You thanks for Your great glory. O Lord God, heavenly King, God the Father almighty. O Lord Jesus Christ, the Only-begotten Son. O Lord God, Lamb of God, Son of the Father: You Who take away the sins of the world, have mercy on us. You Who take away the sins of the world, receive our prayer. You Who sit at the right hand of the Father, have mercy on us. For You alone are holy. You alone are the Lord. You alone, O Jesus Christ, are most high. Together with the Holy Spirit ✠ in the glory of God the Father. Amen.

The Priest kisses the altar and turns to the people, saying:

P. The Lord be with you. *S.* And with your spirit. *P.* Let us pray.

THE PRAYER

Going to the right (Epistle) side, he says:

STIR up, we beseech You, O Lord, the wills of Your faithful people; that more earnestly seeking after the fruit of good works, they may receive more abundant helps from Your mercy. Through our Lord Jesus Christ, Your Son, Who lives and reigns with You in the unity of the Holy Spirit, God, world without end. S. Amen.

THE EPISTLE • Col. 1, 9-14

BRETHREN: We have been praying for you unceasingly, asking that you may be filled with knowledge of God's will, in all spiritual wisdom and understanding. May you walk worthily of God and please Him in all things, bearing fruit in every good work and growing in the knowledge of God. May you be completely strengthened through His glorious power unto perfect patience and long-suffering; joyfully rendering thanks to God the Father, Who has made us worthy to share the lot of the saints in light. He has rescued us from the power of darkness and transferred us into the kingdom of His beloved Son, in Whom we have our redemption, through His Blood, the remission of sins. S. Thanks be to God.

THE GRADUAL • Ps. 43, 8-9

YOU saved us, O Lord, from our foes, and those who hated us You put to shame. ℣. In God we gloried day by day; Your name we praised always.

Alleluia, alleluia. ℣. *Ps. 129, 1.* 2. Out of the depths I cry to You, O Lord; Lord, hear my prayer! Alleluia.

PRAYER BEFORE THE GOSPEL

Bowing down at the center of the altar, he says:

CLEANSE my heart and my lips, O almighty God, Who cleansed the lips of the Prophet

Isaias with a burning coal. In Your gracious mercy deign so to purify me that I may worthily proclaim Your holy Gospel. Through Christ our Lord. Amen.

Lord, grant Your blessing. The Lord be in my heart and on my lips, that I may worthily and fittingly proclaim His holy Gospel. Amen.

THE GOSPEL • Matt. 24, 15-35

Going to the left (Gospel) side of the altar, he says:

P. The Lord be with you. *S.* And with your spirit.
P. ✠ The continuation of the holy Gospel according to Saint Matthew. *S.* Glory be to You, O Lord.

AT THAT time, Jesus said to His disciples: "When you see the abomination of desolation, which was spoken of by Daniel the prophet, standing in the holy place — let him who reads understand — then let those who are in Judea flee to the mountains; and let him who is on the housetop not go down to take anything from his house; and let him who is in the field not turn back to take his cloak. But woe to those who are with child, or have infants at the breast in those days! But pray that your flight may not be in the winter, or on the Sabbath. For then there will be great tribulation, such as has not been from the beginning of the world until now, nor will be. And unless those days had been shortened, no living creature would be saved. But for the sake of the elect those days will be shortened. Then if anyone say to you, 'Behold, here is the Christ,' or, 'There He is,' do not believe it. For false christs and false prophets will arise, and will show great signs and wonders, so as to lead astray, if possible, even the elect. Behold, I have told it to you beforehand. If therefore they say to you, 'Behold, He is in the desert,' do not go forth; 'Behold, He is in the inner chambers,' do not believe it. For as the lightning comes forth from the east and shines even to the west, so also will the coming of the Son of Man be. Wherever the body is, there will the eagles be gathered together. But immediately after the tribulation of those days, the sun will be darkened, and the moon will not give her light, and the stars will fall from heaven, and the powers of heaven will be shaken. And then will appear the sign of the Son of Man in heaven; and then will all tribes of the earth mourn, and they will see the Son of Man coming upon the clouds of heaven with great power and majesty. And He will send forth His angels with a trumpet and a great sound, and they will gather His elect from the four winds, from one end of the heavens to the other. Now from the fig tree learn this parable. When its branch is now tender, and the leaves break forth, you know that summer is near. Even so, when you see all those things, know that it is near, even at the door. Amen I say to you, this generation will not pass away till all these things have been accomplished. Heaven and earth will pass away, but My words will not pass away." *S.* Praise be to You, O Christ.

P. By the words of the Gospel, may our sins be taken away.

THE NICENE CREED

At the center of the altar, he says:

I BELIEVE in one God, the Father almighty, Maker of heaven and earth, and of all things visible and invisible. And in one Lord Jesus Christ, the Only-begotten Son of God. Born of the Father before all ages. God of God; Light of Light; true

God of true God. Begotten not made; of one being with the Father; by Whom all things were made. Who for us men, and for our salvation, came down from heaven. (*Here all genuflect.*) And was made Flesh by the Holy Spirit of the Virgin Mary: AND WAS MADE MAN. He was also crucified for us, suffered under Pontius Pilate and was buried. And on the third day He rose again according to the Scriptures. And ascending into heaven, He sits at the right hand of the Father. And He shall come again in glory to judge the living and the dead; and of His kingdom there shall be no end. And I believe in the Holy Spirit, Lord and Giver of life, Who proceeds from the Father and the Son. Who together with the Father and the Son is no less adored, and glorified: Who spoke by the Prophets. And I believe in One, Holy, Catholic and Apostolic Church. I confess one Baptism for the remission of sins. And I look for the resurrection of the dead. ✠ And the life of the world to come. Amen.

THE OFFERTORY

The Priest turns to the people and says:

P. The Lord be with you. S. And with your spirit.
P. Let us pray.

THE OFFERTORY VERSE • Ps. 129, 1. 2

OUT of the depths I cry to You, O Lord; Lord, hear my prayer! Out of the depths I cry to You, O Lord.

The Priest now uncovers the chalice, places the host on the paten and offering it up, says:

ACCEPT, O holy Father, almighty and eternal God, this spotless host, which I, Your unworthy servant, offer to You, my living and true

God, to atone for my numberless sins, offenses, and negligences; on behalf of all here present and likewise for all faithful Christians living and dead, that it may profit me and them as a means of salvation to life everlasting. Amen.

He pours wine and water into the chalice, blessing the water before it is poured.

O GOD, Who established the nature of man in wondrous dignity, and still more admirably restored it, grant that through the mystery of this water and wine, we may be made partakers of His Divinity, Who has condescended to become partaker of our humanity, Jesus Christ, Your Son, our Lord. Who lives and reigns with You in the unity of the Holy Spirit, God, world without end. Amen.

Offering up the wine, the Priest says:

WE OFFER You, O Lord, the chalice of salvation, humbly begging of Your mercy that it may arise before Your Divine Majesty, with a pleasing fragrance, for our salvation and for that of the whole world. Amen.

Bowing down, the Priest says:

IN A humble spirit and with a contrite heart, may we be accepted by You, O Lord, and may our sacrifice so be offered in Your sight this day as to please You, O Lord God.

Raising his eyes and blessing the offering, he says:

COME, O Sanctifier, almighty and eternal God, and bless ✠ this sacrifice prepared for the glory of Your holy name.

WASHING THE FINGERS

I WASH my hands in innocence, and I go around Your altar, O Lord, giving voice to my thanks,

and recounting all Your wondrous deeds. O Lord, I love the house in which You dwell, the tenting-place of Your glory. Gather not my soul with those of sinners, nor with men of blood my life. On their hands are crimes, and their right hands are full of bribes. But I walk in integrity; redeem me, and have pity on me. My foot stands on level ground; in the assemblies I will bless You, O Lord. Glory be to the Father, and to the Son, and to the Holy Spirit. As it was in the beginning, is now, and ever shall be, world without end. Amen.

ACCEPT, Most Holy Trinity, this offering which we are making to You in remembrance of the Passion, Resurrection, and Ascension of Jesus Christ, our Lord; and in honor of Blessed Mary, ever Virgin, Blessed John the Baptist, the Holy Apostles Peter and Paul, and of these, and of all the Saints; that it may add to their honor and aid our salvation; and may they deign to intercede in heaven for us who honor their memory here on earth. Through the same Christ our Lord. Amen.

The Priest turns toward the people and says:

Pray, brethren, that my sacrifice and yours may become acceptable to God the Father almighty.
S. May the Lord accept this sacrifice from your hands to the praise and glory of His name, for our advantage, and that of all His holy Church.
P. Amen.

THE SECRET

BE PROPITIOUS, O Lord, to our supplications, and accepting the offerings and prayers of Your people, convert the hearts of us all to Yourself, that being freed from earthly desires, we may

pass on to the desires of heaven. Through our Lord Jesus Christ, Your Son, Who lives and reigns with You in the unity of the Holy Spirit, God.
P. World without end. *S.* Amen.

PREFACE—CANON

P. The Lord be with you. *S.* And with your spirit.
P. Lift up your hearts.
S. We have lifted them up to the Lord.
P. Let us give thanks to the Lord, our God.
S. It is fitting and just.

IT IS fitting indeed and just, right and helpful to salvation, for us always and everywhere to give thanks to You, O holy Lord, Father almighty, everlasting God, Who with Your Only-begotten Son and the Holy Spirit are one God, one Lord; not in the unity of a single person, but in the trinity of a single nature. For that which we believe on Your revelation concerning Your glory, that same we believe of Your Son, that same of the Holy Spirit, without difference or discrimination. So that in confessing the true and everlasting Godhead, we shall adore distinction in Persons, oneness in being, and equality in Majesty. This the Angels and Archangels, the Cherubim, too, and the Seraphim do praise; day by day they cease not to cry out as with one voice, saying (*the bell is rung* 3 *times*):

HOLY, HOLY, HOLY, Lord God of Hosts. Heaven and earth are filled with Your glory. Hosanna in the highest. ✠ Blessed is He Who comes in the name of the Lord. Hosanna in the highest.

THE CANON OF THE MASS

THEREFORE, most gracious Father, we humbly beg of You and entreat You through Jesus Christ Your Son, our Lord, (*he kisses the altar*) to deem acceptable and bless these ✠ gifts, these ✠ offerings, these ✠ holy and unspotted oblations which, in the first place, we offer You for Your Holy Catholic Church, that You would deign to give her peace and protection, to unite and guard her throughout the world, together with Your servant N., our Pope, and N., our Bishop; and all true believers who cherish the Catholic and Apostolic Faith.

Commemoration of the Living

REMEMBER, O Lord, Your servants and handmaids, N. and N., (*name them*) and all here present, whose faith and devotion are known to You, on whose behalf we offer to You, or who' themselves offer to You, this sacrifice of praise for themselves, families and friends, for the good of their souls, for their hope of salvation and deliverance from all harm, and who offer their homage to You, eternal, living and true God.

Commemoration of the Saints

IN THE unity of holy fellowship we observe the memory, first of all, of the glorious and ever Virgin Mary, Mother of our Lord and God Jesus Christ; next, that of Your Blessed Apostles and Martyrs, Peter and Paul, Andrew, James, John, Thomas, James, Philip, Bartholomew, Matthew, Simon and Thaddeus; of Linus, Cletus, Clement, Sixtus, Cornelius, Cyprian, Lawrence, Chrysogonus, John and Paul, Cosmas and Damian, and of all

Your Saints, by whose merits and prayers grant that we may be always fortified by the help of Your protection. Through the same Christ our Lord. Amen.

Spreading his hands over the oblation, he says:

GRACIOUSLY accept, then, we beseech You, O Lord, this service of our worship and that of all Your household. Provide that our days be spent in Your peace, save us from everlasting damnation, and cause us to be numbered in the flock You have chosen. Through Christ our Lord. Amen.

O GOD, deign to bless ✠ what we offer, and make it approved, ✠ effective, ✠ right, and wholly pleasing in every way, that it may become for our good, the Body ✠ and Blood ✠ of Your dearly beloved Son, Jesus Christ our Lord.

CONSECRATION—ELEVATION

WHO, the day before He suffered, took bread into His holy and venerable hands, and having raised His eyes to heaven, to You, O God, His almighty Father, giving thanks to You, He blessed it, ✠ broke it, and gave it to His disciples, saying: All of you take and eat of this:

FOR THIS IS MY BODY.

IN LIKE manner, when the supper was done, taking also this goodly chalice into His holy and venerable hands, again giving thanks to You, He blessed ✠ it, and gave it to His disciples, saying: All of you take and drink of this:

FOR THIS IS THE CHALICE OF MY BLOOD OF THE NEW AND ETERNAL COVENANT: THE MYSTERY OF FAITH: WHICH SHALL BE SHED FOR YOU AND FOR MANY UNTO THE FORGIVENESS OF SINS.

After replacing the chalice on the corporal, he says:

As often as you shall do these things, in memory of Me shall you do them.

Offering of the Victim

MINDFUL, therefore, O Lord, not only of the blessed Passion of the same Christ, Your Son, our Lord, but also of His Resurrection from the dead, and finally His glorious Ascension into heaven, we, Your ministers, as also Your holy people, offer to Your supreme Majesty, of the gifts bestowed upon us, the pure ✠ Victim, the holy ✠ Victim, the all-perfect ✠ Victim: the holy ✠ Bread of life eternal and the Chalice ✠ of unending salvation.

AND this deign to regard with gracious and kindly attention and hold acceptable, as You deigned to accept the offerings of Abel, Your just servant, and the sacrifice of Abraham our patriarch, and that which Your chief priest Melchisedec offered to You, a holy sacrifice and a spotless victim.

MOST humbly we implore You, almighty God, bid these offerings to be brought by the hands of Your holy angel to Your altar above; before the face of Your Divine Majesty; that those of us who, by sharing in the Sacrifice of this altar, shall receive the Most Sacred ✠ Body and ✠ Blood of Your Son, may be filled with every grace and heavenly blessing. Through the same Christ our Lord. Amen.

Commemoration of the Dead

REMEMBER also, O Lord, Your servants and handmaids, *N.* and *N.*, who have gone before us with the sign of faith, and rest in the sleep of peace. (*Here pray for the dead*). To these, O Lord,

and to all who rest in Christ, we beseech You to grant of Your goodness, a place of comfort, light and peace. Through the same Christ our Lord. Amen.

TO US sinners also, Your servants, trusting in the greatness of Your mercy, deign to grant some part and fellowship with Your Holy Apostles and Martyrs: with John, Stephen, Matthias, Barnabas, Ignatius, Alexander, Marcellinus, Peter, Felicitas, Perpetua, Agatha, Lucy, Agnes, Cecilia, Anastasia, and all Your Saints; into whose company, we implore You to admit us, not weighing our merits, but freely granting us pardon. Through Christ our Lord.

THROUGH Whom, O Lord, You always create, ✠ sanctify, ✠ fill with life, ✠ bless, and bestow upon us all good things.

The Minor Elevation

THROUGH ✠ Him, and with ✠ Him, and in ✠ Him, is to You, God the Father ✠ almighty, in the unity of the Holy ✠ Spirit, all honor and glory, world without end. S. Amen.

THE COMMUNION AND THANKSGIVING

Let us pray. Prompted by saving precepts, and taught by Your divine teaching, we dare to say:

OUR FATHER, Who art in heaven, hallowed be Thy name: Thy kingdom come: Thy will be done on earth as it is in heaven. Give us this day our daily bread; and forgive us our trespasses, as we forgive those who trespass against us. And lead us not into temptation: S. But deliver us from evil. P. Amen.

DELIVER us, we beseech You, O Lord, from all evils, past, present, and to come; and by the intercession of the Blessed and glorious Mary, ever Virgin, Mother of God, together with Your Blessed Apostles Peter and Paul, and Andrew, and all the Saints, grant of Your goodness, peace in our days, that aided by the riches of Your mercy, we may be always free from sin and safe from all disturbance.

Through the same our Lord Jesus Christ, Your Son, Who lives and reigns with You in the unity of the Holy Spirit, God, world without end. S. Amen.

P. May the peace ✠ of the Lord be ✠ always with ✠ you. *S.* And with your spirit.

The Priest puts a small particle into the chalice, saying:

May this mingling and consecration of the Body and Blood of our Lord Jesus Christ help us who receive it to life everlasting. Amen.

LAMB of God, You Who take away the sins of the world, have mercy on us.

Lamb of God, You Who take away the sins of the world, have mercy on us.

Lamb of God, You Who take away the sins of the world, grant us peace.

PRAYERS BEFORE HOLY COMMUNION

Then inclining toward the altar, he says:

O LORD Jesus Christ, Who said to Your Apostles: "Peace I leave with you, My peace I give to you," regard not my sins but the faith of Your Church, and deign to give her peace and unity according to Your Will: Who live and reign, God, world without end. Amen.

O LORD Jesus Christ, Son of the living God, Who, by the will of the Father, with the cooperation of the Holy Spirit, have by Your death given life to the world, deliver me by this Your Most Sacred Body and Blood from all my sins and from every evil. Make me always cling to Your commandments, and never permit me to be separated from You. Who with the same God the Father and the Holy Spirit, live and reign, God, world without end. Amen.

LET not the partaking of Your Body, O Lord Jesus Christ, which I, though unworthy, presume to receive, turn to my judgment and condemnation; but through Your goodness, may it become a safeguard and an effective remedy, both of soul and body. Who live and reign with God the Father, in the unity of the Holy Spirit, God, world without end. Amen.

COMMUNION OF THE PRIEST

I WILL take the Bread of heaven, and call upon the name of the Lord.

Lord, I am not worthy that You should come under my roof; but only say the word, and my soul will be healed. (3 *times.*)

Making the Sign of the Cross with the Host, he says:

MAY the Body of our Lord Jesus Christ preserve my soul to life everlasting. Amen.

What return shall I make to the Lord for all He has given me? I will take the Chalice of salvation, and I will call upon the name of the Lord. Praising will I call upon the Lord and I shall be saved from my enemies.

Making the Sign of the Cross with the chalice, he says:

MAY the Blood of our Lord Jesus Christ preserve my soul to life everlasting. Amen.

The Priest reverently consumes the Precious Blood.

COMMUNION OF THE FAITHFUL

The Server and people say the "Confiteor."

P. May almighty God have mercy on you, forgive you your sins, and bring you to life everlasting. *S.* Amen.

P. May the almighty and merciful Lord grant you pardon, ✠ absolution and remission of your sins. *S.* Amen.

Holding up a Sacred Host, the Priest says:

Behold the Lamb of God, behold Him Who takes away the sins of the world.

Lord, I am not worthy that You should come under my roof; but only say the word, and my soul will be healed. (3 *times.*)

The Priest says to each communicant:

May the Body of our Lord Jesus Christ preserve your soul to life everlasting. Amen.

The Priest purifies the chalice with wine, saying:

WHAT has passed our lips as food, O Lord, may we possess in purity of heart, that what is given to us in time, be our healing for eternity.

He purifies his fingers with wine and water, saying:

MAY Your Body, O Lord, which I have eaten, and Your Blood which I have drunk, cleave to my very soul, and grant that no trace of sin be found in me, whom these pure and holy mysteries

have renewed. Who live and reign, world without end. Amen.

THE COMMUNION • Mark 11, 24

AMEN I say to you, all things whatever you ask for in prayer, believe that you shall receive, and it shall be done to you.

The Priest, turning to the people, says:

P. The Lord be with you. *S.* And with your spirit.
P. Let us pray.

THE POSTCOMMUNION

GRANT, we beseech You, O Lord, that by this sacrament, which we have received, whatever is corrupted in our souls may be restored by the gift of its efficiency. Through our Lord Jesus Christ, Your Son, Who lives and reigns, etc. *S.* Amen.

FINAL PRAYERS

The Priest turns again to the people, and says:

P. The Lord be with you. *S.* And with your spirit.
P. Go, you are dismissed. *S.* Thanks be to God.

MAY the tribute of my worship be pleasing to You, Most Holy Trinity, and grant that the sacrifice which I, all unworthy, have offered in the presence of Your Majesty, may be acceptable to You, and through Your mercy obtain forgiveness for me and all for whom I have offered it. Through Christ our Lord. Amen.

THE LAST BLESSING

MAY almighty God bless you: ✠ the Father, and the Son, and the Holy Spirit. *S.* Amen.

The Last Gospel and Prayers after Low Mass are conveniently placed inside the back cover.

"You Are the Glory of Jerusalem, You Are the Joy of Israel, You Are the Honor of Our People."

Judith 15, 10.

"Hail, full of grace, the Lord is with you."

Dec. 8—IMMACULATE CONCEPTION

Because Mary was chosen to be the Mother of God, the singular privilege was bestowed upon her by which, in the first instant of her Conception, in view of the merits of Jesus Christ, she was preserved from all stain of original sin. (WHITE VESTMENTS)

PRAYERS AT THE FOOT OF THE ALTAR

IN THE name of the Father, ✠ and of the Son, and of the Holy Spirit. Amen.

Priest. I will go in to the altar of God.

Server. The God of my gladness and joy.

Psalm 42

DO ME justice, O God, and fight my fight against a faithless people; from the deceitful and impious man rescue me.

S. For You, O God, are my strength. Why do You keep me so far away? Why must I go about in mourning, with the enemy oppressing me?

P. Send forth Your light and Your fidelity; they shall lead me on and bring me to Your holy mountain, to Your dwelling-place.

S. Then will I go in to the altar of God, the God of my gladness and joy.
P. Then will I give You thanks upon the harp, O God, my God. Why are you so downcast, O my soul? Why do you sigh within me?
S. Hope in God! For I shall again be thanking Him in the presence of my Savior and my God.
P. Glory be to the Father, and to the Son, and to the Holy Spirit.
S. As it was in the beginning, is now, and ever shall be, world without end. Amen.
P. I will go in to the altar of God.
S. The God of my gladness and joy.
P. Our help ✠ is in the name of the Lord.
S. Who made heaven and earth.
P. I confess to almighty God, etc.
S. May almighty God have mercy on you, forgive you your sins, and bring you to life everlasting.
P. Amen.

The Server, bowing, says the "Confiteor."

I CONFESS to almighty God, to Blessed Mary, ever Virgin, to Blessed Michael the Archangel, to Blessed John the Baptist, to the Holy Apostles Peter and Paul, and to all the Saints, and to you, Father, that I have sinned exceedingly in thought, word and deed, *through my fault, through my fault, through my most grievous fault.* Therefore I beseech Blessed Mary, ever Virgin, Blessed Michael the Archangel, Blessed John the Baptist, the Holy Apostles Peter and Paul, and all the Saints, and you, Father, to pray to the Lord our God for me.
P. May almighty God have mercy on you, forgive you your sins, and bring you to life everlasting.
S. Amen.

MAY the almighty and merciful Lord grant us pardon, ✠ absolution, and remission of our sins. *S.* Amen.

P. Will You not, O God, give us life?
S. And shall not Your people rejoice in You?
P. Show us, O Lord, Your kindness.
S. And grant us Your salvation.
P. O Lord, hear my prayer.
S. And let my cry come to You.
P. The Lord be with you.
S. And with your spirit. *P.* Let us pray.

Going up to the altar, the Priest prays silently:

TAKE away from us our sins, O Lord, we beseech You, that we may enter with pure minds into the Holy of Holies. Through Christ our Lord. Amen.

WE BESEECH You, O Lord, by the merits of Your Saints (*he kisses the altar*) whose relics lie here, and of all the Saints: deign in Your mercy to pardon me all my sins. Amen.

THE INTROIT • Isa. 61, 10

At the right side of the altar, the Priest says:

I WILL greatly rejoice in the Lord, and my soul shall be joyful in my God: for He has clothed me with the garments of salvation, and with the robe of justice He has covered me, as a bride adorned with her jewels. (*P.T.* Alleluia, alleluia.) *Ps.* 29. I will extol You, O Lord, for You drew me clear and did not let my enemies rejoice over me. Glory be to the Father, and to the Son, and to the Holy Spirit. As it was in the beginning, is now, and ever shall be, world without end. Amen. — I will greatly rejoice in the Lord, and my soul shall be joyful in my God: for He has clothed me with the garments of salvation, and with the robe of justice He has covered me, as a bride adorned with her jewels. (*P.T.* Alleluia, alleluia.)

THE KYRIE

P. Lord, have mercy. *S.* Lord, have mercy. *P.* Lord, have mercy. *S.* Christ, have mercy. *P.* Christ, have mercy. *S.* Christ, have mercy. *P.* Lord, have mercy. *S.* Lord, have mercy. *P.* Lord, have mercy.

THE GLORIA

GLORY to God in the highest. And on earth peace to men of good will. We praise You. We bless You. We adore You. We glorify You. We give You thanks for Your great glory. O Lord God, heavenly King, God the Father almighty. O Lord Jesus Christ, the Only-begotten Son. O Lord God, Lamb of God, Son of the Father: You Who take away the sins of the world, have mercy on us. You Who take away the sins of the world, receive our prayer. You Who sit at the right hand of the Father, have mercy on us. For You alone are holy. You alone are the Lord. You alone, O Jesus Christ, are most high. Together with the Holy Spirit ✠ in the glory of God the Father. Amen.

The Priest kisses the altar and turns to the people, saying:

P. The Lord be with you. *S.* And with your spirit. *P.* Let us pray.

THE PRAYER

Going to the right (Epistle) side, he says:

O GOD, by the Immaculate Conception of the Virgin, You prepared a worthy habitation for

Your Son; we beseech You, that, as by the foreseen death of Your same Son You preserved her from all stain of sin, so You would grant us also, through her intercession, to come to You with pure hearts. Through the same our Lord Jesus Christ, Your Son, Who lives and reigns with You in the unity of the Holy Spirit, God, world without end. S. Amen.

THE EPISTLE • Prov. 8, 22-35

THE Lord begot me, the firstborn of His ways, the forerunner of His prodigies of long ago; from of old I was poured forth, at the first, before the earth. When there were no depths I was brought forth, when there were no fountains or springs of water; before the mountains were settled into place, before the hills, I was brought forth; while as yet the earth and the fields were not made, nor the first clods of the world. When He established the heavens I was there, when He marked out the vault over the face of the deep; when He made firm the skies above, and poised the fountains of waters; when He set for the sea its limit, so that the waters should not transgress His command; when He fixed fast the foundations of the earth; then was I beside Him as His craftsman, and I was His delight day by day, playing before Him all the while, playing on the surface of His earth and I found delight in the sons of men. So now, O children, listen to me; happy those who keep my ways. Hear instruction, and be wise, and refuse it not. Happy the man who obeys me, watching daily at my gates, waiting at my doorposts; for he who finds me finds life, and wins favor from the Lord. S. Thanks be to God.

THE GRADUAL • Judith 13, 23

BLESSED are you, O Virgin Mary, by the Lord the most high God, above all women upon the earth. ℣. *Judith 15, 10.* You are the glory of Jerusalem, you are the joy of Israel, you are the honor of our people.

Alleluia, alleluia. ℣. *Cant. 4, 7.* You are all beautiful, O Mary, and there is in you no stain of original sin. Alleluia.

After Septuagesima omit Alleluia and versicle, and say:

THE TRACT • Ps. 86, 1-2. 3. 5

HIS foundation upon the holy mountains the Lord loves: the gates of Sion, more than any dwelling of Jacob. ℣. Glorious things are said of you, O city of God! ℣. A man is born in her, and He Who has established her is the Most High.

During Paschaltime omit Gradual, and say:

Alleluia, alleluia. ℣. *Judith 15, 10.* You are the glory of Jerusalem, you are the joy of Israel, you are the honor of our people. Alleluia. ℣. *Cant. 4, 7.* You are all beautiful, O Mary, and there is in you no stain of original sin. Alleluia.

PRAYER BEFORE THE GOSPEL

Bowing down at the center of the altar, he says:

CLEANSE my heart and my lips, O almighty God, Who cleansed the lips of the Prophet Isaias with a burning coal. In Your gracious mercy deign so to purify me that I may worthily proclaim Your holy Gospel. Through Christ our Lord. Amen.

Lord, grant Your blessing. The Lord be in my heart and on my lips, that I may worthily and fittingly proclaim His holy Gospel. Amen.

THE GOSPEL • Luke 1, 26-28

Going to the left (Gospel) side of the altar, he says:

P. The Lord be with you. *S.* And with your spirit.

P. ✠ The continuation of the holy Gospel according to Saint Luke. *S.* Glory be to You, O Lord.

AT THAT time, the angel Gabriel was sent from God to a town of Galilee called Nazareth, to a virgin betrothed to a man named Joseph, of the house of David, and the virgin's name was Mary. And when the angel had come to her, he said, "Hail, full of grace, the Lord is with you. Blessed are you among women." *S.* Praise be to You, O Christ.

P. By the words of the Gospel, may our sins be taken away.

THE NICENE CREED

At the center of the altar, he says:

I BELIEVE in one God, the Father almighty, Maker of heaven and earth, and of all things visible and invisible. And in one Lord Jesus Christ, the Only-begotten Son of God. Born of the Father before all ages. God of God; Light of Light; true God of true God. Begotten not made; of one being with the Father; by Whom all things were made. Who for us men, and for our salvation, came down from heaven. (*Here all genuflect.*) And was made Flesh by the Holy Spirit of the Virgin Mary: AND WAS MADE MAN. He was also crucified for us, suffered under Pontius Pilate and was buried. And on the third day He rose again according to the Scriptures. And ascending into heaven, He sits at the right hand of the Father. And He shall come again in glory to judge the living and the dead; and of His kingdom there shall be no end. And I believe in the Holy Spirit, Lord and Giver of life, Who proceeds from the Father and the Son. Who together with the Father and the Son is no less adored, and glorified: Who spoke by the Prophets. And I believe in One, Holy, Catholic and Apostolic Church. I confess one Baptism for the remission of sins. And I look for the resurrection of the dead. ✠ And the life of the world to come. Amen.

THE OFFERTORY

The Priest turns to the people and says:

P. The Lord be with you. S. And with your spirit.
P. Let us pray.

THE OFFERTORY VERSE • Luke 1, 28

HAIL, Mary, full of grace, the Lord is with you; blessed are you among women, alleluia.

The Priest now uncovers the chalice, places the host on the paten and offering it up, says:

ACCEPT, O holy Father, almighty and eternal God, this spotless host, which I, Your unworthy servant, offer to You, my living and true God, to atone for my numberless sins, offenses, and negligences; on behalf of all here present and likewise for all faithful Christians living and dead, that it may profit me and them as a means of salvation to life everlasting. Amen.

He pours wine and water into the chalice, blessing the water before it is poured.

O GOD, Who established the nature of man in wondrous dignity, and still more admirably restored it, grant that through the mystery of this water and wine, we may be made partakers of His Divinity, Who has condescended to become par-

taker of our humanity, Jesus Christ, Your Son, our Lord. Who lives and reigns with You in the unity of the Holy Spirit, God, world without end. Amen.

Offering up the wine, the Priest says:

WE OFFER You, O Lord, the chalice of salvation, humbly begging of Your mercy that it may arise before Your Divine Majesty, with a pleasing fragrance, for our salvation and for that of the whole world. Amen.

Bowing down, the Priest says:

IN A humble spirit and with a contrite heart, may we be accepted by You, O Lord, and may our sacrifice so be offered in Your sight this day as to please You, O Lord God.

Raising his eyes and blessing the offering, he says:

COME, O Sanctifier, almighty and eternal God, and bless ✠ this sacrifice prepared for the glory of Your holy name.

WASHING THE FINGERS

I WASH my hands in innocence, and I go around Your altar, O Lord, giving voice to my thanks, and recounting all Your wondrous deeds. O Lord, I love the house in which You dwell, the tenting-place of Your glory. Gather not my soul with those of sinners, nor with men of blood my life. On their hands are crimes, and their right hands are full of bribes. But I walk in integrity; redeem me, and have pity on me. My foot stands on level ground; in the assemblies I will bless You, O Lord. Glory be to the Father, and to the Son, and to the Holy Spirit. As it was in the beginning, is now, and ever shall be, world without end. Amen.

ACCEPT, Most Holy Trinity, this offering which we are making to You in remembrance of the Passion, Resurrection, and Ascension of Jesus Christ, our Lord; and in honor of Blessed Mary, ever Virgin, Blessed John the Baptist, the Holy Apostles Peter and Paul, and of these, and of all the Saints; that it may add to their honor and aid our salvation; and may they deign to intercede in heaven for us who honor their memory here on earth. Through the same Christ our Lord. Amen.

The Priest turns toward the people and says:

Pray, brethren, that my sacrifice and yours may become acceptable to God the Father almighty.

S. May the Lord accept this sacrifice from your hands to the praise and glory of His name, for our advantage, and that of all His holy Church.

P. Amen.

THE SECRET

RECEIVE the saving oblation which we offer to You, O Lord, on the solemn feast of the Immaculate Conception of the Blessed Virgin Mary, and grant that, as we confess that, by Your preventing grace, she was kept free from every stain of sin, so, by her intercession, we may be freed from all sin. Through our Lord Jesus Christ, Your Son, Who lives and reigns with You in the unity of the Holy Spirit, God.

P. World without end. *S.* Amen.

PREFACE—CANON

P. The Lord be with you. *S.* And with your spirit.

P. Lift up your hearts.

S. We have lifted them up to the Lord.

P. Let us give thanks to the Lord, our God.
S. It is fitting and just.

IT IS fitting indeed and just, right and helpful to salvation, for us always and everywhere to give thanks to You, O holy Lord, Father almighty, everlasting God, and that we should praise, bless, and proclaim You in the Immaculate Conception of the Blessed Mary, ever Virgin; for she conceived Your Only-begotten Son by the overshadowing of the Holy Spirit, and, while the glory of her virginity remained, brought forth to the world the Eternal Light, Jesus Christ, our Lord. Through Whom the Angels praise Your Majesty, the Dominations adore it, the Powers are in awe. The heavens and the heavenly hosts and the blessed Seraphim join together in celebrating their joy. With these, we pray You, join our own voices also, while we say with lowly praise (*the bell is rung* 3 *times*):

HOLY, HOLY, HOLY, Lord God of Hosts. Heaven and earth are filled with Your glory. Hosanna in the highest. ✠ Blessed is He Who comes in the name of the Lord. Hosanna in the highest.

THE CANON OF THE MASS

THEREFORE, most gracious Father, we humbly beg of You and entreat You through Jesus Christ Your Son, our Lord, (*he kisses the altar*) to deem acceptable and bless these ✠ gifts, these ✠ offerings, these ✠ holy and unspotted oblations which, in the first place, we offer You for Your Holy Catholic Church, that You would deign to give her peace and protection, to unite and guard her throughout the world, together with Your serv-

ant N., our Pope, and N., our Bishop; and all true believers who cherish the Catholic and Apostolic Faith.

Commemoration of the Living

REMEMBER, O Lord, Your servants and handmaids, N. and N., (*name them*) and all here present, whose faith and devotion are known to You, on whose behalf we offer to You, or who themselves offer to You, this sacrifice of praise for themselves, families and friends, for the good of their souls, for their hope of salvation and deliverance from all harm, and who offer their homage to You, eternal, living and true God.

Commemoration of the Saints

IN THE unity of holy fellowship we observe the memory, first of all, of the glorious and ever Virgin Mary, Mother of our Lord and God Jesus Christ; next, that of Your Blessed Apostles and Martyrs, Peter and Paul, Andrew, James, John, Thomas, James, Philip, Bartholomew, Matthew, Simon and Thaddeus; of Linus, Cletus, Clement, Sixtus, Cornelius, Cyprian, Lawrence, Chrysogonus, John and Paul, Cosmas and Damian, and of all Your Saints, by whose merits and prayers grant that we may be always fortified by the help of Your protection. Through the same Christ our Lord. Amen.

Spreading his hands over the oblation, he says:

GRACIOUSLY accept, then, we beseech You, O Lord, this service of our worship and that of all Your household. Provide that our days be spent in Your peace, save us from everlasting damnation, and cause us to be numbered in the flock You have chosen. Through Christ our Lord. Amen.

O GOD, deign to bless ✠ what we offer, and make it approved, ✠ effective, ✠ right, and wholly pleasing in every way, that it may become for our good, the Body ✠ and Blood ✠ of Your dearly beloved Son, Jesus Christ our Lord.

CONSECRATION—ELEVATION

WHO, the day before He suffered, took bread into His holy and venerable hands, and having raised His eyes to heaven, to You, O God, His almighty Father, giving thanks to You, He blessed it, ✠ broke it, and gave it to His disciples, saying: All of you take and eat of this:

FOR THIS IS MY BODY.

IN LIKE manner, when the supper was done, taking also this goodly chalice into His holy and venerable hands, again giving thanks to You, He blessed ✠ it, and gave it to His disciples, saying: All of you take and drink of this:

FOR THIS IS THE CHALICE OF MY BLOOD OF THE NEW AND ETERNAL COVENANT: THE MYSTERY OF FAITH: WHICH SHALL BE SHED FOR YOU AND FOR MANY UNTO THE FORGIVENESS OF SINS.

After replacing the chalice on the corporal, he says:

As often as you shall do these things, in memory of Me shall you do them.

Offering of the Victim

MINDFUL, therefore, O Lord, not only of the blessed Passion of the same Christ, Your Son, our Lord, but also of His Resurrection from the dead, and finally His glorious Ascension into heav-

en, we, Your ministers, as also Your holy people, offer to Your supreme Majesty, of the gifts bestowed upon us, the pure ✠ Victim, the holy ✠ Victim, the all-perfect ✠ Victim: the holy ✠ Bread of life eternal and the Chalice ✠ of unending salvation.

AND this deign to regard with gracious and kindly attention and hold acceptable, as You deigned to accept the offerings of Abel, Your just servant, and the sacrifice of Abraham our patriarch, and that which Your chief priest Melchisedec offered to You, a holy sacrifice and a spotless victim.

MOST humbly we implore You, almighty God, bid these offerings to be brought by the hands of Your holy angel to Your altar above; before the face of Your Divine Majesty; that those of us who, by sharing in the Sacrifice of this altar, shall receive the Most Sacred ✠ Body and ✠ Blood of Your Son, may be filled with every grace and heavenly blessing. Through the same Christ our Lord. Amen.

Commemoration of the Dead

REMEMBER also, O Lord, Your servants and handmaids, N. and N., who have gone before us with the sign of faith, and rest in the sleep of peace. (*Here pray for the dead*). To these, O Lord, and to all who rest in Christ, we beseech You to grant of Your goodness, a place of comfort, light and peace. Through the same Christ our Lord. Amen.

TO US sinners also, Your servants, trusting in the greatness of Your mercy, deign to grant some part and fellowship with Your Holy Apostles and

Martyrs: with John, Stephen, Matthias, Barnabas, Ignatius, Alexander, Marcellinus, Peter, Felicitas, Perpetua, Agatha, Lucy, Agnes, Cecilia, Anastasia; and all Your Saints; into whose company, we implore You to admit us, not weighing our merits, but freely granting us pardon. Through Christ our Lord.

THROUGH Whom, O Lord, You always create, ✠ sanctify, ✠ fill with life, ✠ bless, and bestow upon us all good things.

The Minor Elevation

THROUGH ✠ Him, and with ✠ Him, and in ✠ Him, is to You, God the Father ✠ almighty, in the unity of the Holy ✠ Spirit, all honor and glory, world without end. S. Amen.

THE COMMUNION AND THANKSGIVING

Let us pray. Prompted by saving precepts, and taught by Your divine teaching, we dare to say:

OUR FATHER, Who art in heaven, hallowed be Thy name: Thy kingdom come: Thy will be done on earth as it is in heaven. Give us this day our daily bread; and forgive us our trespasses, as we forgive those who trespass against us. And lead us not into temptation: S. But deliver us from evil. *P.* Amen.

DELIVER us, we beseech You, O Lord, from all evils, past, present, and to come; and by the intercession of the Blessed and glorious Mary, ever Virgin, Mother of God, together with Your Blessed Apostles Peter and Paul, and Andrew, and all the Saints, grant of Your goodness, peace in our

days, that aided by the riches of Your mercy, we may be always free from sin and safe from all disturbance.

Through the same our Lord Jesus Christ, Your Son, Who lives and reigns with You in the unity of the Holy Spirit, God, world without end. S. Amen.

P. May the peace ✠ of the Lord be ✠ always with ✠ you. S. And with your spirit.

The Priest puts a small particle into the chalice, saying:

May this mingling and consecration of the Body and Blood of our Lord Jesus Christ help us who receive it to life everlasting. Amen.

LAMB of God, You Who take away the sins of the world, have mercy on us.

Lamb of God, You Who take away the sins of the world, have mercy on us.

Lamb of God, You Who take away the sins of the world, grant us peace.

PRAYERS BEFORE HOLY COMMUNION

Then inclining toward the altar, he says:

O LORD Jesus Christ, Who said to Your Apostles: "Peace I leave with you, My peace I give to you," regard not my sins but the faith of Your Church, and deign to give her peace and unity according to Your Will: Who live and reign, God, world without end. Amen.

O LORD Jesus Christ, Son of the living God, Who, by the will of the Father, with the cooperation of the Holy Spirit, have by Your death given life to the world, deliver me by this Your Most Sacred Body and Blood from all my sins and from every evil. Make me always cling to Your commandments, and never permit me to be separated from You. Who with the same God the Father and the Holy Spirit, live and reign, God, world without end. Amen.

LET not the partaking of Your Body, O Lord Jesus Christ, which I, though unworthy, presume to receive, turn to my judgment and condemnation; but through Your goodness, may it become a safeguard and an effective remedy, both of soul and body. Who live and reign with God the Father, in the unity of the Holy Spirit, God, world without end. Amen.

COMMUNION OF THE PRIEST

I WILL take the Bread of heaven, and call upon the name of the Lord.

Lord, I am not worthy that You should come under my roof; but only say the word, and my soul will be healed. (3 *times.*)

Making the Sign of the Cross with the Host, he says:

MAY the Body of our Lord Jesus Christ preserve my soul to life everlasting. Amen.

What return shall I make to the Lord for all He has given me? I will take the Chalice of salvation, and I will call upon the name of the Lord. Praising will I call upon the Lord and I shall be saved from my enemies.

Making the Sign of the Cross with the chalice, he says:

MAY the Blood of our Lord Jesus Christ preserve my soul to life everlasting. Amen.

The Priest reverently consumes the Precious Blood.

COMMUNION OF THE FAITHFUL

The Server and people say the "Confiteor."

P. May almighty God have mercy on you, forgive you your sins, and bring you to life everlasting. **S.** Amen.

P. May the almighty and merciful Lord grant you pardon, ✠ absolution and remission of your sins. **S.** Amen.

Holding up a Sacred Host, the Priest says:

Behold the Lamb of God, behold Him Who takes away the sins of the world.

Lord, I am not worthy that You should come under my roof; but only say the word, and my soul will be healed. (3 *times.*)

The Priest says to each communicant:

May the Body of our Lord Jesus Christ preserve your soul to life everlasting. Amen.

The Priest purifies the chalice with wine, saying:

WHAT has passed our lips as food, O Lord, may we possess in purity of heart, that what is given to us in time, be our healing for eternity.

He purifies his fingers with wine and water, saying:

MAY Your Body, O Lord, which I have eaten, and Your Blood which I have drunk, cleave to my very soul, and grant that no trace of sin be found in me, whom these pure and holy mysteries have renewed. Who live and reign, world without end. Amen.

THE COMMUNION

GLORIOUS things are said of you, O Mary, for He Who is mighty has done great things for you. (*P.T.* Alleluia.)

The Priest, turning to the people, says:

P. The Lord be with you. *S.* And with your spirit.
P. Let us pray.

THE POSTCOMMUNION

MAY the sacrament which we have received, O Lord our God, heal in us the wounds of that sin, from which You, by a singular privilege, preserved Immaculate the Conception of Blessed Mary. Through our Lord Jesus Christ, Your Son, Who lives and reigns with You in the unity of the Holy Spirit, God, world without end. *S.* Amen.

FINAL PRAYERS

The Priest turns again to the people, and says:

P. The Lord be with you. *S.* And with your spirit.
P. Go, you are dismissed. *S.* Thanks be to God.

MAY the tribute of my worship be pleasing to You, Most Holy Trinity, and grant that the sacrifice which I, all unworthy, have offered in the presence of Your Majesty, may be acceptable to You, and through Your mercy obtain forgiveness for me and all for whom I have offered it. Through Christ our Lord. Amen.

THE LAST BLESSING

He kisses the altar, and facing the people, says:

MAY almighty God bless you: ✠ the Father, and the Son, and the Holy Spirit.

S. Amen.

The Last Gospel and Prayers after Low Mass are conveniently placed inside the back cover.

"The Lord . . . clothed him with a robe of glory."

Mar. 19—SAINT JOSEPH

In the eyes of the Jews, St. Joseph was an ordinary carpenter. His greatness lay in his inner life and in his relation to Jesus and Mary. We confidently pray to him for help in temporal needs, for spiritual progress, and for a happy death. (WHITE VESTMENTS)

If the Feast of St. Joseph falls in Holy Week, it is celebrated on the Tuesday after Low Sunday.

PRAYERS AT THE FOOT OF THE ALTAR

IN THE name of the Father, ✠ and of the Son, and of the Holy Spirit. Amen.

Priest. I will go in to the altar of God.

Server. The God of my gladness and joy.

Psalm 42

DO ME justice, O God, and fight my fight against a faithless people; from the deceitful and impious man rescue me.

S. For You, O God, are my strength. Why do You keep me so far away? Why must I go about in mourning, with the enemy oppressing me?

P. Send forth Your light and Your fidelity; they shall lead me on and bring me to Your holy mountain, to Your dwelling-place.

S. Then will I go in to the altar of God, the God of my gladness and joy.
P. Then will I give You thanks upon the harp, O God, my God. Why are you so downcast, O my soul? Why do you sigh within me?
S. Hope in God! For I shall again be thanking Him in the presence of my Savior and my God.
P. Glory be to the Father, and to the Son, and to the Holy Spirit.
S. As it was in the beginning, is now, and ever shall be, world without end. Amen.
P. I will go in to the altar of God.
S. The God of my gladness and joy.
P. Our help ✠ is in the name of the Lord.
S. Who made heaven and earth.
P. I confess to almighty God, etc.
S. May almighty God have mercy on you, forgive you your sins, and bring you to life everlasting.
P. Amen.

The Server, bowing, says the "Confiteor."

I CONFESS to almighty God, to Blessed Mary, ever Virgin, to Blessed Michael the Archangel, to Blessed John the Baptist, to the Holy Apostles Peter and Paul, and to all the Saints, and to you, Father, that I have sinned exceedingly in thought, word and deed, *through my fault, through my fault, through my most grievous fault.* Therefore I beseech Blessed Mary, ever Virgin, Blessed Michael the Archangel, Blessed John the Baptist, the Holy Apostles Peter and Paul, and all the Saints, and you, Father, to pray to the Lord our God for me.
P. May almighty God have mercy on you, forgive you your sins, and bring you to life everlasting.
S. Amen.

MAY the almighty and merciful Lord grant us pardon, ✠ absolution, and remission of our sins. *S.* Amen.

P. Will You not, O God, give us life?
S. And shall not Your people rejoice in You?
P. Show us, O Lord, Your kindness.
S. And grant us Your salvation.
P. O Lord, hear my prayer.
S. And let my cry come to You.
P. The Lord be with you.
S. And with your spirit. *P.* Let us pray.

Going up to the altar, the Priest prays silently:

TAKE away from us our sins, O Lord, we beseech You, that we may enter with pure minds into the Holy of Holies. Through Christ our Lord. Amen.

WE BESEECH You, O Lord, by the merits of Your Saints (*he kisses the altar*) whose relics lie here, and of all the Saints: deign in Your mercy to pardon me all my sins. Amen.

THE INTROIT • Ps. 91, 13-14. 2

At the right side of the altar, the Priest says:

THE just man shall flourish like the palm tree, like a cedar of Lebanon shall he grow: planted in the house of the Lord, in the courts of the house of our God. (*P.T.* Alleluia, alleluia.) *Ps.* It is good to give thanks to the Lord, to sing praise to Your name, Most High. Glory be to the Father, and to the Son, and to the Holy Spirit. As it was in the beginning, is now, and ever shall be, world without end. Amen. — The just man shall flourish like the palm tree, like a cedar of Lebanon shall he grow:

planted in the house of the Lord, in the courts of the house of our God. (*P.T.* Alleluia, alleluia.)

THE KYRIE

P. Lord, have mercy. **S.** Lord, have mercy. **P.** Lord, have mercy. **S.** Christ, have mercy. **P.** Christ, have mercy. **S.** Christ, have mercy. **P.** Lord, have mercy. **S.** Lord, have mercy. **P.** Lord, have mercy.

THE GLORIA

GLORY to God in the highest. And on earth peace to men of good will. We praise You. We bless You. We adore You. We glorify You. We give You thanks for Your great glory. O Lord God, heavenly King, God the Father almighty. O Lord Jesus Christ, the Only-begotten Son. O Lord God, Lamb of God, Son of the Father: You Who take away the sins of the world, have mercy on us. You Who take away the sins of the world, receive our prayer. You Who sit at the right hand of the Father, have mercy on us. For You alone are holy. You alone are the Lord. You alone, O Jesus Christ, are most high. Together with the Holy Spirit ✠ in the glory of God the Father. Amen.

The Priest kisses the altar and turns to the people, saying:

P. The Lord be with you. **S.** And with your spirit. **P.** Let us pray.

THE PRAYER

Going to the right (Epistle) side, he says:

WE BESEECH You, O Lord, that we may be assisted by the merits of the Spouse of Your Most Holy Mother, so that what we cannot obtain by our own power may be given to us through his intercession. Who live and reign with God the

Father, in the unity of the Holy Spirit, God, world without end. S. Amen.

THE EPISTLE • Ecclus. 45, 1-6

BELOVED of God and men, whose memory is held in benediction. He made him like the Saints in glory, and magnified him in the fear of his enemies, and with his words He made prodigies to cease. He glorified him in the sight of kings, and gave him commandments in the sight of his people, and revealed to him His glory. He sanctified him in his faith and meekness, and chose him out of all flesh. For He heard him and his voice, and brought him into a cloud. And, face to face, He gave him the Commandments, the law of life and understanding. S. Thanks be to God.

THE GRADUAL • Ps. 20, 4-5

O LORD, You welcomed him with goodly blessings, You placed on his head a crown of pure gold. ℣. He asked life of You: You gave him length of days forever and ever.

Alleluia, alleluia. ℣. *Ps. 91, 13.* The just man shall flourish like the palm tree, like a cedar of Lebanon shall he grow. Alleluia.

During Paschaltime omit Gradual and Tract, and say:

Alleluia, alleluia. ℣. *Ecclus. 45, 9.* The Lord loved him, and adorned him; He clothed him with a robe of glory. Alleluia. ℣. *Osee 14, 6.* The just shall spring as the lily; and shall flourish forever before the Lord. Alleluia.

PRAYER BEFORE THE GOSPEL

Bowing down at the center of the altar, he says:

CLEANSE my heart and my lips, O almighty God, Who cleansed the lips of the Prophet

Isaias with a burning coal. In Your gracious mercy deign so to purify me that I may worthily proclaim Your holy Gospel. Through Christ our Lord. Amen.

Lord, grant Your blessing. The Lord be in my heart and on my lips, that I may worthily and fittingly proclaim His holy Gospel. Amen.

THE GOSPEL • Matt. 1, 18-21

Going to the left (Gospel) side of the altar, he says:

P. The Lord be with you. S. And with your spirit.
P. ✠ The continuation of the holy Gospel according to Saint Matthew. S. Glory be to You, O Lord.

WHEN Mary the Mother of Jesus had been betrothed to Joseph, before they came together, she was found to be with child by the Holy Spirit. But Joseph her husband, being a just man, and not wishing to expose her to reproach, was minded to put her away privately. But while he thought on these things, behold, an angel of the Lord appeared to him in a dream, saying, "Do not be afraid, Joseph, son of David, to take to you Mary your wife, for that which is begotten in her is of the Holy Spirit. And she shall bring forth a Son, and you shall call His name Jesus; for He shall save His people from their sins." S. Praise be to You, O Christ.

P. By the words of the Gospel, may our sins be taken away.

THE NICENE CREED

At the center of the altar, he says:

I BELIEVE in one God, the Father almighty, Maker of heaven and earth, and of all things visible and invisible. And in one Lord Jesus Christ, the Only-begotten Son of God. Born of the Father before all ages. God of God; Light of Light; true

God of true God. Begotten not made; of one being with the Father; by Whom all things were made. Who for us men, and for our salvation, came down from heaven. (*Here all genuflect.*) And was made Flesh by the Holy Spirit of the Virgin Mary: AND WAS MADE MAN. He was also crucified for us, suffered under Pontius Pilate and was buried. And on the third day He rose again according to the Scriptures. And ascending into heaven, He sits at the right hand of the Father. And He shall come again in glory to judge the living and the dead; and of His kingdom there shall be no end. And I believe in the Holy Spirit, Lord and Giver of life, Who proceeds from the Father and the Son. Who together with the Father and the Son is no less adored, and glorified: Who spoke by the Prophets. And I believe in One, Holy, Catholic and Apostolic Church. I confess one Baptism for the remission of sins. And I look for the resurrection of the dead. ✠ And the life of the world to come. Amen.

THE OFFERTORY

The Priest turns to the people and says:

P. The Lord be with you. *S.* And with your spirit.
P. Let us pray.

THE OFFERTORY VERSE • Ps. 88, 25

MY FAITHFULNESS and My kindness shall be with him, and through My name shall his horn be exalted. (*P.T.* Alleluia.)

The Priest now uncovers the chalice, places the host on the paten and offering it up, says:

ACCEPT, O holy Father, almighty and eternal God, this spotless host, which I, Your unworthy servant, offer to You, my living and true

God, to atone for my numberless sins, offenses, and negligences; on behalf of all here present and likewise for all faithful Christians living and dead, that it may profit me and them as a means of salvation to life everlasting. Amen.

He pours wine and water into the chalice, blessing the water before it is poured.

O GOD, Who established the nature of man in wondrous dignity, and still more admirably restored it, grant that through the mystery of this water and wine, we may be made partakers of His Divinity, Who has condescended to become partaker of our humanity, Jesus Christ, Your Son, our Lord. Who lives and reigns with You in the unity of the Holy Spirit, God, world without end. Amen.

Offering up the wine, the Priest says:

WE OFFER You, O Lord, the chalice of salvation, humbly begging of Your mercy that it may arise before Your Divine Majesty, with a pleasing fragrance, for our salvation and for that of the whole world. Amen.

Bowing down, the Priest says:

IN A humble spirit and with a contrite heart, may we be accepted by You, O Lord, and may our sacrifice so be offered in Your sight this day as to please You, O Lord God.

Raising his eyes and blessing the offering, he says:

COME, O Sanctifier, almighty and eternal God, and bless ✠ this sacrifice prepared for the glory of Your holy name.

WASHING THE FINGERS

I WASH my hands in innocence, and I go around Your altar, O Lord, giving voice to my thanks,

and recounting all Your wondrous deeds. O Lord, I love the house in which You dwell, the tenting-place of Your glory. Gather not my soul with those of sinners, nor with men of blood my life. On their hands are crimes, and their right hands are full of bribes. But I walk in integrity; redeem me, and have pity on me. My foot stands on level ground; in the assemblies I will bless You, O Lord. Glory be to the Father, and to the Son, and to the Holy Spirit. As it was in the beginning, is now, and ever shall be, world without end. Amen.

ACCEPT, Most Holy Trinity, this offering which we are making to You in remembrance of the Passion, Resurrection, and Ascension of Jesus Christ, our Lord; and in honor of Blessed Mary, ever Virgin, Blessed John the Baptist, the Holy Apostles Peter and Paul, and of these, and of all the Saints; that it may add to their honor and aid our salvation; and may they deign to intercede in heaven for us who honor their memory here on earth. Through the same Christ our Lord. Amen.

The Priest turns toward the people and says:

Pray, brethren, that my sacrifice and yours may become acceptable to God the Father almighty.

S. May the Lord accept this sacrifice from your hands to the praise and glory of His name, for our advantage, and that of all His holy Church.

P. Amen.

THE SECRET

WE PAY You, O Lord, the debt of our service, humbly entreating You to guard Your gifts within us by the prayers of Blessed Joseph, Spouse of the Mother of Your Son, Jesus Christ our Lord, on whose holy feast we offer You this sacrifice of praise. Through the same, etc. S. Amen.

PREFACE—CANON

P. The Lord be with you. S. And with your spirit.
P. Lift up your hearts.
S. We have lifted them up to the Lord.
P. Let us give thanks to the Lord, our God.
S. It is fitting and just.

IT IS fitting indeed and just, right and helpful to salvation, for us always and everywhere to give thanks to You, O holy Lord, Father almighty, everlasting God; and magnify You with due praise, bless and proclaim You on the feast of Blessed Joseph; who, as a just man, was given by You to be the spouse of the Virgin Mother of God, and as a faithful and prudent servant, was set over Your family, that with fatherly care he might guard Your Only-begotten Son, Jesus Christ our Lord, conceived by the overshadowing of the Holy Spirit. Through Whom the Angels praise Your Majesty, the Dominations adore it, the Powers are in awe. The heavens and the heavenly hosts and the blessed Seraphim join together in celebrating their joy. With these we pray You, join our own voices also, while we say with lowly praise: Holy, Holy, Holy, Lord God of Hosts. Heaven and earth are filled with Your glory. Hosanna in the highest. ✠ Blessed is He Who comes in the name of the Lord. Hosanna in the highest.

THE CANON OF THE MASS

THEREFORE, most gracious Father, we humbly beg of You and entreat You through Jesus

Christ Your Son, our Lord, (*he kisses the altar*) to deem acceptable and bless these ✠ gifts, these ✠ offerings, these ✠ holy and unspotted oblations which, in the first place, we offer You for Your Holy Catholic Church, that You would deign to give her peace and protection, to unite and guard her throughout the world, together with Your servant N., our Pope, and N., our Bishop; and all true believers who cherish the Catholic and Apostolic Faith.

Commemoration of the Living

REMEMBER, O Lord, Your servants and handmaids, N. and N., (*name them*) and all here present, whose faith and devotion are known to You, on whose behalf we offer to You, or who themselves offer to You, this sacrifice of praise for themselves, families and friends, for the good of their souls, for their hope of salvation and deliverance from all harm, and who offer their homage to You, eternal, living and true God.

Commemoration of the Saints

IN THE unity of holy fellowship we observe the memory, first of all, of the glorious and ever Virgin Mary, Mother of our Lord and God Jesus Christ; next, that of Your Blessed Apostles and Martyrs, Peter and Paul, Andrew, James, John, Thomas, James, Philip, Bartholomew, Matthew, Simon and Thaddeus; of Linus, Cletus, Clement, Sixtus, Cornelius, Cyprian, Lawrence, Chrysogonus, John and Paul, Cosmas and Damian, and of all Your Saints, by whose merits and prayers grant that we may be always fortified by the help of Your protection. Through the same Christ our Lord. Amen.

Spreading his hands over the oblation, he says:

GRACIOUSLY accept, then, we beseech You, O Lord, this service of our worship and that of all Your household. Provide that our days be spent in Your peace, save us from everlasting damnation, and cause us to be numbered in the flock You have chosen. Through Christ our Lord. Amen.

O GOD, deign to bless ✠ what we offer, and make it approved, ✠ effective, ✠ right, and wholly pleasing in every way, that it may become for our good, the Body ✠ and Blood ✠ of Your dearly beloved Son, Jesus Christ our Lord.

CONSECRATION—ELEVATION

WHO, the day before He suffered, took bread into His holy and venerable hands, and having raised His eyes to heaven, to You, O God, His almighty Father, giving thanks to You, He blessed it, ✠ broke it, and gave it to His disciples, saying: All of you take and eat of this:

FOR THIS IS MY BODY.

IN LIKE manner, when the supper was done, taking also this goodly chalice into His holy and venerable hands, again giving thanks to You, He blessed ✠ it, and gave it to His disciples, saying: All of you take and drink of this:

FOR THIS IS THE CHALICE OF MY BLOOD OF THE NEW AND ETERNAL COVENANT: THE MYSTERY OF FAITH: WHICH SHALL BE SHED FOR YOU AND FOR MANY UNTO THE FORGIVENESS OF SINS.

After replacing the chalice on the corporal, he says:

As often as you shall do these things, in memory of Me shall you do them.

Offering of the Victim

MINDFUL, therefore, O Lord, not only of the blessed Passion of the same Christ, Your Son, our Lord, but also of His Resurrection from the dead, and finally His glorious Ascension into heaven, we, Your ministers, as also Your holy people, offer to Your supreme Majesty, of the gifts bestowed upon us, the pure ✠ Victim, the holy ✠ Victim, the all-perfect ✠ Victim: the holy ✠ Bread of life eternal and the Chalice ✠ of unending salvation.

AND this deign to regard with gracious and kindly attention and hold acceptable, as You deigned to accept the offerings of Abel, Your just servant, and the sacrifice of Abraham our patriarch, and that which Your chief priest Melchisedec offered to You, a holy sacrifice and a spotless victim.

MOST humbly we implore You, almighty God, bid these offerings to be brought by the hands of Your holy angel to Your altar above; before the face of Your Divine Majesty; that those of us who, by sharing in the Sacrifice of this altar, shall receive the Most Sacred ✠ Body and ✠ Blood of Your Son, may be filled with every grace and heavenly blessing. Through the same Christ our Lord. Amen.

Commemoration of the Dead

REMEMBER also, O Lord, Your servants and handmaids, *N.* and *N.*, who have gone before us with the sign of faith, and rest in the sleep of

peace. (*Here pray for the dead.*) To these, O Lord, and to all who rest in Christ, we beseech You to grant of Your goodness, a place of comfort, light and peace. Through the same Christ our Lord. Amen.

TO US sinners also, Your servants, trusting in the greatness of Your mercy, deign to grant some part and fellowship with Your Holy Apostles and Martyrs: with John, Stephen, Matthias, Barnabas, Ignatius, Alexander, Marcellinus, Peter, Felicitas, Perpetua, Agatha, Lucy, Agnes, Cecilia, Anastasia, and all Your Saints; into whose company, we implore You to admit us, not weighing our merits, but freely granting us pardon. Through Christ our Lord.

THROUGH Whom, O Lord, You always create, ✠ sanctify, ✠ fill with life, ✠ bless, and bestow upon us all good things.

The Minor Elevation

THROUGH ✠ Him, and with ✠ Him, and in ✠ Him, is to You, God the Father ✠ almighty, in the unity of the Holy ✠ Spirit, all honor and glory, world without end. S. Amen.

THE COMMUNION AND THANKSGIVING

Let us pray. Prompted by saving precepts, and taught by Your divine teaching, we dare to say:

OUR FATHER, Who art in heaven, hallowed be Thy name: Thy kingdom come: Thy will be done on earth as it is in heaven. Give us this day our daily bread; and forgive us our trespasses, as we forgive those who trespass against us. And lead us

not into temptation: S. But deliver us from evil. *P*. Amen.

DELIVER us, we beseech You, O Lord, from all evils, past, present, and to come; and by the intercession of the Blessed and glorious Mary, ever Virgin, Mother of God, together with Your Blessed Apostles Peter and Paul, and Andrew, and all the Saints, grant of Your goodness, peace in our days, that aided by the riches of Your mercy, we may be always free from sin and safe from all disturbance.

Through the same our Lord Jesus Christ, Your Son, Who lives and reigns with You in the unity of the Holy Spirit, God, world without end. *S*. Amen.

P. May the peace ✠ of the Lord be ✠ always with ✠ you. *S*. And with your spirit.

The Priest puts a small particle into the chalice, saying:

May this mingling and consecration of the Body and Blood of our Lord Jesus Christ help us who receive it to life everlasting. Amen.

LAMB of God, You Who take away the sins of the world, have mercy on us.

Lamb of God, You Who take away the sins of the world, have mercy on us.

Lamb of God, You Who take away the sins of the world, grant us peace.

PRAYERS BEFORE HOLY COMMUNION

Then inclining toward the altar, he says:

O LORD Jesus Christ, Who said to Your Apostles: "Peace I leave with you, My peace I give to you," regard not my sins but the faith of Your Church, and deign to give her peace and unity

according to Your Will: Who live and reign, God, world without end. Amen.

O LORD Jesus Christ, Son of the living God, Who, by the will of the Father, with the co-operation of the Holy Spirit, have by Your death given life to the world, deliver me by this Your Most Sacred Body and Blood from all my sins and from every evil. Make me always cling to Your commandments, and never permit me to be separated from You. Who with the same God the Father and the Holy Spirit, live and reign, God, world without end. Amen.

LET not the partaking of Your Body, O Lord Jesus Christ, which I, though unworthy, presume to receive, turn to my judgment and condemnation; but through Your goodness, may it become a safeguard and an effective remedy, both of soul and body. Who live and reign with God the Father, in the unity of the Holy Spirit, God, world without end. Amen.

COMMUNION OF THE PRIEST

I WILL take the Bread of heaven, and call upon the name of the Lord.

Lord, I am not worthy that You should come under my roof; but only say the word, and my soul will be healed. (3 *times.*)

Making the Sign of the Cross with the Host, he says:

MAY the Body of our Lord Jesus Christ preserve my soul to life everlasting. Amen.

What return shall I make to the Lord for all He has given me? I will take the Chalice of salvation, and I will call upon the name of the Lord. Prais-

ing will I call upon the Lord and I shall be saved from my enemies.

Making the Sign of the Cross with the chalice, he says:

MAY the Blood of our Lord Jesus Christ preserve my soul to life everlasting. Amen.

The Priest reverently consumes the Precious Blood.

COMMUNION OF THE FAITHFUL

The Server and people say the "Confiteor."

P. May almighty God have mercy on you, forgive you your sins, and bring you to life everlasting. *S.* Amen.

P. May the almighty and merciful Lord grant you pardon, ✠ absolution and remission of your sins. *S.* Amen.

Holding up a Sacred Host, the Priest says:

Behold the Lamb of God, behold Him Who takes away the sins of the world.

Lord, I am not worthy that You should come under my roof; but only say the word, and my soul will be healed. (3 *times.*)

The Priest says to each communicant:

May the Body of our Lord Jesus Christ preserve your soul to life everlasting. Amen.

The Priest purifies the chalice with wine, saying:

WHAT has passed our lips as food, O Lord, may we possess in purity of heart, that what is given to us in time, be our healing for eternity.

He purifies his fingers with wine and water, saying:

MAY Your Body, O Lord, which I have eaten, and Your Blood which I have drunk, cleave to my very soul, and grant that no trace of sin be found in me, whom these pure and holy mysteries

have renewed. Who live and reign, world without end. Amen.

THE COMMUNION • Matt. 1, 20

DO NOT be afraid, Joseph, son of David, to take to you Mary your wife, for that which is begotten in her is of the Holy Spirit. (*P.T.* Alleluia.)

The Priest, turning to the people, says:

P. The Lord be with you. *S.* And with your spirit.
P. Let us pray.

THE POSTCOMMUNION

BE PRESENT with us, we beseech You, O merciful God, and by the intercession of Blessed Joseph, Your Confessor, mercifully guard Your gifts bestowed upon us. Through our Lord Jesus Christ, Your Son, Who lives and reigns, etc. *S.* Amen.

FINAL PRAYERS

P. The Lord be with you. *S.* And with your spirit.
P. Go, you are dismissed. *S.* Thanks be to God.

MAY the tribute of my worship be pleasing to You, Most Holy Trinity, and grant that the sacrifice which I, all unworthy, have offered in the presence of Your Majesty, may be acceptable to You, and through Your mercy obtain forgiveness for me and all for whom I have offered it. Through Christ our Lord. Amen.

THE LAST BLESSING

MAY almighty God bless you: ✠ the Father, and the Son, and the Holy Spirit. *S.* Amen.

The Last Gospel and Prayers after Low Mass are conveniently placed inside the back cover.

"Mary Is Taken Up into Heaven: the Host of Angels Rejoice."

Aug. 15—THE ASSUMPTION

On November 1, 1950, Pope Pius XII defined as a truth revealed by God that the Immaculate Mother of God, Mary, ever Virgin, when the course of her life on earth was finished, was taken up body and soul into heaven. On this occasion the following Mass of the Assumption was used for the first time by our Holy Father. (WHITE VESTMENTS)

PRAYERS AT THE FOOT OF THE ALTAR

IN THE name of the Father, ✠ and of the Son, and of the Holy Spirit. Amen.

Priest. I will go in to the altar of God.

Server. The God of my gladness and joy.

Psalm 42

DO ME justice, O God, and fight my fight against a faithless people; from the deceitful and impious man rescue me.

S. For You, O God, are my strength. Why do You keep me so far away? Why must I go about in mourning, with the enemy oppressing me?

P. Send forth Your light and Your fidelity; they shall lead me on and bring me to Your holy mountain, to Your dwelling-place.

S. Then will I go in to the altar of God, the God of my gladness and joy.

P. Then will I give You thanks upon the harp, O God, my God. Why are you so downcast, O my soul? Why do you sigh within me?

S. Hope in God! For I shall again be thanking Him in the presence of my Savior and my God.

720-38

P. Glory be to the Father, and to the Son, and to the Holy Spirit.
S. As it was in the beginning, is now, and ever shall be, world without end. Amen.
P. I will go in to the altar of God.
S. The God of my gladness and joy.
P. Our help ✠ is in the name of the Lord.
S. Who made heaven and earth.
P. I confess to almighty God, etc.
S. May almighty God have mercy on you, forgive you your sins, and bring you to life everlasting.
P. Amen.

The Server, bowing, says the "Confiteor."

I CONFESS to almighty God, to Blessed Mary, ever Virgin, to Blessed Michael the Archangel, to Blessed John the Baptist, to the Holy Apostles Peter and Paul, and to all the Saints, and to you, Father, that I have sinned exceedingly in thought, word and deed, *through my fault, through my fault, through my most grievous fault.* Therefore I beseech Blessed Mary, ever Virgin, Blessed Michael the Archangel, Blessed John the Baptist, the Holy Apostles Peter and Paul, and all the Saints, and you, Father, to pray to the Lord our God for me.
P. May almighty God have mercy on you, forgive you your sins, and bring you to life everlasting.
S. Amen.

MAY the almighty and merciful Lord grant us pardon, ✠ absolution, and remission of our sins. S. Amen.
P. Will You not, O God, give us life?
S. And shall not Your people rejoice in You?

P. Show us, O Lord, Your kindness.
S. And grant us Your salvation.
P. O Lord, hear my prayer.
S. And let my cry come to You.
P. The Lord be with you.
S. And with your spirit. *P.* Let us pray.

Going up to the altar, the Priest prays silently:

TAKE away from us our sins, O Lord, we beseech You, that we may enter with pure minds into the Holy of Holies. Through Christ our Lord. Amen.

WE BESEECH You, O Lord, by the merits of Your Saints (*he kisses the altar*) whose relics lie here, and of all the Saints: deign in Your mercy to pardon me all my sins. Amen.

THE INTROIT • Apoc. 12, 1

At the right side of the altar, the Priest says:

A GREAT sign appeared in heaven: a woman clothed with the sun, and the moon was under her feet, and upon her head a crown of twelve stars. *Ps.* 97. Sing to the Lord a new song, for He has done wondrous deeds. Glory be to the Father, and to the Son, and to the Holy Spirit. As it was in the beginning, is now, and ever shall be, world without end. Amen. — A great sign appeared in heaven: a woman clothed with the sun, and the moon was under her feet, and upon her head a crown of twelve stars.

THE KYRIE

P. Lord, have mercy. S. Lord, have mercy. *P.* Lord, have mercy. S. Christ, have mercy. *P.* Christ, have

mercy. *S.* Christ, have mercy. *P.* Lord, have mercy. *S.* Lord, have mercy. *P.* Lord, have mercy.

THE GLORIA

GLORY to God in the highest. And on earth peace to men of good will. We praise You. We bless You. We adore You. We glorify You. We give You thanks for Your great glory. O Lord God, heavenly King, God the Father almighty. O Lord Jesus Christ, the Only-begotten Son. O Lord God, Lamb of God, Son of the Father: You Who take away the sins of the world, have mercy on us. You Who take away the sins of the world, receive our prayer. You Who sit at the right hand of the Father, have mercy on us. For You alone are holy. You alone are the Lord. You alone, O Jesus Christ, are most high. Together with the Holy Spirit ✠ in the glory of God the Father. Amen.

The Priest kisses the altar and turns to the people, saying:

P. The Lord be with you. *S.* And with your spirit. *P.* Let us pray.

THE PRAYER

Going to the right (Epistle) side, he says:

O ALMIGHTY and eternal God, You assumed to celestial glory, in body and soul, the Immaculate Virgin Mary, the Mother of Your Son; grant, we beseech You, that, ever intent on heavenly things, we may be worthy to share in her glory. Through the same our Lord Jesus Christ, Your Son, Who lives and reigns with You in the unity of the Holy Spirit, God, world without end. *S.* Amen.

THE EPISTLE • Judith 13, 22-25; 15, 10

THE Lord has blessed you by His power, because by you He has brought our enemies to naught. Blessed are you, O daughter, by the Lord the Most High God, above all women upon the earth. Blessed be the Lord Who made heaven and earth, Who has directed you to the cutting off the head of the prince of our enemies, because He has so magnified your name this day, that your praise shall not depart out of the mouth of men, who shall be mindful of the power of the Lord forever; for you have not spared your life, by reason of the distress and tribulation of your people, but have prevented our ruin in the presence of our God. You are the glory of Jerusalem, you are the joy of Israel, you are the honor of our people. S. Thanks be to God.

THE GRADUAL • Ps. 44, 11-12. 14

HEAR, O daughter, and see; turn your ear; for the King shall desire your beauty. ℣. All glorious is the King's daughter as she enters; her raiment is threaded with spun gold.

Alleluia, alleluia. ℣. Mary is taken up into heaven: the host of angels rejoice. Alleluia.

PRAYER BEFORE THE GOSPEL

Bowing down at the center of the altar, he says:

CLEANSE my heart and my lips, O almighty God, Who cleansed the lips of the Prophet Isaias with a burning coal. In Your gracious mercy deign so to purify me that I may worthily proclaim Your holy Gospel. Through Christ our Lord. Amen.

Lord, grant Your blessing. The Lord be in my heart and on my lips, that I may worthily and fittingly proclaim His holy Gospel. Amen.

THE GOSPEL • Luke 1, 41-50

Going to the left (Gospel) side of the altar, he says:

P. The Lord be with you. *S.* And with your spirit.
P. ✠ The continuation of the holy Gospel according to Saint Luke. *S.* Glory be to You, O Lord.

AT THAT time, Elizabeth was filled with the Holy Spirit, and cried out with a loud voice, saying, "Blessed are you among women and blessed is the fruit of your womb! And how have I deserved that the Mother of my Lord should come to me? For behold, the moment that the sound of your greeting came to my ears, the babe in my womb leapt for joy. And blessed is she who has believed, because the things promised her by the Lord shall be accomplished." And Mary said, "My soul magnifies the Lord, and my spirit rejoices in God my Savior; because He has regarded the lowliness of His handmaid; for, behold, henceforth all generations shall call me blessed; because He Who is mighty has done great things for me, and holy is His name; and His mercy is from generation to generation on those who fear Him." *S.* Praise be to You, O Christ.

P. By the words of the Gospel, may our sins be taken away.

THE NICENE CREED

At the center of the altar, he says:

I BELIEVE in one God, the Father almighty, Maker of heaven and earth, and of all things visible and invisible. And in one Lord Jesus Christ, the Only-begotten Son of God. Born of the Father before all ages. God of God; Light of Light; true God of true God. Begotten not made; of one being with the Father; by Whom all things were

made. Who for us men, and for our salvation, came down from heaven. (*Here all genuflect.*) And was made Flesh by the Holy Spirit of the Virgin Mary: AND WAS MADE MAN. He was also crucified for us, suffered under Pontius Pilate and was buried. And on the third day He rose again according to the Scriptures. And ascending into heaven, He sits at the right hand of the Father. And He shall come again in glory to judge the living and the dead; and of His kingdom there shall be no end. And I believe in the Holy Spirit, Lord and Giver of life, Who proceeds from the Father and the Son. Who together with the Father and the Son is no less adored, and glorified: Who spoke by the Prophets. And I believe in One, Holy, Catholic and Apostolic Church. I confess one Baptism for the remission of sins. And I look for the resurrection of the dead. ✠ And the life of the world to come. Amen.

THE OFFERTORY

The Priest turns to the people and says:

P. The Lord be with you. *S.* And with your spirit.
P. Let us pray.

THE OFFERTORY VERSE • Gen. 3, 15

I WILL put enmity between you and the Woman, between your seed and her seed.

The Priest now uncovers the chalice, places the host on the paten and offering it up, says:

ACCEPT, O holy Father, almighty and eternal God, this spotless host, which I, Your unworthy servant, offer to You, my living and true God, to atone for my numberless sins, offenses, and negligences; on behalf of all here present and likewise for all faithful Christians living and dead,

that it may profit me and them as a means of salvation to life everlasting. Amen.

He pours wine and water into the chalice, blessing the water before it is poured.

O GOD, Who established the nature of man in wondrous dignity, and still more admirably restored it, grant that through the mystery of this water and wine, we may be made partakers of His Divinity, Who has condescended to become partaker of our humanity, Jesus Christ, Your Son, our Lord. Who lives and reigns with You in the unity of the Holy Spirit, God, world without end. Amen.

Offering up the wine, the Priest says:

WE OFFER You, O Lord, the chalice of salvation, humbly begging of Your mercy that it may arise before Your Divine Majesty, with a pleasing fragrance, for our salvation and for that of the whole world. Amen.

Bowing down, the Priest says:

IN A humble spirit and with a contrite heart, may we be accepted by You, O Lord, and may our sacrifice so be offered in Your sight this day as to please You, O Lord God.

Raising his eyes and blessing the offering, he says:

COME, O Sanctifier, almighty and eternal God, and bless ✠ this sacrifice prepared for the glory of Your holy name.

WASHING THE FINGERS

I WASH my hands in innocence, and I go around Your altar, O Lord, giving voice to my thanks, and recounting all Your wondrous deeds. O Lord, I love the house in which You dwell, the tenting-place of Your glory. Gather not my soul with those of sinners, nor with men of blood my life. On their hands are crimes, and their right hands are full of bribes. But I walk in integrity; redeem me, and have pity on me. My foot stands on level ground; in the assemblies I will bless You, O Lord. Glory be to the Father, and to the Son, and to the Holy Spirit. As it was in the beginning, is now, and ever shall be, world without end. Amen.

ACCEPT, Most Holy Trinity, this offering which we are making to You in remembrance of the Passion, Resurrection, and Ascension of Jesus Christ, our Lord; and in honor of Blessed Mary, ever Virgin, Blessed John the Baptist, the Holy Apostles Peter and Paul, and of these, and of all the Saints; that it may add to their honor and aid our salvation; and may they deign to intercede in heaven for us who honor their memory here on earth. Through the same Christ our Lord. Amen.

The Priest turns toward the people and says:

Pray, brethren, that my sacrifice and yours may become acceptable to God the Father almighty.

S. May the Lord accept this sacrifice from your hands to the praise and glory of His name, for our advantage, and that of all His holy Church.

P. Amen.

THE SECRET

MAY the offering of our devotion ascend to You, O Lord, and through the intercession of the Most Blessed Virgin Mary, assumed into heaven, may our hearts, fired by the flame of charity, incessantly long for You. Through our Lord Jesus Christ, Your Son, Who lives and reigns with You in the unity of the Holy Spirit, God.

P. World without end. *S.* Amen.

PREFACE—CANON

P. The Lord be with you. *S.* And with your spirit.
P. Lift up your hearts.
S. We have lifted them up to the Lord.
P. Let us give thanks to the Lord, our God.
S. It is fitting and just.

IT IS fitting indeed and just, right and helpful to salvation, for us always and everywhere to give thanks to You, O holy Lord, Father almighty, everlasting God, and that we should praise, bless, and proclaim You in the Assumption of the Blessed Mary, ever Virgin; for she conceived Your Only-begotten Son by the overshadowing of the Holy Spirit, and, while the glory of her virginity remained, brought forth to the world the Eternal Light, Jesus Christ, our Lord. Through Whom the Angels praise Your Majesty, the Dominations adore it, the Powers are in awe. The heavens and the heavenly hosts and the blessed Seraphim join together in celebrating their joy. With these, we pray You, join our own voices also, while we say with lowly praise (*the bell is rung* 3 *times*):

HOLY, HOLY, HOLY, Lord God of Hosts. Heaven and earth are filled with Your glory. Hosanna in the highest. ✠ Blessed is He Who comes in the name of the Lord. Hosanna in the highest.

THE CANON OF THE MASS

THEREFORE, most gracious Father, we humbly beg of You and entreat You through Jesus Christ Your Son, our Lord, (*he kisses the altar*) to deem acceptable and bless these ✠ gifts, these ✠ offerings, these ✠ holy and unspotted oblations

which, in the first place, we offer You for Your Holy Catholic Church, that You would deign to give her peace and protection, to unite and guard her throughout the world, together with Your servant N., our Pope, and N., our Bishop; and all true believers who cherish the Catholic and Apostolic Faith.

Commemoration of the Living

REMEMBER, O Lord, Your servants and handmaids, N. and N., (*name them*) and all here present, whose faith and devotion are known to You, on whose behalf we offer to You, or who themselves offer to You, this sacrifice of praise for themselves, families and friends, for the good of their souls, for their hope of salvation and deliverance from all harm, and who offer their homage to You, eternal, living and true God.

Commemoration of the Saints

IN THE unity of holy fellowship we observe the memory, first of all, of the glorious and ever Virgin Mary, Mother of our Lord and God Jesus Christ; next, that of Your Blessed Apostles and Martyrs, Peter and Paul, Andrew, James, John, Thomas, James, Philip, Bartholomew, Matthew, Simon and Thaddeus; of Linus, Cletus, Clement, Sixtus, Cornelius, Cyprian, Lawrence, Chrysogonus, John and Paul, Cosmas and Damian, and of all Your Saints, by whose merits and prayers grant that we may be always fortified by the help of Your protection. Through the same Christ our Lord. Amen.

Spreading his hands over the oblation, he says:

GRACIOUSLY accept, then, we beseech You, O Lord, this service of our worship and that of all Your household. Provide that our days be

spent in Your peace, save us from everlasting damnation, and cause us to be numbered in the flock You have chosen. Through Christ our Lord. Amen.

O GOD, deign to bless ✠ what we offer, and make it approved, ✠ effective, ✠ right, and wholly pleasing in every way, that it may become for our good, the Body ✠ and Blood ✠ of Your dearly beloved Son, Jesus Christ our Lord.

CONSECRATION—ELEVATION

WHO, the day before He suffered, took bread into His holy and venerable hands, and having raised His eyes to heaven, to You, O God, His almighty Father, giving thanks to You, He blessed it, ✠ broke it, and gave it to His disciples, saying: All of you take and eat of this:

FOR THIS IS MY BODY.

IN LIKE manner, when the supper was done, taking also this goodly chalice into His holy and venerable hands, again giving thanks to You, He blessed ✠ it, and gave it to His disciples, saying: All of you take and drink of this:

FOR THIS IS THE CHALICE OF MY BLOOD OF THE NEW AND ETERNAL COVENANT: THE MYSTERY OF FAITH: WHICH SHALL BE SHED FOR YOU AND FOR MANY UNTO THE FORGIVENESS OF SINS.

After replacing the chalice on the corporal, he says:

As often as you shall do these things, in memory of Me shall you do them.

Offering of the Victim

MINDFUL, therefore, O Lord, not only of the blessed Passion of the same Christ, Your Son,

our Lord, but also of His Resurrection from the dead, and finally His glorious Ascension into heaven, we, Your ministers, as also Your holy people, offer to Your supreme Majesty, of the gifts bestowed upon us, the pure ✠ Victim, the holy ✠ Victim, the all-perfect ✠ Victim: the holy ✠ Bread of life eternal and the Chalice ✠ of unending salvation.

AND this deign to regard with gracious and kindly attention and hold acceptable, as You deigned to accept the offerings of Abel, Your just servant, and the sacrifice of Abraham our patriarch, and that which Your chief priest Melchisedec offered to You, a holy sacrifice and a spotless victim.

MOST humbly we implore You, almighty God, bid these offerings to be brought by the hands of Your holy angel to Your altar above; before the face of Your Divine Majesty; that those of us who, by sharing in the Sacrifice of this altar, shall receive the Most Sacred ✠ Body and ✠ Blood of Your Son, may be filled with every grace and heavenly blessing. Through the same Christ our Lord. Amen.

Commemoration of the Dead

REMEMBER also, O Lord, Your servants and handmaids, N. and N., who have gone before us with the sign of faith, and rest in the sleep of peace. (*Here pray for the dead.*) To these, O Lord, and to all who rest in Christ, we beseech You to grant of Your goodness, a place of comfort, light and peace. Through the same Christ our Lord. Amen.

TO US sinners also, Your servants, trusting in the greatness of Your mercy, deign to grant some

part and fellowship with Your Holy Apostles and Martyrs: with John, Stephen, Matthias, Barnabas, Ignatius, Alexander, Marcellinus, Peter, Felicitas, Perpetua, Agatha, Lucy, Agnes, Cecilia, Anastasia, and all Your Saints; into whose company, we implore You to admit us, not weighing our merits, but freely granting us pardon. Through Christ our Lord.

THROUGH Whom, O Lord, You always create, ✠ sanctify, ✠ fill with life, ✠ bless, and bestow upon us all good things.

The Minor Elevation

THROUGH ✠ Him, and with ✠ Him, and in ✠ Him, is to You, God the Father ✠ almighty, in the unity of the Holy ✠ Spirit, all honor and glory, world without end. S. Amen.

THE COMMUNION AND THANKSGIVING

Let us pray. Prompted by saving precepts, and taught by Your divine teaching, we dare to say:

OUR FATHER, Who art in heaven, hallowed be Thy name: Thy kingdom come: Thy will be done on earth as it is in heaven. Give us this day our daily bread; and forgive us our trespasses, as we forgive those who trespass against us. And lead us not into temptation: S. But deliver us from evil. *P.* Amen.

DELIVER us, we beseech You, O Lord, from all evils, past, present, and to come; and by the intercession of the Blessed and glorious Mary, ever Virgin, Mother of God, together with Your Blessed Apostles Peter and Paul, and Andrew, and all the Saints, grant of Your goodness, peace in our

days, that aided by the riches of Your mercy, we may be always free from sin and safe from all disturbance.

Through the same our Lord Jesus Christ, Your Son, Who lives and reigns with You in the unity of the Holy Spirit, God, world without end.

S. Amen.

P. May the peace ✠ of the Lord be ✠ always with ✠ you.

S. And with your spirit.

The Priest puts a small particle into the chalice, saying:

May this mingling and consecration of the Body and Blood of our Lord Jesus Christ help us who receive it to life everlasting. Amen.

LAMB of God, You Who take away the sins of the world, have mercy on us.

Lamb of God, You Who take away the sins of the world, have mercy on us.

Lamb of God, You Who take away the sins of the world, grant us peace.

PRAYERS BEFORE HOLY COMMUNION

Then inclining toward the altar, he says:

O LORD Jesus Christ, Who said to Your Apostles: "Peace I leave with you, My peace I give to you," regard not my sins but the faith of Your Church, and deign to give her peace and unity according to Your Will: Who live and reign, God, world without end. Amen.

O LORD Jesus Christ, Son of the living God, Who, by the will of the Father, with the cooperation of the Holy Spirit, have by Your death given life to the world, deliver me by this Your Most Sacred Body and Blood from all my sins and from every evil. Make me always cling to Your commandments, and never permit me to be separated from You. Who with the same God the Father and the Holy Spirit, live and reign, God, world without end. Amen.

LET not the partaking of Your Body, O Lord Jesus Christ, which I, though unworthy, presume to receive, turn to my judgment and condemnation; but through Your goodness, may it become a safeguard and an effective remedy, both of soul and body. Who live and reign with God the Father, in the unity of the Holy Spirit, God, world without end. Amen.

COMMUNION OF THE PRIEST

I WILL take the Bread of heaven, and call upon the name of the Lord.

Lord, I am not worthy that You should come under my roof; but only say the word, and my soul will be healed. (3 *times.*)

Making the Sign of the Cross with the Host, he says:

MAY the Body of our Lord Jesus Christ preserve my soul to life everlasting. Amen.

What return shall I make to the Lord for all He has given me? I will take the Chalice of salvation, and I will call upon the name of the Lord. Praising will I call upon the Lord and I shall be saved from my enemies.

Making the Sign of the Cross with the chalice, he says:

MAY the Blood of our Lord Jesus Christ preserve my soul to life everlasting. Amen.

The Priest reverently consumes the Precious Blood.

COMMUNION OF THE FAITHFUL

The Server and people say the "Confiteor."

P. May almighty God have mercy on you, forgive you your sins, and bring you to life everlasting. *S.* Amen.

P. May the almighty and merciful Lord grant you pardon, ✠ absolution and remission of your sins. *S.* Amen.

Holding up a Sacred Host, the Priest says:

Behold the Lamb of God, behold Him Who takes away the sins of the world.

Lord, I am not worthy that You should come under my roof; but only say the word, and my soul will be healed. (3 *times.*)

The Priest says to each communicant:

May the Body of our Lord Jesus Christ preserve your soul to life everlasting. Amen.

The Priest purifies the chalice with wine, saying:

WHAT has passed our lips as food, O Lord, may we possess in purity of heart, that what is given to us in time, be our healing for eternity.

He purifies his fingers with wine and water, saying:

MAY Your Body, O Lord, which I have eaten, and Your Blood which I have drunk, cleave to my very soul, and grant that no trace of sin be found in me, whom these pure and holy mysteries have renewed. Who live and reign, world without end. Amen.

THE COMMUNION • Luke 1, 48-49

ALL generations shall call me blessed; because He Who is mighty has done great things for me.

The Priest, turning to the people, says:

P. The Lord be with you. *S.* And with your spirit.
P. Let us pray.

THE POSTCOMMUNION

HAVING received Your salutary sacraments, grant, we beseech You, O Lord, that through the merits and intercession of the Blessed Virgin Mary, assumed into heaven, we may be brought to the glory of the resurrection. Through our Lord Jesus Christ, Your Son, Who lives and reigns with You in the unity of the Holy Spirit, God, world without end. *S.* Amen.

FINAL PRAYERS

The Priest turns again to the people, and says:

P. The Lord be with you. *S.* And with your spirit.
P. Go, you are dismissed. *S.* Thanks be to God.

MAY the tribute of my worship be pleasing to You, Most Holy Trinity, and grant that the sacrifice which I, all unworthy, have offered in the presence of Your Majesty, may be acceptable to You, and through Your mercy obtain forgiveness for me and all for whom I have offered it. Through Christ our Lord. Amen.

THE LAST BLESSING

He kisses the altar, and facing the people, says:

MAY almighty God bless you: ✠ the Father, and the Son, and the Holy Spirit.

S. Amen.

The Last Gospel and Prayers after Low Mass **are** *conveniently placed inside the back cover.*

"Blessed are the clean of heart, for they shall see God."

Nov. 1—FEAST OF ALL SAINTS

Whether or not their names are commemorated in the Liturgy, the Church today honors all Saints, those holy souls who during life loved Jesus and strove to imitate Him. (WHITE VESTMENTS)

PRAYERS AT THE FOOT OF THE ALTAR

IN THE name of the Father, ✠ and of the Son, and of the Holy Spirit. Amen.

Priest. I will go in to the altar of God.

Server. The God of my gladness and joy.

Psalm 42

DO ME justice, O God, and fight my fight against a faithless people; from the deceitful and impious man rescue me.

S. For You, O God, are my strength. Why do You keep me so far away? Why must I go about in mourning, with the enemy oppressing me?

P. Send forth Your light and Your fidelity; they shall lead me on and bring me to Your holy mountain, to Your dwelling-place.

S. Then will I go in to the altar of God, the God of my gladness and joy.
P. Then will I give You thanks upon the harp, O God, my God. Why are you so downcast, O my soul? Why do you sigh within me?
S. Hope in God! For I shall again be thanking Him in the presence of my Savior and my God.
P. Glory be to the Father, and to the Son, and to the Holy Spirit.
S. As it was in the beginning, is now, and ever shall be, world without end. Amen.
P. I will go in to the altar of God.
S. The God of my gladness and joy.
P. Our help ✠ is in the name of the Lord.
S. Who made heaven and earth.
P. I confess to almighty God, etc.
S. May almighty God have mercy on you, forgive you your sins, and bring you to life everlasting.
P. Amen.

The Server, bowing, says the "Confiteor."

I CONFESS to almighty God, to Blessed Mary, ever Virgin, to Blessed Michael the Archangel, to Blessed John the Baptist, to the Holy Apostles Peter and Paul, and to all the Saints, and to you, Father, that I have sinned exceedingly in thought, word and deed, *through my fault, through my fault, through my most grievous fault*. Therefore I beseech Blessed Mary, ever Virgin, Blessed Michael the Archangel, Blessed John the Baptist, the Holy Apostles Peter and Paul, and all the Saints, and you, Father, to pray to the Lord our God for me.
P. May almighty God have mercy on you, forgive you your sins, and bring you to life everlasting.
S. Amen.

MAY the almighty and merciful Lord grant us pardon, ✠ absolution, and remission of our sins. *S.* Amen.

P. Will You not, O God, give us life?
S. And shall not Your people rejoice in You?
P. Show us, O Lord, Your kindness.
S. And grant us Your salvation.
P. O Lord, hear my prayer.
S. And let my cry come to You.
P. The Lord be with you.
S. And with your spirit. *P.* Let us pray.

Going up to the altar, the Priest prays silently:

TAKE away from us our sins, O Lord, we beseech You, that we may enter with pure minds into the Holy of Holies. Through Christ our Lord. Amen.

WE BESEECH You, O Lord, by the merits of Your Saints (*he kisses the altar*) whose relics lie here, and of all the Saints: deign in Your mercy to pardon me all my sins. Amen.

THE INTROIT · Ps. 32, 1

At the right side of the altar, the Priest says:

LET us all rejoice in the Lord, celebrating a feast day in honor of all the Saints, on whose solemnity the angels rejoice, and give praise to the Son of God. *Ps.* Exult, you just, in the Lord; praise from the upright is fitting. Glory be to the Father, and to the Son, and to the Holy Spirit. As it was in the beginning, is now, and ever shall be, world without end. Amen. — Let us all rejoice in the Lord, celebrating a feast day in honor of all the Saints, on whose solemnity the angels rejoice, and give praise to the Son of God.

THE KYRIE

P. Lord, have mercy. *S.* Lord, have mercy. *P.* Lord, have mercy. *S.* Christ, have mercy. *P.* Christ, have mercy. *S.* Christ, have mercy. *P.* Lord, have mercy. *S.* Lord, have mercy. *P.* Lord, have mercy.

THE GLORIA

GLORY to God in the highest. And on earth peace to men of good will. We praise You. We bless You. We adore You. We glorify You. We give You thanks for Your great glory. O Lord God, heavenly King, God the Father almighty. O Lord Jesus Christ, the Only-begotten Son. O Lord God, Lamb of God, Son of the Father: You Who take away the sins of the world, have mercy on us. You Who take away the sins of the world, receive our prayer. You Who sit at the right hand of the Father, have mercy on us. For You alone are holy. You alone are the Lord. You alone, O Jesus Christ, are most high. Together with the Holy Spirit ✠ in the glory of God the Father. Amen.

The Priest kisses the altar and turns to the people, saying:

P. The Lord be with you. *S.* And with your spirit. *P.* Let us pray.

THE PRAYER

Going to the right (Epistle) side, he says:

ALMIGHTY and everlasting God, You have granted us to venerate in one solemn feast the merits of all Your Saints; we beseech You, that, since so many are praying for us, You would pour forth upon us the desired abundance of Your mercy. Through our Lord Jesus Christ, Your Son, Who lives and reigns with You in the unity of the Holy Spirit, God, world without end. *S.* Amen.

THE EPISTLE • Apoc. 7, 2-12

IN THOSE days, behold, I, John, saw another angel ascending from the rising of the sun, having the seal of the living God; and he cried with a loud voice to the four angels, who had it in their power to harm the earth and the sea, saying, "Do not harm the earth or the sea or the trees, till we have sealed the servants of our God on their foreheads." And I heard the number of those who were sealed, a hundred and forty-four thousand sealed, out of every tribe of the children of Israel; of the tribe of Juda, twelve thousand sealed; of the tribe of Ruben, twelve thousand; of the tribe of Gad, twelve thousand; of the tribe of Aser, twelve thousand; of the tribe of Nephthali, twelve thousand; of the tribe of Manasses, twelve thousand; of the tribe of Simeon, twelve thousand; of the tribe of Levi, twelve thousand; of the tribe of Issachar, twelve thousand; of the tribe of Zabulon, twelve thousand; of the tribe of Joseph, twelve thousand; of the tribe of Benjamin, twelve thousand sealed. After this I saw a great multitude which no man could number, out of all nations and tribes and peoples and tongues, standing before the throne and before the Lamb, clothed in white robes, and with palms in their hands. And they cried with a loud voice, saying, "Salvation belongs to our God Who sits upon the throne, and to the Lamb." And all the angels were standing round about the throne, and the elders and the four living creatures; and they fell on their faces before the throne and worshipped God, saying, "Amen. Blessing and glory and wisdom and thanksgiving and honor and power and strength to our God forever and ever. Amen."
S. Thanks be to God.

THE GRADUAL • Ps. 33, 10. 11

FEAR the Lord, you His holy ones, for naught is lacking to those who fear Him. ℣. But those who seek the Lord want for no good thing.

Alleluia, alleluia. ℣. *Matt. 11,* 28. Come to Me, all you who labor and are burdened, and I will give you rest. Alleluia.

PRAYER BEFORE THE GOSPEL

Bowing down at the center of the altar, he says:

CLEANSE my heart and my lips, O almighty God, Who cleansed the lips of the Prophet Isaias with a burning coal. In Your gracious mercy deign so to purify me that I may worthily proclaim Your holy Gospel. Through Christ our Lord. Amen. Lord, grant Your blessing. The Lord be in my heart and on my lips, that I may worthily and fittingly proclaim His holy Gospel. Amen.

THE GOSPEL • Matt. 5, 1-12

Going to the left (Gospel) side of the altar, he says:

P. The Lord be with you. *S.* And with your spirit.
P. ✠ The continuation of the holy Gospel according to Saint Matthew. *S.* Glory be to You, O Lord.

AT THAT time, Jesus, seeing the crowds, went up the mountain. And when He was seated, His disciples came to Him. And opening His mouth He taught them, saying, "Blessed are the poor in spirit, for theirs is the kingdom of heaven. Blessed are the meek, for they shall possess the earth. Blessed are they who mourn, for they shall be comforted. Blessed are they who hunger and thirst for justice, for they shall be satisfied. Blessed are the merciful, for they shall obtain mercy. Blessed are the clean of heart, for they shall see God. Blessed are the peacemakers, for they shall be called children of God. Blessed are they who suffer persecution for justice' sake, for theirs is the kingdom of heaven. Blessed are you when men reproach you, and persecute you, and, speaking falsely, say all manner of evil against you, for My sake. Rejoice and exult, because your reward is great in heaven." *S.* Praise be to You, O Christ.

P. By the words of the Gospel, may our sins be taken away.

THE NICENE CREED

At the center of the altar, he says:

I BELIEVE in one God, the Father almighty, Maker of heaven and earth, and of all things visible and invisible. And in one Lord Jesus Christ, the Only-begotten Son of God. Born of the Father before all ages. God of God; Light of Light; true God of true God. Begotten not made; of one being with the Father; by Whom all things were made. Who for us men, and for our salvation, came down from heaven. (*Here all genuflect.*) And was made Flesh by the Holy Spirit of the Virgin Mary: AND WAS MADE MAN. He was also crucified for us, suffered under Pontius Pilate and was buried. And on the third day He rose again according to the Scriptures. And ascending into heaven, He sits at the right hand of the Father. And He shall come again in glory to judge the living and the dead; and of His kingdom there shall be no end. And I believe in the Holy Spirit, Lord and Giver of life, Who proceeds from the Father and the Son. Who together with the Father and the Son is no less adored, and glorified: Who spoke by

the Prophets. And I believe in One, Holy, Catholic and Apostolic Church. I confess one Baptism for the remission of sins. And I look for the resurrection of the dead. ✠ And the life of the world to come. Amen.

THE OFFERTORY

The Priest turns to the people and says:

P. The Lord be with you. *S.* And with your spirit.
P. Let us pray.

THE OFFERTORY VERSE • Wis. 3, 1. 2. 3

THE souls of the just are in the hand of God, and no torment shall touch them. They seemed, in the view of the foolish, to be dead: but they are in peace. Alleluia.

The Priest now uncovers the chalice, places the host on the paten and offering it up, says:

ACCEPT, O holy Father, almighty and eternal God, this spotless host, which I, Your unworthy servant, offer to You, my living and true God, to atone for my numberless sins, offenses, and negligences; on behalf of all here present and likewise for all faithful Christians living and dead, that it may profit me and them as a means of salvation to life everlasting. Amen.

He pours wine and water into the chalice, blessing the water before it is poured.

O GOD, Who established the nature of man in wondrous dignity, and still more admirably restored it, grant that through the mystery of this water and wine, we may be made partakers of His Divinity, Who has condescended to become partaker of our humanity, Jesus Christ, Your Son, our Lord. Who lives and reigns with You in the unity of the Holy Spirit, God, world without end. Amen.

Offering up the wine, the Priest says:

WE OFFER You, O Lord, the chalice of salvation, humbly begging of Your mercy that it may arise before Your Divine Majesty, with a pleasing fragrance, for our salvation and for that of the whole world. Amen.

Bowing down, the Priest says:

IN A humble spirit and with a contrite heart, may we be accepted by You, O Lord, and may our sacrifice so be offered in Your sight this day as to please You, O Lord God.

Raising his eyes and blessing the offering, he says:

COME, O Sanctifier, almighty and eternal God, and bless ✠ this sacrifice prepared for the glory of Your holy name.

WASHING THE FINGERS

I WASH my hands in innocence, and I go around Your altar, O Lord, giving voice to my thanks, and recounting all Your wondrous deeds. O Lord, I love the house in which You dwell, the tenting-place of Your glory. Gather not my soul with those of sinners, nor with men of blood my life. On their hands are crimes, and their right hands are full of bribes. But I walk in integrity; redeem me, and have pity on me. My foot stands on level ground; in the assemblies I will bless You, O Lord. Glory be to the Father, and to the Son, and to the Holy Spirit. As it was in the beginning, is now, and ever shall be, world without end. Amen.

ACCEPT, Most Holy Trinity, this offering which we are making to You in remembrance of the Passion, Resurrection, and Ascension of Jesus Christ, our Lord; and in honor of Blessed Mary, ever Virgin, Blessed John the Baptist, the Holy Apostles Peter and Paul, and of these, and of all the Saints; that it may add to their honor and aid our salvation; and may they deign to intercede in heaven for us who honor their memory here on earth. Through the same Christ our Lord. Amen.

The Priest turns toward the people and says:

Pray, brethren, that my sacrifice and yours may become acceptable to God the Father almighty.

S. May the Lord accept this sacrifice from your hands to the praise and glory of His name, for our advantage, and that of all His holy Church.

P. Amen.

THE SECRET

WE OFFER You, O Lord, the gifts of our devotion; may they please You for the honor of all the just, and, by Your mercy, profit us to salvation. Through our Lord Jesus Christ, Your Son, Who lives and reigns with You in the unity of the Holy Spirit, God.

P. World without end. *S.* Amen.

PREFACE—CANON

P. The Lord be with you. *S.* And with your spirit.

P. Lift up your hearts.

S. We have lifted them up to the Lord.

P. Let us give thanks to the Lord, our God.

S. It is fitting and just.

IT IS fitting indeed and just, right and helpful to salvation, for us always and everywhere to give thanks to You, O holy Lord, Father almighty, everlasting God, through Christ our Lord. Through Him the Angels praise Your Majesty, the Dominations adore it, the Powers are in awe. The heavens and the heavenly hosts, and the blessed Seraphim, join together in celebrating their joy. With these, we pray You, join our own voices also, while we say with lowly praise (*the bell is rung 3 times*):

HOLY, HOLY, HOLY, Lord God of Hosts. Heaven and earth are filled with Your glory. Hosanna in the highest. ✠ Blessed is He Who comes in the name of the Lord. Hosanna in the highest.

THE CANON OF THE MASS

THEREFORE, most gracious Father, we humbly beg of You and entreat You through Jesus Christ Your Son, our Lord, (*he kisses the altar*) to deem acceptable and bless these ✠ gifts, these ✠ offerings, these ✠ holy and unspotted oblations which, in the first place, we offer You for Your Holy Catholic Church, that You would deign to give her peace and protection, to unite and guard her throughout the world, together with Your servant N., our Pope, and N., our Bishop; and all true believers who cherish the Catholic and Apostolic Faith.

Commemoration of the Living

REMEMBER, O Lord, Your servants and handmaids, N. and N., (*name them*) and all here present, whose faith and devotion are known to You, on whose behalf we offer to You, or who themselves offer to You, this sacrifice of praise for themselves, families and friends, for the good of their souls, for their hope of salvation and deliverance from all harm, and who offer their homage to You, eternal, living and true God.

Commemoration of the Saints

IN THE unity of holy fellowship we observe the memory, first of all, of the glorious and ever

Virgin Mary, Mother of our Lord and God Jesus Christ; next, that of Your Blessed Apostles and Martyrs, Peter and Paul, Andrew, James, John, Thomas, James, Philip, Bartholomew, Matthew, Simon and Thaddeus; of Linus, Cletus, Clement, Sixtus, Cornelius, Cyprian, Lawrence, Chrysogonus, John and Paul, Cosmas and Damian, and of all Your Saints, by whose merits and prayers grant that we may be always fortified by the help of Your protection. Through the same Christ our Lord. Amen.

Spreading his hands over the oblation, he says:

GRACIOUSLY accept, then, we beseech You, O Lord, this service of our worship and that of all Your household. Provide that our days be spent in Your peace, save us from everlasting damnation, and cause us to be numbered in the flock You have chosen. Through Christ our Lord. Amen.

O GOD, deign to bless ✠ what we offer, and make it approved, ✠ effective, ✠ right, and wholly pleasing in every way, that it may become for our good, the Body ✠ and Blood ✠ of Your dearly beloved Son, Jesus Christ our Lord.

CONSECRATION—ELEVATION

WHO, the day before He suffered, took bread into His holy and venerable hands, and having raised His eyes to heaven, to You, O God, His almighty Father, giving thanks to You, He blessed it, ✠ broke it, and gave it to His disciples, saying: All of you take and eat of this:

FOR THIS IS MY BODY.

IN LIKE manner, when the supper was done, taking also this goodly chalice into His holy and

venerable hands, again giving thanks to You, He blessed ✠ it, and gave it to His disciples, saying: All of you take and drink of this:

FOR THIS IS THE CHALICE OF MY BLOOD OF THE NEW AND ETERNAL COVENANT: THE MYSTERY OF FAITH: WHICH SHALL BE SHED FOR YOU AND FOR MANY UNTO THE FORGIVENESS OF SINS.

After replacing the chalice on the corporal, he says:

As often as you shall do these things, in memory of Me shall you do them.

Offering of the Victim

MINDFUL, therefore, O Lord, not only of the blessed Passion of the same Christ, Your Son, our Lord, but also of His Resurrection from the dead, and finally His glorious Ascension into heaven, we, Your ministers, as also Your holy people, offer to Your supreme Majesty, of the gifts bestowed upon us, the pure ✠ Victim, the holy ✠ Victim, the all-perfect ✠ Victim: the holy ✠ Bread of life eternal and the Chalice ✠ of unending salvation.

AND this deign to regard with gracious and kindly attention and hold acceptable, as You deigned to accept the offerings of Abel, Your just servant, and the sacrifice of Abraham our patriarch, and that which Your chief priest Melchisedec offered to You, a holy sacrifice and a spotless victim.

MOST humbly we implore You, almighty God, bid these offerings to be brought by the hands of Your holy angel to Your altar above; before the face of Your Divine Majesty; that those of us who, by sharing in the Sacrifice of this altar, shall receive the Most Sacred ✠ Body and ✠ Blood of Your Son, may be filled with every grace and heavenly blessing. Through the same Christ our Lord. Amen.

Commemoration of the Dead

REMEMBER also, O Lord, Your servants and handmaids, N. and N., who have gone before us with the sign of faith, and rest in the sleep of peace. (*Here pray for the dead.*) To these, O Lord, and to all who rest in Christ, we beseech You to grant of Your goodness, a place of comfort, light and peace. Through the same Christ our Lord. Amen.

TO US sinners also, Your servants, trusting in the greatness of Your mercy, deign to grant some part and fellowship with Your Holy Apostles and Martyrs: with John, Stephen, Matthias, Barnabas, Ignatius, Alexander, Marcellinus, Peter, Felicitas, Perpetua, Agatha, Lucy, Agnes, Cecilia, Anastasia, and all Your Saints; into whose company, we implore You to admit us, not weighing our merits, but freely granting us pardon. Through Christ our Lord.

THROUGH Whom, O Lord, You always create, ✠ sanctify, ✠ fill with life, ✠ bless, and bestow upon us all good things.

The Minor Elevation

THROUGH ✠ Him, and with ✠ Him, and in ✠ Him, is to You, God the Father ✠ almighty, in the unity of the Holy ✠ Spirit, all honor and glory, world without end. S. Amen.

THE COMMUNION AND THANKSGIVING

Let us pray. Prompted by saving precepts, and taught by Your divine teaching, we dare to say:

OUR FATHER, Who art in heaven, hallowed be Thy name: Thy kingdom come: Thy will be done on earth as it is in heaven. Give us this day our daily bread; and forgive us our trespasses, as we forgive those who trespass against us. And lead us not into temptation: S. But deliver us from evil. P. Amen.

DELIVER us, we beseech You, O Lord, from all evils, past, present, and to come; and by the intercession of the Blessed and glorious Mary, ever Virgin, Mother of God, together with Your Blessed Apostles Peter and Paul, and Andrew, and all the Saints, grant of Your goodness, peace in our days, that aided by the riches of Your mercy, we may be always free from sin and safe from all disturbance.

Through the same our Lord Jesus Christ, Your Son, Who lives and reigns with You in the unity of the Holy Spirit, God, world without end.

S. Amen.

P. May the peace ✠ of the Lord be ✠ always with ✠ you.

S. And with your spirit.

The Priest puts a small particle into the chalice, saying:

May this mingling and consecration of the Body and Blood of our Lord Jesus Christ help us who receive it to life everlasting. Amen.

LAMB of God, You Who take away the sins of the world, have mercy on us.

720-39

Lamb of God, You Who take away the sins of the world, have mercy on us.

Lamb of God, You Who take away the sins of the world, grant us peace.

PRAYERS BEFORE HOLY COMMUNION

Then inclining toward the altar, he says:

O LORD Jesus Christ, Who said to Your Apostles: "Peace I leave with you, My peace I give to you," regard not my sins but the faith of Your Church, and deign to give her peace and unity according to Your Will: Who live and reign, God, world without end. Amen.

O LORD Jesus Christ, Son of the living God, Who, by the will of the Father, with the cooperation of the Holy Spirit, have by Your death given life to the world, deliver me by this Your Most Sacred Body and Blood from all my sins and from every evil. Make me always cling to Your commandments, and never permit me to be separated from You. Who with the same God the Father and the Holy Spirit, live and reign, God, world without end. Amen.

LET not the partaking of Your Body, O Lord Jesus Christ, which I, though unworthy, presume to receive, turn to my judgment and condemnation; but through Your goodness, may it become a safeguard and an effective remedy, both of soul and body. Who live and reign with God the Father, in the unity of the Holy Spirit, God, world without end. Amen.

COMMUNION OF THE PRIEST

I WILL take the Bread of heaven, and call upon the name of the Lord.

Lord, I am not worthy that You should come under my roof; but only say the word, and my soul will be healed. (3 *times.*)

Making the Sign of the Cross with the Host, he says:

MAY the Body of our Lord Jesus Christ preserve my soul to life everlasting. Amen.

What return shall I make to the Lord for all He has given me? I will take the Chalice of salvation, and I will call upon the name of the Lord. Praising will I call upon the Lord and I shall be saved from my enemies.

Making the Sign of the Cross with the chalice, he says:

MAY the Blood of our Lord Jesus Christ preserve my soul to life everlasting. Amen.

The Priest reverently consumes the Precious Blood.

COMMUNION OF THE FAITHFUL

The Server and people say the "Confiteor."

P. May almighty God have mercy on you, forgive you your sins, and bring you to life everlasting. ***S.*** Amen.

P. May the almighty and merciful Lord grant you pardon, ✠ absolution and remission of your sins. S. Amen.

Holding up a Sacred Host, the Priest says:

Behold the Lamb of God, behold Him Who takes away the sins of the world.

Lord, I am not worthy that You should come under my roof; but only say the word, and my soul will be healed. (3 *times.*)

The Priest says to each communicant:

May the Body of our Lord Jesus Christ, preserve your soul to life everlasting. Amen.

The Priest purifies the chalice with wine, saying:

WHAT has passed our lips as food, O Lord, may we possess in purity of heart, that what is given to us in time, be our healing for eternity.

He purifies his fingers with wine and water, saying:

MAY Your Body, O Lord, which I have eaten, and Your Blood which I have drunk, cleave to my very soul, and grant that no trace of sin be found in me, whom these pure and holy mysteries have renewed. Who live and reign, world without end. Amen.

THE COMMUNION • Matt. 5, 8-10

BLESSED are the clean of heart, for they shall see God. Blessed are the peacemakers, for they shall be called children of God. Blessed are they who suffer persecution for justice' sake, for theirs is the kingdom of heaven.

The Priest, turning to the people, says:

P. The Lord be with you. *S.* And with your spirit.
P. Let us pray.

THE POSTCOMMUNION

GRANT, we beseech You, O Lord, that Your faithful people may always rejoice in honoring all Your Saints, and may be defended by their unceasing prayers. Through our Lord Jesus Christ, Your Son, Who lives and reigns with You in the unity of the Holy Spirit, God, world without end. S. Amen.

FINAL PRAYERS

The Priest turns again to the people, and says:

P. The Lord be with you. *S.* And with your spirit.
P. Go, you are dismissed. *S.* Thanks be to God.

MAY the tribute of my worship be pleasing to You, Most Holy Trinity, and grant that the sacrifice which I, all unworthy, have offered in the presence of Your Majesty, may be acceptable to You, and through Your mercy obtain forgiveness for me and all for whom I have offered it. Through Christ our Lord. Amen.

THE LAST BLESSING

He kisses the altar, and facing the people, says:

MAY almighty God bless you: ✠ the Father, and the Son, and the Holy Spirit.
S. Amen.

The Last Gospel and Prayers after Low Mass are conveniently placed inside the back cover.

"He is not here, for He has risen . . ."

THE EASTER VIGIL MIDNIGHT MASS

In a Midnight Mass, the Church celebrates the dawn of Easter, honoring the Lord in all His glorious mysteries, and feeding her children once more with the Flesh and Blood of One Who is forever the Conqueror over death and sin, the Savior of all mankind.

(WHITE VESTMENTS)

The Celebrant, with his Ministers, in white vestments, comes to the foot of the altar and makes the proper reverence, omitting the prayers at the foot of the altar. Ascending, he kisses the altar and incenses it, while the Choir sings the "Kyrie." When the Choir finishes the "Kyrie," the Celebrant solemnly intones the "Gloria," and the bells, which have remained silent, are now rung again, and the statues and sacred images are uncovered.

THE GLORIA

GLORY to God in the highest. And on earth peace to men of good will. We praise You. We bless You. We adore You. We glorify You. We give You thanks for Your great glory. O Lord God, heavenly King, God the Father almighty. O Lord Jesus Christ, the Only-begotten Son. O Lord God, Lamb of God, Son of the Father: You Who take away the sins of the world, have mercy on us.

You Who take away the sins of the world, receive our prayer. You Who sit at the right hand of the Father, have mercy on us. For You alone are holy. You alone are the Lord. You alone, O Jesus Christ, are most high. Together with the Holy Spirit ✠ in the glory of God the Father. Amen.

The Celebrant kisses the altar and turns to the people, saying:

P. The Lord be with you. S. And with your spirit.
P. Let us pray.

THE PRAYER

Going to the right (Epistle) side, he says:

O GOD, You illumine this most holy night by the glory of the Lord's Resurrection; preserve in the new children of Your family the spirit of adoption which You have given, that, renewed in body and mind, they may render to You a pure service. Through the same our Lord Jesus Christ, Your Son, Who lives and reigns with You in the unity of the Holy Spirit, God, world without end. S. Amen.

THE EPISTLE • Col. 3, 1-4

BRETHREN: If you have risen with Christ, seek the things that are above, where Christ is seated at the right hand of God. Mind the things that are above, not the things that are on earth. For you have died and your life is hidden with Christ in God. When Christ, your life, shall appear, then you too will appear with Him in glory.

After the Epistle, the Celebrant sings "Alleluia" three times, each time in a higher tone, and all present repeat after him in the same tone as the Celebrant.

Then the Choir continues:

℣. *Ps. 117, 1.* Give thanks to the Lord, for He is good, for His mercy endures forever.

℣. *Ps. 116, 1-2.* Praise the Lord, all you nations; glorify Him, all you peoples! ℣. For steadfast is His kindness toward us, and the fidelity of the Lord endures forever.

PRAYER BEFORE THE GOSPEL

Bowing down at the center of the altar, he says:

CLEANSE my heart and my lips, O almighty God, Who cleansed the lips of the Prophet Isaias with a burning coal. In Your gracious mercy deign so to purify me that I may worthily proclaim Your holy Gospel. Through Christ our Lord. Amen.

Lord, grant Your blessing. The Lord be in my heart and on my lips, that I may worthily and fittingly proclaim His holy Gospel. Amen.

At the Gospel, candles are not carried, but only incense.

THE GOSPEL • Matt. 28, 1-7

Going to the left (Gospel) side of the altar, he says:

P. The Lord be with you. S. And with your spirit.
P. ✠ The continuation of the holy Gospel according to Saint Matthew. S. Glory be to You, O Lord.

NOW late in the night of the Sabbath, as the first day of the week began to dawn, Mary Magdalene and the other Mary came to see the sepulchre. And behold, there was a great earthquake; for an angel of the Lord came down from heaven, and drawing near rolled back the stone, and sat upon it. His countenance was like lightning, and his raiment like snow. And for fear of him the guards were terrified, and became like dead men. But the angel spoke and said to the women, "Do not be afraid; for I know that you seek Jesus, Who was crucified. He is not here, for He has risen even as He said. Come, see the place where the Lord was laid. And go quickly, tell His disciples that He has risen, and behold, He goes before you into Galilee; there you shall see Him. Behold, I have foretold it to you." S. Praise be to You, O Christ.

At Solemn Mass, the Deacon places the Gospel book on the altar and after the Celebrant blesses incense, he kneels and says the "Prayer before the Gospel." He then takes the book, kneels before the Celebrant and asks his blessing, saying:

Father, grant your blessing.

The Celebrant responds:

The Lord be in your heart and on your lips, that you may worthily and fittingly proclaim His holy Gospel: In the name of the Father, and of the Son, ✠ and of the Holy Spirit. Amen.

After the Gospel, the Celebrant kisses the Gospel book, saying: By the words of the Gospel, may our sins be taken away.

P. The Lord be with you. S. And with your spirit.

P. Let us pray.

At Solemn Mass, the Celebrant receives the paten with the host from the Deacon.

ACCEPT, O holy Father, almighty and eternal God, this spotless host, which I, Your unworthy servant, offer to You, my living and true God, to atone for my numberless sins, offenses, and negligences; on behalf of all here present and likewise for all faithful Christians living and dead,

that it may profit me and them as a means of salvation to life everlasting. Amen.

At Solemn Mass, the Deacon pours wine into the chalice and the Subdeacon pours the water which the Celebrant has blessed.

O GOD, Who established the nature of man in wondrous dignity, and still more admirably restored it, grant that through the mystery of this water and wine, we may be made partakers of His Divinity, Who has condescended to become partaker of our humanity, Jesus Christ, Your Son, our Lord. Who lives and reigns with You in the unity of the Holy Spirit, God, world without end. Amen.

Offering up the wine, the Celebrant says:

WE OFFER You, O Lord, the chalice of salvation, humbly begging of Your mercy that it may arise before Your Divine Majesty, with a pleasing fragrance, for our salvation and for that of the whole world. Amen.

At Solemn Mass, the Subdeacon receives the paten from the Deacon and covering it with the ends of the veil worn over his shoulders, he holds it before his eyes and takes his place at the foot of the altar until the conclusion of the "Our Father."

Bowing down, the Celebrant says:

IN A humble spirit and with a contrite heart, may we be accepted by You, O Lord, and may our sacrifice so be offered in Your sight this day as to please You, O Lord God.

Raising his eyes and blessing the offering, he says:

COME, O Sanctifier, almighty and eternal God, and bless ✠ this sacrifice prepared for the glory of Your holy name.

At Solemn Mass, even at a sung Mass, the offerings of bread and wine are incensed, also the altar and all who are present. The Celebrant blesses the incense, saying:

Through the intercession of Blessed Michael the Archangel, standing at the right hand of the altar of incense, and of all His elect may the Lord vouchsafe to bless ✠ this incense and to receive it in the odor of sweetness. Through Christ our Lord. Amen.

Receiving the thurible, he incenses the bread and wine, saying:

May this incense blessed by You, arise before You, O Lord, and may Your mercy come down upon us.

Incensing the altar, he says Psalm 140:

Let my prayer, O Lord, come like incense before You; the lifting up of my hands, like the evening sacrifice. O Lord, set a watch before my mouth, a guard at the door of my lips. Let not my heart incline to the evil of engaging in deeds of wickedness.

Giving the thurible to the Deacon, he says:

May the Lord enkindle in us the fire of His love and the flame of everlasting charity. Amen.

WASHING THE FINGERS

I WASH my hands in innocence, and I go around Your altar, O Lord, giving voice to my thanks, and recounting all Your wondrous deeds. O Lord, I love the house in which You dwell, the tenting-place of Your glory. Gather not my soul with those of sinners, nor with men of blood my life. On their hands are crimes, and their right hands are full of bribes. But I walk in integrity; redeem me, and have pity on me. My foot stands on level ground; in the assemblies I will bless You, O Lord. Glory be to the Father, and to the Son, and to the Holy Spirit. As it was in the beginning, is now, and ever shall be, world without end. Amen.

ACCEPT, Most Holy Trinity, this offering which we are making to You in remembrance of the Passion, Resurrection, and Ascension of Jesus Christ, our Lord; and in honor of Blessed Mary, ever Virgin, Blessed John the Baptist, the Holy Apostles Peter and Paul, and of these, and of all the Saints; that it may add to their honor and aid our salvation; and may they deign to intercede in heaven for us who honor their memory here on earth. Through the same Christ our Lord. Amen.

The Celebrant turns toward the people and says:

Pray, brethren, that my sacrifice and yours may become acceptable to God the Father almighty.
S. May the Lord accept this sacrifice from your hands to the praise and glory of His name, for our advantage, and that of all His holy Church.

P. Amen.

THE SECRET

ACCEPT, we beseech You, O Lord, the prayers of Your people together with the sacrifice they offer, that what has been begun by these Easter mysteries, may by Your working profit us to everlasting salvation. Through our Lord Jesus Christ, Your Son, Who lives and reigns with You in the unity of the Holy Spirit, God.
P. World without end. *S.* Amen.

PREFACE—CANON

P. The Lord be with you. *S.* And with your spirit.
P. Lift up your hearts.
S. We have lifted them up to the Lord.
P. Let us give thanks to the Lord, our God.
S. It is fitting and just.

IT IS fitting indeed and just, right and helpful to salvation for us always to praise You, O Lord, but more gloriously on this night above others when Christ our Passover was sacrificed. For He is the true Lamb Who has taken away the sins of the world: Who by dying has destroyed our death; and by rising again has restored us to life. And therefore with Angels and Archangels, with Thrones and Dominations, and with the whole host of the heavenly army, we sing a hymn to Your glory, saying again and again (*the bell is rung 3 times*):

HOLY, HOLY, HOLY, Lord God of Hosts. Heaven and earth are filled with Your glory. Hosanna in the highest. ✠ Blessed is He Who comes in the name of the Lord. Hosanna in the highest.

THE CANON OF THE MASS

THEREFORE, most gracious Father, we humbly beg of You and entreat You through Jesus Christ Your Son, our Lord, (*he kisses the altar*) to deem acceptable and bless these ✠ gifts, these ✠ offerings, these ✠ holy and unspotted oblations which, in the first place, we offer You for Your Holy Catholic Church, that You would deign to give her peace and protection, to unite and guard her throughout the world, together with Your servant N., our Pope, and N., our Bishop; and all true believers who cherish the Catholic and Apostolic Faith.

Commemoration of the Living

REMEMBER, O Lord, Your servants and handmaids, N. and N., (*name them*) and all here present, whose faith and devotion are known to You, on whose behalf we offer to You, or who themselves offer to You, this sacrifice of praise for themselves, families and friends, for the good of their souls, for their hope of salvation and deliverance from all harm, and who offer their homage to You, eternal, living and true God.

Commemoration of the Saints

IN THE unity of holy fellowship, and keeping the most holy night of the Resurrection of our Lord Jesus Christ according to the flesh, we also observe the memory, first of all, of the glorious and ever Virgin Mary, Mother of our Lord and God Jesus Christ; next, that of Your Blessed Apostles and Martyrs, Peter and Paul, Andrew, James, John, Thomas, James, Philip, Bartholomew, Matthew, Simon and Thaddeus; of Linus, Cletus, Clement, Sixtus, Cornelius, Cyprian, Lawrence, Chrysogonus, John and Paul, Cosmas and Damian, and of all Your Saints, by whose merits and prayers grant that we may be always fortified by the help of Your protection. Through the same Christ our Lord. Amen.

Spreading his hands over the oblation, he says:

GRACIOUSLY accept, then, we beseech You, O Lord, this service of our worship, and that of all Your household, which we make to You in behalf of those whom You have vouchsafed to bring to a new birth by water and the Holy Spirit, giving them remission of all their sins. Provide that our days be spent in Your peace, save us from everlasting damnation, and cause us to be numbered in the flock You have chosen. Through Christ our Lord. Amen.

O GOD, deign to bless ✠ what we offer, and make it approved, ✠ effective, ✠ right, and

wholly pleasing in every way, that it may become for our good, the Body ✠ and Blood ✠ of Your dearly beloved Son, Jesus Christ our Lord.

CONSECRATION—ELEVATION

WHO, the day before He suffered, took bread into His holy and venerable hands, and having raised His eyes to heaven, to You, O God, His almighty Father, giving thanks to You, He blessed it, ✠ broke it, and gave it to His disciples, saying: All of you take and eat of this:

FOR THIS IS MY BODY.

IN LIKE manner, when the supper was done, taking also this goodly chalice into His holy and venerable hands, again giving thanks to You, He blessed ✠ it, and gave it to His disciples, saying: All of you take and drink of this:

FOR THIS IS THE CHALICE OF MY BLOOD OF THE NEW AND ETERNAL COVENANT: THE MYSTERY OF FAITH: WHICH SHALL BE SHED FOR YOU AND FOR MANY UNTO THE FORGIVENESS OF SINS.

After replacing the chalice on the corporal, he says:

As often as you shall do these things, in memory of Me shall you do them.

Offering of the Victim

MINDFUL, therefore, O Lord, not only of the blessed Passion of the same Christ, Your Son, our Lord, but also of His Resurrection from the dead, and finally His glorious Ascension into heaven, we, Your ministers, as also Your holy people, offer to Your supreme Majesty, of the gifts bestowed upon us, the pure ✠ Victim, the holy ✠

Victim, the all-perfect ✠ Victim: the holy ✠ Bread of life eternal and the Chalice ✠ of unending salvation.

AND this deign to regard with gracious and kindly attention and hold acceptable, as You deigned to accept the offerings of Abel, Your just servant, and the sacrifice of Abraham our patriarch, and that which your chief priest Melchisedec offered to You, a holy sacrifice and a spotless victim.

MOST humbly we implore You, almighty God, bid these offerings to be brought by the hands of Your holy angel to Your altar above; before the face of Your Divine Majesty; that those of us who, by sharing in the Sacrifice of this altar, shall receive the Most Sacred ✠ Body and ✠ Blood of Your Son, may be filled with every grace and heavenly blessing. Through the same Christ our Lord. Amen.

Commemoration of the Dead

REMEMBER also, O Lord, Your servants and handmaids, *N.* and *N.*, who have gone before us with the sign of faith, and rest in the sleep of peace. (*Here pray for the dead.*) To these, O Lord, and to all who rest in Christ, we beseech You to grant of Your goodness, a place of comfort, light and peace. Through the same Christ our Lord. Amen.

TO US sinners also, Your servants, trusting in the greatness of Your mercy, deign to grant some part and fellowship with Your Holy Apostles and Martyrs: with John, Stephen, Matthias, Barnabas, Ignatius, Alexander, Marcellinus, Peter, Felicitas, Perpetua, Agatha, Lucy, Agnes, Cecilia, Anastasia, and all Your Saints; into whose company, we implore You to admit us, not weighing our merits, but freely granting us pardon. Through Christ our Lord.

THROUGH Whom, O Lord, You always create, ✠ sanctify, ✠ fill with life, ✠ bless, and bestow upon us all good things.

The Minor Elevation

THROUGH ✠ Him, and with ✠ Him, and in ✠ Him, is to You, God the Father ✠ almighty, in the unity of the Holy ✠ Spirit, all honor and glory, world without end. S. Amen.

THE COMMUNION AND THANKSGIVING

Let us pray. Prompted by saving precepts, and taught by Your divine teaching, we dare to say:

OUR FATHER, Who art in heaven, hallowed be Thy name: Thy kingdom come: Thy will be done on earth as it is in heaven. Give us this day our daily bread; and forgive us our trespasses, as we forgive those who trespass against us. And lead us not into temptation: S. But deliver us from evil. *P.* Amen.

DELIVER us, we beseech You, O Lord, from all evils, past, present, and to come; and by the intercession of the Blessed and glorious Mary, ever Virgin, Mother of God, together with Your Blessed Apostles Peter and Paul, and Andrew, and all the Saints, grant of Your goodness, peace in our days, that aided by the riches of Your mercy, we may be always free from sin and safe from all disturbance.

Through the same our Lord Jesus Christ, Your Son, Who lives and reigns with You in the unity of the Holy Spirit, God, world without end.

S. Amen.

P. May the peace ✠ of the Lord be ✠ always with ✠ you.

S. And with your spirit.

The Celebrant puts a small particle into the chalice, saying:

May this mingling and consecration of the Body and Blood of our Lord Jesus Christ help us who receive it to life everlasting. Amen.

PRAYERS BEFORE HOLY COMMUNION

Then inclining toward the altar, he says:

O LORD Jesus Christ, Son of the living God, Who, by the will of the Father, with the co-operation of the Holy Spirit, have by Your death given life to the world, deliver me by this Your Most Sacred Body and Blood from all my sins and from every evil. Make me always cling to Your commandments, and never permit me to be separated from You. Who with the same God the Father and the Holy Spirit, live and reign, God, world without end. Amen.

LET not the partaking of Your Body, O Lord Jesus Christ, which I, though unworthy, presume to receive, turn to my judgment and condemnation; but through Your goodness, may it become a safeguard and an effective remedy, both of soul and body. Who live and reign with God the Father, in the unity of the Holy Spirit, God, world without end. Amen.

COMMUNION OF THE PRIEST

I WILL take the Bread of heaven, and call upon the name of the Lord.

Lord, I am not worthy that You should come under my roof; but only say the word, and my soul will be healed. (3 *times.*)

Making the Sign of the Cross with the Host, he says:

MAY the Body of our Lord Jesus Christ preserve my soul to life everlasting. Amen.

What return shall I make to the Lord for all He has given me? I will take the Chalice of salvation, and I will call upon the name of the Lord. Praising will I call upon the Lord and I shall be saved from my enemies.

Making the Sign of the Cross with the chalice, he says:

MAY the Blood of our Lord Jesus Christ preserve my soul to life everlasting. Amen.

The Celebrant reverently consumes the Precious Blood.

COMMUNION OF THE FAITHFUL

The Server and people say the "Confiteor."

P. May almighty God have mercy on you, forgive you your sins, and bring you to life everlasting. ***S.*** Amen.

P. May the almighty and merciful Lord grant you pardon, ✠ absolution and remission of your sins. ***S.*** Amen.

Holding up a Sacred Host, the Celebrant says:

Behold the Lamb of God, behold Him Who takes away the sins of the world.

Lord, I am not worthy that You should come under my roof; but only say the word, and my soul will be healed. (3 *times.*)

The Celebrant says to each communicant:

May the Body of our Lord Jesus Christ preserve your soul to life everlasting. Amen.

The Celebrant purifies the chalice with wine, saying:

WHAT has passed our lips as food, O Lord, may we possess in purity of heart, that what is given to us in time, be our healing for eternity.

He purifies his fingers with wine and water, saying:

MAY Your Body, O Lord, which I have eaten, and Your Blood which I have drunk, cleave to my very soul, and grant that no trace of sin be found in me, whom these pure and holy mysteries have renewed. Who live and reign, world without end. Amen.

LAUDS

Ant. Alleluia, alleluia, alleluia.

PSALM 150

PRAISE the Lord in His sanctuary, praise Him in the firmament of His strength. Praise Him for His mighty deeds, praise Him for His sovereign majesty. Praise Him with the blast of the trumpet, praise Him with lyre and harp. Praise Him with timbrel and dance, praise Him with strings and pipe. Praise Him with sounding cymbals, praise Him with clanging cymbals. Let everything that has breath praise the Lord! Glory be to the Father, and to the Son, and to the Holy Spirit. As it was in the beginning, is now, and ever shall be, world without end. Amen.

Ant. Alleluia, alleluia, alleluia.

THE ANTIPHON

AND very early in the morning after the Sabbath, they came to the sepulchre at sunrise, alleluia.

THE BENEDICTUS • Luke 1, 68-79

BLESSED be the Lord, the God of Israel, because He has visited and wrought redemption for His people, and has raised up a horn of salvation for us, in the house of David His servant, as He promised through the mouth of His holy ones, the prophets from of old; salvation from our enemies, and from the hand of all who hate us, to show mercy to our forefathers and to be mindful of His holy covenant, of the oath that He swore to Abraham our father, that He would grant us, that, delivered from the hand of our enemies, we should serve Him without fear, in holiness and justice before Him all our days. And you, child, shall be called the prophet of the Most High, for you shall go before the face of the Lord to prepare His ways, to give to His people knowledge of salvation through forgiveness of their sins, because of the loving-kindness of our God, wherewith the Orient from on high has visited us, to shine on those who sit in darkness and in the shadow of death, to guide our feet into the way of peace. Glory be to the Father, and to the Son, and to the Holy Spirit. As it was in the beginning, is now, and ever shall be, world without end. Amen.

THE ANTIPHON

AND very early in the morning after the Sabbath, they came to the sepulchre at sunrise, alleluia.

P. The Lord be with you. *S.* And with your spirit.
P. Let us pray.

THE POSTCOMMUNION

POUR forth upon us, O Lord, the Spirit of Your love, that those whom You have filled with the Easter sacraments may, by Your goodness, be of one mind. Through our Lord Jesus Christ, Your Son, Who lives and reigns with You in the unity of the Holy Spirit, God, world without end. S. Amen.

P. The Lord be with you. S. And with your spirit.

The Deacon (or Celebrant) turns to the people and says:

P. Go, you are dismissed. Alleluia, alleluia.

S. Thanks be to God. Alleluia, alleluia.

MAY the tribute of my worship be pleasing to You, Most Holy Trinity, and grant that the sacrifice which I, all unworthy, have offered in the presence of Your Majesty, may be acceptable to You, and through Your mercy obtain forgiveness for me and all for whom I have offered it. Through Christ our Lord. Amen.

THE LAST BLESSING

The Celebrant kisses the altar, and facing the people, says:

MAY almighty God bless you: ✠ the Father, and the Son, and the Holy Spirit.

S. Amen.

The Gospel of St. John is omitted, and all return to the sacristy.

"What therefore God has joined together, let no man put asunder."

THE NUPTIAL MASS

For Christians, marriage is not only a very important contract, a source of life, but is the most intimate and sublime union between husband and wife. This union of love and confidence has been raised by our Lord to the dignity of a great Sacrament and, if consummated, can only be dissolved by death. The grace of the Sacrament of Marriage and that of frequent Communion help the married couple to overcome the obstacles to this harmonious life, which is "the symbol of the sacred union of Jesus Christ with His Church."

THE MARRIAGE SERVICE

The Priest first asks the bridegroom, who stands or kneels at the right side of the bride:

N . . . , will you take N . . . , here present, for your lawful wife, according to the rite of our holy Mother, the Church? *Response*: I will.

Then the Priest asks the bride:

N . . . , will you take N . . . , here present, for your lawful husband, according to the rite of our holy Mother, the Church? *Response*: I will.

The bridegroom now holds the bride's right hand in his own right hand, and prompted by the Priest, promises her his troth in these words:

I N . . . take you, N . . . , for my lawful wife, to have and to hold, from this day forward, for better, for worse, for richer, for poorer, in sickness and in health, until death do us part.

Now loosening their hands and joining them again, the bride, prompted by the Priest, says:

I N . . . take you, N . . . , for my lawful husband, to have and to hold, from this day forward, for better, for worse, for richer, for poorer, in sickness and in health, until death do us part.

The bridegroom and bride may kneel or stand and the Priest says:

I JOIN you together in marriage, in the name of the Father, and of the Son, ✠ and of the Holy Spirit. Amen.

He then sprinkles them with holy water. This done, the Priest blesses the ring, saying:

Priest. Our help is in the name of the Lord.

Server. Who made heaven and earth.

P. O Lord, hear my prayer. *S.* And let my cry come to You.

P. The Lord be with you. *S.* And with your spirit.

Let us pray. Bless, ✠ O Lord, this ring, which we bless ✠ in Your name, that she who is to wear it, keeping true faith to her husband, may abide in Your peace and obedience to Your will, and ever live in mutual love. Through Christ our Lord. *S.* Amen.

The Priest sprinkles the ring with holy water in the form of a Cross; and the bridegroom, having received the ring from the hand of the Priest, puts it on the ring finger of the left hand of the bride, saying:

With this ring I wed you, and I pledge you my fidelity.

The Priest then says:

In the name of the Father, and of the Son, ✠ and of the Holy Spirit. Amen.
P. Confirm, O God, that which You have wrought in us.
S. From Your holy temple, which is in Jerusalem.

Lord, have mercy. (3 *times.*) Christ, have mercy (3 *times.*) Lord, have mercy. (3 *times.*) Our Father, etc. (*silently.*)
P. And lead us not into temptation.
S. But deliver us from evil.
P. Save Your servants.
S. Who hope in You, O my God.
P. Send them help, O Lord, from the sanctuary.
S. And defend them out of Sion.
P. Be to them, O Lord, a tower of strength.
S. From the face of the enemy.
P. O Lord, hear my prayer.
S. And let my cry come to You.
P. The Lord be with you.
S. And with your spirit.

Let us pray. Look, O Lord, we beseech You, upon these Your servants, and graciously protect Your own institution, whereby You have provided for the propagation of mankind, that they who are joined together by Your authority may be preserved by Your help. Through Christ our Lord. S. Amen.

THE MASS

IN THE name of the Father, ✠ and of the Son, and of the Holy Spirit. Amen.
Priest. I will go in to the altar of God.
Server. The God of my gladness and joy.

Psalm 42

DO ME justice, O God, and fight my fight against a faithless people; from the deceitful and impious man rescue me.

S. For You, O God, are my strength. Why do You keep me so far away? Why must I go about in mourning, with the enemy oppressing me?

P. Send forth Your light and Your fidelity; they shall lead me on and bring me to Your holy mountain, to Your dwelling-place.

S. Then will I go in to the altar of God, the God of my gladness and joy.

P. Then will I give You thanks upon the harp, O God, my God. Why are you so downcast, O my soul? Why do you sigh within me?

S. Hope in God! For I shall again be thanking Him in the presence of my Savior and my God.

P. Glory be to the Father, and to the Son, and to the Holy Spirit.

S. As it was in the beginning, is now, and ever shall be, world without end. Amen.

P. I will go in to the altar of God.

S. The God of my gladness and joy.

P. Our help ✠ is in the name of the Lord.

S. Who made heaven and earth.

P. I confess to almighty God, etc.

S. May almighty God have mercy on you, forgive you your sins, and bring you to life everlasting.

P. Amen.

The Server, bowing, says the "Confiteor."

I CONFESS to almighty God, to Blessed Mary, ever Virgin, to Blessed Michael the Archangel, to Blessed John the Baptist, to the Holy Apostles Peter and Paul, and to all the Saints, and to you, Father, that I have sinned exceedingly in thought, word and deed, *through my fault, through my fault, through my most grievous fault.* Therefore I beseech Blessed Mary, ever Virgin, Blessed Michael the Archangel, Blessed John the Baptist, the Holy Apostles Peter and Paul, and all the Saints, and you, Father, to pray to the Lord our God for me.

P. May almighty God have mercy on you, forgive you your sins, and bring you to life everlasting.

S. Amen.

MAY the almighty and merciful Lord grant us pardon, ✠ absolution, and remission of our sins. *S.* Amen.

P. Will You not, O God, give us life?

S. And shall not Your people rejoice in You?

P. Show us, O Lord, Your kindness.

S. And grant us Your salvation.

P. O Lord, hear my prayer.

S. And let my cry come to You.

P. The Lord be with you.

S. And with your spirit. *P.* Let us pray.

Going up to the altar, the Priest prays silently:

TAKE away from us our sins, O Lord, we beseech You, that we may enter with pure minds into the Holy of Holies. Through Christ our Lord. Amen.

WE BESEECH You, O Lord, by the merits of Your Saints (*he kisses the altar*) whose relics lie here, and of all the Saints: deign in Your mercy to pardon me all my sins. Amen.

THE INTROIT • Tob. 7, 15; 8, 19

At the right side of the altar, the Priest says:

MAY the God of Israel join you together: and may He be with you, Who was merciful to two only children: and now, O Lord, make them bless You more fully. (*P.T.* Alleluia, alleluia.) *Ps.* 127. Happy are you who fear the Lord, who walk in His ways! Glory be to the Father, and to the Son, and to the Holy Spirit. As it was in the beginning, is now, and ever shall be, world without end. Amen. — May the God of Israel join you together: and may He be with you, Who was merciful to two only children: and now, O Lord, make them bless You more fully. (*P.T.* Alleluia, alleluia.)

THE KYRIE

P. Lord, have mercy. *S.* Lord, have mercy. *P.* Lord, have mercy. *S.* Christ, have mercy. *P.* Christ, have mercy. *S.* Christ, have mercy. *P.* Lord, have mercy. *S.* Lord, have mercy. *P.* Lord, have mercy.

The Priest kisses the altar and turns to the people, saying:

P. The Lord be with you. *S.* And with your spirit.
P. Let us pray.

THE PRAYER

Going to the right (Epistle) side, he says:

GRACIOUSLY hear us, almighty and merciful God, that, what is performed by our ministry may be fulfilled by Your blessing. Through our Lord Jesus Christ, Your Son, Who lives and reigns with You in the unity of the Holy Spirit, God, world without end. *S.* Amen.

THE EPISTLE • Eph. 5, 22-33

BRETHREN: Let wives be subject to their husbands as to the Lord: because a husband is head of the wife, just as Christ is head of the Church, being Himself Savior of the body. But just as the Church is subject to Christ, so also let wives be to their husbands in all things. Husbands, love your wives, just as Christ also loved the Church, and delivered Himself up for her, that He might sanctify her, cleansing her in the bath of water by means of the word; in order that He might present to Himself the Church in all her glory, not having spot or wrinkle or any such thing, but that she might be holy and without blemish. Even thus ought husbands also to love their wives as their own bodies. He who loves his own wife, loves himself. For no one ever hated his own flesh; on the contrary he nourishes and cherishes it, as Christ also does the Church (because we are members of His body, made from His flesh and from His bones). "For this cause a man shall leave his father and mother, and cleave to his wife; and the two shall become one flesh." This is a great mystery — I mean in reference to Christ and to the Church. However, let each one of you also love his wife just as he loves himself; and let the wife respect her husband. *S.* Thanks be to God.

THE GRADUAL • Ps. 127, 3

YOUR wife shall be like a fruitful vine in the recesses of your home. ℣. Your children, like olive plants around your table.

Alleluia, alleluia. ℣. *Ps. 19,* 3. May the Lord send you help from the sanctuary, from Sion may He sustain you. Alleluia.

After Septuagesima omit Alleluia and versicle, and say:

THE TRACT • Ps. 127, 4-6

BEHOLD, thus is the man blessed who fears the Lord. ℣. The Lord bless you from Sion: may you see the prosperity of Jerusalem all the days of your life. ℣. May you see your children's children. Peace be upon Israel!

During Paschaltime omit Gradual, and say:

Alleluia, alleluia. ℣. *Ps. 19, 3.* May the Lord send you help from the sanctuary, from Sion may He sustain you. Alleluia. ℣. *Ps. 133, 3.* May the Lord bless you from Sion, the Maker of heaven and earth. Alleluia.

PRAYER BEFORE THE GOSPEL

Bowing down at the center of the altar, he says:

CLEANSE my heart and my lips, O almighty God, Who cleansed the lips of the Prophet Isaias with a burning coal. In Your gracious mercy deign so to purify me that I may worthily proclaim Your holy Gospel. Through Christ our Lord. Amen.

Lord, grant Your blessing. The Lord be in my heart and on my lips, that I may worthily and fittingly proclaim His holy Gospel. Amen.

THE GOSPEL • Matt. 19, 3-6

Going to the left (Gospel) side of the altar, he says:

P. The Lord be with you. *S.* And with your spirit.
P. ✠ The continuation of the holy Gospel according to Saint Matthew. *S.* Glory be to You, O Lord.

AT THAT time, there came to Jesus some Pharisees, testing Him, and saying, "Is it lawful for a man to put away his wife for any cause?" But He answered and said to them, "Have you not read that the Creator, from the beginning, made them male and female, and said, 'For this cause a man shall leave his father and mother, and cleave to his wife, and the two shall become one flesh'? Therefore now they are no longer two, but one flesh. What therefore God has joined together, let no man put asunder." *S.* Praise be to You, O Christ. *P.* By the words of the Gospel, may our sins be taken away.

THE OFFERTORY

The Priest turns toward the people and says:

P. The Lord be with you. *S.* And with your spirit.
P. Let us pray.

THE OFFERTORY VERSE • Ps. 30, 15. 16

MY TRUST is in You, O Lord; I say, "You are my God." In Your hands is my destiny. (*P.T.* Alleluia.)

The Priest now uncovers the chalice, places the host on the paten and offering it up, says:

ACCEPT, O holy Father, almighty and eternal God, this spotless host, which I, Your unworthy servant, offer to You, my living and true God, to atone for my numberless sins, offenses, and negligences; on behalf of all here present and likewise for all faithful Christians living and dead, that it may profit me and them as a means of salvation to life everlasting. Amen.

He pours wine and water into the chalice, blessing the water before it is poured.

O GOD, Who established the nature of man in wondrous dignity, and still more admirably restored it, grant that through the mystery of this water and wine, we may be made partakers of His Divinity, Who has condescended to become par-

taker of our humanity, Jesus Christ, Your Son, our Lord. Who lives and reigns with You in the unity of the Holy Spirit, God, world without end. Amen.

Offering up the wine, the Priest says:

WE OFFER You, O Lord, the chalice of salvation, humbly begging of Your mercy that it may arise before Your Divine Majesty, with a pleasing fragrance, for our salvation and for that of the whole world. Amen.

Bowing down, the Priest says:

IN A humble spirit and with a contrite heart, may we be accepted by You, O Lord, and may our sacrifice so be offered in Your sight this day as to please You, O Lord God.

Raising his eyes and blessing the offering, he says:

COME, O Sanctifier, almighty and eternal God, and bless ✠ this sacrifice prepared for the glory of Your holy name.

WASHING THE FINGERS

I WASH my hands in innocence, and I go around Your altar, O Lord, giving voice to my thanks, and recounting all Your wondrous deeds. O Lord, I love the house in which You dwell, the tenting-place of Your glory. Gather not my soul with those of sinners, nor with men of blood my life. On their hands are crimes, and their right hands are full of bribes. But I walk in integrity; redeem me, and have pity on me. My foot stands on level ground; in the assemblies I will bless You, O Lord. Glory be to the Father, and to the Son, and to the Holy Spirit. As it was in the beginning, is now, and ever shall be, world without end. Amen.

ACCEPT, Most Holy Trinity, this offering which we are making to You in remembrance of the Passion, Resurrection, and Ascension of Jesus Christ, our Lord; and in honor of Blessed Mary, ever Virgin, Blessed John the Baptist, the Holy Apostles Peter and Paul, and of these, and of all the Saints; that it may add to their honor and aid our salvation; and may they deign to intercede in heaven for us who honor their memory here on earth. Through the same Christ our Lord. Amen.

The Priest turns to the people and says:

Pray, brethren, that my sacrifice and yours may become acceptable to God the Father almighty.

S. May the Lord accept this sacrifice from your hands to the praise and glory of His name, for our advantage, and that of all His holy Church.

P. Amen.

THE SECRET

ACCEPT, we beseech You, O Lord, the gifts offered for the sacred bond of marriage; and dispose according to Your will, that which is instituted by Your bounty. Through our Lord Jesus Christ, Your Son, Who lives and reigns with You in the unity of the Holy Spirit, God.

P. World without end. *S.* Amen.

PREFACE—CANON

P. The Lord be with you. *S.* And with your spirit.
P. Lift up your hearts.
S. We have lifted them up to the Lord.
P. Let us give thanks to the Lord, our God.
S. It is fitting and just.

IT IS fitting indeed and just, right and helpful to salvation, for us always and everywhere to give thanks to You, O holy Lord, Father almighty, everlasting God, through Christ our Lord. Through Him the Angels praise Your Majesty, the Dominations adore it, the Powers are in awe. The heavens and the heavenly hosts, and the blessed Seraphim, join together in celebrating their joy. With these, we pray You, join our own voices also, while we say with lowly praise (*the bell is rung 3 times*):

HOLY, HOLY, HOLY, Lord God of Hosts. Heaven and earth are filled with Your glory. Hosanna in the highest. ✠ Blessed is He Who comes in the name of the Lord. Hosanna in the highest.

THE CANON OF THE MASS

THEREFORE, most gracious Father, we humbly beg of You and entreat You through Jesus Christ Your Son, our Lord, (*he kisses the altar*) to deem acceptable and bless these ✠ gifts, these ✠ offerings, these ✠ holy and unspotted oblations which, in the first place, we offer You for Your Holy Catholic Church, that You would deign to give her peace and protection, to unite and guard her throughout the world, together with Your servant N., our Pope, and N., our Bishop; and all true believers who cherish the Catholic and Apostolic Faith.

Commemoration of the Living

REMEMBER, O Lord, Your servants and handmaids, N. and N., (*name them*) and all here present, whose faith and devotion are known to You, on whose behalf we offer to You, or who themselves offer to You, this sacrifice of praise for themselves, families and friends, for the good of their souls, for their hope of salvation and deliverance from all harm, and who offer their homage to You, eternal, living and true God.

Commemoration of the Saints

IN THE unity of holy fellowship we observe the memory, first of all, of the glorious and ever Virgin Mary, Mother of our Lord and God Jesus Christ; next, that of Your Blessed Apostles and Martyrs, Peter and Paul, Andrew, James, John, Thomas, James, Philip, Bartholomew, Matthew, Simon and Thaddeus; of Linus, Cletus, Clement, Sixtus, Cornelius, Cyprian, Lawrence, Chrysogonus, John and Paul, Cosmas and Damian, and of all Your Saints, by whose merits and prayers grant that we may be always fortified by the help of Your protection. Through the same Christ our Lord. Amen.

Spreading his hands over the oblation, he says:

GRACIOUSLY accept, then, we beseech You, O Lord, this service of our worship and that of all Your household. Provide that our days be spent in Your peace, save us from everlasting damnation, and cause us to be numbered in the flock You have chosen. Through Christ our Lord. Amen.

O GOD, deign to bless ✠ what we offer, and make it approved, ✠ effective, ✠ right, and wholly pleasing in every way, that it may become for our good, the Body ✠ and Blood ✠ of Your dearly beloved Son, Jesus Christ our Lord.

CONSECRATION—ELEVATION

WHO, the day before He suffered, took bread into His holy and venerable hands, and having raised His eyes to heaven, to You, O God, His almighty Father, giving thanks to You, He blessed it, ✠ broke it, and gave it to His disciples, saying: All of you take and eat of this:

FOR THIS IS MY BODY.

IN LIKE manner, when the supper was done, taking also this goodly chalice into His holy and venerable hands, again giving thanks to You, He blessed ✠ it, and gave it to His disciples, saying: All of you take and drink of this:

FOR THIS IS THE CHALICE OF MY BLOOD OF THE NEW AND ETERNAL COVENANT: THE MYSTERY OF FAITH: WHICH SHALL BE SHED FOR YOU AND FOR MANY UNTO THE FORGIVENESS OF SINS.

After replacing the chalice on the corporal, he says:

As often as you shall do these things, in memory of Me shall you do them.

Offering of the Victim

MINDFUL, therefore, O Lord, not only of the blessed Passion of the same Christ, Your Son, our Lord, but also of His Resurrection from the dead, and finally His glorious Ascension into heaven, we, Your ministers, as also Your holy people, offer to Your supreme Majesty, of the gifts bestowed upon us, the pure ✠ Victim, the holy ✠ Victim, the all-perfect ✠ Victim: the holy ✠ Bread of life eternal and the Chalice ✠ of unending salvation.

AND this deign to regard with gracious and kindly attention and hold acceptable, as You deigned to accept the offerings of Abel, Your just servant, and the sacrifice of Abraham our patriarch, and that which Your chief priest Melchisedec offered to You, a holy sacrifice and a spotless victim.

MOST humbly we implore You, almighty God, bid these offerings to be brought by the hands of Your holy angel to Your altar above; before the face of Your Divine Majesty; that those of us who, by sharing in the Sacrifice of this altar, shall receive the Most Sacred ✠ Body and ✠ Blood of Your Son, may be filled with every grace and heavenly blessing. Through the same Christ our Lord. Amen.

Commemoration of the Dead

REMEMBER also, O Lord, Your servants and handmaids, *N.* and *N.*, who have gone before us with the sign of faith, and rest in the sleep of peace. (*Here pray for the dead*). To these, O Lord, and to all who rest in Christ, we beseech You to grant of Your goodness, a place of comfort, light and peace. Through the same Christ our Lord. Amen.

TO US sinners also, Your servants, trusting in the greatness of Your mercy, deign to grant some part and fellowship with Your Holy Apostles and Martyrs: with John, Stephen, Matthias, Barnabas, Ignatius, Alexander, Marcellinus, Peter, Felicitas; Perpetua, Agatha, Lucy, Agnes, Cecilia, Anastasia, and all Your Saints; into whose company, we implore You to admit us, not weighing our merits, but freely granting us pardon. Through Christ our Lord.

THROUGH Whom, O Lord, You always create, ✠ sanctify, ✠ fill with life, ✠ bless, and bestow upon us all good things.

The Minor Elevation

THROUGH ✠ Him, and with ✠ Him, and in ✠ Him, is to You, God the Father ✠ almighty, in the unity of the Holy ✠ Spirit, all honor and glory, world without end. *S.* Amen.

THE COMMUNION AND THANKSGIVING

Let us pray. Prompted by saving precepts, and taught by Your divine teaching, we dare to say:

OUR FATHER, Who art in heaven, hallowed be Thy name: Thy kingdom come: Thy will be done on earth as it is in heaven. Give us this day our daily bread; and forgive us our trespasses, as we forgive those who trespass against us. And lead us not into temptation: *S.* But deliver us from evil. *P.* Amen.

Turning to the bridal couple, who are kneeling before the Altar, the Priest confers the Nuptial Blessing upon them.

Let us pray. Be appeased, O Lord, by our humble prayers, and in Your kindness assist this institution of marriage which You have ordained for the propagation of the human race; so that this union made here, joined by Your authority, may be preserved by Your help. Through our Lord, etc. *S.* Amen.

Let us pray. O God, by Your mighty power You made all things out of nothing. First, You set the beginnings of the universe in order. Then, You made man in Your image, and appointed woman to be his inseparable helpmate. Thus You made woman's body from the flesh of man, thereby teaching that what You have been pleased to institute from one principle might never lawfully be put asunder. O God, You have sanctified marriage by a mystery so excellent that in the marriage union You foreshadowed the union of Christ and the

Church. O God, You join woman to man, and You endow that fellowship with a blessing which was not taken away in punishment for original sin nor by the sentence of the flood. Look, in Your mercy, upon this Your handmaid, about to be joined in wedlock, who entreats You to protect and strengthen her. Let the yoke of marriage to her be one of love and peace. Faithful and chaste, let her marry in Christ. Let her ever follow the model of holy women: let her be dear to her husband like Rachel; wise like Rebecca; long-lived and faithful like Sara. Let the author of sin work none of his evil deeds within her; let her ever keep the Faith and the commandments. Let her be true to one wedlock and shun all sinful embraces; let her strengthen weakness by stern discipline. Let her be grave in demeanor, honorable for her modesty, learned in heavenly doctrine, fruitful in children. Let her life be good and innocent. Let her come finally to the rest of the blessed in the kingdom of heaven. May they both see their children's children to the third and fourth generation, thus attaining the old age which they desire. Through the same, etc. S. Amen.

The Priest then continues the Mass as usual.

DELIVER us, we beseech You, O Lord, from all evils, past, present, and to come; and by the intercession of the Blessed and glorious Mary, ever Virgin, Mother of God, together with Your Blessed Apostles Peter and Paul, and Andrew, and all the Saints, grant of Your goodness, peace in our days, that aided by the riches of Your mercy, we may be always free from sin and safe from all disturbance.

Through the same our Lord Jesus Christ, Your Son, Who lives and reigns with You in the unity of the Holy Spirit, God, world without end. *S.* Amen.

P. May the peace ✠ of the Lord be ✠ always with ✠ you. *S.* And with your spirit.

The Priest puts a small particle into the chalice, saying:

May this mingling and consecration of the Body and Blood of our Lord Jesus Christ help us who receive it to life everlasting. Amen.

LAMB of God, You Who take away the sins of the world, have mercy on us.
Lamb of God, You Who take away the sins of the world, have mercy on us.
Lamb of God, You Who take away the sins of the world, grant us peace.

PRAYERS BEFORE HOLY COMMUNION

Then inclining toward the altar, he says:

O LORD Jesus Christ, Who said to Your Apostles: "Peace I leave with you, My peace I give to you," regard not my sins but the faith of Your Church, and deign to give her peace and unity according to Your Will: Who live and reign, God, world without end. Amen.

O LORD Jesus Christ, Son of the living God, Who, by the will of the Father, with the cooperation of the Holy Spirit, have by Your death given life to the world, deliver me by this Your Most Sacred Body and Blood from all my sins and from every evil. Make me always cling to Your commandments, and never permit me to be separated from You. Who with the same God the Father and the Holy Spirit, live and reign, God, world without end. Amen.

LET not the partaking of Your Body, O Lord Jesus Christ, which I, though unworthy, presume to receive, turn to my judgment and condemnation; but through Your goodness, may it become a safeguard and an effective remedy, both of soul and body. Who live and reign with God the Father, in the unity of the Holy Spirit, God, world without end. Amen.

COMMUNION OF THE PRIEST

I WILL take the Bread of heaven, and call upon the name of the Lord.

Lord, I am not worthy that You should come under my roof; but only say the word, and my soul will be healed. (3 *times.*)

Making the Sign of the Cross with the Host, he says:

MAY the Body of our Lord Jesus Christ preserve my soul to life everlasting. Amen.

What return shall I make to the Lord for all He has given me? I will take the Chalice of salvation, and I will call upon the name of the Lord. Praising will I call upon the Lord and I shall be saved from my enemies.

Making the Sign of the Cross with the chalice, he says:

MAY the Blood of our Lord Jesus Christ preserve my soul to life everlasting. Amen.

The Priest reverently consumes the Precious Blood.

COMMUNION OF THE FAITHFUL

The Server and people say the "Confiteor."

P. May almighty God have mercy on you, forgive you your sins, and bring you to life everlasting. *S.* Amen.

P. May the almighty and merciful Lord grant you

pardon, ✠ absolution and remission of your sins. S. Amen.

Holding up a Sacred Host, the Priest says:

Behold the Lamb of God, behold Him Who takes away the sins of the world.

Lord, I am not worthy that You should come under my roof; but only say the word, and my soul will be healed. (3 *times.*)

The Priest says to each communicant:

May the Body of our Lord Jesus Christ preserve your soul to life everlasting. Amen.

The Priest purifies the chalice with wine, saying:

WHAT has passed our lips as food, O Lord, may we possess in purity of heart, that what is given to us in time, be our healing for eternity.

He purifies his fingers with wine and water, saying:

MAY Your Body, O Lord, which I have eaten, and Your Blood which I have drunk, cleave to my very soul, and grant that no trace of sin be found in me, whom these pure and holy mysteries have renewed. Who live and reign, world without end. Amen.

THE COMMUNION • Ps. 127, 4. 6

BEHOLD, thus is the man blessed who fears the Lord; may you see your children's children. Peace be upon Israel! (*P.T.* Alleluia.)

The Priest, turning to the people, says:

P. The Lord be with you. *S.* And with your spirit.
P. Let us pray.

THE POSTCOMMUNION

WE BESEECH You, almighty God, to accompany the institutions of Your providence with gracious favor; that You may preserve with lasting peace those whom You have joined in lawful union. Through our Lord Jesus Christ, Your Son, Who lives and reigns with You in the unity of the Holy Spirit, God, world without end. S. Amen.

FINAL PRAYERS

The Priest turns again to the people, and says:

P. The Lord be with you. S. And with your spirit.
P. Let us bless the Lord. S. Thanks be to God.

The Priest turns to the Bridegroom and Bride, saying:

MAY the God of Abraham, the God of Isaac, and the God of Jacob be with you: and may He fulfill His blessing in you: that you may see your children's children even to the third and fourth generation, and thereafter may have life everlasting, by the grace of our Lord Jesus Christ. Who with the Father and the Holy Spirit lives and reigns, God, world without end. S. Amen.

MAY the tribute of my worship be pleasing to You, Most Holy Trinity, and grant that the sacrifice which I, all unworthy, have offered in the presence of Your Majesty, may be acceptable to You, and through Your mercy obtain forgiveness for me and all for whom I have offered it. Through Christ our Lord. Amen.

THE LAST BLESSING

He kisses the altar, and facing the people, says:

MAY almighty God bless you: ✠ the Father, and the Son, and the Holy Spirit. S. Amen.

The Last Gospel is conveniently placed inside the back cover. Prayers after Low Mass are not said.

"Eternal rest give to them, O Lord."

DAILY MASS FOR THE DEAD

According to the doctrine and practice of the Church, based on the words of Holy Scripture, "It is a holy and wholesome thought to pray for the dead, that they may be loosed from their sins" (2 Mach. 12, 46). We offer the holy sacrifice for the souls in purgatory. (BLACK VESTMENTS)

PRAYERS AT THE FOOT OF THE ALTAR

IN THE name of the Father, ✠ and of the Son, and of the Holy Spirit. Amen.

Priest. I will go in to the altar of God.

Server. The God of my gladness and joy.

P. Our help ✠ is in the name of the Lord.

S. Who made heaven and earth.

P. I confess to almighty God, etc.

S. May almighty God have mercy on you, forgive you your sins, and bring you to life everlasting.

P. Amen.

The Server, bowing, says the "Confiteor."

I CONFESS to almighty God, to Blessed Mary, ever Virgin, to Blessed Michael the Archangel, to Blessed John the Baptist, to the Holy Apostles Peter and Paul, and to all the Saints, and to you, Father, that I have sinned exceedingly in thought, word and deed, *through my fault, through my fault, through my most grievous fault.* Therefore I beseech Blessed Mary, ever Virgin, Blessed Michael the Archangel, Blessed John the Baptist, the Holy Apostles Peter and Paul, and all the Saints, and you, Father, to pray to the Lord our God for me.

P. May almighty God have mercy on you, forgive you your sins, and bring you to life everlasting.

S. Amen.

MAY the almighty and merciful Lord grant us pardon, ✠ absolution, and remission of our sins. *S.* Amen.

P. Will You not, O God, give us life?
S. And shall not Your people rejoice in You?
P. Show us, O Lord, Your kindness.
S. And grant us Your salvation.
P. O Lord, hear my prayer.
S. And let my cry come to You.
P. The Lord be with you.
S. And with your spirit. *P.* Let us pray.

Going up to the altar, the Priest prays silently:

TAKE away from us our sins, O Lord, we beseech You, that we may enter with pure minds into the Holy of Holies. Through Christ our Lord. Amen.

WE BESEECH You, O Lord, by the merits of Your Saints (*he kisses the altar*) whose relics lie here, and of all the Saints: deign in Your mercy to pardon me all my sins. Amen.

THE INTROIT • 4 Esd. 2, 34. 35

At the right side of the altar, the Priest says:

ETERNAL rest give to them, O Lord; and let perpetual light shine upon them. *Ps. 64.* To You we owe our hymn of praise, O God, in Sion; to You must vows be fulfilled in Jerusalem. Hear my prayer; to You all flesh must come. Eternal rest give to them, O Lord; and let perpetual light shine upon them.

THE KYRIE

P. Lord, have mercy. *S.* Lord, have mercy. *P.* Lord, have mercy. *S.* Christ, have mercy. *P.* Christ, have mercy. *S.* Christ, have mercy. *P.* Lord, have mercy. *S.* Lord, have mercy. *P.* Lord, have mercy.

The Priest kisses the altar and turns to the people, saying:

P. The Lord be with you. *S.* And with your spirit. *P.* Let us pray.

THE PRAYER

For Deceased Bishops and Priests:

O GOD, in the apostolic priesthood, You raised Your servants (N. Your servant) to the dignity of the episcopate (priesthood); grant, we beseech You, that they (he) may be numbered with Your Bishops and Priests forever. Through our Lord Jesus Christ, Your Son, Who lives, etc. Amen.

For Deceased Brethren, Relations and Benefactors:

O GOD, the giver of pardon and the lover of man's salvation, we beseech Your mercy, through the intercession of Blessed Mary ever Virgin and of all Your Saints, to grant to the souls of the brethren, relations and benefactors of our congregation who have passed out of this life, the companionship of everlasting bliss.

For All the Faithful Departed:

O GOD, the Creator and Redeemer of all the faithful, grant to the souls of Your servants and handmaids, the remission of all their sins, that, through devout prayers, they may obtain the pardon they always desired. Who live, etc. S. Amen.

THE EPISTLE • Apoc. 14, 13

IN THOSE days, I heard a voice from heaven saying, "Write: Blessed are the dead who die in the Lord henceforth. Yes, says the Spirit, let them rest from their labors, for their works follow them." S. Thanks be to God.

THE GRADUAL • 4 Esd. 2, 34. 35

ETERNAL rest give to them, O Lord; and let perpetual light shine upon them. ℣. *Ps. 111,* 7. The just man shall be in everlasting remembrance; an evil report he shall not fear.

THE TRACT

ABSOLVE, O Lord, the souls of all the faithful departed from every bond of sin. ℣. And by the help of Your grace may they be enabled to escape the judgment of punishment. ℣. And enjoy the bliss of everlasting light.

PRAYER BEFORE THE GOSPEL

Bowing down at the center of the altar, he says:

CLEANSE my heart and my lips, O almighty God, Who cleansed the lips of the Prophet Isaias with a burning coal. In Your gracious mercy deign so to purify me that I may worthily proclaim Your holy Gospel. Through Christ our Lord. Amen.

THE GOSPEL • John 6, 51-55

Going to the left (Gospel) side of the altar, he says:

P. The Lord be with you. *S*. And with your spirit.
P. ✠ The continuation of the holy Gospel according to Saint John. *S*. Glory be to You, O Lord.

AT THAT time, Jesus said to the multitudes of the Jews, "I am the living bread that has come down from heaven. If anyone eat of this bread he shall live forever; and the bread that I will give is My Flesh for the life of the world." The Jews on that account argued with one another, saying, "How can this Man give us His Flesh to eat?" Jesus therefore said to them, "Amen, amen, I say to you, unless you eat the Flesh of the Son of Man, and drink His Blood, you shall not have life in you. He who eats My Flesh and drinks My Blood has life everlasting and I will raise him up on the last day." *S*. Praise be to You, O Christ.

THE OFFERTORY

The Priest turns to the people and says:

P. The Lord be with you. *S*. And with your spirit.
P. Let us pray.

THE OFFERTORY VERSE

O LORD Jesus Christ, King of glory, deliver the souls of all the faithful departed from the pains of hell and from the bottomless pit; deliver them from the lion's mouth, that hell swallow them not up, that they fall not into darkness, but let the holy standard-bearer Michael bring them into that holy light which You promised of old to Abraham and to his seed. ℣. We offer You, O Lord, sacrifices and prayers of praise; receive them in behalf of those souls we commemorate this day.

Grant them, O Lord, to pass from death to that life which You promised of old to Abraham and to his seed.

The Priest now uncovers the chalice, places the host on the paten and offering it up, says:

ACCEPT, O holy Father, almighty and eternal God, this spotless host, which I, Your unworthy servant, offer to You, my living and true God, to atone for my numberless sins, offenses, and negligences; on behalf of all here present and likewise for all faithful Christians living and dead, that it may profit me and them as a means of salvation to life everlasting. Amen.

He pours wine and water into the chalice, saying:

O GOD, Who established the nature of man in wondrous dignity, and still more admirably restored it, grant that through the mystery of this water and wine, we may be made partakers of His Divinity, Who has condescended to become partaker of our humanity, Jesus Christ, Your Son, our Lord. Who lives and reigns with You in the unity of the Holy Spirit, God, world without end. Amen.

Offering up the wine, the Priest says:

WE OFFER You, O Lord, the chalice of salvation, humbly begging of Your mercy that it may arise before Your Divine Majesty, with a pleasing fragrance, for our salvation and for that of the whole world. Amen.

Bowing down, the Priest says:

IN A humble spirit and with a contrite heart, may we be accepted by You, O Lord, and may our sacrifice so be offered in Your sight this day as to please You, O Lord God.

Raising his eyes and blessing the offering, he says:

COME, O Sanctifier, almighty and eternal God, and bless ✠ this sacrifice prepared for the glory of Your holy name.

WASHING THE FINGERS

I WASH my hands in innocence, and I go around Your altar, O Lord, giving voice to my thanks, and recounting all Your wondrous deeds. O Lord, I love the house in which You dwell, the tenting-place of Your glory. Gather not my soul with those of sinners, nor with men of blood my life. On their hands are crimes, and their right hands are full of bribes. But I walk in integrity; redeem me, and have pity on me. My foot stands on level ground; in the assemblies I will bless You, O Lord.

ACCEPT, Most Holy Trinity, this offering which we are making to You in remembrance of the Passion, Resurrection, and Ascension of Jesus Christ, our Lord; and in honor of Blessed Mary, ever Virgin, Blessed John the Baptist, the Holy Apostles Peter and Paul, and of these, and of all the Saints; that it may add to their honor and aid our salvation; and may they deign to intercede in heaven for us who honor their memory here on earth. Through the same Christ our Lord. Amen.

The Priest turns toward the people and says:

Pray, brethren, that my sacrifice and yours may become acceptable to God the Father almighty.

S. May the Lord accept this sacrifice from your hands to the praise and glory of His name, for our advantage, and that of all His holy Church.

P. Amen.

THE SECRET

For Deceased Bishops and Priests:

ACCEPT, we beseech You, O Lord, for the souls of Your servants, Bishops (Priests), the sacrifice which we offer, and let those whom in this world You raised to episcopal (sacerdotal) rank, be admitted into the company of Your Saints in the kingdom of heaven. Through our Lord Jesus Christ, Your Son, Who lives and reigns with You in the unity of the Holy Spirit, God, world without end. Amen.

For Deceased Brethren, Relations and Benefactors:

O GOD, Whose mercies are numberless, graciously receive our humble prayers, and through these sacraments of our salvation, grant to the souls of our brethren, relations and benefactors, who by Your grace did confess Your name, the remission of all their sins.

For All the Faithful Departed:

MERCIFULLY regard, we beseech You, O Lord, the sacrifice which we offer You for the souls of Your servants and handmaids, that, to those on whom You conferred the favor of the Christian Faith You would also grant its reward. Through our Lord Jesus Christ, Your Son, Who lives and reigns with You in the unity of the Holy Spirit, God.

P. World without end. *S.* Amen.

PREFACE—CANON

P. The Lord be with you. *S.* And with your spirit.
P. Lift up your hearts.
S. We have lifted them up to the Lord.

P. Let us give thanks to the Lord, our God.
S. It is fitting and just.

IT IS fitting indeed and just, right and helpful to salvation, for us always and everywhere to give thanks to You, O holy Lord, Father almighty, everlasting God, through Christ our Lord. In Whom the hope of a blessed resurrection has shone upon us, that those whom the certainty of dying afflicts, may be consoled by the promise of future immortality. For to Your faithful, O Lord, life is changed, not taken away; and the abode of this earthly sojourn being dissolved, an eternal dwelling is prepared in heaven. And therefore with Angels and Archangels, with Thrones and Dominations, and with the whole host of the heavenly army, we sing a hymn to Your glory, saying again and again (*the bell is rung* 3 *times*):

HOLY, HOLY, HOLY, Lord God of Hosts. Heaven and earth are filled with Your glory. Hosanna in the highest. ✠ Blessed is He Who comes in the name of the Lord. Hosanna in the highest.

THE CANON OF THE MASS

THEREFORE, most gracious Father, we humbly beg of You and entreat You through Jesus Christ Your Son, our Lord, (*he kisses the altar*) to deem acceptable and bless these ✠ gifts, these ✠ offerings, these ✠ holy and unspotted oblations which, in the first place, we offer You for Your Holy Catholic Church, that You would deign to give her peace and protection, to unite and guard her throughout the world, together with Your serv-

ant *N.*, our Pope, and *N.*, our Bishop; and all true believers who cherish the Catholic and Apostolic Faith.

Commemoration of the Living

REMEMBER, O Lord, Your servants and handmaids, *N.* and *N.*, (*name them*) and all here present, whose faith and devotion are known to You, on whose behalf we offer to You, or who themselves offer to You, this sacrifice of praise for themselves, families and friends, for the good of their souls, for their hope of salvation and deliverance from all harm, and who offer their homage to You, eternal, living and true God.

Commemoration of the Saints

IN THE unity of holy fellowship we observe the memory, first of all, of the glorious and ever Virgin Mary, Mother of our Lord and God Jesus Christ; next, that of Your Blessed Apostles and Martyrs, Peter and Paul, Andrew, James, John, Thomas, James, Philip, Bartholomew, Matthew, Simon and Thaddeus; of Linus, Cletus, Clement, Sixtus, Cornelius, Cyprian, Lawrence, Chrysogonus, John and Paul, Cosmas and Damian, and of all Your Saints, by whose merits and prayers grant that we may be always fortified by the help of Your protection. Through the same Christ our Lord. Amen.

Spreading his hands over the oblation, he says:

GRACIOUSLY accept, then, we beseech You, O Lord, this service of our worship and that of all Your household. Provide that our days be spent in Your peace, save us from everlasting damnation, and cause us to be numbered in the flock You have chosen. Through Christ our Lord. Amen.

O GOD, deign to bless ✠ what we offer, and make it approved, ✠ effective, ✠ right, and wholly pleasing in every way, that it may become for our good, the Body ✠ and Blood ✠ of Your dearly beloved Son, Jesus Christ our Lord.

CONSECRATION—ELEVATION

WHO, the day before He suffered, took bread into His holy and venerable hands, and having raised His eyes to heaven, to You, O God, His almighty Father, giving thanks to You, He blessed it, ✠ broke it, and gave it to His disciples, saying: All of you take and eat of this:

FOR THIS IS MY BODY.

IN LIKE manner, when the supper was done, taking also this goodly chalice into His holy and venerable hands, again giving thanks to You, He blessed ✠ it, and gave it to His disciples, saying: All of you take and drink of this:

FOR THIS IS THE CHALICE OF MY BLOOD OF THE NEW AND ETERNAL COVENANT: THE MYSTERY OF FAITH: WHICH SHALL BE SHED FOR YOU AND FOR MANY UNTO THE FORGIVENESS OF SINS.

After replacing the chalice on the corporal, he says:

As often as you shall do these things, in memory of Me shall you do them.

Offering of the Victim

MINDFUL, therefore, O Lord, not only of the blessed Passion of the same Christ, Your Son, our Lord, but also of His Resurrection from the dead, and finally His glorious Ascension into heaven, we, Your ministers, as also Your holy people, offer to Your supreme Majesty, of the gifts bestowed upon us, the pure ✠ Victim, the holy ✠ Victim, the all-perfect ✠ Victim: the holy ✠ Bread of life eternal and the Chalice ✠ of unending salvation.

AND this deign to regard with gracious and kindly attention and hold acceptable, as You deigned to accept the offerings of Abel, Your just servant, and the sacrifice of Abraham our patriarch, and that which Your chief priest Melchisedec offered to You, a holy sacrifice and a spotless victim.

MOST humbly we implore You, almighty God, bid these offerings to be brought by the hands of Your holy angel to Your altar above; before the face of Your Divine Majesty; that those of us who, by sharing in the Sacrifice of this altar, shall receive the Most Sacred ✠ Body and ✠ Blood of Your Son, may be filled with every grace and heavenly blessing. Through the same Christ our Lord. Amen.

Commemoration of the Dead

REMEMBER also, O Lord, Your servants and handmaids, *N.* and *N.*, who have gone before us with the sign of faith, and rest in the sleep of peace. (*Here pray for the dead.*) To these, O Lord, and to all who rest in Christ, we beseech You to grant of Your goodness, a place of comfort, light and peace. Through the same Christ our Lord. Amen.

TO US sinners also, Your servants, trusting in the greatness of Your mercy, deign to grant some part and fellowship with Your Holy Apostles and Martyrs: with John, Stephen, Matthias, Barnabas, Ignatius, Alexander, Marcellinus, Peter, Felicitas,

Perpetua, Agatha, Lucy, Agnes, Cecilia, Anastasia, and all Your Saints; into whose company, we implore You to admit us, not weighing our merits, but freely granting us pardon. Through Christ our Lord.

THROUGH Whom, O Lord, You always create, ✠ sanctify, ✠ fill with life, ✠ bless, and bestow upon us all good things.

The Minor Elevation

THROUGH ✠ Him, and with ✠ Him, and in ✠ Him, is to You, God the Father ✠ almighty, in the unity of the Holy ✠ Spirit, all honor and glory, world without end. S. Amen.

THE COMMUNION AND THANKSGIVING

Let us pray. Prompted by saving precepts, and taught by Your divine teaching, we dare to say:

OUR FATHER, Who art in heaven, hallowed be Thy name: Thy kingdom come: Thy will be done on earth as it is in heaven. Give us this day our daily bread; and forgive us our trespasses, as we forgive those who trespass against us. And lead us not into temptation: S. But deliver us from evil. *P.* Amen.

DELIVER us, we beseech You, O Lord, from all evils, past, present, and to come; and by the intercession of the Blessed and glorious Mary, ever Virgin, Mother of God, together with Your Blessed Apostles Peter and Paul, and Andrew, and all the Saints, grant of Your goodness, peace in our days, that aided by the riches of Your mercy, we may be always free from sin and safe from all disturbance.

Through the same our Lord Jesus Christ, Your Son, Who lives and reigns with You in the unity of the Holy Spirit, God, world without end. *S.* Amen.

P. May the peace ✠ of the Lord be ✠ always with ✠ you. *S.* And with your spirit.

The Priest puts a small particle into the chalice, saying:

May this mingling and consecration of the Body and Blood of our Lord Jesus Christ help us who receive it to life everlasting. Amen.

LAMB of God, You Who take away the sins of the world, grant them rest.

Lamb of God, You Who take away the sins of the world, grant them rest.

Lamb of God, You Who take away the sins of the world, grant them eternal rest.

PRAYERS BEFORE HOLY COMMUNION

Then inclining toward the altar, he says:

O LORD Jesus Christ, Son of the living God, Who, by the will of the Father, with the co-operation of the Holy Spirit, have by Your death given life to the world, deliver me by this Your Most Sacred Body and Blood from all my sins and from every evil. Make me always cling to Your commandments, and never permit me to be separated from You. Who with the same God the Father and the Holy Spirit, live and reign, God, world without end. Amen.

LET not the partaking of Your Body, O Lord Jesus Christ, which I, though unworthy, presume to receive, turn to my judgment and condemnation; but through Your goodness, may it become a safeguard and an effective remedy, both of soul and body. Who live and reign with God the Father, in the unity of the Holy Spirit, God, world without end. Amen.

COMMUNION OF THE PRIEST

I WILL take the Bread of heaven, and call upon the name of the Lord.

Lord, I am not worthy that You should come under my roof; but only say the word, and my soul will be healed. (3 *times.*)

Making the Sign of the Cross with the Host, he says:

MAY the Body of our Lord Jesus Christ preserve my soul to life everlasting. Amen.

What return shall I make to the Lord for all He has given me? I will take the Chalice of salvation, and I will call upon the name of the Lord. Praising will I call upon the Lord and I shall be saved from my enemies.

Making the Sign of the Cross with the chalice, he says:

MAY the Blood of our Lord Jesus Christ preserve my soul to life everlasting. Amen.

The Priest reverently consumes the Precious Blood.

COMMUNION OF THE FAITHFUL

The Server and people say the "Confiteor."

P. May almighty God have mercy on you, forgive you your sins, and bring you to life everlasting. S. Amen.

P. May the almighty and merciful Lord grant you pardon, ✠ absolution and remission of your sins. S. Amen.

Behold the Lamb of God, behold Him Who takes away the sins of the world.
Lord, I am not worthy that You should come under my roof; but only say the word, and my soul will be healed. (3 *times.*)

The Priest says to each communicant:

May the Body of our Lord Jesus Christ preserve your soul to life everlasting. Amen.

The Priest purifies the chalice with wine, saying:

WHAT has passed our lips as food, O Lord, may we possess in purity of heart, that what is given to us in time, be our healing for eternity.

He purifies his fingers with wine and water, saying:

MAY Your Body, O Lord, which I have eaten, and Your Blood which I have drunk, cleave to my very soul, and grant that no trace of sin be found in me, whom these pure and holy mysteries have renewed. Who live and reign, world without end. Amen.

THE COMMUNION • 4 Esd. 2, 35. 34

MAY light eternal shine upon them, O Lord, with Your Saints forever, for You are gracious. ℣. Eternal rest give to them, O Lord; and let perpetual light shine upon them: with Your Saints forever, for You are gracious.

The Priest, turning to the people, says:

P. The Lord be with you. *S.* And with your spirit.
P. Let us pray.

THE POSTCOMMUNION

For Deceased Bishops and Priests:

WE BESEECH You, O Lord, that Your mercy, which we implore, may benefit the souls of

Your servants, Bishops (Priests), that, by Your goodness, they may obtain eternal companionship with Him in Whom they hoped and believed. Through our Lord, etc. Amen.

For Deceased Brethren, Relations and Benefactors:

GRANT, we beseech You, almighty and merciful God, that the souls of our brethren, relations and benefactors, for whom we have offered this sacrifice in praise of Your Majesty, by virtue of this sacrament, may be freed from all their sins, and by Your mercy, receive the bliss of eternal light.

For All the Faithful Departed:

MAY the prayer of Your suppliant people, we beseech You, O Lord, benefit the souls of Your servants and handmaids, that You may deliver them from all their sins, and make them share in Your Redemption. Who live, etc. *S.* Amen.

FINAL PRAYERS

P. The Lord be with you. *S.* And with your spirit.
P. May they rest in peace. *S.* Amen.

MAY the tribute of my worship be pleasing to You, Most Holy Trinity, and grant that the sacrifice which I, all unworthy, have offered in the presence of Your Majesty, may be acceptable to You, and through Your mercy obtain forgiveness for me and all for whom I have offered it. Through Christ our Lord. Amen.

The Last Gospel and Prayers after Low Mass are conveniently placed inside the back cover.

PRAYER CONCLUSIONS

The conclusions of the Prayers, Secrets and Postcommunions of the Mass vary according to the rules given below.

For Prayers addressed to God the Father:

Through our Lord Jesus Christ, Your Son, Who lives and reigns with You in the unity of the Holy Spirit, God, world without end. S. Amen.

When our Lord is mentioned at the beginning or body of the Prayer:

Through the same our Lord Jesus Christ, Your Son, Who lives and reigns with You in the unity of the Holy Spirit, God, world without end. S. Amen.

For Prayers mentioning the Holy Spirit:

Through our Lord Jesus Christ, Your Son, Who lives and reigns with You in the unity of the same Holy Spirit, God, world without end. S. Amen.

For Prayers whose final clause mentions our Blessed Lord:

Who with You lives and reigns in the unity of the Holy Spirit, God, world without end. S. Amen.

When the Prayer is addressed to God the Son:

Who live and reign with God the Father, in the unity of the Holy Spirit, God, world without end. S. Amen.

THE ASPERGES BEFORE HIGH MASS

The "Asperges" or sprinkling of holy water takes place before the principal Mass on Sundays.

Antiphon. Cleanse me of sin with hyssop, O Lord, that I may be purified; wash me, and I shall be whiter than snow.

Psalm 50, 3. Have mercy on me, O God, in Your goodness.

℣. Glory be, etc.

On Passion and Palm Sundays the "Glory be" is omitted.

Antiphon. Cleanse me of sin, *as above.*

℣. Show us, O Lord, Your kindness. (*P.T.* Alleluia.)

℟. And grant us Your salvation. (*P.T.* Alleluia.)

℣. O Lord, hear my prayer.

℟. And let my cry come to You.

℣. The Lord be with you.

℟. And with your spirit.

Let us pray. Graciously hear us, O holy Lord, Father almighty, eternal God; and be pleased to send down from heaven Your holy angel, that he may watch over, foster, safeguard, abide with and defend all who dwell in this house. Through Christ our Lord. ℟. Amen.

Asperges from Easter to Pentecost inclusive

Antiphon. I saw water flowing from the temple on the right side, alleluia: and all those to whom this water came were saved, and they shall say: alleluia, alleluia.

Psalm 117. Give thanks to the Lord, for He is good, for His mercy endures forever.

℣. Glory be, etc.

Antiphon. I saw water, *as above.*

℣. Show us, O Lord, Your kindness, *as above.*

EVENING PRAYERS

O ALMIGHTY and eternal God! Prostrate before Your Divine Majesty, I adore You with all possible reverence. I believe and hold for certain all You have revealed to Your holy Church. I hope in Your infinite goodness and mercy, and I love You with all my heart.

O great and almighty God! I kneel before You to thank You with my whole heart for all the favors which You have bestowed upon me this day; for my food and drink, my health and all my powers of body and soul. I thank You for all Your holy lights and inspirations, for Your care and protection, and for all those other mercies which I do not now recall, or which I do not know how to value as I ought. I thank You for them all, O heavenly Father. Through Jesus Christ, Your Son, our Lord.

Say the Act of Contrition, *page* 1248.

Prayer for the Dead

O GOD, the Creator and Redeemer of all the faithful, grant to the souls of Your servants departed full remission of all their sins, that, through our devout prayers, they may obtain the pardon, which they have always desired. Who live and reign, world without end. Amen.

℣. Eternal rest grant to them, O Lord.
℟. And let perpetual light shine upon them.
℣. May they rest in peace. ℟. Amen.

The Memorare

REMEMBER, O most gracious Virgin Mary, that never was it known that anyone who fled to your protection, implored your help, or sought your intercession, was left unaided. Inspired with this confidence, I fly to you, O Virgin of virgins, my Mother! To you I come; before you I stand, sinful and sorrowful. O Mother of the Word Incarnate, despise not my petitions, but, in your mercy, hear and answer me. Amen.

An indulgence of 3 years. A plenary indulgence under the usual conditions, if recited daily for a month. (No. 339.)

THE SACRAMENT OF PENANCE

Prayer before Confession

RECEIVE my confession, O most loving and gracious Lord Jesus Christ, only hope for the salvation of my soul. Grant to me true contrition of soul, so that day and night I may by penance make satisfaction for my many sins. Savior of the world, O good Jesus, Who gave Yourself to the death of the Cross to save sinners, look upon me, most wretched of all sinners; have pity on me, and give me the light to know my sins, true sorrow for them, and a firm purpose of never committing them again.

O gracious Virgin Mary, Immaculate Mother of Jesus, I implore you to obtain for me by your powerful intercession these graces from your Divine Son.

St. Joseph, pray for me.

The Ten Commandments

1st Commandment. Have I wilfully doubted or denied my holy religion? Have I taken part in services other than those of my religion? Have I consulted fortune tellers, or read forbidden books, or despaired of God's mercy? Have I neglected to worship God with prayer and the Mass?

2nd Commandment. Have I made false, unlawful or unnecessary oaths? Have I taken God's name in vain?

3rd Commandment. Have I absented myself without due cause from Mass on Sundays or Holy Days of Obligation? Have I done unnecessary servile work on these days, or caused others to do so?

4th Commandment. Have I neglected my parents in their necessity? Have I been disobedient to them, or displayed anger toward them? Have I fulfilled my obligations toward my children? Instructed them? Reprimanded them when necessary? Watched over their companionships, etc.?

5th Commandment. Have I been angry? Have I been violent toward another, or caused violence without just cause? Have I been jealous of others? Have I been guilty of drinking to excess?

6th and 9th Commandments. Have I deliberately taken pleasure in impure thoughts? Have I committed any wilful impure actions? Have I gone to places of amusement that I knew would lead me into sin? Have I kept away from other occasions of sin?

7th and 10th Commandments. Have I stolen anything? Defrauded others of their just wages? Cheated in prices, weights, etc.? Have I through my own fault caused damage to the property of another? Have I made restitution for past sins of this nature? Have I now any ill-gotten goods?

8th Commandment. Have I injured (without just cause) the name or reputation of another? By telling lies about him? By exposing without necessity his faults? Have I restored his good name when I have by untruth injured it?

The Precepts of the Church

1. Have I attended Mass on Sundays and Holy Days of Obligation?

2. Have I fasted on the days appointed, and abstained from meat on Fridays and other days of abstinence?

3. Have I confessed at least once a year any mortal sins I may have committed?
4. Have I neglected to make my Easter duty?
5. Have I contributed to the support of my Church according to my means?
6. Have I failed in observing Church regulations with reference to the Sacrament of Matrimony?

Form of Confession

Say first: *"Bless me, Father, for I have sinned. It is (state the time) since my last confession"; then, confess your sins. Do not use the words, "several times" or "quite often," or similar expressions. Add at the end*: *"For these, and all the sins of my past life, especially (here mention, in general, sins against charity, obedience, purity, of anger, etc.) I am heartily sorry." Always try to make a perfect act of contrition based upon perfect love of God.*

Prayer after Confession

O ALMIGHTY and most merciful God, I give You thanks with all the powers of my soul for this and all other mercies, graces, and blessings bestowed on me, and prostrating myself at Your sacred feet, I offer myself to be henceforth forever Yours. Let nothing in life or death ever separate me from You! I renounce with my whole soul all my treasons against You, and all the abominations and sins of my past life. I renew my promises made in Baptism, and from this moment I dedicate myself eternally to Your love and service. Grant that for the time to come, I may detest sin more than death itself, and avoid all such occasions and companies as have unhappily brought me to it. This I resolve to do by the aid of Your divine grace, without which I can do nothing. Amen.

PRAYERS BEFORE HOLY COMMUNION

The following indulgenced prayers are usually said by the Priest before celebrating the Holy Sacrifice of the Mass. They may also be said by the laity in preparation for Holy Communion.

Prayer of St. Thomas Aquinas

An indulgence of 3 years. A plenary indulgence once a month, for daily recitation under the usual conditions. (No. 158.)

ALMIGHTY and eternal God, I approach the sacrament of Your Only-begotten Son, our Lord Jesus Christ. As a sick man I approach the physician of life; as a man unclean, I come to the fountain of mercy; blind, to the light of eternal brightness; poor and needy, to the Lord of heaven and earth. I beseech You, therefore, in Your boundless mercy, to heal my sickness, to wash away my defilements, to enlighten my blindness, to enrich my poverty, and to clothe my nakedness; that I may receive the Bread of angels, the King of kings, the Lord of lords, with such reverence and humility, such contrition and faith, such purpose and intention, as may help the salvation of my soul. Grant, I beseech You, that I may receive not only the Sacrament of the Body and Blood of our

Lord, but also the whole grace and virtue of the Sacrament. O most indulgent God, grant me so to receive the Body of Your Only-begotten Son, our Lord Jesus Christ, which He took of the Virgin Mary, that I may be found worthy to be incorporated with His Mystical Body and numbered among His members. O most loving Father, grant that I may one day forever contemplate Him unveiled and face to face, Whom, on my pilgrimage, I receive under a veil, Your beloved Son, Who with You lives and reigns in the unity of the Holy Spirit, God, world without end. Amen.

Prayer to the Blessed Virgin

An indulgence of 3 years. (No. 747.)

O MOST Blessed Virgin Mary, most loving and most merciful Mother, I, a wretched and unworthy sinner, come before you, with the heartfelt prayer, that in your goodness you would deign graciously to be near me and all who throughout the whole Church are to receive the Body and Blood of your Son this day, even as you stood by your most dear Son as He hung on the Cross, that, aided by your gracious help, we may worthily offer up a pure and acceptable sacrifice in the sight of the most high and undivided Trinity. Amen.

Prayer to St. Joseph

An indulgence of 3 years. (No. 747.)

O BLESSED Joseph, happy man, to whom it was given not only to see and to hear that God Whom many kings longed to see, and saw not, to hear, and heard not; but also to carry Him in your arms, to embrace Him, to clothe Him, and to guard and defend Him.

℣. Pray for us, O Blessed Joseph.
℟. That we may be made worthy of the promises of Christ.

Let us pray. O God, Who have given us a royal priesthood, we beseech You, that as Blessed Joseph was found worthy to touch with his hands, and to bear in his arms, Your Only-begotten Son, born of the Virgin Mary, so may we be made fit, by cleanness of heart and blamelessness of life, to minister at Your holy altar; may we, this day, with reverent devotion partake of the Sacred Body and Blood of Your Only-begotten Son, and may we in the world to come be accounted worthy of receiving an everlasting reward. Through the same Christ our Lord. Amen.

Prayer for Peace

O LORD Jesus Christ, Who said to Your Apostles: "Peace I leave with you, My peace I give to you," regard not my sins but the faith of Your Church, and deign to give her peace and unity according to Your Will: Who live and reign, God, world without end. Amen.

Prayer for Holiness

O LORD Jesus Christ, Son of the living God, Who, by the will of the Father, with the cooperation of the Holy Spirit, have by Your death given life to the world, deliver me by this Your Most Sacred Body and Blood from all my sins and from every evil. Make me always cling to Your commandments, and never permit me to be separated from You. Who with the same God the Father and the Holy Spirit, live and reign, God, world without end. Amen.

ACT OF SPIRITUAL COMMUNION

An indulgence of 3 years. A plenary indulgence under the usual conditions, if said daily for a month. (No. 164.)

MY JESUS, I believe that You are in the Blessed Sacrament. I love You above all things, and I long for You in my soul. Since I cannot now receive You sacramentally, come at least spiritually into my heart. As though You have already come, I embrace You and unite myself entirely to You; never permit me to be separated from You.

THANKSGIVING AFTER HOLY COMMUNION

Prayer of St. Thomas Aquinas

An indulgence of 3 years. (No. 160.)

I THANK You, O holy Lord, almighty Father, eternal God, Who have deigned, not through any merits of mine, but out of the condescension of Your goodness, to satisfy me a sinner, Your unworthy servant, with the precious Body and Blood of Your Son, our Lord Jesus Christ. I pray that this holy Communion be not a condemnation to punishment for me, but a saving plea to forgiveness. May it be to me the armor of faith and the shield of a good will. May it be the emptying out of my vices and the extinction of all lustful desires; an increase of charity and patience, of humility and obedience, and of all virtues; a strong defense against the snares of all my enemies, visible and invisible; the perfect quieting of all my evil impulses of flesh and spirit, binding me firmly to You, the one true God; and a happy ending of my life. I pray too that You will deign to bring me a sinner to that ineffable banquet, where You with Your Son and the Holy Spirit, are to Your Saints true light, fulfillment of desires, eternal joy, unalloyed gladness, and perfect bliss. Through the same Christ our Lord. Amen.

Adoro Te

An indulgence of 7 years if this Hymn (or only the last stanza) is said before the Blessed Sacrament. (No. 166.)

O HIDDEN Godhead, humbly I adore You,
Who truly are beneath the forms in view.
To You I bow my heart and bend the knee,
Since, contemplating You, all fails for me.

Sight, touch and taste in You are each deceived:
The ear alone most safely is believed.
I firmly hold whate'er God's Son has spoken,
Than Truth's own word there is no truer token.

God only on the Cross was hid from view,
But here hides Deity and Manhood too;
And I in both professing firm belief,
Make mine the prayer of the repentant thief.

Your wounds, as Thomas saw, I do not see,
Yet You confess my Lord and God to be.
My faith confirm and childlike trust impart,
And may I love You, Lord, with all my heart.

O Blest Memorial of our Lord's own dying:
O Living Bread, to mortals life supplying:
Become indeed the life of my own mind,
So that in You I may all sweetness find.

O Pelican, self-wounding on the Rood,
Me unclean man yet cleanse with Your own Blood,
Of which a single drop, for sinners spilt,
Can purge this wicked world of all its guilt.

O Jesus Whom at present veiled I see,
What I so thirst for, grant to me:
That I may see Your Blessed Self unfolding,
And may find rest Your glory in beholding. Amen.

Offering and Prayer of St. Ignatius Loyola "Suscipe"

An indulgence of 3 years. (No. 52.)

TAKE, O Lord, and receive my entire liberty, my memory, my understanding and my whole will. All that I am and all that I possess You have given me: I surrender it all to You to be disposed of according to Your will. Give me only Your love and Your grace; with these I will be rich enough, and will desire nothing more.

Anima Christi

300 days every time. Seven years after Communion. Plenary indulgence under the usual conditions once a month for those who recite it every day. (No. 131.)

SOUL of Christ, sanctify me.
Body of Christ, save me.
Blood of Christ, inebriate me.
Water from the side of Christ, wash me.
Passion of Christ, strengthen me.
O good Jesus, hear me.
Within Your wounds hide me.

Separated from You let me never be.
From the malignant enemy, defend me.
At the hour of death, call me.
And close to You bid me.
That with Your Saints I may be
Praising You, forever and ever. Amen.

Indulgenced Prayer Before a Crucifix

BEHOLD, O kind and most sweet Jesus, I cast myself upon my knees in Your sight, and with the most fervent desire of my soul I pray and beseech You that You would impress upon my heart lively sentiments of Faith, Hope, and Charity, with true repentance for my sins, and a firm desire of amendment, while with deep affection and grief of soul I ponder within myself and mentally contemplate Your five most precious wounds; having before my eyes that which David spoke in prophecy of You, O good Jesus: They have pierced my hands and feet; they have numbered all my bones.

An indulgence of 10 years. A plenary indulgence may be gained by all, who having confessed and received Holy Communion, recite this prayer before an image of Christ crucified and also pray for the intentions of the Holy Father. (No. 201.)

Petitions of St. Augustine

An indulgence of 500 days. A plenary indulgence if these petitions are repeated daily for a month. (No. 88.)

LORD Jesus, let me know myself; let me know You,
And desire nothing else but You.

Let me hate myself and love You,
And do all things for Your sake.

Let me humble myself and exalt You,
And think of nothing else but You.

Let me die to myself and live in You,
And take whatever happens as coming from You.

Let me forsake myself and walk after You,
And ever desire to follow You.

Let me flee from myself and turn to You,
That so I may merit to be defended by You.

Let me fear for myself, let me fear You,
And be among those that are chosen by You.

Let me distrust myself and trust in You,
And ever obey for the love of You.

Let me cleave to nothing but You,
And ever be poor because of You.

Look upon me that I may love You,
Call me, that I may see You,
And forever possess You, for all eternity. Amen.

Prayer to St. Joseph

An indulgence of 3 years. (No. 473.)

GUARDIAN of virgins, and holy father Joseph, to whose faithful custody Christ Jesus, Innocence itself, and Mary, Virgin of virgins, were committed; I pray and beseech you, by these dear pledges, Jesus and Mary, that, being preserved from all uncleanness, I may with spotless mind, pure heart and chaste body, ever serve Jesus and Mary most chastely all the days of my life. Amen.

THE APPROVED LITANIES

The Litany of the Holy Name of Jesus

An indulgence of 7 years. A plenary indulgence once a month under the usual conditions when this Litany is recited daily for a month. (No. 114.)

LORD, have mercy.
Christ, have mercy.
Lord, have mercy.
Jesus, hear us.
Jesus, graciously hear us.
God the Father of Heaven,*
God the Son, Redeemer of the world,
God the Holy Spirit,
Holy Trinity, One God,
Jesus, Son of the living God,
Jesus, Splendor of the Father,
Jesus, Brightness of eternal Light,
Jesus, King of Glory,
Jesus, Sun of Justice,
Jesus, Son of the Virgin Mary,
Jesus, most amiable,
Jesus, most admirable,
Jesus, the mighty God,
Jesus, Father of the world to come,
Jesus, angel of great counsel,
Jesus, most powerful,
Jesus, most patient,
Jesus, most obedient,
Jesus, meek and humble of heart,
Jesus, Lover of Chastity,
Jesus, our Lover,
Jesus, God of Peace,
Jesus, Author of Life,
Jesus, Model of Virtues,
Jesus, zealous for souls,
Jesus, our God,
Jesus, our Refuge,
Jesus, Father of the Poor,
Jesus, Treasure of the Faithful,
Jesus, good Shepherd,
Jesus, true Light,
Jesus, eternal Wisdom,
Jesus, infinite Goodness,
Jesus, our Way and our Life,
Jesus, joy of Angels,
Jesus, King of the Patriarchs,
Jesus, Master of the Apostles,
Jesus, Teacher of the Evangelists,
Jesus, Strength of Martyrs,
Jesus, Light of Confessors,
Jesus, Purity of Virgins,
Jesus, Crown of all Saints,

Be merciful, *spare us, O Jesus!*

Be merciful, *graciously hear us, O Jesus!*

From all evil,†
From all sin,
From Your wrath,
From the snares of the devil,
From the spirit of fornication,
From everlasting death,
From the neglect of Your inspirations,
Through the mystery of Your holy incarnation,
Through Your nativity,
Through Your infancy,
Through Your most divine life,

**Have mercy on us.*

†*Deliver us, O Jesus.*

Through Your labors,*
Through Your agony and passion,
Through Your cross and dereliction,
Through Your sufferings,
Through Your death and burial,
Through Your resurrection,
Through Your ascension,
Through Your institution of the Most Holy Eucharist,
Through Your joys,
Through Your glory,
Lamb of God, You Who take away the sins of the world, *spare us, O Jesus!*
Lamb of God, You Who take away the sins of the world, *graciously hear us, O Jesus!*
Lamb of God, You Who take away the sins of the world, *have mercy on us, O Jesus!*
Jesus, hear us.
Jesus, graciously hear us.

Deliver us, O Jesus.

Let us pray. O Lord Jesus Christ, You have said, "Ask and you shall receive; seek, and you shall find; knock, and it shall be opened to you"; mercifully attend to our supplications, and grant us the grace of Your most divine love, that we may love You with all our hearts, and in all our words and actions, and never cease to praise You.

Make us, O Lord, to have a perpetual fear and love of Your holy name, for You never fail to govern those whom You solidly establish in Your love. Who live and reign, world without end. ℟. Amen.

The Litany of the Most Sacred Heart of Jesus

An indul. of 7 years. A plenary indulgence once a month under the usual conditions, if the entire Litany with its versicle and prayer is recited daily for a month. (No. 245.)

LORD, have mercy.
Christ, have mercy.
Lord, have mercy.
Christ, hear us.
Christ, graciously hear us.
God the Father of Heaven,*
God the Son, Redeemer of the world,
God the Holy Spirit,
Holy Trinity, One God,
Heart of Jesus, Son of the Eternal Father,
Heart of Jesus, formed by the Holy Spirit in the womb of the Virgin Mother,
Heart of Jesus, substantially united to the Word of God,
Heart of Jesus, of Infinite Majesty,
Heart of Jesus, Sacred Temple of God,
Heart of Jesus, Tabernacle of the Most High,

Have mercy on us.

Heart of Jesus, House of God and Gate of Heaven,*
Heart of Jesus, burning furnace of charity,
Heart of Jesus, abode of justice and love,
Heart of Jesus, full of goodness and love,
Heart of Jesus, abyss of all virtues,
Heart of Jesus, most worthy of all praise,
Heart of Jesus, king and center of all hearts,
Heart of Jesus, in Whom are all the treasures of wisdom and knowledge,
Heart of Jesus, in Whom dwells the fullness of divinity,
Heart of Jesus, in Whom the Father was well pleased,
Heart of Jesus, of Whose fullness we have all received,
Heart of Jesus, desire of the everlasting hills,
Heart of Jesus, patient and most merciful,
Heart of Jesus, enriching all who invoke You,
Heart of Jesus, fountain of life and holiness,
Heart of Jesus, propitiation for our sins,
Heart of Jesus, loaded down with opprobrium,
Heart of Jesus, bruised for our offenses,
Heart of Jesus, obedient to death,
Heart of Jesus, pierced with a lance,
Heart of Jesus, source of all consolation,
Heart of Jesus, our life and resurrection,
Heart of Jesus, our peace and reconciliation,
Heart of Jesus, victim for our sins,
Heart of Jesus, salvation of those who trust in You,
Heart of Jesus, hope of those who die in You,
Heart of Jesus, delight of all the Saints,

Lamb of God, You Who take away the sins of the world, *spare us, O Lord.*

Lamb of God, You Who take away the sins of the world, *graciously hear us, O Lord.*

Lamb of God, You Who take away the sins of the world, *have mercy on us.*

℣. Jesus, meek and humble of heart.

℟. Make our hearts like to Yours.

**Have mercy on us.*

Let us pray. Almighty and eternal God, look upon the Heart of Your most beloved Son and upon the praises and satisfaction which He offers You in the name of sinners; and to those who implore Your mercy, of Your great goodness, grant forgiveness in the name of the same Jesus Christ, Your Son, Who with You lives and reigns, world without end. ℟. Amen.

The Litany of the Blessed Virgin Mary

An indulgence of 7 years. A plenary indulgence once a month under the usual conditions, if this Litany with its versicle and prayer is recited daily for a month. (No. 319.)

LORD, have mercy.
Christ, have mercy.
Lord, have mercy.
Christ, hear us.
Christ, graciously hear us.
God the Father of Heaven, *have mercy on us.*
God the Son, Redeemer of the world, *have mercy on us.*
God the Holy Spirit, *have mercy on us.*
Holy Trinity, One God, *have mercy on us.*
Holy Mary,*
Holy Mother of God,
Holy Virgin of virgins,
Mother of Christ,
Mother of divine grace,
Mother most pure,
Mother most chaste,
Mother inviolate,
Mother undefiled,
Mother most amiable,
Mother most admirable,
Mother of good counsel,
Mother of our Creator,
Mother of our Savior,
Virgin most prudent,
Virgin most venerable,
Virgin most renowned,
Virgin most powerful,
Virgin most merciful,
Virgin most faithful,
Mirror of justice,
Seat of wisdom,
Cause of our joy,
Spiritual vessel,
Vessel of honor,
Singular vessel of devotion,
Mystical rose,
Tower of David,
Tower of ivory,
House of gold,
Ark of the covenant,
Gate of heaven,
Morning star,
Health of the sick,
Refuge of sinners,
Comforter of the afflicted,
Help of Christians,
Queen of Angels,
Queen of Patriarchs,
Queen of Prophets,
Queen of Apostles,
Queen of Martyrs,
Queen of Confessors,
Queen of Virgins,
Queen of all Saints,
Queen conceived without original sin,
Queen assumed into heaven,
Queen of the most holy Rosary,
Queen of Peace,
Lamb of God, You Who take away the sins of the world, *spare us, O Lord!*
Lamb of God, You Who take away the sins of the world, *graciously hear us, O Lord!*
Lamb of God, You Who take away the sins of the world, *have mercy on us.*

℣. Pray for us, O holy Mother of God.

℟. That we may be made worthy of the promises of Christ.

**Pray for us.*

Let us pray. Grant, we beseech You, O Lord God, that we Your servants, may enjoy lasting health of mind and body, and by the glorious intercession of the Blessed Mary, ever Virgin, be delivered from present sorrow and enter into the joy of eternal happiness. Through Christ our Lord. ℟. Amen.

The Litany of St. Joseph

An indulgence of 5 years. A plenary indulgence once a month under the usual conditions, if this Litany with its versicle and prayer is recited daily for a month. (No. 462.)

LORD, have mercy.
Christ, have mercy.
Lord, have mercy.
Christ, hear us.
Christ, graciously hear us.
God the Father of Heaven,*
God the Son, Redeemer of the world,
God the Holy Spirit,
Holy Trinity, One God,
Holy Mary,**
St. Joseph,
Renowned offspring of David,
Light of Patriarchs,
Spouse of the Mother of God,
Chaste guardian of the Virgin,
Foster father of the Son of God,
Diligent protector of Christ,
Head of the Holy Family,
Joseph most just,
Joseph most chaste,
Joseph most prudent,
Joseph most strong,
Joseph most obedient,
Joseph most faithful,
Mirror of patience,
Lover of poverty,
Model of artisans,
Glory of home life,
Guardian of virgins,
Pillar of families,
Solace of the wretched,
Hope of the sick,
Patron of the dying,
Terror of demons,
Protector of Holy Church,
Lamb of God, You Who take away the sins of the world, *spare us, O Lord!*
Lamb of God, You Who take away the sins of the world, *graciously hear us, O Lord!*
Lamb of God, You Who take away the sins of the world, *have mercy on us.*

℣. He made him the lord of His household.

℟. And prince over all His possessions.

**Have mercy on us.*
***Pray for us.*

Let us pray. O God, in Your ineffable providence You were pleased to choose Blessed Joseph to be the spouse of Your most holy Mother; grant, we beseech

You, that we may be worthy to have him for our intercessor in heaven whom on earth we venerate as our Protector. Who live and reign, world without end. ℟. Amen.

The Litany of the Saints

An indulgence of 5 years. A plenary indulgence once a month under the usual conditions, when this Litany is recited daily for a month. (No. 687.)

LORD, have mercy.
Christ, have mercy.
Lord, have mercy.
Christ, hear us.
Christ, graciously hear us.
God the Father of Heaven, *have mercy on us.*
God the Son, Redeemer of the world, *have mercy on us.*
God the Holy Spirit, *have mercy on us.*
Holy Trinity, one God, *have mercy on us.*
Holy Mary,*
Holy Mother of God,
Holy Virgin of virgins,
St. Michael,
St. Gabriel,
St. Raphael,
All you holy Angels and Archangels,
All you holy orders of blessed Spirits,
St. John the Baptist,
St. Joseph,
All you holy Patriarchs and Prophets,
St. Peter,
St. Paul,
St. Andrew,
St. James,
St. John,
St. Thomas,
St. James,
St. Philip,
St. Bartholomew,
St. Matthew,
St. Simon,
St. Thaddeus,
St. Matthias,
St. Barnabas,
St. Luke,
St. Mark,
All you holy Apostles and Evangelists,
All you holy Disciples of our Lord,
All you holy Innocents,
St. Stephen,
St. Lawrence,
St. Vincent,
Sts. Fabian and Sebastian,
Sts. John and Paul,
Sts. Cosmas and Damian,
Sts. Gervase and Protase,
All you holy Martyrs,
St. Sylvester,
St. Gregory,
St. Ambrose,
St. Augustine,
St. Jerome,
St. Martin,
St. Nicholas,
All you holy Bishops and Confessors,
All you holy Doctors,
St. Anthony,
St. Benedict,
St. Bernard,

**Pray for us.*

St. Dominic,*
St. Francis,
All you holy priests and levites,
All you holy monks and hermits,
St. Mary Magdalen,
St. Agatha,
St. Lucy,
St. Agnes,
St. Cecilia,
St. Catherine,
St. Anastasia,
All you holy virgins and widows,
All you holy men and women, Saints of God, *make intercession for us.*
Be merciful, *spare us, O Lord.*
Be merciful, *graciously hear us, O Lord.*
From all evil,**
From all sin,
From Your wrath,
∞From threatening dangers,
∞From the scourge of earthquakes,
∞From plague, famine and war,
From sudden and unprovided death,
From the snares of the devil,
From anger, and hatred, and ill-will,
From the spirit of fornication,
From lightning and tempest,
†From the scourge of earthquake,
†From plague, famine and war,
From everlasting death,
Through the mystery of Your holy Incarnation,
Through Your coming,
Through Your nativity,
Through Your baptism and holy fasting,
Through Your Cross and Passion,
Through Your death and burial,
Through Your holy resurrection,
Through Your admirable ascension,
Through the coming of the Holy Spirit, the Paraclete,
In the day of judgment,
We sinners,††
That You would spare us,
That You would pardon us,
That You would bring us to true penance,
That You would vouchsafe to govern and preserve Your holy Church,
That You would vouchsafe to preserve our Apostolic Prelate, and all orders of the Church in holy religion,
That You would vouchsafe to humble the enemies of Holy Church,
That You would vouchsafe to give peace and true concord to Christian kings and princes,
That You would vouchsafe to grant peace and unity to all Christian people,

**Pray for us.*
***O Lord, deliver us.*
††We beseech You, hear us.

∞ To be said only during the Forty Hours' Exposition.
† Not to be said again during the Forty Hours' Exposition.

That You would vouchsafe to restore to the unity of the Church all who have strayed from the truth and lead all unbelievers to the light of the Gospel,*

That You would vouchsafe to confirm and preserve us in Your holy service,

That You would lift up our minds to heavenly desires,

That You would render eternal blessings to all our benefactors,

That You would deliver our souls and the souls of our brethren, relations and benefactors, from eternal damnation,

That You would vouchsafe to give and preserve the fruits of the earth,

That You would vouchsafe to grant eternal rest to all the faithful departed,

That You would vouchsafe graciously to hear us,

Son of God,

Lamb of God, You Who take away the sins of the world, *spare us, O Lord.*

Lamb of God, You Who take away the sins of the world, *graciously hear us, O Lord.*

Lamb of God, You Who take away the sins of the world, *have mercy on us.*

Christ, hear us.
Christ, graciously hear us.
Lord, have mercy.
Christ, have mercy.
Lord, have mercy.

Our Father, etc. (inaudibly).

℣. And lead us not into temptation.

℟. But deliver us from evil.

**We beseech You, hear us.*

Psalm 69

DEIGN, O God, to rescue me; O Lord, make haste to help me.

Let them be put to shame and confounded who seek my life.

Let them be turned back in disgrace who desire my ruin.

Let them retire in their shame who say to me, "Aha, aha!"

But may all who seek You exult and be glad in You, and may those who love Your salvation say ever, "God be glorified!"

But I am afflicted and poor; O God, hasten to me!

You are my help and my deliverer; O Lord, hold not back!

Glory be to the Father, and to the Son, and to the Holy Spirit.

As it was in the beginning, is now, and ever shall be, world without end. Amen.

℣. Save Your servants.

℟. Who hope in You, O my God.

℣. Be to us, O Lord, a tower of strength.

℟. From the face of the enemy.

℣. Let not the enemy prevail against us.

℟. Nor the son of iniquity have power to hurt us.

℣. O Lord, deal not with us according to our sins.

℟. Neither requite us according to our iniquities.

℣. Let us pray for our Sovereign Pontiff N.

℟. The Lord preserve him, and give him life, and make him blessed upon the earth, and deliver him not up to the will of his enemies.

℣. Let us pray for our benefactors.

℟. Vouchsafe, O Lord, for Your name's sake, to reward with eternal life all those who do us good. Amen.

℣. Let us pray for the faithful departed.

℟. Eternal rest give to them, O Lord; and let perpetual light shine upon them.

℣. May they rest in peace.

℟. Amen.

℣. For our absent brethren.

℟. Save Your servants, who hope in You, O my God.

℣. Send them help, O Lord, from Your holy place.

℟. And from Sion protect them.

℣. O Lord, hear my prayer.

℟. And let my cry come to You.

℣. The Lord be with you.

℟. And with your spirit.

The following prayers are not said after the Litany of the Forty Hours' Devotion.

Let us pray

O GOD, Whose property is always to have mercy and to spare, receive our petition, that we, and all Your servants who are bound by the chains of sin, may, by the compassion of Your goodness, be mercifully absolved.

Graciously hear, we beseech You, O Lord, the prayers of Your suppliants, and pardon the sins of those who confess to You, that in Your bounty You may grant us both pardon and peace.

In Your clemency, O Lord, show us Your ineffable mercy, that You may both free us from all our sins, and deliver us from the punishments which we deserve for them.

O God, Who by sin are offended and by penance pacified, mercifully regard the prayers of Your suppliant people, and turn away the scourges of Your anger, which we deserve for our sins.

Almighty, everlasting God, have mercy upon Your servant N., our Sovereign Pontiff, and direct him according to Your clemency into the way of everlasting salvation, that by Your grace he may desire those things that are pleasing to You, and perform them with all his strength.

O God, from Whom are holy desires, good counsels, and just works, give to Your servants that peace which the world cannot give, that our hearts be set to keep Your commandments, and that, being removed from the fear of our enemies, we may pass our time in peace under Your protection.

Burn our desires and our hearts with the fire of the Holy Spirit, O Lord, that we may serve You with a chaste body, and with a clean heart be pleasing to You.

O God, the Creator and Redeemer of all the faithful, grant to the souls of Your servants and handmaids the remission of all their sins, that, through devout prayers, they may obtain the pardon which they always desired.

Direct, we beseech You, O Lord, our actions by Your holy inspirations, and carry them on by Your gracious assistance, that every prayer and work of ours may begin always with You, and through You be happily ended.

Almighty and everlasting God, You have dominion over the living and the dead, and You are merciful to all who You foreknow will be Yours by faith and good works; we humbly beseech You that those for whom we intend to pour forth our prayers, whether this present world still detain them in the flesh, or the world to come has already received them out of their bodies, may, through the intercession of all Your Saints, by the clemency of Your goodness, obtain the remission of all their sins. Through our Lord, etc. ℟. Amen.

℣. The Lord be with you. ℟. And with your spirit.

℣. May the almighty and merciful Lord graciously hear us. ℟. Amen.

℣. And may the souls of the faithful departed, through the mercy of God, rest in peace. ℟. Amen.

PRAYERS TO SAINT JOSEPH

Prayer to St. Joseph, Patron of the Universal Church

An indulgence of 500 days. (No. 474.)

O GLORIOUS St. Joseph, you were chosen by God to be the reputed father of Jesus, the most pure Spouse of Mary, ever Virgin, and the Head of the Holy Family. You have been chosen by Christ's Vicar as the heavenly Patron and Protector of the Church founded by Christ. Therefore, with the greatest confidence I implore your powerful assistance for the whole Church Militant. Protect, in a special manner, with true fatherly love, the Sovereign Pontiff and all the bishops and priests in communion with the See of Peter. Be the protector of all who labor for souls amid the trials and tribulations of this life; and grant that all the nations of the earth may submit with docility to that Church out of which there is no salvation.

Dearest St. Joseph, accept the offering I now make of myself to you. I dedicate myself to your service, that you may ever be my Father, my Protector and my Guide in the way of salvation. Obtain for me great purity of heart and a fervent love for the interior life. Grant that, after your example, all my actions may be directed to the greater glory of God, in union with the divine Heart of Jesus, the Immaculate Heart of Mary, and your own paternal heart. Finally, pray for me that I may share in the peace and joy of your holy death. Amen.

Memorare to St. Joseph

An indulgence of 500 days. (No. 472.)

REMEMBER, O most chaste Spouse of the Virgin Mary, that never was it known that anyone who implored your help and sought your intercession was left unassisted. Full of confidence in your power, I fly unto you, and beg your protection. Despise not, O foster-father of the Redeemer, my humble supplication, but in your bounty, hear and answer me. Amen.

BENEDICTION OF THE BLESSED SACRAMENT

O Salutaris

O SALUTARIS Hostia	O SAVING Victim, opening wide
Quæ cœli pandis ostium:	The gate of heav'n to man below:
Bella premunt hostilia,	Our foes press on from every side;
Da robur, fer auxilium.	Your aid supply, Your strength bestow.
Uni trinoque Domino,	To Your great name be endless praise,
Sit sempiterna gloria,	Immortal Godhead, One in Three!
Qui vitam sine termino	O grant us endless length of days
Nobis donet in patria. Amen.	With You in our true country. Amen.

Before the "Tantum Ergo," any number of hymns may be sung together with prayers in conformity with the custom of the particular church.

Tantum Ergo

TANTUM ergo Sacramentum,	DOWN in adoration falling,
Veneremur cernui:	Lo! the Sacred Host we hail;

Et antiquum documentum	Lo! o'er ancient forms departing
Novo cedat ritui;	Newer rites of grace prevail;
Præstet fides supplementum	Faith for all defects supplying
Sensuum defectui.	Where the feeble senses fail.
Genitori, Genitoque Laus et jubilatio, Salus, honor, virtus quoque, Sit et benedictio: Procedenti ab utroque Compar sit laudatio. Amen.	To the everlasting Father, And the Son Who reigns on high, With the Holy Spirit proceeding Forth from each eternally, Be salvation, honor, blessing, Might and endless majesty! Amen.
℣. Panem de cœlo præstitisti eis. (Alleluia.)	℣. You gave them bread from heaven. (Alleluia.)
℟. Omne delectamentum in se habentem. (Alleluia.)	℟. Containing in itself all sweetness. (Alleluia.)

Let us pray. O God, under a marvelous sacrament You have left us the memorial of Your Passion; grant us, we beseech You, so to venerate the sacred mysteries of Your Body and Blood, that we may ever perceive within us the fruit of Your Redemption. Who live and reign, world without end. ℟. Amen.

The Divine Praises

An indulgence of 3 years. An indulgence of 5 years, if said publicly. A plenary indulgence under the usual conditions, if said daily for a month. (No. 696.)

BLESSED be God. Blessed be His Holy Name. Blessed be Jesus Christ, true God and true Man. Blessed be the Name of Jesus. Blessed be His Most Sacred Heart. Blessed be Jesus in the Most Holy Sacrament of the Altar. Blessed be the great Mother of God, Mary most Holy. Blessed be her Holy and Immaculate Conception. Blessed be her Glorious Assumption. Blessed be the Name of Mary, Virgin and Mother. Blessed be St. Joseph, her most chaste spouse. Blessed be God in His Angels and in His Saints.

I. HOLY DAYS OF OBLIGATION

In U.S.A.: All Sundays. — The Circumcision, *Jan. 1st.* — Ascension Day. — The Assumption, *Aug. 15th.* — All Saints, *Nov. 1st.* — Immaculate Conception, *Dec. 8th.* — Christmas, *Dec. 25th.*

In Canada: All Sundays. — The Circumcision, *Jan. 1st.* — The Epiphany, *Jan. 6th.* — The Ascension. — All Saints, *Nov. 1st.* — The Immaculate Conception, *Dec. 8th.* — Christmas Day, *Dec. 25th.*

In Australia: Same as U.S.A., except Immaculate Conception.

II. Fasting and Abstinence-Days

Abstinence—Everyone over seven years of age is bound to observe the law of abstinence.

Complete abstinence is to be observed on Fridays, Ash Wednesday, the Vigils of the Immaculate Conception and Christmas, and on Holy Saturday until midnight. On days of complete abstinence meat, and soup or gravy made from meat, may not be used at all.

Partial abstinence is to be observed on Ember Wednesdays and Saturdays and on the Vigil of Pentecost. On days of partial abstinence meat, and soup or gravy made from meat, may be taken only once a day at the principal meal.

Fast—Everyone over 21 and under 59 years of age is also bound to observe the law of fast on the weekdays of Lent, Holy Saturday, Ember Days, Vigils of Pentecost, Immaculate Conception and Christmas.

On days of fast only one full meal is allowed. Two other meatless meals, sufficient to maintain strength, may be taken according to each one's needs; but together they should not equal another full meal.

Meat may be taken at the principal meal on a day of fast except on Fridays, Ash Wednesday, Holy Saturday, the Vigils of Immaculate Conception and Christmas.

Eating between meals is not permitted; but liquids, including milk and fruit juices, are allowed.

When health or ability to work would be seriously affected, the law does not oblige. In doubt concerning fast or abstinence, a parish priest or confessor should be consulted.

New Law of Eucharistic Fast

(From the Motu Proprio issued by His Holiness Pope Pius XII, March 19, 1957)

1. Priests and faithful, before Holy Mass or Holy Communion, respectively, must abstain for three hours from solid foods and alcoholic beverages, and for one hour from non-alcoholic beverages. Water does not break the fast.

2. From now on, the fast must be observed for the period of time indicated in Number One, even by those who celebrate or receive Holy Communion at midnight or in the first hours of the day.

3. The infirm, even if not bedridden, may take non-alcoholic beverages and that which is really and properly medicine, either in liquid or solid form, before Mass or Holy Communion without any time limit.

We strongly exhort priests and faithful who are able to do so to observe the old and venerable form of the Eucharistic fast before Mass and Holy Communion. All those who will make use of these concessions must compensate for the good received by becoming shining examples of a Christian life and principally with works of penance and charity.

The dispositions of this Motu Proprio will go into effect on March 25, 1957, the Feast of the Annunciation of the Blessed Virgin Mary. Every disposition whatsoever to the contrary is abrogated, even if it is worthy of special mention.

Given at Rome at St. Peter's, March 19, the Feast of St. Joseph, Patron of the Universal Church, 1957, the 19th year of Our pontificate.

Page	SUNDAY OR FEASTDAY	YEAR					
		1958	1959	1960	1961	1962	1963
118	Circumcision........	1 Jan.	1 Jan.	1 Jan.	1 Jan.	1 Jan.	1 Jan.
136	Holy Name..........	5 Jan.	4 Jan.	3 Jan.	2 Jan.	2 Jan.	2 Jan.
154	Epiphany............	6 Jan.	6 Jan.	6 Jan.	6 Jan.	6 Jan.	6 Jan.
173	Feast of Holy Family.	12 Jan.	11 Jan.	10 Jan.	8 Jan.	7 Jan.	13 Jan.
191	2nd Sun. aft. Epiph...	19 Jan.	18 Jan.	17 Jan.	15 Jan.	14 Jan.	20 Jan.
209	3rd Sun. aft. Epiph...	26 Jan.	....	24 Jan.	22 Jan.	21 Jan.	27 Jan.
227	4th Sun. aft. Epiph...	....	....	31 Jan.	....	28 Jan.	3 Feb.
246	5th Sun. aft. Epiph...	....	....	7 Feb.	....	4 Feb.	....
265	6th Sun. aft. Epiph...	....	....	....	....	11 Feb.	....
284	Septuagesima........	2 Feb.	25 Jan.	14 Feb.	29 Jan.	18 Feb.	10 Feb.
302	Sexagesima..........	9 Feb.	1 Feb.	21 Feb.	5 Feb.	25 Feb.	17 Feb.
321	Quinquagesima......	16 Feb.	8 Feb.	28 Feb.	12 Feb.	4 Mar.	24 Feb.
339	1st Sun. of Lent.....	23 Feb.	15 Feb.	6 Mar.	19 Feb.	11 Mar.	3 Mar.
357	2nd Sun. of Lent.....	2 Mar.	22 Feb.	13 Mar.	26 Feb.	18 Mar.	10 Mar.
375	3rd Sun. of Lent.....	9 Mar.	1 Mar.	20 Mar.	5 Mar.	25 Mar.	17 Mar.
393	4th Sun. of Lent.....	16 Mar.	8 Mar.	27 Mar.	12 Mar.	1 Apr.	24 Mar.
411	Passion Sunday......	23 Mar.	15 Mar.	3 Apr.	19 Mar.	8 Apr.	31 Mar.
429	Palm Sunday........	30 Mar.	22 Mar.	10 Apr.	26 Mar.	15 Apr.	7 Apr.
1190	Easter Vigil.........	6 Apr.	29 Mar.	17 Apr.	2 Apr.	22 Apr.	14 Apr.
455	Easter Sunday.......	6 Apr.	29 Mar.	17 Apr.	2 Apr.	22 Apr.	14 Apr.
474	1st Sun. aft. Easter..	13 Apr.	5 Apr.	24 Apr.	9 Apr.	29 Apr.	21 Apr.
492	2nd Sun. aft. Easter..	20 Apr.	12 Apr.	1 May	16 Apr.	6 May	28 Apr.
510	3rd Sun. aft. Easter..	27 Apr.	19 Apr.	8 May	23 Apr.	13 May	5 May
528	4th Sun. aft. Easter..	4 May	26 Apr.	15 May	30 Apr.	20 May	12 May
546	5th Sun. aft. Easter..	11 May	3 May	22 May	7 May	27 May	19 May
564	Ascension Day.......	15 May	7 May	26 May	11 May	31 May	23 May
582	Sun. aft. Ascension..	18 May	10 May	29 May	14 May	3 June	26 May
601	Pentecost...........	25 May	17 May	5 June	21 May	10 June	2 June
620	Trinity Sunday......	1 June	24 May	12 June	28 May	17 June	9 June
638	Corpus Christi.......	5 June	28 May	16 June	1 June	21 June	13 June
657	2nd Sun. aft. Pent....	8 June	31 May	19 June	4 June	24 June	16 June
675	Sacred Heart........	13 June	5 June	24 June	9 June	29 June	21 June
694	3rd Sun. aft. Pent....	15 June	7 June	26 June	11 June	1 July	23 June
712	4th Sun. aft. Pent....	22 June	14 June	3 July	18 June	8 July	30 June

Page	SUNDAY OR FEASTDAY	YEAR					
		1958	1959	1960	1961	1962	1963
731	5th Sun. aft. Pent....	29 June	21 June	10 July	25 June	15 July	7 July
749	6th Sun. aft. Pent....	6 July	28 June	17 July	2 July	22 July	14 July
768	7th Sun. aft. Pent....	13 July	5 July	24 July	9 July	29 July	21 July
786	8th Sun. aft. Pent....	20 July	12 July	31 July	16 July	5 Aug.	28 July
804	9th Sun. aft. Pent....	27 July	19 July	7 Aug.	23 July	12 Aug.	4 Aug.
822	10th Sun. aft. Pent...	3 Aug.	26 July	14 Aug.	30 July	19 Aug.	11 Aug.
1153	Assumption.........	15 Aug.	15 Aug.	15 Aug.	15 Aug.	15 Aug.	15 Aug.
840	11th Sun. aft. Pent...	10 Aug.	2 Aug.	21 Aug.	6 Aug.	26 Aug.	18 Aug.
858	12th Sun. aft. Pent...	17 Aug.	9 Aug.	28 Aug.	13 Aug.	2 Sept.	25 Aug.
877	13th Sun. aft. Pent...	24 Aug.	16 Aug.	4 Sept.	20 Aug.	9 Sept.	1 Sept.
895	14th Sun. aft. Pent...	31 Aug.	23 Aug.	11 Sept.	27 Aug.	16 Sept.	8 Sept.
913	15th Sun. aft. Pent...	7 Sept.	30 Aug.	18 Sept.	3 Sept.	23 Sept.	15 Sept.
931	16th Sun. aft. Pent...	14 Sept.	6 Sept.	25 Sept.	10 Sept.	30 Sept.	22 Sept.
949	17th Sun. aft. Pent...	21 Sept.	13 Sept.	2 Oct.	17 Sept.	7 Oct.	29 Sept.
967	18th Sun. aft. Pent...	28 Sept.	20 Sept.	9 Oct.	24 Sept.	14 Oct.	6 Oct.
985	19th Sun. aft. Pent...	5 Oct.	27 Sept.	16 Oct.	1 Oct.	21 Oct.	13 Oct.
1003	20th Sun. aft. Pent...	12 Oct.	4 Oct.	23 Oct.	8 Oct.	....	20 Oct.
1040	21st Sun. aft. Pent....	19 Oct.	11 Oct.	....	15 Oct.	4 Nov.	....
1021	Christ the King......	26 Oct.	25 Oct.	30 Oct.	29 Oct.	28 Oct.	27 Oct.
1171	All Saints...........	1 Nov.	1 Nov.	1 Nov.	1 Nov.	1 Nov.	1 Nov.
1059	22nd Sun. aft. Pent...	....	18 Oct.	6 Nov.	22 Oct.	11 Nov.	3 Nov.
1077	23rd Sun. aft. Pent...	2 Nov.	....	13 Nov.	....	18 Nov.	10 Nov.
265	24th Sun. aft. Pent...	**9 Nov.	....	....	*5 Nov.	....	17 Nov.
265	25th Sun. aft. Pent...	16 Nov.	**8 Nov.	....	**12Nov	....	....
265	26th Sun. aft. Pent...	....	15 Nov.	....	19 Nov.	....	....
1095	Last Sun. aft. Pent...	23 Nov.	22 Nov.	20 Nov.	26 Nov.	25 Nov.	24 Nov.
3	1st Sun. of Advent...	30 Nov.	29 Nov.	27 Nov.	3 Dec.	2 Dec.	1 Dec.
21	2nd Sun. of Advent...	7 Dec.	6 Dec.	4 Dec.	10 Dec.	9 Dec.	....
1115	Immaculate Concep...	8 Dec.	8 Dec.	8 Dec.	8 Dec.	8 Dec.	8 Dec.
39	3rd Sun. of Advent...	14 Dec.	13 Dec.	11 Dec.	17 Dec.	16 Dec.	15 Dec.
57	4th Sun. of Advent...	21 Dec.	20 Dec.	18 Dec.	24 Dec.	23 Dec.	22 Dec.
76	Christmas...........	25 Dec.	25 Dec.	25 Dec.	25 Dec.	25 Dec.	25 Dec.
100	Sun. btw. Chr. & N.Y.	28 Dec.	27 Dec.	....	31 Dec.	30 Dec.	29 Dec.
	*Page 227 **Page 246						

Page	SUNDAY OR FEASTDAY	YEAR					
		1964	1965	1966	1967	1968	1969
118	Circumcision........	1 Jan.	1 Jan.	1 Jan.	1 Jan.	1 Jan.	1 Jan.
136	Holy Name.........	5 Jan.	3 Jan.	2 Jan.	2 Jan.	2 Jan.	5 Jan.
154	Epiphany	6 Jan.	6 Jan.	6 Jan.	6 Jan.	6 Jan.	6 Jan.
173	Feast of Holy Family.	12 Jan.	10 Jan.	9 Jan.	8 Jan.	7 Jan.	12 Jan.
191	2nd Sun. aft. Epiph...	19 Jan.	17 Jan.	16 Jan.	15 Jan.	14 Jan.	19 Jan.
209	3rd Sun. aft. Epiph...	....	24 Jan.	23 Jan.	....	21 Jan.	26 Jan.
227	4th Sun. aft. Epiph...	....	31 Jan.	30 Jan.	....	28 Jan.	....
246	5th Sun. aft. Epiph...	....	7 Feb.	....	....	4 Feb.	....
284	Septuagesima.......	26 Jan.	14 Feb.	6 Feb.	22 Jan.	11 Feb.	2 Feb.
302	Sexagesima.........	2 Feb.	21 Feb.	13 Feb.	29 Jan.	18 Feb.	9 Feb.
321	Quinquagesima......	9 Feb.	28 Feb.	20 Feb.	5 Feb.	25 Feb.	16 Feb.
339	1st Sun. of Lent.....	16 Feb.	7 Mar.	27 Feb.	12 Feb.	3 Mar.	23 Feb.
357	2nd Sun. of Lent.....	23 Feb.	14 Mar.	6 Mar.	19 Feb.	10 Mar.	2 Mar.
375	3rd Sun. of Lent.....	1 Mar.	21 Mar.	13 Mar.	26 Feb.	17 Mar.	9 Mar.
393	4th Sun. of Lent..	8 Mar.	28 Mar.	20 Mar.	5 Mar.	24 Mar.	16 Mar.
411	Passion Sunday......	15 Mar.	4 Apr.	27 Mar.	12 Mar.	31 Mar.	23 Mar.
429	Palm Sunday.......	22 Mar.	11 Apr.	3 Apr.	19 Mar.	7 Apr.	30 Mar.
1190	Easter Vigil.........	29 Mar.	18 Apr.	10 Apr.	26 Mar.	14 Apr.	6 Apr.
455	Easter Sunday.......	29 Mar.	18 Apr.	10 Apr.	26 Mar.	14 Apr.	6 Apr.
474	1st Sun. aft. Easter..	5 Apr.	25 Apr.	17 Apr.	2 Apr.	21 Apr.	13 Apr.
492	2nd Sun. aft. Easter..	12 Apr.	2 May	24 Apr.	9 Apr.	28 Apr.	20 Apr.
510	3rd Sun. aft. Easter..	19 Apr.	9 May	1 May	16 Apr.	5 May	27 Apr.
528	4th Sun. aft. Easter..	26 Apr.	16 May	8 May	23 Apr.	12 May	4 May
546	5th Sun. aft. Easter..	3 May	23 May	15 May	30 Apr.	19 May	11 May
564	Ascension Day.......	7 May	27 May	19 May	4 May	23 May	15 May
582	Sun. aft. Ascension...	10 May	30 May	22 May	7 May	26 May	18 May
601	Pentecost..........	17 May	6 June	29 May	14 May	2 June	25 May
620	Trinity Sunday......	24 May	13 June	5 June	21 May	9 June	1 June
638	Corpus Christi......	28 May	17 June	9 June	25 May	13 June	5 June
657	2nd Sun. aft. Pent....	31 May	20 June	12 June	28 May	16 June	8 June
675	Sacred Heart.......	5 June	25 June	17 June	2 June	21 June	13 June
694	3rd Sun. aft. Pent....	7 June	27 June	19 June	4 June	23 June	15 June
712	4th Sun. aft. Pent....	14 June	4 July	26 June	11 June	30 June	22 June
731	5th Sun. aft. Pent....	21 June	11 July	3 July	18 June	7 July	29 June

PROMISES OF OUR LORD
'O SAINT MARGARET MARY

(E Office which the Church has prescribed he Feast of the Sacred Heart of Jesus, we of the apparitions granted by our Divine St. Margaret Mary Alacoque, and special n is called to the apparition on the day the Octave of Corpus Christi, during which nmissioned the Saint to have the Feast hed throughout the world. When she ob- because she realized that humanly speaking task was beyond her power, she was assured is was the very reason why she had been , that thus all men might understand that opagation of the devotion to the Sacred was the work of God.

world-wide spread of the devotion to the Heart, as made known to St. Margaret is one of the marvels of modern Catholicity. less souls have been moved, by the tender aints of our Lord, to make reparation for own sins and for the sins of all who neglect especially in the Sacrament of His love. ially in June the appeal for reparation is made Catholics.

Page	SUNDAY OR FEASTDAY	YEAR 1964	1965	1966	1967	1968	1969
749	6th Sun. aft. Pent....	28 June	18 July	10 July	25 June	14 July	6 July
768	7th Sun. aft. Pent....	5 July	25 July	17 July	2 July	21 July	13 July
786	8th Sun. aft. Pent....	12 July	1 Aug.	24 July	9 July	28 July	20 July
804	9th Sun. aft. Pent....	19 July	8 Aug.	31 July	16 July	4 Aug.	27 July
822	10th Sun. aft. Pent...	26 July	....	7 Aug.	23 July	11 Aug.	3 Aug.
1153	Assumption.........	15 Aug.	15 Aug.	15 Aug.	15 Aug.	15 Aug.	15 Aug.
840	11th Sun. aft. Pent...	2 Aug.	22 Aug.	14 Aug.	30 July	18 Aug.	10 Aug.
858	12th Sun. aft. Pent...	9 Aug.	29 Aug.	21 Aug.	6 Aug.	25 Aug.	17 Aug.
877	13th Sun. aft. Pent...	16 Aug.	5 Sept.	28 Aug.	13 Aug.	1 Sept.	24 Aug.
895	14th Sun. aft. Pent...	23 Aug.	12 Sept.	4 Sept.	20 Aug.	8 Sept.	31 Aug.
913	15th Sun. aft. Pent...	30 Aug.	19 Sept.	11 Sept.	27 Aug.	15 Sept.	7 Sept.
931	16th Sun. aft. Pent...	6 Sept.	26 Sept.	18 Sept.	3 Sept.	22 Sept.	14 Sept.
949	17th Sun. aft. Pent...	13 Sept.	3 Oct.	25 Sept.	10 Sept.	29 Sept.	21 Sept.
967	18th Sun. aft. Pent...	20 Sept.	10 Oct.	2 Oct.	17 Sept.	6 Oct.	28 Sept.
985	19th Sun. aft. Pent...	27 Sept.	17 Oct.	9 Oct.	24 Sept.	13 Oct.	5 Oct.
1003	20th Sun. aft. Pent...	4 Oct.	24 Oct.	16 Oct.	1 Oct.	20 Oct.	12 Oct.
1021	Christ the King......	25 Oct.	31 Oct.	30 Oct.	29 Oct.	27 Oct.	19 Oct.
1171	All Saints...........	1 Nov.	1 Nov.	1 Nov.	1 Nov.	1 Nov.	1 Nov.
1040	21st Sun. aft. Pent...	11 Oct.	....	23 Oct.	8 Oct.	....	26 Oct.
1059	22nd Sun. aft. Pent...	18 Oct.	7 Nov.	....	15 Oct.	3 Nov.	....
1077	23rd Sun. aft. Pent...	....	14 Nov.	6 Nov.	22 Oct.	10 Nov.	2 Nov.
265	24th Sun. aft. Pent...	....	....	13 Nov.	....	17 Nov.	9 Nov.
265	25th Sun. aft. Pent...	**8 Nov.	....	....	*5 Nov.	....	16 Nov.
265	26th Sun. aft. Pent...	15 Nov.	....	....	**12Nov	....	....
265	27th Sun. aft. Pent...	....	....	....	19 Nov.	....	....
1095	Last Sun. aft. Pent....	22 Nov.	21 Nov.	20 Nov.	26 Nov.	24 Nov.	23 Nov.
3	1st Sun. of Advent...	29 Nov.	28 Nov.	27 Nov.	3 Dec.	1 Dec.	30 Nov.
21	2nd Sun. of Advent...	6 Dec.	5 Dec.	4 Dec.	10 Dec.	....	7 Dec.
1115	Immaculate Concep...	8 Dec.	8 Dec.	8 Dec.	8 Dec.	8 Dec.	8 Dec.
39	3rd Sun. of Advent...	13 Dec.	12 Dec.	11 Dec.	17 Dec.	15 Dec.	14 Dec.
57	4th Sun. of Advent...	20 Dec.	19 Dec.	18 Dec.	24 Dec.	22 Dec.	21 Dec.
76	Christmas...........	25 Dec.	25 Dec.	25 Dec.	25 Dec.	25 Dec.	25 Dec.
100	Sun. btw. Chr. & N.Y.	27 Dec.	26 Dec.	....	31 Dec.	29 Dec.	28 Dec.
	*Page 227 **Page 246						

✠

The Promise of the Sacred Heart

✠

720-42

IN f
are
Lor
atte
with
He
esta
jecte
such
that
chos
the
Hea

Th
Sacr
Mar
Cou
com
thei
Him
Esp
to a

FIRST PROMISE

"I will give to My faithful all the graces necessary in their state of life."

SECOND PROMISE

"I will establish peace in their homes."

THIRD PROMISE

"I will comfort them in all their afflictions."

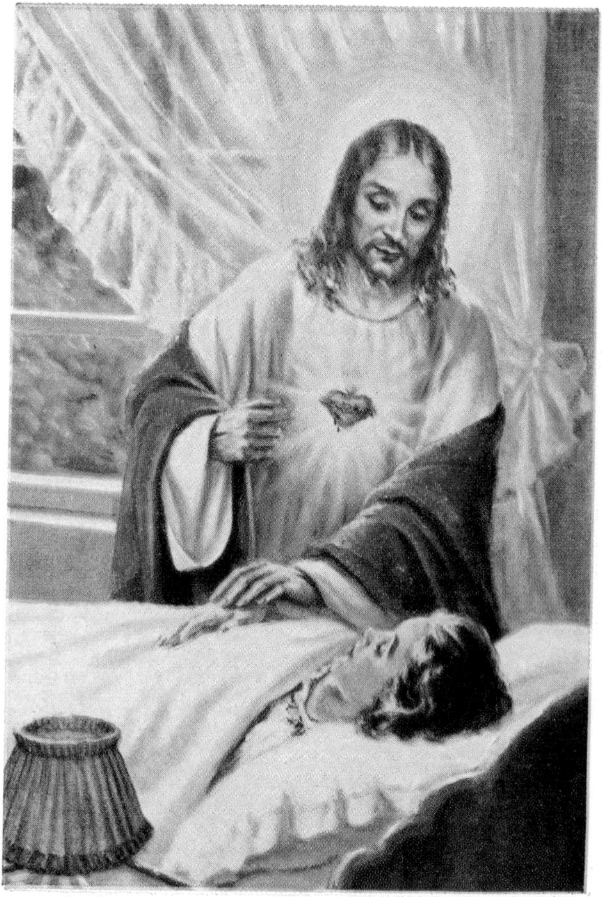

FOURTH PROMISE

"I will be their secure refuge in life, and above all in death."

FIFTH PROMISE

"I will bestow abundant blessings upon all their undertakings."

SIXTH PROMISE

"Sinners shall find in My Heart the source and the infinite ocean of mercy."

SEVENTH PROMISE

"Tepid souls shall become fervent."

EIGHTH PROMISE

"Fervent souls shall quickly mount to high perfection."

Page	SUNDAY OR FEASTDAY	YEAR					
		1964	1965	1966	1967	1968	1969
749	6th Sun. aft. Pent....	28 June	18 July	10 July	25 June	14 July	6 July
768	7th Sun. aft. Pent....	5 July	25 July	17 July	2 July	21 July	13 July
786	8th Sun. aft. Pent....	12 July	1 Aug.	24 July	9 July	28 July	20 July
804	9th Sun. aft. Pent....	19 July	8 Aug.	31 July	16 July	4 Aug.	27 July
822	10th Sun. aft. Pent...	26 July	....	7 Aug.	23 July	11 Aug.	3 Aug.
1153	Assumption.........	15 Aug.	15 Aug.	15 Aug.	15 Aug.	15 Aug.	15 Aug.
840	11th Sun. aft. Pent...	2 Aug.	22 Aug.	14 Aug.	30 July	18 Aug.	10 Aug.
858	12th Sun. aft. Pent...	9 Aug.	29 Aug.	21 Aug.	6 Aug.	25 Aug.	17 Aug.
877	13th Sun. aft. Pent...	16 Aug.	5 Sept.	28 Aug.	13 Aug.	1 Sept.	24 Aug.
895	14th Sun. aft. Pent...	23 Aug.	12 Sept.	4 Sept.	20 Aug.	8 Sept.	31 Aug.
913	15th Sun. aft. Pent...	30 Aug.	19 Sept.	11 Sept.	27 Aug.	15 Sept.	7 Sept.
931	16th Sun. aft. Pent...	6 Sept.	26 Sept.	18 Sept.	3 Sept.	22 Sept.	14 Sept.
949	17th Sun. aft. Pent...	13 Sept.	3 Oct.	25 Sept.	10 Sept.	29 Sept.	21 Sept.
967	18th Sun. aft. Pent...	20 Sept.	10 Oct.	2 Oct.	17 Sept.	6 Oct.	28 Sept.
985	19th Sun. aft. Pent...	27 Sept.	17 Oct.	9 Oct.	24 Sept.	13 Oct.	5 Oct.
1003	20th Sun. aft. Pent...	4 Oct.	24 Oct.	16 Oct.	1 Oct.	20 Oct.	12 Oct.
1021	Christ the King......	25 Oct.	31 Oct.	30 Oct.	29 Oct.	27 Oct.	19 Oct.
1171	All Saints...........	1 Nov.	1 Nov.	1 Nov.	1 Nov.	1 Nov.	1 Nov.
1040	21st Sun. aft. Pent....	11 Oct.	....	23 Oct.	8 Oct.	....	26 Oct.
1059	22nd Sun. aft. Pent...	18 Oct.	7 Nov.	....	15 Oct.	3 Nov.	....
1077	23rd Sun. aft. Pent...	....	14 Nov.	6 Nov.	22 Oct.	10 Nov.	2 Nov.
265	24th Sun. aft. Pent...	....	....	13 Nov.	....	17 Nov.	9 Nov.
265	25th Sun. aft. Pent...	**8 Nov.	....	....	*5 Nov.	....	16 Nov.
265	26th Sun. aft. Pent...	15 Nov.	....	....	**12Nov	....	....
265	27th Sun. aft. Pent...	....	....	....	19 Nov.	....	....
1095	Last Sun. aft. Pent....	22 Nov.	21 Nov.	20 Nov.	26 Nov.	24 Nov.	23 Nov.
3	1st Sun. of Advent...	29 Nov.	28 Nov.	27 Nov.	3 Dec.	1 Dec.	30 Nov.
21	2nd Sun. of Advent...	6 Dec.	5 Dec.	4 Dec.	10 Dec.	....	7 Dec.
1115	Immaculate Concep...	8 Dec.	8 Dec.	8 Dec.	8 Dec.	8 Dec.	8 Dec.
39	3rd Sun. of Advent...	13 Dec.	12 Dec.	11 Dec.	17 Dec.	15 Dec.	14 Dec.
57	4th Sun. of Advent...	20 Dec.	19 Dec.	18 Dec.	24 Dec.	22 Dec.	21 Dec.
76	Christmas...........	25 Dec.	25 Dec.	25 Dec.	25 Dec.	25 Dec.	25 Dec.
100	Sun. btw. Chr. & N.Y.	27 Dec.	26 Dec.	....	31 Dec.	29 Dec.	28 Dec.
	*Page 227 **Page 246						

✠

The Promises of the Sacred Heart

✠

720-42

PROMISES OF OUR LORD TO SAINT MARGARET MARY

IN THE Office which the Church has prescribed for the Feast of the Sacred Heart of Jesus, we are told of the apparitions granted by our Divine Lord to St. Margaret Mary Alacoque, and special attention is called to the apparition on the day within the Octave of Corpus Christi, during which He commissioned the Saint to have the Feast established throughout the world. When she objected, because she realized that humanly speaking such a task was beyond her power, she was assured that this was the very reason why she had been chosen, that thus all men might understand that the propagation of the devotion to the Sacred Heart was the work of God.

The world-wide spread of the devotion to the Sacred Heart, as made known to St. Margaret Mary, is one of the marvels of modern Catholicity. Countless souls have been moved, by the tender complaints of our Lord, to make reparation for their own sins and for the sins of all who neglect Him, especially in the Sacrament of His love. Especially in June the appeal for reparation is made to all Catholics.

FIRST PROMISE

"I will give to My faithful all the graces necessary in their state of life."

SECOND PROMISE

"I will establish peace in their homes."

THIRD PROMISE

"I will comfort them in all their afflictions."

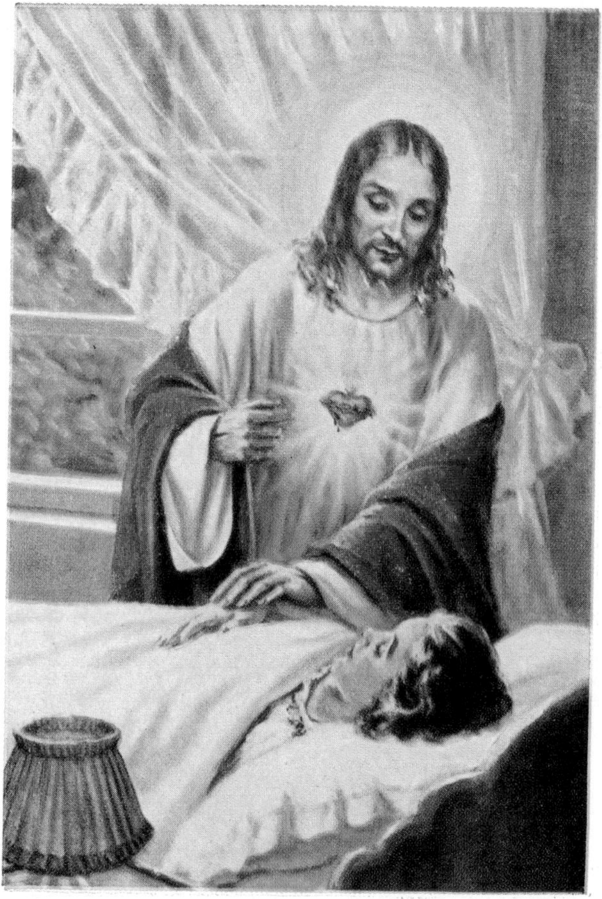

FOURTH PROMISE

"I will be their secure refuge in life, and above all in death."

FIFTH PROMISE

"I will bestow abundant blessings upon all their undertakings."

SIXTH PROMISE

"Sinners shall find in My Heart the source and the infinite ocean of mercy."

SEVENTH PROMISE

"Tepid souls shall become fervent."

EIGHTH PROMISE

"Fervent souls shall quickly mount to high perfection."

NINTH PROMISE

"I will bless every place in which an image of My Heart shall be exposed and honored."

TENTH PROMISE

"I will give to priests the gift of touching the most hardened hearts."

ELEVENTH PROMISE

"Those who promote this devotion shall have their names written in My Heart, never to be effaced."

TWELFTH PROMISE

"To those who shall communicate on the First Friday, for nine consecutive months, I will grant the grace of final penitence."

Consecration of the Human Race to the Sacred Heart of Jesus

MOST sweet Jesus, Redeemer of the human race, look down upon us humbly prostrate before Your altar. We are Yours, and Yours we wish to be; but, to be more surely united with You, behold each one of us freely consecrates himself today to Your Most Sacred Heart. Many indeed have never known You; many too, despising Your precepts, have rejected You. Have mercy on them all, most merciful Jesus, and draw them to Your Sacred Heart.

You are King, O Lord, not only of the faithful who have never forsaken You, but also of the prodigal children who have abandoned You; grant that they may quickly return to their Father's house lest they die of wretchedness and hunger.

You are King of those who are deceived by erroneous opinions, or whom discord keeps aloof; call them back to the harbor of truth and unity of faith, so that soon there may be but one flock and one Shepherd.

You are King of all those who are still involved in the darkness of idolatry or of Islamism; refuse not to draw them all into the light and kingdom of God. Turn Your eyes of mercy toward the children of that race, once Your chosen people. Of old they called down upon themselves the Blood of the Savior; may it now descend upon them a laver of redemption and of life.

Grant, O Lord, to Your Church assurance of freedom and immunity from harm; give peace and order to all nations, and make the earth resound from pole to pole with one cry: Praise to the Divine Heart that wrought our salvation; to It be glory and honor forever. Amen.

FIRST FRIDAY DEVOTIONS

Those who receive Holy Communion on the First Friday of the month and who assist at the public exercises in honor of the Sacred Heart, may gain: A plenary indulgence with the addition of Confession, Communion and prayers for the intentions of the Holy Father.

Those who receive Holy Communion on the First Friday, and recite privately some prayers in reparation for the injuries against the Sacred Heart, may gain: A plenary indulgence under the usual conditions. If, moreover, a public service is held, this latter indulgence can be gained only by those who are lawfully prevented from assisting at such a service.

Those who recite devout prayers of reparation on other Fridays of the year, may gain: An indulgence of 7 years once on each Friday. (No. 252.)
